Managing Human Resources

Productivity, Quality of Work Life, Profits

Fifth Edition

Wayne F. Cascio
University of Colorado at Denver

Boston Burr Ridge, IL Dubuque, IA Madison, WI New York San Francisco St. Louis
Bangkok Bogotá Caracas Lisbon London Madrid
Mexico City Milan New Delhi Seoul Singapore Sydney Taipei Toronto

Irwin/McGraw-Hill

A Division of The ***McGraw·Hill*** *Companies*

MANAGING HUMAN RESOURCES: PRODUCTIVITY, QUALITY OF WORK LIFE, PROFITS

This book is printed on acid-free paper.

4 5 6 7 8 9 0 DOW/DOW 9 0 9

ISBN 0-07-011944-9

Publisher: *Craig Beytien*
Senior sponsoring editor: *John E. Biernat*
Developmental editor: *Maryellen Krammer*
Marketing manager: *Ellen Cleary*
Project manager: *Pat Frederickson*
Production supervisor: *Michael R. McCormick*
Designer: *Larry J. Cope*
Cover art: *Paul Klee.* A Sportive Lady, 1938. *Private collection, Milan, Italy. Eric Lessing/Art Resource, NY*
Photo research coordinator: *Sharon Miller*
Compositor: *GAC/Shepard Poorman*
Typeface: *10/12 Melior*
Printer: *R. R. Donnelley & Sons Company*

Library of Congress Cataloging-in-Publication Data

Cascio, Wayne F.
Managing human resources : productivity, quality of work life, profits / Wayne F. Cascio. — 5th ed., International ed.
p. cm.
Includes index.
ISBN 0-07-011944-9
1. Personnel management I. Title.
HF5549.C2975 1998
658.3—dc21 97-30865

INTERNATIONAL EDITION

When ordering the title, use ISBN 0-07-115224-5.

http://www.mhhe.com

TO MY SON, JOE,

the choicest blessing life has provided;
constant reminder of what really counts.

About the Author

WAYNE F. CASCIO earned his B.A. degree from Holy Cross College in 1968, his M.A. degree from Emory University in 1969, and his Ph.D. in industrial/organizational psychology from the University of Rochester in 1973. Since that time he has taught at Florida International University, the University of California–Berkeley, and the University of Colorado–Denver, where he is at present Professor of Management.

Professor Cascio is past president of both the Human Resources Division of the Academy of Management and the Society for Industrial and Organizational Psychology. He is a Fellow of the American Psychological Association and a Diplomate in industrial/organizational psychology of the American Board of Professional Psychology. His editorial board memberships have included the *Journal of Applied Psychology, Academy of Management Review, Journal of Management, International Journal of Selection and Assessment, Human Performance, Organizational Dynamics,* and *Asia-Pacific Journal of Human Resources.* He has consulted on six continents with a wide variety of organizations in both the public and private sectors on HR matters, and periodically he testifies as an expert witness in employment discrimination cases. Professor Cascio is an active researcher and is the author or editor of five books on human resource management.

CONTENTS IN BRIEF

CONTENTS

Part Six SUPPORT, EVALUATION, AND INTERNATIONAL IMPLICATIONS 563

Chapter 14 SAFETY, HEALTH, AND EMPLOYEE ASSISTANCE PROGRAMS 564

BOXES AND SPECIAL FEATURES

PREFACE

This book was not written for aspiring human resource management (HRM) specialists. It was written for the student of general management whose job inevitably will involve responsibility for managing people, along with other organizational assets. A fundamental assumption, then, is that all managers are accountable to their organizations in terms of the impact of their HRM activities, and they are expected to add value by managing their people effectively. They also are accountable to their peers and to their subordinates in terms of the quality of work life they are providing.

As a unifying theme for the text, I have tried to link the content of each chapter to three key outcome variables—productivity, quality of work life, and profits. This relationship should strengthen the student's perception of HRM as an important function affecting individuals, organizations, and society.

Each chapter incorporates the following distinguishing features:

- In keeping with the general management orientation of the book, each chapter opens with "Questions This Chapter Will Help Managers Answer." This section provides a broad outline of the topics to be covered in the chapter.
- Following the chapter opener is a split-sequential vignette, often from the popular press, that illustrates "Human Resource Management in Action." Events in the vignette are designed to sensitize the reader to the subject matter of the chapter. The events lead to a climax, but then the vignette stops—like a two-part television drama. The reader is asked to predict what will happen next and to anticipate the impact of alternative courses of action.
- Then the text for the chapter appears, replete with concepts, research findings, court decisions, company examples, and international comparisons.
- Within each chapter is an "Ethical Dilemma." The purpose of this feature is to identify issues relevant to the topic under discussion where different courses of action may be desirable and possible. The student must choose a course of action and defend the reason for doing so.
- As in the fourth edition, "Implications for Management Practice" provides insights into the ways in which the issues presented in the chapter affect the decisions that managers must make. "Impact" boxes in each chapter reinforce the link between the chapter content and the strategic objectives—

productivity, quality of work life, and the bottom line—that influence all HR functions.
- Near the end of the chapter, the vignette introduced at the outset is continued, allowing the reader to compare his or her predictions with what actually happened.

Ultimately, the aim of each chapter is to teach prospective managers to *make decisions* based on accurate diagnoses of situations that involve people—in both domestic and global contexts. Students' ability to do this is enhanced by familiarity with theory, research, and practice. The numerous real-world applications of concepts allow the student to learn from the experience of others, and the dynamic design of the chapter allows the student to move back and forth from concept to evidence to practice—then back to evaluating concepts—in a continuous learning loop.

What's New in the Fifth Edition?

HRM texts have sometimes been criticized for overemphasizing the HR practices of large businesses. There is often scant advice for the manager of a small business who "wears many hats" and whose capital resources are limited. To address this issue explicitly, I have made a conscious effort to provide examples of effective HRM practices in small businesses in almost every chapter.

This was no cosmetic revision. I examined every topic and every example, in each chapter, for its continued relevance and appropriateness. I added dozens of new company examples, updated legal requirements in each area, and cited new findings from research in every chapter. Fully one-third of the references are new since the previous edition of the book. As in the previous editions, I have tried to make the text readable, neither too simplistic nor too complex.

Many instructors commented that it is difficult to cover 18 chapters in the course of a one-semester course; they also asked for cases and exercises to be included in the text. In response, I collapsed 18 chapters into 16 and added a case or exercise at the end of each chapter. In addition, each of the six major parts of the text ends with a full-length article from *Business Week*, together with a set of discussion questions to complement the article. New to this edition is a glossary at the back of the book to help the student locate definitions of important terms quickly.

A final issue concerns the treatment of international issues. While there are merits to including a separate chapter on this topic, as well as interspersing international content in each chapter, I do not see this as an either-or matter. I have done both, recognizing the need to frame domestic HR issues in a global context (e.g., staffing, compensation, labor-management relations), as well as to treat international HR issues (e.g., cultural differences, selection, training, and compensation of expatriates) in more depth in a separate chapter.

New Topics in the Fifth Edition

- People as a source of competitive advantage, new forms of organization (modular, virtual) to leverage the impact of people in the contexts of strategic HRM and global competition (Chapter 1).

- Latest court rulings on affirmative action, age discrimination, sexual harassment, drug and alcohol testing, the Americans with Disabilities Act, and the Family and Medical Leave Act (Chapter 2).
- The business-related reasons why managers should pay attention to managing diversity effectively, the linkage between managing diversity and HR strategy, and practices at leading companies, such as Xerox, Pacific Bell, J.C. Penney, Banker's Trust, Ford, and Levi Strauss & Company, which illustrate how to capitalize on diversity in age, gender, ethnicity, and sexual orientation (Chapter 3).
- The challenges of analyzing jobs and work as firms move from a task-based to a process-based organization of work; in addition, the special problems of succession planning in small businesses, to illustrate the role of HR planning in firms of all sizes (Chapter 4).
- Managing recruiting in the information age, enhanced discussion of job search strategies (i.e., how to find a job), and company examples that show how companies and job applicants are using the Internet to advertise, learn about, and apply for open jobs (Chapter 5).
- The impact of strategy and organizational culture on staffing decisions, as well as revised discussions of all screening and selection methods (Chapter 6).
- Company examples that show how Intel redeploys people displaced as a result of new technology and Marriott's approach to new-employee orientation, and an "International Application" on German apprenticeship programs (Chapter 7).
- The performance management process; development of a simple, workable approach to use in practice; and a discussion of the pros and cons of using multirater or 360-degree feedback (Chapter 8).
- Major emphasis on self-reliance as the key to career management for the twenty-first century, restructuring and the demise of corporate loyalty, plus bottom-line benefits for family-friendly companies (Chapter 9).
- How small businesses cope with tight labor markets; Liberty Mutual's use of a Windows-based decision-support system to guide pay decisions; team-based performance incentives at XEL; and premium stock options at Monsanto (Chapter 10).
- The Health Insurance Portability and Accountability Act of 1997, health-care cost-containment strategies, how Coca-Cola controls the cost of workers' compensation, retirement benefits and small business, and alternative proposals to save Social Security (Chapter 11).
- The changing nature of industrial relations in the United States, the 1997 changes to Australian labor law, seniority and the Americans with Disabilities Act, and new models of labor-management cooperation (Chapter 12).
- New chapter opener on alternative dispute resolution, as well as updated treatment of employment-at-will, employment contracts, and whistle-blowing (Chapter 13).
- Unsafe conditions at foreign sweatshops that make high-fashion clothes for U.S. consumers, plus updated treatments of AIDS and business, violence at work, EAPs, and wellness programs—e.g., how Johnson & Johnson and Quaker Oats reach high-risk employees (Chapter 14).
- Firm-level assessments of the effectiveness of HR systems and the financial impact of high-performance work practices (Chapter 15).

- Differences between international and domestic HR, Asea Brown Boveri's "global paradox"—at once international and local—the balance-sheet approach to international compensation, the pros and cons of working for a foreign-owned company in the United States, and the ethics of using bribery to win business (Chapter 16).

Help for Instructors

Several important supplements are available to help you use this book more effectively:

- **Instructor's Manual/Test Bank** (prepared by Glenn McEvoy, Utah State University). The comprehensive instructor's manual includes suggested course outlines for both 10- and 16-week terms, chapter outlines (in transparency master form), answers to "Challenge" questions that follow the chapter opening vignette, answers to end-of-chapter discussion questions, and comments on end-of-chapter cases and exercises. The test bank contains true-false, multiple-choice, fill-in-the-blank, and short-answer questions for each chapter. Approximately 1200 questions are included. Each question is classified according to level of difficulty and includes a text page reference.
- **Computerized Testing Software.** The most recent version of Irwin/McGraw-Hill's test-generation software, this program includes advanced features that allow the instructor to add and edit questions on-line, save and reload tests, create up to 99 versions of each test, attach graphics to questions, import and export ASCII files, and select questions on the basis of type, level of difficulty, or key word. The program allows password protection of saved test and question databases and is networkable.
- **PowerPoint Presentation Software.** New to this edition are PowerPoint slides (prepared by Rhonda Carlson). The software contains tables and figures from the text, plus additional graphic material. A self-contained viewer is packaged with each disk so that those who do not have the PowerPoint software can easily view the presentation.
- **Color Acetates** (prepared by Rhonda Carlson). Approximately 50 color transparencies are available, consisting of reproductions of key exhibits from the text as well as other graphic material.

Organization and Plan of the Book

The chart on the inside of the front cover provides an organizing framework for the book. The organization of the parts is designed to reflect the fact that HRM is an integrated, goal-directed set of managerial functions, not just a collection of techniques.

The text is based on the premise that three critical strategic objectives guide all HR functions: productivity, quality of work life, and profits. The functions (employment; development; compensation; labor-management accommodation; and support, evaluation, and international implications) in turn are carried out in the context of multiple environments: competitive, social, legal, and organizational.

Part 1, "Environment," includes Chapters 1 through 3. It provides the backdrop against which students will explore the nature and content of each HRM function. These first three chapters paint a broad picture of the competitive, social, legal, and organizational environments of HR. They also describe key economic and noneconomic factors that affect productivity, quality of work life, and profits. The remaining five parts (13 chapters) in the book are presented in the context of this conceptual framework.

Logically, "Employment" (Part 2) is the first step in the HRM process. Analyzing work, planning for people, recruiting, and staffing are key components of the employment process. Once employees are on board, the process of "Development" (Part 3) begins, with workplace training, performance management, and career management activities.

Parts 4, 5, and 6 present concurrent processes. That is, "Compensation" (Part 4), "Labor-Management Accommodation" (Part 5), and "Support, Evaluation, and International Implications" (Part 6) are all closely intertwined, conceptually and in practice. They represent a network of interacting activities, such that a change in one of them (e.g., a new pay system or collective bargaining contract) inevitably will have an impact on all other components of the HRM system. It is only for ease of exposition that they are considered separately in Parts 4, 5, and 6.

In teaching HRM courses at both graduate and undergraduate levels, I use this conceptual framework as a road map throughout the course. I believe that it is important for students to grasp the big picture, as well as to understand how the topics in question fit into the broader scheme of HRM functions. I have found that referring to the framework frequently throughout the course, to show students where we have been and where we are going, helps them adopt a more systematic, strategic perspective in addressing any given HRM issue.

Acknowledgments

Many people played important roles in the development of this edition of the book, and I am deeply grateful to them. Ultimately, of course, any errors of omission or commission are mine, and I bear responsibility for them.

Three people at Irwin/McGraw-Hill were especially helpful. Senior Sponsoring Editor John Biernat and Developmental Editor Maryellen Krammer provided continual advice, support, and encouragement. Project Manager Pat Frederickson was ever vigilant to ensure that all phases of the book's production stayed on schedule. All three were a pleasure to work with. Finally, the many reviewers of various portions of the fifth edition provided important insights that helped improve the final product. They deserve special thanks: Stephen P. Schappe, Pennsylvania State University–Harrisburg; James C. Wimbush, Indiana University; Nancy E. Day, University of Missouri–Kansas City; Satish P. Deshpande, Western Michigan University; Gary Pieroni, California State University–Hayward; and Kenneth A. Kovach, George Mason University. I would also like to acknowledge reviewers of previous editions whose guidance and feedback have helped make this text what it is today: Richard Alpert, Esq., Employment Discrimination Specialist; Christy L. DeVader, Loyola College in Maryland; Diane Dodd-McCue, University of Virginia; Jeremy Fox, Appalachian State University; David A. Gray, University of Texas at Arlington; W. Roy Johnson, Iowa State University; Allen I. Kraut, Baruch College; Glenn M. McEvoy, Utah State University; Carolyn Wiley, University of Tennessee at Chattanooga; and Kevin C. Wooten, University of Houston–Clear Lake.

Wayne F. Cascio

PART 1

ENVIRONMENT

An essential part of managing people effectively in today's world of work is understanding and appreciating the significant competitive, legal, and social issues. The purpose of Chapters 1, 2, and 3 is to provide insight into these issues. They provide both direction for and perspective on the management of human resources in the late 1990s.

1 HUMAN RESOURCES IN A GLOBALLY COMPETITIVE BUSINESS ENVIRONMENT

Questions This Chapter Will Help Managers Answer

1. Given the changes in workforce demographics, what can our firm do to be a beneficiary, rather than a victim, of these changes?
2. What people-related problems are likely to arise as a result of changes in the forms of organizations? How can we avoid these problems?
3. How are the various factors of production affected by global competition? Do we manage people any differently in a globally competitive environment?
4. How might the productivity of the workforce be affected by changes in the quality of work life?
5. From a strategic perspective, how can senior management make the best use of the human resource (HR) function?

*PARADIGMS FOR POSTMODERN MANAGERS**

Human Resource Management in Action

If we don't change our direction, we might end up where we're headed.
Ancient Chinese proverb

The modern corporation is a thing of the past. The twentieth-century enterprise was defined by Alfred P. Sloan, the legendary chairman of General Motors Corporation and the most influential professional manager of our time. His classic work, *My Years with General Motors,* set forth a management philosophy that has dominated U.S. corporations for decades. Company success, he argued, was based on efficiency and economies of scale—he never once mentioned the word "creativity" or "flexibility." Large, efficient organizations, he theorized, must decentralize manufacturing while centralizing corporate policy and financial controls in hierarchical structures.

For decades, that model remained intact—even as managers challenged, debated, and refined it. Today, so many management gurus and corporate executives have abandoned Sloan's tenets that they are increasingly speaking of a "paradigm shift" in management thought—a dramatic change in the way we think about business problems and organizations.

Key Values. This new paradigm values teamwork over individualism, seeks global markets over domestic ones, and focuses on customers rather than on short-term profits. It views time, rather than a single minded focus on costs, as the key competitive advantage. It recognizes the value of a multicultural workforce in an increasingly diverse labor pool and customer base. The new form of organization is based on a network of alliances and partnerships, not on Sloan's self-sufficient hierarchy. It is governed by an independent board with a broad view of the company's constituents—not just shareholders, but also employees, suppliers, customers, and the local community. A synopsis of these and other changes is presented in Table 1-1.

If GM once defined the shape of the old model, no existing organization serves as the prototype of this twenty-first-century corporation. And no company is likely to assume the ideal shape, because the successful company of the future will be an adaptive one in which change replaces stability as a key trait. What is right today is not likely to be right tomorrow or the next day. Says a senior consultant, "There's an awareness that the re-invention of the corporation is going to go on forever. That's a new feeling. Not long ago, executives thought this thing called change was an event."

If no one corporation does it all, certain innovators have come up with exceptionally effective approaches to managing some aspects of change. These are the strategies that will help their practitioners thrive in the global economy of the twenty-first century. In the case conclusion at the end of the chapter, we will see what some of these strategies look like.

*Adapted from: Paradigms for postmodern managers, *Business Week*, 1992 Bonus Issue (Nov. 30), "Reinventing America," pp. 69 ff. Reprinted from November 30, 1992, issue of *Business Week* by special permission, copyright ©1992 by McGraw-Hill, Inc.

Table 1-1

REINVENTING THE CORPORATION

What shape will the twenty-first-century corporation take? How will its culture and the way it competes differ from today's model? Here are a dozen characteristics common to most organizations and the ways in which many theorists and management experts expect the characteristics to change.

Current model		Twenty-first-century prototype
Hierarchy	ORGANIZATION	Network
Self-sufficiency	STRUCTURE	Interdependencies
Security	WORKER EXPECTATIONS	Personal growth
Homogeneous	WORKFORCE	Culturally diverse
By individuals	WORK	By teams
Domestic	MARKETS	Global
Cost	COMPETITIVE ADVANTAGE	Time
Profits	FOCUS	Customers
Capital	RESOURCES	Information
Board of directors	GOVERNANCE	Varied constituents
Affordability	QUALITY	No compromises
Autocratic	LEADERSHIP	Inspirational

Challenges

1. In Table 1-1, which dimensions of the twenty-first-century prototype model require effective skills in managing people?
2. If change is an ongoing process rather than a one-time event, what must managers and employees do to deal effectively with change?
3. If the twenty-first-century prototype model of organizations is to be successful, how must companies change their approaches to managing people?

THE ENTERPRISE IS THE PEOPLE

Organizations are managed and staffed by people. Without people, organizations cannot exist. Indeed, the challenge, the opportunity, and also the frustration of creating and managing organizations frequently stem from the people-related problems that arise within them. People-related problems, in turn, frequently stem from the mistaken belief that people are all alike, that they can be treated identically. Nothing could be further from the truth. Like snowflakes, no two people are exactly alike, and everyone differs physically and psychologically from everyone else. Sitting in a sports arena, for example, will be tall people, small people, fat people, thin people, people of color, white people, elderly people, young people, and so on. Even within any single physical category there will be enormous variability in psychological characteristics. Some will be outgoing, others reserved; some will be intelligent, others not so intelligent; some will prefer indoor activities, others outdoor activities. The point is that these differences demand attention so that each person can maximize his or her potential, so that organizations can maximize their effectiveness, and so that society as a whole can make the wisest use of its human resources.

Some managers place greater emphasis than do others on developing employees' potential. For example, Mr. Konosuke Matsushita, founder of the giant electronics firm that bears his name and markets its products under the brand names National, Panasonic, Technics, and Quasar, was a lifelong believer in the notion that "the enterprise is the people." Here is a brief excerpt from his written philosophy of management as stated in the 1950s:

> When my company was still small I often told my employees that when customers asked, "What does your company make?" they should answer, "Matsushita Electric is making men. We also make electrical appliances, but first and foremost our company makes men."[1]

This book is about managing people, the most vital of all resources, in work settings. Rather than focus exclusively on issues of concern to the human resource specialist, however, we will examine human resource management (HRM) issues in terms of their impact on management in general. A changing world order has forced us to take a hard look at the ways we manage people. Research has shown time and again that HRM practices can make an important, practical difference in terms of three key organizational outcomes: productivity, quality of work life, and profit. This is healthy. Each chapter in this book considers the impact of a different aspect of human resource management on these three broad themes. To study these impacts, we will look at the latest theory and research in each topical area, plus examples of actual company practices.

In this chapter we will examine some general issues related to productivity and quality of work life. In subsequent chapters we will focus on the relationship between competent human resource (HR) practices and profits. Let's begin by considering some basic ideas about organizations.

ORGANIZATIONS: WHY DO THEY EXIST AND HOW DO THEY WORK?

As our wants and needs grow, so do the ways of satisfying them. Consider the growth of the home-computer industry, for example, and how the firms within it are racing to deliver software—games, puzzles, educational exercises—to meet consumer demands for such products. None of our wants and needs is satisfied randomly or haphazardly. When you go to a store that sells computers, for example, the store will be open, and you will be able to buy the product of your choice even though the salesperson who helped you last time has the day off. In the process of satisfying needs and wants, continuity and predictability are essential in the delivery of goods and services. In modern society, continuity and predictability are made possible by organizations.

A traditional office workplace of the 1950s.

Some of the organizations that accommodate our wants and needs are fast-food restaurants, movie theaters, sporting goods stores, hospitals, universities, accounting firms, and antique stores, to name just a few. Each of these organizations exists because consumers demand its products or services, and because what must be done, the task to be accomplished, is too large or complex for one person to accomplish alone. So a number of people are brought together, and each is assigned a part of the total task. It is most efficient to divide a large task (such as building a house) into its component parts so that specially qualified individuals can perform the subfunctions. Specialization by subfunction and coordination among all the tasks to be accomplished make the largest-scale task possible.

Although there are great differences among the organizations in our society, they also have much in common. Every organization is (1) made up of people (2) who perform specialized tasks (3) that are coordinated (4) to enhance the value or utility (5) of some good or service (6) that is wanted by and provided to a set of customers or clients.

The Traditional Approach to Organizing

In the simplest terms, a formal organization exists by virtue of two factors: the work it does and the technology it embraces to do that work. However, these are not the only elements of a formal organization. The key elements of a formal organization, in the traditional view, are related as follows (Figure 1-1): All organizations have objectives (e.g., to provide high-quality goods and services at competitive prices) that are based on some perceived unfulfilled demand in the outside environment. Attaining these objectives requires that certain tasks be done (e.g., processing canceled checks, assembling parts of an appliance, checking a patient's vital signs). Indeed, formal organizations are defined by the kind of work they do. Technology determines the nature of the work processes since it includes all the aspects of knowledge that are related to the attainment of a firm's objectives (e.g., employee skills, machines, and facilities). Organizational structure supports and facilitates technology by designing jobs and grouping tasks in order to optimize control, coordination, and productivity. This, for example, is why some firms organize by function—production, marketing, sales, and distri-

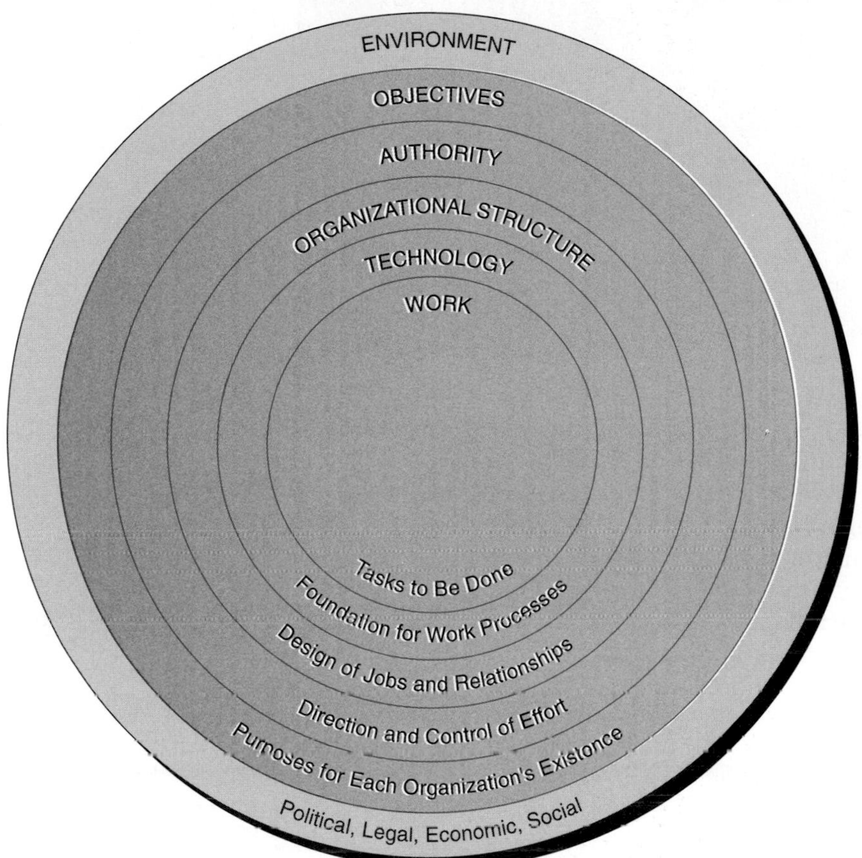

Figure 1-1
Key elements of formal organization, from specific to general.

bution. To attain the benefits of specialization and efficiency, they use authority to ensure adequate role performance and direction of efforts. Some workers are bosses (in whom authority is formally vested by the organization), while others are subordinates. Today, these key elements are being redefined.

New Forms of Organization

In today's world of fast-moving global markets and fierce competition, the windows of opportunity are often frustratingly brief.[2] "Three-C" (i.e., command, control, compartmentalization) logic dominated industrial society's approach to organizational design throughout the nineteenth and twentieth centuries, but trends such as the following are accelerating the shift toward new forms of organization for the twenty-first:[3]

- Smaller companies that employ fewer people
- The shift from vertically integrated hierarchies to networks of specialists
- Technicians, ranging from computer repair specialists to radiation therapists, replacing manufacturing operatives as the worker elite

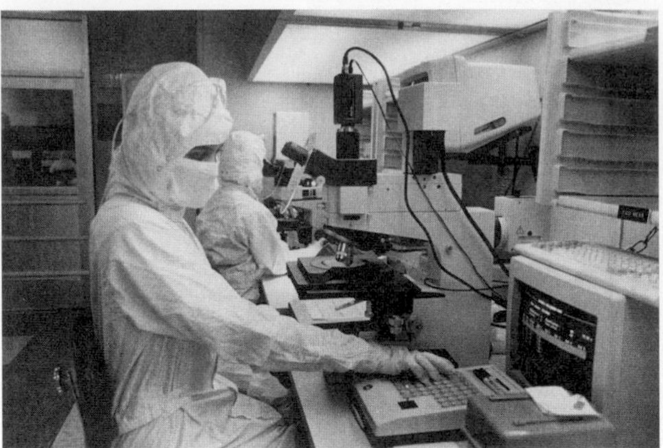

In many modern organizations, technicians are the worker elite.

- Pay tied less to a person's position or tenure in an organization and more to the market value of his or her skills
- A change in the paradigm of doing business from making a product to providing a service, often by part-time or temporary employees
- Outsourcing of activities that are not core competencies of a firm (e.g., payroll)
- The redefinition of work itself: constant learning, more higher-order thinking, less nine-to-five mentality

One example of a new organizational form that is evolving from these changes is the *virtual corporation,* where teams of specialists come together to work on a project—as in the movie industry—and disband when the project is finished. Virtual corporations are already quite popular in consulting, in legal defense, and in sponsored research. More common in the information age, however, is the *virtual workplace*—work anytime, anywhere—in real space or in cyberspace. The widespread availability of e-mail, teleconferencing, faxes, and intranets (within-company information networks) facilitates such arrangements. Compelling business reasons drive their implementation. Consider the benefits to companies and their employees:[4]

- Hewlett-Packard doubled its revenue per salesperson. Even though employees put in more hours, they still have more time available at home, and job satisfaction is up.
- Andersen Consulting found that it could manage its growth and its overhead for a staff that spent little time in the office: entry-level consultants (10–15%), managers (35%), and partners (70% or more). Today the only people with offices are the equity partners and staff. Others reserve space in the company's business center by accessing a custom-developed software program that allows for reservations in 2-hour blocks of time.
- A similar approach among IBM's 20,000 mobile employees has reduced real estate costs by 40 to 60 percent per site, for an annual savings of $35 million. Meanwhile, productivity is up 15 percent, and both customer satisfaction and employee satisfaction have improved.

A third example of a new organizational form is the *modular corporation*—that's right, modular. The basic idea is to focus on a few core competencies—those a company does best, such as designing and marketing computers or copiers—and to outsource everything else to a network of suppliers.[5] If design and marketing are core competencies, then manufacturing or service units are modular components. They can be added or taken away with the flexibility of switching parts in a child's Lego set.

Does the modular corporation work? As an example, consider Dell Computer.

COMPANY EXAMPLE

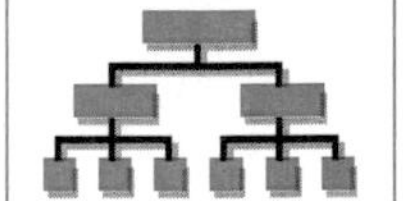

DELL COMPUTER—THE MODULAR CORPORATION IN ACTION

Dell prospers by concentrating on only two aspects of the business: marketing and service. Says CEO Michael Dell, "We can grow at a rapid rate by focusing on our core business." Grow it has, at twice the rate of the personal-computer industry in 6 of the last 7 years, and from $3.4 billion in sales in fiscal 1995 to over $7 billion in fiscal 1996.[6]

Instead of spending heavily on plants, Dell lavishes money on training salespeople and service technicians and on furnishing them with the best computers, databases, and software. Those investments generate terrific returns. Dell sells IBM-compatible personal computers (PCs) in competition with Compaq, Digital, and IBM. But while others rely primarily on computer stores or dealers, Dell sells directly to consumers, who read about the products in newspaper ads or catalogues. Buyers call a toll-free number and place their orders with a staff of 1300 well-trained salespeople.

Dell assembles a machine only after a customer has ordered one. Soon, for instance, Dell will cut out a step in the delivery of monitors made by other firms. Instead of going to a Dell distribution center, the monitors will be shipped from a supplier's factory in Mexico at the same time that a finished computer leaves Dell's factory in Texas, meeting for the first time in a delivery van just before reaching the customer.[7] By eliminating intermediaries—and the retailer's typical 13 percent markup—Dell can charge lower prices than its rivals.[8]

Modular companies are flourishing in two industries that sell trendy products in a fast-changing marketplace: apparel (Nike and Reebok are modular pioneers) and electronics. Such companies work best when they accomplish two objectives: (1) collaborating smoothly with suppliers and (2) choosing the right specialty. Companies need to find loyal, reliable vendors they can trust with trade secrets, and they need the vision to identify what customers will want, not just what the company is technically good at.

Is this just a fad? Hardly. Such a streamlined structure fits today's tumultuous, fast-moving marketplace. According to the CEO of defense contractor and auto-parts producer Rockwell International: "Without a doubt—focusing on a core competency—and outsourcing the rest—is a major trend of the 1990s."[9] It is important to note that this trend has both advantages and disadvantages. The major advantage for companies is that by shifting work to suppliers and contractors, they can pay local market rates, rather than those of the industry they are in. The disadvantage is that by failing to invest in developing new skills among current workers, firms may lock themselves out of participating in future technologies and new industries.[10]

Organizations Need People, and People Need Organizations

Without people, organizations could not function. Even in highly automated plants, such as the one designed and built by Yamazaki (a large Japanese company that makes machine tools) to run smoothly using only 12 workers, people are still required to coordinate and control the plant's operations. Accounts payable departments, after slashing large numbers of workers, found that their computers, unlike people, could not spot a lot of errors and fraud.[11] Conversely, people need organizations so that they can satisfy their needs and wants, so that they can maintain their standard of living (by working in organizations), and so that modern society can continue to function.

These needs (organizations for people, people for organizations) will be ever more difficult to satisfy in the context of today's competitive business environment. That environment is defined by characteristics such as the following.

SOME KEY CHARACTERISTICS OF THE COMPETITIVE BUSINESS ENVIRONMENT

Demographic Changes and Increasing Cultural Diversity

In the last decade of the twentieth century, 88 percent of workforce growth in the United States will come from these groups: women, African Americans, and people of Hispanic or Asian origin, including immigrants. White men, meanwhile, account for most retirees and are leaving the workforce in record numbers. These trends are shown graphically in Figure 1-2.

Figure 1-2
The changing labor pool.

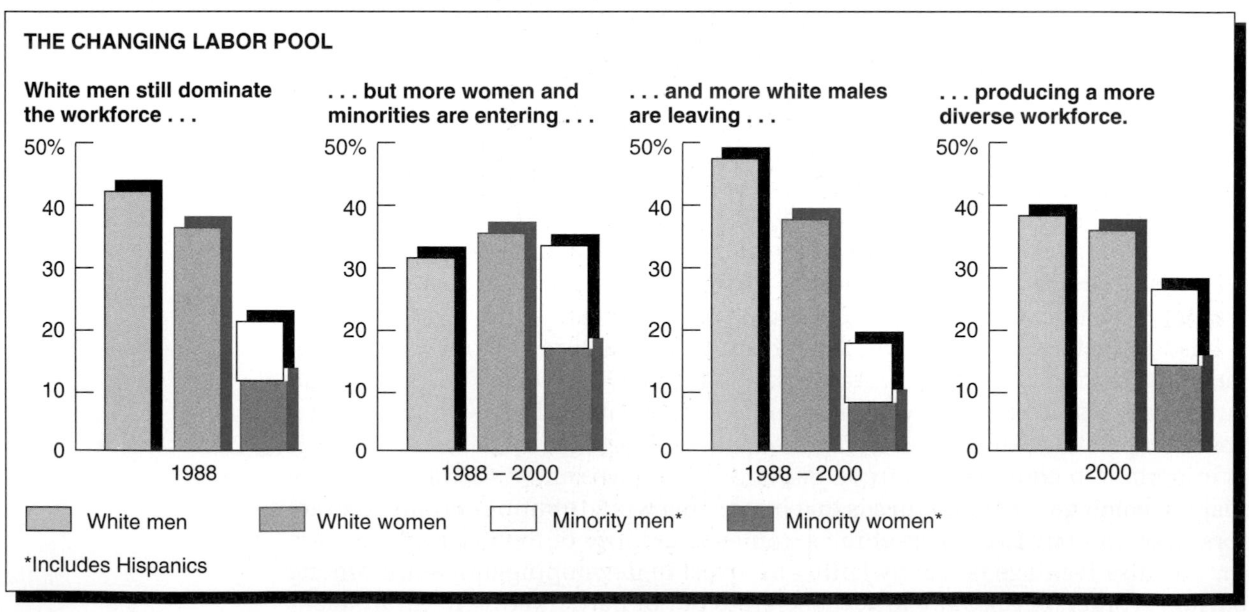

By 2005, the U.S. workforce will clearly be far older and more heterogeneous than ever before. Nearly half of all workers will be women, and more than a quarter will likely be members of minority races. About 40 percent of the workforce will be over 45 years of age—a dramatic jump from 31 percent in 1996—and only about 15 percent of new entrants will be the young, white males who once were the main engine of American commerce.[12]

These trends have two key implications for managers: (1) The reduced supply of entry-level workers will make finding and keeping employees a top priority in the decade ahead. Companies that once reluctantly accepted women and minorities into their ranks now find them indispensable.[13] (2) The task of managing a culturally diverse workforce, of harnessing the motivation and efforts of a wide variety of workers, will present managers with one of their biggest challenges throughout the rest of the 1990s and beyond.

The Skills Gap

The high level of change and the need for flexibility experienced in organizations around the world suggest that basic skills common to a wide range of jobs are important, and that a solid grounding in reading, writing, arithmetic, and communication skills will help graduates learn how to learn and how to adapt to changing demands in their jobs.[14]

Although in the last decade the overall education level of Americans has increased in terms of schooling and even fundamental literacy, so also have the demands of the workplace. As a group, high school graduates are simply not keeping pace with the kinds of skills required in the new economy, and U.S. firms are feeling these effects now. Scott Paper Company is typical. It spent $100,000 to search for workers for its new tissue-products plant in Owensboro, Kentucky. Managers screened 14,176 applicants to come up with 174 new hires. Of the 10,000 people who made it through the preliminary screening, 4000 failed a standardized English and high school algebra test. The rest went through 28 hours of testing.[15]

To deal with these problems, business is following two broad strategies. One of these is illustrated by the Boston Compact, an agreement in which 600 Boston-area companies joined with the public schools to form a compact that reserves jobs for high school graduates who meet academic and attendance requirements. Seven other cities followed Boston's example and now have similar compacts in existence.[16]

A second strategy is in-house training for current or prospective employees. Among firms of all sizes in the manufacturing sector, 75 percent provide formal training programs to their employees, and 99 percent provide informal (on-the-job) training. However, smaller establishments (20 to 49 employees) are much less likely than larger establishments (1000 employees or more) to provide some type of formal training program (60% versus 98%, respectively). Likewise, firms in the chemicals, petroleum products, and primary metals industries are more likely to provide formal training (88% of establishments) than are firms in the textile and apparel sector (61%).[19]

Although both of these strategies are expensive, the alternative—not having a competent workforce that will enable firms to compete in world markets—is unthinkable. For U.S. business, this is a "must win" situation. Our standard of living and our very way of life are at stake.

ETHICAL DILEMMA
Should Schools Teach Attitudes?[17]

Each chapter of this book contains a brief scenario that illustrates a decision-making situation that could result in a breach of acceptable behavior. Such situations pose ethical dilemmas. To be ethical is to conform to moral standards or to conform to the standards of conduct of a given profession or group (e.g., medicine, auditing). Ethical behavior is not governed by hard-and-fast rules; rather, it adapts and changes in response to social norms and in response to the needs and interests of those served by a profession (e.g., management). Ethical decisions about behavior take account not only of one's own interests but also, equally, the interests of those affected by a decision. What would you recommend in response to the following scenario?

A recent survey of small employers revealed that their top priority in seeking applicants was "a sense of responsibility, self-discipline, pride, teamwork, and enthusiasm." Dedication to work and discipline in work habits were the biggest deficits that employers saw in high school graduates who were applying for jobs. Another survey found that the most common reason for rejecting job applicants (other than a lack of prior work experience) was the belief that they did not have the work attitudes and behaviors to adapt successfully to the work environment. The most common reasons for firing new hires were absenteeism and failure to adapt to the work environment. Only 9 percent of workers were dismissed because of difficulties in learning how to perform their jobs.

In the opinion of many employers, the most significant deficit in new entrants to the workforce is in their attitudes, not their skills. Indeed, the influential SCANS report (Secretary's Commission on Achieving Necessary Skills)[18] identified a set of personal qualities (e.g., responsibility, sociability) that constitute one-third of the basic-skills foundation required for a quality workforce.

Should the schools teach values? Opponents object on philosophical grounds (government-induced paternalism), and they question which set of values should be taught. Proponents counter that characteristics such as consistency and prosocial behavior ("going the extra mile" for the good of the organization or for those in it) are of broad benefit to individuals and to society and do more than simply aid employers. What do you think?

Global Competition

As citizens of the twentieth century, we have witnessed more change in our daily existence and in our environment than anyone else who ever walked the planet. But if you think the pace of change was fast in this century, fasten your seat belts. The twenty-first century will be even more complex, fast-paced, and turbulent. It will also be very different.

Just as wars—two world wars, the Korean conflict, Vietnam, and Desert Storm—dominated the geopolitical map of the twentieth century, economics will rule the twenty-first. The competition that is normal and inevitable among nations increasingly will be played out not in aggression or war, but in the economic sphere. The weapons used will be those of commerce: growth rates, investments, trade blocs, imports and exports.[20]

What is behind all this change? Global competition—the single most powerful economic fact of life in the 1990s. In the relatively sheltered era of the 1960s, a mere 6 percent of the U.S. economy was exposed to international competition. In the 1980s, that number zoomed past 70 percent, and it will keep climbing. U.S. exports now generate one in six jobs; as recently as 1986, exports generated only one in eight.[21]

Global economic competition is a powerful economic fact of life.

To be sure, the fall of communism has accelerated the forces of global competition. As an ideology, communism began to unravel with the June 1989 elections in Poland—the first Communist state to evolve into a democracy. Subsequently, Communist regimes all across central and eastern Europe began to fall like dominoes.

The results of accelerated global competition have been almost beyond comprehension—free political debate throughout the former Soviet empire, democratic reforms in South and Central America, the integration of the European Community, peace pacts between Israel and its neighbors, the signing of the North American Free Trade Agreement, and an explosion of free-market entrepreneurship in southern China. In short, the free markets and free labor markets that we in the United States have enjoyed throughout our national history have now become a global passion.[22]

In fact, as nations around the world make the transition from wartime to peacetime economies, from industrial societies to information-based societies, we are witnessing profound, wrenching structural changes brought about by a number of factors. In the United States, two such factors are:

1. **Falling real wages.** As global competition has increased, corporations have been able to boost productivity using a combination of restructuring, downsizing, and investment in new technology. And while unemployment has fallen, all of these factors have combined to hold down wage growth. In fact, Americans have suffered a steady decline in their average income for nearly two decades. From 1989 to 1994, for example, average family income declined by 5.2 percent.[23] In short, in the 1990s, economic growth has been a spectator sport for most working Americans.

2. **Downsizing.** Downsizing, the planned elimination of positions or jobs, has had, and will continue to have, profound effects on organizations, managers at all levels, employees, labor markets, customers, and shareholders. These are just the direct effects. They do not address the effects on families and communities. In the United States, 43 million jobs were erased between 1979 and 1995, according to an analysis by *The New York Times* of U.S. Labor Department data.[24] While far more jobs were created than lost over that period, a net increase of 27 million, the real story lies in the types of jobs that are disappearing. Increasingly, it is the higher-paid, white-collar jobs, and, along with them, the careers of women and men, many of whom are in their peak earning years. According to the Labor Department, only about 35 percent of laid-off workers end up in equally remunerative or better-paying jobs. Indeed, the torrent of downsizing companies has produced fundamental, structural changes in our economy, and in the minds and hearts of the workforce that drives it. Consider just five statistics that characterize the revolution that is taking place:[25]
   - Nearly three-quarters of all U.S. households have had a close encounter with layoffs since 1980. In one-third of all households, a family member has lost a job, and nearly 40 percent more know a relative, a friend, or a neighbor who was laid off.
   - About 19 million people—1 in 10 adults—acknowledged that a lost job in their household had precipitated a major crisis in their lives.
   - While permanent layoffs have been symptomatic of most recessions, now they are occurring in the same large numbers even during an economic recovery that has lasted 5 years and even at companies that are doing well.[26]
   - In the 1990s, better-paid workers—those earning at least $50,000—account for twice the share of the lost jobs (12%) that they did in the 1980s (6%).
   - Roughly 50 percent more people—about 3 million—are affected by layoffs each year than the 2 million victims of violent crimes.

Perhaps the most disquieting result of downsizing is that our views of organizational life, managing as a career, hard work, rewards, and loyalty will never be the same.[27]

Impact and Effect of the Economic Changes

Studies show that, on average, workers who lose their jobs in downsizings earn about 10 percent less in their next jobs.[28] As a result, both their spending power and their standard of living have dropped. What is happening here? In a nutshell, as an executive in the pharmaceutical industry noted recently, we are moving from an economy in which there are a lot of hardworking people to one in which there are fewer smarter-working people.[29] Jobs are not being lost temporarily; rather, they are being wiped out permanently as a result of computerization, improved machinery, and new ways of organizing work.

Here's the problem: displaced workers must now reintegrate themselves into an economy that increasingly rewards only highly skilled labor. What has happened to the United States is not that people are a lot less educated than they were 20 years ago; it is that we live in a very different world. New technology, the pace of change, and global competition have "raised the bar"—that is, jobs require a higher level of skill.

While part of the problem of increasing productivity is on the supply side—the quality of the workforce—the more subtle story is on the demand side. Does downsizing work? While it may give a short-term boost to a firm's stock price, research on the 500 largest firms traded on the New York Stock Exchange (Standard & Poor's 500) over a 15-year period revealed that at the end of the year of downsizing and in the subsequent 2 years, companies that used a pure downsizing strategy were never better off than companies with stable employment in terms of profitability or total return on common stock. Firms that did best did so by growing their businesses, not by cutting workers.[30] To be sure, the shift from a cost-cutting to a revenue-growing strategy is not easy,[31] but in an age of global competition, it is just not possible for a firm to save its way into prosperity.

People as a Source of Competitive Advantage

As every advanced economy becomes global, a nation's most important competitive asset becomes the skills and cumulative learning of its workforce. Globalization, almost by definition, makes this true. Virtually all developed countries can design, produce, and distribute goods and services equally well and equally fast. Every factor of production other than workforce skills can be duplicated anywhere in the world. Capital moves freely across international boundaries, seeking the lowest costs. State-of-the-art factories can be erected anywhere. The latest technologies move from computers in one nation, up to satellites parked in space, and back down to computers in another nation—all at the speed of electronic impulses. It is all fungible—capital, technology, raw materials, information—all except for one thing, the most critical part, the one element that is unique about a nation or a company: its workforce. A workforce that is knowledgeable and skilled at doing complex things keeps a company competitive and attracts foreign investment.[32]

In fact, the relationship forms a virtuous circle: well-trained workers attract global corporations, which invest and give the workers good jobs; the good jobs, in turn, generate additional training and experience. We must face the fact that, regardless of the shifting political winds in Tokyo, Berlin, Washington, Beijing, or Budapest, the shrunken globe is here to stay. Today Tokyo is closer than the town 100 miles away was 30 years ago (after all, routine long-distance phone use did not begin until the 1970s).

And tomorrow? Our networks of suppliers, producers, distributors, service companies, and customers will be so tightly linked that we literally will not be able to tell one locale from another. No political force can stop, or even slow down for long, the borderless economy.[33] The lesson for managers is clear: be ready or be lost.

We noted at the beginning of this section that people make organizations go. How the people are selected, trained, and managed determines to a large extent how successful an organization will be. As you can certainly appreciate by now, the task of managing people in today's world of work is particularly challenging in light of the changes we have discussed. Indeed, one of the most pressing concerns that organizations face is productivity improvement.

PRODUCTIVITY: WHAT IS IT AND WHY IS IT IMPORTANT?

A popular buzzword in American industry today is "productivity." Although people talk about it as though they know precisely what it means, it is surprisingly difficult to define and measure, especially in highly diversified firms. As examples, consider a computer factory, where every year the products improve and the prices drop, or a hospital, where no one is even sure what output means. Even more perplexing, how does one identify the productivity improvement associated with outsourcing—that is, turning to outside service firms for work that ultimately raises output?[34] Theorists generally agree that productivity concepts, definitions, and measures are arbitrary. Their relevance depends on the purpose for which they are developed—for example, comparing individuals, work groups, companies, or the competitive positions of nations.[35]

In general, however, productivity is a measure of the output of goods and services relative to the input of labor, material, and equipment. The more productive an industry, the better its competitive position because its unit costs are lower. When productivity increases, businesses can pay higher wages without boosting inflation. That is the way standards of living improve.[36] Improving productivity simply means getting more out of what is put in. It does not mean increasing production through the addition of resources, such as time, money, materials, or people. It is doing better with what you have. Improving productivity is not working harder; it is working smarter. Today's world demands that we do more with less—fewer people, less money, less time, less space, and fewer resources in general. These ideas are shown graphically in Figure 1-3.

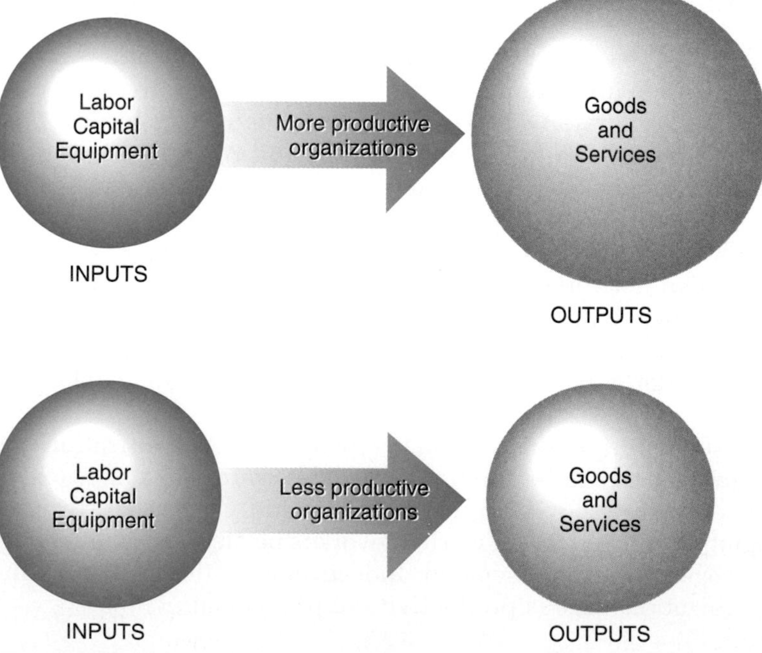

Figure 1-3
More productive organizations get more goods and services out of a given amount of labor, capital, and equipment than do less productive organizations.

COMPANY EXAMPLE

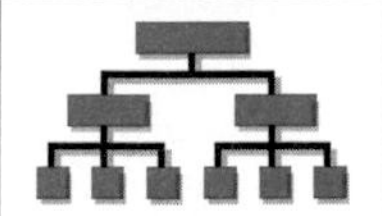

IMPROVING PRODUCTIVITY AT GTE CORPORATION[37]

Evidence from a wide range of industries shows that productivity gains are real and ongoing. Whether it is manufacturing semiconductors, offering banking services, or keeping track of medical records, U.S. companies are doing more with less. GTE Corporation's operations in Florida's Tampa-Sarasota region are more the rule than the exception. Over the past 5 years, the area's population and telephone system have grown by about 7 percent annually, yet GTE still employs the same number of service people, about 250. Laptops let repair crews plan their daily schedules efficiently and allow customers to get a more accurate time of arrival from the repair folks. The staff backing up these technicians has dropped from 45 to 11 as software-driven "expert" systems take customer requests and arrange them in the most efficient order. Indeed, one survey of nearly 400 companies found that the return on investment in information systems could exceed 50 percent.

PRODUCTIVITY IMPROVEMENT: LESSONS WE HAVE LEARNED

Among the hundreds of economists, think tanks, professors, politicians, and management consultants who ponder this issue full-time, there is a surprising convergence of views, regardless of their political persuasion. Most would agree that we need:

- Steps by the government to allow and encourage businesses to make capital investments and to be more flexible as a result of less government regulation.
- Steps by organizations to rebuild employee loyalty that has been eroded by downsizing, restructuring, and mergers. Firms like Xerox, Monsanto, and United Technologies are doing it by boosting training budgets for survivors and overhauling pay plans to give survivors a bigger stake in the company's success.[38]
- To make both unionized and nonunionized workers, as well as managers, aware that their rewards depend ultimately on production.
- Recognition that there is no "quick fix" approach. Worker training, work redesign, product reengineering—all must be linked to the priorities of the business plan and integrated into a comprehensive productivity-improvement strategy.
- Recognition of the crucial importance of continuous improvements in quality (an important aspect of productivity improvement) through prevention. Doing so requires a reshaping of attitudes from the boardroom to the loading dock, so that quality becomes more important than simply getting a product out the door.
- Public investment in highways, bridges, railways, and airports, which will raise productivity by reducing transportation delays and costs.

Former Labor Secretary Robert Reich described the challenge clearly: "If we have an adequately educated and trained workforce and a state-of-the-art infrastructure linking them together and with the rest of the world, then global capital will come here to create good jobs. If we don't, the only way global capital will be invested here is if we promise low wages."[39]

Is this just academic theory? Hardly. Well-trained trades workers who can adapt to change are a big attraction to the more than 200 German companies that have invested over $4 billion in North and South Carolina.[40] As we noted earlier, greater productivity benefits organizations directly (i.e., it improves their competitive position relative to that of rivals), and it benefits workers indirectly (e.g., in higher pay and improved purchasing power). But many workers want to see a tighter connection between working smarter and the tangible and psychological rewards they receive from doing their jobs well. They want to see significant improvements in their quality of work life.

QUALITY OF WORK LIFE: WHAT IS IT?

There are two ways of looking at what quality of work life (QWL) means.[41] One way equates QWL with a set of objective organizational conditions and practices (e.g., promotion-from-within policies, democratic supervision, employee involvement, safe working conditions). An example of this approach is shown in Figure 1-4. The other way equates QWL with employees' perceptions that

Figure 1-4
Quality of work life through quality relationships, as practiced by the Adolph Coors Company of Golden, Colorado.

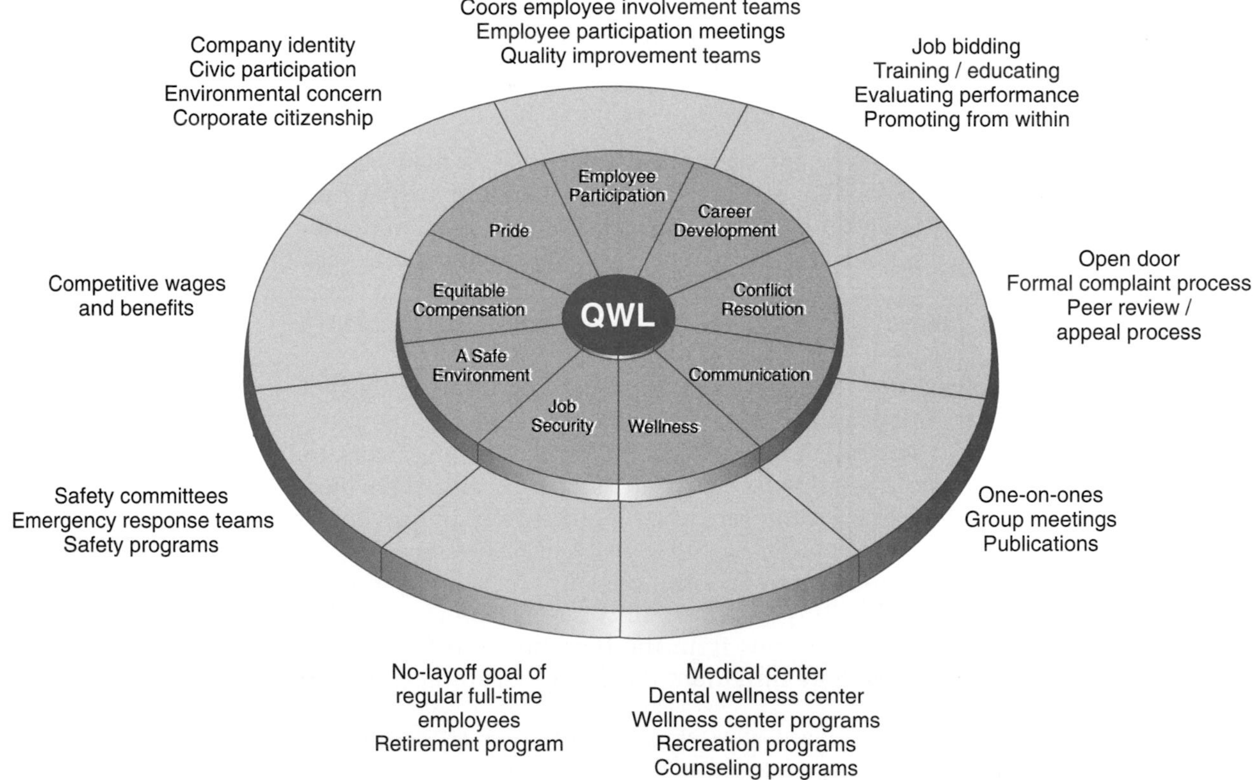

they are safe, relatively well satisfied, and able to grow and develop as human beings. This way relates QWL to the degree to which the full range of human needs is met.

In many cases these two views merge: workers who like their organizations and the ways their jobs are structured will feel that their work fulfills them. In such cases, either way of looking at one's quality of work life will lead to a common determination of whether a good QWL exists. However, because of the differences between people and because the second view is quite subjective—it concedes, for example, that not everyone finds such things as democratic decision making and self-managed work teams to be important components of a good QWL—we will define QWL in terms of employees' perceptions of their physical and mental well-being at work.

Current Status of QWL Efforts

In theory, QWL is simple—it involves giving workers the opportunity to make decisions about their jobs, the design of their workplaces, and what they need to make products or to deliver services most effectively. It requires managers to treat workers with dignity. Its focus is on employees and management operating the business together.

In practice, its best illustrations can be found in the auto, steel, food, electronics, and consumer products industries, in plants characterized by self-managing work teams, flat organizational structures, and challenging roles for all. It requires a willingness to share power, extensive training for workers and managers, and considerable patience by all involved. Workers must get to know the basics of cost, quality, profits, losses, and customer satisfaction by being exposed to more than a narrowly defined job—they must learn to think and act like businesspeople.[42] Managers must come to understand their new role: leaders, helpers, and information gatherers. None of this is simple or easily done, and it may take several years to become fully integrated into a business. Here are some other things that successful QWL efforts require:

- Managers must become leaders and coaches, not bosses and dictators.
- Openness and trust are necessary. QWL cannot be used as a tool to break unions or keep them out. It must remain separate from the collective bargaining contract. And it cannot be used by unions as a tool against management.
- Information typically held by management alone must be shared, and suggestions made by nonmanagers must be taken seriously.
- QWL must change continually and go forward from initial problem solving to an actual partnership between management and workers.[43]
- QWL cannot be mandated unilaterally by management.

Thus far we have been talking about improving productivity and quality, and the crucial role that people play in that process. The next section will describe more specifically the linkages between human resource strategies and general business strategies.

MANAGING PEOPLE: A CRITICAL ROLE FOR EVERY MANAGER

When it comes to managing people, all managers must be concerned to some degree with the following five activities: staffing, retention, development, adjustment, and managing change.

Staffing comprises the activities of (1) identifying work requirements within an organization, (2) determining the numbers of people and the skills mix necessary to do the work, and (3) recruiting, selecting, and promoting qualified candidates.

Retention comprises the activities of (1) rewarding employees for performing their jobs effectively, (2) ensuring harmonious working relations between employees and managers, and (3) maintaining a safe, healthy work environment.

Development is a function whose objective is to preserve and enhance employees' competence in their jobs through improving their knowledge, skills, abilities, and other characteristics; HR specialists use the term "competencies" to refer to these items.

Adjustment comprises activities intended to maintain compliance with the organization's HR policies (e.g., through discipline) and business strategies (e.g., cost leadership).

Managing change is an ongoing process whose objective is to enhance the ability of an organization to anticipate and respond to developments in its external and internal environments, and to enable employees at all levels to cope with the changes.

Needless to say, these activities can be carried out at the individual, work-team, or larger organizational unit (e.g., department) level. Sometimes they are initiated by the organization (e.g., recruitment efforts or management development programs), and sometimes they are initiated by the individual or work team (e.g., voluntary retirement, safety improvements). Whatever the case, the responsibilities for carrying out these activities are highly interrelated. Together, these activities constitute the HRM system. To understand how each of the major activities within HRM relates to every other one, consider the following scenario.

As a result of a large number of unexpected early retirements, the Hand Corporation finds that it must recruit extensively to fill the vacated jobs. The firm is well aware of the rapid changes that will be occurring in its business over the next 5 to 10 years, so it must change its recruiting strategy in accordance with the expected changes in job requirements. It also must develop selection procedures that will identify the kinds of competencies required of future employees. Compensation policies and procedures may have to change because job requirements will change, and new incentive systems will probably have to be developed. Since the firm cannot identify all the competencies that will be required 5 to 10 years from now, it will have to offer new training and development programs along the way to satisfy those needs. Assessment procedures will necessarily change as well, since different competencies will be required in order to function effectively at work. As a result of carrying out all this activity, the firm may need to discharge, promote, or transfer some employees to accomplish its mission, and it will have to provide mechanisms to enable all remaining employees to cope effectively with the changed environment.

It is surprising how that single event, an unexpectedly large number of early retirees, can change the whole ballgame. So it is with any system or network of interrelated components. Changes in any single part of the system have a reverberating effect on all other parts of the system. Simply knowing that this will occur is healthy, because then we will not make the mistake of confining our problems to only one part. We will recognize and expect that whether we are dealing with problems of staffing, training, compensation, or labor relations, all parts are interrelated. In short, the systems approach provides a conceptual framework for integrating the various components within the system and for linking the HRM system with larger organizational needs. Consider the practical example of two successful companies—FedEx and UPS—whose HRM systems differ dramatically.

COMPANY EXAMPLE

EMPLOYMENT SYSTEMS AND BUSINESS STRATEGIES AT FEDERAL EXPRESS (FedEx) AND UNITED PARCEL SERVICE (UPS)[44]

Explanations for what makes firms competitive are turning more frequently to the notion of "core competencies" that are unique to firms.[45] In this example, let us consider some unique competencies that differentiate services and, in turn, drive the competitiveness of the two firms in question.

Although both FedEx and UPS are in the shipping business, it is difficult to find two companies with people-management practices that are more different. FedEx has no union, and its workforce is managed using the latest HRM tools. For example, both individual and group performance are assessed, and both influence pay. The company has pay-for-suggestion systems, quality-of-work-life programs, and a variety of other arrangements that empower employees and increase their involvement. Employees at FedEx have played an important role in helping design the organization of work and the way technology has been used.

UPS, on the other hand, uses none of these HRM practices. Employees have no direct say over issues regarding how work is organized. Their jobs are designed by industrial engineers according to time-and-motion studies. The performance of each employee is measured and evaluated against company standards for each task, and employees receive daily feedback on their performance. The only effort at employee involvement is collective bargaining over contract terms through the Teamsters' Union, which represents drivers. Management, rather than the union, appears to be the force maintaining this system of work organization. It has shown little interest in moving toward work systems such as the kind used at FedEx.

The material rewards for working at UPS are substantial, and may more than offset the low levels of job enrichment and the tight supervision. The company pays the highest wages and benefits in the industry. It also offers employees gain-sharing and stock ownership plans. UPS is privately held and is owned by its employees. In contrast to FedEx, UPS fills virtually all promotions (98%) from within the company, offering entry-level drivers excellent long-term prospects for advancement.

As a result of these material rewards, UPS employees are highly motivated and loyal to the company, despite the 16-day strike in 1997. The productivity of UPS drivers, the most important work group in the delivery business, is about 3 times higher (measured by deliveries and packages) than productivity at FedEx.

Why does it make sense for UPS to rely on highly engineered systems that are generally thought to contribute to poor morale and motivation, but then to offset the negative effects with strong material rewards? FedEx, in contrast, offers an alternative model with high levels of morale and motivation and lower material rewards. Differences in technology do not explain it. FedEx is known for its pioneering investments in information systems, but UPS has responded recently with its own wave of computerized operations. Yet the basic organization of work at UPS has not changed.

In fact, the employment systems in these two companies are driven by their business strategies. FedEx is the smaller of the two, operating until recently with only one hub in Memphis and focusing on the overnight package delivery service as its platform product. UPS, in contrast, has a much wider range of products. While its overnight delivery volume is only 60 percent of FedEx's, its total business is 9 times as large (11.5 million deliveries per day at UPS versus 1.2 million at FedEx).

The scale and scope of business at UPS demand an extremely high level of coordination across its network of delivery hubs, coordination that is achievable only through a highly regimented and standardized approach to job design. Changes in practices and procedures essentially have to be systemwide to be effective. Such coordination is compatible with the systemwide process of collective bargaining but not with significant levels of autonomy of the kind associated with shop-floor decision making by employees.

FedEx, on the other hand, historically had only one hub, which meant that there were fewer coordination problems. This allowed considerable scope for autonomy and participation in shaping work decisions at the group level.

What is the lesson in this example? When it comes to managing people, there can be no single set of "best practices" for all employers. Firms that are in competition with one another work hard to differentiate their products and services and to find niches in markets where they are protected from competition. Differentiating products and services is one of the essential functions of strategic management. Distinctive human resource practices encourage differentiation by shaping the core competencies that determine how firms compete.

To some, the activities of staffing, retention, development, and adjustment are the special responsibilities of the HR department. But these responsibilities also lie within the core of every manager's job throughout any organization—and because line managers have authority (the organizationally granted right to influence the actions and behavior of the workers they manage), they have considerable impact on the ways workers actually behave. This implies two things: (1) a broad objective of HRM is to optimize the usefulness (i.e., the productivity) of all workers in an organization, and (2) a special objective of the HR department is to help line managers manage those workers more effectively. The HR department accomplishes this special objective through policy initiation and formulation, advice, service, and control in close communication and coordina-

Table 1-2

HRM ACTIVITIES AND THE RESPONSIBILITIES OF LINE MANAGERS AND THE HR DEPARTMENT

Activity	Line management responsibility	HR department responsibility
Staffing	Providing data for job analyses and minimum qualifications; integrating strategic plans with HR plans at the unit level (e.g., department, division); interviewing candidates, integrating information collected by the HR department, making final decisions on entry-level hires and promotions	Job analysis, human resource planning, recruitment; compliance with civil rights laws and regulations; application blanks, written tests, performance tests, interviews, background investigations, reference checks, physical examinations
Retention	Fair treatment of employees, open communication, face-to-face resolution of conflict, promotion of teamwork, respect for the dignity of each individual, pay increases based on merit	Compensation and benefits, employee relations, health and safety, employee services
Development	On-the-job training, job enrichment, coaching, applied motivational strategies, performance feedback to subordinates	Development of legally sound performance management systems, morale surveys, technical training; management and organizational development; career planning, counseling; HR research
Adjustment	Discipline, discharge, layoffs, transfers	Investigation of employee complaints, outplacement services, retirement counseling
Managing change	Provide a vision of where the company or unit is going and the resources to make the vision a reality	Provide expertise to facilitate the overall process of managing change

tion with line managers. To be sure, each of the responsibilities of HRM is shared by the HR department and the line managers, as shown in Table 1-2.

In the context of Table 1-2, note how line and HR managers share people-related business activities. Generally speaking, HR provides the technical expertise in each area, while line managers (or, in some cases, self-directed work teams) use this expertise in order to manage people effectively. In a small business, however, line managers are responsible for both the technical and managerial aspects of HRM. For example, in the area of retention, line managers are responsible for treating employees fairly, resolving conflicts, promoting teamwork, and providing pay increases based on merit. In order to do these things effectively, the HR department has the responsibility to devise a compensation and benefits system that employees will perceive as attractive and fair, to establish merit-increase guidelines that will apply across departments, and to provide training and consultation to line managers on all employee relations issues—such as conflict resolution and team building.

Using the HRM Function Strategically

Chief executive officers need HR executives who have a clear sense of strategic direction, know the services required by the business, and understand the initiatives the business should be taking toward organizational change.[46] In order to use the HRM function most effectively as a corporate resource, therefore, top management should consider doing the following:

1. Require that HR executives be experienced businesspeople, for example, through job rotation policies and by extensive interaction with managers in all other functional areas. Unless these executives are perceived as equals by their corporate peers, their ability to make significant contributions to the firm will be diminished.[47]
2. Require the senior HR executive to report directly to the CEO. At present this occurs in about 70 percent of companies nationwide. Consider whether any corporate resource is more important than its people. Suppose a fire destroyed all the plant and equipment of a 1000-employee firm; how long would it take to rebuild the plant and replace the equipment? A year? Now suppose the same firm lost all its employees; how long would it take to replace the same level of competence and commitment? Considerably longer. Indeed, is any management function more important than managing the people who constitute the organization? HR policy cannot have any real meaning unless the CEO is intimately involved in its development.
3. Ensure that the top HR officer is a key player in the development and implementation of business plans—providing early warning regarding their acceptance and serving as the CEO's "window" on the organization and as a sounding board.
4. Define the HR department's responsibility as the maximization of corporate profits through the better management and use of people. The key issues are time and money. Concentrate the HRM function on ways to make people more productive—especially on ways of improving the employees' job skills, improving their motivation by improving their quality of work life (QWL), and improving the professional skills of managers.
5. Do not dilute the HRM function by saddling the HR department with unrelated responsibilities, such as the mailroom and public relations. Consider moving productivity functions, such as industrial engineering, into the HR department. In today's climate of increased competition and cost control, there is simply no room for people who cannot have a significant impact on the firm's productivity and profitability. HR is no exception.[48]

Strategic Human Resource Management

In practical terms, strategic HRM means getting everybody from the top of the organization to the bottom doing things to implement the strategy of the business effectively. The idea is to use people most wisely with respect to the strategic needs of the organization. This does not just happen. An integrative framework that systematically links HR activities with strategic business needs can help. Consider one such approach, the "Human Resources Strategic Blueprint."[49]

The goal of this approach is to develop a map and a time line to ensure alignment between HR strategy and general business strategy. To make that happen, Megrez Corporation (a fictitious company) takes the following steps:

1. Representatives from HR and line managers from the business unit generate key business strategies for the coming year. To do so, they identify major external and internal factors that may have an impact on the future of the business, together with future customer requirements. The result? A business-unit annual plan that outlines
   - Major driving forces in the business unit.
   - Major business initiatives in the business unit.
   - Primary directions.
   - Major priorities for key executives of the business unit.
2. The HR manager at Megrez assembles a cross-functional team (e.g., a finance analyst, a staffing expert, a quality manager, an organization development consultant, and an operations training manager) whose members will be instrumental in leading the business unit toward its productivity goals.
3. Beginning with the business needs identified from the business-unit plan, the cross-functional team has the objective of identifying HR implications. For example, if the business objective is to increase production by 50 percent in 6 months, major implications for HR include the development of fully competent skill sets by all workers, additional staffing, and team development (i.e., better communication between production teams and design teams).
4. With the problem diagnosed (at Megrez, 80 percent of the manufacturing unit's managers have less than 18 months' tenure, and therefore are ill-prepared to increase productivity by 50 percent in 6 months), the cross-functional team brainstorms possible options to deal with the problem. These include (1) a training program for new managers on how to produce during peak periods; (2) on-the-job observations of managers to assess their weaknesses; (3) a mandatory mentoring program for all novice managers; and (4) the hiring of managers (either from internal or external sources) who have the requisite skills.
5. A designated team member returns to his or her own unit to research the feasibility of each option, then "makes the case" for the best option with the cross-functional team (in this case, the establishment of the mentoring program because it can be developed quickly).

6. HR presents the first draft of its blueprint to senior managers. They either agree or disagree on substance with each element of the blueprint. Where there is disagreement on substance, senior managers return these items to the cross-functional team for reconsideration or rework. Thus the blueprint emerges through multiple iterations with managers responsible for operations.
7. The critical element in the blueprint process is the assignment to individuals of responsibility for specific actions with target completion dates (e.g., in the areas of management development, employee development, staffing, and the drafting of new competency profiles for various grade levels of workers).
8. Every 6 months, the HR manager meets with the business-unit manager to consider two key questions: (1) how important is the strategy we are pursuing? and (2) how well are we executing that strategy? If business conditions have changed, then HR needs to adjust or redirect its priorities and change its blueprint. If conditions have not changed, then management assesses the extent to which strategies being pursued are aligned properly with business-unit objectives and if HR's delivery of services is complete and timely. HR receives a grade for delivery.
9. To provide an incentive for superior performance, business-unit management at Megrez (managers in marketing, operations, finance, product development, and manufacturing) rigorously assess HR's performance against its blueprint objectives. If HR meets its goals by year-end, all HR managers receive additional bonus compensation.

Managers who have used the strategic blueprint process emphasize that its single greatest benefit is this: *it forces HR managers to concentrate solely on critical, value-adding activities.* Such an approach is sorely needed, as a recent American Management survey of 1500 HR managers found. When asked how well HR strategy is linked to business results, 6 out of 10 respondents said it was either not effective or just somewhat effective. Only 3 percent characterized the linkage as "world class."[50]

Evaluating the HRM Function

It has been said many times that if HR people are to make meaningful contributions to an enterprise, they must think and act like businesspeople. To promote this sort of outlook, it is useful to ask "How much profit must a profit center make to keep an HR department going?"

Suppose you run an HR department for a firm that makes bicycles. Last year the total cost to the company for your department's services was $1 million. How many bikes does the company have to sell to pay your way? Let's say that on a $200 bicycle, your company makes a profit of $20. Dividing this $20 into $1 million shows that 50,000 bikes must be sold to keep the HR department in business.

The point of this exercise is not to argue for the abolition of HR departments in order to save profits or to save selling more bikes. Certainly, if the HR department was not doing its work, somebody else would be doing much of it. Rather, the point is that there is an important connection between human resource management and profits. It is seldom discussed, but it should be, in order to promote increased awareness of how time and money are spent. Imagine an HR director asking how many bikes will have to be sold to support a new orientation program.

A second important question that management should ask and that HR people should be prepared to answer is "How much more product can be sold because of your services?" While many HR contributions are not related directly to the bottom line, it is important to promote increased awareness of how HR activities relate to the purposes of the organization.[51] Here are some possible HR department responses in some key areas:

- "Here's what we did for you [in recruiting, say], here's what it cost, and here's what you would have done without us and what it would have cost you."
- "Here's how much money we saved you by changing insurers in our benefits package."
- "Here's an idea that workers developed in a training program we were leading. It's now working and saving you $50,000 per year."
- "If you had not asked us to do this executive search, you would have had to go outside, at a cost of $30,000. We did it for $5000."
- "You used to have an unhappy person doing this job for $40,000 per year. As a result of our work redesign, you now have a motivated person doing the same work for $20,000."
- "In working with the union on a new contract, we found a new way to reduce grievances by 30 percent, saving the company 6429 hours per year in management time."

Even though precise bottom-line numbers might be hard to come by for many HR activities, it is important to encourage HR people to think in these terms. This is just a brief glimpse into several areas where effective HRM can make a substantial contribution to the improvement of productivity, the quality of work life, and the bottom line. Although we have discussed each area separately, the overall objective is to develop a uniform financial reporting system for the entire HRM subsystem. Significant and timely information can be produced, both line managers and HR staff can see how their work is interconnected, and over time such a measurement system can become a very powerful tool.

Business Trends and HR Competencies

A 1996 study identified the following six trends as most critical for HRM to address over the next 10 years:[53]

- **Globalization** involves commerce without borders, interdependence of business operations internationally, and the necessity to use human knowledge to gain a competitive edge.
- **Technology** is vital because the need for information drives the expectation to perform anytime, anywhere.
- **Change** drives the need for continuous learning, may result in increased stress, calls for redefinition of careers, and provides opportunities for new products and services.

IMPACT OF EFFECTIVE HRM ON PRODUCTIVITY, QUALITY OF WORK LIFE, AND THE BOTTOM LINE

Employees are well aware that the U.S. workplace is in a state of turbulence. Many have been through multiple waves of downsizing, and they have seen careers and work lives jolted from stability to uncertainty. As a result, according to a recent survey, employees are less loyal to their companies, and they tend to put their own needs and interests above those of their employers. More often they are willing to trade off higher wages and benefits for flexibility and autonomy, job characteristics that allow them to balance their lives on and off the job. Almost 9 out of every 10 workers live with family members, and nearly half care for dependents, including children, elderly parents, or ailing spouses. Among employees who switched jobs in the last 5 years, pay and benefits rated in the bottom half of 20 possible reasons why they did so. Factors rated highest were "nature of work," "open communication," and "effect on personal/family life." What are the implications of these results for organizations that depend on workforces made docile by fear? When companies fail to factor in quality-of-work-life issues and quality-of-life issues when introducing any of the popular schemes for improving productivity, the only thing they may gain is a view of the backs of their best people leaving for friendlier employers.[52]

- **Knowledge capital,** i.e., valuing what people know, will result in the need to distinguish between technical and managerial competency.
- **Speed in market change** will result in the need to be in constant touch with customers and the need for more strategic partnering.
- **Cost control** means keeping business costs at the lowest possible level in order to be competitive.

The same study also identified emerging leadership competencies HR professionals will need to demonstrate 10 years from now:

- **Credibility.** In the mind of the beholder, the perception that the HR professional is helpful in meeting the needs of others in the organization.
- **People skills.** The commitment to build increased appreciation for diversity and the ability to do business cross-culturally.
- **Understanding the business of business.** A general understanding of how to compete, how to market, how to finance, how to manage people, and how to make a product or offer a service.
- **A consultative approach.** The ability to work effectively with all levels of managers, employees, and stakeholders to anticipate issues, troubleshoot problems, and find solutions.
- **Comfort with change.** The ability to cope effectively with, and even thrive on, change and ambiguity.
- **Visioning.** The ability to conceptualize what should be happening in the future, and to excite and inspire others in making that vision a reality.

Indeed, as people-related business issues continue to increase, professional *certification* in the HR field is becoming more important. Individuals become certified by demonstrating mastery of the defined body of knowledge required for success in a field. In HRM, two designations are available: Professional in Human Resources (PHR) and Senior Professional in Human Resources (SPHR).

IMPLICATIONS FOR MANAGEMENT PRACTICE

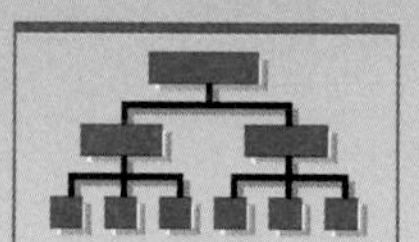

The trends we have reviewed in this chapter suggest that the old approaches to managing people may no longer be appropriate responses to economic or social reality. A willingness to experiment with new approaches to managing people is healthy. To the extent that the newer approaches do enhance productivity and QWL, everybody wins. The competitive problems facing us cannot simply be willed away, and because of this we may see even more radical experiments in organizations. The traditional role of the manager may be blurred further as workers take a greater and greater part in planning and controlling work, not simply doing what managers tell them to do. For example, under its "Work-Out" program, General Electric holds corporate "town meetings" at which lower-level blue- and white-collar employees and even customers grill bosses and suggest ways to improve efficiency. The boss is supposed to approve or deny most suggestions immediately. The aim isn't to reduce the number of employees, but to get every employee involved in improving efficiency. Jack Welch, CEO of General Electric, contends that "Work-Out" is the key to the company's sustained productivity growth in the 1990s. Programs such as GE's suggest that human resource management, an essential part of the jobs of all managers, will play an even more crucial role in the future world of work.

Each requires one comprehensive exam that covers six areas: staffing, labor relations, compensation, training, safety, and management practice. Other types of certification are available (see Figure 1-5) within more specialized areas in HR and related fields. Certification has enhanced the credibility of the profession, and today more than 19,000 HRM professionals have completed the certification process.[54]

PARADIGMS FOR POSTMODERN MANAGERS

Human Resource Management in Action: Conclusion

As we noted at the beginning of this case, organizations of tomorrow will be characterized by values such as teamwork, empowerment, cultural diversity, global focus, and customer orientation. Consider some examples of each of these. In the twenty-first-century prototype corporation, a key component of managing people will be empowering them to make decisions that affect them. And when it comes to employee empowerment, it is Saturn Corporation—a GM division, ironically enough—that is leading the way. Saturn's teams of workers manage everything from budgets to inventory control, often without direct oversight from top management.[55] Both Procter & Gamble and du Pont are demonstrating that recruiting, retaining, and promoting a culturally diverse workforce is a strategic advantage in serving culturally diverse markets.[56]

As for the global focus that will be needed in a worldwide economy, Loctite Corporation, a small maker of adhesives and sealants, is showing all companies why they should never define their markets narrowly.[57] Loctite earns $8 of every $10 of profit outside its U.S. base. For focus on the customer, 7-Eleven Japan Company has few rivals. It took an American concept, the convenience store, and made it an overwhelming success in Japan. A $200-million computer system monitors inventory and tracks customer preferences. Clerks even key in the sex and approximate age of each customer to monitor buying patterns. Orders

CERTIFYING AGENCY	CERTIFICATION DESIGNATION
Human Resource Certification Institute	Professional in Human Resources
	Senior Professional in Human Resources
American Compensation Association	Certified Compensation Professional
International Foundation of Employee Benefit Plans	Certified Employee Benefit Specialist
Board of Certified Safety Professionals	Associate Safety Professional
	Certified Safety Professional
American Board of Industrial Hygiene / Board of Certified Safety Professionals	Occupational Health and Safety Technologist

Figure 1-5
Options for professional certification in human resource management. (*Source:* C. Wiley, The certified HR professional, *HRMagazine*, Aug. 1992, p. 79.)

are transmitted instantly via satellite to distribution centers and manufacturers. Anything that does not move is discontinued immediately: of the 3000 items each franchisee carries, 70 percent are replaced annually. A bare-bones inventory saves money by allowing for the allocation of shelf space to only what local shoppers really want.[58]

Each of these companies has mastered at least one of the attributes of the organization of tomorrow. What many of them have found, however, is that even a single change poses new challenges to management and has implications that reach far beyond the concept itself. Perhaps the most basic element of the new paradigm is quality. Most senior managers now view quality not as a competitive advantage but as a competitive necessity. Says the CEO of Wausau Paper Mills: "Quality is your ticket into the stadium. You can't even come to the game unless you have a quality product and process in place. You have to compete on other dimensions."[59] As you can see from this case, managing twenty-first-century organizations will be fast-paced, exciting, and full of people-related business challenges.

SUMMARY

In a fast-paced, globally competitive economy, efforts to boost productivity and quality never end. To make organizations more responsive to the demands of the marketplace, new organization forms, such as the virtual corporation, the virtual workplace, and the modular corporation, are appearing. The new forms imply a redistribution of power, greater participation by workers, and more teamwork. These changes are necessary, for the competitive business environment of the 1990s will be characterized by factors such as an aging and changing workforce in a high-tech workplace that demands and rewards ever-increasing skill; workers who have been scarred by the unpleasant side effects of downsizing; and increasing global competition in almost every sector of the economy. The challenge of managing people effectively has never been greater.

One of the most pressing demands we face today is for productivity improvement—getting more out of what is put in, doing better with what we have, and working smarter, not harder. Nevertheless, increased productivity does not preclude a high quality of work life (QWL). QWL refers to employees' perceptions of their physical and psychological well-being at work. It involves giving workers the opportunity to make decisions about their jobs, the design of their workplaces, and what they need to make products or to deliver services most effectively. Its focus is on employees and management operating a business together.

People are a major component of any business, and the management of people (or human resource management, HRM) is a major part of every manager's job. It is also the specialized responsibility of the HR department. In fact, we use the term "strategic HRM" to refer to the wisest possible use of people with respect to the strategic needs of the organization. HRM involves five major areas: staffing, retention, development, adjustment, and managing change. Together they compose the HRM system, for they describe a network of interrelated components. The HRM function is responsible for maximizing productivity, quality of work life, and profits through better management of people. To fulfill this responsibility, HR people should above all be businesspeople, accountable, just as employees from any other function, in terms of their overall contributions to enhancing productivity and controlling costs.

DISCUSSION QUESTIONS

1-1 How are the demographic trends of the 1990s, the skills gap, downsizing, and the global competition for high-quality workers interrelated?

1-2 What common characteristics do the following organizations share: a hospital, a school, an auto repair shop, a baseball team?

1-3 Considering everything we have discussed in this chapter, describe management styles and practices that will be effective for U.S. businesses in the next decade.

1-4 What difficulties do you see in shifting from a hierarchical, departmentalized organization to a leaner, flatter one in which power is shared between workers and managers?

1-5 How can effective HRM contribute to profits?

APPLYING YOUR KNOWLEDGE

*Employee Participation and Customer Satisfaction** — *Case 1-1*

"Joe and I virtually share everything. We sit together. We're in meetings together. We're together even when we're apart." So says R. Timothy Epps, vice president of people systems at Saturn Corporation. The partner to which he refers is Joseph D. Rypkowski, a vice president of the United Auto Workers (UAW). This partnering between management and labor is the crux of Saturn Corporation's revolutionary idea. Not only are Epps and Rypkowski "paired," but so are Skip LeFauve, Saturn's president, and Dick Hoalcraft, the UAW's top boss. From the top management level down through the ranks, both represented and nonrepresented workers have partners, and, unlike many other organizations with adversarial labor-management relations, the UAW and Saturn's management work together as teams in virtually every facet of the operation. According to Epps, "We're committed to an entirely different set of beliefs. One is to have UAW involvement in all aspects of the business. The other crucial principle is that we believe those people affected by a decision should be involved in that decision."

Saturn Corporation is a wholly owned subsidiary of General Motors (GM). Its market share in the U.S. is down to 31.5 percent, and GM, the largest industrial corporation in the world, has been struggling of late. GM is Detroit's high-cost producer. Saturn is part of GM's strategy to get its North American automobile business back in gear.

The genesis of the Saturn experiment in teamwork occurred in February of 1984 with the establishment of Group 99. This group consisted of 99 employees representing a broad cross section of UAW members, GM managers, and staff from over 50 plants around the country.

The goal of Group 99 was to study other top-performing, globally successful corporations, and create a new approach to building a small car in the United States. The hope was that this step would enable GM to compete effectively in the small-car market, something it had been unable to do in the past.

After visiting and studying about 60 benchmark companies, Group 99 concluded that employees did their best work and were most committed when they felt they were part of the decision-making process. Their recommendation was that Saturn, with its headquarters in Troy, Michigan, and its manufacturing operations in Spring Hill, Tennessee, would have to operate with a totally new and different philosophy. According to Epps, "The primary goal is to create a culture in which employees accept ownership for the direct labor functions they perform, but to also create a culture that reaches out and helps them understand the systems that support them."

To enable Saturn to operate with a completely new philosophy, GM created Saturn as a separate subsidiary on January 7, 1985. This autonomy allowed a new structure to be put into place and is a crucial step in Saturn's success.

General Motors sees Saturn as a possible model for future GM plants. Former chairman Roger Smith indicated that the techniques that GM would learn from the Saturn experiment would eventually be replicated throughout the company, "improving the efficiency and competitiveness of every plant we operate. . . . Saturn is the key to GM's long-term competitiveness, survival, and success as a domestic producer."

Along with a different approach to its employees, Saturn has taken a much different approach toward its customers. It begins with the now-famous "no-dicker-sticker"—a fixed price for each automobile sold. This eliminates the price haggling many customers resent. Saturn salespeople are called "sales consultants" and they do not work on commission. These "consultants" receive considerable training, including team-building skills and orientation toward partnering with the factory and treating customers as intelligent human beings.

Saturn's customer orientation is illustrated in the way it handled a recall in June of 1993. At that time, the company discovered that a wire may not have been properly grounded on all models produced prior to April 1993. The publicity surrounding the recall was generally positive. For one thing, the recall was not mandated by the government. Instead, it was voluntary. And the recall was handled expeditiously. After two weeks, about half of the cars were repaired. By comparison, a major recall by a competi-

---

*Adapted from: D. A. Aaker, Building a brand: The Saturn story, *California Management Review, 36*(2), 1994, 114–133; R. Blumenstein. GM's first-quarter profit soared 76%, aided by strength in North America, *The Wall Street Journal*, Apr. 15, 1997 pp. A3, A5; S. Rubinstein, M. Bennett, & T. Kochan, The Saturn partnership: Co-management and the reinvention of the local union, in B. E. Kaufman & M. M. Kleiner (eds.), *Employment representation*, Ithaca, NY: ILR Press, 1992; C. M. Solomon, Behind the wheel at Saturn, *Personnel Journal, 70*(6), 1991, 72–74.

tor about the same time was only about one-third complete after a year. Finally, Saturn dealers handled the recall with grace and good humor. One chartered a bus to a local baseball game. When the bus returned, the cars had been repaired and washed. Another had a barbecue for customers while their cars were being fixed. A third offered theater tickets. The result of all this? Marketing studies undertaken by the J. D. Power Company showed that customer satisfaction did not decline at all as a result of the recall. In fact, several dimensions of customer satisfaction (e.g., "takes care of customers," "good dealer") ratings actually improved.

One key is that the UAW has also committed to the Saturn experiment, and has signed a historic labor agreement in an attempt to minimize confrontation. "Traditionally, in my experience," explains Rypkowski, "production employees felt that the corporation had very deep pockets and that their input wasn't welcome. It didn't matter whether they provided input. Therefore, who cared if the systems that supported them or the operations around them were inefficient because it didn't matter."

The UAW has accepted some fundamental philosophical approaches to running the Saturn plant that are quite different. "We are trying to get more involvement in decision making and ownership for activities that have traditionally been performed by management or resource people," explains Rypkowski.

In the new approach to management at Saturn, these tasks are performed by people who produce the product. For example, assembly line workers are responsible for quality control, budgeting, materials handling, and to some degree, ordering their own materials. Team members even hire their own new team members.

"We've broadened the scope of their responsibilities so they have a bigger and better picture of what it takes to run the business," says Rypkowski. "Even though their piece of running the business may be relatively small, they gain a better appreciation for what the organization has to do and what it costs in dollars."

The ultimate goal at Saturn is to have self-directed work teams in which consensus is used to make decisions. Currently, there are about 150 work teams, consisting of approximately 15 people each.

Saturn's mission statement makes it clear that the intent is to allow employees to be involved in decision making in areas that affect them. Presently, decisions are reached by the "70 percent comfortable" rule of consensus: each team member must feel at least 70 percent comfortable with a decision.

"All you have to do is tell somebody that once," says Rypkowski. "They hear that, and they're going to hold you to it. Once you make that statement, you had better be prepared to follow through because people take it very seriously."

At Saturn, there is no shortage of interest and involvement. In fact, it is not uncommon now for employees to ask how their input was taken into consideration any time a decision is made that affects them. But people's willingness to take responsibility and their ability to do so can be two different things. Employees may *want* to be involved, but are they *able* to perform in these tasks?

Questions

1. What aspects of quality-of-work-life (QWL) programs does the experiment at the Saturn plant illustrate?
2. How can Saturn ensure that employees have not only the willingness to take responsibility but also the ability to do so?
3. In this case, a completely new company was started with considerable autonomy from General Motors. Why do you think so many large organizations turn to "green field" operations such as this when undertaking major changes in corporate culture and operations? Do you foresee any problems down the road for GM in this regard?

REFERENCES

1. Matsushita, K. (1978). *My management philosophy.* Tokyo: PHP Institute, Inc., p. 45.
2. Byrne, J. A. (1993, Feb. 8). The virtual corporation. *Business Week,* pp. 98–103.
3. Kiechel, W., III (1993, May 17). How we will work in the year 2000. *Fortune,* pp. 38–52.
4. O'Connell, S. E. (1996, Mar.). The virtual workplace moves at warp speed. *HRMagazine,* pp. 51–57.
5. Spee, J. C. (1995, Mar.). Addition by subtraction: Outsourcing strengthens business focus. *HRMagazine,* pp. 38–43. See also Tully, S. (1993, Feb. 8). The modular corporation. *Fortune,* pp. 106–108, 112–114.
6. McWilliams, G. (1997, Apr. 7). Whirlwind on the web. *Business Week,* pp. 132, 134, 136. See also Double barrels aimed at Dell. (1996, Dec. 9). *Business Week,* p. 6.
7. Ramstad, E. (1996, Dec. 16). Dell takes another shot at selling to home-PC users. The *Wall Street Journal,* p. B4.
8. Dial Dell for servers. (1996, Sept. 16). *Business Week,* p. 102. See also The computer is in the mail (really). (1995, Jan. 23). *Business Week,* pp. 76, 77. See also Tully, loc. cit.
9. Beall, D. in Tully, op. cit., p. 106.
10. Lei, D., & Hitt, M. A. (1995). Strategic restructuring and outsourcing: The effect of mergers and acquisitions and LBOs on building firm skills and capabilities. *Journal of Management,* **21**, 835–859. See also Outsourced—and out of luck. (1995, July 17). *Business Week,* pp. 60, 61.
11. Berton, L. (1996, Sept. 5). Downsize danger: Many firms cut staff in accounts payable and pay a steep price. *The Wall Street Journal,* pp. A1, A6.
12. Labich, K. (1996, Sept. 9). Making diversity pay. *Fortune,* pp. 177–180.
13. Sanchez, J. I., & Brock, P. (1996). Outcomes of perceived discrimination among Hispanic employees: Is diversity management a luxury or a necessity? *Academy of Management Journal,* **39**, 704–719. See also Thaler-Carter, R. E. (1996, Jan.). Survey finds growing workplace recognition of work/life diversity. *Mosaics,* pp. 1–2. See also Diversity: Beyond the numbers game. (1995, Aug. 14). *Business Week,* pp. 60, 61.
14. Cappelli, P. (1995). Is the "skills gap" really about attitudes? *California Management Review,* **37**(4), 108–124.
15. Narisetti, R. (1995, Sept. 8). Job paradox: Manufacturers decry a shortage of workers while rejecting many. *The Wall Street Journal,* pp. A1, A4.
16. Kruger, P. (1990, Jan.). A game plan for the future. *Working Woman,* pp. 67–71.
17. Cappelli, loc. cit.
18. Secretary's Commission on Achieving Necessary Skills (SCANS). (1991). *What work requires of schools: A SCANS report for America 2000.* Washington, DC: U.S. Department of Labor.
19. Lynch, L. M., & Black, S. E. (1996). *Employer-provided training in the manufacturing sector: First results from the United States.* Philadelphia: National Center on the Educational Quality of the Workforce, WP34.
20. Nelan, B. W. (1992, Fall). How the world will look in 50 years. *Time* (Special Issue: Beyond the Year 2000), pp. 36–38.
21. Cascio, W. F. (1995). Whither industrial and organizational psychology in a changing world of work? *American Psychologist,* **50**(11), 928–939.
22. Doyle, F. P. (1992, June). Keynote address. National Academy of Human Resources, Santa Fe, NM.
23. Kuttner, R. (1996, Sept. 9). Happy labor day, Joe six-pack. Have some crumbs. *Business Week,* p. 26. See also The wage squeeze. (1995, July 17). *Business Week,* pp. 54–62.

24. Uchitelle, L., & Kleinfield, N. R. (1996, Mar. 3). On the battlefields of business, millions of casualties. *The New York Times*, pp. 1, 14, 15.
25. Ibid.
26. Cascio, W. F., & Young, C. E. (1996, Feb.). Corporate downsizing: A look at the last 15 years. Washington, DC: U.S. Department of Labor.
27. Cascio, W. F. (1993). Downsizing: What do we know? What have we learned? *Academy of Management Executive*, 7(1), 95–104.
28. Bernstein, A. (1996, June 24). This job market still has plenty of slack. *Business Week*, p. 36.
29. Pilon, L. J. Quoted in Jobs, jobs. (1993, Feb. 22). *Business Week*, p. 74.
30. Cascio, W. F., Young, C. E., & Morris, J. (In press). Financial consequences of employment-change decisions in major U.S. corporations. *Academy of Management Journal*.
31. Bleakley, F. R. (1996, July 5). Going for growth: Many firms see gains of cost-cutting over, push to lift revenues. *The Wall Street Journal*, pp. A1, A2.
32. Reich, R. B. (1990, Jan.–Feb.). Who is us? *Harvard Business Review*, pp. 53–64.
33. Borderless management: Companies strive to become truly stateless. (1994, May 23). *Business Week*, pp. 24–26.
34. Malabre, A. L., Jr., & Clark, L. H., Jr. (1992, Aug. 12). Dubious figures: Productivity statistics for the service sector may understate gains. *The Wall Street Journal*, pp. A1, A5. See also Wildstrom, S. H. (1993, June 14). Gauging output: It's not just counting widgets anymore. *Business Week*, p. 68.
35. Mahoney, T. A. (1988). Productivity defined: The relativity of efficiency, effectiveness, and change. In J. P. Campbell & R. J. Campbell (eds.), *Productivity in organizations*. San Francisco: Jossey-Bass, pp. 13–39. See also Pritchard, R. D., Jones, S. D., Roth, P. L., Stuebing, K. K., & Ekeberg, S. E. (1989). The evaluation of an integrated approach to measuring organizational productivity. *Personnel Psychology*, 42, 69–115.
36. Farrell, C. (1995, Oct. 9). Why the productivity tide will lift all boats. *Business Week*, pp. 136, 137.
37. Riding high: Corporate America now has an edge over its global rivals. (1995, Oct. 9). *Business Week*, p. 142.
38. White, J. B., & Lublin, J. S. (1996, Sept. 27). Some companies try to rebuild loyalty. *The Wall Street Journal*, pp. B1, B2.
39. Reich, R. In Greenhouse, S. (1992, Feb. 9). Attention, America! Snap out of it! *The New York Times*, pp. 1F, 8F.
40. McCarthy, M. J. (1993, May 4). Unlikely sites: Why German firms choose the Carolinas to build U.S. plants. *The Wall Street Journal*, pp. A1, A6.
41. Lawler, E. E., & Mohrman, S. A. (1985, Jan.–Feb.). Quality circles: After the fad. *Harvard Business Review*, pp. 65–71.
42. Case, J. (1995, June). The open-book revolution. *Inc.*, pp. 26–43.
43. Bassin, M. (1996, Jan.). From teams to partnerships. *HRMagazine*, pp. 84–86.
44. Cappelli, P., & Crocker-Hefter, A. (1996, Winter). Distinctive human resources are firms' core competencies. *Organizational Dynamics*, pp. 7–22.
45. Prahalad, C. K., & Hamel, G. (1990, May–June). The core competencies of the corporation. *Harvard Business Review*, pp. 79–91.
46. *Futures study: HR's survival depends on developing competencies to manage future issues.* (1996, June). Washington, DC: Society for Human Resource Management/Commerce Clearing House.
47. Mike Bowlin started his path to Arco CEO from a personnel job. (1996, Sept.3). *The Wall Street Journal*, p. B1. See also Leonard, B. (1994, Dec.). HR vet leads ARCO. *HRMagazine*, pp. 46–51.
48. Sheley, E. (1996, June). Share your worth: Talking numbers with the CEO. *HRMagazine*, pp. 86–95.

49. Human resources strategic blueprint. (1995). In *Vision of the future: Role of human resources in the new corporate headquarters.* Washington, DC: The Advisory Board Company, pp. 193–210.
50. American Management Association. (1995). *Business goals and strategies: The human resources perspective.* New York: Author.
51. Sheley, loc. cit.
52. Noble, B. P. (1993, Sept. 11). Quality-of-life is getting to be key work issue. *The New York Times*, p. A6.
53. Futures study, op. cit.
54. Downey, K. (1996, Sept. 10). Personal communication. Human Resource Certification Institute, Alexandria, VA.
55. Overman, S. (1995, Mar.). Saturn teams working and profiting. *HRMagazine*, pp. 72–74.
56. Labich, loc. cit.
57. Why ignore 95% of the world's market? Loctite thinks globally, profits locally. (1992, Nov. 30). *Business Week* (1992 Bonus Issue: Reinventing America), p. 65.
58. Listening to shoppers' voices: 7-Eleven Japan's common sense principles. (1992, Nov. 30). *Business Week* (1992 Bonus Issue: Reinventing America), p. 62.
59. Nemirow, A. In Paradigms for postmodern managers. (1992, Nov. 30). *Business Week* (1992 Bonus Issue: Reinventing America), p. 70.

2 THE LEGAL CONTEXT OF EMPLOYMENT DECISIONS

Questions This Chapter Will Help Managers Answer

1 How are employment practices affected by the civil rights laws and Supreme Court interpretations of those laws?
2 What should be the components of an effective policy to prevent sexual harassment?
3 What obligations does the Family and Medical Leave Act impose on employers? What rights does it grant to employees?
4 When a company is in the process of downsizing, what strategies can be used to avoid complaints of age discrimination?
5 What should senior management do to ensure that job applicants or employees with disabilities receive "reasonable accommodation"?

DISABILITY DISCRIMINATION—CAN AN EMPLOYEE WHO SEEKS TREATMENT FOR ALCOHOL ABUSE BE FIRED?*

Shortly after the Exxon *Valdez* struck a reef off the Alaskan coast in 1989, Exxon Shipping Company adopted a new policy barring any employee who had ever participated in an alcohol rehabilitation program from holding designated jobs within the company. In accordance with this policy, Theodore Ellenwood, who had no connection to the *Valdez* incident, was removed from his position as chief engineer of another Exxon oil tanker, the Exxon *Wilmington*. Ellenwood had voluntarily entered, and had successfully completed, a month-long alcohol rehabilitation program a year before the *Valdez* accident. Despite his concerns about his drinking, Ellenwood had never had an on-the-job problem with alcohol. A psychiatrist who examined Ellenwood in connection with this case concluded that he had never been an alcoholic.

Relying primarily on the company's previous written policy that "no employees with alcoholism will have their job security or future opportunities jeopardized due to a request for help or involvement in a rehabilitation effort," Ellenwood and his wife brought suit against Exxon alleging that the company breached an agreement not to discriminate on the basis of Ellenwood's "disability" of alcohol abuse, as well as violations of state statutes prohibiting discrimination against the disabled. The Ellenwoods also alleged, among other claims, wrongful discharge in violation of the public policy promoting responsible treatment of alcoholism.

In response, Exxon raised three issues. First, it argued that Congress has a unique interest in regulating federal contractors like Exxon. It cited a passage from a Senate report that stated: "Congress intended that the federal Rehabilitation Act of 1973 be administered in such a manner that a consistent, uniform, and effective Federal approach to discrimination against disabled persons would result. Thus, Federal agencies and departments should cooperate in developing standards and policies so that there is a uniform, consistent Federal approach to these sections." Exxon claimed this passage demonstrated that Congress was seeking an exclusive approach to discrimination against persons with disabilities by federal contractors (that is, there should be no "overlapping remedies"), and consequently, that it must have intended the federal law to displace parallel state laws governing the same conduct. Hence the Ellenwoods' claim of violation of state laws prohibiting discrimination against persons with disabilities should be dismissed.

Second, Exxon claimed that the area of discrimination against persons with disabilities requires an extraordinary balancing of competing interests that distinguishes it from other types of employment discrimination, such as those involving race, gender, and age. In this area, Exxon maintained, the possibility of conflicting judgments is much greater because courts in different jurisdictions could reach widely disparate conclusions on such basic questions as what constitutes a "disability" and which persons with disabilities are "qualified" to

**Ellenwood et al. v. Exxon Shipping Co.*, U.S. Court of Appeals for the First Circuit, No. 92–1473, 1993 U.S. App. Lexis 362, January 14, 1993.

hold particular positions. Restricting individuals to the remedies specified under federal law would ensure that a federal contractor doing business in more than one state would face uniform obligations nationwide. Moreover, even if federal law does not preempt claims of violations of state law barring discrimination against persons with disabilities, maritime law, which governs all issues surrounding Ellenwood's employment as a chief engineer on board ship, does.

Finally, Exxon contended that in allowing the jury to consider Ellenwood's claim of wrongful discharge in violation of the public policy promoting responsible treatment of alcoholism, the district court improperly created an exception to the well-established rule that maritime employment is terminable at will by either party in the absence of a contract setting a specific term.

Challenges

1. Should aggrieved parties be able to take advantage of "overlapping remedies" such as state and federal laws?
2. Is discrimination on the basis of disability different in kind from discrimination on the basis of age, race, gender, or religion?
3. In the interest of promoting safety in the operation of its tankers, should Exxon be allowed to terminate employees for substance abuse problems, even if treated?

SOCIETAL OBJECTIVES

As a society, we espouse equality of opportunity, rather than equality of outcomes. That is, the broad goal is to provide for all Americans, regardless of race, age, gender, religion, national origin, or disability, an equal opportunity to compete for jobs for which they are qualified. The objective, therefore, is EEO (equal employment opportunity), not EE (equal employment, or equal numbers of employees from various subgroups). For Americans with disabilities, the nation's goals are to ensure equality of opportunity, full participation, independent living, and economic self-sufficiency.

The United States population, as well as its workforce, is a diverse lot. Even among native-born English speakers, at least 22 different dialects of English are spoken in the United States! Whenever the members of such heterogeneous groups must work together, the possibility of unfair discrimination exists. Civil rights laws have been passed at the federal and state levels to provide remedies for job applicants or employees who feel they have been victims of unfair discrimination. From a managerial perspective, it is important to understand the rights as well as the obligations of employers, job candidates, and employees. Indeed, understanding these laws and their management implications is critical for all managers, not just for HR professionals. As we will see, ignorance in this area can turn out to be very expensive. Let's begin by considering the meaning of EEO and the forms of unfair discrimination.

EEO AND UNFAIR DISCRIMINATION: WHAT ARE THEY?

Civil rights laws, judicial interpretations of the laws, and the many sets of guidelines issued by state and federal regulatory agencies have outlawed discrimination based on race, religion, national origin, age, sex, and physical disability. In short, they have attempted to frame national policy on *equal employment opportunity (EEO)*. Although no law has ever attempted to define precisely the term *discrimination*, in the employment context it can be viewed broadly as the giving of an unfair advantage (or disadvantage) to the members of a particular group in comparison with the members of other groups.[1] The disadvantage usually results in a denial or restriction of employment opportunities, or in an inequality in the terms or benefits of employment.

It is important to note that whenever there are more candidates than available positions, it is necessary to select some candidates in preference to others. Selection implies exclusion. And as long as the exclusion is based on what can be demonstrated to be job-related criteria, that kind of discrimination is entirely proper. It is only when candidates are excluded on a prohibited basis, one that is not related to the job (e.g., age, race, sex), that unlawful and unfair discrimination exists. In short, EEO implies at least two things:

1. *Evaluation of candidates for jobs in terms of characteristics that really do make a difference between success and failure* (e.g., in selection, promotion, performance appraisal, or layoff)
2. *Fair and equal treatment of employees on the job* (e.g., equal pay for equal work, equal benefits, freedom from sexual harassment)

Despite federal and state laws on these issues, they represent the basis of an enormous volume of court cases, indicating that stereotypes and prejudices do not die quickly or easily. Discrimination is a subtle and complex phenomenon that may assume two broad forms:

1. **Unequal (disparate) treatment** is based on an intention to discriminate, including the intention to retaliate against a person who opposes discrimination, has brought charges, or has participated in an investigation or a hearing. There are three major subtheories of discrimination within the disparate treatment theory:
   a. Cases that rely on *direct evidence* of the intention to discriminate. Such cases are proved with direct evidence of:
      - Pure bias based on an open expression of hatred, disrespect, or inequality, knowingly directed against members of a particular group.
      - Blanket exclusionary policies—for example, deliberate exclusion of an individual whose disability (e.g., an inability to walk) has nothing to do with the requirements of the job she is applying for (financial analyst).
   b. Cases that are proved through *circumstantial evidence* of the intention to discriminate (see *McDonnell Douglas v. Green* test, p. 47), including those that rely on statistical evidence as a method of circumstantially proving the intention to discriminate systematically against classes of individuals.
   c. *Mixed-motive cases* (a hybrid theory) that often rely on both direct evidence of the intention to discriminate on some impermissible basis (e.g.,

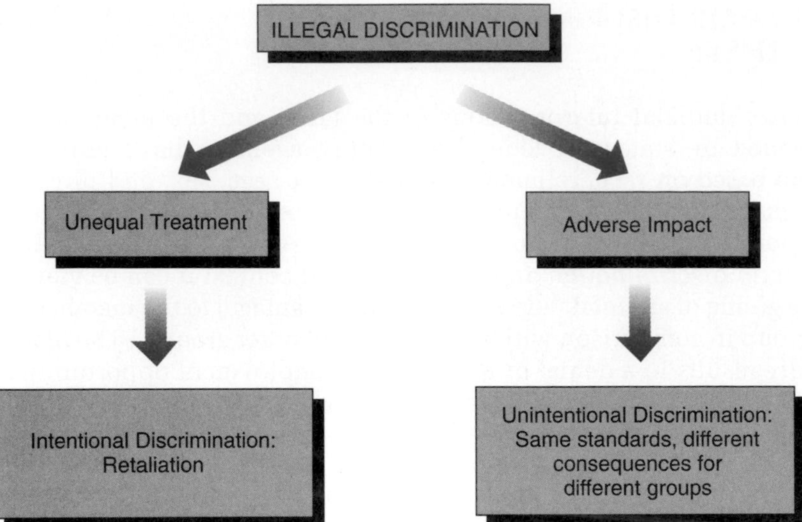

FIGURE 2-1
Major forms of illegal discrimination.

sex, race, disability) and proof that the employer's stated legitimate basis for its employment decision is actually just a pretext for illegal discrimination.

2. **Adverse impact (unintentional) discrimination** occurs when identical standards or procedures are applied to everyone, despite the fact that they lead to a substantial difference in employment outcomes (e.g., selection, promotion, layoffs) for the members of a particular group, and they are unrelated to success on a job. For example:
   - Use of a minimum height requirement of 5 feet 8 inches for police cadets. That requirement would have an adverse impact on Asians, Hispanics, and women. The policy is neutral on its face but has an adverse impact. To use it, an employer would need to show that the height requirement is necessary to perform the job.

These two forms of illegal discrimination are illustrated graphically in Figure 2-1.

THE LEGAL CONTEXT OF HUMAN RESOURCE DECISIONS

Now that we understand the forms that illegal discrimination can take, let's consider the major federal laws governing employment. Then we will consider the agencies that enforce the laws, as well as some important court cases that have interpreted them. The federal laws that we will discuss fall into two broad classes:

1. Laws of broad scope that prohibit unfair discrimination
2. Laws of limited application, for example, those that require nondiscrimination as a condition for receiving federal funds (contracts, grants, revenue-sharing entitlements)

The particular laws to be discussed within each category are the following:

Laws of broad scope	Laws of limited application
Thirteenth and Fourteenth Amendments to the U.S. Constitution	Executive Orders 11246, 11375, and 11478
Civil Rights Acts of 1866 and 1871	Rehabilitation Act of 1973
Equal Pay Act of 1963	Vietnam Era Veterans Readjustment Act of 1974
Title VII of the Civil Rights Act of 1964	Uniformed Services Employment and Reemployment Rights Act of 1994
Civil Rights Act of 1991	
Age Discrimination in Employment Act of 1967, as amended in 1986	
Immigration Reform and Control Act of 1986	
Americans with Disabilities Act of 1990	
Family and Medical Leave Act of 1993	

The Thirteenth and Fourteenth Amendments

The Thirteenth Amendment prohibits slavery and involuntary servitude. Any form of discrimination may be considered an incident of slavery or involutary servitude and thus be liable to legal action under this amendment.[2] The Fourteenth Amendment guarantees equal protection of the law for all citizens. Both the Thirteenth and Fourteenth Amendments granted to Congress the constitutional power to enact legislation to enforce their provisions. It is from this source of constitutional power that all subsequent civil rights legislation originates.

The Civil Rights Acts of 1866 and 1871

These laws were enacted on the basis of the provisions of the Thirteenth and Fourteenth Amendments. The Civil Rights Act of 1866 grants all citizens the right to make and enforce contracts for employment, and the Civil Rights Act of 1871 grants all citizens the right to sue in federal court if they feel they have been deprived of any rights or privileges guaranteed by the Constitution and other laws.

Until recently, both of these civil rights acts were viewed narrowly as tools for solving Reconstruction-era racial problems. This is no longer so. In *Johnson v. Railway Express Agency, Inc.*, the Supreme Court held that while the Civil Rights Act of 1866 on its face relates primarily to racial discrimination in the making and enforcement of contracts, it also provides a federal remedy against racial discrimination in private employment.[3] It is a powerful remedy. The Civil Rights Act of 1991 amended the Civil Rights Act of 1866 so that workers are protected from intentional discrimination in all aspects of employment, not just hiring and promotion. Thus racial harassment is covered by this civil rights law. The Civil Rights Act of 1866 allows for jury trials and for compensatory and punitive damages* for victims of intentional racial and ethnic discrimination, and it covers both large and small employers, even those with fewer than 15 employees.

The 1866 law also has been used recently to broaden the definition of racial discrimination originally applied to African Americans. In a unanimous decision, the Supreme Court ruled that race was equated with ethnicity during the legislative debate after the Civil War, and therefore Arabs, Jews, and other ethnic groups thought of as "white" are not barred from suing under the 1866 act. The Court held that Congress intended to protect identifiable classes of persons who are subjected to intentional discrimination solely because of their ancestry or ethnic characteristics. Under the law, therefore, race involves more than just skin pigment.[4]

The Equal Pay Act of 1963

This act was passed as an amendment to an earlier compensation-related law, the Fair Labor Standards Act of 1938. For those employees covered by the Fair Labor Standards Act, the Equal Pay Act requires that men and women working for the same establishment be paid the same rate of pay for work that is substantially equal in skill, effort, responsibility, and working conditions. Pay differentials are legal and appropriate if they are based on seniority, merit, systems that measure the quality or quantity of work, or any factor other than sex. Moreover, in correcting any inequity under the Equal Pay Act, employers must raise the rate of lower-paid employees, not lower the rate of higher-paid employees.

Hundreds of equal-pay suits were filed (predominantly by women) during the 1970s and the 1980s. For individual companies the price can be quite high. For example, at Chicago's Harris Trust, the company agreed to pay $14 million in back wages to thousands of female workers in order to settle a 12-year-old lawsuit. The women claimed they had been treated differently solely because of their sex (i.e., unequal treatment discrimination). For example, female trainees were required to type, but male trainees were not.

Even before the decision, however, the bank had come a long way. When the suit was filed in 1977, Harris had 5 female vice presidents. By 1989, out of 380 vice presidents, 102 were female.[5]

Title VII of the Civil Rights Act of 1964

The Civil Rights Act of 1964 is divided into several sections, or titles, each dealing with a particular facet of discrimination (e.g., voting rights, public accommodations, public education). Title VII is most relevant to the employment context, for it prohibits discrimination on the basis of race, color, religion, sex, or national origin in all aspects of employment (including apprenticeship programs). Title VII is the most important federal EEO law because it contains the broadest coverage, prohibitions, and remedies. Through it, the Equal Employ-

*Punitive damages are awarded in civil cases to punish or deter a defendant's conduct and are separate from compensatory damages, which are intended to reimburse a plaintiff for injuries or harm.

ment Opportunity Commission (EEOC) was created to ensure that employers, employment agencies, and labor organizations comply with Title VII.

Some may ask why we need such a law. As an expression of social policy, the law was passed to guarantee that people would be considered for jobs not on the basis of the color of their skin, their religion, their gender, or their national origin, but rather, on the basis of the individual abilities and talents that are necessary to perform a job.

In 1972, the coverage of Title VII was expanded. It now includes almost all public and private employers with 15 or more employees, except (1) private clubs, (2) religious organizations (which are allowed to discriminate on the basis of religion in certain circumstances), and (3) places of employment connected with an Indian reservation. The 1972 amendments also prohibit the denial, termination, or suspension of government contracts (without a special hearing) if an employer has followed and is now following an affirmative action plan accepted by the federal government for the same facility within the past 12 months. "Affirmative action" refers to *those actions appropriate to overcome the effects of past or present policies, practices, or other barriers to equal employment opportunity.*[6]

Finally, back-pay awards in Title VII cases are limited to 2 years prior to the filing of a charge. For example, if a woman filed a Title VII claim in 1991, and the matter continued through investigation, conciliation, trial, and appeal until 1996, she might be entitled to as much as 7 years' back pay, from 1989 (2 years prior to the filing of the charge) until the matter was resolved in her favor. The 2-year statute of limitations begins with the *filing* of a charge of discrimination.

Elected officials and their appointees are excluded from Title VII coverage, but they are still subject to the Fourteenth Amendment, to the Civil Rights Acts of 1866 and 1871, and to the Civil Rights Act of 1991. The following are also specifically exempted from Title VII coverage:

1. **Bona fide occupational qualifications (BFOQs)**. Discrimination is permissible when a prohibited factor (e.g., gender) is a bona fide occupational qualification for employment, that is, when it is considered "reasonably necessary to the operation of that particular business or enterprise." The burden of proof rests with the employer to demonstrate this. (According to one HR director, the only legitimate BFOQs that she could think of are sperm donor and wet nurse!) Both the EEOC and the courts interpret BFOQs quite narrowly.[7] The preferences of the employer, coworkers, or clients are irrelevant and do not constitute BFOQs. Moreover, BFOQ is not a viable defense to a Title VII race claim.

2. **Seniority systems**. Although there are a number of legal questions associated with their use, Title VII explicitly permits bona fide seniority, merit, or incentive systems "provided that such differences are not the result of an intention to discriminate."

3. **Preemployment inquiries**. Inquiries regarding such matters as race, sex, or ethnic group are permissible as long as they can be shown to be job-related. Even if not job-related, some inquiries (e.g., regarding race or sex) are necessary to meet the reporting requirements of federal regulatory agencies. Applicants provide this information on a voluntary basis.

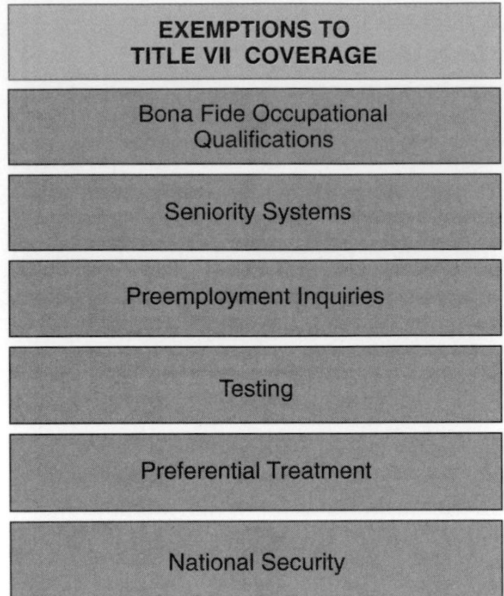

FIGURE 2-2
The six exemptions to Title VII coverage.

4. **Testing**. An employer may give or act upon any professionally developed ability test. If the results demonstrate adverse impact against a protected group, then the test itself must be shown to be job-related (i.e., valid) for the position in question.

5. **Preferential treatment**. The Supreme Court has ruled that Title VII does not require the granting of preferential treatment to individuals or groups because of their race, sex, religion, or national origin on account of existing imbalances:

> The burden which shifts to the employer is merely that of proving that he based his employment decision on a legitimate consideration, and not an illegitimate one such as race . . . . Title VII forbids him from having as a goal a work force selected by any proscribed discriminatory practice, but it does not impose a duty to adopt a hiring procedure that maximizes hiring of minority employees.[8]

6. **National security**. Discrimination is permitted under Title VII when it is deemed necessary to protect the national security (e.g., against members of groups whose avowed aim is to overthrow the U.S. government).

Initially it appeared that these exemptions (summarized in Figure 2-2) would blunt the overall impact of the law significantly. However, it soon became clear that they would be interpreted very narrowly both by the EEOC and by the courts.

Litigating Claims of Unfair Discrimination

If someone decides to bring suit under Title VII, the first step is to establish a prima facie case of discrimination (i.e., a body of facts presumed to be true until proved otherwise). However, the nature of prima facie evidence differs depending on the type of case brought before the court. If an individual alleges that a particular employment practice had an *adverse impact* on all members of a class that he or she represents, prima facie evidence is presented when adverse impact is shown to exist. Usually this is demonstrated by showing that the selection rate for the group in question is less than 80 percent of the rate of the dominant group (e.g., white males), and that the difference is statistically significant. If the individual alleges that he or she was treated differently from others in the context of some employment practice (i.e., *unequal treatment discrimination*), a prima facie case is usually presented either through direct evidence of the intention to discriminate or by circumstantial evidence. The legal standard for circumstantial evidence is a four-part test first specified in the *McDonnell Douglas v. Green* case,[9] wherein a plaintiff must be able to demonstrate that:

1. She or he has asserted a basis protected by Title VII, the Age Discrimination in Employment Act, or the Americans with Disabilities Act.
2. She or he was somehow harmed or disadvantaged (e.g., by not receiving a job offer or a promotion).
3. She or he was qualified to do the job or to perform the job in a satisfactory manner.
4. Either a similarly situated individual (or a group other than that of the plaintiff) was treated more favorably than the plaintiff, or the matter complained of involved an actual (rather than a nonexistent) employment opportunity.

Once the court accepts prima facie evidence, the burden of producing evidence shifts back and forth from plaintiff (the complaining party) to defendant (the employer). First, the employer is given the opportunity to articulate a legitimate, nondiscriminatory reason for the practice in question. Following that, in an unequal treatment case, the burden then shifts back to the plaintiff to show that the employer's reason is a pretext for illegal discrimination. In an adverse impact case, the plaintiff's burden is to show that a less discriminatory alternative practice exists and that the employer failed to use it. A similar process is followed in age discrimination cases.

The Civil Rights Act of 1991[10]

This act overturned six Supreme Court decisions issued in 1989. Following are some key provisions that are likely to have the greatest impact in the context of employment.

Monetary Damages and Jury Trials

A major effect of this act is to expand the remedies in discrimination cases. Individuals who feel they are the victims of intentional discrimination based on race, gender (including sexual harassment), religion, or disability can ask for compensatory damages for pain and suffering, as well as for punitive damages, and they may demand a jury trial. In the past, only plaintiffs in age discrimination cases had the right to demand a jury.

Compensatory and punitive damages are available only from nonpublic employers (public employers are still subject to compensatory damages up to $300,000), and not for adverse impact (unintentional discrimination) cases. Moreover, they may not be awarded in an Americans with Disabilities Act (ADA) case when an employer has engaged in good-faith efforts to provide a reasonable accommodation. The total amount of damages that can be awarded depends on the size of the employer's workforce:

Number of employees	Maximum combined damages per complaint
15 to 100	$ 50,000
101 to 200	$100,000
201 to 500	$200,000
More than 500	$300,000

As we noted earlier, victims of intentional discrimination by race or national origin may sue under the Civil Rights Act of 1866, in which case there are no limits to compensatory and punitive damages. Note also that since intentional discrimination by reason of disability is a basis for compensatory and punitive damages (unless the employer makes a good-faith effort to provide reasonable accommodation), the 1991 Civil Rights Act provides the sanctions for violations of the Americans with Disabilities Act of 1990.

Adverse Impact (Unintentional Discrimination) Cases

The act clarifies each party's obligation in such cases. As we noted earlier, when an adverse impact charge is made, the plaintiff must identify a specific employment practice as the cause of discrimination. If the plaintiff is successful in demonstrating adverse impact, the burden of producing evidence shifts to the employer, who must prove that the challenged practice is "job-related for the position in question and consistent with business necessity."

Protection in Foreign Countries

Protection from discrimination in employment, under Title VII of the 1964 Civil Rights Act and the Americans with Disabilities Act, is extended to U.S. citizens employed in a foreign facility owned or controlled by a U.S. company. However, the employer does not have to comply with U.S. discrimination law if to do so would violate the law of the foreign country.

Racial Harassment

As we noted earlier, the act amended the Civil Rights Act of 1866 so that workers are protected from intentional discrimination in all aspects of employment, not just hiring and promotion.

Challenges to Consent Decrees

Once a court order or consent decree is entered to resolve a lawsuit, nonparties to the original suit cannot challenge such enforcement actions.

Mixed-Motive Cases

In a mixed-motive case, an employment decision was based on a combination of job-related factors as well as unlawful factors, such as race, gender, religion, or disability. Under the Civil Rights Act of 1991, an employer is guilty of discrimination if it can be shown that a prohibited consideration was a motivating factor in a decision, even though other factors, which are lawful, also were used. However, if the employer can show that the same decision would have been reached even without the unlawful considerations, the court may not assess damages or require hiring, reinstatement, or promotion.

Seniority Systems

The act provides that a seniority system that intentionally discriminates against the members of a protected group can be challenged (within 180 days) at any of three points: (1) when the system is adopted, (2) when an individual becomes subject to the system, or (3) when a person is injured by the system.

"Race Norming" and Affirmative Action

The act makes it unlawful "to adjust the scores of, use different cutoff scores for, or otherwise alter the results of employment-related tests on the basis of race, color, religion, sex, or national origin." Prior to the passage of this act, within-group percentile scoring (so-called race norming) had been used extensively to adjust the test scores of minority candidates to make them more comparable to those of nonminority candidates. Under race norming, each individual's percentile score on a selection test was computed relative only to others in his or her race/ethnic group, and not relative to the scores of all examinees who took the test. The percentile scores (high to low) were then merged into a single list, and the single list of percentiles was presented to those responsible for hiring decisions.

Extension to U.S. Senate and Appointed Officials

The act extends protection from discrimination on the basis of race, color, religion, gender, national origin, age, and disability to employees of the U.S. Senate, political appointees of the President, and staff members employed by elected officials at the state level. Employees of the U.S. House of Representatives are covered by a House resolution adopted in 1988.

The Age Discrimination in Employment Act of 1967 (ADEA)

As amended in 1986, this act prohibits discrimination in pay, benefits, or continued employment for employees age 40 and over, unless an employer can demonstrate that age is a BFOQ for the job in question. Like Title VII, this law is administered by the EEOC. A key objective of the law is to prevent financially troubled companies from singling out older employees when there are cutbacks. In a 1996 ruling, the Supreme Court made clear that an employee over 40 is not required to show that he or she was replaced by a person under 40 in order to bring a claim of age discrimination.[11] However, the EEOC has ruled that when there are cutbacks, older workers can waive their rights to sue under this law (e.g., in return for sweetened benefits for early retirement). Under the Older Workers Benefit Protection Act, which took effect in 1990, employees have 45 days to consider such waivers, and 7 days after signing to revoke them.

Increasingly, older workers are being asked to sign such waivers in exchange for enhanced retirement benefits. For example, at AT&T Communications, Inc., employees who signed waivers received severance pay equal to 5 percent of current pay times the number of years of service. For those without waivers, the company offered a multiplier of 3 percent.

The Immigration Reform and Control Act of 1986 (IRCA)

This law applies to every employer in the United States, even to those with only one employee. It also applies to every employee—whether full-time, part-time, temporary, or seasonal. This act makes the enforcement of national immigration policy the job of every employer. While its provisions are complex, the basic features of the law fall into four broad categories:[12]

1. Employers may not hire or continue to employ "unauthorized aliens" (that is, those not legally authorized to work in this country).
2. Employers must verify the identity and work authorization of every new employee. Employers may not require any particular form of documentation but must examine documents provided by job applicants (e.g., U.S. passports for U.S. citizens; "green cards" for resident aliens) showing identity and work authorization. Both employer and employee then sign a form (I-9), attesting under penalty of perjury that the employee is lawfully eligible to work in the United States.
3. Employers with 4 to 14 employees may not discriminate on the basis of citizenship or national origin. Those with 15 or more employees are already prohibited from national origin discrimination by Title VII. However, this prohibition is tempered by an exception that allows employers to select an applicant who is a U.S. citizen over an alien when the two applicants are equally qualified.
4. Certain illegal aliens have "amnesty" rights. Those who can prove that they resided in the United States continuously from January 1982 to November 6, 1986 (the date of the law's enactment), are eligible for temporary, and ultimately permanent, resident status.

Penalties for noncompliance are severe. For example, for failure to comply with the verification rules, fines range from $100 to $1000 for each employee whose identity and work authorization have not been verified. The act also provides for criminal sanctions for employers who engage in a pattern or practice of violations, and a 1996 Executive Order prohibits companies that knowingly hire illegal aliens from receiving federal contracts.[13]

The Americans with Disabilities Act of 1990 (ADA)

Passed to protect the estimated 43 million Americans with disabilities, this law applies to all employers with 15 or more employees. People with disabilities are protected from discrimination in employment, transportation, and public accommodation. Title I of the ADA, the employment section, protects approximately 86 percent of the American workforce.[14]

As a general rule, the ADA prohibits an employer from discriminating against a "qualified individual with a disability." A qualified individual is one who is able to perform the "essential" (i.e., primary) functions of a job with or without accommodation. "Disability" is a physical or mental impairment that substantially limits one or more major life activities, such as walking, talking, seeing, hearing, or learning. People are protected if they currently have an impairment, have a record of such impairment, or if the employer thinks they have an impairment (e.g., a person with diabetes under control).[15] Rehabilitated drug and alcohol abusers are protected, but current drug abusers may be fired. The alcoholic, in contrast, is covered and must be reasonably accommodated by being given a firm choice to rehabilitate himself or herself or face career-threatening consequences.[16] The law also protects people who have tested positive for the AIDS virus.[17] Here are five major implications for employers:

1. Any factory, office, retail store, bank, hotel, or other building open to the public will have to be made accessible to those with physical disabilities (e.g., by installing ramps, elevators, telephones with amplifiers). "Expensive" will be no excuse, unless such modifications will lead an employer to suffer an "undue hardship."

2. Employers must make "reasonable accommodations" for job applicants or employees with disabilities (e.g., by restructuring job and training programs, modifying work schedules, or purchasing new equipment that is "user friendly" to sight- or hearing-impaired people). Qualified job applicants (i.e., individuals with disabilities who can perform the essential functions of a job with or without reasonable accommodation) must be considered for employment. Practices such as the following may facilitate the process:[18]
   - Expressions of commitment by top management to accommodate workers with disabilities
   - Assignment of a specialist within the "EEO/Affirmative Action" section to focus on "equal access" for people with disabilities
   - Centralizing recruiting, intake, and monitoring of hiring decisions
   - Identifying jobs or task assignments where a specific disability is not a bar to employment
   - Developing an orientation process for workers with disabilities, supervisors, and coworkers
   - Publicizing successful accommodation experiences within the organization and among outside organizations
   - Providing in-service training to all employees and managers about the firm's "equal access" policy, and about how to distinguish "essential" from "marginal" job functions
   - Outreach recruitment to organizations that can refer job applicants with disabilities
   - Reevaluating accommodations on a regular basis

3. Preemployment physicals will now be permissible only if all employees are subject to them, and they cannot be given until after a conditional offer of employment is made. That is, the employment offer is made conditional upon passing of the physical examination. Further, employers are not permitted to ask about past workers' compensation claims or disabilities in general. However, after describing essential job functions, an employer can ask whether the applicant can perform the job in question.

   Here is an example of the difference between these two types of inquiries: "Do you have any back problems?" clearly violates the ADA because it is not job-specific. However, the employer could state the following: "This job involves lifting equipment weighing up to 50 pounds at least once every hour of an 8-hour shift. Can you do that?"

4. Medical information on employees must be kept separate from other personal or work-related information about them.
5. Drug testing rules remain intact. An employer can still prohibit the use of alcohol and illegal drugs at the workplace and continue to give alcohol and drug tests.

Enforcement

This law is enforced according to the same procedures currently applicable to race, gender, national origin, and religious discrimination under Title VII of the Civil Rights Act of 1964. The enforcement agency is the Equal Employment Opportunity Commission (EEOC). In cases of intentional discrimination, individuals with disabilities may be awarded both compensatory and punitive damages up to $300,000 (depending on the size of the employer's workforce). In the first 3 years after the law took effect, 54,690 discrimination complaints were filed with the agency. Of these, back impairments were cited most often (19%), and wrongful discharge (51%) and lack of reasonable accommodation (27%) were the violations alleged most often.[19] As the chapter-opening vignette illustrates, this area will be a "hot" one for allegations of illegal discrimination for some time to come.

What will the cost to employers be? According to the EEOC, making such accommodations will cost employers $16 million a year, while providing productivity gains among people with disabilities of $164 million, reduced government support payments, and higher tax revenues of $222 million a year.[20]

The Family and Medical Leave Act of 1993 (FMLA)

The FMLA covers all private-sector employers with 50 or more employees, including part-timers, who work 1250 hours over a 12-month period (an average of 25 hours per week). The law gives workers up to 12 weeks' unpaid leave each year for birth, adoption, or foster care of a child within a year of the child's arrival; care for a spouse, parent, or child with a serious health condition; or the employee's own serious health condition if it prevents him or her from working. The employer is responsible for designating an absence or leave as FMLA leave, on the basis of information provided by the employee.[21] Employers can require workers to provide medical certification of such serious illnesses and can require a second medical opinion. Employers also can exempt from the FMLA key salaried employees who are among their highest-paid 10 percent. For leave takers, however, employers must maintain health insurance benefits and give the workers their previous jobs (or comparable positions) when their leaves are over. Enforcement provisions of the FMLA are administered by the U.S. Department of Labor.[22] The overall impact of this law was softened considerably by the exemption of some of its fiercest opponents—companies with fewer than 50 employees, or 95 percent of all businesses.[23] Nevertheless, the law still covers about 300,000 employers and 45 million employees in the private sector, and about 15 million more in state and local governments.[24]

This completes the discussion of "absolute prohibitions" against discrimination. The following sections discuss nondiscrimination as a basis for eligibility for federal funds.

Executive Orders 11246, 11375, and 11478

Presidential Executive Orders in the realm of employment and discrimination are aimed specifically at federal agencies, contractors, and subcontractors. They have the force of law, even though they are issued unilaterally by the President without congressional approval, and they can be altered unilaterally as well. The requirements of these orders are parallel to those of Title VII.

In 1965, President Johnson issued Executive Order 11246, prohibiting discrimination on the basis of race, color, religion, or national origin as a condition of employment by federal agencies, contractors, and subcontractors with contracts of $10,000 or more. Those covered are required to establish and maintain a program of equal employment opportunity in every facility of 50 or more people. Such programs include employment, upgrading, demotion, transfer, recruitment or recruitment advertising, layoff or termination, pay rates, and selection for training.

In 1967, Executive Order 11375 prohibited discrimination in employment based on sex. Executive Order 11478, issued by President Nixon in 1969, went even further, for it prohibited discrimination in employment based on all the previous factors, plus political affiliation, marital status, or physical handicap.

Enforcement of Executive Orders

Executive Order 11246 provides considerable enforcement power, administered by the Department of Labor through its Office of Federal Contract Compliance Programs (OFCCP). Upon a finding by the OFCCP of noncompliance with the order, the Department of Justice may be advised to institute criminal proceedings, and the secretary of labor may cancel or suspend current contracts as well as the right to bid on future contracts. Needless to say, noncompliance can be very expensive.

The Rehabilitation Act of 1973

This act requires federal contractors (those receiving more than $2500 in federal contracts annually) and subcontractors to actively recruit qualified people with disabilities and to use their talents to the fullest extent possible. The legal requirements are similar to those of the Americans with Disabilities Act.

The purpose of this act is to eliminate *systemic discrimination*, i.e., any business practice that results in the denial of equal employment opportunity.[25] Hence the act emphasizes "screening in" applicants, not screening them out. It is enforced by the OFCCP.

The Vietnam Era Veterans Readjustment Act of 1974

Federal contractors and subcontractors are required under this act to take affirmative action to ensure equal employment opportunity for Vietnam-era veterans (August 5, 1964, to May 7, 1975). The OFCCP enforces it.

Uniformed Services Employment and Reemployment Rights Act of 1994

Regardless of the size of its organization, an employer may not deny a person initial employment, reemployment, promotion, or benefits on the basis of that person's membership or potential membership in the armed service. To be protected, the employee must provide advance notice. Employers need not always rehire a returning service member (e.g., if the employee received a dishonorable discharge, or if changed circumstances at the workplace make reemployment impossible or unreasonable), but the burden of proof will almost always be on the employer.

This law is administered by the U. S. Department of Labor.[26]

FEDERAL ENFORCEMENT AGENCIES: EEOC AND OFCCP

The Equal Employment Opportunity Commission is an independent regulatory agency whose five commissioners (one of whom is chairperson) are appointed by the President and confirmed by the Senate for terms of 5 years. No more than three of the commissioners may be from the same political party. Like the OFCCP, the EEOC sets policy and in individual cases determines whether there is "reasonable cause" to believe that unlawful discrimination has occurred. If reasonable cause is found, the EEOC can sue either on its own behalf or on behalf of a claimant. As far as the employer is concerned, the simplest and least costly procedure is to establish a system to resolve complaints internally. However, if this system fails or if the employer does not make available an avenue for such complaints, an aggrieved individual (or group) can file a formal complaint with the EEOC. The process is shown graphically in Figure 2–3.

Once it receives a complaint of discrimination, the EEOC follows a three-step process: investigation, conciliation, and litigation.[27] As Figure 2–3 indicates, complaints must be filed within 180 days of an alleged violation (300 days if the same basis of discrimination is prohibited by either state or local laws). If that requirement is satisfied, the EEOC immediately refers the complaint to a state agency charged with enforcement of fair employment laws (if one exists) for resolution within 60 days. If the complaint cannot be resolved within that time, the state agency can file suit in a state district court and appeal any decision to a state appellate court, the state supreme court, or the U.S. Supreme Court. As an alternative to filing suit, the state agency may redefer to the EEOC. Again, voluntary reconciliation is sought, but if this fails, the EEOC may refer the case to the Justice Department (if the defendant is a public employer) or file suit in federal district court (if the defendant is a private employer). Like state court decisions, federal court decisions may be appealed to one of the 12 U.S. Courts of Appeal (corresponding to the geographical region, or "circuit," in which the case arose). In turn, these decisions may be appealed to the U.S. Supreme Court, although very few cases are actually heard by the Supreme Court. Generally the Court will grant certiorari (discretionary review) when two or more circuit courts have reached different conclusions on the same point of law or when a major question of constitutional interpretation is involved. If certiorari is denied, the lower court's decision is binding.

EEOC Guidelines

The EEOC has issued a number of guidelines for Title VII compliance. Among these are guidelines on discrimination because of religion, national origin, gender, and pregnancy; guidelines on affirmative action programs; guidelines on employee selection procedures; and a policy statement on preemployment in-

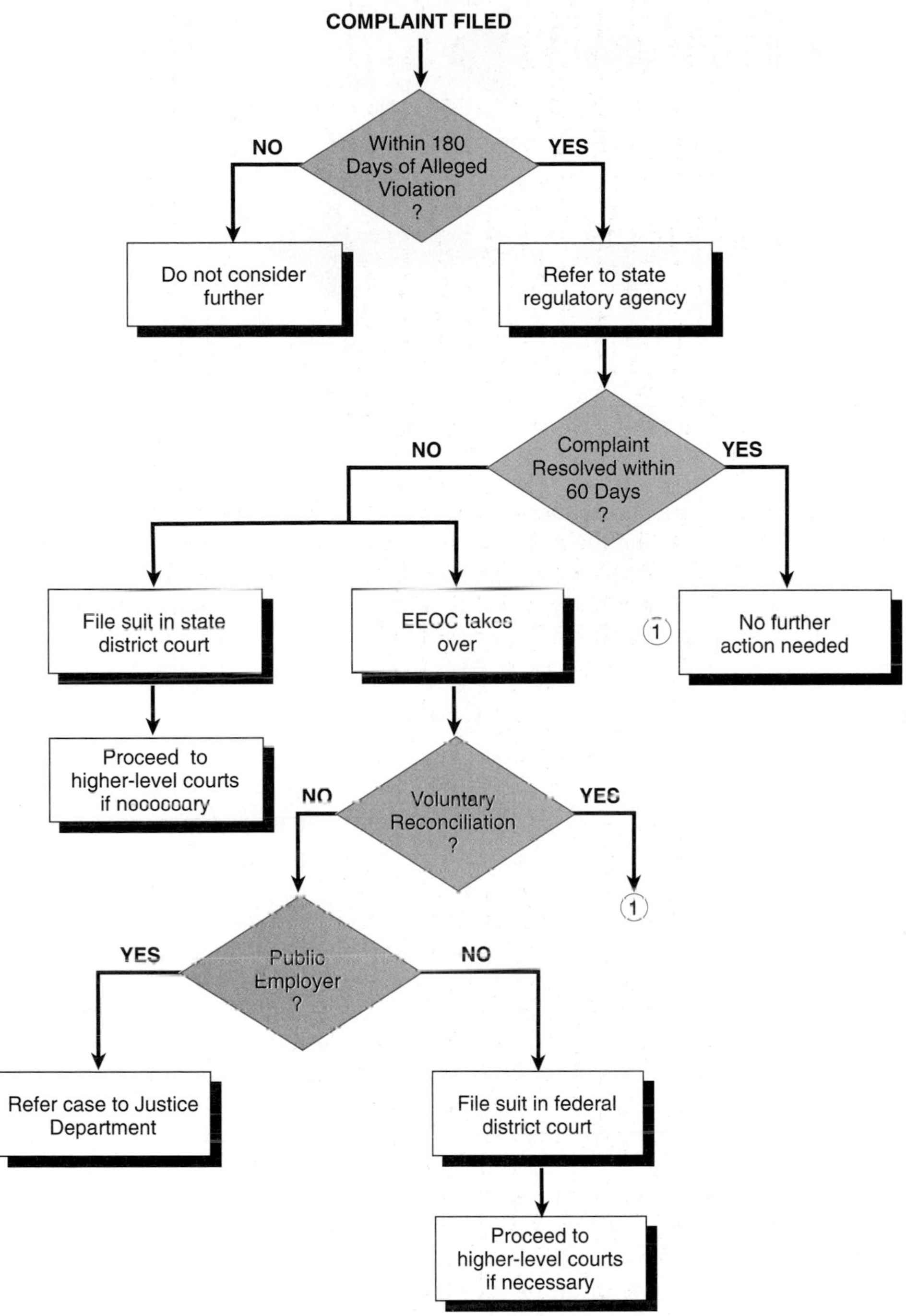

FIGURE 2-3
Discrimination complaints: the formal process.

quiries. These guidelines are not laws, although the Supreme Court has indicated that they are entitled to "great deference."[28]

Information Gathering

This is another major EEOC function, for each organization in the United States with 100 or more employees must file an annual report (EEO-1) detailing the number of women and minorities employed in nine different job categories

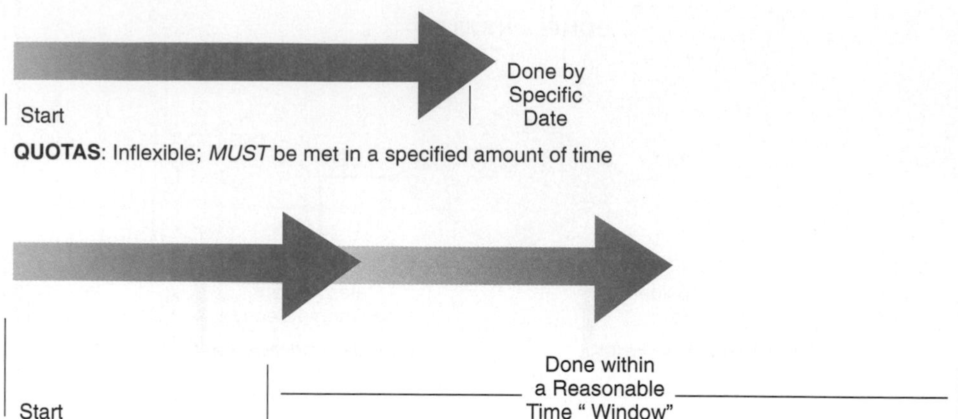

FIGURE 2-4
The distinction between rigid quotas and goals and timetables.

ranging from laborers to managers and professionals. Through computerized analysis of the forms, the EEOC is able to identify broad patterns of discrimination (systemic discrimination) and to attack them through class actions. In any given year the EEOC typically receives more than 95,000 complaints and has about 500 class action suits in progress.[29]

The Office of Federal Contract Compliance Programs (OFCCP)

Contract compliance means that in addition to quality, timeliness, and other requirements of federal contract work, contractors and subcontractors must meet EEO and affirmative action requirements. As we have seen, these requirements cover all aspects of employment.

Companies are willing to go to considerable lengths to avoid the loss of government contracts. More than a quarter of a million companies, employing 27 million workers and providing the government with more than $100 billion in construction, supplies, equipment, and services, are subject to contract compliance enforcement by the OFCCP.[30] Contractors and subcontractors with more than $50,000 in government business and with 50 or more employees must prepare and implement written affirmative action plans.

In jobs where women and minorities are underrepresented in the workforce relative to their availability in the labor force, employers must establish goals and timetables for hiring and promotion. Theoretically, goals and timetables are distinguishable from rigid quotas in that they are flexible objectives that can be met in a realistic amount of time (Figure 2–4). Goals and timetables are not required under the Rehabilitation Act and Vietnam veterans law.

From the employer's perspective, compliance reviews are costly. Thus City Utilities of Springfield, Missouri, spent $26,500 and 734 hours of employee time. The OFCCP found no evidence of discriminatory hiring practices.[31] However, when a compliance review by the OFCCP does indicate problems that cannot be resolved easily, it tries to reach a conciliation agreement with the employer. Such an agreement might include back pay, seniority credit, special recruitment efforts, promotion, or other forms of relief for the victims of unlawful discrimination.

The conciliation agreement is the OFCCP's preferred route, but if such efforts are unsuccessful, formal enforcement action is necessary. Contractors and subcontractors are entitled to a hearing before a judge. If conciliation is not reached before or after the hearing, employers may lose their government contracts, their payments may be withheld by the government, or they may be debarred from any government contract work. Debarment is the OFCCP's ultimate weapon, for it indicates in the most direct way possible that the U.S. government is serious about equal employment opportunity programs.

Affirmative Action Remedies

In three different cases, the Supreme Court found that Congress specifically endorsed the concept of non-victim-specific racial hiring goals to achieve compliance.[32] Further, the Court noted the benefits of flexible affirmative action rather than rigid application of a color-blind policy that would deprive employers of flexibility in administering human resources. How do employers do in practice? One 7-year study of companies that set annual goals for increasing African-American male employment found that only one-tenth of the goals were achieved. Some may see this as a sign of failure, but it also reflects the fact that the goals were not rigid quotas. "Companies promise more than they can deliver, . . . but the ones that promise more do deliver more."[33]

EMPLOYMENT CASE LAW: SOME GENERAL PRINCIPLES

Although Congress enacts laws, the courts interpret the laws and determine how they will be enforced. Such interpretations define what is called *case law*, which serves as a precedent to guide future legal decisions. And, of course, precedents are regularly subject to reinterpretation.

In the area of employment, a considerable body of case law has accumulated since 1964. Figure 2–5 illustrates areas in which case law is developed most extensively. Lawsuits affecting virtually every aspect of employment have been filed, and in the following sections we will consider some of the most significant decisions to date.

Sex Discrimination

Suppose you run an organization that has 238 managerial positions—all filled by men. Only one promotional opportunity to a managerial position is available. Suppose that only a 2-point difference in test scores separates the best-qualified man from the best-qualified woman. What do you do? Until a landmark Supreme Court decision in 1987 (*Johnson v. Santa Clara Transportation Agency*[34]), if you promoted the woman you invited a lawsuit by the man. If you promoted the woman to correct past discrimination (thereby acknowledging past bias), you would invite discrimination suits by women. No longer. The Supreme Court ruled unambiguously that in traditionally sex-segregated jobs, a qualified woman can be promoted over a marginally better-qualified man to promote more balanced representation. The Court stressed the need for affirmative action plans to be flexible, gradual, and limited in their effect on whites and

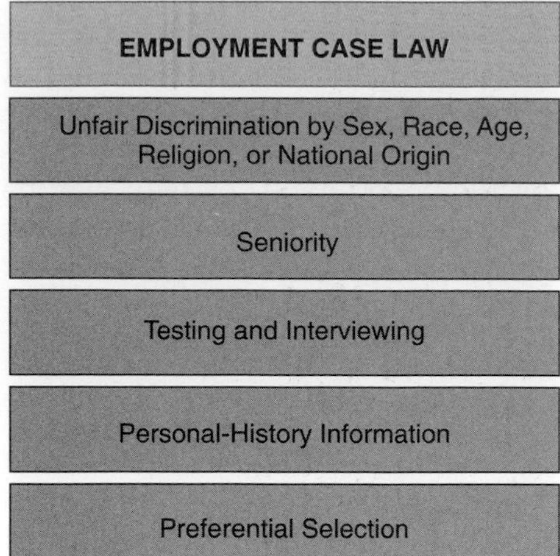

FIGURE 2-5
Areas making up the main body of employment case law.

men. The Court also expressed disapproval of strict numerical quotas except where necessary (on a temporary basis) to remedy severe past discrimination.

Many employers are in similar positions. That is, they have not been proved guilty of past discrimination, but they have a significant underrepresentation of women or other protected groups in various job categories. This decision clearly put pressure on employers to institute voluntary affirmative action programs, but at the same time it also provided some welcome guidance on what they were permitted to do.

Pregnancy

The Equal Employment Opportunity Commission's guidelines on the Pregnancy Discrimination Act of 1978 state:

> The basic principle of the Act is that women affected by pregnancy and related conditions must be treated the same as other applicants and employees on the basis of their ability or inability to work. A woman is therefore protected against such practices as being fired, or refused a job or promotion, merely because she is pregnant or has had an abortion. She usually cannot be forced to go on leave as long as she can still work. If other employees who take disability leave are entitled to get their jobs back when they are able to work again, so are women who have been unable to work because of pregnancy.[35]

Each year, the EEOC receives about 3600 complaints related to pregnancy (about 1 out of every 50 complaints the commission receives).[36] However, this may be only the tip of the iceberg. For example, the National Association of Working Women in Cleveland handles 15,000 calls a year from women claiming gender-based discrimination, including pregnancy.[37]

Under the law, an employer is never *required* to give pregnant employees special treatment. If an organization provides no disability benefits or sick leave to other employees, it is not required to provide them for pregnant employees.[38] While the actual length of maternity leave is now an issue to be determined by the woman's and/or the company's physician, a 1987 Supreme Court decision in *California Federal Savings & Loan Association v. Guerra* upheld a California law that provides for up to 4 months of unpaid leave for pregnancy disability.[39]

Economic pressures on employers may make legal action unnecessary in the future. Evidence now indicates that many employers are doing their best to accommodate pregnant women through flexible work scheduling and generous maternity leave policies.[40] Given the number of women of childbearing age in the workforce and the fact that 85 percent of all women have children,[41] combined with the fact that two out of every three people who will fill new jobs by the year 2000 will be women, there really is no other choice.

One large survey of company practices found that new mothers typically spend 1 to 3 months at home following childbirth, that job guarantees for returning mothers were provided by 35 percent of the companies, and that employers of 501 to 1000 employees are most likely to provide full pay.[42]

What percentage of women use disability benefits fully and then decide not to return to work? At Corning Glass, Inc., First Bank of Minneapolis, and Levi Straus & Co., more than 80 percent do return to work. Moreover, the provision of maternity leave benefits has helped establish good rapport with employees.[43]

How much do these extra benefits cost? The Health Insurance Association of America estimated that the extension of health insurance coverage to pregnancy-related conditions of women employees and employees' spouses would increase premiums by an average of 13 percent.[44]

Reproductive Hazards

Another way sex discrimination may be perpetuated is by barring women from competing for jobs that pose occupational health hazards to their reproductive systems. In a landmark 1991 decision (*UAW v. Johnson Controls, Inc.*) the Supreme Court ruled that such "fetal protection" policies, which had been used by more than a dozen major companies, including General Motors, du Pont, Monsanto, Olin, Firestone, and B. F. Goodrich, are a form of illegal sex discrimination that is prohibited by Title VII. At issue was the policy of Johnson Controls, Inc., a car battery manufacturer, that excluded women of childbearing age from jobs involving exposure to lead.[45] The company argued that its policy was based on the BFOQ exception to Title VII, because it was essential to a safe workplace.

The High Court disagreed, ruling that the BFOQ exception is a narrow one, limited to policies that are directly related to a worker's ability to do the job. "Women as capable of doing their jobs as their male counterparts may not be forced to choose between having a child and having a job. . . . Decisions about the welfare of future children must be left to the parents who conceive, bear, support, and raise them rather than to the employers who hire those parents," said the Court.[46]

What are businesses to do? Clearly, they will have to provide more complete information to inform and warn female (and male) workers about fetal health risks on the job. They may also urge women to consult their physicians before starting such assignments. However, the Supreme Court noted that it would be difficult to sue a company for negligence after it abandoned its fetal protection policy if (1) the employer fully informs women of the risk, and (2) it has not acted negligently.[47] Mere exclusion of workers, both unions and managers agree, does not address chemicals remaining in the workplace to which other workers may be exposed. Nor are women more sensitive to reproductive hazards than men. Changing the workplace, rather than the workforce, is a more enlightened policy.

ETHICAL DILEMMA
Secret Taping of Supervisors: It May Be Legal, but Is It Ethical?

Employees who think a supervisor is out to get them have something new up their sleeves: hidden tape recorders. Secret tapings are on the rise, often by employees trying to protect their jobs, and aided by the availability of cheap, miniature recorders. Such taping, often done to support legal claims, outrages and exasperates employers. Defenders counter that secret recording sometimes is the only way to bring out the truth.

Federal law allows secret taping, as long as one of the people being recorded knows about it. At least a dozen states, including New York, have similar state laws. However, in about 14 other states, including California, the law requires that everyone being taped must know that he or she is being recorded.

Most companies confronted with a tape quickly settle out of court. In one case, for example, a pregnant saleswoman's coworkers told her outright that they would force her off the job by making life hard on her at work. The workers were afraid the pregnancy would stop the woman from racking up sales, and they all would lose a bonus as a result. Once the woman sued for pregnancy discrimination, the coworkers lied about threatening her. They said, "We were all happy for her—we gave her a big hug when we found out she was pregnant." But the woman produced a secret tape she had made of the threats and won a $180,000 settlement.

What is a business to do? Issue a policy against covert recording. That way, employees who tape can be fired for breaking company rules. In states where secret taping is illegal, companies can turn the tables on employees by using the recordings against them. Employment lawyers also advise companies to hire experts to make sure the tapes are authentic and have not been edited. How about coworkers and managers? The cheapest and best protection of all is to avoid saying things you would be embarrassed to go into on a witness stand . . . or to see on the evening news.[48]

Sexual Harassment

This is not really about sex. It's about power—more to the point, the abuse of power.[49] In the vast majority of cases on this issue, females rather than males have suffered from sexual abuse at work. Such abuse may constitute illegal sex discrimination, a form of unequal treatment on the job. How prevalent is it? More than 12,500 complaints are filed annually with the EEOC, 90 percent of Fortune 500 companies have dealt with sexual harassment complaints, and more than a third have been sued at least once. The cost? An average of $200,000 on each complaint that is investigated in-house and found to be valid. In fact, one consulting firm estimates that the problem costs the average large corporation $6.7 million a year.[50] It is perilous self-deception for a manager to believe that sexual harassment does not exist in his or her own organization.

What is sexual harassment? Although opinions differ,[51] perhaps the clearest definition is that provided by the EEOC: "unwelcome sexual advances, requests for sexual favors, and other verbal or physical conduct of a sexual nature when submission to or rejection of this conduct explicitly or implicitly affects an individual's employment, unreasonably interferes with an individual's work performance, or creates an intimidating, hostile, or offensive work environment."[52]

Actually, the "no frills" definition can be put into one word: "unwelcome." According to the courts, for behavior to be treated as sexual harassment, the offender has to know that the behavior is unwelcome. If a person wants to file a grievance, therefore, it is important to be able to prove either that he or she told the perpetrator to back off or that the action was so offensive the harasser should have known it was unwelcome.

While many behaviors can constitute sexual harassment, there are two main types:

1. Quid pro quo (you give me this; I'll give you that)
2. Hostile work environment (an intimidating, hostile, or offensive atmosphere)

Quid pro quo harassment exists when the harassment is a condition of employment. For example, consider the case of *Barnes v. Costle:* The plaintiff rebuffed her director's repeated sexual overtures. She ignored his advice that sexual intimacy was the path she should take to improve her career opportunities. Subsequently the director abolished her job. The court of appeals found that sexual cooperation was a condition of her employment, a condition the director did not impose upon males. Therefore, sex discrimination occurred and the employer was liable.[53]

The courts have gone even further, holding employers responsible even if they knew nothing about a supervisor's conduct. For example, a federal appeals court held Avco Corporation of Nashville, Tennessee, liable for the sexually harassing actions of one of its supervisors against two female secretaries working under his supervision. The court found that the employer had a policy against sexual harassment but failed to enforce it effectively. Both the company *and* the supervisor were held liable. Regarding the company's liability, the court noted: "Although Avco took remedial action once the plaintiffs registered complaints, its duty to remedy the problem, or at a minimum, inquire, was created earlier when the initial allegations of harassment were reported."[54]

Hostile environment harassment was defined by the Supreme Court in the case of *Meritor Savings Bank v. Vinson.*[55] Vinson's boss had abused her verbally as well as sexually. However, since Vinson was making good career progress, the district court ruled that the relationship was a voluntary one having nothing to do with her continued employment or advancement. The Supreme Court disagreed, ruling that whether the relationship was "voluntary" is irrelevant. The key question was whether the sexual advances from the supervisor were "unwelcome." If so, and if they are "sufficiently severe or pervasive to be abusive,"[56] then they are illegal. This case was groundbreaking because it expanded the definition of harassment to include verbal or physical conduct that creates an intimidating, hostile, or offensive work environment or interferes with an employee's job performance.

In a 1993 case, *Harris v. Forklift Systems, Inc.*, the Supreme Court ruled that plaintiffs in such suits need not show psychological injury to prevail. While a victim's emotional state may be relevant, she or he need not prove extreme distress. In considering whether illegal harassment has occurred, juries must consider factors such as the frequency and severity of the harassment, whether it is physically threatening or humiliating, and whether it interferes with an employee's work performance.[57]

As we noted earlier, the Civil Rights Act of 1991 permits victims of sexual harassment—who previously could be awarded only missed wages—to collect a wide range of punitive damages and attorney's fees from employers who mishandled a complaint.

Preventive Actions by Employers

What can an employer do to escape, or to at least limit, its liability for the sexually harassing acts of its managers or workers? An effective policy should include the following features:[58]

- A statement from the chief executive officer that states firmly that sexual harassment will not be tolerated
- A workable definition of sexual harassment that is publicized via staff meetings, bulletin boards, handbooks, and new-employee orientation programs
- An established complaint procedure to provide a vehicle for employees to report claims of harassment to their supervisors or to a neutral third party, such as the HR department
- A clear statement of sanctions for violators and protection for those who make charges
- Prompt, confidential investigation of every claim of harassment, no matter how trivial
- Preservation of all investigative information, with records of all such complaints kept in a central location
- Training of all managers and supervisors to recognize and respond to complaints, giving them written materials outlining their responsibilities and obligations when a complaint is made
- Follow-up to determine if harassment has stopped[59]

Age Discrimination

The Equal Employment Opportunity Commission's guidelines on age discrimination emphasize that in order to defend an adverse employment action against employees age 40 and over, an employer must be able to demonstrate a "business necessity" for doing so. That is, it must be shown that age is a factor directly related to the safe, efficient operation of a business. To establish a prima facie case of age discrimination with respect to termination, for example, an individual must show that:[60]

1. She or he is within the protected age group (40 years of age and over).
2. She or he is doing satisfactory work.
3. She or he was discharged despite satisfactory work performance.
4. The position was filled by a person younger than the person replaced.

For example, an employee named Schwager had worked for Sun Oil Ltd. for 18 years, and his retirement benefits were to be vested (i.e., not contingent on future service) at 20 years. When the company reorganized and had to reduce the size of its workforce, the average age of those retained was 35 years, while the average age of those terminated was 45.7 years. The company was able to demonstrate, however, that economic considerations prompted the reorganization and that factors other than age were considered in Schwager's termination. The local manager had to let one person go, and he chose Schwager because he ranked lowest in overall job performance among salespeople in his district and did not measure up to their standards. Job performance, not age, was the reason for Schwager's termination. Employers can still fire unproductive workers, but the key is to base employment decisions on ability, not on age.[61]

"ENGLISH-ONLY" RULES—NATIONAL ORIGIN DISCRIMINATION?

Rules that require employees to speak only English in the workplace have come under fire in recent years. Employees who speak a language other than English claim that such rules are not related to the ability to do a job and have a harsh impact on them because of their national origin.

In a recent case, an employer applied an "English-only" rule while employees were on the premises of the company. Non-Spanish-speaking employees complained that they were being talked about by the plaintiff and others who spoke Spanish. The Eleventh Circuit Court of Appeals ruled in favor of the employer. The court noted that the rule in this case was job-related in that supervisors and other employees who spoke only English had a need to know what was being said in the workplace.

Employers should be careful when instituting an English-only rule. While it is not necessarily illegal to make fluency in English a job requirement, or to discipline an employee for violating an English-only rule, employers must be able to show there is a legitimate business need for it. Then they must inform employees in advance of the circumstances where speaking only in English is required, and of the consequences of violating the rule. (Conversely, many employers would be delighted to have a worker who can speak the language of a non-English-speaking customer.) Otherwise, the employer may be subject to discrimination complaints on the basis of national origin.[62]

"Overqualified" Job Applicants

Employers sometimes hesitate to hire an individual who has a great deal of experience for a job that requires few qualifications and may be only an entry-level job. They assume that an overqualified individual will be bored in such a job or is using the job only to get a foot in the door so he or she can apply for another job at a later time. Beware of violating the Age Discrimination in Employment Act! An appeals court recently ruled that rejection of an older worker because he or she is overqualified may be a pretext to mask the real reason for rejection—the employee's age. In the words of the court: "How can a person overqualified by experience and training be turned down for a position given to a younger person deemed better qualified?"[63]

Seniority

"Seniority" is a term that connotes length of employment. A "seniority system" is a scheme that, alone or in tandem with "nonseniority" criteria, allots to employees ever-improving employment rights and benefits as their relative lengths of pertinent employment increase.[64]

Various features of seniority systems have been challenged in the courts for many years.[65] However, one of the most nettlesome issues is the impact of established seniority systems on programs designed to ensure equal employment opportunity. Employers often work hard to hire and promote members of protected groups. If layoffs become necessary, however, those individuals may be lost because of their low seniority. As a result, the employer takes a step backward in terms of workforce diversity. What is the employer to do when seniority conflicts with EEO?

The courts have been quite clear in their rulings on this issue. In two landmark decisions, *Firefighters Local Union No. 1784 v. Stotts*[66] (decided under

Title VII) and *Wygant v. Jackson Board of Education*[67] (decided under the equal protection clause of the Fourteenth Amendment), the Supreme Court ruled that an employer may not protect the jobs of recently hired African-American employees at the expense of whites who have more seniority.[68]

Voluntary modifications of seniority policies for affirmative action purposes remain proper, but where a collective bargaining agreement exists, the consent of the union is required. Moreover, in the unionized setting, courts have made it clear that the union must be a party to any decree that modifies a bona fide seniority system.[69]

Testing and Interviewing

Title VII clearly sanctions the use of "professionally developed" ability tests. Nevertheless, it took several landmark Supreme Court cases to clarify the proper role and use of tests. The first of these was *Griggs v. Duke Power Co.*, the most significant EEO case ever, which was decided in favor of Griggs.[70] The employer was prohibited from requiring a high school education or the passing of an intelligence test as a condition of employment or job transfer where neither standard was shown to be significantly related to job performance:

> What Congress has forbidden is giving these devices and mechanisms controlling force unless they are demonstrably a reasonable measure of job performance. . . . What Congress has commanded is that any tests used must measure the person for the job and not the person in the abstract.[71]

The ruling also included four other general principles:

1. The law prohibits not only open and deliberate discrimination but also practices that are fair in form but discriminatory in operation. That is, Title VII prohibits practices having an adverse impact on protected groups, unless they are job-related. This is a landmark pronouncement because it officially established adverse impact as a category of illegal discrimination.

   For example, suppose an organization wants to use prior arrests as a basis for selection. In theory, arrests are a "neutral" practice since all persons are equally subject to arrest if they violate the law. However, if arrests cannot be shown to be job-related, and, in addition, if a significantly higher proportion of African Americans than whites is arrested, the use of arrests as a basis for selection is discriminatory in operation.

2. The employer bears the burden of proof that any requirement for employment is related to job performance. As affirmed by the Civil Rights Act of 1991, when a charge of adverse impact is made, the plaintiff must identify a specific employment practice as the cause of the discrimination. If the plaintiff is successful, the burden shifts to the employer.

3. It is not necessary for the plaintiff to prove that the discrimination was intentional; intent is irrelevant. If the standards result in discrimination, they are unlawful.

4. Job-related tests and other employment selection procedures are legal and useful.

The confidentiality of individual test scores has also been addressed both by the profession[72] and by the courts. Thus the Supreme Court affirmed the right of the Detroit Edison Company to refuse to hand over to a labor union copies of aptitude tests taken by job applicants and to refuse to disclose individual test scores without the written consent of employees.[73]

As is well known, interviews are commonly used as bases for employment decisions to hire or to promote certain candidates in preference to others. Must such "subjective" assessment procedures satisfy the same standards of job-relatedness as more "objective" procedures, such as written tests? If they produce an adverse impact against a protected group, the answer is yes, according to the Supreme Court in *Watson v. Fort Worth Bank & Trust.*[74]

As in its *Griggs* ruling, the Court held that it is not necessary for the plaintiff to prove that the discrimination was intentional. If the interview ratings result in adverse impact, they are presumed to be unlawful, unless the employer can show some relationship between the content of the ratings and the requirements of a given job. This need not involve a formal validation study, although the Court agreed unanimously that it is possible to conduct such studies when subjective assessment devices are used.[75] The lesson for employers? Be sure that there is a legitimate, job-related reason for every question raised in an employment or promotional interview. Limit questioning to "need to know," rather than "nice to know," information and monitor interview outcomes for adverse impact. Validate this selection method. It would be unwise to wait until the selection system is challenged.

Personal History

Frequently, job qualification requirements involve personal background information. If the requirements have the effect of denying or restricting equal employment opportunity, they may violate Title VII. For example, in the *Griggs v. Duke Power Co.* case, a purportedly neutral practice (the high school education requirement that excluded a higher proportion of African Americans than whites from employment) was ruled unlawful because it had not been shown to be related to job performance. Other allegedly neutral practices that have been struck down by the courts on the basis of non-job relevance include:

- Recruitment practices based on present employee referrals, where the workforce is nearly all white to begin with.[76]
- Height and weight requirements.[77]
- Arrest records, because they show only that a person has been accused of a crime, not that she or he was guilty of it; thus arrests may not be used as a basis for selection decisions,[78] except in certain sensitive and responsible positions (e.g., police officer, school principal).[79]
- Conviction records, unless the conviction is directly related to the work to be performed—for example, a person convicted of embezzlement applying for a job as a bank teller.[80]

Despite such decisions, personal-history items are not unlawfully discriminatory per se, but to use them you must show that they are relevant to the job in question. Just as with employment interviews, collect this information on a "need to know," not on a "nice to know," basis.

These people are protesting the passage of California's 1996 anti-affirmative action law.

Preferential Selection

In an ideal world, selection and promotion decisions would be color-blind. That is, social policy as embodied in Title VII emphasizes that so-called reverse discrimination (discrimination against whites and in favor of members of protected groups) is just as unacceptable as is discrimination by whites against members of protected groups.[81] In an effort to improve the prospects for advancement of members of protected groups, such as African Americans, can an employer grant them preference in admission to a training program? The case of *United Steelworkers of America v. Weber* addressed this issue.

Brian Weber, a white lab analyst at Kaiser Aluminum & Chemical Company's Gramercy, Louisiana, plant, sued his company and his union under Title VII after he was bypassed for a crafts retraining program in which the company and the union had jointly agreed to reserve 50 percent of the available places for African Americans.[82] Although there had been years of exclusion of African Americans from such training programs, there was no proven record of bias at the plant on which to justify such a quota. Thus the company and the union were caught in a dilemma. To eliminate the affirmative action plan was to run the risk of suits by minority employees and the loss of government contracts. To

IMPACT OF LEGAL FACTORS ON PRODUCTIVITY, QUALITY OF WORK LIFE, AND THE BOTTOM LINE

There are both direct and indirect costs associated with unlawful discrimination. For example, sexual harassment can create high levels of stress and anxiety for both the victim and the perpetrator. These psychological reactions can lead to outcomes that increase labor costs for employers. Job performance may suffer, and absenteeism, sick leave, and turnover may increase. Both internal discrimination against present employees and external discrimination against job applicants can lead to costly lawsuits. Litigation is a time-consuming, expensive exercise that no organization wants. Yet organizations have been hit with lawsuits affecting virtually every aspect of the employment relationship, and many well-publicized awards to victims have reached millions of dollars.

Let's not view the legal and social aspects of the HR management process exclusively in negative terms. Most of the present civil rights laws and regulations were enacted as a result of gross violations of individual rights. In most instances, the flip side of unlawful discrimination is good HR practice. For example, it is good practice to use properly developed and validated employment selection procedures and performance appraisal systems. It is good HR practice to treat people as individuals and not to rely on stereotyped group membership characteristics (e.g., stereotypes about women, ethnic groups, older workers, workers with disabilities). Finally, it just makes good sense to pay people equally, regardless of gender, if they are equally qualified and are doing the same work. These kinds of HR practices can enhance productivity, provide a richer quality of work life, and contribute directly to the overall profitability of any enterprise.

retain the plan when there was no previous history of proven discrimination was to run the risk of reverse discrimination suits by white employees. And to admit previous discrimination at the plant in order to justify the affirmative action plan was to invite suits by minority applicants and employees.

The Supreme Court ruled that employers can give preference to minorities and women in hiring for "traditionally segregated job categories" (i.e., where there has been a societal history of purposeful exclusion of these individuals from the job category). Employers need not admit past discrimination in order to establish voluntary affirmative action programs. The Court also noted that the Kaiser plan was a "temporary measure" designed simply to eliminate a manifest racial imbalance.[83]

Subsequent cases, together with the Civil Rights Act of 1991, have clarified a number of issues left unresolved by Weber:

1. Courts may order, and employers voluntarily may establish, affirmative action plans, including goals and timetables, to address problems of underutilization of women and minorities. Court-approved affirmative action settlements may not be reopened by individuals who were not parties to the original suit.
2. The plans need not be directed solely to identified victims of discrimination but may include general, classwide relief.
3. While the courts will almost never approve a plan that would result in whites' losing their jobs through layoffs, they may sanction plans that impose limited burdens on whites in hiring and promotions (i.e., plans that postpone hiring and promotion).
4. Numerically based preferential programs should not be used in every instance, and they need not be based on an actual finding of discrimination.[84]

Social policy, as articulated in pronouncements by Congress and the courts, clearly reflects an effort to provide a "more level playing field" that allows women, minorities, and nonminorities to compete for jobs on the basis of merit alone. As Eleanor Holmes Norton, former chair of the EEOC, noted: "Affirmative action alone cannot cure age-old disparities based on race or sex. But if Title VII is allowed to do its work, it will speed the time when it has outlived its usefulness and our country has lived up to its promises."[85]

Human Resource Management in Action: Conclusion

CAN AN EMPLOYEE WHO SEEKS TREATMENT FOR ALCOHOL ABUSE BE FIRED?

"Overlapping Remedies"

In its decision, the appeals court noted that in the Americans with Disabilities Act of 1990, which amended the Rehabilitation Act and extended remedies for discrimination on the basis of disability to many more private employers, Congress stated explicitly that the legislation did not "limit the remedies, rights, and procedures of any . . . law of any State . . . or jurisdiction that provides greater or equal protection for the rights of individuals with disabilities than are afforded by this chapter." The court noted: "While this provision obviously can have no effect on our view of Congressional intent in 1973, it is a particularly pertinent example of Congress's historical practice of allowing overlapping remedies for employment discrimination."

Disability Discrimination as a "Special Case"

The court stated:

> We think it unlikely that Congress has a special interest in immunizing federal contractors from obligations otherwise applicable to them under state [disability] discrimination statutes. These companies may do only $2500 in business with the federal government, with the bulk of their enterprise devoted to commerce within a single state. This division gives the state a substantial interest in protecting the employment interests of its disabled citizens. The developing nature of the issues raised in the field of disability discrimination strikes us as insufficient justification for excusing these employers from obligations imposed on others who differ only in that the federal government is not one of their customers.

In sum, the court found no "clear and manifest" intent on the part of Congress to treat disability discrimination claims against federal contractors any differently from other types of discrimination claims or to exempt them from state laws.

Maritime versus State Law

The court ruled that a state law claim should not be dismissed simply because it would result in differing remedies for plaintiffs in different parts of the country. "As a general matter, however, we conclude that state human rights statutes may be applied in maritime cases. Indeed, it would be anomalous for maritime law, which has always shown 'a special solicitude for the welfare of seamen and their families,' to reject such an employee-sensitive provision."

Wrongful Discharge of Ellenwood

The appeals court noted that the district court did not devise a new "wrongful discharge" cause of action on behalf of Ellenwood. It simply recognized the obvious fact that—notwithstanding the general rule that a seaman's employment is at will—a maritime employer may make a contractual agreement with, or an enforceable promise to, its employees:

> In this case, Ellenwood claimed that Exxon had promised that his job security and future opportunities would not be jeopardized if he sought treatment for alcoholism. The jury found that the requirements for establishing a binding obligation were met. We see no reason why maritime law would invalidate this self-imposed obligation.

Ultimately, the jury awarded Ellenwood a judgment of $677,648 for his claims.

SUMMARY

Congress enacted the following laws to promote fair employment. They provide the basis for discrimination suits and subsequent judicial rulings:

- Thirteenth and Fourteenth Amendments to the U.S. Constitution
- Civil Rights Acts of 1866 and 1871
- Equal Pay Act of 1963
- Title VII of the Civil Rights Act of 1964
- Age Discrimination in Employment Act of 1967 (as amended in 1986)
- Immigration Reform and Control Act of 1986
- Americans with Disabilities Act of 1990
- Civil Rights Act of 1991
- Family and Medical Leave Act of 1993
- Executive Orders 11246, 11375, and 11478
- Rehabilitation Act of 1973
- Uniformed Services Employment and Reemployment Rights Act of 1994

The Equal Employment Opportunity Commission (EEOC) and the Office of Federal Contract Compliance Programs (OFCCP) are the two major federal regulatory agencies charged with enforcing these nondiscrimination laws. The EEOC is responsible for both private and public nonfederal employers, unions, and employment agencies. The OFCCP is responsible for ensuring compliance from government contractors and subcontractors.

A considerable body of case law has developed, affecting almost all aspects of the employment relationship. Case law in the following areas was discussed:

- Sex discrimination, sexual harassment, reproductive hazards, and pregnancy
- Age discrimination
- National origin discrimination
- Seniority
- Testing and interviewing
- Personal history (specifically, preemployment inquiries)
- Preferential selection

IMPLICATIONS FOR MANAGEMENT PRACTICE

A manager can easily feel swamped by the maze of laws, court rulings, and regulatory agency pronouncements that organizations must navigate through. While it is true that in the foreseeable future there will continue to be legal pressure to avoid unlawful discrimination, there will be great economic pressure to find and retain top talent.[86] Workforce diversity is a competitive necessity, and employers know it. Progressive managers recognize that now is the time to begin developing the kinds of corporate policies and interpersonal skills that will enable them to operate effectively in multicultural work environments.

The bottom line in all these cases is that, as managers, we need to be very clear about job requirements and performance standards, we need to treat people as individuals, and we must evaluate each individual fairly relative to job requirements and performance standards.

DISCUSSION QUESTIONS

2-1 If you were asked to advise a private employer (with no government contracts) of its equal employment opportunity responsibilities, what would you say?

2-2 As a manager, what steps can you take to deal with the organizational impact of the Family and Medical Leave Act?

2-3 Prepare a brief outline of an organizational policy on sexual harassment. Be sure to include grievance, counseling, and enforcement procedures.

2-4 What steps would you take as a manager to ensure fair treatment for older employees?

2-5 Collect two policies on EEO, sexual harassment, or family and medical leave from two different employers in your area. How are they similar (or different)? Which aspects of the policies support the appropriate law?

APPLYING YOUR KNOWLEDGE

Case 2-1 *A Case of Harassment?*

Erin Dempsey was working late trying to finish the analysis of the ticket report for her boss, Ron Hanson. The deadline was tomorrow, and she still had several hours of work to do before the analysis would be finished. Erin did not particularly enjoy working late, but she knew Ron would be expecting the report first thing in the morning. She had been working very hard recently, hoping that she would earn a promotion to senior travel agent at the large urban travel agency where she was employed. Getting the ticket report done on time would be absolutely essential for any promotion opportunities.

Matt Owens, a coworker at the travel agency, was also working late that evening. Suddenly, he appeared in her office uninvited and sat down in the side chair. "Got a big date tonight, eh Erin?" Matt said with a touch of sarcasm in his voice.

"I'm working very hard on the ticket report tonight Matt, and I really could use a bit of privacy." Erin had sensed before that Matt was a pest and she hoped that by being rather direct with him he would leave her alone.

"A cute chick like you shouldn't waste a perfectly good Wednesday evening working late."

"Please Matt, I've got work to do."

"Oh come on Erin. I've noticed the way you act when you walk by my office or when we pass in the halls. It's clear that you're dying to go out with me. Some things a guy can just sense. This is your big chance. I'll tell you what. Let's go to dinner at that new intimate French restaurant up on the hill. Afterwards we can stop by my place for some music, a fire in the fireplace, and a nightcap. I make a great Black Russian. What do you say?"

Erin was furious. "I say you're an egotistical, self-centered, obnoxious, dirty old man. If you don't get out of here right now, I'm going to call Ron Hanson at home and tell him that you're keeping me from finishing the ticket report."

"Oh my, you're even sexier when you're angry. I like that in a woman."

Erin could see that she was getting nowhere fast with this approach, so she decided to leave the room in hopes that Matt would get the hint and go home. As she stormed through the door, Matt mockingly held the door ajar, said "after you, sweet thing," and then patted Erin on the backside as she passed. Erin stopped in her tracks, turned to Matt, and said, "If you *ever* do that again, I'll . . . " She was so mad that she couldn't think of an appropriate threat. So instead she just stormed off down the hall and left the building.

The next morning, Erin was waiting in the office of Daryl Kolendich, the owner of the travel agency, when he arrived at work. Erin knew that Ron Hanson would probably be angry that she had gone over his head to the agency owner, but she was so furious with Matt Owens that she wanted immediate action. She described the incident to Daryl and demanded that some sort of disciplinary action be taken with Matt.

"Now calm down, Erin. Let's think through this problem a bit first. Isn't it possible that you can handle this sort of problem yourself? Is it possible that you may in fact have been encouraging Matt to act this way? Look, I understand that you're upset. I would be too, if I were in your shoes. But look at it this way. We've been hiring male travel agents for only the last few years now. Prior to that time there were only female agents, so problems like these never arose. Matt is from an older generation than yours. It takes time for men like him to get used to working on an equal basis with women. Can't you just try to make sure over the next few weeks that you give him no encouragement at all? If you do, I'm sure this problem will take care of itself."

Erin was not at all convinced. "But I *did* make it very clear I was not interested in him. It seemed to make him even more persistent. You're the owner and the boss here, and I'll do what you ask, but it seems to me that it's your responsibility to make sure this kind of sexual harassment doesn't take place in this agency."

"Erin, has your supervisor Ron Hanson ever suggested that your job opportunities here would be improved if you went out with him? Have I ever in any way intimated that a date with me could lead to a promotion for you?"

Erin was silent. It was true that none of the management staff at the agency had been guilty of sexual harassment. In fact, both Ron and Daryl had been highly supportive of her work ever since she arrived. Her annual pay raises had been higher than those of most other coworkers, both male and female.

Daryl broke the silence. "I guess my point is that we don't have a sexual harassment situation here. Please try what I've suggested and let me know in a couple of weeks if you feel it hasn't worked."

Questions

1. What is sexual harassment in the workplace? Was Matt Owens guilty of sexual harassment?
2. If you were Erin Dempsey, what would you do?

3. What is an organization's responsibility in regard to sexual harassment among co-workers or supervisor-subordinate pairs? Do you think that Daryl Kolendich responded appropriately to the problem?
4. Outline a brief personnel policy that an organization could adopt to protect itself from sexual harassment lawsuits.

REFERENCES

1. Jones, J. E., Jr., Murphy, W. P., & Belton, R. (1987). *Discrimination in employment* (5th ed.). St. Paul, MN: West.
2. Friedman, A. (1972). Attacking discrimination through the Thirteenth Amendment. *Cleveland State Law Review*, **21**, 165–178.
3. *Johnson v. Railway Express Agency, Inc.* (1975). 95 S. Ct. 1716.
4. Civil rights statutes extended to Arabs, Jews. (1987, May 19). *Daily Labor Report*, pp. 1, 2, 6.
5. Boys Club pays its dues. (1989, Jan. 23). *Time*, p. 47.
6. Jones et al., op. cit. See also *Bakke v. Regents of the University of California* (1978). 17 FEPC 1000.
7. Privacy and sex discrimination. (1992, Apr.). *Bulletin*. Denver: Mountain States Employers Council, Inc., p. 3.
8. *Furnco Construction Corp. v. Waters* (1978). 438 U.S. 567.
9. *McDonnell Douglas v. Green* (1973). 411 U.S. 972.
10. Civil Rights Act of 1991, Public Law No. 102–166, 105 Stat. 1071 (1991). Codified as amended at 42 U.S.C., Section 1981, 2000e *et seq.*
11. Age discrimination. (1996, May). *Bulletin*. Denver: Mountain States Employers Council, Inc., pp. 3, 4.
12. Pitfalls of verifying a worker's employment authorization: Are your I-9 forms up to snuff? (1996, Apr.). *Bulletin*. Denver: Mountain States Employers Council, Inc., p. 2. See also Bradshaw, D. S. (1987). Immigration reform: This one's for you. *Personnel Administrator*, **32**(4), 37–40.
13. Pitfalls, loc. cit.
14. Four years after the ADA. (1996, Nov./Dec.). *Working Age*, p. 2.
15. EEOC definition of term "disability." (1995, May). *Bulletin*. Denver: Mountain States Employers Council, Inc., pp. 1, 3.
16. Drug and alcohol testing: 1996 overview for employers. *Bulletin*. Denver: Mountain States Employers Council, Inc., pp. 1, 3.
17. Americans with Disabilities Act of 1990, Public Law No. 101–336, 104 Stat. 328 (1990). Codified at 42 U.S.C., Section 12101 *et seq.*
18. Cascio, W. F. (1994). The 1991 Civil Rights Act and the Americans with Disabilities Act of 1990: Requirements for psychological practice in the workplace. In B. D. Sales & G. R. VandenBos (eds.), *Psychology in litigation and legislation*. Washington, DC: American Psychological Association, pp. 175–211.
19. Update on EEOC ADA charges. (1996, May). *PTC Newsletter*. p. 3.
20. Karr, A. R. (1991, Feb. 28). EEOC clarifies law on rights of handicapped. *The Wall Street Journal*, p. A12.
21. FMLA—The supervisor's role. (1996, Aug.). *Bulletin*. Denver: Mountain States Employers Council, Inc., p. 1.
22. Family and Medical Leave Act—The regulations. (1993, Aug.). *Bulletin*. Denver: Mountain States Employers Council, Inc., p. 1.
23. Most small businesses appear prepared to cope with new family-leave rules. (1993, Feb. 8). *The Wall Street Journal*, pp. B1, B2.

24. Brotherton, P. (1996, Apr.). HR exec, FMLA officials disagree on law's impact. *HR News*, p. 10.
25. Jackson, D. J. (1978). Update on handicapped discrimination. *Personnel Journal*, **57**, 488–491.
26. The Uniformed Services Employment and Reemployment Rights Act of 1994, Public Law 102–353; H. R. 995.
27. Ledvinka, J., & Scarpello, V. G. (1991). *Federal regulation of personnel and human resource management* (2d ed.). Boston: PWS-Kent.
28. *Albemarle Paper Company v. Moody* (1975). 442 U.S. 407.
29. EEOC—ADR. (1995, June). *Bulletin*. Denver: Mountain States Employers Council, Inc., p. 2.
30. Lublin, J. S., & Pasztor, A. (1985, Dec. 11). Tentative affirmative action accord is reached by top Reagan officials. *The Wall Street Journal*, p. 4.
31. Leonard, B. (1996, Apr.). Affirmative action debated in hearings, conference panel. *HR News*, pp. 1, 11.
32. *Wygant v. Jackson Board of Education* (1986). 106 S. Ct. 1842; *Local 28 Sheet Metal Workers v. E.E.O.C.* (1986). 106 S. Ct. 3019; *Local 93 Firefighters v. Cleveland* (1986). 106 S. Ct. 3063.
33. Pear, R. (1985, Oct. 27). The cabinet searches for consensus on affirmative action. *The New York Times*, p. E5.
34. *Johnson v. Santa Clara Transportation Agency* (1987, Mar. 26). 107 S. Ct. 1442, 43 FEP Cases 411; *Daily Labor Report*, pp. A1, D1–D19.
35. Equal Employment Opportunity Commission (EEOC). (1979, Mar. 9). Pregnancy Discrimination Act: Adoption of interim interpretive guidelines, questions, and answers. *Federal Register*, 44, 13277–13281.
36. Cowan, A. L. (1989, Aug. 21). Women's gains on the job: Not without a heavy toll. *The New York Times*, pp. A1, A14.
37. Fernandez, J. P. (1993). *The diversity advantage*. New York: Lexington.
38. Trotter, R., Zacur, S. R., & Greenwood, W. (1982). The pregnancy disability amendment: What the law provides. Part II. *Personnel Administrator*, **27**, 55–58.
39. *California Federal Savings & Loan Association v. Guerra* (1987). 42 FEP Cases 1073.
40. Balancing work and family. (1996, Sept. 16). *Business Week*, pp. 74–80.
41. Schwartz, F. N. (1992, Mar.–Apr.). Women as a business imperative. *Harvard Business Review*, pp. 105–113.
42. *Pregnancy and employment: The complete handbook on discrimination, maternity leave, and health and safety*. (1987). Washington, DC: Bureau of National Affairs.
43. Ibid.
44. Trotter et al., loc. cit.
45. Kilborn, P. (1990, Sept. 2). Manufacturer's policy, women's job rights clash. *Denver Post*, p. 2A.
46. Wermiel, S. (1991, Mar. 21). Justices bar "fetal protection" policies. *The Wall Street Journal*, pp. B1, B8. See also Epstein, A. (1991, Mar. 21). Ruling called women's rights victory. *Denver Post*, pp. 1A, 16A.
47. Fetal protection policy voided. (1991, May). *Bulletin*. Denver: Mountain States Employers Council, p. 2
48. Woo, J. (1992, Nov. 3). Secret taping of supervisors is on the rise, lawyers say. *The Wall Street Journal*, pp. B1, B5.
49. Fisher, A. B. (1993, Aug. 23). Sexual harassment: What to do. *Fortune*, pp. 84–88.
50. Ibid. See also Yang, C. (1996, May 13). Getting justice is no easy task. *Business Week*, p. 98.
51. York, K. M. (1989). Defining sexual harassment in workplaces: A policy-capturing approach. *Academy of Management Journal*, **32**, 830–850.
52. EEOC. (1980). *Guidelines on discrimination because of sex*. 29 C.F.R., Part 1604 (11)(a).

53. *Barnes v. Costle* (1977). 561 F. 2d 983 (D.C. Cir.).
54. Court holds employer liable for harassment by supervisor. (1987, June 1). *Daily Labor Report*, pp. A1, D1–D5.
55. *Meritor Savings Bank v. Vinson* (1986). 477 U.S. 57.
56. Ibid.
57. Barrett, P. M. (1993, Nov. 10). Justices make it easier to prove sex harassment. *The Wall Street Journal*, pp. A3, A4.
58. McMorris, F. A. (1995, Aug. 15). Sexual-harassment ruling limits employers' liability. *The Wall Street Journal*, p. B3. See also Johnson, C. (1995, May 17). Court cases give firms guidance on sexual harassment. *The Wall Street Journal*, p. B2.
59. Lessons learned: The hard way. (1996, Apr.). *Bulletin*. Denver: Mountain States Employers Council, pp. 2, 3. See also Sexual Harassment: Preventive measures. (1992, Jan.). *Bulletin*. Denver: Mountain States Employers Council, p. 2.
60. *Schwager v. Sun Oil Company of PA* (1979). 591 F. 2d 58 (10th Cir.).
61. Miller, C. S., Kaspin, J. A., & Schuster, M. H. (1990). The impact of performance appraisal methods on age discrimination in employment act cases. *Personnel Psychology*, **43**, 555–578.
62. Leonard, B. (1995, Sept.). English-only rules. *HR News*, pp. 1, 6; *Garcia v. Gloor* (1980). 618 F. 2d 264 (5th Cir.); *Jurado v. Eleven-Fifty Corporation* (1987). 813 F. 2d 1406 (9th Cir.). See also English only. (1993, July). *Bulletin*. Denver: Mountain States Employers Council, Inc., p. 3.
63. Over qualified. (1991, Nov.–Dec.). *Bulletin*. Denver: Mountain States Employers Council, Inc., p. 3. See also Age discrimination—Overqualified. (1993, July). *Bulletin*. Denver: Mountain States Employers Council, Inc., p. 2.
64. *California Brewers Association v. Bryant* (1982). 444 U.S. 598, p. 605.
65. See, for example, *Franks v. Bowman Transportation Co.* (1976). 424 U.S. 747; *International Brotherhood of Teamsters v. United States* (1977). 432 U.S. 324; *American Tobacco Company v. Patterson* (1982). 535 F. 2d 257 (CA-4). See also Gordon, M. E., & Johnson, W. A. (1982). Seniority: A review of its legal and scientific standing. *Personnel Psychology*, **35**, 255–280.
66. *Firefighters Local Union No. 1784 v. Stotts* (1984). 104 S. Ct. 2576.
67. *Wygant v. Jackson Board of Education* (1986). 106 S. Ct. 1842.
68. Greenhouse, L. (1984, June 13). Seniority is held to outweigh race as a layoff guide. *The New York Times*, pp. A1, B12.
69. Britt, L. P., III (1984). Affirmative action: Is there life after Stotts? *Personnel Administrator*, **29**(9), 96–100.
70. *Griggs v. Duke Power Company* (1971). 402 U.S. 424.
71. Ibid., p. 428.
72. Committee on Psychological Tests and Assessment, American Psychological Association. (1996, June). Statement on the disclosure of test data. *American Psychologist*. **51**, 644–648.
73. Justices uphold utility's stand on job testing. (1979, Mar. 6). *The Wall Street Journal*, p. 4.
74. *Watson v. Fort Worth Bank & Trust* (1988). 108 S. Ct. 299.
75. Bersoff, D. N. (1988). Should subjective employment devices be scrutinized? *American Psychologist*, **43**, 1016–1018.
76. *EEOC v. Radiator Specialty Company* (1979). 610 F. 2d 178 (4th Cir.).
77. *Dothard v. Rawlinson* (1977). 433 U.S. 321.
78. *Gregory v. Litton Systems, Inc.* (1972). 472 F. 2d 631 (9th Cir.).
79. *Webster v. Redmond* (1979). 599 F. 2d 793 (7th Cir.).
80. *Hyland v. Fukada* (1978). 580 F. 2d 977 (9th Cir.).
81. *McDonald v. Santa Fe Transportation Co.* (1976). 427 U.S. 273.
82. *United Steelworkers of America v. Weber* (1979). 99 S. Ct. 2721.

83. Beyond Bakke: High Court approves affirmative action in hiring, promotion. (1979, June 28). *The Wall Street Journal*, pp. 1, 30.
84. Replying in the affirmative. (1987, Mar. 9). *Time*, p. 66.
85. Norton, E. H. (1987, May 13). Step by step, the Court helps affirmative action. *The New York Times*, p. A27.
86. Labich, K. (1996, Sept. 9). Making diversity pay. *Fortune*, pp. 177–180.

3 DIVERSITY AT WORK

Questions This Chapter Will Help Managers Answer

1 Are there business reasons why I should pay attention to "managing diversity"?
2 What are leading companies doing in this area?
3 What can I do to reverse the perception among many managers that the growing diversity of the workforce is a problem?
4 How can I maximize the potential of a racially and ethnically diverse workforce?
5 What can I do to accommodate women and older workers?

ON MANAGING A MULTICULTURAL WORKFORCE*

- A manager born and raised in the United States sees two Arab Americans in his group arguing—and figures he'd better stay out of it. What started as a small disagreement escalates into a conflict requiring formal disciplinary action. Both employees had in fact expected a third-party intermediary, or *wasta* in Arabic. Without one, the incident blows up. This expectation goes back to the Koran and to Bedouin tradition. The dominant American culture (that is, the one traditionally defined by the most populous group in organizations—white males) tends to assume an individualistic, win-lose approach and to emphasize privacy. What the manager doesn't understand is that Arab Americans tend to value a win-win result that preserves group harmony even if it requires mediation.
- A Latino manager starts a budget-planning meeting by chatting casually and checking with his new staff on whether everyone can get together after work. His own boss frets over the delay and wonders why he doesn't get straight to the numbers. What his boss doesn't understand is that in the Latino culture, building relationships is crucial to working together. It's the boss's American culture that wants the manager to "get right down to business."
- An Asian American woman is being interviewed for employment. Deferring to authority, she keeps her eyes down, rarely meeting the interviewer's eyes. The interviewer, a white American male, thinks, "She's not assertive, not strong enough, maybe she's hiding something or is insecure." What the interviewer doesn't understand is that the Asian-American woman views the persistent eye contact of the interviewer as domineering, invasive, and controlling. The result: neither trusts the other.
- In a corporate setting, one manager, who is an African American, shows up a bit late for a meeting. Everyone notices. He is on time for the next meeting, when three other managers, who are white, are late. Their lateness is tolerated and not much of an issue. What is going on here is the exaggerated way in which the behavior of nonwhite people is often perceived, relative to that of white people.

These four scenarios are not blatant cases of unlawful discrimination. Nor are such incidents usually so overt as suggested here. But they do represent what happens every day in the workplace because cultural differences are not understood or appreciated.

*Adapted from J. Solomon, As cultural diversity of workers grows, experts urge appreciation of differences, *The Wall Street Journal*, Sept. 12, 1990, pp. B1, B12. Reprinted by permission of *The Wall Street Journal*, (c) 1990 Dow Jones & Company, Inc. All rights reserved worldwide.

Challenges

1. What is the objective of effective cross-cultural communication?
2. In light of the massive restructuring and downsizing that has occurred in large organizations, are employees from different cultures in a position to demand more flexibility from management?
3. What steps can you take to become more effective as a manager in a multicultural work environment?

The United States workforce is diverse—and becoming more so every year.

- More than half the U.S. workforce now consists of racial (i.e., nonwhite) and ethnic (i.e., groups of people classified according to common traits and customs) minorities, immigrants, and women.
- White, native-born males, though still dominant, are themselves a statistical minority. From 1982 to 1994, the percentage of white male professionals and managers in companies with more than 100 employees dropped from 73 percent to 61 percent.[1]
- Women will fill almost two-thirds of the new jobs created during this decade, and by 2005, projections indicate 6 in 10 new workers will be female.[2]
- The so-called mainstream is now almost as diverse as the society at large. Today more than 20 million Americans were born in another country.[3]
- White males will make up only 15 percent of the increase in the workforce over the next decade, and about 40 percent of the workforce will be over 45 years of age—a dramatic jump from 31 percent today.[4]

These demographic facts do not indicate that a diverse workforce is something a company ought to have. Rather, they tell us that all companies already do have or soon will have diverse workforces.

Unfortunately, the attitudes and beliefs about the groups contributing to the diversity change only slowly. To some, workers and managers alike, workforce diversity is simply a problem that will not go away. Nothing can be gained with this perspective. To others, diversity represents an opportunity, an advantage that can be used to compete and win in the global marketplace, as we will now see.

WORKFORCE DIVERSITY: AN ESSENTIAL COMPONENT OF HR STRATEGY

Managing diversity means establishing a heterogeneous workforce (including white men) to perform to its potential in an equitable work environment where no member or group of members has an advantage or a disadvantage.[5] Managing diversity is not the same thing as managing affirmative action. Affirmative action refers to actions taken to overcome the effects of past or present practices, policies, or other barriers to equal employment opportunity.[6] It is a first step that gives managers the opportunity to correct imbalances, injustices, and past mistakes. Over the long term, however, the challenge is to create a work setting in which each person can perform to his or her full potential and therefore compete for promotions and other rewards on merit alone. Key differences between managing diversity and managing affirmative action/equal employment opportunity are shown in Table 3-1.

There are five reasons why diversity has become a dominant activity in managing an organization's human resources (see Figure 3-1):

1. The shift from a manufacturing to a service economy
2. The globalization of markets
3. New business strategies that require more teamwork
4. Mergers and alliances that require different corporate cultures to work together
5. The changing labor market[7]

The Service Economy

Roughly 84 percent of U.S. employees work in service-based industries (see Table 3-2).[8] Service-industry jobs, such as in banking, financial services, tourism, and retailing, imply lots of interaction with customers. Service employees need to be able to "read" their customers—to understand them, to anticipate and monitor their needs and expectations, and to respond sensitively and appropriately to those needs and expectations. In the service game, "customer

Figure 3-1
Increased diversity in the workforce meshes well with the evolving changes in organizations and markets.

Table 3-1

THE DIFFERENCES BETWEEN MANAGING DIVERSITY AND MANAGING AFFIRMATIVE ACTION/EQUAL EMPLOYMENT OPPORTUNITY (AA/EEO)

Managing diversity

Reason: Proactive—based on reality and anticipated needs

1. Top management leads by example.
2. AA/EEO is an important part of the strategy for managing a diverse workforce.
3. Strategic part of the business plan to help the organization survive, adapt (to changes in markets, customers, products, and services), and grow.
4. Strong link to managerial performance appraisals and rewards.
5. Linked to team building and quality efforts.
6. Wide variety of programs that affect the organization's cultural values and norms (e.g., "family-friendly" policies, formal mentoring programs for all new hires).
7. Long-term linked commitments that use ongoing acquired knowledge as building blocks for future strategies, plans, and goals.
8. Emphasizes strategies to manage more effectively a diverse customer base, a more diverse employee body, and a more diverse stakeholder base.
9. Inclusive (focuses on all employees regardless of race, ethnicity, gender, age, religion, language, personality, sexual orientation, physical or mental limitations).
10. Respects, values, understands, and appreciates differences.
11. Produces significant change in reward, recognition, and benefit programs.
12. Both an internal and external strategy, that is, actively involved in community and societal issues involving diversity.

(continued)

literacy" is an essential skill. Racial- and ethnic-minority customers, in particular, represent a large market segment that accounts for $600 billion in purchases every year. Almost half of all Fortune 1000 companies have some type of ethnic-marketing campaign, and by the year 2000, minorities may account for 30 percent of the U.S. economy.[9]

A growing number of companies now realize that their workforces should mirror their customers. Similarities in culture, dress, and language between service workers and customers creates more efficient interactions between them and better business for the firm. Maryland National Bank in Baltimore discovered this when it studied the customer-retention records for its branches. The branches showing highest customer loyalty recruited locally to hire tellers, who could swap neighborhood gossip. The best of 20 branch managers was located in a distant suburb and was described as dressing "very blue collar. She doesn't look like a typical manager of people. But this woman is totally committed to her customers."[10]

When companies discover they can communicate better with their customers through employees who are similar to their customers, those companies then realize they have increased their internal diversity. And that means they have to manage and retain their new, diverse workforce. There is no going back; diversity breeds diversity. Managing it well is an essential part of HR strategy.

Table 3-1 (continued)

THE DIFFERENCES BETWEEN MANAGING DIVERSITY AND MANAGING AFFIRMATIVE ACTION/EQUAL EMPLOYMENT OPPORTUNITY (AA/EEO)
Managing AA/EEO
Reason: Reactive and based on law and moral imperatives (i.e., "it's the right thing to do")
1. Top management delegates the leading roles to AA/EEO administrators.
2. AA/EEO is a separate activity.
3. Nonstrategic, not tied into the business plan.
4. No formal link to managerial performance appraisals and rewards.
5. Not linked to team building and quality efforts.
6. Targeted special programs that have no significant impact on the organization's cultural values (e.g., "affirmative action recruiting").
7. Short-term, unlinked commitments with little building on acquired knowledge for the next steps.
8. Emphasizes strategies to deal primarily with employees, not customers and stakeholders.
9. Exclusive (focuses primarily on women and people of color).
10. Attempts to make individuals conform to organizational norms.
11. Rewards, recognition, and benefit programs not changed.
12. Primarily an internal strategy, that is, only a limited involvement in community and societal issues to meet governmental requirements.

Source: Adapted from J. P. Fernandez, with M. Barr, *The diversity advantage*. New York: Lexington Books, 1993, pp. 294, 295.

The Globalization of Markets

As organizations around the world compete for customers, they offer customers choices unavailable to them domestically. With more options to choose from, customers have more power to insist that their needs and preferences be satisfied. To satisfy them, firms have to get closer and closer to their customers. Some firms have established a strong local presence (e.g., advertisements for Japanese-made cars that showcase local dealerships and satisfied American owners); others have forged strategic international alliances (e.g., Apple Computer and Sony). Either way, diversity must be managed: by working through domestic diversity (local presence) or by merging national as well as corporate cultures (international alliances).

New Business Strategies That Require More Teamwork

To survive, to serve, and to succeed, organizations need to accomplish goals that are defined more broadly than ever before (e.g., world-class quality, reliability, and customer service). That means carrying out strategies that no single part of the organization can execute. For example, if a firm's business strategy emphasizes speed in every function (in developing new products, producing them, distributing them, and responding to feedback from customers), the firm needs

In many companies, diverse work teams execute business strategy.

Table 3-2

THE SHIFT FROM MANUFACTURING TO SERVICE JOBS, 1973–1993

Year	Manufacturing jobs (%)	Service jobs (%)
1973	26	74
1983	20	80
1993	16	84

Source: Adapted from The perplexing case of the plummeting payrolls, *Business Week*, Sept. 20, 1993, p. 27.

to rely on teams of workers. Teams mean diverse workforces, whether as a result of drawing from the most talented or experienced staff or through deliberately structuring diversity to stimulate creativity.

Firms have found that only through work teams can they execute newly adopted strategies stressing better quality, innovation, cost control, or speed.[11] For example, Ford Motor Company was able to execute its "Quality Is Job One" strategy by getting its employees' commitment to this strategy through team-based work that gave shop-floor workers the opportunity to suggest and implement changes that would improve the quality and efficiency of the production process. Such changes saved Ford over $73 million in production costs for its 1996 model Taurus, and companywide profit sharing has given the teams an incentive to be more efficient. To produce quality products, Ford believes, employees must be involved in and committed to their jobs, and team-based work fosters such commitment.[12] Indeed, thousands of companies, such as General Mills, Corning, Federal Express, Westinghouse, and Dana Corporation, have found that work teams promote greater flexibility, reduced operating costs, faster response to technological change, fewer job classifications, better response to new worker values (e.g., empowerment of lower-level workers, increased autonomy and responsibility), and the ability to attract and retain top talent.[13] Teams also facilitate innovation by bringing together experts with different knowledge bases and perspectives,[14] such as in concurrent engineering—a design process that relies on teams of experts from design, manufacturing, and marketing.

Diversity is an inevitable by-product of teamwork, especially when teams are drawn from a diverse base of employees. Young and old, male and female, American-born and non-American-born, better and less well educated—these are just some of the dimensions along which team members may differ. Coordinating team talents to develop new products, better customer service, or ways of working more efficiently is a difficult, yet essential, aspect of business strategy. As the national director of HR for Deloitte & Touche LLP, a management consulting firm, says, "Diversity is good business. If you don't use the best of all talent, you don't make money."[15]

Mergers and Strategic International Alliances

The managers who have worked out the results of all the mergers, acquisitions, and strategic international alliances occurring over the past 20 years know how important it is to knit together the new partners' financial, technological, production, and marketing resources.[16] However, the resources of the new enterprise also include people, and this means creating a partnership that spans different corporate cultures. A key source of problems in mergers, acquisitions, and strategic international alliances is differences in corporate cultures.[17] According to a *Harvard Business Review* survey of 12,000 managers from 25 different countries, corporate cultures have created problems in 59 percent of the companies creating such alliances.[18] Corporate cultures may differ in many ways, such as the customs used in conducting business, the ways people are expected to behave, and the kinds of behaviors that get rewarded.

When two foreign businesses attempt a long-distance marriage, the obstacles include national cultures as well as corporate cultures. Fifty percent of U.S. managers either resign or are fired within 18 months of a foreign takeover.[19] Many of the managers report a kind of "culture shock." As one manager put it, "You don't quite know their values, where they're coming from, or what they really have in mind for you."[20] Both workers and managers need to understand and capitalize on diversity as companies combine their efforts to offer products and services to customers in far-flung markets.

The Changing Labor Market

You can be sure of this: The U.S. workforce will comprise more women, more immigrants, more people of color, and more older workers as we move into the twenty-first century.[21] Our workplaces will be characterized by more diversity in every respect. The first step to attaining the advantages of diversity is to teach all employees to understand and value different races, ethnic groups, cultures, languages, religions, sexual orientations, levels of physical ability, and family structures. Skeptical managers, supervisors, and policymakers need to understand that different does not mean deficient.[22] For example, in attempting to resolve a conflict between two employees, workers or managers from different

A WORD ABOUT TERMINOLOGY

In recent years, few topics have sparked as much debate as "politically correct" language. Choosing the right words may take a bit more thought and effort, but it is imperative to do so in business communication. After all, it makes no sense to alienate employees and customers by using words that show a lack of respect or sensitivity. Consider just two examples. Instead of referring to dark-skinned people as blacks (whose ethnic origins may be Hispanic or African), it is more appropriate to refer to them as Hispanic Americans or African Americans. Instead of referring to people with physical or mental impairments as "the disabled' or "the handicapped" (terms that suggest a general inability to perform work), it is more appropriate to refer to them as "people with disabilities," thus emphasizing that they can perform some types of work). Showing respect and sensitivity to differences by means of the language we use in business is the first step toward building upon the capabilities of a diverse workforce.

cultures might (1) dictate a solution; (2) serve as referees, issuing rulings only after hearing from both sides; or (3) stay out of the conflict altogether. Each of these strategies can work under certain circumstances. The use of different styles does not mean that one style is necessarily better than another. Only when employees understand and value differences will the corporation they work for be able to build the trust that is essential among the members of high-performance work teams. Such teams incorporate practices that provide their members with the information, skills, incentives, and responsibility to make decisions that are essential to innovate, to improve quality, and to respond rapidly to change.[23]

DIVERSITY AT WORK—A PROBLEM FOR MANY ORGANIZATIONS

Recent studies of the U.S. workforce indicate widespread perceptions of racial and sexual discrimination in the workplace—perceptions that take a heavy toll on job performance. Thus in a 1995 study by the National Black MBA Association, 51 percent of its members said that discrimination was one of several factors hurting their chances for success.[24] A study by the *Los Angeles Times* reported that 75 percent of Hispanics feel there is too much immigration—which leads to discrimination.[25] Reports of discrimination correlate with a tendency to feel "burned out," a reduced willingness to take initiative on the job, and a greater likelihood of planning to change jobs. Not surprisingly, therefore, minorities and women quit companies up to 2.5 times as often as white males, costing employers millions of dollars in lost training and productivity.[26] At Digital Equipment Corporation, more than 70 percent of buyouts in some plants have been taken by women and African Americans, many of whom felt frustrated in their progress up the corporate ladder.[27] This is hardly the way to build a productive workforce.

Studies also challenge the notion that younger workers cope better with a more diverse workplace. Workers under 25 years of age show no greater preference than older workers do for working with people of other races, ages, or

Valuing and respecting differences are keys to success in multicultural business environments.

ethnic groups. Just over half of surveyed workers of all ages said they prefer to work with people of the same race, ethnic group, gender, and education. However, employees who had already lived or worked with people of other races, ethnic groups, or ages showed a stronger preference for diversity in the workplace. Unfortunately, few employees have had this experience. Even workers under 25 had little contact with people of different ethnic and cultural backgrounds in the neighborhoods where they grew up.[28] These responses suggest that the workplace is the main arena for racial and social interaction. If employers want to promote healthy, cooperative interaction, they must assume the leadership to do so.

To begin to promote such interaction, employers must understand the concept of culture and its impact on thought and action. Culture is the foundation of group differences. In the following sections we will examine the concept of culture and then focus briefly on some key issues that characterize three racial/ethnic groups (African Americans, Hispanic Americans, and Asian Americans), women, and the six generations that make up the U.S. workforce. As in other chapters, examples will be presented of companies that have provided progressive leadership.

Culture—The Foundation of Group Differences

Culture refers to the characteristic behavior of people in a country or region. Culture helps people make sense of their part of the world. It provides them with an identity—one they retain even when they emigrate and that is retained by their children and grandchildren as well.[29]

When we talk about culture, we include, for example, family patterns, customs, social classes, religions, political systems, clothing, music, food, literature, and laws.[30] Understanding the things that make up a person's culture helps

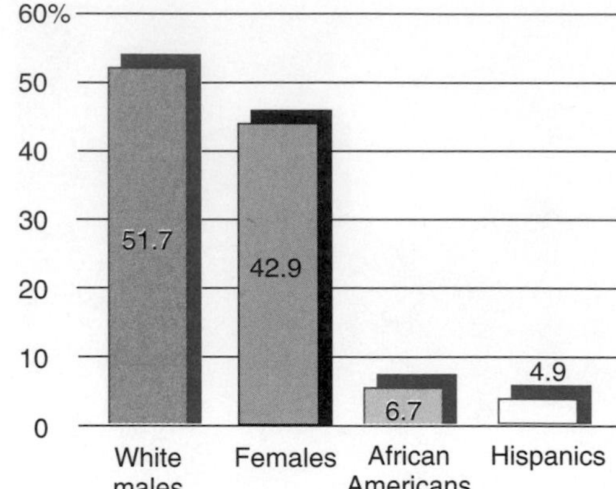

Figure 3-2
Who holds executive, managerial, and administrative jobs? (*Source*: U.S. Department of Labor, 1995.)

diverse people deal more constructively with one another. Conversely, misunderstandings among people of goodwill often cause unnecessary interpersonal problems and have undone countless business deals. The concept of culture will be examined more fully in the final chapter of this text.

"Accepting diversity" means more than feeling comfortable with employees whose race, ethnicity, or gender differ from your own.[31] It means more than accepting their accents or language, their dress or food. What it does mean is learning to value and respect styles and ways of behaving that differ from yours. In a diverse workforce, there is no room for inflexibility and intolerance—they must be displaced by adaptability and acceptance.

African Americans in the Workforce

African Americans will make up 16 percent of the U.S. civilian workforce in 2000.[32] Since the early 1970s, the economic status of African Americans, relative to that of white Americans, has stagnated or deteriorated.[33] Studies indicate that some of the reasons are the following:

1. A shift in the industrial base of the U.S. economy from blue-collar manufacturing to service industries
2. A falling percentage of employed African Americans of all ages, relative to that of whites
3. An enormous increase in nonworkers among African-American men in the prime working age group
4. An increase in poverty rates associated with an increase in the number of African-American families headed by females (80 percent of African-American families with children were headed by married couples in 1890; in 1990, that percentage was down to 39 percent[34])
5. Large occupational differences between African Americans and white Americans, with proportionally more African Americans in low-wage–low-skill jobs. As Figure 3-2 shows, only 6.7 percent held executive, managerial, or administrative jobs in 1994.[35]

Why do these occupational differences persist? Don't companies know about the underrepresentation of African Americans in their ranks? The answer is that companies are offering equitable, not preferential, treatment. Managers are held accountable for their overall minority employment record and for attaining workforce diversity, rather than for the representation of specific racial or ethnic minority groups.[36]

Ceridian Corporation is a good example of this approach. Throughout the company, high-potential women and minorities are selected for succession planning—and all employees get help with career development. Ceridian provides internships to inner-city teenagers and recruits at African-American colleges. Every year managers must set diversity goals, and 10 percent of their bonuses reflect whether those goals were met. Of Ceridian's 7500 employees, 50 percent are women and 19 percent are minorities. At the managerial and executive levels, 36 percent are women and 10 percent are minorities.[37] As these results demonstrate, Ceridian is going a long way to reach out to attract and retain a diverse workforce at all levels of the company.

There are additional options to reduce barriers to occupational advancement among African Americans and other minorities. One of these is public- and private-sector investments in training to enhance skills and productive capabilities. For example, Toyota Motor Sales USA invested $3 million in a minority automotive job training program, donating the money to the Los Angeles Urban League's Automotive Training Center. The center recruits, trains, and places unemployed minority workers in automotive repair jobs.[38] Other options include the promotion of economic growth and new job opportunities (for example, through tax incentives to businesses that invest in inner-city enterprise zones), and a reduction in discrimination (including subtle racism at work and in social situations[39]) and involuntary segregation.

At a societal level, efforts such as these seem to be paying off. Thirty years ago, just 18 percent of African-American families had attained middle-class living standards. Today that figure is 40 percent.[40]

COMPANY EXAMPLE

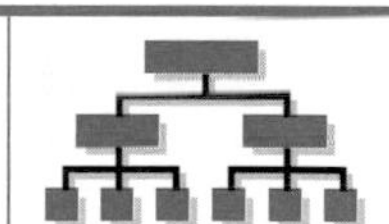

COMMITMENT TO DIVERSITY AT XEROX[41]

The philosophy at Xerox is simple: "If you don't value diversity, you can't manage it." This attitude can be traced to Joseph C. Wilson, who founded Xerox and who regularly stressed its social responsibilities and community involvement. David Kearns, the firm's former CEO, expressed the company's stance: "At Xerox, affirmative action is not a platitude, nor is it a special program. It is a clear-cut, plainly stated corporate business objective." One of the ways in which the company supports diversity is its recognition and encouragement of a network of local and regional caucus groups (for African Americans, women, and Hispanic Americans). The groups meet on their own time and set their own rules and agendas, serving their members in these ways: (1) as a communication link between the members and upper management; (2) as a vehicle for personal and professional development (e.g., through workshops on topics such as presentation skills or how to run a meeting); (3) as a forum for networking and support within the caucus group (e.g., women relating to women on issues of common concern); (4) by giving members a chance to serve as role models to majority employees for managing diversity; and (5) by representing the corporation in community activities, such as outreach recruitment or presentations to schools or civic associations.

Another diversity strategy at Xerox focuses on how to get minority employees and women into jobs that are pivotal to further advancement. The idea here is to examine the backgrounds of all top executives and identify the key positions they held at lower levels—that is, positions that get people noticed—and to set goals for getting minorities and women into those jobs.

A third goal at Xerox is to transform its total employment from a male-dominated to a fully diverse workforce. This means that Xerox is actively striving to achieve and then maintain equitable representation of all employee groups—majority males and females as well as minority males and females—at all grade bands, in all functions, and in all organizations. To accomplish this, Xerox has incorporated these objectives into its corporate HR planning, and especially into all decisions regarding hiring, developing, and moving employees at all levels.

Has this approach worked? Yes; Xerox won the 1995 Commerce Department glass ceiling award for removing barriers to minorities and women. Despite dropping 7800 employees between 1992 and 1995, the company maintained—and in some categories increased—minority representation. Thus the share of African-American officers and managers rose from 11.7 percent in 1992 to 12.1 percent in 1995. Xerox's layoffs were achieved without racial imbalance because minorities were not concentrated in any one area that would make them vulnerable in a workforce reduction.[42]

Hispanics in the Workforce

Hispanics, who will constitute over 14 percent of the civilian labor force in the year 2000,[43] experience many of the same disadvantages as African Americans. Hispanics are the second largest minority group in the United States. However, the term "Hispanic" encompasses a large, diverse group of people who come from distinctively different ethnic and racial backgrounds and who have achieved various economic and educational levels. For example, a third-generation, educated, white Cuban American has little in common with an uneducated Central American immigrant of mainly Native American ancestry who has fled civil upheaval and political persecution. Despite the fact that their differences far outweigh their similarities, both are classified as Hispanic. Why? Largely because of the language they speak (Spanish) or because of their surnames or because of their geographical origins.

Mexicans, Puerto Ricans, and Cubans constitute the three largest groups classified as Hispanic.[44] They are concentrated in four geographic areas: Mexican Americans reside mostly in California and Texas, Puerto Ricans mostly in New York, and a majority of Cuban Americans in Florida. Labor force participation rates for Hispanics (as a group) are growing rapidly (as Figure 3-3 shows), although in the best-paid and most prestigious professions they are woefully underrepresented at present. Hispanics currently hold less than half of their proportional share (7.5 percent) of the best-paying types of jobs (managerial and professional occupations). Take engineering, for example. In 1993, only 2.4 percent of engineers in the United States were Hispanics, up slightly from 2.2 percent in 1983. That means, of course, that they are overrepresented in service and blue-collar jobs.

Other occupations in which there are relatively few Hispanics include physicians (4.4 percent), college and university professors (2.9 percent), dentists

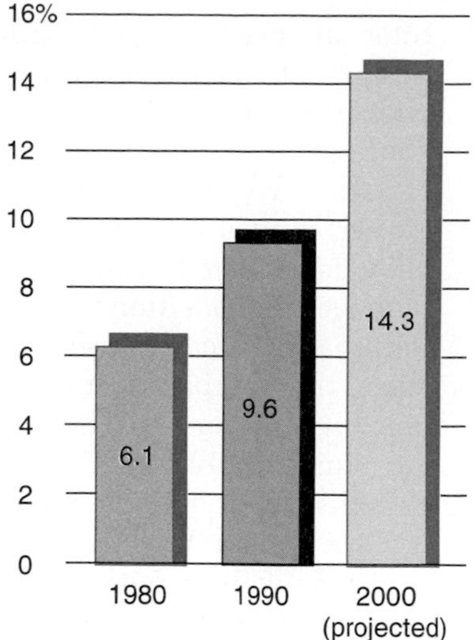

Figure 3-3
Growth of the civilian Hispanic labor force (in millions), 1980–2000. (*Source*: Statistical Abstract of the United States, 1995.)

(2.7 percent), computer systems analysts and scientists (2.6 percent), authors (1 percent), and geologists (0.6 percent). However, there are some bright spots. By 1993, for example, 25 percent of Cuban Americans in the labor force were employed as managers, executives, or professionals.[45]

To encourage greater representation of Hispanics throughout the corporate structure, companies like Pacific Bell have initiated aggressive recruitment and retention programs.

COMPANY EXAMPLE

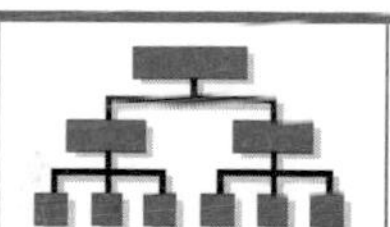

MANAGEMENT DIVERSITY AT PACIFIC BELL[46]

Pacific Bell, a telecommunications company operating in California, realized for two basic reasons that it had to change the way it traditionally recruited employees and managers. For one, the population of Hispanics, African Americans, and Asian Americans was increasing rapidly in California, but only a small percentage of these minorities attended college. If Pacific Bell continued to hire only through college and university campuses, its minority employee percentage of total employees would most likely shrink. This would be especially true for Hispanics, because their population was growing at the fastest rate. Hence while the percentage of Hispanics in California was growing, the percentage of Hispanics on the payroll of Pacific Bell was decreasing.

The other reason Pacific Bell decided to change its recruitment was based on forecasts by the company's planners that its largest growth in management jobs would be in the high-technology areas of engineering, marketing, and data systems. The work in these management jobs requires advanced technical skills and formal education, and they had traditionally been filled via promotion from lower levels. But the company recognized that promotions could not produce the number of skilled managers needed in the near future. So Pacific Bell developed a new recruitment strategy comprising four components:

1. Internal networking by a group called the Management Recruitment District designed to generate employee referrals, to establish networks of employees who had contacts in the minority communities, to identify employees who could serve as guest speakers for external presentations, and to make presentations at regularly scheduled departmental staff meetings.
2. Advertising directed toward specific ethnic groups. The advertisements showed a diverse group of people employed in marketing, engineering, and management positions. These ads were placed on a regular basis in local and national publications serving the targeted minority communities to demonstrate the company's interest in minority hiring and the fact that it valued employee diversity. The same ads were placed in campus publications to announce appointments for employment interviews.
3. Establishment of contact with small institutions in the California State University system, which tended to enroll a higher proportion of minority students, as well as with Arizona State University and the University of New Mexico, both of which have large Hispanic enrollments. The company established relationships with minority student organizations and faculty (particularly those identified with business or technical fields) to identify issues and to offer support. For example, Pacific Bell developed a video, "Engineering Your Management Future," to tell engineering majors about career paths in management.
4. Search for advisors at the local or national level of minority professional organizations, such as the National Hispanic Council for High Technology Careers, to help develop management candidates. The company even hosted a 3-day conference to address the alarming underrepresentation of Hispanics in the teaching and practice of sciences and engineering.

Pacific Bell also established an internship program (the Summer Management Program) for third-year college students, making them student ambassadors representing Pacific Bell's career opportunities. For the company's managers from minority groups, Pacific Bell offered 6-day, off-site training programs conducted by external consultants and designed to help further develop employees' skills. The programs also provided a safe place for participants to talk about sensitive issues such as covert racism and prejudice, topics not likely to be discussed in the work setting.

Over the program's first 11 years, 1980 through 1990, the percentage of minority managers increased from 17.5 to 28.2 percent (even after the significant downsizing that followed the AT&T divestiture in 1984). As of 1996, 70 percent of the company's workforce was minority or female.[47] Pacific Bell has won many awards for its recruitment among minorities, including the Exemplary Voluntary Efforts (EVE) award from the Department of Labor's Office of Federal Contract Compliance Programs, for its long-term commitment to equal employment opportunity.

Women in the Workforce

Over the past 30 years, women have raised their expectations and levels of aspiration sharply higher, largely because of the women's movement (sparked by Betty Friedan's 1963 book, *The Feminine Mystique*), coupled with landmark civil rights legislation and well-publicized judgments against large companies for gender discrimination in hiring, promotion, and pay. Feminism was the last focus of the civil rights movement. Its constituency was the broadest and deepest, and so were the problems it addressed. In 1972, women questioned the possibility of having a family and holding a job at the same time. By the mid-1980s, they took it for granted that they could manage both, and by the mid-1990s, 89 percent of young women said they expect to have both a family and a job.[48] Five forces account for the changes:

1. **Changes in the family**. Legalized abortion, contraception, divorce, and a declining birthrate have all contributed to a decrease in the number of years of their lives most women devote to rearing children. Of all women, 85 percent have babies,[49] but 55 percent of mothers with children under 3 years of age now work, as do 75 percent of those whose youngest child is under 18.[50] The older the youngest child is, the more likely the mother is to work. Women are also significant providers of family income, with more than 55 percent of employed women bringing in half or more.[51]

   The proportion of single-parent family groups with children under age 18 has increased dramatically, such that more than half of all children born in the United States after 1980 will probably spend some time living in a single-parent household before reaching age 18.[52] Most single-parent families are headed by women, and most working women have little choice except to work.

2. **Changes in education**. Since World War II, increasing numbers of women have been attending college. Women now earn 52 percent of all undergraduate degrees, 55 percent of all undergraduate accounting degrees, 51 percent of all master's degrees, and 35 percent of MBAs.[53] In engineering, however, women are still far behind. The percentage of female engineers increased just 1 percent—from 2.7 to 3.7—from 1983 to 1993.

3. **Changes in self-perception**. Many women juggle work and family roles. This often causes personal conflict, and the higher they rise in an organization, the more that work demands of them in terms of time and commitment. Many women executives pay a high personal price for their organizational status; some are faced with broken marriages, while others choose never marrying at all.[54] These kinds of personal conflicts have been termed the "mommy wars."[55] Thus *a major goal of EEO for women is to raise the awareness of these issues among both women and men so that women can be given fair chances to think about their interests and potential, to investigate other possibilities, to make intelligent choices, and then to be considered for openings or promotions on an equal basis with men.*[56]

4. **Changes in technology**. Advances in technology, both in the home (e.g., frozen foods, microwave ovens) and in the workplace (e.g., robotics), have reduced the physical effort and time required to accomplish tasks. Through technology, more women can now qualify for formerly all-male jobs. In some occupations though, the ability to meet physical demands is the price of respect and acceptance. For example, labor unions will accept women painters if they carry their own ladders. And men do not harass a woman who is willing to climb a 35-foot telephone pole to hook up a transformer.[57]

5. **Changes in the economy**. Although there has been an increasing shift away from goods production and toward service-related industries, there are increasing numbers of female employees in all types of industries. Here are some statistics characterizing these changes:[58]
   - 6.5 million businesses with fewer than 500 employees (roughly 33 percent of all U.S. companies) are owned and managed by women, and 1 in 10 American workers is employed by a woman-owned company.[59]
   - Women-owned businesses include the same types of industries as are in the Fortune 500.
   - The number of jobs in businesses owned by women now surpasses the number of jobs in the businesses represented on the Fortune 500 list.
   - Women held 42.9 percent of executive, managerial, and administrative jobs in 1994.
   - Only 7 percent of working women now drop out of the workforce in any given year, down from 12 percent in the mid-1970s.
   - 70 percent of families having annual incomes that reach $40,000 to $50,000 include working wives.
   - By 2001, women are expected to hold about a third of the top jobs in major concerns and to head 10 percent of all companies.

The statistics presented thus far imply that women have made considerable economic gains over the past three decades. However, there are also some disturbing facts that moderate any broad conclusions about women's social and economic progress:

- A 1992 report by the U.S. Department of Labor indicated that little progress had been made by women in breaking through to senior management positions in the country's 1000 largest corporations.[60] Women therefore failed to crack the "glass ceiling" (i.e., although they can see the top jobs, they cannot actually reach them). Women represented less than 2 percent of all corporate officers and accounted for only 2.6 percent of executives (vice president and up) at Fortune 500 firms. Of 1315 board members of the 100 largest American corporations, only 7.5 percent were women. And only 11.5 percent of top union leaders were women. The situation is even worse in Europe, where women make up 41 percent of the workforce, but hold only 29 percent of all management jobs, less than 2 percent of senior management jobs, and less than 1 percent of board seats.[61]
- Today, U.S. women make 76 cents for every dollar earned by men. At the current rate of increase, women will not reach wage parity with men until 2017. Although the gap is decreasing, at every educational level women make less than men at the same level, and female-dominated fields do not pay as well as male-dominated fields.[62]
- As a group, women who interrupt their careers for family reasons never again make as much money as women who stay on the job. A study of over 2400 women aged 30 to 64 (each with one or more gaps in work of at least 6 months) found that those who took a break of 1 year or so lost the same ground in salary as women who dropped out for longer periods. Compared with women who stayed on the job, women who took breaks earned 33 percent less, on average, during the year they returned to work. And the stigma persists: despite working continuously for 11 to 20 years after the dropout interval, these

women still earned 10 percent less.[63] (However, women who stay on the job, and do not have children, suffer almost no gender gap in pay, relative to men of the same age[64])

- Women in paid jobs still bear most of the responsibility for family care and housework.

Conclusions Regarding Women in the Workforce

The clearest picture we need to see from the data reflecting all these changes is this: If all the working women in the United States were to quit their jobs tomorrow, businesses would disintegrate. There is no going back to the way things were before women entered the workforce. What many people tend to think of as "women's issues" really are business issues, competitiveness issues. Examples: Companies that routinely do not offer child care and flexibility in work scheduling will suffer along with their deprived workers.[65] Women are not less committed employees; working mothers especially are not less committed to their work. Three-quarters of professional women who quit large companies did so because of lack of career progress; only 7 percent left to stay at home with their children.[66] Businesses should react to the kinds of issues reflected in these examples not on the basis of what is the right or wrong thing to do, but on the basis of what makes economic sense to do—which usually is also the right thing to do.

The people who make the decisions about what makes economic sense from the perspective of their new workforces have to learn how to be more creative. For example, not many executives understand that skillfully managing time between the needs and responsibilities of the home and the needs and responsibilities of the office can provide enhanced productivity, which certainly makes good economic sense. It is important that executives see that creative responses to work/family dilemmas are in the best interests of both employers and employees. Adjustments to work schedules (flextime), extended maternity and paternity leaves, and quality day care based near the job come a little closer to workable solutions. Chapter 9 will consider work and family issues in greater detail, but for now let's consider some practical steps that two companies are taking.

COMPANY EXAMPLE

WOMEN'S ADVISORY COMMITTEES AT J.C. PENNEY AND BANKERS TRUST[67]

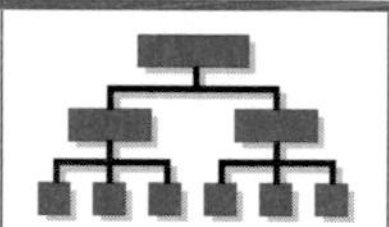

Women employees first began to form groups within their firms during the feminist movement of the mid-1970s. Initially, management perceived such groups to be adversarial and discouraged them, but eventually management accepted the groups, once it understood why they were formed and that there were solid business reasons for their existence. Here are two examples:

Sometime during 1990, J.C. Penney realized there were few women in its senior management positions. So the firm assembled a women's advisory committee, consisting of women employees from all departments. The committee members meet regularly to discuss issues ranging from long-term career goals to the details of how they balance job and family. As a result of what the women had to say at these meetings, there are now four additional women in senior management positions, and the firm has regular programs to train its store managers and executives in all aspects of a diverse workforce.

At Bankers Trust in New York City, a women's group started at about the same time, for the same purposes, and developed in the same way. At many of the regularly scheduled meetings, the group speakers and seminars addressed issues of special relevance to women, such as mentoring, career management, and creative approaches to work/family dilemmas. Membership has grown to 600 and has the full support of management because "management believes that to be successful the company has to be global, that workforce demographics are changing, and that we have to be diverse. Diversity breeds creativity."

Age-Based Diversity

At present, the U.S. workforce is populated by six different generations of workers, each with different, often conflicting, values and attitudes.[68] Here is a brief sketch of each:

- The *swing generation* (born roughly 1910 to 1929) struggled through the Great Depression, fought the "good war" (World War II), and, following that war, rebuilt the American economy, which would dominate the world for more than 30 years. Most, but not all, members of the swing generation have retired.
- The *silent generation* (born 1930 to1945) is demographically smaller. Born in the middle of the Great Depression, too young to have fought in World War II, they were influenced by the swing generation. Because members of the silent generation represented a scarcer resource (i.e., they were in relatively short supply), they were more heavily in demand. Many went to the best colleges, were courted by corporations, rose rapidly, and were paid more than any other group in history. In return, they embraced their elders' values and became good "Organization Men" (i.e., they gave their hearts and souls to their employers and made whatever sacrifices were necessary to get ahead; in return, employers gave them increasing job responsibility, pay, and benefits). The silent generation currently holds most positions of power (e.g., corporate leaders, members of Congress).
- The *baby-boom generation* (born 1946 to 1964) currently accounts for 78 million people and 55 percent of the workforce. Many boomers do not share their parents' attitudes about much of anything. "Big business" still carries a negative connotation among many baby boomers. They believe that the business of business includes leadership in redressing social inequities.

  The boomers believe in rights to privacy, due process, and freedom of speech in the workplace; that employees should not be fired without just cause; and that the best should be rewarded without regard to age, gender, race, position, or seniority. Downsizing (the planned elimination of positions or jobs) has shocked and frustrated many boomers because of shrinking advancement opportunities for themselves and has created a sense of betrayal as their parents were fired or rushed into early retirement. Nevertheless, only 3 percent of employees 50 or over change jobs in any given year, compared with 10 percent of the entire labor force, and 12 percent of workers ages 25 to 34.[69]
- Members of the *lost generation* (born 1965 to 1969) feel disenfranchised because they grew up in the boomers' shadow. Hurt more by parental divorce,

they are waiting for life to get better and are not affluent. Not surprisingly, therefore, they are marrying later than any previous generation in this century (26.5 years for men, 24.1 years for women).[70]

- The *birth dearth generation* (born 1970 to 1977) grew up in the rich 1980s and acquired a taste for excellence, but their jobs will not support that lifestyle. They have become practical, focused, and future-oriented. Members are distinctly divided between those who have knowledge and skills and expect to do well and those who do not have knowledge and skills and have no hopes for the future. Nevertheless, this is a computer-literate generation. Its members are the most skeptical about society's institutions and their own ability to solve problems.

  Collectively, those born from 1965 to 1976 are also known as the *baby-bust generation*. Busters do not invest loyalty in a large corporation, they see work as a means to an end, and they seek jobs more than careers. Raised in shopping malls, which were the centers of their social lives, they are rabid consumers.[71] Their greatest value is quality of life, and they believe strongly in the family, particularly that family comes before work. They probably will be conscientious parents and spend lots of time with their children.

- The *baby boomlet* (born 1978 to the present) comprises children of the baby boomers. They have a strong desire for the affluence of their parents' generation, though they are unlikely to have as much money. Still forming, this generation will be nearly as big as that of their parents. It will have a huge impact on future products and marketing.

COMPANY EXAMPLE

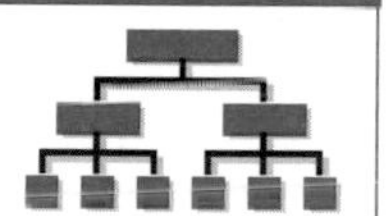

HOW FORD USES GENERATIONAL VALUES TO REDESIGN CARS[72]

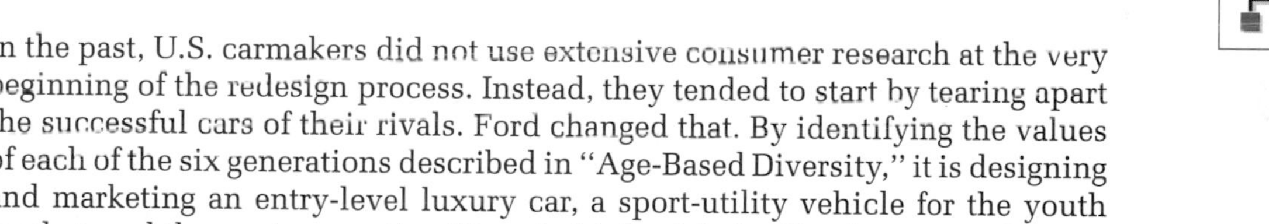

In the past, U.S. carmakers did not use extensive consumer research at the very beginning of the redesign process. Instead, they tended to start by tearing apart the successful cars of their rivals. Ford changed that. By identifying the values of each of the six generations described in "Age-Based Diversity," it is designing and marketing an entry-level luxury car, a sport-utility vehicle for the youth market, and the next-generation Thunderbird to hit the "hot buttons" of different generations. While the approach sounds kooky, insiders say it could completely change how Ford develops and markets its cars.

The approach is founded on the assumption that the basic values that motivate purchases are instilled in each generation between the teens to mid-twenties, formed by everything from relationships with parents to whether their lives were touched by war and the movie stars they worshipped. Says James Bulin, the designer who developed the generational value groups strategy, "The growing-up experience of each generation establishes the rules they live by."[73] Has the approach worked? Consider the newly redesigned F-150 pickup truck, designed to appeal particularly to baby boomers. Sales are up 18 percent, allowing the F-150 easily to retain its lead as America's top-selling vehicle. Says the Ford Truck Division's general manager: "This launch has exceeded our wildest expectations."[74]

MANAGING DIVERSITY

Racial and ethnic minorities, women, and immigrants will account for 80 percent of the growth in the U.S. labor force by the year 2000. And there are other large and growing groups—older workers, workers with disabilities, and gay and lesbian workers—that will soon affect the overall makeup of the workforce. Businesses that want to grow will have to rely on this diversity. Let us consider some practical steps that managers can take to prepare for these forthcoming changes.

Racial and Ethnic Minorities

To derive maximum value from a diverse workforce, not merely to tolerate it, corporations now realize that it is not enough just to start a mentoring program or put a woman on the board of directors. Rather, they have to undertake a host of programs—and not just inside the company. Texaco and Dow Chemical are building ties with minorities as early as high school. Polaroid and Ameritech are investing in employee organizations that monitor corporate policies and work with community groups. For example, Ameritech's Black Advocacy Panel reviews corporate policy on such things as downsizing, and works to improve diversity at top levels by meeting periodically with top management. More specifically, to attract and retain racial and ethnic minorities, consider taking the following steps:[75]

- **Focus** on bringing in the best talent, not on meeting numerical goals.
- **Establish** mentoring programs among employees of same and different races.
- **Hold** managers accountable for meeting diversity goals.
- **Develop** career plans for employees as part of performance reviews.
- **Promote** minorities to decision-making positions, not just to staff jobs.
- **Diversify** the company's board of directors.

Diversity should be linked to every business strategy—e.g., recruiting, selection, placement (after identifying high-visibility jobs that lead to other opportunities within the firm), succession planning, performance appraisal, and reward systems. Northern States Power in Minneapolis is an example of a company that is doing just that.[76] None of these approaches will work unless a majority of employees wants them to work and their cooperative efforts are spearheaded by top management. Levi Strauss & Company is an example of one company that uses a strategic approach.

COMPANY EXAMPLE

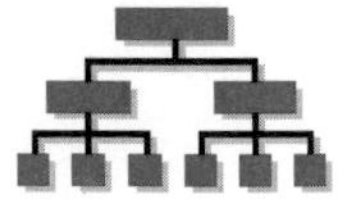

LEVI STRAUSS & COMPANY—DIVERSE BY DESIGN[77]

CEO Robert D. Haas is proud of Levi Strauss & Company's (LS&CO.'s) 7 consecutive years of record sales. But he's just as proud that the company today is recognized as one of the most ethnically and culturally diverse companies in the United States, if not the world. Fully 56 percent of its 23,000 U.S. employees belong to minority groups. Its top management level is 14 percent nonwhite and 30 percent female.

Education is the cornerstone of Haas's efforts. The company invests in its employees through its Valuing Diversity educational programs, one of which lasts 3½-days. The program is designed to get employees thinking about how to become more tolerant of personal differences and to see the importance of those differences.

The company's ads for job openings encourage minorities and women to apply. When job seekers interview at the company, they often find a person who looks like them on the other side of the desk. Says the African-American manager of internal audits: "You get a feeling that there's opportunity here because of the diversity at senior levels."

LS&CO. also supports in-house networking groups of African Americans, Hispanics, Asian-Pacific Islanders, women, lesbians, and gay men. A Diversity Council, made up of two members of every group, meets regularly with members of the executive committee to raise awareness of diversity issues. Finally, part of every manager's bonus is tied to specific activities and accomplishments that meet the goals of the company's Aspiration Statement, which encourages all employees to aspire to appreciate diversity.

Promoting diversity in the workforce makes good marketing sense for LS&CO. too. As an Asian-American manager of corporate marketing noted: "It's tough to design and develop merchandise for markets you don't understand." On the flip side: when you make a point of valuing other people's contributions, some good ideas for products make their way back to headquarters. The company credits an Argentine employee for coming up with the idea of its Dockers® brand of casual pants, now with more than $1 billion a year in revenues.

Alas, diversity also has its downside: costly and time-consuming disagreements abound in a company where everyone's ideas are encouraged. And some managers who feel they need command and control become uncomfortable in a less structured, more open and egalitarian organization—which Haas thinks harnesses diversity—and they leave.

Female Workers

Here are six ways that firms today provide women with opportunities not previously available to them:[78]

1. **Alternative career paths**. This option is especially popular in law and accounting firms that have sanctioned part-time work for professionals.

2. **Extended leave.** IBM, for example, grants up to 3 years off with benefits and the guarantee of a comparable job on return. However, leave takers must be on call for part-time work during 2 of the 3 years.

3. **Flexible scheduling**. At NCNB, a bank based in North Carolina, employees create their own schedules and work at home. After 6 months' maternity leave, new mothers can increase their hours at work gradually. Most who choose to cut their hours work two-thirds time and receive two-thirds pay.

4. **Flextime**. Although flextime may take a variety of forms, a common arrangement allows any employee the right to shift the standard workday forward or backward by 1 hour. Thousands of public and private employers now allow flextime.

5. **Job sharing**. This approach is not for everyone, but it may work especially well with clerical positions where the need for coordination of the overall workload is minimal. That is, activities such as filing, faxing, word processing, and photocopying are relatively independent tasks that workers can share. However, development of a new product or a new marketing campaign, for example, often requires a continuity of thought and coordinated action that cannot easily be assigned to different workers or managers. At Steelcase, the office equipment manufacturer, for example, two employees can share title, workload, salary, health benefits, and vacation.
6. **Telecommuting**. A high-tech solution for high-tech working moms. Employers such as the California-based telecommunications firm Pacific Telesis allow employees to limit the time they spend in the office and to work at home using personal computers, fax machines, and electronic mail. Today, millions of employees of business or government agencies work at home, either part-time or full-time.[79]

Flexible approaches like these will be enhanced, revised, and extended as firms compete to attract and retain top female talent.

Older Workers

Within 20 years, more than a third of all workers will be 50 or older.[80] To be sure, their experience, wisdom, and institutional memories (memories of traditions, of how and why things are done as they are in an organization) represent important assets to firms. As important elements of the diversity "mix," these assets should continue to be developed and used effectively. Here are six priorities to consider in order to maximize the use of older workers and to prepare more generally for coming changes in the internal environments of many organizations:[81]

1. **Age/experience profile**. Executives should look at the age distribution across jobs, as compared with performance measures, to see what career paths for older workers might open in the future and what past performance measures have indicated about the kinds of knowledge, skills, abilities, and other characteristics necessary to hold these positions. Why do this? Because it is important to identify types of jobs where older workers can use their experience and talents most effectively.
2. **Job performance requirements**. Companies should then define more precisely the types of abilities and skills needed for various posts. While physical abilities decline with age, especially for heavy lifting, running, or sustained physical exertion (which are needed in jobs such as firefighting and law enforcement), mental abilities generally remain stable well into the eighties. Clear job specifications must serve as the basis for improved personnel selection, job design, and performance appraisal systems. For example, jobs may be designed for self-pacing, may require periodic updating, or may require staffing by people with certain physical abilities.
3. **Performance appraisal**. Not only must a firm analyze the requirements of jobs better; there must also be improved ways of analyzing the performance of workers in those jobs. For example, age biases may be reflected in managers' attitudes. This is known as age grading: subconscious expectations about

what people can and cannot do at particular times of their lives. Both Banker's Life and Casualty Company and Polaroid have teams that audit the appraisals of older workers to check for unfair evaluations. These teams also attempt to redress general age prejudice in the workplace by working with employees and managers at all levels to replace myths about older workers with facts based on evidence.

4. **Workforce interest surveys**. Once management understands the abilities its older workers have, it must determine what they want. The idea is to survey workers to determine their career goals so that the ones who are capable of achieving their goals will not stall. Not only must management decide that it wants to encourage selectively some older workers to continue with the organization; it must also consider encouraging turnover of workers it does not want to continue. And, of course, management must evaluate what effects different incentives will have on the workers it wants to continue and on the ones it does not want to continue.

5. **Training and counseling**. To meet the needs of the workforce remaining on the job, firms need to develop training programs to avoid midcareer plateauing (i.e., performance at an acceptable but not outstanding level, coupled with little or no effort to improve one's current performance), as well as training programs to reduce obsolescence (the tendency for knowledge or skills to become out of date). These programs must reflect the special needs of older workers, who can learn but may need to be taught differently (for example, by means of self-paced programs instead of lectures).

6. **The structure of jobs**. To whatever degree management may consider changing older workers' work conditions, such as work pace or the length or timing of the workday, it should explore the proposed changes jointly with the workforce. Says Marilyn Joyce, who heads up an Arthur D. Little unit that consults with companies on ergonomic issues: "You simply have to adapt your workplace to the labor force; ignore it, and you could be sacrificing quality and productivity."[82]

Workers with Disabilities

A 30-year-old war veteran with a disability called a radio talk show recently to complain that prospective employers would not consider him for jobs despite his outstanding credentials. "How many interviews have you had?" asked the talk show host, who heads a nonprofit organization dedicated to placing people with disabilities in jobs. "Not one," he admitted. "As soon as I tell them I can't walk, type, and other things I can't do, they get off the telephone as quickly as possible."

"I'm not surprised," said the host, "Prospective employers want to know what job applicants can do for them, not what their limitations are. If you can show a prospective employer that you will bring in customers, design a new product, or do something else that makes a contribution, employers will hire you. Your disability won't matter if you can prove that you will contribute to the employer's bottom line."[83]

The fact is that poll after poll of employers demonstrates that they regard most people with disabilities as good workers—punctual, conscientious, and competent—if those workers are given reasonable accommodation. Despite this evidence, people with disabilities are less likely to be working than any other demographic group under age 65. One survey found that two-thirds of those between the ages of 16 and 64 with disabilities are unemployed. Of the 12.4 million unemployed people with disabilities, 8.4 million want jobs. What can be done?

Perhaps the biggest barrier is employers' lack of knowledge. For example, many are concerned about financial hardship because they assume it will be costly to make architectural changes to accommodate wheelchairs and add equipment to aid workers who are sight- or hearing-impaired. In fact, statistics show that most accommodations cost less than $1000 per employee, and 15 percent cost nothing.[84] Consider several possible modifications:

- Placing a desk on blocks, lowering shelves, and using a carousel for files. Such inexpensive accommodations enable people in wheelchairs to be employed.
- Installing telephone amplifiers for hearing-impaired individuals or magnifying glasses for sight-impaired individuals. Much to their delight, employers have found that these systems helped them gain new customers with hearing or sight impairments.[85]
- Introducing flextime, job sharing, and other modifications to the work schedule. Such approaches, which enabled mothers with young children to continue to work in the 1980s, are being used to help employees with AIDS, cancer, and other life-threatening diseases to continue to work.

Actions like these enable people with disabilities to work, to gain self-esteem, and to reach their full potential. That is a key objective of diversity at work.

Gay and Lesbian Employees

Throughout this chapter we have emphasized that workforce diversity is a business issue—either you attract, retain, and motivate the best talent or you lose business. This fact of business life is one reason why, in late 1996, IBM joined the ranks of nearly 470 other large corporations, governments, and universities to extend the same benefits to the partners of its same-sex couples as to heterosexual couples.[86] Well-known companies such as Apple Computer, Fox Broadcasting, Glaxo-Wellcome, Microsoft, Time Warner, and The Walt Disney Company have the same policy.

American Express Financial Advisors goes one step further. It has established 15 diversity learning labs in its field locations. The labs receive concentrated funding, resource, and training support from the regional and corporate offices. They focus on diverse segments in the African-American, gay and lesbian, Hispanic, and women's markets. Not only are the labs helping employees acquire a more diverse base of clients for the company, but they also are revealing some key lessons:

- Targeting diverse clients drives the need for a similarly diverse workforce.
- To drive the diversity initiative throughout the company, managers must integrate it into business plans, with a requirement to measure specific results.

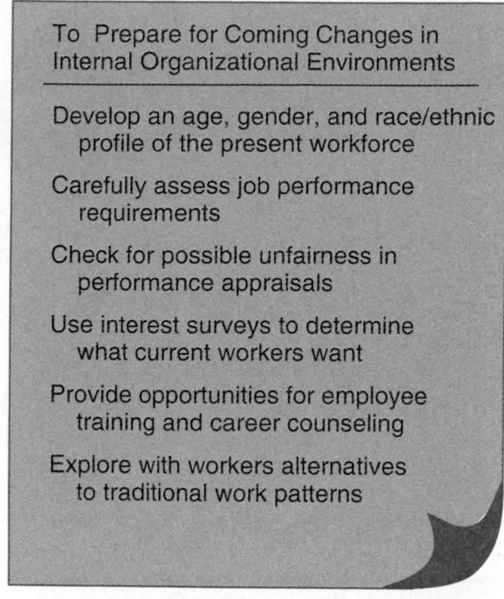

Figure 3-4
Priority listing of suggested actions to manage effectively the internal organizational environments of the future.

- Leaders of the efforts to acquire diverse clients must have not only client-acquisition expertise in that specific market segment, but also strong project-management experience.

The labs have grown from 5 in 1995 to 15 in 1996. With two additional lab start-ups in 1997, plans are to keep the lab level at 17, implement the lessons learned, and eventually weave the funding support from the corporate office into the field offices. The internal expertise and competence fostered by the learning labs is also helping American Express prosper in its business on a global scale.[87]

As we have seen, the workforce is now and will continue to be more and more diverse. A list of actions that managers can take to deal with these changes is presented in Figure 3-4.

ON MANAGING A MULTICULTURAL WORKFORCE

Human Resource Management in Action: Conclusion

Managing a diverse workforce to derive the benefits it is capable of producing depends on one fundamental thing—communication among the cultures that make up the diversity, communication that makes it possible for someone from each culture to understand the perspectives engendered by the culture of others and through that understanding to become comfortable with perspectives different from one's own. This is what managing a workforce is all about today—quite different from yesterday, when managers were taught to ignore differences or regard them as irrelevant. Today, we recognize that cultural differences exist, that they are relevant, and that they reflect values. Rather than suppress cultural differences at work, managers are being taught how to respect them and how to work with them to maximize the contribution of each employee.

Today, both managers and employees are being encouraged to explore their own culture and the cultures of those around them, and to talk about the differences. Nevertheless, many people are uncomfortable doing this. They fear it

ETHICAL DILEMMA
Does Diversity Management Conflict with Maximizing Shareholder Value?

The main objective of profit-making businesses is to maximize overall returns to shareholders (increases in stock prices plus dividends). Since earnings affect this objective, management needs to determine the extent to which any new program—including any new workforce program—will affect the bottom line. There are sound business reasons why having a diverse workforce and managing it properly can increase shareholder value. However, companies generally tend to measure success in these programs by looking at indicators other than the bottom line. Affirmative action programs have been criticized strongly for adding costs to firms but few or no financial benefits.[88] Given the costs involved, can diversity programs be justified over time purely on philosophical and moral grounds (i.e., it's the right thing to do)?

IMPACT OF DIVERSITY ON PRODUCTIVITY, QUALITY OF WORK LIFE, AND THE BOTTOM LINE

All employees, no matter who, no matter at what level, want to be treated with respect. They want to know that their employer values the work they do. That is the most basic thing you must do in managing diversity. And when diversity is managed well, as at du Pont, Procter & Gamble, Monsanto, and Allied Signal, productivity and the quality of work life improve. So do stock prices. A recent study examined the effect on stock prices of announcements of U.S. Department of Labor awards for exemplary diversity programs, and of announcements of damage awards from the settlement of discrimination lawsuits. Announcements of awards were associated with significant, positive excess returns that represent the capitalization of positive information concerning improved business prospects. Conversely, damage awards were associated with significant negative stock price changes, which represent the capitalization of negative economic implications associated with discriminatory corporate practices.[89] In terms of specific payoffs, a multicultural team at du Pont gained about $45 million in new business worldwide by changing the way du Pont develops and markets decorating materials, such as its Corian countertops. Among other things, the team recommended an array of new colors that appealed to overseas customers.[90] Said the chief executive officer of Nutrasweet: "You can't send someone from the north side of Chicago to sell Nutrasweet in Singapore. You need a team to reflect the markets you're going to serve."[91]

will arouse suppressed tensions that could disrupt a system that appears to be functioning smoothly.

And when managers and employees do recognize differences, they have to be careful that they are perceived clearly and objectively. For example, during a training program on workforce diversity, a group of executives of a large oil company received kits containing, among other items, a *Harvard Business Review* article, "Black Managers: The Dream Deferred," which described African Americans' corporate experiences. Without reading the article, dozens of white managers sent their copies to the one African-American manager in the firm with the earnest thought that it would interest him. When the African-American

IMPLICATIONS FOR MANAGEMENT PRACTICE

1. Workforce diversity is here to stay. There is no going back to the demographic makeup of organizations 20 years ago. To be successful in this new environment, learn to value and respect cultural styles and ways of behaving that differ from your own.
2. Recognize that there are tangible business reasons why managing workforce diversity effectively should be a high priority: (a) it is an opportunity to serve the needs of customers better and to penetrate new markets, and (b) diverse teams make it possible to enhance creativity, flexibility, and rapid response to change.
3. To maximize the potential of all members of the workforce, link concerns for diversity to every business strategy: recruitment, selection, placement, succession planning, performance management, and rewards.
4. To retain talented women and minorities, follow the lead of Procter & Gamble in developing long-term career plans that include multiple assignments—and do not be afraid to share the plan with the employees in question. Says CEO John Pepper: "So often, people don't know how you feel about them until it's too late."[92]

manager glanced through the article, he thought, "Those white executives need to read this. I know what it's like."

Not only do managers need to learn about various cultures, they also have to be aware of differences within a culture and of personal idiosyncrasies and preferences. For example, many people assume that all Americans want to be recognized publicly for their accomplishments. Suppose, however, that the person who wants private recognition is a blond California woman who just happens to be shy. What is the bottom line in dealing with diversity in the workforce? According to many experts the solution is simple: ask, do not just assume.

SUMMARY

More than half the U.S. workforce now consists of racial and ethnic minorities, immigrants, and women. White, native-born males, as a group, are still dominant in numbers over any other group, but women will fill almost two-thirds of the new jobs created during the 1990s, and by the year 2000, nearly half the entire workforce will be female. White males will make up only 15 percent of the increase in the workforce over the next decade.

Managing diversity means encouraging a heterogeneous workforce, which includes white men, to perform to its potential in an equitable work environment in which no one group enjoys an advantage or suffers a disadvantage. At least five factors account for the increasing attention companies are paying to diversity: (1) the shift from a manufacturing to a service economy, (2) the globalization of markets, (3) new business strategies that require more teamwork, (4) mergers and alliances that require different corporate cultures to work together, and (5) the changing labor market. Each of these factors can represent opportunities for firms whose managers and employees understand what culture is and the cultural differences among employees and managers, and especially, the differences within the firm's markets.

To attract and retain women, as well as people with disabilities, companies are making available to them alternative career paths, extended leaves, flexible scheduling, flextime, job sharing, and opportunities to telecommute. In addition, many companies now offer the same benefits to same-sex couples as to heterosexual couples. A different aspect of diversity is generational diversity—important differences in values, aspirations, and beliefs that characterize the swing generation, the silent generation, the baby boomers, the lost generation, the birth dearth, and the baby boomlet. To manage older workers effectively, managers should develop an age profile of the workforce, monitor job performance requirements for the kinds of characteristics people need to do their jobs well, develop safeguards against age bias in performance appraisal, conduct workforce interest surveys, provide education and counseling, and consider modifying the structure of jobs.

Finally, to manage diversity effectively, do the following things well: focus on bringing in the best talent, not on meeting numerical goals; establish mentoring programs among employees of the same and different races; hold managers accountable for meeting diversity goals; develop career plans for employees as part of performance reviews; promote women and minorities to decision-making positions, not just to staff jobs; and diversify the company's board of directors.

DISCUSSION QUESTIONS

3-1 In your opinion, what are some key business reasons for emphasizing the effective management of a diverse workforce?

3-2 Discuss some possible reasons why deep divisions in the workforce still remain between and among racial and ethnic minorities, between women and men, and across generations.

3-3 What would the broad elements of a company policy include if the objective was to emphasize the management of diversity?

3-4 How should the outcomes of diversity programs be measured?

3-5 Suppose you were asked to enter a debate in which your task was to argue against any special effort to manage workforce diversity. What would you say?

APPLYING YOUR KNOWLEDGE

Case 3-1 *The Challenge of Diversity**

Talk, talk, talk. As Ken Hartman, an African-American midlevel manager at Blahna, Inc., recalls, that's all he got from the white men above him in top management—despite the fact that Blahna had long enjoyed a reputation as a socially responsible company. But that reputation didn't mean much to Hartman as he watched other African-American

---

**Source:* Diversity management: Beyond awareness, *Employee Relations Bulletin*, Aug. 7, 1994, pp. 1–7; R. Mitchell & M. Oneal, Managing by values, *Business Week*, Aug. 1, 1994, pp. 46–52; F. Rice, How to make diversity pay, *Fortune*, Aug. 8, 1994, pp. 78–86.

managers he thought were highly qualified get passed over for plum jobs, and his own career seemed stalled on a lonely plateau. Top management always mouthed diversity, Hartman said, "but in the end, they chose people they were comfortable with for key positions."

The Diversity Track Record

Is this situation uncommon? Not at all. Human resource experts estimate that only 3 percent to 5 percent of U.S. corporations are diversifying their workforces effectively. Employers agree with this assessment. A 1992 survey by the Hay Group showed that only 5 percent of 1405 participating companies thought they were doing a "very good job" of managing the diversity of their workforces.

Such results might surprise those who remember how loudly the diversity drum was beaten several years ago when the Labor Department released its study entitled *Workforce 2000.* This study reported that only 15 percent of the new entrants into the workforce by the year 2000 would be white males. At the time, many companies vowed to master the management of diversity. They spent large sums of money on consultants to whip it into the corporate culture mix. Yet in most cases, the changes never took hold. At many companies, downsizing became the more urgent imperative. At others, the commitment was never really there.

Examples are provided by Maybelline, Microsoft, and advertising agencies. At the former, a new line of cosmetics for women of darker hues was launched in 1990. It was called "Shades of You." The product was a clear winner, garnering about 35 percent of the ethnic cosmetics market despite the fact that few people of color are employed by Maybelline. Maybelline CEO Robert Hiatt asserts, "It is not the makeup of our management that is important; it is paying attention to the market and our customers. We don't even keep track of the number of minorities in our company."

Microsoft fails to push diversity as well. Says Randy Massengale, who heads Microsoft's 2-year-old diversity effort, "The company has been so focused on growth that we have not built all of the human resources infrastructure we need." The result? A much more homogeneous staff than the hip culture at Microsoft might suggest.

Ad agencies, in particular, don't seem to have caught on. A recent survey reveals that fewer than 1 percent of media managers are African American, 2 percent are Hispanic, 3 percent are Asian, and Native Americans are too few to count. This lack of diversity is particularly ironic for an industry that is supposed to know consumer markets.

The way a company deals with a crisis is often what marks it as a leader. AT&T, lavishly praised for its management of diversity during the past decade, was hit hard by a headline-making incident last fall. The company's employee magazine featured a cartoon of customers on various continents making phone calls. The caller in Africa was depicted as an animal. Immediately upon dissemination of the newsletter, the company's switchboard lit up with calls from irate employees, customers, civil rights groups, and legislators.

Tackling the problem head on, AT&T Chairman Robert Allen apologized to all for the "racist" illustration and noted that it was drawn by a freelancer. He vowed to turn the ugly incident into an opportunity to accelerate the pace of workforce diversity at AT&T and immediately went to work developing an action plan to make it happen. The plan appeared in less than 2 months, with a mission "to create a work environment that sets the world-class standard for valuing diversity." Among the steps listed in the six-page plan, all 13 top officers at AT&T will increase their direct interactions with minority employee caucus groups.

The Strategy at Blahna, Inc.

Ken Hartman's firm, Blahna, Inc., has finally gotten the message. The company is now using diversity management strategies to head off conflict and reduce turnover among employees it can ill afford to lose.

Several years ago, Blahna formed a 20-member Committee for Workplace Diversity, chaired by a vice president. The commitee was chartered to consider why women and minorities weren't better represented at all levels of the organization. Although the company had a good record of hiring women and minorities, the committee discovered that turnover was 2 to 3 times higher for these groups than it was for white males.

Sample exit interviews revealed that women and minorities left for culture-related reasons—for instance, because they didn't feel valued in their day-to-day work, didn't have effective working relationships, or didn't sense that the work they were being given to do would lead to the fulfillment of their career goals. White males, on the other hand, left for business-related reasons, such as limited opportunities for future advancement.

As a result of this initial investigation, Blahna formed a 25-person Diversity Advisory Committee. The committee determined to take a two-step approach to dealing with diversity issues. The first step was to increase awareness; the second was to build skills for dealing with diversity-related challenges. Both steps involved training conducted by diversity consultants, Hope & Associates.

To date, 60 percent of Blahna's 11,000 employees have gone through a 2-day diversity seminar. Forty percent have gone through a more extensive 6-day training program as well. "The premise of the training is that the more different you are, the more barriers there can be to working well together," explains Blahna's diversity development director. Training sessions do not offer advice on how to get along with Asian Americans, women, or other specific groups. Rather, the emphasis is on learning skills that will make it easier to relate to and communicate with others.

A key part of the training offered by Hope & Associates is the implementation of a "consulting pairs" process. The consulting pairs approach is designed to help trainees take what they've learned in training and apply it on the job. When a conflict—which may or may not be related to diversity—first arises between two peers or a manager and employee, a consulting pair is called in to facilitate discussion and problem solving. The unique feature of this approach is that the consulting pair is selected to match as closely as possible the backgrounds of the individuals who are involved in the conflict. Of course, all proceedings are strictly confidential.

The result? Ken Hartman is a happier guy these days. As president of one of Blahna's divisions, the 48-year-old executive is a step away from joining the ranks of senior management. Life has changed for him since Blahna "stopped talking about values like diversity and began behaving that way."

Questions

1. Why do many companies find increasing and managing diversity to be difficult challenges?
2. What were the key elements in Blahna's successful diversity strategy?
3. Under what circumstances might the consulting pairs approach be most useful?
4. What steps should management take to ensure that the consulting pairs approach is working?

REFERENCES

1. Kaufman, J. (1996, Sept. 5). Mood swing: White men shake off that losing feeling on affirmative action. *The Wall Street Journal*, pp. A1, A4. See also White, male, and worried (1994, Jan. 31). *Business Week*, pp. 50–55.

2. Affirmative action on the edge (1995, Feb. 13). *U.S. News & World Report*, pp. 33–47.
3. The new face of America: How immigrants are shaping the world's first multicultural society (1993, Fall). *Time*, Special Issue, p. 3.
4. Labich, K. (1996, Sept. 9). Making diversity pay. *Fortune*, pp. 177–180.
5. Torres, C., & Bruxelles, M. (1992, Dec.). Capitalizing on global diversity. *HRMagazine*, pp. 30–33.
6. Equal Employment Opportunity Commission (1979, Jan. 19). *Affirmative action guidelines*. Pub. no. 44 FR 4421. Washington, DC: U.S. Government Printing Office.
7. Jackson, S. E., & Alvarez, E. B. (1992). Working through diversity as a strategic imperative. In S. E. Jackson (ed.), *Diversity in the workplace*. New York: Guilford, pp. 13–35.
8. The data for Table 3-2 come from The perplexing case of the plummeting payrolls (1993, Sept. 20). *Business Week*, p. 27.
9. The new face of America, loc. cit.
10. Sellers, P. (1990, June 4). What customers really want. *Fortune*, pp. 58–68.
11. Petzinger, T., Jr. (1996, Sept. 13). Charlene Pedrolie rearranged furniture and lifted a business. *The Wall Street Journal*, p. B1.
12. NBC Nightly News, Sept. 17, 1996. See also Banas, P. A. (1988). Employee involvement: A sustained labor-management initiative at the Ford Motor Company. In J. P. Campbell and R. J. Campbell (eds.), *Productivity in organizations: New perspectives from industrial and organizational psychology*. San Francisco: Jossey-Bass, pp. 348–416.
13. Huszczo, G. E. (1996). *Tools for team excellence: Getting your team into high gear and keeping it there*. Palo Alta, CA: Davies-Black. See also Wellins, R. S., Byham, W. C., & Wilson, J. M. (1991). *Empowered teams*. San Francisco: Jossey-Bass.
14. Watson, W. E., Kumar, K., & Michaelson, L. K. (1993). Cultural diversity's impact on interaction process and performance: Comparing homogeneous and diverse task groups. *Academy of Management Journal*, **36**(3), 590–602.
15. Wall, J. In Affirmative action on the edge, op. cit., p. 37.
16. Cascio, W. F., & Serapio, M. G., Jr. (1991, Winter). Human resources systems in an international alliance: The undoing of a done deal? *Organizational Dynamics*, pp. 63–74.
17. Serapio, M. G., Jr., & Cascio, W. F. (1996). End-games in international alliances. *Academy of Management Executive*, **10**(1), 63–73.
18. Kanter, R. M. (1991, May–June). Transcending business boundaries: 12,000 world managers view change. *Harvard Business Review*, pp. 151–164.
19. McWhirter, W. (1989, Oct. 9). I came, I saw, I blundered. *Time*, pp. 72, 77.
20. Ibid.
21. *Workplace Visions: Demographics* (1996, Sept./Oct.). Alexandria, VA: Society for Human Resource Management.
22. Jackson, S. E. (1992). Preview of the road to be traveled. In S. E. Jackson (ed.), *Diversity in the workplace*. New York: Guilford, pp. 4–12.
23. *High-performance work practices and firm performance* (1993, Aug.). Washington DC: U.S. Department of Labor.
24. Diversity: Beyond the numbers game (1995, Aug. 14). *Business Week*, pp. 60, 61.
25. Thiederman, S. (1996, Sept.). Regaining our balance: A look at diversity backlash. *Mosaics*, **2**(5), 1, 2. See also Glazer, N. (1995, Apr. 23). Debate on aliens flares beyond the melting pot. *The New York Times*, p. E3.
26. Diversity: Beyond the numbers game, loc. cit.
27. Kaufman, loc. cit.
28. Shellenbarger, S. (1993, Sept. 3). Work-force study finds loyalty is weak, divisions of race and gender are deep. *The Wall Street Journal*, pp. B1, B5.
29. Boyacigiller, N. A., Kleinberg, M. J., Phillips, M. E., & Sackman, S. A. (1996). Conceptualizing culture. In B. J. Punnett & O. Shenkar (eds.), *Handbook for international management research*. Cambridge, MA: Blackwell, pp. 157–208.

30. Harris, P. R., & Moran, R. T. (1990). *Managing cultural differences* (3d ed.). Houston: Gulf Publishing.
31. Fernandez, J. P., with Barr, M. (1993). *The diversity advantage*. New York: Lexington Books.
32. *Statistical Abstract of the United States* (1995). Washington DC: U.S. Government Printing Office.
33. Brief, A. P., & Hayes, E. L. (1996). The continuing American dilemma: Studying racism in organizations. New Orleans, Tulane University, Working Paper 96-OBHR-02. See also Sharpe, R. (1993, Sept. 14). Losing ground: In latest recession, only blacks suffered net employment loss. *The Wall Street Journal*, pp. A1, A14, A15.
34. Civil rights: The next generation (1993, Aug. 31). *The Wall Street Journal*, p. A10.
35. Diversity: Beyond the numbers game, loc. cit.
36. Labich, loc. cit.
37. Diversity: Beyond the numbers game, loc. cit.
38. *Workplace Visions: Demographics*, op. cit.
39. Brief & Hayes, op. cit.
40. Affirmative action on the edge, loc. cit.
41. Sessa, V. J. (1992). Managing diversity at the Xerox Corporation: Balanced workforce goals and caucus groups. In S. E. Jackson (ed.), *Diversity in the workplace*. New York: Guilford, pp. 37–64.
42. Wynter, L. E. (1996, Feb. 7). Business and race. *The Wall Street Journal*, p. B1.
43. *Statistical Abstract of the United States* (1995). Washington DC: U.S. Government Printing Office.
44. Fernandez, with Barr, op. cit.
45. Castro, M. J. (1993, Oct. 3). Hispanics and the new workforce. *Vista*, pp. 8, 10.
46. Roberson, L., & Gutierrez, N. (1992). Beyond good faith: Commitment to recruiting management diversity at Pacific Bell. In S. E. Jackson (ed.), *Diversity in the workplace*. New York: Guilford, pp. 65–68.
47. Work Week (1996, Sept. 24). *The Wall Street Journal*, p. A1.
48. Shellenbarger, S. (1995, May 11). Women indicate satisfaction with role of big breadwinner. *The Wall Street Journal*, pp. B1, B2.
49. Schwartz, F. N. (1992, Mar.–Apr.). Women as a business imperative. *Harvard Business Review*, pp. 105–113.
50. *Workplace Visions: Demographics*, op. cit. See also Richardson, L. (1992, Sept. 2). No cookie cutter answers in "mommy wars." *The New York Times*, pp. B1, B5.
51. Shellenbarger, loc. cit.
52. Lewin, T. (1992, Oct. 5). Rise in single parenthood is reshaping U.S. *The New York Times*, pp. B1, B6. See also Chira, S. (1992, Oct. 4). New realities fight old images of mother. *The New York Times*, pp. 1, 32.
53. Schwartz, loc. cit.
54. Sellers, P. (1996, Aug. 5). Women, sex, and power. *Fortune*, pp. 43–57.
55. Richardson, loc. cit.
56. Boyle, M. B. (1975). Equal opportunity for women is smart business. *Harvard Business Review*, **51,** 85–95.
57. Women in hard hats (1995, Feb. 13). *U.S. News & World Report*, pp. 39, 40.
58. Roberts, S. (1995, Apr. 27). Women's work: What's new, what isn't. *The New York Times*, p. B6. See also Dobrzynski, J. H. (1995, Apr. 20). Some action, little talk: Companies embrace diversity but are reluctant to discuss it. *The New York Times*, pp. D1, D4. See also Sharpe, R. (1994, Mar. 29). The waiting game: Women make strides, but men stay firmly in top company jobs. *The Wall Street Journal*, pp. A1, A8. See also Nasar, S. (1992, Oct. 18). Women's progress stalled? Just not so. *The New York Times*, pp. 1F, 10F.
59. Women entrepreneurs (1994, Apr. 18). *Business Week*, pp. 104–110.

60. *Pipelines of progress: A status report on the glass ceiling* (1992). Washington, DC: U.S. Department of Labor.
61. Europe: Out of the typing pool, into career limbo (1996, Apr. 15). *Business Week*, pp. 93–94.
62. Crittenden, D. (1995, Aug. 22). Yes, motherhood lowers pay. *The New York Times*, p. A15. See also Fernandez, with Barr, op. cit; and Roberts, loc. cit.
63. Rowland, M. (1992, Aug. 23). Strategies for stay-at-home moms. *The New York Times*, p. 16F.
64. Crittenden, loc. cit.
65. Balancing work and family (1996, Sept. 16). *Business Week*, pp. 74–80.
66. Women entrepreneurs, loc. cit.
67. Genasci, L. (1993, Sept. 6). U.S. women at work organizing into groups. *The Denver Post*, pp. 1F, 4F.
68. The framework for this section was drawn from the following sources: How Ford's F-150 lapped the competition (1996, July 29). *Business Week*, pp. 74–76; Managing generational diversity (1991, Apr.). *HRMagazine*, pp. 91, 92; Ratan, S. (1993, Oct. 4). Generational tension in the office: Why busters hate boomers. *Fortune*, pp. 56–70.
69. Fisher, A. (1996, Sept. 30). Wanted: Aging baby-boomers. *Fortune*, p. 204.
70. Ibid.
71. Peterson, K. S. (1993, Sept. 23). Baby busters rise above elders' scorn. *USA Today*, pp. 1D, 2D.
72. How Ford's F-150 lapped the competition, loc. cit.
73. Ibid., p. 75.
74. Ibid., p. 74.
75. Diversity: Beyond the numbers game, loc. cit.
76. Northern States Power Company (1993). *Capitalizing on diversity*. Minneapolis: Author.
77. Cuneo, A. (1992, Nov. 15). Diverse by design: How good intentions make good business. *Business Week*, p. 72.
78. Balancing work and family (1996, Sept. 16). *Business Week*, pp. 74–80. See also Wentling, R. M. (1995, May). Breaking down barriers to women's success. *HRMagazine*, pp. 79–85.
79. Calem, R. E. (1993, Apr. 18). Working at home, for better or worse. *The New York Times*, pp. 1F, 6F.
80. Thornburg, L. (1995, Feb.). The age wave hits: What older workers want and need. *HRMagazine*, pp. 40–45.
81. Ibid. See also Andrews, E. S. (1992, Winter). Expanding opportunities for older workers. *Journal of Labor Research*, **13**(1), 55–65. See also Lefkovich, J. L. (1992, Spring). Older workers: Why and how to capitalize on their powers. *Employment Relations Today*, **19**(1), 63–79.
82. Labich, op. cit., p. 178.
83. Just one break changes lives of disabled (1994, Oct. 23). *The New York Times*, Special Supplement, "The diversity challenge," p. 11.
84. Disabled succeed in the workplace (1994, Oct. 23). *The New York Times*, Special Supplement, "The diversity challenge," pp. 10–11.
85. Ibid. See also Cascio, W. F. (1994). The Americans with Disabilities Act of 1990 and the 1991 Civil Rights Act: Requirements for psychological practice in the workplace. In B. D. Sales & G. R. VandenBos (eds.), *Psychology in litigation and legislation*. Washington DC: American Psychological Association, pp. 175–211.
86. IBM's decision expected to influence other firms (1996, Sept. 21). *The Miami Herald*, p. 1C.
87. Diversity: Making the business case (1996, Dec. 9). *Business Week*, Special Advertising Section, p. 7.

88. Brimelow, P., & Spencer, L. (1993, Feb. 15). When quotas replace merit, everybody suffers. *Forbes*, pp. 80–102.
89. Wright, P., Ferris, S. P., Hiller, J. S., & Kroll. M. (1995). Competitiveness through management of diversity: Effects on stock price valuation. *Academy of Management Journal*, **38**, 273–287.
90. Labich, loc. cit.
91. Dobrzynski, loc. cit.
92. Labich, loc. cit.

Abuse of Power

By Mark Maremont

THE ASTONISHING TALE OF SEXUAL HARASSMENT AT ASTRA USA

The lights were dim, the music was softly romantic. It was the final night of the Astra USA Inc. national sales meeting last June, and pairs of employees were dancing in the ballroom of a suburban Boston hotel. Astra President and Chief Executive Officer Lars Bildman, then 49, was entwined with a 25-year-old sales representative, Pamela L. Zortman. Two onlookers notice that Bildman, extremely drunk, was running his hands along her back and nibbling at her neck.

Suddenly, Zortman rushed into a nearby rest room. Sobbing, she told other women there that Bildman had tried to kiss her. Zortman, who had worked at the company less than a year, apparently didn't get much sympathy from two longtime female managers present. According to accounts Zortman later gave to two sources, the women told her, in effect: "That's the way it is at Astra, and you'd better get used to it."

Not anymore. On Apr. 29, as *Business Week* was about to publish the results of a six-month investigation into allegations of rampant sexual harassment at Astra, Bildman was suspended and relieved of his responsibilities by Astra's parent, giant Swedish drugmaker Astra AB. The parent company appointed one of its most senior executives, Jan Larsson, to replace Bildman and hired outside counsel to perform a thorough probe.

Senior Astra executives acknowledge that *Business Week*'s investigation sparked the abrupt action. Although Bildman had told superiors about the investigation months ago, Carl-Gustav Johansson, a member of Swedish Astra's executive committee, says the company was unaware of the full scope of the allegations until it received a lengthy letter from *Business Week* on Apr. 19. "We hadn't heard anything this detailed—and certainly not that Mr. Bildman himself was the focus" of some allegations, says Johansson. Refusing further comment on Astra's own preliminary inquiries—which also now include allegations of minor financial improprieties by Bildman—Johansson says Astra suspended its U.S. CEO because "we lost some trust in him."

The *Business Week* investigation, which involved interviews with more than 70 former and current employees, uncovered a disturbing pattern of complaints during much of Bildman's 15-year tenure as CEO of Astra USA. *Business Week* found a dozen cases of women who claimed they were either fondled or solicited for sexual favors by Bildman or other executives. Many women described evenings in which they were expected to escort senior executives to bars and dancing clubs. Others received frequent invitations to join the often inebriated managers in their hotel suites for more intimate late-night gatherings. Until recently, company parties were raucous affairs at which heavy drinking and dancing were virtually mandated. "Guys were encouraged to get as drunk as they could—and do whatever they could to the women," recalls Kimberley A. Cote, a former Astra sales rep who obtained an out-of-court settlement of harassment charges in 1994. "If they felt like grabbing a woman by the boob or by the ass, that was O.K."

"If they felt like grabbing a woman by the boob or by the ass, that was O.K."

Ex-Rep Cote settled her harassment case out of court in 1994.

Even many male employees were appalled. "I've never seen anything as blatant and untoward," says Mashaan Guy, an Astra rep who quit in 1992 because he disliked the culture. Adds David G. Thurston, a respected district sales manager who quit last September in disgust: "If ever there was a company where sexual harassment was rampant, this is it."

Bildman and other senior managers at Astra USA did not respond to *Business Week*'s repeated requests for interviews over the course of two weeks. On May 1, as the article was going to press, Bildman categorically denied the allegations in a written statement. An attorney for Bildman claimed his client hadn't had enough time to respond. In a preliminary interview one week before Bildman's suspension, Astra USA General Counsel Charles E. Yon and national sales manager Robert Vogel vehemently denied the allegations of excessive drinking and widespread sexual harassment. Yon refused, however, to talk about complaints that had been settled, and he declined to respond to numerous specific allegations. Now, as executives from Sweden take charge of the investigation, Johansson says he cannot comment on whether earlier denials still stand.

Some of the individual allegations may be difficult to prove conclusively. That's the nature of sexual harrassment, which is partly a question of perception: What one woman might believe is harmless fun, another might find grossly offensive. Plus, some of the incidents took place with just the supposed harasser and his accuser present. But in many cases, the alleged harassment at Astra was witnessed by more than one person or experienced by more than one woman in an evening. And the sheer number of complaints centering on the same male executives, as well as the widely held view among both current and former employees that the environment was generally hostile to women, suggests Astra has a serious problem.

The Astra example comes on the heels of the sexual-harassment scandal at the Normal (Ill.) factory of Mitsubishi Motor Manufacturing of America Inc. There, 15 women allege they were groped and subjected to demeaning and offensive comments. The Equal Employment Opportunity Commission, which brought its largest suit of this kind against the company, alleges Mitsubishi did not respond to the repeated complaints. Mitsubishi denies wrongdoing and, at least initially, mounted an aggressive public-relations campaign designed to show that its employees disputed the EEOC's charges.

While Mitsubishi and Astra are extraordinary for the breadth and depth of their problems, many companies are struggling with sexual-harassment claims. Since the issue burst upon the public's awareness four years ago with Anita Hill's challenges at Clarence Thomas' confirmation hearings, complaints to the EEOC have more than doubled—to 15,549—while monetary awards have more than tripled. In response, many employers have introduced sensitivity training and instituted clear policies for handling complaints.

What is sexual harassment, exactly? EEOC guidelines define it as "unwelcome" sexual attention in the workplace. At the extreme, that means the demand or hint that job benefits will be gained in return for favors. But federal law also bans any conduct that creates "an intimidating, hostile, or offensive working environment."

Trickle Down

What is especially disturbing about Astra is the way the alleged harassment emanated from the top—then coursed its way down through the organization. Legions of women who felt embarrassed and angry nonetheless conformed to an unacceptable standard of behavior set by the subsidiary's very own CEO. So, too, did their male colleagues, many of whom later said they also considered Astra's conduct offensive.

As the Astra case suggests, few people have the fortitude or the financial wherewithal to blow the proverbial whistle. Some Astra employees were daunted by the prospect of taking on a deep-pocketed corporation—especially since those who did complain allege they were targeted for retaliation. Economic need meant others put up with behavior they felt was degrading. Many of those interviewed also said they feared complaints would only result in a reputation as a troublemaker—something that would haunt them in the job market. "If another pharmaceutical company knows you're involved in something like that, your chances of being hired are slim," says Mary Ann Lowe, a former rep who left in 1991. "Plus, it's very personal. Nobody wants to go public with sexual harassment. You know that if it ever went to trial, you'd be on trial, not the harasser." With the alleged harassment sanctioned at the top, many women who felt harassed—and the men who sympathized with them—simply quit.

Where were the legal deterrents? Former employees say that in many cases where women with evidence of harassment or retaliation threatened suits, Astra settled to avoid legal sanction. It has paid cash sums ranging from $20,000 to about $100,000 to five women that *Business Week* knows of. In return, those women agreed to keep silent. "When women won't back off, they pay them off," says former district manager Thurston. As a result, for the executives charged with harassment, there was no real penalty. Worse, they appear to have used shareholder funds to protect themselves.

Yon denies that Astra paid off women in exchange for their silence. Astra says there have been only a few settlements, and that the majority of the claims came from people fired for poor performance. Though it says most of the claims were baseless, it insists the settlements were made primarily to avoid costly litigation. From the outside, Astra appears to have a clean record. The company says it has won the only harassment case to go to a jury, and there's only one serious complaint in Massachusetts files since 1990. As for the EEOC, Astra says it has faced just four claims, two of which are pending.

Militaristic

Insiders ascribe much of the responsibility for the harassing environment to Bildman, a 22-year Astra veteran. The Swedish-born executive has run the U.S. arm since the early 1980s and is credited with its financial success. "He's a very disciplined, goal-oriented guy," says Stefan Solvell, Astra USA's No. 2 executive for years until he quit to run another company last year. With campuslike headquarters in the Boston suburb of Westborough, Mass., the company has grown to 1,500 employees and $323 million in revenues. Its products include the local anesthetic Xylocaine and the allergy medication Rhinocort. A hot new asthma drug, Pulmicort, is expected to hit the market soon. Bildman's bosses in Sweden, meanwhile, have also engineered fast growth: Parent Astra had $5.3 billion in sales last year, triple that of 1991.

Lanky, with longish hair, a shaggy mustache, and piercing eyes, Bildman is a charismatic, if somewhat quirky, leader. He favors suits in unusual colors: purple, coral, or traffic-cone orange. Those who've worked for him describe Bildman as obsessed with youth, beauty, and health. He also has a taste for the high life. According to Massachusetts records, among his six vehicles are a 1967 Lamborghini Miura and a 1967 Ferrari GT. Married, with children, insiders say he's a connoisseur of caviar, fine wine, and Dom Perignon champagne.

Inside Astra, say many sources, Bildman was an autocrat. He established a rigid, almost militaristic atmosphere at Astra's stark offices. Most staffers were required to go to lunch at precisely the same time every day and had to get permission to hang anything personal on their cubicle walls. Another oddity: All but the highest-ranking executives had to use one centralized fax number, and many former insiders say Bildman received copies of all incoming and outgoing messages. "He has total control of the company; everybody's afraid of him," says a former manager who left on good terms two years ago.

Numerous sources say Bildman would exercise power in capricious ways. At one meeting, recalls a sales rep, Bildman didn't like the suit a high-ranking executive was wearing and told him to change it. The executive quickly obliged. Bildman insisted on other unusual rules about attire, including one mandating that an Astra pin had to be worn at all company functions. People who forgot their pins were severely reprimanded. "I used to carry extra pins around," says a former manager. "The fear got so out of hand that I recall at least six times that I gave somebody an extra pin and they were literally shaken by the fact that they had lost theirs."

Astra Way

To fuel its fast growth, Astra has hired hundreds of young salespeople, both men and women, since the late 1980s. For female recruits, say numerous sources, appearance seemed inordinately important. One male sales rep who quit early this year recalls being asked by two senior male managers to help persuade a wavering candidate to join the company. "They told me in no uncertain terms why they wanted her hired—because she was extremely attractive," he says. Another ex-manager recalls George Roadman, a vice-president then running Astra's fastest-growing unit, rejecting an unattractive candidate by saying: "We're not hiring her. I can't see me sitting at a bar having a drink with her." In an interview before Bildman's suspension, Vogel, Astra's national sales manager, denied that looks played any role in selection. Roadman, in a written statement, denied allegations that he had behaved inappropriately. He said he did have a drinking problem but that he had gone for voluntary counseling and had not consumed alcohol at Astra functions since 1994.

To many recruits, the job was a dream come true. Selling pharmaceuticals is a high-paying, much-sought-after profession. Starting at $35,000, plus a car and hefty bonuses, compensation at Astra was better than at most rivals. But before going out into the field, newly hired reps—few of whom had prior pharmaceutical experience—attended Astra's rigorous nine-week training course, which included in-depth sales instruction as well as subjects such as anatomy and physiology. Trainees had to study hard and were tested often.

The training also offered an immersion in Astra's unique culture, known as the Astra Way. Each class of up to 100 people was billeted for the entire nine weeks at the Westborough Marriott near Astra headquarters. The company paid for just one plane ticket home and discouraged trainees from taking other trips or receiving visitors. Trainees soon learned that the Astra Way included a rigid set of rules covering everything from sales techniques—presentations had to be memorized and delivered to doctors virtually by rote—to acceptable casual dress. (No jeans. No shorts. Socks required.) Some rules seemed petty. Others added polish to the new recruits. Trainees were taught how to hold their silverware European style and how to drink wine.

Dozens of sources who went through the training describe it as all-encompassing—and isolating. Cut off from family and friends and frequently reprimanded if they didn't adapt fast to the extensive new rules, many say Astra's training bore more than a passing resemblance to military basic training. Some new recruits were even marched around the building in sweats for a day, as managers dressed in fatigues barked questions. Those who flubbed the answers had to do push-ups. Others add it was almost like a cult. "They tell you how to eat, drink, and sleep," says Kristina K. Bell, an Astra rep who quit last year. "It was a very controlling, domineering atmosphere—like Astra owned me."

Open-Bar Nights

Socializing also appeared to play a key role in the Astra Way. Over and over, recruits were told that to succeed, they had to play hard as well as work hard. "Work eight hours, play eight hours, sleep eight hours," was a phrase Bildman and other top managers frequently used. "Part of being a successful rep is to be with your customers—and not just nine to five," explains Solvell, the former No. 2. "It means entertaining."

Of course, good social skills are key to many sales jobs. But at the open-bar nights that managers would host three or four nights a week, the social skills of attractive women drew most of the attention. "Upper management was barely paying attention to the male students, but they were all over the female students," says Kendra Kurz, a 1993 trainee who left Astra a year later. Yon and Vogel deny that socializing or drinking played an inappropriate role at Astra.

"Upper management was . . . all over the female students."

Kurz, a trainee at the company in 1993, left Astra a year later.

Nevertheless, trainees from four different classes say the bar nights were common—and that Bildman and Roadman were frequent revelers. "Bildman would sit in on meetings," recalls one former rep who left in 1993 because of the environment. "He'd go to the bar afterwards, when everybody else went." Numerous others say Roadman would often stay at the bar until late at night—and pressure others to do the same.

Race Matters

Frequently, Roadman and other managers would call female trainees in their rooms to ask them down to the bar. Such invitations were hard to refuse. According to Terrance Leahy, who recently retired after years as Astra's director of training, roughly 15% of new recruits were fired during training. Participants say they were repeatedly told that social skills were key to evaluations. Moreover, the managers hanging out in the bar could make the difference between being assigned to San Francisco or Fargo, N.D. "You had to go to the bar," says a female rep still with the company. Adds another who quit Astra last year: "They would use their power and authority to make you think you didn't have a job if you didn't go along."

"They would use their power and authority to make you think you didn't have a job if you didn't go along."

Trainees say they were often offended by what went on down in the bar. Lelia Bush, a black woman who trained in late 1992, says that Roadman called her in her room several times inviting her to join him at the bar. She and another black ex-rep, Cordelia E. Webb, who has also filed an EEOC complaint, claim Roadman liked to talk about racial differences in sexuality. "He said black women were stallions compared to white women, sexually," Bush alleges. "He said he was a black man in a white man's body." Both women were terminated in circumstances that are under dispute.

Upstairs, the drinking and dancing continued. "I didn't feel I could say no," Bell says. Bildman was dancing "way too close," she alleges, and kept steering her near the bed. When Bildman remarked that she seemed tense, she told him she was uncomfortable. Bildman's alleged response: "We're very open here at Astra." After she escaped to the couch, Bell alleges Bildman came and "put his arms around me, pulling me toward him. I kept thinking: 'He's the president of the company. Is there any way to get out of this discreetly?'"

Not long after, Bell moved to her new territory in Cincinnati. At her first meeting with her new manager, Thurston, she started crying and told him the entire story. He filed a formal harassment complaint on her behalf. Astra's Yon says the company investigated and concluded that Bell's claim had no merit. The investigation, he says, involved taking sworn statements from the other five trainees. "The other five," he says, "swore that they saw nothing inappropriate, nothing offensive."

But the way in which Astra seemingly conducted its investigation raises questions. For one thing, Bildman got directly involved. Not long after Bell filed her complaint, she says Bildman called her at her hotel. "Lars was very concerned about that night," Bell recalls. "He asked me: 'Did I feel my job was in jeopardy? Did I feel pressured?'" Bell says that Bildman even told her not to tell Thurston he had called. It was clear, Bell says, that Bildman "was trying to cover himself."

At a national sales meeting soon after, Kurz was called out of a meeting and ushered into Bildman's penthouse hotel suite. "It was very intimidating," she recalls, "just me and Lars."

Allegations Center on U.S. Execs, but Swedes Visiting from Headquarters Got Involved, Too

Bildman, Roadman, and other managers would also invite women out on the town for more intimate excursions. After rebuffing him repeatedly, Kurz recalls finally agreeing to join Bildman when he organized a night out with six trainees—four women and two men. Also joining them was Edward Aarons, a senior executive in charge of institutional business. After dinner, the group retired to a darkly lit piano bar, where Bildman ordered up dancing and Dom Perignon. Trainee Bell remembers it as a "come-on" bar, "the type of place where you'd meet somebody, have a steamy dance, and go home."

As the party moved to a raucous nightclub, Bell remembers Aarons "pawing me," and alleges that both executives were "dancing very close to me. I kept thinking: 'How do I get out of this?'" she says. In a written statement, Aarons denied that he ever harassed any women, terming such allegations "completely false."

The group arrived back at the Westborough Marriott after 2 a.m. Although Bildman lived nearby, he had taken a suite for the night and wanted everybody to join him. "We didn't want to go up," says Bell. "But we felt we should make an appearance." Only Kurz slipped away.

During a long discussion, she says Bildman told her he was going to fire somebody else who had vocally pursued a separate harassment complaint. Then, he directed her into another room to meet Yon, the general counsel, and to sign an affidavit about the dinner-and-dancing evening. The affidavit, Kurz says, merely stated that she hadn't been harassed by Bildman himself that evening. "They were very careful in the questions they asked," says Kurz, who felt she had no choice but to sign. "It was clear they were trying to protect Lars."

Few women protested such treatment during training. Most were in their mid-20s, and Astra was their first or second job after college. "People were inexperienced," says Ann Marie Nowak, who left in 1991. "They don't really know what's appropriate or inappropriate in a business setting."

Still others say they believed complaining would be tantamount to quitting. Just weeks into a new job, most weren't prepared to do so. "I kept telling myself: 'The training is only for two months, and then I'll be out in the field,'" recalls one ex-rep.

Of course, some women who gave top execs the cold shoulder found that their careers did not suffer. And there were others who openly responded to the attention from senior managers. Some were naturally flirtatious and enjoyed the party atmosphere. A few perhaps hoped to improve their careers in the age-old tradition of the casting couch. Inside Astra, these women became known as The Chosen. Long after training was over, they were frequently seen with senior managers at dinners and other corporate functions. Vogel insists that reps who sat with Bildman were chosen "strictly based on performance."

"I'd get my package in the mail [for meetings], and I'd start feeling sick."
Former Astra employee Webb filed a complaint with the EEOC.

But those who thought the harassment would end with training soon found they were mistaken. For each of its two main divisions, Astra held three national sales meetings each year. With Bildman and other top executives typically attending each weeklong meeting, the drunken partying and harassment began anew. "I'd get my package in the mail, and I'd start feeling sick," says Webb.

The gung-ho partying often turned boisterous. At one Fort Lauderdale meeting, dozens of men in tuxedos and women ended up in the hotel swimming pool. Many ended up sleeping on the pool lounge chairs that night. At another meeting, held at the exclusive Sagamore resort in upstate New York in 1991, the partying got so out of control, say several people present, that people threw dishes out the window and burned furnishings in the fireplace. After hotel managers threatened to call the police, the group checked out the next morning.

"Their behavior was unbelievably unprofessional," says a hotel official. "I've never known this to happen with a corporate group."

At other meetings, much of the late-night action took place at invitation-only parties in managers' suites. Michelle Porter, a former rep who left in 1991, recalls going to one such party in Bildman's quarters. After much eating and drinking, Porter started to leave when everyone else did. Bildman asked her to stay, and he ducked into another room. "All of a sudden, he came out wearing a robe," she recalls. "I said: 'I want to leave.' He grabbed my arm, and said: 'I want to talk to you.'" Porter quickly left.

"This One's Mine"

Ed Aarons was another object of many complaints. During one late-night party at a 1993 sales meeting, Webb recalls, Aarons grabbed her by the neck in a corridor, tried to kiss her, and bellowed: "Hands off. This one's mine." Aarons, she says, "was reeking of alcohol. I kept thinking: 'I've got to get away.'" But when she tried to leave, Aarons became belligerent and berated her manager for giving her permission to leave. In his written statement, Aarons denied that he was drunk or that he had tried to kiss Webb or harass her in any way.

Although Astra's parent insists it didn't know about the goings-on at its U.S. subsidiary, many sources say that when Europeans visited from headquarters, they, too, became involved. Lisa D. Hall, a 1992 trainee, recalls that Roadman asked her to come to the bar to entertain visiting execs. "These were VPs, high-level people," says Hall, a black former rep who left in 1994 after twice taking disability leave; the circumstances are under dispute. "Roadman told me to be friendly to them." The Swedes, she says, "liked black girls."

Several people also remember a 1994 visit of Andreas Feulner, president of Astra's German subsidiary and a member of the company's executive committee. At one evening function, a former rep says Feulner came up behind her, "grabbed my butt, and pulled me toward him. He said: 'I want you to come sit with me.'" She says she had never met Feulner before. Later that night, after being pressured to have her picture taken with him, former rep Webb claims that Feulner "tried to put his room passkey into my hand. He told me to wait up there." Webb says she refused to take the key. Feulner denies all the allegations: "I can assure you that I never grabbed any women . . . on the buttocks," he said in a written response, adding that he had also not asked any women to join him in his room or given them his key.

DENIAL: Feulner, with former sales rep Webb, says he "never grabbed any women . . . by the buttocks."

Obsession

Webb says she later told her manager about the incident and asked him to file a complaint. He agreed to do so, she says, but "he told me a lot of people had filed complaints in the past and it hadn't worked." She says she never heard another word about her complaint.

Although the obsession with sex was strongest during training and sales meetings, former staffers say its influence spread throughout the culture. Women who were Bildman's favorites would often deal with him directly, say several former male managers, while higher-level male managers rarely talked to the CEO. Others say they didn't dare discipline laggard female reps with links to the top for fear of losing their own jobs. "If someone in your district is close to Lars, it's hands off," alleges one longtime insider who recently left.

Many sources also contend that women who were either physically attractive or close to top managers seemed to get bigger bonuses and do better generally in their careers. Bush, for instance, complains in her EEOC filing that she was fired for poor performance at the same time that another female rep, with worse sales figures, was retained. This rep, Bush alleges, was having an affair with a regional manager. And in her EEOC filing, Webb charges that her roommate during training had an affair with Roadman. The woman later was among the first in her class to be promoted to district manager. Although several reps say the woman was a good performer who may have deserved the promotion, the appearance of favoritism remained.

There were other problems as well. Given the signals from the top, some lower-level male managers allegedly took them as a license to act in a similar manner. After Kim Cote began working in the Boston area in late 1992, her then-manager, Mark Hollands, began traveling in her car as she made her rounds. She claims Hollands would touch her inappropriately and could recount scenes from lurid novels he read, suggesting that Cote "could fit nicely in this" scene. Although he praised her performance in person, Cote claims, when she didn't respond, Hollands began criticizing her in written evaluations. When she didn't receive a raise she says she had been promised earlier, Cote says she finally confronted Hollands. According to Cote, Hollands responded: "You know what I want. I know what you want. What are you going to do about it?" Cote's reaction: "I said: 'I'm not going to sleep with you.'" In a written statement, Hollands proclaimed his "absolute and complete denial of those allegations."

Cote says she protested to Vogel but never heard anything about her complaint again. Vogel agrees that Cote lodged a complaint and says he investigated, following Astra's complaint procedure. After interviewing Hollands and Cote, he says he passed the complaint on to personnel, where Cote's allegation was found to have "no basis in reality." Yet Vogel concedes he only phoned personnel and never filed a written complaint. Nor did he speak to Cote further or follow up. She left the company two months later under conditions that are under dispute. Cote reached a partial settlement with Astra in 1994 and on Apr. 29 filed a follow-up suit against Hollands.

Of course, many other lower-level male managers were appalled by such behavior. The conundrum they faced, however, was what to do. Former rep Mashaan Guy says that if he saw a woman in an awkward situation, for example, he would join the conversation. He also counseled women on how to deflect the attention. But the culture left him so angry he eventually quit. "A few times, I wanted to deck one of these guys," he says. "I felt powerless and embarrassed as a man."

"What you wanted to say was: 'Lars, keep your pants on, and we wouldn't have this problem.'"

Former manager Thurston says he and a small group of male managers frequently discussed the impact harassment was having on morale. In part, they were also worried for their own reputations: They feared that all men at Astra would be tagged as harassers. Finally, Thurston says he approached his boss, Vogel, and told him the harassment was harming the company. But Thurston says the male managers had little ability to force change. "What you wanted to say was: 'Lars, keep your pants on, and we wouldn't have this problem,'" he says. "But you couldn't do it. It was a totally autocratic company. Whatever Lars said, goes." Vogel denies that there is any generalized harassment problem at Astra or that any manager ever spoke to him about it.

With most of the female reps out in the field, there were fewer overt problems at headquarters. But similar attitudes toward women seemed to prevail. One notable example: a glossy calendar distributed through the building in early 1991, called The Astra Glamour Girls. It featured photos of home-office employees in suggestive poses, complete with makeup, fancy clothes, and come-hither looks. Four sources involved, including the photographer who took the pictures, say the calendar was created as a gift for Bildman, though Astra denies that allegation.

Stifled

Women who objected to Astra's climate soon found their own conduct under scrutiny. About a year after the calendar appeared, one of the women in it, Nanette Corcoran, filed a gender discrimination complaint with the Massachusetts Commission Against Discrimination in which she alleged that "women at Astra have been continually subjected to sexual harassment." In response, Astra denied that Corcoran had ever been harassed. Instead, the company attacked Corcoran for what it called "inappropriate and unprofessional conduct." In one incident, Astra stated, "it was reported to Corcoran's superiors that Corcoran would socialize with various [trainees] following training sessions," and that she once had hosted a party at her apartment during which "there was excessive consumption of alcohol—as a result of which a fight broke out" between two trainees.

Indeed, there is ample evidence that people who brought harassment complaints found their careers stifled or became targets for dismissal. At a September, 1991, sales meeting, a Boston-area rep named Maura Lynch called an informal meeting of female reps to discuss ways to improve Astra's hostile environment. Top management soon found out about the meeting, and Lynch, who had been a rep for several years, suddenly came under a microscope. According to people close to Lynch, her manager began making surprise visits and finding fault with small things. By December, he said she had to leave. She hired a lawyer to file a complaint with the MCAD, but Astra quickly settled. She, too, signed a confidentiality clause. The women's group never met again.

Sabotage Scheme

Perhaps the most serious case of alleged retaliation resulted from an incident in late 1993 involving a young trainee, Laura Moore. According to people familiar with the situation, Moore claimed that Roadman approached her in the hotel bar one night and asked her to go to another bar. Afraid to refuse, she dragged two male friends along. Roadman was allegedly all over her in the car on the way back from the bar. After she returned to her room well after midnight, Moore told friends, Roadman knocked on the door and talked his way in. Although she repeatedly asked him to leave, he allegedly pinned her against the wall and kissed her. He also allegedly asked her to sleep with him. Roadman "was lucky the cops weren't called," says one person familiar with the episode.

Moore finally got Roadman out of her room and immediately called the manager in her soon-to-be-assigned territory, Jennifer Price. An experienced manager hired from outside Astra, Price agreed to pursue the complaint aggressively. Once again, Bildman got involved in the inquiries. One of those he quizzed was Kurz, a friend and fellow trainee of Moore's. "Lars was telling me . . . he was concerned that Jennifer Price had a scheme to sabotage people in the company," Kurz claims. "Lars told me he was planning to fire Jennifer."

Not long afterward, Price was fired. The official reason: poor performance. Convinced she was fired in retaliation, Price threatened to sue. The company quickly settled in return for Price's silence. Astra refused to discuss allegations concerning Price.

In the past 18 months, Astra has toned down its rambunctious culture. Now, sales reps are issued a limited number of drink tickets at meetings, and recent training courses have been quieter. But heavy drinking remains a staple—and the old Astra shows through when the liquor flows, as last June's incident with Zortman demonstrated.

Moreover, until Bildman's forced suspension, Astra continued to deny it had any problems. At the initial interview with *Business Week,* Yon paraded out a host of mostly low-level female staffers. Their stories, told in the presence of three Astra legal representatives and two outside public-relations executives, flatly contradicted those told to *Business Week* by numerous independent sources. Those efforts appeared to be part of a much broader strategy to discredit the *Business Week* article and those who've raised allegations of harassment. Indeed, after Astra executives became aware of the investigation in mid-January, the company asked female sales reps to sign a letter denying they had seen or experienced any harassment. Ostensibly a grassroots effort organized by loyal female sales managers, insiders say many employees believe the action originated from a panicky executive suite. Most women signed; some feared they would lose their jobs if they didn't.

Although many of the women subjected to the worst of Astra's harassment have left the company, some remain scarred by their experiences. Leaving Astra abruptly has often made finding another job hard. Prospective employers always ask why they left. "It's difficult, because you want to tell them what happened at Astra but you don't know if they'll understand," says Kurz. At one interview, Kurz says, she told the female interviewer some of her story. "You could tell by the look on her face," says Kurz. "She was thinking: 'Scandal, stay away from us.'" Many others say they lie about the reasons they left in order to get a job.

Some claim they still suffer from psychological trauma. Former rep Yvonne Stokes says the combination of extreme stress and sexual harassment got so bad that she started crying one day in front of a doctor she had called on as a sales rep. He referred her to a psychiatrist. Still taking antidepressant drugs, she says: "I just want to be me again. I look back and say: 'How could I have let this company do this to me?'"

Webb claims Astra turned her from a happy-go-lucky and deeply religious young woman into an emotional basket case. She says the toll from 2½ years of harassment was so bad that her hair started to fall out, she was often sick to her stomach, and she started to scratch her back and chest until the skin was raw. Her doctor ordered her to go on disability leave last May, and she is still under psychiatric care.

Nearly a year after going on leave, Webb's perceptions of normal, everyday events are still warped by her Astra experience. A regular in her church choir,

Webb says: "There's something wrong when I think the people in my church are hugging me wrong." And at a recent job interview, she says the male interviewer asked her a perfectly innocent question: Was she willing to travel? But Webb says her instinctive reaction was: "He wants to get me into a hotel room." The happiest day of her life, Webb says, came when Astra finally fired her a few months ago. Now preparing a lawsuit, she vows: "If I have to lose every penny I have, I'll do it to show them that what they do isn't right."

With Jane A. Sasseen in New York

GETTING JUSTICE IS NO EASY TASK

For workers who have endured sexual harassment, the Equal Employment Opportunity Commission is supposed to be their champion. That's why the suit against Mitsubishi Motor Manufacturing of America Inc.—potentially the largest EEOC case ever—has brought praise from civil rights groups and uneasiness from business groups.

But for such victims, a search for justice is no simple task. Overcoming fear and embarrassment to confront a lecher is hard. But even those who clear that hurdle don't easily find vindication when the two best avenues for help—law-enforcement agencies and the courts—are fraught with delay. The underfunded EEOC is struggling to stay on top of a heavy caseload. State agencies take up some of the slack but face budget constraints, too. And private lawsuits are costly.

Holdups

Result: When fresh evidence can make or break a case, "justice delayed is justice denied," says Gary E. Phelan, a plaintiffs' attorney in New Haven. To get recourse, workers facing alleged harassment can first turn to their employers or unions for help. If those channels don't pan out, they can sue their employers and co-workers in court or turn to the government to pursue a case on their behalf. Either way, they must first file a complaint at the EEOC or a state antibias agency within 180 days of the alleged discriminatory act.

Even those who want to pursue their own lawsuits must first get a so-called right-to-sue letter from a government agency—a step meant to keep complaints from clogging the courts. The EEOC is required to issue such approvals within 180 days of the charge. In reality, the process averages eight months, even though complainants can ask for a go-ahead earlier. After approval, plaintiffs have 90 days to file in court.

Workers who press their complaints through the EEOC face a backlog of 97,000 cases. In the past five years, the workload has exploded. Sexual-harassment charges alone rose by 150% from 1990, to 15,549 last year—driven in part by publicity over allegations by law professor Anita Hill against Supreme Court appointee Clarence Thomas during his 1991 confirmation hearings. Yet the agency's budget rose by only 26%, to $232.6 million, during that period. New EEOC Chairman Gilbert Casellas is pushing an overhaul of agency procedures and is giving charges of systemic bias priority.

Hard To Win

There's always the option of hiring a lawyer to pursue a grievance in court. But they're expensive. Fees vary, but some charge $2,500 to $7,500 to go on retainer, according to Phelan. For many women with harassment complaints, a government-run case is often the only recourse.

Like all bias complaints, sexual-harassment cases are difficult to win. Under the law, "a stray remark or a cross-eyed look" does not make a case, says Ellen J. Vargyas, EEOC general counsel. And sexual-harassment cases often boil down to the credibility of accuser and accused. If a victim does win, there's a cap on damages. Plaintiffs can recover a maximum of $50,000, including compensatory and punitive damages, from employers with fewer than 100 workers and $300,000 maximum from those with more than 500 workers.

For harassment victims, an EEOC overhaul can't come soon enough. Speedy resolution of such painful cases is the best way to deliver justice—to all parties involved.

By Catherine Yang in Washington

EDITORIALS

The Cult Of Astra

When does a company become a cult? A six-month investigation by *Business Week* into Astra USA Inc., the American arm of Swedish pharmaceutical company Astra, reveals that the transition can occur when a corporate culture gets hijacked at the top. A bizarre case of abuse of power appears to have taken place at Astra, where a 15-year pattern of sexual harassment emanated from the president's office and worked its way down through the organization. On Apr. 29, the president was suspended by the Swedish parent just days before *Business Week* went to press with the story.

Astra is a striking example of how vulnerable a corporate culture can be to its leaders' cues. To many who worked there, Astra was a cult led by an autocratic, charismatic leader who established an almost militaristic atmosphere at headquarters. Staffers had to eat lunch at precisely the same time each day. Permission was needed to hang anything personal on cubicle walls. A nine-week training period cut people off from their families. Young trainees were drilled in a rigid set of rules covering everything from sales techniques to dress.

Then there was the drinking and partying. Trainees were indoctrinated with the idea that success in sales required heavy socializing both inside and outside Astra. Bar nights were part of training and sales conferences. Managers, led by the president and including visiting Astra officials from Europe, asked young women to bars and back to their hotel suites. Advancement in Astra appeared to go to those who cooperated. Women who responded favorably to the attention from senior managers were called "The Chosen," and their careers prospered. It was a sales culture gone mad.

Some women did well in this environment. Others felt harassed by managers but kept silent. A few protested loudly, and there were financial settlements. In exchange for money, these women promised to be silent about their grievances. Astra says it settled only to avoid costly court procedures.

To the outside world, Astra was a successful corporation. Because most of the women who felt sexually harassed didn't go to the Equal Employment Opportunity Commission, the company appeared to be in good standing. Because the sales force was effective in selling Astra's pharmaceuticals to doctors, the home office perceived it as a winner.

What lessons can be drawn from this strange situation? In the recent case of Mitsubishi Motors Corp., alleged victims of sexual harassment went to the EEOC, which sued the company. An investigation will reveal what really happened there. But at Astra, there was no government intervention. Female employees didn't have the financial resources, resolve, or courage to risk their jobs and reputations battling harassment.

In the end, harassment is simply bullying by another name. One can see why its victims, in this case, might wish to remain silent. After all, it appeared to be encouraged from the top down. One cannot, however, absolve Astra in Stockholm, owned largely by the Wallenbergs, who failed to supervise its subsidiary adequately as it careened out of control.

It may be mere coincidence that two foreign companies in the U.S. in recent weeks experienced serious problems with the alleged sexual harassment of their employees. But in this era of economic globalization, where companies operate in dozens of cultures around the world, corporations everywhere must look beyond the financials in supervising their farflung operations. Corporations, not governments, are primarily responsible for the people who work for them—and they must act to protect their dignity wherever they live.

INVESTIGATIONS

Aftershocks Are Rumbling through Astra

An EEOC sexual-harassment probe could be in the works

After 18 months as a sales rep for Astra USA Inc., Melanie J. Strobel, 27, had finally had enough of what she says was widespread sexual harassment and a bizarrely controlling culture. She quit on Mar. 31, hoping to erase the memory of what she calls "a sick company."

Then came *Business Week*'s May 13 cover story exposing claims of rampant sexual harassment at Astra. Reading the claims of female former employees, who said they were fondled or required to accompany male executives to bars, nightclubs, and hotel suites, Strobel says her anger reached the boiling point. "There it was, in writing. It was exactly the company I worked for." Although she had feared taking on Astra because of what she saw as an intimidating management style, she's now thinking about suing or joining a class action. "They robbed me of a year and a half of my life. They caused me psychological trauma that I'm still struggling with."

Broken Pact?

Strobel isn't the only former Astra employee looking for legal relief. The drug company, which suspended CEO Lars Bildman on Apr. 28 and two other top executives, George W. Roadman and Edward Aarons, on May 3, now may face a blizzard of lawsuits from former and current employees claiming sexual harassment and other wrongdoing. "Their exposure is probably immense," says Eric J. Wallach, a New York attorney who specializes in defending companies against harassment suits. It would be particularly damaging to Astra if the suits show that the company knew about the problems but did nothing, Wallach says. "That's what really triggers the big awards," he says.

What's more, the Equal Employment Opportunity Commission may already have launched its own investigation into Astra, a unit of Swedish drugmaker Astra AB. James L. Lee, chief attorney for the EEOC's Northeast region, won't directly confirm the investigation. But, he says, "when egregious cases of sexual harassment are brought to the attention of the agency, it's our practice to fully investigate the matter." Printed allegations suggest that, "on a scale of sexual harassment cases, this one seems to rank on up there," he says.

Even some former employees who have already settled cases against Astra are coming back for more. One is Pamela L. Zortman, a former sales rep who filed a claim charging that Bildman had kissed and fondled her while dancing at an Astra party. Zortman agreed to a $100,000 settlement from Astra in January. But on May 8, she filed a follow-up suit. Among her claims: breach of contract. In the original agreement, each party pledged not to disparage the other. Zortman's attorney, James F. Champa, says Bildman's lawyer broke that pact and cast doubt on her honesty by telling the press that an unnamed claim that sounded like Zortman's was baseless.

Legal experts say that reopening cases will be difficult. "It sounds to me like a desperate attempt to withdraw from a mutually bargained-for agreement now that the company is in the public eye," says Philip M. Berkowitz, an employment attorney at Epstein, Becker & Green in New York.

Eeric Atmosphere

Even so, Astra could still suffer more fallout. Newly named top managers say a rigorous investigation is under way—and hint that more executives will be implicated. Harassment experts say anyone found to be directly involved clearly must go but that casualties should also include executives who simply allowed such behavior to continue. Bildman remains on suspension pending the probe's outcome, but insiders say the company has made it clear that he won't return. Bildman's attorney, Roderick MacLeish Jr., says "there is nothing independent about this investigation, and the results have been predetermined." He denies the allegations against Bildman. And on May 8, as this article was going to press, MacLeish phoned Astra to say that Bildman had just filed a lawsuit against the company.

The probe, which is also examining possible financial improprieties, already is taking some bizarre turns. On Apr. 29, two Astra lawyers went to the hotel room of consultant Lars Magnusson, who was helping Bildman respond to *Business Week*'s investigation. Magnusson says they were seeking a missing Astra safe and computer about which he knows nothing. Jan Larsson, Astra USA's new CEO, confirms that "we have heard rumors of a safe or documents" being missing and says the lawyers "wanted to talk" to Magnusson about them.

Not long after new management took over, sources say, high-level staffers about to attend a meeting were suddenly warned not to use a conference room because it was bugged. One source says Astra then swept for electronic listening devices several times. They didn't find any. But the scare has added to the eerie, siege-like atmosphere at Astra's headquarters in suburban Westborough, Mass. The Astra saga is hardly over yet.

By Mark Maremont in Boston

NEWS: ANALYSIS & COMMENTARY

Follow-ups

Day of Reckoning at Astra
Bildman, Accused of Sexual Harassment, and Three Others Are Out

Most companies try to sweep scandal under the carpet. Not Astra, the giant Swedish drugmaker. Confronted by allegations in a May 13 *Business Week* cover story of widespread sexual harassment and other abuses at its Astra USA Inc. subsidiary, the company quickly suspended three top executives and launched an internal probe.

Just weeks later, on June 26, the parent company took decisive action: It announced that it had fired Astra USA President and CEO Lars Bildman without paying him any severance. Although Astra won't comment on specific sexual-harassment allegations, Carl-Gustav Johansson, an Astra executive vice-president, says the investigation found that Bildman had "exhibited inappropriate behavior at company functions" and had "abused his power." Another suspended executive, George Roadman, also was shown the door, while a third, Edward Aarons, resigned. A senior executive in Sweden, Anders Lönner, was asked to resign for failing to report the misconduct to superiors, Astra says.

INVESTIGATOR JOHANSSON Astra also alleges that Bildman used about $2 million for personal expenses.

Airing yet more dirty linen, Astra also disclosed that it believes Bildman used company funds to pay for about $2 million worth of personal expenses during the past decade. The bulk of the money supposedly came in the form of renovations done on three Bildman houses by Astra-paid contractors. Bildman allegedly also used company money to pay for lavish vacations and other personal expenses. The U.S. Attorney's office and Massachusetts Revenue Dept. officials have opened probes of the alleged misappropriation of funds, Astra says.

In a statement issued by his attorney, Bildman denied personal involvement in sexual harassment and "categorically denied" the allegations of financial improprieties. He also claimed to have canceled checks proving he paid for the renovations and called the decision to fire him a "cowardly and disloyal" action. Astra says Bildman did pay for some, though not all, of the renovations.

Disputed Documents

To some degree, demonizing Bildman may serve to deflect blame from Astra itself. Many outsiders believe Bildman could not have run amok for most of his 15 years at the helm of the U.S. unit if he had been properly supervised by the parent company. Johansson hotly disputes that. Bildman was "expert at handling these things within the organization," so the parent company "had no chance" of finding out about the improprieties, he contends.

Indeed, in the weeks before the *Business Week* story was published, the Astra investigators say, Bildman was trying to hide information from the parent company. He hired a consultant, Lars Magnusson, allegedly to help with the coverup. During at least two weekends, the investigators contend, the two men were seen shredding documents at headquarters. Magnusson, they say, also allegedly spirited away documents that are now the subject of a legal battle between Astra and Bildman. Magnusson did not respond to requests for comment. Bildman's attorney denies any coverup or shredding of documents.

Bildman and Magnusson also allegedly conducted a secret campaign to discredit or deflect the *Business Week* story before it appeared. Two Astra insiders say they were asked by Magnusson and an executive to secretly tape phone conversations with *Business Week.* Both say they refused.

Secret Office

Bildman seemed to suspect that the article was being orchestrated by enemies within Astra, the investigators claim—an idea Bildman's lawyer calls "ridiculous." Whatever the reason, Bildman and Magnusson set up a secret office in a nondescript building not far from Astra USA's headquarters in Westborough, Mass. Staffed with computers and paralegals, the office apparently was intended "to be a nerve center for the effort to prove that *Business Week* was a tool of Astra USA's enemies," says Francis Carling, a New York lawyer who helped conduct the internal probe.

Is the misconduct at Astra USA really over? Several staffers say a recent national sales meeting was the quietest in memory, with limited alcohol and no dancing. But some insiders contend the housecleaning should have gone much deeper. "The mentality is still there," says one female sales rep. "A lot of people who should still be looked at [by investigators] haven't changed. They're just quiet for the time being."

Maybe so. But experts say that if Astra does any more housecleaning, it's likely to do so more discreetly over the next 6 to 12 months. Meanwhile, it already has done more than most companies in similar circumstances.

By Mark Maremont in Westborough, Mass.

Discussion Questions

1. At Astra, harassment originated from the top of the organization, and permeated lower levels as well. Outline specific steps that employees (male or female) might take in a similar situation to bring about changes in the organization's culture.
2. According to *Business Week,* "the way in which Astra investigated complaints raises questions. For one thing, Bildman got directly involved." Develop a timeline of events that illustrates explicitly how such investigations should be conducted.
3. American citizens are protected by U.S. civil rights laws when employed by U.S.-owned multinational companies (MNCs) overseas. MNCs may operate in dozens of cultures around the world. How can MNCs ensure that their far-flung operations are in compliance with company policies and U.S. civil rights laws (if American citizens are employed in an overseas locale)?

PART

2 EMPLOYMENT

Now that you understand the competitive, legal, and social environments within which HR management activities take place, it is time to address three major aspects of the employment process: analyzing the work to be done, determining the kinds of skills needed to do the work, and hiring employees. Logically, before an organization can select employees, it needs to be able to specify the kind of work that needs to be done, how it should be done, the number of people needed, and the personal characteristics required of those who will do the work. Chapter 4 addresses these issues. Chapter 5 considers the planning, implementation, and evaluation of recruitment operations. Finally, Chapter 6 examines initial screening and personnel selection—why they are done, how they are done, and how they can be evaluated.

4 ANALYZING WORK AND PLANNING FOR PEOPLE

Questions This Chapter Will Help Managers Answer

1 How can job analysis information be useful to the operating manager?
2 How can HR planning be integrated most effectively with general business planning?
3 What should be the components of a fair policy with regard to collecting, maintaining, and disseminating information about employees?
4 How can human resource forecasts be most useful?
5 What control mechanisms might be most appropriate to ensure that action plans match targeted needs?

THE ANALYSIS OF WORK—FOUNDATION FOR EMPLOYMENT PRACTICES

Situation: You are Pat Evans, chief engineer at Western Water Company. Western Water is a small, investor-owned utility company that provides water treatment, water distribution, and water use planning for a small, but growing, area. Each year, Western hires about six junior civil engineers to work in any of the following areas: water service planning, wastewater treatment, facilities planning, design engineering, or construction engineering. However, the number of new hires among civil engineers is expected to grow larger in the coming years, as the population density (and thus the demand for water service) increases in the area served by Western Water.

As chief engineer, you are responsible for all hiring of new engineers. You are concerned that past hiring procedures have been pretty slack—basically, a cursory review of courses taken in the engineering curriculum plus an unstructured interview. As a result, Western really does not know what its new junior civil engineers can do, what they are looking for in a company, and what particular assignments they are best suited for. To make matters worse, an average of 50 percent of the newly hired junior civil engineers leave the company within 3 years. You are determined to change current practices. As a start, you have asked your HR department to analyze each of the possible job assignments for junior civil engineers and to report back to you with a list of "common denominators" that seem to cut across all the assignments. That study was begun in July, it is now November 1, and you have just received the results. Western will begin recruiting in earnest next February, and most hiring decisions will be made in March and April, primarily from among engineering students who will graduate in May and June. Thus you have several months to develop new hiring procedures to be put into place before the screening and selection of the next group of candidates actually begin.

Here is the summary that you just received from HR of the broad job dimensions of junior civil engineers, along with a statement of the personal characteristics necessary for each job dimension.

1. **Modeling and calculations**. Applications of professional engineering knowledge in order to develop and test mathematical models of civil engineering activities (e.g., models dealing with water distribution, quality, and treatment; hydraulic models; structural models). Knowledge required: civil engineering principles, including mathematics through advanced calculus; statics; dynamics; basic water and wastewater chemistry; engineering economics; structural systems; surveying principles; and construction methods.
2. **Computer software applications**. Use and application of computer software tools ranging from word processing to spreadsheet-based economic analyses to modeling proposed projects. Abilities required: use of computer-based spreadsheets, graphics, word processing, and database management programs. Ability to use civil engineering modeling software, applications-development software, project scheduling, and computer-aided drafting is desirable.

3. **Project planning and management**. Identification of project objectives, scope, feasibility, milestones, and completion schedules, together with preparation of supporting documentation. Monitor and coordinate project activities in order to meet time and cost parameters. Knowledge and abilities required: engineering standard practices, formats of technical reports, water distribution systems, methods of effective presentations, whether oral or written. Must be able to develop cost analyses for projects, set priorities, and schedule activities in a logical, organized manner. Must be able to coordinate activities and work with other engineering sections, vendors, consultants, and contractors.

4. **Written communications**. Preparation of memos, letters, and engineering reports designed to address a variety of audiences, including other engineers; staff members working in maintenance, operations, or clerical positions; public agencies; government bodies; and members of the general public. Knowledge and abilities required: proper English grammar, spelling, punctuation, and sentence structure; ability to organize and compile relevant information to be used in reports; ability to communicate effectively in English in a clear, concise, organized manner, taking into account the abilities and needs of the audience.

5. **Individual and group interactions**. Provision of technical expertise, either by telephone or face-to-face, to contractors, other engineers, members of the board of directors, government agencies, and applicants for water service. Knowledge and abilities required: engineering terminology; ability to establish and maintain effective working relationships in a variety of contexts (one-on-one or group) and with people from a variety of backgrounds (technical as well as nontechnical); ability to communicate orally in English in a clear, understandable, concise manner, taking into account the needs and abilities of the audience.

6. **Data summary and synthesis**. Integration of information from a variety of sources (e.g., maps, calculations, environmental reports, feasibility studies) in order to provide a basis for technical recommendations or project planning. Abilities required: organize data in order to assemble a written memo; modify existing maps to help visualize a site and surrounding conditions; summarize assumptions used in project design in order to recommend a course of action to superiors.

7. **Problem resolution**. Use of technical and interpersonal skills in order to achieve workable solutions to civil engineering, economic, or people-related problems. Abilities required: negotiate effectively with a variety of constituencies; listen actively in order to clarify issues and to ask for appropriate information; express one's own position—orally as well as in writing—including supporting logic and arguments, in order to communicate one's position to other parties.

Just as you finish reading the report, Tracy Garcia, a senior civil engineer at Western, knocks on your door. "Have you read that job analysis report on junior civils yet, Pat?" You reply, "I sure have, and boy, has it given me ideas about new ways of selecting, training, and judging the performance of our new hires."

Challenges

1. How might the information presented in the job analysis help Western do a better job of recruiting new junior civil engineers?
2. As Pat Evans, what specific selection procedures would you like to see put into place?
3. How might the information in the job analysis report be useful in judging the performance of new hires?

In order to make intelligent decisions about the people-related needs of a business, two types of information are essential: (1) a description of the work to be done, the skills needed, and the training and experience required for various jobs, and (2) a description of the future direction of a business. Once this information is known, it makes sense to forecast the numbers and the skills mix of people required at some future time period. We consider the first of these needs, job analysis, in the early sections of the chapter, and the second, human resource planning, in the latter part of the chapter.

ALTERNATIVE PERSPECTIVES ON JOBS

Jobs are frequently the subject of conversation: "I'm trying to get a job"; "I'm being promoted to a new job"; "I'd sure like to have my boss's job." Or, as Samuel Gompers, first president of the American Federation of Labor, once said, "A job's a job; if it doesn't pay enough, it's a lousy job."

Jobs are important to individuals: they help determine standards of living, places of residence, status (value ascribed to individuals because of their position), and even one's sense of self-worth. Jobs are important to organizations because they are the vehicles through which work (and thus organizational objectives) are accomplished. The way to manage people to work efficiently is through answers to such questions as:

- Who specifies the content of each job?
- Who decides how many jobs are necessary?
- How are the interrelationships among jobs determined and communicated?
- Has anyone looked at the number, design, and content of jobs from the perspective of the entire organization, the "big picture"?
- What are the minimum qualifications for each job?
- What should training programs stress?
- How should performance on each job be measured?
- How much is each job worth?

Unfortunately, there is often a tendency, even an urgency, to get on with work itself ("get the job done!") rather than to take the time to think through these basic questions. But this tendency is changing as firms struggle to raise productivity and to cope with such problems as deregulation and global economic competition.

In the spirit of continuous improvement, firms in every developed country around the world are rethinking the fundamental principles that underlie the design of work and the required numbers and skills of people to do the work. For example, in an effort to get a better return on its enormous capital investment, General Motors has instituted round-the-clock production and flexible, lean manufacturing at its Lordstown, Ohio, plant. To do so, it retrained workers to handle a variety of jobs, instead of endlessly repeating a few rote tasks.[1] Job analysis was essential to understand the relationships among the newly enlarged jobs.

The term *job analysis* describes the process of obtaining information about jobs. As the chapter opening vignette illustrates, this information is useful for a number of business purposes. Regardless of how it is collected, it usually includes information about the tasks to be done on the job, as well as the personal characteristics (education, experience, specialized training) necessary to do the tasks.

An overall written summary of task requirements is called a job description, and an overall written summary of worker requirements is called a job specification. The result of the process of job analysis is a job description and a job specification. In the past, such job definitions often tended to be quite narrow in scope. Today's organizations, however, emphasize flexibility and more critical thinking in jobs. As an example, consider a job description developed by Mazda executives of assembly line work at their Flat Rock, Michigan, plant:

> They want their new employees to be able to work in teams, to rotate through various jobs, to understand how their tasks fit into the entire process, to spot problems in production, to troubleshoot, articulate the problems to others, suggest improvements, and write detailed charts and memos that serve as a road map in the assembly of the car.[2]

Does that sound like a traditional description of assembly line work? Hardly. Yet it is typical of the increased mental demands being placed on workers at all levels. Instead of being responsible for simple procedures and predictable tasks, workers are now expected to draw inferences and render diagnoses, judgments, and decisions, often under severe time pressure.[3]

Why Study Job Requirements?

Sound HR management practice dictates that thorough job analyses always be done, for they provide a deeper understanding of the behavioral requirements of jobs. This in turn creates a solid basis on which to make job-related employment decisions.[4] Legally, job analyses play a major role in the defense of employment practices (e.g., interviews, tests, performance appraisal systems) that are challenged, for they demonstrate that the practices in question are "job-related." Unfortunately, job analyses are often done for a specific purpose (e.g., training design) without consideration of the many other uses of this information. Some of these other uses, along with a brief description of each, are listed below and shown graphically in Figure 4-1.

Organizational structure and design. Through clarification of job requirements and the interrelationships among jobs, responsibilities at all levels can be specified, promoting efficiency and minimizing overlap or duplication.

Figure 4-1
Job analysis is the foundation of many human resource management programs. (*Source*: R. C. Page and D. M. Van De Voort, Human resource planning and job analysis. In W. F. Cascio (ed.), *Planning, employment, and placement*, vol. 2 of the ASPA/BNA *Human resource management series*. Washington, DC: Bureau of National Affairs, 1989.)

Human resource planning. Job analysis is the foundation for forecasting the need for human resources as well as for plans for such activities as training, transfer, or promotion. Frequently, job analysis information is incorporated into a human resource information system (HRIS).

Job evaluation and compensation. Before jobs can be ranked in terms of their overall worth to an organization or compared with jobs in other firms for purposes of pay surveys, it is important to understand what the jobs require. Job descriptions and specifications provide such understanding to those who must make job evaluation and compensation decisions.

Recruitment. The most important information an executive recruiter ("headhunter") or company recruiter needs is full knowledge of the job(s) in question.

Selection. Any method used to select or promote applicants must be based on a keen, meaningful forecast of job performance. An understanding of just what a worker is expected to do on the job, as reflected in job-related interviews or test questions, is necessary for such a meaningful forecast.

Placement. In many cases, applicants are first selected and then placed in one of many possible jobs. When there is a clear picture of the needs of a job and the abilities of workers to fulfill those needs, selection decisions will be accurate and workers will be placed in jobs where they will be the most productive. That is, selection and placement tend to go hand in hand. On the other side of the selection-placement coin, when there is a blurred picture of the needs of a job, selection decisions will not be accurate, and placement will probably be worse.

Orientation, training, and development. Training a worker can be very costly, as we will see later. Up-to-date job descriptions and specifications help ensure that training programs reflect actual job requirements. In other words, "What you learn in training today, you'll use on the job tomorrow."

Performance appraisal. If employees are to be judged in terms of how well they do those parts of their jobs that really matter, those that distinguish effective from ineffective performers, it is important to specify critical and noncritical job requirements. Job analysis does this.

Career path planning. If the organization (as well as the individual) does not have a thorough understanding of the requirements of available jobs and how jobs at succeeding levels relate to one another, effective career path planning is impossible.

Labor relations. The information provided by job analysis is helpful to both management and unions for contract negotiations, as well as for resolving grievances and jurisdictional disputes.

Engineering design and methods improvement. To design equipment to perform a specific task reliably and efficiently, engineers must understand exactly the capabilities of the operator and what he or she is expected to do. Similarly, any improvements or proposed new working methods must be evaluated relative to their impact on overall job objectives.

Job design. As with methods improvement, changes in the way work is accomplished must be evaluated through a job analysis, focusing on the tasks to be done and on the behaviors required of the people doing the tasks.

Safety. Frequently, in the course of doing a job analysis, unsafe conditions (environmental conditions or personal habits) are discovered and thus may lead to safety improvements.

Vocational guidance and rehabilitation counseling. It is possible to make informed decisions regarding career choices from comprehensive job descriptions and specifications.

Job classification systems. Selection, training, and pay systems are often keyed to job classification systems, also referred to as "job families." Without job analysis information, it is impossible to determine reliably the structure of the relationships among jobs in an organization.

Dynamic Characteristics of Jobs

There are two basic things to keep in mind when thinking about what job analysis is and what it should accomplish:

One, as time goes on, everything changes, including jobs. This changing nature of jobs has been recognized only recently. The former popular view of a job was that what it required did not change; a job was a static thing, designed to be consistent although the workers who passed through it were different. Now we know that for a job to produce efficient output, it must change according to the workers who do it. In fact, the nature of jobs might change for three reasons:

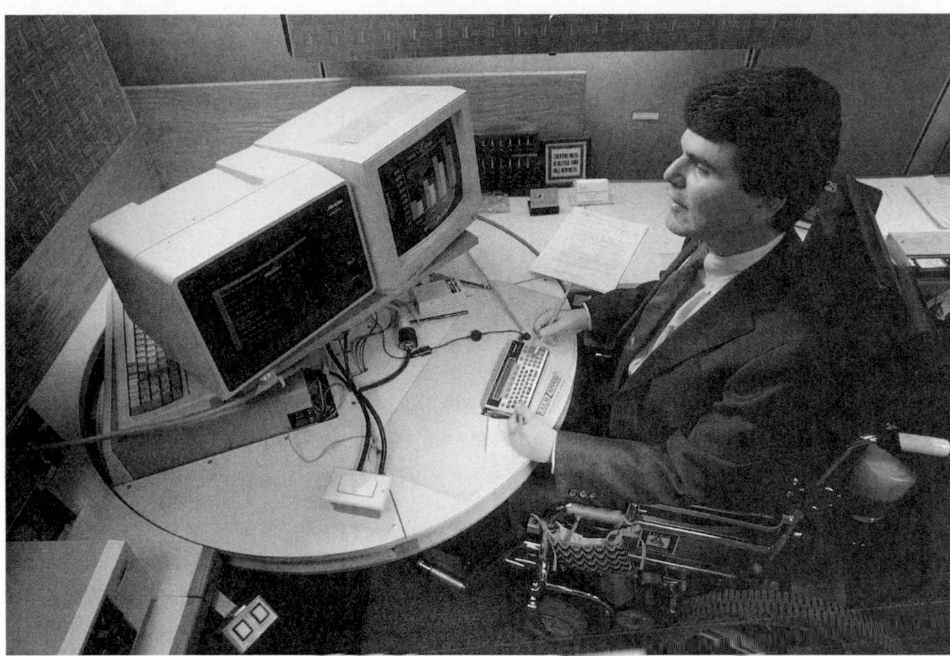

New developments in computer technology permit persons with disabilities to perform many kinds of work.

- **Time**. For example, lifeguards, ski instructors, and accountants do different things at different times of the year.
- **People**. Particularly in management jobs but also in teaching or coaching, the job is what the incumbent makes of it.
- **Environment**. Such changes may be technological—for example, word processing has drastically changed the nature of many secretarial jobs. Or the changes may be situational, as in a recent collective bargaining agreement between Gulf Oil Corporation and the Oil, Chemical, and Atomic Workers Union in which the company has "total flexibility" in assigning work across traditional craft lines; thus welders may be assigned as helpers to pipe fitters, boilermakers, and forklift operators.

Two, job analysis comprises job specifications and people requirements that should reflect *minimally* acceptable qualifications for job holders. Frequently, they do not, reflecting instead a profile of the *ideal* job holder.

How are job specifications set? Typically by consensus among experts—immediate supervisors, job incumbents, and job analysts. Such a procedure is professionally acceptable, but care must be taken to distinguish between required and desirable qualifications. The term "required" denotes inflexibility; that is, it is assumed that without this qualification, an individual absolutely would be unable to do the job. "Desirable" implies flexibility; it is "nice to have" this ability, but it is not a "need-to-have" (see job dimension 2 in the chapter opening vignette). To be sure, required qualifications will exist in almost all jobs, but care must be exercised in establishing them, for such requirements must meet a higher standard.

LEGALITIES

JOB ANALYSIS AND THE AMERICANS WITH DISABILITIES ACT OF 1990

Job analyses are not legally required under the ADA, but sound professional practice suggests that they be done—for three reasons. One, the law makes it clear that job applicants must be able to understand what the essential functions of a job are before they can respond to the question "Can you perform the essential functions of the job for which you are applying?" Essential functions are those that require relatively more time and have serious consequences of error or nonperformance associated with them. A function may be essential because the reason the position exists at all is to perform that function (e.g., a baggage handler at an airport must be able to lift bags weighing up to 70 pounds repeatedly throughout an 8-hour shift). Alternatively, the function may be so highly specialized that it cannot be shifted to others (e.g., in a nuclear power plant, a nuclear engineer must perform inspections, often by crawling through tight spaces). Job analysis is a systematic procedure that can help identify essential job functions.

Two, existing job analyses may need to be updated to reflect additional dimensions of jobs, namely, the physical demands, environmental demands, and mental abilities required to perform essential functions. Figure 4-2 shows a portion of a checklist of physical demands.

Three, once job analyses are updated as described, a summary of the results is normally prepared in writing in the form of a job description. What may work even better under the ADA, however, is a video job description, to provide concrete evidence to applicants of the physical, environmental (e.g., temperatures, noise level, working space), or mental (e.g., irate customers calling with complaints) demands of jobs. Candidates who are unable to perform a job because of a physical or mental disability may self-select out, thereby minimizing the likelihood of a legal challenge.

To ensure job-relatedness, be able to link required knowledge, skills, abilities, and other characteristics (measures of which candidates actually are assessed on) to essential job functions. Finally, recognize that under the ADA it is imperative to distinguish "essential" from "nonessential" functions *prior* to announcing a job opening or interviewing applicants.[5] If a candidate with a disability can perform the essential functions of a job and is hired, the employer must be willing to make "reasonable accommodations" to enable the person to work. Here are some examples that the ADA defines as "reasonable" accommodation efforts:

- Restructuring a job so that someone else does the nonessential tasks a person with a disability cannot do
- Modifying work hours or work schedules so that a person with a disability can commute during off-peak periods
- Reassigning a worker who becomes disabled to a vacant position
- Acquiring or modifying equipment or devices (e.g., a telecommunications device for the hearing-impaired)

Use the symbols below to rate the following activities:

NP	Not present	Activity does not exist
O	Occasionally	Activity exists up to 1/3 of the time
F	Frequently	Activity exists from 1/3 to 2/3 of the time
C	Constantly	Activity exists 2/3 or more of the time

1a. Strength (also enter the percentage of time spent in each activity)

_____ Standing _____ percent
_____ Walking _____ percent
_____ Sitting _____ percent

1b. Also indicate the number of pounds that must be lifted, carried, pushed, or pulled.

_____ Lifting _____ (weight)
_____ Carrying _____ (weight)
_____ Pushing _____ (weight)
_____ Pulling _____ (weight)

2. Climbing _____
3. Balancing _____
4. Stooping _____
5. Kneeling _____
6. Crouching _____
7. Crawling _____
8. Reaching _____
9. Talking (Ordinary) _____ (Other) _____
10. Hearing (Ordinary conversation) _____ (Other) _____

Figure 4-2
Portion of a physical abilities checklist.

- Adjusting or modifying examinations, training materials, or HR policies
- Providing qualified readers or interpreters

From a Task-Based to a Process-Based Organization of Work

Traditional task-based jobs were packaged into clusters of similar tasks and assigned to specialist workers. Today many firms have no reason to package work that way. Instead, they are unbundling tasks into broader chunks of work that change over time. Such shifting clusters of tasks make it difficult to define a "job," at least in the traditional sense. Practices such as flextime, job sharing, and telecommuting, not to mention temporary workers, part-timers, and consultants, have compounded the definitional problem.

Today there is a detectable shift away from a task-based toward a process-based organization of work. A process is a collection of activities (such as procurement, order fulfillment, product development, or credit issuance) that takes one or more kinds of input and creates an output that is of value to a customer.[6] Individual tasks are important parts of the process, but the process itself cuts across organizational boundaries and traditional functions, such as engineering, production, marketing, and finance.

Consider credit issuance as an example. Instead of the separate jobs of credit checker and pricer, the two may be combined into one "deal structurer." Such integrated processes may cut response time and increase efficiency and productivity. Bell Atlantic created a "case team"—a group of people who, as a whole, have all the skills necessary to handle an installation order. Members of the team—who previously were located in different departments and in different geographical areas—were brought together into a single unit and given total responsibility for installing the equipment. Such a process operates, on average, 10 times faster than the assembly line version it replaces. Bell Atlantic, for example, reduced the time it takes to install a high-speed digital service link from 30 days to 3 days.[7]

Employees involved in the process are responsible for ensuring that customers' requirements are met on time and with no defects, and they are empowered to experiment in ways that will cut cycle time and reduce costs. Result: less supervision is needed, while workers take on broader responsibilities and a wider purview of activities. Moreover, the kinds of activities that each worker does are likely to shift over time.

In a process-based organization of work, three kinds of information are important:

- Identification of job specifications (i.e., the personal characteristics—knowledge, skills, abilities, and other characteristics—necessary to do the work)
- Identification of the environment, context, and social aspects of work
- Change in emphasis from describing jobs to describing roles

Keep these ideas in mind as you continue reading about the analysis of jobs and work.

How Do We Study Job Requirements?

A number of methods are available to study jobs. At the outset it is important to note that no one of them is sufficient. Rather, it is important to use a combination of them to obtain a total picture of the task and the physical, mental, social, and environmental demands of a job. Here are five common methods of job analysis:

1. **Job performance**. With this approach, an analyst actually does the job under study to get firsthand exposure to what it demands.
2. **Observation**. The analyst simply observes a worker or group of workers doing a job. Without interfering, the analyst records the what, why, and how of the various parts of the job. Usually this information is recorded in a standard format.

3. **Interviews.** In many jobs in which it is not possible for the analyst actually to perform the job (e.g., airline pilot) or where observation is impractical (e.g., architect), it is necessary to rely on workers' own descriptions of what they do, and why, and how they do it. As with recordings of observations, a standard format is used to collect input from all workers sampled to interview. In this way all questions and responses can be restricted to job-related topics. More importantly, standardization makes it possible to compare what different people are saying about the job in question.

4. **Critical incidents.** These are vignettes consisting of brief actual reports that illustrate particularly effective or ineffective worker behaviors. For example:

   > On January 14, Mr. Vin, the restaurant's wine steward, was asked about an obscure bottle of wine. Without hesitation, he described the place of vintage and bottling, the meaning of the symbols on the label, and the characteristics of the grapes in the year of vintage.

   After collecting many of these little incidents from knowledgeable individuals, the analyst abstracts and categorizes them according to the general job area they describe. The result is a fairly clear picture of actual job requirements.

5. **Structured questionnaires.** These questionnaires list tasks, behaviors (e.g., negotiating, coordinating, using both hands), or both. Items relating to tasks focus on *what* gets done—a job-oriented approach. Items relating to behaviors, on the other hand, focus on *how* a job is done—a worker-oriented, or ability-requirements, approach. Workers rate each task or behavior in terms of whether or not it is performed; if it is, they rate characteristics such as frequency, importance, level of difficulty, and relationship to overall performance. The ratings provide a basis for scoring the questionnaires and for developing a profile of actual job requirements.[8] The ability to represent job content in terms of numbers allows relatively precise comparisons across different jobs.[9] One of the most popular structured questionnaires is the Position Analysis Questionnaire (PAQ).

   The PAQ is a behavior-oriented job analysis questionnaire.[10] It consists of 194 items that fall into the following categories:

   - **Information input**—where and how the worker gets the information to do her or his job
   - **Mental processes**—the reasoning, planning, and decision making involved in a job
   - **Work output**—physical activities as well as the tools or devices used
   - **Relationships with other people**
   - **Job context**—physical and social
   - **Other job characteristics**—for example, apparel, work continuity, licensing, hours, and responsibility

   The items provide for either checking a job element if it applies or rating it on a scale, such as in terms of importance, time, or difficulty. An example of some PAQ items is shown in Figure 4-3. While structured job analysis questionnaires are growing in popularity, the newest applications use computer-generated graphics to help illustrate similarities and differences across jobs and organizational units.[11]

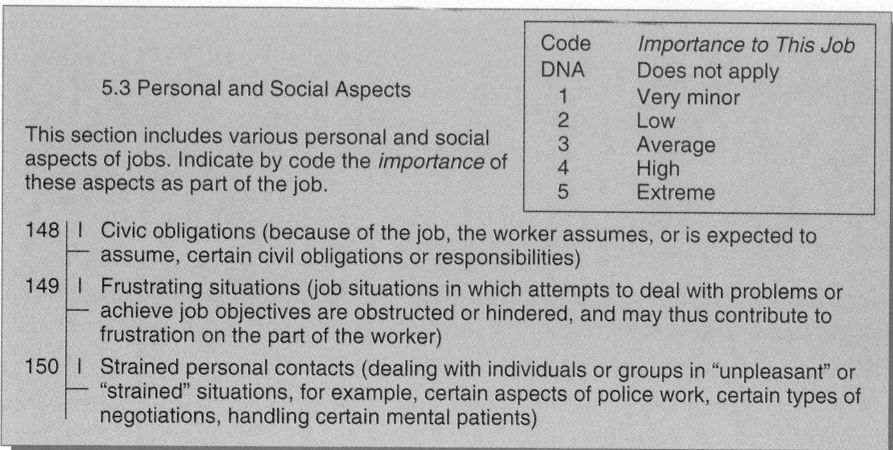
5.3 Personal and Social Aspects

This section includes various personal and social aspects of jobs. Indicate by code the *importance* of these aspects as part of the job.

Code	*Importance to This Job*
DNA	Does not apply
1	Very minor
2	Low
3	Average
4	High
5	Extreme

148 I Civic obligations (because of the job, the worker assumes, or is expected to assume, certain civil obligations or responsibilities)

149 I Frustrating situations (job situations in which attempts to deal with problems or achieve job objectives are obstructed or hindered, and may thus contribute to frustration on the part of the worker)

150 I Strained personal contacts (dealing with individuals or groups in "unpleasant" or "strained" situations, for example, certain aspects of police work, certain types of negotiations, handling certain mental patients)

Figure 4-3
Sample PAQ items.

The preceding five methods of job analysis represent the popular ones in use today. Table 4-1 considers the pros and cons of each method. Regardless of the method used, the workers providing job information to the analyst must be experienced and knowledgeable about the jobs in question;[12] however, there seem to be no differences in the quality of information provided by members of different gender or racial/ethnic subgroups,[13] or by high as opposed to low performers.[14] Nevertheless, it may well be that in relatively autonomous jobs, such as those of stockbrokers, high and low performers allocate their time quite differently.[15] In terms of the types of data actually collected, the most popular methods today are observation, interviews, and structured questionnaires.

Analyzing Managerial Jobs

Analysis of managerial jobs requires some special considerations. One is that managers tend to adjust the content of their jobs to fit their own style rather than to fit the needs of the work to be done. The result of this tendency is that when it comes to querying them about their work, they will describe what they actually do, having lost sight of what they should be doing. Another consideration is that it is difficult to identify what a manager does over time because her or his activity differs from time to time, perhaps one activity one month or week or day and then some other activity the following day or week or month. Indeed, managers' activities change throughout the day. As immediate situations or general environments change, so will the content of a manager's job, and each such change will affect managers differently in different functional areas, different geographical areas, and different organizational levels (e.g., first-line supervisors versus divisional vice presidents). To analyze managerial jobs, we must identify and measure the fundamental dimensions along which they differ and change. That is, we must identify what managers actually do on their jobs, and then we must specify behavioral differences due to time, person, and environmental changes.

The Management Position Description Questionnaire (MPDQ) is a 197-item, behaviorally based instrument for describing, comparing, classifying, and evaluating executive positions in terms of their content.[16] An example of one portion of the MPDQ is shown in Figure 4-4.

Table 4-1

ADVANTAGES AND DISADVANTAGES OF FIVE POPULAR JOB ANALYSIS METHODS

Method	Advantages	Disadvantages
Job performance	With this method there is exposure to actual job tasks, as well as to the physical, environmental, and social demands of the job. It is appropriate for jobs that can be learned in a relatively short period of time.	This method is inappropriate for jobs that require extensive training or are hazardous to perform.
Observation	Direct exposure to jobs can provide a richer, deeper understanding of job requirements than workers' descriptions of what they do.	If the work in question is primarily mental, observations alone may reveal little useful information. Critical yet rare job requirements (e.g., "copes with emergencies") simply may not be observed.
Interviews	This method can provide information about standard as well as nonstandard activities and about physical as well as mental work. Since the worker is also his or her own observer, he or she can report on activities that would not be observed often. In short, the worker can provide the analyst with information that might not be available from any other source.	Workers may be suspicious of interviewers and their motives; interviewers may ask ambiguous questions. Thus distortion of information (either as a result of honest misunderstanding or as a result of purposeful misrepresentation) is a real possibility. For this reason, the interview should never be used as the sole job analysis method.
Critical incidents	This method focuses directly on what people do in their jobs, and thus it provides insight into job dynamics. Since the behaviors in question are observable and measurable, information derived from this method can be used for most possible applications of job analysis.	It takes considerable time to gather, abstract, and categorize the incidents. Also, since by definition the incidents describe particularly effective or ineffective behavior, it may be difficult to develop a profile of average job behavior—the main objective in job analysis.
Structured questionnaires	This method is generally cheaper and quicker to administer than other methods. Questionnaires can be completed off the job, thus avoiding lost productive time. Also, where there are large numbers of job incumbents, this method allows an analyst to survey all of them, thus providing a breadth of coverage that is impossible to obtain otherwise. Furthermore, such survey data often can be quantified and processed by computer, which opens up vast analytical possibilities.	Questionnaires are often time-consuming and expensive to develop. Rapport between analyst and respondent is not possible unless the analyst is present to explain items and clarify misunderstandings. Such an impersonal approach may have adverse effects on respondent cooperation and motivation.

Job Analysis: Relating Method to Purpose

With such a wide variety of available job analysis methods, the combination of methods to use is the one that best fits the *purpose* of the job analysis research (e.g., staffing, training design, performance appraisal). Table 4-2 is a matrix that suggests some possible match-ups between job analysis methods and various purposes. The table simply illustrates the relative strengths of each method

Part 8 Contacts

To achieve organizational goals, managers and consultants may be required to communicate with employees at many levels within the company and with influential people outside of the company. This part of the questionnaire addresses the nature and level of these contacts.

Directions:

Step 1—Significance

For each contact and purpose of contact noted, indicate how significant a part of your position each represents by assigning a number between 0 to 4 to each block. Remember to consider both the importance and frequency of the contact.

0–**Definitely not** a part of the position.

1–**Minor significance** to the position.

2–**Moderate significance** to the position.

3–**Substantial significance** to the position.

4–**Crucial significance** to the position.

Step 2—Other Contacts

If you have any other contacts, please elaborate on their nature and purpose below.

____

____

____

____

____

____

____

____

____

____

____

Purpose of Contact

	Share Information regarding past, present, or anticipated activities or decisions.	Influence others to act or decide in a manner consistent with your objectives	Direct the plans, activities, or decisions of others
1. Executives.	10	11	12
2. Group managers (managers report to position).	13	14	15
3. Managers (supervisors report to position).	16	14	18
4. Supervisors (no supervisors report to position).	19	20	21
5. Professional/administrative exempt.	22	23	24
6. Clerical or support staff (nonexempt)	25	26	27
7. Other nonexempt employees.	28	29	30

	Provide/gather Information or promote the organization or its products/services.	Resolve problems.	Sell products/ services.	Negotiate contracts/ settlements, etc.
8. Customers of the company's products or services.	31	32	33	34
9. Representatives of vendors/subcontractors.	35	36	37	38
10. Representatives of other companies or professional organizations and institutions.	39	40	41	42
11. Representatives of labor unions.	43	44	45	46
12. Representatives of influential community organizations.	47	48	49	50
13. Individuals such as applicants or shareholders.	51	52	53	54
14. Representatives of the media, including the press, radio, television, etc.	55	56	57	58
15. National, state, or regional elected government representatives and/or lobbyists.	59	60	61	62
16. Local government officials and/or representatives of departments such as customs, tax, revenue, traffic, procurement, law enforcement, and environment.	63	64	65	66

Figure 4-4
Sample Management Position Description Questionnaire items.

Table 4-2

JOB ANALYSIS METHODS AND THE PURPOSE(S) *BEST* SUITED TO EACH

Method	Job descriptions	Development of tests	Development of interviews	Job evaluation	Training design	Performance appraisal design	Career path planning
Job performance		X	X		X	X	
Observation	X	X	X				
Interviews	X	X	X	X	X	X	
Critical incidents	X	X	X		X	X	
Questionnaires:							
Task checklists	X	X	X	X	X	X	
Behavior checklists			X	X	X	X	X

when used for each purpose. For example, the job performance method of job analysis is most appropriate for the development of tests and interviews, training design, and performance appraisal system design.

COSTS AND BENEFITS OF ALTERNATIVE JOB ANALYSIS METHODS

Key considerations in the choice of job analysis methods are the method-purpose fit, cost, practicality, and an overall judgment of their appropriateness for the situation in question. Comparative research based on the purposes and practicality of these five job analysis methods has yielded a pattern of results similar to that shown in Table 4-2.[17] In terms of costs, the PAQ (a behavior checklist) was the least costly method to use, while critical incidents was the most costly. However, cost is not the only consideration in choosing a job analysis method. Appropriateness for the situation is another. While the PAQ is used widely, unless a trained analyst actually interviews job incumbents, the PAQ may be more appropriate for analyzing higher-level jobs since a college-graduate reading level is required to comprehend the items.[18] Related to the issue of appropriateness is an awareness that behavioral similarities in jobs may mask genuine task differences between them. For example, on the surface the jobs of pianist and eye surgeon may appear quite similar—both require fine motor movements!

A thorough job analysis may require a considerable investment of time, effort, and money. Choices must be made among methods. If the choices are based on a rational consideration of the trade-offs involved, they will result in the wisest use of time *and* effort *and* money.

As an example, consider a job analysis approach called JobScope, used by Nationwide Insurance Companies. As a result of improved accuracy in job evaluation (assessment of the relative worth of jobs to the firm), the system is saving the company more than $60,000 in salary and benefits *each year*. The company recouped the entire cost of developing JobScope during its first 2 years of operation and used it as the basis for developing an integrated HR system.[19]

THE RELATIONSHIP OF JOB ANALYSIS TO HUMAN RESOURCE PLANNING

Having identified the behavioral requirements of jobs, the organization is in a position to identify the numbers of employees and the skills required to do those jobs, at least in the short term. Further, an understanding of available competencies is necessary to allow the organization to plan for the changes to new jobs required by corporate goals. This process is known as human resource planning (HRP). HRP is becoming more important in firms as a result of globalization, new technologies, organizational restructuring, and diversity in the workforce. All these factors produce uncertainty—and since it is difficult to be efficient in an uncertain environment, firms develop business and HR plans to reduce the impact of uncertainty. The plans may be short-term or long-term in nature, but if they are to have a meaningful impact on future operations, both business and HR plans must be linked tightly to each other. To understand why, let's consider how HRP in the 1990s differs from HRP in earlier time periods.

HRP in the 1990s

In the past, HRP tended to be a reactive process because business needs usually defined human resource needs. For example, in the past, a bank might decide to acquire a rival bank because it made good economic sense. Only after that decision was made would the bank worry about deploying talent in the two firms and integrating the two workforces. Today, major changes in business, economic, and social environments are forcing organizations to integrate business planning with HRP and to adopt a longer-term, proactive perspective.[20] For example, according to the vice president of human resources at Liz Claiborne, Inc.:

> Human resources is part of the strategic [business] planning process. It's part of policy development, line extension planning, and merger and acquisition processes. Little is done in the company that doesn't involve us in the planning, policy, or finalization stages of any deal.[21]

The extent, as well as the pace, of change, is accelerating. Thus, in a recent survey of 400 executives of large firms, 79 percent reported that change in their companies is rapid or extremely rapid, and 61 percent believed the pace of change will accelerate.[22] To address human resource concerns systematically, firms now recognize that they need short-term as well as long-term solutions. As usually practiced, job analysis identifies qualities that employees need to perform existing jobs. Yet rapid changes in technology mean that the jobs of the future will differ radically from those of the present.[23] Methods are available now for identifying skill and ability requirements for jobs that do not yet exist. These are known as future-oriented, or "strategic," job analyses.[24] They can provide additional, relevant information to general business plans. General business plans, in turn, may be strategic or tactical in nature.

Types of Plans: Strategic, Tactical, and Human Resources

Strategic Planning

Strategic planning is not about how to position products and businesses within an industry. Rather, it is about changing industry rules or creating tomorrow's industries, much as Wal-Mart Stores, Inc. did in retailing or Charles Schwab did in the brokerage and mutual fund businesses.[25] Strategic planning for an organization includes:

Defining philosophy. Why does the organization exist? What unique contribution does it make?

Formulating statements of identity, purpose, and objectives. What is the overall mission of the organization? What are its goals? Are the missions and goals of strategic business units consistent with the mission of the organization?

Evaluating strengths, weaknesses, and competitive dynamics. What factors, internal or external, may enhance or inhibit the ability of the organization to achieve its objectives?

Determining design. What are the components of the organization, what should they do, and how should they relate to one another toward achieving objectives and fulfilling the organization's mission?

Developing strategies. How will the objectives, at every level, be achieved? How will they be measured, not only in quantitative terms of what is to be achieved, but also in terms of time?

Devising programs. What will be the components of each program, and how will the effectiveness of each program be measured?

The biggest benefit of strategic planning is its emphasis on growth, for it encourages managers to look for new opportunities, rather than simply cutting more workers. But the danger of strategic planning is that it may lock companies into a particular vision of the future—one that may not come to pass. This poses a problem: how to plan for the future when the future changes so quickly. The answer is to make the planning process more democratic. Instead of being relegated to a separate staff—as in the past—the responsibility for strategic planning needs to involve a wide range of people, from line managers to customers to suppliers. Top managers must listen and be prepared to shift plans in midstream, if conditions demand such a response.

Hewlett-Packard CEO Lewis Platt typifies the new approach: "My role is to encourage discussion of the white spaces, the overlap and gaps among business strategies, the important areas that are not addressed by the strategies of individual HR businesses."[26] To bridge those gaps, HP now brings its customers and suppliers together with the general managers of its many business units in strategy sessions aimed at creating new market opportunities.

Strategic planning differs considerably from short-range tactical (or operational) planning. It involves fundamental decisions about the very nature of the business. Strategic planning may result in new business acquisitions, divestitures of current (profitable or unprofitable) product lines, new capital investments, or new management approaches.[27] It provides direction and scope to tactical planning.

Tactical, or Operational, Planning

This aspect of planning addresses issues associated with the growth of current or new operations, as well as with any specific problems that might disrupt the pace of planned growth. Purchasing new or additional office equipment to enhance efficiency (e.g., computer hardware or software), coping with the recall of a defective product (e.g., defective brakes in cars), and dealing with the need for a new design (e.g., tamper-proof bottle caps in the pharmaceutical industry) are examples of tactical planning problems. Beyond the obvious difference in the time frames distinguishing strategic planning and tactical planning is the difference in the degree of change resulting from the planning—and hence the degree of impact on human resource planning.

Human Resource Planning

Human resource planning parallels the plans for the business as a whole. HRP focuses on questions such as these: What do the proposed business strategies imply with respect to human resources? What kinds of internal and external constraints will (or do) we face? For example, restrictive work rules in a collective bargaining contract are an internal constraint, while a projected shortfall in the supply of college graduate electrical engineers (relative to the demand for them by employers) is an external constraint. What are the implications for staffing, compensation practices, training and development, and management succession? What can be done in the short run (tactically) to prepare for long-term (strategic) needs?

More on Human Resource Planning

Although HRP means different things to different people, general agreement exists on its ultimate objective—namely, the most effective use of scarce talent in the interests of the worker and the organization. Thus we may define HRP broadly as an effort to anticipate future business and environmental demands on an organization, and to provide qualified people to fulfill that business and satisfy those demands.[28] This general view suggests several specific, interrelated activities that together constitute an HRP system. They include:

- **A talent inventory** to assess current human resources (skills, abilities, and potential) and to analyze how they are currently being used.
- **A human resource forecast** to predict future HR requirements (the number of workers needed, the number expected to be available based on labor market characteristics, the skills mix required, internal versus external labor supply).
- **Action plans** to enlarge the pool of people qualified to fill the projected vacancies through such actions as recruitment, selection, training, placement, transfer, promotion, development, and compensation.
- **Control and evaluation** to provide feedback on the overall effectiveness of the human resource planning system by monitoring the degree of attainment of HR objectives.

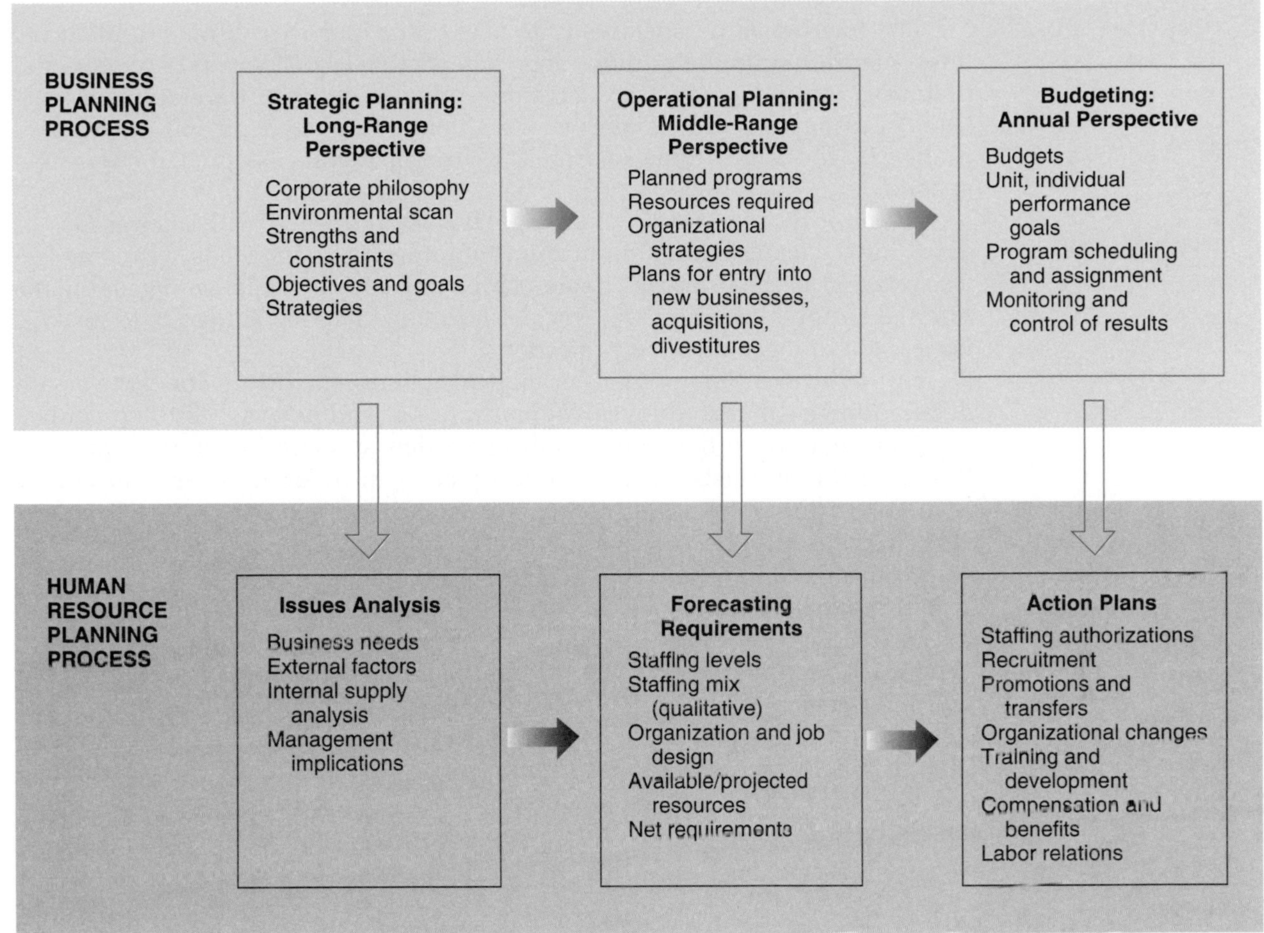

Figure 4-5
Impact of three levels of business planning on human resource planning.

THE RELATIONSHIP OF HUMAN RESOURCE PLANNING TO STRATEGIC AND TACTICAL PLANNING

A variety of HRP applications exists.[29] For example, HRP itself can be strategic (long-term and general) or tactical (short-term and specific). It may be done organizationwide, or it may be restricted to divisions, departments, or any common employee groups. It may be carried out on a recurring basis (e.g., annually) or only sporadically (e.g., when launching a new product line or at the outset of a capital expansion project). Regardless of the specific HRP application, almost all experts agree that if HRP is to be genuinely effective, it must be linked with the different levels of general business planning, not as an end or goal in and of itself, but rather as a means to the end of building more competitive organizations. The overall process is directed by line managers. When line managers perceive that HR practices help them achieve their goals, they are more likely to initiate and support HRP efforts. Furthermore, the business-planning process raises important human resource questions,[30] as Figure 4-5 shows.

The long-range perspective (2 to 5 years or longer) of strategic planning flows naturally into the middle-range perspective (1 to 2 years) of operational planning. Annual budgeting decisions provide specific timetables, allocations of resources, and standards for implementing strategic and operational plans. As the time frame shortens, planning details become increasingly specific.

At the level of strategic planning, HRP is concerned with such issues as assessing the management implications of future business needs, assessing factors external to the firm (e.g., demographic and social trends), and gauging the internal supply of employees over the long run. The focus here is to analyze issues, not to make detailed projections.

At the level of operational, or tactical, planning, HRP is concerned with detailed forecasts of employee supply (internal and external to the organization) and employee demand (numbers needed at some future time period). Based on the forecasts, specific action plans can be undertaken. These may involve recruitment, changes in incentives, promotions, training, or transfers. Procedures must be established to control and evaluate progress toward targeted objectives.

Of necessity, Figure 4-5 is an oversimplification. In practice, business objectives (needs) may be long- or short-term in nature, and HR forecasts and programs (action plans) must address both types. As a simple example, consider that the personal characteristics of managers that lead to success during the start-up and early growth phases of an organization's life cycle (i.e., short- and intermediate-term horizons) may inhibit performance as the organization matures and stabilizes (i.e., the long-term horizon). To appreciate such a situation, consider the experience of Apple Computer, Inc.

COMPANY EXAMPLE

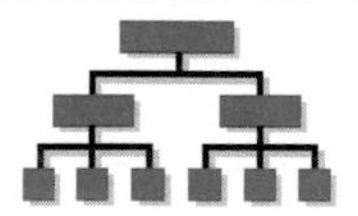

CHANGING BUSINESS AND HR NEEDS AT APPLE COMPUTER, INC.

Apple experienced dramatic changes as a company as it moved from an entrepreneurial start-up in the 1970s, through a high-growth phase tied to its Macintosh computers in the 1980s, to a mature, stable competitor in the globally competitive personal computer market in the mid-1990s. In the 1970s, Apple was launched by technical whizzes and young dreamers, led by Steven Jobs. The major objective was to produce a commercially viable product. In the 1980s, Apple hired John Sculley as CEO to provide marketing savvy and technological vision as the company showed the masses that computing with a graphical user interface could be fun. The Macintosh line had arrived, as had the need for professional marketing expertise. Unfortunately, Sculley's decision not to license the Macintosh operating system in the mid-1980s cost Apple an estimated \$20 to \$40 billion in value. In the 1990s, therefore, Apple realized that it needed a CEO with a proven ability to cut costs, to shorten product development cycles, and to penetrate new markets. The current CEO recognizes that Apple's challenge in the 1990s, as it was in the 1970s, is once again to make and market commercially viable products—in a business environment totally different from that of the 1970s.[31]

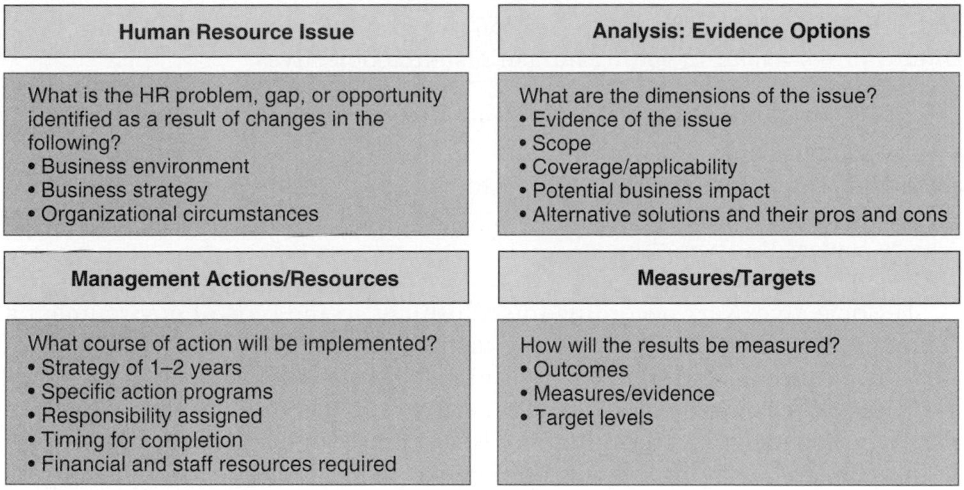

Human Resource Issue	Analysis: Evidence Options
What is the HR problem, gap, or opportunity identified as a result of changes in the following? • Business environment • Business strategy • Organizational circumstances	What are the dimensions of the issue? • Evidence of the issue • Scope • Coverage/applicability • Potential business impact • Alternative solutions and their pros and cons
Management Actions/Resources	**Measures/Targets**
What course of action will be implemented? • Strategy of 1–2 years • Specific action programs • Responsibility assigned • Timing for completion • Financial and staff resources required	How will the results be measured? • Outcomes • Measures/evidence • Target levels

Figure 4-6
Data to include on an HR strategy worksheet. (*Source*: R. S. Schuler & J. W. Walker, Human resources strategy: Focusing on issues and actions. *Organizational Dynamics,* Summer 1990, p. 14.)

As Figure 4-5 shows, human resource planning focuses on firm-level responses to people-related business issues over multiple time horizons. What are some examples of such issues, and how can managers identify them? People-related business concerns, or issues, might include, for example, "What types of managers will we need to run the business in the early twenty-first century, and how do we make sure we'll have them?" At a broader level, issues include the impact of rapid technological change, more complex organizations (in terms of products, locations, customers, and markets), more frequent responses to external forces such as legislation and litigation, demographic changes, and increasing multinational competition. In this scenario, environmental changes drive issues, issues drive actions, and actions encompass programs and processes used to design and implement them.[32] Issues themselves may be identified with the aid of an HR strategy worksheet, such as that shown in Figure 4-6.

Realistically, HR concerns become business concerns and are dealt with only when they affect the line manager's ability to function effectively. Such concerns may result from an immediate issue, such as downsizing or a labor shortage, or from a longer-term issue that can be felt as if it were an immediate issue, such as management development and succession planning.[33] On the other hand, HR issues such as workforce diversity, changing requirements for managerial skills, no-growth assumptions, mergers, retraining needs, and health and safety are issues that relate directly to the competitiveness of an organization and threaten its ability to survive. In short, progressive firms regard HR issues as people-related business issues that will have powerful impacts on their strategic business and HR planning.

HR Objectives—Foundation for Human Resource Planning

Objectives can be expressed either in behavioral terms ("By the third week of training, you should be able to do these things . . . ") or in end-result terms ("By the end of the next fiscal year, five new retail stores should be open, and each should be staffed by a manager, an assistant manager, and three clerks"). In the context of cost control in compensation, for example, the following questions should prove useful in setting human resource objectives:

- What level will the wage rate for an occupation be?
- How many people will we employ?
- How much more will our firm have to pay to attract more employees?
- How would the number of people our company employs change if the wage were lower? If it were higher?

HR objectives vary according to such things as the type of environment a company operates in, its strategic and tactical plans, and the current design of jobs and employee work behaviors. As examples, consider some of McDonald's human resource objectives: define jobs narrowly so that they are easy to learn in a short period of time; pay minimum wages to most nonmanagement employees so that the cost of turnover is low; design jobs to minimize decision making by the human operator (e.g., computer-controlled cooking operations, item labeling on cash registers).[34]

To be sure, objectives will differ depending on the time frame they represent. Examples of short-term HR objectives include increasing the breadth and depth of the applicant pool, increasing the length of time new hires stay with the organization, and decreasing the amount of time undesirable hires stay with the organization. In the longer term, HR objectives are more likely to include readjusting employees' skills, attitudes, and behaviors to fit major changes in the needs of the business. This happened, for example, as heavily regulated industries, such as cable television, were given the freedom to compete for business in open markets. Different kinds of competencies were needed. Of course, HR practices also must change to fit changes in the needs of employees.

In sum, differences in the types of objectives established for the short and long terms reflect differences in the types of changes that are feasible with 2 or 3 additional years of time. Setting human resource objectives is art as much as it is science. It requires conscious forethought based on the kind of future the firm wants to create for itself. It requires teamwork, and it cannot be left to serendipity.

TALENT INVENTORIES

Once HR objectives are set, it then becomes useful to compare the numbers, skills, and experience of the current workforce with those desired at some future time period. A talent inventory facilitates assessment of the current workforce; HR forecasts of supply and demand help determine future needs. In combination, they provide powerful planning information for the development of action programs. In both large and small organizations, such information is often computerized. When combined with other databases, it can be used to form a complete human resource information system (HRIS) that is useful in a variety of situations.[35] Information such as the following is typically included in a profile developed for each manager or nonmanager:

- Current position information
- Previous positions in the company
- Other significant work experience (e.g., other companies, military)

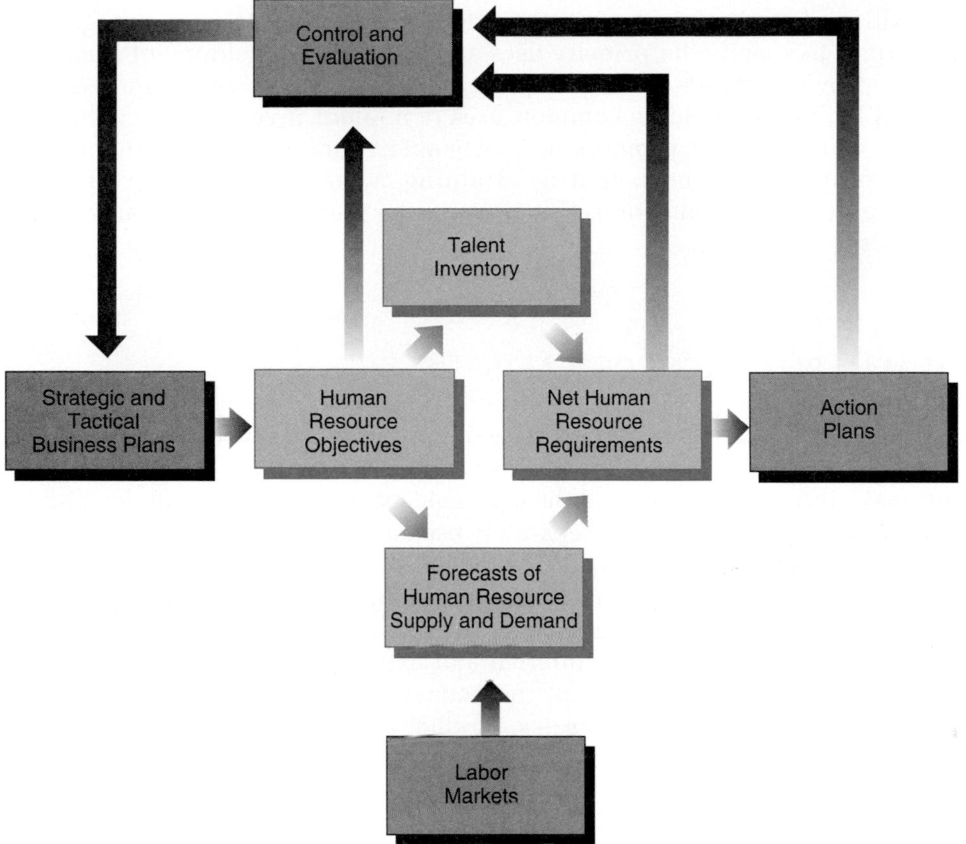

Figure 4-7
An integrated human resource planning system.

- Education (including degrees, licenses, certifications)
- Language skills and relevant international experience
- Training and development programs attended
- Community or industry leadership responsibilities
- Current and past performance appraisal data
- Disciplinary actions
- Awards received

Information provided by individuals may also be included. A major retailer, for example, includes factors that may limit an employee's mobility (e.g., health, family circumstances), as well as willingness to relocate. IBM includes the individual's expressed preference for future assignments and locations, including interest in staff or line positions in other IBM locations and divisions.[36]

Talent inventories and HR forecasts must complement each other; an inventory of present talent is not particularly useful for planning purposes unless it can be analyzed in terms of future HR requirements. On the other hand, a forecast of HR requirements is useless unless it can be evaluated relative to the current and projected future supply of workers available internally. Only at that time, when we have a clear understanding of the projected surpluses or deficits of employees in terms of their numbers, their skills, and their experience, does it make sense to initiate action plans to rectify projected problems. Figure 4-7 illustrates such an integrated HRP system.

Although secondary uses of the talent inventory data may emerge, it is important to specify the primary uses at the concept-development stage. Doing so provides direction and scope regarding who and what kinds of data should be included. Some common uses of a talent inventory are identification of candidates for promotion, management succession planning, assignment to special projects, transfer, training, workforce diversity planning and reporting, compensation planning, career planning, and organizational analysis.

HUMAN RESOURCE FORECASTS

The purpose of human resource forecasting is to estimate labor requirements at some future time period. Such forecasts are of two types: (1) the external and internal supply of labor and (2) the aggregate external and internal demand for labor. Each type is considered separately because each rests on a different set of assumptions and depends on a different set of variables.[37]

Internal supply forecasts relate to conditions *inside* the organization, such as the age distribution of the workforce, terminations, retirements, and new hires within job classes. Both internal and external demand forecasts, on the other hand, depend primarily on the behavior of some business factor (e.g., student enrollments, projected sales, product volume) to which HR needs can be related. Unlike internal and external supply forecasts, demand forecasts are subject to many uncertainties—in domestic or worldwide economic conditions, in technology, and in consumer behavior, to name just a few. The *Occupational Outlook Handbook*, published by the U.S. Department of Labor, focuses on macroforecasts of aggregate demand for various occupations. Figure 4-8 shows an excerpt of one such forecast for the fastest-growing occupations. In the following sections we will consider several micro- or firm-level HR forecasting techniques that have proven practical and useful.

Forecasting External Human Resource Supply

Recruiting and hiring new employees are essential activities for virtually all firms, at least over the long run. Whether they are due to projected expansion of operations or to normal workforce attrition, forays into the labor market are necessary.

Several agencies regularly make projections of external labor market conditions and estimates of the supply of labor to be available in general categories. These include the Bureau of Labor Statistics of the U.S. Department of Labor, the Engineering Manpower Commission, and the Public Health Service of the Department of Health and Human Services. For new college and university graduates, the Northwestern Endicott-Lindquist Report is one of the most respected barometers of future hiring decisions. Organizations in both the public and private sectors are finding such projections of the external labor market to be helpful in preventing surpluses or deficits of employees.

Managers in Japan pay especially close attention to forecasts of HR supply, because among blue-chip employers, it is taboo to lay off workers. While

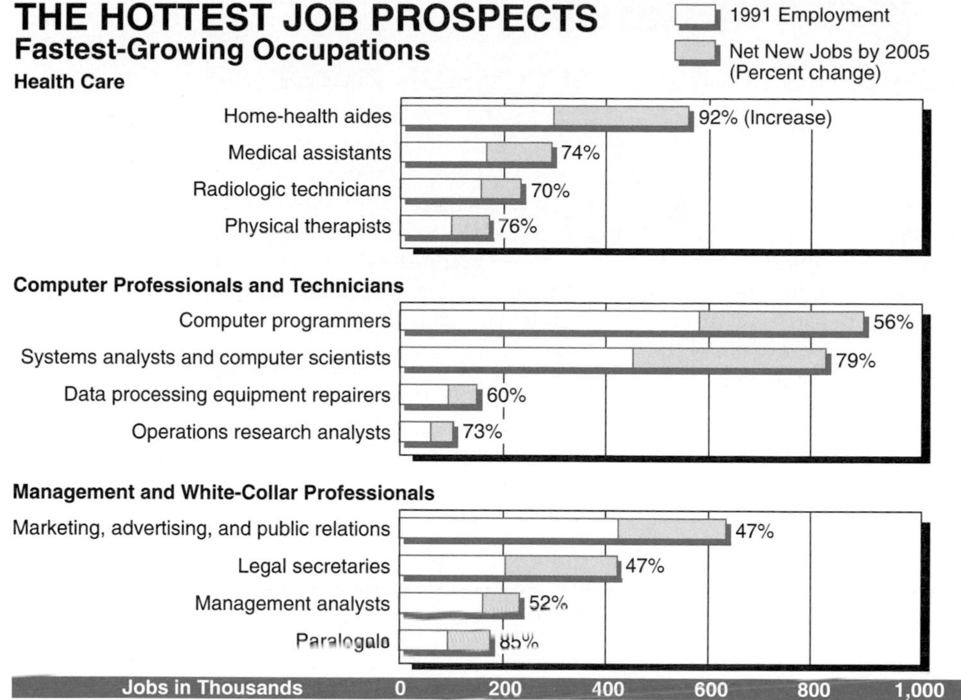

Figure 4-8
The fastest-growing occupations, 1991–2005. (*Source:* L. S. Richman, Jobs that are growing and slowing, *Fortune,* July 12, 1993, p. 53.)

Western governments give money to workers after they lose their jobs, the Japanese government pays distressed companies not to lay off workers.[38] It was no surprise, therefore, to find that in a poll of senior HR executives taken in the United States and Japan, managers from both countries gave top priority to executive development and recruiting. However, while a third major concern of the Americans was compensation, for the Japanese it was workforce planning.[39]

Forecasting Internal Human Resource Supply

A reasonable starting point for projecting a firm's future supply of labor is its current supply of labor. Perhaps the simplest type of internal supply forecast is the succession plan, a concept that has been discussed in the planning literature for over 25 years. Succession plans may be developed for management employees, nonmanagement employees, or both. The process for developing such a plan includes setting a planning horizon, identifying replacement candidates for each key position, assessing current performance and readiness for promotion, identifying career development needs, and integrating the career goals of individuals with company goals. The overall objective, of course, is to ensure the availability of competent executive talent in the future or, in some cases, immediately, as when a key executive dies suddenly.[40] Consider the succession planning undertaken by the Ministry of Transportation and Communications in the Province of Ontario.

SMALL BUSINESSES CONFRONT SUCCESSION PLANNING[41]

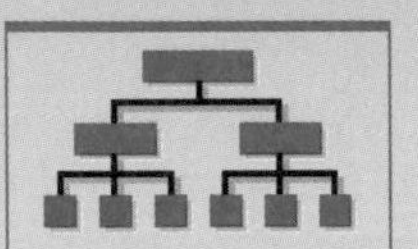

What happens with regard to succession planning in small firms, such as family-owned businesses? Only about 30 percent of family businesses outlive their founders, usually for lack of planning. Since many founders of small companies started in the post-World War II boom are now retiring, the question of succession is becoming more pressing. Here are some of the ways families are trying to solve the problem:

- 35 percent plan to groom one child from an early age to take over.
- 25 percent plan to let the children compete and choose one or more successors with help from the board of directors.
- 15 percent plan to let the children compete and choose one or more successors without input from a third party.
- 15 percent plan to form an "executive committee" of two or more children.
- 10 percent plan to let the children choose their own leader, or leaders.

Suppose the CEO dies suddenly. Plan to establish a committee that would assume immediate control of the company while it searches for a permanent successor. Experts say that naming a successor too quickly can anger employees still coping with the loss of their boss.

COMPANY EXAMPLE

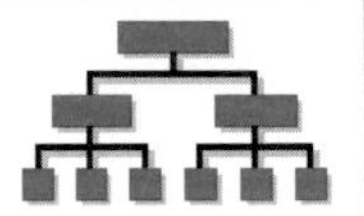

SUCCESSION PLANNING IN THE MINISTRY OF TRANSPORTATION AND COMMUNICATIONS (MTC), PROVINCE OF ONTARIO

MTC, one of the leading transportation authorities in North America, is responsible for the management of a highway network comprising approximately 13,000 miles of provincial roads. It also manages the subsidy allocation for an additional 62,500 miles of municipal roads and is involved in the planning for provincial commuter rail and air services. Major operational activities include planning, design, construction, maintenance, and research related to transportation systems and facilities.

The full-time workforce consists of approximately 2600 management and 7700 bargaining-unit employees, although for practical reasons, succession planning has been limited to middle and senior management (about 1300 positions). Succession planning is one of the responsibilities of every manager.

Current and future business plans and the assessed skills and potential of the management workforce provide the main inputs to the planning system. Meaningful forecasts can be done only for large job families. Hence, MTC's operations have been divided into five primary and eight secondary functions, and separate analyses are done for each of these functions. Figure 4-9 illustrates the various data that are used in the forecast to determine potential shortages, surpluses, numbers of promotable staff blocked from promotion (e.g., because there is no higher-level job to progress to in a particular job family), and annual training and development effort required to maintain backup strength.

- Current strength is determined from a talent inventory maintained by the corporate planning group.

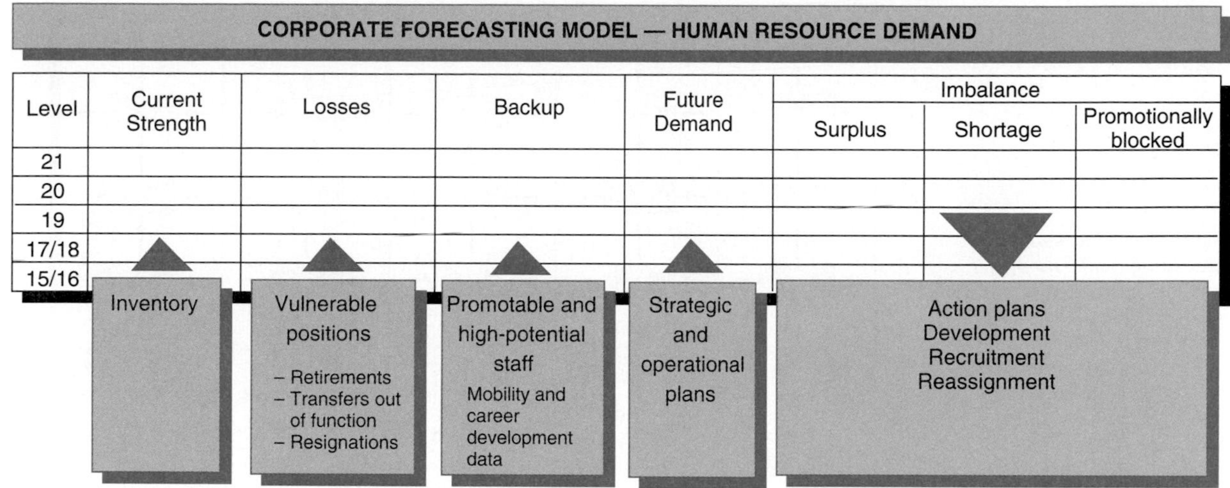

Figure 4-9
Corporate human resource demand forecasting model used at the Ontario Ministry of Transportation and Communications. See text explanations of the data that go into each column.

- Losses are made up of resignations, dismissals, transfers, and retirements. Resignations, dismissals, and transfers are assessed from historical data, modified by current and future trends. Retirement figures are based on a review of individual retirement ranges.
- Backup is determined from two sources: (1) As part of the annual appraisal process, managers identify those employees who are considered promotable within the next 1-year planning cycle; and (2) in a separate annual process, managers identify high-potential individuals who have the ability to progress to two responsibility levels higher—in more than one function—during a 4-year forecast period.
- Future demand is forecast on the basis of current as well as future business plans. These are determined by MTC's strategic policy committee (composed of the CEO and senior executives) with input from six planning groups.
- Finally, the data for succession planning for each function are manipulated by means of a computerized forecasting model (Figure 4-10). The model was chosen because it is simple to use and flexible enough to be able to provide data for use in analyzing situations that vary according to staffing levels, turnover rates, and replacement strategies.[42]

What is different about succession planning in today's turbulent business environment? In a nutshell, in specifying position requirements, companies are defining more generic competencies (e.g., ability to cut costs and to work with diverse constituencies), rather than specific knowledge and skills. They also are making it clear to individuals that they are responsible for their own career development, with no explicit or implicit promises made to them about future opportunities by the firm.[43]

Forecasting Human Resource Demand

In contrast to supply forecasting, demand forecasting is beset with multiple uncertainties—changes in technology; consumer attitudes and patterns of buying behavior; local, national, and international economies; number, size, and types of contracts won or lost; and government regulations that might open new

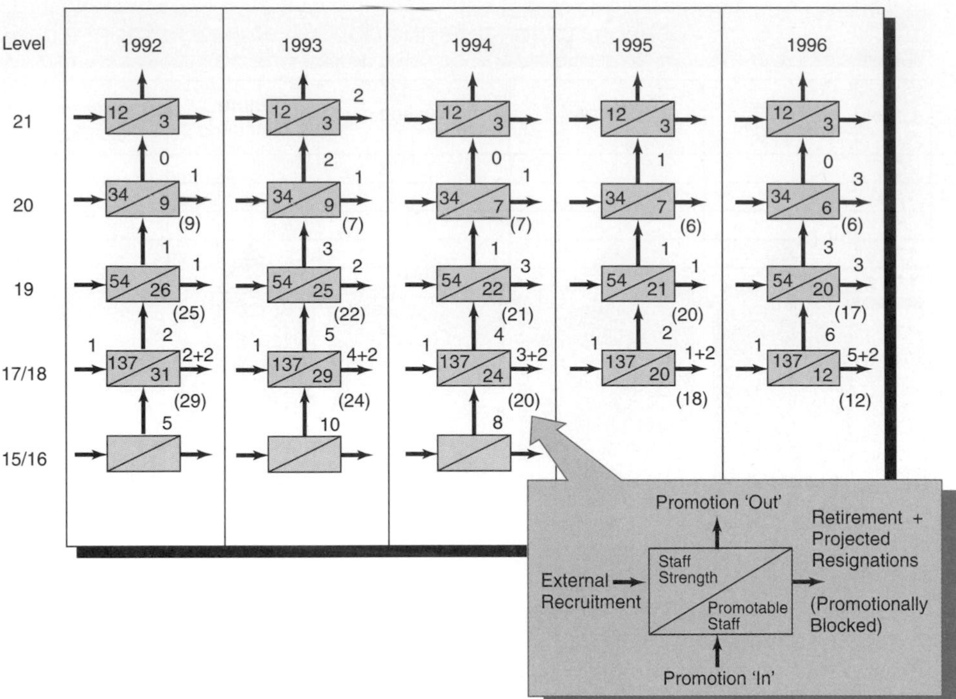

Figure 4-10

Management succession forecasting model used at the Ontario Ministry of Transportation and Communications. An explanation of the numbers in each box is contained in the lower right corner of the figure. For example, at job level 17/18 in 1994, staff strength is 137 persons, of whom 24 are promotable. Four persons were promoted "out," 8 were promoted "in," 1 was recruited externally, 3 retired, 2 were projected to resign, and 20 were promotionally blocked.

markets or close off old ones, just to name a few. Consequently, forecasts of HR demand are often more subjective than quantitative, although in practice a combination of the two is often used. One popular approach to demand forecasting is the Delphi technique.

The Delphi Technique

Delphi is a structured approach for reaching a consensus judgment among experts about future developments in any area that might affect a business (e.g., the level of a firm's future demand for labor). Originally developed as a method to facilitate group decision making, it has also been used in HR forecasting. Experts are chosen on the basis of their knowledge of internal factors that might affect a business (e.g., projected retirements), their knowledge of the general business plans of the organization, or their knowledge of external factors that might affect demand for the firm's product or service and hence its internal demand for labor. Experts may range from first-line supervisors to top-level managers. Sometimes experts internal to the firm are used, but if the required expertise is not available internally, then one or more outside experts may be brought in to contribute their opinions. To estimate the level of future demand for labor, an organization might select as experts, for example, managers from corporate planning, human resources, marketing, production, and sales.

The Delphi technique was developed during the late 1940s at the Rand Corporation's think tank in Santa Monica, California. Its objective is to predict future developments in a particular area by integrating the independent opinions of experts.[44] Face-to-face group discussion among the experts is avoided since differences in job status among group members may lead some individuals to avoid criticizing others and to compromise on their good ideas. Instead, an intermediary is used. The intermediary's job is to pool, summarize, and then

ETHICAL DILEMMA
Should Succession Plans Be Secret?

The issue of secrecy versus openness with regard to succession plans is a thorny one. If firms keep HR planning information about specific candidates secret, planning may have limited value. Thus at a software company, a senior executive on her way out the door for a president's job at a competitor was told that the firm had expected her to be its next president. Her response? "If I'd known, I would have stayed."

A somewhat different course of events transpired at another firm, whose policy was to talk openly about prospective candidates. There, employees learned what the company had in mind for them over the next 3 to 5 years. Subsequently, when they did not get the jobs they thought they were entitled to, employees felt betrayed. Some sued; others left.

In your view, is it unethical to share planning information with employees and then not follow the plan? Conversely, do employees have a right to see such information?

feed back to the experts the information generated independently by all the other experts during the first round of forecasting. The cycle is then repeated, so that the experts are given the opportunity to revise their forecasts and the reasons behind their revised forecasts. Successive rounds usually lead to a convergence of expert opinion within three to five rounds.

In one application, Delphi did provide an accurate 1-year demand forecast for the number of buyers needed for a retailing firm.[45] Here is a set of guidelines to make the Delphi process most useful:

- Give the expert enough information to make an informed judgment. That is, give him or her the historical data that have been collected, as well as the results of any relevant statistical analysis that has been conducted, such as staffing patterns and productivity trends.
- Ask the kinds of questions a unit manager can answer. For example, instead of asking for total staffing requirements, ask by what percentage staffing is likely to increase or ask only about anticipated increases in key employee groups, such as marketing managers or engineers.
- Do not require precision. Allow the experts to round off figures, and give them the opportunity to indicate how sure they are of the forecasted figures.
- Keep the exercise as simple as possible, and, especially, avoid questions that are not absolutely necessary.
- Be sure that all experts have a common understanding of classifications of employees and other definitions.
- Enlist top management's and experts' support for the Delphi process by showing how good forecasts will benefit the organization and small-unit operations, and how they will affect profitability and workforce productivity.[46]

How Accurate Is Accurate?

Accuracy in forecasting the demand for labor varies considerably by firm and by industry type (e.g., utilities versus women's fashions): roughly from 2 to 20 percent error. Certainly, factors such as the duration of the planning period, the quality of the data on which forecasts are based (e.g., expected changes in the business factor and labor productivity), and the degree of integration of HRP with strategic business planning all affect accuracy. How accurate a labor demand forecast should be depends on the degree of flexibility in staffing the workforce. That is, to the extent that people are geographically mobile, multiskilled, and easily hired, there is no need for precise forecasts.[47]

Matching Forecast Results to Action Plans

Labor demand forecasts affect a firm's programs in many different areas, including recruitment, selection, performance appraisal, training, transfer, and many other types of career-enhancement activities. These activities all constitute action programs. Action programs help organizations adapt to changes in their environments. In the past decade or so, one of the most obvious changes in the business environment has been the large influx of women, minorities, and immigrants into the workforce. To adapt to these changes, organizations have provided extensive training programs designed to develop these individuals' management skills. Also, they have provided training programs for supervisors and coworkers in human relations skills to deal effectively with members of these underrepresented groups.[48]

Assuming a firm has a choice, however, is it better to select workers who *already have developed the skills* necessary to perform competently or to train workers who do not have the skills immediately but who can learn to perform competently? This is the same type of "make-or-buy" decision that managers often face in so many other areas of business. Managers have found that it is often more cost-effective to buy, rather than to make. This is also true in the context of selection versus training.[49] Put your money and resources into selection. Always strive *first* to develop the most accurate, the most valid selection process that you can, for it will yield higher-ability workers. *Then* apply those action programs that are most appropriate in further increasing the performance of your employees. With high-ability employees, the productivity gain from a training program in, say, spreadsheets might be greater than the gain from the same program with lower-ability employees. Further, even if the training is about equally effective with well-selected, higher-ability employees and poorly selected, lower-ability employees, the *time* required for training may be less for higher-ability employees. Thus training costs will be reduced, and the net effectiveness of training will be greater when applied along with a highly valid personnel selection process. This point becomes even more relevant if one views training as a strategy for building sustained competitive advantage. Firms that select high-caliber employees, and then commit resources to develop them continually, gain a competitive advantage that no other organization can match: a deep reservoir of firm-specific human capital.

CONTROL AND EVALUATION OF HRP SYSTEMS

The purpose of control and evaluation is to guide HRP activities, identifying deviations from the plan and the causes of those deviations. For this reason, we need yardsticks to measure performance. Qualitative and quantitative objectives can both play useful roles in HRP. Quantitative objectives make

IMPACT OF JOB ANALYSIS AND HRP ON PRODUCTIVITY, QUALITY OF WORK LIFE, AND THE BOTTOM LINE

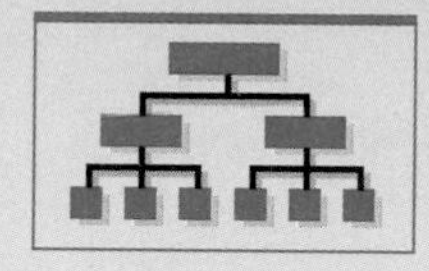

As noted earlier, jobs are dynamic, not static, in their requirements. This is especially true of jobs at the bottom and at the top of today's organizations. Entry-level jobs now demand workers with new and different kinds of skills. Even simple clerical work now requires computer knowledge, bank tellers need more knowledge of financial transactions and sales techniques, and foreign competition means that assembly line workers need more sophisticated understanding of mathematics and better reading and reasoning skills in order to cut costs and improve quality.

Current information on the behavioral requirements of jobs is critically important if firms are to develop meaningful specifications for selecting, training, and appraising the performance of employees in them and if employees are to perform their jobs successfully. HR planning information is no less important so that firms can institute action plans now to cope with projected HR needs in the future.

What are firms actually doing? A recent survey of 2100 firms by the Hay Group found that HR planning was formal and well developed at only 21 percent of the firms. It was undeveloped or rudimentary at another 30 percent. Most firms said that finding and keeping key people is a top priority.[50] However, without solid planning they may miss seeing the need for new talent and the need to develop new ways of selecting and training that talent.

the control and evaluation process more objective and measure deviations from desired performance more precisely. Nevertheless, the nature of evaluation and control should always match the degree of development of the rest of the HRP process. In newly instituted HRP systems, for example, evaluation is likely to be more qualitative than quantitative, with little emphasis placed on control. This is because supply-and-demand forecasts are likely to be based more on hunches and subjective opinions than on hard data. Under these circumstances, human resource planners should attempt to assess the following:[51]

- The extent to which they are tuned in to human resource problems and opportunities and the extent to which their priorities are sound
- The quality of their working relationships with staff specialists and line managers who supply data and use HRP results (how closely do the human resource planners work with these specialists and line managers on a day-to-day basis?)
- The extent to which decision makers, from line managers who hire employees to top managers who develop long-term business strategy, are making use of HRP forecasts, action plans, and recommendations
- The perceived value of HRP among decision makers (do they view the information provided by human resource planners as useful to them in their own jobs?)

In more established HRP systems, in which objectives and action plans are both underpinned by measured performance standards, key comparisons might include the following:[52]

IMPLICATIONS FOR MANAGEMENT PRACTICE

More and more, HR issues are seen as people-related business issues. This approach suggests that as a manager you should do the following:

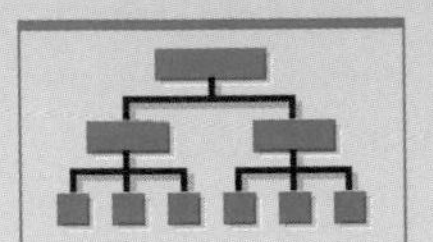

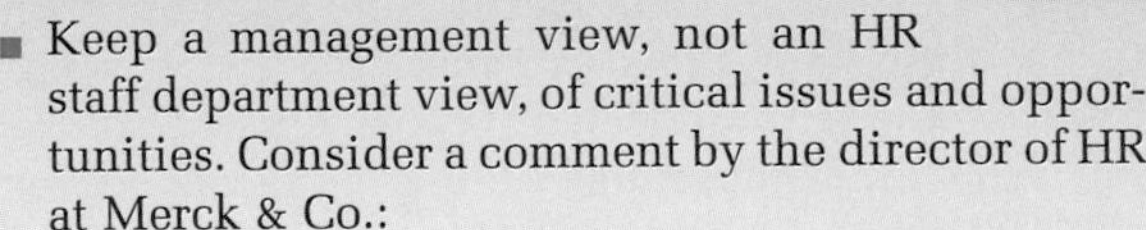

- Keep a management view, not an HR staff department view, of critical issues and opportunities. Consider a comment by the director of HR at Merck & Co.:

  > Line managers are starting to address the needs of individual and organizational performance—e.g., they know why every job exists in the organization, who the people in these jobs are, and how competent they are; and they know it is important to keep their skills updated. There is a saying at Merck: "Human resources are too important to be left to the HR department." Fully one-third of the performance evaluation of line managers is related to people management.[53]

- Plan within the context of managing the business strategically.
- Execute the strategy—doing so requires effective management consensus, communications designed to educate, and involvement of all parties. This is not a "pie in the sky" recommendation. In a recent survey, almost 60 percent of managers felt that the linkage between HR strategy and business results was either not effective or just "somewhat effective." Only 3 percent rated it "world class."[54] On the other hand, tight linkage, as at Northwestern Mutual Life Insurance, Mary Kay Cosmetics, and Tandy Corporation—can lead to consistent levels of high performance. As one CEO noted: "We don't make financial, marketing, technical, or human resources decisions—we make business decisions [and] we routinely involve all the functions."[55]

- Actual staffing levels against forecast staffing requirements
- Actual levels of labor productivity against anticipated levels of labor productivity
- Actual personnel flow rates against desired rates
- Action programs implemented against action programs planned (were there more or fewer? why?)
- Actual results of the action programs implemented against expected results (e.g., improved applicant flows, lower quit rates, improved replacement ratios)
- Labor and action program costs against budgets
- Ratios of action program benefits to action program costs

The advantage of quantitative information is that it highlights potential problem areas and can provide the basis for constructive discussion of the issues.

Human Resource Management in Action: Conclusion

THE ANALYSIS OF WORK—FOUNDATION FOR EMPLOYMENT PRACTICES

One of the new ideas that you, as Pat Evans, had for recruiting junior civil engineers was to develop a video that illustrated each of the seven essential functions of the job: modeling and calculations, computer software applications, project planning and management, written communications, individual and group interactions, summary and synthesis of data, and problem resolution.

Using a narrator, a script, and actual engineers at Western, the video would, in your opinion, ensure that job applicants developed a realistic picture of what it is like to work at Western. Since the company always seemed to have many more applicants than positions, you thought that perhaps the video might help reduce turnover among new hires; if they could get a good idea ahead of time of what they would be getting into, they would be less likely to leave the company. Just as the company was selective about whom it chose to hire, the video would provide job applicants with information that would allow them to be selective by helping them make informed decisions about their future employer.

Another application of the job dimensions and the video was in the selection process. You could visualize a "technical oral interview" in which candidates would be asked to describe their experiences in dealing with each of the seven major areas revealed by the job analysis. Interviewers would then ask follow-up questions in a systematic manner in order to elicit relevant information, and, on the basis of the recruiting video they had seen, job applicants could ask meaningful questions of the interviewers. Finally, it occurred to you that the very same job dimensions identified by the job analysis could, with a little elaboration, also be used as bases for judging the performance of junior civil engineers. You thought: "I love to mine information from a report, and that job analysis report has really been a gold mine for me and for engineering at Western."

SUMMARY

We are witnessing vast changes in the very nature of work itself, as well as in the types and numbers of jobs available. In an effort to reduce uncertainty and increase efficiency, careful attention needs to be paid to a thorough understanding of the behavioral requirements of jobs and the determination of human resource needs.

A written summary of the task requirements for a particular job is called a job description, and a written summary of worker requirements is called a job specification. Together, they constitute a job analysis. This information is useful for a variety of organizational purposes ranging from HR planning to career counseling.

Some combination of available job analysis methods (job performance, observation, interviews, critical incidents, structured questionnaires) should be used, for all have both advantages and disadvantages. Key considerations in the choice of methods are the method-purpose fit, cost, and practicality, along with an overall judgment of the appropriateness of the methods for the situation in question.

Job analysis provides one input to the HR planning process. Strategic and operational planning provides others. Strategic business planning is the long-range process of setting organizational objectives and deciding on action programs to achieve those objectives. Operational, or tactical, planning deals with the normal, ongoing growth of current operations or with specific problems that temporarily disrupt the pace of normal growth. Annual budgeting decisions provide specific timetables, allocations of resources, and implementation standards. The shorter the planning time frame, the more specific the planning details must be.

Strategic and operational business objectives dictate what HR objectives must be. So also do internal and external labor markets. Human resource planning (HRP) parallels general business planning. Broadly speaking, HRP is an effort to anticipate future business and environmental demands on an organization and to meet the human resource requirements dictated by those conditions. This general view suggests several interrelated activities that together make up an integrated HRP system. These include (1) an inventory of talent currently on hand, (2) forecasts of human resource supply and demand over short- and long-term periods, (3) action plans such as training or job transfer to meet forecasted HR needs, and (4) control and evaluation procedures.

DISCUSSION QUESTIONS

4-1 In your opinion, what are some of the key reasons for the deep changes we are seeing in the way jobs are done?

4-2 Choose a business process, e.g., order fulfillment, and identify the flow of work. How do task-based and process-based work flows differ?

4-3 For purposes of succession planning, what information would you want in order to evaluate "potential"?

4-4 In your opinion, is it more cost-effective to "buy" or to "make" competent employees?

4-5 Why should the output from forecasting models be tempered with the judgment of experienced line managers?

APPLYING YOUR KNOWLEDGE

Case 4-1 *HRP at First Bank*

First Bank is a large federally chartered bank located in a rapidly growing area in the southwestern United States. Over the past several years, First Bank experienced a significant expansion in size and operations, and a rapid influx of new personnel at all organizational levels. As it expanded and matured, the bank began to recognize its pressing need for talented, knowledgeable management personnel. Much talent had been hired from outside the bank over the past several years, but top management had become convinced that the long-run health of the bank depended on being able to develop managerial talent internally.

Linda Bishop had recently been hired to develop and install a new human resource planning (HRP) system at First Bank. She had previous experience both in banking and in human resource planning, so she seemed like a logical choice for the job. On the basis of her prior experience, Linda knew that many banking functions cross divisional lines and require managers with broad exposure to important areas within the bank. Further, she knew that division heads operate with a high degree of autonomy, and that divisional and corporate objectives are not always directly aligned. Therefore, Linda knew that the new HRP process would have to be corporatewide in scope. Only from that perspective could a planner assess bankwide, long-run human resource needs.

When Linda arrived at her new job, her boss had informed her that the focus of the HRP system was to be on management development and succession planning. To emphasize that focus, she was given the title of Director of Management Development and

Human Resource Planning. The position had corporatewide staff authority over all presently existing activities that related to management development and human resource planning. Today, Linda is thinking about a briefing that she is to give the executive officers of the bank next week. They have asked her to provide them with a statement of the objectives of the new HRP system as she sees it, an outline of the potential benefits that might accrue to the bank, and a list of suggested steps in the implementation of the HRP system.

Questions

If you were Linda Bishop, what would you be prepared to say to the executive officers in terms of:

1. The objectives of HRP?
2. The potential benefits of HRP?
3. Important steps in the implementation of the HRP system?

REFERENCES

1. General Motors: Open all night (1992, June 1). *Business Week*, pp. 82, 83.
2. Vobejda, B. (1987, Apr. 4). The new cutting edge in factories. *The Washington Post*, p. A14.
3. Goldstein, I. L., & Gilliam, P. (1990). Training system issues in the year 2000. *American Psychologist*, **45**, 134–143.
4. Landy, F. J., Shankster-Cawley, L., & Moran, S. K. (1995). Advancing personnel selection and placement methods. In A. Howard (ed.), *The changing nature of work*. San Francisco: Jossey-Bass, pp. 252–289.
5. Cascio, W. F. (1994). The Americans with Disabilities Act of 1990 and the 1991 Civil Rights Act: Requirements for psychological practice in the workplace. In B. D. Sales & G. R. VandenBos (eds.), *Psychology in litigation and legislation*. Washington, DC: American Psychological Association, pp. 175–211.
6. Hammer, M., & Champy, J. (1993). *Reengineering the corporation*. New York: Harper Business.
7. Ibid.
8. Fleishman, E. A., & Mumford, M. D. (1991). Evaluating classifications of job behavior: A construct validation of the ability requirements scales. *Personnel Psychology*, **44**, 523–575.
9. Harvey, R. J. (1991). Job analysis. In M. D. Dunnette & L. M. Hough (eds.), *Handbook of industrial and organizational psychology*, Vol. 2. Palo Alto, CA: Consulting Psychologists Press, pp. 71–163.
10. McCormick, E. J., Jeanneret, P. R., & Mecham, R. C. (1972). A study of job characteristics and job dimensions as based on the Position Analysis Questionnaire (PAQ). *Journal of Applied Psychology*, **56**, 347–368.
11. *Fleishman Job Analysis Survey* (1992). Palo Alto, CA: Consulting Psychologists Press. See also Page, R. C., & Van De Voort, D. M. (1989). Job analysis and HR planning. In W. F. Cascio (ed.), *Human resource planning, employment, and placement*. Washington, DC: Bureau of National Affairs, pp. 2-34 to 2-72.

12. Landy, F. J., & Vasey, J. (1991). Job analysis: The composition of SME samples. *Personnel Psychology*, **44**, 27–50. See also DiNisi, A. S., Cornelius, E. T., III, & Blencoe, A. G. (1987). Further investigation of common knowledge effects on job analysis ratings. *Journal of Applied Psychology*, **72**, 262–268. See also Friedman, L., & Harvey, R. J. (1986). Can raters with reduced job descriptive information provide accurate Position Analysis Questionnaire (PAQ) ratings? *Personnel Psychology*, **39**, 779–789.
13. Schmitt, N., & Cohen, S. A. (1989). Internal analyses of task ratings by job incumbents. *Journal of Applied Psychology*, **73**, 96–104.
14. Conley, P. R., & Sackett, P. R. (1987). Effects of using high- versus low-performing job incumbents as sources of job-analysis information. *Journal of Applied Psychology*, **72**, 434–437.
15. Borman, W. C., Dorsey, D., & Ackerman, L. (1992). Time-spent responses as time-allocation strategies: Relations with sales performance in a stockbroker sample. *Personnel Psychology*, **45**, 763–777.
16. Tornow, W. W., & Pinto, P. R. (1976). The development of a managerial taxonomy: A system for describing, classifying, and evaluating executive positions. *Journal of Applied Psychology*, **61**, 410–418.
17. Levine, E. L., Ash, R. A., & Bennett, N. (1980). Exploratory comparative study of four job analysis methods. *Journal of Applied Psychology*, **65**, 524–535. See also Levine, E. L., Ash, R. A., Hall, H., & Sistrunk, F. (1983). Evaluation of job analysis methods by experienced job analysts. *Academy of Management Journal*, **26**(2), 339–348.
18. Ash, R. A., & Edgell, S. L. (1975). A note on the readability of the Position Analysis Questionnaire (PAQ). *Journal of Applied Psychology*, **60**, 765–766.
19. Page & Van De Voort, loc. cit.
20. Morgan, R. B., & Smith, J. E. (1996). *Staffing the new workplace.* Chicago: CCH. See also Jackson, S. E., & Schuler, R. S. (1990). Human resource planning: Challenges for industrial/organizational psychologists. *American Psychologist*, **45**, 223–239.
21. Connors, K., cited in Lawrence, S. (1989, Apr.). Voice of HR experience. *Personnel Journal*, p. 70.
22. Changing, but not happy about it (1993, Sept. 20). *Business Week*, p. 44.
23. Richman, L. S. (1993, July 12). Jobs that are growing and slowing. *Fortune*, pp. 52–55.
24. Arvey, R. D., Salas, E., & Gialluca, K. A. (1992). Using task inventories to forecast skills and abilities. *Human Performance*, **5**, 171–190. See also Schneider, B., & Konz, A. M. (1989). Strategic job analysis. *Human Resource Management*, **38**, 51–64.
25. Prahalad, C. K., & Hamel, G. (1994). *Competing for the future.* Boston: Harvard Business School Press.
26. Strategic planning (1996, Aug. 26). *Business Week*, p. 50.
27. Ibid., pp. 46–52. See also Walker, J. W. (1992). *Human resource strategy.* New York: McGraw-Hill.
28. Cascio, W. F. (1998). Applied psychology in personnel management (5th ed.). Englewood Cliffs, NJ: Prentice-Hall.
29. Jackson & Schuler, loc. cit.
30. Ulrich, D. (1986). Human resource planning as a competitive edge. *Human Resource Planning*, **9**(2), 41–50.
31. Apple articulates its internet plans (1996, Aug.). *Macworld*, pp. 27, 28; Apple's CEO gets tough (1996, July). *Macworld*, pp. 35–37; Strategic planning (1996, Aug. 26), loc. cit.
32. Schuler, R. S., & Walker, J. W. (1990, Summer). Human resources strategy: Focusing on issues and actions. *Organizational Dynamics*, pp. 5–19.
33. Ibid.
34. The man who McDonaldized Burger King (1979, Oct. 8). *Business Week*, pp. 132, 136.

35. See, for example, Kavanagh, M. J., Geutal, H. G., & Tannenbaum, S. I. (1990). *Human resource information systems: Development and application.* Boston: PWS-Kent.
36. Walker, op. cit.
37. Ibid.
38. Schlesinger, J. M. (1993, Sept. 16). Japan begins to confront job insecurity. *The Wall Street Journal*, p. A20.
39. Labor letter (1990, May 22). *The Wall Street Journal*, p. A1.
40. Wing, J. (1996, May). Succession planning smooths return to business-as-usual. *HR News*, p. 11; Bennett, A. (1988, Apr. 29). Many companies aren't prepared to deal with sudden death of chief executive. *The Wall Street Journal*, p. 25.
41. Nothing succeeds like a succession plan (1991, Sept. 30). *Business Week*, pp. 126, 127. Wing, loc. cit; Bennett, A., & Lublin, J. S. (1992, Mar. 17). Predecessor's presence clouds succession plan. *The Wall Street Journal*, pp. B1, B8; Brown, B. (1988, Aug. 4). Succession strategies for family firms. *The Wall Street Journal*, p. 23.
42. Reypert, L. J. (1981). Succession planning in the Ministry of Transportation and Communications, Province of Ontario. *Human Resource Planning*, **4**, 151–156.
43. For more on this issue, see Borwick, C. (1993, May). Eight ways to assess succession plans. *HRMagazine*, pp. 109–114.
44. Dalkey, N. (1969). *The Delphi method: An experimental study of group opinion.* Santa Monica, CA: Rand.
45. Milkovich, G. T., Annoni, A. J., & Mahoney, T. A. (1972). The use of the Delphi procedure in manpower forecasting. *Management Science*, **19**, 381–388.
46. Frantzreb, R. B. (1981). Human resource planning: Forecasting manpower needs. *Personnel Journal*, **60**, 850–857.
47. Ibid.
48. Labich, K. (1996, Sept. 9). Making diversity pay. *Fortune*, pp. 177–180.
49. Schmidt, F. L., Hunter, J. E., & Pearlman, K. (1982). Assessing the economic impact of personnel programs on workforce productivity. *Personnel Psychology*, **35**, 333–347.
50. Lopez, J. A. (1993, Jan. 5). Bosses seek ways to hold onto workers as recovery encourages job hopping. *The Wall Street Journal*, pp. B1, B4.
51. Walker, J. W. (1980). *Human resource planning.* New York: McGraw-Hill.
52. Dyer, L., & Holder, G. W. (1988). A strategic perspective of human resource management. In L. Dyer & G. W. Holder (eds.), *Human resource management: Evolving roles and responsibilities.* Washington, DC: Bureau of National Affairs, pp. 1-1 to 1-46.
53. Schuler & Walker, op. cit., p. 13.
54. American Management Association (1995). *Human resource management survey.* New York: Author.
55. Buller, P. F. (1993). Successful partnerships: HR and strategic planning at eight top firms. In R. S. Schuler (ed.), *Strategic human resources management.* New York: American Management Association, p. 23.

5 RECRUITING

Questions This Chapter Will Help Managers Answer

1 What factors are most important to consider in developing a recruitment policy?
2 Under what circumstances does it make sense to retain an executive search firm?
3 Do alternative recruitment sources yield differences in the quality of employees and in their "survival" rates on the job?
4 How can we communicate as realistic a picture as possible of a job and of the organization to prospective employees? What kinds of issues are most crucial to them?
5 If I lose my current job in management, what is the most efficient strategy for finding a new one?

RÉSUMÉ DATABASES—RECRUITMENT METHOD OF CHOICE IN THE FUTURE?*

Human Resource Management in Action

To many professionals in the recruitment industry, résumé databases are on the edge of an explosive growth in popularity. They believe that the cost- and time-efficient nature of the database will make most other recruiting methods obsolete. Says the director of communications for a Chicago-based database company that currently has more than 175,000 résumés on file: "Ten years from now, [résumé databases] will be the primary method of recruiting. I liken it to word processing software; 10 years ago, very few people used it."

Such databases have already begun to shape the ways that corporations approach recruiting college graduates. By using a database system, corporate recruiters can receive copies of students' résumés before they visit a campus. By specifying the kinds of characteristics they are looking for in successful candidates (e.g., bachelor's degree in chemistry, specialization in plastics), recruiters can use the power and speed of the computer to scan thousands of résumés to identify candidates who meet such criteria. Quickly and inexpensively, recruiters can make a list of which schools they want to visit and which students they want to interview. Not only are the numbers of people enrolling in résumé database systems growing, but so are the numbers of employers interested in using databases to conduct recruitment searches.

According to the president of University ProNet in Palo Alto, California (owned by the alumni associations of such top-tier universities as Stanford and MIT), employers' interest in recruitment databases is increasing because they are realizing major cost savings in job searches. Although it typically costs a company $1000 to conduct a job search through a ProNet database, that search usually will net three or four qualified candidates. The cost of using an executive search firm can average between 20 and 35 percent of an employee's first-year salary, costing an employer as much as $35,000 to hire an executive at a salary of $100,000 per year. "Even if the employer conducts 15 searches through the database, the cost of using a search firm only once is still 100 percent higher than using the database 15 times," he said.

Challenges

1. Proponents make the use of résumé databases sound almost too good to be true. Do you see any disadvantages to using this approach?
2. Are there aspects of recruitment for which résumé databases are not suitable?
3. In your opinion, is a résumé database search appropriate for jobs at all levels?

*Adapted from B. Leonard, Résumé databases to dominate field, *HRMagazine*, April 1993, pp. 59–60. Reprinted with the permission of *HRMagazine*, published by the Society for Human Resource Management, Alexandria, VA.

RECRUITMENT AS A STRATEGIC IMPERATIVE

Recruitment is a form of business competition. Just as corporations compete to develop, manufacture, and market the best product or service, so they must also compete to identify, attract, and hire the most qualified people. Recruitment is a business, and it is big business.[1] It demands serious attention from management, for any business strategy will falter without the talent to execute it. Certainly, the range of recruitment needs is broad. A small manufacturer in a well-populated rural area faces recruitment challenges that are far different from those of a high-technology firm operating in global markets. Nevertheless, both need talent, although different types of talent, to be successful in their respective markets. Regardless of the size of a firm or what industry it is in, recruitment and selection of people with strategically relevant abilities is more important than ever. Let's begin by examining the big picture of the employee recruitment and selection process, along with some important legal issues. Then we will focus specifically on the processes of planning, managing, and evaluating recruitment efforts. We will address the special issues associated with recruiting people for international assignments in Chapter 16.

THE EMPLOYEE RECRUITMENT AND SELECTION PROCESS

Recruitment begins, as Figure 5-1 indicates, by specifying human resource requirements (numbers, skills mix, levels, time frame), which are the typical result of job analysis and HR planning activities. Conceptually (and logically), job analysis precedes HR planning in Figure 5-1, because, as we noted in Chapter 4, it is necessary to specify the work to be done and the personal characteristics necessary to do the work (knowledge, skills, abilities, and other characteristics) before one can specify the numbers and types of people needed to do the work. Not shown in Figure 5-1, although critically important to the overall recruitment and selection process, are strategic business objectives. For example, recruitment and selection strategies for new employees are likely to differ considerably depending on whether a company's objective in hiring, say, new salespeople, is to identify candidates who are able to execute "cold calls" for new customers or to service existing, long-term customers.

The step following recruitment is *initial screening*, which is basically a rapid, rough "selection" process. Sixty years ago, when line supervisors hired factory workers outside the gates of a plant, they simply looked over the candidates and then, pointing to various people, would say, "You, you, and you—the rest of you come back another day." That is an example of initial screening, and it was probably done only on the basis of physical characteristics. The *selection process* following initial screening is more rigorous. For example, physical characteristics alone do not provide many clues about a person's potential for management, or for any other kind of work for that matter. What is needed, of course, are samples of behavior, either through tests and personal interviews or through the testimony of others about a candidate, as with reference checks.

Past the selection stage, we are no longer dealing with job candidates; we are dealing with new employees. Typically, the first step in their introduction to

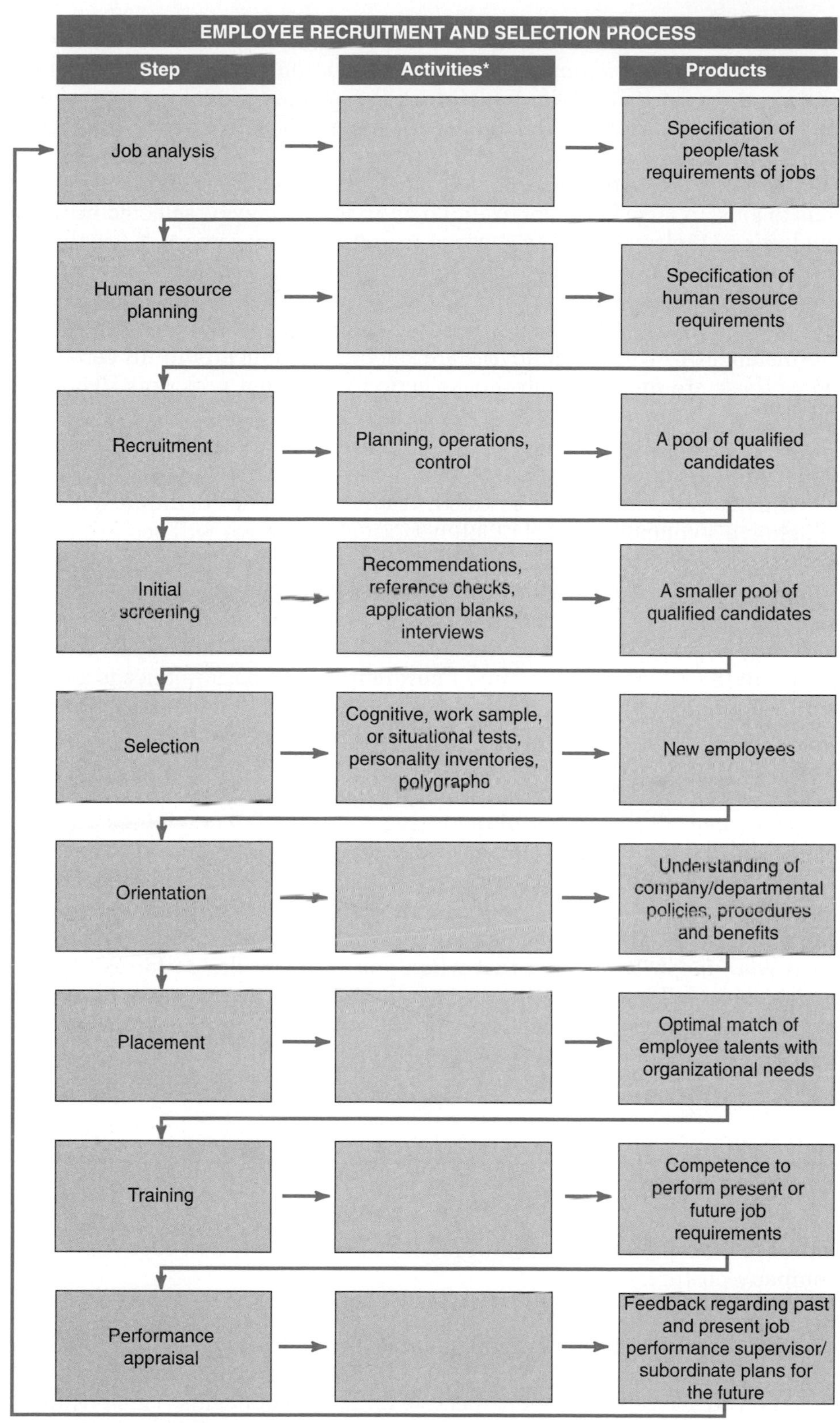

Figure 5-1
The employee recruitment and selection process.

company policies, practices, and benefits (technically, this step is called "socialization") is an *orientation program.* Orientation may take up several hours or several weeks; it may be formal, informal, or some combination of the two. As we will see in Chapter 7, orientation has more significant and lasting effects than most people might expect.

Placement occurs after orientation; placement is the assignment of individuals to jobs. In large firms, for example, individuals may be selected initially on the basis of their potential to succeed in general management. After they have been observed and assessed during an intensive management training program, however, the organization is in a much better position to assign them to specific jobs within broader job families, such as marketing, production, or sales. (There are instances in which employees are selected specifically to fill certain positions; these are so-called one-shot selection-placement programs.) The technical expertise and the resources necessary to implement optimal placement programs (select, orient, then place) are found mostly in very large organizations, such as the military.

Once new employees are selected, oriented, and placed, they can be *trained* to achieve a competent level of job performance. As we will see in Chapter 7, training is very big business.

Finally, *performance appraisal,* one component of a performance-management system, provides feedback to employees regarding their past and present job performance proficiency, as well as a basis for improving performance in the future. The first time a new employee's performance is appraised, it is like pushing the button that starts a continuous loop—more precisely, a continuous feedback loop comprising the employee's performance, the manager's appraisal of it, and the communication between the two about performance and appraisal.

Of course, all the phases of recruiting and selecting employees are interrelated. But the final test of all phases comes with the appraisal of job performance. There is no point in reporting that, say, 150 possible candidates were recruited and screened, that 90 offers were extended, and that 65 candidates were hired and trained, if the first appraisal of their performance indicates that most were inept. Remember that when you evaluate the performance of new hires, you are doing so within the context of a system, a network of human resource activities, and you are really appraising recruitment, selection, and training, among other HRM activities.

LEGALITIES

RECRUITMENT POLICIES

As a framework for setting recruitment policies, let us consider four possible company postures:[2]

1. **Passive nondiscrimination** is a commitment to treat all races and both sexes equally in all decisions about hiring, promotion, and pay. No attempt is made to recruit actively among prospective minority applicants. This posture fails to recognize that discriminatory practices in the past may block prospective applicants from seeking present job opportunities.

2. **Pure diversity-based recruitment** is a concerted effort by the organization to actively expand the pool of applicants so that no one is excluded because of past or present discrimination. However, the decision to hire or to promote is based on the best-qualified individual, regardless of race or sex.

3. **Diversity-based recruitment with preferential hiring** goes further than pure diversity-based recruitment; it systematically favors women and minorities in hiring and promotion decisions. This approach is known as a "soft-quota" system.

4. **Hard quotas** represent a mandate to hire or promote specific numbers or proportions of women or minority-group members.

Both private and government employers find hard quotas an unsavory strategy for rectifying the effects of past or present unfair discrimination. Nevertheless, the courts have ordered "temporary" quotas in instances where unfair discrimination has obviously taken place and where no other remedy is feasible.[3] Temporary quotas have bounds placed on them. For example, a judge might order an employer to hire two African-American employees for every white employee until the number of African-American employees reaches a certain percent of the employer's workforce.

Passive nondiscrimination misses the mark. This became obvious as far back as 1968, when the secretary of labor publicly cited the Allen-Bradley Company of Milwaukee for failure to comply with Executive Order 11246 by not actively recruiting African Americans. The company was so well known in Milwaukee as a good place to work that it usually had a long waiting list of friends and relatives of current employees. As a matter of established business practice, the company preferred to hire referrals from current employees; almost no public recruiting was done for entry-level job openings. As a result, because almost all the present employees were white, so were almost all the referrals.

As noted in Chapter 2's discussion of legal issues in employment, preferential selection is a sticky issue. However, in several landmark cases the Supreme Court established the following principle:[4] Staffing decisions must be made on a case-by-case basis; race or sex may be taken into account as one factor in an applicant's favor, but the overall decision to select or reject must be made on the basis of a combination of factors, such as entrance test scores and previous performance. That guideline leaves us with pure diversity-based recruitment as a recruitment and selection strategy. Indeed, in a free and open competitive labor market, that is the way it ought to be.

Recruitment policies ultimately depend on the structure and functioning of internal and external labor markets. Let us therefore discuss labor market issues in some detail.

Developing Recruitment Policies: Labor Market Issues

A labor market is a geographical area within which the forces of supply (people looking for work) interact with the forces of demand (employers looking for people) and thereby determine the price of labor.[5] In a tight labor market, demand by employers exceeds the available supply of workers, which tends to exert upward pressure on wages. In a loose labor market, the reverse is true: the supply of workers exceeds employer demand, exerting downward pressure on wages. In recent years the labor market for software developers, computer and electrical engineers, and aircraft mechanics has been fairly tight; wages for these jobs have been increasing steadily.[6] On the other hand, the labor market for lawyers, steelworkers, and unskilled labor has been fairly loose in recent years, reducing pressure for wage increases for these workers.

Unfortunately, it is not possible to define the geographical boundaries of a labor market in any clear-cut manner.[7] Employers needing key employees will recruit far and wide if necessary. In short, employers do not face a single, homogeneous market for labor, but rather a series of discontinuous, segmented labor markets over which supply-and-demand conditions vary substantially.[8] Economists focus on this fact as the major explanation for wage differences among occupations and among geographical areas.

Of practical concern to managers, however, is a reasonably accurate definition of labor markets for planning purposes. Here are some factors that are important for defining the limits of a labor market:[9]

- Geography
- Education and/or technical background required to perform a job
- Industry
- Licensing or certification requirements
- Union membership

Companies may use one or more of these factors to help define their labor markets. Thus an agricultural research firm that needs to hire four veterinarians cannot restrict its search to a local area, since the market is national or international in scope. Union membership is not a concern in this market, but licensing and/or certification is. Typically, a doctor of veterinary medicine degree is required, along with state licensure to practice. Applicants are likely to be less concerned with where the job is located and more concerned with job design and career opportunities. On the other hand, suppose a brewery is trying to hire a journey-level plumber. The brewery will be looking at a labor market defined primarily by geographic proximity and secondarily by people whose experience, technical background, and (possibly) willingness to join a union after employment qualify them for the job.

Internal versus External Labor Markets

The discussion thus far has concerned the structure and function of external labor markets. Internal labor markets also affect recruitment policies, in many cases more directly, because firms often give preference to present employees in promotions, transfers, and other career-enhancing opportunities. Each employing unit is a separate market. At Delta Air Lines, for example, virtually all jobs above the entry level are filled by internal promotion rather than by outside recruitment. Delta looks to its present employees as its source of labor supply, and workers look to this internal labor market to advance their careers. In the internal labor markets of most organizations, employees peddle their talents to available "buyers."[10] Three elements constitute the internal labor market:

- Formal and informal practices that determine how jobs are organized and described
- Methods for choosing among candidates
- Procedures and authorities through which potential candidates are generated by those responsible for filling open jobs

In an open internal labor market, every available job is advertised throughout the organization, and anyone can apply. Preference is given to internal candidates by withholding outside advertising until the job has been on the internal market for a specified length of time, from several days to several weeks. Finally, each candidate for a job receives an interview.

Recruitment Policies and Labor Market Characteristics

A great deal of research suggests that employers change their policies in response to changes in market conditions.[11] For example, as labor becomes increasingly scarce, employers may change their policies in the following ways:

- Improving the characteristics of vacant positions, for example, by raising salaries or increasing training and educational benefits
- Reducing hiring standards
- Using more (and more expensive) recruiting methods
- Extending searches over a wider geographical area

As we have seen, legal considerations are an important component of recruitment policies. Workforce utilization is a central issue in this area.

LEGALITIES

WORKFORCE UTILIZATION

Workforce utilization is simply a way of identifying whether or not the composition of the workforce—measured by race and sex—employed in a particular job category in a particular firm is representative of the composition of the entire labor market available to perform that job. To see what considerations this implies, let's consider this situation: There is a town where the percentage of qualified arc welders is 10 percent females and 15 percent African Americans. Now let's say that a firm in this town needs and has on staff 20 arc welders, of whom none are female and 3 are African American. If the representation of the workforce reflects the representation of qualified arc welders in the town, we should expect to find 3 (20×0.15) African-American arc welders and 2 (20×0.10) female arc welders. Yet no female arc welders are employed at the firm. Now can you begin to see what workforce utilization is all about?

One of the main considerations in workforce utilization is the available labor market, which the courts refer to as the "relevant labor market." In practice, some courts have defined the relevant labor market for jobs that require skills not possessed by the general population as those living within a reasonable commuting or recruiting area for the facility who are in the same occupational classification as the job in question.[12]

Table 5-1

AFRICAN-AMERICAN AND FEMALE UTILIZATION ANALYSIS FOR MANAGERIAL JOBS

Managers employed by the firm			Percent available in relevant labor market		Utilization*		Goal	
Total	African Americans	Females	African Americans	Females	African Americans	Females	African Americans	Females
90	20	15	30	10	− 7 (22%)	+ 6 (17%)	27	9

*Under the "utilization" column, the − 7 for African Americans means that according to the relevant labor market, the African Americans are underrepresented by 7 managers, and the + 6 for females means that not only are the females adequately represented, but there are 6 more female managers than needed to meet parity according to the relevant labor market.

In computing workforce-utilization statistics, one begins by preparing a table, such as Table 5-1, which examines the job group "managers." (Similar analyses must also be done for eight other categories of employees specified by the EEOC.) This table shows that of 90 managers, 20 are African-American and 15 are female. However, labor market data indicate that 30 percent and 10 percent of the available labor market for managers are African-American and female, respectively. Hence, for workforce representation to reach parity with labor market representation, 27 (0.30 × 90) of the managers should be African-American and 9 (0.10 × 90) should be female. The recruitment goal, therefore, is to hire 7 more African Americans to reach parity with the available labor force. What about the 6 excess female managers? The utilization analysis serves simply as a "red flag," calling attention to recruitment needs. The extra female managers will not be furloughed or fired. However, they may be given additional training, or they may be transferred to other jobs that might provide them with greater breadth of experience, particularly if utilization analyses for those other jobs indicate a need to recruit additional females.

At this point, a logical question is how large a disparity between the composition of the workforce employed and the composition of the available labor market constitutes a prima facie case of unfair discrimination by the employer. Fortunately, the Supreme Court has provided some guidance on this question in its ruling in *Hazelwood School District v. United States.*[13] Appreciating the Court's ruling requires an understanding of the reasoning behind it. The first step in an examination of disparities between workforce representation and labor force representation is to compute the difference between the actual number of employees in a particular job category (e.g., the 20 African-American managers in Table 5-1) and the number expected if the workforce were truly representative of the labor force (27 African-American managers). The Court ruled that if the difference between the actual number and the expected number is so large that the difference would have only 1 chance in 20 of occurring by chance alone, it is reasonable to conclude that race was a factor in the hiring decisions made. If the odds of the difference's occurring by chance alone are greater than 1 in 20 (e.g., 1 in 10), it is reasonable to conclude that race was not a factor in the hiring decisions. Statistical tests can be used to compute the probability that the difference occurred by chance.

RECRUITMENT—A TWO-WAY PROCESS

Recruitment frequently is treated as if it were a one-way process—something organizations do to search for prospective employees. This approach may be termed a "prospecting" theory of recruitment. In practice, however, prospective employees seek out organizations just as organizations seek them out. This view, termed a "mating" theory of recruitment, appears more realistic. Recruitment success (from the organization's perspective) and job search success (from the candidate's perspective) both depend on timing. If there is a match between organizational recruitment efforts and a candidate's job search efforts, conditions are ripe for the two to meet.

In order for organizations and candidates actually to meet, however, three other conditions must be satisfied: (1) there must be a common communication medium (e.g., the organization advertises in a trade journal read by the candidate), (2) the candidate perceives a match between his or her personal characteristics and the organization's stated job requirements, and (3) the candidate is motivated to apply for the job. Comprehensive recruitment-planning efforts must address these issues.

RECRUITMENT PLANNING

Recruitment begins with a clear specification of (1) the number of people needed (e.g., through HR forecasts and workforce-utilization analyses) and (2) when they are needed. Implicit in the latter is a time frame—the duration between the receipt of a résumé and the time a new hire starts work. This time frame is sometimes referred to as "the recruitment pipeline." The "flow" of events through the pipeline is represented in Table 5-2. The table shows that if an operating manager sends a requisition for a new hire to the HR department today, it will take almost a month and a half, 43 days on average, before an employee fulfilling that requisition actually starts work. Among 1- to 500-employee organizations, a recent survey found that, in practice, the average length of the pipeline is 41 days.[14] The HR department must make sure that operating and staff managers realize and understand information such as is represented by this pipeline.

One of the ways that operating and staff managers can be sure that their recruitment needs will fit the length of the recruitment pipeline is by examining the segments of the overall workforce by job group (e.g., clerical, sales, production, engineering, managers). For each of these job groups, the HR department, with the cooperation of operating managers who represent each job group, should examine what has occurred over the past several years in terms of new hires, promotions, transfers, and turnover. This review will help provide an index of what to expect in the coming year, if past trends continue.

Table 5-2

AVERAGE TIME SPAN FOR EVENTS IN A RECRUITMENT PIPELINE

Sequence of events		
From	To	Average number of days
Résumé	Invitation	5
Invitation	Interview	6
Interview	Offer	4
Offer	Acceptance	7
Acceptance	Report to work	21
Total length of the pipeline		43

INTERNAL RECRUITMENT

In the decision-making process regarding where, when, and how to implement recruitment activities, initial consideration should be given to a company's current employees, especially for filling jobs above the entry level. If external recruitment efforts are undertaken without considering the desires, capabilities, and potential of present employees (e.g., the six excess female managers shown in Table 5-1), a firm may incur both short- and long-run costs. In the short run, morale may degenerate; in the long run, firms with a reputation for consistent neglect of in-house talent may find it difficult to attract new employees and to retain experienced ones. This is why soundly conceived action plans (that incorporate developmental and training needs) and management succession plans are so important.

One of the thorniest issues confronting internal recruitment is the reluctance of managers to grant permission for their subordinates to be interviewed for potential transfer or promotion. As one reviewer put it, "Most supervisors are about as reluctant to release a current employee as they are to take a cut in pay."[15] In order for managers to overcome this aversion, promotion-from-within policies must receive strong top-management support, coupled with a company philosophy that permits employees to consider available opportunities within the organization.

Among the channels available for internal recruitment, the most popular ones are succession plans (discussed in Chapter 4), job posting, employee referrals, and temporary worker pools.

Job Posting

Advertising available jobs internally began in the early days of affirmative action, as a means of providing equal opportunity for women and minorities to compete. It served as a method of getting around the "old boy" network, where jobs sometimes were filled on the basis of *who* you knew more than *what* you knew. Today job posting is an established practice in many organizations, especially for filling jobs up to the lower executive level.

Openings are published on bulletin boards (electronic or hard-copy) or in lists available to all employees. Interested employees must reply within a specified number of days, and they may or may not have to obtain the consent of their immediate supervisors.[16] Some job posting systems apply only to the plant or office in which a job is located, while such systems in other companies will relocate employees.

An example of the latter practice occurred when the Gannett Company, Inc., inaugurated its national newspaper, *USA Today*. It filled 50 positions at the new office with experienced people from the chain's other 133 newspapers. Employees who worked on the start-up had the option of staying with *USA Today* once it was under way or returning to their previous job assignments.

While there are clear advantages to job posting, potential disadvantages arise if employees "game" the system by transferring to new jobs that do not require different or additional skills, in other company departments or locations, simply as a way of obtaining grade or salary increases. To avoid this problem, companies must establish consistent pay policies across jobs and locations. Further, if no limits are placed on the bidding process, job posting systems can impose substantial administrative costs. Thus, at some firms, employees cannot bid on a new job until at least 1 year after hire, and they must have accrued at least 6 months' tenure in their current jobs before becoming eligible to bid for new ones.[17]

Another problem might arise from poor communication. For example, if employees who unsuccessfully apply for open jobs do not receive feedback that might help them be more competitive in the future, and if they have to find out through the grapevine that someone else got the job they applied for, a job posting program cannot be successful. The lesson for managers is obvious: regular communication and follow-up feedback are essential if job posting is to work properly.

Employee Referrals

Referral of job candidates by present employees has been and continues to be a major source of new hires at many levels, including professional levels. It is an internal recruitment method, since internal rather than external sources are used to attract candidates. Typically, such programs offer a cash or merchandise bonus when a current employee refers a successful candidate to fill a job opening. The logic behind employee referral is that "it takes one to know one." Interestingly, the rate of employee participation seems to remain unaffected by such incentives as higher cash bonuses, cars, or expense-paid trips.[18] This suggests that good employees will not refer potentially undesirable candidates even if the rewards are outstanding.

The Apple Bank for Savings in New York City has a typical referral program. Current employees who recruit new workers receive $250 after the new recruits have remained with the bank for 3 months and an additional $250 when the recruits have been employed for 1 year. The employee who recruits the new worker also must remain with the bank to receive the payment. Thus the program incorporates the twin advantage of attracting new employees and retaining old ones. The bank hires about 50 percent of the candidates referred by current employees.[19] High-technology firms are a bit more generous. Cognos Corporation, a maker of business-intelligence tools, offers $4000 to employees who refer new hires; other companies pay as much as $10,000 for referrals.[20]

Three factors seem to be instrumental in the prescreening process of referrals: the morale of present employees, the accuracy of job information, and the closeness of the intermediary friend.[21] While employee referrals clearly have advantages, it is important to note that from an EEO perspective, employee referrals are fine only as long as the workforce is diverse in gender, race, and ethnicity to begin with. A potential disadvantage, at least for some firms, is that employee referrals tend to perpetuate the perspective and belief systems of the current workforce. Thus an employee referral system may not be the best approach for organizations that are trying to promote changes in strategy, outlook, or orientation.

Temporary Worker Pools

Unlike workers supplied from temporary agencies, in-house "temporaries" work directly for the hiring organization and may receive benefits, depending on the number of scheduled hours worked per week. Temporary workers (e.g., in clerical jobs, accounting, word processing) help meet fluctuating labor demands due to such factors as illness, vacations, terminations, and resignations. Companies save on commissions to outside agencies, which may be as high as 50 percent or more of a temporary employee's hourly wages.[22]

In the health-care field, Hospital Corporation of America began in 1990 to employ an internal pool of 2000 itinerant registered nurses who circulated among the company's 83 hospitals in 19 cities on 13-week assignments. The nurses got a monthly housing allowance, even if they stayed with their families or friends, and they kept accruing benefits and seniority rather than starting anew each time they took an assignment.[23]

The Travelers Corporation established a pool of temporaries made up of its own retirees. A recent survey showed the growing popularity of this practice. Almost half the firms surveyed used retirees under some contractual arrangement, about 10 percent allowed retirees to share jobs with other employees, and most retirees continued to receive pension and insurance benefits when they came back to work. About 40 percent of the respondents paid market rates for jobs performed by retirees, while 26 percent paid retirees what they had received at the time they retired.[24]

EXTERNAL RECRUITMENT

To meet demands for talent brought about by business growth, to seek fresh ideas, or to replace employees who leave, organizations periodically turn to the outside labor market. In doing so, they may employ a variety of recruitment sources. Four of the most popular ones are university relations, executive search firms, employment agencies, and recruitment advertising.

University Relations

What used to be known as "college recruiting" is now considerably broader in many companies. The companies have targeted certain schools that best meet their needs and have broadened the scope of their interactions with them. Such activities may now include, in addition to recruitment, gifts and grants to the institutions, summer employment and consulting projects for faculty, and invitations to placement officers to visit company plants and offices.

Mobil is a good example of this trend. The company now deals with only about 50 colleges and universities, instead of the 200 or so on its list a few years ago. It also uses separate teams (made up of six to eight people from various Mobil units) for each school. Many of the team members are graduates of the school they are assigned to, and they help plan the dozen or so campus activities each year, such as providing talent for student organizations, conducting career information days, holding receptions, and sponsoring ceremonies at which recruiters present Mobil Foundation checks to support some campus activity. The recruitment team strategy has already helped increase the number of graduates hired from targeted schools.[25]

COMPANY EXAMPLE

HOW BRISTOL-MYERS SQUIBB USES COMPUTER TECHNOLOGY TO FIND TOP MBA STUDENTS

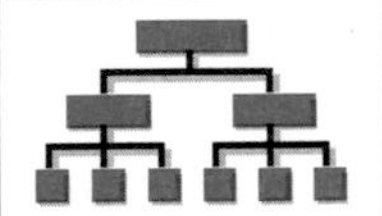

In order to get itself noticed by MBA students at some of the best schools in the country, Bristol-Myers Squibb distributed an interactive computer diskette that conveyed its recruitment message. That message included information about the company, positions available at the company, and case histories of Squibb managers, specifically, case histories of difficult business problems faced by recent MBAs who worked for Squibb. After the description of a problem, the diskette provided several options for solving it. Viewers were asked which solution they would choose. Subsequently, they were told which option actually was chosen and why.

Squibb chose to use these interactive quizzes so that viewers would get involved in the recruitment information it provided. In designing the diskette, Squibb provided a menu so that MBAs could access the information they were interested in and skip the rest. To set itself apart from other companies, Squibb injected humor into its "otherwise information-laden message."

Was the recruitment diskette effective? On the basis of follow-up research, Squibb found that 33 percent of those who received the diskette viewed it once, 29 percent viewed it twice, and 18 percent viewed it three times or more.[26] As this example shows, employers are becoming more sophisticated in deciding where, when, and how to approach markets they have targeted.

To enhance the yield from campus recruitment efforts, employers should consider the following research-based guidelines:[27]

1. Establish a "presence" on college campuses beyond just the on-campus interviewing period (as Mobil has done).
2. Upgrade the content and specificity of recruiting brochures. Many are far too general in nature. Instead, provide more detailed information about the characteristics of entry-level jobs, especially those that have had a significant positive effect on the decisions of prior applicants to join the organization.
3. Devote more time and resources to training on-campus interviewers to answer specific job-related questions from applicants.
4. For those candidates who are invited for on-site company visits, provide itineraries and agendas prior to their arrival. Written materials should

answer candidates' questions dealing with travel arrangements, expense reimbursements, and whom to contact at the company and how.

5. Ensure that the attributes of vacant positions are comparable to those of competitors. This is as true for large as for small organizations. Some of the key job attributes that influence the decisions of applicants, according to a Roper poll of 1000 college students, are promotional opportunities, job security, and long-term income potential. They ranked starting salary in sixth place, after "opportunities for creativity or to exercise initiative" and employee benefits packages.[28]

Executive Search Firms

Such firms are retained typically to recruit for senior-level positions that command salaries over $70,000 and total compensation packages worth in excess of $100,000. The reasons for retaining an executive search firm may include a need to maintain confidentiality (to prevent the news of the search from reaching an incumbent or a competitor), a lack of local resources to recruit executive-level individuals, or insufficient time. To use an executive search consultant most effectively requires time and commitment from the hiring organization. It must allow the consultant to become a company "insider," to develop knowledge and familiarity with the business, its strategic plans, and key players.[29] Although using an executive search firm has advantages, firms must consider the following facts: only 55 to 60 percent of all contracts to search for qualified candidates are fulfilled; of those fulfilled, only 40 percent are fulfilled within the promised time estimate. Some 50 percent of the fulfilled searches take 2 or 3 times longer than originally estimated.[30] In short, many employers are being sold recruitment services that will never be provided. Employers evaluating a search firm should carefully consider the following indications that the firms can do competent work:[31]

- The firm has defined its market position by industries rather than by disciplines or as a jack-of-all-trades.
- The firm understands how your organization functions within the industries served.
- The firm is performance-oriented and compensates the search salesperson substantially on the basis of assignment completion.
- The firm combines the research and recruiting responsibilities into one function. Doing so allows the researcher-recruiter to make a more comprehensive and knowledgeable presentation to targeted candidates on behalf of the client.
- The firm uses primary research techniques for locating sources. Secondary research techniques in the form of computerized databases, files of unsolicited résumés, and directories can identify qualified candidates, but finding top performers requires a more personalized approach. In fact, only 1 in 300 unsolicited résumés is likely to be shown to a client, and only 1 in 3000 of these job seekers may get a job.[32]
- The firm is organized to function as a task force in the search for candidates, particularly where they are being recruited for multiple assignments or when placement speed is essential.

Compared with other recruitment sources, executive search firms are quite expensive. Total fees may reach 30 to 35 percent of the compensation package of

Figure 5-2
A Burger King franchise in Michigan uses billboards to advertise a benefit designed to help employees earn money for college tuition.

the new hire. Fees are often paid as follows: a retainer amounting to one-third the total fee as soon as the search is commissioned; another one-third 60 days into the assignment; and a final third upon completion. If an organization hires a candidate on its own prior to the completion of the search, it still must pay all or some portion of the search firm's fee, unless it makes other arrangements.[33]

Employment Agencies

These are some of the most widely available and used outside sources. However, there is great variability in size and quality across agencies. To achieve best results from this channel, cultivate a small number of firms and thoroughly describe the characteristics (e.g., education, training, experience) of candidates needed, the fee structure, and the method of resolving disputes.[34]

Agency fees generally vary from 10 percent of the starting salary for clerical and support staff to 20 to 30 percent of the starting salary for professional, exempt-level hires. Unlike executive search firms, however, employment agencies receive payment only if one of their referrals results in a hire. In addition, most agencies offer prorated refunds if a candidate proves unacceptable. For example, an agency might return 90 percent of its fee if a candidate leaves within 30 days, 60 percent if the new hire leaves between 30 and 60 days, and 30 percent if the new hire leaves after 60 to 90 days on the job.[35] Table 5-3 summarizes the differences between executive search firms and employment agencies.

Recruitment Advertising

When this medium is mentioned, most people think of want ads in the local newspaper. But think again. This medium has become just as colorful, lively, and imaginative as consumer advertising. In addition to newspapers, such advertising media include magazines, direct mail, radio and television, and even billboards (see Figure 5-2).

Sybase, Inc. recently hired a biplane to fly over rival Oracle's headquarters, trailing a banner reading: "Sybase Wants You." The flight was retaliation for an

Table 5-3

DIFFERENCES BETWEEN EXECUTIVE SEARCH FIRMS AND EMPLOYMENT AGENCIES

Services	Executive search firms	Employment agencies
Financial arrangements	Fees based on 30 to 35 percent of candidate's salary and time needed to recruit, or a flat rate plus expenses.	Fees based on 20 to 35 percent of candidate's starting salary.
	Retainer fee required; payment due even if opening filled through other sources.	No retainer fee; fee due only if position filled by agency.
	Staff compensation may include salary, bonus, profit sharing, and incentives for business generation.	Staff compensation usually depends on commissions for placements made.
Caseload	Personal consultant handles only three to five cases at once.	Agent works with many open job orders at one time.
	Firms usually handle openings at higher levels of organization.	Agencies typically assigned lower-level vacancies.
Relationship with clients	Firms represent employers only.	Agencies represent employers and job seekers.
	General management involved in decision to retain search firm.	HR department makes decision to use agency.
	Consultant thoroughly researches client organization and position requirements before search.	Agents spend less time on initial research and job specifications. Some assignments handled by phone with no personal contact.
	Firms conduct assignments on an exclusive basis.	Agencies compete with similar companies for placements.
Time commitment	Consultant invests 40 to 50 hours per month on each search.	Limited investment of time on any client, due to lack of guaranteed payment.
Referral rates and guarantees	Two to four highly qualified candidates recommended to each client.	Large numbers of applicants referred to increase odds of a placement.
	Recruitment and evaluation efforts target broad range of candidates, most of whom are not in job market.	Recruitment focuses mainly on candidates actively seeking new employment.
	Process- and results-oriented.	Placement-oriented.
	Reputable firms offer a professional guarantee and commitment to thorough, ethical practices.	Contingency fee arrangement eliminates any obligation to produce results.
Level of client involvement	Minimal HR and management time involvement required.	Considerable HR time required to screen, interview, and evaluate candidates.

Source: J. S. Lord, External and internal recruitment. In W. F. Cascio (ed.), *Human resource planning, employment, and placement.* Washington, DC: Bureau of National Affairs, 1989, pp. 2-87, 2-88.

earlier stunt in which Oracle's Bracknell, England, office mounted an 8-foot by 40-foot placard on a flatbed truck and parked it outside the offices of Sybase. "Make the Move to Oracle," the sign said.[36]

COMPANY EXAMPLE

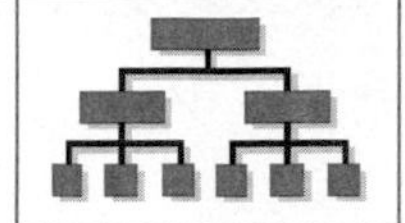

HELP WANTED: ON-LINE JOB SEARCH[37]

When Wheat Belt Public Power District in Sidney, Nebraska, needed an experienced line supervisor, it listed the position on America's Job Bank, an Internet job site sponsored by the U.S. Labor Department and funded by each state's unemployment insurance program. It got 12 responses, including the person it needed for the job. Such on-line job sites have boomed recently, with roughly 1 in 4 employers using the Internet to list job openings or to recruit. Virtually every profession has a bulletin board, and most major corporations have World Wide Web sites on the Internet. However, none of these job sites approaches the size of America's Job Bank.

The job bank contains over 500,000 job openings, and more than 6 million Internet "hits" (i.e., the number of times users access a given Internet site) were recorded for the site in 1 month alone! America's Job Bank features all listings from all state employment agencies. IBM also lists 24,000 job openings a year in the job bank, and this has challenged other private employers to post their openings there too. The service is free for both employers and job seekers.

For job seekers without Internet access, the service is available through public libraries, community colleges, and local unemployment offices. Applicants are asked to contact employers directly from information provided on the job bank. America's Job Bank address on the Internet is http://www.ajb.dni.us.

The preceding sections provide just a glimpse into external recruitment sources. Others include career fairs, outplacement firms, former employees, trade shows, co-op and work-study programs, government employment agencies, alumni associations, racial and ethnic organizations, and free-standing, computer-based name banks. With respect to the latter, some, such as Career Placement Registry and College Recruitment Database, are generalized lists of job seekers. Others, such as Bank Executive Network, specialize. Both get used a lot; Career Placement says employers order 1800 résumés a month from its lists.[38]

OTHER RECRUITMENT ISSUES

Special Inducements

Three other recruitment issues deserve special treatment—relocation aid, help for the trailing spouse, and sign-on bonuses. We consider each of these in the paragraphs that follow.

1. **Relocation aid**. Especially with higher-level jobs, newly recruited managers expect some form of relocation assistance. Such assistance may include disposal of the residence left behind, as well as payment of lease-breaking

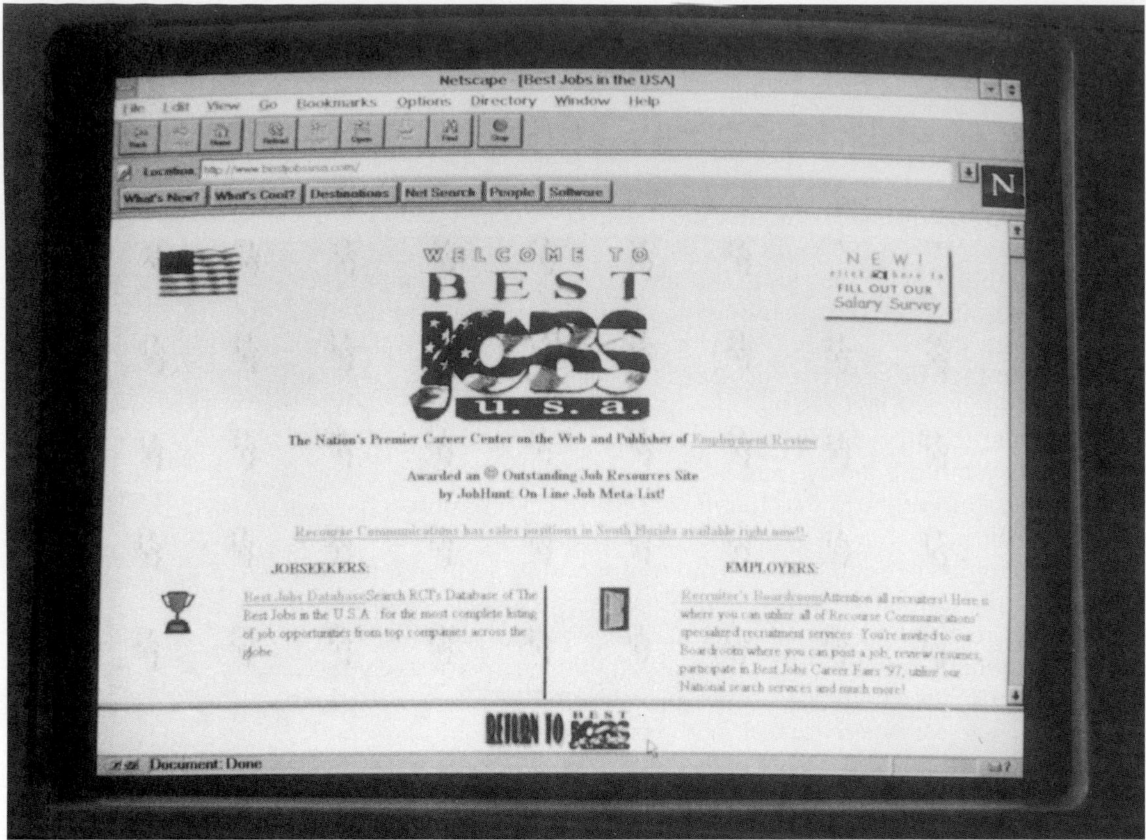

Computer-based recruitment is fast becoming a popular way to attract applicants for both technical and non-technical jobs.

expenses, temporary living expenses, and moving costs, to name just a few. Such costs add up quickly. The average cost of relocating a homeowning employee is about $45,000.[39]

2. **Help for the trailing spouse**. Prodded by the emergence of the dual-career family (51 percent of all families by the year 2000[40]), firms are finding that many managers and professionals, men and women alike, are reluctant to relocate unless the spouse will be able to find suitable employment in a new location. In 1996, companies spent an average of $52,100 in aid to trailing spouses, primarily directed to job-finding assistance or to retraining those who found their existing skills were not required in their new location. That figure is 75 percent higher than the average amount spent on trailing-spouse resettlement in 1994.[41]

3. **Sign-on bonuses**. Another recruiting inducement, independent of any relocation assistance, is the sign-on bonus. Originally used in the sports world, signing bonuses are now common among executives, professionals (particularly in high-technology firms), and middle-level executives, as companies seek to buttress the eroding bonds between them and their employees.

   What is a company to do if things do not work out and the new person simply walks away with the cash? Firms such as General Electric and Owens-Corning require that the entire amount be repaid if the person leaves within 1 year, and 50 percent of it if he or she leaves within 2 years. After that, the repayment gradually drops to zero.[42]

With the explosion of new technologies being developed for internal computer networks and the Internet, high-technology companies are going after all the talent they can find. In fact, competition for experienced workers is so intense that "you have to treat your current employees as though you were recruiting them" [to stave off raids by rivals] says the chief technology officer at Sun Microsystems, Inc.[43] He's right. A project leader at Sun with 6 years' experience recently left to join a rival firm. Why? It offered a $6000 signing bonus plus 1500 shares of the company's stock.[44]

Summary Findings Regarding Recruitment Sources

Now that we have examined some of the most popular sources for internal and external recruiting, it seems reasonable to ask, "Which sources are most popular with employers and job applicants?" Among employers, evidence indicates that:

- Informal contacts are used widely and effectively at all occupational levels.
- Use of public employment services declines as required skills levels increase.
- The internal market is a major recruitment source except for entry-level, unskilled, and semiskilled workers.
- Larger firms are the most frequent users of walk-ins, write-ins, and the internal market.[45]

With regard to recruiting workers from underrepresented groups, a study of 20,000 applicants in a major insurance company revealed that female and African-American applicants consistently used formal recruitment sources (employment agencies, advertising) rather than informal ones (walk-ins, write-ins, employee referrals). Nevertheless, informal sources produced the best-quality applicants for all groups (males, females, African Americans, Hispanics, and both younger and older workers) and led to proportionately more hires.[46]

Factors Affecting Recruitment Success

A recent survey of 500 companies revealed how factors such as the source of résumés, type of position, geographic location, and time constraints all can influence recruitment success.[47] With regard to résumés, managers surveyed judged only about 7 percent of incoming résumés to be worth routing to hiring managers. However, those from employment agencies generated more qualified applicants than did general inquiries or advertisements.

The rate of invitations to visit varied markedly (from 8 to 60 percent), depending on the type of position in question. Generally, candidates for technical and lower-level positions had the highest invitation rates. However, the invitation rate fell as the level of position rose. About 40 percent of those interviewed received job offers, with candidates for lower-level positions earning the highest offer rates. Nontechnical positions generated twice as many acceptances (82 percent) as technical positions (41 percent).

With respect to geographical location, positions requiring relocation generated fewer acceptances to interview requests and (not surprisingly) fewer employment offers. A final factor that affects recruitment needs is time. Adequate assessment of recruitment needs begins with accurate staffing analysis and forecasting. However, a large number of unexpected retirements, resignations, or terminations may place unrealistic time demands on recruiters. Although time frames differ from job to job and industry to industry, 3 months from the receipt of a requisition to the new employee's start date is considered an acceptable time period for recruiting a journey-level professional.[48]

Diversity-Oriented Recruiting

Special measures are called for in diversity-oriented recruiting: employers should use women and members of underrepresented groups (1) in their HR offices as interviewers; (2) on recruiting trips to high schools, colleges, and job fairs; and (3) in employment advertisements.

Employers need to establish contacts in the groups targeted for recruitment based on credibility between the employer and the contact, and credibility between the contact and the targeted groups. Allow plenty of lead time for the contacts in the targeted groups to notify prospective applicants and for the applicants to apply for available positions.

Various community or professional organizations might be contacted (e.g., Society of Mexican-American Engineers and Scientists, National Society of Black Engineers), and leaders of those organizations should be encouraged to visit the employer and to talk with employees. As we saw in Chapter 3, this strategy was used successfully by Pacific Bell in its effort to recruit high-potential Hispanic candidates.[49] Another source is *Outreach and Recruitment Directory: A Resource for Diversity-Related Recruitment Needs.*[50] The directory is available as a hardcover book or as software, and the database can be sorted by a variety of factors, such as job type, location, target population, or specific types of organizations.

For companies that use search firms to recruit executives, some offer an additional 5 percent of the first year's salary—in addition to the usual 30 percent fee—if the search consultant can find qualified minorities to fill a position.[51] Frequent use of the phrase "an equal opportunity–equal access employer" is a "must" in diversity-oriented recruiting. Finally, recognize that (1) it will take time to establish a credible, workable diversity-oriented recruitment program, and (2) there is no payoff from passive nondiscrimination.

What are firms actually doing in this area to increase workforce diversity? Kraft General Foods, Philip Morris, and Dun & Bradstreet are typical. They are revamping their decentralized recruitment systems in order to develop a coordinated recruitment effort. They have begun by gathering data on who, when, and where they recruit, and how they fare with different groups. The goal is to create a consistent corporate image that will support recruiting efforts across the board.[52]

MANAGING RECRUITMENT OPERATIONS

Administratively, recruitment is one of the easiest activities to foul up—with potentially long-term negative publicity for the firm. Traditionally, recruitment was intensively paper-based. It proceeded as shown in Figure 5-3.

A traditional employment department receives paper résumés, date-stamps them, and distributes them to individual recruiters. The recruiters then man-

Figure 5-3
Traditional approach to résumé processing.

ually code, categorize, and file each individual résumé, frequently repeating this manual process hundreds of times a day.

Finding and matching candidates to open requisitions entails more manual paper processing. Papers must then be copied and forwarded to hiring managers for review, tracked manually with notes and comments, and refiled manually. Individuals are identified as future candidates or as employees, if they have been hired. The process is cumbersome and time-consuming.

Reengineered Recruitment in the Information Age

With the Resumix Human Skills Management System, automation replaces the entire manual process (see Figure 5-4). The Resumix system:

- Employs advanced scanning, optical character recognition (OCR), and imaging technologies to capture an exact on-line image of the original résumé.
- Extracts key résumé information and inputs it into an applicant résumé database.
- Provides instant on-line access to résumé and skills information in the database.

The system can scan and process up to 2000 pages of résumés daily per scanner. Résumés can also be faxed or e-mailed into Resumix for processing. After a résumé is processed, Resumix creates a résumé summary, containing the key information extracted from the résumé, including name, addresses, telephone numbers; degrees, schools, grade-point averages; work history, including dates, companies, job titles; and up to 80 skills.

Information in the résumé summary is stored in the applicant résumé database. The user searches against the database by building requisitions containing specific skill and experience criteria, and then accessing the search function. Resumix then provides a prioritized list of qualified applicants for review.

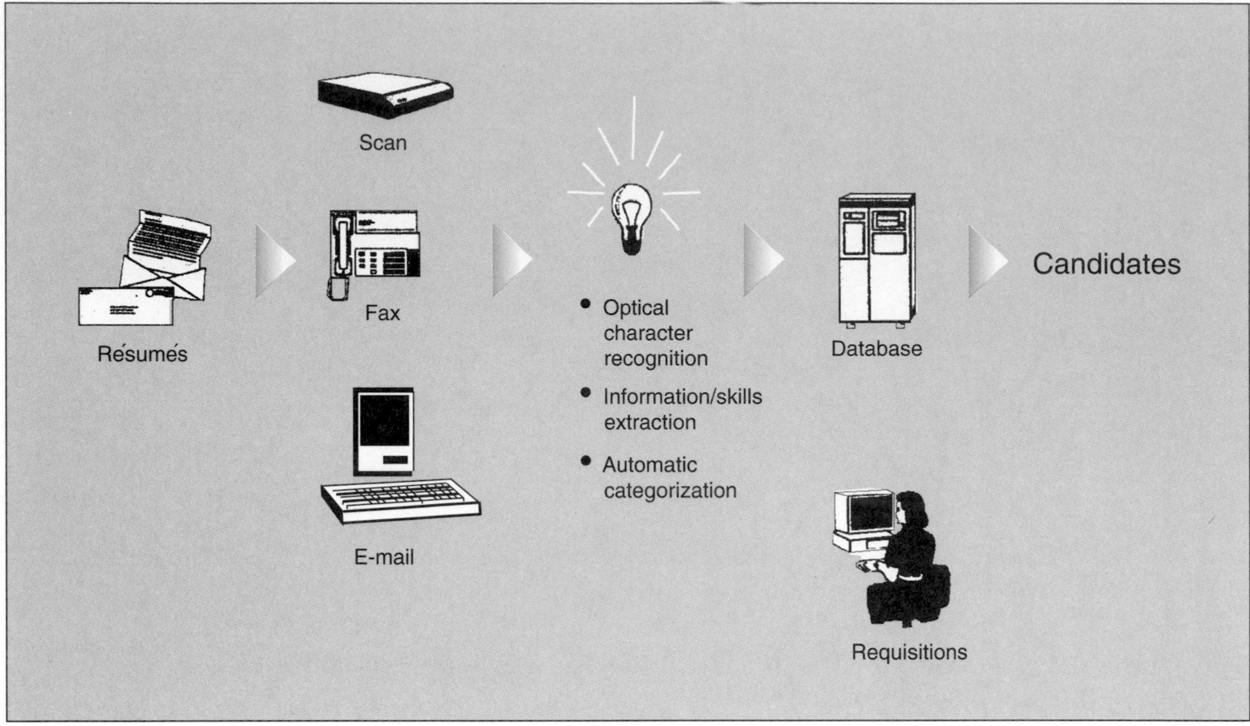

Figure 5-4
Reengineered résumé processing with Resumix.

How does the system work in practice? Firms such as Texas Instruments, The Walt Disney Company, Vanguard Group, and United Parcel Service Airlines have found that Resumix has cut résumé-processing time by up to 80 percent.[53] That's a competitive advantage!

Evaluation and Control of Recruitment Operations

The reason for evaluating past and current recruitment operations is simple: to improve the efficiency of future recruitment efforts. Accomplishing that goal requires systematically analyzing the performance of the various recruitment sources. Consider collecting the following kinds of information:

- Cost of operations, that is, labor costs of company recruitment staff, operational costs (e.g., recruiting staff's travel and living expenses, agency fees, advertising expenses, brochures, supplies, and postage), and overhead expenses (e.g., rental of temporary facilities and equipment)
- Cost per hire, by source
- Number and quality of résumés by source
- Acceptance-to-offer ratio
- Analysis of postvisit and rejection questionnaires
- Salary offered—acceptances versus rejections

Evidence indicates, unfortunately, that the evaluation of recruitment activities by large organizations is honored more in the breach than in the observance. Few firms link their recruitment practices to posthire effectiveness, and evaluation is more subjective than quantitative.[54] In one study, for example, just over half the firms even bothered to calculate the average cost per hire in their college recruitment operations (over $2700 in 1996 dollars).[55] As a general benchmark, other research suggests one-third of annual first-year salary.[56] Given the rapid proliferation of human resource information systems, with at least a dozen that provide applicant-tracking features (e.g., PeopleSoft, Revelation Technologies, Resumix),[57] there is no excuse for not evaluating this costly activity.

Which recruitment sources are most *effective*? According to a survey of 245 firms, newspaper advertisements are the most effective sources for recruiting office/clerical, professional/technical, and commissioned sales workers. For recruiting managers, promotion from within is most effective, followed by newspaper ads. Walk-ins are the most popular method for recruiting production/service workers.[58]

However, a study of 10 different recruitment sources used by more than 20,000 applicants for the job of insurance agent showed that recruiting source explained only 5 percent of the variation in applicant quality, 1 percent of the variation in the survival of new hires, and none of the variation in commissions.[59] If sources do not differ appreciably on these important characteristics, organizations probably should rely on those that are less costly (e.g., newspaper ads) and produce higher-quality applicants (informal sources) than more expensive sources (employment agencies). Later research generally has supported these findings. Thus, regardless of the recruitment sources used to generate applicants, once a final applicant pool has been assembled, organizations can maximize the economic returns of selection by ignoring recruitment sources and using a top-down (i.e., rank order from best to least qualified) selection strategy.[60]

Several studies have examined the recruitment process from the perspective of applicants—how applicants regarded the various sources of information (on-campus interviewer-recruiter, friend, job incumbent, professor) about a job opportunity.[61] The studies investigated whether applicants regarded the information source as credible or not, which sources provided favorable or unfavorable job information, and which sources led to greater acceptances of job offers.

Findings indicated that the on-campus interviewer-recruiter, the first and often the only representative of a company seen by applicants, often was not liked, not trusted, and not perceived as knowing much about the job. Furthermore, applicants were more inclined to believe unfavorable information than favorable information, and they were more likely to accept jobs when the source of information about the job was not the interviewer. Other research has shown that job attributes (supervision, job challenge, location, salary, title) *as well as* recruitment activities (e.g., gender and educational characteristics of recruiter, behavior during the interview) are important to applicants' reactions. In short, recruitment may be viewed as a market exchange process in which employers attempt to differentiate their "products" (job opportunities) among "consumers" (job applicants) who vary in their levels of job-relevant knowledge, abilities, and skills.[62]

Timing issues in recruitment, particularly delays, are important factors in the job choice decisions of applicants.[63] Research indicates that (1) long delays between recruitment phases are not uncommon; (2) applicants react to such delays very negatively, often perceiving that "something is wrong" with the organization; and (3) regardless of their inferences, the most marketable candidates accept other offers if delays become extended. What are the implications

ETHICAL DILEMMA
Must a Company Tell a Job Applicant about Potential Layoffs?

Does a company have an obligation to tell job applicants if it is on shaky financial ground and plans to cut back? Some managers argue that such disclosure is not necessary since the layoffs may never materialize. Moreover, they say, "You don't want to scare off top talent, do you?"

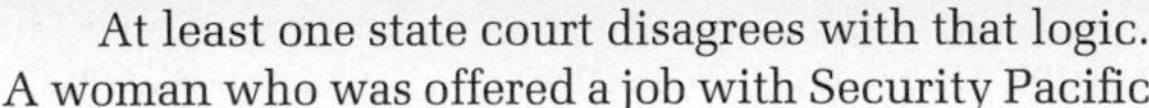

At least one state court disagrees with that logic. A woman who was offered a job with Security Pacific Information Services, Inc., relocated from New Orleans to Denver. Seven weeks after she started work, the unit she worked for collapsed for lack of business. A jury awarded her $250,000 for actual and punitive damages, and the Colorado Court of Appeals upheld the jury's verdict.[70] As a general matter, do you agree with the jury's verdict?

of these findings? In a competitive marketplace, top talent disappears quickly. If you want to compete for it, streamline the decision-making process so that you can move fast.

Realistic Job Previews

A conceptual framework that might help explain some of these research findings is that of the realistic job preview (RJP).[64] An RJP requires that, in addition to telling applicants about the nice things a job has to offer (e.g., pay, benefits, opportunities for advancement), recruiters must also tell applicants about the unpleasant aspects of the job. For example, "It's hot and dirty, and sometimes you'll have to work on weekends." Research in actual company settings has indicated consistent results.[65] That is, when the unrealistically positive expectations of job applicants prior to hire are lowered to match the reality of the actual work setting, job acceptance rates may be lower and job performance is unaffected, but job satisfaction and survival are higher for those who receive an RJP. These conclusions have held up in different organizational settings (e.g., manufacturing versus service jobs) and when different RJP techniques are used (e.g., plant tours versus slide presentations versus written descriptions of the work). In fact, RJPs improve retention rates, on average, by 9 percent.[66]

Longitudinal research shows that RJPs should be balanced in their orientation. That is, they should enhance overly pessimistic expectations and reduce overly optimistic expectations. Doing so helps bolster the applicant's perceptions of the organization as caring, trustworthy, and honest.[67]

A final recommendation is to develop RJPs even when there is no turnover problem (proactively rather than reactively). RJPs should employ an audiovisual medium and, where possible, show actual job incumbents.[68]

Nevertheless, RJPs are not appropriate for all types of jobs. They seem to work best (1) when few applicants are actually hired (that is, the selection ratio is low), (2) when used with entry-level positions (since those coming from outside to inside the organization tend to have more inflated expectations than those who make changes internally), and (3) when unemployment is low (since job candidates are more likely to have alternative jobs to choose from).[69]

THE OTHER SIDE OF RECRUITMENT—JOB SEARCH

At some time or another, whether voluntarily or otherwise, almost everyone faces the difficult task of finding a job. Much of this chapter has emphasized recruitment from the organization's perspective. But as we noted at the outset, a mating theory of recruitment—in which organizations search for qualified candidates just as candidates search for organizations—is more realistic. How do people find jobs? Research shows that 70 percent land a job through personal contacts, 15 percent through placement agencies, 10 percent through direct mailings of their résumés, and only 5 percent through published job openings.[71]

Consider the following scenario, which has happened all too frequently over the last decade (as a result of mergers, restructurings, and downsizings) and is expected to occur often this decade as economic conditions change.[72] You are a midlevel executive, well regarded, well paid, and seemingly well established in your chosen field. Then—whammo!—a change in business strategy or a change in economic conditions results in your layoff from the firm you hoped to retire from. What do you do? How do you go about finding another job? According to management consultants and executive recruiters, the following are some of the key things *not* to do:[73]

- **Don't panic**. A search takes time, even for well-qualified middle- and upper-level managers. Seven months to a year is not unusual. Be prepared to wait it out.
- **Don't be bitter**. Bitterness makes it harder to begin to search; it also turns off potential employers.
- **Don't kid yourself**. Do a thorough self-appraisal of your strengths and weaknesses, your likes and dislikes about jobs and organizations. Face up to what has happened, decide if you want to switch fields, figure out where you and your family want to live, and don't delay the search itself for long.
- **Don't drift**. Develop a plan, target companies, and go after them relentlessly. Realize that your job is to find a new job. Cast a wide net; consider industries other than your own.
- **Don't be lazy**. The heart of a good job hunt is research. Use reference books, public filings, and annual reports when drawing up a list of target companies. If negotiations get serious, talk to a range of insiders and knowledgeable outsiders to learn about politics and practices. You don't want to wind up in a worse fix than the one you left. Unfortunately, research indicates that only about 5 percent of job applicants do any research on a company before an interview.[74]
- **Don't be shy or overeager**. Since personal contacts are the most effective means to land a job, pull out all the stops to get the word out that you are available. At the same time, resist the temptation to accept the first job that comes along. Unless that job is absolutely right for you, continue your search. The chances of making a mistake by taking the first job offered are quite high.
- **Don't ignore your family**. Some executives are embarrassed and don't tell their families what's going on. A better approach, experts say, is to bring the family into the process and deal with issues honestly.

IMPACT OF RECRUITMENT ON PRODUCTIVITY, QUALITY OF WORK LIFE, AND THE BOTTOM LINE

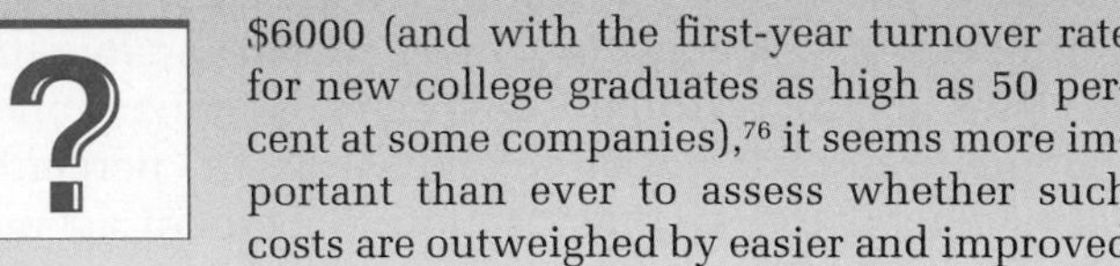

A close fit between individual strengths and interests and organizational and job characteristics almost guarantees a happy "marriage." On the other hand, since the bottom line of recruitment success lies in the number of successful placements made, the effects of ineffective recruitment may not appear for years. For this reason alone, a regular system for measuring and evaluating recruitment efforts is essential. Moreover, it is difficult to manage what you cannot measure.[75] With the cost of new college hires between $1500 and $6000 (and with the first-year turnover rate for new college graduates as high as 50 percent at some companies),[76] it seems more important than ever to assess whether such costs are outweighed by easier and improved selection procedures, better employee retention, lower training needs and costs, or higher levels of productivity. Finding, attracting, and retaining top talent is now and will continue to be an important management challenge with direct impacts on productivity, quality of work life, and the bottom line.

- **Don't lie**. Experts are unanimous on this point. Don't lie, and don't stretch a point—either on résumés or in interviews. Be willing to address failures as well as strengths. Discuss openly and fully what went wrong at the old job.
- **Don't jump the gun on salary**. Always let the potential employer bring this subject up first. But once it surfaces, thoroughly explore all aspects of your future compensation and benefits package.

Those who have been through the trauma of job loss and the challenge of finding a job often describe the entire process as a wrenching, stressful one. Avoiding the mistakes shown above can ensure that finding a new job need not take any longer than necessary.

Human Resource Management in Action: Conclusion

RÉSUMÉ DATABASES—RECRUITMENT METHOD OF CHOICE IN THE FUTURE?

Generally speaking, there are two disadvantages to such databases.[77] One, many individuals who currently are employed will not list themselves in a database to which the public can have access. The last thing they want their current employers to know is that they are looking for another job. Thus such databases might best be used to locate individuals who are not currently employed, such as new college graduates. Two, some employers do not use public-access databases because they believe that when the objective is to hire experienced individuals, the best candidates are those that are not really "in the market." That is, they have to be "sold" before they will leave their current jobs.

Thus while résumé databases may become an integral part of recruitment cycles, they will probably supplement, but not replace completely, the recruitment systems that most employers now use. After all, no recruitment effort would be complete without an interview that allows a prospective employer to see and interact with a candidate and allows the candidate an opportunity to

IMPLICATIONS FOR MANAGEMENT PRACTICE

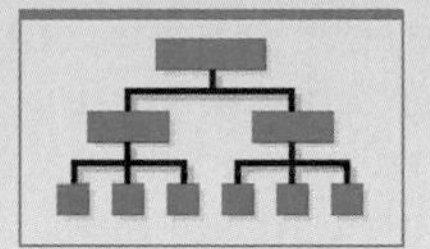

Wave after wave of downsizings and restructurings, predominately at large firms, indicates that in many fields job hunting has become a buyer's market in the late 1990s. Talent is what makes firms go. Recruitment is therefore a strategic imperative. Given the substantial costs of recruitment and training, employers must consider the needs of employees if they wish to attract and retain top talent. American Express Travel-Related Services adopted this view in introducing its KidsCheque and FamilyCheque programs to subsidize child care and elder care for employees, over 70 percent of whom are female.[78] Its experience suggests that the following elements should be part of any successful recruitment program:

- Always view recruitment as a long-term strategy.
- Be responsive to employees' needs.
- Develop benefits that genuinely appeal to the employees being hired.
- Promote recruitment benefits to the target audience.
- Audit the recruitment programs in place.

How did the senior HR officer at American Express Travel-Related Services sell the program to hard-nosed senior managers? By emphasizing its business advantages; that is, he presented it less like a typical human resource plan and more like a marketing plan—focusing on the goal of differentiating the company in the labor market and placing it ahead of the competition. He emphasized again and again the importance of acting immediately to obtain a first-mover advantage.

What were the results of the program? Within weeks of introducing the program in Jacksonville, Florida, for example, almost 80 percent of eligible employees had signed up. In addition, the company began to receive résumés from people who had heard about KidsCheque from the local media and who were interested in joining American Express as a result. It also received telephone calls from HR managers at other companies that were interested in instituting similar programs.[79]

learn more about the prospective job and organization. Moreover, the terms and conditions of employment are usually negotiated face to face, not by computer.

According to the president of a résumé database firm in Boston, The Executives' Network, "We have found that our database works best in finding that elusive, qualified mid-level manager. Top-level management searches such as CEOs will always be politically sensitive and will need special handling. Those searches will likely remain in the realm of the executive search firm."

SUMMARY

Recruitment begins with a clear statement of objectives, based on the types of knowledge, skills, abilities, and other characteristics that an organization needs. Objectives are also based on a consideration of the gender and ethnic-group representation of the workforce, relative to that of the surrounding labor force. Finally, a recruitment policy must spell out clearly an organization's intention to evaluate and screen candidates without regard to factors such as race, gender, age, or disability, where those characteristics are unrelated to a person's ability to do a job successfully. The actual process of recruitment begins with a specification of HR requirements—numbers, skills mix, levels, and the time frame within which such needs must be met.

Recruitment may involve internal, external, or both kinds of labor markets. Internal recruitment often relies on succession plans, job posting, employee referrals, or temporary worker pools. Many external recruitment sources are also available. In this chapter we discussed four such sources: university relations, executive search firms, employment agencies, and recruitment advertising. In managing and controlling recruitment operations, consider calculating the cost of operations and analyzing the performance of each recruitment source, since recruitment success is determined by the number of hires who actually perform their jobs successfully.

DISCUSSION QUESTIONS

5-1 What special measures might be necessary for a successful diversity-oriented recruitment effort?

5-2 Discuss the conditions under which realistic job previews are and are not appropriate.

5-3 How would you advise a firm that wants to improve its college recruitment efforts?

5-4 Draft a recruitment ad for a trade journal to advertise a job opening at your company. Have a friend as well as, if possible, a knowledgeable HR professional from a local company critique it. Summarize their suggestions for improvement and incorporate them into a final draft.

5-5 You have just lost your middle-management job. Outline a procedure to follow in trying to land a new one.

APPLYING YOUR KNOWLEDGE

Case 5-1 *Recruiting at Sandmeyer Steel Company*

Kenneth T. Sandmeyer, a man who patrols the shop floor in a three-piece suit and provides holiday turkeys to all hands, exudes old-school attitudes about how to run a business. But that does not extend to having unusually high employee recruitment standards.

"Don't give us your best and brightest," the 57-year-old head of Sandmeyer Steel Company tells people who may know someone looking for a job. "Give us the people who are average or mediocre and don't know what they want to do with their lives."

Yet Mr. Sandmeyer has trouble finding workers to meet even his modest standards. His predicament is a measure of how hard it is for many American manufacturers to find workers these days, for reasons that embrace culture, education, and demographics.

Indeed, what Mr. Sandmeyer calls the people problem is getting worse in many parts of the country, hastening America's decline as a manufacturer and undermining the ability to compete against countries like Japan and Germany, where factory work has higher status and the numbers of skilled workers are larger.

The problem is particularly bad in urban areas like Philadelphia, where the middle class has higher aspirations, the poor have no skills, and the television-weaned youth of both groups are shocked to discover that the modern factory is still often noisy, smelly, dirty, and uncomfortably hot or cold.

Mr. Sandmeyer calls the people problem his biggest worry in managing his family's stainless steel company in the northeast corner of the city: "It's held down our growth. We have not been able to gain as much market share as we would have, had we had more productive and capable employees."

With imaginative searching that enlisted the aid of a local priest—and has resulted in 30 to 40 percent of its workforce being foreign-born—Sandmeyer Steel has largely managed to fill its ranks. It has succeeded despite stiff competition from large employers that typically offer similar pay but more training, more prestige, better fringe benefits, and less physical discomfort.

A newly hired employee with no previous work experience is paid $6.50 an hour. Someone with a year or two of experience and a record of dependability might get $7.50 to $9.50. Mr. Sandmeyer said the tight labor situation has bid up the company's wage costs.

"It's hot and dirty work; it's heavy manufacturing," Sandmeyer acknowledged of his plant. "Instead of air conditioning," he said, "we open every window and door when it gets over 90, and everybody gets free soda."

Questions

1. Serious labor shortages do exist in many places, but these are not the only reasons for the recruiting problems experienced by many small businesses. What are some others?
2. As a manager in such a small business, what sources might you use to find new workers?
3. What special advantages does a small business have over a large one? How can you incorporate these into the recruitment process?

REFERENCES

1. Lord, J. S. (1989). External and internal recruitment. In W. F. Cascio (ed.), *Human resource planning, employment, and placement*. Washington, DC: Bureau of National Affairs, pp. 2-73 to 2-102.
2. Seligman, D. (1973, Mar.). How "equal opportunity" turned into employment quotas. *Fortune*, pp. 160–168.
3. Replying in the affirmative (1987, Mar. 9). *Time*, p. 66.
4. *Officers for Justice v. Civil Service Commission* (1992). 979 F. 2d 721 (9th Cir.), cert. denied, 61 U.S.L.W. 3667, 113 S. Ct. 1645 (Mar. 29, 1993). See also Affirmative action upheld by High Court as a remedy for past job discrimination (1986, July 3). *The New York Times*, pp. A1, B9.
5. Reynolds, L. G., Masters, S. H., & Moser, C. H. (1986). *Labor economics and labor relations* (9th ed.). Englewood Cliffs, NJ: Prentice-Hall.
6. Booming Boeing (1996, Sept. 30). *Business Week*, pp. 118–125. See also Chan, S. (1996, Aug. 9). In frenzy to recruit, high-tech concerns try gimmicks, songs. *The Wall Street Journal*, pp. B1, B3.
7. Reynolds et al., op. cit.
8. Sebastian, P. (1988, Sept. 16). Labor pains. *The Wall Street Journal*, pp. 1, 12.
9. Milkovich, G. T., & Newman, J. G. (1996). Compensation (5th ed.). Homewood, IL: Irwin. See also Wallace, M. J., & Fay, C. H. (1988). Compensation theory and practice (2d ed.). Boston: PWS-Kent.
10. Baron, J. N., Davis-Blake, A., & Bielby, W. T. (1986). The structure of opportunity: How promotion ladders vary within and among organizations. *Administrative*

Science Quarterly, **31**, 248–273. See also Stewman, S. (1986). Demographic models of internal labor markets. *Administrative Science Quarterly*, **31**, 212–247.

11. For an excellent summary of this research, see Rynes, S. L. (1991). Recruitment, job choice, and post-hire consequences: A call for new research directions. In M. D. Dunnette & L. M. Hough (eds.), *Handbook of industrial and organizational psychology*, Vol. 2 (2d ed). Palo Alto, CA: Consulting Psychologists Press, pp. 399–444.
12. *Wards Cove Packing Co. v. Antonio*, 109 S. Ct. 2115 (1989). See also Ledvinka, J., & Scarpello, V. G. (1991). *Federal regulation of personnel and human resource management* (2d ed.). Boston: PWS-Kent.
13. *Hazelwood School District v. United States* (1977). 433 U.S. 299.
14. Staffing efficiency quantified (1995, Oct.). *Bulletin*. Denver: Mountain States Employers Council, p. 5.
15. Lord, loc. cit.
16. Farish, P. (1989). Recruitment sources. In W. F. Cascio (ed.), *Human resource planning, employment, and placement*. Washington, DC: Bureau of National Affairs, pp. 2-103 to 2-134.
17. Breaugh, J. A. (1992). *Recruitment: Science and practice*. Boston: PWS-Kent.
18. Lord, loc. cit.
19. Amante, L. (1989). Help wanted: Creative recruitment tactics. *Personnel*, **66**(10), 32–36.
20. Chan, loc. cit.
21. Kirnan, J. P., Farley, J. A., & Geisinger, K. F. (1989). The relationship between recruiting source, applicant quality, and hire performance: An analysis by sex, ethnicity, and age. *Personnel Psychology*, **42**, 293–308.
22. Lord, loc. cit.
23. Kilborn, P. T. (1990, May 6). Nurses get V.I.P. treatment, easing shortage. *The New York Times*, pp. 1, 28.
24. Farish, loc. cit.
25. Ibid.
26. Koch, J. (1990, Winter). Desktop recruiting. *Recruitment Today*, **3**, pp. 32–37.
27. Kolenko, T. A. (1990). College recruiting: Models, myths, and management. In G. R. Ferris, K. M. Rowland, & M. R. Buckley (eds.), *Human resource management: Perspectives and issues* (2d ed.). Boston: Allyn & Bacon, pp. 109–121.
28. Employee priorities shifting (1992, Sept. 7). *The Denver Post*, p. 19A. See also Today's students say money isn't everything (1988, Sept. 7). *The Wall Street Journal*, p. 27.
29. Lord, loc. cit.
30. Dee, W. (1983). Evaluating a search firm. *Personnel Administrator*, **28**(3), 41–43, 99–100.
31. Lord, loc. cit. See also LoPresto, R. (1986). Ethical recruiting. *Personnel Administrator*, **31**(11), 90–91.
32. Labor letter (1988, May 10). *The Wall Street Journal*, p. 1.
33. Lord, loc. cit.
34. Farish, loc. cit.
35. Lord, loc. cit.
36. Chan, loc. cit.
37. Ottinger, R. (1996, Aug.). America's Job Bank adds IBM, expands listings. *HR News*, p. 24; On-line job search: Help wanted (1996, July 29). *The Colombian Post*, p. 3B.
38. Labor letter (1989, Dec. 5). *The Wall Street Journal*, p. A1.
39. Labor letter (1992, Apr. 14). *The Wall Street Journal*, p. A1.
40. Two-income couples in the U.S. make changes at work and home (1996, June). *Manpower Argus*, p. 2.
41. Pope, H. (1996, Sept.). Trailing-spouse costs rise. *Chartered Secretary* (UK), p. 26.

42. Markels, A. (1996, Aug. 21). Signing bonuses rise to counter rich pay plans. *The Wall Street Journal*, pp. B1, B4.
43. Chan, loc. cit.
44. Ibid.
45. Bureau of National Affairs (1988, May). *Recruiting and selection procedures* (PPF Survey 146). Washington, DC: Author.
46. Kirnan et al., loc. cit.
47. Lord, loc. cit.
48. Ibid.
49. Roberson, L., & Gutierrez, N. C. (1992). Beyond good faith: Commitment to recruiting management diversity at Pacific Bell. In S. E. Jackson (ed.), *Diversity in the workplace*. New York: Guilford, pp. 65–88.
50. *Outreach and recruitment directory: A resource for diversity-related recruitment needs* (1995). Columbia, MD: Berkshire Associates, Inc.
51. Labor letter (1989, Mar. 21). *The Wall Street Journal*, p. A1.
52. Employers go to school on minority recruiting (1992, Dec. 15). *The Wall Street Journal*, p. B1.
53. *Reengineering the workforce with human skills management* (1996). Santa Clara, CA: Resumix.
54. Kolenko, loc. cit.
55. Rynes, S. L., & Boudreau, J. W. (1986). College recruiting in large organizations: Practice, evaluation, and research implications. *Personnel Psychology*, **39**, 729–757. See also Martin, S. L., & Raju, N. S. (1992). Determining cutoff scores that optimize utility: A recognition of recruiting costs. *Journal of Applied Psychology*, **77**, 15–23.
56. Staffing efficiency quantified, loc. cit. See also Breaugh, op. cit.
57. O'Connell, S. E. (1996, Aug.). HR productivity software dominates IHRIM exhibits. *HR News*, pp. 10, 20. See also Polilli, S. (1992, Feb.). Applicant tracking tools automate résumé review. *Software Magazine*, pp. 8–14.
58. Bureau of National Affairs, op. cit.
59. Kirnan et al., loc. cit.
60. Williams, C. R., Labig, C. E., Jr., & Stone, T. H. (1993). Recruitment sources and posthire outcomes for job applicants and new hires: A test of two hypotheses. *Journal of Applied Psychology*, **78**, 163–172.
61. Rynes, S. L., Bretz, R. D., Jr., & Gerhart, B. (1991). The importance of recruitment in job choice: A different way of looking. *Personnel Psychology*, **44**, 487–521. See also Fisher, C. D., Ilgen, D. R., & Hoyer, W. D. (1979). Source credibility, information favorability, and job offer acceptance. *Academy of Management Journal*, **22**, 94–103.
62. Maurer, S. D., Howe, V., & Lee, T. W. (1992). Organizational recruiting as marketing management: An interdisciplinary study of engineering graduates. *Personnel Psychology*, **45**, 807–833.
63. Rynes et al., loc. cit.
64. Popovich, P., & Wanous, J. P. (1982). The realistic job preview as a persuasive communication. *Academy of Management Review*, **7**, 570–578.
65. Breaugh, op. cit. See also Premack, S. L., & Wanous, J. P. (1985). A meta-analysis of realistic job preview experiments. *Journal of Applied Psychology*, **70**, 706–719.
66. McEvoy, G. M., & Cascio, W. F. (1985). Strategies for reducing employee turnover. A meta-analysis. *Journal of Applied Psychology*, **70**, 342–353.
67. Meglino, B. M., De Nisi, A. S., Youngblood, S. A., & Williams, K. J. (1988). Effects of realistic job previews: A comparison using an enhancement and a reduction preview. *Journal of Applied Psychology*, **73**, 259–266.
68. Wanous, J. P. (1989). Installing a realistic job preview: Ten tough choices. *Personnel Psychology*, **42**, 117–134.
69. Wanous, J. P. (1980). *Organizational entry: Recruitment, selection and socialization of newcomers*. Reading, MA: Addison-Wesley.

70. Menter, E. (1990, Fall). Company must disclose problems to applicants. *The Legal Vantage.* Denver: Pryor, Garney and Johnson.
71. Falvey, J. (1991, Fall). A new set of rules for the "real world." *Managing Your Career.* Chicopee, MA: special section of *The Wall Street Journal*, pp. 39, 41. See also Cohn, G. (1985, Nov. 19). Advice on what not to do as the search continues. *The Wall Street Journal*, p. 37.
72. Uchitelle, L., & Kleinfeld, N. R. (1996, Mar. 3). On the battlefields of business, millions of casualties. *The New York Times*, pp. 1, 14–17.
73. When a recruiter comes knocking, be ready to respond. (1996, Aug. 6). *The Wall Street Journal*, p. B1. See also Rigdon, J. E. (1992, June 17). Deceptive résumés can be door openers but can become an employee's undoing. *The Wall Street Journal*, pp. B1, B7. See also Cohn, loc. cit.
74. Work week (1995, Oct. 31). *The Wall Street Journal*, p. A1.
75. Kolenko, loc. cit.
76. Breaugh, op. cit.
77. Willis, R. (1990, May). Recruitment: Playing the database game. *Personnel*, **67**, 25–29.
78. Morrison, E. W., & Herlihy, J. M. (1992). Becoming the best place to work: Managing diversity at American Express Travel-Related Services. In S. E. Jackson (ed.), *Diversity in the workplace.* New York: Guilford, pp. 203–226.
79. Ibid.

STAFFING

6

Questions This Chapter Will Help Managers Answer

1 In what ways do business strategy and organizational culture affect staffing decisions?
2 What screening and selection methods are available, and which ones are most accurate?
3 What should be done to improve preemployment interviews?
4 Can work-sample tests improve staffing decisions?
5 What are some advantages and potential problems to consider in using assessment centers to select managers?

CEO SELECTION CRITERIA—IN THE THROES OF CHANGE*

Human Resource Management in Action

According to management experts, many of today's top executives are the right people, but for the wrong time. The quickening pace of corporate change means growing numbers of managers who are well groomed for the wrong race. This, apparently, was the case for Robert Stempel, former chairman of General Motors Corporation, who resigned in 1992 under pressure from outside directors of the company.

By most accounts, Mr. Stempel was a competent manager who inspired strong loyalty in his staff. His grooming by the ponderous GM management system was thorough and meticulous. Yet the very skills that propel managers such as Mr. Stempel to the top of large, successful companies—conciliation, deliberateness, relationship-building, loyalty—can prove to be their undoing. Boards often compound the problem by choosing chief executives groomed in yesterday's corporate cultures to solve yesterday's problems. The result? Boards often select the right leaders—but for the wrong time.

Mr. Stempel is not alone. At about the same time, both Tom H. Barrett of Goodyear Tire & Rubber Co. and Kenneth H. Olsen of Digital Equipment Corporation also resigned under intense pressure from their boards of directors. Like Mr. Stempel, who had been with GM for 34 years, both were old-time company men. Mr. Barrett had spent 38 years with Goodyear, and Mr. Olsen, who founded Digital, stayed with the company for 35 years. All three faced sharp changes in market demand and competition.

What is the problem? Management experts say that most CEOs of big companies are products of long, ponderous, and often very highly structured management succession systems. Especially at old-line industrial companies, these individuals often joined the company right out of school and worked their way up through the ranks, assuming greater and greater management responsibility along the way.

Such systems worked well during an epoch of stable markets and increasing consumer demand, but they may prove inadequate for a more rapidly changing environment. Leaders groomed in one business environment thus wind up ill-prepared for another. Experts generally agree that there are three flaws in the current system: (1) the process takes too long, (2) the system produces leaders who are too insular in their contacts and their views, and (3) the current approach ties executives too closely to tradition.

Challenges

1. What kinds of experience and personal characteristics should boards be looking for in today's top executives?
2. How should companies address the flaws in the current system?
3. Are there "seasons" for leaders?

*Adapted from A. Bennett, Many of today's top corporate officers are the right people for the wrong time, *The Wall Street Journal*, Oct. 27, 1992, pp. B1, B12. Reprinted by permission of *The Wall Street Journal*,

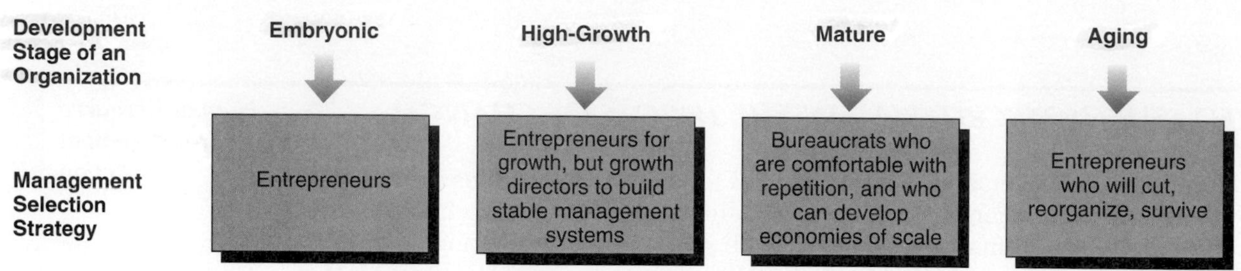

Figure 6-1
The relationship between the development stage of an organization and the management selection strategy that best fits each stage.

The chapter opening vignette describes how the changing business environment affects the process of selecting a top manager. In fact, management-selection decisions are some of the most important and most difficult staffing decisions that organizations face. Compounding the difficulties is the constant need to align staffing decisions with business strategy and organizational culture. As we will see in this chapter, there is a wide variety of tools for initial screening and selection decisions, and much is known about each one. We will examine the evidence of the relative effectiveness of the tools; such knowledge allows decision makers to choose those tools that best fit their long- and short-range objectives.

ORGANIZATIONAL CONSIDERATIONS IN STAFFING DECISIONS

Business Strategy

Clearly, there should be a fit between the intended strategy of an enterprise and the characteristics of the people who are expected to implement it. Unfortunately, very few firms actually link strategy and staffing decisions in a structured, logical way. Nevertheless, we can learn how to effect such a fit by considering a two-dimensional model that relates an organization's strategy during the stages of its development to the style of its managers during each stage.[1]

For strategic reasons, it is important to consider the stage of development of a business, because many characteristics of a business—such as its growth rate, product lines, market share, entry opportunity, and technology—change as the organization changes. One possible set of relationships between the development stage and the management-selection strategies is shown in Figure 6-1. While a model such as this is useful conceptually, in practice, the stages might not be so clearly defined, and there are many exceptions.

Organizations that are just starting out are in the *embryonic* stage. They are characterized by high growth rates, basic product lines, heavy emphasis on product engineering, and little or no customer loyalty.

Organizations in the *high-growth* stage are concerned with two things: fighting for market share and building excellence in their management teams. They focus on refining and extending product lines, and on building customer loyalty.

Mature organizations emphasize the maintenance of market share, cost reductions through economies of scale, more rigid management controls over workers' actions, and the generation of cash to develop new product lines. In contrast to the freewheeling style of an embryonic organization, there is much less flexibility and variability in a mature organization.

Finally, an *aging* organization struggles to hold market share in a declining market, and it demands extreme cost control obtained through consistency and centralized procedures. Economic survival becomes the primary motivation.

Different management styles seem to fit each of these development stages best. In the embryonic stage there is a need for enterprising managers who can thrive in high-risk environments. Such managers are known as entrepreneurs (see Figure 6-1). They are decisive individuals who can respond rapidly to changing conditions.

During the high-growth stage there is still a need for entrepreneurs, but it is also important to select the kinds of managers who can develop stable management systems to preserve the gains achieved during the embryonic stage. We might call these managers "growth directors."

As an organization matures, there is a need to select the kind of manager who does not need lots of variety in her or his work, who can oversee repetitive daily operations, and who can search continually for economies of scale. Individuals who fit best into mature organizations have a "bureaucratic" style of management.

Finally, an aging organization needs "movers and shakers" to reinvigorate it. Strategically, it becomes important to select (again) entrepreneurs capable of doing whatever is necessary to ensure the economic survival of the firm. This may involve divesting unprofitable operations, firing unproductive workers, or eliminating practices that are considered extravagant.

Admittedly, these characterizations are coarse, but they provide a starting point in the construction of an important link between the development stage of an organization and its staffing strategy. Such strategic concerns may be used to supplement job analyses as bases for staffing. The incorporation of strategic concerns into job analyses also suggests that *job* descriptions, which standardize and formalize behavior, should be broadened into *role* descriptions, which reflect the broader and more changeable strategic requirements of an organization.

Organizational Culture

A logical extension of the mating theory of recruitment (i.e., concurrent search efforts for a match by organizations and individuals) is the mating theory of selection. That is, just as organizations choose people, people choose jobs and organizations that fit their personalities and career objectives and in which they can satisfy needs that are important to them.[2]

In the context of selection, it is important for an organization to describe the dimensions of its culture. *Culture* is the pattern of basic assumptions a given group has invented, discovered, or developed in learning to adapt to both its external environment and its internal environment. The pattern of assumptions has worked well enough to be considered valid and, therefore, to be taught to new members as the correct way to perceive, think, and feel in relation to those problems. Organizational culture is embedded and transmitted through mechanisms such as the following:

1. Formal statements of organizational philosophy and materials used for recruitment, selection, and socialization of new employees
2. Promotion criteria
3. Stories, legends, and myths about key people and events
4. Aspects of performance or experience leaders pay attention to, measure, and control
5. Implicit and possibly unconscious criteria that leaders use to determine who fits into key slots in the organization

Organizational culture has two implications for staffing decisions. One, cultures vary across organizations; individuals will consider this information in their job-search process if it is available to them.[3] Companies such as IBM and Procter & Gamble have a strong marketing orientation, and their staffing decisions tend to reflect this value. Other companies, such as Sun Microsystems and Hewlett-Packard, are oriented toward R&D and engineering, while still others, such as McDonald's, concentrate on consistency and efficiency. By linking staffing decisions to cultural factors, companies try to ensure that their employees have internalized the strategic intent and core values of the enterprise. In this way they will be more likely to act in the interest of the company and as dedicated team members, regardless of their formal job duties.[4]

Two, other things being equal, individuals who choose jobs and organizations that are consistent with their own values, beliefs, and attitudes are more likely to be productive, satisfied employees. This was demonstrated in a study of 904 college graduates hired by six public accounting firms over a 6-year period. Those hired by firms that emphasized interpersonal-relationship values (team orientation, respect for people) stayed an average of 45 months. Those hired by firms that emphasized work-task values (detail, stability, innovation) stayed with their firms an average of 31 months. This 14-month difference in survival rates translated into an opportunity loss of at least $6 million for each firm that emphasized work-task values.

While the firms that emphasized interpersonal-relationship values were uniformly more attractive to both strong and weak performers, strong performers stayed an average of 13 months longer in firms that emphasized work-task values (39 months versus 26 months for weak performers). The lesson for managers? Promote cultural values that are attractive to most new employees; do not just select individuals who fit a predetermined profile of cultural values.[5]

The Logic of Personnel Selection

If variability in physical and psychological characteristics were not so prevalent, there would be little need for selection of people to fill various jobs. Without variability among individuals in abilities, aptitudes, interests, and personality traits, we would expect all job candidates to perform comparably. Research shows clearly that as jobs become more complex, individual differences in output variability increase.[6] Likewise, if there were 10 job openings available and only 10 qualified candidates, selection again would not be a significant issue since all 10 candidates would have to be hired. Selection becomes a relevant concern only when there are more qualified candidates than there are positions to be filled, for selection implies choice and choice means exclusion.

Since practical considerations (safety, time, cost) make job tryouts for all candidates infeasible in most selection situations, it is necessary to *predict* the relative level of job performance of each candidate on the basis of available information. As we will see, some methods for doing this are more accurate than others. However, before considering them, we need to focus on the fundamental technical requirements of all such methods—reliability and validity.

Reliability of Measurement

The goal of any selection program is to identify applicants who score high on measures that purport to assess knowledge, skills, abilities, or other characteristics that are critical for job performance. Yet we always run the risk of making errors in employee-selection decisions. Selection errors are of two types: selecting someone who should be rejected (erroneous acceptance) and rejecting someone who should be accepted (erroneous rejection). These kinds of errors can be avoided by using measurement procedures that are reliable and valid.

A measurement is considered reliable if it is consistent or stable, for example, in the following ways:

- **Over time**—such as on a hearing test administered first on Monday morning and then again on Friday night
- **Across different samples of items**—say, on form A and form B of a test of mathematical aptitude; or on a measure of vocational interests administered at the beginning of a student's sophomore year in college and then again at the end of her or his senior year
- **Across different raters or judges working independently**—as in a gymnastics competition

As you might suspect, inconsistency is present to some degree in all measurement situations. In employment settings, people generally are assessed only once. That is, organizations give them, for example, one test of their knowledge of a job or one application form or one interview. The procedures through which these assessments are made must be standardized in terms of content, administration, and scoring. Only then can the results of the assessments be compared meaningfully with one another. Those who desire more specific information about how reliability is estimated in quantitative terms should consult the Technical Appendix at the end of this chapter.

Validity of Measurement

Reliability is certainly an important characteristic of any measurement procedure, but it is simply a means to an end, a step along the way to a goal. Unless a measure is reliable, it cannot be valid. This is so because unless a measure produces consistent, dependable, stable scores, we cannot begin to understand what implications high versus low scores have for later job performance and economic returns to the organization. Such understanding is the goal of the validation process. From a practical point of view, validity refers to the job-relatedness of a measure—that is, the strength of the relationship between scores from the measure and some indicator or rating of actual job performance.[7]

Although evidence of validity may be accumulated in many ways, validity always refers to the degree to which the evidence supports inferences that are drawn from scores or ratings on a selection procedure. It is the inferences regarding the specific use of a selection procedure that are validated, not the procedure itself.[8] Hence a user must first specify exactly why he or she intends to use a particular selection procedure (that is, what inferences he or she intends to draw from it). Then the user can make an informed judgment about the adequacy of the available evidence of validity in support of that particular selection procedure when used for a particular purpose.

Scientific standards for validation are described in greater detail in *Principles for the Validation and Use of Personnel Selection Procedures*,[9] and legal standards for validation are contained in the *Uniform Guidelines on Employee Selection Procedures*.[10] For those who desire an overview of the various strategies used to validate employee selection procedures, see the Technical Appendix at the end of the chapter.

Quantitative evidence of validity is often expressed in terms of a correlation coefficient (that may assume values between –1 and +1) between scores on a predictor of later job performance (e.g., a test or an interview) and a criterion that reflects actual job performance (e.g., supervisory ratings, dollar volume of sales). In employment contexts, predictor validities typically vary between about .20 and .50. In the following sections we will consider some of the most commonly used methods for screening and selection decisions, together with validity evidence for each one.

SCREENING AND SELECTION METHODS

Employment Application Forms

Particularly when unemployment is high, organizations find themselves deluged with applications for employment for only a small number of available jobs. As an example, consider that a typical public utility company receives about 75 applications a day (each of which must be screened), interviews about 4 of the 75 applicants, and selects maybe 1 of the 4. A considerable number of staff-hours are required just for screening these applications. Alaska Airlines attempted to cause applicants to screen themselves before applying for 40 jobs as flight attendants. How did it do that? By charging applicants a $10 fee for filing an application for employment. More than 5000 people applied and paid the filing fee![11] Other airlines noticed. Now they too charge each job applicant a $10 "processing fee."[12] It is not clear whether such fees discourage any applicants, but at least the companies can recover some of the costs associated with screening them.

An important requirement of all employment application forms is that they ask only for information that is valid and fair with respect to the nature of the job. Studies of application forms used by more than 200 organizations indicated that, for the most part, the questions required information that was job-related and necessary for the employment decision.[13] On the other hand, more than 95 percent of the forms included one or more legally indefensible questions.

Companies must review employment application forms regularly to be sure that the information they require complies with equal employment opportunity

ETHICAL DILEMMA
Are Work History Omissions Unethical?

Consider this situation: A job applicant knowingly omits some previous work history on a company's application form, even though the form asks applicants to provide a complete list of previous jobs. However, the applicant is truthful about the dates of previous jobs he does report. He leaves it to the interviewer to discover and to ask about the gaps in his work history. The interviewer fails to ask about the gaps. Is the job applicant's behavior unethical?

guidelines and case law. For example, under the Americans with Disabilities Act of 1990, an employer may not ask a general question about disabilities on an application form, or whether an applicant has ever filed a workers' compensation claim. However, at a preemployment interview, after describing the essential functions of a job, an employer may ask if there is any physical or mental reason why the candidate cannot perform the essential functions. Consider deleting the following types of questions from application forms:[14]

- Any question that might lead to an adverse impact on the employment of members of groups protected under civil rights law
- Any question that cannot be demonstrated to be job-related or that does not concern a bona fide occupational qualification
- Any question that could possibly constitute an invasion of privacy

Some organizations have sought to identify statistically significant relationships between responses to questions on application forms and later measures of job performance (e.g., tenure, absenteeism, theft). Such "weighted application blanks" (WABs) are often highly predictive, yielding validities in the range of .25 to .50.[15] In one study, for example, researchers examined 28 objective questions for a random sample of the employment applications representing 243 current and former circulation-route managers at a metropolitan daily newspaper.[16] A statistical procedure (multiple regression analysis) was used to identify which people were most likely to stay on the job for more than 1 year (the break-even point for employee orientation and training costs). Several interesting findings resulted from the study:

1. Questions on the WAB that best predicted time on the job at the beginning of the study did not predict time on the job several years later. Hence, it is necessary to recheck WAB questions periodically.
2. The statistical analysis showed that items that "conventional wisdom" might suggest or those used by interviewers did not predict employee turnover accurately.
3. An independent check of a new sample of job candidates showed that the WAB was able to identify employees who would stay on the job longer than 1 year in 83 percent of the cases.

VIDEO RÉSUMÉS?

Yes, they're here—but maybe not to stay. With the popularity of videocassette recorders at home and at work, the video résumé may seem like an inevitable development. Candidates can look their best, rehearse answers to questions, and, in general, present themselves in the "best possible light."

These efforts, however, get mixed reviews from employers and recruiters, many of whom consider video résumés to be costly gimmicks that fail to provide as much useful information as an ordinary résumé. Here are some of their objections: answers are shallow rather than in-depth, the videos take considerable time to review, and they could cause legal problems for employers who reject candidates from protected groups. As the director of human resources for Apple Computer noted: "We get 9000 résumés a month; we don't have time to watch videos when we're going through our screening process."[17] Stay tuned for future developments.

4. The length of the time employees stayed on previous jobs was unrelated to their length of stay on their current job.
5. The best predictors were "experience as a sales representative," "business school education," and "never previously worked for this company."

Executives balk at spending time and money on human resource research. Nevertheless, poor hires are expensive. SmithKline Beecham Corporation spends an average of $10,000 to recruit and train each worker.[18] That's $1 million for every 100 workers hired. Those kinds of numbers often tend to cast new light on this neglected area.

Recommendations and Reference Checks

Recommendations and reference checks are commonly used to screen outside job applicants. They can provide four kinds of information about a job applicant: (1) education and employment history, (2) character and interpersonal competence, (3) ability to perform the job, and (4) the willingness of the past or current employer to rehire the applicant.

A recommendation or reference check will be meaningful, however, only if the person providing it (1) has had an adequate opportunity to observe the applicant in job-relevant situations, (2) is competent to evaluate the applicant's job performance, (3) can express such an evaluation in a way that is meaningful to the prospective employer, and (4) is completely candid.[19]

Unfortunately, evidence is beginning to show that there is little candor, and thus little value, in written recommendations and referrals, especially those that must, by law, be revealed to applicants if they petition to see them. Specifically, the Family Educational Rights and Privacy Act of 1974 (the Buckley amendment) gives students the legal right to see all letters of recommendation written about them. It also permits release of information about a student only to people approved by the student at the time of the request.

Research suggests that if letters of recommendation are to be meaningful, they should contain the following information:[20]

1. Degree of writer familiarity with the candidate—time known, and time observed per week.
2. Degree of writer familiarity with the job in question. To help the writer make this judgment, the reader should supply to the writer a description of the job in question.
3. Specific examples of performance—goals, task difficulty, work environment, and extent of cooperation from coworkers.
4. Individuals or groups to whom the candidate is compared.

When seeking information about a candidate from references, consider the following guidelines:[21]

- Request job-related information only; put it in written form to prove that your hire or no-hire decision was based on relevant information.
- Obtain job candidates' written permission to check references prior to doing so.
- Stay away from subjective areas, such as the candidate's personality.
- Evaluate the credibility of the source of the reference material. Under most circumstances, an evaluation by a past immediate supervisor will be more credible than an evaluation by an HR representative.
- Wherever possible, use public records to evaluate on-the-job behavior or personal conduct—e.g., records regarding criminal and civil litigation, driving, or bankruptcy.
- Remember that the courts have ruled that a reference check of an applicant's prior employment record does not violate his or her civil rights as long as the information provided relates solely to work behavior and to reasons for leaving a previous job.

What should you do if you are asked to provide reference information? Here are some useful guidelines:

- Obtain written consent from the employee prior to providing reference data. Fully 89 percent of respondents in a recent survey said they do this now.[22]
- Do not blacklist former employees.
- Keep a written record of all released information.
- Make no subjective statements, such as "He's got a bad attitude." Be specific, such as "He was formally disciplined three times last year for fighting at work."
- So long as you know the facts and have records to back you up, you can feel free to challenge an ex-employee's ability or integrity. But official records are not always candid. A file might show that an executive "resigned," but not that the company avoided a scandal by letting him quit instead of firing him for dishonesty. When there is no supporting data, never even whisper about the employee's "sticky fingers."[23]
- If you are contacted by phone, use a telephone "call-back" procedure to verify information provided on a job application by a former employee. Ask the caller to give her or his name, title, company name, and the nature and purpose of the request. Next, obtain the written consent of the employee to release the information. Finally, call back the company by phone. Do not

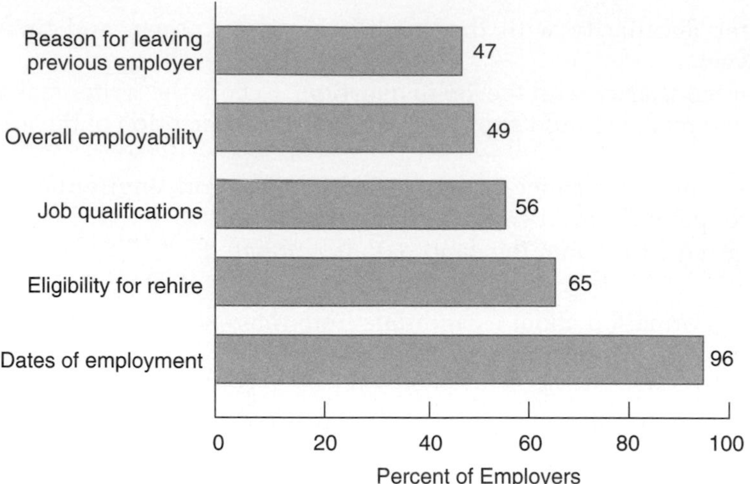

Figure 6-2
Information most commonly sought in a reference check. For example, 65 percent of the employers sampled reported that they ask specifically whether a candidate is eligible to be rehired by a former employer. (*Source:* J. Click, SHRM survey highlights dilemmas of reference checks, *HR News,* July 1995, p. 13.)

volunteer any information; say only whether or not the information the caller already has is correct.

- Release only the following general types of information (subject to written consent of the employee): dates of employment, job titles during employment and time in each position, promotions, demotions, attendance record, salary, and reason for termination (no details, just the reason).

Sweetening of résumés and previous work history is common. How common? It has been reported that 20 to 25 percent of all résumés and job applications include at least one major fabrication.[24] The lesson: Always verify key aspects of previous history.

What is the current status of reference checking in practice? In a recent survey, fully two-thirds of companies reported that it has become harder to check applicants' references. Some 44 percent said that a former employer's reluctance to comment hurts applicants' chances of being hired.[25] In large measure this reluctance is due to a series of well-publicized suits for slander, such as the $25 million in punitive damages received by a former employee of John Hancock Company and the $250,000 award upheld by a federal appeals court in Washington, D.C., against a construction company for giving a poor job reference based on hearsay.[26]

On the other hand, employers can be held liable for negligent hiring if they fail to check closely enough on a prospective employee who then commits a crime in the course of performing his or her job duties. The employer becomes liable if it knew, or should have known, about the applicant's unfitness to perform the job in question.[27]

Currently, an employer has no legal duty or obligation to provide information to prospective employers. However, if an employer's policy is to disclose reference information, providing false or speculative information could be grounds for a lawsuit.[28] Reference checking is not an infringement on privacy when fair reference-checking practices are used. It is a sound evaluative tool that can provide objectivity for employers and fairness for job applicants. Figure 6-2 shows the kinds of employment information checked most often.

THE USE OF TESTS AND INVENTORIES IN SELECTION

Organizations evaluate and select job candidates on the basis of the results of psychological measurements. The term "measurements" is used here in the broad sense, to include tests and inventories. Tests are standardized measures of behavior (e.g., math, vocabulary) that have right and wrong answers, while inventories are standardized measures of behavior (e.g., interests, attitudes, opinions) that do not have right and wrong answers. Inventories can be falsified to present an image that a candidate thinks a prospective employer is looking for. Tests cannot be falsified. In the context of personnel selection, tests are preferable, for obvious reasons. Inventories are probably best used for purposes of placement or development because in those contexts there is less motivation for a job candidate to present an image other than what he or she really is. Nevertheless, as we will see, inventories have been used (with modest success) in selection. Following is a brief description of available methods and techniques, together with an assessment of their track records to date.

Drug Testing

Drug screening tests, which began in the military and spread to the sports world, are now becoming more common in employment. Fully 70 percent of large companies now make preemployment drug testing a regular part of their prehire procedures.[29]

Critics charge that such screening violates an individual's right to privacy and that frequently the tests are inaccurate.[30] Employers counter that the widespread abuse of drugs is reason enough for wider testing.

Do the results of such drug tests forecast certain aspects of later job performance? In the largest reported study of its kind, the U.S. Postal Service took urine samples from 5465 job applicants. It never used the results to make hiring decisions and did not tell local managers of the findings. When the data were examined 6 months to a year later, workers who had tested positive prior to employment were absent 41 percent more often and were fired 38 percent more often than those who had not tested positive. There were no differences in turnover between those who tested positive and those who did not. These results held up even after adjustment for factors such as age, sex, and race. As a result, the Postal Service is now implementing preemployment drug testing nationwide.[31] A later review found that absenteeism and involuntary turnover are the outcomes that drug testing forecasts most accurately.[32]

Is such drug testing legal? In two rulings in 1989, the Supreme Court upheld the constitutionality of (1) the government regulations that require railroad crews involved in accidents to submit to prompt urinalysis and blood tests and (2) urine tests for U.S. Customs Service employees seeking drug enforcement posts. The extent to which such rulings will be limited to safety-sensitive positions has yet to be clarified by the Court. Nevertheless, an employer has a legal right to ensure that employees perform their jobs competently and that no employee endangers the safety of other workers. So if illegal drug use either on or off the job may reduce job performance and endanger coworkers, the employer has adequate legal grounds for conducting drug tests.

To avoid legal challenge, companies should consider instituting the following commonsense procedures:[33]

1. Inform all employees and job applicants, in writing, of the company's policy regarding drug use.
2. Include the policy, and the possibility of testing, in all employment contracts.
3. Present the program in a medical and safety context. That is, state that drug screening will help improve the health of employees and will also help ensure a safer workplace.
4. Check the testing laboratory's experience, its analytical methods, and the way it protects the security and identity of each sample.
5. If drug testing will be used with employees as well as job applicants, tell employees in advance that it will be a routine part of their employment.
6. If drug testing is done, it should be uniform—that is, it should apply to managers as well as nonmanagers.

COMPANY EXAMPLE

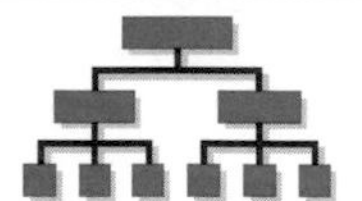

PERFORMANCE FACTORS INC. (PFI)

PFI has designed an innovative, computer-based assessment program to determine an employee's fitness for work. PFI's Factor 1000 software, which tests a worker's hand-eye coordination, could provide an effective alternative to blood tests and urinalysis, which many regard as an invasion of personal privacy. The test, which demands considerable concentration and skill, requires the employee to center a moving object between two posts on the computer screen; employees are able to manipulate the object by turning a small knob while the computer monitors and records their performance. Results of each employee's performance are compared with a companywide baseline average.

One company that uses Factor 1000 is Silicon Valley's Ion Implant Services, Inc. Each day before work, delivery drivers line up to stand in front of a computer to play the short video game. But it is not a game. Unless the machine prints a receipt confirming that the drivers have passed the video test, they cannot climb behind the wheel.

Does Factor 1000 work? According to *Business Week*, R. F. White, a California petroleum distributor, used Factor 1000 for a year and found that accidents dropped 67 percent, errors fell 92 percent, and workers' compensation claims declined 64 percent. Not surprisingly, PFI's business has been good. It now tests workers who perform a range of tasks, from machine tooling to driving tour buses to handling poisonous gases and high-voltage equipment (*Business Week*, June 3, 1996, p. 36).

Two Controversial Selection Techniques

Handwriting Analysis

Handwriting analysis (graphology) is reportedly used as a hiring tool by 85 percent of all European companies.[34] In Israel, graphology is more widespread than any other personality measurement. Its use is clearly not as widespread in the United States, although sources estimate that more than 3000 U.S. firms retain handwriting analysts as employment consultants. Such firms generally require job applicants to provide a one-page writing sample. Experts then examine it (at a cost of $60 to $500) for 3 to 10 hours. They assess more than 300 personality traits, including enthusiasm, imagination, and ambition.[35] Are the analysts' predictions valid? In one study involving the prediction of sales success, 103 writers supplied two samples of their handwriting—one "neutral" in content, the second autobiographical. The data were then analyzed by 20 professional graphologists to predict supervisors' ratings of each salesperson's job performance, each salesperson's own ratings of his or her job performance, and sales productivity. The results indicated that the type of script sample did not make any difference. There was some evidence of interrater agreement, but there was no evidence for the validity of the graphologists' predictions.[36] Similar findings have been reported in other well-controlled studies.[37] In short, there is little to recommend the use of handwriting analysis as a predictor of job performance.

Polygraph Examinations

Polygraph (literally, "many pens") examinations are quick and inexpensive ($25 to $50 per person) in comparison with reference checks or background investigations ($100 to $500 and up, depending on the degree of detail required). Professional polygraphers claim their tests are accurate in more than 90 percent of criminal and employment cases if interpreted by a competent examiner. Critics claim that the tests are accurate only two-thirds of the time and are far more likely to be unreliable for a subject who is telling the truth.[38]

Prior to 1988, some 2 million polygraph tests were administered each year, 98 percent in private industry.[39] However, a federal law passed in 1988, the Employee Polygraph Protection Act, severely restricts the use of polygraphs in the employment context (except in the case of firms providing security services and those manufacturing controlled substances). It permits polygraph examinations of current employees only under very restricted circumstances. The prohibition is a huge setback for the polygraph industry, causing it to lose about 85 percent of its $100 million in annual revenues.[40] Indeed, arbitrators had long held that the refusal of an employee to submit to a polygraph exam does not constitute "just cause" for discharge, even when the employee has agreed in advance (e.g., on a job application) to do so on request.[41]

Integrity Tests

According to a congressional study, crime increases retail prices by 15 percent.[42] "Shrinkage"—an industry term for losses due to bookkeeping errors and employee, customer, and vendor theft—is estimated to make up almost 2 percent of annual sales.[43] With statistics like these, it should come as no surprise that written integrity tests are being used by an estimated 25 percent of employers.[44] They are of two types.[45] Overt integrity tests (clear-purpose tests) are designed to assess directly attitudes toward dishonest behaviors. The second type, personality-based measures (disguised-purpose tests) aim to predict a broad range of counterproductive behaviors at work (disciplinary problems, violence on the job, excessive absenteeism, and drug abuse, in addition to theft).

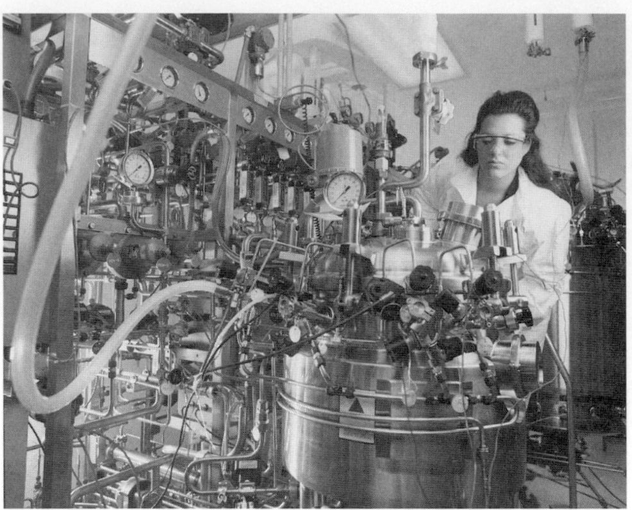

High levels of mental ability are important for knowledge workers.

Do they work? Yes—as a meta-analysis (a statistical cumulation of research results across studies) of 665 validity coefficients that used 576,460 test takers demonstrated. The average validity of the tests, when used to predict supervisory ratings of performance, was .41. The results for overt integrity and personality-based tests were similar. However, the average validity of overt tests for predicting theft per se was much lower—.13. For personality-based tests, there were no validity estimates available for the prediction of theft alone. Thus theft appears to be less predictable than broadly counterproductive behaviors, at least by overt integrity tests. Finally, since there is no correlation between race and integrity test scores, such tests might well be used in combination with general mental ability test scores to constitute a broader selection procedure.[46]

Despite these encouraging findings, at least three key issues have yet to be resolved:[47] (1) there are almost no data regarding the types of classification errors made by these measures; (2) while fakability or impression management has been observed on honesty tests,[48] many such tests do not contain lie scales to detect response distortion; and (3) many writers in the field apply the same language and logic to integrity testing as to ability testing. Yet there is an important difference: while it is possible for an individual with poor moral behavior to "go straight," it is certainly less likely that an individual who has demonstrated a lack of intelligence will "go smart." If they are honest about their past, therefore, reformed individuals with a criminal past may be "locked into" low scores on integrity tests (and therefore be subject to classification error). Thus the broad validation evidence that is often acceptable for cognitive ability tests may not hold up in the public policy domain for integrity tests.

Mental Ability Tests

The major types of mental ability tests used in business today include measures of general intelligence; verbal, nonverbal, and numerical skills; spatial relations ability (the ability to visualize the effects of manipulating or changing the position of objects); motor functions (speed, coordination); mechanical information, reasoning, and comprehension; clerical aptitudes (perceptual speed tests); and

Well-developed social skills coupled with moderate levels of mental ability are important for workers in customer-service jobs.

inductive reasoning (the ability to draw general conclusions on the basis of specific facts). When job analysis shows that the abilities or aptitudes measured by such tests are important for successful job performance, the tests are among the most valid predictors currently available (see Figure 6-3 and Table 6-1). For administrative convenience and for reasons of efficiency, many tests today are administered on personal computers. While there are obvious advantages to computer-based tests, it is important to ensure that they measure the same characteristics as the paper-and-pencil versions of the same tests.[49]

With respect to the selection of managers, 70 years of research indicate that successful managers are forecast most accurately by tests of their intellectual ability, by their ability to draw conclusions from verbal or numerical information, and by their interests.[50] Further research has found two other types of mental abilities that are related to successful performance as a manager: fluency with words and spatial relations ability.[51]

Validity Generalization

A traditional belief of testing experts is that validity is situation-specific. That is, a test with a demonstrated validity in one setting (e.g., selecting bus drivers in St. Louis) might not be valid in another, similar setting (e.g., selecting bus drivers in Atlanta), possibly as a result of differences in specific job tasks, duties, and behaviors. Thus it would seem that the same test used to predict bus driver success in St. Louis and in Atlanta would have to be validated separately in each city.

Two decades of research have cast serious doubt on this assumption.[52] In fact, it has been shown that the major reason for the variation in validity coefficients across settings is the size of the samples—they were too small. When the effect of sampling error is removed, the validities observed for similar test-job combinations across settings do not differ significantly. In short, the results of a validity study conducted in one situation can be generalized to other situations as long as it can be shown that jobs in the two situations are similar.

Since thousands of studies have been done on the prediction of job performance, validity generalization allows us to use this database to establish definite values for the average validity of most predictors. The average validities for predictors commonly in use are shown in Table 6-1.

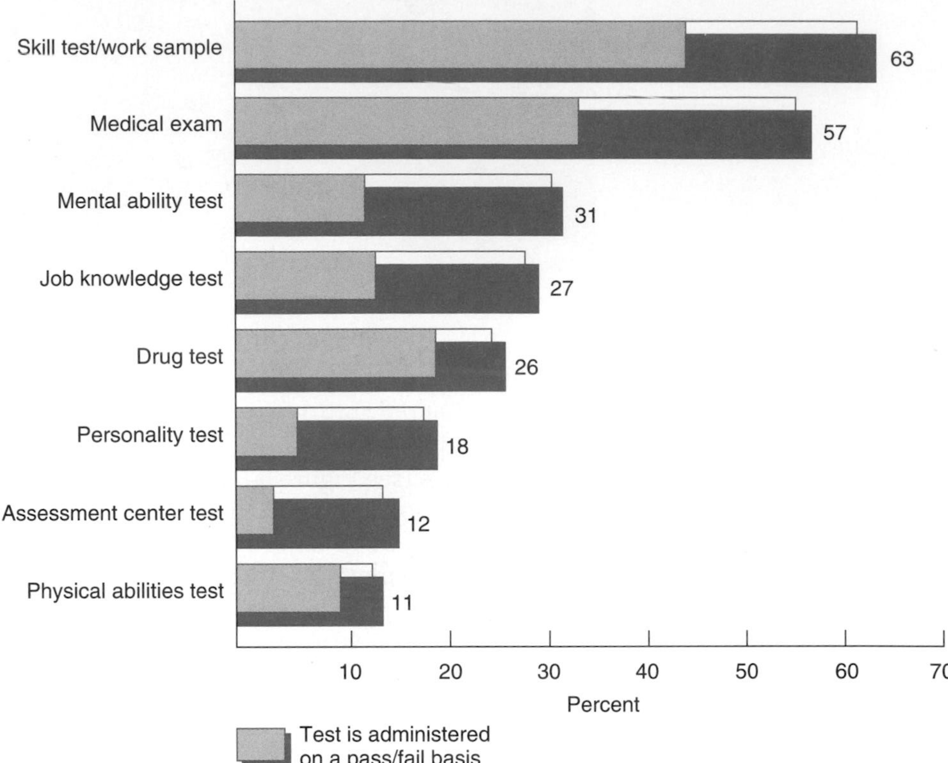

Figure 6-3
Most common tests and examinations used for selection. Note that the white rectangles within each category of test indicate the percentage of companies using pass/fail scoring. (*Source:* Bureau of National Affairs, Recruiting and selection procedures, *PPF Survey 146*, May 1988, Washington, DC: Bureau of National Affairs, p. 18.)

Objective Personality and Interest Inventories

Objective personality and interest inventories provide a clear stimulus, such as statements about preferences for various ways of behaving, and a clear set of responses from which to choose. Here is an example of an objective measure of personality; the examinee's task is to select the alternatives that are most (M) and least (L) descriptive of herself or himself:

Prefers to get up early in the morning	M	L
Does not get enough exercise	M	L
Follows a well-balanced diet	M	L
Does not care for popular music	M	L

Ever since 1944, Sears has used objective personality and interest inventories as part of a larger "executive battery" of measures to predict management success. It has done so very successfully.[53] Measures of "general activity" have proved especially accurate, as have measures of conscientiousness, dependability, imagination, ambition, and sociability.[54] In fact, when job analysis informa-

Table 6-1

AVERAGE VALIDITIES OF ALTERNATIVE PREDICTORS OF JOB PERFORMANCE

Entry level + training		Current performance used to predict future performance	
Cognitive ability tests	.53	Work-sample tests	.54
Job tryout	.44	Cognitive ability tests	.53
Biographical inventories	.37	Peer ratings	.49
Reference checks	.26	Ratings of the quality of performance in past work experience (behavioral consistency ratings)	
Experience	.18	Job knowledge tests	.48
Interview	.14	Assessment centers	.43
Ratings of training and experience	.13		
Academic achievement	.11		
Amount of education	.10		
Interest	.10		
Age	−.01		

Source: J. E. Hunter & R. E. Hunter, Validity and utility of alternative predictors of job performance, *Psychological Bulletin*, *96*, 1984, 72–98.

tion is used explicitly to select personality measures, their average validity is a respectable .38.[55]

Projective Measures

Projective measures present an individual with ambiguous stimuli (primarily visual) and allow him or her to respond in an open-ended fashion (Figure 6-4), for example, by telling a story regarding what is happening in the picture. Based on how the individual structures the situation through the story he or she tells, an examiner (usually a clinical psychologist) makes inferences concerning the individual's personality structure.

Basically, the difference between an objective and a projective test is this: in an objective test, the test taker tries to guess what the examiner is thinking; in a projective test, the examiner tries to guess what the test taker is thinking.[56]

Although early research showed projective measures not to be accurate predictors of management success,[57] they can provide useful results when the examinee's responses are related to motivation to manage (e.g., achievement motivation, willingness to accept a leadership role).[58] Moreover, measures of intelligence are unrelated to scores on projective tests. So a combination of both types of instruments can provide a fuller picture of individual "can-do" (intelligence) and "will-do" (motivational) factors than can either one used alone.

Measures of Leadership Ability

At first glance, one might suspect that measures of leadership ability are highly predictive of managerial success since they appear to tap a critical management job requirement directly. Scales designed to measure two key aspects of leadership behavior, consideration and initiating structure, have been developed and

Figure 6-4
Sample projective stimulus. Candidates are told to look at the picture briefly and then to write the story it suggests. Stories are scored in terms of the key themes expressed.

used in many situations. Consideration reflects management actions oriented toward developing mutual trust, respect for subordinates' ideas, and consideration of their feelings. Initiating structure, on the other hand, reflects the extent to which an individual defines and structures her or his role and those of her or his subordinates toward task accomplishment.

Unfortunately, questionnaires designed to measure consideration and initiating structure have been inaccurate predictors of success in management.[59] This is not to imply that leadership is unimportant in managerial jobs. Rather, it may be that the majority of such jobs are designed to encourage and reward managing (doing things right) rather than leading (doing the right things).

Personal-History Data

On the basis of the assumption that one of the best predictors of what a person will do in the future is what he or she has done in the past, biographical information has been used widely and successfully as one basis for staffing decisions. As with any other method, careful, competent research is necessary if "biodata" are to prove genuinely useful as predictors of job success.[60] For example, items that are more objective and verifiable are less likely to be faked.[61]

Many professionals resist taking preemployment tests, arguing "My record speaks for itself." The accomplishment record inventory, a biodata instrument, lets those records speak systematically.[62] Job candidates describe their accomplishments, in writing, in each job dimension that job analysis shows to be essential (e.g., for attorneys, technical knowledge, research/investigating, assertive advocacy). Raters then use scales developed (by incumbents) for each dimension to evaluate the accomplishments. Research with five types of jobs (attorneys, librarians, economists, research analysts, and supervisors) yielded validities ranging from .22 to .45 and no adverse impact against protected groups.[63] The approach is legally defensible, results-oriented, and highly job-related, and it elicits unique, job-relevant information from each person. Not surprisingly, therefore, it is getting lots of attention.

Employment Interviews

Employment interviewing is a difficult mental and social task. Managing a smooth social exchange while instantaneously processing information about a job candidate makes interviewing uniquely difficult among all managerial tasks.[64] Researchers have been studying the employment interview for more than 60 years for two purposes: (1) to determine the reliability (consistency) and validity (accuracy) of employment decisions based on assessments derived from interviews, and (2) to discover the various psychological factors that influence interviewer judgments. Hundreds of research articles on these issues have been published, along with periodic reviews of the "state of the art" of interviewing research and practice.[65] Until recently, the employment interview was considered an unreliable basis for employment decisions (note that in Table 6-1 the average validity for interviews is only .14). However, research is beginning to indicate that the interview works well when:

1. The interview is limited to information that a prior job analysis indicates is important for successful job performance.
2. Interviewers are trained to evaluate behavior objectively.
3. The interview is conducted along a specific set of guidelines.[66]

The interview remains a poor basis for employment decisions to the extent that interviewers' decisions are overly influenced by such factors as first impressions, personal feelings about the kinds of characteristics that lead to success on the job, and contrast effects, among other nonobjective factors. *Contrast effects* describe a tendency among interviewers to evaluate a current candidate's interview performance relative to those that immediately preceded it. If a first candidate received a very positive evaluation and a second candidate is just "average," interviewers tend to evaluate the second candidate more negatively than is deserved. The second candidate's performance is "contrasted" to that of the first.

Finally, research indicates that when interviewers' evaluations of job candidates are in the form of specific predictions of job behavior rather than in terms of general impressions about each candidate, less distortion between actual and perceived interview behavior is found. Employers are therefore likely to achieve nonbiased hiring decisions if they concentrate on shaping interviewer behavior.[67]

One way to shape interviewer behavior is to establish a specific system for conducting the employment interview. Here are some factors to consider in setting up such a system:[68]

- Determine the requirements of the job through a job analysis that considers the input of the incumbent along with the inputs of the supervisor and the HR representative.
- To know what to look for in applicants, focus only on the competencies necessary for the job. Be sure to distinguish between entry-level and full-performance competencies.
- Screen résumés and application forms by focusing on (1) key words that match job requirements, (2) quantifiers and qualifiers that show whether applicants have these requirements, and (3) skills that might transfer from previous jobs to the new job.
- Develop interview questions that are based strictly on the job analysis results; use open-ended questions (those that cannot be answered with a simple yes or no response); and use questions relevant to the individual's ability to perform, motivation to do a good job, and overall fit with the firm.
- Consider asking "What would you do if . . . ?" questions. Such questions constitute the situational interview, which is based on the assumption that a person's expressed behavioral intentions are related to subsequent behavior. In the situational interview, candidates are asked to describe how they think they would respond in certain job-related situations. Alternatively, in an experience-based interview, they are asked to provide detailed accounts of actual situations. For example, instead of asking "How would you reprimand an employee?" the interviewer might say, "Give me a specific example of a time you had to reprimand an employee. What action did you take, and what was the result?" Answers tend to be remarkably consistent with actual (subsequent) job behavior.[69] Validities for both types of interviews vary from about .22 to .28.[70]
- Conduct the interview in a relaxed physical setting. Begin by putting the applicant at ease with simple questions and general information about the organization and the position being filled. Throughout, note all nonverbal cues, such as "body language" and type of facial expressions, as possible indicators of the candidate's interest in and ability to do the job.
- To evaluate applicants, develop a form containing a list of competencies weighted for overall importance to the job, and evaluate each applicant relative to each competency.

A systematic interview developed along these lines will minimize the uncertainty so inherent in decision making that is based predominantly on "gut feeling." Table 6-2 shows some examples of proper and improper interview questions, along with several examples of situational-type questions.

Peer Assessment

In the typical peer assessment procedure, raters are asked to predict how well a peer will do if placed in a leadership or managerial role. Such information can be enlightening, since peers evaluate managerial behavior from a different perspective than do managers themselves. Actually, the term *peer assessment* is a general term denoting three basic methods that members of a well-defined group use in judging each other's performance. *Peer nomination* requires each group member to designate a certain number of group members as highest or lowest on a performance dimension. *Peer rating* requires each group member to

Table 6-2

EXAMPLES OF PROPER AND IMPROPER QUESTIONS IN EMPLOYMENT INTERVIEWS

Issue	Proper	Improper
Criminal history	Have you ever been convicted of a violation of a law?	Have you ever been arrested?
Marital status	None	Are you married? Do you prefer Ms., Miss, or Mrs.? What does your spouse do for a living?
National origin	None	Where were you born? Where were your parents born?
Disability	None	Do you have any disabilities or handicaps? Do you have any health problems?
Sexual orientation	None	Whom do you live with? Do you ever intend to marry?
Citizenship status	Do you have a legal right to work in the United States?	Are you a U.S. citizen? Are you an alien?
Situational questions	(Assumption: Job analysis has shown such questions to be job-related) How do you plan to keep up with current developments in your field? How do you measure your customers' satisfaction with your product or services? If you were a product, how would you position yourself?	

rate the performance of every other group member. *Peer ranking* requires each group member to rank the performance of all other members from best to worst.

Reviews of more than 50 studies found all three methods of peer assessment to be reliable, valid, and free from bias.[71] Peer assessments do predict job advancement.[72] However, since implicitly, they require people to consider privileged information about their coworkers, it is essential that peers be thoroughly involved in the planning and design of the peer assessment method to be used.

Work-Sample Tests

Work-sample, or situational, tests are standardized measures of behavior whose primary objective is to assess the ability to do rather than the ability to know. Such tests may assess motor skills, involving physical manipulation of things (e.g., trade tests for carpenters, plumbers, electricians), or verbal skills, involving problem situations that are primarily language-oriented or people-oriented (e.g., situational tests for supervisory jobs).[73] Since work samples are miniature replicas of actual job requirements, they are difficult to fake, and they are unlikely to lead to charges of discrimination or invasion of privacy. Moreover, since the content of the test reflects the essential content of the job, the tests have content-oriented evidence of validity. Their use in one study of 263 applicants for city government jobs led to a reduction of turnover from 40 percent to less than 3 percent in the 9 to 26 months following their introduction. The reduction in turnover saved the city more than $720,000 in 1996 dollars.[74]

Nevertheless, since each candidate must be tested individually, work-sample tests are probably not cost-effective when large numbers of people must be evaluated.

Two types of situational tests are used to evaluate and select managers: group exercises, in which participants are placed in a situation where the successful completion of a task requires interaction among the participants, and individual exercises, in which participants complete a task independently. The following sections consider three of the most popular situational tests: the leaderless group discussion, the in-basket test, and the business game.

Leaderless Group Discussion (LGD)

The LGD is simple and has been used for decades. A group of participants is given a job-related topic and is asked simply to carry on a discussion about it for a period of time. No one is appointed leader, nor is anyone told where to sit. Instead of a rectangular table (with a "head" at each end), a circular table is often used so that each position carries equal weight. Observers rate the performance of each participant.

For example, IBM uses an LGD in which each participant is required to make a 5-minute oral presentation of a candidate for promotion and then subsequently defend her or his candidate in a group discussion with five other participants. All roles are well defined and structured. Seven characteristics are rated, each on a 5-point scale of effectiveness: aggressiveness, persuasiveness or selling ability, oral communication, self-confidence, resistance to stress, energy level, and interpersonal contact.[75]

LGD ratings have forecast managerial performance accurately in virtually all the functional areas of business.[76] Previous LGD experience appears to have little effect on present LGD performance, although prior training clearly does.[77] Individuals in one study who received a 15-minute briefing on the history, development, rating instruments, and research relative to the LGD were rated significantly higher than untrained individuals. To control for this, all those with prior training in LGD should be put into the same groups.

In-Basket Test

A situational test designed to simulate important aspects of a position, the in-basket tests an individual's ability to work independently. In general, it takes the following form:

> It consists of the letters, memoranda, notes of incoming telephone calls, and other materials which have supposedly collected in the in-basket of an administrative officer. The subject who takes the test is given appropriate background information concerning the school, business, military unit, or whatever institution is involved. He is told that he is the new incumbent of the administrative position and that he is to deal with the material in the in-basket. The background information is sufficiently detailed that the subject can reasonably be expected to take action on many of the problems presented by the in-basket documents. The subject is instructed that he is not to play a role, he is not to pretend to be someone else. He is to bring to the new job his own background of knowledge and experience, his own personality, and he is to deal with the problems as though he were really the incumbent of the administrative position. He is not to say what he would do; he is actually to write letters and memoranda, prepare agenda for meetings, make notes and reminders for himself, as though he were actually on the job.[78]

Some sample in-basket items are shown in Figure 6-5.

Although the situation is relatively unstructured, each candidate faces the same complex set of materials. At the conclusion of the in-basket test, each candidate leaves behind a packet full of notes, memos, letters, etc., that provide a record of his or her behavior. The test is then scored by describing (if the purpose is development) or evaluating (if the purpose is selection for promotion) what the candidate did in terms of such dimensions as self-confidence, organizational and planning abilities, written communications, decision making, risk taking, and administrative abilities. The dimensions to be evaluated are identified through job analysis prior to designing or selecting the exercise. The major advantages of the in-basket, therefore, are its flexibility (it can be designed to fit many different types of situations and modes of administration, such as via computer[79]) and the fact that it permits direct observation of individual behavior within the context of a job-relevant, standardized problem situation.

More than 25 years of research on the in-basket indicate that it validly forecasts subsequent job behavior and promotion.[80] Moreover, since performance on the LGD is not strongly related to performance on the in-basket, in combination they are potentially powerful predictors of managerial success.

Business Games

The business game is a situational test, a living case in which candidates play themselves, not an assigned role, and are evaluated within a group. Like the in-basket, business games are available for a wide variety of executive activities, from marketing to capital asset management. They may be simple (focusing on very specific activities) or complex models of complete organizational systems. They may be computer-based or manually operated, rigidly programmed or flexible.[81] They will probably be used more frequently for training purposes, given the continued development and availability of personal computers and simulation software—for example, stock market simulations and battle simulations for military academies.

COMPANY EXAMPLE

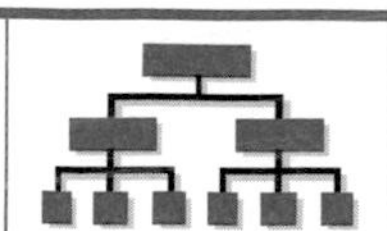

IBM'S MANUFACTURING PROBLEM

In the exercise used at IBM, six participants must work together as a group to operate a manufacturing company. They must purchase raw materials, manufacture a product, and sell it in the market. Included in the exercise are a product forecast and specific prices (that fluctuate during the exercise) for raw materials and completed products. No preassigned roles are given to the participants, but each one is rated in terms of aggressiveness, persuasiveness or selling ability, resistance to stress, energy level, interpersonal contact, administrative ability, and risk taking. In one IBM study, performance on the manufacturing problem accurately forecast changes in position level for 94 middle managers 3 years later.[82] When the in-basket score was added as an additional predictor, the forecast was even more accurate.

Business games have several advantages. One, they compress time; events that might not actually occur for months or years are made to occur in a matter

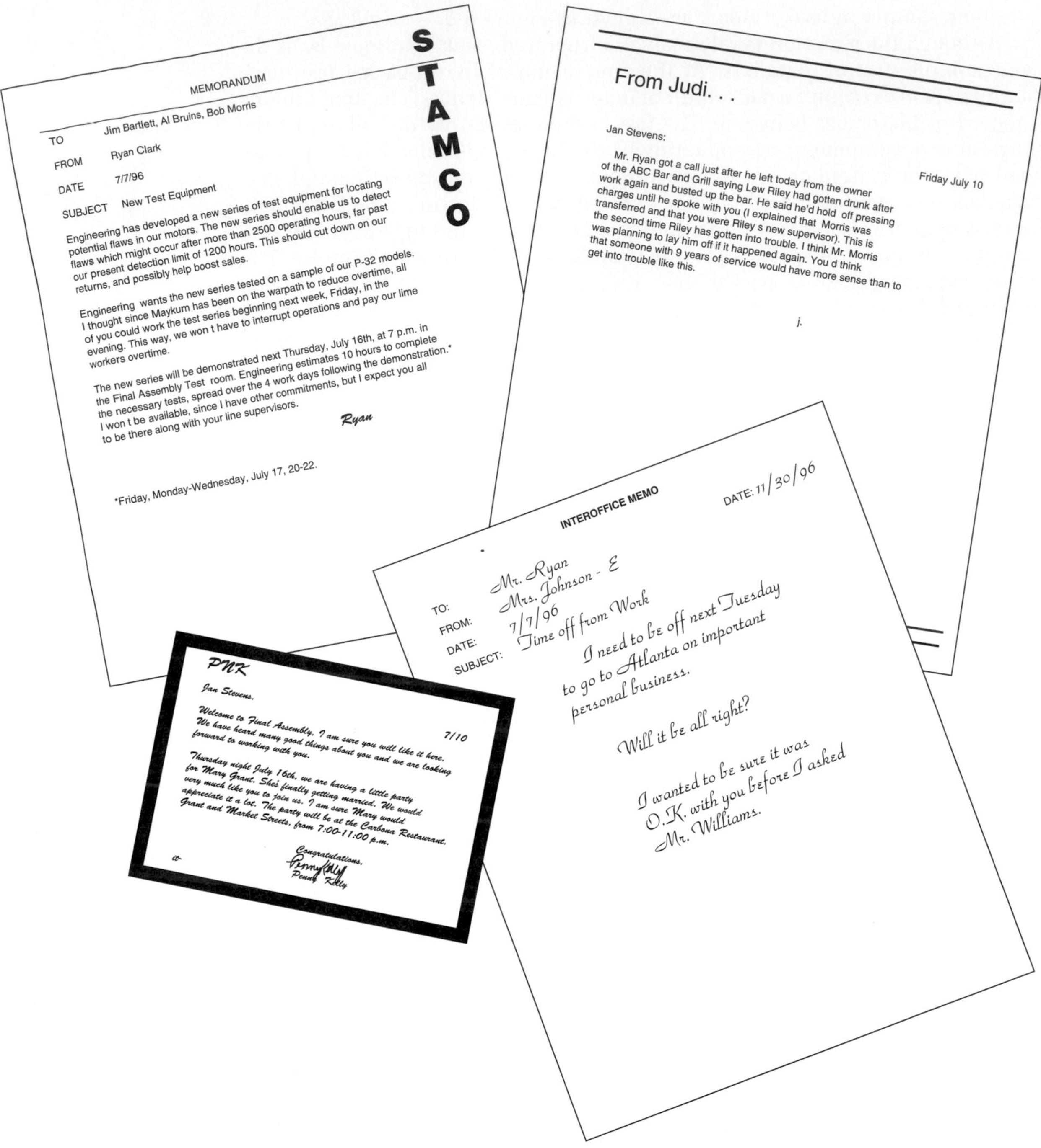

MEMORANDUM

STAMCO

TO Jim Bartlett, Al Bruins, Bob Morris
FROM Ryan Clark
DATE 7/7/96
SUBJECT New Test Equipment

Engineering has developed a new series of test equipment for locating potential flaws in our motors. The new series should enable us to detect flaws which might occur after more than 2500 operating hours, far past our present detection limit of 1200 hours. This should cut down on our returns, and possibly help boost sales.

Engineering wants the new series tested on a sample of our P-32 models. I thought since Maykum has been on the warpath to reduce overtime, all of you could work the test series beginning next week, Friday, in the evening. This way, we won t have to interrupt operations and pay our lime workers overtime.

The new series will be demonstrated next Thursday, July 16th, at 7 p.m. in the Final Assembly Test room. Engineering estimates 10 hours to complete the necessary tests, spread over the 4 work days following the demonstration.* I won t be available, since I have other commitments, but I expect you all to be there along with your line supervisors.

Ryan

*Friday, Monday-Wednesday, July 17, 20-22.

From Judi. . .

Jan Stevens: Friday July 10

Mr. Ryan got a call just after he left today from the owner of the ABC Bar and Grill saying Lew Riley had gotten drunk after work again and busted up the bar. He said he'd hold off pressing charges until he spoke with you (I explained that Morris was transferred and that you were Riley s new supervisor). This is the second time Riley has gotten into trouble. I think Mr. Morris was planning to lay him off if it happened again. You d think that someone with 9 years of service would have more sense than to get into trouble like this.

j.

INTEROFFICE MEMO DATE: 11/30/96

TO: Mr. Ryan
FROM: Mrs. Johnson - E
DATE: 7/7/96
SUBJECT: Time off from Work

I need to be off next Tuesday to go to Atlanta on important personal business.

Will it be all right?

I wanted to be sure it was O.K. with you before I asked Mr. Williams.

PNK

Jan Stevens, 7/10

Welcome to Final Assembly. I am sure you will like it here. We have heard many good things about you and we are looking forward to working with you.

Thursday night July 16th, we are having a little party for Mary Grant. Shes finally getting married. We would very much like you to join us. I am sure Mary would appreciate it a lot. The party will be at the Carbona Restaurant, Grant and Market Streets, from 7:00-11:00 p.m.

Congratulations,
Penny Kelly

of hours. Two, the games are interesting because of their realism, competitive nature, and the immediacy and objectivity of feedback. And three, such games promote increased understanding of complex interrelationships among organizational units.

Business games also have several drawbacks. One, in the context of training, some participants may become so engrossed in "beating the system" that they fail to grasp the underlying management principles being taught. And two,

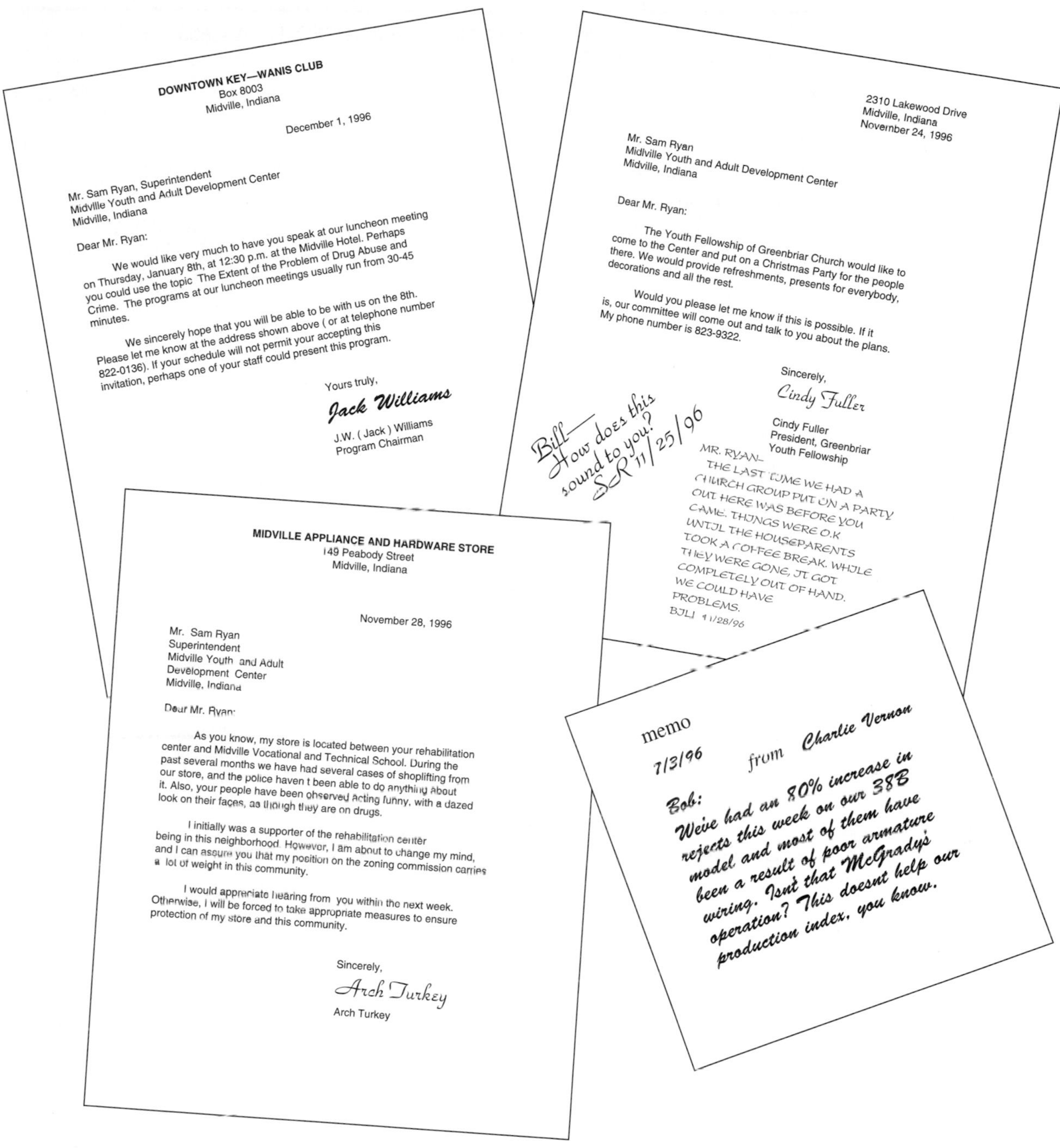

DOWNTOWN KEY—WANIS CLUB
Box 8003
Midville, Indiana

December 1, 1996

Mr. Sam Ryan, Superintendent
Midville Youth and Adult Development Center
Midville, Indiana

Dear Mr. Ryan:

We would like very much to have you speak at our luncheon meeting on Thursday, January 8th, at 12:30 p.m. at the Midville Hotel. Perhaps you could use the topic The Extent of the Problem of Drug Abuse and Crime. The programs at our luncheon meetings usually run from 30-45 minutes.

We sincerely hope that you will be able to be with us on the 8th. Please let me know at the address shown above (or at telephone number 822-0136). If your schedule will not permit your accepting this invitation, perhaps one of your staff could present this program.

Yours truly,

Jack Williams

J.W. (Jack) Williams
Program Chairman

2310 Lakewood Drive
Midville, Indiana
November 24, 1996

Mr. Sam Ryan
Midville Youth and Adult Development Center
Midville, Indiana

Dear Mr. Ryan:

The Youth Fellowship of Greenbriar Church would like to come to the Center and put on a Christmas Party for the people there. We would provide refreshments, presents for everybody, decorations and all the rest.

Would you please let me know if this is possible. If it is, our committee will come out and talk to you about the plans. My phone number is 823-9322.

Sincerely,

Cindy Fuller

Cindy Fuller
President, Greenbriar
Youth Fellowship

Bill—
How does this
sound to you?
SR 11/25/96

MR. RYAN—
THE LAST TIME WE HAD A CHURCH GROUP PUT ON A PARTY OUT HERE WAS BEFORE YOU CAME. THINGS WERE O.K UNTIL THE HOUSEPARENTS TOOK A COFFEE BREAK. WHILE THEY WERE GONE, IT GOT COMPLETELY OUT OF HAND. WE COULD HAVE PROBLEMS.
BJL 11/28/96

MIDVILLE APPLIANCE AND HARDWARE STORE
149 Peabody Street
Midville, Indiana

November 28, 1996

Mr. Sam Ryan
Superintendent
Midville Youth and Adult
Development Center
Midville, Indiana

Dear Mr. Ryan:

As you know, my store is located between your rehabilitation center and Midville Vocational and Technical School. During the past several months we have had several cases of shoplifting from our store, and the police haven t been able to do anything about it. Also, your people have been observed acting funny, with a dazed look on their faces, as though they are on drugs.

I initially was a supporter of the rehabilitation center being in this neighborhood. However, I am about to change my mind, and I can assure you that my position on the zoning commission carries a lot of weight in this community.

I would appreciate hearing from you within the next week. Otherwise, I will be forced to take appropriate measures to ensure protection of my store and this community.

Sincerely,

Arch Turkey

Arch Turkey

memo

7/3/96 from Charlie Vernon

Bob:
Weive had an 80% increase in rejects this week on our 38B model and most of them have been a result of poor armature wiring. Isnt that McGradys operation? This doesnt help our production index, you know.

Figure 6-5
Sample in-basket items.

creative approaches to solving problems presented by the game may be stifled, particularly if the highly innovative manager is penalized financially during the game for her or his unorthodox strategies.[83]

Table 6-3 presents a rough "scorecard," based on available research, indicating the overall effectiveness of predictors commonly used to assess managerial potential.

Table 6-3

ACCURACY OF VARIOUS PROCEDURES USED TO ASSESS MANAGERIAL POTENTIAL

Procedure	Accuracy
Mental ability tests	5
Objective personality and interest inventories	4
Projective techniques	3
Measures of leadership ability	1
Interviews	2
Personal history data	4
Peer assessment	4
Situational tests (when used in combination, as in an assessment center)	5

Procedures are rated on a 1-to-5 scale, where 1 = poor prediction and 5 = accurate prediction. It is important to stress, however, that no single procedure or combination of procedures is perfectly accurate. Even the most accurate procedures available account for only about 25 percent of the variability in actual job performance among managers. The following rating scheme, based on the average correlation between scores on the procedure and measures of actual job performance, was used therefore for each procedure:

Average correlation	Accuracy score
.00 to .10	1
.11 to .20	2
.21 to .30	3
.31 to .40	4
.41 to .50	5

Assessment Centers

The assessment center approach was first used by German military psychologists during World War II to select officers. They felt that paper-and-pencil tests took too narrow a view of human nature; therefore, they chose to observe each candidate's behavior in a complex situation to develop a broader appraisal of his reactions. Borrowing from this work and from that of the War Office Selection Board of the British army during the early 1940s, the U.S. Office of Strategic Services used the method to select spies during World War II. Each candidate had to develop a cover story that would hide her or his identity during the assessment. Testing for the ability to maintain cover was crucial, and ingenious situational tests were designed to seduce candidates into breaking cover.[84]

After World War II many military psychologists and officers joined private companies, where they started small-scale assessment centers. In 1956, AT&T was the first to use the method as the basis of a large-scale study of managerial progress and career development. As a result of extensive research conducted over 25 years, AT&T found that managerial skills and abilities are best measured by the following procedures:[85]

1. **Administrative skills**—performance on the in-basket test
2. **Interpersonal skills**—LGD, manufacturing problem
3. **Intellectual ability**—paper-and-pencil ability tests
4. **Stability of performance**—in-basket, LGD, manufacturing problem
5. **Work-oriented motivation**—projective tests, interviews, simulations
6. **Career orientation**—projective tests, interviews, personality inventories
7. **Dependency on others**—projective tests

Assessment centers do more than just test people. The assessment center method is a process that evaluates a candidate's potential for management on the basis of three sources: (1) multiple assessment techniques, such as situational tests, tests of mental abilities, and interest inventories; (2) standardized methods of making inferences from such techniques, because assessors are trained to distinguish between effective and ineffective behaviors by the candidates; and (3) pooled judgments from multiple assessors to rate each candidate's behavior.

Today assessment centers take many different forms, for they are used in a wide variety of settings and for a variety of purposes. Thousands of organizations in countries around the world are now using the assessment center method, and more are doing so every year. In addition to its use in evaluating and selecting managers, the method is being used to train and upgrade management skills, to encourage creativity among research and engineering professionals, to resolve interpersonal and interdepartmental conflicts, to assist individuals in career planning, to train managers in performance appraisal, and to provide information for human resource planning and organization design.

The assessment center method offers great flexibility. The specific content and design of a center can be tailored to the characteristics of the job in question. For example, when used for management selection, the assessment center method should be designed to predict how a person would behave in the next-higher-level management job. By relating each candidate's overall performance on the assessment center exercises to such indicators as the management level subsequently achieved 2 (or more) years later or to current salary, researchers have shown that the predictions for each candidate are very accurate. An accurate reading of each candidate's behavior before the promotion decision is made can help avoid potentially costly selection errors (erroneous acceptances as well as erroneous rejections).

As a specific example of the flexibility of the assessment center method in using multiple assessment techniques, consider the following six types of exercises used to help select U.S. Army recruiters:[86]

- **Structured interview**. Assessors ask a series of questions targeted at the subject's level of achievement motivation, potential for being a self-starter, and commitment to the Army.
- **Cold calls**. The subject has an opportunity to learn a little about three prospects and must phone each of them for the purpose of getting them to come into the office. Assessor role players have well-defined characters (prospects) to portray.
- **Interviews**. Two of the three cold-call prospects agree to come in for an interview. The subject's job is to follow up on what was learned in the cold-call conversations and to begin promoting Army enlistment to these people. A third walk-in prospect also appears for an interview with the subject.

- **Interview with concerned parent**. The subject is asked to prepare for and conduct an interview with the father of one of the prospects that he or she interviewed previously.
- **Five-minute speech about the Army**. The subject prepares a short talk about an Army career that she or he delivers to the rest of the group and to the assessors.
- **In-basket**. The subject is given an in-basket filled with notes, phone messages, and letters on which he or she must take some action.

The third feature of the assessment center method is assessor training. Assessors are typically line managers two or more levels above the candidates, trained (from 2 days to several weeks, depending on the complexity of the center) in interviewing techniques, behavior observation, and in-basket performance. In addition, assessors usually go through the exercises as participants before rating others. This experience, plus the development of a consensus by assessors on effective versus ineffective responses by candidates to the situations presented, enables the assessors to standardize their interpretations of each candidate's behavior. Standardization ensures that each candidate will be assessed fairly, that is, in terms of the same "yardstick." Instead of professional psychologists, line managers are often used as assessors for several reasons:

1. They are thoroughly familiar with the jobs for which candidates are being assessed.
2. Their involvement in the assessment process contributes to its acceptance by participants as well as by line managers.
3. Participation by line managers is a developmental experience for them and may contribute to the identification of areas in which they need improvement themselves.[87]
4. Line managers can be more objective in evaluating candidate performance since they usually do not know the candidates personally.[88]

Despite these potential advantages, cumulative evidence across assessment center studies indicates that professional psychologists who are trained to interpret behaviors in the assessment center relative to the requirements of specific jobs provide more valid assessment center ratings than do managers.[89]

In order to rate each candidate's behavior, organizations pool the judgments of multiple assessors. The advantage of pooling is that no candidate is subject to ratings from only one assessor. Since judgments from more than one source tend to be more reliable and valid, pooling enhances the overall accuracy of the judgments made. Each candidate is usually evaluated by a different assessor on each exercise. Although assessors make their judgments independently, the judgments must be combined into an overall rating on each dimension of interest. A summary report is then prepared and shared with each candidate.

These features of the assessment center method—flexibility of form and content, the use of multiple assessment techniques, standardized methods of interpreting behavior, and pooled assessor judgments—account for the successful track record of this approach over the past four decades. It has consistently demonstrated high validity, with correlations between assessment center performance and later job performance as a manager sometimes reaching the .50s and .60s.[90] Both minorities and nonminorities and men and women acknowledge that the method provides them a fair opportunity to demonstrate what they are capable of doing in a management job.[91]

In terms of its bottom-line impact, two studies have shown that assessment centers are cost-effective, even though the per-candidate cost may vary from as little as $50 to more than $2000. Using the general utility equation (Equation 6-1 in the Technical Appendix, page 242), both studies have demonstrated that the assessment center method should not be measured against the cost of implementing it, but rather against the cost (in lost sales and declining productivity) of promoting the wrong person into a management job.[92] In a first-level management job, the gain in improved job performance as a result of promoting people via the assessment center method is about $3700 per year (in 1996 dollars). However, if the average tenure of first-level managers is, say, 5 years, the gain per person is about $18,500 (in 1996 dollars).

Despite its advantages, the method is not without potential problems. These include:[93]

- Adoption of the assessment center method without carefully analyzing the need for it and without adequate preparations to use it wisely.
- Blind acceptance of assessment data without considering other information on candidates, such as past and current performance.
- The tendency to rate only general exercise effectiveness, rather than performance relative to individual behavioral dimensions (e.g., by using a behavioral checklist), as the number of dimensions exceeds the ability of assessors to evaluate each dimension individually.
- Lack of control over the information generated during assessment, for example, leaking of assessment ratings to operating managers.
- Failure to evaluate the utility of the program in terms of dollar benefits relative to costs.
- Inadequate feedback to participants.

Here is an interesting finding: ratings of management potential made after a review of employee files correlated significantly (.46) with assessment ratings, suggesting that assessment might to some extent duplicate a much simpler and less costly process.[94] This conclusion held true for predictions made regarding each candidate's progress in management 1 and 8 years after assessment.[95] However, when the rating of management potential was added to the assessment center prediction, the validity of the two together (.58) was higher than that of either one alone. What does the assessment center prediction add? Not much if we are simply trying to predict each candidate's rate and level of advancement. But if we are trying to predict performance in management—that is, to clarify and evaluate the promotion system in an organization—assessment centers can be of considerable help, even if they serve only to capture the promotion policy of the organization.[96]

Choosing the Right Predictor

Determining the right predictor depends on the following:

- *The nature of the job*
- An estimate of the *validity of the predictor* in terms of the size of the correlation coefficient that summarizes the strength of the relationship between

INTERNATIONAL APPLICATION
The Japanese Approach to Staffing

Soon after Toyota announced that it would build an auto assembly plant in Kentucky, some 90,000 job applications poured in for the 2700 production jobs and 300 office jobs available. To narrow the field of applicants, Toyota uses common tests to an uncommon degree. Even someone applying for the lowest-paying job on the shop floor goes through at least 14 hours of testing, administered on Toyota's behalf by state employment offices and Kentucky State University.

Rigorous testing is also standard procedure for the U.S. auto plants of Mazda Motor Corporation; for a joint venture of Isuzu Motors, Ltd., and Fuji Heavy Industries, Ltd.; and for Diamond-Star Motors Corporation, a joint venture of Mitsubishi and Chrysler.

Initial tests cover reading and mathematics, manual dexterity, "job fitness," and, for skilled trades, technical knowledge. Job fitness is actually an attitude measure in which applicants are asked whether they agree or disagree with 100 different statements. Here are two examples: "It's important for workers to work past quitting time to get the job done when necessary"; "Management will take advantage of employees whenever possible."

Next come workplace simulations. Groups of applicants are assigned such problems as ranking the features of a hypothetical auto according to how well the market would accept them. As the job seekers discuss the options, trained assessors record their observations and later pool their findings in order to assess each candidate. Other problems focus on manufacturing and making repairs—though not of or on autos, since Toyota is interested in aptitude more than experience.

There are also mock production lines, where applicants assemble tubes or circuit boards. The objective is to identify applicants who can keep to a fast pace, endure tedious repetition, and yet stay alert. The tube-assembly procedure is intentionally flawed, and applicants are asked how they would improve it.

Only 1 applicant in 20 makes it to an interview, which is conducted by a panel representing various Toyota departments. By then, says an HRM staffer, "we're going to know more about these people than perhaps any company has ever known about people." The final steps are a physical examination and a drug test.

For all the testing being done by many of the Japanese automakers, there are others that use different methods. Honda, for example, uses few tests at its Marysville, Ohio, plant. Instead, it puts every potential hire through three interviews. And Nissan Motor Company, which has been operating in Smyrna, Tennessee, since the early 1980s, prefers to give probable hires at least 40 hours of "preemployment" training—without pay. The training is intended partly as a final check on whether the company and those in training are really right for each other.[97]

applicants' scores on the predictor and their corresponding scores on some measure of performance

- *The selection ratio*, or percentage of applicants selected
- *The cost of the predictor*

To the extent that job performance is multidimensional (as indicated in job analysis results), multiple predictors, each focused on critical competencies, might be used. Other things being equal, use predictors with the highest estimated validities; they will tend to minimize the number of erroneous acceptances and rejections, and they will tend to maximize workforce productivity. Table 6-1 summarizes the accumulated validity evidence for a number of potential predictors. The predictors fall into two categories: those that can be used for entry-level hiring into jobs that require subsequent training, and those that depend on the use of current job performance or job knowledge to predict future job performance.

It is important to take into account the selection ratio (the percentage of applicants hired) in evaluating the overall usefulness of any predictor, regardless of its validity. On the one hand, low selection ratios mean that more applicants must be evaluated; on the other hand, low selection ratios also mean that only the cream of the applicant crop will be selected. Hence predictors with lower validity may be used when the selection ratio is low since it is necessary only to distinguish the very best qualified from everyone else.

Finally, the cost of selection is a consideration, but not a major one. Of course, if two predictors are roughly equal in estimated validity, then use the less costly procedure. However, the trade-off between cost and validity should almost always be resolved in favor of validity. Choose the more valid procedure, because the major concern is not the cost of the procedure, but rather the cost of a mistake if the wrong candidate is selected or promoted. In management jobs, such mistakes are likely to be particularly costly.[98]

CEO SELECTION CRITERIA—IN THE THROES OF CHANGE

Human Resource Management in Action: Conclusion

Listed below are three flaws in the current systems for developing managers and some suggested improvements to correct those flaws:

1. **The process takes too long**. Instead of identifying potential leaders early in their careers, perhaps limiting choices for chief executives later on, some boards of directors are building in more flexibility. That is, they are hiring search firms to identify new board members who can step in as CEO if necessary.
2. **The system produces leaders who are too insular**. As an engineer and long-time GM insider, Mr. Stempel was well respected inside the company. But he apparently lacked the outside contacts and experience to make him an effective peer to a strong board. The antidote? The experience of would-be CEOs should be broad enough to give them visibility outside the organization so that they do not have to rely only on their internal authority in the enterprise. As an example, consider IBM's chairman, Louis Gerstner, Jr. After graduating from the Harvard Business School in 1965, he became one of the youngest directors ever of McKinsey & Company, a management consulting firm. A hard-charging corporate strategist, he moved to American Express Company in 1978 and eventually rose to its presidency. In 1989, he left to take the chairman's job at RJR Nabisco, then in the spotlight as it went through the biggest leveraged buyout ever. Finally, in 1993, at the age of 51, Mr. Gerstner was named chairman of IBM.[99] No one would ever accuse him of being too insular!
3. **The method ties executives too closely to tradition**. Experts say that the grooming process for CEOs should focus more on the ability to adapt to change than on a specific skill, such as engineering or finance. Indeed, when major change is needed, it is almost impossible for long-term internal people to do it. Says a New York executive recruiter: "Sometimes they just can't see the solution. Sometimes they can see it but can't face it emotionally. The people whose lives and careers they are affecting are close friends. It is their entire network and support system."

What is the bottom line in all of this? According to Warren Bennis, an expert on leadership, "With the galloping changes that are taking place—demographic, geopolitical, global—if you think you can run the business in the next 10 years the way you did in the last 10 years, you are crazy." In short, there are seasons for leaders.

SUMMARY

In the staffing of an organization or an organizational unit, it is important to consider its developmental stage—embryonic, high-growth, mature, or aging—in order to align staffing decisions with business strategy. It also is important to communicate an organization's culture, since research shows that applicants will consider this information, if it is available to them, to choose among jobs. In order to use selection techniques meaningfully, however, organizations must specify the kinds of competencies that are necessary for success.

Organizations commonly screen applicants through recommendations and reference checks, information on application forms, or employment interviews. In addition, some firms use written ability or integrity tests, work-sample tests, drug tests, polygraph examinations, or handwriting analysis. In each case, it is important to pay careful attention to the reliability and validity of the information obtained. *Reliability* refers to the consistency or stability of scores over time, across different samples of items, or across different raters or judges. *Validity* refers to the job-relatedness of a measure—that is, the strength of the relationship between scores from the measure and some indicator or rating of actual job performance.

In the context of managerial selection, numerous techniques are available, but the research literature indicates that the most effective ones have been mental ability tests, objective personality and interest inventories, peer assessments, personal-history data, and situational tests. Projective techniques and leadership ability tests have been less effective. The use of situational tests, such as the leaderless group discussion, the in-basket, and the business game, lies at the heart of the assessment center method. Key advantages of the method are its high validity, fair evaluation of each candidate's ability, and flexibility of form and content. Other features include the use of multiple assessment techniques, assessor training, and pooled assessor judgments in rating each candidate's behavior.

Recent research indicates, at least for ability tests, that a test that accurately forecasts performance on a particular job in one situation will also forecast performance on the same job in other situations. Hence it may not be necessary to conduct a new validity study each time a predictor is used. Recent research has also demonstrated that the dollar benefits to an organization that uses valid selection procedures may be substantial. In choosing the right predictors for a given situation, pay careful attention to four factors: the nature of the job, the estimated validity of the predictor(s), the selection ratio, and the cost of the predictor(s). Doing so can pay handsome dividends to organizations and employees alike.

IMPACT OF STAFFING DECISIONS ON PRODUCTIVITY, QUALITY OF WORK LIFE, AND THE BOTTOM LINE

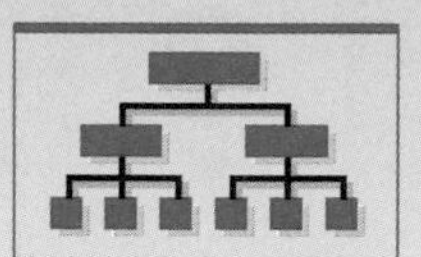

Some companies avoid validating their screening and selection procedures because they think validation is too costly—and its benefits too elusive. Alternatively, scare tactics ("validate or else lose in court") have not encouraged widespread validation efforts either. However, a large body of research has shown that the dollar gains in productivity associated with the use of valid selection and promotion procedures far outweigh the cost of those procedures.[100] Think about that. If people who score high (low) on selection procedures also do well (poorly) on their jobs, high scores suggest a close fit between individual capabilities and organizational needs. Low scores, on the other hand, suggest a poor fit. In both cases, productivity, quality of work life, and the bottom line stand to gain from the use of valid selection procedures. Thus a study of firms in the service and financial industries reported correlations ranging from .71 to .86 between the use of progressive staffing practices (e.g., validation studies, use of structured interviews, biodata, and mental ability tests) and measures of organizational performance over a 5-year period (annual profit, profit growth, sales growth, and overall performance).[101]

DISCUSSION QUESTIONS

6-1 How can the accuracy of preemployment interviews be improved?
6-2 Why are reliability and validity key considerations for all assessment methods?
6-3 How does business strategy affect management selection?
6-4 "At lower levels, managers do basically the same things regardless of functional specialty." Do you agree or disagree with this statement, and why?
6-5 As jobs become more team-oriented, assessment centers will be used more often for nonmanagement jobs. Do you agree or disagree?

APPLYING YOUR KNOWLEDGE

An In-Basket and an LGD for Selecting Managers — *Exercise 6-1*

There are several means by which an organization can attempt to determine the right choices in the managerial selection process. An approach that is growing rapidly in popularity is to attempt to assess what a managerial candidate can *do*, rather than what he or she *knows*.

Various kinds of work samples or situational tests can be used to assess what a candidate can do. In this exercise, you will have an opportunity to see how two of the most valid managerial work samples—in-baskets and leaderless group discussions (LGDs)—operate. An attractive feature of this combination of predictors is that while both are valid, the scores on each do not correlate highly with each other. This suggests that in-baskets and LGDs tap a different, but important, subset of the managerial performance domain.

Part A: In-Basket Exercise

An in-basket exercise is designed to assess a candidate's problem-solving, decision-making, and administrative skills. Further, because all responses are written ones, the exercise can also assess written communication ability.

IMPLICATIONS FOR MANAGEMENT PRACTICE

The research evidence is clear: valid selection procedures can produce substantial economic gains for organizations. The implication for policymakers also is clear:

- Select the highest-caliber managers and lower-level employees, for they are most likely to profit from development programs.
- Do not assume that a large investment in training can transform marginally competent performers into innovative, motivated top performers.
- A wide variety of screening and selection procedures is available. It is your responsibility to ask tough questions of staff specialists about the reliability, job-relatedness, and validity of each procedure proposed for use.
- Recognize that no one predictor is perfectly valid and therefore that some mistakes in selection (erroneous acceptances or erroneous rejections) are inevitable. By consciously selecting managers and lower-level employees based on their fit with demonstrated job requirements, the strategic direction of a business, and organizational culture, you will minimize mistakes and make optimum choices.

An in-basket consists of a set of letters, notes, memos, and telephone messages to which a candidate must respond. To give you a sense of how an in-basket operates, a sample set of such stimuli is provided below. The set is similar to the one in the text, except that for ease of administration, all items are stated in memorandum form.

Procedure. You are to assume that you have just been appointed director of human resources at Ace Manufacturing Company and that your name is George Ryan. The president of the firm is Arnold ("Arnie") Ace. You were to replace the current HR director, John Armstrong, in 2 weeks, when he was scheduled to be transferred to Hong Kong. However, a family emergency in South Africa has required that John leave the country immediately and you must fill in for him as best as you can. You have taken an alternate flight on an important business trip to Washington, D.C., and have stopped over in Lompoc, where Ace's headquarters is located. It is Saturday morning and no one else is available in the office. You must resume your flight to Washington, D.C., within an hour.

Read through the items in your in-basket, decide what to do with each item, and record your decision on a separate sheet of paper. If any decisions require writing a letter or memo, you are to draft the response in the space provided. You are not to role-play how you think someone else might behave in this situation. Rather, you are to behave exactly as you yourself would in each situation.

Item 1

MEMO TO: John Armstrong, HR Director
FROM: Jackie Williams, Downtown Business Club
SUBJECT: Speaking engagement next week

Thanks again for your willingness to speak to our Business Club next week. As you know, this group represents a good cross section of the Lompoc business community as well as a number of Ace's best customers. We are all looking forward to what you have to say regarding the relationship between strategic planning and human resource information systems.

Item 2

MEMO TO: Mr. Ryan
FROM: Judy [secretary to the director of human resources]
SUBJECT: Tom Tipster's employment status

Just after Mr. Armstrong left yesterday, we received a call from the owner of Stockman's Bar and Grill saying that Tom Tipster had gotten drunk in the middle of the day again and busted up the bar. He said he'd hold off pressing charges until he talked to you (I explained that you were Mr. Armstrong's replacement). This is the third time that Mr. Tipster has gotten in trouble over his drinking problem. I think Mr. Armstrong was planning to fire him if he had another problem like this. You'd think that someone with 17 years of service at Ace would have more sense than to get into trouble like this—especially with 7 kids at home to feed!

Item 3

MEMO TO: John
FROM: Arnie
SUBJECT: EEO Report

Where is that EEO report you promised me? There's no way I want to face the investigators from Denver Wednesday without it!

Item 4

MEMO TO: John Armstrong
FROM: Lisa Buller, Administrator of Training Programs
SUBJECT: Time off

I need to take next Thursday off to fly to San Francisco on important personal business. Will this be OK?

Item 5

MEMO TO: Mr. John Armstrong
FROM: Arch Turkey
SUBJECT: Thefts

As you know, my store is located between your downtown office extension and that of Deuce's. During the past several months we have had several cases of shoplifting from our store, and the police haven't been able to do anything about it. Further, several custodians from your facility have been observed acting funny (with dazed looks on their faces) and wandering around outside my store looking in. I think that your people may be responsible for the recent shoplifting losses I have suffered. I would appreciate hearing from you within the next week. Otherwise, I will be forced to take appropriate measures to ensure protection of my store.

Item 6

MEMO TO: John
FROM: Alice Calmers, Director of Manufacturing
SUBJECT: Thursday's training program

I finally got everything rearranged for that training program on Thursday. You can't imagine how difficult it is to try to rearrange the schedules of 15 very busy supervisors to attend anything at the same time. I certainly hope that Lisa's presentation is going to be worth all this juggling of schedules!

Item 7

MEMO TO: John Armstrong
FROM: Ralph Herzberg, Manager of Customer Relations
SUBJECT: New training program

We have a serious problem in the customer relations department. It is quite common for a large number of calls to come in all at once. When this happens, the customer relations contact employee is supposed to take the customer's phone number and get back to him or her within an hour. We've found in the past that this is a reasonable target since, after a big rush of calls, things usually settle down for a while. But when we check up on the contact employees, we find that they get back to the customer within an hour only about 1/3 of the time. Sometimes they don't get back to the customer until the next day! I sent a memo to all contact employees about a month ago reminding them of the importance of prompt responses on their parts, but it did very little good. We need a training program from your department to improve this critical performance area. Can we get together early next week?

Responses

On a separate sheet of paper, provide your responses to the in-basket items.

Item 1: Speaking engagement next week

Item 2: Tom Tipster's employment status

Item 3: EEO Report

Item 4: Time off

Item 5: Thefts

Item 6: Thursday's training program

Item 7: New training program

Part B: Leaderless Group Discussion (LGD)

Unlike the in-basket exercise, a leaderless group discussion exercise involves groups of managerial candidates working together on a job-related problem. The problem is usually designed to be as realistic as possible, and it is often tackled in groups of five or six candidates. No one in the group is appointed leader, nor is anyone told where to sit or how to act. Candidates are instructed simply to solve the problem to the best of their ability in the time allotted.

The LGD is used to assess such managerial traits and skills as aggressiveness, interpersonal skills, persuasive ability, oral communication skills, self-confidence, energy level, and resistance to stress.

Procedure. The problem that follows is typical of those in an LGD. However, to conserve time, we have simplified it somewhat. Read the statement of the problem and then, working in groups of five or six students, arrive at a consensus regarding the solution to the problem. When finished, be prepared to discuss the kinds of management skills exhibited by students in your group.

Bonus Allocation Problem

Your organization has recently instituted an incentive bonus in an attempt to stimulate and reward key employee behaviors. The company has budgeted $40,000 for this purpose, to be spent every 6 months. You have been appointed to a committee charged with the responsibility of determining the allocation of bonus funds to deserving employees over the previous 6-month period. A total of 25 employees were recommended by their supervisors. Decisions have already been made on 20 of them, and $32,000 of the original sum has been expended. Your task today is to decide on the size of the bonuses (if any) to be received by the remaining five employees. Summaries of the qualifications for the five employees are presented below:

Virginia Dewey. Head custodian. 15 years with the firm. High school diploma. 22 years of relevant job experience. Manages a flawless custodial staff with low turnover and few union grievances. Present salary below average in most recent salary survey. Supports a family of six. Overlooked for salary increase last year.

Alfred Newman. Accounting clerk. 3 years with the firm. 2-year college degree. 3 years of relevant work experience. Performs well under pressure of deadlines. Present salary is average in recent salary survey. Is known to be looking for other jobs.

Augusta Nie. Manager of corporate data analysis. 7 years with the firm. Master's degree in computer science. 14 years of relevant work experience. Has developed the data analysis department into one of the most efficient in the company. Present salary is above average in recent salary survey. Has leadership potential and may be offered jobs from other firms. Difficult to replace good data processing personnel.

Barry Barngrover. Machinist. 11 years with the firm. High school diploma. 11 years relevant job experience. Is the top performer in the milling machine department, and exhibits a positive company attitude. Present salary is average in a recent salary survey. Is single and seems to have all the money he needs to support his chosen lifestyle.

Harvey Slack. Personnel administrator. 1 year with the firm. College degree from prestigious Ivy League school. 3 years of relevant work experience. Very knowledgeable in subject matter, but has trouble getting along with older coworkers. Present salary is above average in a recent salary survey. His mentor is the firm's vice president for human resources, who is said to be grooming Harvey for the VP position. Has received several offers from other firms recently.

Table 6-4

HYPOTHETICAL SCORES FOR THE SAME INDIVIDUALS ON FORM A AND FORM B OF A MATHEMATICAL APTITUDE TEST

Person number	Form A	Form B
1	75	82
2	85	84
3	72	77
4	96	90
5	65	68
6	81	82
7	93	95
8	59	52
9	67	60
10	87	89

The coefficient of correlation between these sets of scores is .93. It is computed from the following formula:

$$r = \frac{\Sigma Z_x Z_y}{N}$$

where r = correlation coefficient
Σ = sum of
Z_x = standard score on form A, where $Z = x$, each person's raw score on form A minus $\bar{X}$, the mean score on form A, divided by the standard deviation of form A scores
Z_y = standard score on form B
N = number of persons in the sample (10 in this case)

TECHNICAL APPENDIX

The Estimation of Reliability

A quantitative estimate of the reliability of each measure used as a basis for employment decisions is important for two reasons: (1) if any measure is challenged legally, reliability estimates are important in establishing a defense, and (2) a measurement procedure cannot be any more valid (accurate) than it is reliable (consistent and stable). To estimate reliability, compute a coefficient of correlation (a measure of the degree of relationship between two variables) between two sets of scores obtained independently. As an example, consider the sets of scores shown in Table 6-4.

Table 6-4 shows two sets of scores obtained from two forms of the same test. The resulting correlation coefficient is called a parallel forms reliability estimate. By the way, the correlation coefficient for the two sets of scores shown in Table 6-4 is .93, a very strong relationship. (The word "test" is used in the broad sense here to include any physical or psychological measurement instrument, technique, or procedure.) However, the scores in Table 6-4 could just as easily have been obtained from two administrations of the same test at two different times (test-retest reliability) or from independent ratings of the same test by two different scorers (interrater reliability).

Finally, in situations where it is not practical to use any of the preceding procedures and where a test can be administered only once, use a procedure known as split-half reliability. With this procedure, split a test statistically into two halves (e.g., odd items and even items) after it has been given. This yields two scores for each individual. In effect, therefore, one creates two sets of scores (so-called parallel forms) from the same test for each individual. Then correlate scores on the two "half tests." However, since reliability increases as we sample larger and larger portions of a particular area of knowledge, skill, or ability, and since we have cut the length of the original test in half, the correlation between the two half tests underestimates the true reliability of the total test. Fortunately, formulas are available to correct such underestimates.

Validation Strategies

Although a number of procedures are available for evaluating evidence of validity, three of the best-known strategies are construct-oriented, content-oriented, and criterion-related. The three differ in terms of the conclusions and inferences that may be drawn, but they are interrelated logically and also in terms of the operations used to measure them.

Evaluation of *construct-oriented evidence of validity* begins by formulating hypotheses about the characteristics of those with high scores on a particular measurement procedure, in contrast to those with low scores. For example, we might hypothesize that sales managers will score significantly higher on the managerial interests scale of the California Psychological Inventory (CPI) than will pharmacy students (in fact, they do), and that they will also be more decisive and more apt to take risks as well. The hypotheses form a tentative theory about the nature of the psychological construct, or trait, that the CPI is believed to be measuring. These hypotheses may then be used to predict how people at different score levels on the CPI will behave on other tests or in other situations during their careers. Construct validation is not accomplished in a single study. It requires that evidence be accumulated from different sources to determine the meaning of the test scores in terms of how people actually behave. It is a logical as well as an empirical process.

Content-oriented evidence of validity is also a judgmental, rational process. It requires an answer to the following question: *Is the content of the measurement procedure a fair, representative sample of the content of the job it is supposed to represent?* Such judgments can be made rather easily by job incumbents, supervisors, or other job experts when job knowledge or work-sample tests are used (e.g., typing tests and tests for electricians, plumbers, and computer programmers). However, content-oriented evidence becomes less appropriate as the behaviors in question become less observable and more abstract (e.g., the ability to draw conclusions from a written sample of material). In addition, since such judgments are not expressed in quantitative terms, it is difficult to justify ranking applicants in terms of predicted job performance, and it is difficult to estimate directly the dollar benefits to the firm from using such a procedure. To overcome these problems, we need a criterion-related validity strategy.

The term "criterion-related evidence of validity" calls attention to the fact that the chief concern is with the relationship between predictor (the selection procedure[s] used) and criterion (job performance) scores, not with predictor scores per se. Indeed, the content of the predictor measure is relatively unimportant, for it serves only as a vehicle to predict actual job performance.

There are two strategies of criterion-related validation: *concurrent* and *predictive.* A *concurrent strategy* is used to measure job incumbents. Job performance (criterion) measures for this group are already available; so immediately after administration of a selection measure to this group, it is possible to compute a correlation coefficient between predictor scores and criterion scores (over all individuals in the group). A procedure identical to that shown in Table 6-4 is used. If the selection measure is valid, those employees with the highest (or lowest) job performance scores should also score highest (or lowest) on the selection measure. In short, if the selection measure is valid, there should exist a systematic relationship between scores on that measure and job performance. The higher the test score, the better the job performance (and vice versa).

When a *predictive strategy* is used, the procedure is identical, except that we measure job candidates. We use the same methods that currently are used to select employees, and simply add the new selection procedure to the overall process. However, we select candidates without using the results of the new procedure. At a later date (e.g., 6 months to a year), when it becomes possible to develop a meaningful measure of job performance for each new hire, scores on the new selection procedure are correlated with job performance scores. We then assess the strength of the predictor-criterion relationship in terms of the size of the correlation coefficient.

Estimating the Economic Benefits of Selection Programs

If we assume that n workers are hired during a given year and that the average job tenure of those workers is t years, the dollar increase in productivity can be determined from Equation 6-1. Admittedly, this is a "cookbook recipe," but the formula was derived more than 45 years ago and is well established in applied psychology:[102]

$$\Delta U = ntr_{xy}SD_y\bar{Z}_x \qquad (6\text{-}1)$$

where ΔU = increase in productivity in dollars
n = number of persons hired
t = average job tenure in years of those hired
r_{xy} = validity coefficient representing the correlation between the predictor and job performance in the applicant population
SD_y = standard deviation of job performance in dollars (roughly 40 percent of annual wage)[103]
$\bar{Z}_x$ = average predictor score of those selected in the applicant population, expressed in terms of standard scores

When Equation 6-1 was used to estimate the dollar gains in productivity associated with use of the Programmer Aptitude Test (PAT) to select computer programmers for federal government jobs, given that an average of 618 programmers per year are selected, each with an average job tenure of 9.69 years, the payoff per selectee was $64,725 over his or her tenure on the job. This represents a per-year productivity gain of $6679 for each new programmer.[104] Clearly, the dollar gains in increased productivity associated with the use of valid selection procedures (the estimated true validity of the PAT is .76) are not trivial. Indeed, in a globally competitive environment, businesses need to take advantage of every possible strategy for improving productivity. The widespread use of valid selection and promotion procedures should be a high-priority consideration in this effort.

Valid selection and promotion procedures also benefit applicants in several ways. A more accurate matching of applicant knowledge, skills, ability, and other characteristics to job requirements helps enhance the likelihood of successful performance. This, in turn, helps workers feel better about their jobs and adjust to changes in them, because they are doing the kinds of things they do best. Moreover, since we know that there is a positive spillover effect between job satisfaction and life satisfaction, the accurate matching of people and jobs will also foster an improved quality of life, not just an improved quality of work life, for all concerned.

REFERENCES

1. Snow, C. C., & Snell, S. A. (1993). Staffing as strategy. In N. Schmitt & W. C. Borman (eds.), *Personnel selection in organizations.* San Francisco: Jossey-Bass, pp. 448–478. See also Smith, E. C. (1982). Strategic business planning and human resources: Part I. *Personnel Journal,* **61**, 606–610.
2. Schneider, B. (ed.) (1990). *Organizational climate and culture.* San Francisco: Jossey-Bass. See also Schneider, B. (1987). The people make the place. *Personnel Psychology,* **40**, 437–453.
3. Power, D. J., & Aldag, R. J. (1985). Soelberg's job search and choice model: A clarification, review, and critique. *Academy of Management Review,* **10**, 48–58.
4. Snow & Snell, loc. cit.
5. Sheridan, J. E. (1992). Organizational culture and employee retention. *Academy of Management Journal,* **35**, 1036–1056.
6. Hunter, J. E., Schmidt, F. L., & Judiesch, M. K. (1990). Individual differences in output variability as a function of job complexity. *Journal of Applied Psychology,* **75**, 28–42.
7. Messick, S. (1995). Validity of psychological assessment. *American Psychologist,* **50**, 741–749.
8. Schmitt, N., & Landy, F. J. (1993). The concept of validity. In N. Schmitt & W. C. Borman (eds.), *Personnel selection in organizations.* San Francisco: Jossey-Bass, pp. 275–309.
9. *Principles for the validation and use of personnel selection procedures* (3d ed.) (1987). College Park, MD: Society of Industrial-Organizational Psychology.
10. Uniform guidelines on employee selection procedures (1978). *Federal Register,* **43**, 38290–38315.
11. Alaska Airlines sets job application handling fee (1983, Jan. 19). *Aviation Daily,* p. 1.
12. Labor letter (1988, Oct. 18). *The Wall Street Journal,* p. 1. See also Labor letter (1986, May 13). *The Wall Street Journal,* p. 1.
13. Lowell, R. S., & DeLoach, J. A. (1982). Equal employment opportunity: Are you overlooking the application form? *Personnel,* **59**(4), 49–55. See also Miller, E. C. (1980). An EEO examination of employment applications. *Personnel Administrator,* **25**(3), 63–69, 81.

14. Bahnsen, E. (1996, Nov.). Questions to ask, and not ask, job applicants. *HR News*, pp. 10, 11. See also Boas, K. M. (1996, Summer). Ask an expert. *Business Briefs*, **15**, 1–2.
15. Klimoski, R. J. (1993). Predictor constructs and their measurement. In N. Schmitt & W. C. Borman (eds.), *Personnel selection in organizations.* San Francisco: Jossey-Bass, pp. 99–134. See also Hunter, J. E., & Hunter, R. F. (1984). Validity and utility of alternative predictors of job performance. *Psychological Bulletin*, **96**, 72–98.
16. Lawrence, D. G., Salsburg, B. L., Dawson, J. G., & Fasman, Z. D. (1982). Design and use of weighted application blanks. *Personnel Administrator*, **27**(3), 47–53, 101.
17. Knowlton, J. (1987, June 22). Smile for the camera: Job seekers make more use of video résumés. *The Wall Street Journal*, p. 29.
18. Labor letter (1987, June 30). *The Wall Street Journal*, p. 1.
19. McCormick, E. J., & Ilgen, D. R. (1985). *Industrial psychology* (8th ed.). Englewood Cliffs, NJ: Prentice-Hall.
20. Knouse, S. B. (1987). An attribution theory approach to the letter of recommendation. *International Journal of Management*, **4**(1), 5–13.
21. LoPresto, R. L., Mitcham, D. E., & Ripley, D. E. (1993). *Reference checking handbook* (Rev. ed.). Alexandria, VA: Society for Human Resource Management. See also Munchus, G. (1992, June). Check references for safer selection. *HRMagazine*, pp. 75–77. See also Rice, J. D. (1978). Privacy legislation: Its effect on pre-employment reference checking. *Personnel Administrator*, **23**, 46–51.
22. Click, J. (1995, July). SHRM survey highlights dilemmas of reference checks. *HR News*, p. 13.
23. Job references: Handle with care (1987, Mar. 9). *Business Week*, p. 124.
24. Rigdon, J. E. (1992, June 17). Deceptive résumés can be door openers but can become an employee's undoing. *The Wall Street Journal*, pp. B1, B7. See also LoPresto et al., op. cit.
25. Reliable references are getting difficult to find (1993, Feb. 23). *The Wall Street Journal*, p. A1.
26. Weiner, T. (1993, May 16). Firms tighten reference policies. *The Denver Post*, p. 5G. See also Reference preference: Employers button lips (1990, Jan. 4). *The Wall Street Journal*, p. B1. See also Revenge of the fired (1987, Feb. 16). *Newsweek*, pp. 46, 47.
27. Ryan, A. M., & Lasek, M. (1991). Negligent hiring and defamation: Areas of liability related to pre-employment inquiries. *Personnel Psychology*, **44**, 293–319.
28. Arnold, D. W. (1996, Feb.). Providing references. *HR News*, p. 16.
29. Brokaw, T. (1996, Oct. 31). *NBC Nightly News.*
30. Morgan, J. P. (1989, Aug. 20). Employee drug tests are unreliable and intrusive. *Hospitals*, p. 42. See also Bogdanich, W. (1987, Feb. 2). False negative: Medical labs, trusted as largely error-free, are far from infallible. *The Wall Street Journal*, pp. 1, 14.
31. Normand, J., Salyards, S., and Mahoney, J. (1990). An evaluation of pre-employment drug testing. *Journal of Applied Psychology*, **75**, 629–639.
32. Harris, M. M., & Heft, L. L. (1993). Preemployment urinalysis drug testing: A critical review of psychometric and legal issues and effects on applicants. *Human Resource Management Review*, **3**, 271–291.
33. Limit drug tests in the workplace (1991, Nov. 20). *The Rocky Mountain News*, p. 50. See also Stone, D. L., & Kotch, D. A. (1989). Individuals' attitudes toward organizational drug testing policies and practices. *Journal of Applied Psychology*, **74**, 518–521.
34. Levy, L. (1979). Handwriting and hiring. *Dun's Review*, **113**, 72–79.
35. Gorman, C. (1989, Jan. 23). Honestly, can we trust you? *Time*, p. 44. See also McCarthy, M. J. (1988, Aug. 25). Handwriting analysis as personnel tool. *The Wall Street Journal*, p. B1.
36. Rafaeli, A., & Klimoski, R. J. (1983). Predicting sales success through handwriting analysis: An evaluation of the effects of training and handwriting sample content. *Journal of Applied Psychology*, **68**, 212–217.

37. Ben-Shakhar, G., Bar-Hillel, M., Bilu, Y., Ben-Abba, E., & Flug, A. (1986). Can graphology predict occupational success? Two empirical studies and some methodological ruminations. *Journal of Applied Psychology*, **71**, 645–653.
38. Kleinmutz, B. (1985, July–Aug.). Lie detectors fail the truth test. *Harvard Business Review*, **63**, 36–42. See also Patrick, C. J., & Iacono, W. G. (1989). Psychopathy, threat, and polygraph test accuracy. *Journal of Applied Psychology*, **74**, 347–355. See also Saxe, L., Dougherty, D., & Cross, T. (1985). The validity of polygraph testing. *American Psychologist*, **40**, 355–356.
39. Polygraph testing hit (1986, Oct.). *Resource*, p. 13.
40. Gorman, loc. cit.
41. Susser, P. A. (1986). Update on polygraphs and employment. *Personnel Administrator*, **31**(2), 28, 32.
42. Jacobs, S. L. (1985, Mar. 11). Owners who ignore security make worker dishonesty easy. *The Wall Street Journal*, p. 25.
43. Conner, C. (1992, Dec. 5). Shoplifting, theft losses decline but U.S. retailers still vigilant. *The Denver Post*, p. 4.
44. Yandrick, R. M. (1995, Nov.). Employers turn to psychological tests to predict applicants' work behavior. *HR News*, pp. 2, 13.
45. Camara, W. J., & Schneider, D. L. (1994). Integrity tests: Facts and unresolved issues. *American Psychologist*, **49**(2), 112–119. See also Sackett, P. R., Burris, L. R., & Callahan, C. (1989). Integrity testing for personnel selection: An update. *Personnel Psychology*, **42**, 491–529.
46. Ones, D. S., Viswesvaran, C., & Schmidt, F. L. (1993). Comprehensive meta-analysis of integrity test validities: Findings and implications for personnel selection and theories of job performance. *Journal of Applied Psychology Monograph*, **78**, 679–703.
47. Lilienfeld, S. O., Alliger, G., & Mitchell, K. (1995). Why integrity testing remains controversial. *American Psychologist*, **50**, 457–458.
48. Cunningham, M. R., Wong, D. T., & Barbee, A. P. (1994). Self-presentation dynamics on overt integrity tests: Experimental studies of the Reid Report. *Journal of Applied Psychology*, **79**, 643–658.
49. Drasgow, F. (1995, July). *Computer versus paper-and-pencil assessment*. Washington, DC: Personnel Testing Council of Metropolitan Washington. See also Burke, M. J. (1993). Computerized psychological testing: Impacts on measuring predictor constructs and future job behavior. In N. Schmitt & W. C. Borman (eds.), *Personnel selection in organizations*. San Francisco: Jossey-Bass, pp. 203–239.
50. Ghiselli, E. E. (1973). The validity of aptitude tests in personnel selection. *Personnel Psychology*, **26**, 461–467. See also Klimoski, R., & Brickner, M. (1987). Why do assessment centers work? The puzzle of assessment center validity. *Personnel Psychology*, **40**, 243–260. See also Lord, R. G., DeVader, C. L., & Alliger, G. M. (1986). A meta-analysis of the relationship between personality traits and leadership perceptions: An application of validity generalization procedures. *Journal of Applied Psychology*, **71**, 402–410.
51. Grimsley, G., & Jarrett, H. F. (1975). The relation of past managerial achievement to test measures obtained in the employment situation: Methodology and results—II. *Personnel Psychology*, **28**, 215–231. See also Korman, A. K. (1968). The prediction of managerial performance: A review. *Personnel Psychology*, **21**, 295–322. See also Kraut, A. I. (1969). Intellectual ability and promotional success among high-level managers. *Personnel Psychology*, **22**, 281–290.
52. Schmidt, F. L. (1992). What do data really mean? *American Psychologist*, **47**, 1173–1181. See also Schmidt, F. L., Pearlman, K., Hunter, J. E., & Hirsch, H. R. (1985). Forty questions about validity generalization and meta-analysis. *Personnel Psychology*, **38**, 697–798.

53. Bentz, V. J. (1985). Executive selection at Sears: An update. In H. J. Bernardin & D. A. Bownas (eds.), *Personality assessment in organizations.* New York: Praeger, pp. 82–144.
54. Hogan, R. T. (1991). Personality and personality measurement. In M. D. Dunnette & L. M. Hough (eds.), *Handbook of industrial and organizational psychology* (Vol. 2). Palo Alto, CA: Consulting Psychologists Press, pp. 873–919. See also Barrick, M. R., & Mount, M. K. (1991). The big five personality dimensions and job performance: A meta-analysis. *Personnel Psychology*, **44**, 1–26. See also Hough, L. M., Eaton, N. K., Dunnette, M. D., Kamp, J. D., & McCloy, R. A. (1990). Criterion-related validities of personality constructs and the effect of response distortion on those validities. *Journal of Applied Psychology Monograph*, **75**, 581–595.
55. Tett, R. P., Jackson, D. N., & Rothstein, M. (1991). Personality measures as predictors of job performance: A meta-analytic review. *Personnel Psychology*, **44**, 703–742.
56. Kelly, G. A. (1958). The theory and technique of assessment. *Annual Review of Psychology*, **9**, 323–352.
57. Kinslinger, H. J. (1966). Application of projective techniques in personnel psychology since 1940. *Psychological Bulletin*, **66**, 134–150.
58. Hogan, loc. cit.
59. Kerr, S., & Schriesheim, C. (1974). Consideration, initiating structure, and organizational criteria—an update of Korman's 1966 review. *Personnel Psychology*, **27**, 555–568. See also Schriesheim, C., House, R. A., & Kerr, S. (1976). Leader initiating structure: A reconciliation of discrepant research results and some empirical tests. *Organizational Behavior and Human Performance*, **15**, 297–321.
60. Kluger, A. N., Reilly, R. R., & Russell, C. J. (1991). Faking biodata tests: Are option-keyed instruments more resistant? *Journal of Applied Psychology*, **76**, 889–896.
61. Becker, T. E., & Colquitt, A. L. (1992). Potential versus actual faking of a biodata form: An analysis along several dimensions of item type. *Personnel Psychology*, **45**, 389–406.
62. Hough, L. M. (1984). Development and evaluation of the "accomplishment record" method of selecting and promoting professionals. *Journal of Applied Psychology*, **69**, 135–146.
63. Hough, L. M. (1985, Nov.). *The accomplishment record method of selecting, promoting, and appraising professionals.* Paper presented at the conference on Selection Guidelines, Testing, and the EEOC: An Update. Berkeley: University of California, Institute for Industrial Relations.
64. Hakel, M. D. (1989). Merit-based selection: Measuring the person for the job. In W. F. Cascio (ed.), *Human resource planning, employment, and placement.* Washington, DC: Bureau of National Affairs, pp. 2-135 to 2-158.
65. Conway, J. M., Jako, R. A., & Goodman, D. F. (1995). A meta-analysis of interrater and internal consistency reliability of selection interviews. *Journal of Applied Psychology*, **80**, 565–579. See also McDaniel, M. A., Whetzel, D. L., Schmidt, F. L., & Maurer, S. (1994). The validity of employment interviews: A comprehensive review and meta-analysis. *Journal of Applied Psychology*, **79** , 599–616. See also Bulkeley, W. (1994, Aug. 22). Replaced by technology: Job interviews. *The Wall Street Journal*, pp. B1, B5.
66. Arvey, R. D., Miller, H. E., Gould, R., & Burch, P. (1987). Interview validity for selecting sales clerks. *Personnel Psychology*, **40**, 1–12. See also Campion, M. A., Pursell, E. D., & Brown, B. K. (1988). Structured interviewing: Raising the psychometric properties of the employment interview. *Personnel Psychology*, **41**, 25–42. See also Harris, M. M. (1989). Reconsidering the employment interview: A review of recent literature and suggestions for future research. *Personnel Psychology*, **42**, 691–726.
67. Dipboye, R. L., & Gaugler, B. B. (1993). Cognitive and behavioral processes in the selection interview. In N. Schmitt & W. C. Borman (eds), *Personnel Selection in Organizations.* San Francisco: Jossey-Bass, pp. 135–170. See also Phillips, A. P., &

Dipboye, R. L. (1989). Correlational tests of a prediction from a process model of the interview. *Journal of Applied Psychology*, **74**, 41–52.

68. Campion et al., loc. cit.
69. Dipboye & Gaugler, loc. cit. See also Weekley, J. A., & Gier, J. A. (1987). Reliability and validity of the situational interview for a sales position. *Journal of Applied Psychology*, **72**, 484–487.
70. Motowidlo, S. J., Carter, G. W., Dunnette, M. D., Tippins, N., Werner, S., Burnett, J. R., & Vaughan, M. J. (1992). Studies of the structured behavioral interview. *Journal of Applied Psychology*, **77**, 571–587.
71. Schmitt, N., Gooding, R. Z., Noe, R. A., & Kirsch, M. (1984). Meta-analysis of validity studies published between 1964 and 1982 and the investigation of study characteristics. *Personnel Psychology*, **37**, 407–422.
72. Shore, T. H., Shore, L. M., & Thornton, G. C., III. (1992). Construct validity of self- and peer evaluations of performance dimensions in an assessment center. *Journal of Applied Psychology*, **77**, 42–54.
73. Asher, J. J., & Sciarrino, J. A. (1974). Realistic work sample tests: A review. *Personnel Psychology*, **27**, 519–533.
74. Cascio, W. F., & Phillips, N. (1979). Performance testing: A rose among thorns? *Personnel Psychology*, **32**, 751–766.
75. Wollowick, H. B., & McNamara, W. J. (1969). Relationship of the components of an assessment center to management success. *Journal of Applied Psychology*, **53**, 348–352.
76. Bass, B. M. (1954). The leaderless group discussion. *Psychological Bulletin*, **51**, 465–492. See also Tziner, A., & Dolan, S. (1982). Validity of an assessment center for identifying future female officers in the military. *Journal of Applied Psychology*, **67**, 728–736.
77. Kurecka, P. M., Austin, J. M., Jr., Johnson, W., & Mendoza, J. L. (1982). Full and errant coaching effects on assigned role leaderless group discussion performance. *Personnel Psychology*, **35**, 805–812. See also Petty, M. M. (1974). A multivariate analysis of the effects of experience and training upon performance in a leaderless group discussion. *Personnel Psychology*, **27**, 271–282.
78. Fredericksen, N. (1962). Factors in in-basket performance. *Psychological Monographs*, **76**(22, whole no. 541), 1.
79. Drasgow, op. cit.
80. See, for example, Brass, G. J., & Oldham, G. R. (1976). Validating an in-basket test using an alternative set of leadership scoring dimensions. *Journal of Applied Psychology*, **61**, 652–657. See also Tziner & Dolan, loc. cit.
81. Goldstein, I. L. (1993). *Training in organizations: Needs assessment, development, and evaluation* (3d ed.). Monterey, CA: Brooks/Cole.
82. Wollowick & McNamara, loc. cit.
83. Wexley, K. N., & Latham, G. P. (1991). *Developing and training human resources in organizations* (2d ed.). Glenview, IL: Scott, Foresman.
84. McKinnon, D. W. (1975). Assessment centers then and now. *Assessment and Development*, **2**, 8–9. See also Office of Strategic Services (OSS) Assessment Staff (1948). Assessment of men. New York: Rinehart.
85. Bray, D. W. (1976). The assessment center method. In R. L. Craig (ed.), *Training and development handbook* (2d ed.). New York: McGraw-Hill, pp. 16-1 to 16-15.
86. Borman, W. C. (1982). Validity of behavioral assessment for predicting military recruiter performance. *Journal of Applied Psychology*, **67**, 3–9. See also Pulakos, E. D., Borman, W. C., & Hough, L. M. (1988). Test validation for scientific understanding: Two demonstrations of an approach to studying predictor-criterion linkages. *Personnel Psychology*, **41**, 703–716.

87. Lorenzo, R. V. (1984). Effects of assessorship on managers' proficiency in acquiring, evaluating, and communicating information about people. *Personnel Psychology*, **37**, 617–634.
88. Byham, W. C. (1970). Assessment centers for spotting future managers. *Harvard Business Review*, **48**, 150–160.
89. Gaugler, B. B., Rosenthal, D. B., Thornton, G. C., III, & Bentson, C. (1987). Meta-analysis of assessment center validity. *Journal of Applied Psychology*, **72**, 493-511.
90. Ibid. See also Howard, A. (1974). An assessment of assessment centers. *Academy of Management Journal*, **17**, 115–134. See also Klimoski & Brickner, loc. cit.
91. Thornton, G. C., III, & Byham, W. C. (1982). *Assessment centers and managerial performance*. New York: Academic Press. See also Huck, J. R., & Bray, D. W. (1976). Management assessment center evaluations and subsequent job performance of white and black females. *Personnel Psychology*, **29**, 13–30.
92. Cascio, W. F., & Ramos, R. A. (1986). Development and application of a new method for assessing job performance in behavioral/economic terms. *Journal of Applied Psychology*, **71**, 20–28. See also Cascio, W. F., & Silbey, V. (1979). Utility of the assessment center as a selection device. *Journal of Applied Psychology*, **64**, 107–118.
93. Klimoski, loc. cit. See also Gaugler, B. B., & Thornton, G. C., III (1989). Number of assessment center dimensions as a determinant of assessor accuracy. *Journal of Applied Psychology*, **74**, 611–618. See also Reilly, R. R., Henry, S., & Smither, J. W. (1990). An examination of the effects of using behavior checklists on the construct validity of assessment center dimensions. *Journal of Applied Psychology*, **43**, 71–84.
94. Hinrichs, J. R. (1969). Comparison of "real life" assessments of management potential with situational exercises, paper-and-pencil ability tests, and personality inventories. *Journal of Applied Psychology*, **53**, 425–433.
95. Hinrichs, J. R. (1978). An eight-year follow-up of a management assessment center. *Journal of Applied Psychology*, **63**, 596–601.
96. Ibid.
97. Koenig, R. (1987, Dec. 1). Exacting employer: Toyota takes pains, and time, filling jobs at its Kentucky plant. *The Wall Street Journal*, pp. 1, 31.
98. Cascio & Ramos, loc. cit.
99. Miller, M. W. (1993, Aug. 2). Fate seemed to have a Gerstner in mind for top job at IBM. *The Wall Street Journal*, pp. A1, A13.
100. Boudreau, J. W. (1991). Utility analysis for decisions in human resource management. In M. D. Dunnette & L. M. Hough (eds.), *Handbook of industrial and organizational psychology* (Vol. 2). Palo Alto, CA: Consulting Psychologists Press, pp. 621–745.
101. Terpstra, D. E., & Rozell, E. J. (1993). The relationship of staffing practices to organizational-level measures of performance. *Personnel Psychology*, **46**, 27–48.
102. Cascio, W. F. (1991). *Costing human resources: The financial impact of behavior in organizations* (3d ed.). Boston: PWS-Kent. See also Boudreau, loc. cit.
103. Hunter, J. E., & Schmidt, F. L. (1983). Quantifying the effects of psychological interventions on employee job performance and workforce productivity. *American Psychologist*, **38**, 473–478.
104. Schmidt, F. L., Hunter, J. E., McKenzie, R., & Muldrow, T. (1979). The impact of valid selection procedures on workforce productivity. *Journal of Applied Psychology*, **64**, 609–626.

CASE IN THE NEWS

Balancing Work And Family

By Keith H. Hammonds

BIG RETURNS FOR COMPANIES WILLING TO GIVE FAMILY STRATEGIES A CHANCE

You're a solid manager and, word has it, a decent guy to work for. You treat your people well. But you've also got product to move—and since last year's restructuring, the proposals and requests have come at you like a wicked tsunami. Your staff seems a little frayed at the edges—no surprise, really, since they're in at 7:30 a.m. for the daily briefing and don't leave until past six. You're still trying to make just one of your kid's soccer games. And you can't remember the last long talk you had with your wife (though you do swap E-mail).

"Work and family"? Yeah, right. You've heard about some program the company offers. Child care, flexible hours, that sort of thing. A few employees actually use it, but they're mainly women with young kids—not people who want a career. Not your boss. And not your staff. Frankly, you think it's a load of hooey.

Clear Gains

You might want to talk to the folks at First Tennessee National Corp. Three years ago, they started taking family issues seriously, treating them as strategic business questions. The bank got rid of a lot of work rules and let employees figure out which schedules worked best—"because they know what needs to be done" both on and off the job, says Becky Tipton, a department supervisor. Then it carted in a kitchen-sink-load of programs to ease family distractions, marketed them relentlessly, and sent Tipton and 1,000 other managers through 3½ days of training.

In short order, clear gains in productivity and customer service emerged. As employees got control over their workplace, "managers had to change the way they did business," says CEO Ralph Horn. Ultimately, though, supervisors rated by their subordinates as supportive of work-family balance retained employees twice as long as the bank average and kept 7% more retail customers. Higher retention rates, First Tennessee says, contributed to a 55% profit gain over two years, to $106 million.

DUPONT

SUMMER CAMP

Work-family programs at DuPont range from on-site camp for kids to in-home emergency elder care.

Disbelievers, skeptics, working stiffs, take note: Work-family strategies haven't just hit the corporate mainstream—they've become a competitive advantage. The exclusive province of working mothers a decade ago, such benefits now extend to elder-care assistance, flexible scheduling, job-sharing, adoption benefits, on-site summer camp, employee help lines, even—no joke—pet-care and lawn-service referrals. The titles "work/life coordinator" and "director of diversity" have entered the bureaucratic lexicon; the ranks of consultants in the field have mushroomed. At the political conventions in August, family-friendliness was all the rage.

It is a phenomenon, in other words, that executives deny at their own risk, now that the two-income family is a fact of life. So *Business Week,* together with the Center on Work & Family at Boston University, has embarked on a new initiative to rate companies on their family-friendly strategies. The nearly year-long study's goal: to identify employers' best practices by asking both companies and employees to describe their work-family balancing acts. How do employers keep productivity growing while addressing family concerns? Can employees have a life and still get ahead?

The results add up to a compelling agenda for corporate managers. Yet they also reflect a yawning divide between family-friendliness in theory and in practice. While 48% of the 8,000 employees in *Business Week*'s survey said they could "have a good family life and still get ahead" in their company, 60% reported that management didn't, or only "somewhat" did, take people into account when making decisions. More telling, more than two-fifths said that work had a negative impact on their home lives. "I may have flexibility to accommodate family needs . . . but I'm home working until midnight to get my job done," wrote one employee. Indeed, says Bradley K. Googins, director of the Center on Work & Family, "while many companies offer benefits and programs, the underlying cultural issues still aren't very well addressed."

Ten companies with impressive strategies and results did emerge from *Business Week*'s study (table, page 255). Some of the leaders were hardly surprises: DuPont, Hewlett-Packard, and Motorola, among others, have led innovation in the work-family arena for a decade or longer. Others aren't as well-known. Eddie Bauer Inc., for one, combines a strong people-oriented culture with a host of leading-edge benefits. And Marriott International Inc. heads a small group of employers seeking solutions for the problems presented by a predominantly low-wage workforce.

What impact does your work have on your home life?

Negative impact 42%

Neutral 26%

Positive impact 32%

The biggest surprise, though, was the company that won the highest overall grades: First Tennessee, a midsize regional bank that only recently has won attention for its progressive work-family response. First Tennessee offers luxurious benefits such as on-site child care or vouchers, job-sharing, and fitness centers. But it also demonstrates an intelligent strategic view of the problem. Work and family, it argues, are not discrete phenomena. They necessarily touch one another, often profoundly. The solution, then, is to build consideration of family issues into job design, work processes, and organizational structures—just as one would consider marketing concerns, say, or engineering input.

In practice, that means that Constance E. Wimbley and her seven co-workers in the bank's Alcoa (Tenn.) account reconcilement department determine work-family balance for themselves. Freed from attendance guidelines, the clerks adjust their schedules to match the work—and their lives. "We're all grown adults," Wimbley says. "It makes me feel good about working here."

When Wimbley works overtime, her team members let her 4-year-old daughter, Chelsie, wait in the office while they finish. Another clerical group opted to work fewer hours in the middle of each month to balance the overtime they put in when month-end account statements went in the mail. Turnaround time on statements was cut in half.

FIRST TENNESSEE
JOB REDESIGN
Constance Wimbley's co-workers let her daughter, Chelsie, hang out during overtime.

First Tennessee's premise—and that of other leaders in the *Business Week* ranking—is that family concerns affect business results. Yet that thinking, while simple, escapes many companies. Typically, executives view work-family initiatives as inexpensive, politically correct gestures, easy accommodations to workers who otherwise have been slammed by stagnant wages, benefit cuts, and layoffs. Managers fail to buy in, and workers fear torpedoing their careers by appearing less than completely committed to their jobs.

Employees acknowledge their companies' wealth of family-oriented programs but say they often don't do the job. Half of the respondents, and even more of high-paid managers and professionals, said they felt "a lot" of stress and pressure at work. Men were more likely than women to say their employer expected long hours no matter how it affected personal life. Production and clerical workers, meanwhile, gave generally lower ratings, reflecting an undercurrent of tension distinctly at odds with the friendly cultures most participating companies say they promote. "Most benefits are offered to managers, technical and office staff," wrote one worker. "Shift employees have *no* options."

Does your company have high-quality programs for people who have to care for children or elder family members?

Not at all/ Not much 23%

Somewhat 26%

Considerably/ A great deal 51%

The study rated work-family policies and benefits at 37 publicly traded companies from the *Business Week* 1000, ranging in size from 1,243 to 218,000 U.S. employees. An initial survey, designed by the Center on Work & Family with Philip H. Mirvis, adjunct professor of organizational behavior at the University of Michigan, graded employers on their self-described breadth of programs, flexible work arrangements, and organizational infrastructure. A second questionnaire, delivered to 500 randomly selected employees at each company, asked workers to assess the results. (Some of the questions, and employees' responses, are found on these pages.)

The project provoked considerable curiosity and angst. Several large employers well-known for enlightened work-family strategies—notably, IBM, Corning, and Johnson & Johnson—declined to participate, as did The McGraw-Hill Companies, *Business Week*'s parent. Most commonly, companies said they were wary, understandably, of exposing employees' views to the world's scrutiny. Indeed, GTE Corp. and AT&T, both known for rigorous consideration of work-family balance, were knocked off the list of leaders by relatively weak employee responses—a function, at least in part, of the seismic restructuring that has shaken the telecommunications industry and destroyed workers' sense of job security. In contrast, MBNA America Bank won the highest employee rating despite the limited group receiving its benefits. Employees cited a culture that, while formal and demanding, addressed the needs of a workforce whose average age is 28.

Other employers cited a conflict between *Business Week*'s project and their own internal surveys, or said they simply had no time. "We're in the business of making hamburgers," said a McDonald's Corp. executive. "We don't do surveys." And some questioned the survey's methodology, especially the lack of complete assurance that everyone would play by the same rules. (In fact, one company was disqualified when 145 of the 216 surveys its employees returned were found to contain nearly identical—and optimal—answers.)

DUPONT
FLEXTIME
With a new schedule, Kevin Murphy cares for his 86-year-old aunt. "I feel I owe them something back," he says.

Ultimately, companies expressed discomfort in publicly exploring a phenomenon still in its adolescence—and one still built on "a little more than faith and a little less than pure science," as MBNA Vice-Chairman Lance L. Weaver says. As recently as 1984, after all, "there was little or no general awareness" of work and family issues, recalls Faith A. Wohl, who led many of DuPont's early initiatives and now oversees day-care and telecommuting efforts for the U.S. General Services Administration. Around that time, DuPont, AT&T, IBM, and a few other large employers began grappling with the need for quality day care presented by an influx of women into the workforce.

Employers had traveled this road before, funding on-site day-care centers, for example, when women took over American factories during World War II. This time, though, the need didn't dissipate as it had when the boys came home—and the agenda quickly broadened. Employers discovered workers such as Kevin Murphy, a 48-year-old distribution planner in DuPont's floor products division in Wilmington, Del. Four years ago, Murphy's 86-year-old aunt, Catherine Boyle, had a stroke that left her unable to care for herself. Murphy was the only relative left to help her.

"It was something totally new," Murphy recalls. It took two months to place Boyle in a nursing home, which he found through a DuPont-contracted referral agency. He worked half-days through that time. After that, Murphy arranged with his supervisor to work a flexible shift that typically starts at 6:30 a.m. That allows him to visit his aunt as she rises, put in a full day, then return to the nursing home to feed her dinner and put her to bed.

Can you have a good family life and still get ahead in your company?

Not at all/ Not much 22%

Somewhat 30%

Considerably/ A great deal 48%

DuPont's return on such flexibility: Commitment. "I feel like I owe them something back," Murphy says. Evidence is mounting that such loyalty has a tangible effect on profitability. At Fel-Pro Inc., a private automotive gasket manufacturer in Skokie, Ill., University of Chicago Associate Professor Susan J. Lambert found that workers who took advantage of family-friendly programs were more likely to participate in team problem-solving, and nearly twice as likely to suggest product or process improvements.

Hitting Home

Reductions in absenteeism and turnover are even more manifest. Aetna Life & Casualty Co. halved the rate of resignations among new mothers by extending its unpaid parental leave to six months, saving it $1 million a year in hiring and training expenses. The Families & Work Institute found that a raft of family programs introduced en masse at Johnson & Johnson in 1992 reduced the number of days absent among all workers. In a broader 1993 study, the institute determined that workers with access to flexible time and leave were more likely to remain at their employers.

Such numbers are swaying some top executives. "The impact we're having on morale and our ability to attract and retain the people we want is clearly going to give us an economic payback," says Eli Lilly CEO Randall L. Tobias. Personal experience is moving other leaders to act. Hewlett-Packard Co.'s embrace of family-friendliness firmed after Lewis E. Platt became CEO in 1992. Platt's first wife had died of cancer 11 years earlier, leaving him responsible for the care of two young daughters. For J. Randall MacDonald, GTE's senior vice-president for human resources, the question hit home, literally, when his wife had to care for an elderly relative. Trying to rush his daughter off to school, he was informed it was a holiday; MacDonald ended up taking her along to a business meeting in Boston.

Awareness and acceptance of family issues at the top is a starting point, and 54% of survey respondents indicated their top brass do, in fact, demonstrate support for family balance. But the question remains: How can you turn that glowing CEO speech into something more than lip service? "This is a jugular issue being treated in a marginal way," says Fran Rogers, CEO of Work/Family Directions, the field's biggest consultancy. Most companies, experts say, have limited their efforts to child-care and elder-care referral services. At a cost of $2 to $3 per employee per year, they're a cheap fix. Instituting *flextime,* likewise, is literally as easy as inserting a paragraph in the employee handbook, and by 1995, 73% of large companies had done so, according to the benefits consultant Hewitt Associates.

Is your supervisor flexible when it comes to responding to your work-family needs?

Not at all/ Not much 8%

Somewhat 16%

Considerably/ A great deal 76%

Such programs don't work, though, unless managers let them. Lisa Latno, rated an "outstanding" performer by superiors, nonetheless was ready to quit her job in Unum Corp.'s policy-adjustment department seven years ago after a supervisor turned down her request to work 10 fewer hours a week. She was commuting three hours a day, and raising a 2-year-old son. "I did it for one year, and found it unbearable," she says. Finally, another manager, Diane Rogers, invited Latno to take a 30-hour-a-week job in her department. Even Rogers was wary: "I might not have bought in that quickly if it was someone I didn't know as well."

Vision Thing

Commitment from managers and employees alike comes from a culture where the embrace of family balance is pervasive and consistent. At Motorola, which placed second in *Business Week*'s survey, a work-life vision statement is reinforced by regular training for supervisors and seminars for the rank and file, and by 50 professionals responsible for programs worldwide. It is translated into a set of benefits offered to workers across the company that reflects the company's values and business goals: "Special Delivery" gives expectant parents a 24-hour nurse hotline, and a pager for dad in the last trimester; long-term care insurance provides security for employees' extended families.

And at Eddie Bauer, as annual sales growth of 20% threatens to bureaucratize the retailer's traditionally informal environment, "work-life programs allow us to keep it personal," says President Richard Fersch. So the headquarters café stays open late to prepare take-out meals for harried employees to take home, and a paid "balance day" off a year is meant to ease workers' juggling.

EDDIE BAUER MEALS-TO-GO The headquarters café is open late, with take-out food for rushed workers such as Laura and Bart Brosten.

Companies that truly get it go a step further, integrating family support into the business itself. At Hewlett-Packard, CEO Platt demands that every business unit identify work-family issues and propose an action plan as part of its annual business review. So when HP's printer group, facing higher consumer demand, had to increase the number of shifts its manufacturing employees worked, it also investigated alternatives for round-the-clock child care. Financial managers recently won approval of a plan to get work done more efficiently by rescheduling activities that cause peak-period bottlenecks, avoiding staffing gaps, and providing technology to allow work from home and other sites. The goal is to encourage more effective work, with less employee burn-out.

A striking study of Xerox, Corning, and Tandem Computer to be released in early October by the Ford Foundation underscores HP's approach. A team of researchers found that successful solutions involved rethinking work processes, rather than finding ways to make people's lives fit the work. "The usual way of dealing with families, individual negotiations between manager and employee, was incomplete," Massachusetts Institute of Technology Professor Lotte Bailyn says. "We had to look at how work was structured, at the culture around work, the norms, from the point of view of people's families."

Just as at First Tennessee, managers at Xerox Corp.'s Dallas customer-administration center handed over responsibility for scheduling shifts to workers themselves and saw an overnight drop in absenteeism—and then, higher productivity. A product-development team in Webster, N.Y., banned early-morning and late-night meetings, which had pushed into family time, and eliminated reports to give engineers more time to think. Result: happier engineers, and the first on-time launch of a new product in the business' history.

UNUM
SUPPORTIVE BOSS Lisa Latno was able to work less to accommodate a toddler and a three-hour commute.

Slowly, employers are beginning to grasp the importance of examples such as Xerox, Hewlett-Packard, and First Tennessee. They had better. Poll after poll indicates that U.S. workers feel a loss of control over their lives. "Companies are seeing they have all these programs, but people are still really stressed out," says Ellen Galinsky, the Families & Work Institute's director. Certainly, employees bear some responsibility for determining their own family balance. But they need help. Companies that recognize the need and adapt work to peoples' lives will win workers' loyalty—and, with that, a competitive edge.

AN INAUGURAL *BUSINESS WEEK* SURVEY ASKS BOTH WORKERS AND EMPLOYERS TO GRADE FAMILY-FRIENDLINESS

Grading Family-Friendliness

Here are the 10 top-scoring companies in *Business Week*'s first-ever rating of work and family strategies. Many employers extend workers some child-care assistance and flexible work options, among other family-friendly programs. This study, though, assessed not only what companies offer but also whether employees feel they're able to use such benefits without putting their careers at risk. These leading companies lived up to their promises.

DuPont

A child-care pioneer in 1984, the chemical giant now has work-life committees at 15 sites. Offers flextime, job-sharing, and telecommuting across its workforce. Employees praise supervisors for flexibility on family needs but cite low job security.

Eddie Bauer

The pay isn't great, but employees like the hours and say management demonstrates impressive family support. A host of innovative programs, including lactation rooms, take-out dinners, and one paid "Balance Day" off a year.

Eli Lilly

CEO Randall Tobias has been an aggressive champion of work-family balance as a business strategy. His message is reinforced by many task forces and employee surveys. Yet workers say having a family life and getting ahead professionally still isn't easy.

	1995 Sales, billions	U.S. employees	Strategy & programs	Employee rating
DUPONT	$42.2	56,825	A	B+
EDDIE BAUER	1.4	9,238	B+	A–
ELI LILLY	6.8	12,826	A–	B
FIRST TENNESSEE BANK	0.4	8,000	A–	A
HEWLETT-PACKARD	31.5	60,000	B+	A–
MARRIOTT INTERNATIONAL	0.9	175,000	B+	B+
MBNA AMERICA BANK	2.6	12,495	C+	A
MERRILL LYNCH	21.5	40,000	B	B+
MOTOROLA	27.0	75,000	A	A–
UNUM LIFE INSURANCE	4.1	4,456	B+	A–

NOTES: Letter grades approximate quantitative scores from two surveys. "Strategy and programs" grades reflect results from questionnaires completed by human resources executives at 37 companies, counting for 40% of the total score. Employers were graded on the percentage of workforce to which a range of programs was available. Flexible work arrangements counted for 8% of the score; family and dependent care, 8%; and health and wellness programs, 8%. Companies were awarded up to 4 points for offering programs to hourly and part-time workers, and 8 more points for a work-family organizational infrastructure. An assessment of strategy and culture counted for 8 points. A letter grade of "A" on this portion corresponds to a score of at least 32 on the 40-point scale. "Employee rating" reflects the combined results from a multiple-choice questionnaire sent to 500 randomly selected workers at each company, of which an average of 44% were returned. Employees were asked to rate various attributes of their companies on a five-point scale. This survey counted for 60% of the total score, as follows: Quality of work life, including hours and pay, 18%; flexibility in practice, 18%; family-friendly culture, 18%; overall assessment of work-family environment, 6%. A letter of "A" on this portion corresponds to a score of at least 45 on the 60-point scale. Certain survey responses that did not meet tests for statistical viability were removed from the results.

First Tennessee Bank
A powerful companywide commitment to family issues, employees say, despite pay and benefits below that of other leaders. Worker teams set their own schedules and say flexibility is central to company culture. Family-friendliness, the bank says, produces better customer service.

Hewlett-Packard
The technology blue chip integrates family support into business strategies at the business unit level, spurred by CEO Lewis Platt. Managers take work-life training. Employees say they feel comfortable taking time off for family problems. The downside: Lots of stress.

MBNA America Bank
It offers a plethora of family programs and benefits—but typically not to the majority of workers. Nonetheless, the bank won the highest grades from employees, who cited both strong programs and job flexibility. Weakness: Spillover from work into home life.

Marriott International
Workers show high job satisfaction, despite low marks for pay and benefits. The hotelier is rolling out a national Associate Resource Line to address family concerns of its hourly workers. So far, employees say programs are good, but not great, at meeting their needs.

Merrill Lynch
A relative latecomer to work-family strategies, the investment bank is still ramping up programs and training. Employees recognize this weakness, but say that despite high stress, the company doesn't ask too much at the expense of family.

Motorola

Executives recognize that work-life balance plays a strategic role in long-term financial success. Management and employee training on family issues is pervasive. Upshot: Employees laud programs and job flexibility, but aren't as happy with their hours and pay.

UNUM Life Insurance

Strong employee orientation is ingrained in the company culture, and programs respond to many task forces and regular surveys. Workers report long hours and relatively low job security but say family programs and flexibility meet their needs.

Data: Boston University Center on Work & Family; *Business Week*, Research Assistants: Susan Brandner, Melissa Eddy.

EDITORIAL

Like It or Not, Work Is a Family Affair

What is Corporate America's responsibility to the family? While Republicans and Democrats at their conventions prattled on about the government helping the family, it is the workplace that has the bigger impact on family life in the U.S. Wages, schedules, benefits, job security or insecurity—all affect the quality of family life. The stresses of technological change and global competition can be seen on the faces of husbands, wives, and children everywhere. After downsizing, reengineering, and getting their employees to work harder and better, companies might do well to tackle work and family issues. It just might give them an even greater competitive edge.

A yearlong project between *Business Week* and the Center on Work & Family on employers' best practices underscores the benefits that accrue to companies that treat work and family issues as strategic business questions. Flexible scheduling, job-sharing, and on-site child care or vouchers cut absenteeism and turnover, boosting productivity. The key is for managers to give up control of the process of work and empower employees to determine how it gets done. *Business Week*'s top 10 family-friendly companies include Eddie Bauer, Motorola, and Hewlett-Packard (page 255).

Corporations, however, should be wary about delving too deeply in family life. There are now "work/life coordinators" and "directors of diversity" who are extending work/family programs to include pet care and lawn service. That's ridiculous. What companies can provide is flexibility in time and good compensation so that families can buy services in the marketplace. Providing quality health care, as part of compensation, is especially important. In their successful drive to reduce medical costs (where inflation is the lowest in 20 years), some companies have allowed the quality of care to diminish.

Thoughtful, focused work/family programs can be competitive assets for many companies. As for the politicians helping the family this election season, we have one suggestion: Start by lifting the marriage penalty in the tax code.

Discussion Questions

1. Develop a presentation to convince skeptical senior managers that work-family strategies are a competitive advantage. Cite specific company examples.
2. Develop a presentation to convince skeptical workers that they should "buy in" to work-family strategies. What might a company do to convince them that they will not damage their careers by doing so?
3. You work for a cable television company's round-the-clock customer-support group that responds to customer inquiries by phone. Develop an action plan that integrates family support into the work of this unit.

PART 3

DEVELOPMENT

Once employees are on board, their personal growth and development over time become a major concern. Change is a fact of organizational life, and coping with it effectively requires planned programs of employee training, development, and career management. We address these issues in Chapters 7 through 9. Chapter 7 examines what is known about training and developing management and nonmanagement employees. Chapter 8 is concerned with performance management—particularly with the design, implementation, and evaluation of such systems. Finally, Chapter 9 considers the many issues involved in managing careers—from the perspective of individuals at different career stages and from the perspective of organizational staffing decisions. The overall objective of Part 3 is to establish a framework for managing the development process of employees as their careers in organizations unfold.

7 WORKPLACE TRAINING

Questions This Chapter Will Help Managers Answer

1. Why should firms expect to expand their training outlays and their menu of choices for employees at all levels?
2. What kind of evidence is necessary to justify investments in training programs?
3. What are the key issues that should be addressed in the design, conduct, and evaluation of training programs?
4. Why should we invest time and money on new-employee orientation? Is there a payoff?
5. How should new-employee orientation be managed for maximum positive impact?

*THE NEW EDUCATORS: COMPANY-BASED SCHOOLS**

Human Resource Management in Action

The news hit the floor of the Collins & Aikman carpet plant in Dalton, Georgia, with a thud: the massive tufting machines and shearing equipment that lined the factory floor were being hooked up to computers. More than a third of the 560 workers at the plant were high school dropouts; a few could not read or write. The prospect of working with a computer was terrifying. Said a plant serviceman who depended on a pocket calculator to tally the weights of various yarns: "I was scared to death."

So are companies across the United States that are trying to join the race for global markets. They are discovering that many of their employees, as well as students fresh from the nation's schools, cannot meet the demands of high-tech jobs. The consequences are not pleasant: declining productivity, an inability to generate new business, and a possible loss of existing business. Some firms have opted for cheap labor instead of advanced technology, moving across the border to Mexico or overseas to Taiwan.

But a growing number of businesses, including Collins & Aikman, are taking another tack: trying to do educational makeovers of their own workforces. Unable to wait for public schools or vocational schools to catch up with their corporate needs, these employers are taking on the role of educators. They are pouring millions of dollars and thousands of hours into high school equivalency courses and basic skill training. Much of it is being taught inside company walls on company time.

As recently as the early 1980s, education was hardly a priority at the carpet plants in the area. For decades, a strong back and nimble hands were enough. HR officers simply smiled to themselves when applicants who were asked to fill out forms suddenly would say, "Can I take this home? I forgot my glasses." Then, because they actually were unable to read or write, they would get someone else to fill out the forms for them.

By 1989, however, the smiles were disappearing fast. The company was buying more sophisticated equipment designed to meet the needs of a changing business. In addition to wanting more types of carpets and more colors in shorter periods of time, customers were demanding floor coverings, with, say, their company logos woven into the fabric. Collins & Aikman installed new tufting machines that can weave elaborate patterns, new automated shearers that work 80 times faster than their predecessors, and new yarn machines that spin out precisely the amount of material needed for each run—all controlled by computer keyboards and all thoroughly intimidating to many workers.

Meanwhile, management had done a study of educational backgrounds and found that fully one-third of the staff had not graduated from high school and only 8 percent of the laborers had the skills the company expected to need in the twenty-first century. These include the ability to analyze machine performance and to make on-the-spot production decisions, tasks that currently are performed by plant supervisors.

*Adapted from H. Cooper, The new educators, *The Wall Street Journal*, Oct. 5, 1992, pp. A1, A6.

So a year ago the company hired an adult education teacher and set up classes on the plant floor. Eighty workers signed up. For 2 hours a day, 2 days a week, on each of three shifts, the new teacher taught reading, writing, science, social studies, and math. The company spent an average of $1200 for each worker's training, including lost work time. The employees themselves often found the task daunting. After a full day's work, they had to spend hours in the evening on homework. Was the effort worth it?

Challenges

1. What are the key distinguishing features of this approach to training?
2. How can the company determine whether or not its training is effective?
3. What obstacles to the success of such a program can you identify?

Traditionally, lower-level employees were "trained," while higher-level employees were "developed." This distinction, focusing on the learning of hands-on skills versus interpersonal and decision-making skills, has become too blurry in practice to be useful. Throughout the remainder of this chapter, therefore, we will use the terms "training" and "development" interchangeably. In the United States, as in many other countries, training is big business, and the first half of this chapter examines some current issues in the design, conduct, and evaluation of training programs.

Change, growth, and sometimes displacement are facts of modern organizational life. The stock market crash of October 19, 1987, vividly illustrated this fact. In the wave of layoffs following the crash, more than 18,000 professionals in the financial services industry lost their jobs. As they found new jobs, they discovered what all new employees do: one has to "relearn the ropes" in the new job setting. Orientation training, the subject of the second part of this chapter, can ease that process considerably, with positive results for both the new employee and the company. Trends such as leased employees, disposable managers, and free-agent workers will make orientation even more important in the future. Let's begin by defining training, and considering some emerging trends in this area.

EMPLOYEE TRAINING

What Is Training?

Training consists of planned programs designed to improve performance at the individual, group, and/or organizational levels. Improved performance, in turn, implies that there have been measurable changes in knowledge, skills, attitudes, and/or social behavior.

When we examine the training enterprise as a whole, it is clear that training issues can be addressed from at least two perspectives. At the structural level, one can examine issues such as the aggregate level of expenditures by the various providers of training (e.g., federal, state, and local governments, educational institutions, private-sector businesses), the degree of cooperation among the providers, incentives (or lack of incentives) for providing training, who gets training, and the economic impact of training. These are macrolevel concerns.

At the micro level, one may choose to examine issues such as what types of training seem to yield positive outcomes for organizations and trainees (i.e., what "works"); how to identify if training is needed and, if so, what type of training best fits the needs that have been identified; how to structure the delivery of training programs; and how to evaluate the outcomes of training efforts.

Unfortunately, organizations sometimes place too much emphasis on the techniques and methods of training and not enough on first defining what the employee should learn in relation to desired job behaviors. In addition, very few organizations make an effort to determine whether the training objectives were met.

In this section, we will do two things: (1) discuss several structural issues at the macro level, and (2) illustrate research-based findings that might lead to improvements in the design, delivery, and evaluation of training systems. Before we do so, however, let's consider some important training trends.

Training Trends

Both economic and demographic trends suggest radical changes in the composition of the workforce of the 1990s.[1] Other factors that affect the number, types, and requirements of available jobs include automation; continuing worker displacement as a function of mergers, acquisitions, and downsizing; and the shift from manufacturing to service jobs.[2] In the mid-1990s, for example, 84 percent of U.S. employees worked in service-based industries.[3]

These issues suggest five reasons why the time and money budgeted for training will increase during the next decade:[4]

1. The number of unskilled and undereducated youth who will be needed for entry-level jobs
2. Increasingly sophisticated technological systems that will impose training and retraining requirements on the existing workforce
3. The need to train currently underutilized groups of racial and ethnic minorities, women, and older workers
4. The need, as more firms move to employee involvement and teams in the workplace, for team members to learn behaviors such as asking for ideas, offering help without being asked, using listening and feedback skills, and recognizing and considering the ideas of others[5]
5. Training needs stimulated by the internationally competitive environments of many organizations

Former Labor Secretary Robert Reich described the challenge clearly: "If we have an adequately educated and trained workforce and a state-of-the-art infrastructure linking them together and with the rest of the world, then global capital will come here to create good jobs. If we don't, the only way global capital will be invested here is if we promise low wages."[6]

Indeed, as the demands of the second industrial revolution spread, companies are coming to regard training expenses as no less a part of their capital costs than plants and equipment. Direct training outlays by U.S. firms now exceed $50 billion per year—and they are rising.[7] At the individual-firm level, Motorola is exemplary. It budgets about 1 percent of annual sales (2.6 percent of payroll) for training. It even trains workers for its key suppliers, many of them small- to medium-size firms without the resources to train their own people in such advanced specialties as computer-aided design and defect control. Taking into account training expenses, wages, and benefits, the total cost to Motorola amounts to about $90 million. The results have been dramatic, according to a company spokesperson: "We've documented the savings from the statistical process control methods and problem-solving methods we've trained our people in. We're running a rate of return of about 30 times the dollars invested—which is why we've gotten pretty good support from senior management."[8]

Retraining, too, can pay off. A study by the Work in America Institute found that retraining current workers for new jobs is more cost-effective than firing them and hiring new ones—not to mention the difference that retraining makes to employee morale.[9] Intel illustrates this approach nicely.

COMPANY EXAMPLE

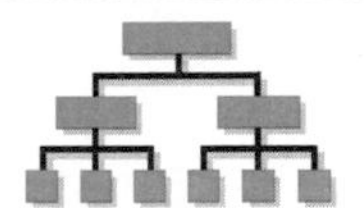

REDEPLOYMENT AT INTEL[10]

Intel, the company that invented the microchip, and whose average product lifecycle is just 2.5 years, has avoided major layoffs through a strong in-house redeployment policy. Every employee receives a brochure entitled "Owning Your Own Employability," and is afforded tools and resources to take advantage of the redeployment option. A redeployment event occurs when there is a business downturn or lack of a need for a particular skill. It does not replace performance management, as Intel's Marile Robinson, corporate manager of redeployment, points out: "It's not meant to shift around people with poor skills, poor performers, or those with behavioral problems."[11] To qualify, a full-time employee must have 2 consecutive years of performance reviews that "meet requirements."

Should an employee become eligible for redeployment, he or she is given options, tools, and resources. The company has five employee development centers offering self-assessment tools, career counseling, educational opportunities, and job listings within Intel. Job skills have been redefined to encourage people to find new places within the company, and temporary assignments (as many as two assignments for a total of 12 months) and up to $8000 of training are provided to prepare them for new positions. Funds are also available for relocation. The entire process is managed through a system that provides centralized tracking and reporting of all redeployment activity.

The ranks of Intel employees are filled with those who have made successful transitions from shop floor to sales and public relations positions, or from obsolete technology divisions to high-margin technology centers within the company. If none of this works, the company pays for outplacement assistance for affected employees. Redeployment is a continuing challenge at Intel because the company's competitive strategy is to stay ahead of its rivals by making its products obsolete!

Between 1989 and 1991, Intel closed plants employing 2000 people, and redeployed approximately 80 percent of the affected workers. From 1991 to 1994, redeployment events affected 3409 employees. The company placed 90 percent of them internally, and in 1994 there was no litigation as a result of plant closures.[12]

Structural Issues in the Delivery of Training

Despite compelling arguments for training, at least nine structural issues must be addressed if training systems are to reach their full potential. Here are some problems often identified at the macro level:[13]

1. **Corporate commitment is lacking and uneven.** Most companies spend nothing at all on training. Those that do tend to concentrate on managers, technicians, and professionals, not rank-and-file workers. Fortunately, this situation is changing; as a result of the rapid pace of introduction of new technology, combined with new approaches to organization design and production management, many companies simply cannot afford not to train.[14] Workers have to learn three kinds of new skills: (1) the ability to use the new technology, (2) the ability to maintain it, and (3) the ability to diagnose system problems.[15] In an increasingly competitive marketplace, the ability to implement rapid changes in products and technologies is often a key requirement to preserve the competitive edge.

2. **Aggregate expenditures by business on training are inadequate.** Thus the American Society for Training and Development urges businesses to increase training expenditures to at least 2 percent of their annual payrolls—up from the current U.S. industry average of 1.2 percent. Leading companies invest much more: General Electric (4.6 percent of payroll), U.S. Robotics (4.2 percent), Motorola (4 percent), Texas Instruments (3 percent).[16]

3. **Businesses complain that schools award degrees, but the degrees are no guarantee that graduates have mastered skills.** As a result, business must spend large amounts of money to retrain workers in basic skills. In a recent survey, business executives said about 37 percent of their workforces lack fundamental math and writing skills. However, only about 15 percent of the companies provide training in mathematics, and only 10 percent aid in reading.[17]

4. **Poaching trained workers is a major problem for U.S. businesses, and provides a strong disincentive for training.** Unlike Germany, where local business groups pressure companies not to steal one another's employees, the United States has no such system.[18] Despite this problem, business may have no choice but to train. As Gary Tooker, CEO of Motorola, says, "If knowledge is becoming antiquated at a faster rate, we have no choice but to spend on education."[19] Such "knowledge obsolescence" has profound consequences for "selling" senior managers on the value of training in the United States.

5. **Despite the rhetoric about training being viewed as an investment, current accounting rules require that it be treated as an expense.** Businesses might spend more on training if accounting rules were revised. Unlike investments in plant and equipment, which show up on the books as assets, training expenditures are seen merely as expenses to be deducted in the year in which they are incurred.[20]

6. **Government is not providing enough funds for retraining to help workers displaced as a result of downsizing or of the defense contraction.** The issue is difficult to address objectively, for what is "enough"? It is a problem not just in the United States. Throughout the industrialized world, government

INTERNATIONAL APPLICATION
In Germany, Apprenticeship Training + College = Job Success

Young adults in Germany who opt for apprenticeship training before entering college tend to make a smoother transition into the job market than those who do not. A recent survey by Hochshule Information Systems in Hanover found that 80 percent of those with the combined training find a full-time job compared with 74 percent of youths with only a college education. Among new college students in Germany, 62 percent of young men and 50 percent of young women are former apprentices. Prior apprenticeship training also pays off when one has to find a new job. Thus, nearly 50 percent of those with apprenticeship training had no problem finding new employment when they lost their jobs, compared with 38 percent of those with only a college degree.[24]

leaders are focusing on one of the most corrosive, dangerous trends of the 1990s: the inability of modern economies to ease the transitions that the young, the poor, and older workers must make to keep up with rapid technological changes in the workplace.[21]

7. **Businesses, with help from the government, need to focus on the 70 percent of non-college graduates who enter the U.S. workforce.** At most, 30 percent of the future workforce will need a college degree. Marriott International, Inc. focuses on non-college graduates now. It targets welfare recipients for its 6-week Pathways to Independence program that teaches business basics, such as showing up on time, and life lessons, such as self-esteem and personal financial management. Marriott works with federally funded local organizations to split the $5500 per-person costs. Over 600 Pathways graduates now work at Marriott as housekeepers, laundry workers, and dishwashers, and in other hourly jobs. Their 13 percent annual turnover rate is far below the company's national average.[22]

8. **Employers and schools must develop closer ties.** Schools are often seen as not being responsive to labor market demands. Business is seen as not communicating its demands to schools. Fortunately, this situation is changing. Sematech, the semiconductor industry association, is working with Maricopa Community Colleges in Phoenix to develop a national curriculum for training entry-level manufacturing technicians. Aegon US, an insurer in Cedar Rapids, Iowa, built a $10 million corporate data center at Kirkwood Community College to be shared by company employees and college students.[23] In Germany, combining education and apprenticeship is the pathway to success on the job (see boxed insert above).

9. **Organized labor can help.** Unions have developed first-rate apprenticeship programs in a number of crafts. Now they are getting involved in "soft skills" training as well. In San Francisco, 12 unionized hotels agreed, as part of a contract with the Hotel Employees and Restaurant Employees International Union, to a $3 million training program designed to teach problem-solving, communication, and conflict-resolution skills. The training program is being designed jointly by the union and the hotels.[25]

CHARACTERISTICS OF EFFECTIVE TRAINING PRACTICE

One survey of corporate training and development practices found that four characteristics seemed to distinguish companies with the most effective training practices:[26]

- Top management is committed to training and development;[27] training is part of the corporate culture. This is especially true of leading companies such as The Walt Disney Company, Marriott, Hewlett-Packard, and Xerox.
- Training is tied to business strategy and objectives and is linked to bottom-line results.
- A comprehensive, systematic approach to training exists; training and retraining are done at all levels on an ongoing basis.
- There is a commitment to invest the necessary resources and to provide sufficient time and money for training.

The Training Paradox

Some businesses, small and large, shy away from training because they think that by upgrading the skills of the workforce, their employees will be more marketable to competitors. That is true. However, it also constitutes an interesting paradox that affects both employee and employer. That is, if an employee takes charge of her own employability by keeping her skills updated and varied so she can work for anyone, she also builds more security with her current employer—assuming the company values highly skilled, motivated employees. As Hewlett-Packard's director of education noted, "What's going to entice them away? Money? Maybe you can buy them for a short time, but what keeps people excited is growing and learning."[28]

At the same time, if a company provides lots of training and learning opportunities, it is more likely to retain workers because it creates an interesting and challenging environment. In short, increasing an individual's employability outside the company simultaneously increases his job security and desire to stay with his current employer.

How Does Training Relate to Competitive Strategies?

The means that firms use to compete for business in the marketplace and to gain competitive advantage are known as competitive strategies.[29] A key objective of any training program, therefore, is to tie workplace training to business targets. Motorola is especially adept at this. For instance, it will set a goal to reduce product-development cycle time (i.e., to increase speed), and then create a course on how to do it. This is not learning for its own sake: trainers drill students in specific tasks until they get them right, whether it is operating a tool or being more persuasive with customers.[30] While the potential returns from well-conducted training programs are hefty, considerable planning and evaluation are necessary in order to realize these returns. The remainder of this chapter examines some key issues that managers need to consider. Let us begin by examining the broad phases that make up training systems.

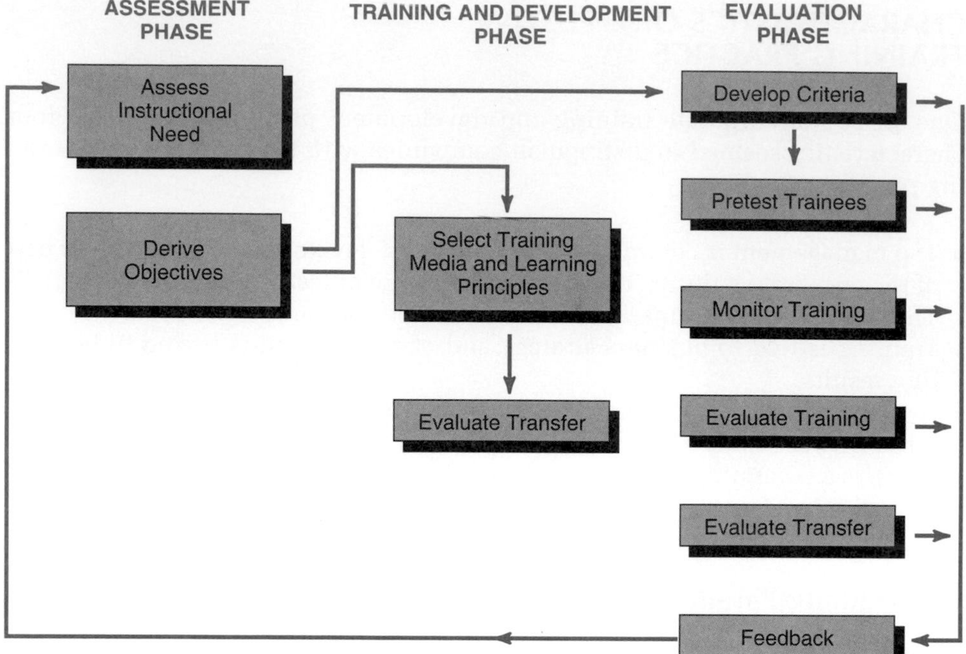

Figure 7-1
A general systems model of the training and development process. Note how information developed during the evaluation phase provides feedback, and therefore new input, to the assessment phase. This initiates a new cycle of assessment, training and development, and evaluation.

ASSESSING TRAINING NEEDS AND DESIGNING TRAINING PROGRAMS

One way to keep in mind the phases of training is to portray them graphically, in the form of a model that illustrates the interaction among the phases. One such model is shown in Figure 7-1.

The *assessment* (or planning) *phase* serves as a foundation for the entire training effort. As Figure 7-1 shows, both the *training and development phase* and the *evaluation phase* depend on inputs from assessment. The purpose of the assessment phase is to define what it is the employee should learn in relation to desired job behaviors. If this phase is not carefully done, the training program as a whole will have little chance of achieving what it is intended to do.

Assuming that managers specify the objectives of the training program carefully, the next task is to design the environment in which to achieve those objectives. This is the purpose of the training phase. Choose methods and techniques carefully and deliver them systematically in a supportive, encouraging environment, based on sound principles of learning.

Finally, if both the assessment phase and the training and development phase have been done competently, evaluation should present few problems. Evaluation is a twofold process that involves (1) establishing indicators of success in training, as well as on the job, and (2) determining exactly what job-related changes have occurred as a result of the training. Evaluation must provide a continuous stream of feedback that can be used to reassess training needs, thereby creating input for the next stage of employee development.

Now that we have a broad overview of the training process, let us consider the elements of Figure 7-1 in greater detail.

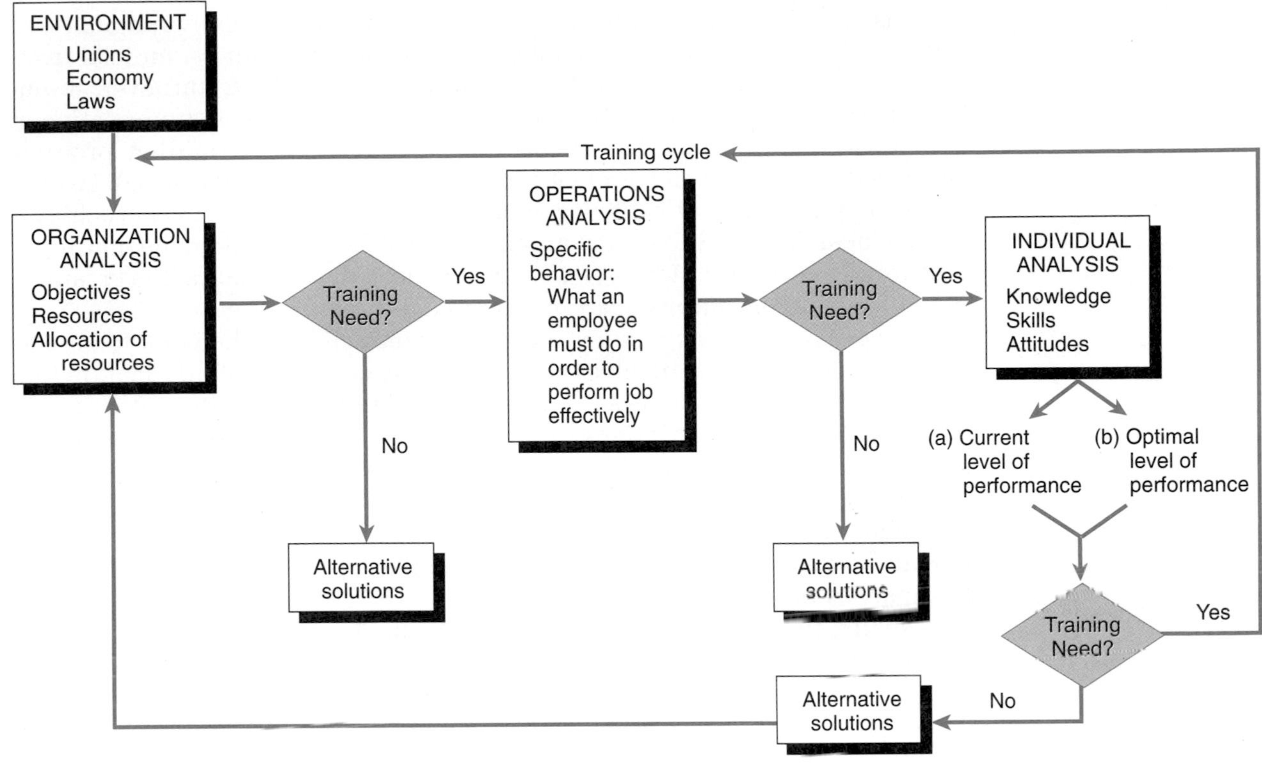

Figure 7-2
Training needs assessment model.

Assessing Training Needs

There are three levels of analysis for determining the needs that training can fulfill:[31]

- **Organization analysis** focuses on identifying where within the organization training is needed.
- **Operations analysis** attempts to identify the content of training—what an employee must do in order to perform competently.
- **Individual analysis** determines how well each employee is performing the tasks that make up his or her job.

Training needs might surface in any one of these three broad areas. But to ask productive questions regarding training needs, managers often find that an integrative model such as that shown in Figure 7-2 is helpful.

At a general level, it is important to analyze training needs against the backdrop of organizational objectives and strategies. Unless you do this, you may waste time and money on training programs that do not advance the cause of the company.[32] People may be trained in skills they already possess (as happened to members of a machinists' union of a major airline not long ago); the training budget may be squandered on "rest and recuperation" sessions, where employees are entertained but learn little in the way of required job skills or job knowledge; or the budget may be spent on glittering hardware that meets the training director's needs but not the organization's.

It is also essential to analyze the organization's external environment and internal climate. Trends in the strategic priorities of a business, judicial decisions, civil rights laws, union activity, productivity, accidents, turnover, absenteeism, and on-the-job employee behavior will provide relevant information at this level. The important question then becomes "Will training produce changes in employee behavior that will contribute to our organization's goals?"

In summary, the critical first step is to relate training needs to the achievement of organizational goals. If you cannot make that connection, the training is probably unnecessary. However, if a training need does surface at the organizational level, an operations analysis is the next step.

Operations analysis requires a careful examination of the work to be performed after training. It involves (1) a systematic collection of information that describes how work is done, so that standards of performance for that work can be determined; (2) descriptions of how tasks are to be performed to meet the standards; and (3) the competencies necessary for effective task performance. Job analyses, performance appraisals, interviews (with jobholders, supervisors, and higher management), and analyses of operating problems (quality control, downtime reports, and customer complaints) all provide important inputs to the analysis of training needs.

Finally, there is *individual analysis*. At this level, training needs may be defined in terms of the following general idea: the difference between desired performance and actual performance is the individual's training need. Performance standards, identified in the operations analysis phase, constitute desired performance. Individual performance data; diagnostic ratings of employees by their supervisors, peers, or customers; records of performance kept by workers in diary form; attitude surveys; interviews; or tests (job knowledge, work-sample, or situational) can provide information on actual performance against which each employee can be compared with regard to desired performance standards. A gap between actual and desired performance may be filled by training.

However, assessing the needs for training does not end here. It is important to analyze needs regularly and at all three levels in order to evaluate the results of training and to assess what training is needed in the future.

- At the organizational level, senior managers who set the organization's goals should analyze needs.
- At the operations level, the managers (or teams) who specify how the organization's goals are going to be achieved should analyze needs.
- At the individual level, the managers and workers who do the work to achieve those goals should analyze needs, keeping in mind that performance is a function both of ability (hence, training) and motivation (the desire to perform well).

COMPANY EXAMPLE

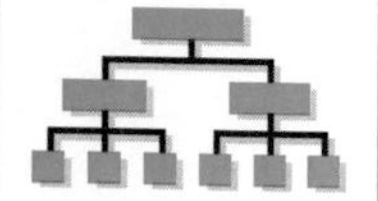

FROM NEEDS ANALYSIS TO TRAINING TO RESULTS!

At Pacific Northwest Bell, installers were uncertain about whether and how much they could charge for work on noncompany equipment and wiring, so they were billing very little. The company, in turn, seeing little revenue generated by the labor-hours spent, had stopped marketing the technicians' services.

A team of internal consultants—a company manager, a representative of the International Brotherhood of Electrical Workers, and a representative of the Communications Workers of America—recognized this problem and tried to solve it by involving a cross section of interested parties. The new task force agreed on two goals: increasing revenues and increasing job security.

A subcommittee of two task developers and two technicians developed a training program designed to teach installers how and what to charge, and also why they should keep accurate records: to increase their job security. The committee agreed to measure the revenues generated by time and materials charging so that those revenues could be weighed against labor costs in layoff decisions.

The training consisted of two 6-hour days and was presented by technicians to about 400 installers throughout Washington State and Oregon. In addition to setting up the course, the task force identified a need for a hot line that technicians could call when bidding for a job. The line was set up, and one of the course instructors was promoted to a management position for answering calls.

The results of the training and hot line were phenomenal, as shown by the pattern of revenues from work on noncompany equipment. In January, prior to the training course, the installers had billed for $589. In April, when half the workers had completed the training, they billed for $21,000 in outside work. By the following February, billings for customized work and charges reached $180,000. Total revenues over the 14-month period were about $1.4 million, or nearly twice the task force's projection of $831,000.

In light of these results, the company now markets the installers' services aggressively. For example, if an installation crew drives by a construction site on their way from another job, they stop and bid on the work. The hot line receives about 50 calls per day from systems technicians, installers, the business office, and customers.

The efforts of the task force increased company revenues, as well as the job security of the installers. Demand for their services grew with increased bidding on jobs, and more installers were added, providing union members in other job titles with opportunities for promotions or transfers into this work group. Future layoffs are unlikely, since the savings in labor costs must be weighed against the revenues generated by the installers.[33] Careful assessment of the need for training, coupled with the delivery of a training program that met targeted needs, produced results that startled management, the union, and the installation technicians. Everybody won!

After training needs have been identified, the next step is to structure the training environment for maximum learning. Careful attention to the fundamental principles of learning will enhance this process.

Principles of Learning

To promote efficient learning, long-term retention, and application of the skills or factual information learned in training to the job situation, training programs should incorporate principles of learning developed over the past century. Which principles should be considered? It depends on whether the trainees are learning skills (e.g., drafting) or factual material (e.g., principles of life insurance).[34]

To be most effective, *skill learning* should include four essential ingredients: (1) goal setting, (2) behavior modeling, (3) practice, and (4) feedback. However, when the focus is on *learning facts*, the sequence should change slightly: namely, (1) goal setting, (2) meaningfulness of material, (3) practice, and (4) feedback. Let's consider each of these in greater detail.

Motivating the Trainee: Goal Setting

A person who wants to develop herself or himself will do so; a person who wants to be developed rarely is. This statement illustrates the role that motivation plays in training—to learn, you must want to learn. And it appears from evidence that the most effective way to raise a trainee's motivation is by setting goals. Goal setting has a proven track record of success in improving employee performance in a variety of settings and cultures.[35] On average, goal setting leads to a 10 percent improvement in productivity, and it works best with tasks of low complexity.[36]

Goal theory is founded on the premise that an individual's conscious goals or intentions regulate her or his behavior.[37] Research indicates that once an individual accepts a goal, difficult but attainable goals result in higher levels of performance than do easy goals or even a generalized goal such as "do your best."[38] These findings have three important implications for motivating trainees:

1. Make the objectives of the training program clear at the outset.
2. Set goals that are challenging and difficult enough that the trainees can derive personal satisfaction from achieving them, but not so difficult that they are perceived as impossible to reach.
3. Supplement the ultimate goal of "finishing the program" with subgoals during training, such as trainer evaluations, work-sample tests, and periodic quizzes. As trainees clear each hurdle successfully, their confidence about attaining the ultimate goal increases.

While goal setting clearly affects trainees' motivation, so also do the expectations of the trainer. In fact, expectations have a way of becoming self-fulfilling prophecies, so that the higher the expectations, the better the trainees perform. Conversely, the lower the expectations, the worse the trainees perform. This phenomenon of the self-fulfilling prophecy is known as the *Pygmalion effect.* Legend has it that Pygmalion, a king of Cyprus, sculpted an ivory statue of a maiden named Galatea. Pygmalion fell in love with the statue, and, in answer to his prayer, Aphrodite, the goddess of love and beauty, gave it life. Pygmalion's fondest wish—his expectation—came true.

Behavior Modeling

Much of what we learn is acquired by observing others. We will imitate other people's actions when they lead to desirable outcomes (e.g., promotions, increased sales, or more accurate tennis serves). The models' actions serve as a cue as to what constitutes appropriate behavior.[39] A model is someone who is seen as competent, powerful, and friendly and has high status within an organization. We try to identify with this model because her or his behavior is seen as

PYGMALION IN ACTION: MANAGERS GET THE KIND OF PERFORMANCE THEY EXPECT

To test the Pygmalion effect and to examine the impact of instructors' prior expectations about trainees on the instructors' subsequent style of leadership toward the trainees, researchers conducted a field experiment at a military training base.[40] In a 15-week combat command course, 105 trainees were matched on aptitude and assigned randomly to one of three experimental groups. Each group corresponded to a particular level of expectation that was communicated to the instructors: high, average, or no prespecified level of expectation (a result of insufficient information). Four days before the trainees arrived at the base, and prior to any acquaintance between instructors and trainees, the instructors were assembled and given a score (known as command potential, or CP) for each trainee, which represented the trainee's potential to command others. The instructors were told that the CP score had been developed on the basis of psychological test scores, data from a previous course on leadership, and ratings by previous commanders. The instructors were also told that course grades predict CP in 95 percent of the cases. The instructors were then given a list of the trainees assigned to them, along with their CPs, and asked to copy each trainee's CP into his or her personal record. The instructors were also requested to learn their trainees' names and their CPs before the beginning of the course.

The Pygmalion hypothesis that the instructor's prior expectation influences the trainee's performance was confirmed. Trainees of whom instructors expected better performance scored significantly higher on objective achievement tests, exhibited more positive attitudes, and were perceived as better leaders. In fact, the prior expectations of the instructors explained 73 percent of the variability in the trainees' performance, 66 percent in their attitudes, and 28 percent in leadership. The lesson to be learned from these results is unmistakable: trainers (and managers) get the kind of performance they expect.

desirable and appropriate. Modeling tends to increase when the model is rewarded for behavior and when the rewards (e.g., influence, pay) are things the imitator would like to have. In the context of training (or coaching or teaching), we attempt to maximize trainees' identification with a model. For us to do this well, research suggests the following:

1. The model should be similar to the observer in age, gender, and race. If the observer sees little similarity between himself or herself and the model, it is unlikely that he or she will imitate the model's behaviors.
2. Portray the behaviors to be modeled clearly and in detail. To focus the trainees' attention on specific behaviors to imitate, provide them with a list of key behaviors to attend to when observing the model and allow them to express the behaviors in language that is most comfortable for them. For example, when one group of supervisors was being taught how to "coach" employees, the supervisors received a list of the following key behaviors:[41] (1) focus on the problem, not on the person; (2) ask for the employees' suggestions, and get their ideas on how to solve the problem; (3) listen openly; (4) agree on the steps that each of you will take to solve the problem; and (5) plan a specific follow-up date.
3. Rank the behaviors to be modeled in a sequence from least to most difficult, and be sure the trainees observe lots of repetitions of the behaviors being modeled.
4. Finally, have several models portray the behaviors, not just one.[42]

Research continues to demonstrate the effectiveness of behavior modeling over other approaches to training.[43] To a large extent, this is because behavior modeling overcomes one of the shortcomings of earlier approaches to training: telling instead of showing.

Meaningfulness of the Material

It is easier to learn and remember factual material when it is meaningful. Meaningfulness refers to material that is rich in associations for the trainees and is therefore easily understood by them. To structure material to maximize its meaningfulness:

1. Provide trainees with an overview of the material to be presented during the training. Seeing the overall picture helps trainees understand how each unit of the program fits together and how it contributes to the overall training objectives.[44]
2. Present the material by using examples, terms, and concepts that are familiar to the trainees in order to clarify and reinforce key learning points. Such a strategy is essential when training the hard-core unemployed.[45]
3. As complex intellectual skills are invariably made up of simpler ones, teach the simpler skills before the complex ones.[46] This is true whether one is teaching accounting, computer programming, or X-ray technology.

Practice (Makes Perfect)

Anyone learning a new skill or acquiring factual knowledge must have an opportunity to practice what he or she is learning. Practice has three aspects: active practice, overlearning, and the length of the practice session. Let's consider each of these:

- **Active practice.** During the early stages of learning, the trainer should be available to oversee the trainee's practice directly. If the trainee begins to "get off the track," the inappropriate behaviors can be corrected immediately, before they become ingrained in the trainee's behavior. This is why low instructor-trainee (or teacher-pupil) ratios are so desirable. It also explains why so many people opt for private lessons when trying to learn or master a sport such as tennis, golf, skiing, or horseback riding.
- **Overlearning.** When trainees are given the opportunity to practice far beyond the point where they have performed a task correctly several times, the task becomes "second nature" and is said to be "overlearned." For some tasks, overlearning is critical.[47] This is true of any task that must be performed infrequently and under great stress: for example, attempting to kick a winning field goal with only seconds left in a football game. It is less important in types of work where an individual practices his or her skills on a daily basis (e.g., auto mechanics, electronics technicians, assemblers).
- **Length of the practice session.** Suppose you have only 1 week to memorize the lines of a play, and during that week, you have only 12 hours available to practice. What practice schedule will produce the greatest improvement? Should you practice 2 hours a day for 6 days, should you practice for 6 hours each of the final 2 days before the deadline, or should you adopt some other schedule? The two extremes represent *distributed* practice (which implies

Immediate feedback on performance encourages both motivation and efficient learning by trainees.

rest intervals between sessions) and *massed* practice (in which the practice sessions are crowded together). Although there are exceptions, most of the research evidence on this question indicates that for the same amount of practice, learning is better when practice is distributed rather than massed.[48] One exception to this rule occurs when one must learn difficult material, such as hard puzzles or other "thought" problems. There seems to be an advantage in staying with the problem for a few massed practice sessions at first, rather than spending a day or more between sessions.

Feedback

This is a form of information about one's attempts to improve. Feedback is essential both for learning and for trainee motivation.[49] The emphasis should be on when and how the trainee has done something correctly, for example, "You did a good job on that report you turned in yesterday—it was brief and to the heart of the issues." It is also important to emphasize that feedback affects group, as well as individual, performance.[50] For example, application of performance-based feedback in a small fast-food store over a 1-year period led to a 15 percent decrease in food costs and a 193 percent increase in profits.[51]

To have the greatest impact, feedback should be provided as soon as possible after the trainee demonstrates good performance. It need not be instantaneous, but there should be no confusion regarding exactly what the trainee did and the trainer's reaction to it. Feedback need not always be positive, but keep in mind that the most powerful rewards are likely to be those provided by the trainee's immediate supervisor. In fact, if the supervisor does not reinforce what is learned in training, the training will be transferred ineffectively to the job—if at all.

Transfer of Training

Transfer refers to the extent to which competencies learned in training can be applied on the job. Transfer may be positive (i.e., it enhances job performance), negative (i.e., it hampers job performance), or neutral. Long-term training or retraining probably includes segments that contain all three of these conditions. Training that results in negative transfer is costly in two ways—the cost of the training (which proved to be useless) and the cost of hampered performance.

TRW's strategic management seminar provides an example of how one company facilitates positive transfer from learning to doing. TRW's approach to "systems learning" suggests that transfer of training (that is, the adoption of concepts and practices learned in training to practice on the job) will be greatest when trainees:

- Are confident in using their newly learned skills.
- Are aware of work situations where demonstration of the new skills is appropriate.
- Perceive that their job performance will improve if they use the new skills.
- Believe that the knowledge and skills emphasized in the training program are helpful in solving work-related problems.[53]

COMPANY EXAMPLE

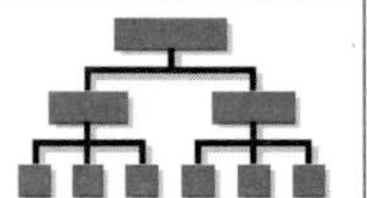

TRW'S STRATEGIC MANAGEMENT SEMINAR

At TRW, systems learning helps focus attention on the important concept of "transfer of training."[52] All training activities are designed with a built-in compatibility between what managers are expected to learn and what they are expected to do on their jobs. Here is an example:

Following instruction in the concepts of competitive strategy, TRW presented a three-phase strategic management seminar to natural business teams within the company: for example, a division vice president and his or her staff. In phase I, each team receives (1) more instruction in the concepts of competitive strategy and (2) a detailed assignment. The teams must apply the concepts to their business and develop an action strategy. Each team must plan a maximum of six actions that it will take over the next 18 months, and it must designate responsibility to particular team members for each action. The teams then "go home" to work on their strategies for about 8 weeks.

Phase II of the seminar is called the "midterm review." A seminar faculty member visits each team to review its progress on the assignment and provides detailed feedback on how well the team is applying the concepts. Sometimes teams make major changes at this point as they recognize, for example, that their competitive analysis is not thorough enough.

Over the following 8 weeks, phase III of the program, each team prepares its final strategic presentation—to be delivered in the presence of two or three other teams. After each team presents its strategy, the audience provides constructive comments and criticisms. Next, the audience votes on whether to accept or reject the strategy, indicating on their ballots what they like and dislike about the strategy. The votes and comments are collected and offered to the presenting team, along with comments and concerns from the faculty member. What is happening here? A powerful peer review process.

Ensuring a tight "fit" between training and application required that some changes be made in TRW's organizational practices, such as changing the process of developing strategic plans, modifying the compensation system so that long-term success is rewarded, and changing the performance appraisal process to emphasize long-term thinking, planning, and action. However, the biggest change of all was senior management's willingness to encourage the kind of risk taking required to implement some of the strategies. This is the essence of systems learning.

Team Training

Up to this point, we have been discussing training and development as an individual enterprise. Yet today there is an increasing emphasis on *team* performance. Cross-functional teams, intact or virtual, are common features of many organizations. *A team is a group of individuals who are working together toward a common goal.* It is this common goal that really defines a team, and if team members have opposite or conflicting goals, the efficiency of the total unit is likely to suffer. For example, consider the effects on a basketball team when one of the players always tries to score, regardless of the team's situation.

There is a core set of skills that characterize effective teamwork. These skills include adaptability, shared awareness of situations, performance monitoring and feedback, leadership/team management, interpersonal skills, coordination, communication, and decision-making skills. Attitudinal skills that characterize effective teamwork include beliefs about the importance of teamwork skills, belief in placing the team's goals above those of individual members, mutual trust, and shared vision.[54] When teams work effectively, these characteristics seem to coalesce into seven key components:[55]

- A clear sense of direction
- Talented members
- Clear and enticing responsibilities
- Reasonable and efficient operating procedures
- Constructive interpersonal relationships
- Active reinforcement systems
- Constructive relationships with other teams and key organizational players who are not members

Training can modify and enhance each of these components. Moreover, research has revealed two broad principles regarding the composition and management of teams. One, the overall performance of a team strongly depends on the individual expertise of its members.[56] Thus individual training and development are still important. But individual training is only a partial solution, for interaction among team members must also be addressed. This interaction is what makes team training unique—it always uses some form of simulation or real-life practice, and it always focuses on the interaction of team members, equipment, and work procedures.[57] For example, Subaru-Isuzu uses a manufacturing simulation in which individuals role-play team members of a small-parts assembly firm. Jobs are self-assigned within teams, and team members make their own decisions about planning and allocating resources.[58]

Two, managers of effective work groups tend to monitor the performance of their team members regularly, and they provide frequent feedback to them.[59] In fact, as much as 35 percent of the variability in team performance can be explained by the frequency of use of monitors and consequences. Incorporating these findings into the training of team members and their managers should lead to better overall team performance.

Selecting Training Methods

New training methods appear every year. While some are well founded in learning theory or models of behavior change (e.g., behavior modeling), others result more from technological than theoretical developments (e.g., videotapes, computer-based business games). Training methods can be classified in three ways: information presentation, simulation methods, and on-the-job training:[60]

- **Information presentation techniques** include lectures, conferences, correspondence courses, videos, reading lists, closed-circuit TV, behavior modeling and systematic observation, programmed instruction, computer-assisted instruction, sensitivity training, and organization development—systematic, long-range programs of organizational improvement.
- **Simulation methods** include the case method, role playing, programmed group exercises, the in-basket technique, and business games.
- **On-the-job training methods** include orientation training, apprenticeships, on-the-job training, near-the-job training (using identical equipment but away from the job itself), job rotation, committee assignments (or junior executive boards), understudy assignments, on-the-job coaching, and performance appraisal.

In the context of developing interpersonal skills, training methods are typically chosen to achieve one or more of three objectives:

- Promoting self-insight and environmental awareness—that is, an understanding of how one's actions affect others and how one is viewed by others. For example, at Parfums Stern, staffers act out customer-salesperson roles to better understand customers' emotions. Wendy's International videotapes customers with disabilities; in one video a blind person asks that change be counted out loud. Meridian Bancorp has workers walk with seeds in their shoes to simulate older customers' corns and calluses.[61]
- Improving the ability of managers and lower-level employees to make decisions and to solve job-related problems in a constructive fashion.
- Maximizing the desire to perform well.

To choose the training method (or combination of methods) that best fits a given situation, first *define carefully what you wish to teach.* That is the purpose of the needs assessment phase. Only then can you choose a method that best fits these requirements. To be useful, the method should meet the minimal conditions needed for effective learning to take place; that is, the training method should:

ETHICAL DILEMMA
Diversity Training—Fad or Here to Stay?

Diversity training is flourishing at the highest reaches of U.S. business. American Airlines, Coca-Cola, Procter & Gamble, and *The New York Times* (which reports that 40 percent of U.S. companies have instituted some form of diversity training) are all engaged in one form or another. All are built on the assumption that "understanding breeds better relationships."[62] Diversity consultants promise corporations they will increase their profits by "empowering their whole workforce," according to the corporate diversity programs manager at Digital Equipment Corporation. Is there any truth to this claim?

Beyond the rhetoric, there is little evidence that such training can solve the problems it purports to address. Proponents acknowledge that they are unable to document the advantages of diversity training or even describe what "managing-diversity heaven" would look like. To some, the preferred solution to the problems of measurement and description is to declare them irrelevant and proceed on faith alone.[63] Is this ethically justifiable in light of the principles of sound training practice—needs assessment, careful specification of objectives, and then evaluation of training in terms of the original objectives?

- Motivate the trainee to improve his or her performance.
- Clearly illustrate desired skills.
- Allow the trainee to participate actively.
- Provide an opportunity to practice.
- Provide timely feedback on the trainee's performance.
- Provide some means for reinforcement while the trainee learns.
- Be structured from simple to complex tasks.
- Be adaptable to specific problems.
- Encourage positive transfer from the training to the job.

EVALUATING TRAINING PROGRAMS

To evaluate training, you must systematically document the outcomes of the training in terms of how trainees actually behave back on their jobs and the relevance of that behavior to the objectives of the organization.[64] To assess the utility or value of training, we seek answers to questions such as the following:

1. Have trainees achieved a specific level of skill, knowledge, or performance?
2. Did change occur?
3. Is the change due to training?
4. Is the change positively related to the achievement of organizational goals?
5. Will similar changes occur with new participants in the same training program?[65]

In the evaluation of training programs, it is possible to measure change in terms of four levels of rigor:[66]

Table 7-1

A TYPICAL BEFORE-AFTER DESIGN FOR ASSESSING TRAINING OUTCOME

	Trained group	Untrained group
Pretest	Yes	Yes
Training	Yes	No
Posttest	Yes	Yes

- **Reaction**—how do the participants feel about the training program?
- **Learning**—to what extent have the trainees learned what was taught?
- **Behavior**—what on-the-job changes in behavior have occurred because of attendance at the training program?
- **Results**—to what extent has training produced cost-related behavioral outcomes (e.g., productivity or quality improvements, reductions in turnover or accidents)?

Since measures of reaction and learning are concerned with outcomes of the training program per se, they are referred to as *internal* criteria. Measures of behavior and results indicate the impact of training on the job environment; they are referred to as *external* criteria.

Measures of reaction typically focus on participants' feelings about the subject and the speaker, suggested improvements in the program, and the extent to which they feel that the training will help them do their jobs better. Assess trainee learning, which may focus on changing knowledge, skills, attitudes, or motivation, by giving a paper-and-pencil or performance test.

Assessing changes in on-the-job behavior is more difficult than measuring reaction or learning, because factors other than the training program (e.g., lengthened job experience, outside economic events, changes in supervision or performance incentives) may also improve performance. To rule out these rival hypotheses, design a plan for evaluation that includes *before* and *after* measurement of the trained group's performance relative to that of one or more untrained control groups. (However, when it is relatively costly to bring subjects to an evaluation and administration costs are particularly high, after-only measurement of trained and untrained groups is best.[67]) To rule out alternative explanations for the changes that occurred, match members of the untrained control group as closely as possible to those in the trained group. Table 7-1 shows a standard design for such a study. If the outcomes of the training are positive, the untrained control group at Time 1 may become the trained group at a later time. It is important to note that the posttraining appraisal of performance should not be done sooner than 3 months (or more) following the training so that the trainees have an opportunity to put into practice what they have learned.

Finally, the impact of training on organizational results is the most significant but most difficult measure to make. *Measures of results are the bottom line of training success.* Exciting developments in this area have come from recent research showing how the general utility equation (Equation 6-1 on page 242) can be modified to reflect the dollar value of improved job performance resulting from training.[68] Utility formulas are now available for evaluating the dollar value of a single training program compared with a control group, a training program readministered periodically (e.g., annually), and a comparison between two or more different training programs.

COMPANY EXAMPLE

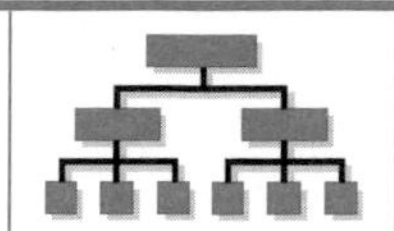

EVALUATING THE BUSINESS IMPACT OF MANAGEMENT TRAINING AT CIGNA CORPORATION

Cigna, an insurance company, set out to demonstrate the impact on productivity and performance of a 7-day training program in basic management skills.[69] The evaluations were based on repeated measures of work-unit performance both before and after training. Some specific features of the program were the following:

- Productivity was a central focus of the program.
- As part of their training, the participants were taught how to create productivity measures.
- The participants were taught how to use productivity data as performance feedback and as support for performance goal setting.
- The participants wrote a productivity action plan as part of the training, and they agreed to bring back measurable results to a follow-up session.
- Individualized productivity measures were put into place as part of the action plan.

These plans were tailored to measure results in specific, objective terms.

The results of the training in basic management skills were evaluated, of necessity, in individual work units. Let us consider one such unit—that of a premium-collections manager. Collecting premiums on time is important in the insurance business, because late premiums represent lost investment opportunities. Through survey feedback from her subordinates, the manager of this unit found that her problems (only 75 percent of the premiums were collected on time) stemmed from poor HRM skills, coupled with a failure to set clear performance goals.

After the training, this manager dramatically altered many of her management behaviors. One year later her unit was collecting 96 percent of the premiums on time. This improvement yielded extra investment income of $150,000 per year. What was the return on the fully loaded cost of training her? The training costs included the costs of facilities, program development amortized over 25 programs, trainer preparation time, general administration, corporate overhead, and the salaries plus benefits of the participants over the 7-day program. These costs amounted to $1600 per participant. It looks as though the returns generated by the collections manager as a result of the action plan ($150,000) relative to the training's cost ($1600) were phenomenal. But were all these gains due to her training? Probably not.

What would have happened had training not occurred? Extrapolating from the rate of improvement prior to training, the researchers concluded that the collections rate would have been up to about 84 percent, from 75 percent. The additional 12-point improvement that was provided—in part—by the program (which generated about $85,000 in extra investment income) represents the upper boundary of the effects of the training program. (Other economic factors, such as lower unemployment among policyholders, may also have contributed to the gain.) Nevertheless, it represents about a 50-to-1 return on the dollars invested.

An often-neglected part of the training enterprise is the orientation of new employees to the company and its culture. Since most turnover occurs during the first few months on the job (at Marriott, 40 percent of the new employees who leave do so during the first 3 months[70]), failure to provide a thorough orientation can be a very expensive mistake. Let's consider what progressive companies are doing in this area.

NEW-EMPLOYEE ORIENTATION: AN OVERVIEW

One definition of *orientation* is "familiarization with and adaptation to a situation or an environment." While 8 out of every 10 organizations in the United States that have more than 50 employees provide orientation, the time and effort devoted to its design, conduct, and evaluation are woefully inadequate. In practice, orientation is often just a superficial indoctrination into company philosophy, policies, and rules; sometimes it includes the presentation of an employee handbook and a quick tour of the office or plant. This approach can be costly. Here is why.

In one way, a displaced worker from the factory who is hired into another environment is similar to a new college graduate. Upon starting a new job, both will face a kind of culture shock. As they are exposed for the first time to a new organizational culture, both find that the new job is not quite what they imagined it to be. In fact, coming to work at a new company is not unlike visiting a foreign country. Either you are told about the local customs, or else you learn them on your own by a process of trial and error. An effective orientation program can help lessen the impact of this shock. But there must be more, such as a period of socialization, or learning to function as a contributing member of the corporate "family."

The cost of hiring, training, and orienting a new person is far higher than most of us realize. For example, Merck & Company, the pharmaceutical giant, found that, depending on the job, turnover costs 1.5 to 2.5 times the annual salary paid for the job.[71] Moreover, since the turnover rate among new college hires can be as great as 50 percent during the first 12 months, such costs can be considerable.

A new employee's experiences during the initial period with an organization can have a major impact on his or her career. A new hire stands on the "boundary" of the organization—certainly no longer an outsider but not yet embraced by those within. There is great stress. The new hire wants to reduce this stress by becoming incorporated into the "interior" as quickly as possible. Consequently, during this period an employee is more receptive to cues from the organizational environment than she or he is ever likely to be again. Such cues to proper behavior may come from a variety of sources, for example:

- Official literature of the organization
- Examples set by senior people
- Formal instructions given by senior people
- Examples given by peers
- Rewards and punishments that flow from the employee's efforts

- Responses to the employee's ideas
- Degree of challenge in the assignments the employee receives

Special problems may arise for new employees whose young lives have been spent mainly in educational settings. As they approach their first jobs, recent graduates may feel motivated entirely by personal creativity. They are information-rich but experience-poor, eager to apply their knowledge to new processes and problems. Unfortunately, there are conditions that may stifle that creative urge. During their undergraduate days, the new employees exercised direct control over their work. But now they face regular hours, greater restrictions, possibly a less pleasant environment, and a need to work through other people—often finding that most of the work is mundane and unchallenging. In short, three typical problems face new employees:

1. **Problems in entering a group**. New employees ask themselves whether they will (a) be acceptable to the other group members, (b) be liked, and (c) be safe—that is, free from physical and psychological harm. These issues must be resolved before they can feel comfortable and productive in the new situation.
2. **Naive expectations**. Organizations find it much easier to communicate factual information about pay and benefits, vacations, and company policies than information about employee norms (rules or guides to acceptable behavior), company attitudes, or "what it really takes to get ahead around here." Simple fairness suggests that employees ought to be told about these intangibles. The bonus is that being up-front and honest with job candidates produces positive results. As we saw in Chapter 5, the research on realistic job previews (RJPs) indicates that job acceptance rates will likely be lower for those who receive an RJP, but job survival rates will be higher.
3. **First-job environment**. Does the new environment help or hinder new employees trying to climb aboard? Can peers be counted on to socialize new employees to desired job standards? How and why were the first job assignments chosen? Is it clear to new employees what they can expect to get out of their first job assignments?

The first year with an organization is the critical period during which an employee will or will not learn to become a high performer. The careful matching of company and employee expectations during this period can result in positive job attitudes and high standards, which then can be reinforced in new and more demanding jobs.

PLANNING, PACKAGING, AND EVALUATING AN ORIENTATION PROGRAM

New employees need specific information in three major areas:

- Company standards, expectations, norms, traditions, and policies
- Social behavior, such as approved conduct, the work climate, and getting to know fellow workers and supervisors
- Technical aspects of the job

Keep in mind that the most common reasons for firing new hires are absenteeism and failure to adapt to the work environment. Fewer than 10 percent of employees are dismissed because of difficulties in learning how to perform their jobs.[72] These results suggest two levels of orientation: company and departmental. There will be some matters of general interest and importance to all new employees, regardless of department, and there will also be matters relevant only to each department. The HR department should have overall responsibility for program planning and follow-up (subject to top-management review and approval), but the specific responsibilities of the HR department and the immediate supervisor should be made very clear to avoid duplication or omission of important information.

Be sure to avoid these approaches to orientation:[73]

- **An emphasis on paperwork**. After completing forms required by the HR department, the new employee is given a cursory welcome. Then the employee is directed to his or her immediate supervisor. The likely result: The employee does not feel like part of the company.
- **A sketchy overview of the basics**. A quick, superficial orientation, and the new employee is immediately put to work—sink or swim.
- "**Mickey Mouse" assignments**. The new employee's first tasks are insignificant duties, supposedly intended to teach the job "from the ground up."
- **Suffocation**. Giving too much information too fast is a well-intentioned but disastrous approach, causing the new employee to feel overwhelmed and "suffocated."

We know from other companies' mistakes what works and what does not. For example, consider how the Marriott Corporation handles new-employee orientation.

COMPANY EXAMPLE

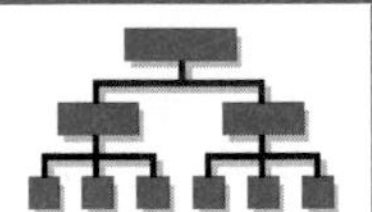

ORIENTATION AT MARRIOTT HOTELS

At Marriott, all new recruits attend an 8-hour initial training session, the highlight of which is an elegant lunch, served by hotel veterans. To guide them through the next 90 days, each associate is assigned a mentor, known as a "buddy." Every member of the entering class attends refresher courses after the first and second months. Finally, once the new hires reach day 90, the hotel treats the whole class to a banquet.

As you can see, Marriott puts less emphasis on policies and procedures and more on emotion. Why? Because the company recognizes that excellent service is more than just a transaction. It is an experience, one that ought to satisfy the employee as well as the customer. As one observer noted, "You can't expect your employees to delight your customers unless you as an employer delight your employees."[74]

Orientation Follow-up

The worst mistake a company can make is to ignore the new employee after orientation. Almost as bad is an informal open-door policy: "Come see me sometime if you have any questions." Many new employees are simply not assertive enough to seek out the supervisor or HR representative—more than likely, they fear looking "dumb." What is needed is formal and systematic orientation follow-up: for example, National Semiconductor uses focus groups of randomly selected new employees to find out what they like and do not like.[75] It found that many of the topics covered during orientation need to be explained briefly again, once the employee has had the opportunity to experience them firsthand. This is natural and understandable in view of the blizzard of information that often is communicated during orientation. In completing the orientation follow-up, review a checklist of items covered with each new employee or small group of employees to ensure that all items were in fact covered. Then make sure that the completed checklist is signed by the supervisor, the HR representative, and the new employee.

Evaluation of the Orientation Program

At least once a year, review the orientation program to determine if it is meeting its objectives and to identify future improvements. To improve orientation, you need candid, comprehensive feedback from everyone involved in the program. There are several ways to provide this kind of feedback: through roundtable discussions with new employees after their first year on the job, through in-depth interviews with randomly selected employees and supervisors, and through questionnaires for mass coverage of all recent hires. Corning's approach to the overall orientation process serves as a valuable case study.

COMPANY EXAMPLE

NEW-EMPLOYEE ORIENTATION AT CORNING, INC.[76]

Corning, like many other firms, faced a difficult problem: new people were getting the red-carpet treatment while being recruited, but once they started work, it was often a different story—a letdown. Often their first day on the job was disorganized and confusing, and sometimes this continued for weeks. One new employee said, "You're planting the seeds of turnover right at the beginning."

Managers at Corning realized that they needed a better way to help new employees make the transition to their new company and community. Corning needed a better way to help these new people get off on the right foot—to learn the how-tos, the wheres, and the whys, and to learn about the company's culture and its philosophies. And the company had to ensure the same support for newly hired secretaries in a district office, sales representatives working out of their homes, or engineers in a plant.

The Corning Orientation System and How it Works

Three features distinguish the Corning approach from others:

1. It is an orientation process, not a program.
2. It is based on guided self-learning. New people have responsibility for their own learning.
3. It is long-term (15 to 18 months), and it is in-depth.

Material distribution. As soon as possible after a hiring decision is made, orientation material is distributed:

- The new person's supervisor gets a pamphlet entitled *A Guide for Supervisors*.
- The new person gets an orientation plan.

The prearrival period. During this period, the supervisor maintains contact with the new person, helps with housing problems, designs the job, makes a preliminary MBO (management by objectives) list after discussing this with the new person, gets the office ready, notifies the organization that this has been done, and sets the interview schedule.

The 1st day. On this important day, new employees have breakfast with their supervisors, go through processing in the personnel department, attend a *Corning and You* seminar, have lunch with the seminar leader, read the workbook for new employees, are given a tour of the building, and are introduced to coworkers.

The 1st week. During this week, the new employee (1) has one-to-one interviews with the supervisors, coworkers, and specialists; (2) learns the how-tos, wheres, and whys connected with the job; (3) answers questions in the workbook; (4) gets settled in the community; and (5) participates with the supervisor in firming up the MBO plan.

The 2nd week. The new person begins regular assignments.

The 3rd and 4th weeks. The new person attends a community seminar and an employee benefits seminar (a spouse or guest may be invited).

The 2nd through 5th months. During this period, assignments are intensified and new people have biweekly progress reviews with their supervisors, attend six 2-hour seminars and intervals (on quality and productivity, technology, performance management and salaried compensation plans, financial and strategic management, employee relations and EEO, and social change), answer workbook questions about each seminar, and review answers with their supervisor.

The 6th month. The new employee completes the workbook questions, reviews the MBO list with the supervisor, participates in a performance review with the supervisor, receives a certification of completion for Phase I orientation, and makes plans for Phase II orientation.

The 7th through 15th months. This period features Phase II orientation: division orientation, function orientation, education programs, MBO reviews, performance reviews, and salary reviews.

Figure 7-3
Timetable of events in the Corning, Inc., orientation system.

The new person learns with help and information from:

- The immediate supervisor, who has guidelines and checklists.
- Colleagues, whom the new person interviews before starting regular assignments.
- Attendance at nine 2-hour seminars at intervals during the first 6 months.
- Answers to questions in a workbook for new employees.

Figure 7-3 provides an overview of how the system works.

Objectives of the Program

Corning set four objectives, each aimed at improving productivity. The first was to reduce voluntary turnover in the first 3 years of employment by 17 percent. The second was to shorten by 17 percent the time it takes a new person to learn the job. The third was to foster a uniform understanding among employees about the company: its objectives, its principles, its strategies, and what the

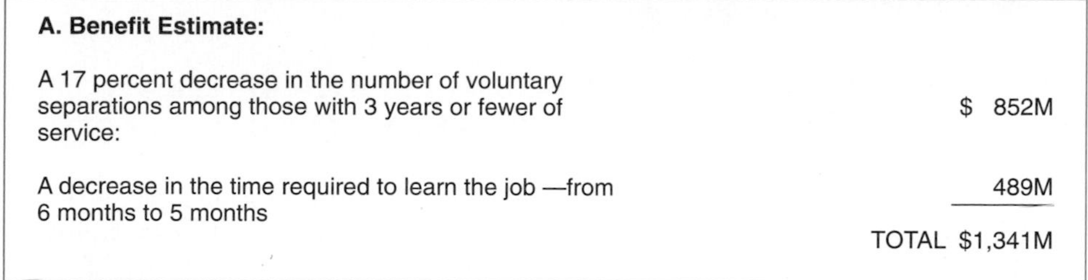

A. Benefit Estimate:

A 17 percent decrease in the number of voluntary separations among those with 3 years or fewer of service:	$ 852M
A decrease in the time required to learn the job —from 6 months to 5 months	489M
	TOTAL $1,341M

B. Cost Estimate

	First Year Only	Ongoing Annual
Materials and salaries of developers, instructors, administrators	$171M	$95M

C. Benefit/Cost Ratio:

First year: $1,341M : 171M = 8 : 1
Ongoing annual: $1,341M : 95M = 14 : 1

The following formula was used to estimate productivity gains per year.

Improved Retention Rate:

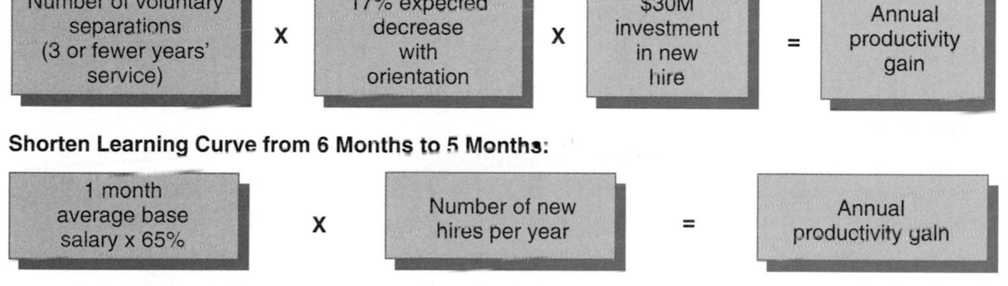

Figure 7-4 Calculation of benefits and costs in the Corning, Inc., orientation program. (*Note:* "M" denotes thousands.)

company expects of its people. The fourth was to build a positive attitude toward the company and its surrounding communities.

Measuring Results

After 2 years, voluntary turnover among new hires was reduced by 69 percent—far greater than the 17 percent expected after 3 years. Corning also anticipates a major payback on its investment in the orientation system: an 8:1 benefit/cost ratio in the first year and a 14:1 ratio annually thereafter. These computations are shown in Figure 7-4.

Lessons Learned

As a result of the 2 years it took to develop the system, Corning's 2 years of experience with it, and the recent experiences of many other companies, we offer the following considerations to guide the process of orienting new employees. They apply to any type of organization, large or small, and to any function or level of job:[77]

IMPACT OF TRAINING AND DEVELOPMENT ON PRODUCTIVITY, QUALITY OF WORK LIFE, AND THE BOTTOM LINE

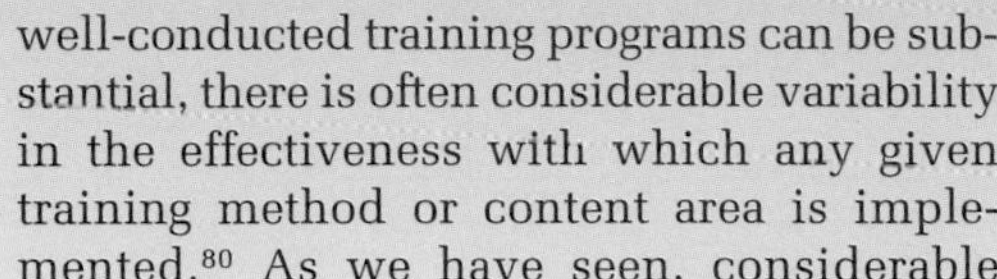

Does training "work"? One investigation used quantitative procedures to summarize the results of 70 studies that had the following characteristics: (1) each study involved managers, (2) each evaluated the effectiveness of one or more training programs, and (3) each included at least one control or comparison group. Results indicated that management training and development efforts are, in general, moderately effective. In terms of objective measures of training results over all content areas, training improved job performance by almost 20 percent, although there was considerable variability around this estimate.[79] At a more general level, the literature on training evaluation shows that while the potential returns from well-conducted training programs can be substantial, there is often considerable variability in the effectiveness with which any given training method or content area is implemented.[80] As we have seen, considerable planning (through needs analysis) and follow-up program evaluation efforts are necessary in order to realize these returns. Given the pace of change in modern society and technology, retraining is imperative to enable individuals to compete for or retain their jobs and to enable organizations to compete in the marketplace. Continual investment in training and learning is therefore essential, because it has such a direct impact on the productivity of organizations and on the quality of work life of those who work in them.

1. The impressions formed by new employees within their first 60 to 90 days on a job are lasting.
2. Day 1 is crucial—new employees remember it for years. It must be managed well.
3. New employees are interested in learning about the total organization—and how they and their unit fit into the "big picture." This is just as important as is specific information about the new employee's own job and department.
4. Give new employees major responsibility for their own orientation, through guided self-learning, but with direction and support. For example, AT&T has its orientation program on CD-ROM so that employees can self-pace their learning.[78]
5. Avoid information overload—provide it in reasonable amounts.
6. Recognize that community, social, and family adjustment is a critical aspect of orientation for new employees.
7. Make the immediate supervisor ultimately responsible for the success of the orientation process.
8. Thorough orientation is a "must" for productivity improvement. It is a vital part of the total management system—and therefore the foundation of any effort to improve employee productivity.

The results of Corning's research are exciting and provocative. They suggest that we should be at least as concerned with preparing the new employee for the social context of his or her job and for coping with the insecurities and frustrations of a new learning situation as with the development of the technical skills necessary for job performance.

IMPLICATIONS FOR MANAGEMENT PRACTICE

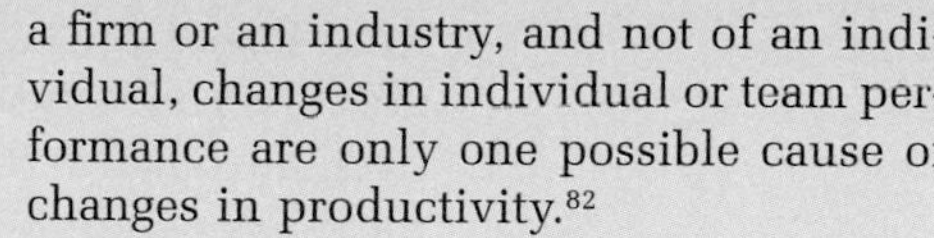

One of the greatest fears of managers and lower-level employees is obsolescence. Perhaps the Paul Principle expresses this phenomenon most aptly: Over time, people become uneducated, and therefore incompetent, to perform at a level they once performed at adequately.[81] Training is an important antidote to obsolescence, but it is important to be realistic about what training can and cannot accomplish:

1. Training cannot solve all kinds of performance problems. In some cases, transfer, job redesign, changes in selection or reward systems, or discipline may be more appropriate.
2. Since productivity (the value of outputs per unit of labor) is a characteristic of a system, such as a firm or an industry, and not of an individual, changes in individual or team performance are only one possible cause of changes in productivity.[82]
3. As a manager, you need to ask yourself three key questions:

- "Do we have an actual or a potential performance problem for which training is the answer?"
- "Have we defined what is to be learned and what the content of training should be before we choose a particular training method or technique?"
- "What kind of evaluation procedure will we use to determine if the benefits of the training outweigh its costs?"

THE NEW EDUCATORS: COMPANY-BASED SCHOOLS

Human Resource Management in Action: Conclusion

Has Collins & Aikman's in-house training paid off? The answer is a tentative yes, although the links between training and some measures of performance are somewhat tenuous. Within tufting operations, productivity, or the amount of carpet stitched, rose 10 percent over a 2-year period. The company also cut the number of returns—carpets sent back to the plant because of problems—in half over the same period. Workers at Collins & Aikman say they are more confident about the new machinery. Some 56 of them have earned high school diplomas through courses taught at the plant. Some have stopped constantly asking supervisors for help, because they know the answers themselves—e.g., how to tally the various weights of yarns. Within a year after the program began, 1230 suggestions poured in from workers on ways the company could improve itself. Workers are encouraging their own children to stay in school. Morale is up—and perhaps that is the reason for a sudden outbreak of health. When the program began, an average of 14 workers were absent each day. Two years later, the average was down to 8.

Not all employees are sold on the idea, though. For some, the level of commitment required to complete the training is too high. For others, the idea of going back to school is so unnerving that, even though they know they need to upgrade their skills in order to keep their old jobs, they willingly accept lower-paying jobs instead. As one manager noted, "For capable human beings to take cuts in pay because they don't have the literacy skills they need—that's really sad." For companies to survive, their choices have really come down to two: either they have to compete with higher technology and smart workers or they have to move overseas and compete with cheaper labor.

SUMMARY

The pace of change in our society is forcing both employed and displaced workers continually to acquire new knowledge and skills. In most organizations, therefore, lifelong training is essential. To be maximally effective, training programs should follow a three-phase sequence: needs assessment, implementation, and evaluation. First define clearly what is to be learned before choosing a particular method or technique. Defining what is to be learned requires a continuous cycle of organization analysis, operations analysis, and analysis of the training needs of employees.

Then relate training needs to the achievement of broader organizational goals and ensure that they are consistent with management's perceptions of strategy and tactics. Beyond these fundamental concerns, principles of learning—goal setting, behavior modeling, meaningfulness of material, practice, feedback, and transfer of training—are essential considerations in the design of any training program. Choose a particular technique according to the degree to which it fits identified needs and incorporates the learning principles.

In evaluating training programs, we measure change in terms of four categories: reaction, learning, behavior, and results. Measures of the impact of training on organizational results are the bottom line of training success. Fortunately, advances in utility analysis now make evaluations possible in terms of dollar benefits and dollar costs.

One of the most neglected areas of training is new-employee orientation. Clearly, a new employee's initial experience with a firm can have a major effect on his or her later career. To maximize the impact of orientation, organizations must recognize that new employees need specific information in three major areas: (1) company standards, traditions, and policies; (2) social behavior, and (3) technical aspects of the job. This suggests two levels of orientation: company, conducted by an HR representative, and departmental, conducted by the immediate supervisor. An orientation follow-up is essential (e.g., after 1 week by the supervisor and after 1 month by an HR representative) to ensure proper quality control plus continual improvement.

DISCUSSION QUESTIONS

7-1 Training has been described by some as intensely "faddish." As an advisor to management, describe how the firm can avoid succumbing to training fads.

7-2 How does goal setting affect trainee learning and motivation?

7-3 Outline an evaluation procedure for a training program designed to teach sales principles and strategies.

7-4 Why is orientation so often overlooked by organizations?

7-5 Think back to your first day on the most recent job you have held. What could the organization have done to hasten your socialization and your adjustment to the job?

APPLYING YOUR KNOWLEDGE

Case 7-1 *Evaluating Training at Hutchinson Inc.*

Hutchinson Inc. is a large insurance brokerage firm operating out of Seattle, Washington. The company was founded in 1922 by John Hutchinson, Sr., father of the current president. Hutchinson offers a complete line of insurance services for both individuals and business firms. As is true with other insurance companies, Hutchinson emphasizes sales. In fact, over half of all corporate employees are involved in sales to some degree.

Because the sales activity is so important to Hutchinson, the company spends a considerable amount of time, effort, and money in sales training. Its training director, Tom Jordan, is constantly on the lookout for new training techniques that can improve sales and profits. He recently uncovered one that he had never heard of before, but which seemed to have some promise. He immediately scheduled a meeting with his boss, Cathy Archer, vice president for human resources at Hutchinson, to discuss the possibility of sending some salespeople to this new training course.

Cathy: Come in Tom. What's this I hear about a new sales training course?

Tom: Well, as you know Cathy, I always try to keep up-to-date on the latest in training techniques so that we can remain competitive. I got a flyer yesterday in the mail announcing a new approach to sales training. The course is offered by a guy named Bagwan Shri Lansig. Apparently, the course involves flying trainees off to a secluded spot in the mountains of Oregon where they undergo a week of intensive training, personal growth exercises, synchronized chanting, and transcendental meditation. The brochure is brimming with personal testimonials from "million-dollar" salespeople who claim to have been helped immeasurably by the training. I already have 10 people in mind to send to the training session next month, but before I speak with them, I thought I'd run it by you.

Cathy: How much does it cost?

Tom: It's not bad. Only $2500 per person. And there's a 10 percent discount if we send over five people.

Cathy: I don't know Tom. That sounds a little steep to me. Besides, John has been bugging me again about the results of our last training effort. He wants to know whether all the money we're spending on sales training is really paying off. As you know, sales and profits are down this quarter, and John is looking for places to cut corners. I'm afraid that if we can't demonstrate a payoff somehow for our training courses, he is going to pull the rug out from under us.

Tom: But we evaluate all our training programs! The last one got rave reviews from all the participants. Remember how they said that they hardly had time to enjoy Hawaii because they were so busy learning about proper closing techniques?

Cathy: That's true, Tom. But John wants more proof than just the reactions of the salespeople. He wants something more tangible. Now before we buy into any more sales training programs, I want you to develop a plan for evaluation of the training effort.

Questions

1. What is meant by the statement that training is extremely "faddish"?
2. How can Hutchinson Inc. avoid becoming a victim of the faddishness of the training business?
3. Develop a detailed training evaluation strategy that Tom can present to Cathy, which would provide evidence of the effectiveness of a particular training technique.

REFERENCES

1. Kaufman, J. (1996, Sept. 5). Mood swing: White men shake off that losing feeling on affirmative action. *The Wall Street Journal*, pp. A1, A4. See also Affirmative action on the edge (1995, Feb. 13). *U. S. News & World Report*, pp. 32–47.
2. Uchitelle, L, & Kleinfield, N. R. (1996, Mar. 3). On the battlefields of business, millions of casualties. *The New York Times*, pp. 1, 14–17.
3. The perplexing case of the plummeting payrolls (1993, Sept. 20). *Business Week*, p. 27.
4. Goldstein, I. L., & Gilliam, P. (1990). Training system issues in the year 2000. *American Psychologist*, **45,** 134–143.
5. Huszczo, G. E. (1996). *Tools for team excellence*. Palo Alto, CA: Davies-Black.
6. Reich, R., in Greenhouse, S. (1992, Feb. 9). Attention America! Snap out of it! *The New York Times*, pp. 1F, 8F.
7. Performance consulting—moving beyond training (1995, Aug.). *Bulletin*. Denver: Mountain States Employers Council, p. 1. See also Cascio, W. F. (1993a, Nov.). *Public investments in training: Perspectives on macro-level structural issues and micro-level delivery systems*. Philadelphia: University of Pennsylvania, National Center on the Educational Quality of the Workforce.
8. Brody, M. (1987, June 8). Helping workers to work smarter. *Fortune*, pp. 86–88.
9. Ibid.
10. Cascio, W. F. (1995, May). *Guide to responsible restructuring*. Washington, DC: U.S. Department of Labor, Office of the American Workplace.
11. Robinson, in Stuller, J. (1993, June). Why not "inplacement"? *Training*, p. 40.
12. Robinson, M., Corporate Redeployment Manager, Intel. (1995, Mar.). Personal communication, plus briefing materials.
13. Cascio, (1993a), op. cit.
14. The new factory worker (1996, Sept. 30). *Business Week*, pp. 59–68.
15. Hodson, R., Hooks, G., & Rieble, S. (1992). Customized training in the workplace. *Work and Occupations*, **19**(3), 272–292.
16. Motorola: Training for the millenium (1994, Mar. 28). *Business Week*, pp. 158–162.
17. Work week. (1996, Oct. 1). *The Wall Street Journal*, p. A1.
18. Salwen, K. G. (1993, Apr. 19). The cutting edge: German-owned maker of power tools finds job training pays off. *The Wall Street Journal*, pp. A1, A7.
19. Tooker, in Motorola: Training for the millenium, op. cit., p. 158.
20. Labor letter (1991, Oct. 22). *The Wall Street Journal*, p. A1.
21. Risen, J. (1994, Mar. 17). Nations struggle to retrain workers as times change. *Los Angeles Times*, p. A9.
22. Low-wage lessons (1996, Nov. 11). *Business Week*, pp. 108–116.
23. Your local campus: Training ground zero (1996, Sept. 30). *Business Week*, p. 68.
24. Apprenticeship training and college combine for success in Germany (1996, Mar.). *Manpower Argus*, No. 330, p. 8.
25. Low-wage lessons. loc. cit.
26. Sirota, Alper, & Pfau, Inc. (1989). *Report to respondents: Survey of views toward corporate education and training practices*. New York: Author.
27. Rodgers, R., Hunter, J. E., & Rogers, D. L. (1993). Influence of top management commitment on management program success. *Journal of Applied Psychology*, **78,** 151–155.
28. Davis, C. in Filipczak, B. (1995, Jan.). You're on your own: Training, employability, and the new employment contract. *Training*, pp. 29–36.
29. Porter, M. E. (1985). *Competitive advantage*. New York: Free Press.
30. Motorola: Training for the millenium, loc. cit.
31. Goldstein, I. L. (1991). Training in work organizations. In M. D. Dunnette & L. M. Hough (eds.), *Handbook of industrial and organizational psychology*. Palo Alto, CA:

Consulting Psychologists Press, pp. 507–619. See also Ostroff, C., & Ford, J. K. (1989). Assessing training needs: Critical levels of analysis. In I. L. Goldstein (ed.), *Training and development in organizations.* San Francisco: Jossey-Bass, pp. 25–62.

32. Moore, M. L., & Dutton, P. (1978). Training needs analysis: Review and critique. *Academy of Management Review,* **3,** 532–454.
33. Hilton, M. (1987). Union and management: A strong case for cooperation. *Training and Development Journal,* **41**(1), 54–55.
34. Wexley, K. N., & Latham, G. P. (1991). *Developing and training human resources in organizations.* New York: HarperCollins.
35. Matsui, T., Kakuyama, T., & Onglatco, M. L. U. (1987). Effects of goals and feedback on performance in groups. *Journal of Applied Psychology,* **72,** 407–415. See also Mento, A. J., Steel, R. P., & Karren, R. J. (1987). A meta-analytic study of the effects of goal setting on performance: 1966–1984. *Organizational Behavior and Human Decision Processes,* **39,** 52–83.
36. Wood, R. E., Mento, A. J., & Locke, E. A. (1987). Task complexity as a moderator of goal effects: A meta-analysis. *Journal of Applied Psychology,* **72,** 416–425.
37. Locke, E. A. (1968). Toward a theory of task motivation and incentives. *Organizational Behavior and Human Performance,* **3,** 157–189.
38. Locke, E. A., Latham, G. P., & Erez, M. (1988). The determinants of goal commitment. *Academy of Management Review,* **13,** 23–39.
39. Bandura, A. (1986). *Social foundations of thought and action: A social cognitive theory.* Englewood Cliffs, NJ: Prentice-Hall.
40. Eden, D., & Shani, A. B. (1982). Pygmalion goes to boot camp: Expectancy, leadership, and trainee performance. *Journal of Applied Psychology,* **67,** 194–199.
41. Hogan, P. M., Hakel, M. D., & Decker, P. J. (1986). Effects of trainee-generated versus trainer-provided rule codes on generalization in behavior-modeling training. *Journal of Applied Psychology,* **71,** 469–473.
42. Goldstein, A. P., & Sorcher, M. (1974). *Changing supervisor behavior.* New York: Pergamon Press. See also Latham, G. P., & Saari, L. M. (1979). The application of social learning theory to training supervisors through behavior modeling. *Journal of Applied Psychology,* **64,** 239–246.
43. Cascio, W. F. (1993b). *Documenting training effectiveness in terms of worker performance and adaptability.* Philadelphia: University of Pennsylvania, National Center on the Educational Quality of the Workforce. See also Baldwin, T. T. (1992). Effects of alternative modeling strategies on outcomes of interpersonal-skills training. *Journal of Applied Psychology,* **77,** 147–154.
44. Wexley & Latham, op. cit.
45. Low-wage lessons, loc. cit. See also Gray, I., & Borecki, T. B. (1970). Training programs for the hard-core: What the trainer has to learn. *Personnel,* **47,** 23–29.
46. Gagné, R. M. (1977). *The conditions of learning.* New York: Holt, Rinehart & Winston.
47. Driskell, J. E., Willis, R. P., & Copper, C. (1992). Effect of overlearning on retention. *Journal of Applied Psychology,* **77,** 615–622.
48. Goldstein, I. L. (1993). *Training in organizations: Needs assessment, development, and evaluation* (3d ed.). Monterey, CA: Brooks/Cole.
49. Latham, G. P. (1989). Behavioral approaches to the training and learning process. In I. L. Goldstein (ed.), *Training and development in organizations.* San Francisco: Jossey-Bass, pp. 256–295.
50. Pritchard, R. D., Jones, S. D., Roth, P. L., Steubing, K. K., & Ekeberg, S. E. (1988). Effects of group feedback, goal setting, and incentives on organizational productivity. *Journal of Applied Psychology,* **73,** 337–358.
51. Florin-Thuma, B. C., & Boudreau, J. W. (1987). Performance feedback utility in a small organization: Effects on organizational outcomes and managerial decision processes. *Personnel Psychology,* **40,** 693–713.

52. Cascio, W. F. (1998). Applied psychology in human resource management (5th ed.). Englewood Cliffs, NJ: Prentice-Hall.
53. Eastburn, R. A. (1986). Developing tomorrow's managers. *Personnel Administrator,* **31**(3), 71–76.
54. Cannon-Bowers, J. A., Tannenbaum, S. I., Salas, E., & Volpe, C. E. (1995). Defining competencies and establishing team training requirements. In R. A. Guzzo & E. Salas (eds.), *Team effectiveness and decision making in organizations.* San Francisco: Jossey-Bass, pp. 333–380.
55. Huszczo, op. cit.
56. Ganster, D. C., Williams, S., & Poppler, P. (1991). Does training in problem solving improve the quality of group decisions? *Journal of Applied Psychology,* **76,** 479–483.
57. Bass, B. M. (1980). Team productivity and individual member competence. *Small Group Behavior,* **11,** 431–504.
58. Wellins, R. S., Byham, W. C., & Wilson, J. M. (1991). *Empowered teams.* San Francisco: Jossey-Bass.
59. Komaki, J. L., Desselles, J. L., & Bowman, E. D. (1989). Definitely not a breeze: Extending an operant model of supervision to teams. *Journal of Applied Psychology,* **74,** 522–529.
60. Campbell, J. P., Dunnette, M. D., Lawler, E. E., & Weick, K. E. (1970). *Managerial behavior, performance, and effectiveness.* New York: McGraw-Hill.
61. Labor letter (1990, May 8). *The Wall Street Journal,* p. A1.
62. Lee, M. (1993, Sept. 2). Diversity training grows at small firms. *The Wall Street Journal,* p. B2.
63. MacDonald, H. (1993, July 5). The diversity industry. *The New Republic,* pp. 22–25.
64. Kraiger, K., Ford, J. K., & Salas, E. (1993). Application of cognitive, skill-based, and affective theories of learning outcomes to new methods of training evaluation. *Journal of Applied Psychology Monograph,* **78,** 311–328.
65. Sackett, P. R., & Mullen, E. J. (1993). Beyond formal experimental design: Towards an expanded view of the training evaluation process. *Personnel Psychology,* **46,** 613–627. See also Goldstein, I. L. (1993), op. cit.
66. Kirkpatrick, D. L. (1983). Four steps to measuring training effectiveness. *Personnel Administrator,* **28**(11), 19–25.
67. Arvey, R. D., Maxwell, S. E., & Salas, E. (1992). The relative power of training evaluation designs under different cost configurations. *Journal of Applied Psychology,* **77,** 155–160.
68. Cascio, W. F. (1989). Using utility analysis to assess training outcomes. In I. L. Goldstein (ed.), *Training and development in organizations.* San Francisco: Jossey-Bass, pp. 63–88. See also Cascio, W. F. (1991). *Costing human resources: The financial impact of behavior in organizations* (3d ed.). Boston: PWS-Kent.
69. Paquet, B., Kasl, E., Weinstein, L., & Waite, W. (1987). The bottom line. *Training and Development Journal,* **41**(6), 27–33.
70. Henkoff, R. (1994, Oct. 3). Finding, training, and keeping the best service workers. *Fortune,* pp. 110–122.
71. Solomon, J. (1988, Dec. 29). Companies try measuring cost savings from new types of corporate benefits. *The Wall Street Journal,* p. B1.
72. Cappelli, P. (1995). Is the "skills gap" really about attitudes? *California Management Review,* **37,** 108–124.
73. St. John, W. D. (1980, May). The complete employee orientation program. *Personnel Journal,* pp. 373–378.
74. Henkoff, loc. cit.
75. Starcke, A. M. (1996). Building a better orientation program. *HRMagazine,* **41**(11), 107–114.
76. McGarrell, E. J., Jr. (1984). An orientation system that builds productivity. *Personnel Administrator,* **29**(10), 75–85.

77. Ibid. See also Starcke, loc. cit.
78. Finney, M. I. (1996, Oct.). Employee orientation programs can help introduce success. *HR News*, p. 2.
79. Burke, M. J., & Day, R. R. (1986). A cumulative study of the effectiveness of managerial training. *Journal of Applied Psychology*, **71**, 232–245.
80. Cascio (1993b), op. cit.
81. Armer, P. (1970). The individual: His privacy, self-image, and obsolescence. *Proceedings of the meeting of the panel on science and technology, 11th "Science and Astronautics."* Washington, DC: U.S. Government Printing Office.
82. Campbell, J. P. (1988). Training design for performance improvement. In J. P. Campbell & R. J. Campbell (eds.), *Productivity in organizations.* San Francisco: Jossey-Bass, pp. 177–215.

8 PERFORMANCE MANAGEMENT

Questions This Chapter Will Help Managers Answer

1. What steps can I, as a manager, take to make the performance management process more relevant and acceptable to those who will be affected by it?
2. How can we best fit our approach to performance management with the strategic direction of our department and business?
3. Should managers and nonmanagers be appraised from multiple perspectives—for example, by those above, by those below, by coequals, and by customers?
4. What strategy should we use to train raters at all levels in the mechanics of performance management and in the art of giving feedback?
5. What would an effective performance management process look like?

*THE EXECUTIVE APPRAISAL PARADOX**

"It just doesn't make any sense. The higher you climb the ladder in this organization, the less chance you have of getting feedback about your performance. . . . We seem to have time for everything else, but not time to give our top people the kind of reviews they need to help them develop."

This observation from an executive-level controller typifies the type of performance feedback most executives receive. With each promotion, reviews become less frequent, systematic, informative, and useful. At the executive level, there often is almost no regular performance feedback other than superficial praise or criticism for some crisis. This suggests an apparent paradox in performance appraisal: the higher managers rise in an organization, the lower the likelihood that they will receive quality feedback on their job performance. For some obscure but apparently pervasive reason, executive appraisal seems to have become a taboo topic in many organizations. This is a serious issue, for executives perform the most uncertain, unstructured, ill-defined, and often most important work in an enterprise.

Recent research (a total of 118 hours of in-depth interviews with 84 executives from 11 major organizations spanning 12 different functional areas) suggests that the widespread disappointment with the quality of executive appraisals is traceable to a series of myths surrounding the process. Together, they contribute to the paradox that those who could most use performance feedback to enhance their effectiveness are often the least likely to get it. The myths turn out to be surprisingly common. We will examine them in the first part of this case, and in the second part, at the end of the chapter, we will identify what can be done to debunk these myths.

Myth #1: Executives neither need nor want structured performance reviews. This belief stems from a widely shared premise that the higher an individual's level in an organization, the lower should be the need for feedback. Paradoxically, this is not the way executives themselves see the need for feedback. Every executive interviewed said that systematic feedback in some form was crucial in order to help him or her grow.

Myth #2: A formal review is beneath the dignity of an executive. The fallacy here is the presumption that appraisal is somehow a sign that one is still on professional probation, that it is a demeaning, aversive experience that managers mercifully can outgrow. Naturally, appraisal at any level can produce anxiety—"there is a need to know and a fear of knowing." But executives insisted that their need to know far outweighed their fear. They preferred to know where they stood.

Myth #3: Top-level executives are too busy to conduct appraisals. Often "too busy" is a smoke screen for some less mundane reason—such as a belief that appraisals are not worth doing. Said one executive who had been burned by this attitude: "It seems like we have time for lots of things that are a lot less important than talking about improving performance and executive development. There

*Adapted from C. O. Longenecker & D. A. Gioia, The executive appraisal paradox, *Academy of Management Executive*, *6*(2), 1992, 18–28. Used by permission.

should always be time for a process that contributes to higher performance and productivity and, paradoxically, the saving of time."

Myth #4: A lack of feedback fosters autonomy and creativity in executives. This approach to executive development is attractive because it affirms the admired notion of "pulling yourself up by your bootstraps." To some degree, it can facilitate autonomy and creativity. There is ample evidence, however, that the same goal can be accomplished—faster—with good feedback. Said one executive: "A lack of performance feedback keeps people in the dark about how others view their performance. That breeds doubt and frustration and, maybe worse, allows little problems to fester into big ones."

Myth #5: Results are the only basis for assessing executive performance. As a division manager put it: "Sure, you have to get results; that's why we're in business. But you also need to look at the road you took to get the results. You need feedback on process and style and the intangibles that you can't quantify." Said another vice president: "Isolating on results is a formula for long-term trouble." An example from the service industry illustrates this nicely. An executive used hard-nosed methods to build his track record as a troubleshooter, one who could turn divisions around. In one division, however, although he did shore up its bottom line, his severe tactics and caustic style nearly incited an employee rebellion. As a result, he was called to headquarters and given an ultimatum to "improve your human relations skills right now or else." It was the first time he had received any formal feedback other than praise.

Myth #6: Comprehensive evaluation of executive performance simply cannot be captured via formal performance appraisal. Intuition, gut feelings, flashes of insight, and other nonmeasurable attributes are hallmarks of high-performing managers. As a result, some executives want the evaluation of executive performance to be considered an intangible domain also. Can you appreciate the exasperation of this disgruntled veteran of ambiguous performance standards? "You never really knew where you stood. You could do exactly what you thought you were supposed to do and get burned, or hit the right number in one column, screw up the rest, and be a saint. Performance at the upper levels is subjective, but sometimes it seems like it's kept that way for some suspicious reasons."

Challenges

1. In your opinion, why do these six myths persist?
2. If standards of performance are ambiguous, does this undermine the philosophy that "rewards are based on performance"?
3. Should the process an executive uses be just as important as the outcomes she or he achieves?

The chapter opening vignette reveals just how complex performance management can be, for it includes both developmental (feedback) and administrative (pay, promotions) issues, as well as both technical aspects (design of an appraisal system) and interpersonal aspects (appraisal interviews). This chapter's objective is to present a balanced view of the performance management process, considering both its technical and its interpersonal aspects. Let's begin by examining the nature of this process.

MANAGING FOR MAXIMUM PERFORMANCE[1]

Consider the following situations:

- The athlete searching for a coach who really understands her
- The student waiting to see his guidance counselor at school
- The worker who has just begun working for a new boss
- A self-managing work team and a supervisor about to meet to discuss objectives for the next quarter

What do these situations all have in common? The need to manage performance effectively—at the level of either the individual or the work team. Think of performance management as a kind of compass—one that indicates an individual's or a team's actual direction as well as the desired direction. Like a compass, the job of the manager (or athletic coach or school guidance counselor) is to indicate where the individual or team is now, and to help focus attention and effort on the desired direction.

Unfortunately, the concept of performance *management* means something very specific, and much too narrow, to many managers. They tend to equate it with performance *appraisal*—an exercise they typically do once a year to identify and discuss job-relevant strengths and weaknesses of individuals or work teams. This approach is a mistake. Would it surprise you to learn that employees often react to appraisal interviews in the following ways?

- Employees are often less certain about where they stood *after* the appraisal interview than before it.
- Employees tend to evaluate their supervisors less favorably after the interview than before it.
- Employees often report that few constructive actions or significant improvements resulted from appraisal interviews.
- Employees feel that the authoritarian "tell and sell" approach, so common in appraisal interviews, is completely out of step with today's emphases on empowerment and workplace democracy.

These are discouraging findings that certainly run counter to what we know about performance management. And what do we know about this concept? We know that performance management is part of a continuous process of improvement over time, that it demands daily, not annual, attention. Think of it this way. Why is the weekend tennis player willing to pay handsomely for private lessons? So that he or she can have a professional who understands and can demonstrate what good performance looks like, observe the player's performance, make an appraisal of it, and then provide real-time feedback to build sound habits and eliminate unsound ones. Subsequent lessons stay focused on the overall objective (a smooth, accurate serve, for example), while recalling information about performance that builds on the foundation of earlier lessons. That is managing for maximum performance.

So what is the role of performance appraisal in the overall performance management process? Performance appraisal is a necessary, but far from sufficient, part of performance management. Managers who are committed to moving from a performance appraisal orientation to one of performance management tell us that the first step is probably the hardest, for it involves a break with tradition. Typically, appraisal is done annually, or in some firms, quarterly. *Performance management requires a willingness and a commitment to focus on improving performance at the level of the individual or team every day.* A compass provides instantaneous, real-time information that describes the difference between the current and the desired course. To practice sound performance management, managers must do the same thing—provide timely feedback about performance, while constantly focusing everyone's attention on the ultimate objective (e.g., world-class customer service).

At a general level, the broad process of performance management requires that managers do three things well:

1. Define performance.
2. Facilitate performance.
3. Encourage performance.

Let's explore each of these ideas briefly.

Define Performance

A manager who defines performance ensures that individual employees or teams know what is expected of them, and that they stay focused on effective performance. How does the manager do this? By paying careful attention to three key elements: *goals, measures,* and *assessment.*

Goal setting has a proven track record of success in improving performance in a variety of settings and cultures.[2] How does it improve performance? Studies show that goals direct attention to the specific performance in question (e.g., percentage of satisfied customers), they mobilize effort to accomplish higher levels of performance, and they foster persistence for higher levels of performance.[3] The practical implications of research on goal setting are clear: set specific, challenging goals, for this clarifies precisely what is expected and leads to high levels of performance. On average, studies show you can expect to improve productivity 10 percent by using goal setting.[4]

The mere presence of goals, however, is not sufficient. Managers must also be able to *measure* the extent to which goals have been accomplished. Goals such as "make the company successful" are too vague to be useful. Measures such as the number of defective parts produced per million or the average time to respond to a customer's inquiry are much more tangible.

The third requirement for defining performance is *assessment.* Here is where performance appraisal comes in. Regular assessment of progress toward goals focuses the attention and efforts of an employee or a team. If a manager takes the time to identify measurable goals, but then fails to assess progress toward them, he or she is asking for trouble.

To define performance properly, therefore, you must do three things well: set goals, decide how to measure accomplishment, and provide regular assessments of progress. Doing so will leave no doubt in the minds of your people as to what is expected of them, how it will be measured, and where they stand at any given time. There should be no surprises in the performance management process—and regular appraisals help ensure that there will not be.

Facilitate Performance

Managers who are committed to managing for maximum performance recognize that one of their major responsibilities is to eliminate roadblocks to successful performance. Another is to provide adequate resources to get a job done right and on time, and a third is to pay careful attention to selecting employees.

What are some examples of *obstacles* that can inhibit maximum performance? Consider just a few: outdated or poorly maintained equipment, delays in receiving supplies, inefficient design of work spaces, and ineffective work methods. Employees are well aware of these, and they are only too willing to identify them—if managers will only ask for their input. Then it's the manager's job to eliminate these obstacles.

Once roadblocks to successful performance have been eliminated, the next step is to *provide adequate resources*—capital resources, material resources, or human resources. After all, if employees lack the tools to reach the challenging goals they have set, they will become frustrated and disenchanted. Indeed, one observer has gone so far as to say, "It's immoral not to give people tools to meet tough goals."[5] Conversely, employees really appreciate it when their employer provides everything they need to perform well. Not surprisingly, they usually do perform well under those circumstances.

A final aspect of performance facilitation is the *careful selection of employees.* After all, the last thing any manager wants is to have people who are ill-suited to their jobs (e.g., by temperament or training), because this often leads to overstaffing, excessive labor costs, and reduced productivity. In leading companies, even top managers often get involved in selecting new employees. Microsoft, with over 15,000 employees, hires software writers "like we're a ten-person company hiring an 11th," with CEO Bill Gates enticing senior engineers, and requiring even experienced software developers to go through 5 or 6 hours of intense interviews.[6] If you are truly committed to managing for maximum performance, you pay attention to all the details—all the factors that might affect performance—and leave nothing to chance. That does not mean that you are constantly looking over everyone's shoulder. On the contrary, it implies greater self-management, more autonomy, and lots of opportunities to experiment, take risks, and be entrepreneurial.

Encourage Performance

This is the last area of management responsibility in a coordinated approach to performance management. To encourage performance, especially repeated good performance, managers must *provide a sufficient number of rewards that employees really value, and do so in a timely and fair manner.*

Do not bother offering rewards that nobody cares about, like a gift certificate to see a fortune-teller. On the contrary, to determine the types of *rewards employees value*, begin by asking your people what is most important to them—for example, pay, benefits, free time, merchandise, or special privileges. Then consider tailoring your awards program so that employees or teams can choose from a menu of similarly valued options.

Next, *provide rewards in a timely manner*, soon after major accomplishments. For example, a metal-stamping plant in San Leandro, California, North American Tool & Die, Inc., provides monthly cash awards for creativity. In one instance, an employee earned $500 for installing an oil-recycling machine.

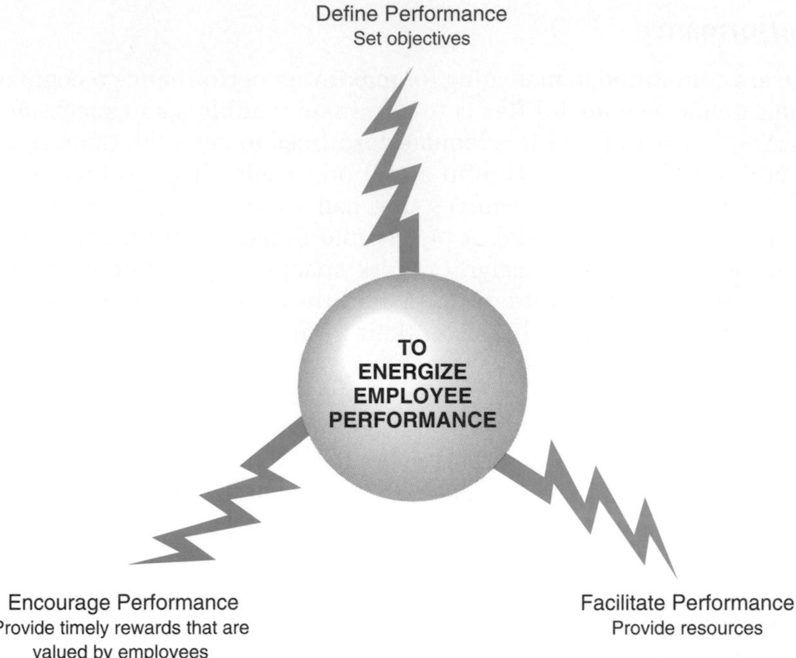

Figure 8-1
Elements of a performance management system.

The company uses large amounts of oil in 55-gallon drums to lubricate its giant metal-stamping machinery. One employee purchased a $900 oil-recycling machine to filter the dirty oil so that it could be reused. The machine paid for itself in 1 month, and the company avoided potential toxic-waste problems associated with disposal of the dirty oil. The employee received the reward within 2 weeks after the recycling machine began to operate. Timing is important; if there is an excessive delay between effective performance and receipt of the reward, then the reward loses its potential to motivate subsequent high performance.

Finally, *provide rewards in a manner that employees consider to be fair*. Fairness is a subjective concept, and it depends on a comparison between the rewards a person receives for his or her contributions to the organization and some comparison standard. Such standards might be:

- Others—a comparison with what others in similar situations received, either inside or outside the organization.
- Self—a comparison with one's own rewards and contributions at a different time or with one's evolving views of self-worth.
- Systems—a comparison with what the organization has promised.

Not surprisingly, employees often behave very responsibly when they are asked in advance for their opinions about what is fair. Indeed, it seems only fair to ask them.

In summary, managing for maximum performance requires that you do three things well: define performance, facilitate performance, and encourage performance. Like a compass, the role of the manager is to provide orientation, direction, and feedback. These ideas are shown graphically in Figure 8-1.

PURPOSES OF PERFORMANCE APPRAISAL SYSTEMS

As we have seen, performance appraisal plays an important part in the overall process of performance management. Hence it is important that we examine it in some detail. Performance appraisal has many facets. It is an exercise in observation and judgment, it is a feedback process, and it is an organizational intervention. It is a measurement process as well as an intensely emotional process. Above all, it is an inexact, human process. Not surprisingly, therefore, it is judged effective in less than 10 percent of the organizations that use it.[7] In view of such widespread dissatisfaction, why do appraisals continue to be used? What purposes do they serve?

In general, appraisal serves a twofold purpose: (1) to improve employees' work performance by helping them realize and use their full potential in carrying out their firms' missions, and (2) to provide information to employees and managers for use in making work-related decisions. More specifically, appraisals serve the following purposes:

1. **Appraisals provide legal and formal organizational justification for employment decisions** to promote outstanding performers; to weed out marginal or low performers; to train, transfer, or discipline others; and to justify merit increases (or no increases). They may also serve as one basis for reducing the size of the workforce. In short, appraisal serves as a key input for administering a formal organizational reward and punishment system.
2. **Appraisals are used as criteria in test validation.** That is, test results are correlated with appraisal results to evaluate the hypothesis that test scores predict job performance.[8] However, if appraisals are not done carefully, or if considerations other than performance influence appraisal results, the appraisals cannot be used legitimately for any purpose.
3. **Appraisals provide feedback to employees** and thereby serve as vehicles for personal and career development.
4. Once the development needs of employees are identified, **appraisals can help establish objectives for training programs.**
5. As a result of the proper specifications of performance levels, **appraisals can help diagnose organizational problems.** They do so by identifying training needs and the knowledge, abilities, skills, and other characteristics to consider in hiring, and they also provide a basis for distinguishing between effective and ineffective performers. Appraisal therefore represents the beginning of a process, rather than an end product.[9] These ideas are shown graphically in Figure 8-2.

Despite their shortcomings, appraisals continue to be used widely, especially as a basis for tying pay to performance.[10] To attempt to avoid these shortcomings by doing away with appraisals is no solution, for whenever people interact in organized settings, appraisals will be made—formally or informally. The real challenge, then, is to identify appraisal techniques and practices that (1) are most likely to achieve a particular objective and (2) are least vulnerable to the obstacles listed above. Let us begin by considering some of the fundamental requirements that determine whether a performance appraisal system will succeed or fail.

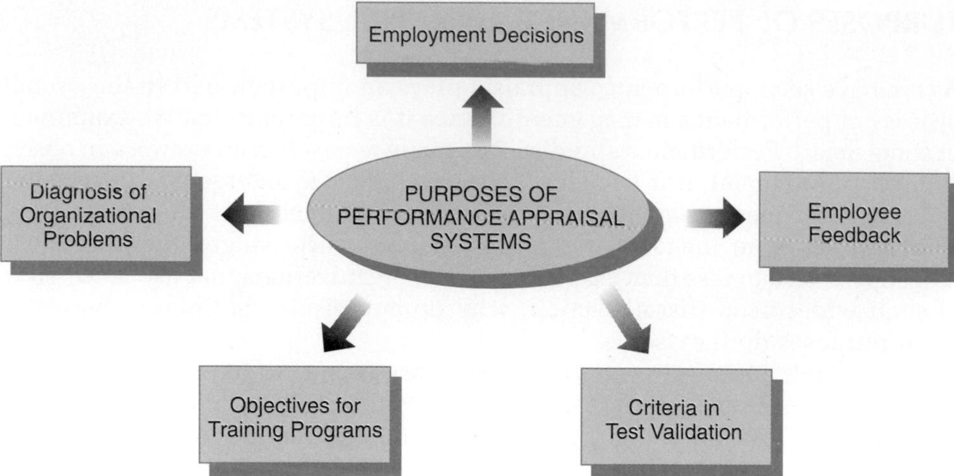

Figure 8-2
Purposes of performance appraisal systems.

Requirements of Effective Appraisal Systems

Legally and scientifically, the key requirements of any appraisal system are relevance, sensitivity, and reliability. In the context of ongoing operations, the key requirements are acceptability and practicality.[11] Let's consider each of these.

Relevance

This requirement implies that there are clear links (1) between the performance standards for a particular job and an organization's goals and (2) between the critical job elements identified through a job analysis and the dimensions to be rated on an appraisal form. In short, relevance is determined by answering the question "What really makes the difference between success and failure on a particular job, and according to whom?" The answer to the latter question is simple: the customer. Customers may be internal (e.g., your immediate boss, workers in another department) or external (those who buy your company's products or services). In all cases, it is important to pay attention to the things that the customer believes are important (e.g., on-time delivery, zero defects, information to solve business problems).

Performance standards translate job requirements into levels of acceptable or unacceptable employee behavior. They play a critical role in the job analysis–performance appraisal linkage, as Figure 8-3 indicates. Job analysis identifies

ETHICAL DILEMMAS IN PERFORMANCE APPRAISAL

Performance appraisal actually encompasses two distinct processes: observation and judgment. Managers must observe performance if they are to be competent to judge its effectiveness. Yet some managers assign performance ratings on the basis of small (and perhaps unrepresentative) samples of their subordinates' work. Is this ethical? And further, is it ethical to assign performance ratings (either good or bad) that differ from what a manager knows a subordinate deserves?

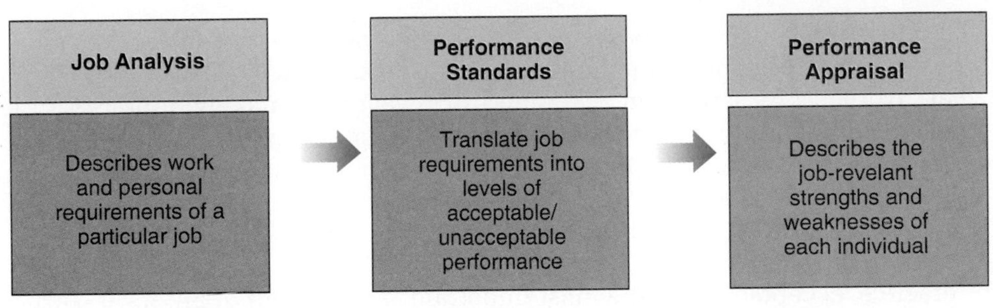

Figure 8-3
Relationship of performance standards to job analysis and performance appraisal.

what is to be done. Performance standards specify *how well* work is to be done. Such standards may be quantitative (e.g., time, errors) or qualitative (e.g., quality of work, ability to analyze, say, market research data or a machine malfunction).

Relevance also implies the periodic maintenance and updating of job analyses, performance standards, and appraisal systems. Should the system be challenged in court, relevance will be a fundamental consideration in the arguments presented by both sides.

Sensitivity

This requirement implies that a performance appraisal system is capable of distinguishing effective from ineffective performers. If it is not, and the best employees are rated no differently from the worst employees, then the appraisal system cannot be used for any administrative purpose, it certainly will not help employees develop, and it will undermine the motivation of both supervisors (who will view appraisals as "pointless paperwork") and subordinates.

A major concern here is the purpose of the rating. One study found that raters process identical sets of performance appraisal information differently, depending on whether a merit pay raise, a recommendation for further development, or the retention of a probationary employee is involved.[12] These results highlight the conflict between appraisals made for administrative purposes and those made for employee development. Appraisal systems designed for administrative purposes demand performance information about differences *between* individuals, while systems designed to promote employee growth demand information about differences *within* individuals. The two different types of information are not interchangeable in terms of purposes, and that is why performance management systems designed to meet both purposes are more complex and costly.

Reliability

A third requirement of sound appraisal systems is reliability. In this context, reliability refers to consistency of judgment. For any given employee, appraisals made by raters working independently of one another should agree closely. In practice, ratings made by supervisors tend to be more reliable than those made by peers.[13] Certainly raters with different perspectives (e.g., supervisors, peers, subordinates) may see the same individual's job performance very differently.[14] To provide reliable data, each rater must have an adequate opportunity to observe what the employee has done and the conditions under which he or she has done it; otherwise, unreliability may be confused with unfamiliarity.

Note that throughout this discussion there has been no mention of the validity or accuracy of appraisal judgments. This is because we really do not know what "truth" is in performance appraisal. However, by making appraisal systems relevant, sensitive, and reliable—by satisfying the scientific and legal requirements for workable appraisal systems—we can assume that the resulting judgments are valid as well.

Acceptability

In practice, acceptability is the most important requirement of all, for it is true that human resource programs must have the support of those who will use them, or else human ingenuity will be used to thwart them. Unfortunately, many organizations have not put much effort into garnering the front-end support and participation of those who will use the appraisal system. We know this in theory, but practice is another matter. Experts say that appraisal systems often do not work because most were designed primarily by HR specialists with limited input from managers and even less input from the employees.[15]

How much simpler it is to enlist the active support and cooperation of subordinates or teams by making explicit exactly what aspects of job performance they will be evaluated on. As we have seen, performance definition is the first step in performance management. Only after managers and subordinates or team members define performance clearly can we hope for the kind of acceptability and commitment that is so sorely needed in performance appraisal.

Practicality

This requirement implies that appraisal instruments are easy for managers and employees to understand and use. The importance of this requirement was brought home forcefully to me in the course of mediating a conflict between a county's Metropolitan Transit Authority (MTA) and its human resource (HR) unit (see the Company Example "Practical Performance Appraisal for Bus Drivers").

COMPANY EXAMPLE

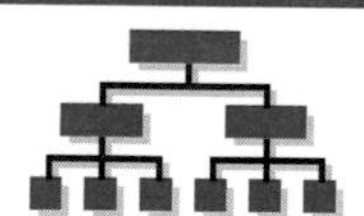

PRACTICAL PERFORMANCE APPRAISAL FOR BUS DRIVERS

The conflict erupted over the HR unit's *imposition* of a new appraisal system on all county departments regardless of each department's need for the new system. Metropolitan Transit Authority (MTA) had developed an appraisal system jointly with its union 5 years earlier, and the system was working fine. In brief, each MTA supervisor (high school–educated) was responsible for about 30 subordinates (a total of 890 bus drivers, some of whom were high school–educated and others who were not). The "old" appraisal system was based on a checklist of infractions (e.g., reporting late for work, being charged with a preventable traffic accident), each of which carried a specified number of points. Appraisals were done quarterly, with each driver assigned 100 points at the beginning of each quarter. A driver's quarterly appraisal was simply the number of points remaining after all penalty points had been deducted during the quarter. Her or his annual appraisal (used as a basis for decisions regarding merit pay, promotions, and special assignments) was simply the average of the four quarterly ratings. Both supervisors and subordinates liked the old system because it was understandable and practical, and also because it had been shown to be workable over a 5-year period.

The new appraisal system required MTA supervisors to write quarterly narrative reports on each of their 30-odd subordinates. The HR unit had made no effort to determine the ratio of supervisors to subordinates in the various departments. Not surprisingly, therefore, objections to the new system surfaced almost immediately. MTA supervisors had neither the time nor the inclination to write quarterly narratives on each of their subordinates. The new system was highly impractical. Furthermore, the old appraisal system was working fine and was endorsed by MTA management, employees, and the union. MTA managers therefore refused to adopt the new system. To dramatize their point, they developed a single, long, detailed narrative on an outstanding bus driver. Then they made 890 copies of the narrative (one for each driver), placed a different driver's name at the top of each "appraisal," and sent the 2-foot-high stack of appraisals to the HR unit. MTA made its point. After considerable haggling by both sides, the HR unit backed down and allowed MTA to continue to use its old (but acceptable and eminently practical) appraisal system. That system was not perfect (e.g., drivers could only lose points for poor performance, not earn points for good performance), but it illustrates how strongly the parties in the appraisal process will fight for a system that they find acceptable.

In a broader context, we are concerned with developing decision systems. From this perspective, relevance, sensitivity, and reliability are simply technical components of a system designed to make decisions about employees. As we have seen, just as much attention needs to be paid to ensuring the acceptability and practicality of appraisal systems. These are the five basic requirements of performance appraisal systems, and none of them can be ignored. However, since some degree of error is inevitable in all employment decisions, the crucial question to be answered in regard to each appraisal system is whether its use results in less human, social, and organizational cost than is currently paid for these errors. The answers to that question can result only in a wiser, fuller utilization of our human resources.

LEGALITIES OF PERFORMANCE APPRAISAL

There is a rich body of case law on performance appraisal, and three reviews of it reached similar conclusions.[16] To avoid legal difficulties, consider taking the following steps:

1. Conduct a job analysis to determine the characteristics necessary for successful job performance.
2. Incorporate these characteristics into a rating instrument. This may be done by tying rating instruments to specific job behaviors (e.g., BARSs, see page 313), but the courts routinely accept less sophisticated approaches, such as simple graphic rating scales. Regardless of the method used, provide written standards to all raters.
3. Train supervisors to use the rating instrument properly, including how to apply performance standards when making judgments. The uniform application of standards is very important. The vast majority of cases lost by organizations have involved evidence that subjective standards were applied

unevenly to members of protected groups versus all other employees. Often, performance appraisal results are used in the selection process to establish the validity of selection instruments. Steps 1, 2, and 3 are identical to those in that process.

4. Include formal appeal mechanisms, coupled with higher-level review of appraisals.
5. Document the appraisals and the reason for any termination decisions. This information may prove decisive in court. Credibility is enhanced by documented appraisal ratings that describe instances of poor performance.[17]
6. Provide some form of performance counseling or corrective guidance to assist poor performers.

Here is a good example of step 6. In *Stone v. Xerox* the organization had a fairly elaborate procedure for assisting poor performers.[18] Stone was employed as a sales representative and in fewer than 6 months had been given several written reprimands concerning customer complaints about his selling methods and failure to develop adequate written selling proposals. As a result, he was placed on a 1-month performance improvement program designed to correct these deficiencies. This program was extended 30 days at Stone's request. When his performance still did not improve, he was placed on probation and told that failure to improve substantially would result in termination. Stone's performance continued to be substandard, and he was discharged at the end of the probationary period. When he sued Xerox, he lost.

Certainly, the type of evidence required to defend performance ratings is linked to the *purposes* for which the ratings are made. For example, if appraisal of past performance is to be used as a predictor of future performance (i.e., promotions), evidence must be presented to show (1) that the ratings of past performance are, in fact, valid and (2) that the ratings of past performance are statistically related to *future* performance in another job.[19] At the very least, this latter step should include job analysis results indicating the extent to which the requirements of the lower- and higher-level jobs overlap. Finally, to assess adverse impact, organizations should keep accurate records of who is eligible for and interested in promotion. These two factors, *eligibility* and *interest*, define the "applicant group."

In summary, it is not difficult to offer prescriptions for scientifically sound, court-proof appraisal systems, but as we have seen, implementing them requires diligent attention by organizations, plus a commitment to making them work. In the development of a performance appraisal system, the most basic requirement is to determine what you want the system to accomplish. This requires a strategy for the management of performance.

The Strategic Dimension of Performance Appraisal

In the study of work motivation, a fairly well established principle is that the things that get rewarded get done. At least one author has termed this "the greatest management principle in the world."[20] So a fundamental issue for managers is "What kind of behavior do I want to encourage in my subordinates?" If employees are rewarded for generating short-term results, they will generate short-term results. If they are rewarded (e.g., through progressively higher commissions or bonuses) for generating repeat business or for reaching quality standards over long periods of time, then they will do those things.

Managers therefore have choices. They can emphasize short- or long-term objectives in the appraisal process, or some combination of the two. Short-term objectives emphasize outcomes such as bottom-line results for the current quarter. Long-term objectives emphasize outcomes such as increasing market share and securing repeat business from customers. To be most useful, however, the strategic management of performance must be linked to the strategies an organization (or strategic business unit) uses to gain competitive advantage—for example, innovation, speed, quality enhancement, or cost control.[21]

Some appraisal systems that are popular in the United States, such as management by objectives (MBO), are less popular in other parts of the world, for example, in Japan and France. MBO focuses primarily on results, rather than on how the results were accomplished. Typically it has a short-term focus, although this need not always be the case.

In Japan, greater emphasis is placed on the psychological and behavioral sides of performance appraisal than on objective outcomes. Thus an employee will be rated in terms of the effort he or she puts into a job; on integrity, loyalty, and cooperative spirit; and on how well he or she serves the customer. Short-term results tend to be much less important than long-term personal development, the establishment and maintenance of long-term relationships with customers (that is, behaviors), and increasing market share.[22]

Once managers decide what they want the appraisal system to accomplish, their next question is "What is the best method of performance appraisal—which technique should I use?" As in so many other areas of HR management, there is no simple answer. The following section considers some alternative methods, along with their strengths and weaknesses. Since readers of this text are more likely to be users of appraisal systems than developers of them, the following will focus most on describing and illustrating them. For more detailed information, consult the references at the end of the chapter.

ALTERNATIVE METHODS OF APPRAISING EMPLOYEE PERFORMANCE

Many regard rating methods or formats as the central issue in performance appraisal; this, however, is not the case.[23] Broader issues must also be considered—such as *trust* in the appraisal system; the *attitudes* of managers and employees; the *purpose*, *frequency*, and *source* of appraisal data; and rater *training*. Viewed in this light, rating formats play only a supporting role in the overall appraisal process.

Many rating formats focus on employee behaviors, either by comparing the performance of employees to that of other employees (so-called relative rating systems) or by evaluating each employee in terms of performance standards without reference to others (so-called absolute rating systems). Other rating formats place primary emphasis on what an employee produces (so-called results-oriented systems); dollar volume of sales, number of units produced, and number of interceptions during a football season are examples. Management by objectives (MBO) and work planning and review use this results-oriented approach.

Evidence indicates that ratings (that is, judgments about performance) are not strongly related to results.[24] Why? Ratings depend heavily on the mental processes of the rater. Because these processes are complex, there may be errors of judgment in the ratings. Conversely, results depend heavily on conditions that may be outside the control of the individual worker, such as the availability of supplies or the contributions of others. Thus most measures of results provide only partial coverage of the overall domain of job performance. With these considerations in mind, let's examine the behavior- and results-oriented systems more fully.

Behavior-Oriented Rating Methods

Narrative Essay

The simplest type of absolute rating system is the narrative essay, in which a rater describes, in writing, an employee's strengths, weaknesses, and potential, together with suggestions for improvement. This approach assumes that a candid statement from a rater who is knowledgeable about an employee's performance is just as valid as more formal and more complicated rating methods. The case of the MTA bus drivers, presented earlier, illustrated this approach.

If essays are done well, they can provide detailed feedback to subordinates regarding their performance. On the other hand, comparisons across individuals, groups, or departments are almost impossible since different essays touch on different aspects of each subordinate's performance. This makes it difficult to use essay information for employment decisions since subordinates are not compared objectively and are not ranked relative to one another. Methods that compare employees with one another are more useful for this purpose.

Ranking

Simple ranking requires only that a rater order all employees from highest to lowest, from "best" employee to "worst" employee. *Alternation ranking* requires that a rater initially list all employees on a sheet of paper. From this list he or she first chooses the best employee (No. 1), then the worst employee (No. n), then the second best (No. 2), then the second worst (No. $n - 1$), and so forth, alternating from the top to the bottom of the list until all employees have been ranked.

Paired Comparisons

This is a more systematic method for comparing employees with one another. Here each employee is compared with every other employee, usually in terms of an overall category such as "present value to the organization." The rater's task is simply to choose the "better" of each pair, and each employee's rank is determined by counting the number of times she or he was rated superior. However, since these comparisons are made on an overall basis (that is, "Who is better?") and not in terms of specific job behaviors or outcomes, they may be subject to legal challenge.[25] On the other hand, methods that compare employees with one another are useful for generating initial rankings for purposes of salary administration.

Forced Distribution

This is another method of comparing employees with one another. As the name "forced distribution" implies, the overall distribution of ratings is forced into a normal, or bell-shaped, curve under the assumption that a relatively small

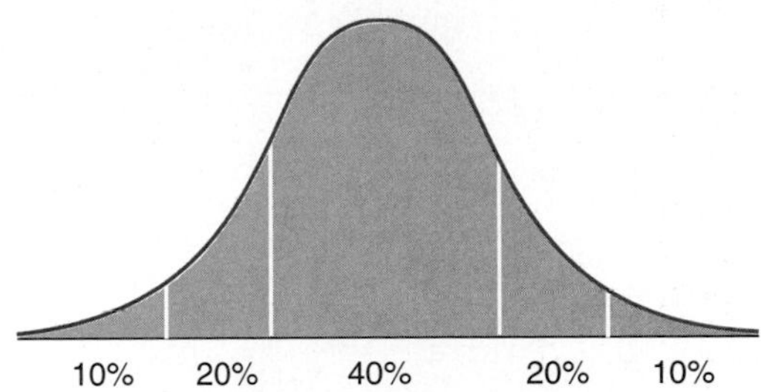

Figure 8-4
Example of a forced distribution. Forty percent of the rates must be rated "average," 20 percent "above average," 20 percent "below average," 10 percent "outstanding," and 10 percent "unsatisfactory."

portion of employees is truly outstanding, a relatively small portion is unsatisfactory, and everybody else falls in between. Figure 8-4 illustrates this method, assuming that five rating categories are used.

Forced distribution does eliminate clustering almost all employees at the top of the distribution (rater *leniency*), at the bottom of the distribution (rater *severity*), or in the middle (*central tendency*). However, it can foster a great deal of employee resentment if an entire group of employees *as a group* is either superior or substandard. It is most useful when a large number of employees must be rated and there is more than one rater.

Behavioral Checklist

Here the rater is provided with a series of statements that describe job-related behavior. His or her task is simply to "check" which of the statements, or the extent to which each statement, describes the employee. In this approach raters are not so much evaluators as reporters or describers of job behavior. And descriptive ratings are likely to be more reliable than evaluative (good-bad) ratings.[26] In one such method, the Likert method of *summed ratings*, a declarative statement (e.g., "She or he follows up on customer complaints") is followed by several response categories, such as "always," "very often," "fairly often," "occasionally," and "never." The rater checks the response category that he or she thinks best describes the employee. Each category is weighted, for example, from 5 ("always") to 1 ("never") if the statement describes desirable behavior. An overall numerical rating (or score) for each employee is then derived by *summing* the weights of the responses that were checked for each item. Figure 8-5 shows a portion of a summed rating scale for appraising teacher performance.

Critical Incidents

These are brief anecdotal reports by supervisors of things employees do that are particularly effective or ineffective in accomplishing parts of their jobs. They focus on behaviors, not traits. For example, a store manager in a retail computer store observed Mr. Wang, a salesperson, do the following:

> Mr. Wang encouraged the customer to try our new word processing package by having the customer sit down at the computer and write a letter. The finished product was full of typographical and spelling errors, each of which was highlighted for the customer when Mr. Wang applied a "spelling checker" to the written material. As a result, Mr. Wang sold the customer the word processing program plus a typing tutor and a spelling checker program.

Such anecdotes force attention on the ways in which situations determine job behavior and also on ways of doing the job successfully that may be unique to the

	Strongly Agree	Agree	Neutral	Disagree	Strongly Disagree
The teacher was well prepared.					
The teacher used understandable language.					
The teacher made me think.					
The teacher's feedback on students' work aided learning.					
The teacher knew his or her field well.					

Figure 8-5
A portion of a summed rating scale. The rater simply checks the response category that best describes the teacher's behavior. Response categories vary in scale value from 5 points (Strongly Agree) to 1 point (Strongly Disagree). A total score is computed by summing the points associated with each item.

person described. Hence they can provide the basis for training programs. Critical incidents also lend themselves nicely to appraisal interviews because supervisors can focus on actual job behaviors rather than on vaguely defined traits. They are judging performance, not personality. On the other hand, supervisors may find that recording incidents for their subordinates on a daily or even a weekly basis is burdensome. Moreover, incidents alone do not permit comparisons across individuals or departments. Graphic rating scales may overcome this problem.

Graphic Rating Scales

Many organizations use graphic rating scales.[27] Figure 8-6 shows a portion of one such scale. Many different forms of graphic rating scales exist. In terms of the amount of structure provided, the scales differ in three ways:

1. The degree to which the meaning of the response categories is defined (in Figure 8-6, what does "conditional" mean?)
2. The degree to which the individual who is interpreting the ratings (e.g., a higher-level reviewing official) can tell clearly what response was intended
3. The degree to which the performance dimensions are defined for the rater (in Figure 8-6, for example, what does "dependability" mean?)

Graphic rating scales may not yield the depth of essays or critical incidents, but they are less time-consuming to develop and administer, they allow results to be expressed in quantitative terms, they consider more than one performance

Figure 8-6
A portion of a graphic rating scale.

	Level of Performance				
Rating Factors	Unsatisfactory	Conditional	Satisfactory	Above Satisfactory	Outstanding
Attendance					
Appearance					
Dependability					
Quality of work					
Quantity of work					
Relationship with people					
Job knowledge					

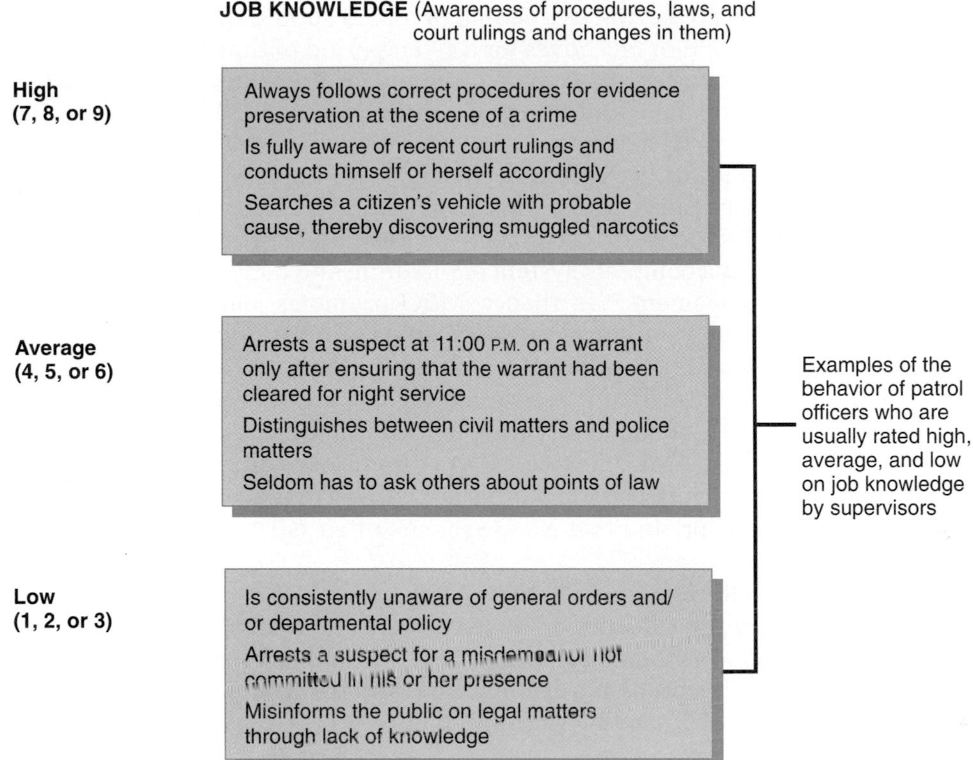

Figure 8-7
A behaviorally anchored rating scale to assess the job knowledge of police patrol officers.

dimension, and, since the scales are standardized, they facilitate comparisons across employees. Graphic rating scales have come under frequent attack, but when compared with more sophisticated forced-choice scales, the graphic scales have proved just as reliable and valid and are more acceptable to raters.[28]

Behaviorally Anchored Rating Scales (BARSs)

These are a variation of the simple graphic rating scale. Their major advantage is that they define the dimensions to be rated in behavioral terms and use critical incidents to describe various levels of performance. BARSs therefore provide a common frame of reference for raters. An example of the job knowledge portion of a BARS for police patrol officers is shown in Figure 8-7. BARSs require considerable effort to develop,[29] yet there is little research evidence to support the superiority of BARSs over other types of rating systems.[30] Nevertheless, the participative process required to develop them provides information that is useful for other organizational purposes, such as communicating clearly to employees exactly what "good performance" means in the context of their jobs.

Results-Oriented Rating Methods

Management by Objectives (MBO)

This is a well-known process of managing that relies on goal setting to establish objectives for the organization as a whole, for each department, for each manager within each department, and for each employee. MBO is not a measure of employee behavior; rather, it is a measure of each employee's contribution to the success of the organization.[31]

To establish objectives, the key people involved should do three things: (1) meet to *agree on the major objectives* for a given period of time (e.g., every year, every 6 months, or quarterly), (2) *develop plans* for how and when the objectives will be accomplished, and (3) *agree on the "yardsticks"* for determining whether the objectives have been met. Progress reviews are held regularly until the end of the period for which the objectives were established. At that time, those who established objectives at each level in the organization meet to evaluate the results and to agree on the objectives for the next period.[32]

To some, MBO is a complete system of planning and control and a complete philosophy of management.[33] In theory, MBO promotes success in each employee because, as each employee succeeds, so do that employee's manager, the department, and the organization. But this is true only to the extent that the individual, departmental, and organizational goals are compatible.[34] Very few applications of MBO have actually adopted a formal "cascading process" to ensure such a linkage. An effective MBO system takes from 3 to 5 years to implement, and since relatively few firms are willing to make that kind of commitment, it is not surprising that MBO systems often fail.[35]

Work Planning and Review

This approach is similar to MBO; however, it places greater emphasis on the periodic review of work plans by both supervisor and subordinate in order to identify goals attained, problems encountered, and the need for training.[36] This approach has long been used by Corning, Inc.

Table 8-1 presents a summary of the appraisal methods we have just discussed.

When Should Each Technique Be Used?

You have just read about a number of alternative appraisal formats, each with its own advantages and disadvantages. At this point you are probably asking yourself, "What's the bottom line? I know that no method is perfect, but what should I do?" First, remember that the rating format is not as important as the relevance and acceptability of the rating system. Second, consider the advice noted below, which is based on systematic comparisons of the various methods.

An extensive review of the research literature that relates the various rating methods to indicators of performance appraisal effectiveness found no clear "winner."[37] However, the researchers were able to provide several "if . . . then" propositions and general statements based on their study. Among these are the following:

- If the objective is to compare employees across raters for important employment decisions (e.g., promotion, merit pay), do not use MBO and work planning and review. They are not based on a standardized rating scheme for all employees.
- If you use a BARS, also make diary keeping a part of the process. This will improve the accuracy of the ratings, and it also will help supervisors distinguish between effective and ineffective employees.
- If objective performance data are available, MBO is the best strategy to use. Work planning and review is not as effective as MBO under these circumstances.

Table 8-1

A SNAPSHOT OF THE ADVANTAGES AND DISADVANTAGES OF ALTERNATIVE APPRAISAL METHODS

Behavior-oriented methods

Narrative essay—Good for individual feedback and development but difficult to use for making comparisons across employees.

Ranking and paired comparisons—Good for making comparisons across employees but provides little basis for individual feedback and development.

Forced distribution—Forces raters to make distinctions among employees but may be unfair and inaccurate if a group of employees, as a group, is either very effective or very ineffective.

Behavioral checklist—Easy to use, provides a direct link between job analysis and performance appraisal, can be numerically scored, and facilitates comparisons across employees. However, the meaning of response categories may be interpreted differently by different raters.

Critical incidents—Focuses directly on job behaviors, emphasizes what employees did that was effective or ineffective, but can be very time-consuming to develop.

Graphic rating scales (including BARSs)—Easy to use, very helpful for providing feedback for individual development, and facilitates comparisons across employees. BARSs are very time-consuming to develop, but dimensions and scale points are defined clearly. Graphic rating scales often do not define dimensions or scale points clearly.

Results-oriented methods

Management by objectives—Focuses on results and on identifying each employee's contribution to the success of the unit or organization. However, MBO is generally short-term-oriented, provides few insights into employee behavior, and does not facilitate comparisons across employees.

Work planning and review—In contrast to MBO, emphasizes process over outcomes. Requires frequent supervisor–subordinate review of work plans. Is time-consuming to implement properly and does not facilitate comparisons across employees.

- In general, appraisal methods that are best in a broad, organizational sense—BARSs and MBO—are the most difficult to use and maintain. Recognize, however, that no rating method is foolproof.
- Methods that focus on describing, rather than evaluating, behavior (e.g., BARSs, summed rating scales) produce results that are the most interpretable across raters. They help remove the effects of individual differences in raters.[38]
- No rating method has been an unqualified success when used as a basis for merit pay or promotional decisions.
- When certain statistical corrections are made, the correlations between scores on alternative rating formats are very high. Hence all the formats measure essentially the same thing.

Which techniques are most popular? A survey of 324 organizations in southern California found that among larger organizations, 51 percent use rating scales of some sort, 23 percent use essays, 17 percent use MBO, and 9 percent use all other forms of appraisal systems, which include behavioral checklists, forced choice, and rankings.[39]

WHO SHOULD EVALUATE PERFORMANCE?

The most fundamental requirement for any rater is that he or she has an adequate opportunity to observe the ratee's job performance over a reasonable period of time (e.g., 6 months). This requirement suggests several possible raters.

The Immediate Supervisor. If appraisal is done at all, it will probably be done by this person. She or he is probably most familiar with the individual's performance and, in most jobs, has had the best opportunity to observe actual job performance. Furthermore, the immediate supervisor is probably best able to relate the individual's performance to what the department and organization are trying to accomplish. Since she or he also is responsible for reward (and punishment) decisions, and for managing the overall performance management process,[40] it is not surprising that feedback from supervisors is more highly related to performance than that from any other source.[41]

Peers. In some jobs, such as outside sales, and in some environments, such as self-managed work teams, the immediate supervisor may observe a subordinate's actual job performance only rarely (and indirectly, through written reports). Sometimes objective indicators, such as number of units sold, can provide useful performance-related information, but in other circumstances the judgment of peers is even better. Peers can provide a perspective on performance that is different from that of immediate supervisors. Thus a member of a cross-functional team may be in a better position to rate another team member than that team member's immediate supervisor. However, to reduce potential friendship bias while simultaneously increasing the feedback value of the information provided, those responsible for the implementation of the peer assessment system must specify exactly what the peers are to evaluate[42]—for example, "the quality of her help on technical problems."

Another approach is to require input from a number of colleagues. Thus, at Harley-Davidson, salaried workers have five colleagues critique their work.[43] Even when done well, however, peer assessments are probably best considered as only part of a performance appraisal system that includes input from all sources that have unique information or perspectives to offer concerning the job performance of an individual or a work group.

Subordinates. Appraisal by subordinates can be a useful input to the immediate supervisor's development.[44] Subordinates know firsthand the extent to which the supervisor *actually* delegates, how well he or she communicates, the type of leadership style he or she is most comfortable with, and the extent to which he or she plans and organizes. Should subordinate ratings be anonymous? Managers want to know who said what, but subordinates prefer to remain anonymous to avoid retribution. To address these concerns, collect and combine the ratings in such a manner that a manager's overall rating is not distorted by an extremely divergent opinion.[45] Like peer assessments, subordinate ratings provide only one piece of the appraisal puzzle.

Self-appraisal. There are several arguments to recommend wider use of self-appraisals. The opportunity to participate in the performance appraisal process, particularly if appraisal is combined with goal setting, improves the ratee's

Customers are often able to rate important aspects of the performance of employees in front-line customer contact positions.

motivation and reduces her or his defensiveness during the appraisal interview.[46] On the other hand, self-appraisals tend to be more lenient, less variable, more biased, and to show less agreement with the judgments of others.[47] Since U.S. employees tend to give themselves higher marks than their supervisors do (conflicting findings have been found with mainland Chinese and Taiwanese employees),[48] self-appraisals are probably more appropriate for counseling and development than for employment decisions.

Customers Served. In some situations the "consumers" of an individual's or organization's services can provide a unique perspective on job performance. Examples abound: subscribers to a cable television service, bank customers, clients of a brokerage house, and citizens of a local police or fire-protection district. Although the customers' objectives cannot be expected to correspond completely with the organization's objectives, the information that customers provide can serve as useful input for employment decisions, such as those regarding promotion, transfer, and need for training. It can also be used to assess the impact of training or as a basis for self-development. At General Electric, for example, the customers of senior managers are interviewed formally and regularly as part of the managers' appraisal process. Their evaluations are important in appraisal, but at the same time they also build commitment, because customers are giving time and information to help GE.[49]

Computers. As noted earlier, employees spend a lot of time unsupervised by their bosses. Now technology has made continuous supervision possible—and very real for millions of workers. What sort of technology? Computer software that monitors employee performance.

COMPANY EXAMPLE

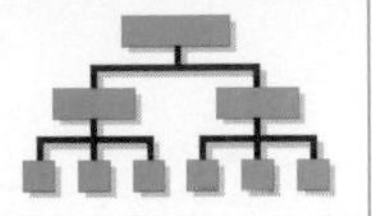

USING COMPUTERS TO MONITOR JOB PERFORMANCE

To proponents, it is a great new application of technology to improve productivity. To critics, it represents the ultimate intrusion of Big Brother in the workplace. For several million workers today, being monitored on the job by a computer is a fact of life.[50]

Computers measure quantifiable tasks performed by secretaries, factory and postal workers, grocery clerks, and airline reservation sales agents. For example, major airlines regularly monitor the time reservation sales agents spend on each call. Until now, lower-level jobs have been affected most directly by computer monitoring. But as software becomes more sophisticated, even engineers, accountants, and doctors are expected to face electronic scrutiny.

Critics feel that overzealous employers will get carried away with information gathering and overstep the boundary between work performance and privacy. Moreover, being watched every second can be stressful, thereby stifling worker creativity, initiative, and morale.

Not everyone views monitoring as a modern-day version of *Modern Times*, the Charlie Chaplin movie in which the hapless hero was tyrannized by automation. At the Third National Bank of Nashville, for example, encoding clerks can earn up to 25 percent more than their base pay if their output is high—and they like that system.

To be sure, monitoring itself is neither good nor bad; how managers use it determines its acceptance in the workplace. Practices such as giving employees access to data collected on them, establishing procedures for challenging erroneous records, and training supervisors to base actions and decisions on actual observation of employees, not just on computer-generated records, can alleviate the fears of employees.[51] At American Express, for example, monitored employees are given feedback about their performance every 2 weeks.

Managers who impose monitoring standards without asking employees what is reasonable may be surprised at the responses of employees. Tactics can include VDT operators' pounding the space bar or holding down the underlining bar while chatting, and telephone operators' hanging up on customers with complicated problems. The lesson, perhaps, is that even the most sophisticated technology can be thwarted by human beings who feel they are being pushed beyond acceptable limits.[52]

Multi-Rater or 360-Degree Feedback

Many organizations, including Alcoa, Lockheed-Martin, DuPont, and Wells Fargo Bank now use input from managers, subordinates, peers, and customers to provide a perspective on performance from all angles (360 degrees).[53] While multi-rater feedback can be helpful, it is not without problems. Here are some key reasons why such programs often fail:[54]

1. **Ambiguous objectives.** What do you want this process to accomplish? What do you want participants and the organization to get out of it? Do not do it just because everyone else is.

2. **Only "problem" employees get 360-degree feedback.** To leverage the full impact of this process, provide it to all key people.
3. **Changing the ground rules after the process has begun.** Changing who gets the results or how the data will be used after the fact undermines the whole process.
4. **Inadequate attention to identifying what each rater should rate.** Make ratings job-specific to ensure that they are relevant. In addition, be sure to include the opportunity for raters to assess characteristics that they are uniquely positioned to rate; e.g., subordinates should rate the extent to which the manager shares information with them.
5. **Failing to develop an action plan following feedback.** Each participant should build an action plan, perhaps with the help of a supervisor or an HR specialist.
6. **Lack of follow-through.** Expectations set by the organization, and its support in prodding and aiding each participant's efforts to improve, will make the difference between an assessment event and a successful, ongoing development process.

To overcome these potential problems, use a *tailored*, multisource feedback process, which includes three steps:[55]

- Employee and manager identify key customers (internal or external) for each of the employee's goals and commitments.
- Contract with each customer regarding his or her expectations. The objective is to pay attention to the same things that the customer thinks are important.
- Meet regularly with each customer to assess progress, to plan for future performance, and to receive feedback during the performance period.

Careful attention to these three action steps is an integral component of performance management. Another important consideration is the timing and frequency of performance appraisal.

WHEN AND HOW OFTEN SHOULD APPRAISAL BE DONE?

Traditionally, formal appraisal is done once, or at best twice, a year. Research, however, has indicated that once or twice a year is far too infrequent.[56] Unless he or she keeps a diary, considerable difficulties face a rater who is asked to remember what several employees did over the previous 6 or 12 months. This is why firms such as Western Digital, Southern California Gas, and Fluor add frequent, informal "progress" reviews between the annual ones.[57]

Research indicates that if a rater is asked to assess an employee's performance over a 6- to 12-month period, biased ratings may result, especially if information has been stored in the rater's memory according to irrelevant, oversimplistic, or otherwise faulty categories.[58] Unfortunately, faulty categorization seems to be the rule more often than the exception.

For example, consider the impact of prior expectations on ratings.[59] Supervisors of tellers at a large West Coast bank provided predictions about the future job performance of their new tellers. Six months later they rated the job performance of each teller. The result? Inconsistencies between prior expectations and later performance clearly affected the judgments of the raters. Thus when a teller's actual performance disappointed or exceeded a supervisor's prior expectations about that performance, ratings were lower than warranted by actual performance. The lesson to be learned is that it is unwise to assume that raters are faulty, but motivationally neutral, observers of on-the-job behavior.

More and more companies are realizing that once-a-year reviews do not work very well. Many now require managers to review employees formally at least twice a year, and talk with them informally even more often about how they are doing. At Sibson & Company, a management consulting concern, employees get formal reviews every 6 months or at the end of each project.[60] Such an approach has merit because the appraisals are likely to provide more accurate inputs to employment decisions, and they have the additional advantage of sending clear messages to employees about where they stand. There should be no "surprises" in appraisals, and one way to ensure this is to do them frequently. A study of 437 companies by Hewitt Associates may provide some incentive to do so. Companies with year-round performance management systems (as opposed to once-a-year performance appraisal systems or no systems) outperformed competitors without such systems on every financial and productivity measure used in the study, including profits, cash flow, and stock market performance.[61]

PERFORMANCE APPRAISAL AND TOTAL QUALITY MANAGEMENT (TQM)

TQM emphasizes the continuous improvement of products and processes to ensure long-term customer satisfaction. Its group problem-solving focus encourages employee empowerment by using the job-related expertise and ingenuity of the workforce. Cross-functional teams develop solutions to complex problems, often shortening the time taken to design, develop, or produce products and services. Since a team may not include a representative of management, the dividing line between labor and management often becomes blurred in practice, as workers themselves begin to solve organizational problems. Thus adoption of TQM generally requires cultural change within the organization as management reexamines its past methods and practices in light of the demands of the new philosophy.[62]

If the "father of TQM," W. Edwards Deming, had his way, appraisal systems that tie individual performance to salary adjustments would be eliminated. In his view, such systems hinder teamwork, create fear and mistrust, and discourage risk-taking behavior, thereby stifling innovation. Worse yet, Deming argues, most appraisal systems are based on the faulty assumption that individuals have significant control over their own performance—that is, that most individuals can improve if they choose to do so by putting forth the necessary effort.[63]

Here is the basis for his argument. Everything done in an organization is done within the framework of one or more systems (e.g., accounting, purchasing, production, sales). The systems provide limits on the activities of machines, processes, employees, and even managers. In a well-designed system, it will be nearly impossible to do a job improperly. Conversely, a poor system can thwart the best efforts of the best employee. If the system itself prevents good work (e.g., outdated technology that makes it impossible to meet current quality standards), performance appraisal cannot serve its intended purpose of differentiating among individuals for purposes of salary adjustments. Further, since employees (and most lower-level managers as well) have little opportunity to change those systems, they may become frustrated and demoralized.

What is the bottom line in all of this? As a basis for implementing a "pay-for-performance" philosophy, performance appraisal is a meaningful tool only if workers have significant control over the variables that affect their individual performance.[64] If not, then it is true, as Deming argues, that appraisals measure only random statistical variation within a particular system.

How Performance Appraisals Can Incorporate Key Elements of TQM

Organizations need not sacrifice their performance appraisal programs on the altar of total quality management. Here are three suggestions for harmonizing these two processes:[65]

1. **Let customer expectations generate individual or team performance expectations.** Start by identifying customer expectations by product or service. Customers may be internal or external. Then individuals or teams can begin to assess their performance against those expectations. Using this baseline of achievement, individuals, teams, and managers can develop continuous improvement targets. Comparing actual performance against expected performance helps avoid detrimental intrateam competition, because individuals or teams are compared against their own benchmarks, rather than against the accomplishments of others.
2. **Include results-expectations that identify actions to meet or exceed those expectations.** Employee (or team) and supervisor together consider these customer expectations in conjunction with the business plan and begin to establish priorities for improvement opportunities.
3. **Include behavioral skills that make a real difference in achieving quality performance and total customer satisfaction.** For example, effective customer service requires "attention to detail," "initiative," and "listening skills." These continuous-improvement skills are as important to total quality as are results-oriented targets.

When performance expectations focus on process improvements as well as on the behavioral skills needed to provide a product or service, total quality, excellent customer service, and appraisal of individual or team performance become "the way we do business."

APPRAISAL ERRORS AND RATER-TRAINING STRATEGIES

The use of ratings assumes that the human observer is reasonably objective and accurate. As we have seen, however, raters' memories are quite fallible, and raters subscribe to their own sets of likes, dislikes, and expectations about people, expectations that may or may not be valid.[66] These biases produce rating

INTERNATIONAL APPLICATION
The Impact of National Culture on Performance Appraisals

Western expatriate managers are often surprised to learn that their management practices have unintended consequences when applied in non-Western cultures. Consider the results of a study of Taiwanese and U.S. business students that examined preferences for various performance appraisal practices.[67]

Compared with American students, Taiwanese students indicated the following:

- Less support for performance appraisal as practiced in Western cultures
- More focus on group rather than individual performance
- Greater willingness to consider nonperformance factors (e.g., off-the-job behaviors, age) as criteria in appraisal
- Less willingness to attribute performance levels to the skills and efforts of particular individuals
- Less open and direct relations between supervisor and subordinate
- An expectation of closer supervisory styles

These results suggest that U.S. managers will need to modify the performance appraisal process that is familiar to them when working with Taiwanese subordinates in order to make it more consistent with Taiwanese values and culture. Such a process recognizes the importance of groups as well as individuals in the organization and honors the criteria of cooperation, loyalty, and attitudes toward superiors, as well as individual goal accomplishment.

errors, or deviations between the "true" rating an employee deserves and the actual rating assigned.[68] We discussed some of the most common types of rating errors previously: leniency, severity, and central tendency. Three other types are halo, contrast, and recency errors.

1. **Halo error** is not as prevalent as is commonly believed.[69] Raters who commit this error assign their ratings on the basis of global (good or bad) impressions of ratees. An employee is rated either high or low on many aspects of job performance because the rater knows (or thinks she or he knows) that the employee is high or low on some specific aspect. In practice, halo is probably due to situational factors or to the interaction of a rater and a situation (e.g., a supervisor who has limited opportunity to observe her subordinates because they are in the field dealing with customers).[70] Thus halo is probably a better indicator of how raters process cognitive information than it is as a measure of rating validity or accuracy.[71]
2. **Contrast error** results when a rater compares several employees with one another rather than with an objective standard of performance.[72] If, say, the first two workers are unsatisfactory while the third is average, the third worker may well be rated outstanding because in contrast to the first two, her or his "average" level of job performance is magnified. Likewise, "average" performance could be downgraded unfairly if the first few workers are outstanding. In both cases, the "average" worker receives a biased rating.
3. **Recency error** results when a rater assigns his or her ratings on the basis of the employee's most recent performance. It is most likely to occur when appraisals are done only after long periods. Here is how one manager described the dilemma of the recency error: "Many of us have trouble rating for the entire year. If one of my people has a stellar three months prior to the

IMPACT OF PERFORMANCE MANAGEMENT ON PRODUCTIVITY, QUALITY OF WORK LIFE, AND THE BOTTOM LINE

Performance management is fundamentally a feedback process. And research indicates that feedback may result in increases in performance varying from 10 to 30 percent.[78] That is a fairly inexpensive way to improve productivity; but, to work effectively, feedback programs require sustained commitment. The challenge for managers, then, is to provide feedback regularly to all their employees.

The cost of failure to provide such feedback may result in the loss of key professional employees, the continued poor performance of employees who are not meeting performance standards, and a loss of commitment by all employees. In sum, the myth that employees know how they are doing without adequate feedback from management can be an expensive fantasy.[79]

review . . . [I] don't want to do anything that impedes that person's momentum and progress."[73] Of course, if the subordinate's performance peaks 3 months prior to appraisal *every year*, that suggests a different problem!

Traditionally, rater training has focused on teaching raters to eliminate errors. Unfortunately, such programs usually have only short-term effects. Worse yet, training raters to reduce errors may actually reduce the accuracy of the ratings.[74] What can be done? First, rater training should emphasize how to observe behavior more accurately, not how to or how not to rate. Such an appraisal might proceed as follows:[75]

1. Show participants a videotape of an employee performing his or her job.
2. Ask participants to evaluate the employee on the videotape using rating scales that the trainer provides.
3. Place each participant's ratings on a flip chart.
4. The trainer leads a discussion among participants about the differences between ratings and reasons for them.
5. Ask the raters to reach a consensus regarding performance standards and relative levels of effective or ineffective behavior.
6. Show the videotape again.
7. Have the participants reassign ratings, this time on the basis of specific examples of behavior that each rater records.
8. Evaluate the ratings relative to the earlier consensus judgments of participants.
9. Provide specific feedback to each participant.

Second, encourage raters to become actively involved in the training process, because, in general, the more actively involved raters become, the better the outcome.[76] Third, encourage raters to discuss the performance dimensions on which they will be rating *before* they observe and evaluate the performance of others. Fourth, give them the opportunity to practice rating a sample of job performance. Finally, provide them with "true" (or expert) ratings with which they can compare their own ratings. Rater training is clearly worth the effort, and research indicates that the kind of approach advocated here is especially effective in improving the meaningfulness and usefulness of the performance appraisal process.[77]

Table 8-2

SUPERVISORY ACTIVITIES BEFORE, DURING, AND AFTER PERFORMANCE FEEDBACK INTERVIEWS

Before
Communicate frequently with subordinates about their performance.
Get training in performance appraisal interviewing.
Plan to use a problem-solving approach rather than "tell and sell."
Encourage subordinates to prepare for performance feedback interviews.
During
Encourage subordinates to participate.
Judge performance, not personality and mannerisms.
Be specific.
Be an active listener.
Avoid destructive criticism.
Set mutually agreeable goals for future improvements.
After
Communicate frequently with subordinates about their performance.
Periodically assess progress toward goals.
Make organizational rewards contingent on performance.

SECRETS OF EFFECTIVE PERFORMANCE FEEDBACK INTERVIEWS

The use of performance feedback, at least in terms of company policies on the subject, is widespread. Most companies require that appraisal results be discussed with employees.[80] As is well known, however, the existence of a policy is no guarantee that it will be implemented, or implemented effectively. Consider just two examples. First, we know that feedback is most effective when it is given immediately following the behavior in question.[81] How effective can feedback be if it is given only once a year during an appraisal interview?

Second, for more than two decades we have known that when managers use a problem-solving approach, subordinates express a stronger motivation to improve performance than when other approaches are used.[82] Yet evidence indicates that most organizations still use a "tell and sell" approach, in which a manager completes an appraisal independently, shows it to the subordinate, justifies the rating, discusses what must be done to improve performance, and then asks for the subordinate's reaction and sign-off on the appraisal.[83] Are the negative reactions of subordinates really that surprising?

If organizations really are serious about fostering improved job performance as a result of performance feedback interviews, the kinds of activities shown in Table 8-2 are essential before, during, and after the interview. Let's briefly examine each of these important activities.

Communicate Frequently. Research on the appraisal interview at General Electric indicated clearly that once-a-year performance appraisals are of questionable value and that coaching should be a day-to-day activity[84]—particularly with poor performers or new employees.[85] Feedback has maximum impact when it is given as close as possible to the action. If a subordinate behaves effectively (or ineffectively), tell him or her immediately. Do not file incidents away so that they can be discussed in 6 to 9 months.

Research strongly supports this view. Thus one study found that communication of performance feedback in an interview is most effective when the subordinate already has relatively accurate perceptions of her or his performance before the session.[86]

Get Training in Performance Feedback and Appraisal Interviewing. As we noted earlier, training allows raters to observe behavior more accurately and fairly. Rater training should focus on managerial characteristics that are difficult to rate and on characteristics that people think are easy to rate but which generally result in disagreements. Such factors include risk taking and development of subordinates.[87] Use a problem-solving, rather than a "tell and sell," approach, as noted earlier.

Encourage Subordinates to Prepare. Research conducted in hospitals, among clerical workers, and in sales organizations has indicated consistently that subordinates who spend more time prior to performance feedback interviews analyzing their job responsibilities and duties, problems they encounter on the job, and the quality of their performance are more likely to be satisfied with the performance management process, more likely to be motivated to improve their performance, and more likely actually to improve.[88]

Encourage Participation. A perception of ownership—a feeling by the subordinate that his or her ideas are genuinely welcomed by the manager—is related strongly to subordinates' satisfaction with the appraisal interview. Participation encourages the belief that the interview was a constructive activity, that some current job problems were cleared up, and that future goals were set.[89]

Judge Performance, Not Personality. In addition to the potential legal liability of dwelling on personality rather than on job performance, supervisors are far less likely to change a subordinate's personality than they are his or her job performance. Maintain the problem-solving, job-related focus established earlier, for evidence indicates that supervisory support enhances employees' motivation to improve.[90]

Be Specific, and Be an Active Listener. By being candid and specific, the supervisor offers clear feedback to the subordinate concerning past actions. She or he also demonstrates knowledge of the subordinate's level of performance and job duties. By being an active listener, the supervisor demonstrates genuine interest in the subordinate's ideas. Active listening requires that you do the following things well: (1) take the time to listen—hold all phone calls and do not allow interruptions; (2) communicate verbally and nonverbally (e.g., by maintaining eye contact) that you genuinely want to help; (3) as the subordinate begins to tell his or her side of the story, do not interrupt and do not argue; (4) watch for verbal as well as nonverbal cues regarding the subordinate's agreement or disagreement with your message; and (5) summarize what was said and what was agreed to. Specific feedback and active listening are essential to subordinates' perceptions of the fairness and accuracy of the process.[91]

Avoid Destructive Criticism. Destructive criticism is general in nature, frequently delivered in a biting, sarcastic tone, and often attributes poor performance to internal causes (e.g., lack of motivation or ability). It leads to three predictable consequences: (1) it produces negative feelings among recipients and can initiate or intensify conflict; (2) it reduces the preference of individuals for handling future disagreements with the giver of the feedback in a conciliatory manner (e.g., compromise, collaboration); and (3) it has negative effects on self-set goals and on feelings of self-confidence.[92] Needless to say, this is one type of communication to avoid.

Set Mutually Agreeable Goals. Earlier in the chapter, we noted that goals direct attention to the specific performance in question, that they mobilize effort to accomplish higher levels of performance, and that they foster persistence for higher levels of performance.[93] The practical implications are clear: set specific, challenging goals, for this clarifies for the subordinate precisely what is expected and leads to high levels of performance. We cannot change the past, but interviews that include goal setting and specific feedback can affect future job performance.

Continue to Communicate, and Assess Progress toward Goals Regularly. Periodic tracking of progress toward goals has three advantages: (1) it helps keep behavior on target, (2) it provides a better understanding of the reasons behind a given level of performance, and (3) it enhances the subordinate's commitment to perform effectively. In short, tracking helps improve supervisor-subordinate work relationships. Improving supervisor-subordinate work relationships, in turn, has positive effects on performance.[94]

Make Organizational Rewards Contingent on Performance. Research results are clear-cut on this point. If subordinates see a link between appraisal results and employment decisions regarding issues like merit pay and promotion, they are more likely to prepare for performance feedback interviews, to participate actively in them, and to be satisfied with the overall performance management system.[95] Furthermore, managers who base employment decisions on the results of appraisals are likely to overcome their subordinates' negative perceptions of the appraisal process.

Human Resource Management in Action: Conclusion

THE EXECUTIVE APPRAISAL PARADOX

Debunking the Myths

It is not possible to design a perfect or ideal performance appraisal program. However, for any such program to be of benefit to all parties in the process, some important items must be in place. These include clearly specified goals and standards, ongoing performance feedback, and an interactive feedback session between superior and subordinate.

Organizations with effective executive appraisals almost invariably cite the involvement of top management as the dominant factor in the success of the process. Senior executives need to articulate and enact the practices discussed below because they are the key players in institutionalizing sound appraisal processes as part of the organization's culture.

1. **Construct a formal, systematic executive appraisal process.** It should be formal so that the process is taken seriously by all parties; it should be systematic so that it provides the executive with useful feedback and guidance.
2. **Incorporate performance planning,** which is essential at the executive level, into the executive review and appraisal process. Essentially, this is strategic planning for individual executives. Such planning should include the following elements: (1) a flexibly framed description of the executive's mission, along with primary and secondary responsibilities; (2) clarification of division/departmental goals and the executive's role in accomplishing them; (3) discussion of management style issues as well as strategies for accomplishing goals; and (4) agreement about what constitutes "successful" performance, given current strategic and operational goals.
3. **Make performance review and appraisal an ongoing process.** As a means to facilitate this process, senior executives suggest the following four steps: (1) make notes on critical instances of effective and ineffective performance, based on personal observations; (2) obtain regular financial and productivity indicators; (3) check the executive's performance with clients, customers, and other departments to assess external relations and teamwork abilities; and (4) use subordinates' appraisals of executives to provide a different perspective on executive performance.
4. **Focus on process as well as outcomes during the executive review.** Process issues are more difficult to address than bottom-line issues, but they are hallmarks of good executive mentors. Striking a balance between means and ends, processes and outcomes, is a wise strategy.
5. **Be as specific and thorough as possible.** Consider doing the following: (1) to supplement the senior executive's judgments, have subordinate executives provide written self-appraisals that focus on achievements, areas needing improvement, and plans for development; (2) as the basis for the formal review, use the responsibilities, goals, and processes that were agreed upon previously; (3) avoid nebulous language when giving performance feedback; (4) strengthen the link between performance and reward by citing specific reasons for any merit raises, bonuses, or perks; and (5) allow time for the subordinate executive to air concerns and to discuss his or her personal development. After all, the review is a forum for developing a blueprint for the coming year.

Executive appraisal can help decrease job-role ambiguity. It can also be the key vehicle for communicating the firm's culture, values, and operating philosophy. It gives executives a feel for the firm's bigger picture, how they fit into that picture, and what they have to do to reach their goals. Treating the appraisal of executives as a positive action should be a high priority.

IMPLICATIONS FOR MANAGEMENT PRACTICE

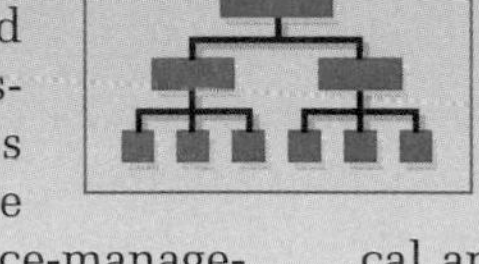

Throughout this chapter we have emphasized the difficulty of implementing and sustaining performance management systems. A basic issue for every manager is "What's in it for me?" If organizations are serious about improving the performance-management process, top management must consider the following policy changes:

- Make "quality of performance feedback to subordinates" and "development of subordinates" integral parts of every manager's job description.
- Tie rewards to effective performance in these areas.
- Recognize that performance management and appraisal constitute a dialogue involving people and data; both political and interpersonal issues are involved. No appraisal method is perfect, but with management commitment and employee "buy-in," performance management can be a very useful and powerful tool.

SUMMARY

Performance management requires a willingness and a commitment to focus on improving performance at the level of the individual or team *every day*. Like a compass, an ongoing performance management system provides instantaneous, real-time information that describes the difference between one's current and desired courses. To practice sound performance management, managers must do the same thing—provide timely feedback about performance, while constantly focusing everyone's attention on the ultimate objective (e.g., world-class customer service).

At a general level, the broad process of performance management requires that managers do three things well: define performance (through goals, measures, and assessments), facilitate performance (by identifying obstacles to good performance and providing resources to accomplish objectives), and encourage performance (by providing a sufficient number of rewards that people care about and doing so in a timely and fair manner).

Performance appraisal (the systematic description of the job-relevant strengths and weaknesses of an individual or a team) is a necessary, but not sufficient, part of the performance management process. It serves two major purposes in organizations: (1) to improve the job performance of employees, and (2) to provide information to employees and managers for use in making decisions. In practice, many performance appraisal systems fail because they do not satisfy one or more of the following requirements: relevance, sensitivity, reliability, acceptability, and practicality. The failure is frequently accompanied by legal challenges to the system based on the system's adverse impact on one or more protected groups.

Performance appraisal is done once or twice a year in most organizations, but research indicates that this is far too infrequent. Do it upon the completion of projects or upon the achievement of important milestones. The rating method used depends on the purpose for which the appraisal is intended. Thus comparisons among employees are most appropriate for generating rankings for salary administration purposes, while MBO, work planning and review, and narrative essays are least appropriate for this purpose. For purposes of employee development, critical incidents or behaviorally anchored rating scales are most appropriate. Finally, rating methods that focus on describing rather than evaluating behavior (e.g., BARSs, behavioral checklists) are the most interpretable across raters.

Rater judgments are subject to various types of biases: leniency, severity, and central tendency, as well as halo, contrast, and recency errors. To improve the reliability and validity of ratings, however, train raters to observe behavior more accurately rather than showing them how to or how not to rate. To improve the value of performance feedback interviews, communicate frequently with subordinates; encourage them to prepare and to participate in the process; judge performance, not personality; be specific; avoid destructive criticism; set goals; assess progress toward goals regularly; and make rewards contingent on performance.

DISCUSSION QUESTIONS

8-1 What would an effective performance management system look like?

8-2 Working in small groups, develop a performance management system for a cashier in a neighborhood grocery with little technology but lots of personal attention given to customers.

8-3 The chief counsel for a large corporation comes to you for advice. She wants to know what makes a firm's appraisal system legally vulnerable. What would you tell her?

8-4 How can we overcome employee defensiveness in performance feedback interviews?

8-5 Can discussions of employee job performance be separated from salary considerations? If so, how?

APPLYING YOUR KNOWLEDGE

Problems in Appraisal at Peak Power — *Case 8-1*

Peak Power, a medium-size hydroelectric power plant near Seattle, Washington, has been having difficulty with its performance appraisal system. The plant's present appraisal system has been in existence for about 10 years and was designed by the head of performance appraisal operations, a clerk who had been promoted into the position without any professional training in human resource management. Presently, all operating personnel are evaluated once a year by their supervisors, using the following form:

PEAK POWER PERFORMANCE APPRAISAL FORM

General Instructions: This form is to be completed in triplicate, and all entries should be typewritten or printed in ink. After the employee's performance has been evaluated by the supervisor and reviewed by higher-level supervision, the employee will be informed of his or her performance rating and will sign all copies of the form indicating that he or she has been so informed. The employee's signature does not necessarily indicate that he or she agrees with the ratings given. Send one completed form to the human resources office, and allow the employee to keep a copy for his or her files. The other copy is the supervisor's.

Complete the form by marking an "X" in the appropriate locations below.

Performance dimension	Excellent	Above average	Average	Below average	Poor
Quantity of work					
Quality of work					
Dependability					
Initiative					
Cooperativeness					
Leadership potential					

"Excellent" is worth 5 points, "Above average" is worth 4 points, "Average" is worth 3 points, "Below average" is worth 2 points, and "Poor" is worth 1 point. Determine the employee's overall evaluation by summing the appropriate number of points from each of the six dimension scores above, and place the total here ______.

Supervisor's signature ______________________

Employee's signature ______________________

Ratings from each year are maintained in employee files in the HR department. If promotions come up, the cumulative ratings are considered at that time. Further, ratings are supposed to be used as a check when raises are given. In practice, little use is made of the ratings, either for determination of promotions or for salary decisions. Employee feelings about the appraisal system range from indifference to outright hostility. A small, informal survey 2 years ago determined that supervisors spent on average about 3 minutes filling out the form, and less than 10 minutes discussing it with employees.

Recent problems in other areas of HR management at the plant and the fear of potential lawsuits led Peak's president to consider hiring an experienced HR professional to upgrade all HR systems. You are being interviewed for the job, and have just been presented with the above information.

Questions

1. The president asks you for your general evaluation of this appraisal system. What is your response?
2. The president asks you for some suggestions for ways in which the present system can be improved. How do you respond?
3. If you should be selected for this position, outline some steps you would take to ensure that a new performance management system would be accepted by its users.

REFERENCES

1. Cascio, W. F. (1996, Sept.). Managing for maximum performance. *HRMonthly* (Australia), pp. 10–13.
2. Matsui, T., Kakuyama, T., & Onglatco, M. L. T. (1987). Effects of goals and feedback on performance in groups. *Journal of Applied Psychology*, **72**, 407–415.
3. Tubbs, M. E. (1986). Goal setting: A meta-analytic examination of the empirical evidence. *Journal of Applied Psychology*, **71**, 474–483.
4. Wood, R. E., Mento, A. J., & Locke, E. A. (1987). Task complexity as a moderator of goal effects: A meta-analysis. *Journal of Applied Psychology*, **72**, 416–425.
5. Kerr, S., in Sherman, S. (1995, Nov. 13). Stretch goals: The dark side of asking for miracles. *Fortune*, p. 31.
6. Deutschman, A. (1994, Oct. 17). The managing wisdom of high-tech superstars. *Fortune*, pp. 197–205.
7. Schellhardt, T. D. (1996, Nov. 19). Annual agony: It's time to evaluate your work, and all involved are groaning. *The Wall Street Journal*, pp. A1, A5.
8. Cascio, W. F. (1998). Applied psychology in human resource management (5th ed.). Upper Saddle River, NJ: Prentice-Hall.
9. Jacobs, R., Kafry, D., & Zedeck, S. (1980). Expectations of behaviorally anchored rating scales. *Personnel Psychology*, **33**, 595–640.
10. Schellhardt, loc. cit. See also Cleveland, J. N., Murphy, K. R., & Williams, R. E. (1989). Multiple uses of performance appraisal: Prevalence and correlates. *Journal of Applied Psychology*, **74**, 130–135.
11. Cascio, W. F. (1982). Scientific, legal, and operational imperatives of workable performance appraisal systems. *Public Personnel Management*, **11**, 367–375.
12. Zedeck, S., & Cascio, W. F. (1982). Performance appraisal decisions as a function of rater training and purpose of the appraisal. *Journal of Applied Psychology*, **67**, 752–758.
13. Viswesvaran, C., Ones, D. S., & Schmidt, F. L. (1996). Comparative analysis of the reliability of job performance ratings. *Journal of Applied Psychology*, **81**, 557–574.
14. Borman, W. C. (1991). Job behavior, performance, and effectiveness. In M. D. Dunnette & L. M. Hough, (eds.), *Handbook of industrial and organizational psychology*, vol. 2. Palo Alto, CA: Consulting Psychologists Press, pp. 271–326.
15. Schellhardt, loc. cit.
16. Barrett, G. V., & Kernan, M. C. (1987). Performance appraisal and terminations: A review of court decisions since *Brito v. Zia* with implications for personnel practices. *Personnel Psychology*, **40**, 489–503. See also Cascio, W. F., & Bernardin, H. J. (1981). Implications of performance appraisal litigation for personnel decisions. *Personnel Psychology*, **34**, 211–226. See also Feild, H. S., & Holley, W. H. (1982). The relationship of performance appraisal system characteristics to verdicts in selected employment discrimination cases. *Academy of Management Journal*, **25**, 392–406.
17. *Paquin v. Federal National Mortgage Association*, (1996, July 31). Civil Action No. 94-1261 SSH.
18. *Stone v. Xerox* (1982). 685 F. 2d 1387 (11th Cir.).
19. *United States v. City of Chicago* (1978). 573 F. 2d 416 (7th Cir.).
20. LeBoeuf, M. (1987). *The greatest management principle in the world.* New York: Berkley Publishing Co.
21. Beatty, R. W. (1989). Competitive human resource advantage through the strategic management of performance. *Human Resource Planning*, **12**, 179–194.
22. Cascio, W. F., & Serapio, M. G., Jr. (1991, Winter). Human resource systems in an international alliance: The undoing of a done deal? *Organizational Dynamics*, pp. 63–74. See also Schneider, S. C. (1988). National versus corporate culture: Implications for human resource management. *Human Resource Management*, **27**, 231–246.

23. Guion, R. M. (1986). Personnel evaluation. In R. A. Berk (ed.), *Performance assessment.* Baltimore: Johns Hopkins University Press, pp. 345–360. See also Bernardin, H. J., & Beatty, R. W. (1984). Performance appraisal: Assessing human behavior at work. Boston: PWS-Kent.
24. Murphy, K. R., & Cleveland, J. N. (1991). *Performance appraisal: An organizational perspective.* Boston: Allyn & Bacon. See also Heneman, R. L. (1986). The relationship between supervisory ratings and results-oriented measures of performance: A meta-analysis. *Personnel Psychology,* **39**, 811–826.
25. Cascio & Bernardin, loc. cit.
26. Stockford, L., & Bissell, H. W. (1949). Factors involved in establishing a merit rating scale. *Personnel,* **26**, 94–116.
27. Landy, F. J., & Rastegary, H. (1988). Criteria for selection. In M. Smith & I. Robertson (eds.), *Advances in personnel selection and assessment.* New York: Wiley, pp. 68–115.
28. Cascio (1998), op. cit.
29. Bernardin, H. J., & Smith, P. C. (1981). A clarification of some issues regarding the development and use of behaviorally anchored rating scales. *Journal of Applied Psychology,* **66**, 458–463.
30. Borman, W. C. (1991). Job behavior, performance, and effectiveness. In M. D. Dunnette & L. M. Hough, (eds.), *Handbook of industrial and organizational psychology,* vol. 2. Palo Alto, CA: Consulting Psychologists Press, pp. 271–326.
31. Campbell, J. P., Dunnette, M. D., Lawler, E. E., & Weick, K. E. (1970). *Managerial behavior, performance, and effectiveness.* New York: McGraw-Hill.
32. McConkie, M. L. (1979). A clarification of the goal-setting and appraisal process in MBO. *Academy of Management Review,* **4**, 29–40.
33. Albrecht, K. (1978). *Successful management by objectives: An action manual.* Englewood Cliffs, NJ: Prentice-Hall. See also Odiorne, G. S. (1965). *Management by objectives: A system of managerial leadership.* Belmont, CA: Fearon.
34. Barton, R. F. (1981). An MCDM approach for resolving goal conflict in MBO. *Academy of Management Review,* **6**, 231–241.
35. Kondrasuk, J. N. (1981). Studies in MBO effectiveness. *Academy of Management Review,* **6**, 419–430.
36. Meyer, H. H., Kay, E., & French, J. R. P. (1965). Split roles in performance appraisal. *Harvard Business Review,* **43**, 123–129.
37. Bernardin & Beatty, op. cit.
38. Hartel, C. E. J. (1993). Rating format research revisited: Format effectiveness and acceptability depend on rater characteristics. *Journal of Applied Psychology,* **78**, 212–217.
39. Locher, A. H., & Teel, K. S. (1988, Sept.). Appraisal trends. *Personnel Journal,* pp. 139–145.
40. Ghorpade, J., & Chen, M. M. (1995). Creating quality-driven performance appraisal systems. *Academy of Management Executive,* **9**(1), 32–39.
41. Becker, T. E., & Klimoski, R. J. (1989). A field study of the relationship between the organizational feedback environment and performance. *Personnel Psychology,* **42**, 353–358.
42. McEvoy, G. M., & Buller, P. F. (1987). User acceptance of peer appraisals in an industrial setting. *Personnel Psychology,* **40**, 785–787.
43. Labor letter (1990, Oct. 16), *The Wall Street Journal,* p. A1.
44. Reilly, R. R., Smither, J. W., & Vasilopoulos, N. L. (1996). A longitudinal study of upward feedback. *Personnel Psychology,* **49**, 599–612. See also Smither, J. W., London, M., Vasilopoulos, N. L., Reilly, R. R., Millsap, R., & Salvemini, N. (1995). An examination of the effects of an upward feedback program over time. *Personnel Psychology,* **48**, 1–34.

45. Antonioni, D. (1994). The effects of feedback accountability on upward appraisal ratings. *Personnel Psychology*, **47**, 249–256.
46. Campbell, D. J., & Lee, C. (1988). Self-appraisal in performance evaluation: Development versus evaluation. *Academy of Management Review*, **13**, 302–314.
47. Fox, S., & Dinur, Y. (1988). Validity of self-assessment: A field evaluation. *Personnel Psychology*, **41**, 581–592. See also Harris, M., & Schaubroeck, J. (1988). A meta-analysis of self-supervisory, self-peer, and peer-supervisory ratings. *Personnel Psychology*, **41**, 43–62.
48. Yu, J., & Murphy, K. R. (1993). Modesty bias in self-ratings of performance: A test of the cultural relativity hypothesis. *Personnel Psychology*, **46**, 357–363. But see also Farh, J. L., Dobbins, G. H., & Cheng, B. S. (1991). Cultural relativity in action: A comparison of self-ratings made by Chinese and U.S. workers. *Personnel Psychology*, **44**, 129–147.
49. Ulrich, D. (1989, Summer). Tie the corporate knot: Gaining complete customer commitment. *Sloan Management Review*, **10**(4), 19–27, 63.
50. Piller, C. (1993, July). Privacy in peril. *Macworld*, pp. 124–130. See also Brophy, B. (1986, Sept. 29). New technology, high anxiety. *U.S. News & World Report*, pp. 54, 55.
51. Nebeker, D. M., & Tatum, C. B. (1993). The effects of computer monitoring, standards, and rewards on work performance and stress. *Journal of Applied Social Psychology*, **28**, 508–534. See also Chalykoff, J., & Kochan, T. A. (1989). Computer-aided monitoring: Its influence on employee job satisfaction and turnover. *Personnel Psychology*, **42**, 807–834.
52. Brophy, loc. cit.
53. Yammarino, F. J., & Atwater, L. E. (1997, Spring). Do managers see themselves as others see them? *Organization Dynamics*, **25**(4), 35–44. See also Hoffman, R. (1995, Apr.). Ten reasons you should be using 360-degree feedback. *HRMagazine*, pp. 82–85.
54. Cheney, A., & Bremley, M. (1996). *The pitfalls of 360-degree feedback*. St. Louis, MO: Psychological Associates.
55. Campbell, R. B., & Garfinkel, L. M. (1996, June). Strategies for success in measuring performance. *HRMagazine*, pp. 98–104.
56. Schellhardt, loc. cit. See also Meyer et al., loc. cit.
57. Labor letter, loc. cit.
58. Mount, M. K., & Thompson, D. E. (1987). Cognitive categorization and quality of performance ratings. *Journal of Applied Psychology*, **72**, 240–246.
59. Hogan, E. A. (1987). Effects of prior expectations on performance ratings: A longitudinal study. *Academy of Management Journal*, **30**, 354–368.
60. Schellhardt, loc. cit.
61. Campbell & Garfinkel, loc. cit.
62. Wiedman, T. G. (1993, October). Performance appraisal in a total quality management environment. *The Industrial-Organizational Psychologist*, **31**(2), 64–66.
63. Deming, W. E. (1986). *Out of the crisis*. Cambridge, MA: MIT Center for Advanced Engineering Study.
64. Wiedman, loc. cit.
65. Total quality and performance appraisal (1992, Oct.). *Bulletin*. Denver: Mountain States Employers Council, Inc., p. 5.
66. Varma, A., DeNisi, A., & Peters, L. M. (1996). Interpersonal affect and performance appraisal: A field study. *Personnel Psychology*, **49**, 341–360.
67. McEvoy, G. M., & Cascio, W. F. (1990). The United States and Taiwan: Two different cultures look at performance appraisal. *Research in Personnel and Human Resources Management* (Supplement 2), pp. 201–219.
68. Hogan, loc. cit.

69. Murphy, K. R., Jako, R. A., & Anhalt, R. L. (1993). Nature and consequences of halo error: A critical analysis. *Journal of Applied Psychology*, **78**, 218–225.
70. Murphy, K. R., & Anhalt, R. L. (1992). Is halo error a property of the rater, ratees, or the specific behavior observed? *Journal of Applied Psychology*, **77**, 494–500.
71. Balzer, W. K., & Sulsky, L. M. (1992). Halo and performance appraisal research: A critical examination. *Journal of Applied Psychology*, **77**, 975–985.
72. Sumer, H. C., & Knight, P. A. (1996). Assimilation and contrast effects in performance ratings: Effects of rating the previous performance on rating subsequent performance. *Journal of Applied Psychology*, **81**, 436–442. See also Maurer, T. J., Palmer, J. K., & Ashe, D. K. (1993). Diaries, checklists, evaluations, and contrast effects in the measurement of behavior. *Journal of Applied Psychology*, **78**, 226–231.
73. Longenecker, C. O., Sims, H. P., Jr., & Gioia, D. A. (1987). Behind the mask: The politics of employee appraisal. *Academy of Management Executive*, **1**, 183–193.
74. Murphy, K. R., & Balzer, W. K. (1989). Rater errors and rating accuracy. *Journal of Applied Psychology*, **74**, 619–624. See also Smith, D. E. (1986). Training programs for performance appraisal: A review. *Academy of Management Review*, **11**, 22–40.
75. Pulakos, E. D. (1986). The development of training programs to increase accuracy with different rating tasks. *Organizational Behavior and Human Decision Processes*, **38**, 76–91. See also Latham, G. P., Wexley, K. N., & Pursell, E. D. (1975). Training managers to minimize rating errors in the observation of behavior. *Journal of Applied Psychology*, **60**, 550–555.
76. Smith, loc. cit.
77. Sanchez, J. I., & DeLaTorre, P. (1996). A second look at the relationship between rating and behavioral accuracy in performance appraisal. *Journal of Applied Psychology*, **81**, 3–10. See also Day, D. V., & Sulsky, L. M. (1995). Effects of frame-of-reference training and information configuration on memory organization and rating accuracy. *Journal of Applied Psychology*, **80**, 158–167.
78. Landy, F. J., Farr, J. L., & Jacobs, R. R. (1982). Utility concepts in performance measurement. *Organizational Behavior and Human Performance*, **30**, 15–40.
79. Joinson, C. (1996, Aug.). Re-creating the indifferent employee. *HRMagazine*, pp. 77–80. See also Darling, M. J. (1994, Nov.). Coaching people through difficult times. *HRMagazine*, pp. 70–73.
80. Schellhardt, loc. cit.
81. Murphy & Cleveland, op. cit.
82. Wexley, K. N., Singh, V. P., & Yukl, G. A. (1973). Subordinate participation in three types of appraisal interviews. *Journal of Applied Psychology*, **58**, 54–57.
83. Schellhardt, loc. cit. See also Wexley, K. N. (1986). Appraisal interview. In R. A. Berk (ed.), *Performance assessment*. Baltimore: Johns Hopkins University Press, pp. 167–185.
84. Meyer et al., loc. cit.
85. Cederblom, D. (1982). The performance appraisal interview: A review, implications, and suggestions. *Academy of Management Review*, **7**, 219–227.
86. Ilgen, D. R., Mitchell, T. R., & Frederickson, J. W. (1981). Poor performers: Supervisors' and subordinates' responses. *Organizational Behavior and Human Performance*, **27**, 386–410.
87. Wohlers, A. J., & London, M. (1989). Ratings of managerial characteristics: Evaluation, difficulty, co-worker agreement, and self-awareness. *Personnel Psychology*, **42**, 235–261.
88. Meyer, H. H. (1991). A solution to the performance appraisal feedback enigma. *Academy of Management Executive*, **5**(1), 68–76. See also Burke, R. S., Weitzel, W., & Weir, T. (1978). Characteristics of effective employee performance review and development interviews: Replication and extension. *Personnel Psychology*, **31**, 903–919.

89. Nathan, B. R., Mohrman, A. M., Jr., & Milliman, J. (1991). Interpersonal relations as a context for the effects of appraisal interviews on performance and satisfaction: A longitudinal study. *Academy of Management Journal*, **34**(2), 352–369.
90. Dorfman, P. W., Stephan, W. G., & Loveland, J. (1986). Performance appraisal behaviors: Supervisor perceptions and subordinate reactions. *Personnel Psychology*, **39**, 579–597.
91. Landy, F. J., Barnes-Farrell, J., & Cleveland, J. N. (1980). Perceived fairness and accuracy of performance evaluation: A follow-up. *Journal of Applied Psychology*, **65**, 355–356.
92. Baron, R. A. (1988). Negative effects of destructive criticism: Impact on conflict, self-efficacy, and task performance. *Journal of Applied Psychology*, **73**, 199–207.
93. Locke, E. A., & Latham, G. P. (1990). *A theory of goal setting and task performance.* Upper Saddle River, NJ: Prentice-Hall. See also Tubbs, M. E. (1986). Goal setting: A meta-analytic examination of the empirical evidence. *Journal of Applied Psychology*, **71**, 474–483.
94. Judge, T. A., & Ferris, G. R. (1993). Social context of performance evaluation decisions. *Academy of Management Journal*, **36**, 80–105.
95. Burke et al., loc. cit.

9 MANAGING CAREERS

Questions This Chapter Will Help Managers Answer

1 What strategies might be used to help employees self-manage their careers?
2 What can supervisors do to improve their management of dual-career couples?
3 Why are the characteristics and environment of an employee's first job so important?
4 What steps can managers take to do a better job of responding to the special needs of workers in their early, middle, and late career stages?
5 How can layoffs be handled in the most humane way?

*SELF-RELIANCE: KEY TO CAREER MANAGEMENT FOR THE TWENTY-FIRST CENTURY**

Consider this stark fact: in today's corporate environment, you are ever more likely to crash into the ranks of the unemployed with no safety net, and it could happen over and over again. Moreover, candor about career issues is in short supply at many companies these days. Bottom line: career survival is up to you—not the company. Consider yourself to be self-employed, responsible for your own career development, CEO of You, Inc. This new approach is based on an underlying assumption that would have been considered heresy 10 or 20 years ago in the paternalistic, "We'll take care of you" environments of many companies—that self-reliance is the key to career management in the twenty-first century.

In the past, many companies assumed responsibility for the career paths and growth of their employees. The company determined to what position, and at what speed, people would advance. That approach worked reasonably well in the corporate climate of the last three decades. However, the corporate disruptions of the 1990s have rendered this approach to employee career development largely unworkable.

Acquisitions, divestitures, rapid growth, and downsizing have left many companies unable to deliver on the implicit career promises made to their employees. Organizations find themselves in the painful position of having to renege on career mobility opportunities their employees had come to expect. In extreme cases, employees who expected career growth no longer even have jobs.

Increasingly, corporations have come to realize that they cannot win if they take total responsibility for the career development of their employees. No matter what happens, employees often blame top management or "the company" for their lack of career growth.

One company changed its approach to career growth as a result of pressure from its professional workforce. Employees felt suffocated by 20-plus years of management's determining people's career progress for them. Task teams worked with top management to develop career self-management training for employees and career counseling skills for managers. The resulting increases in employee productivity, enhanced morale, and decreased turnover of key employees have more than justified the new approach to employee career management.

Characteristics of the New Approach

Although the primary and final responsibility for career development rests with each employee, the company has complementary responsibilities. The company is responsible for communicating to employees where it wants to go and

*For more information on the new approach to career self-management, see W. J. Morin, (1996, December 9), You are absolutely, positively on your own, *Fortune*, p. 222; T. D. Hall, (1996). Protean careers of the 21st century, *Academy of Management Executive*, *10*(4), 8–16; and E. H. Schein, (1996), Career anchors revisited: Implications for career development in the 21st century, *Academy of Management Executive*, *10*(4), 80–88.

how it plans to get there (the corporate strategy), providing employees with as much information about the business as possible, and responding to the career initiatives of employees with candid, complete information. One of the most important contributions a company can make to each employee's development is to provide him or her with honest performance feedback about current job performance. Employees, in turn, are responsible for knowing what their skills and capabilities are and what assistance they need from their employers, asking for that assistance, and preparing themselves to assume new responsibilities.

This approach to career management can be summed up as follows: assign employees the responsibility for managing their own careers; then provide the support they need to do it. This support takes different forms in different companies but usually contains several core components—as we will see in the conclusion to this vignette.

Challenges

1. Should employees be responsible for their own career development?
2. Is the new approach to corporate career management likely to be a fad, or is it here to stay?
3. What kinds of support mechanisms are necessary to make career self-management work?

As the chapter opening vignette demonstrates, corporate career management has come a long way in the last several decades. This chapter presents a number of topics that have sparked this reevaluation. We will consider the impact of mergers, acquisitions, and downsizing on corporate loyalty; the impact of dual-career couples on the career management process; and the major issues that workers and managers must deal with during the early, middle, and late career stages of the adult life cycle. Finally, we will examine alternative patterns of career change: promotions, demotions, lateral transfers, relocations, layoffs, and retirements. Career management has many facets, for both the individual and the organization. The chapter opening vignette emphasized that in the new concept of career management, the company and the employee are partners in career development. This chapter reinforces that theme. Let's begin by attempting to define the word "career."

TOWARD A DEFINITION OF "CAREER"

In everyday parlance, the word "career" is used in a number of different ways. People speak of "pursuing a career"; "career planning" workshops are common; colleges and universities hold "career days" during which they publicize jobs in different fields and assist individuals through "career counseling." A person may be characterized as a "career" woman or man who shops in a store that specializes in "career clothing." Likewise, a person may be characterized as a "career military officer." We may overhear a person say, "That movie made his career" (i.e., it enhanced his reputation), or in a derogatory tone, after a subordinate has insulted the CEO, "She can kiss her career good-bye" (i.e., she has tarnished her reputation). Finally, an angry supervisor may remark to her dawdling subordinate, "Watney, are you going to make a career out of changing that light bulb?"

As these examples illustrate, the word "career" can be viewed from a number of different perspectives. From one perspective *a career is a sequence of positions occupied by a person during the course of a lifetime.* This is the *objective* career. From another perspective, though, *a career consists of a sense of where one is going in one's work life.* This is the *subjective* career, and it is held together by a self-concept that consists of (1) perceived talents and abilities, (2) basic values, and (3) career motives and needs.[1] Both of these perspectives, objective and subjective, focus on the individual. Both assume that people have some degree of control over their destinies and that they can manipulate opportunities in order to maximize the success and satisfaction derived from their careers.[2] They assume further that HR activities should recognize career stages and assist employees with the development tasks they face at each stage. Career planning is important because the consequences of career success or failure are linked closely to each individual's self-concept, identity, and satisfaction with career and life.

Given the downsizing mentality that has characterized most large organizations over the past several years, career development and planning have been deemphasized in some firms as employees wondered if they would even have jobs, much less careers. Companies that ignore career issues are mistaken if they think those issues will somehow go away. They won't. Here are some reasons why:[3]

1. Rising concerns for quality of work life and for personal life planning
2. Pressures to expand workforce diversity throughout all levels of an organization[4]
3. Rising educational levels and occupational aspirations
4. Slow economic growth and reduced opportunities for advancement

PROACTIVE CAREER MANAGEMENT

A career is not something that should be left to chance; instead, in the evolving world of work it should be shaped and managed more by the individual than by the organization.[5] But what is the meaning of "career success"?

Toward a Definition of "Career Success"

The tradition-oriented "organization man" of the 1950s had a clear definition of success and a stable model for achieving it. However, the constant threat of restructuring or downsizing in the late 1990s has forced employees at all levels to explore alternative models of career success, and they are confronted with a variety of possibilities. As a consequence, organizations are finding today's employees harder to manage. But they are also finding them to be highly motivated and committed to tasks they value.[6]

In practical terms, what does all this mean for the concept of development and success in the work career? Is it occupational success? Job satisfaction? Growth and development of skills? Successful movement through various life stages? Traditionally, career development and success have been defined in terms of occupational advancement, which is clear and easy to measure. However,

Career progress in today's world requires continual learning, relearning, and cross-functional experience.

throughout the 1990s, in response to tougher global competition and the threat of being taken over, companies have thinned out their ranks to become more efficient and profitable. That means less hierarchy and fewer rungs on the corporate ladder.[7] At the same time, the large number of baby boomers (those born between 1946 and 1964) and baby busters (born between 1965 and 1976), including record numbers of business school graduates, have come of age and are competing for the remaining rungs. The result: HR management problems that organizations have never faced before. The impact on employees will be more stress, more burnout, and more psychological withdrawal. Alternative means of satisfying employees' career aspirations will be needed. Consider a new model of career progress: in the future more careers will be cyclical—involving periodic cycles of skill apprenticeship, mastery, and reskilling. Lateral, rather than upward movement will constitute career development; cross-functional experience will be essential to multiskilling and continued employability. Late careers increasingly will be defined in terms of phased retirement.[8] In this new world, the ultimate goal is *psychological success,* the feeling of pride and personal accomplishment that comes from achieving one's most important goals in life, be they achievement, family happiness, inner peace, or something else.[9] Before we examine career management in more detail, as background to the discussion, let's consider the adult life-cycle stages.

Adult Life-Cycle Stages

For years, researchers have attempted to identify the major developmental tasks that employees face during their working lives and to organize these tasks into broader career stages (such as early, middle, and late career). Although a number of models have been proposed, very little research has tested

MERGERS, ACQUISITIONS, RESTRUCTURINGS, AND THE DEMISE OF CORPORATE LOYALTY

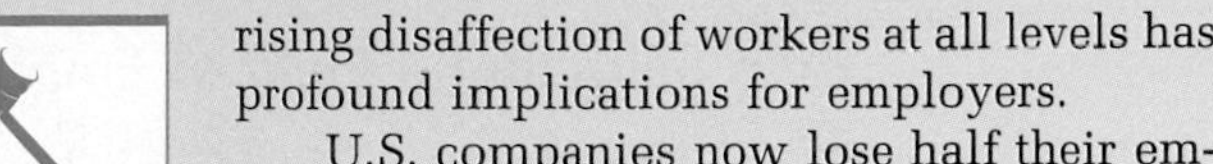

Thousands of mergers and acquisitions have taken place over the past decade among both large and small companies. In general, after a buyout, the merged company eliminates staff duplications and unprofitable divisions. Restructuring, including downsizing, often leads to similar effects—diminished loyalty from employees. In the wave of takeovers, mergers, downsizings, and layoffs, thousands of workers have discovered that years of service mean little to a struggling management or a new corporate parent. This leads to a rise in stress and a decrease in satisfaction, commitment, intentions to stay, and perceptions of an organization's trustworthiness, honesty, and caring about its employees.[11]

Companies counter that today's competitive business environment makes it difficult to protect workers. Understandably, organizations are streamlining in order to become more competitive by cutting labor costs and to become more flexible in their response to the demands of the marketplace. But the rising disaffection of workers at all levels has profound implications for employers.

U.S. companies now lose half their employees every 4 years, half their customers in 5 years, and half their investors in less than 12 months.[12] Median time on the job for all ages was about 4 years in 1996.[13] Furthermore, employee turnover is expensive. It costs as much as $75,000 in the case of a middle manager, and 3 to 5 times annual salary for a CEO.[14] Soon managers will hold 7 to 10 jobs in a lifetime, up from 3 to 4 in the 1970s. Some 10 percent of the American workforce actually switch occupations every year.[15] Yet there is hope, as companies like Monsanto, United Technologies, and Xerox recognize an opportunity to create value in the midst of such turmoil. How? By understanding that they can retain loyal customers only with a base of loyal employees.[16] Decreasing defection rates of customers, employees, and investors can lead to substantial growth, profits, and lasting value. That is a win-win situation for all concerned.

their accuracy. Moreover, there is little, if any, agreement about whether career stages are linked to age or not. Most theorists give age ranges for each stage, but these vary widely. Consequently, it may make more sense to think in terms of career stages linked to time. This approach would allow a "career clock" to begin at different points for different individuals, according to their personal backgrounds and experiences.[10]

Such an approach allows for differences in the number of distinct stages through which individuals may pass, the overlapping tasks and issues they may face at each stage, and the role of transition periods between stages. The lesson for managers is that all models of adult life-cycle stages should be viewed as broad guidelines rather than as exact representations of reality.

CAREER MANAGEMENT: INDIVIDUALS FOCUSING ON THEMSELVES

In discussions of career management, it is important to emphasize the increasingly *temporary* relationships between individuals and organizations. Said a victim of three corporate downsizings in 4 years: "A job is just an opportunity to learn new skills that you can then peddle elsewhere in the marketplace."[17] While such a view might appear cynical to some, the fact is that responsibility for career development belongs ultimately to each individual. Unfortunately, few individuals are technically prepared (and willing) to handle this assignment. This is not surprising, for very few college programs specifically address the problems of managing one's own career. However, as long as it remains difficult for organizations to match the career expectations of their employees, one option for employees will be to switch organizations. Guidelines for doing this fall into the following three major categories.[18]

Selecting a Field of Employment and an Employer

1. You cannot manage your career unless you have a macro, long-range objective. The first step, therefore, is to think in terms of where you ultimately want to be, recognizing, of course, that your career goals will change over time.
2. View every potential employer and position in terms of your long-range career goal. That is, how well does this job serve to position me in terms of my ultimate objective? For example, if you aspire to reach senior management by the year 2000, consider the extent to which your current job helps you develop a global orientation, develop public speaking skills, practice the "bring out the best in people" leadership style, and learn to manage cultural diversity. These are now, and will continue to be, key requirements for senior positions.[19]
3. Accept short-term trade-offs for long-term benefits. Certain lateral moves or low-paying jobs can provide extremely valuable training opportunities or career contacts.
4. Consider carefully whether to accept highly specialized jobs or isolated job assignments that might restrict or impede your visibility and career development.

Knowing Where You Are

1. Always be aware of opportunities available to you in your current position—e.g., training programs that might further your career development.
2. Carefully and honestly assess your current performance. How do you see yourself, and how do you think higher management sees your performance?
3. Try to recognize when you and your organization have outlived your utility for each other. This is not an admission of failure but rather an honest reflection of the fact that there is little more the organization can do for you and, in turn, that your contribution to the organization has reached a point of diminishing returns.

Here are five important symptoms: you are not excited by what you are doing, advancement is blocked, your organization is poorly managed and is losing market share, you feel you are not adequately rewarded for your work, or you are not fulfilling your dreams.[20]

Planning Your Exit

1. Try to leave at your convenience, not the organization's. To do this, you must do two things well: (a) know when it is time to leave (as before), and (b) since downsizing can come at any time, establish networking relationships while you still have a job.
2. Leave your current organization on good terms and not under questionable circumstances.

3. Do not leave your current job until you have landed another one; it is easier to find a new job when you are currently employed. Like bank loans, jobs often go to people who do not seem to need them.[21]

The Role of the Organization

Up to this point it may sound as though managing your career is all one-sided. This is not true; the organization should be a proactive force in this process. To do so, organizations must think and plan in terms of shorter employment relationships. This can be done, as it often is in professional sports, through fixed-term employment contracts with options for renegotiation and extension.

A second strategy for organizations is to invest adequate time and energy in job design and equipment. Given that mobility among workers is expected to increase, careful attention to these elements will make it easier to make replacements fully productive as soon as possible. How does the self-management of careers work in practice? If Hewlett-Packard's experience is any indication, we can expect to see more of it in the future.

COMPANY EXAMPLE

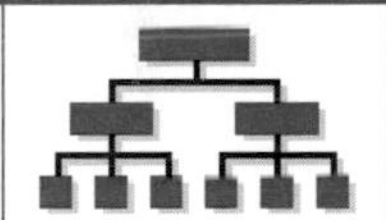

HEWLETT-PACKARD HELPS EMPLOYEES SELF-MANAGE THEIR CAREERS

A 3-month course in personal career management was developed at Hewlett-Packard's Colorado Springs Division. The two methods used in the course were self-assessment and subsequent application of findings to the workplace to chart a career path for each employee.[22]

The idea of self-assessment as the first step toward career planning is certainly not new. Self-help books have flooded the market for years. However, books by themselves lack a critical ingredient for success: the emotional support of a group setting in which momentum and motivation can be shared and maintained. Make no mistake about it, self-assessment can be a grueling process.

Hewlett-Packard uses six devices to generate data for self-assessment (based on earlier work for a second-year Harvard MBA course in career development). These include:

- **A written self-interview.** Participants are given 11 questions about themselves, they are asked to provide facts about their lives (people, places, events), and they are asked to discuss the future and the transitions they have made. This autobiographical sketch provides core data for the subsequent analysis.
- **Strong Vocational Interest Inventory.** Participants complete this 325-item instrument to determine their preferences about occupations, academic subjects, types of people, and so forth. An interest profile is developed for each individual by comparing her or his responses with those of successful people in a wide range of occupations.
- **Allport-Vernon-Lindzey Study of Values.** Each participant makes 45 choices among competing values in order to measure the relative strength of theoretical, economic, aesthetic, social, political, and religious values.

- **24-hour diaries.** Participants log their activities during one workday and also during one nonworkday. This information is used to confirm, or occasionally to contradict, information from the other sources.
- **Interviews with two "significant others."** Each participant asks a friend, spouse, relative, coworker, or someone else of importance questions about himself or herself. The two interviews are tape-recorded.
- **Lifestyle representations.** Participants depict their lifestyles using words, photos, drawings, or any other medium they choose.

A key ingredient in this program is its emphasis on an inductive approach. That is, the program begins by generating new data about each participant, rather than by starting with generalizations and deducing from them more specific information about each person. The process proceeds from the specific to the general (inductive), rather than from the general to the specific (deductive). Participants slowly recognize generalizations or themes within the large amounts of information they have produced. They come to tentative conclusions about these themes—first, in each device individually, and then, in all the workshop's instruments as a whole—by analyzing the data they have collected.

Following the self-assessment, department managers interview subordinates to learn about their career objectives. They record these objectives and describe the people and positions currently in their departments. This information is then available for senior management to use in devising an overall human resource plan, which defines the skills required and includes a timetable. When data on the company's future needs are matched against each employee's career objectives, department managers can help employees chart a career course in the company (e.g., through training or additional job experience). Career development objectives for each employee are incorporated into performance objectives for future performance appraisals. The department head monitors the employee's career progress as part of the review process, and she or he is responsible for offering all possible support.

Results of the Career Self-Management Program

Senior managers at Hewlett-Packard found that after the workshops, they had far more flexibility in moving employees than was previously the case. The company was able either to give employees reasons to stay where they were, to develop a new path for them in the company, or to help them move out. Significantly, the Colorado Springs Division's overall turnover rate was unchanged in the year following the workshops. At an estimated $66,000 replacement cost (in 1996 dollars) for a departing middle manager, this was a welcome finding.

Within 6 months after the course, 37 percent of the participants had advanced to new jobs within the company, while 40 percent planned moves within the following 6 months. Of those who advanced, 74 percent credited the program for playing a significant part in their job change. The workshops also promoted workforce diversity since the sessions were open to all employees who expressed an interest in career development.

Perhaps the most persuasive reason for helping employees manage their own careers is the need to remain competitive. Although it might seem like a contradiction, such efforts can enhance a company's stability by developing more purposeful, self-assured employees. As noted earlier, today's employees are more difficult to manage. Companies that recognize the need to provide employees with satisfying opportunities will have the decided advantage of a loyal and industrious workforce.

One of the most challenging career management problems organizations face today is that of the dual-career couple. Let's examine this issue in detail.

Dual-Career Couples: Problems and Opportunities

Today, two of every three employed men have wives employed in the workforce.[23] Dual-career couples face the problems of managing work and family responsibilities. Furthermore, it appears that there may be an interaction effect that compounds the problems and stresses of each separate career.[24] This implies that, by itself, career planning and development may be meaningless unless an employee's role as a family member also is considered, particularly when this role conflicts with work activities.[25] What can be done?

Research indicates that if dual-career couples are to manage their family responsibilities successfully, they (and their managers) must be flexible; they must be mutually committed to both careers; and they must develop the competencies to manage their careers through planning, goal setting, and problem solving.[26]

From an organizational perspective, successful management of the dual-career couple requires (1) flexible work schedules (now offered by 73 percent of large companies), (2) special counseling, (3) training for supervisors in career counseling skills, and (4) the establishment of support structures for transfers and relocations. What have organizations actually done?

As part of a package deal, roughly 50 percent of U.S. companies provide assistance to the "trailing" spouse in finding a suitable job consistent with the spouse's career plans.[27] Unisys pays up to $500 for résumé writing and job-hunting help for a trailing spouse. U.S. West offers as much as $2500, including insuring against home-sale losses. Cigna will cover a month's pay at the spouse's former salary while he or she seeks a new job.[28]

COMPANY EXAMPLE

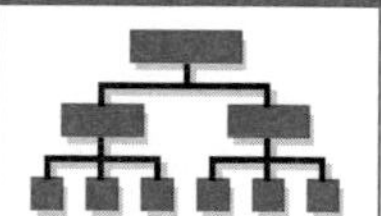

BOTTOM-LINE BENEFITS FOR FAMILY-FRIENDLY COMPANIES[29]

Companies that truly "get it" actually go further and integrate family-support mechanisms into the business itself. Thus Hewlett-Packard requires that every business unit identify work-family issues and propose an action plan as part of its annual business review. A Ford Foundation study found that successful solutions involved rethinking work processes, rather than finding ways to make people's lives fit the work. Thus when Xerox's Dallas customer-administration center handed over responsibility for scheduling shifts to workers themselves, it saw an overnight drop in absenteeism, followed by a rise in productivity. First Tennessee National Corporation found that supervisors rated by their subordinates as supportive of work-family balance retained employees twice as long as the bank average, and kept 7 percent more retail customers. Higher retention rates, according to the company, contributed to a 55 percent profit gain over 2 years, to $106 million. Bottom line: work-family strategies have not just hit the corporate mainstream—they have become a competitive advantage.

For all the talk about family-friendly policies, however, only about 25 percent of large employers actually provide on-site or near-site child-care programs.[30] Yet demand for the service has never been greater. Families nationwide pay an average of about 7.5 percent of their annual pretax income for child care.[31] Here are some reasons why employer-supported child care will continue to grow:

- Dual-career couples now constitute a preponderance of the workforce.
- There has been a significant rise in the number of single parents, over half of whom use child-care facilities.[32]
- More and more, career-oriented women are arranging their lives to include motherhood and professional goals.

Employer-sponsored dependent care is no longer limited just to on-site or near-site child-care centers, however. The concept has expanded to include elder care, intergenerational care, sick-child care, and programs for school-age children (before- and after-school as well as holiday programs). Other variations include centers located in office and industrial parks for use by all tenants, and centers sponsored by networks of businesses.[33]

Data from a national random sample indicate that *providing family benefits promotes a dedicated, loyal workforce among people who benefit directly from the policies, as well as among those who do not.*[34] However, the lesson from two other studies is clear: do not expect that a day-care center or a flexible schedule will keep women managers from leaving corporations. They may be quite willing to throw corporate loyalty to the wind if they are not getting adequate opportunities for career growth and job satisfaction.[35]

Managing dual-career couples, from an individual as well as from an organizational perspective, is difficult. But if current conditions are any indication of long-term trends, we can be quite sure of one thing: this "problem" is not going to go away.

CAREER MANAGEMENT: ORGANIZATIONS FOCUSING ON INDIVIDUALS

In this section we will examine current organizational practices used to manage workers at various stages of their careers. Let's begin by considering organizational entry.

Organizational Entry

Once a person has entered the workforce, the next stage is to enter a specific organization, to settle down, and to begin establishing a career there. Entry refers to the process of "moving inside," or becoming more involved in a particular organization.[36] For entry to be successful, a process known as socialization

ETHICAL DILEMMA
Bringing Mentors and Protégés Together

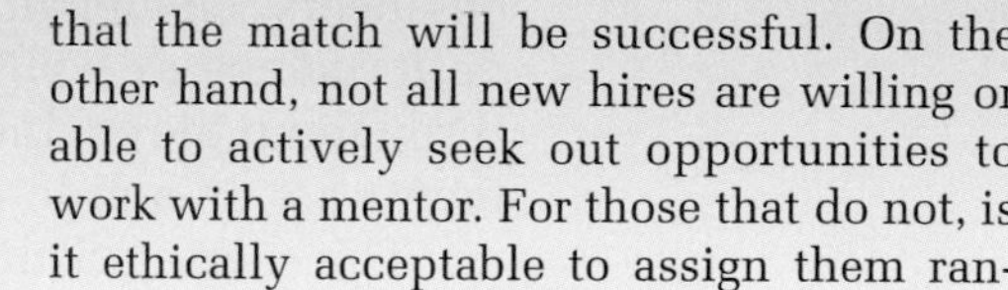

Recent research indicates that informal mentorships (spontaneous relationships that occur without involvement from the organization) lead to more positive career outcomes than do formal mentorships (programs that are managed and sanctioned by the organization).[41] Random assignment of protégés to mentors is like arranging a blind date—there is only a small chance that the match will be successful. On the other hand, not all new hires are willing or able to actively seek out opportunities to work with a mentor. For those that do not, is it ethically acceptable to assign them randomly to mentors, or to let them "sink or swim"? How would you advise an organization to proceed when faced with this dilemma?

is essential. *Socialization* refers to the mutual adaptation of the new employee and the new employer to one another. Learning organizational policies, norms, traditions, and values is an important part of the process. Getting to know one's peers, supervisor, and subordinates is another important part. All of this enhances the newcomer's desire for personal control.[37] Since most turnover occurs early in a person's tenure with an organization, programs that accelerate socialization will tend also to reduce early turnover (i.e., at entry) and therefore reduce a company's overall turnover rate. Two of the most effective methods for doing this are realistic job previews (see Chapter 5) and new-employee orientation (see Chapter 7). A third is mentoring.

Mentoring

A mentor is a teacher, an advisor, a sponsor, and a confidant.[38] He or she should be bright and well seasoned enough to understand the dynamics of power and politics in the organization and also be willing to share this knowledge with one or more new hires. Indeed, to overcome the potential problems associated with one-on-one, male-female mentoring relationships, some firms have established "quad squads" that consist of a mentor plus three new hires: a male, a female, and a member of a protected group. Bank of America is typical. It assigns mentors to three or four promising young executives for a year at a time. There are also benefits for the mentor. For example, just being chosen as a mentor, according to one 35-year-old female branch bank manager, boosted her self-esteem. This is a central goal of any mentoring effort.

Organizations should actively promote such relationships and provide sufficient time for mentors and new hires (or promising young executives) to meet on a regularly scheduled basis, at least initially. The mentor's role is to be a "culture carrier," to teach new hires the ropes, to provide candid feedback on how they are being perceived by others, and to serve as a confidential sounding board for dealing with work-related problems. That sounding board may even be a computer-based bulletin board, such as America Online or CompuServe, that provides a forum for discussing specific workplace issues.[39] If successful, mentor relationships can help reduce the inflated expectations that newcomers often have about organizations, can relieve the stress experienced by all new hires, and, best of all, can improve the newcomer's chances for survival and growth in the organization.[40]

Early Career: The Impact of the First Job

Many studies of early careers focus on the first jobs to which new employees are assigned. The positive impact of initial job challenge upon later career success and retention has been found many times in a wide variety of settings. Among engineers, challenging early work assignments were related to strong initial performance as well as to the maintenance of competence and performance throughout the engineer's career.[42] In other words, challenging initial job assignments are an antidote to career obsolescence.

The characteristics of the first supervisor are also critical. He or she must be personally secure; unthreatened by the new subordinate's training, ambition, and energy; and able to communicate company norms and values.[43] Beyond that, the supervisor ideally should be able to play the roles of coach, feedback provider, trainer, role model, and protector in an accepting, esteem-building manner.

One other variable affects the likelihood of obtaining a high-level job later in one's career: *initial aspirations*.[44] Employees should be encouraged to aim high because, in general, higher aspirations lead to higher performance. Parents, teachers, employers, and friends should therefore avoid discouraging so-called impractical aspirations.

COMPANY EXAMPLE

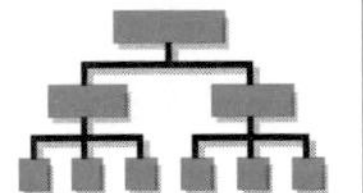

IMPACT OF THE FIRST JOB ON LATER CAREER SUCCESS

For more than 20 years researchers generally accepted the view that unless an individual has a challenging first job and receives quick, early promotions, her or his entire career will suffer. This is a "tournament" model of upward mobility. It assumes that everyone has an equal chance in the early contests but that the losers are not eligible for later contests, at least not those of the major tournament. An alternative model is called "signaling" theory. It suggests three cues ("signals") that those responsible for promotion may use: (1) prior history of promotions (a signal of ability), (2) functional-area background, and (3) number of different jobs held.

A study of the patterns of early upward mobility for 180 employees of an oil company over an 11-year period are enlightening.[45] The company's very detailed job classification systems and actual salary grades served as measures of career attainment. The results generally did not support the tournament model of career mobility, because the losers—those passed over in the early periods—were later able to move up quickly. Rather, the results were more analogous to a horse race: position out of the gate had relatively little effect in comparison with position entering the home stretch.

Different mobility patterns for administration and technical personnel helped explain why the pattern of the early years did not always persist. Those who started early in administrative positions began to move up early but also plateaued early. A technical background meant a longer wait before upward movement, followed by relatively rapid promotion. The number of different positions held also predicted higher attainment.

In summary, one's past position, functional background, and number of different jobs all seem to act as signals to those making decisions about promotions. All were related strongly to career attainment. Together they accounted for more than 60 percent of the variability in promotions.

Managing Men and Women in Midcareer

To a large extent, middle age is still a mystery. Myths about psychological landmarks of midlife, such as the empty-nest syndrome, the midlife crisis, and the menopausal change of life have little scientific basis.[46] Nevertheless, the following issues may arise at some point during the ages of 35 to 55:[47]

- An awareness of advancing age and an awareness of death
- An awareness of bodily changes related to aging
- Knowing how many career goals have been or will be attained
- A search for new life goals
- A marked change in family relationships
- A change in work relationships (one is now more of a "coach" than a novice or "rookie")
- A growing sense of obsolescence at work (as Satchel Paige once said, "Never look back; someone may be gaining on you")
- A feeling of decreased job mobility and increased concern for job security[48]

One's career is a major consideration during this period. If a person has been in the same job for 10 years or more (sometimes less), he or she must face the facts of corporate politics, of changing job requirements, and of possibilities of promotion, demotion, or job loss altogether. The fact of the matter is, over the next decade promotions will slow down markedly as middle-level managers are put into "holding patterns."

While career success traditionally has been defined in terms of upward mobility, in the 1990s, more and more leading corporations are encouraging employees to step off the fast track and convincing them that they can find rewards and happiness in lateral mobility. In lectures and newsletters, the companies are trying to convince employees that "plateauing" is a fact of life, not a measure of personal failure, and that success depends on lateral integration of the business. Does such a move make sense? Yes, if it puts a person into a core business, gives that person closer contact with customers, or teaches new skills that will increase marketability (both inside and outside one's present company) in case the person is fired.[49] Companies that are moving this way are still in the minority, but they include such giants as Monsanto, Motorola, BellSouth, General Electric, and RJR Nabisco.

Others note that while there are fewer middle managers at medium and large companies as a result of the reductions in layers of managers during the corporate restructurings of the last decade, their jobs are more important. Middle managers now focus less on supervision and more on decision making.[50] However, for those who simply cannot accept lateral mobility, there is still hope. In the coming years, according to the Bureau of Labor Statistics, many firms will face shortages of managers with leadership and technical knowledge (such as engineers with MBA degrees) and of managers with expertise in human resource management and computer matters.[51]

What can a middle-aged man or woman do? The rapid growth of technology and the accelerating development of new knowledge require that a person in midlife make some sort of *change* for her or his own survival. A 30-year-old might make the statement, "I can afford to change jobs or careers a few more times before I have to settle down." But a 50-year-old faces the possibility that there is only one chance left for change, and now may be the time to take it.[52]

Not everyone who goes through this period in life is destined to experience problems, but everyone does go through the transition, and some are better equipped to cope than are others. Evidence now indicates that the older people are, the more control they feel in their work, finances, and marriages, but the less control they feel over health, children, and sex.[53] Life planning and career planning exercises are available that encourage employees to face up to feelings of restlessness and insecurity, to reexamine their values and life goals, and to set new ones or to recommit themselves to old ones.

One strategy is to *train midcareer employees to develop younger employees* (i.e., to serve as coaches or mentors). Both parties can win under such an arrangement. The midcareer employee keeps himself or herself fresh, energetic, and up to date, while the younger employee learns to see the big picture and to profit from the experience of the older employee. An important psychological need at midcareer is to build something lasting, something that will be a permanent contribution to one's organization or profession. The development of a future generation of leaders could be a significant, lasting, and highly satisfying contribution.

Another strategy for coping with midcareer problems is to *deal with or prevent obsolescence.* To deal with the problem, some firms send their employees to seminars, workshops, university courses, and other forms of "retooling." But a better solution is to prevent obsolescence from occurring in the first place. Research with engineers indicated that this can be done through challenging initial jobs; periodic changes in assignments, projects, or jobs; work climates that contain frequent, relevant communications; rewards that are closely tied to performance; and participative styles of leadership.[54] Furthermore, three personal characteristics tend to be associated with low obsolescence: high intellectual ability, high self-motivation, and personal flexibility (lack of rigidity).

COMPANY EXAMPLE

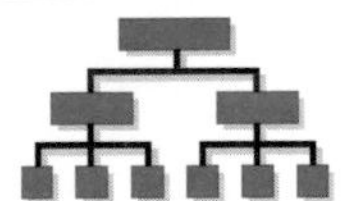

STRATEGIES FOR COPING WITH "PLATEAUED" WORKERS[55]

Chevron, General Motors, and Chicago's Continental Bank are encouraging employees to move across departmental lines on a horizontal basis since restructuring has made vertical promotions less frequent. In banking, for example, someone from auditing might switch to commercial training; someone from systems research and development might move into international development. The inflexible HRM policies of the past are rapidly fading to accommodate present and future problems. Another strategy is to create dual technical/management ladders. New "technical executive" positions are equal to management jobs in title and dollars. For example, Continental Bank has created senior lending positions and positions for accounting and systems specialists that are equivalent to senior managerial posts in those departments.

An alternative way to placate people who do not move up is to pay them more for jobs well done. For years, companies that rely heavily for growth on creative people—scientists, engineers, writers, artists—have provided incentives for them to stay on. Companies are now offering such incentives to a broader spectrum of employees. For example, at Monsanto, favored scientists can now climb a university-like track of associate fellow, fellow, senior fellow, distinguished fellow. The company has 130 fellows, and they earn from $65,000 a year to well over $100,000.

At General Electric, employees who are "plateaued" (either organizationally, through a lack of available promotions, or personally, through lack of ability or desire) are sometimes assigned to task forces or study teams. These employees have not been promoted in a technical sense, but at least they have gotten a new assignment, a fresh perspective, and a change in their daily work.

Finally, Prudential Life Insurance Company rotates managers to improve their performance. Rockwell International uses task forces, where possible, to "recharge" managers so they do not feel a loss of self-worth if they do not move up as fast as they think they should.

Actually, there may be a bright side to all of this. Because of increased competition for fewer jobs, the *quality* of middle managers should increase. Those unwilling to wait for promotions in large corporations may become entrepreneurs and start their own businesses. Others may simply accept the status quo, readjust their life and career goals, and attempt to satisfy their needs for achievement, recognition, and personal growth off the job. Research at AT&T supports this proposition. By the time managers were interviewed after 20 years on the job, most had long ago given up their early dreams, and many could not even remember how high they had aspired to go in the first place. At least on the surface, most had accepted their career plateaus and adjusted to them. Midlife was indeed a crisis to some of the managers, but not to the majority.[56]

It is possible to move through the middle years of life without reevaluation of one's goals and life. But it is probably healthier to develop a new or revised "game plan" during this period.

Managing the Older Worker

"Work is life" is a phrase philosophers throughout the ages have emphasized. Today, advances in health and medicine make it possible for the average male to live for more than 72 years and for the average female to live for more than 79 years.[57] Expected life span has increased by 27 years in this century. The result: an army of healthy, over-65, unemployed adults. The elimination of mandatory retirement has made this issue even more significant. As managers, what can we expect in terms of demographic trends?

Post-World War II baby boomers (those born between 1946 and 1964) are passing into middle life. The Census Bureau predicts that the number of new workers ages 16 to 24 will drop by 16 percent between 1990 and 2010. Meanwhile, by the year 2010 all the people born during the baby-boom years will be age 45 and older; those born in 1946 will be 64. In the year 2020, the oldest "baby boomers" will be 75 and the youngest will be 56.[58] Figure 9-1 graphically illustrates these trends. In short, the baby boom of the postwar period will become the "rocking-chair boom" of the twenty-first century.

Myths versus Facts about Older Workers

Age stereotypes are an unfortunate impediment to the continued growth and development of workers over the age of 55. Here are some common myths about age, along with the facts:

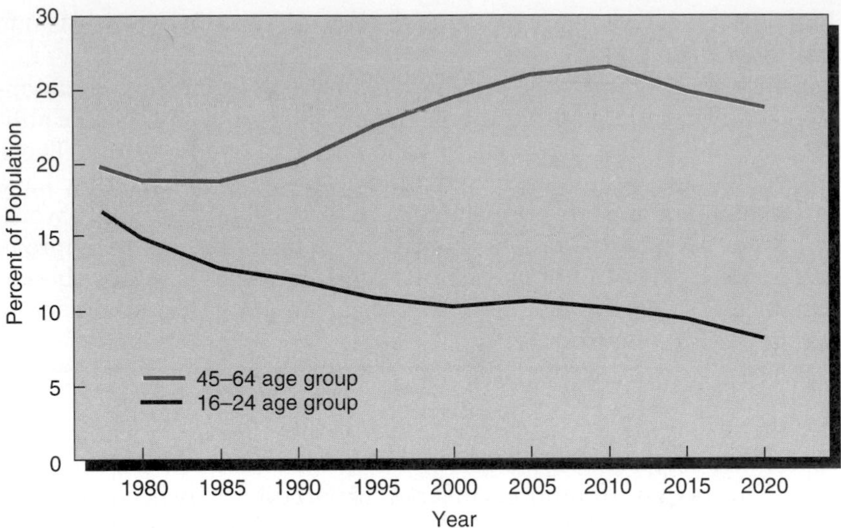

Figure 9-1
Population distribution by age group, ages 16–24 and 45–65. (*Source:* U.S. Bureau of the Census, "Estimates of the Population of the United States, by Age, Sex, and Race: 1980 to 1983," *Current Population Reports,* Series P-25, No. 949, May 1984; U.S. Bureau of the Census, "Projections of the Population of the United States, by Age, Sex, and Race: 1983 to 2080," *Current Population Reports,* Series P-25, No. 952, May 1984.)

Myth. Older workers are less productive than younger workers.

Fact. Cumulative research evidence on almost 39,000 individuals indicates that in both professional and nonprofessional jobs, age and job performance are generally unrelated.[59] The relationship of aging to the ability to function, and the implication of aging for job performance, is complex. Overwhelming evidence contradicts simple notions that rate of decline is tied in some linear or direct fashion to chronological age. Rather, the effects of aging on performance can be characterized by stability and growth, as well as decline, with large individual differences in the timing and amount of change in the ability to function.[60]

Myth. It costs more to prepare older workers for a job.

Fact. Studies show that mental abilities, such as verbal, numerical, and reasoning skills, remain stable into the seventies.[61]

Myth. Older workers are absent more often because of age-related infirmities and above-average rates of illness.

Fact. Cumulative research has found that older workers tend to be absent less frequently, at least in nonillness situations, but the duration of the absences that do take place tends to be longer.[62]

Myth. Older workers have an unacceptably high rate of accidents on the job.

Fact. According to a study by the Department of Health and Human Services, workers age 55 and over had only 9.7 percent of all workplace injuries, even though they made up 13.6 percent of the workforce at the time of the study.[63] The data are even more compelling when only healthy workers are considered (i.e., as a result of a thorough medical screening). Among healthy workers age 23 to 75, age was not associated with increased accidents and illnesses at work.[64]

One might argue that this is because older workers have more experience on a job. But regardless of length of experience, the younger the employee, the higher the accident rate (see Chapter 14).

Myth. Older workers do not get along well with other employees.

Fact. Owners of small and large businesses alike agree that older employees bring stability and relate well. Indeed, the over-55 worker's sense of responsibility and consistent job performance provide a positive role model for younger workers.[65]

Myth. The cost of employee benefits outweighs any other possible benefits from hiring older workers.

Fact. True, when older people get sick, the illness is often chronic and requires repeated doctor's visits and hospitalization. However, the costs of health care for an older worker are lower than those for a younger, married worker with several children.[66]

Myth. Older people are inflexible about the type of work they will perform.

Fact. A study of job candidates by Right Associates, placement counselors, found that 55 percent of those under age 50, but 63 percent of those age 50 to 59 and 78 percent of those over age 60, changed industries. Many older workers saw difficulties in being rehired by their old industries.

Myth. Older people do not function well if constantly interrupted.

Fact. Neither do younger people.

Implications of the Aging Workforce for HRM

Certainly not all older workers are model employees, just as not all older workers fit traditional stereotypes. What are the implications of this growing group of able-bodied individuals for human resource management?

We know what the future labor market will look like in general terms: both the demand for and the supply of older workers will continue to expand. To capitalize on these trends, one approach is to recruit workers from those individuals who would otherwise retire. *Make the job more attractive than retirement, and keep employees who would otherwise need replacing*[67] Some companies, in fact, are rehiring their own retirees.

COMPANY EXAMPLE

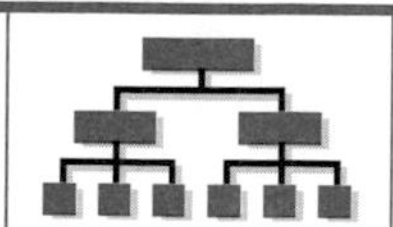

"UNRETIREES"

Travelers Corporation is one of a growing number of companies that are finding their own retirees to be a valuable source of experienced, dependable, and motivated help. The retirees meet seasonal or sporadic employment needs for the company, and the company gets a tax break. In 1980, Travelers invited all of its 5000 retirees to enroll in its Retirees Job Bank in Hartford, Connecticut. By 1990,

In many fields, older workers are especially valuable because they have a lifetime of experience to draw from.

more than 750 did. They fill a variety of jobs, including typists, data-entry operators, systems analysts, underwriters, and accountants. Working a maximum of 40 hours per month, retirees are paid at the midpoint of the salary range for their job classifications. If they work more than half a standard workweek, they risk losing their pension benefits. Nevertheless, retirees generally like the program, for it keeps them in better physical, mental, and financial shape than full-time retirement does.[68]

With a smaller cohort of young workers entering the workforce, other companies are also seeking workers who once would have been considered "over the hill." McDonald's prints applications for "McMasters" on its tray liners. Days Inns of America holds Senior Power job fairs. One such effort attracted 634 companies and 5000 older people in 26 states. The Polaroid Corporation offers gradual retirement for those who want to continue working part-time.[69] According to Chicago's Harris Trust and Savings Bank, which has been rehiring its retirees since the 1940s, the savings from its program come to $3 to $5 per hour when compared with the fees charged by temporary help agencies.

A second approach is to *survey the needs of older workers and, where feasible, adjust HRM practices and policies to accommodate those needs:*

1. Keep records on why employees retire and on why they continue to work.[70]
2. Implement flexible work patterns and options. For example, older workers might work on Mondays and Fridays and on days before and after holidays, when so many other employees fail to show up.
3. Where possible, redesign jobs to match the physical capabilities of the aging worker.
4. At a broader level, develop career paths that consider the physical capabilities of workers at various stages of their careers.[71]
5. Provide opportunities for retraining in technical and managerial skills. Particularly with older workers, it is important to provide a nonthreatening training environment that does not emphasize speed and does not expose the older learner to unfavorable comparisons with younger learners. Verbal assurances, ample time, and privacy are key ingredients for successfully training older workers.[72]
6. Examine the suitability of performance appraisal systems as bases for employment decisions affecting older workers. To avoid age discrimination suits, be able to provide documented evidence of ineffective job performance.
7. Despite the encouraging findings presented earlier, in the section "Myths versus Facts about Older Workers," research has indicated no overall improvement in attitudes toward older workers over a 40-year period.[73] Characteristics employers consider most desirable in employees—flexibility, adaptability to change, capacity and willingness to exercise independent judgment—are not commonly associated with older workers.[74]

For their part, older workers say their biggest problem is discrimination by would-be employers who underestimate their skills. They say they must convince supervisors and coworkers, not to mention some customers, that they are not stubborn, persnickety, or feeble.[75] To change this trend, workers and managers alike need to know the facts about older workers so that they do not continue to espouse myths.

CAREER MANAGEMENT: ORGANIZATIONS FOCUSING ON THEIR OWN MAINTENANCE AND GROWTH

Ultimately, it is top management's responsibility to develop and implement a cost-effective career planning program. The program must fit the nature of the business, its competitive employment practices, and the current (or desired) organizational structure. This process is complex because organizational career management combines areas that previously have been regarded as individual issues: performance appraisal, development, transfer, and promotion. Before coaching and counseling take place, however, it is important to identify characteristic career paths that employees tend to follow.

Career paths represent logical and possible sequences of positions that could be held, based on an analysis of what people actually do in an organization.[76] Career paths should:

- Represent real progression possibilities, whether lateral or upward, without implied "normal" rates of progress or forced specialization in a technical area.

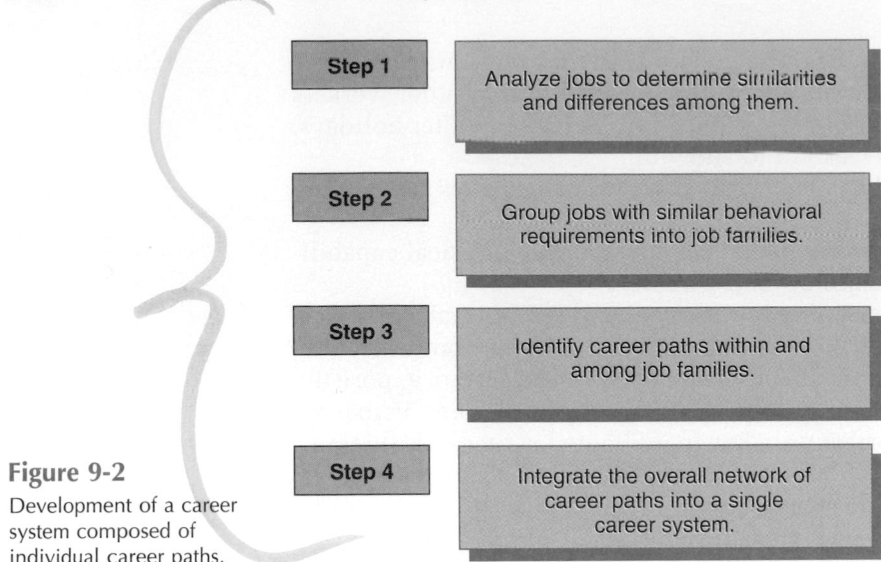

Figure 9-2
Development of a career system composed of individual career paths.

- Be tentative and responsive to changes in job content, work priorities, organizational patterns, and management needs.
- Be flexible, taking into consideration the compensating qualities of a particular employee, managers, subordinates, or others who influence the way that work is performed.
- Specify the skills, knowledge, and other attributes required to perform effectively at each position along the paths and specify how they can be acquired. (If specifications are limited to educational credentials, age, and experience, some capable performers may be excluded from career opportunities.)

Data derived from HRM research are needed to define career paths in this manner. Behaviorally based job analyses (see Chapter 4) that can be expressed in quantitative terms are well suited to this task since they focus directly on what people must do effectively in each job. Clusters or families of jobs requiring similar patterns of behavior can then be identified.

Once this is done, the next task is to identify career paths within and among the job families and to integrate the overall network of these paths into a single career system. The process is shown graphically in Figure 9-2.

Federal guidelines on employee selection require a job-related basis for all employment decisions. Career paths based on job analyses of employee behaviors provide a documented, defensible basis for organizational career management and a strong reference point for individual career planning and development activities.

In practice, organizational career management systems sometimes fail for the following reasons: (1) employees believe that supervisors do not care about their career development, (2) neither the employee nor the organization is fully aware of the employee's needs and organizational constraints, and (3) career plans are developed without regard for the support systems necessary to fulfill the plans.[77] The following section gives examples of several companies that avoided these pitfalls.

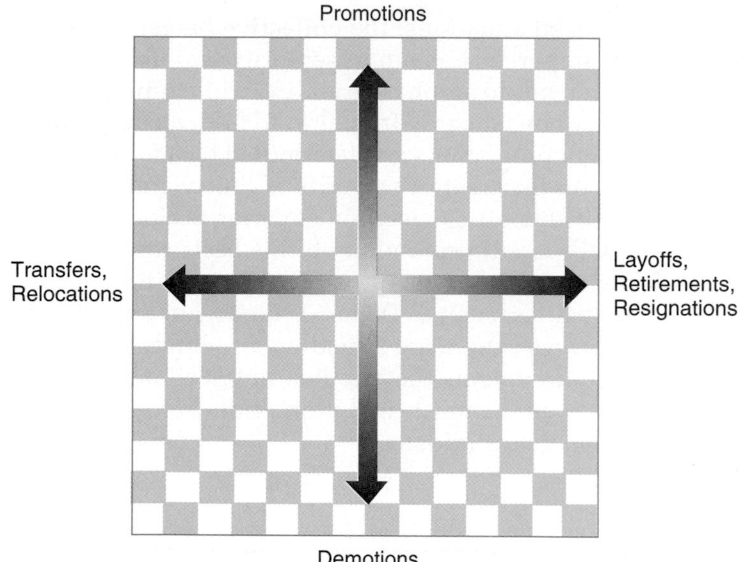

Figure 9-3
As in chess, people can make a variety of internal moves in an organization.

Internal Staffing Decisions: Patterns of Career Change

From the organization's point of view, there are four broad types of internal moves: up, down, over, and out (Figure 9-3). These moves correspond to promotions (up), demotions (down), transfers and relocations (over), and layoffs, retirements, and resignations (out). Technically, dismissals also fall into the last category, but we will consider them in the context of disciplinary actions and procedural justice. Briefly, let's consider each of these patterns of movement.

Promotions

Promoted employees usually assume greater responsibility and authority in return for higher pay, benefits, and privileges. Psychologically, promotions help satisfy employees' needs for security, belonging, and personal growth. Promotions are important organizational decisions that should receive the same careful attention as any other employment decision. They are more likely to be successful to the extent that firms:

1. Conduct an extensive search for candidates.
2. Make standardized, clearly understandable information available on all candidates.[78]

Organizations must continue to live with those who are bypassed for promotion. Research indicates that these individuals often feel they have not been treated fairly, with the result that their commitment decreases and their absenteeism increases. Conversely, promoted individuals tend to increase their commitment.[79] Minimizing defensive behavior requires that the procedures used for promotion decisions (e.g., assessment centers plus performance appraisals) be acceptable, valid, and fair to the unsuccessful candidates. Further, the greater merits of the promoted candidates, relative to those who were not promoted, should be emphasized.

In unionized situations, the collective bargaining contract will determine the relative importance given to seniority and ability in promotion decisions. Management tends to emphasize ability, while unions favor seniority. Although practices vary considerably from firm to firm, a compromise is usually reached through which promotions are determined by a formula, such as promoting the employee with the greatest seniority *if* ability and experience are equal. However, if one candidate is clearly a superior performer relative to others, many contracts will permit promotion on this basis regardless of seniority.

A further issue concerns promotion from within versus outside the organization. Many firms, such as Delta Air Lines, have strict promotion-from-within policies. However, there are situations in which high-level jobs or newly created jobs require talents that are just not available in-house. Under these circumstances, even the most rigid promotion-from-within policy must yield to a search for outside candidates.

COMPANY EXAMPLE

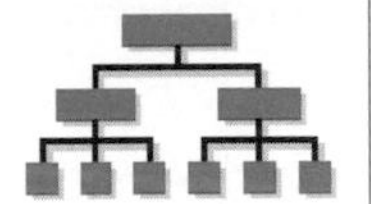

PROMOTIONS TO PARTNER AT GOLDMAN, SACHS & COMPANY

Goldman, Sachs & Company is one of the last of Wall Street's major private partnerships. Each year, the firm picks a small number of new partners from among its hundreds of young executives. Winners are set for life and typically retire as multimillionaires after only a decade or so. But it is getting harder to decide who gets the prize.

Exactly what goes on behind the scenes of the 2-month-long competition is a closely held secret. Current partners describe it, of course, as a rigorous but fair process in which politics are unimportant. The process certainly is rigorous. It starts with a winnowing down of the worldwide workforce of 6600 to a list of 50 to 60 serious candidates. Each potential new partner must then be nominated by a current partner.

What do partners look for? In addition to keen business judgment and a proven track record of success, partners look for team players and "culture carriers." Such people fit Goldman's conservative style and its customer-oriented tradition, which dates back to the 1860s, when Marcus Goldman began hawking commercial paper on the streets of New York.

Partners, who are expected to back their nominees' causes throughout the process, then file mountains of endorsement letters. For the next several weeks, an eight-member management committee reviews these materials and checks out the nominees. Members of the committee who are not in a candidate's division grill department heads and other partners about the candidate's qualifications and then report back. Candidates themselves are never interviewed. In fact, they are not even supposed to know that they are candidates. But of course they do.

After a dizzying round of management-committee summit meetings, a final "town meeting" of all current partners is held, at which the management committee presents its final list for discussion and debate—even though it is pretty clear that the committee's list is final. Following the town meeting, the partners announce the list of newly minted millionaires. In 1990, Goldman added 32 members to its exclusive club, which now numbers 148.[80]

Demotions

Employee demotions usually involve a cut in pay, status, privilege, or opportunity. They occur infrequently since they tend to be accompanied by problems of employee apathy, depression, and inefficiency that can undermine the morale of a work group. For these reasons, many managers prefer to discharge or to move employees laterally rather than demote them. In either case, careful planning, documentation, and concern for the employee should precede such moves.

What causes demotion? It could be a disciplinary action, inability of an employee to handle the requirements of a higher-level job, health problems, or changing interests (e.g., a desire to move from production to sales). Demotions also may result from structural changes, as one-time managers are recast into project leaders, technical specialists, or internal consultants by companies in the throes of reorganization. In many cases, demotion is mutually satisfactory to the organization and to the affected employee.[81]

Transfers and Relocations

Who is most likely to be transferred? A survey by the Employee Relocation Council found that the prototypical transferee is a married 37-year-old male with children. Female workers are less likely to be transferred, although this situation is changing.[82] Reduced mobility, in turn, tends to retard women's salary progression relative to that of similarly situated men.[83]

With respect to relocations, senior management sometimes faces resistance from employees. The effect of a move on a family can be profound. For the employee, relocation often means increased prestige and income. However, the costs of moving and the complications resulting from upsetting routines, losing friends, and changing schools and jobs are borne by the family. Uprooted family members often suffer from loss of credentials as well. They do not enjoy the built-in status that awaits the transferred employee at the new job; they must start from scratch. Wives may become more dependent on their husbands for social contacts (or vice versa, depending on who is transferred). Women now account for about 25 percent of corporate moves, up from 5 percent in 1980. By the year 2000, a third of transferees will be female, and one in four trailing spouses may be men. Do such moves work out? Mobil Corporation finds that a man generally will follow his wife only if she earns at least 25 percent to 40 percent a year more than he does.[84]

There is one bright side to all of this, however. Research has shown that transfers produce little short-term impact on the mental or physical health of children.[85]

Transferred employees who are promoted estimate that it will take them a full 9 months to get up to speed in their new posts. Lateral transfers take an average of 7.8 months. However, the actual time taken to reach competency varies with (1) the degree of similarity between the old and new jobs and (2) the amount of support from peers and superiors at the new job.[86]

To reduce this "downtime," companies are taking some unusual steps. Thus Sprint Corporation spends up to $4000 to replace a relocated spouse's income for 60 days. That has helped transferees return to full productivity in about 3 months; previously, the process had taken 6 months. Marriott Corporation installed a computerized job-posting system that tracks its managerial vacancies nationwide. Both employees and their trailing spouses can apply for the openings.[87] In sum, personal adjustments—not problems with housing—are the biggest obstacles to relocation.[88] As an overall strategy on relocation, some companies have developed frequency standards whereby no manager can be relocated more than once in 2 years or three times in 10 years. Another firm has set up one-stop rotational programs at its larger facilities to replace what used to be four stints of 6 months each at different plants over a 2-year training period.

The financial implications of relocation are another major consideration. In 1970, most relocation programs consisted of a few cost categories: house-hunting trips, the shipment of household goods, temporary living expenses at the new location, and often 1 month's salary bonus to cover other incidentals. In the 1990s, typical relocation expenses and services included all those offered in 1970 plus ongoing cost-of-living differentials; mortgage interest differentials; home-disposal and home-finding expenses; expenses to help defray losses on home sales; real estate commissions; home purchase expenses; home maintenance, repair, and refurbishing costs; equity loans; and, for renters, lease-breaking expenses. Employees on temporary assignments often receive home-property-management expenses. All of these expenses add up. According to the Employee Relocation Council, the average cost of moving a home-owning employee is about $45,000.[89]

Organizations are well aware of these social and financial problems and in many cases they are responding by providing improved support systems to make the process easier. These include special online relocation programs, intranets, house-hunting on the Internet, and electronic data interchange (EDI) that lets relocation professionals keep track of every detail of every move.[90]

Layoffs, Retirements, and Resignations

These all involve employees moving *out* of the organization.

Layoffs. How safe is my job? For many people, that is the issue of the late 1990s. It is becoming clear that corporate cutbacks were not an oddity of the 1980s and 1990s, but rather are likely to persist.[91]

Involuntary layoffs are never pleasant, and management policies must consider the impacts on those who leave, on those who stay, on the local community, and on the company. For laid-off workers, efforts should be directed toward a rapid, successful, and orderly career transition.[92] How long does it take on average to find a new job? While it depends a great deal on the amount of effort put into the job search, a rough rule of thumb for managers is 1 month for every $10,000 in salary.[93] Firms should emphasize outplacement programs that help laid-off employees deal with the psychological stages of career transition (anger, grief, depression, family stress), assess individual strengths and weaknesses, and develop support networks.[94]

Termination is a traumatic experience. Egos are shattered, and employees may become bitter and angry. Family problems may also occur because of the added emotional and financial strain.[95] It is important that those who remain retain the highest level of loyalty, trust, teamwork, motivation, and productivity possible. This does not just happen—and unless there is a good deal of face-to-face, candid, open communication between senior management and "survivors," it probably will not happen. Layoff policies should consider the company's reputation and image within the community, in addition to the impact of the layoff on the local economy and social service agencies. Although layoffs are intended to reduce costs, some costs may in fact increase, as noted in the following table:

Direct costs	Indirect costs
Severance pay, pay in lieu of notice	Recruiting and employment cost of new hires
Accrued vacation and sick pay	Training and retraining
Supplemental unemployment benefits	Increase in unemployment tax rate
Outplacement	Potential charges of unfair discrimination
Pension and benefit payoffs	Low morale among remaining employees
Administrative processing costs	Heightened insecurity and reduced productivity

What are the options? One approach is to initiate a program of job sharing to perform the reduced workload. While no one is laid off, everyone's workweek and pay are reduced. This helps the company reduce labor costs. In an area experiencing high unemployment, it may be better to have all employees share the "misery" rather than to lay off selected ones. Some of the benefits of job sharing are as follows:[96]

- Twice as much talent and creativity is available.
- Benefits continue.
- Overtime is reduced.
- Workers retain a career orientation and the potential for upward mobility.
- It eliminates the need for training a temporary employee, for example, when one employee is sick or is on vacation, because the other can take over.

Job sharing is not without its drawbacks:[97]

- There is a lack of job continuity.
- Supervision is inconsistent.
- Accountability is not centered in one person.
- Nonsalary expenses do not decrease, because many benefits are a function of the employee, not the amount of pay.
- When workers are represented by a union, seniority is bypassed, and senior workers may resist sharing jobs.[98]

However, when Motorola reviewed job sharing at its facilities in Arizona, it found that avoiding layoffs saved an average of $1868 per employee—for a total savings of $975,000.[99]

Retirements. For selected employees, early retirement is a possible alternative to being laid off. Early retirement programs take many forms, but typically they involve partial pay stretched over several years, along with extended benefits. Early retirement programs are intended to provide incentives to terminate; they are not intended to replace regular retirement benefits.[100] Any losses in pension resulting from early retirement are usually offset by attractive incentive payments.

IMPACT OF CAREER MANAGEMENT ON PRODUCTIVITY, QUALITY OF WORK LIFE, AND THE BOTTOM LINE

From first job effects through midcareer transition to preretirement counseling, career management has a direct bearing on productivity, quality of work life, and the bottom line. It is precisely because organizations are sensitive to these concerns that career management activities have become as popular as they are. The saying "organizations have many jobs, but individuals have only one career" is as true today as it ever was. While organizations find themselves in worldwide competition, most individuals are striving for achievement, recognition, personal growth, and "the good life." Unless careers are managed actively by both individuals and organizations, neither can achieve their goals.

For example, in 1988, IBM offered workers at its Boca Raton, Florida, plant a voluntary severance program that included up to 2 years' pay, with benefits, plus a $25,000 bonus. In 1990, Digital Equipment offered thousands of workers voluntary severance packages of between 40 weeks and 2 years of pay, plus benefits. Those kinds of packages are disappearing fast. In the mid-1990s, for example, IBM gave departing employees a maximum of 26 weeks of pay plus 6 months of medical coverage.[101]

Yet some voluntary severance and early retirement programs backfire. Both Kodak and IBM lost skilled, senior-level employees in past cutbacks. To overcome that problem, the firms targeted subsequent programs to specific groups of employees, such as those in manufacturing and in some administrative jobs.[102] The keys to success are to *identify, before the incentives are offered, exactly which jobs are targeted for attrition and to understand the needs of the employees targeted to leave.*

Since mandatory retirement at a specified age can no longer be required legally, most employees will choose their own times to retire. More of them are choosing to retire earlier than age 65. In 1948, for example, 50 percent of males and 9 percent of females continued to work past the age of 65. By 2005, those numbers are expected to drop to 16 percent and 8 percent, respectively.[103]

Research indicates that both personal and situational factors affect retirement decisions. Personally, individuals with type A behavior patterns (hard-driving, aggressive, impatient) are less likely to prefer to retire, while those with obsolete job skills, chronic health problems, and sufficient financial resources are more likely to retire. Situationally, employees are more likely to retire to the extent that they have reached their occupational goals, that their jobs have undesirable characteristics, that home life is seen as preferable to work life, and that there are attractive alternative (leisure) activities.[104]

While retirement is certainly attractive to some, many retirees are returning to the workforce. In fact, retirees are the fastest-growing part of the temporary workforce. Many are bored with retirement, have high energy levels, and can maintain flexible schedules.[105] Others need the money, and they need health benefits to compensate for those they have lost. Many want in retirement what they do not currently have: *balance.* They want what aging

IMPLICATIONS FOR MANAGEMENT PRACTICE

To profit from current workforce trends, managers should consider taking the following steps:

- Develop explicit policies to attract and retain dual-career couples.
- Plan for more effective use of "plateaued" workers as well as those who are in midcareer transitions.
- Educate other managers and workers in the facts about older workers; where possible, hire older workers for full-time or part-time work.
- Commit to broadening career opportunities for women and members of protected groups.

experts now call a *blended life course*—an ongoing mix of work, leisure, and education.[106]

Resignations. Resignation, or voluntary worker turnover, has been increasing steadily over the past 15 years, particularly among white-collar and professional workers.[107] Employees who resign should avoid burning their bridges behind them, leaving anger and resentment in their wake; instead, they should leave gracefully and responsibly, stressing the value of their experience in the company.

SELF-RELIANCE: KEY TO CAREER MANAGEMENT FOR THE TWENTY-FIRST CENTURY

Human Resource Management in Action: Conclusion

Corporate career management programs often include one or more of the following support mechanisms:

Self-assessment. The goal of self-assessment is to help employees focus on appropriate career goals. For example, Career Architect is a deck of 67 skills cards that each employee sorts into three piles: greatest strengths, strengths, and weaknesses. The system, also available in software form, helps employees walk themselves through the difficult and sometimes emotional process of assessing their own skills—for example, dealing with new technology or working in teams. It is a process of identifying and calibrating one's professional aptitudes and capabilities and of identifying improvements that will enhance one's career growth. As we saw in the Hewlett-Packard example, that company has pioneered in offering self-assessment training to its employees at all levels.

Career planning. Bell Atlantic uses the results of Career Architect to chart the skills the company most needs for future business and to forge career development plans for its high-potential managers. Royal Insurance created a series of success profiles for important jobs using the cards.[108] The companies then teach employees how to plan their career growth once they have determined where they want to go. Employees learn what they need as well as how to "read" the corporate environment and to become savvy about how to get ahead in their own companies.

Supervisory training. Employees frequently turn first to their immediate supervisors for help with career management. At Sikorsky Aircraft, for example, supervisors are taught how to provide relevant information and to question the logic of each employee's career plans, but not to give specific career advice. Giving advice relieves the employee of responsibility for managing his or her own career.

Succession planning. Simply designating replacements for key managers and executives is no guarantee that those replacements will be ready when needed. Enlightened companies are adopting an approach to succession planning that is consistent with the concept of career self-management. They develop their employees broadly to prepare them for any of several positions that may become available. As business needs change, broadly developed people can be moved into positions that are critical to the success of the business.

The practice of making career self-management part of the corporate culture has spread rapidly over the past several years. Companies are using this approach to build a significant competitive advantage. Given today's turbulent, sometimes convulsive corporate environments, along with workers who seek greater control over their own destinies, it may be the only approach that can succeed over the long term.

SUMMARY

A career is a sequence of positions occupied by a person during the course of a lifetime. Career planning is important because the consequences of career success or failure are closely linked to an individual's self-concept and identity, as well as to career and life satisfaction. This chapter addresses career management from three perspectives. The first is that of individuals focusing on themselves: self-management of one's own career, establishment of career objectives, and dual-career couples. The second perspective is that of organizations focusing on individuals: that is, managing individuals during early career (organizational entry, impact of the first job); midcareer, including strategies for coping with midlife transitions and "plateaued" workers; and late career (age 50 and over) stages. We considered the implications of each of these stages for human resource management. Finally, a third perspective is that of organizations focusing on their own maintenance and growth. This requires the development of career management systems based on career paths defined in terms of employee behaviors. It involves the management of patterns of career movement up, down, over, and out.

DISCUSSION QUESTIONS

9-1 Why is the design of one's first permanent job so important?
9-2 What practical steps can you suggest to minimize midcareer crises?
9-3 How can an organization avoid the problems associated with older workers' clogging the career paths of younger workers?
9-4 Discuss the special problems faced by dual-career couples.

9-5 Working in small groups, develop a corporate policy that specifies how training, performance appraisal, and reward systems might integrate career planning considerations.

APPLYING YOUR KNOWLEDGE

Self-Assessment and Career Planning — *Exercise 9-1*

Awareness of both the job market and your own strengths, weaknesses, needs, and desires is required to make an effective career choice. This exercise focuses on the second part of the equation: personal traits, interests, needs, and aspirations as they relate to the choice of a career. Professionally developed interest inventories and personality tests can help in this diagnosis. They are usually available through college placement offices.

Following are three exercises designed to help you discover how your personal characteristics relate to your career choices. A sample self-assessment exercise is followed by an exercise providing guidelines for discussing and evaluating answers to the self-assessment questions. The final exercise provides additional ways to examine self-perceptions and interests.

A. Self-Assessment

An approach that has proved useful is that of answering a series of probing questions. A list of typical questions is provided below. Answer them as honestly as you can.

1. List five words that describe my personality best (not roles such as student, husband, daughter).
   a.
   b.
   c.
   d.
   e.
2. Who am I? List five statements that answer this question.
   a.
   b.
   c.
   d.
   e.
3. My best childhood memory is:
4. The single achievement in my life of which I am most proud is:
5. The type of people I like best are:
6. When I have 15 minutes to do anything I want, I most enjoy:
7. When I think about making changes, I feel:
8. My overriding goal in life is to:
9. My greatest strengths in the following work-related areas are (list specific strengths):
   a. Intellectual abilities
   b. Social skills
   c. Leadership skills
   d. Communication skills
10. My greatest weaknesses in the following work-related areas are (list specific weaknesses):
    a. Intellectual abilities

b. Social skills
c. Leadership skills
d. Communication skills

11. Ranking values. Rank the following 16 values in terms of their importance to you (1 is most important, 2 is second most important, etc.).

a. ____ Family security	i. ____ A world at peace
b. ____ Social recognition	j. ____ Self-respect
c. ____ Salvation	k. ____ True friendship
d. ____ An exciting life	l. ____ Happiness
e. ____ A world of beauty	m. ____ Equality
f. ____ Inner harmony	n. ____ Wisdom
g. ____ Mature love	o. ____ Freedom
h. ____ Accomplishment	p. ____ Pleasure

12. Ranking job outcomes. Rank the following 14 job outcomes in terms of their importance to you (1 is most important, 2 is second most important, etc.).

a. ____ Status	h. ____ Travel
b. ____ Money	i. ____ Respect
c. ____ Security	j. ____ Flexible hours
d. ____ Variety	k. ____ Working conditions
e. ____ Independence	l. ____ Socially important work
f. ____ Power	m. ____ Self-actualization
g. ____ Challenge	n. ____ Achievement

13. Life line. Draw a line representing your life. Use peaks and valleys to represent positive and negative periods or events in your life. Mark an "X" where you are now; then project your life line out to the end. At the end of your life line, write the epitaph that you think will best summarize your life's work.

B. Discussion and Career Planning

The class should now divide into groups of two (dyads). Each individual in turn should explain to the other what insights were gained about himself or herself from answering the questions in Part A. Then the dyads should discuss appropriate career options based on the answers. Finally, using the insights and information gained from the responses to the questions and from the discussions, each student should answer the following questions individually.

1. What are my three major career strengths?
2. What characteristics of jobs are most important to me?
3. What occupations, jobs, and types of organizations seem most suitable for me?
4. What career goals should I set for myself, both long-term and short-term?
5. What steps should I take, and by when should I take them, to accomplish these goals?

Further Exploration of Self-Perceptions and Interests

1. It is frequently helpful in career planning to get others' perspectives on you to compare with your self-perceptions. One way to do this involves interviewing one or two people who know you very well, such as a parent, spouse, or best friend. Ask them the same questions you asked yourself in Part A of this exercise. Then compare their responses with your own. What are the similarities and differences? What explains the differences?
2. Another way to get a different perspective beyond your own is to take an interest inventory. Such questionnaires typically assess your career interests according to

some underlying model of careers and compare your responses with those of individuals in a variety of career fields. Your career development office on campus should be able to administer an instrument such as the Strong Vocational Interest Inventory or the Kuder Preference Scale.

3. It is also sometimes useful to keep a 24-hour diary. For one full school day, keep track of how you spend your time. Then repeat the process for a weekend day or some other day when you do no schoolwork. What did you learn about how you like to spend your time? What does this indicate about your interests.

REFERENCES

1. Schein, E. H. (1996). Career anchors revisited: Implications for career development in the 21st century. *Academy of Management Executive*, **10**(4), 80–88.
2. Greenhaus, J. H. (1987). *Career management.* Chicago: Dryden.
3. Hall, D. T. (1996). Protean careers of the 21st century. *Academy of Management Executive*, **10**(4), 8–16. See also Nicholson, N. (1996). Career systems in crisis: Change and opportunity in the information age. *Academy of Management Executive*, **10**(4), 40–51. See also Quaintance, M. K. (1989). *Internal placement and career management.* In W. F. Cascio (ed.), *Human resource planning, employment, and placement.* Washington, DC: Bureau of National Affairs, pp. 2-200 to 2-235.
4. Lublin, J. S. (1996, Nov. 22). Texaco case causes a stir in boardrooms. *The Wall Street Journal*, pp. B1, B2.
5. Hall, D. T., & Mirvis, P. H. (1995). Careers as lifelong learning. In A. Howard (ed.), *The changing nature of work.* San Francisco: Jossey-Bass, pp. 323–361.
6. Rousseau, D. M., & Wade-Benzoni, K. A. (1995). Changing individual-organizational attachments. In A. Howard (ed.), *The changing nature of work.* San Francisco: Jossey-Bass, pp. 290–322.
7. Byrne, J. A. (1993). Belt-tightening the smart way. *Business Week, Special 1993 Bonus Issue: Enterprise*, pp. 34–38.
8. Hall & Mirvis, loc. cit.
9. Hall, loc. cit.
10. Milkovich, G. T., & Anderson, J. C. (1982). Career planning and development systems. In K. M. Rowland & G. R. Ferris (eds.), *Personnel management.* Boston: Allyn & Bacon, pp. 364–389.
11. Kleinfeld, N. R. (1996, Mar. 4). The company as family no more. *The New York Times*, pp. A1, A8–A11. See also Gutknecht, J. E., & Keys, J. B. (1993). Mergers, acquisitions, and takeovers: Maintaining morale of survivors and protecting employees. *Academy of Management Executive*, **7**(3), 26–36. See also Schweiger, D. M., & Denisi, A. S. (1991). Communication with employees following a merger: A longitudinal field experiment. *Academy of Management Journal*, **34**, 110–135.
12. Reichheld, F. F. (1996). *The loyalty effect.* Boston: Harvard Business School Press.
13. Work week (1997, Feb. 11). *The Wall Street Journal*, p. A1. See also Job mobility, American-style (1997, Jan. 27). *Business Week*, p. 20.
14. Dalton, D. R., Daily, C. M., & Kesner, I. F. (1993). Executive severance agreements: Benefit or burglary? *Academy of Management Executive*, **7**(4), 69–76.
15. Henkoff, R. (1996, Jan. 15). So, you want to change your job. *Fortune*, pp. 52–56.

16. Reichheld, op. cit. See also White, J. B., & Lublin, J. S. (1996, Sept. 27). Some companies try to rebuild loyalty. *The Wall Street Journal*, pp. B1, B2.
17. Working scared (1993, Apr. 17). *NBC News*.
18. Bolles, R. N. (1996). *The 1996 What color is your parachute?* Berkeley, CA: Ten-Speed Press. See also Henkoff, loc. cit. See also Farnham, A. (1996, Jan. 15). Casting off: Three who did it right. *Fortune*, pp. 60–64.
19. Aburdene, P. (1990, Sept.). How to think like a CEO for the 1990s. *Working Woman*, pp. 134–137.
20. Petras, K., & Petras, R. (1989). *The only job book you'll ever need.* New York: Simon & Schuster.
21. Ibid.
22. Wilhelm, W. R. (1983). Helping workers to self-manage their careers. *Personnel Administrator*, **28**(8), 83–89.
23. Laquer, M, & Dickinson, D. (1994). *Breaking out of 9 to 5.* Princeton, NJ: Peterson's. See also Shellenbarger, S. (1993, June 21). So much talk, so little action. *The Wall Street Journal*, pp. R1, R4.
24. Greenhaus, op. cit.
25. Balancing work and family (1996, Sept. 16). *Business Week*, pp. 74–80.
26. Work & family (1993, June 28). *Business Week*, pp. 80–88. See also Sekaran, U. (1986). *Dual-career families.* San Francisco: Jossey-Bass.
27. Lublin, J. S. (1993, Apr. 13). Husbands in limbo. *The Wall Street Journal*, pp. A1, A8.
28. Labor letter (1989, Apr. 11).*The Wall Street Journal*, p. A1.
29. Balancing work and family, loc. cit.
30. Flynn, G. (1995, Oct.). Deciding how to provide dependent care isn't child's play. *Personnel Journal*, pp. 92–94.
31. Asinof, L. (1996, Dec. 12). The nanny facts. *The Wall Street Journal*, p. R26.
32. Lewin, T. (1992, Oct. 5). Rise in single parenthood is reshaping U.S. *The New York Times*, pp. B1, B6.
33. Ritter, B. (1996, Dec.). *Work-family conflicts.* Unpublished manuscript, Graduate School of Business, University of Colorado-Denver.
34. Grover, S. L., & Crooker, K. J. (1995). Who appreciates family-responsive human resource policies: The impact of family friendly policies on the organizational attachments of parents and non-parents. *Personnel Psychology*, **48**, 271–288.
35. Trost, C. (1990, May 2). Women managers quit not for family but to advance their corporate climb. *The Wall Street Journal*, pp. B1, B8.
36. Breaugh, J. A. (1992). *Recruitment: Science and practice.* Boston: PWS-Kent.
37. Ashford, S. J., & Black, J. S. (1996). Proactivity during organizational entry: The role of desire for control. *Journal of Applied Psychology*, **81**, 199–214.
38. Whitely, W., Dougherty, T. W., & Dreher, G. F. (1991). Relationship of career mentoring and socioeconomic origin to managers' and professionals' early career progress. *Academy of Management Journal*, **34**, 331–351. See also Wilson, J. A., & Elman, N. S. (1990). Organizational benefits of mentoring. *Academy of Management Executive*, **4**(4), 88–94.
39. Rigdon, J. E. (1993, Dec. 1). You're not all alone if there's a mentor just a keyboard away. *The Wall Street Journal*, p. B1.
40. Dreher, G. F., & Cox, T. H., Jr. (1996). Race, gender, and opportunity: A study of compensation attainment and the establishment of mentoring relationships. *Journal of Applied Psychology*, **81**, 297–308. See also Whitely et al., loc. cit.
41. Chao, G. T., Walz, P. M., & Gardner, P. D. (1992). Formal and informal mentorships: A comparison of mentoring functions and contrast with nonmentored counterparts. *Personnel Psychology*, **45**, 619–636.
42. Northrup, H. R., & Malin, M. E. (1986). *Personnel policies for engineers and scientists.* Philadelphia: Industrial Research Unit, The Wharton School, University of Pennsylvania.

43. Schein, E. H. (1978). *Career dynamics: Matching individual and organizational needs.* Reading, MA: Addison-Wesley.
44. Raelin, J. A. (1983). First-job effects on career development. *Personnel Administrator,* **28**(8), 71–76, 92.
45. Forbes, J. B. (1987). Early intraorganizational mobility: Patterns and influences. *Academy of Management Journal,* **30**, 110–125.
46. Azar, B. (1996, Nov.). Project explores landscape of midlife. *Monitor,* p. 26.
47. Bell, J. E. (1982, Aug.). Mid-life transition in career men. *AMA Management Digest,* pp. 8–10.
48. Bennett, A. (1990, Sept. 11). A white-collar guide to job security. *The Wall Street Journal,* pp. B1, B12.
49. Lublin, J. S. (1993, Aug. 4). Strategic sliding: Lateral moves aren't always a mistake. *The Wall Street Journal,* p. B1. See also Rigdon, loc. cit.
50. Floyd, S. W., & Woolridge, B. (1996). *The strategic middle manager.* San Francisco: Jossey-Bass.
51. Richman, L. S. (1993, July 12). Jobs that are growing and slowing. *Fortune,* pp. 52–54.
52. Bell, loc. cit.
53. Azar, loc. cit.
54. Northrup & Malin, op. cit.
55. London, M. (1996). Redeployment and continuous learning in the 21st century: Hard lessons and positive examples from the downsizing era. *Academy of Management Executive,* **10**(4), pp. 67–79; Fierman, J. (1993, Sept. 6). Beating the midlife career crisis. *Fortune,* pp. 52–60. Ference, T. P., Stoner, J. A., & Warren, E. K. (1977). Managing the career plateau. *Academy of Management Review,* **2**, 602–612. Labor letter (1991, Feb. 19). *The Wall Street Journal,* p. A1.
56. Howard, A., & Bray, D. W. (1982, Mar. 21). AT&T: The hopes of middle managers. *The New York Times,* p. F1
57. *The aging workforce.* (1995). Washington, D.C.: American Association of Retired Persons.
58. Belous, R. S. (1991, Sept.). *Demographic currents.* Washington D.C.: National Planning Association, Occasional Paper No. 7.
59. McEvoy, G. M., & Cascio, W. F. (1989). Cumulative evidence of the relationship between employee age and job performance. *Journal of Applied Psychology,* 74, 11–20.
60. Czaja, S. J. (1995, Spring). Aging and work performance. *Review of Public Personnel Administration,* pp. 46–61. See also Sterns, H. L., & Miklos, S. M. (1995). The aging worker in a changing environment: Organizational and individual issues. *Journal of Vocational Behavior,* **47**, 248–268. See also Landy, F. J., et al. (1992, Jan.). *Alternatives to chronological age in determining standards of suitability for public safety jobs.* Report submitted to the U.S. Equal Employment Opportunity Commission, Washington, D.C.
61. Cascio, W. F. (1996). *Is age a proxy for declines in performance among workers over age 65?* Working Paper 96-09, Graduate School of Business, University of Colorado-Denver.
62. Martocchio, J. J. (1989). Age-related differences in employee absenteeism: A meta-analysis. *Psychology and Aging,* **4**, 409–414. See also Berkowitz, M. (1988). Functioning ability and job performance as workers age. In Borus, M. E., Parnes, H. S., Sandell, S. H., & Seidman, B. (eds.), *The older worker.* Madison, WI: Industrial Relations Research Association, pp. 87–114.
63. Bureau of National Affairs (1987). *Older Americans in the workforce: Challenges and solutions.* Washington, D.C.: Bureau of National Affairs.
64. Farrimond, T. (1989). Accident and illness rates for younger and older workers when employment is based on medical examination. *Psychological Reports,* **65**, 556–558.

65. American Association of Retired Persons (1993a). *America's changing work force.* Washington, D.C.: Author.
66. New study cracks myth about the costs of older workers. (1995). *Working Age,* **11**(4), 2, 3. See also Bureau of National Affairs, loc. cit.
67. *The aging workforce,* op. cit. See also American Association of Retired Persons (1993b). *The older workforce: Recruitment and retention.* Washington, D.C.: Author.
68. Solomon, J., & Fuchsberg, G. (1990, Jan. 26). Great number of older Americans seem ready to work. *The Wall Street Journal,* p. B1. See also Brooks, A. (1985, Dec. 2). Quitting a job gracefully. *The New York Times,* p. B12.
69. More retirees choose to work (1989, Sept. 7). *The New York Times,* p. C13.
70. Lefkovich, J. L. (1992). Older workers: Why and how to capitalize on their powers. *Employment Relations Today,* **19**(1), 63–79.
71. Paul, R. J., & Townsend, J. B. (1993). Managing the older worker—Don't just rinse away the gray. *Academy of Management Executive,* **7**(3), 67–74. See also Labich, K. (1993, Mar. 8). The new unemployed. *Fortune,* pp. 40–49.
72. Simon, R. (1996, July). "Too damn old." *Money,* pp. 118–126. See also *Vitality for life: Psychological research for productive aging* (1993). Washington, D.C.: American Psychological Association.
73. Simon, loc. cit. See also Bird, C. P., & Fisher, T. D. (1986). Thirty years later: Attitudes toward the employment of older workers. *Journal of Applied Psychology,* **71**, 315–317.
74. New study cracks myth about the costs of older workers, loc. cit.
75. Hirsch, J. S. (1990, Feb. 26). Older workers chafe under younger managers. *The Wall Street Journal,* pp. B1, B6.
76. Walker, J. W. (1992). *Human resource strategy.* New York: McGraw-Hill.
77. Quaintance, loc. cit.
78. Stumpf, S. A., & London, M. (1981). Management promotions: Individual and organizational factors influencing the decision process. *Academy of Management Review,* **6**, 539–549.
79. Schwarzwald, J., Koslowsky, M., & Shalit, B. (1992). A field study of employees' attitudes and behaviors after promotion decisions. *Journal of Applied Psychology,* **77**, 511–514.
80. Power, W., & Siconolfi, M. (1990, Oct. 19). Who will be rich? How Goldman, Sachs chooses new partners: With a lot of angst. *The Wall Street Journal,* pp. A1, A8.
81. Lancaster, H. (1996, Nov. 19). A demotion does not have to mean the end of a fulfilling career. *The Wall Street Journal,* p. B1.
82. Auerbach, J. (1996, April 5). Executive relocations—and hassles—increase. *The Wall Street Journal,* p. B8.
83. Stroh, L. K., Brett, J. M., & Reilly, A. H. (1992). All the right stuff: A comparison of female and male managers' career progression. *Journal of Applied Psychology,* **77**, 251–260.
84. Lublin, 1993, Apr. 13, loc. cit.
85. Labor letter (1989, Nov. 17). *The Wall Street Journal,* p. A1.
86. Pinder, C. C., & Schroeder, K. G. (1987). Time to proficiency following job transfers. *Academy of Management Journal,* **30**, 336–353.
87. Lublin, 1993, Apr. 13, loc. cit.
88. Driessnack, C. H. (1987). Spouse relocation: A moving experience. *Personnel Administrator,* **32**(8), 94–102.
89. Auerbach, loc. cit.
90. Mumma, J. S. (1996, Oct.). New technologies speed relocation process. *HRMagazine,* pp. 55–60.
91. Uchitelle, L., & Kleinfeld, N. R. (1996, Mar. 3). On the battlefields of business, millions of casualties. *The New York Times,* pp. 1, 14–17. See also Sanger, D. E., & Lohr, S. (1995, Mar. 9). A search for answers to avoid the layoffs. *The New York Times,* pp. 1, 10–12.

92. Bragg, R. (1996, Mar. 5). Big holes where the dignity used to be. *The New York Times*, pp. 1, 8–10. See also, Rimer, S. (1996, Mar. 6). A hometown feels less like home. *The New York Times*, pp. 1, 8–10. See also Kozlowski, S. W. J., Chao, G. T., Smith, E. M., & Hedlund, J. (1993). Organizational downsizing: Strategies, interventions, and research implications. *International Review of Industrial and Organizational Psychology*, **8**, 263–332.
93. The higher the pay, the longer the job hunt (1989, Dec. 15). *The Wall Street Journal*, p. B1.
94. Knowdell, R. L., Branstead, E., & Moravec, M. (1994). *From downsizing to recovery.* Palo Alto, CA: Consulting Psychologists Press. See also Collarelli, S. M., & Beehr, T. A. (1993). Selection out: Firings, layoffs, and retirement. In N. Schmitt & W. C. Borman (eds.), *Personnel selection in organizations.* San Francisco: Jossey-Bass, pp. 341–384. See also Sweet, D. H. (1989). Outplacement. In W. F. Cascio (ed.), *Human resource planning, employment, and placement.* Washington, DC: Bureau of National Affairs, pp. 2-236 to 2-261.
95. Leana, C. R. (1996, Apr. 14). Why downsizing won't work. *Chicago Tribune Magazine*, pp. 15–18.
96. Sheley, E. (1996, Jan.). Job-sharing offers unique challenges. *HRMagazine*, pp. 46–49.
97. Solomon, C. M. (1994, Sept.). Job-sharing: One job, double headache? *Personnel Journal*, pp. 88–93.
98. Noble, K. B. (1990, Mar. 15). Union experiment provokes a fight. *The New York Times*, pp. A1, B20.
99. Labor letter (1986, Apr. 1). *The Wall Street Journal*, p. A1.
100. Damato, K. (1995, Apr. 14). Retire with the biggest pension check you can get. *The Wall Street Journal*, p. C1.
101. Lopez, J. A. (1993, Oct. 25). Out in the cold: Many early retirees find the good deals not so good after all. *The Wall Street Journal*, pp. A1, A4.
102. Take the money and run—or take your chances (1993, Aug. 16). *Business Week*, pp. 28, 29.
103. American Association of Retired Persons, 1993a, op. cit.
104. Greene, M. S. (1992). *Retirement: A new beginning.* St. John's, Newfoundland, Canada: Jesperson Press.
105. Andrews, E. S. (1992). Expanding opportunities for older workers. *Journal of Labor Research*, **13**(1), 55–65.
106. Morris, B. (1996, Aug. 19). The future of retirement. *Fortune*, pp. 86–94.
107. Take the money and run—or take your chances, loc. cit.
108. Lancaster, H. (1995, Aug. 29). Professionals try new way to assess and develop skills. *The Wall Street Journal*, p. B1.

CASE IN THE NEWS

The New Factory Worker

By Stephen Baker
Larry Armstrong

Today, life on the line requires more brains than brawn—so laborers are heading for the classroom.

Fred Price gropes his way downstairs in the dark, grabs a Danish, and races off to work at 4 A.M. Today is a special day for the 29-year-old North Carolina factory hand. On the job, he will schedule orders as usual for the tiny tool-and-die shop where he doubles as a supervisor when he's not bending metal himself. But at midday, test results are coming in from the state Labor Dept. in Raleigh. These aptitude exams for all 43 workers at Northeast Tool & Manufacturing Co., outside Charlotte, measure everything from math and mechanical skills to leadership and adaptability. And they come with a prescription. Now it appears that Price will have to pull back from the bird hunting a little and spend less time with the kids' go-cart. Like tens of thousands of factory workers across America, Fred Price is going back to school.

FRED PRICE Northeast Tool, *Charlotte, N.C.:* Part supervisor, part metal worker, Price is aiming for a two-year degree in metallurgy. "Someday," he says, "I hope to manage the plant."

Growing up, Price liked to work with his hands more than his head. He would help his father fix the family's old Ford pickup, and once they rigged up a hydraulic log-splitter. In high school, he excelled in shop class but sat toward the back in English and math. These days, in an economy where even factory work increasingly is defined by blips on a computer screen, more schooling is the only road ahead. Northeast Tool, for one, will use the employee tests over the next several months to develop customized training for each worker. Some will enroll at a nearby community college. Others will take remote courses through computers set up at the plant. A few will attend afternoon classes with professors brought right into the mill. Price wants to pursue a two-year degree in metallurgy, even if it means putting in long hours on weekends. "Someday I hope to manage the plant," he says.

Until recently, Americans often divided ranks in high school between shop kids such as Price, who went on to industrial or service work, and college-bound students headed for white-collar professional jobs. They parted ways at graduation and would move into distinct categories of manual and knowledge workers.

In the Loop

But over the past decade, thinned-out ranks of managers have been equipping factory workers with industrial robots and teaching them to use computer controls to operate massive steel casters and stamp presses. At the same time, managers are funneling reams of information through the computers, bringing employees into the data loop. Workers are trained to watch inventories, to know suppliers and customers, costs and prices. Knowledge that long separated brain workers from hand workers is now available via computer on the factory floor. At Northeast Tool, Rusty Arant, Fred Price's manager, points to a powerful computer he rigged up to a milling machine and says: "I crammed it with memory because I want these guys to be managing the business from the shop floor."

The trend toward high-skills manufacturing began in the mid-1980s with innovative companies such as Corning, Motorola, and Xerox. They replaced rote assembly-line work with an industrial vision that requires skilled and nimble workers to think while they work. In the 1990s, what was once the industrial avant-garde is now mainstream as its practices spread across the manufacturing sector. Large, old-line companies finally are learning the lesson that investments in training boost productivity, often at less cost than capital investments. And as the big guys push suppliers and subcontractors on quality, price, and just-in-time delivery, even little shops such as Northeast Tool see high skills as essential for competition.

The result is an intensifying transformation of the American factory, The ranks of manufacturers that put a majority of their workers through different types of training have doubled or tripled in the past decade, according to surveys of large companies by the University of California's Center for Effective Organizations. At the same time, the share of the country's 19 million factory workers with a year or two of college has jumped to 25% vs. 17% in 1985, according to the Bureau of Labor Statistics. An additional 19% have college diplomas today, up from 16% a decade ago. "There's a real rise in companies' willingness to invest in their workforces," says Pamela J. Tate, president of the Council for Adult & Experiential Learning, a Chicago consulting group.

This investment, though, carries a none-too-subtle message for America's manufacturing workers: hone your skills or risk being left behind. U.S. workers are being pushed to raise their technical savvy to the level of the best Japanese and German workers. At the same time, many are being asked to develop leadership skills and to take a role in managing that 's rare in the top-down structures found in Asia and Europe.

Indeed, the old formula of company loyalty, a strong back, and showing up on time no longer guarantees job security, or even a decent paycheck. Today, industrial workers will thrive only if they use their wits and keep adding to their skills base. It's a rich irony: Millions of Americans who headed for the factory because they didn't like school, among other reasons, are now faced with a career-long dose of it. "It isn't whether you can hoist 100-pound sacks anymore," says Anthony Carnevale, a training expert at Educational Testing Service in Princeton, N.J. "Most of the work is mental."

Demanding as it is, the high-skills factory represents blue-collar America's best hope for retaining high wages in a world teeming with workers. Across the economy, in manufacturing and services alike, there has been a surge in demand for higher skills as employers reorganize work around new technologies and human capital-investments. Recently, the pressure for more capable workers has even begun to generate skills shortages in pockets around the country.

Skills Gap

But many companies still need to catch up: Only 10% to 20% of large companies have adopted high-performance techniques, surveys show, including a third of large manufacturers, according to the National Association of Manufacturers. Others are actually going in the opposite direction. In industries as diverse as apparel making, telemarketing, and chicken processing, many employers continue to slice pay, avoid unions, and outsource work to lower-wage subcontractors. These trends have led to a growing inequality along skill and education lines, similar to the one cleaving society at large. So far, the net result has weighed more heavily downward, even in manufacturing, where average pay lagged inflation by 3% from 1989 to 1995, according to the BLS.

In this cutthroat environment, an individual worker's best chance of getting ahead now lies in advancing his or her skills whenever the opportunity arises. And plenty of workers are jumping at the chance. From downsized defense-industry hands in Long Beach, Calif., to white-smocked pharmaceutical workers in the Delaware Valley, they are studying for new factory jobs.

JOHN WARNER Acme Metals, *Chicago:* When steelmaker Acme saw a need for more skilled workers, Warner, a pipe fitter, jumped at the chance. Now he's studying to be a maintenance technician.

This even includes veterans in old-line smokestack companies. Take Adlai John Warner, 44, who put in 25 years at Acme Metals Inc., a specialty steelmaker outside Chicago. Warner always enjoyed learning and was quick with facts—quick enough to be given top security clearance as a U.S. Marine intelligence specialist in Vietnam. He had planned to attend college when he returned to Chicago after the war. Instead, he started a family and wound up making good money as a laborer at Acme.

No-Brainer

Warner found the work tedious. Acme, like most other manufacturers, was organized for a low-skilled force and used Warner's body but not much of his brain. Even after he jumped a few rungs on the job ladder by apprenticing as a pipe fitter, the work required more endurance than thought. Warner describes long empty days of sitting around, waiting for pipe-fitting jobs, making time and a half with gobs of overtime. Despite pay that eventually reached $60,000 a year, the boredom prompted Warner to pursue a bachelor's degree in psychology at night at Chicago State University in the hopes of moving into human resources. He got his BA in 1978, but it never led anywhere.

Meanwhile, the world was closing in on Acme. Low-cost minimills and foreign mills threatened its niche in super-high-carbon steel, which is used in knife blades, tools, and critical machine parts. Its old equipment was falling apart. In 1994, management launched a $400 million redesign of the mill with a high-tech German caster—an audacious move for a $560 million company. But operation of the finicky caster, which converts molten steel into a two-inch-thick band, is fast and dangerous. If workers can't make quick decisions, they risk a "breakout," when hot liquid steel spills from the mold all over the machinery. To date, only minimill leader Nucor Corp. and its offspring, Steel Dynamics Inc., with skilled and flexible workforces, have made money with the new technology.

In effect, Acme is betting the company on its workers' brains—and Warner has leaped at the opportunity. Last year, the company brought in scads of consultants to test those who volunteered among its 1,100 unionized ranks. They used an exhaustive battery of exams to look for reading, math, technical, and communication skills. Some workers weren't interested and took early retirement. About 750 were chosen to create an entirely new, team-oriented system. Warner qualified for an advanced job as a maintenance technician and last September promptly hit the books.

Acme set up classroom trailers next to the mill and brought in teachers from Detroit, Georgia, even Germany. The company paid Warner and 130 others to spend nine months, full-time, learning everything from metallurgy, math, and computers to a piece-by-piece study of the new machinery. The total cost to upgrade the workforce, including employee salaries, came to some $8 million, or just 2% of the amount Acme spent on the new caster. "We're being exposed to things we've never been exposed to before," says Warner appreciatively.

New Standards

Warner and his colleagues also are involved in reinventing Acme's entire work system. In the spring, he and five other workers were selected to sit down with managers and consultants for weeks on end at the nearby Ramada Inn. There, they hung poster paper all over the walls and blackboards, marking up a scheme for the new workplace, from devising a pay system pegged to profits to redefining supervisors' roles. "The people working there have to make the decisions," says Anthony C. Capito, Acme's vice-president for steel production. The new system, including the training received by Warner and his colleagues, will be put to the test when the new caster is brought on line this fall.

Workers at small manufacturers are facing similar tests. In 1985, when the then 18-year-old Fred Price landed his job at Northeast Tool, the job shop sold custom-made metal pieces primarily to local Carolina customers. Today, as regional markets meld into national and global ones, Northeast must boost quality enough to land contracts from the likes of BMW and Siemens. These companies want metal fashioned to precise tolerances that only statistical quality-control methods can achieve. Many demand that suppliers be certified to tough European standards, a goal Northeast is pursuing.

All this requires more training than Price, a high school graduate, had gained through work experience. For him, the payoff comes in getting a shot at advancement and improving his $15-an-hour pay. From manager Arant's perspective, there's no choice at all. Arant plans to use his higher-skilled workforce to bid for more lucrative business and expand. If he didn't, Northeast could fall behind, as Arant thinks some rivals may do. "They'll run the machines as long as they can and then close," he predicts.

Opportunity Costs

Until recently, workers such as Price probably would have been out of luck. Northeast, a flyspeck of a company with annual revenues of less than $5 million, simply wouldn't have had the wherewithal to launch its ambitious training program. And many companies, large and small, were loath to invest too much in workers, only to lose them later. Now, though, more companies feel they can't afford not to train. And Northeast, like other small companies, has been able to tap into a growing network of local and state training initiatives. Often, these are cobbled together with regional or state development funds and community-college training programs.

As a result, Northeast is spending just $35,000 for its entire training plan. North Carolina has set up programs to assist small companies, helped out with staff advice, software, and access to the nearby community college. Such state programs are growing fast. "If we don't invest in higher skills, we relegate ourselves to low-wage jobs," says Eric Butler, president of Bay States Skills Corp., which coordinates training programs in Boston.

The education message rings so loudly today that some job-seekers actually target high-performance employers just to get the schooling. In fact, in the post-cold-war era, such companies are replacing the military as a blue-collar training ground as a way to get some college education, or its equivalent, inexpensively. Many companies are willing to sink money into training if they feel confident the employee has the profile of a lifelong learner. "We look for people who want change, who don't see it as troublesome, but as an opportunity," says David P. Jones, an official of Aon Consulting, a Chicago firm that assists manufacturers in testing and hiring.

RACHELLE COOK, Medrad, *Pittsburgh:* Cook took a job at the medical-equipment maker because she heard it invested in its workers—and last year, managers chose her for a career-development program.

Rachelle Cook, 36, fits that description. Cook worked at a Pittsburgh nursing home for six years while she pursued an associate degree at Westmoreland County Community College. But to get anywhere in nursing, she says, requires at least a four-year degree, and the mother of two was having enough trouble freeing up study time after work. So in 1992, when a friend told her that Medrad Inc., a Pittsburgh medical-equipment maker, invested in its workers, she applied for a job.

Medrad didn't seem at all promising at first. Cook found herself working as a temp, up all night assembling syringes, and making less than $10 per hour. "Everyone could see I was miserable," she recalls. "Working that shift, I had no life." But she had good communications skills and loads of ambition. She applied for every job she saw posted.

Gung Ho

Fortunately, Medrad was instituting teams in its 250-employee factory and giving workers more say in how their jobs are done. Cook was part of a pilot project that offered courses in conflict resolution, problem solving, and customer and supplier relations. A few times, the team stayed up all night debating how to reorganize manufacturing and quality-control systems.

Cook excelled, primarily because of a gung ho attitude and her sense of teamwork. The result: Last year, company managers selected her for a career development program. Now, she fills in as a substitute to learn different jobs and takes a slew of in-house computer courses. Once a week, she commutes into downtown Pittsburgh for a Dale Carnegie course on public speaking. When she's done in a year or two, Medrad will place her in a higher-paying job that best uses her abilities—possibly as a trainer or a customer service supervisor.

Unfortunately, plenty of the most flexible factory workers wind up running in place. Or worse, they take on new responsibilities and get a pay cut for their trouble. That's Phil Waccary's problem. In 1992, defense cuts prompted Allied Signal Inc. to shutter the aerospace plant in Torrance, Calif., where he had earned $19 an hour as a supervisor. Waccary found part-time jobs driving freight trucks and loading planes for a United Parcel Service Inc. subcontractor. Next came a full-time post in a shipping and receiving department. But none paid close to what he had made building medical instruments for Hewlett-Packard, F-18 fighters for Northrop Grumman, and aircraft parts for Allied.

So Waccary took a monthlong federally funded course that teaches job-seekers how to write résumés and start businesses. But a host of job interviews led to nothing with much promise. He suspected that part of the problem may have been his age, 57. Then, finally, in 1994, Waccary won a spot on the graveyard shift at Kinetic Parts Manufacturing Inc., a high-tech auto parts factory in Harbor City.

PHIL WACCARY Kinetic Parts Manufacturing, *Harbor City, Calif.:* Waccary, a former defense industry worker, has gotten plenty of training at auto-parts maker Kinetic, but his wages remain low.

The plant was opened that year by Autospecialty, a privately owned, $75 million importer of brake parts. Autospecialty had gone into manufacturing after industry consolidation left it chronically short of critical parts. The company's founders traversed the globe to study brake manufacturing and designed a high-tech plant based on heavy training and job rotation.

"Starting Over"

But while Kinetic is high-performance, it's not exactly high-wage. It set up shop in the Southern California town and hired lots of laid-off defense and aerospace workers such as Waccary for $9 an hour. By now, Waccary has gone through the same kind of extensive training that has helped Price, Warner, and Cook. Armed with state funds, Kinetic paid him and other new hires to put in a month of eight-hour days learning basic math, algebra, and blueprint reading with instructors from nearby El Camino College.

The company also has given Waccary and his fellow employees doses of upgrade training on the job, including more math, supervisory skills, office automation, and computer-aided design. Now, Kinetic is setting up classes for total quality management and statistical process control.

But fierce competition from the Chinese has left Kinetic barely profitable so far. And even though recent U.S. trade threats against China for dumping brake parts has the company mulling a major expansion, Waccary is not likely ever to come close to his old wage. So far, he has received only a 50¢-an-hour raise for the training he has gone through. "No one in this building can take pride in their salaries," concedes Kinetic plant manager Stephen J. Ruiz. Says Waccary: "I feel like I'm starting over again. But I'm not sure I have any other choice."

The same could be said for many other blue-collar Americans. To earn a higher paycheck or save their jobs from rivals abroad, U.S. factory workers are under the gun to add value. This relentless atmosphere is far less forgiving than the seniority-based assembly line it replaces. But talk to these men and women about their work, their class load, the software they have to reconfigure, or the inventory that should show up in, oh, three minutes, and many seem happy for the chance to stake out a new path. Most realize that they're helping to carry U.S. industry. This time, though, it's not on their shoulders, but with their heads.

By Stephen Baker in Pittsburgh, with Larry Armstrong in Los Angeles

YOUR LOCAL CAMPUS: TRAINING GROUND ZERO

The six guys clustered around a transmission hardly look like state-of-the-art high-skilled workers. Yet these students are toiling at a potent nexus of academia and business. They're ripping apart General Motors Corp. cars with sophisticated GM equipment, working toward associate degrees at Gateway

Community-Technical College—and to careers as technicians of GM-made natural-gas-powered cars.

Over the past seven years, GM has donated $2 million of equipment and 75 demonstration cars to the college's North Haven (Conn.) campus. And when the auto maker started investing in alternative-powered cars, Gateway sought out a federal grant to run its technician training. "Satisfying the needs of the community is one of our goals, but now we're finding this other [business] market, and we're pushing the envelope to get into it," says Roy C. Francis, coordinator of the auto program at Gateway.

Welcome Business

In accepting his party's renomination Aug. 29 in Chicago, President Bill Clinton vowed to "make the typical community-college education available to every American"—with, among other proposals, a $1,500-a-year tuition tax credit. The pledge acknowledged a new reality: Community colleges, long the humble stepsisters of U.S. higher education, are in demand.

"In the past, community colleges didn't seem to have that strong an interest in working with [companies], and we weren't that easy to work with," says Stan Horner, senior manager of training and education at chipmaker AMD. These days, though, community colleges are awash in corporate contracts. With government funding dwindling and their full-time student base stagnating, the institutions welcome the business. Local governments see the programs as engines for business development. Employers, meanwhile, have discovered that the colleges are better at most sorts of training—and cheaper, too.

Community colleges were born after World War II, and they multiplied through the 1960s and 1970s. Today, some 5 million students are enrolled in degree programs, paying average tuition of $1,492. But deeper ties with business and industry "are the future of the community-college movement," says George Baker, who studies community colleges at North Carolina State University in Raleigh. "Business and industry have to have training because technology is changing so rapidly," he says. Massive restructuring, moreover, has left thousands of displaced workers in need of new skills.

In the Chips

Look at Austin Community College (ACC) in Texas. A sleepy 1,800-student two-year institution when it opened in 1973, it now serves 26,000 for-credit students. On top of that, 18,000 employees get training through $2.7 million in annual contracts with local businesses such as AMD. The chipmaker gave the college $400,000 in equipment; ACC, which already had worked with AMD and other technology companies to create programs for semiconductor manufacturing technicians, put in $2 million. The result: a new facility that ultimately could train up to 350 chip workers a year.

Most contracts are more modest, lasting less than three months and costing under $10,000—far less than companies typically would pay elsewhere. In Pittsfield, Mass., papermaker Crane & Co. pays Berkshire Community College an average of $400 per student, a fraction of the $1,500 it once spent on commercial courses. "Because we do it every day, we think we can be more cost-effective," says Robert J. Kopecek, president of Northampton Community College in Bethlehem, Pa. That's compelling logic—for employers and colleges alike.

Community Colleges Go Corporate

Training partnerships between community colleges and corporate employers are growing:

Sematech
The semiconductor industry association is working with Maricopa Community Colleges in Phoenix to develop a national curriculum for training entry-level manufacturing technicians.

Pennsylvania Power & Light
The utility has created a technology demonstration center with Northampton Community College in Bethlehem, Pa., to test-run new developments.

Aegon US
In Cedar Rapids, Iowa, the insurer built a $10 million corporate data center at Kirkwood Community College, to be shared by company employees and college students.

GM
With Toyota, it has donated equipment to laboratories at Gateway Community-Technical College in North Haven, Conn., to prepare service technicians for work at area dealerships. GM has similar programs at more than 50 other schools.

By Susan Jackson in North Haven, Conn.

Discussion Questions

1. Develop a menu of options for a small business that wants to provide regular training opportunities for its employees.
2. If a company was interested in using training as a recruitment and retention tool, how should it communicate that in multiple ways to current employees and job applicants? Develop a persuasive message that encourages employees and applicants to buy in.
3. Develop a set of interview questions to help screen prospective factory employees for their interest in pursuing career-long training opportunities.

PART 4

COMPENSATION

Compensation, which includes direct cash payments, indirect payments in the form of employee benefits, and incentives to motivate employees to strive for higher levels of productivity, is a critical component of the employment relationship. Compensation is affected by forces as diverse as labor market factors, collective bargaining, government legislation, and top management's philosophy regarding pay and benefits. This is a dynamic area, and Chapters 10 and 11 present the latest developments in compensation theory and examples of company practices. Chapter 10 is a nontechnical introduction to the subject of pay and incentive systems; Chapter 11 focuses on employee benefits. You will find that the material in both chapters has direct implications for sound management practice.

10 PAY AND INCENTIVE SYSTEMS

Questions This Chapter Will Help Managers Answer

1. How can we tie compensation strategy to general business strategy?
2. What economic and legal factors should be considered in establishing pay levels for different jobs?
3. What is the best way to develop pay systems that are understandable, workable, and acceptable to employees at all levels?
4. How can we tie incentives to individual, team, or organizationwide performance?
5. In implementing a pay-for-performance system, what key traps must we avoid to make the system work as planned?

THE TRUST GAP*

Human Resource Management in Action

Among chief executive officers, three of today's most popular buzzwords are "employee involvement" and "empowerment" of employees. CEOs say, "We're a team; we're all in this together." But employees look at the difference between their pay and that of the CEOs. They also compare top management's perks—oak dining rooms and heated garages—with the conditions of their work environment—cafeterias for lower-level workers and parking spaces a half mile from the plant. And they wonder, "Is this togetherness?" As the disparity in pay widens (some heads of major U.S. companies receive compensation that is more than 200 times higher than the pay of the average American), the wonder grows. Hourly workers and supervisors indeed agree that "we're all in this together," but what they are in turns out to be a frame of mind that mistrusts senior management's intentions, doubts its competence, and resents its self-congratulatory pay. Indeed, the widening gulf has ignited a political firestorm and raised the specter of social turmoil.

Study after study, involving hundreds of companies and thousands of workers, has found evidence of a trust gap—and it is growing. Indeed, the attitudes of middle managers and professionals toward the workplace are becoming more like those of hourly workers, historically the most disaffected group.

As an example, consider American Telephone & Telegraph chief Robert E. Allen. Last year he received a $1.5 million bonus and a 10-fold increase in stock options, although AT&T barely broke even, a result of $5.4 billion in restructuring charges. Soon after, Mr. Allen announced plans to eliminate 40,000 jobs.

By contrast, Peggy McMullen, a $15-an-hour equipment operator, has moved and taken pay cuts twice since 1990 to remain employed by AT&T. Last year her "bonus" consisted of a T-shirt, a tote bag, and a week of free meals at the Reading, Pennsylvania, microelectronics plant where she works the evening shift.

To be sure, much of the trust gap can be traced to inconsistencies between what management says and what it does—between saying "people are our most important asset" and in the next breath ordering layoffs, or between sloganeering about quality while continuing to evaluate workers by how many pieces they push out the door. The result is a world in which top management thinks it is sending crucial messages, but employees never hear a word. Thus a recent survey found that 82 percent of *Fortune* 500 executives believe their corporate strategy is understood by everyone who needs to know. Unfortunately, less than a third of employees in the same companies say management provides clear goals and direction.

Confidence in top management's competence is collapsing. The days when top management could say, "Trust us; this is for your own good" are over. Employees have seen that if the company embarks on a new strategic tack and it does not work, employees—not management—are the ones who lose their jobs.

**Sources:* J. S. Lublin, The great divide, *The Wall Street Journal*, Apr. 11, 1996, pp. R1, R4; A. Farnham, The trust gap, *Fortune*, Dec. 4, 1989, pp. 56–78; Gross compensation? *Business Week*, Mar. 18, 1996, pp. 32, 33.

Michael Eisner, CEO of Disney, is one of the highest-paid CEOs in the United States.

While competence may be hard to judge, pay is known, and to the penny. The rate of increase in top management's pay split from workers' in 1979 and has rocketed upward ever since. CEOs who make 100 times the average hourly worker's pay are no longer rare. European and Japanese CEOs, who seldom earn

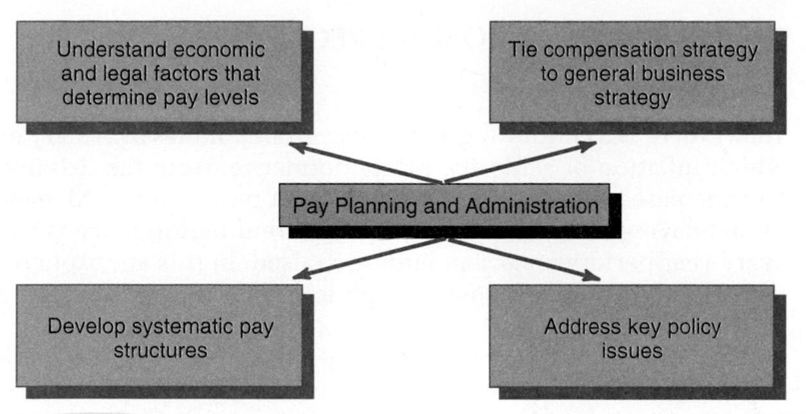

Figure 10-1
Four key challenges in planning and administering a pay system.

more than 15 times the employee average, look on in amazement. Said one observer, "The gap is widening beyond what the guy at the bottom can even understand. . . . There's very little common ground left in terms of the experience of the average worker and the CEO."

While most U.S. workers are willing to accept substantial differentials in pay between corporate top management and lower-level workers and acknowledge top-level managers should receive their just rewards, more and more of the lower-level—and the middle-level—employees are asking, "Just how just is just?"

Challenges

1. To many people, a deep-seated sense of unfairness lies at the heart of the trust gap. How might perceptions of unfairness develop?
2. What are some of the predictable consequences of a trust gap?
3. Can you suggest alternative strategies for reducing the trust gap?

The chapter opening vignette illustrates important changes in the current thinking about pay: levels of pay will always be evaluated by employees in terms of "fairness," and unless pay systems are acceptable to those affected by them, they will breed mistrust and lack of commitment. Pay policies and practices are critically important, for they affect every single employee, from the janitor to the CEO. The first part of this chapter will explore four major questions: (1) How do firms tie compensation strategy to general business strategy? (2) What economic and legal factors determine pay levels within a firm? (3) How do firms develop systematic pay structures that reflect different levels of pay for different jobs? (4) What key policy issues in pay planning and administration must managers address? These challenges are shown graphically in Figure 10-1.

We will then consider what is known about incentives at the individual, team, and organizationwide levels. As an educated worker or manager, you must become knowledgeable about these important issues. This chapter will help you develop that knowledge base.

CHANGING PHILOSOPHIES REGARDING PAY SYSTEMS

Today there is a continuing move away from policies of "salary entitlement," in which inflation or seniority, not performance, were the driving forces behind pay increases. Pay-for-performance is the new mantra. Managers are asking, "What have you done for me lately?" Current performance is what counts, and every year performance standards are raised. In this atmosphere, we are seeing three major changes in company philosophies concerning pay and benefits:

1. Increased willingness to reduce the size of the workforce and to restrict pay to control the costs of wages, salaries, and benefits.
2. Less concern with pay position relative to that of competitors and more concern with what the company can afford.
3. Implementation of programs to encourage and reward performance—thereby making pay more variable. In fact, a recent study revealed that this is one of the most critical compensation issues facing large companies today.[1]

We will consider each of these changes as well as other material, in this and the following chapter, from the perspective of the line manager, not from that of the technical compensation specialist.

Cost-Containment Actions

Given that wage and salary payments constitute about 60 percent of the costs of nonfinancial corporations, employers have an obvious interest in controlling them.[2] To do so, they are attempting to contain staff sizes, payrolls, and benefits costs. Some of the cutbacks are only temporary, such as pay freezes and postponements of raises. Other changes are meant to be permanent: firing executives or offering them early retirement; asking employees to work longer hours, to take fewer days off, and to shorten their vacations; reducing the coverage of medical plans or asking employees to pay part of the cost; trimming expense accounts, with bans on first-class travel and restrictions on phone calls and entertainment. If such a strategy is to work, however, CEOs will first need to demonstrate to employees at all levels, by means of tangible actions, that they are serious about closing the "trust gap" (see chapter opening vignette).

Paying What the Company Can Afford

To cover its labor costs and other expenses, a company must earn sufficient revenues through the sales of its products or services. It follows, then, that an employer's ability to pay is constrained by its ability to compete. The nature of the product or service markets affects a firm's external competitiveness and the pay level it sets.[3]

Key factors in the product and service markets are the degree of competition among producers (e.g., fast-food outlets) and the level of demand for the products or services (e.g., the number of customers in a given area). Both of these affect the ability of a firm to change the prices of its products or services. If an employer cannot change prices without suffering a loss of revenues due to decreased sales, that employer's ability to raise the level of pay is constrained. If the employer does pay more, it has two options: to try to pass the increased costs

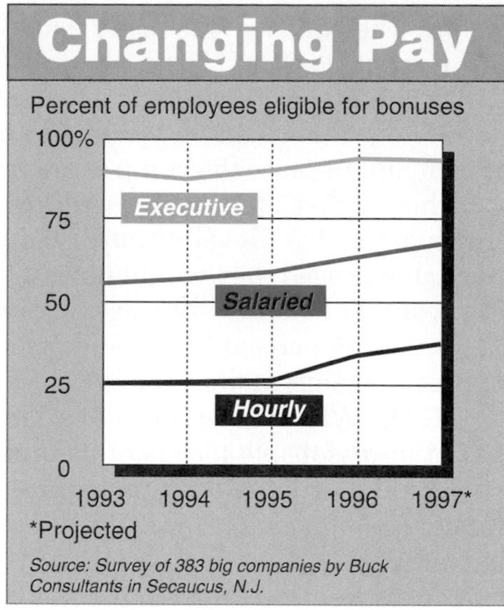

Figure 10-2
The trend toward making pay more variable affects all levels of employees. (*Source:* J. S. Lublin, Why more people are battling over bonuses, *The Wall Street Journal*, Jan. 8, 1997, p. B1.)

on to consumers or to hold prices fixed and allocate a greater portion of revenues to cover labor costs.[4]

Programs That Encourage and Reward Performance

Firms are continuing to relocate to areas where organized labor is weak and pay rates are low. They are developing pay plans that channel more dollars into incentive awards and fewer into fixed salaries. Entrepreneurs in start-up, high-risk organizations; salespeople; piecework factory workers; and rock stars have long lived with erratic incomes.[5] People in other jobs are used to fairly fixed paychecks that grow a bit every year. The program of fairly fixed incomes has been a bedrock of the U.S. compensation system, but it is gradually being nudged aside by programs that put more pay at risk.[6] (See Figure 10-2.) These programs are being linked to profit and productivity gains—usually a moving, ever-rising target.

Such variable-pay systems almost guarantee cost control. In many new plans any productivity gains are shared 25 percent by the employees and 75 percent by the company. If business takes off, more pay goes to workers. If it does not, the company is not locked into high fixed costs of labor. In the U.S., about 61 percent of large- and medium-size companies now offer some kind of variable pay—such as profit sharing and bonus awards—up from 47 percent in 1990.[7] Later in this chapter we will discuss more fully the pay-for-performance theme and how it can be put into effect.

COMPANY EXAMPLE

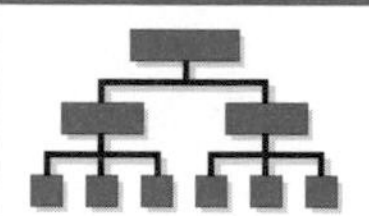

TYING PAY TO PERFORMANCE IN THE UNITED STATES AND JAPAN[8]

In an effort to hold down labor costs, thousands of U.S. companies are changing the way they increase workers' pay. Instead of the traditional annual increase, millions of workers in industries as diverse as supermarkets and aircraft manufacturing are receiving cash bonuses. For most workers, the plans mean less money. The bonuses take many names: "profit sharing" at Abbott Laboratories and Hewlett-Packard, "gain sharing" at Mack Trucks and Panhandle Eastern Corporation, and "lump-sum payments" at Boeing. All have two elements in common: (1) they can vary with the company's fortunes, and (2) they are not permanent. Because the bonuses are not folded into base pay (as merit increases are), there is no compounding effect over time. They are simply provided on top of a constant base level of pay. This means that both wages and benefits rise more slowly than they would have if the base level of pay was rising each year. The result: a flattening of wages nationally.

Today, 40 percent of all workers covered by major union agreements have bonus provisions in their contracts. How have unions reacted? In the view of the AFL-CIO, "Where there is justification for belt-tightening, then profit-sharing is not an unreasonable means of passing on earnings when times improve."[9]

Flexible pay—tied mostly to profitability and promising better job security, but not guaranteeing it—is at the heart of the evolving bonus system. Employees are being asked to share the risks of the new global marketplace. How large must the rewards be? MIT economist Martin Weitzman estimates that over the long run the proper bonus level is 20 to 25 percent of total compensation, because that would give workers a pay increase equal to the rate of inflation plus productivity gains. But in the United States most bonus payments have been averaging about 10 percent of a worker's base pay annually. Conversely, the Japanese currently pay many workers a bonus that represents about 25 percent of base pay. For workers in both nations, a significant amount of their pay is "at risk."

Have such plans generated greater productivity in the U.S. manufacturing sector in recent years? Maybe, but an equally plausible explanation is that the gains were due to automation, to company efforts to give workers more of a say in how they do their jobs, and to workers' fear that if they did not improve their productivity, their plants would become uncompetitive and be closed. In short, the jury is still out on the productivity impact of bonus systems as well as on their effect on worker motivation and commitment to the organization.

COMPONENTS AND OBJECTIVES OF ORGANIZATIONAL REWARD SYSTEMS

At a broad level, an organizational reward system includes anything an employee values and desires that an employer is able and willing to offer in exchange for employee contributions. More specifically, the reward system includes both financial and nonfinancial rewards. Financial rewards include direct payments (e.g., salary) plus indirect payments in the form of employee benefits (see Chapter 11). Nonfinancial rewards include everything in a work environment that enhances a worker's sense of self-respect and esteem by others (e.g., work environments that are physically, socially, and mentally healthy; opportunities for training and personal development; effective supervision; recognition). These ideas are shown graphically in Figure 10-3.

Although money is obviously a powerful tool to capture the minds and hearts of workers and to maximize their productivity, do not underestimate the

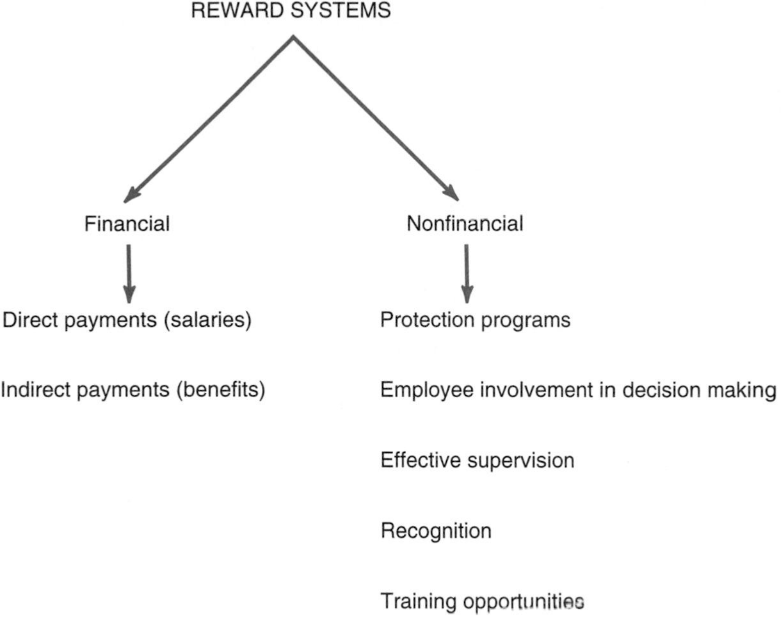

Figure 10-3 Organizational reward systems include financial as well as nonfinancial components.

impact of nonfinancial rewards. As an example, consider Wilton Connor Packaging Inc. in Charlotte, North Carolina. In addition to offering on-site laundry service, it has a handyman on staff who does free minor household repairs for employees while they are at work—thus cutting down on excuses for missing work. If there is a major problem, say, a toilet that needs to be replaced—the handyman orders it from Home Depot and charges it to the company's account there. The employee repays the company a few dollars a month.

"We have virtually no turnover, we have no quality problems, we have very few supervisors," asserts Wilton Connor, the company's chief executive. "Those are the hard-nosed business reasons for doing these things."[10] Companies are doing these things because they do not have much choice. Giving their workers more ease and freedom is simply enlightened self-interest. As one executive noted, "The demand for brains is higher than it's ever been." Satisfying this demand will require radical rethinking of employment practices that have served organizations reasonably well in the past.[11]

Rewards bridge the gap between organizational objectives and individual expectations and aspirations. To be effective, organizational reward systems should provide four things: (1) a sufficient level of rewards to fulfill basic needs, (2) equity with the external labor market, (3) equity within the organization, and (4) treatment of each member of the organization in terms of his or her individual needs.[12] In a broader sense, pay systems are designed to attract, retain, and motivate employees. This is the ARM (attraction, retention, and motivation) concept. Indeed, much of the design of compensation systems involves working out trade-offs among more or less seriously conflicting objectives.[13]

Perhaps the most important objective of any pay system is fairness, or equity. Equity can be assessed on at least three dimensions:

ETHICAL DILEMMA
Should Board Members Who Set CEO Pay Be Independent?

At Citizens Utilities, based in Stamford, Connecticut, the firm's chief executive officer received $21.6 million in pay in 1992. That is about $26 from each of more than 800,000 Citizens customers in 13 states who get their electricity, water, and gas from the company. All three members of the board of directors who negotiated the CEO's employment contract had close ties to the company. One of them made more than $500,000 in consulting fees. The second benefited from legal work at Citizens. And the third received 7271 stock options in a cellular-phone subsidiary of Citizens that sold stock, netting him a $123,000 paper profit.[17] In the late 1990s, however, powerful institutional investors and money managers are demanding that such cozy relationships be disclosed, because, to quote former Supreme Court Justice Louis D. Brandeis, "sunlight is the best disinfectant."[18] At Citizens Utilities, the board members' actions were legal, but were they ethical? Whose interests should be considered in matters such as these?

1. **Internal equity.** In terms of the relative worth of individual jobs to an organization, are pay rates fair?
2. **External equity.** Are the wages paid by an organization fair in terms of competitive market rates outside the organization?
3. **Individual equity.** Is each individual's pay fair relative to that of other individuals doing the same or similar jobs?

Researchers have proposed several bases for determining equitable payment for work.[14] The bases have three points in common:

1. Each assumes that employees perceive a fair return for what they contribute to their jobs.
2. All include the concept of social comparison, whereby employees determine what their equitable return should be after comparing their inputs (e.g., skills, education, effort) and outcomes (e.g., pay, promotion, job status) with those of their peers or coworkers (comparison persons).
3. The theories assume that employees who perceive themselves to be in an inequitable situation will seek to reduce that inequity. They may do so by mentally distorting their inputs or outcomes, by directly altering their inputs or outcomes, or by leaving the organization.

Reviews of both laboratory and field tests of equity theory are quite consistent: individuals tend to follow the equity norm and to use it as a basis for distributing rewards. They report inequitable conditions as distressing, although there may be individual differences in sensitivity to equity.[15]

A final objective is *balance*—the relative size of pay differentials among different segments of the workforce. If pay systems are to accomplish the objectives set for them, ultimately they must be perceived as adequate and equitable. For example, there should be a balance in pay relationships between supervisors and the highest-paid subordinates reporting to them. According to the public accounting firm Coopers & Lybrand, among companies judged to be well managed, this differential is generally 15 percent.[16] As the chapter opening vignette illustrated, ratios of 100 to 1 (or greater) between the highest- and lowest-paid employees are generally regarded as out of balance.

STRATEGIC INTEGRATION OF COMPENSATION PLANS AND BUSINESS PLANS

Unfortunately, the rationale behind many compensation programs is "Two-thirds of our competitors do it" or "That is corporate policy." Compensation plans need to be tied to an organization's strategic mission and should take their direction from that mission. They must support the general business strategy—e.g., innovation, cost leadership.[19] Further, evidence now shows that inferior performance by a firm is associated with a lack of fit between its pay policy and its business strategy.[20] From a managerial perspective, therefore, the most fundamental question is "What do you want your pay system to accomplish?"

As an example, consider Dial Corporation, the big consumer-products maker. Over the 3-year period 1997 to 1999 the company will do away with merit raises for its 1400 nonunion staffers. Instead, they will be eligible for annual cash bonuses, which primarily will reflect three measures of corporate financial performance—net revenue growth, operating margin, and asset turnover. These measures reflect business strategies of cost leadership and differentiation (setting oneself apart from the competition). Potential bonuses (11.25 percent in 1997) will rise as merit raises are phased out.[21]

This approach to managing compensation and business strategies dictates that actual levels of compensation should not be strictly a matter of what is being paid in the marketplace. Instead, compensation levels derive from an assessment of what must be paid to attract and retain the right people, what the organization can afford, and what will be required to meet the organization's strategic goals. The idea is to align the interests of managers and employees.

When compensation is viewed from a strategic perspective, therefore, firms do the following:

1. They recognize compensation as a pivotal control and incentive mechanism that can be used flexibly by management to attain business objectives.
2. They make the pay system an integral part of strategy formulation.
3. They integrate pay considerations into strategic decision-making processes, such as those that involve planning and control.
4. They view the firm's performance as the ultimate criterion of the success of strategic pay decisions and operational compensation programs.[22]

DETERMINANTS OF PAY STRUCTURE AND LEVEL

In the simplest terms, marginal revenue product theory in labor economics holds that the value of a person's labor is what someone is willing to pay for it.[23] In practice, a number of factors interact to determine wage levels. Some of the most influential of these are labor market conditions, legislation, collective bargaining, managerial attitudes, and an organization's ability to pay. Let us examine each of these factors.

Labor Market Conditions

As noted in Chapter 5, whether a labor market is "tight" or "loose" has a major impact on wage structures and levels. Thus, if the demand for certain skills is high, while the supply is low (a "tight" market), there tends to be an increase in the price paid for these skills. Conversely, if the supply of labor is plentiful, relative to the demand for it, wages tend to decrease. As an example, consider Jordan Machine Company.

COMPANY EXAMPLE

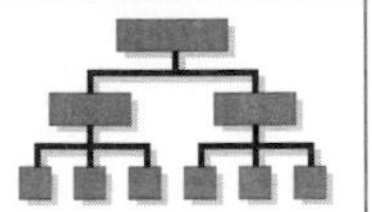

SMALL BUSINESS CONTENDS WITH TIGHT LABOR MARKETS

Jordan Machine Company of Birmingham, Alabama, has never worked so hard to find so few employees. "We've turned over barrels and drums and searched just about everywhere we can think," says Jerry Edwards, chief executive officer. The company needs skilled machinists to help manufacture molds for everything from fishing lures to submarine hatch covers.

Despite his efforts—including offers of annual wages that exceeded $20,000, full health benefits, and a company-sponsored savings program—Mr. Edwards estimated that his company lost more than $400,000 in sales in 1996, simply because it could not find enough workers to meet the demand for new orders.

Jordan Machine Company is not alone, as companies, high-tech and low-tech alike, simply cannot find workers. The difficulty in finding workers is all part of the economic boom in major metropolitan areas of the South (Georgia, Alabama, North Carolina, South Carolina, Tennessee, Virginia, West Virginia, and Florida). In Birmingham, the unemployment rate in the third quarter of 1996 was just 2.9 percent, compared with a national average of 5.2 percent. Not surprisingly, therefore, wages have risen 24 percent in Birmingham since 1990, compared with 19 percent for the United States as a whole.[24]

Another labor market phenomenon that causes substantial differences in pay rates, even among people who work in the same field and are of similar age and education, is the payment of wage premiums by some employers to attract the best talent available, and to enhance productivity in order to offset any increase in labor costs. This is known as the "efficiency wage hypothesis" in labor economics, and it has received considerable support among economic researchers.[25] The forces discussed thus far affect pay levels to a considerable extent. So also does government legislation.

Legislation

As in other areas, legislation related to pay plays a vital role in determining internal organization practices. Because we cannot analyze all the relevant laws here, Table 10-1 presents a summary of the coverage, major provisions, and federal agencies charged with administering four major federal wage-hour laws. Wage-hour laws set limits on minimum wages to be paid and maximum hours to be worked. Of the four laws shown in Table 10-1, only the Fair Labor Standards Act (FLSA) affects almost every organization in the United States. It is the

TABLE 10-1

FOUR MAJOR FEDERAL WAGE-HOUR LAWS.

	Scope of coverage	Major provisions	Administrative agency
Fair Labor Standards Act (FLSA) of 1938 (as amended)	Employers involved in interstate commerce with two or more employees and annual revenues greater than $500,000. Exemption from overtime provisions for managers, supervisors, executives, outside salespersons, and professional workers.	Minimum wage of $5.15 per hour for covered employees (as of September 1997); time-and-a-half pay for over 40 hours per week; restrictions by occupation or industry on the employment of persons under 18; prohibits wage differentials based exclusively on sex—equal pay for equal work. No extra pay required for weekends, vacations, holidays, or severance.	Wage and Hour Division of the Employment Standards Administration, U.S. Department of Labor
Davis-Bacon Act (1931)	Federal contractors involved in the construction or repair of federal buildings and public works with a contract value over $2000.	Employees on the project must be paid prevailing community wage rates for the type of employment used. Overtime of time and one-half for more than 40 hours per week. Three-year blacklisting of contractors who violate this act.	Comptroller General and Wage and Hour Division
Walsh-Healy Act (1936)	Federal contractors manufacturing or supplying materials, articles, or equipment to the federal government with a value exceeding $10,000 annually.	Same as Davis-Bacon. Under the Defense Authorization Act of 1986, overtime is required only for hours worked in excess of 40 per week, not 8 per day, as previously.	Same as FLSA
McNamara-O'Hara Service Contract Act (1965)	Federal contractors who provide services to the federal government with a value in excess of $2500.	Same as Davis-Bacon.	Same as Davis-Bacon

source of the terms "exempt employees" (exempt from the overtime provisions of the law) and "nonexempt employees." It established the first national minimum wage (25 cents an hour) in 1938; subsequent changes in the minimum wage and in national policy on equal pay for equal work for both sexes (the Equal Pay Act of 1963) were passed as amendments to this law.

There are many loopholes in FLSA minimum-wage coverage.[26] Certain workers, including casual baby-sitters and most farm workers, are excluded, as are employees of small businesses and firms not engaged in interstate commerce. State minimum-wage laws are intended to cover these workers. At the same time, if a state's minimum is higher than the federal minimum, the state minimum applies. For example, while the federal minimum wage is $5.15 per hour in 1997, California's will rise to $5.75 by 1998, which would give one-sixth of its labor force a raise.[27]

An important feature of the FLSA is its provision regarding the employment of young workers. On school days, 14-year-olds and 15-year-olds are allowed to work no more than 3 hours (no more than 8 hours on nonschool days), or a total of 18 hours a week when school is in session. They may work 40-hour weeks during the summer and during school vacations, but they may not work outside the hours of 7 a.m. to 7 p.m. (or 9 p.m. June 1 to Labor Day). Both federal and state laws allow 16-year-olds and 17-year-olds to work any hours but forbid them to work in hazardous occupations, such as driving or working with power-driven meat slicers.

The remaining three laws shown in Table 10-1 apply only to organizations that do business with the federal government in the form of construction or by supplying goods and services.

Collective Bargaining

Another major influence on wages in unionized as well as nonunionized firms is collective bargaining. Nonunionized firms are affected by collective bargaining agreements made elsewhere since they must compete with unionized firms for the services and loyalties of workers. Collective bargaining affects two key factors: (1) the level of wages, and (2) the behavior of workers in relevant labor markets. In an open, competitive market, workers tend to gravitate toward higher-paying jobs. To the extent that nonunionized firms fail to match the wages of unionized firms, they may have difficulty attracting and keeping workers. Furthermore, benefits negotiated under union agreements have had the effect of increasing the "package" of benefits in firms that have attempted to avoid unionization. In addition to wages and benefits, collective bargaining is also used to negotiate procedures for administering pay, procedures for resolving grievances regarding compensation decisions, and methods used to determine the relative worth of jobs.[28]

Managerial Attitudes and an Organization's Ability to Pay

These factors have a major impact on wage structures and levels. Earlier we noted that an organization's ability to pay depends, to a large extent, on the competitive dynamics it faces in its product or service markets. Therefore, regardless of its espoused competitive position on wages, an organization's ability to pay ultimately will be a key factor that limits actual wages.

This is not to downplay the role of management philosophy and attitudes on pay. On the contrary, management's desire to maintain or to improve morale, to attract high-caliber employees, to reduce turnover, and to improve employees' standards of living also affect wages, as does the relative importance of a given position to a firm.[29] A safety engineer is more important to a chemical company than to a bank. Wage structures tend to vary across firms to the extent that managers view any given position as more or less critical to their firms. Thus compensation administration reflects management judgment to a considerable degree. Ultimately, top management renders judgments regarding the overall competitive pay position of the firm (above-market, at-market, or below-market rates), factors to be considered in determining job worth, and the relative weight to be given seniority and performance in pay decisions. Such judgments are key determinants of the structure and level of wages.

AN OVERVIEW OF PAY SYSTEM MECHANICS

The procedures described below for developing pay systems help those involved in the development process to apply their judgments in a systematic manner. The hallmarks of success in compensation management, as in other areas, are understandability, workability, and acceptability. The broad objective in developing pay systems is to assign a monetary value to each job in the organization (a base rate) and to develop an orderly procedure for increasing the base rate (e.g., based on merit, inflation, or some combination of the two). To develop such a system, we need four basic tools:

1. Updated job descriptions
2. A job evaluation method (i.e., one that will rank jobs in terms of their overall worth to the organization)
3. Pay surveys
4. A pay structure

Figure 10-4 presents an overview of this process.

Job descriptions are key tools in the design of pay systems, for they serve two purposes:

1. They identify important characteristics of each job so that the relative worth of jobs can be determined.
2. From them we can identify, define, and weight compensable factors (common job characteristics that an organization is willing to pay for, such as skill, effort, responsibility, and working conditions).

Once job descriptions have been established or updated, the next step is to rate the worth of all jobs using a predetermined system.

A number of job evaluation methods have been developed since the 1920s, and many, if not most, of them are still used. They all have the same final objective—ranking jobs in terms of their relative worth to the organization so that an equitable rate of pay can be determined for each job. Moreover, they all yield similar results.[30]

For example, in the point-factor method of job evaluation, each job is analyzed and defined in terms of the compensable factors an organization has agreed

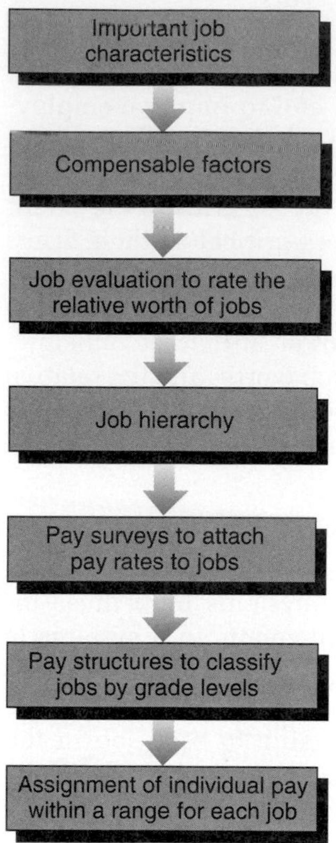

Figure 10-4
Traditional job-based compensation model.

to adopt. Points are assigned to each level (or degree) of a compensable factor, such as responsibility. The total points assigned to each job across each compensable factor are then summed. A hierarchy of job worth is therefore defined when jobs are rank-ordered from highest point total to lowest point total.

Job evaluation is used widely, but not universally, among firms. One reason firms may not use job evaluation is that several policy issues must be resolved first:[31]

- Does management perceive meaningful differences among jobs?
- Is it possible to identify and operationalize meaningful criteria for distinguishing among jobs?
- Will job evaluation result in meaningful distinctions in the eyes of employees?
- Are jobs stable, and will they remain stable in the future?
- Is job evaluation consistent with the organization's goals and strategies? For example, if the goal is to ensure maximum flexibility among job assignments, a knowledge- or skill-based pay system may be most appropriate. That topic is addressed more fully in a later section.

Linking Internal Pay Relationships to Market Data

In the point-factor method of job evaluation, the next task is to translate the point totals into a pay structure. Two key components of this process are identifying and surveying pay rates in relevant labor markets. This can often be a complex task since employers must pay attention not only to labor markets but also to product markets.[32] Pay practices must be designed not only to attract and retain employees, but also to ensure that labor costs (as part of the overall costs of production) do not become excessive in relation to those of competing employers.

The definition of relevant labor markets requires two key decisions: which jobs to survey and which markets are relevant for each job. Jobs selected for a survey are generally characterized by stable tasks and stable job specifications (e.g., computer programmers, purchasing managers). Jobs with these characteristics are known as "key" or "benchmark" jobs. Jobs that do not meet these criteria, but that are characterized by high turnover or are difficult to fill, should also be included.

As we noted earlier, the definition of relevant labor markets should consider geographical boundaries (local, regional, national, or international) as well as product-market competitors. Such an approach might begin with product-market competitors as the initial market, followed by adjustments downward (e.g., from national to regional markets) on the basis of geographical considerations.

Once target populations and relevant markets have been identified, the next task is to obtain survey data. Surveys are available from a variety of sources, including the federal government (Bureau of Labor Statistics), employers' associations, trade and professional associations, users of a given job evaluation system (e.g., the Hay Group's point-factor system), and compensation consulting firms.

Managers should be aware of two potential problems with pay survey data.[33] The most serious is the assurance of an accurate job match. If only a "thumbnail sketch" (i.e., a very brief description) is used to characterize a job, there is always the possibility of legitimate misunderstanding among survey respondents. To deal with this, some surveys ask respondents if their salary data for a job are direct matches, or somewhat higher or lower than those described (and therefore worthy of more or less pay).

A second problem has resulted from the explosion of at-risk forms of pay, some of which are based on individual performance and some on the profitability of an organization. As we noted earlier, base pay is becoming a smaller part of the total compensation package for a broad range of employees. This makes it difficult to determine the actual pay of job incumbents, and can make survey results difficult to interpret. For example, how does one compare salary figures that include only base pay or direct cash payouts with at-risk pay that may take the form of a lump-sum bonus, additional time off with pay, or an employee stock-ownership plan?

Despite these potential problems, all indications are that pay surveys will continue to be used widely. One example is the system used by Liberty Mutual.

COMPANY EXAMPLE

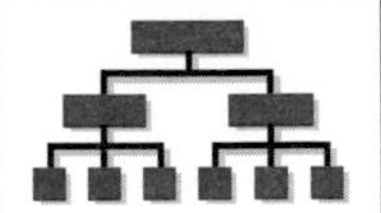

LIBERTY MUTUAL INSURANCE GROUP OF BOSTON'S S.M.A.R.T. SYSTEM[34]

Liberty Mutual uses a Windows-based decision-support system called the Survey, Market Analysis, and Reporting Tool (S.M.A.R.T.). The company's need to respond to change, with more than 21,000 employees located in more than 400 offices in the United States and abroad, prompted development of the

ANALYZING THE COMPETITION

Market Analysis Report – Cut 1

Grade: 02 Midpoint: $17,700 Lo Salary: $15,200 Hi Salary: $20,000 Avg Salary: $16,500

Company Data				**Survey Data**									
Job	**Title**	**#Incs**	**Avg Salary**	**Surv#**	**Title**	**#Cos**	**Aged Wtd #Incs**	**Avg**	**Aging**	**%**	**Avg to MKT**	**Mid to MKT**
8633	File Processor	146	$16,775	TSGB	FILE CLERK, JUNIOR	317	1719	$17,609	6/1/94	4	–5.2%	0.1%
3535	Financial Assistant	26	$17,500	TSGB	FINANCIAL CLERK	734	437	$18,700	6/1/94	4	–6.4%	–5.3%
Bench Avg: weighted by co bench of incs		172	$16,885				1,719	$17,842			–5.3%	0.7%
Grade Avg: weighted by co grade of incs		200	$17,500					$17,842			–1.9%	

Note: All data shown are dummy data. Bench = Benchmark.

Figure 10-5
Liberty Mutual's market analysis report. Codes: #Incs = number of incumbents; TSGB = The Survey Group Benchmark; #Cos = number of companies; Aged Wtd Avg = weighted-average pay, adjusted for a 4% increase as of 6/1/94; Avg to MKT = company-average pay relative to market-average pay; Mid to MKT = midpoint salary paid by company relative to market-average pay. (*Source:* D. Barry & K. McLaughlin, A S.M.A.R.T. method for comp analysis, *HRMagazine*, May, 1996, p. 82. Used with permission.)

S.M.A.R.T. system. As the company moved to a decentralized structure, it found that managers needed additional compensation information and consulting services. S.M.A.R.T., a multiuser system on a local-area network, responds to that need. Here are several defining features of the system:

- Automated access to and summaries of employee and job information and market data
- The ability to input data either manually or electronically
- Standardized forms for entering and viewing information
- Standardized reports to support job evaluation and market analysis
- Ad-hoc reporting capabilities
- A user-friendly interface

Figure 10-5 presents one such report, a market analysis report, based on the results of about 15 pay surveys. Analysts or line managers can produce alternative versions of the report—for example, a report sorted by job family, a report based on specific industry surveys, or a report that includes only Canadian jobs. This feature allows analysts to ask what-if questions, and to identify quickly areas that require special attention. The time saved by running market analysis reports with S.M.A.R.T., rather than producing them with spreadsheets, is especially valuable during the busy market analysis season.

The result of a pay survey is often a chart, as in Figure 10-6, that relates current wage rates to the total points assigned to each job. For each point total, a trend line is fitted to indicate the average relationship between points assigned to the benchmark jobs and the hourly wages paid for those jobs. Once a midpoint trend line is fitted, two others are also drawn: (1) a trend line that represents the minimum rate of pay for each point total and (2) a trend line that represents the maximum rate of pay for each point total.[35]

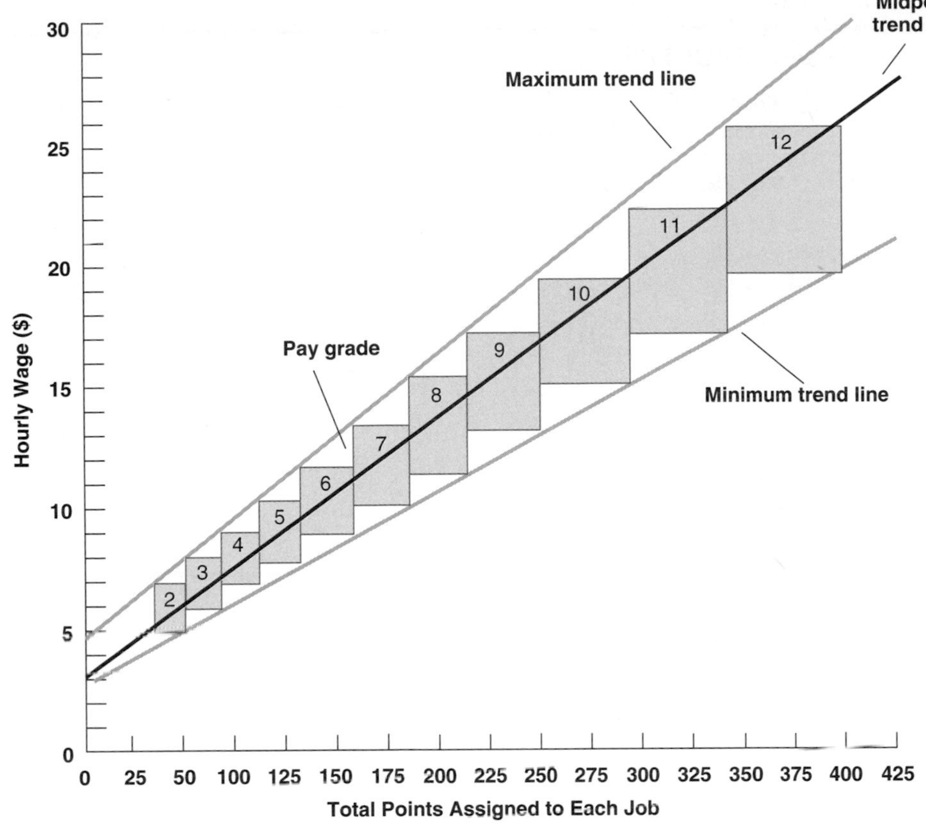

Figure 10-6
Chart relating hourly wage rates to the total points assigned to each job. Three trend lines are shown – minimum, midpoint, and maximum—as well as 11 pay grades. Within each pay grade there is a 30 percent spread from minimum to maximum and a 50 percent overlap from one pay grade to the next.

Developing a Pay Structure

The final step in attaching dollar values to jobs using the point method is to establish pay grades, or ranges, characterized by a point spread from minimum to maximum for each grade. Starting wages are given by the trend line that represents the minimum rate of pay for each pay grade, while the highest wages that can be earned within a grade are given by the trend line that represents the maximum rate of pay. The pay structure is described numerically in Table 10-2.

For example, consider the job of "administrative clerk." Let's assume that the job evaluation committee arrived at a total allocation of 142 points across all compensable factors. The job therefore falls into pay grade 6. Starting pay is $9.75 per hour, with a maximum pay rate of $12.37 per hour.

The actual development of a pay structure is a complex process, but there are certain rules of thumb to follow:

- Jobs of the same general value should be clustered into the same pay grade.
- Jobs that clearly differ in value should be in different pay grades.
- There should be a smooth progression of point groupings.
- The new system should fit realistically into the existing allocation of pay within a company.
- The pay grades should conform reasonably well to pay patterns in the relevant labor markets.[36]

Table 10-2

SAMPLE PAY STRUCTURE

Pay grade	Point spread	Midpoint	Minimum rate of pay	Maximum rate of pay
2	62– 75	68	$ 6.00	$ 7.50
3	76– 91	83	6.75	8.47
4	92–110	101	7.61	9.60
5	110–132	121	8.60	10.89
6	133–157	145	9.75	12.37
7	158–186	172	11.06	14.07
8	187–219	203	12.57	16.03
9	220–257	238	14.30	18.29
10	258–300	279	16.30	20.88
11	301–350	325	18.59	23.87
12	351–407	379	21.23	27.30

Once such a pay structure is in place, the determination of each individual's pay (based on experience, seniority, and performance) becomes a more systematic, orderly procedure. A compensation planning worksheet, such as that shown in Figure 10-7, can be very useful to managers confronted with these weighty decisions.

Alternatives to Pay Systems Based on Job Evaluation

There are at least two such alternatives. These are market-based pay and skill- or knowledge-based pay, also referred to as competency-based pay.

Market-Based Pay

This system uses a direct market-pricing approach for all of a firm's jobs. This type of pay structure is feasible if all jobs are benchmark jobs and direct matches can be found in the market. Pay surveys can then be used to determine the market prices of the jobs in question. This type of pay system may be used in entrepreneurial start-up firms, research and development units, and sales organizations.[37] Larger firms with more diverse jobs, however, may have to rely on market pricing only for benchmark jobs and use job evaluation in order to price nonbenchmark jobs.

Competency-Based Pay

Under such a system, workers are paid not on the basis of the job they currently are doing but, rather, on the basis of the number of jobs they are capable of doing, that is, on the basis of their skills or their depth of knowledge, both of which are termed "competencies." In a world of slimmed-down big companies and agile small ones, the last thing any manager wants to hear from an employee is "It's not my job." To see how such a system might work in practice, consider Polaroid's pay system.

ORG. UNIT ____________
MGR. OR SUPV. ____________

ANNUAL COMPENSATION PLANNING WORKSHEET

EMPLOYEE NAME	JOB TITLE	LAST SALARY ADJUSTMENT				CURRENT SALARY	RANGE MINIMUM	RANGE MIDPOINT	RANGE MAXIMUM	PERFORMANCE APPRAISAL	FORECAST SALARY ADJUSTMENT (If Any)				
		Amt.	%	Date	Type*						Amt.	%	Date	New Salary	Inter-val

*Code for "Type"
1—Promotion
2—Merit

PREPARED BY ____________

Figure 10-7
Sample annual compensation planning worksheet.

COMPANY EXAMPLE

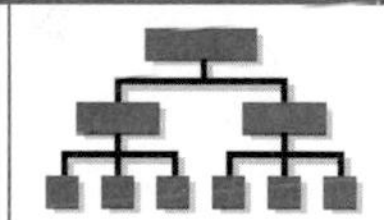

COMPETENCY-BASED PAY AT POLAROID CORPORATION[38]

Polaroid initiated a companywide, competency-based pay system in April 1990. Polaroid employees are encouraged to form work teams and to redesign their work functions in order to make them more efficient, according to Richard G. Terry, compensation manager at Polaroid, which is based in Cambridge, Massachusetts. Although Polaroid's system includes everyone from the mailroom clerk to the chief executive officer, it has been more effective in the manufacturing part of the business.

Polaroid's manufacturing employees have learned skills in a number of different areas, rather than focusing on a single job. In addition, the work teams have picked up some of the responsibilities of supervisors, such as scheduling assignments and overtime. Employees who have succeeded at the new jobs have received more money. "Their pay has gone beyond what was traditionally the top," Mr. Terry said.

The focus of Polaroid's white-collar employees has been on learning new technologies. But here, the process has not worked as smoothly. Part of the problem is that skills, or competencies, are not so easy to measure in managerial jobs. But that will not stop companies from attempting to apply this scheme to their white-collar workforces. "Slowly, but surely, we're becoming a skill-based society where your market value is tied to what you can do and what your skill set is. . . . In this new world, where skills and knowledge are what really count, it doesn't make sense to treat people as jobholders. It makes sense to treat them as people with specific skills, and to pay them for those skills."

In such a "learning environment," the more workers learn, the more they earn. Of 22 Corning plants, 9 are on competency-based pay. At one, workers can lift their base pay from $9.50 an hour to almost $13.50. Workers at American Steel & Wire can boost their annual salaries by up to $12,480 by acquiring as many as 10 skills. Is there any impact on productivity or morale? A recent survey of 27 companies with such programs revealed that 70 to 88 percent reported higher job satisfaction, product quality, or productivity. Some 70 to 75 percent reported lower operating costs or reduced turnover.[39] In another survey of 150 compensation professionals, three-fourths of the respondents reported a surge in interest in such pay plans.[40]

Companies view competency-based pay plans as a way to develop the critical behaviors and abilities employees need to achieve specific business results. By linking compensation directly to individual contributions that make a difference to the organization, a company can maintain the highest caliber of workers, regardless of their particular specialty or role. Such plans also provide a mechanism for cross-training employees to ensure that people in different functional areas have the behavioral or technical skills to take on additional responsibilities as needed.[41] Competency-based pay systems work best when the following conditions exist:[42]

1. A supportive HRM philosophy underpins all employment activities. Such a philosophy is characterized by mutual trust and the conviction that employees have the ability and motivation to perform well.
2. HRM programs such as profit sharing, participative management, empowerment, and job enrichment complement the competency-based pay system.
3. Technology and organization structure change frequently.
4. Employee exchanges (i.e., assignment, rotation) are common.
5. There are opportunities to learn new skills.
6. Employee turnover is relatively high.
7. Workers value teamwork and the opportunity to participate.

In summary, if compensation systems are to be used strategically, it is important that management (1) understand clearly what types of behavior it wants the compensation system to reinforce, (2) recognize that compensation systems are integral components of planning and control, and (3) view the firm's performance as the ultimate criterion of the success of strategic pay decisions and operational compensation programs. Now let us consider some key policy issues.

POLICY ISSUES IN PAY PLANNING AND ADMINISTRATION

Pay Secrecy

The extent to which information on pay is public or private is a basic issue that needs to be addressed by management. The U.S. courts have generally supported companies in their view that salary information, like a product formula or a marketing strategy, is confidential and the property of management. An employee who ferrets out and releases such data can be discharged for "willful misconduct."[43] However, a 1992 ruling by the National Labor Relations Board makes such a company policy illegal. In its ruling the Board noted:

> It is elemental that these activities encompass the ability of employees to discuss amongst themselves any quarrel that they may have concerning their wages in an effort to obtain a change in this condition of employment. Moreover, this is so regardless of whether a labor organization is on the scene to serve as the proponent of that change.[44]

Pay secrecy is a difficult policy to maintain, particularly as companies look to strengthen the link between pay and performance. For example, research with bank managers found that when pay systems are open, managers tend to award higher pay raises to subordinates on whom they depend heavily. Apparently they do so because they need the subordinates' cooperation, and subordinates can check on pay allocations.[45]

Openness versus secrecy is not an either/or phenomenon. Rather, it is a matter of degree. For example, organizations may choose to disclose one or more of the following: (1) the work- and business-related rationale on which the system is based, (2) pay ranges, (3) pay-increase schedules, and (4) the availability of pay-related data from the compensation department.[46] There is also a downside to pay openness:

1. It forces managers to defend their pay decisions and practices publicly. Since the process is inherently subjective, there is no guarantee that satisfactory answers will ever be found that can please all concerned parties.
2. The cost of a mistaken pay decision escalates, since all the system's inconsistencies and weaknesses become visible once the cloak of secrecy is lifted.
3. Open pay might induce some managers to reduce differences in pay among subordinates in order to avoid conflict and the need to explain such differences to disappointed employees.[47]

In general, open-pay systems tend to work best under the following circumstances: individual or team performance can be measured objectively, performance measures can be developed for all the important aspects of a job, and effort and performance are related closely over a relatively short time span.

The Effect of Inflation

All organizations must make some allowance for inflation in their salary programs. Given an inflation rate of 5 percent, for example, the firm that fails to increase its salary ranges at all over a 2-year period will be 10 percent behind its competitors. Needless to say, it becomes difficult to recruit new employees under these circumstances, and it becomes difficult to motivate present employees to remain and, if they do remain, to produce.

How do firms cope? Automatic pay raises for nonunion employees have almost disappeared at most major concerns. Average increases for salaried employees sank to 3.9 percent in 1996, down from 5 percent in 1990.[48] As we have seen, companies such as Dial, Corning, Du Pont, Merck, and America West Airlines are tying pay more to performance in an attempt to make the costs of labor more variable and less fixed. At Dial, for example, "Employees have gotten merit increases irrespective of company performance. . . . We can't afford to go on doing business through [that] kind of pay program."[49] More and more companies, large and small, feel the same way.

Pay Compression

Pay compression is related to the general problem of inflation. It is a narrowing of the ratios of pay between jobs or pay grades in a firm's pay structure.[50] Pay compression exists in many forms, including (1) higher starting salaries for new hires, which lead long-term employees to see only a slight difference between their current pay and that of new hires; (2) hourly pay increases for unionized employees that exceed those of salaried and nonunion employees; (3) recruitment of new college graduates for management or professional jobs at salaries above those of current jobholders; and (4) excessive overtime payments to some employees or payment of different overtime rates (e.g., time and a half for some, double time for others). However, first-line supervisors, unlike middle managers, may actually benefit from pay inflation among nonmanagement employees since companies generally maintain a differential between the supervisors' pay and that of their highest-paid subordinates. As we noted earlier, these differentials average 15 percent.[51]

One solution to the problem of pay compression is to institute equity adjustments; that is, give increases in pay to employees to maintain differences in job worth between their jobs and those of others. Some companies provide for equity adjustments through a constantly changing pay scale. Thus Aluminum Company of America (ALCOA) surveys its competitors' pay every 3 months and adjusts its pay rates accordingly. ALCOA strives to maintain at least a 20 percent differential between employees and their supervisors.[52]

Another approach is to grant sign-on bonuses to new hires in order to offer a competitive total compensation package, especially to those with scarce skills. Since bonuses do not increase base salaries, the structure of differences in pay between new hires and experienced employees does not change. Alternatively, some firms provide benefits that increase gradually to more senior employees. Thus, although the difference between the direct pay of this group and that of their shorter-service coworkers may be slim, senior employees have a distinct advantage when the entire compensation package is considered.

Overtime as a cause of compression can be dealt with in two ways. First, it can be rotated among employees so that all share overtime equally. However, in situations where this kind of arrangement is not feasible, firms might consider establishing an overtime pay policy for management employees; for example, a supervisor may be paid an overtime rate after he or she works a minimum number of overtime hours. Such a practice does not violate the Fair Labor Standards Act, for under the law overtime pay is not required for exempt jobs,[53] although it may be adopted voluntarily, as it is at some public-accounting firms.

Pay compression is certainly a difficult problem—but not so difficult that it cannot be managed. Indeed, it must be managed if companies are to achieve their goal of providing pay that is perceived as fair.

Pay Raises

Coping with inflation is the biggest hurdle to overcome in a pay-for-performance plan. On the other hand, the only measure of a raise is how much it exceeds the increase in the cost of living: the 12.4 percent inflation of 1980 more than wiped out the average raise. However, the average 3.9 percent increase that white-collar workers received in 1996 matched inflation and therefore maintained the purchasing power of their dollars.[54]

The simplest, most effective method for dealing with inflation in a merit-pay system is to increase salary ranges. By raising salary ranges (e.g., based on a survey of average increases in starting salaries for the coming year) without giving general increases, a firm can maintain competitive hiring rates and at the same time maintain the merit concept surrounding salary increases. Since a raise in minimum pay for each salary range creates an employee group that falls below the new minimum, it is necessary to raise those employees to the new minimum. Such adjustments technically violate the merit philosophy, but the advantages gained by keeping employees in the salary range and at a rate that is sufficient to retain them clearly outweigh the disadvantages.[55]

The size of the merit increase for a given level of performance should decrease as the employee moves farther up the salary range. Merit guide charts provide a means for doing this. Guide charts identify (1) an employee's current performance rating and (2) his or her location in a pay grade. The intersection of these two dimensions identifies a percentage of pay increase based on the performance level and location of the employee in the pay grade. Figure 10-8 shows an example of such a chart. The rationale for the merit guide chart approach is that a person at the top of the range is already making more than the "going rate" for that job. Hence she or he should have to demonstrate more than satisfactory performance in order to continue moving farther above the going rate. Performance incentives, one-time awards that must be reearned each year, allow employees to supplement their income.

PERFORMANCE INCENTIVES

Over the past decade, incentive awards that once were reserved for upper management have boomed in popularity. As of 1997, about 34 percent of 383 major companies offer formal bonus plans to hourly workers, up from 27 percent in 1995. Nearly two-thirds do so for salaried employees, up from about 57 percent in 1993.[56] Evidence indicates that incentives work.[57] Workers feel the same way. In a recent survey, fully 86 percent of 1200 workers said they could boost their productivity by an average of 26 percent given the right incentives. The biggest barriers: inadequate supervision and employee involvement in decision making (nonfinancial rewards), too much work, and insufficient financial rewards and chances to advance.[58]

EMPLOYEE PERFORMANCE	PERCENT INCREASE				
Distinguished	14%	12%	11%	10%	9%
Commendable	11%	10%	9%	8%	Ceiling
Competent	9%	8%	7%	Ceiling	
Adequate	5%	0	Ceiling		
Provisional	0	Ceiling			
Salary (as % of midpoint) is:	80% → 88%	→ 96%	→ 104%	→ 112%	→ 120%

Figure 10-8
Sample merit guide chart.

Performance incentives comprise many different approaches. Since each has different consequences, each needs special treatment.[59] One way to classify them is according to the level of performance targeted—individual, team, or total organization. Within these broad categories, literally hundreds of different approaches for relating pay to performance exist. In this chapter we will consider the three categories described above, beginning with merit pay for individuals—both executives and lower-level workers. First, however, let's consider some fundamental requirements of all incentive programs.

REQUIREMENTS OF EFFECTIVE INCENTIVE SYSTEMS

At the outset it is important to distinguish merit systems from incentive systems. Both are designed to motivate employees to improve their job performance. Most commonly, merit systems are applied to exempt employees in the form of permanent increases to their base pay. The goal is to tie pay increases to each employee's level of job performance. Incentives (e.g., sales commissions, profit sharing) are one-time supplements to base pay. They are also awarded on the basis of job performance, and they are applied to broader segments of the labor force, including nonexempt and unionized employees.

Properly designed incentive programs work because they are based on two well-accepted psychological principles: (1) increased motivation improves performance, and (2) recognition is a major factor in motivation.[60] Unfortunately, however, many incentive programs are improperly designed, and they do not work. They violate one or more of the following rules (shown graphically in Figure 10-9):

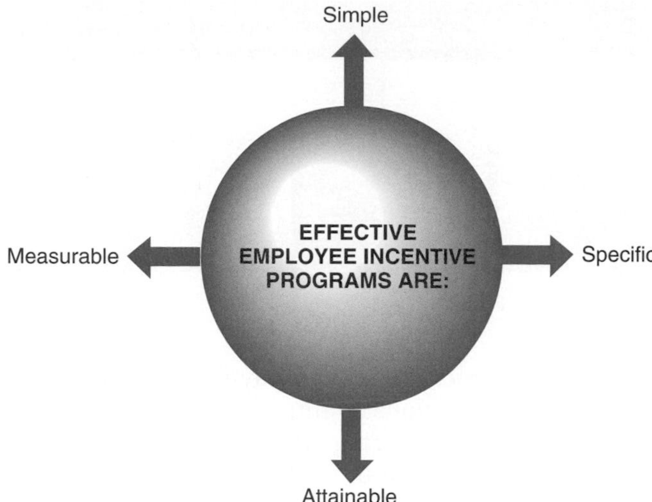

Figure 10-9
Requirements of effective incentive systems.

- **Be simple**. The rules of the system should be brief, clear, and understandable.
- **Be specific**. It is not sufficient to say "produce more" or "stop accidents." Employees need to know precisely what they are expected to do.
- **Be attainable**. Every employee should have a reasonable chance to gain something.
- **Be measurable**. Measurable objectives are the foundation on which incentive plans are built. Program dollars will be wasted (and program evaluation hampered) if specific accomplishments cannot be related to dollars spent.

MERIT-PAY SYSTEMS

In one survey of 2400 employers, 94 percent said that at least part of their employees' pay was based on performance.[61] Unfortunately, many of the plans do not work. Here are some reasons why:[62]

1. **The incentive value of the reward offered is too low**. Give someone a $5000 raise and she keeps $250 a month after taxes. The "stakes," after taxes, are nominal.[63]

2. **The link between performance and rewards is weak**. If performance is measured annually on a one-dimensional scale, employees will remain unclear about just what is being rewarded. In addition, the timing of a merit-pay award may have little or no correlation with the timing of desirable behaviors.[64] If such conditions prevail, and cannot be fixed, then do not use financial incentives.

3. **Supervisors often resist performance appraisal**. Few supervisors are trained in the art of giving feedback accurately, comfortably, and with a minimum likelihood of creating other problems (see Chapter 8). As a result, many are afraid to make distinctions among workers—and they do not. When the best performers receive rewards that are no higher than the worst performers, motivation plummets.

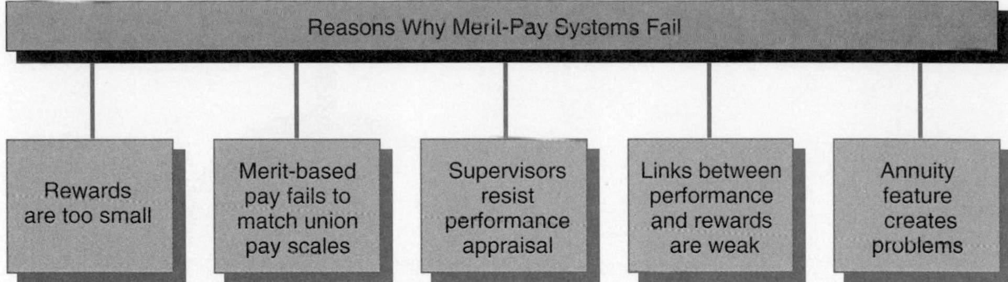

Figure 10-10
Why merit-pay systems fail.

4. **Union contracts influence pay-for-performance decisions within and between organizations**. Failure to match union wages over a 3- or 4-year period (especially during periods of high inflation) invites dissension and turnover among nonunion employees.
5. **The "annuity" problem**. As past "merit payments" are incorporated into an individual's base salary, the payments form an annuity (a sum of money received at regular intervals) and allow formerly productive individuals to slack off for several years and still earn high pay. The annuity feature also leads to another problem: topping out. After a long period in a job, individuals often reach the top of the pay range for their jobs. As a result, pay no longer serves as a motivator because it cannot increase as a result of performance.[65]

These reasons are shown graphically in Figure 10-10.

Barriers Can Be Overcome

Lincoln Electric, a Cleveland-based manufacturer of welding machines and motors, boasts a productivity rate more than double that of other manufacturers in its industry. It follows two cardinal rules:

1. Pay employees for productivity, and only for productivity.
2. Promote employees for productivity, and only for productivity.[66]

Furthermore, research on the effect of merit-pay practices on performance in white-collar jobs indicates that not all merit reward systems are equal. Those that tie performance more closely to rewards are likely to generate higher levels of performance, particularly after a year or two. In addition, merit systems that incorporate a wide range of possible increases tend to generate higher levels of job performance after 1 year. Some typical ranges used in successful merit systems are as follows: Digital Equipment, 0 to 30 percent; Xerox, 0 to 13 percent; and Westinghouse, 0 to 19 percent.[67]

GUIDELINES FOR EFFECTIVE MERIT-PAY SYSTEMS

Those affected by the merit-pay system must support it if it is to work as designed. This is in addition to the requirements for incentive programs shown in Figure 10-9. From the very inception of a merit-pay system, it is important that employees feel a sense of "ownership" of the system. To accomplish this goal,

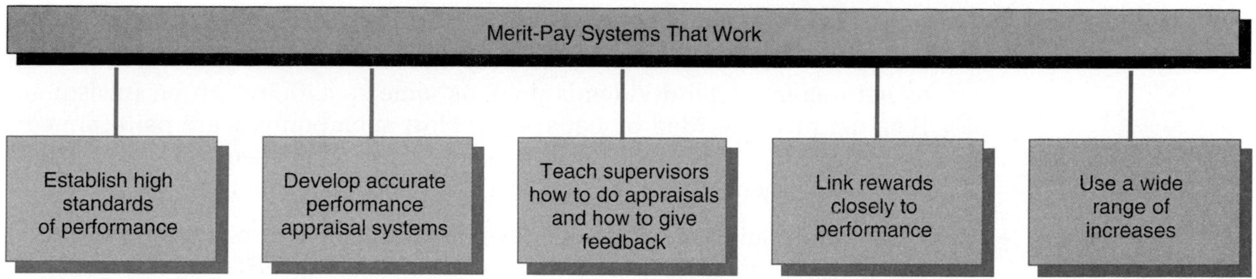

Figure 10-11
Guidelines for effective merit-pay systems.

consider implementing a merit-pay system on a step-by-step basis (for example, over a 2-year period), coupled with continued review and revision. Here are five steps to follow:

1. **Establish high standards of performance.** Low expectations tend to be self-fulfilling prophecies. In the world of sports, successful coaches such as Vince Lombardi, John Wooden, and Don Shula have demanded excellence. Excellence rarely results from expectations of mediocrity.
2. **Develop accurate performance appraisal systems.** Focus on job-specific, results-oriented criteria (outcomes) as well as on employees' behavior (processes).
3. **Train supervisors in the mechanics of performance appraisal and in the art of giving feedback to subordinates.** Train them to manage ineffective performance constructively.
4. **Tie rewards closely to performance.** For example, use semiannual performance appraisals as bases for merit increases (or lack of increases).
5. **Use a wide range of increases.** Make pay increases meaningful.

Merit-pay systems can work, but they need to follow these guidelines if they are to work effectively. Figure 10-11 depicts these guidelines graphically.

INCENTIVES FOR EXECUTIVES

"It took me a long while to learn that people do what you pay them to do, not what you ask them to do," says Hicks Waldron, former chairman and CEO of Avon Products, Inc.[68]

Companies with a history of outperforming their rivals, regardless of industry or economic climate, have two common characteristics: (1) a long-term, strategic view of their executives, and (2) stability in their executive groups.[69] It makes sense, therefore, to develop integrated plans for total executive compensation so that rewards are based on achieving the company's long-term strategic goals. This may require a rebalancing of the elements of executive reward systems: base salary, annual (short-term) incentives, and long-term incentives.

Regardless of the exact form of rebalancing, base salaries (more than $1 million a year for CEOs of the largest American corporations[70]) will continue to be the center point of executive compensation. This is because they generally serve as an index for benefit values. Objectives for short- and long-term incentives frequently are defined as a percentage of base salary. However, incentives are likely to become more long- than short-term-oriented. Here's why:

1. Annual, or short-term, incentive plans encourage the efficient use of existing assets. They are usually based on indicators of corporate performance, such as net income, total dividends paid, or some specific return on investment (i.e., net profit divided by net assets). Most such bonuses are paid immediately in cash, with CEOs receiving an average of 48 percent of their base pay, senior management 35 percent, and middle management 22 percent.[71]

2. Long-term plans encourage the development of new processes, plants, and products that open new markets and restore old ones. Hence long-term performance encompasses qualitative progress as well as quantitative accomplishments. Long-term incentive plans are designed to reward strategic gains rather than short-term contributions to profits. They are as common in owner-controlled firms (where at least 5 percent of outstanding stock is held by an individual or organization not involved in the actual management of a company) as they are in management-controlled firms (where no individual or organization controls more than 5 percent of the stock).[72] We should be encouraging such a long-term view among executives, for it relates consistently to company success.

In the face of widespread criticism of executive pay practices, some firms are rethinking the way they reward top executives.[73] Take stock options, for example. Executives are granted the right to buy the company's stock sometime in the future at a fixed price, usually the price on the day the options are granted. Options are popular because they allow issuing companies to contend that the executives will not benefit unless the shareholders do. However, even enthusiasts cannot prove that options motivate executives to perform better. Critics contend that stock options reward executives not just for their own performance but for a booming stock market. To a large extent, they are right, for as much as 70 percent of the change in a company's stock price depends only on changes in the overall market.[74] In response, some companies now grant stock options not at the market price but at some higher price. These are known as "premium-price options."[75] Thus executives will profit only after the stock has risen substantially, as is the case at Monsanto, for example.

COMPANY EXAMPLE

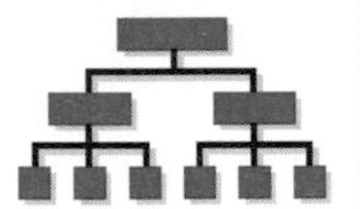

PREMIUM-PRICE OPTIONS AT MONSANTO

At Monsanto, executives receive options to purchase stock at prices that *ascend* over time. In other words, they profit only to the extent that the stock price clears a hurdle rate. Thus executives will be able to purchase stock at four prices: $150, $175, $200, and $225 a share. When chief executive officer Robert Shapiro signed off on the plan, the stock was trading at $116. Therefore, the price would have to increase by 30 percent before he started to profit on the least expensive options, and by 90 percent for the dearest options.

Four months after the plan was set, the stock hit the first hurdle, trading at $153. Monsanto is now being run as though its managers have a stake in it. In the past year, as its genetically engineered seed business has taken off, Monsanto unloaded its plastics unit at the top of the cycle, and bought into seed companies on the cheap. If Shapiro and his top executives are right, they will be richly rewarded.

INCENTIVES FOR LOWER-LEVEL EMPLOYEES

As noted earlier in this chapter, a common practice is to supplement employees' pay with increments related to improvements in job performance. Most such plans have a "baseline," or normal, work standard; performance above this standard is rewarded. The baseline should be high enough so that employees are not given extra rewards for what is really just a normal day's work. On the other hand, the baseline should not be so high that it is impossible to earn additional pay.

It is more difficult to specify work standards in some jobs than in others. At the top management level, for instance, what constitutes a "normal" day's output? As one moves down the organizational hierarchy, however, jobs can be defined more clearly, and shorter-run goals and targets can be established.

Setting Workload Standards

All incentive systems depend on workload standards. The standards provide a relatively objective definition of the job, they give employees targets to shoot for, and they make it easier for supervisors to assign work equitably. Make no mistake about it, though, effective performance is often hard to define. For example, when a Corning group set up a trial program to reward workers for improving their efficiency, a team struggled to figure out "What's a meaningful thing to measure? What's reasonable?" The measures finally settled on included safety, quality, shipping efficiency, and forecast accuracy.[76] Once workload standards are set, employees have an opportunity to earn more than their base salaries, often as much as 20 to 25 percent more. In short, they have an incentive to work both harder and smarter.

When workload standards are set for production work, the ideal job (ideal only in terms of the ability to measure performance, not in terms of improving work motivation or job satisfaction) should (1) be highly repetitive, (2) have a short job cycle, and (3) produce a clear, measurable output. However, before explicit workload standards can be set, management must do the following:

- Describe the job by means of job analysis.
- Decide *how* the job is to be done (motion study).
- Decide *how fast* the job should be done (time study).

The standards themselves will vary, of course, according to the *type* of product or service (e.g., a hospital, a factory, a cable television company), the *method of service delivery*, the degree to which service can be *quantified*, and *organizational needs*, including legal and social pressures. In fact, the many different forms of incentive plans for lower-level employees really differ along only two dimensions:

1. How premium rates are determined
2. How the extra payments are made

To be sure, incentives oriented toward individuals are becoming less popular as work increasingly becomes interdependent in nature. Nevertheless, individual incentives remain popular in some industries, particularly manufacturing. Lincoln Electric is a prime example.

COMPANY EXAMPLE

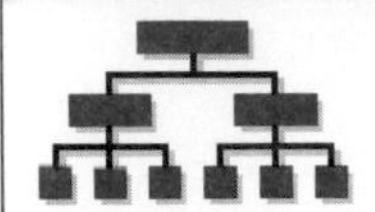

INDIVIDUAL INCENTIVES AT LINCOLN ELECTRIC[77]

From its earliest years, 100-year-old Lincoln Electric Company of Cleveland, Ohio, has charted a unique path in worker-management relations, featuring high wages, guaranteed employment, few supervisors, a lucrative bonus-incentive system, and piecework compensation. The company is the world's largest maker of arc-welding equipment; it has 3400 U.S. employees, 23 plants in 17 countries, and no unions. Among the innovative management practices that set Lincoln apart are these:

- Guaranteed employment for all full-time workers with more than 2 years' service, and no mandatory retirement. No worker has been laid off since 1948, and turnover is less than 4 percent for those with more than 180 days on the job.
- High wages (an average of $35,000), including a substantial annual bonus (up to 100 percent of base pay) based on the company's profits. Wages at Lincoln ($16.54 an hour) are roughly equivalent to wages for similar work elsewhere in the Cleveland area ($14.25), but the bonuses the company pays make its compensation substantially higher. For example, in 1995 the average worker at Lincoln earned a bonus of 56 percent of his or her base pay, for total earnings of almost $54,000. (The most hard-driving workers made over $100,000.) Lincoln has never had a strike and has not missed a bonus payment since the system was instituted in 1934. Individual bonuses are set by a formula that judges workers on five dimensions: quality, output, dependability, ideas, and cooperation. The ratings determine how much of the total corporate bonus pool each worker will get, on top of his or her hourly wage.
- Piecework—more than half of Lincoln's workers are paid according to what they produce, rather than an hourly or weekly wage. If a worker is sick, he or she does not get paid.
- Promotion is almost exclusively from within, according to merit, not seniority.
- Few supervisors, with a supervisor-to-worker ratio of 1 to 100, far lower than in much of the industry. Each employee is supposed to be a self-managing entrepreneur, and each is accountable for the quality of his or her own work.
- No break periods, and mandatory overtime. Workers must work overtime, if ordered to, during peak production periods and must agree to change jobs to meet production schedules or to maintain the company's guaranteed employment program.

While the company insists on individual initiative—and pays according to individual effort—it works diligently to foster the notion of teamwork. And it did so long before the Japanese became known for emphasizing such concepts. If a worker is overly competitive with fellow employees, he or she is rated poorly in terms of cooperation and team play on his or her semiannual rating reports. Thus that worker's bonus will be smaller. Says one company official: "This is not an easy style to manage; it takes a lot of time and a willingness to work with people."

Union Attitudes

A unionized employer may establish an incentive system, but it will be subject to negotiation through collective bargaining. Unions may also wish to participate in the day-to-day management of the incentive system, and management ought to consider that demand seriously. Employees often fear that management will manipulate the system to the disadvantage of employees. Joint participation helps reassure employees that the plan is fair.

Union attitudes toward incentives vary with the type of incentive offered. Unions tend to oppose individual piece-rate systems because they pit worker against worker and can create unfavorable intergroup conflict. However, unions tend to support organizationwide systems, such as profit sharing, because of the extra earnings they provide to their members.[78] In one experiment, for example, an electric utility instituted a division-level incentive plan in one division but not in others. The incentive payout was based on equal percentage shares based on salary. Relative to a control division, the one operating under the incentive plan performed significantly better in reduction of unit cost, in budget performance, and on 9 of 10 other objective indicators. Nevertheless, union employees helped kill the plan for two reasons: (1) negative reactions from union members in other divisions who did not operate under the incentive plan; and (2) a preference for equal dollar shares, rather than equal percentage shares, because the earnings of bargaining-unit employees were lower, on average, than those of managers and staff employees.[79]

TEAM INCENTIVES

To provide broader motivation than is furnished by incentive plans geared to individual employees, firms have tried several other approaches. The aim of such plans is twofold: to increase productivity and to improve morale by giving employees a feeling of participation in and identification with the company. Team incentives are one such plan.

Team incentives provide an opportunity for each team member to receive a bonus based on the output of the team as a whole. Teams may be as small as 4 to 7 employees or as large as 35 to 40 employees. Team incentives are most appropriate when jobs are highly interrelated. In fact, highly interrelated jobs are the wave of the future and, in many cases, the wave of the present. In the past, relatively few firms used team incentives. In the future, they will need to be more creative in using team performance appraisal and team incentives.[80] For example, XEL uses a team-based variable-pay system as part of its compensation plan.

COMPANY EXAMPLE

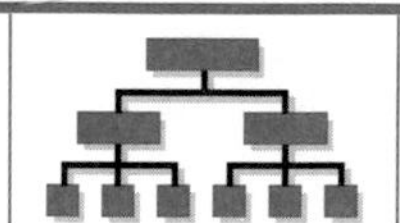

TEAM INCENTIVES IN A SMALL BUSINESS[81]

XEL, a manufacturer of electronic equipment for the telecommunications industry, uses a three-tier incentive compensation plan to complement its use of self-managed work teams: a lump-sum profit sharing plan, a pay-for-skills program, and a team-based variable-pay system. For the team-based pay system, XEL sets aside a percentage of its total payroll, and payouts are determined by team rankings. A team's ranking is based on three criteria: ratings by internal and external customers, achievement of quarterly team objectives, and management input recognizing special circumstances.

In this system, members on the same team do not all receive the same payout, since the final payout is adjusted to reflect peer evaluations. For example, if the overall merit-pay budget is 5 percent of payroll, the top-ranked team might get 8 percent; a midranked team, 5 percent; and a bottom-ranked team, nothing. Further, within the top team there may be a spread of 5 to 10 percent among individual members' ratings. The major benefit of such a system: team deficiencies get quick attention.

Team incentives have the following advantages:

1. They make it possible to reward workers who provide essential services to line workers (so-called indirect labor), yet who are paid only their regular base pay. These employees do things like transport supplies and materials, maintain equipment, or inspect work output.
2. They encourage cooperation, not competition, among workers.

On the other hand, team incentives also have disadvantages, which are as follows:

1. Fear that management will cut rates (or employees) if employees produce too much.
2. Competition between teams, to the detriment of the organization as a whole.
3. Inability of workers to see their individual contributions to the output of the team. If they do not see the link between their individual effort and increased rewards, they will not be motivated to produce more.

To overcome some of the first two disadvantages of team incentives, many firms have introduced organizationwide incentives.

ORGANIZATIONWIDE INCENTIVES

In this final section, we will consider three broad classes of organizationwide incentives: profit sharing, gain sharing, and employee stock ownership plans. As we will see, each is different in its objectives and implementation.

Profit Sharing

In the United States, firms use profit sharing for one or more of the following reasons: to provide a group incentive for increased productivity, to institute a flexible reward structure that reflects a company's actual economic position, to enhance employees' security and identification with the company, to attract and retain workers more easily, and/or to educate individuals about the factors that underlie business success and the capitalistic system.[82]

Employees receive a bonus that is normally based on some percentage (e.g., 10 to 30 percent) of the company's profits beyond some minimum level. In 1994, for example, each of 81,000 Chrysler workers received a profit sharing bonus of $4300. Does profit sharing improve productivity? One review of 27 econometric studies found that profit sharing was positively related to productivity in better than 9 of every 10 instances. Productivity was generally 3 to 5 percent higher in firms with profit sharing plans than in those without such plans.[83]

A most ambitious profit sharing program was started by Du Pont in 1988 for nearly all of its 20,000 managers and employees in the fibers business in the United States. Under the plan, employees could earn up to 12 percent of their base pay if the business exceeded its profit goals, but they could also lose part of their original increase if the profit goals were not met.[84] In late 1990, when it appeared that workers would lose as much as 4 percent of their base pay as a result of poor sales in the fibers unit, discontent among workers was so high that Du Pont canceled the plan.[85] Although there were many reasons for the plan's failure, two of the most telling were (1) the fact that employees felt powerless to influence profits, and (2) employee resentment over loopholes for high-level managers in the fibers unit, who were still able to benefit from Du Pont's companywide bonus program. That program was geared to the company's total profits, not just to the profits of the fibers unit.

This case illustrates the two-sided nature of profit sharing. On the one hand, compensation costs become more variable, since a company pays only if it makes a profit. On the other hand, from the employee's perspective, benefits and pensions are insecure. Certainly, the success of profit sharing plans depends on the company's overall human resource management policy and on the state of labor-management relations. This is even more true of gain-sharing plans.

Gain Sharing

Gain sharing is a formal reward system that has existed in a variety of forms for more than 50 years. Sometimes known as the Scanlon plan, the Rucker plan, or Improshare (improved productivity through sharing), gain sharing comprises three elements:[86]

1. A philosophy of cooperation
2. An involvement system
3. A financial bonus

The philosophy of cooperation refers to an organizational climate characterized by high levels of trust, two-way communication, participation, and harmonious industrial relations. The involvement system refers to the structure and process for improving organizational productivity. Typically, it is a broadly based suggestion system implemented by an employee-staffed committee structure that usually reaches all areas of the organization. Sometimes this structure involves work teams, but usually it is simply an employee-based suggestion system. The employees involved develop and implement ideas related to productivity. The third component, the financial bonus, is determined by a calculation that measures the difference between expected and actual costs during a bonus period.

The three components mutually reinforce one another.[87] High levels of cooperation lead to information sharing, which in turn leads to employee involvement, which leads to new behaviors, such as offering suggestions to improve organizational productivity. This increase in productivity then results in a financial bonus (based on the amount of the productivity increase), which rewards and reinforces the philosophy of cooperation.

It is important to distinguish gain sharing from profit sharing. The two approaches differ in three important ways:[88]

1. Gain sharing is based on a measure of productivity. Profit sharing is based on a global profitability measure.
2. Gain sharing, productivity measurement, and bonus payments are frequent events, distributed monthly or quarterly, in contrast to the annual measures and rewards of profit sharing plans.
3. Gain-sharing plans are current distribution plans, in contrast to most profit sharing plans, which have deferred payments. Hence gain-sharing plans are true incentive plans rather than employee benefits. As such, they are more directly related to individual behavior and therefore can motivate worker productivity.

When gain-sharing plans such as the Scanlon plan work, they work well. For example, consider a 17-year evaluation of such a plan in a manufacturing operation, DeSoto, Inc., of Garland, Texas. The bonus formula, which measures labor productivity, revealed that average bonuses ranged from 2.5 percent to more than 22 percent, with an overall average of 9.6 percent. Moreover, over the 17-year period of the study, output (as measured by gallons of paint) increased by 78 percent.[89] Nevertheless, in the 50 years since the inception of gain sharing, it has been abandoned by firms about as often as it has been retained. Here are some reasons why:

1. Generally, it does not work well in piecework operations.
2. Some firms are uncomfortable about bringing unions into business planning.
3. Some managers may feel they are giving up their prerogatives.[90]

Neither the size of a company nor the type of technology it employs seems to be related to Scanlon plan success. However, employee participation, positive managerial attitudes, the number of years a company has had a Scanlon plan, favorable and realistic employee attitudes, and involvement by a high-level executive are strongly related to the success of a Scanlon plan.[91] In the development of an organizationwide incentive plan that has a chance to survive, let alone succeed, careful in-depth planning must precede implementation. It is true of all incentive plans, though, that *none will work well except in a climate of trustworthy labor-management relations and sound human resource management practices.*

Employee Stock Ownership Plans (ESOPs)

ESOPs have become popular in both large and small companies in the United States, as they have in western Europe, some countries in central Europe, and China.[92] About 10,000 U.S. firms now share ownership with 10 million employees. Employees own an average of 13 percent of the stock at 562 public companies. However, they have board seats at fewer than a dozen of them, and most of

IMPACT OF PAY AND INCENTIVES ON PRODUCTIVITY, QUALITY OF WORK LIFE, AND THE BOTTOM LINE

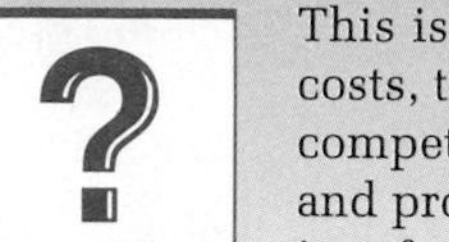

High salary levels alone do not ensure a productive, motivated workforce. This is evident in the auto industry, where wages are among the highest in the country, yet quality problems and high absenteeism persist. A critical factor, then, is not *how much* a company pays its workers but, more important, *how the pay system is designed, communicated, and managed.* Excessively high labor costs can bankrupt a company.[97] This is especially likely if, to cover its labor costs, the company cannot price its products competitively. If that happens, productivity and profits both suffer directly, and the quality of work life suffers indirectly. When sensible policies on pay and incentives are established using the principles discussed in this chapter, everybody wins: the company, the employees, and employees' families as well.

those are unionized.[93] Employee ownership can be found in every industry, in every size firm, and in every part of the country.[94]

Generally, ESOPs are established for any of the following reasons:

- As a means of tax-favored, company-financed transfer of ownership from a departing owner to a firm's employees. This is often done in small firms with closely held stock.[95]
- As a way of borrowing money relatively inexpensively. A firm borrows money from a bank using its stock as collateral, places the stock in an employee stock ownership trust, and, as the loan is repaid, distributes the stock at no cost to employees. Companies can deduct the principal as well as interest on the amount borrowed, and lenders pay taxes on only 50 percent of their income from ESOP loans.
- To fulfill a philosophical belief in employee ownership. For example, at 22,000-employee Science Applications International Corporation, a $2.1 billion high-tech research and engineering concern, founder J. Robert Beyster began giving employees stock in the company every time they landed a new contract. That was 27 years ago, and he has never stopped. Beyster attributes much of the company's growth not to management skills or to an overarching strategy, but to his ownership philosophy. He says, "Employee-ownership really did it. Who has a better right to own the company than the people who make it worth something?" So far that has proved to be a winning formula.[96]
- As an additional employee benefit.

Do ESOPs improve employee motivation and satisfaction? Longitudinal research spanning 45 case studies found that stock ownership alone does not make employees work harder or enjoy their day-to-day work more.[98] Nor does it promote an increase in perceived employee influence in company decisions or status on the job. Nevertheless, certain features do affect employee motivation, satisfaction, and commitment through stock ownership:

1. ESOP satisfaction tends to be highest in companies where (a) the company makes relatively large annual contributions to the plan; (b) management is committed to employee ownership and is willing to share power and

IMPLICATIONS FOR MANAGEMENT PRACTICE

With regard to pay and incentives, expect to see three trends continue:

1. The movement to performance-based pay plans, in which workers put more of their pay "at risk" in return for potentially higher rewards
2. The movement toward the use of teamwide or organizationwide incentive plans at all levels
3. Use of a wide range of pay increases, in an effort to make distinctions in performance as meaningful as possible.

decision-making authority with employees, and (c) there are extensive company communications about the ESOP, the company's current performance, and its long-range plans.[99]

2. Employees tend to be most satisfied with stock ownership when the company established its ESOP for employee-centered reasons (management was committed to employee ownership) rather than for strategic or financial reasons (e.g., as an antitakeover device or to gain tax savings).
3. Satisfaction breeds satisfaction. That is, the same individual-level and ESOP characteristics that lead to ESOP satisfaction also lead (somewhat less strongly) to organizational commitment.

How does employee stock ownership affect economic performance? When the above three conditions are met, employee-owned firms have been 150 percent as profitable, have had twice the productivity growth, and have generated three times more new jobs than their competitors. High-tech companies that share ownership widely grow 2 to 4 times as fast as those that do not. Publicly held companies that are at least 10 percent employee-owned outperform 62 to 75 percent of their competitors, depending on the measure used.[100] On an aggregate level, between 1979 and 1992, a portfolio of companies that were at least 10 percent employee-owned would have produced an annualized return of 27.17 percent, against 16.54 percent for Standard & Poor's 500-stock index.[101]

While such data do not prove that employee stock ownership causes success (it may be that successful firms are more likely to make employees part owners), they do suggest that if implemented properly, such plans can improve employee attitudes and economic productivity. Nevertheless, ESOPs are not risk-free to employees. ESOPs are not insured, and if a company goes bankrupt, its stock may be worthless.

Human Resource Management in Action: Conclusion

THE TRUST GAP

What steps can companies take to sew corporate top and bottom back together? Here are seven suggestions. One, start with the obvious. Tie the financial interests of high- and low-level workers closer together by making exposure to risks *and* rewards more equitable. Thus, when NUCOR, a steel company in Charlotte, North Carolina, went through tough times, its president took a 60 percent cut in pay. Said a compensation consultant, "How often do you see that? . . . It makes a real difference if employees see that their CEO is willing to take it in the shorts along with them."[102] Conversely, First Bank reaped a $190 million windfall when its deal to buy First Interstate collapsed in 1996. Management awarded $11 million to 12,000 employees, or about $750 each. Said one teller, "I think it's awesome . . . it was very unexpected."[103]

Two, consider instituting profit sharing, a Scanlon plan, gain sharing, or some other program that lets employees profit from their efforts. Make sure, however, that incentive pay is linked to performance over which the beneficiaries have control.

Three, rethink perquisites. Now that perks come under taxable income, they just do not have the same appeal to executives as they used to. Yet they still have at least the same downside with the rank and file.

Four, look at the office layout with an eye toward equity. In Sweden, for example, same-size offices are the norm. When an American visitor asked his Swedish corporate hosts how they could give the same amount of space to a secretary as to an engineer, they said, "How can we hire a secretary and expect her to be committed to our company, when, by the size of the office we give her, we tell her she's a second-class citizen?"[104]

Five, make sure your door is really open. If that means meeting with employees at unorthodox times, such as when their shifts end, then do it. Not a single one of the CEOs interviewed by *Fortune* could recall employees ever abusing an open-door policy. The lesson is clear for managers at all levels: employees do not walk through your door unless they have to.

Six, if you do not survey employee attitudes now, start to do so. What you find can help identify problems before they become crises. Share findings, and be sure employees know how subsequent decisions may be related to them. Do not worry about raising expectations too high. As one executive commented, "Employees by and large are reasonable people. They understand you can't do everything they want. As long as they know their views are being considered and they get some feedback from you to that effect, you will be meeting their expectations."[105]

Seven, explain things—personally. While one study found that 97 percent of CEOs believe that communicating with employees has a positive impact on job satisfaction and 79 percent think it benefits the bottom line, only 22 percent do it weekly or more often.

There is no doubt that these seven steps can help close the trust gap that exists in so many U.S. organizations today. On the other hand, virtually all experts cite one important qualification: it is suicidal to start down this road unless you are absolutely sincere.

SUMMARY

Contemporary pay systems (outside the entertainment and professional sports fields) are characterized by cost containment, pay and benefit levels commensurate with what a company can afford, and programs that encourage and reward performance.

Generally speaking, pay systems are designed to attract, retain, and motivate employees; to achieve internal, external, and individual equity; and to maintain a balance in relationships between direct and indirect forms of compensation and between the pay rates of supervisory and nonsupervisory employees. Pay systems need to be tied to the strategic mission of an organization, and they should take their direction from that strategic mission. However, actual wage levels depend on labor market conditions, legislation, collective bargaining, management attitudes, and an organization's ability to pay. The broad objective in developing pay systems is to assign a monetary value to each job or skill set in the organization (a base rate) and to establish an orderly procedure for increasing the base rate. To develop a job-based system, we need four basic tools: job analyses and job descriptions, a job evaluation plan, pay surveys, and a pay structure. In addition, the following pay policy issues are important: pay secrecy versus openness, the effect of inflation on pay systems, pay compression, and pay raises.

In terms of incentive plans, the most effective ones are simple, specific, attainable, and measurable. Consider merit pay, for example. Merit pay works best when these guidelines are followed: (1) establish high standards of performance, (2) develop appraisal systems that focus on job-specific, results-oriented criteria; (3) train supervisors in the mechanics of performance appraisal and in the art of giving constructive feedback; (4) tie rewards closely to performance; and (5) provide a wide range of possible pay increases.

Long-term incentives, mostly in the form of stock options, are becoming a larger proportion of executives' pay packages. Finally, there is a wide variety of individual, group, and organizationwide incentive plans (e.g., profit sharing, gain sharing, employee stock ownership plans) with different impacts on employee motivation and economic outcomes. Blending fixed versus variable pay in a manner that is understandable and acceptable to employees will present a management challenge for years to come.

DISCUSSION QUESTIONS

10-1 What steps can a company take to integrate its compensation system with its general business strategy?

10-2 What can companies do to ensure internal, external, and individual equity for all employees?

10-3 Discuss the advantages and disadvantages of skill-based pay systems.

10-4 How has "strategic thinking" affected executive incentives?

10-5 If you were implementing an employee stock ownership plan, what key factors would you consider?

APPLYING YOUR KNOWLEDGE

Case 10-1 *Compensation and Incentive Pay at Shaver, Inc.*

"I don't understand it. We're a successful company that pays well, and we have a reputation to uphold. Now you tell me that last year most of the raises employees got were *not* given on the basis of performance. How can that be?" So asked Shaver, Inc.'s chief executive officer Phyllis Johnstone. Mike Mercer, Shaver, Inc.'s vice president for human resources, fumbled for an answer. "Well, we've got a darn good compensation system. The problem is simply that managers don't know how to use it effectively."

This exchange of views prompted Mike Mercer to return to his office and think about the journey that he and his Salary Review Task Force had begun several years ago. This task force, which involved employees from virtually every division at Shaver, Inc. had reviewed the earlier compensation system and had instituted a series of changes designed to make the system more effective. But apparently the changes had not been very successful, and Mike Mercer was on the horns of a dilemma.

Company Background

Shaver, Inc., a manufacturer of all kinds of wood and steel tables for business and industry, was headquartered in Eugene, Oregon. Its roots date back to 1907, when founder Jason Bishop started up a new business near a saw mill on the outskirts of Eugene and developed a uniquely crafted writing table for bookkeepers. The business initially was family-owned and remained relatively small until the 1940s. By then, however, outside investors had begun to take an interest in the quality of workmanship that was demonstrated by the Bishop family, and they purchased the business and began to expand its operations both domestically and overseas. The organization was incorporated in 1952 and continued to expand rapidly throughout the 1950s and 1960s. Today, Shaver, Inc. manufactures and markets more than 40 varieties of tables and is the leader in the western United States in this particular business.

Shaver, Inc. enjoys a reputation for excellent management practice and has been written up in numerous business magazines over the years. It consistently receives high ratings for product innovation, return on stockholder investment, product quality, and financial acumen. It also receives high marks for its ability to attract, develop, and retain talented employees.

Shaver, Inc. has also traditionally been a very profitable organization, which is what attracted the initial investor interest in the 1940s. Until 1992, Shaver, Inc. had always outperformed its competitors in terms of return on investment for its shareholders. For instance, in 1988, Shaver's return on assets averaged 15 percent while its largest competitor's in the same year averaged only 11 percent. However, in 1992 the situation began to change. Shaver's traditional lead over its competitors deteriorated, possibly due to changes in organizational structure or to a set of disappointments in new product innovations in the marketplace. But CEO Phyllis Johnstone was not convinced that only factors such as these were to blame for some of Shaver's problems. She was concerned that perhaps employee motivation was deteriorating as well, and her impressions of the salary and compensation system did not provide her with any comfort in this regard.

Compensation Policy at Shaver, Inc.

Shaver, Inc. employs about 16,000 people, roughly half of whom are hourly manufacturing or clerical employees. The other half are salaried exempt employees, including salespeople, engineers, technicians, supervisors and managers, and others. Compensation for the 8000 exempt salaried employees at Shaver, Inc. has historically ranked among the top 33 percent of midsize U.S. corporations. These progressive HR policies and pay practices have contributed to inordinately high levels of employee commitment and loyalty, as characterized by historically low voluntary turnover rates (averaging less than 2 percent of the workforce per year).

As with other companies, the salary determination process at Shaver, Inc. was built upon the annual performance review. Shaver's existing performance appraisal process had been designed and developed by Mike Mercer's Salary Review Task Force in 1992. Under this plan, supervisors rated employees on a scale from 1 to 5, with 5 designating exceptional performance and 1 indicating unacceptable performance. Plus and minus ratings were allowed, with the exception that no one with a 5 could earn a plus and no one with a 1 could earn a minus. Thus, managers could choose from 13 different rating categories in assigning an overall performance evaluation for a particular employee (5, 5–, 4+, 4, 4–, etc.).

Salaries for the 8000 exempt employees at Shaver, Inc. were based on a combination of job characteristics and merit. The job characteristics were measured using "Hay points." Hay points were determined by evaluating each position at Shaver, Inc. in terms of the three Hay factors—know-how, problem solving, and accountability. For each job, numerical scores were assigned to each of the three factors according to guide charts provided by Hay Associates. The guide charts revealed what was meant by "know-how" or one of the other compensable factors. Each compensable factor was broken down in terms of more specific building blocks to make the process as objective as possible. The total number of Hay points for each position in the organization was calculated by summing the points given on each of the three compensable factors. At Shaver, Inc., Hay points were then converted to a "a control point" (which equated roughly to an average monthly salary) using a "salary line formula." For example, in 1994, the salary line formula was as follows: control point = \$1462 + \$3.23 X (where X = number of Hay points).

With this formula, an employee with 550 Hay points had a 1994 control point of \$3238 per month. At Shaver, Inc., the employee's actual salary could range from 80 percent to 125 percent of the control point. Actual salary as a percentage of the control point is called the employee's "compa-ratio." For example, an employee with 550 Hay points and a compa-ratio of 110 would have a 1994 monthly salary of \$3562. On the other hand, an employee with 550 Hay points and a compa-ratio of 80 would have a 1994 monthly salary of \$2591. Each employee's compa-ratio goes down whenever the salary line formula is moved upward, and goes up each time he or she gets a merit salary increase.

Shaver, Inc. has always prided itself on being an organization that pays above-average salaries. It sets its salary line formula so that employees with compa-ratios of 100 earn approximately 10 percent more than the average compensation in other medium-size organizations. This means that an employee at Shaver, Inc. in a position with 550 Hay points would earn roughly 10 percent more than a similarly situated employee with 550 Hay points at another organization, assuming that both had similar compa-ratios. In order to guarantee that Shaver, Inc. is paying about 10 percent above market, it takes part in a variety of salary surveys each year. In these surveys, it sends it salary data in and receives reports back from the surveying organization showing how its salaries compare with those of other organizations.

The salary line formula is revised annually on July 1, the beginning of Shaver's fiscal year. The salary line formula is adjusted upward so that control points for particular positions approximate 10 percent above the market salary goal that Shaver sets for itself. However, the salaries themselves are not automatically adjusted when the salary line formula changes. Instead, individual compa-ratios decline every July 1st when control points are increased.

Merit-Pay Increases

Salary revisions themselves are linked to both control-point increases and performance appraisal ratings through guidelines established by Mike Mercer's human resource management department. Theoretically, employees with higher performance appraisal ratings should get larger pay increases, and raises for a given performance rating should be smaller for employees with higher compa-ratios. For example, the salary increase for an employee receiving a performance rating of 4 might be in the 5 to 7 percent range if his or her compa-ratio is 90, but only in the 3 to 5 percent range if his or her compa-ratio is 110.

Employees who achieve compa-ratios considerably above 100 over an extended period of time are generally viewed as the star performers at Shaver, Inc. This level of sustained performance suggests that the individual is a clear candidate for promotion. In addition, since salaries are rarely decreased, compa-ratios may be above 100 in the short run for employees who are not performing particularly well and, therefore, not actually candidates for promotion.

The maximum obtainable compa-ratio is 125. Thus, salaries are effectively capped at 125 percent of the control point, and employees near the cap can receive up to, but cannot surpass, the cap during each annual merit-salary increase. In practice, however, only a few employees achieve and maintain compa-ratios exceeding 115. One reason is that the salary line formula is adjusted prior to salary revisions each year. Therefore, even employees hitting the cap in a particular year will likely be well below the cap after the salary line changes on July 1st. The second reason that few employees maintain a salary close to 125 percent of the control point is that those with high compa-ratios are frequently promoted once they attain that level of salary. Since it takes time to learn the skills necessary in a new position, the starting compa-ratio for a newly promoted employee is almost always lower than his or her final compa-ratio in the previous position. For example, in 1993 the average starting compa-ratio for all employees promoted into positions with 500 Hay points was 85.

Performance Appraisal at Shaver

Back in 1992 when Mike Mercer and his Salary Review Task Force had looked into the problems associated with compensation and the performance appraisal system, they had discovered through interviews that there was general agreement that rewards for excellent performance were inadequate. Outstanding performers were getting salary increases that were in many cases only marginally better than those given to average and below-average performers. And in many cases, outstanding performance was not even being identified through the appraisal system.

The Salary Review Task Force had redesigned the appraisal system so that it looked like the one described earlier in the case, and this revision had been implemented in 1992. It was the hope of the task force that this redesigned system would help overcome some of the problems that were uncovered during the interviews. According to Mike Mercer, "One thing that really hit home for us was the negative feeling of some of our best performers concerning the reward system here at Shaver. The key issue seemed to be the appraisal system itself and it simply had to be dealt with."

The problem was that everyone seemed to have different ideas about how to restructure the performance appraisal system. The Salary Review Task Force got a variety of opinions, mostly negative, about the existing appraisal system. Many pointed out that managers were afraid to give experienced people ratings below 8 (the old system had been based on a 10-point rating scale). They also pointed out that it was very difficult to get a rating of 10. In many cases the supervisor had never received a rating of 10 and was not about to give that rating to a subordinate. Some other quotes that were representative of problems uncovered included:

"What's the use of working hard? You still get the same rating everyone else does, and you still get the same 4 percent salary increase. It's demoralizing and demotivating."

"Sharlene has been in that job for 11 years and hasn't done anything extraordinary for the last 8. But do you think my boss would give her a 7? No way! If he did, he'd spend the next year listening to Sharlene complain about her rating."

"How can I evaluate my direct reports fairly and objectively when the other managers are giving all their people 8s? A 7 simply isn't acceptable. The system would be okay if everyone played by the same rules, but they don't."

"It's getting to the point where many of the best people are going to leave Shaver unless they get the right kinds of rewards. Now, who do you want to do the walking? Your best people or your worst?"

It was with these problems in mind that the Salary Review Task Force undertook the redesign of the performance appraisal system in 1992. The recent results of appraisal ratings distribution and salary increases in 1994 for all salaried exempt employees are presented in the following table. It was the information in this table that Mike Mercer presented to Phyllis Johnstone which created the incident described at the beginning of the case.

1994 RATING DISTRIBUTION AND AVERAGE PAY INCREASE UNDER THE 1992 PERFORMANCE APPRAISAL AND SALARY ADMINISTRATION PROGRAM

			Average 1994 pay increase		
1994 rating	Number of employees	Percentage distribution	Compa-ratio 80–94	Compa-ratio 95–109	Compa-ratio 110–125
5	16	0.2			
5–	49	0.6	9.3%	8.7%	6.5%
4+	1,421	17.6			
4	2,447	30.4	6.5%	5.5%	4.8%
4–	1,471	18.3			
3+	1,394	17.3			
3	876	10.9	5.9%	4.8%	4.1%
3–	281	3.5			
2+	63	0.8			
2	27	0.3	4.4%	1.9%	0.1%
2–	1				
1+	1				
1	4				

Questions

1. What are the problems with Shaver, Inc.'s present performance appraisal and salary review program?
2. What changes in Shaver, Inc.'s performance appraisal and salary review system would you recommend?
3. Discuss the rationale and relative advantages of each of the changes you recommend.

REFERENCES

1. Unstable pay becomes ever more common (1995, Dec. 4). *The Wall Street Journal*, p. A1.
2. Mahoney, T. A. (1989). Employment compensation planning and strategy. In L. R. Gomez-Mejia (ed.), *Compensation and benefits.* Washington, DC: Bureau of National Affairs, pp. 3-1 to 3-28.
3. Milkovich, G. T., & Newman, J. M. (1996). *Compensation* (5th ed.). Homewood, IL: BPI-Irwin.
4. Ibid.

5. Stroh, L. K., Brett, J. M., Baumann, J. P., & Reilly, A. H. (1996). Agency theory and variable pay compensation strategies. *Academy of Management Journal*, **39**, 751–767.
6. Grib, G. (1995, July). Pay plans that reward employee achievement. *HRMagazine*, pp. 49, 50.
7. Lublin, J. S. (1997, Jan. 7). Don't count on that merit raise this year. *The Wall Street Journal*, pp. B1, B6.
8. Nelson, E. (1995, Sept. 29). Gas company's gain-sharing plan turns employees into cost-cutting vigilantes. *The Wall Street Journal*, pp. B1, B4; Uchitelle, L. (1987, June 26). Bonuses replace wage raises and workers are the losers.*The New York Times*, pp. A1, D3; Lublin, J. S. (1995, Apr. 12). My colleague, my boss. *The Wall Street Journal*, pp. R4, R12.
9. Uchitelle, op. cit., p. D3.
10. Dolan, K. A. (1996, Nov. 18). When money isn't enough. *Forbes*, pp. 164–170.
11. Ibid., p. 166.
12. Lawler, E. E., III (1989). Pay for performance: A strategic analysis. In L. R. Gomez-Mejia (ed.), *Compensation and benefits*. Washington, DC: Bureau of National Affairs, pp. 3-136 to 3-181. See also Lawler, E. E., III (1977). Reward systems. In J. R. Hackman & J. L. Suttle, *Improving life at work: Behavioral science approaches to organizational change*. Santa Monica, CA: Goodyear, pp. 163–226.
13. Foulkes, F. K., & Livernash, E. R. (1989). *Human resources management: Cases and text* (2d ed.). Englewood Cliffs, NJ: Prentice-Hall.
14. Thierry, H. (1992). Pay and payment systems. In J. F. Hartley & S. M. Stephenson (eds.), *Managing employment relations*. Oxford: Basil Blackwell, pp. 136–160. See also Sweeney, P. D., McFarlin, D. B., & Inderrieden, E. J. (1990). Using relative deprivation theory to explain satisfaction with income and pay level: A multistudy examination. *Academy of Management Journal*, **33**, 423–436.
15. Huseman, R. C., Hatfield, J. D., & Miles, E. W (1987). A new perspective on equity theory: The equity sensitivity construct. *Academy of Management Review*, **12**, 222–234.
16. Labor letter (1990, Oct. 2). *The Wall Street Journal*, p. A1.
17. Cowan, A. L. (1993, May 21). At what point is pay too high? *The New York Times*, pp. D1, D2.
18. The best and worst boards (1996, Nov. 25). *Business Week*, p. 94.
19. Gomez-Mejia, L. R., & Balkin, D. B. (1992). *Compensation, organizational strategy, and firm performance*. Cincinnati, OH: South-Western.
20. Montemayor, E. (1996). Congruence between pay policy and competitive strategy in high-performing firms. *Journal of Management*, **22**, 889–908.
21. Lublin (1997, Jan. 7), loc. cit.
22. Gomez-Mejia & Balkin, op. cit.
23. Milkovich & Newman. op. cit.
24. Jaffe, G. (1997, Jan. 15). South's growth rate hits speed bump. *The Wall Street Journal*, p. A2.
25. Klaas, B. S., & Ullman, J. C. (1995). Sticky wages revisited: Organizational responses to a declining market-clearing wage. *Academy of Management Review*, **20**, 281–310. See also Cappelli, P., & Chauvin, K. (1991). An interplant test of the efficiency wage hypothesis. *Quarterly Journal of Economics*, **106**, 769–794. See also Holzer, H. J. (1990). Wages, employer costs, and employee performance in the firm. *Industrial and Labor Relations Review*, **43**, 147S–164S.
26. Ormiston, K. A. (1988, May 10). States know best what labor's worth. *The Wall Street Journal*, p. 38.
27. Work week (1996, Aug. 27). *The Wall Street Journal*, p. A1.
28. Mills, D. Q. (1994). *Labor-management relations* (5th ed.). New York: McGraw-Hill.

29. Pfeffer, J., & Davis-Blake, A. (1987). Understanding organizational wage structures: A resource dependence approach. *Academy of Management Journal*, 30, 437–455.
30. Gomez, L. R., Page, R. C., & Tornow, W. W. (1982). A comparison of the practical utility of traditional, statistical, and hybrid job evaluation approaches. *Academy of Management Journal*, **25**, 790–809.
31. Gerhart, B., & Milkovich, G. T. (1992). Employee compensation: Research and practice. In M. D. Dunnette & L. M. Hough (eds.), *Handbook of industrial and organizational psychology*. Palo Alto, CA: Consulting Psychologists Press, pp. 481–569. See also Hills, F. S. (1989). Internal pay relationships. In L. R. Gomez-Mejia (ed.), *Compensation and benefits*. Washington, DC: Bureau of National Affairs, pp. 3-29 to 3-69.
32. Rynes, S. L., & Milkovich, G. T. (1986). Wage surveys: Dispelling some myths about the "market wage." *Personnel Psychology*, **39**, 71–90.
33. Fay, C. H. (1989). External pay relationships. In L. R. Gomez-Mejia (ed.), *Compensation and benefits*. Washington, DC: Bureau of National Affairs, pp. 3-70 to 3-100.
34. Barry, D., & McLaughlin, K. (1996, May). A S.M.A.R.T method for comp analysis. *HRMagazine*, pp. 80–83.
35. Wallace, M. J., Jr., & Fay, C. H. (1988). *Compensation theory and practice* (2d ed.). Boston: PWS-Kent.
36. Sibson, R. E. (1991). *Compensation* (5th ed.). New York: American Management Association.
37. Balkin, D. B., & Logan, J. W. (1988). Reward policies that support entrepreneurship. *Compensation and Benefits Review*, **20**(1), 18–25.
38. Rowland, M. (1993, June 6). It's what you can do that counts. *The New York Times*, p. F17.
39. Skill-based pay boosts worker productivity and morale (1992, Apr. 18). *The Wall Street Journal*, p. A1.
40. Grib, G., & O'Donnell, S. (1995, July). Pay plans that reward employee achievement. *HRMagazine*, pp. 49, 50.
41. Ibid. See also Leonard, B. (1995, Feb.). Creating opportunities to excel. *HRMagazine*, pp. 47–51.
42. Gomez-Mejia & Balkin, op. cit.
43. Solomon, J. (1990, Apr. 18). Hush money. *The Wall Street Journal Supplement*, pp. R22–R24.
44. Handbook rule against wage discussion illegal (1992, Feb.) Bulletin. Denver: Mountain States Employers Council, p. 1.
45. Bartol, K. M., & Martin, D. C. (1988). Influences on managerial pay allocations: A dependency perspective. *Personnel Psychology*, **41**, 361–378.
46. Milkovich & Newman, op. cit.
47. Markels, A., & Berton, L. (1996, Apr. 11). Something to talk about. *The Wall Street Journal Supplement*, p. R10. See also Gomez-Mejia & Balkin, op. cit.
48. Lublin (1997, Jan. 7), loc. cit.
49. Casner, in Lublin (1997, Jan. 7), op. cit., p. B1.
50. Gomez-Mejia & Balkin, op. cit.
51. Labor letter, loc. cit. See also Kanter, R. M. (1987, Mar.–Apr.). The attack on pay. *Harvard Business Review*, pp. 60–67.
52. Bergmann, T. J., Hills, F. S., & Priefert, L. (1983, Second Quarter). Pay compression: Causes, results, and possible solutions. *Compensation Review*, **6**, 17–26.
53. Zacharay, G. P. (1996, June 24). Shortchanged: Many firms refuse to pay for overtime, employees complain. *The Wall Street Journal*, pp. A1, A6.
54. Lublin (1997, Jan. 7), loc. cit.
55. Schwartz, J. D. (1982, Feb.). Maintaining merit compensation in a high-inflation economy. *Personnel Journal*, pp. 147–152.
56. Lublin, J. S. (1997, Jan. 8). Why more people are battling over bonuses. *The Wall Street Journal*, pp. B1, B6.

57. Banker, R. D., Lee, S. Y., Potter, G., & Srinivasan, D. (1996). Contextual analysis of performance impacts of outcome-based incentive compensation. *Academy of Management Journal*, **39**, 920–948. See also Kaufman, R. T. (1992). The effects of improshare on productivity. *Industrial and Labor Relations Review*, **45**, 311–322.
58. Sweet carrots, big gains: Workers say incentives work (1995, July 10). *Business Week*, p. 24.
59. Lawler (1989), loc. cit.
60. Rethinking rewards (1993, Nov.–Dec.). *Harvard Business Review*, pp. 37–49.
61. Bennett, A. (1991, Sept. 10). Paying workers to meet goals spreads, but gauging performance proves tough. *The Wall Street Journal*, pp. B1, B2.
62. Waldman, S., & Roberts, B. (1988, Nov. 14). Grading "merit pay." *Newsweek*, pp. 45, 46.
63. Dolan, loc. cit.
64. Rollins, T. (1987, June). Pay for performance: The pros and cons. *Personnel Journal*, pp. 104–107.
65. Lawler (1989), loc. cit.
66. A model incentive plan gets caught in a vise (1996, Jan. 22). *Business Week*, pp. 89, 92. See also Wiley, C. (1993, Aug.). Incentive plan pushes production. *Personnel Journal*, pp. 86–91.
67. Kopelman, R. E., & Reinharth, L. (1982, Fourth Quarter). Research results: The effect of merit-pay practices on white-collar performance. *Compensation Review*, **5**, 30–40.
68. Bennett, A. (1991, Apr. 17). The hot seat: Talking to the people responsible for setting pay. *The Wall Street Journal*, p. R3.
69. Meyer, P. (1983). Executive compensation must promote long-term commitment. *Personnel Administrator*, **28**(5), 37–42.
70. The boss's pay. (1996, Apr. 11). *The Wall Street Journal Supplement*, pp. 15–17.
71. Kanter, loc. cit.
72. Gomez-Mejia, L. R., Tosi, H., & Hinkin, T. (1987). Managerial control, performance, and executive compensation. *Academy of Management Journal*, **30**, 51–70.
73. Lowenstein, R. (1996, Apr. 4). Renegade firms redefine executive pay. *The Wall Street Journal*, p. B1.
74. Bennett, A. (1992, Mar. 11). Taking stock: Big firms rely more on options but fail to end pay criticism. *The Wall Street Journal*, pp. A1, A8.
75. Share the wealth with the workforce (1996, Apr. 22). *Business Week*, p. 158.
76. Bennett (1991, Apr. 17), loc. cit.
77. A model incentive plan gets caught in a vise (1996, Jan. 22). *Business Week*, pp. 89, 92; Wiley, C. (1993, Aug.). Incentive plan pushes production. *Personnel Journal*, pp. 86–91; Serrin, W. (1984, Jan. 15). The way that works at Lincoln. *The New York Times*, p. D1.
78. M. Smith, Director of Hose Manufacturing, and T. Cecil, Manufacturing Supervisor, Gates Rubber Company, Denver. Personal interviews, Dec. 1996.
79. Petty, M. M., Singleton, B., & Connell, D. W. (1992). An experimental evaluation of an organizational incentive plan in the electric utility industry. *Journal of Applied Psychology*, **77**, 427–436.
80. Norman, C. A., & Zawacki, R. A. (1991, Sept.). Team appraisals—team approach. *Personnel Journal*, pp. 101–104. See also Rowland, M. (1992, Feb. 9). Pay for quality, by the group. *The New York Times*, p. D6.
81. Sheudan, J. H. (1996, Mar. 4). Yes: To team incentives. *Industry Week*, p. 63.
82. Schroeder, M. (1988, Nov. 7). Watching the bottom line instead of the clock. *Business Week*, pp. 134, 136. See also Florkowski, G. W. (1987). The organizational impact of profit sharing. *Academy of Management Review*, **12**, 622–636.
83. Banerjee, N. (1994, Apr. 12). Rebounding earnings stir old debate on productivity's tip to profit-sharing. *The Wall Street Journal*, pp. A2, A12. See also U.S. Department

of Labor (1993, Aug.). *High performance work practices and firm performance.* Washington, DC: Author.

84. Hays, L. (1988, Dec. 5). All eyes on Du Pont's incentive-pay plan. *The Wall Street Journal*, p. B1.
85. Koenig, R. (1990, Oct. 25). Du Pont plan linking pay to fibers profit unravels. *The Wall Street Journal*, pp. B1, B5.
86. Collins, D., Hatcher, L., & Ross, T. L. (1993). The decision to implement gainsharing: Role of work climate, expected outcomes, and union status. *Personnel Psychology*, **46**, 77–104. See also Graham-Moore, B., & Ross, T. L. (1990). Understanding gainsharing. In B. Graham-Moore & T. L. Ross (eds.), *Gainsharing*. Washington, DC: Bureau of National Affairs, pp. 3–18.
87. Graham-Moore & Ross, loc. cit.
88. Hammer, T. H. (1988). New developments in profit sharing, gainsharing, and employee ownership. In J. P. Campbell & R. J. Campbell (eds.), *Productivity in organizations*. San Francisco: Jossey-Bass, pp. 328–366.
89. Graham-Moore, B. (1990). Seventeen years of experience with the Scanlon plan: DeSoto revisited. In B. Graham-Moore & T. L. Ross (eds.), *Gainsharing*. Washington, DC: Bureau of National Affairs, pp. 139–173.
90. Tyler, L. S., & Fisher, B. (1983). The Scanlon concept: A philosophy as much as a system. *Personnel Administrator*, **29**(7), 33–37. See also Moore, B., & Ross, T. (1978). *The Scanlon way to improved productivity*. New York: Wiley.
91. White, J. K. (1979). The Scanlon plan: Causes and consequences of success. *Academy of Management Journal*, **22**, 292–312.
92. Becker, G. S. (1989, Oct. 23). ESOPs aren't the magic key to anything. *Business Week*, p. 20.
93. Why ESOP deals have slowed to a crawl (1996, Mar. 18). *Business Week*, pp. 101, 102.
94. Jones, D., & Schmitt, J. (1993, Dec. 20). UAL plan may put industry in new hands. *USA Today*, pp. 1B, 2B.
95. ESOPs offer way to sell stakes in small firms (1988, May 3). *The Wall Street Journal*, p. 33.
96. Happy fallout down at the nuke lab (1996, Oct. 7). *Business Week*, p. 42.
97. Northwest's sigh of relief has rivals groaning (1993, July 26). *Business Week*, p. 84.
98. Klein, K. J., & Hall, R. J. (1988). Correlates of employee satisfaction with stock ownership: Who likes an ESOP most? *Journal of Applied Psychology*, **73**, 630–638. See also Klein, K. J. (1987). Employee stock ownership and employee attitudes: A test of three models. *Journal of Applied Psychology*, **72**, 319–332. See also Rosen, C., Klein, K. J., & Young, K. M. (1986). When employees share the profits. *Psychology Today*, **20**, 30–36.
99. Labich, K. (1996, Oct. 14). When workers really count. *Fortune*, pp. 212–214. See also United we own: Employee ownership is working at the airline. Can it travel? (1996, Mar. 18). *Business Week*, pp. 96–100.
100. Rosen et al., loc. cit.
101. White, J. A. (1992, Feb. 13). When employees own big stake, it's a buy signal for investors. *The Wall Street Journal*, pp. C1, C9.
102. Farnham, A. (1989, Dec. 4). The trust gap. *Fortune,* p. 66.
103. Berenson, A. (1996, Feb. 3). First Bank's windfall means bonus for workers. *The Denver Post*, p. B1.
104. Farnham, loc. cit.
105. Farnham, op. cit., p. 70.

11 INDIRECT COMPENSATION: EMPLOYEE BENEFITS PLANS

Questions This Chapter Will Help Managers Answer

1 What strategic considerations should guide the design of benefits programs?
2 What options are available to help a business control the rapid escalation of health-care costs?
3 Should companies offer a uniform package of benefits, or should they move to a flexible plan that allows employees to choose the benefits that are most meaningful to them, up to a certain dollar amount?
4 What cost-effective benefits options are available to a small business?
5 In view of the considerable sums of money that are spent each year on employee benefits, communicating their value to employees is vital. What is the best way to do so?

*THE NEW WORLD OF EMPLOYEE BENEFITS**

Human Resource Management in Action

In the early 1990s, experts predicted that benefits packages would become ever more generous as companies competed for a shrinking pool of workers. Today, that forecast seems as outdated as the notion that computers would create a paperless society. Struggling to deal with benefits costs that seem to rise relentlessly, many firms are eliminating benefits or asking employees to pay more for them. Plans that allow employees to choose among alternative benefits choices, so-called flexible benefits, force employees to make trade-offs—and profoundly affect how they think about security, company loyalty, and employment itself. The world of benefits was not always this way.

In the past, major corporations offered their employees a wide array of company-paid insurance and retirement benefits. Corporations decided what was best for their employees. Now, however, most employers are not only changing the range of benefit choices they offer, but also changing the basic structure of their benefits.

Economics and demographics are driving these changes. Economically, most employers realize that the traditional blanket approach to benefits—total coverage for everyone—would subject them to unbearable expense. Benefits are no longer the "fringe" of compensation. Today they often constitute 35 to 40 percent of wages. As a result of unending increases in the price of medical care, for example, health-care expenses now consume an average of 56 percent of pretax profits of U.S. corporations. Increasing life expectancy has made pensions more costly as well. And the combination of increased longevity, rising health-care costs, and an accounting standard that requires firms to report the cost of future retiree health-care benefits on their balance sheets—thereby reducing profits—has led employers to rethink dramatically their entire approach to employee benefits.

Demographically, the United States now has a much more diverse workforce than it has had in the past. As a result, the one-size-fits-all approach to employee benefits does not work. Employees who have working spouses covered by health insurance have insurance needs that differ from those of employees who are sole breadwinners. Single parents and childless couples place very different priorities on child-care benefits. So rather than attempt to fashion a single approach that suits all these interests, many employers determine a sum they will spend on each employee, establish a menu of benefits, and then let each employee choose the benefits he or she wants or needs. At the same time, such plans allow employers to trim benefits merely by raising the prices of the various options on the benefits menu. Such "life-cycle benefits plans" represent the next generation of full-blown flexible benefits.

These changes reflect more than demographic diversity, however. A fundamental change in philosophy is taking place as employees are forced to take more responsibility. Part of this is a movement toward employee self-management. Indeed, the new approach might well be described as one of "sharing costs, sharing risks."

**Sources:* E. P. Gunn, How to maximize your pension payout, *Fortune*, Oct. 28, 1996, p. 233; B. Leonard, Perks give way to life-cycle benefits plans, *HRMagazine*, Mar. 1995, pp. 45–48; L. Luciano, How companies are slashing benefits, *Money*, May 1993, pp. 128–138.

Challenges

1. Do you think companies should provide a broader menu of "exotic" benefits (e.g., veterinary care, dietary counseling) or improve the menu of "core" benefits (e.g., health care, insurance, pensions)? Why?
2. How might employees' preferences for various benefits change as they grow older or as their family situations change?
3. Do employees' risks (e.g., with respect to sickness or disability) change over the course of their working lives?

Benefits currently account for almost 40 percent of the total compensation costs for each employee. Yesterday's fringes have become today's expected benefits and services. Here are some reasons why benefits have grown:

- The imposition of wage ceilings during World War II forced organizations to offer more benefits in place of wage increases to attract, retain, and motivate employees.
- The interest by unions in bargaining over benefits has grown, particularly since employers are pushing for more cost sharing by employees.[1]
- The tax treatment of benefits makes them preferable to wages. Many benefits remain nontaxable to the employee and are deductible by the employer. With other benefits, taxes are deferred. Hence employees' disposable income increases since they are receiving benefits and services that they would otherwise have to purchase with after-tax dollars.
- Granting benefits (in a nonunionized firm) or bargaining over them (in a unionized firm) confers an aura of social responsibility on employers; they are "taking care" of their employees. This sense of social responsibility is important, for evidence indicates that employees retain a strong sense of entitlement to benefits.[2]

STRATEGIC CONSIDERATIONS IN THE DESIGN OF BENEFITS PROGRAMS

As is the case with compensation systems in general, managers need to think carefully about what they wish to accomplish by means of their benefits programs. On average, firms spend over $15,000 in benefits for each worker on the payroll.[3] General Motors, for example, spends about $1200 for every car it builds in the United States, $700 more than it spends on the car's steel, just to provide health benefits to active and retired workers.[4] It is no exaggeration to say that for most firms, benefits represent substantial annual expenditures, for they constitute fully 28 percent of the overall costs of doing business.[5] In order to leverage the impact of these expenditures, managers should be prepared to answer questions such as the following:

- Are the type and level of our benefits coverage consistent with our long-term strategic business plans?
- Given the characteristics of our workforce, are we meeting the needs of our employees?
- What legal requirements must we satisfy in the benefits we offer?
- Are our benefits competitive in cost, structure, and value to employees and their dependents?
- Is our benefits package consistent with the key objectives of our total compensation strategy, namely, adequacy, equity, cost control, and balance?

In the following sections, we will examine each of these points.

Long-Term Strategic Business Plans

Such plans outline the basic directions in which an organization wishes to move in the next 3 to 5 years. One strategic issue that should influence the design of benefits is an organization's stage of development. For example, a start-up venture probably will offer low base pay and benefits, but high incentives; a mature firm with well-established products and substantial market share will probably offer much more generous pay and benefits combined with moderate incentives.

Other strategic considerations include the projected rate of employment growth or downsizing, geographic redeployment, acquisitions, and expected changes in profitability.[6] Each of these conditions suggests a change in the optimum mix of benefits in order to be most consistent with an organization's business plans.

COMPANY EXAMPLE

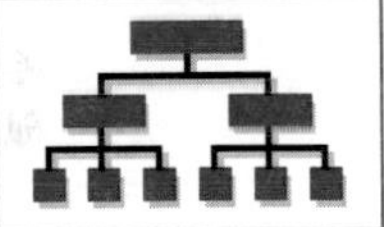

IBM'S NEW PRODUCT—EMPLOYEE BENEFITS[7]

Like most other companies, IBM has been looking for cost-effective ways to cut its annual cost of employee benefits (more than $1 billion per year). In 1992, it found one that is consistent with its long-term business plan to make each of its independent units a profit center. It spun off its huge human resource operation into a separate company called Workforce Solutions, which is now saving IBM more than $45 million annually in the form of reduced staffing, consolidation of offices, and use of new technology, such as automated telephones. In fact, the overall HR staff has shrunk by about a third, to 1500 employees. Whereas IBM previously took a one-size-fits-all approach to benefits, the spin-off provides customized services to each of IBM's 13 independent business units. In addition, Workforce Solutions handles business for other companies, such as the National Geographic Society, capitalizing on IBM's reputation for excellence and lots of practical experience in the benefits area. Beginning in 1994, each IBM unit was free to choose its own provider of benefits and HR functions. Workforce Solutions has had to compete for that business. Its success shows that marketing internal operations to outsiders can turn benefits departments from drains on the bottom line to profit centers in their own right.

Characteristics of the Workforce

Young employees who are just starting out are likely to be more concerned with direct pay (e.g., for a house purchase) than with a generous pension program. Older workers may desire the reverse. Unionized workers may prefer a uniform benefits package, while single parents, older workers, or workers with disabilities may place heavy emphasis on flexible work schedules. Employers that hire large numbers of temporary or part-time workers may offer entirely different benefits to those groups. Among temporary employees, while 56 percent receive holiday pay, 46 percent skills training, and 22 percent performance bonuses, only 8 percent get health-care benefits.[8]

Legal Requirements

The government plays a central role in the design of any benefits package. While controlling the cost of benefits is a major concern of employers, the social and economic welfare of citizens is the major concern of government.[9] As examples of such concern, consider the four income-maintenance laws shown in Table 11-1.

Income-maintenance laws were enacted to provide employees and their families with income security in case of death, disability, unemployment, or retirement. At a broad level, government tax policy has had, and will continue to have, a major impact on the design of benefits programs. Two principles have had the greatest impact on benefits.[10] One is the *doctrine of constructive receipt*, which holds that an individual must pay taxes on benefits that have monetary value when the individual receives them. The other principle is the *antidiscrimination rule*, which holds that employers can obtain tax advantages only for those benefits that do not discriminate in favor of highly compensated employees. Such an employee is one who owns at least 5 percent of company stock or partnership rights, a company officer who earns more than $45,000 a year, or an employee who earns more than $50,000 a year and has income in the top 20 percent of the general workforce. These dollar amounts are adjusted periodically.

These two tax-policy principles define the conditions for the preferential tax treatment of benefits. Together they hold that if benefits discriminate in favor of highly paid or "key" employees, both the employer and the employee receiving those benefits may have to pay taxes on the benefits when they are transferred.

Social Security, which accounts for $1 of every $5 spent by the federal government, has had, and will continue to have, an effect on the growth, development, and design of employee benefits. National health policy increasingly is shifting costs to the private sector and emphasizing cost containment; such pressures will intensify. Finally, national policy on unfair discrimination, particularly through the civil rights laws, has caused firms to reexamine their benefit policies.

Competitiveness of the Benefits Offered

The issue of benefits-program competitiveness is much more complicated than that of salary competitiveness.[11] In the case of salary, both employees and management focus on the same item: direct pay. However, in determining the competitiveness of benefits, senior management tends to focus mainly on cost, while employees are more interested in value. The two may conflict. Thus employees'

Table 11-1

FOUR MAJOR INCOME-MAINTENANCE LAWS

Law	Scope of coverage	Funding	Benefits	Administrative agency
Social Security Act (1935)	Full coverage for retirees, dependent survivors, and disabled persons insured by 40 quarters of payroll taxes on their past earnings or earnings of heads of households. Federal government employees hired prior to January 1, 1984, and railroad workers are excluded.	For 1997, payroll tax of 7.65% for employees and 7.65% for employers on the first $65,400 in earnings. Self-employed persons pay 15.3% of this wage base. Of the 7.65%, 6.2% is allocated for retirement, survivors, and disability insurance, and 1.45% for Medicare. The Omnibus Budget Reconciliation Act of 1993 extended the 1.45% Medicare payroll tax to all wages and self-employment income.	Full *retirement payments* after age 65, or at reduced rates after 62, to worker and spouse. Size of payment depends on past earnings. *Survivor benefits* for the family of a deceased worker or retiree. At age 65 a widow or widower receives the full age-65 pension granted to the deceased. A widow or widower of any age with dependent children under 16, and each unmarried child under 18, receives a 75% benefit check. *Disability benefits* to totally disabled workers, after a 5-month waiting period, as well as to their spouses and children. *Health insurance* for persons over 65 (Medicare). All benefits are adjusted upward whenever the consumer price index (CPI) increases more than 3% in a calendar year and trust funds are at a specified level. Otherwise the adjustment is based on the lower of the CPI increase or the increase in average national wages (1983 amendments).	Social Security Administration
Federal Unemployment Tax Act (1935)	All employees except some state and local government workers, domestic and farm workers, railroad workers, and some nonprofit employees.	Payroll tax of at least 3.4% of first $7000 of earnings paid by employer. (Employees also taxed in Alaska, Alabama, and New Jersey.) States may raise both the percentage and base earnings taxed through legislation. Employer contributions may be reduced if state experience ratings for them are low.	Benefits average roughly 50% of average weekly earnings and are available for up to 26 weeks. Those eligible for benefits have been employed for some specified minimum period and have lost their jobs through no fault of their own. Most states exclude strikers. During periods of high unemployment, benefits may be extended for up to 52 weeks.	U.S. Bureau of Employment Security, U.S. Training and Employment Service, and the several state employment security commissions

(continues)

Table 11-1 (cont.)

FOUR MAJOR INCOME-MAINTENANCE LAWS

Law	Scope of coverage	Funding	Benefits	Administrative agency
Workers' compensation (state laws)	Generally, employees of nonagricultural, private-sector firms are entitled to benefits for work-related accidents and illnesses leading to temporary or permanent disabilities.	One of the following options, depending on state law: self-insurance, insurance through a private carrier, or payroll-based payments to a state insurance system. Premiums depend on the riskiness of the occupation and the experience rating of the insured.	Benefits average about two-thirds of an employee's weekly wage and continue for the term of the disability. Supplemental payments are made for medical care and rehabilitative services. In case of a fatal accident, survivor benefits are payable.	Various state commissions
Employee Retirement Income Security Act (ERISA) (1974)	Private-sector employees over age 21 enrolled in noncontributory (100% employer-paid) retirement plans who have 1 year's service	Employer contributions.	The 1986 Tax Reform Act authorizes several formulas to provide vesting of retirement benefits after a certain length of service (5–7 years). Once an employee is "vested," receipt of the pension is not contingent on future service. Authorizes tax-free transfer of vested benefits to another employer or to an individual retirement account ("portability") if a vested employee changes jobs and if the present employer agrees. Employers must fund plans on an actuarially sound basis. Pension trustees ("fiduciaries") must make prudent investments. Employers may insure vested benefits through the federal Pension Benefit Guaranty Corporation.	Department of Labor, Internal Revenue Service, Pension Benefit Guaranty Corporation

perceptions of the value of their benefits as competitive may lead to excessive costs, in the view of top management. On the other hand, achieving cost competitiveness provides no assurance that employees will perceive the benefits program as valuable to them.

COMPANY EXAMPLE

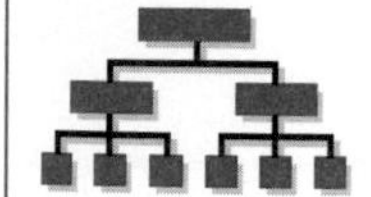

HOW NIKE MATCHES PEOPLE WITH BENEFITS[12]

To attract and retain skilled workers, Nike enlists current employees to help enrich its benefits offerings. It starts by probing workers' fears, needs, and desires in focus groups and surveys, in which employees often express worries about not being able to buy a house, send their children to college, or care for elderly parents. Then Nike asks employee teams to design new benefits packages that offer more choices without raising costs. Some of the choices the teams come up with include company-matching funds for college tuition, subsidies for child care or elder care, paid time off for family leave, group discounts on auto or home insurance, discounted mortgages, legal services, and financial planning advice.

Many of the new offerings are relatively cheap for the company. To contain costs further, Nike gives employees incentives to make health-benefits tradeoffs, such as pledging to stop smoking or using company-chosen physician networks. By tailoring its benefits to those that employees really need and care deeply about, Nike is maximizing the return on its "benefits bucks."

Total Compensation Strategy

The broad objective of the design of compensation programs (that is, direct as well as indirect compensation) is to integrate salary and benefits into a package that will encourage the achievement of an organization's goals. For example, while a generous pension plan may help retain employees, it probably does little to motivate them to perform on a day-to-day basis. This is because the length of time between performance and reward is too great. On the other hand, a generous severance package offered to targeted segments of the employee population may facilitate an organization's objective of downsizing to a specified staffing level. In all cases, considerations of adequacy, equity, cost control, and balance should guide decision making in the context of a total compensation strategy.

With these considerations in mind, let us now examine some key components of the benefits package.

COMPONENTS OF THE BENEFITS PACKAGE

There are many ways to classify benefits, but we will follow the classification scheme used by the U.S. Chamber of Commerce. According to this system, benefits fall into three categories: security and health, payments for time not worked, and employee services. Within each of these categories there is a bewildering array of options. The following discussions consider only the most popular options and cover only those that have not been mentioned previously.

As we begin, consider how the costs of employer payments for benefits as a percentage of payroll have changed over time:[13]

	1955	1965	1975	1985	1994
Percent of payroll	20.3	24.7	35.4	37.7	40.7

Security and Health Benefits

This category of benefits includes:

- Life insurance
- Workers' compensation
- Disability insurance
- Hospitalization, surgical, and maternity coverage

- Health maintenance organizations (HMOs)
- Other medical coverage
- Sick leave
- Pension plans
- Social Security
- Unemployment insurance
- Supplemental unemployment insurance
- Severance pay

Insurance is the basic building block of almost all benefits packages, for it protects employees against income loss caused by death, accident, or ill health. Most organizations provide group coverage for their employees. The plans may be contributory (in which employees share in the cost of the premiums) or noncontributory.

It used to be that when a worker switched jobs, he or she lost health insurance coverage. The worker had to "go naked" for months until coverage began at a new employer. That is no longer the case. Under the Consolidated Omnibus Budget Reconciliation Act (COBRA) of 1986, companies with at least 20 employees must make medical coverage available at group insurance rates for as long as 18 months after the employee leaves—whether the worker left voluntarily, retired, or was dismissed. The law also provides that following a worker's death or divorce, the employee's family has the right to buy group-rate health insurance for as long as 3 years. Employers who do not comply can be sued and denied corporate tax deductions related to health benefits.[14]

However, since some corporate medical plans do not cover preexisting conditions, some employees have found that when they changed jobs (and health plans), their benefits were reduced sharply. To alleviate that problem, Congress passed the Health Insurance Portability and Accountability Act (HIPAA), effective June 30, 1997. In general, HIPAA includes the following provisions:

1. Exclusions for preexisting conditions are limited to 12 months.
2. If employees do not enroll as soon as they become eligible, employers may impose exclusions for preexisting conditions of up to 18 months.
3. Companies must reduce the 12-month cap by 1 month for each month of prior continuous coverage. Thus if an employee has had prior continuous coverage for more than 12 months, the new employer may not claim any exclusion for preexisting conditions.
4. If there is a break in coverage of more than 63 days, employers need not count prior continuous coverage before that time against the 12-month cap.[15]

With these provisions in mind, let us consider the major forms of security and health benefits commonly provided to employees.

Group Life Insurance

This type of insurance is usually yearly-renewable term insurance; that is, each employee is insured 1 year at a time. The actual amounts of coverage vary, but one rule of thumb is to have coverage equal roughly 2 years' income. This amount provides a reasonable financial cushion to the surviving spouse during the difficult transition to a different way of life. Thus a manager making $40,000 per year may have a group term-life policy with a face value of $80,000 or

CONTROLLING THE COSTS OF WORKERS' COMPENSATION

More than $70 billion is paid out to public and private insurers each year for workers' compensation costs. Some of the driving forces behind these costs are higher medical costs, the increasing involvement of attorneys, and widespread fraud. Recent studies indicate that as much as 20 percent or more of claims may involve cheating.[21] Figure 11-1 shows the differences in medical charges and days of treatment for identical conditions handled by ordinary health insurers, such as Blue Cross, and under the workers' compensation system. For back disorders, for example, the cost under workers' compensation was more than twice as high and treatment lasted more than twice as long. What are states and companies doing to control costs?

California set up a fund, financed by employers, that pays for special teams to go after fraud. Job-injury claims declined from nearly 10 to 8.4 per 100 workers within 2 years. Connecticut no longer awards disability benefits for mental or psychological disorders unless they are the result of an injury. It has eliminated cost-of-living adjustments on disability benefits, and has cut some benefits by a third. Insurance premiums in the state have fallen 24 percent in the last 2 years.

Finally, workers' compensation insurers are forming alliances with managed-care providers in order to take advantage of case-management methods and volume-discounting. At Coca-Cola Bottling Company of New York, the company paid an average of $3164 in workers' compensation claims in 1989. Then it turned to managed care and addressed longstanding safety issues in its plants. Today its average claim is $1257—a 60 percent reduction.[22]

Is there an underlying theme in these approaches? Yes, and it is simple: aggressive management of workplace safety issues pays dividends for workers and for their employers as well.

$100,000. To discourage turnover, almost all companies cancel this benefit if an employee terminates.

Life insurance has been heavily affected by flexible benefits programs. Typically such programs provide a core of basic life coverage (e.g., $25,000) and then permit employees to choose greater coverage (e.g., in increments of $10,000 to $25,000) as part of their optional package.[16] Employees purchase the additional insurance through payroll deductions.[17]

Workers' Compensation

As shown in Table 11-1, these payments vary by state. Disability benefits, which have been extended to cover stress (in four states) and occupational disease, tend to be highest in states where organized labor is strong.[18] With regard to stress, California now requires that the workplace be the *predominant* cause of the stress cited in a disability claim, not just a contributing factor of 10 percent or more.[19]

A state's industrial structure also plays a big part in setting disability-insurance rates. Thus serious injuries are more common and costly among Oregon loggers and Michigan machinists than among assembly line workers in a Texas semiconductor plant. Sometimes the costs can get out of hand, especially for small businesses. Consider Bartow, Florida, construction contractor Jean Stinson. Her company's liability insurance costs—of which workers' compensation is the biggest part—jumped 187 percent in 1 year, to $250,000. When she raised her bids to recoup the higher costs, customers put their projects on hold.[20] Trends such as these have prompted high-cost states, such as California, Florida, Michigan, and Maine, to lower workers' compensation premiums so that they can continue to attract and retain businesses in their states.

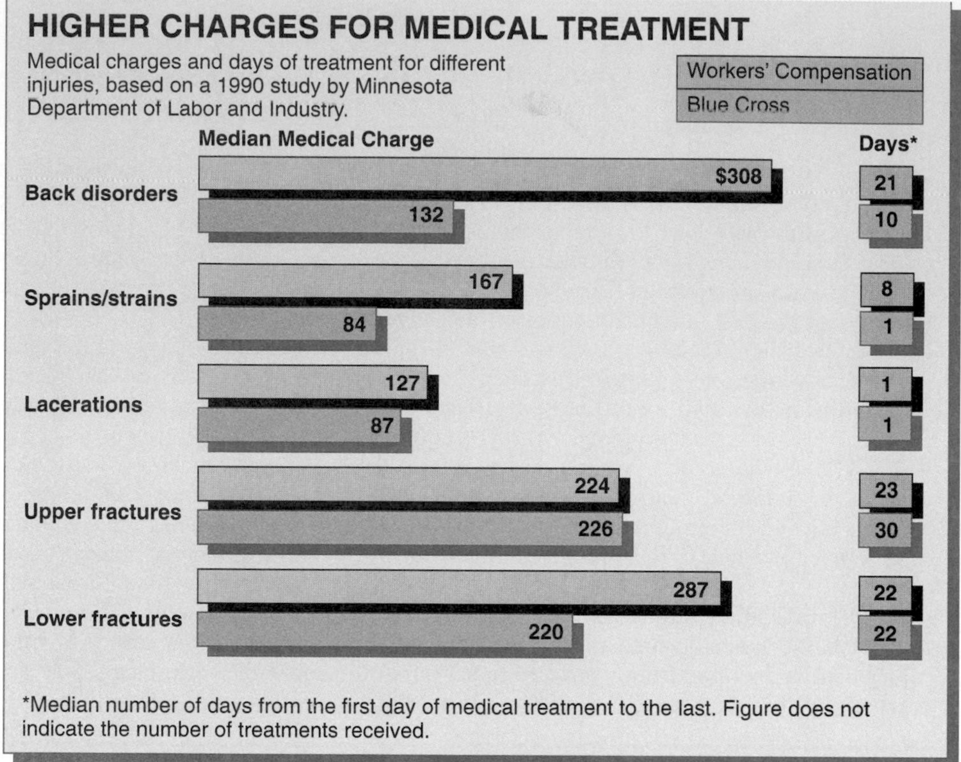

Figure 11-1

Comparisons of medical costs: workers' compensation versus Blue Cross. (*Source:* P. Kerr, Vast amount of fraud discovered in workers' compensation system, *The New York Times*, Dec. 29, 1991, p. 14.)

At present, all 50 states have workers' compensation laws. While specific terms and levels of coverage vary by state, all state laws share the following features:[23]

- All job-related injuries and illnesses are covered.
- Coverage is provided regardless of who caused the injury or illness (i.e., regardless of who was "at fault").
- Payments are usually made through an insurance program financed by employer-paid premiums.
- A worker's loss is usually not covered fully by the insurance program. Most cash payments are at least two-thirds of the worker's weekly wage, but, together with disability benefits from Social Security, the payments may not exceed 80 percent of the worker's weekly wage.

Workers' compensation programs protect employees, dependents, and survivors against income loss resulting from total disability, partial disability, or death; from medical expenses; and from rehabilitation expenses.

Disability Insurance

Such coverage provides a supplemental, one-time payment when death is accidental, and it provides a range of benefits when employees are disabled—that is, when they cannot perform the "main functions" of their occupations.[24] Long-term disability (LTD) plans cover employees who are disabled 6 months or longer, usually at no more than 60 percent of their base pay, until they begin receiving pension benefits.

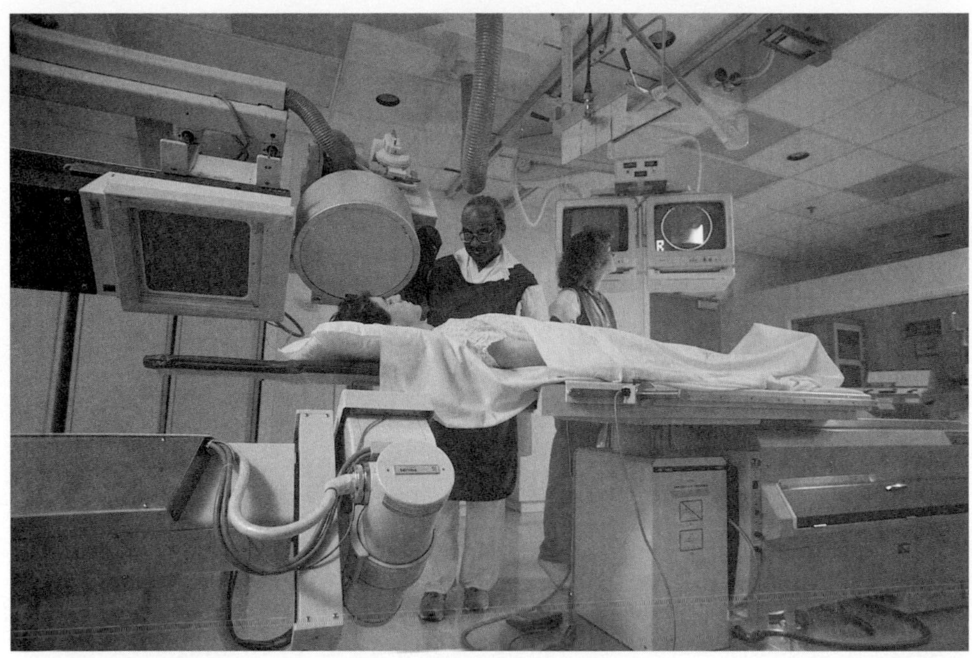

New technology has helped make medical care better—and more expensive—than ever.

Disability leaves shot up over 14 percent from 1992 to 1996, and they are growing at 4 times the rate of the gross national product. They cost companies between 8 and 20 percent of payroll annually.[25] To control these costs, firms such as Cable Systems International and Eastman Chemical are turning to "managed-disability" programs. Much like managed health care, such programs focus on making sure that employees with disabilities receive the care and rehabilitation they need to help them return to work quickly.[26]

Although disability benefits traditionally were divided into salary continuation, short-term disability, and long-term disability, combined managed-disability programs now merge all three. Doing so allows for a single claim-application process and uniform case management. An employee whose short-term illness turns into a lengthy disability does not have to reapply for benefits or start over with a new case manager; the process is uniform and seamless, regardless of the length of the disability.

Another developing trend is toward integrating disability coverage with workers' compensation, and, eventually, with group health care. Under this scenario, patients would be treated under the same health-care delivery system, regardless of whether they became ill or were injured at work or on their own time. This concept, called "managed health" or "total health and productivity management," is still in its infancy but holds great potential.[27]

Hospitalization, Surgical, and Maternity Coverage

These are essential benefits for most working Americans. Self-insurance is out of the question since the costs incurred by one serious, prolonged illness could easily wipe out a lifetime of savings and assets and place a family in debt for years to come. The U.S. health insurance system is based primarily on group coverage provided by employers. At a general level, the system is characterized by statistics such as the following:[28]

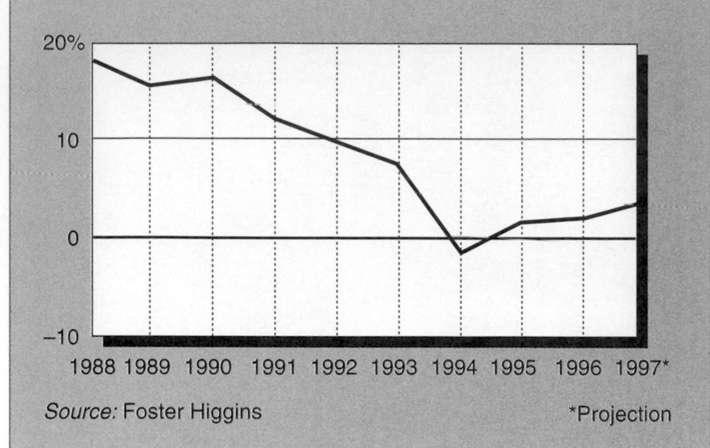

Figure 11-2
Rebounding costs: Average annual increase in health-benefit costs per employee. (*Source:* R. Winslow, Health-care costs may be heading up again, *The Wall Street Journal,* Jan. 21, 1997, p. B1.)

- Most Americans have health insurance and receive excellent care. Except for the poor, especially in inner cities, Americans are healthier than ever.
- Those over age 65 are covered by Medicare, but less than half of those living below the poverty line are covered by Medicaid. About 40 million Americans have no health insurance.[29]
- Contrary to popular belief, most of the uninsured are jobholders—part-timers and per-day workers—the working poor. Small businesses and service businesses are especially likely not to provide insurance.
- Insurance rates have climbed faster for small businesses than for large ones.
- Whether employed or not, younger people, as well as African-American and Hispanic people, are most likely to lack health insurance. Americans with chronic diseases or a history of serious illness have trouble obtaining affordable insurance.
- Figures on the number of uninsured people understate the extent of vulnerability. Over a recent 28-month period, one in four Americans spent at least a month without health insurance.
- Polls indicate that most Americans are pleased with their doctors and hospitals. Yet there is widespread anxiety about the reliability of the system. Despite the fact that medical-care *inflation* was only 4 percent in 1995 (the lowest level since 1973), health-benefit *costs* (up 2.5 percent to $3915 for coverage and care in 1996) are expected to escalate from an estimated 4 percent in 1997 to 10 percent in 1998 (see Figure 11-2).[30]

In 1996, for example, the United States medical tab exceeded $700 billion.[31] To put this into perspective, let us return to an example cited earlier, namely, that General Motors spends $1200 per car to provide health benefits to its active and retired workers in the United States. Chrysler spends $700 a car, and Ford $510. Both have fewer retirees than GM does. However, those outlays compare with as little as $100 per car at the U.S. factories of foreign automakers, which have younger, healthier workers and hardly any retirees.[32]

Both management and labor in the United States worry that a gap that large makes U.S. companies less competitive. Competitiveness issues arising from health-care costs are particularly acute at companies with the following three characteristics:

1. Their workforces are made up largely of people in their forties and fifties, who require more health care than younger workers do.
2. Their health plans cover a much larger number of retired workers than do those of newer companies, like computer or airline concerns.
3. They make products that must compete on world markets.[33]

For workers, the rise in health-care costs has direct consequences. Namely, there is less money for pay increases. How much less? A study funded by the Service Employees International Union found that working families lost an average of $8398 in forgone wages between 1980 and 1992. In fact, every dollar increase in employer health premiums costs U.S. workers 88 cents in wages.[34]

Why is this happening? What is driving these increases in the cost of health care? In addition to population changes, general inflation, and excess medical inflation (including administrative costs that add millions to the country's health-care spending[35]), a key factor is the cost of new technology.

The United States relies far more heavily on health-care technology than do other advanced nations. On a per capita basis, for example, the United States has 4 times as many diagnostic imaging machines (magnetic resonance imaging) as Germany and 8 times as many as Canada. U.S. doctors perform open-heart surgery 2.6 times as often as Canadian doctors and 4.4 times as often as German doctors. When it comes to the use of "smart" machines to perform medical tests, one expert noted: "There's no way to shut it off. The doctors crave it, it's reassuring, and patients crave it."[36] On top of that, hospitals often push to buy the latest machines in order to retain their competitive status as full-service, modern health-care centers.

Cost-Containment Strategies. Strategies to contain the high costs of health care are taking center stage in the boardroom as well as in the health-care industry itself. Here are some measures that firms have taken to gain tighter management control over the cost of health care:

1. **Deal with hospitals and insurers as with any other suppliers**. The auto companies set quality and cost standards for qualifying for their business. For example, Ford is joining with utility companies and other employers to use their own claims data to negotiate with hospitals and insurers. Recently it started distributing a ranking of hospitals on quality and costs to Detroit-area employees in hopes of steering them to the most responsive providers.[37]

2. **Induce employees to voluntarily choose reduced medical coverage through flexible benefits plans.**

3. **Combine self-care literature with 24-hour nurse counseling**. In a controlled experiment among employees and their dependents in selected Wisconsin school districts, one group had access to the self-care literature and the telephone counseling, plus additional maternity-education information. A second group had no such access. Costs for the group with access to self-care services averaged $46.16 less for the year per plan member than for those with no access. Total savings: over $1 million, or $4.75 for each dollar of program costs.[38]

4. **Take advantage of focused providers.** They handle only certain patients in strictly defined settings and markets. Intensiva HealthCare is a good example.

Specializing in long-term, acute cases and operating independently within 10 hospitals (by leasing space), it takes on patients that most hospitals cannot afford to keep. Its costs are 50 percent lower than those of a typical intensive-care ward. How are costs kept so low? Says the firm's CEO: "We treat [patients] more aggressively and get them out of the hospital quicker." And, he says, more patients leave in better health.[39] This latest step in health care's evolution promises to alter once more the way Americans are treated for a broad range of medical conditions.

5. **Require preadmission certification**, that is, doctor's clearance for the treatment desired for the employee before he or she enters the hospital. If the medical staff gives additional treatment or tests, refuse to pay bills unless doctors can confirm that a deviation from the original plan was necessary. For example, Merrill Lynch pays doctors to review other doctors' medical-procedure recommendations.[40]

This strategy has been termed "managed care," and it is being offered by large insurers such as Cigna Corporation. One of its clients is Allied Signal Corporation and its 86,500 employees and their dependents. Managed care relies on a "gatekeeper" system of cost controls. The gatekeeper is a primary-care physician who monitors the medical history and care of each employee and his or her family. The doctor orders testing, makes referrals to specialists, and recommends hospitalization, surgery, or outpatient care, as appropriate. To make this approach pay off, Cigna must deliver high-quality medical care and still keep a tight lid on medical expenses. Yet Allied Signal embraced the plan. Why? Its health-care bill escalated 39 percent in the year before it adopted managed care.[41] Managed care may take a variety of forms. The following section examines one of the most popular, the health maintenance organization (HMO).

HMOs

An HMO is an organized system of health care that ensures the delivery of services to employees who enroll voluntarily under a prepayment plan. The emphasis is on preventive medicine, that is, maintaining the health of each employee. Legally, HMOs are authorized under the HMO Act of 1973.

The objective of HMOs is to control health-care costs by keeping people out of the hospital. Deere & Company, the agricultural-equipment manufacturer, used to pay for a staggering 1400 hospital days each year for every 1000 workers. Then, in 1980, Deere took the lead in helping local doctors establish an HMO, and annual hospitalization has since dropped to 500 days per thousand workers. Deere's HMO was so successful that Deere began selling its service to other companies. Today only 22 percent of the HMO's 290,000 members have any relation to Deere & Company. Most work at 300 other client companies, including Chrysler, Eastman Chemical, and Woolworth.[42]

Yet there are drawbacks. Plan members give up the freedom to choose their doctors, and for companies with scattered employment sites, the location of the HMO may be inconvenient. Nevertheless, 77 percent of workers were in some form of managed-care program in 1996, up sharply from 49 percent in 1992.[43]

While the HMO industry is dominated by independent companies such as Kaiser Permanente and U.S. Healthcare Corporation, insurance companies have invested billions to set up HMOs. In fact, insurance companies operate 4 of every 10 HMOs nationwide. Do HMOs save employers money? A recent study by Northwestern National Life Insurance analyzed $556 million in claims and

Table 11-2

THE ABCs OF MANAGED CARE

Plan	How it works	What you pay	Benefits
Health maintenance organization (HMO)	A specified group of doctors and hospitals provide the care. A gatekeeper must approve all services before they are performed.	There is no deductible. The nominal fees generally range from nothing to $15 a visit depending on the service performed.	Virtually all services are covered, including preventive care. Out-of-pocket costs tend to be lower then for any other managed-care plan.
Preferred-provider organization (PPO)	In-network care comes from a specified group of physicians and hospitals. You can pay extra to get care from outside the network. There generally is no gatekeeper.	The typical yearly family deductible is $400. The plan pays 80% to 100% for what is done within the network but only 50% to 70% for services rendered outside it.	Preventive services may be covered. There are lower deductibles and copayments for in-network care than for out-of-network care.
Point-of-service (POS) plan	POSs combine the features of HMOs and PPOs. Patients can get care in or out of the network, but there is an in-network gatekeeper who must approve all services.	In addition to a deductible, there is a flat $5 to $15 fee for in-network care, and you pay 20% to 50% of the bills for care you get outside the network.	Preventive services are generally covered. And there are low out-of-pocket costs for the care you get in the network.

found that employers saved $400 per employee annually, or as much as 11 percent on health-care costs, if they used HMOs or preferred providers and explored alternative treatments at lower costs.[44] Their relatively low out-of-pocket costs make them popular among employees.

To overcome some employees' complaints about the lack of freedom to choose their doctors in an HMO, some firms offer point-of-service plans. Such plans offer you, the patient, a choice every time you seek medical care. You can use the plan's network of doctors and hospitals and pay no deductibles, with only a $5 to $10 copayment for office visits, as with a traditional HMO. Or you can see a physician outside the network, and pay 30 to 40 percent of the total cost, just like traditional health coverage.[45] Table 11-2 presents a summary of alternative types of managed-care plans: HMOs, preferred-provider organizations, and point-of-service plans.

Other Medical Coverage

Medical coverage in areas such as dental care, vision care, drug abuse, alcoholism, and mental illness is decreasing, despite a 205 percent increase in psychiatric claims between 1989 and 1994. Big insurers often limit coverage for most psychiatric benefits to just 2 years for all ailments for the lifetime of an insured individual. The benefits can be used all at once or broken up over a period of time.[46] As for dental care, dental HMOs are growing fast. As with medical HMOs, a dental plan is usually paid a set annual fee per employee (usually about 10 to 15 percent of the amounts paid for medical benefits). Dental coverage is a standard inclusion for about 84 percent of U.S. employers, covering about 100 million workers.[47]

Sick-Leave Programs

These programs provide short-term insurance to workers against loss of wages due to short-term illness. However, in many firms such well-intentioned programs have often *added* to labor costs because of abuse by employees and because of the widespread perception that sick leave is a right and that if it is not used, it will be lost. From the employer's perspective, such unscheduled absences cost between 8 and 20 percent of payroll annually. As noted earlier, some firms are turning to managed-disability programs to control these costs.[48] Others, like Garden Valley Telephone Company of Minnesota, have taken a different tack. Garden Valley reduced discretionary sick-leave time from 12 days to 5 days. Unused benefits at year-end are paid to employees at their current wage rates. Extended sick-leave benefits (8 to 12 weeks, based on years of service) are available after the 5-day waiting period. Over a 10-year period, paid absences decreased by 22,000 hours.[49]

Pensions

A pension is a sum of money paid at regular intervals to an employee (or to his or her dependents) who has retired from a company and is eligible to receive such benefits. Before World War II, private pensions were rare. However, two developments in the late 1940s stimulated their growth: (1) clarification of the tax treatment of employer contributions and (2) the 1948 Inland Steel case, in which the National Labor Relations Board ruled that pensions were subject to compulsory collective bargaining.[50]

For a time, there were no standards and little regulation, which led to abuses in funding many pension plans and to the denial of pension benefits to employees who had worked many years. Perhaps the most notorious example of abuses occurred in 1963, when Studebaker closed its South Bend, Indiana, car factory and stopped payments to the seriously underfunded plan that covered the workers. Only those already retired or on the verge of retirement received the pension benefits they expected. Others got only a fraction—or nothing.[51]

Incidents like the one involving the Studebaker employees led to the passage of the Employee Retirement Income Security Act (ERISA; see Table 11-1) in 1974. Despite increased regulation, ERISA has generally been beneficial. In 1960, only 9 percent of retirees received a private pension. In 1993, about 30 percent did, and projections indicate that by 2004, 88 percent will.[52]

Money set aside by employers to cover pension obligations has become the nation's largest source of capital.[53] Pension funds hold 26 percent of the company equity and 15 percent of the taxable bonds in the U.S. economy, for a total of $2.5 trillion.[54] That is roughly $8000 for every man, woman, and child in the United States! Pension funds are an enormous force in the nation's (and the world's) capital markets. Pension-fund managers tend to invest for the long term, and the big corporate pension funds (95 percent of pension fund assets are covered by 5 percent of the plans) have less than 1 percent of their assets invested in leveraged buyouts or high-risk, high-yield junk bonds.[55]

In general, the financial health of most private pension plans is good.[56] However, to ensure that covered workers will receive their accrued benefits even if their companies fail, ERISA created the Pension Benefit Guaranty

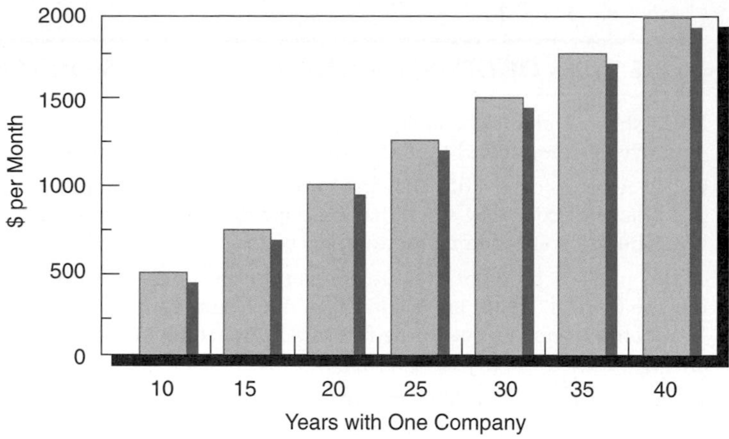

Figure 11-3
Monthly pension for a worker whose final average pay is $40,000 per year.

Corporation (PBGC). This agency acts as an insurance company, collecting annual premiums from companies with defined-benefit plans that spell out specific payments upon retirement. A company can still walk away from its obligation to pay pension benefits to employees entitled to receive them, but it must then hand over up to 30 percent of its net worth to the PBGC for distribution to the affected employees.

The PBGC insures the pensions of 42 million U.S. workers.[57] Typically it takes over about 100 underfunded plans a year, and it currently oversees 2084 pension plans.[58] For plans terminating in 1996, the PBGC pays a maximum personal benefit of anywhere from $11,096 to $31,704 annually, depending on the age when the employees begin to receive their payments.[59]

Despite these protections, the consequences of pension plan termination can still be devastating to some pensioners. Executives whose accrued benefits are bigger than the PBGC's guaranteed limits can see their monthly checks shrivel. Employees who have not worked at a company long enough to be vested (typically 5 years[60]) are not entitled to any benefits, and all workers lose the ability to accrue credits toward future benefits. So retirees may wind up having to get by with less to support them than they had planned. Nevertheless, as a matter of social policy, most retirees end up getting nearly all that is promised to them.

How Pension Plans Work. Contributions to pension funds typically are managed by trustees or outside financial institutions, frequently insurance companies. As an incentive for employers to begin and maintain such plans, the government defers taxes on the pension contributions and their earnings. Retirees pay taxes on the money as they receive it.

Traditionally, most big corporate plans have been *defined-benefit plans*, under which an employer promises to pay a retiree a stated pension, often expressed as a percentage of preretirement pay. In 1996, 80 percent of large companies offered such plans.[61] The most common formula is 1.5 percent of average salary over the last 5 years prior to retirement ("final average pay") times the number of years employed. In determining final average pay, the company may use base pay alone or base pay plus bonuses and other compensation. An example of a monthly pension for a worker earning final average pay of $40,000 a year, as a function of years of service, is shown in Figure 11-3. When

Table 11-3

FIVE TYPES OF DEFINED-CONTRIBUTION PENSION PLANS

- **Profit sharing plan.** The company puts a designated amount of its profits into each employee's account and then invests the money. ESOPs are a form of profit sharing.
- **ESOP.** An employee stock ownership plan pays off in company stock. Each employee gets shares of company stock that are deposited into a retirement account. Dividends from the stock are then added to the account.
- **401(k) plan.** A program in which an employee can deduct up to $9500 of his or her income (in 1997) from taxes and place the money into a personal retirement account. Many employers add matching funds, and the combined sums grow tax-free until they are withdrawn, usually at retirement.
- **Money-purchase plan.** The employer contributes a set percentage of each employee's salary, up to 25 percent in an incorporated business (20 percent if self-employed), to each employee's account. Employees must be vested. Annual investment earnings and losses are added to or subtracted from the account balances.
- **Simplified employee pension.** Under SEP, a small-business employer can contribute up to 15 percent, but no more than $30,000, of an employee's salary tax-free to an Individual Retirement Account. The employee is vested immediately for the amount paid into the account. The employee cannot withdraw any funds before age 59½ without penalty.

combined with Social Security benefits, that percentage is often about 50 percent of final average pay. The company then pays into the fund each year whatever is needed to cover expected benefit payments.

A second type of pension plan, popular either as a support to an existing defined-benefit plan or as a stand-alone retirement-savings vehicle, is called a *defined-contribution plan*. Examples include stock bonuses, savings plans, profit sharing, and various kinds of employee stock ownership plans. Brief descriptions of five types of such plans are shown in Table 11-3.

Defined-contribution plans fix a rate for employer contributions to the fund. Future benefits depend on how fast the fund grows. Such plans therefore favor young employees who are just beginning their careers (because they contribute for many years). Defined-benefit plans favor older, long-service workers.

Defined-contribution plans have great appeal for employers because a company will never owe more than what was contributed. However, since the amount of benefits received depends on the investment performance of the monies contributed, employees cannot be sure of the size of their retirement checks. In fact, regardless of whether a plan is a defined-benefit or defined-contribution plan, employees will not know what the purchasing power of their pension checks will be, because the inflation rate is variable.

What appears to be evolving is a system that will make employees (instead of employers) more responsible for how much money they have for retirement. Suppose employees are disappointed with the returns on their investments. Can they sue? Yes, but the Labor Department has adopted rules that provide at least some protection for employers. Employers are protected if (1) they give workers a choice of at least three investment vehicles, each of which differs in risk and return; and (2) they communicate with workers about the relative performance of each option at least quarterly. Information about options allows each employee to decide whether to switch from one vehicle to another if, say,

RETIREMENT BENEFITS AND SMALL BUSINESSES[63]

For most small-business employers, the administrative costs associated with a traditional defined-benefit plan are simply too high. Fortunately, there are alternatives that need not cost owners a bundle. One of these is a simplified version of the well-known 401(k) plan. For an annual administrative fee of $700 plus $10 per participant in excess of 10, the 401(k) Association of Langhorne, Pennsylvania, will administer a simple starter plan for businesses with fewer than 25 employees. Participants receive performance statements quarterly, and they direct how their contributions are invested. Although employees may invest in only three mutual funds from within a mutual-fund family, and there are no provisions for loans or hardship withdrawals, these features keep administrative costs down. As the business grows larger or employees amass larger sums of money in their savings plans, the firm may gravitate to a full-featured 401(k).

the stock market is slumping and he or she wants to move into fixed-income securities.[62]

Unisex Pensions. Nathalie Norris, an employee of the state of Arizona, paid $199 per month into an annuity retirement plan offered by the state—the amount deducted from the paychecks of both male and female state employees earning the same salary. But Norris discovered that upon retirement she would get $34 per month less than male employees. This figure was based on actuarial tables showing that women, on average, live longer than men. Norris sued the state, and in a 1983 Supreme Court ruling, she won. The Court ruled that (1) federal laws prohibiting sex discrimination in employment also bar employee-sponsored retirement plans that pay men higher benefits than women; and (2) all contributions to such plans must be used to finance a system of equal payments to employees of both sexes. However, the Court denied retroactive relief to women, which could have cost insurance companies as much as $1.2 billion annually.[64] As a result of this ruling, many insurance companies have developed "merged-gender mortality tables," which show the combined number of persons living, the combined number of persons dying, and the merged-gender mortality rate for each age. The effect on benefits depends on the income option(s) elected at the time retirement income begins. For men aged 65, this could mean a monthly income decrease of up to 8 percent, while for women aged 65, it could mean a monthly income increase of up to 8 percent.[65]

Pension Reforms That Benefit Women. These reforms were incorporated into the Retirement Equity Act of 1984. Corporate pension plans must now include younger workers and permit longer breaks in service. Women typically start work at a younger age than do men, and they are more likely to stop working for several years in order to have and care for children. However, since the new rules apply to both sexes, men also will accrue larger benefits. There are five major changes under the act:[66]

1. As of January 1, 1985, pension plans must include all employees 21 or older (down from 25). This provision extended pension coverage to an additional 600,000 women and 500,000 men.

Table 11-4

1996 SOCIAL SECURITY BENEFITS—MONTHLY	
Maximum monthly benefit for a person retiring in 1997 at age 65	$1284
Average benefit for:	
All retired workers	740
Retired couples	1250
Young widows with two eligible children	1448
Older widows without children	700

2. Employers must use 18 rather than 22 as the starting age for counting years of service. Employees at some firms need 10 years of service to be fully vested, or entitled to receive their pensions regardless of any future service. Thus a worker hired at age 19 can join a plan at 21 and can be fully vested by age 29.
3. Employees may have breaks in service of as long as 5 years before losing credit for prior years of work. In addition, a year of maternity or paternity leave cannot be considered a break in service.
4. Pension benefits may now be considered a joint asset in divorce settlements. State courts can award part of an individual's pension to the ex-spouse.
5. Employers must provide survivor benefits to spouses of fully vested employees who die before reaching the minimum retirement age.

Social Security

Table 11-1 outlined provisions for this program. Social Security is an income-maintenance program, not a pension program. It is the nation's best defense against poverty for the elderly, and it has worked well. Without it, according to one study, the poverty rate among the elderly would have jumped from 12.4 to 47.6 percent.[67] Table 11-4 shows maximum and average Social Security benefits for 1996.

Current Social Security beneficiaries get back what they paid in, many times over. Including matching payments by employers, the average worker retiring in 1996 at age 65 paid $43,000 into the system, and will receive between $150,000 and $200,000 in total benefits.[68] Sound too good to be true? It is.

Social Security is a pay-as-you-go system; payroll taxes earned by current workers are distributed to pay benefits for those who are already retired. Right now there are more than three workers for every retiree in our society, but when the first of the 77 million baby boomers, those born between 1946 and 1964, become eligible for benefits, there will be about two workers per retiree. In addition, people are living substantially longer—by 2020 the life expectancy for 65-year-old men and women will be 16.5 and 20 years, respectively.[69]

While the system will be solvent through the year 2030, at that time, given the large number of retirements by baby boomers, Social Security taxes will cover only 75 percent of promised benefits.[70] To meet such long-term funding needs, the system will have to be reformed soon—by raising payroll taxes or retirement ages, by cutting benefits, or by investing a portion of the current surplus in the stock market.[71]

This last alternative raises several vexing policy arguments:[72]

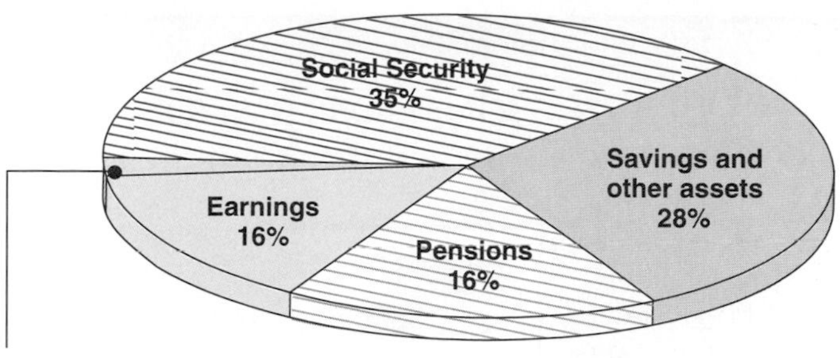

Figure 11-4
Where retirees get their income. (*Source:* Supplementing Social Security, *USA Today*, Apr. 7, 1992, p. 11A.)

- Should workers' retirement be built on government guarantees or the economy's health?
- Should the government own one-sixth of the stock market?
- Should Washington expose workers' retirement funds to market fluctuations?

Keep in mind, however, that Social Security was never intended to cover 100 percent of retirement expenses. For a worker earning $60,000 a year, for example, experts estimate that he or she will need about 75 percent of that in retirement. Social Security will replace about 30 percent of preretirement income; pensions and personal savings will have to make up the rest. How does this estimate compare with the actual distribution of retirees' income?

Figure 11-4 shows the current distribution of retirees' income, on average. Just over half (54 percent) comes from Social Security and pensions; the rest comes primarily from personal savings and current earnings in retirement. In combination, Social Security and private pensions typically provide just 67 percent of preretirement income for middle-income Americans who are covered by employer pension plans. That is well below the coverage in western European countries, which ranges from 74 percent in Germany to 92 percent in the Netherlands. In Japan, the rate is 79 percent.[73]

Unemployment Insurance

Although 97 percent of the workforce is covered by federal and state unemployment-insurance laws, each worker must meet eligibility requirements in order to receive benefits. That is, an unemployed worker must (1) be able and available to work and be actively seeking work, (2) not have refused suitable employment, (3) not be unemployed because of a labor dispute (except in Rhode Island and New York), (4) not have left a job voluntarily, (5) not have been terminated for gross misconduct, and (6) have been employed previously in a covered industry or occupation, earning a designated minimum amount for a specific minimum amount of time. Many claims are disallowed for failure to satisfy one or more of these requirements.

Every unemployed worker's benefits are "charged" against one or more companies. The more money paid out on behalf of a firm, the higher is the unemployment insurance rate for that firm.

The tax in most states amounts to 6.2 percent of the first $7000 earned by each worker. The state receives 5.4 percent of this 6.2 percent, and the remainder goes to the federal government. However, the tax rate may fall to zero percent in some states for employers who have had no recent claims by former employees, and it may rise to 10 percent for organizations with large numbers of layoffs.

INTERNATIONAL APPLICATION
Social Security in Other Countries

Many countries outside the United States have adopted pension programs that combine Social Security with private retirement accounts. In Britain, for example, workers can opt out of part of the state pension system by applying up to 44 percent of their social security tax to their own private individual investment accounts. Japan, Finland, Sweden, France, and Switzerland have similar programs. In these countries, the social security component of the pension system remains on a pay-as-you-go basis in which current tax receipts are used to pay for both current benefits and other government programs.

In contrast, Chile's retirement system is 100 percent privatized, with a mandatory 10 percent of employees' pay going into individual accounts. Australia is moving to a privatization plan that calls for 9 percent of workers' pay to go into private retirement accounts, up from 6 percent previously. The employer chooses a menu of investment options that employees can use to allocate their retirement savings.

Singapore uses a payroll tax to fund retirement, but it works like a private pension system. The revenues are invested in individually owned accounts; unlike U.S. social security taxes, they are tax-deductible and not subject to income taxes.

Employees can withdraw money from their retirement funds to purchase housing; as a result, 80 percent of Singapore's citizens own their own residences. If an employee is dissatisfied with the return earned by the public fund, he or she can transfer the account to investments in the Singapore stock market or other approved vehicles. The asset balance in a Singaporean's retirement fund passes to his or her beneficiaries upon death. Among the countries that have systems similar to Singapore's are India, Kenya, Malaysia, Zambia, and Indonesia.[74]

There is a growing sensitivity by state governments that high unemployment-insurance taxes can be a black eye on a state's business climate. In 1997, for example, Kansas, its unemployment-insurance fund bulging, enjoyed a fourth straight year of no such tax for many employers. State officials credited the moratorium with helping to add 37,000 new jobs in 1996.[75] Benefit levels have generally kept up with inflation. They average about 35 percent of what workers were earning at their last jobs.[76]

Supplemental Unemployment Insurance

This type of insurance is common in the auto, steel, rubber, flat glass, and farm equipment industries. Employers contribute to a special fund for this purpose. Initially, the primary purpose of such plans was to replace employees' pay during seasonal layoffs, but the provisions also apply in the case of permanent layoffs. Such plans, when combined with unemployment compensation, usually replace nearly all after-tax base wages for 6 months, with extensions under certain conditions. Only 8 percent of employees are covered by supplemental unemployment insurance plans, but most others are protected by some form of severance pay. Both types of arrangements are covered by ERISA, and this point has been affirmed by the Supreme Court.[77]

Severance Pay

Such pay is not legally required, and, because of unemployment compensation, many firms do not offer it. However, severance pay has been used extensively by firms that are downsizing in order to provide a smooth outflow of

Unemployment insurance benefits provide a "safety net" for individuals who qualify. These people are standing in line to receive benefits from the New York State Department of Labor.

employees.[78] This is a good example of the strategic use of compensation. Thus Philadelphia Electric Company gave an extra 9 months' severance pay to 1859 older workers who agreed to stagger their early retirements over a 2-year period. Roughly 17 percent of the workforce took advantage of the offer.[79] Said an executive of the firm: "If we lost all of them at once, we couldn't keep our electricity going."

Length of service, organization level, and the cause of the termination are key factors that affect the size of severance agreements. Most lower-level employees receive 1 week of pay for each year they work for a company.[80] Midlevel executives with median salaries of $60,000 can expect 3 or more weeks of pay for each year worked (an average of 12.7 months' pay in 1996), while chief executive officers with management contracts may receive 2 to 3 years of salary in the event of a takeover.[81] Besides wages, today's severance packages may also include outplacement counseling, extended health coverage, loans of computers or other equipment, free retraining courses, and sometimes a bargain deal on a company car.[82]

Payments for Time Not Worked

Included in this category are such benefits as the following:

Vacations	Personal excused absences
Holidays	Grievances and negotiations
Reporting time	Sabbatical leaves

COMPANY EXAMPLE

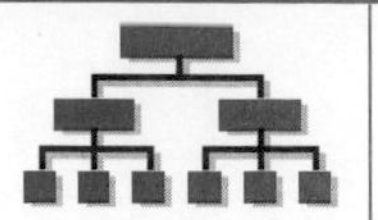

SABBATICAL LEAVES AT XEROX AND WELLS FARGO[83]

Some employees work with people with disabilities, others do alcohol and drug counseling, and still others do preretirement counseling. All are Xerox employees on 1-year leaves with full pay. Social commitment is a driving force behind the Xerox program, begun in 1971, but it is not the only rationale for the leaves. Public-service leaves boost the morale and skills of employees, according to those responsible for the program, and they make Xerox a more desirable place to work. Former leave takers say their careers were not affected by the leaves, and many feel their careers were advanced. Nevertheless, the program has its problems. Fully 40 percent of the leave takers reported major or moderate reentry difficulties on returning to work. More than one-third have quit, regarding their Xerox work as "not very rewarding or extremely unrewarding," in contrast with their high opinion of volunteer work. Despite these problems, Xerox aims to continue the program, at a direct cost of about $500,000 per year. Employees want such a program, and society needs them.

Wells Fargo Bank in San Francisco offers both 3-month and 6-month paid leaves. A selection committee receives about 40 proposals per year, most of which they reject. The committee uses two criteria in its decisions: (1) the sabbaticals must fit into a budget; highly paid employees deplete the budget faster than lower-paid employees; and (2) projects must really require a full-time commitment; those that an employee could do while working full- or part-time are less likely to be chosen.

About 10 percent of large employers in the United States currently offer sabbaticals. While companies of all sizes offer unpaid leave with job security on an informal basis, sabbaticals are most popular at law firms, computer firms, and consulting companies, where burnout is often a problem.

Employee Services

A broad group of benefits falls into the employee services category. Employees qualify for them purely by virtue of their membership in the organization, and not because of merit. Some examples are:

- Tuition aid
- Credit unions
- Auto insurance
- Food service
- Company car
- Career clothing
- Legal services
- Counseling
- Child adoption
- Child care
- Elder care
- Gift matching
- Charter flights
- Flexible work arrangements
- Thrift and short-term savings plans
- Stock purchase plans
- Fitness and wellness programs
- Moving and transfer allowances
- Transportation and parking
- Merchandise purchasing
- Christmas bonuses
- Service and seniority awards
- Umbrella liability coverage
- Social activities
- Referral awards
- Purchase of used equipment
- Family leaves

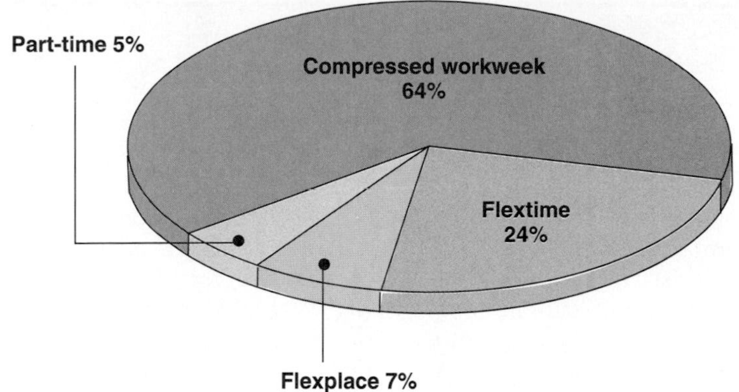

Figure 11-5
Distribution of requests for flexible work arrangements. (*Source:* S. Shellenbarger, The keys to successful flexibility, *The Wall Street Journal,* Jan. 13, 1994, p. B1.)

National survey data now indicate that people are more attached and committed to organizations that offer family-friendly policies, regardless of the extent to which they benefit personally from the policies.[84] Benefits that define family-friendly firms include on-site child care, subsidized child care on-site and off-site, flexible work schedules, and the ability to convert sick days into personal days off that employees can use to care for a sick child. The issue has taken on added importance as increasing numbers of women with children younger than age 6 have joined the workforce. In 1975 that figure was 39 percent; today it is more than 60 percent.[85] Figure 11-5 shows the distribution of requests for flexible work arrangements.

Once viewed as an expense with little return, such policies are now endorsed by a growing number of executives as an investment that pays dividends in morale, productivity, and ability to attract and retain top-notch talent. Du Pont's experience is typical. The firm estimated that it received a 637 percent return on its family-friendly spending. The payback came from improved performance, employee retention, reduced stress, and reduced absenteeism.[86] Said an executive at Du Pont: "If we don't have programs that will encourage our people to stay, then somebody else is going to invent the next breakthrough product."[87]

BENEFITS ADMINISTRATION

Benefits and Equal Employment Opportunity

In addition to the factors already noted, equal employment opportunity requirements affect the administration of benefits. Consider as examples health-care coverage and pensions. Effective in 1987, an amendment to the Age Discrimination in Employment Act eliminated mandatory retirement at any age. It also requires employers to continue the same group health-insurance coverage offered to younger employees to employees over the age of 70. Medicare payments are limited to what Medicare would have paid for in the absence of a group health plan and to the actual charge for the services. This is another example of government "cost shifting" to the private sector.

As noted in Chapter 2, the Older Workers Benefit Protection Act of 1990 restored age-discrimination protection to employee benefits. Early retirement offers are now legal if they are offered at least 45 days prior to the decision, and, if they are accepted, employees are given 7 days to revoke them. Employers were also granted some flexibility in plant closings to offset retiree health benefits or

ETHICAL DILEMMA
To Accept or Not to Accept Gifts

Nearly 9 out of every 10 companies surveyed by the Bureau of National Affairs limit employees' abilities to accept gifts from clients and outside business contacts. They do so to avoid even the appearance of a conflict of interest. At Price Waterhouse, such gifts may not exceed $50 in value, while policies at Aetna, 3M, and Motorola do not set specific limits, thus leaving the appropriateness to the judgment of the recipient.

However, even as companies broadcast their policies to the rank and file, some top executives may be participating in golf tournaments, sitting in stadium skyboxes, and riding chartered jets courtesy of clients and suppliers. Said one observer: "People have come to look on these things as perquisites—untaxed compensation that you get when you're in the right job."[88] Is this a double standard? Is it a conflict of interest? If your answer to these questions is yes, develop a policy that takes into account the interest of all parties and that, in your view, is ethical and just.

pension sweeteners against severance pay. That is, an employer is entitled to deny severance pay if an employee is eligible for retiree health benefits.

With regard to pensions, the IRS considers a plan *discriminatory* unless the employer's contribution for the benefit of lower-paid employees covered by the plan is comparable to contributions for the benefit of higher-paid employees. An example of this is the 401(k) salary-reduction plan described briefly in Table 11-3. The plan permits significant savings out of pretax compensation, produces higher take-home pay, and results in lower Social Security taxes. The catch: *the plan has to be available to everyone in any company that implements it.* Maximum employee contributions each year ($9500 in 1997) are based on average company participation. Thus poor participation by lower-paid employees curbs the ability of the higher-paid employees to make full use of the 401(k).[89]

Costing Benefits

Despite the high cost of benefits, many employees take them for granted. A major reason for this is that employers have failed to do in-depth cost analyses of their benefits programs and thus have not communicated the value of their benefits programs to employees. Four approaches are widely used to express the costs of employee benefits and services. Although each has value individually, a combination of all four often enhances their impact on employees. The four methods are:[90]

- **Annual cost of benefits for all employees**—valuable for developing budgets and for describing the total cost of the benefits program
- **Cost per employee per year**—the total annual cost of each benefits program divided by the number of employees participating in it
- **Percentage of payroll**—the total annual cost divided by total annual payroll (this figure is valuable in comparing benefits costs across organizations)
- **Cents per hour**—the total annual cost of benefits divided by the total number of hours worked by all employees during the year

Table 11-5 presents an example of benefits costs for a fictitious firm named Sun, Inc. The table includes all four methods of costing benefits. Can you find an example of each?

Table 11-5

EMPLOYEE BENEFITS: THE FORGOTTEN EXTRAS

Listed below are the benefits for the average full-time employee of Sun, Inc. (annual salary $34,000*).

Benefit	Who pays	Sun's annual cost	Percentage of base earnings	What the employee receives
Health, dental, and life insurance	Sun and employee	$ 2,723.40	8.01	Comprehensive health and dental plus life insurance equivalent to the employee's salary
Holidays	Sun	1,700.00	5.00	13 paid holidays
Annual leave (vacation)	Sun	1,309.00	3.85	10 days of vacation per year (additional days starting with sixth year of service)
Sick days	Sun	1,567.40	4.61	12 days annually
Company retirement	Sun	3,716.20	10.93	Vested after 5 years of service
Social Security	Sun and employee	2,278.00	6.70	Retirement and disability benefits as provided by law
Workers' compensation and unemployment insurance	Sun	340.00	1.00	Compensation if injured on duty and if eligible; income while seeking employment
Total		$13,634.00 or $6.55 per hour	40.10	

*The dollar amount and percentages will differ slightly depending upon the employee's salary. If an employee's annual salary is less than $34,000, the percentage of base pay will be greater. If the employee's salary is greater than $34,000, the percentage will be less but the dollar amount will be greater. Benefit costs to Sun, Inc., on behalf of 5480 employees are more than $74,680,000 per year.

Cafeteria, or Flexible, Benefits

The theory underlying this approach to benefits is simple: instead of offering all workers at a company the same benefits, the benefits program allows each worker to pick and choose among alternative options "cafeteria-style." Thus the elderly bachelor might pass up maternity coverage for additional pension contributions. The mother whose children are covered under her husband's health insurance may choose legal and auto insurance instead.

The typical plan works like this: workers are offered a package of benefits that includes "basic" and "optional" items. Basics might include modest medical coverage, life insurance equal to a year's salary, vacation time based on length of service, and some retirement pay. But then employees can use "flexible credits" to choose among such additional benefits as full medical coverage, dental and eye care, more vacation time, additional disability income, and higher company payments to the retirement fund. Nationwide, about 27 percent of large firms have flexible benefits plans, up from 18 percent in 1987.[91] The plans were devised largely in response to the rise in the number of two-income families. When working spouses both have conventional plans, their basic benefits, such as health and life insurance, tend to overlap. Couples rarely can use both plans fully. But if at least one spouse is covered by a "flex" plan, the couple can add benefits, such as child care, prepaid legal fees, and dental coverage, that it might otherwise have to buy on its own. Two studies have now examined employees' satisfaction with their benefits and understanding of them both

IMPACT OF BENEFITS ON PRODUCTIVITY, QUALITY OF WORK LIFE, AND THE BOTTOM LINE

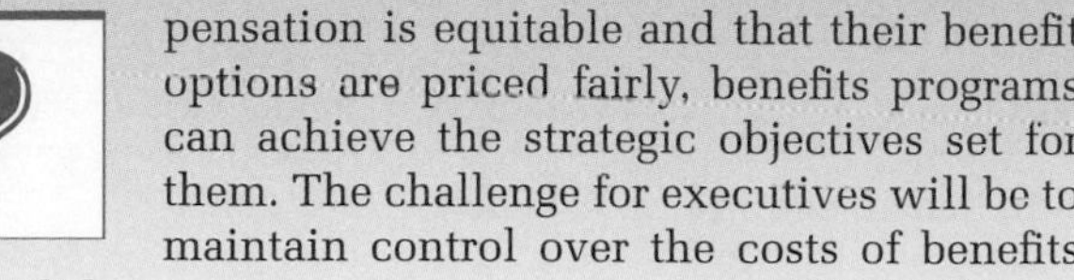

Generally speaking, employee benefits do not enhance productivity. Their major impact is on attraction and retention and on improving the quality of life for employees and their dependents. Today there is widespread recognition among employers and employees that benefits are an important component of total compensation. As long as employees perceive that their total compensation is equitable and that their benefit options are priced fairly, benefits programs can achieve the strategic objectives set for them. The challenge for executives will be to maintain control over the costs of benefits while providing genuine value to employees in the benefits offered. If they can do this, everybody wins.

before and after the introduction of a flexible benefits plan. Both found substantial improvements in satisfaction and understanding after the plan was implemented.[92]

There are advantages for employers as well. Under conventional plans, employers risked alienating employees if they cut benefits, regardless of increases in the costs of coverage. Flexible plans allow them to pass some of the increases on to workers more easily. Instead of providing employees a set package of benefits, the employer says, "On the basis of your $35,000 annual salary, I promise you $7000 to spend any way you want." If health-care costs soar, the employee—not the employer—decides whether to pay more or to take less coverage.

There is help for employees even under these circumstances if they work for firms that sponsor "flexible-spending accounts" (about 80 percent of all large firms). Employees can save for expenses such as additional health insurance or day care with pretax dollars, up to a specified amount (e.g., in a dependent-care spending account, up to $5000 for child or elder care). The result is a win-win situation for both employer and employee.[93]

To realize these potential advantages, companies must use major communications efforts to help employees fully understand their benefits. Since employees have more choices, they often experience anxiety about making the "right" choices. In addition, they need benefits information on a continuing basis to ensure that their choices continue to support their changing needs. Careful attention to communication can enhance recruitment efforts, help cut turnover, and make employees more aware of their total package of benefits.

Communicating the Benefits

Try to make a list of good reasons why any company should not make a deliberate effort to market its benefits package effectively. It will be a short list. Generally speaking, there are four broad objectives in communicating benefits:

1. To make employees *aware* of them. This can be done by reminding them of their coverages periodically and of how to apply for benefits when needed.
2. To help employees *understand* the benefits information they receive in order to take full advantage of the plans.
3. To make employees confident that they can *trust* the information they receive.

4. To convince present and future employees of the *worth* or value of the benefits package. After all, it is their "hidden paycheck."[94]

Traditionally, employers concentrated their communications about benefits at the start of employment and assumed that was sufficient in relation to future events. Today firms provide their employees "the benefits information you need, when you need it." Company-based intranets, with ready access by all employees to benefits information, make "HR on the desktop" a reality for many firms.

As an example, consider the use of a decision support system (DSS) and an expert system (ES) to communicate benefits information, as recently applied in a *Fortune* 500 company.[95] DSSs are interactive computer programs designed to do two things: (1) provide relevant information, and (2) answer what-if questions. ESs capture and combine the knowledge of subject matter experts (e.g., benefits specialists) and use this information to recommend a solution for the user. There is growing use of ESs in human resource management.[96]

The ES, called Personal Choice Expert, generated recommendations for each of nine categories of benefits and two spending accounts. The DSS, called Choice Maker, computed the cost of each choice and deducted it from the total credits provided to the employee. A typical user session consisted of four phases:

- **Introduction**—informing the user about what the system does, how to use the on-line help screen, and how to proceed.
- **Questioning**—capturing information about the employee (age, gender, income) and his or her family (marital status, spouse income, number of children, spending habits, alternative sources of health and life insurance).
- **Recommendations**—combining the employee's inputs with the decision schemes embedded in the ES to generate a set of recommended decisions. Outcomes are displayed on the screen and printed out on the company's actual enrollment-benefit forms.
- **Modifications**—allowing the employee to ask what-if questions, recompute costs, and update enrollment forms.

The ES also included hypertext information. Key words and phrases were underlined, and at any time, users could click on these underlined words and phrases. The system then provides more in-depth information. Results of the study indicated that employees who used the ES and DSS were 25 percent more satisfied with their benefits than those who did not, and made choices that converged toward those the ES recommended. Perhaps most encouraging was the fact that the development cost of this custom system was less than $8000. With results like these, we can expect many more employers to begin using ES and DSS to communicate their benefits packages.

THE NEW WORLD OF EMPLOYEE BENEFITS

Human Resource Management in Action: Conclusion

In this new world of sharing costs and sharing risks, there are four major areas that change has affected most profoundly: health insurance, programs to promote healthy lifestyles, retirement programs, and employee savings programs.

Health Insurance

There are no more blank checks. Employers and insurers are both taking an aggressive role in shifting from reimbursement plans (in which employees or medical providers receive direct payments for medical expenses) to a managed-care approach (e.g., health maintenance organizations). Fully 77 percent of all workers were in managed-care programs in 1996, up sharply from 49 percent 4 years earlier.[97] At the same time, firms as varied as IBM, Harley Davidson, Charles Schwab, The Walt Disney Company, and Microsoft have extended medical benefits to same-sex couples. In an effort to recruit and retain the best talent in their industries, they offer the same compensation and benefits to people doing the same work.[98]

Keeping Employees Healthier

One of the most important themes in employee benefits is now prevention: limiting health-care claims by keeping employees and their families healthier. The Travelers Insurance Company thoroughly studied its own programs in this area and found that the funds it spent on health promotion helped the company save $7.8 million in employee benefits costs. That is a savings of $3.40 for every dollar spent. The biggest payoffs came from education programs, including efforts to discourage smoking and drinking and to encourage healthier diets.

Some companies have added new benefits, even as they eliminated others. Johnson & Johnson and Hewlett-Packard began paying for routine checkups and tests for infants, while AT&T launched a prenatal care program.

Retirement Programs—Sharing the Risk

More employers are now shifting to defined-contribution pension plans, in which the employee shares the investment risk. In return, however, employees have a larger voice in choosing how the funds will be invested. Employees also have greater "portability"—due largely to the meteoric growth of 401(k) plans.[99] In 1984, for example, only 36 percent of employers offered such plans. Today, almost all employers offer them, and by 2001 nearly 30 million workers at some 340,000 companies will be able to join one.[100] Nine out of ten companies that offer 401(k)s provide a partial matching (up to $5000 a year or more) of employees' savings, and nearly 80 percent of eligible employees participate in them. Such plans provide a true incentive to save because they are easily funded through payroll deductions.

Meanwhile, sophisticated companies like IBM, BankAmerica, and Xerox are developing "cash-balance" plans that combine elements of defined-benefit and defined-contribution plans. Since they are funded on the basis of a worker's current salary, not his or her final average salary, they cost companies about a third less than traditional defined-benefit plans do. Funding such plans on the basis of a worker's current salary also simplifies and improves retirement planning.[101]

Expanding the 401(k) Concept

To many observers, the kind of sharing and choice embodied in 401(k) plans is the wave of the future in employee benefits. Companies want plans that give employees choices to suit their needs, incentives to conserve funds, and risks to

IMPLICATIONS FOR MANAGEMENT PRACTICE

As you think about the design and implementation of employee benefits plans, consider three practical issues:

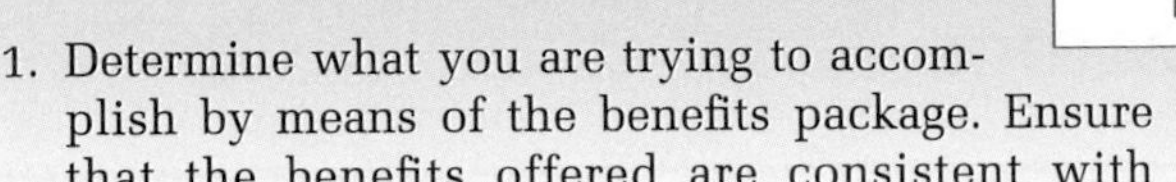

1. Determine what you are trying to accomplish by means of the benefits package. Ensure that the benefits offered are consistent with the strategic objectives of the unit or organization as a whole.
2. Take the time to learn about alternative benefit arrangements. Doing so can save large amounts of money.
3. Develop an effective strategy for communicating benefits regularly to all employees.

share with the company. For example, it is possible that the 401(k) concept of individual and corporate partnership will be expanded to assist in saving for long-term medical care.

Of one thing we can be sure, however. During the next decade the number of choices available to employees seems likely to expand and become more complicated. Advice on how to make informed choices will itself become an increasingly popular employee benefit.

SUMMARY

Managers need to think carefully about what they wish to accomplish by means of their benefits programs. At a cost of about 40 percent of base pay for every employee on the payroll, benefits represent substantial annual expenditures. Factors such as the following are important strategic considerations in the design of benefits programs: the long-term plans of a business, its stage of development, its projected rate of growth or downsizing, characteristics of its workforce, legal requirements, competitiveness of its overall benefits package, and its total compensation strategy.

There are three major components of the benefits package: security and health benefits, payments for time not worked, and employee services. Despite the high cost of benefits, many employees take them for granted. A major reason for this is that employers have not done in-depth cost analyses or communicated the value of their benefits programs. This is a multimillion-dollar oversight. Certainly the counseling that must accompany the implementation of a flexible-benefits program, coupled with the use of computer-based expert systems and decision support systems, can do much to alleviate this problem.

DISCUSSION QUESTIONS

11-1 What should a company do over both the short term and the long term to maximize the use and value of its benefits choices to employees?

11-2 Should employees have more or less control over how their company-sponsored retirement funds are invested?

11-3 In terms of the "attract-retain-motivate" philosophy, how do benefits affect employee behavior?
11-4 What can firms do to control health-care costs?
11-5 Your company has just developed a new, company-sponsored savings plan for employees. Develop a strategy to publicize the program and to encourage employees to participate in it.

APPLYING YOUR KNOWLEDGE

Case 11-1 *Reducing Health-Care Costs*

In the Spring of 1995, Ron McGee, vice president of group insurance and labor relations at Polson Corporation, delivered the bad news to top management. Medical insurance premiums for the following fiscal year were expected to increase approximately 40 percent, up dramatically from the 8 percent increase of the previous year. And future cost projections were equally grim. It was estimated that by 1999, the company's $355 million annual health-care bill would increase to a staggering $613 million.

Polson is a large high technology automotive and electronics products company that employs about 70,000 people in the United States. It decided not to tinker with traditional remedies to escalating health-care costs, such as increasing deductibles and shifting larger copayments to employees. Instead, it decided to develop one of the few nationwide, managed health-care networks then in existence. It did so by contracting with Whitefish Corporation, a large employee benefits company specializing in such managed health-care plans.

A task force was formed in 1995, under the direction of Ron McGee. The task force included human resource executives from the corporate office of Polson in Morristown, New Jersey. This group was given the challenge of developing a custom-designed program that would hold down health-care premium costs to a reasonable level. The group decided that the new program would be built on the following foundation:

1. The insurance carrier, Whitefish Corporation, would be a partner in the program and would carry a financial risk, not merely be an administrator that paid the bills as they came in.
2. The insurance carrier would use its buying power to establish a network of highly qualified primary-care physicians and specialists throughout the United States, coinciding with the company's primary locations.
3. The insurance carrier would guarantee a high level of quality care to be provided to Polson's employees.
4. Unlike other health maintenance organization (HMO) plans, under the new Polson Plan employees would be able to switch from managed care to a traditional indemnity plan at will, but would pay extra for exercising this option.

"We sought to change the way health care was delivered to our employees," says Al Gesler, corporate director of human resources for Polson. "The net result was a hybrid program, taking into account the best features of HMOs and indemnity plans and combining that with a partnership arrangement between Whitefish, Polson, and its employees." Whitefish was chosen because it was a large and experienced insurance carrier and had a health-care network in place across the United States that pretty well coincided with major locations where Polson had operations.

In March 1996, Polson signed a 3-year agreement with Whitefish for a managed-care program which was called "The Health-Care Connection." This plan covered medical, dental, vision, and hearing care, as well as prescription medications. It also included a well-care program covering such items as an annual physical exam and prenatal care. An important feature of the plan was that Whitefish guaranteed annual premium increases of less than 10 percent during each of the 3 contract years on the managed-care side of the program. No similar guarantee was provided on the indemnity side. The actual figure would depend on the number of employees using the indemnity portion of the program.

"We wanted a very strong gatekeeper system," says McGee. "For our employees to take advantage of the extremely comprehensive benefits found on the in-network side of The Health-Care Connection program, as well as the modest $10 copayment feature, they had to agree to choose a primary-care physician from within the closed panel and visit specialists in hospitals only when referred by their primary-care physicians. That was the trade-off." Where employees stayed in the network, the costs were very modest: a $10 copayment per office visit and $5 per prescription. If employees chose to go outside the network, they could switch to the indemnity side of the plan at any time for any particular illness or injury with no restrictions. Those who did, however, paid an annual deductible equal to 1 percent of their annual salaries and then were subject to an 80/20 copayment split (in other words, employees paid 20 percent of the medical-care costs after the deductible was met).

"The basic concept behind managed care is just that, managing it," says McGee. "By staying in the network, everyone saves money. We felt this was a major effort aimed at limiting unnecessary care."

For its part, Whitefish is responsible for guaranteeing the quality of the managed-care side of the network. It is responsible for using its buying power to ensure that hospitals in the plan attract an adequate supply of high-quality physicians. It also means continual monitoring of employee usage of different types of medical care through "utilization studies."

Questions

1. How should Polson communicate its new health-benefits plan to employees?
2. What results in terms of cost reduction do you anticipate Polson will achieve through the implementation of its new health-care program?
3. What additional follow-up should the benefits administration people at Polson take now that the program has been in effect for several years?
4. To what extent do you believe managed health-care plans such as those at Polson are the wave of the future for health-benefits plans in major American corporations?

REFERENCES

1. Bennet, J. (1993, Sept. 5). Auto talks hang on health costs, but workers are loath to chip in. *The New York Times*, pp. 1, 8–10.
2. Leonard, B. (1995, Mar.). Perks give way to life-cycle benefits plans. *HRMagazine*, pp. 45–48.
3. Benefits costs (1996, Apr.). *MSEC Bulletin*. Denver: Mountain States Employers Council, Inc.
4. Blumenstein, R. (1996, Dec. 9). Seeking a cure: Auto makers attack high health-care bills with a new approach. *The Wall Street Journal*, pp. A1, A4.

5. Trouble ahead in the battle to contain labor costs (1997, Feb. 10). *Business Week*, p. 29.
6. McCaffery, R. M. (1989). Employee benefits and services. In L. R. Gomez-Mejia (ed.), *Compensation and benefits*. Washington, DC: Bureau of National Affairs, pp. 3-101 to 3-135.
7. Smart, T. (1993, May 10). IBM has a new product: Employee benefits. *Business Week*, p. 58.
8. Rubis, L. (1995, Jan.). Benefits boost appeal of temporary work. *HRMagazine*, pp. 54–58.
9. Ledvinka, J., & Scarpello, V. G. (1991). *Federal regulation of personnel and human resource management* (2d ed.). Boston: PWS-Kent.
10. Ibid.
11. McCaffery (1989), loc. cit.
12. Shellenbarger, S. (1993, Dec. 17). Firms try to match people with benefits. *The Wall Street Journal*, p. B1
13. Benefits costs—What happened in 1994? (1996, Apr.). *MSEC Bulletin*. Denver: Mountain States Employers Council, Inc., p. 5 See also U.S. Chamber of Commerce (1995). *Employee benefits, 1995*. Washington, DC: Author.
14. Peers, A. (1987, June 29). Firms now must offer health insurance to some ex-workers—but at what price? *The Wall Street Journal*, p. 29.
15. Williams, P., II. (1996, Oct.). Law enhances portability of health benefits. *HRNews*, pp. 4, 5. See also Jeffrey, N. A. (1996, Aug. 30). Healthy switch: New law eases job-hops, sometimes. *The Wall Street Journal*, p. C1.
16. McCaffery, R. M. (1992). *Employee benefit programs: A total compensation perspective* (2d ed.). Boston: PWS-Kent.
17. Leonard, loc. cit.
18. Say, does workers' comp cover wretched excess? (1991, July 22). *Business Week*, p. 23.
19. Crackdown on job-injury costs: New workers' compensation rules have double edge (1995, Mar. 16). *The New York Times*, pp. D1, D7.
20. Marsh, B. (1991, Dec. 31). Rising worker compensation costs worry small firms. *The Wall Street Journal*, p. B2.
21. Kerr, P. (1991, Dec. 29). Vast amount of fraud discovered in workers' compensation system. *The New York Times*, pp. 1, 14.
22. First aid for workers comp (1996, Mar. 18). *Business Week*, p. 106; Crackdown on job-injury costs, loc. cit.; Evangelista-Uhl, G. A. (1995, June). Avoid the workers' comp crunch. *HRMagazine*, pp. 95–99; Fefer, M. D. (1994, Oct. 3). Taking control of your workers' comp costs. *Fortune*, pp. 131–136.
23. McCaffery (1992), op. cit.
24. There when you need it: Disability coverage. (1996, Oct.). *USAA Magazine*, p. 5; Schultz, E. E. (1990, Apr. 17). Disability coverage? Well, I have some. *The Wall Street Journal*, pp. C1, C23.
25. King, D. (1996, Oct.). A comprehensive approach to disability management. *HRMagazine*, pp. 97–102.
26. Jeffrey, N. A. (1996, Oct. 28). Employers aggressively attack disability costs. *The Wall Street Journal*, pp. B1, B5.
27. Ibid.
28. Kuttner, R. (1995, Aug. 7). The lethal side effects of managed care. *Business Week*, p. 166. See also Lewin, T. (1991, Apr. 28). High medical costs affect broad areas of daily life. *The New York Times*, pp. 1, 28–32.
29. DePalma, A. (1996, Dec. 15). Doctor, what's the prognosis? Crisis for Canada. *The New York Times*, p. 3.
30. Winslow, R. (1997, Jan. 21). Health-care costs may be heading up again. *The Wall Street Journal*, pp. B1, B7. See also Feel better? (1996, Feb. 26). *Business Week*, p. 8.

31. Health care (1997, Jan. 13). *Business Week*, pp. 114, 115.
32. Blumenstein, loc. cit.
33. Uchitelle, L. (1991, May 1). Insurance as a job benefit shows signs of overwork. *The New York Times*, pp. A1, D23.
34. Labor letter (1992, Nov. 3). *The Wall Street Journal*, p. A1.
35. Stodghill, R. (1997, Jan. 13). Minnesota's HMO-ectomy. *Business Week*, p. 115.
36. A crisis of medical success (1993, Mar. 15). *Business Week*, pp. 78–80. See also Pollack, A. (1991, Apr. 29). Medical technology "arms race" adds billions to the nation's bills. *The New York Times*, pp. A1, B8–B10.
37. Blumenstein, loc. cit.
38. Thornburg, L. (1995, Aug.). Teach employees self-care to cut costs. *HRMagazine*, pp. 36–43.
39. Medical lessons from the big Mac (1997, Feb. 10). *Business Week*, pp. 94, 98.
40. Labor letter (1991, Aug. 13). *The Wall Street Journal*, p. A1.
41. Garcia, B. E. (1989, Feb. 16). Cigna's "managed" health care is all-or-nothing game. *The Wall Street Journal*, p. A6.
42. Deere's surprising harvest in health care (1994, July 11). *Business Week*, pp. 107, 111.
43. Trouble ahead in the battle to contain labor costs, loc. cit.
44. Khanna, P. M. (1992, Aug. 17). Health costs. *The Wall Street Journal*, p. B1.
45. Jeffrey, N. A. (1996, Dec. 2). Bills and costs lurk within HMO options. *The Wall Street Journal*, pp. C1, C19.
46. Stressed out over stress benefits? (1997, Feb. 10). *Business Week*, p. 132.
47. Milkovich, G. T., & Newman, J. M. (1996). *Compensation* (5th ed.). Chicago: Irwin. See also Dental HMO enrollment rising (1993, Apr.). *HRMagazine*, p. 31. See also Freudenheim, M. (1992, May 12). Business and health. *The New York Times*, p. D2.
48. King, loc. cit.
49. Howe, R. C. (1995, Mar.). Rx for an ailing sick-leave plan. *HRMagazine*, pp. 67–69.
50. Widder, P. (1982, May 31). Individuals gain more control over their pensions. *The Denver Post*, pp. 1C, 8C.
51. Colvin, G. (1982, Oct. 4). How sick companies are endangering the pension system. *Fortune*, pp. 72–78.
52. Topolnicki, D. M. (1993, Nov.). Beat the five threats to your retirement. *Money*, pp. 66–73. See also Widder, loc. cit.
53. White, J. A. (1990, Mar. 20). Pension funds try to retire idea that they are villains. *The Wall Street Journal*, pp. C1, C8.
54. The smart 401(k) (1995, July 3). *Business Week*, pp. 58–62. See also Salwen, K. G., & Scism, L. (1993, Dec. 14). Corporate pensions face proxy rules. *The Wall Street Journal*, pp. C1, C6.
55. White, loc. cit.
56. Work week (1997, Jan. 14). *The Wall Street Journal*, p. A1.
57. Burkins, G. (1996, Oct. 4). Pension Benefit Guaranty reaches pact with men's suit industry to rescue fund. *The Wall Street Journal*, pp. A2, A10.
58. O'Connell, V. (1996, Aug. 8). Smith Corona acts to end pension plans; move would reduce benefits to many. *The Wall Street Journal*, pp. A2, A4.
59. O'Connell, V. (1996, Aug. 13). Salvaging your troubled pension plan. *The Wall Street Journal*, pp. C1, C27.
60. Gunn, E. P. (1996, Oct. 28). How to maximize your pension payout. *Fortune*, p. 233. See also When 401(k) benefits vest (1996, May). *HRMagazine*, p. 65.
61. Ibid.
62. The smart 401(k), loc. cit.
63. Zall, M. (1995, July). Retirement benefits small employers can afford. *HRMagazine*, pp. 53–56.
64. A bow to unisex pensions (1983, July 18). *Newsweek*, p. 66.

65. The *Norris* decision and merged-gender annuity rates (1983, Aug.). TIAA-CREF, Notice to annuity owners.
66. Pension reform has something for everyone (1984, Aug. 27). *U.S. News & World Report*, p. 67.
67. *Older Americans in the workforce: Challenges and solutions* (1987). Washington, DC: Bureau of National Affairs.
68. Richards, P. (1997, Winter). Social Security: Will it be there? *Stages*, pp. 5–9.
69. Ibid. See also Shoven, J. (1996, Aug.). Should Social Security be privatized? *USAA Financial Spectrum*, pp. 1–3.
70. How should we fix Social Security? (1997, Jan. 20). *Business Week*, pp. 24–26.
71. Carter, M. N., & Shipman, W. G. (1996). *Saving Social Security's dream*. Washington, DC: Regnery Publishing.
72. How should we fix Social Security? loc. cit.
73. Labor letter (1992, June 21). *The Wall Street Journal*, p. A1.
74. Shoven, loc. cit.; Roberts, P. C. (1990, Feb. 1). Let workers own their own retirement funds . . . that's how it's done in other countries. *The Wall Street Journal*, p. A21; Riley, B. (1996, Oct. 29). All work and no pension. *Financial Times*, p. 12.
75. Work week (1997, Feb. 11). *The Wall Street Journal*, p. A1.
76. Rosenbaum, D. E. (1990, Dec. 2). Unemployment insurance aiding fewer workers. *The New York Times*, pp. 1, 38.
77. McCaffery (1992), op. cit.
78. Capell, P. (1996, Feb. 26). Take the money and run. *The Wall Street Journal*, pp. R1, R11.
79. Lublin, J. S. (1991, Apr. 1). Bosses alter early-retirement windows to be less coercive—and less generous. *The Wall Street Journal*, pp. B1, B7.
80. Take my job, please! (1996, July 8). *Business Week*, p. 6. See also Schultz, E. E. (1990, Oct. 17). A financial survival guide for the newly unemployed. *The Wall Street Journal*, pp. C1, C17.
81. Work week (1996, Aug. 13). *The Wall Street Journal*, p. A1. See also Alderman, L. (1996, Aug.). Walk out the door with all the money you deserve. *Money*, pp. 66–68.
82. Alderman, loc. cit.
83. Sheley, E. (1996, Mar.). Why give employees sabbaticals? To reward, relax, and recharge. *HRMagazine,* pp. 58–70; Tannenbaum, J. A. (1981, May 6). Paid public-service leaves buoy workers, but return to old jobs can be wrenching. *The Wall Street Journal,* p. 29; Axel, H. (1992). *Company sabbatical policies.* New York: Conference Board.
84. Grover, S. L., & Crooker, K. J. (1995). Who appreciates family responsive human resource policies: The impact of family-friendly policies on the organizational attachment of parents and non-parents. *Personnel Psychology*, 48, 271–288.
85. Leib, J. (1997, Feb. 16). Family-friendly nets bottom-line gains. *The Denver Post*, pp. 1J, 19J.
86. Ibid.
87. Gardner, J., in Sheley, E. (1996, Feb.). Flexible work options: Beyond 9 to 5. *HRMagazine*, p. 53.
88. Jacobs, D. L. (1993, Dec. 5). The rules for giving, and for giving back. *The New York Times*, p. 25.
89. The smart 401(k), loc. cit.
90. McCaffery (1992), op. cit.
91. Luciano, L. (1993, May). How companies are slashing benefits. *Money,* pp. 128–138.
92. Sturman, M. C., Hannon, J. M., & Milkovich, G. T. (1996). Computerized decision aids for flexible-benefits decisions: The effects of an expert system and decision-support system on employee intentions and satisfaction with benefits. *Personnel Psychology*, **49,** 883–908. See also Barber, A. E., Dunham, R. B., & Formisano, R. A.

(1992). The impact of flexible benefits on employee satisfaction: A field study. *Personnel Psychology*, **45,** 55–75.

93. Labor letter (1993, Dec. 14). *The Wall Street Journal*, p. A1.
94. Markowich, M. M. (1992, Oct.). 25 ways to save a bundle. *HRMagazine*, pp. 48–57.
95. Sturman et al., loc. cit.
96. Lawler, J. J., & Elliot, R. (1996). Artificial intelligence in HRM: An experimental study of an expert system. *Journal of Management*, **22,** 85–111.
97. Trouble ahead in the battle to contain labor costs, loc. cit.
98. Gay rights, corporate style (1996, Oct. 7). *Business Week*, p. 170.
99. How to take your 401(k) on the road (1995, June 5). *Business Week*, p. 132.
100. Special 401(k) report (1996, June). *Money*, pp. 95–100.
101. McLean, B. (1996, Oct. 28). The latest twist: Cash-balance plans. *Fortune*, p. 234.

CASE IN THE NEWS

Executive Pay: A Special Report

By Jennifer Reingold,
with bureau reports

It seems to have worked like a charm. In recent years, as boards shifted the mix of executive pay away from cash and toward stock options, corporate profits and the stock market have vaulted to record levels. It's exactly the win-win situation that pay for performance was expected to bring: more reward for the leaders and better returns for shareholders, who can sleep well knowing that executives feel the same pain they do if their companies underperform.

Tying pay to performance is a great idea. But stock-option deals have compensation out of control.

It's a soothing lullaby, but shareholders are starting to wake up to some sour notes. The explosion of executive pay—propelled by huge option grants, easy performance provisos, and a bull market—has created a windfall for all. Star CEOs are winning big, but so are many second-stringers. Even for the success stories, the CEO's gains often exceed the company's own strong year proportionally. And while the mass embrace of options has helped shareholders, options have hidden costs and are diluting those gains to the tune of tens of millions of dollars.

Few doubt 1996 was a stellar year. The Standard & Poor's 500-stock index rose a stunning 23%. Corporate profits rose, too—an impressive 11%. Who would begrudge U.S. chieftains a healthy raise?

For CEOs, an average 54% raise. For factory workers, 3%.

Apparently, no one. But many CEOs took that—and a good deal more. For 1996, CEO pay gains far outstripped the roaring economy or shareholder returns. The average salary and bonus for a chief executive rose a phenomenal 39%, to $2.3 million. Add to that retirement benefits, incentive plans, and gains from stock options, and the numbers hit the roof. CEOs' average total compensation rose an astounding 54% last year, to $5,781,300. That largesse came on top of a 30% rise in total pay in 1995—yet it was hardly spread down the line. The average compensation of the top dog was 209 times that of a factory employee, who garnered a tiny 3% raise in 1996. White-collar workers eked out just 3.2%, though many now get options too.

It all adds up to quite a payday—and one that's raising a storm of criticism. "We've got terrible tensions this year" with institutional investors, says Pearl Meyer, president of pay specialist Pearl Meyer & Partners. Even many shareholder advocates who pushed for the move to pay for performance in the early 1990s question whether the approach is working. As once-outsize options packages become the norm, many CEOs are taking the lion's share. Far smaller gains are going to managers and other key employees. The disturbing message: The CEO deserves nearly all the credit for the company's success. Worse, there's very little downside to many CEO pay deals. Many executives are negotiating big guaranteed payouts in case they stumble. And if the market drops, some pay experts worry that executives will demand—and get—options at lower prices to ensure that their pay packets remain full.

High pay packages may just be "the cost of finding brains."

What are the main results of *Business Week*'s 47th annual Executive Pay Scoreboard? Compiled with Standard & Poor's Compustat, a division of The McGraw-Hill Companies, the survey examines the compensation of the two highest-paid executives at 365 of the country's largest companies. In comparing pay with performance over three years, *Business Week* found that Microsoft's William H. Gates III and Avon Products' James E. Preston gave investors the best results for their pay (page 474). Conseco's Stephen C. Hilbert and America Online's Stephen M. Case were the worst-performing CEOs relative to payouts.

Despite the soaring pay, many experts argue that the system is working better than ever. They see the bull market and healthy corporate sector as proof positive that companies get what they pay for. They argue that as long as CEOs continue to turn in strong results for their shareholders, the absolute level of executive pay is irrelevant. "You can't legislate morality," says James E. McKinney, consultant at pay experts Hirschfeld, Stern, Moyer & Ross Inc. "The U.S. is the most exciting economy the world has ever seen." Adds Charles W. Sweet, president of A. T. Kearney Executive Search: It's simply "the cost of finding brains."

Little-Known Leader

In many cases last year, those brains cost a lot more. The top ranks were peopled by such corporate standouts as Intel's Andrew S. Grove, who earned $97.6 million, and Travelers Group's Sanford I. Weill, who made $94.2 million, most of which remains in Travelers stock that he can't sell until he retires. Heading our list for the second straight year was Lawrence M. Coss, the little-known CEO and chairman of Green Tree Financial Corp., based in St. Paul, Minn. Thanks to a five-year deal set in 1991 that paid him 2.5% of pretax income, Coss made $102.4 million last year—a 56% rise over the $65.6 million he earned in 1995.

By any standard, Coss's paycheck is huge. And for many investors and pay experts, he remains the poster boy for all that is right with pay for performance. Coss himself makes no apologies. "Indeed it is a huge number," he says, "but I'd rather talk about the success of the company." That's easy to do. Between 1991 and 1996, Green Tree's share had compounded annual returns of 53% as it became the largest lender to the manufactured-home sector. Although two small pension plans recently sued Coss and the board for excessive compensation, most big shareholders appear satisfied. "In no way would I consider him overpaid," says Thomas W. Smith, partner at Prescott Investors Inc., which holds 2.7 million shares.

Like Coss, most well-paid execs point to stock gains as proof that their pay is richly deserved. Ask Sam Wyly, chairman of Sterling Software Inc., about the fact that his $439 million company produced three of the biggest pay packages in Corporate America last year, and he lets out a belly laugh. "We should," he says, pointing to the company's 673% stock price rise since its 1983 initial public offering. The payouts—which totaled $69.6 million for Wyly, $34.7 million for his brother, vice-chairman Charles J. Wyly Jr., and $58.2 million for CEO Sterling L. Williams—came mostly from option exercises.

Yet if few would dispute the success of such fast-growing companies, investors are increasingly asking how much is enough to get top performance. Again, take Coss. His pay is so gargantuan that it dwarfs his stellar performance. The ratio between his three-year pay and the shareholders' return puts Coss third on *Business Week*'s list of CEOs who gave shareholders the least for their buck. Moreover, the huge award significantly diluted other shareholders' gains: Coss's payouts cut Green Tree's 1996 earnings 16%, to $308.7 million.

"Performance criteria are almost like intellectual Silly Putty," says professor Warren Bennis of USC.

Because he received shares directly, rather than options, Coss's compensation differs from that of most CEOs. But as the sheer number of options has soared, shareholder dilution is proving an unanticipated by-product. Companies use options in part to align executives' interests with shareholders. But they also favor them because—unlike other forms of pay—they never show up on an income statement. Instead, starting this year, companies must footnote them in their annual reports using the Black-Scholes fair value option pricing model.

It takes some digging, but those footnotes provide plenty of surprise. For all the benefits that options create, they're not free. PepsiCo Inc., for example, reported that its option grants would have reduced earnings by $68 million, or 6% last year, had they been counted as compensation. Medical-equipment maker Guidant Corp.'s earnings after charges would have taken an 11% hit. By putting more potential shares into circulation, options reduce every shareholder's slice of the earnings pie. And because the footnotes include only options granted since 1995, Bear, Stearns & Co. accounting analyst Pat McConnell estimates they understate the impact by at least 50%.

Concerned Investors

Companies with broad-based option plans say the dilution is a small cost next to the benefit of motivating employees. But the largest share of those new options goes to the corner office. According to *Executive Compensation Reports,* a Fairfax Station (Va.) newsletter and database, 51% of companies that have reported granting options for 1996 have given 10% or more of them to the CEO. In 1993, only 18% of companies did so.

But that's not the only hidden cost of options. Companies have been buying back shares in record numbers, even as many sell discounted shares back to executives when they cash in their options. With many shares trading near record highs, those companies are paying top dollar to buy back stock—while execs pocket the aftertax difference between the option price and the market price. That often results in large cash outlays, and it also means executives end up with an ever higher percentage of outstanding shares. "Want to talk about the largest social welfare transfer program in the world?" says Patrick S. McGurn, director of corporate programs at Institutional Shareholder Services Inc., a proxy advisory service based in Bethesda, Md. "It's from shareholders into the pockets of executives."

So far, investors have been relatively quiet on dilution. But now they're taking notice. Institutional Shareholder Services is recommending "no" votes against at least 20% of new stock-option plans, including those at Starbucks

Corp. and Sprint Corp. And the five New York City pension funds will oppose some one-third of plans this year, primarily because of concerns over dilution. Options "do come home to roost," says Jon Lukomnik, New York City Deputy Controller for pensions.

Another unwelcome result of the shift to pay for performance: It's not just the best who are pulling in giant pay. Performance targets are often set so low—or so loosely—that they're virtually meaningless. "Performance criteria are almost like intellectual Silly Putty," says Warren Bennis, Distinguished Professor of Business Administration at the University of Southern California's Marshall School of Business.

According to *Executive Compensation Reports,* of proxies examined so far this year, only 6.6% of option-granting companies issued any "premium-priced" options—those with prices above market value on the day of issue. And though the number is up from last year's 3.5%, most companies boasting premium-priced options make them only a small portion of the package. Just 20% of PepsiCo CEO Roger Enrico's 1.7 million stock-option awards in 1996 were made at prices above then-current market value, for example. And of last year's record-setting grant of 8 million options to Walt Disney CEO Michael D. Eisner, only 3 million were awarded at above-market prices.

Shareholder advocates say that tougher targets are necessary to keep from rewarding average CEOs who are simply riding a bull market. Nell Minow, a principal in LENS, an activist investor group, argues, for example, that executives should outperform the market or their peer group to receive big packages.

Instead, with grants in the hundreds of thousands of shares now commonplace, managers can earn a big payday even if their stocks rise only slightly. In Eisner's case, if Disney shares rise a tiny $2 annually—a poor performance by Disney's standards—the value of his market-priced options would increase $10 million annually. And there's little real downside. Few executives suffer financially if the stock drops. "One of my biggest complaints is there's not much risk" with options, says Anne Yerger, director of research at the Council of Institutional Investors. "In a bull market, most executives are going to get money."

Losing the Balance?

As a result, many execs whose performance trailed their peers' have also benefited. Typical was H. J. Heinz's Anthony F. J. O'Reilly, who made $64.2 million last year. His company's stock performance rose just 11%, trailing both the S&P and other food companies. O'Reilly defends his huge option grants as part of a generous incentive scheme. "There can be no more honorable or fairer way" to compensate CEOs, O'Reilly argues.

The staggering rise in pay for the good, the bad, and the indifferent has left even some advocates of pay for performance wondering whether the balance between the CEO and the shareholder is tilting the wrong way. "I've been consulting for over 20 years and have seen options accepted carte blanche as a good thing," says George B. Paulin, president of compensation consultancy Frederic W. Cook & Co. "Now, boards and investors are starting to question the structure of option deals."

In the meantime, many top execs have amassed vast troves of options that have yet to be exercised (page 477). Among those with the largest potential jackpots: Disney CEO Eisner, who holds some $364.4 million in unexercised stock options. The gains are so enormous that AOL's Case, who cashed in most of his $27.4 million in options before growing pains and accounting changes beat up the stock last year, is still sitting on options worth an additional $116.6 million. And topping the list is HFS CEO Henry R. Silverman, with $544.3 million in exercisable stock options.

The question, of course, is why boards don't set the performance bar higher. While compensation committees are much more vigilant than they've ever been, Kayla J. Gillan, general counsel at the California Public Employees' Retirement System, a $110 billion pension fund, points out that about 25% of the companies in the S&P still have an insider on the compensation committee. And companies fear they'll lose talent if their executive pay falls below that of their peers. That helps to inflate compensation. Says Howard B. Edelstein, a principal of the Todd Organization, a benefits consulting firm: "Companies are saying, 'Take me to the middle.'"

Despite recent requirements that boards disclose the criteria they use to set pay, there's plenty of wiggle room. At Mattel Inc., for example, newly named CEO Jill E. Barad wasn't eligible for a bonus in 1996 because the company missed internal targets. So instead, the board awarded her a $280,000 "special achievement bonus" for progress made in 1995. And like many executives, Barad has also negotiated protection should things at Mattel go wrong. If Barad is dismissed or leaves for "good reason," she'll receive five times her last salary plus average bonus, become vested in an executive retirement plan at the age of 50, and have a $3 million loan forgiven.

Seller's Market

Even those whose subpar performance makes their options worthless have recourse. For example, in 1995 Digital Equipment CEO Robert B. Palmer was granted 300,000 options at the then-market price of $48. The next year the package was smaller, but the exercise price fell to $37.75 to match the swooning stock. If the stock returns to its already depressed 1995 price, Palmer will pocket nearly $2 million.

Many consultants say companies, faced with executives who are more willing to job-hop, must dole out juicy options packages and guarantees to get the execs they want. It's a seller's market, with CEOs in demand holding most of the cards. "In many cases," says Peter T. Chingos, national practice director of compensation at KPMG Peat Marwick: "You don't have a choice."

And if the recent tremors in the stock market turn into an earthquake? With shareholder returns increasingly the gauge for setting executive compensation, the truest test of pay for performance may come in a bear, not a bull, market. Yet few expect CEOs, now accustomed to supercharged awards, to cut back. Instead, experts anticipate demands for lower-priced options or for more cash. "When stock prices go down [CEOs argue], it's purely the vagaries of the market," says Kevin Murphy, a professor of business administration at USC. "But when they go up, it's what they did to create value."

Already, the pressure to reprice has begun. After a difficult few years in the trucking industry, Jerry W. Walton, chief financial officer at J. B. Hunt Transport Services Inc. in Lowell, Ark., says he tried to get the top brass to reprice their options, which have fallen below market value, on condition that they surrender some of the stock. Included: a grant of 2.5 million options for Chairman Wayne Garrison. "Everybody thought it was a good idea to reprice," Walton says with a laugh. "Nobody thought it was a good idea to surrender [the options]."

Will executive pay ever descend from the heavens? Some who helped push the early-1990s reforms aimed at trimming exorbitant executive pay—and tying it more closely to performance—are cynical. "I wouldn't say the glass is half full; I'd say it's one-millionth full," says Minow. "I do think things have improved. But a lot of the reforms we thought would happen with executive pay have been ineffective." For shareholders, 1996 was a good year indeed. But it was a far better year for the boss.

By Jennifer Reingold in New York, with bureau reports

WHICH BOSSES EARNED THEIR PAY, AND WHICH DIDN'T?

Microsoft Corp. Chairman William H. Gates III doesn't fuss about the size of his salary. In fact, he even jokes about lowering it. But as the software giant's largest shareholder, Gates certainly doesn't need a megapay package. His 23.7% stake in Microsoft is worth a colossal $27.7 billion. Salary or not, he comes out a big winner.

And his shareholders haven't done so badly either. Gates is one of this year's two pay-for-performance winners. A *Business Week* analysis shows that Gates gave shareholders the highest return relative to his pay. And for the second year, James E. Preston, chief executive of Avon Products Inc., delivered the highest return on equity (ROE) relative to his pay (table, page 479).

Network

Gates has driven Microsoft to develop one success after another. Windows 95, along with applications such as Office, lofted sales to $8.7 billion last year, up from $5.9 billion in 1995. Gates also engineered a wrenching change last year, making the Net central to all new products. Microsoft's Web browser, Internet Explorer, has now racked up more than a 20% market share. Since 1994, Gates's total pay has been just $1.4 million, while shareholder returns have jumped 310%.

Preston is the CEO whose company performed best relative to his pay. To align his pay with performance, Preston froze his $610,000 salary five years ago and began taking most of his compensation in stock options. Over the past three years, Preston has earned $8 million. Avon's average ROE is 141%. In part, that reflects Avon's renewed growth, although an aggressive stock-buyback program has also left Avon with a small equity base. This year, Preston's salary will jump to $1 million. But with $22 million in options yet unexercised, he insists he's still a big advocate of pay for performance. "I will do well or not well depending on how the stock does," he says.

On the other side of the ledger, Conseco Inc.'s Stephen C. Hilbert gave shareholders the least for the $165 million he's collected since 1994. Most came from a $107 million stock-option exercise in 1994 and a $23 million exercise last year. Since 1994, shareholder return has been 133%. A company spokesman argues it's unfair to compare the value of Hilbert's options with performance over the past three years. He says it should be compared with the 3,100% return created over the 10 years since the first option grant. Adds Hilbert: "I'm certainly not embarrassed about our success or mine personally."

Stephen M. Case, CEO of America Online Inc., provided the worst corporate performance relative to his pay. During the past three years, Case earned $33.5 million, while the ROE was negative 413%. Most of his gains came from exercising $27.4 million in options last year. Last summer, the stock was driven down by growing pains and a restructuring to change AOL's controversial accounting practices. CFO Lennert J. Leader says AOL is concentrating on growing its customer base and revenues, as opposed to short-term profits. But as Case struggles to get AOL back in the black, the payoff—for the company, if not for him—appears far away.

By Lori Bongiorno in New York, with bureau reports

The Overachievers

Gates
Since 1994, his total pay has been $1.4 million—while Microsoft shareholders have reaped returns of 310%.

Preston
Avon had the highest ROE of any company relative to the CEO's pay.

The Underperformers

Hilbert
$165 million since 1994—while Conseco stock returned 133%.

Case
He got $33.5 million, but AOL's stock tanked.

OPTIONS: THE HIDDEN COSTS

In a footnote in this year's annual reports, companies are required to disclose—for the first time—the cost of options. Although current accounting rules treat options as cost-free, here's what a handful of companies would have to deduct from 1996 earnings if options were accounted for:

	Millions
MCI COMMUNICATIONS	$97
PEPSICO	68
BRISTOL-MYERS SQUIBB	55
J. P. MORGAN	52
TRAVELERS	51
GILLETTE	47
MORGAN STANLEY	43
RAYTHEON	29
COMPAQ	21
REPUBLIC INDUSTRIES	18
USAIRWAYS	15

Data: Pearl Meyer & Partners Inc.; Bear, Stearns & Co.; Company Reports; *Business Week.*

AN EMBARRASSMENT OF RICHES?

When Union Pacific Corp. stockholders gather for the annual meeting in Salt Lake City on Apr. 18, they'll run a gauntlet of noisy Teamsters protesting high executive pay. Their target: Drew Lewis, who received $21.5 million last year as UP CEO and retired in January with a five-year, $3.75 million consulting contract that required him to work one week a month. "We're trying to raise the issue of CEO pay any way we can," says Bart Naylor, head of the union's corporate affairs unit. UP says Lewis' compensation was recognition for his role in the merger with Southern Pacific.

CEOs will see a lot more challenges to their pay packages this year, mostly from unions and religious groups. So far, 112 proxy resolutions on the issue have been filed, up from 63 in 1996, according to Investor Responsibility Research Center Inc. (IRRC), a proxy research firm in Washington. And on Apr. 10, the AFL-CIO was due to launch a site on the World Wide Web that tells workers and investors how to combat high CEO paychecks (www.ctsg.com/ceopay). While the protests haven't cut executive pay, the share of stockholders voting against new executive pay plans jumped to 19% last year, up from 3.5% in 1988, according to the IRRC. "We have absolutely been voting 'no' more on CEO pay packages," says Peter Collins, a spokesman for Florida's $80 billion pension fund.

Although the public outcry that met last year's proxy season has died down, it hasn't gone away. Instead, it has gone grassroots. One way unions try to embarrass CEOs is by publicizing their pay. The United Farm Workers plans a campaign against Monsanto CEO Robert B. Shapiro, who earned $4.4 million in '96. Monsanto owns strawberry farms that pay pickers less than $10,000 a year.

Other groups are filing proxy resolutions to limit executive pay. In May, for example, AT&T stockholders will vote on whether the company should consider an executive pay cap at some level and a freeze during downsizings. The resolution is sponsored by the United States Trust Co. of Boston, whose investment arm runs socially responsible investment funds. The move was sparked by the $10 million in options CEO Robert E. Allen was granted in late 1995 as part of the restructuring that led to 40,000 job cuts. An AT&T spokeswoman says the board already considers these issues.

While management almost always prevails on such votes, many companies talk to the filing group. Some give ground. For example, the Teamsters, which has $60 billion in pension assets, filed a resolution last fall at RJR Nabisco Inc. to stop the company from repricing executive options when the stock falls. In 1995, RJR let execs swap options priced at up to $50 for new ones priced at $27 after its stock dropped to $27. After talks with the Teamsters, RJR agreed in February, 1997, to a new policy restricting repricing. The union withdrew its resolution. RJR says it wasn't planning to reprice more options anyway.

The AFL-CIO's Web site aims to spur attacks on high CEO pay. The target audience ranges from fund managers who invest $250 billion of union pension money to union leaders and members who own company stock, 401(k)s, or mutual funds. The Web site lets them look at a CEO's pay and chart it against average wages—or their own pay. It also tells investors how to dig up dirt on corporate directors' conflicts of interest with the CEO and how to file proxy resolutions. "We want to arm people so they can battle to have their money represented differently," says William Patterson, director of the AFL-CIO's office of investments. If he succeeds, CEOs may be fighting off more pay complaints than ever.

By Aaron Bernstein in Washington

Target: CEO Pay

AFL-CIO

The labor federation is launching a Web page that details CEO pay and shows how to file proxies and complain to directors.

Demonstrations

The Teamsters will picket Union Pacific's annual meeting, while the United Farm Workers are planning attacks against Monsanto.

Proxy Battles

More than 110 proxies attempting to restrict executive pay have been filed at large companies.

Fortunes in the Future

These chief executives still have huge rewards to reap from stock options that have yet to be exercised. The top 20 treasure chests:

Executive/Company	Value of Nonexercised Stock Options,* Thousands of Dollars
HENRY SILVERMAN, HFS	$544,284
MICHAEL EISNER, WALT DISNEY	364,360
CHARLES WANG, COMPUTER ASSOCIATES	248,928
RICHARD SCRUSHY, HEALTHSOUTH	188,044
STEPHEN HILBERT, CONSECO	145,860
ROBERTO GOIZUETA, COCA-COLA	134,059
WAYNE CALLOWAY, PEPSICO	123,785
LAWRENCE ELLISON, ORACLE	121,178
STEPHEN CASE, AMERICA ONLINE	116,592
DANIEL TULLY, MERRILL LYNCH	111,387
JOHN WELCH, GENERAL ELECTRIC	107,310
SANFORD WEILL, TRAVELERS GROUP	101,547
ECKHARD PFEIFFER, COMPAQ COMPUTER	97,381
STEPHEN WIGGINS, OXFORD HEALTH PLANS	81,514
LOUIS GERSTNER, IBM	81,183
STEVEN BURD, SAFEWAY	80,938
LAWRENCE BOSSIDY, ALLIEDSIGNAL	79,101
SCOTT McNEALY, SUN MICROSYSTEMS	78,228
CASEY COWELL, U.S. ROBOTICS	72,833
ANDREW GROVE, INTEL	72,280

*Based on stock price at end of company's fiscal year.
Data: Standard & Poor's Compustat.

Discussion Questions

1. What's right and what's wrong with stock options?
2. According to *Business Week,* the salary of the CEO of a large American company was, on average, 209 times that of a factory employee. How can balance be restored?
3. What specifically should companies do to provide incentives with real motivational pull for executives, while at the same time not rewarding average executives who are simply riding a bull market?

THE TOP-PAID CHIEF EXECUTIVES . . .

	1996 Salary and Bonus, Thousands of Dollars	Long-Term Compensation	Total Pay
1. LAWRENCE COSS, Green Tree Financial	$102,449	none	$102,449
2. ANDREW GROVE, Intel	3,003	$94,587	97,590
3. SANFORD WEILL, Travelers Group	6,330	87,828	94,157
4. THEODORE WAITT, Gateway 2000	965	80,361	81,326
5. ANTHONY O'REILLY, H. J. Heinz	2,736	61,500	64,236
6. STERLING WILLIAMS, Sterling Software	1,448	56,801	58,249
7. JOHN REED, Citicorp	3,467	40,143	43,610
8. STEPHEN HILBERT, Conseco	13,962	23,450	37,412
9. CASEY COWELL, U.S. Robotics	3,430	30,522	33,952
10. JAMES MOFFETT, Freeport-McMoran C&G	6,956	26,776	33,732
11. JOHN CHAMBERS, Cisco Systems	619	32,594	33,213
12. STEPHEN WIGGINS, Oxford Health Plans	1,738	27,270	29,008
13. ECKHARD PFEIFFER, Compaq Computer	4,250	23,546	27,796
14. STEPHEN CASE, America Online	200	27,439	27,639
15. JOHN WELCH, General Electric	6,300	21,321	27,621
16. RICHARD SCRUSHY, Healthsouth	11,380	16,197	27,577
17. HENRY SILVERMAN, HFS	3,752	19,990	23,742
18. NORMAN AUGUSTINE, Lockheed Martin	2,781	20,324	23,105
19. JOHN AMERMAN, Mattel	3,732	18,923	22,655
20. DREW LEWIS, Union Pacific	3,131	18,320	21,452

. . . AND TEN WHO AREN'T CEOS

	1996 Salary and Bonus, Thousands of Dollars	Long-Term Compensation	Total Pay
1. SAM WYLY, Sterling Software	$ 1,571	$68,036	$69,608
2. FRANK LANZA, Lockheed Martin	1,947	48,918	50,865
3. RICHARD KINDER, Enron	2,458	35,238	37,697
4. JAMES CROWE,* Worldcom	1,497	34,280	35,777
5. CHARLES WYLY JR., Sterling Software	816	33,870	34,686
6. JOE ROBY, Donaldson, Lufkin, Jenrette	8,773	24,220	32,992
7. SHIGERU MYOJIN, Salomon	10,558	20,873	31,431
8. FRANK MARSHALL, Cisco Systems	490	27,879	28,369
9. WILLIAM RHODES, Citicorp	1,300	22,189	23,489
10. JOEL ALVORD, Fleet Financial Group	3,040	19,409	22,449

*Former CEO of MFS Communications.
Data: Execucomp by Standard & Poor's Compustat, a Division of The McGraw-Hill Companies.

PAY FOR PERFORMANCE: WHO MEASURES UP . . . AND WHO DOESN'T

To see how pay matches up to performance, *Business Week* uses two measurement systems. One relates to how good a job the boss did for shareholders. The other compares what the boss made with how well the company did.

1994–96	Total pay,* Thousands of dollars	Shareholder return**	Relative index
Executives Who Gave Shareholders the Most for Their Pay . . .			
1. WILLIAM GATES, Microsoft	$ 1,436	310%	286
2. WARREN BUFFETT, Berkshire Hathaway	904	109	231
3. THOMAS GOLISANO, Paychex	1,475	238	229
4. MICHAEL BIRCK, Tellabs	3,369	537	189
5. RICHARD USSERY, Total Systems Service	2,454	315	169
. . . And Those Who Gave Shareholders the Least			
1. STEPHEN HILBERT, Conseco	165,223	133	1.4
2. SANFORD WEILL, Travelers	156,166	140	1.6
3. LAWRENCE COSS, Green Tree Financial	197,007	230	1.7
4. ANTHONY O'REILLY, H. J. Heinz	68,179	66	2.4
5. JOHN WELCH, General Electric	57,292	104	3.6

	Total pay,* Thousands of dollars	Avg. Return on Equity	Relative index
Executives Whose Companies Did The Best Relative To Their Pay . . .			
1 JAMES PRESTON, Avon Products	$ 7,907	141%	107
2 B. THOMAS GOLISANO, Paychex	1,475	28	102
3 WILLIAM GATES, Microsoft	1,436	27	93
4 MITCHELL FROMSTEIN, Manpower	10,415	32	84
5 C. RUSSELL LUIGS, Global Marine	4,851	20	83
. . . And Those Whose Companies Did The Worst			
1 STEPHEN CASE, America Online	33,460	–413	–226
2 ROBERT PALMER, Digital Equipment	3,840	–25	–40
3 ANDREW LUDWICK, Bay Networks	1,512	14	–39
4 JAMES ROBBINS, Cox Communications	3,991	2	–13
5 JOHN ROACH, Tandy	3,967	7	–12

*Salary, bonus, and long-term compensation paid for the entire three-year period. **Stock price at the end of 1996, plus dividends reinvested for three years, divided by stock price at the end of 1993.
Data: Standard & Poor's Compustat.

PART 5

LABOR-MANAGEMENT ACCOMMODATION

Harmonious working relations between labor and management are critical to organizations. Traditionally both parties have assumed a win-lose, adversarial posture toward each other. This must change if U.S. firms are to remain competitive in the international marketplace. Part Five is entitled "Labor-Management Accommodation" to emphasize a general theme: to achieve long-term success, labor and management must learn to accommodate one another's needs, rather than repudiate them. By doing so, management and labor can achieve two goals at once: increase productivity and improve the quality of work life. In the current climate of wants and needs, there is no other alternative.

The focus of Chapter 12 is on union representation and collective bargaining. Chapter 13 focuses on procedural justice, ethics, and concerns for privacy in employee relations. These are currently some of the most dominant issues in this field. As managers, you must develop and implement sound practices with respect to them. Chapters 12 and 13 will help you do that.

12 UNION REPRESENTATION AND COLLECTIVE BARGAINING

Questions This Chapter Will Help Managers Answer

1 How have changes in product and service markets affected the way labor and management relate to each other?
2 How should management respond to a union organizing campaign?
3 To what extent should labor-management cooperative efforts be encouraged?
4 What kinds of dispute resolution mechanisms should be established in order to guarantee due process for all employees?

IMPROVING PRODUCTIVITY, QWL, AND PROFITS THROUGH LABOR-MANAGEMENT COOPERATION*

Human Resource Management in Action

Many managers see unions as a major stumbling block to the implementation of workplace changes that are essential to increased competitiveness. To them, unions are a problem. To others, unions can be and should be part of the solution to problems of workplace competitiveness. Many union leaders and members, in turn, deeply distrust management's motives. They see "enhanced competitiveness" as thinly veiled code words for downsizing. Who is right? Is it possible for a well-established union to take a leadership role in workplace innovation and imaginative approaches to enhancing competitiveness? Is it possible for management to allow creative approaches to more efficient operations without cutting workers as a result of the increases in efficiency?

To be sure, management and workers have ample reason to distrust each other. While Ford, Chrysler, and GM's Saturn Division pay salaried and hourly employees the same amount in profit sharing ($1800, $3700, and $10,000, respectively, in 1997), General Motors pays different bonuses to hourly workers ($300 each in 1997) and to its salaried employees (1 percent of annual salary, with a $300 minimum). Management argues that wildcat strikes are not the fault of salaried employees, but union members complain that it is hypocritical for management to preach teamwork on the one hand, and then proceed to reward different classes of workers unevenly.

Many union leaders fear cooperative work systems, because they suspect that management's real intention is to circumvent lawfully designated unions. In some cases this has occurred, as in a recent decision by the National Labor Relations Board that Electromation, Inc., used teams to create a company-dominated union.

Despite such potential problems, some employee-involvement plans have worked brilliantly. For example, the United Auto Workers played a key role in the improvement of productivity and quality at Ford Motor Company during the early 1980s. Ford has improved its assembly line productivity by 36 percent since 1980, at least in part because of its employee-involvement system. Today some Ford plants are as productive as Japanese automakers. Is this just an isolated example, or are there other success stories?

Challenges

1. What are some key obstacles that stand in the way of true cooperation by labor and management?
2. Is labor-management cooperation just a short-term solution to economic problems, or can it become institutionalized into the very culture of an organization?
3. Will widespread labor-management cooperation lead to a loss of union power?

**Source:* M. Maynard, GM doles out uneven bonuses, *USA Today,* Feb. 21, 1997, p. 1B; A. Bernstein, Why America needs unions—but not the kind it has now, *Business Week,* May 23, 1994, pp. 70–82; A. Bernstein, Now labor can be part of the solution, *Business Week,* Mar. 1, 1993, p. 35; Xerox and the ACTWU: Tracing a transformation in industrial relations. In F. K. Foulkes & E. R. Livernash, *Human resources management: Cases and text* (2d ed.), 1989, Englewood Cliffs, NJ: Prentice-Hall, pp. 348–373.

WHY DO EMPLOYEES JOIN UNIONS?

Beliefs about the effects of a union at a person's own workplace are critical determinants of intentions to vote for or against union representation.[1] Visualize this scenario: It's 7:30 on a cool December evening in Las Vegas, and 105 off-duty hotel maids, cooks, and bellhops are waiting for their monthly union meeting to start. It has been a long day working in the big casino hotels, but still the room buzzes with energy. One by one, a dozen or so members recount their success in recruiting 2700 new colleagues at the MGM Grand, the world's largest hotel. After a 3-year campaign of street demonstrations, mass arrests, and attacks on the company's HR practices that helped oust the stridently anti-labor CEO in 1995, MGM Grand recognized the union in November 1996 without an election. Another group reports on the victory at New York, New York, a new hotel that agreed to the unionization of 900 workers.

Much of the credit for these successes lies with the spirited rank and file. Indeed, the day after the meetings, some members gathered—on their day off—to sign up recruits outside the New York, New York hiring office. Says Edelisa Wolf, an $11.25-an-hour waitress at the MGM Grand: "I spend a day a week volunteering for the union, because otherwise we would earn $7.50 an hour and no benefits."[2]

On the other hand, it is pure folly to assume that pro-union attitudes are based simply on expected economic gains; much deeper values are at stake.[3] As one author noted:

> If one talks to any worker long enough, and candidly enough, one discovers that his loyalty to the union is not simply economic. One may even be able to show him that, on a strictly cost-benefit analysis, measuring income lost from strikes, and jobs lost as a result of contract terms, the cumulative economic benefits are delusions. It won't matter. In the end, he will tell you, the union is the only institution that insures and protects his "dignity" as a worker, that prevents him from losing his personal identity, and from being transformed into an infinitesimal unit in one huge and abstract "factor of production."[4]

This conclusion that values deeper than money are at stake was illustrated in the 11-year battle to organize workers at the J. P. Stevens plant in North Carolina. The organizing drive was much publicized—the award-winning movie *Norma Rae* was based on it—and the settlement was heralded widely as a historic breakthrough in a decades-old attempt to organize southern industry. Even though the wages at the unionized Stevens plant are not substantially higher now than at the company's nonunionized plants or than at other nonunion textile plants in the South, the wage level was never the biggest issue. The union contract has meant expanded benefits, a seniority system to protect workers when jobs are lost and to provide opportunities when jobs open, and a grievance procedure with access to binding arbitration. For the company, the settlement allowed it to put its past squabbles with the workers behind and to concentrate on battling foreign textile imports. Among union members, however, worker after worker echoes the same sentiment: the collective bargaining agreement has meant that they are treated with new dignity on the job.[5]

Managers who fail to treat workers with respect, or companies that view workers only as costs to be cut rather than as assets to be developed, *invite* collective action by employees to remedy these conditions. However, unions

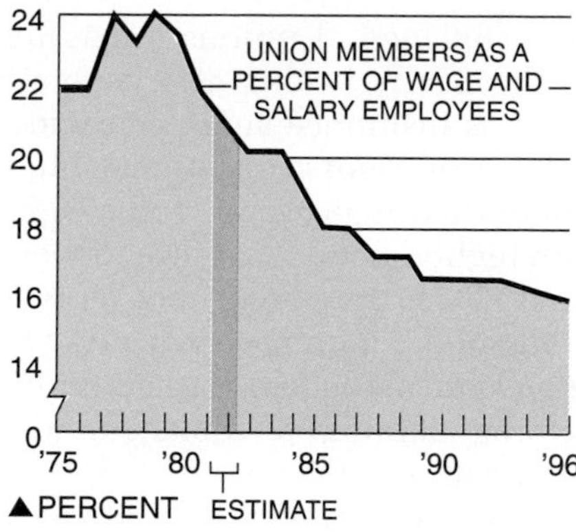

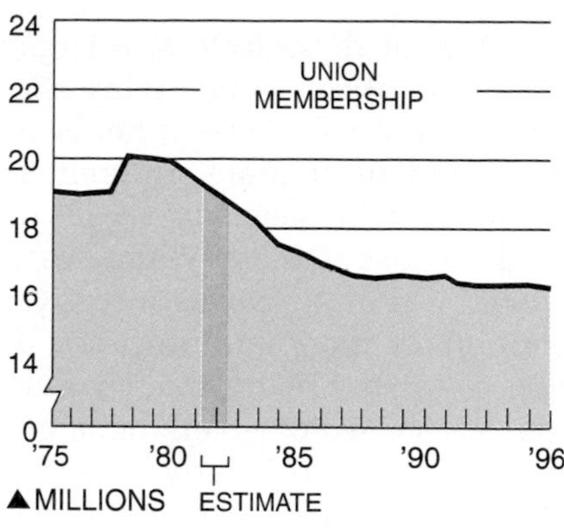

Figure 12-1
Decline in union membership, 1975 to 1996. (*Source:* Sweeney's blitz, *Business Week,* Feb. 17, 1997, p. 58.)

are not without sin either, and workers will vote against them to the extent that the unions are seen as unsympathetic to a company's need to remain viable, or if they feel unions abuse their power by calling strikes, or have fat-cat leaders who selfishly promote their own interests at the expense of the members' interests.[6]

UNION MEMBERSHIP IN THE UNITED STATES

Union membership has shrunk from a high of 35 percent of the workforce in 1945 to 22 percent in 1980 to 14.5 percent in 1996. Excluding public-sector membership, unions represented just 10 percent of private-sector employees in 1996.[7] Figure 12-1 shows the drop-off in membership between 1975 and 1996 in percentage terms and also in terms of the number of members.

Several economic and demographic forces favor a resurgence of unions. The same trends toward globalization and corporate downsizing that have sharply cut union membership have also crated a new receptiveness for union organizers among surviving employees, who find themselves overworked and under excessive stress. And it is not just blue-collar workers who are organizing. Managed-care pressures prompted over 10,000 physicians in northeastern states to join the Office and Professional Employees International Union in 1997.[8] Further, while labor productivity has increased 25 percent over the past 22 years, wage growth has been stagnant over the same time period. For example, after adjustment for inflation, median family income declined by 5.2 percent between 1989 and 1994. In 1996, compensation growth still trailed the growth of consumer prices.[9] To add insult to injury, the gap between the pay of executives at large firms has grown from 33 times the average income of U.S. workers in 1973 to 187 times the average in 1996.[10]

Finally, both women and other minority-group members, who are expected to continue entering the workforce at a high rate, tend to favor unions. Evidence indicates that women's participation is likely to be enhanced to the extent that there is greater representation of women in local union offices.[11] However, organized labor's biggest untapped strength is its 16 million members. If 5 percent of them volunteer a day a month, according to one calculation, labor's effective spending on recruitment would jump to $4 billion a year (assuming professional organizers cost a total of $75,000 a year). That would dwarf the estimated $1 billion employers spend annually to thwart unionization.[12]

Despite these factors, a large-scale resurgence of unions seems unlikely. What complicates organizing efforts is that many in this new generation are white-collar workers—in fields as diverse as insurance and electronics. Their goals and desires are different from those of labor's traditional blue-collar stalwarts, who seemed to want little more than high wages and steady work. And because so many young workers are highly mobile (average job tenure for workers of all ages was just 4 years in 1996[13]), they might not be willing to support a 6-month unionization drive that might culminate in a strike to win a first contract. Finally, many young workers are taking jobs in the rapidly growing service sector—banking, computer programming, financial services—jobs that unions traditionally have not penetrated.

The very nature of high-tech industry also hampers organizing efforts. Many software designers and biotechnical engineers work for small, start-up companies that unions find difficult and expensive to organize. Among larger firms like Compaq Computer, which has no production unions, workers are often parts of flexible teams that change tasks from month to month and work closely with management. Such teamwork creates a sense of empowerment that can leave unions with little role to play. As one observer noted: "The new industries in the U.S. are evolving so rapidly that there is no stable craft pattern for a union to represent."[14]

Despite the drop-off in membership, unions are a powerful social, political, and organizational force. In the unionized firm, managers must deal with the union rather than directly with employees on many issues. Indeed, the "rules of the game" regarding wages, hours, and conditions of employment are described in a collective bargaining agreement (or contract) between management and labor. Although it need not always be so, adversarial "us" and "them" feelings are frequently an unfortunate by-product of this process.

Economic and working conditions in unionized firms directly affect those in nonunionized firms, as managers strive to provide competitive working conditions for their employees. Yet the nature of the internal and external environments of most U.S. firms differs dramatically in the late 1990s relative to that of earlier periods. This difference has lead to fundamental changes in labor-management relations, as we will see in the next section.

THE CHANGING NATURE OF INDUSTRIAL RELATIONS IN THE UNITED STATES

Fundamentally, labor-management relations are about power—who has it and how they use it. As we will see, both parties are finding that they achieve the best results when they share power rather than revert to a win-lose orientation.[15] In recent years, unions have lost power as a result of four interrelated factors: global competition, growth of service industries, corporate downsizing (which has depleted the membership of many unions), and the willingness of firms to move operations overseas. In today's world, firms face more competitive pressures than ever before. That competition arises from abroad (e.g., Toyota, Nissan, Hyundai, Sanyo, Pohang, and third-world steelmakers); from domestic, nonunion operators (e.g., Nucor in steel); and from nonregulated new entities (e.g., dozens of new telecommunications companies).

These competitive pressures have forced business to develop the ability to shift rapidly, to cut costs, to innovate, to enter new markets, and to devise a flexible labor force strategy. As managers seek to make the most cost-effective use of their human resources, the old "rules of the labor-management game" are changing.[16]

Traditionally, the power of unions to set industrywide wage levels and to relate these in "patterns" was based on the market power of strong domestic producers or industries sheltered by regulation. As employers lost their market power in the 1970s and 1980s, union wage dominance shrank and fragmented. One union segment had to compete with another and with nonunion labor both in the United States and abroad. Management's objective was (and is) to get labor costs per unit of output to a point below that of the competition at the product-line level. Out of this approach have come wage-level differences and, with them, the breakdown of pattern bargaining. As a result, even under union bargaining pressures, wages are now far more responsive to economic conditions at the industry and firm levels, and even at the product-line level, than they traditionally have been.[17]

Related to wage-level flexibility is employment-level flexibility. By contracting out work more freely, outsourcing business services, and using more part-time and temporary workers, management is trying to make employment levels more fluid and adjustable, to make labor costs even more variable, and to gain power for rapid downsizing and cost cutting. This approach has been termed "kanban employment," using the Japanese term for just-in-time delivery and no stockpiling or inventorying of resources.[18] In the auto industry it has led to crippling strikes, as workers feared for their job security.[19]

The labor relations system that evolved during the 1940s and lasted until the early 1980s was institutionalized around the market power of the firm and around those unions that had come to represent large proportions, if not nearly all, of an industry's domestic workforce. The driving force for change in the 1990s has been business conditions in the firm. Those conditions have changed for good—and so must the U.S. industrial relations system. In order to put that system into better perspective, let us examine the approach taken in other countries. Keep in mind, however, that direct comparisons are difficult. The next section shows why.

DIFFICULTIES IN COMPARING INDUSTRIAL RELATIONS SYSTEMS

Three reasons explain the difficulties involved in making comparisons:[20]

1. **The same concept may be interpreted differently in different industrial relations contexts.** For example, consider the concept of collective bargaining. In the United States it is understood to mean negotiations between a labor union local and management. In Sweden and Germany, however, the term refers to negotiation between an employers' organization and a trade union at the industry level.

2. **The objectives of the bargaining process may differ in different countries.** For example, European unions view collective bargaining as a form of class

struggle, but in the United States collective bargaining is viewed mainly in economic terms.

3. **No industrial relations system can be understood without an appreciation of its historical origin.** Such historical differences may be due to managerial strategies for labor relations in large companies, ideological divisions within the trade union movement, the influence of religious organizations on the development of trade unions, methods of union regulation by governments, or the mode of technology and industrial organization at critical stages of union development.[21]

The following brief overview of the Japanese system will illustrate such differences in industrial relations systems.

The Japanese Industrial Relations System*

Although the Trade Union Act was passed in December 1945, the basic framework of the industrial relations system was not implemented until 1956, after the economic boom of the Korean War. Under the Trade Union Act workers in the private sector were guaranteed three basic rights: to organize labor unions, to bargain collectively, and to take industrial action to insist on their interests. Union membership peaked in 1949 at 58.9 percent of the workforce. By 1975, it had fallen to 34.4 percent, and to 24.4 percent in 1992. Membership in unions is expected to fall below 20 percent by the end of the decade, largely because of the growth in nonunion, part-time jobs.[22] These features and trends are similar to those of the U.S. system.

Forms of Trade Unions

Most Japanese unions in the private sector are enterprise unions. This concept, based on the idea of *groupism,* has its roots in the lifestyle and social values of farmers and fishers. Workers moving from rural areas to large cities expected (correctly) that their idea of groupism would be maintained even in the context of manufacturing operations.

Union membership is limited to regular employees of a single company regardless of whether they are blue-collar or white-collar employees. Subcontractors and temporary workers are not eligible for membership, but supervisors of blue-collar workers and subsection heads of white-collar workers may be union members if the company-level collective bargaining agreement permits. Top executives and middle managers are often former members of their company's labor union, because they usually have worked their way up through the ranks.

An enterprise union usually joins one of four so-called national centers of labor unions. These centers play an important role in developing policies of their member labor unions, in coordinating interests of the member unions, and in influencing government economic and industrial relations policies. They also play a leading role in directing the Spring Labor Offensive, which usually determines the main direction of collective bargaining at each company.

*Much of the material in this section has been adapted from K. Okubayashi, The Japanese industrial relations system, *Journal of General Management, 14,* 1989, 67–88.

The Spring Labor Offensive (*Shunto-hoshiki*) was established in 1956 to overcome the weakness of enterprise unionism. About 80 percent of all labor negotiations take place at the beginning of the spring, especially in March and April. This time was chosen because April is the beginning of the accounting term and the month when new school graduates come into companies. One of the main reasons that employers accept the coordinated wage settlement is that they can avoid severe competition among themselves on wages and other benefits under the guidance of their trade association.

Employers' Organizations

Of the four main employers' associations, Keidanren (Japan Federations of Economic Organization) is the most influential with respect to labor relations issues. It includes 54 trade associations and all the regional employers' associations. Keidanren's main function is to coordinate employers' opinions on economic policies and labor problems and to present these to both the public and the government.

The Structure of Collective Bargaining

For the most part, as noted, collective bargaining is based on negotiations between an enterprise union and its employer. Contents of the collective agreement include clauses dealing with topics such as wages, annual wage increases, benefits, working hours, and criteria for dismissal. The agreement also includes sections dealing with issues such as union membership as a condition of continued employment, time-card stamping at the beginning and end of work, and the conduct of union activities during working hours. Finally, the agreement includes sections dealing with joint consultation and grievance resolution procedures.

The Joint Consultation System

This system, in addition to collective bargaining, plays a very important role in promoting industrial democracy in Japanese industrial relations. About 71 percent of companies with more than 1000 employees have adopted such a system. Employee representatives at each level of a company (shop floor, factory, and the company as a whole) meet monthly with their counterparts in management to exchange information about the company's policies, production schedule, and changes of practices on the shop floor. At these meetings, management often shares confidential information concerning production plans, financial conditions, staffing plans, and the introduction of new technology, for example. Union representatives can express their opinions on this information and provide counterproposals to management. Differences between the two groups are handled in one of two ways: management subsequently may modify its proposal, or execution of the original proposal is suspended for a cooling-off period. These mechanisms help avoid severe conflicts or strikes.

In practice, employee representatives are union officials. Therefore rigid differentiation between collective bargaining and the joint consultation system is very difficult in the sense that both work effectively to promote communication between management and employees.

The idea of participative management is supported by labor unions, employers, and workers themselves. However, the main forms of participation in Japanese industrial systems are collective bargaining, the joint consultation system, suggestion systems, and small-group activities such as quality circles. Employee representation on boards of directors and participation in high-level strategic business decisions, which are usual in Germany, are not practiced in Japan.

Worker Participation at Industrial and National Levels

The activities of enterprise unions extend beyond their companies to include joint consultation between representatives of confederations of labor unions and corresponding associations of employers. Such systems exist in industries such as mining, textiles, iron and steel, electric power, machinery and metal fabrication, shipbuilding, automobile, chemical, plastics, and oil. Representatives exchange opinions on general industrial policies, business trends, and the main strategies of the Spring Labor Offensive, as well as employment security within their own industries, safety, work hours, and minimum wages. Although the participants in these meetings do not have the authority to conclude industrywide collective agreements concerning industrial policies, the meetings are very effective mechanisms for the exchange of perceptions about industrial situations. This exchange of ideas facilitates consensus between enterprise unions and employers.

In summary, the Japanese industrial relations system consists of enterprise unions that work with company managers to conclude collective bargaining agreements during the Spring Labor Offensive and to promote industrial democracy through the joint consultation system, as well as through union-management discussions at the industrial and national levels.

As noted earlier, examination of another country's industrial relations system, such as that of Japan, helps put the U.S. system into better perspective. The remainder of this chapter will examine that U.S. system in greater detail.

Fundamental Features of the U.S. Industrial Relations System

Six distinctive features of the U.S. system, compared with those in other countries, are as follows:[23]

1. **Exclusive representation**—one and only one union in a given job territory, selected by majority vote. However, multiple unions may represent different groups of employees who work for the same employer (e.g., pilots, flight attendants, and machinists at an airline). This situation is in contrast to that existing in continental Europe, where affiliations by religious and ideological attachment exist in the same job territory.
2. **Collective agreements that embody a sharp distinction between negotiation of and interpretation of an agreement.** Most agreements are of fixed duration, often 2 or 3 years, and they result from legitimate, overt conflict that is confined to a negotiations period. They incorporate no-strike (by employees) and no-lockout (by employer) provisions during the term of the agreement, as well as interpretation of the agreement by private arbitrators or umpires. In contrast, the British system features open-ended, nonenforceable agreements.

3. **Decentralized collective bargaining,** largely due to the size of the United States, the diversity of its economic activity, and the historic role of product markets in shaping the contours of collective bargaining. By contract, in Sweden the government establishes wage rates, and in Australia, most wages are set by arbitration councils,[24] although new federal legislation encourages bargaining at the enterprise level.[25]
4. **Relatively high union dues and large union staffs** to negotiate and administer private, decentralized agreements, including grievance arbitration to organize against massive employer opposition and to lobby before legislative and administrative tribunals.
5. **Opposition by both large and small employers to union organization,** compared with countries such as France and Germany, which has been modified in terms of the constraints placed on management only slightly by 50 years of legislation.
6. **The role of government** in the U.S. industrial relations system as compared with other systems, such as those of Mexico and Australia. The U.S. government has been relatively passive in dispute resolution and highly legalistic both in administrative procedures and in the courts. As regulation has expanded to cover health and safety, pension benefits, and equal employment opportunity, the litigious quality of relations has grown in many relationships.

THE UNIONIZATION PROCESS

The Legal Basis

The Wagner Act, or National Labor Relations Act, of 1935 affirmed the right of all employees to engage in union activities, to organize, and to bargain collectively without interference or coercion from management. It also created the National Labor Relations Board (NLRB) to supervise representation elections and to investigate charges of unfair labor practices by management. The Taft-Hartley Act of 1947 reaffirmed those rights and, in addition, specified unfair labor practices for both management and unions. The unfair labor practices are shown in Table 12-1. The act was later amended (by the Landrum-Griffin Act of 1959) to add the *secondary boycott* as an unfair labor practice. A secondary boycott occurs when a union appeals to firms or other unions to stop doing business with an employer who sells or handles a struck product.

A so-called free-speech clause in the act specifies that management has the right to express its opinion about unions or unionism to employees, provided that it does not threaten or promise favors to employees to obtain anti-union actions. The Taft-Hartley Act covers most private-sector employers and nonmanagerial employees, except railroad and airline employees (they are covered under the Railway Labor Act of 1926). Federal government employees are covered by the Civil Service Reform Act of 1978. That act affirmed their right to organize and to bargain collectively over working conditions, established unfair labor practices for both management and unions, established the Federal Labor Relations Authority to administer the act, authorized the Federal Services

Table 12-1

UNFAIR LABOR PRACTICES FOR MANAGEMENT AND UNIONS UNDER THE TAFT-HARTLEY ACT OF 1947

Management

1. Interference with, coercion of, or restraint of employees in their right to organize
2. Domination of, interference with, or illegal assistance of a labor organization
3. Discrimination in employment because of union activities
4. Discrimination because the employee has filed charges or given testimony under the act
5. Refusal to bargain in good faith
6. "Hot cargo" agreements: refusals to handle another employer's products because of that employer's relationship with the union

Union

1. Restraint or coercion of employees who do not want to participate in union activities
2. Any attempt to influence an employer to discriminate against an employee
3. Refusal to bargain in good faith
4. Excessive, discriminatory membership fees
5. Make-work or featherbedding provisions in labor contracts that require employers to pay for services that are not performed
6. Use of pickets to force an organization to bargain with a union, when the organization already has a lawfully recognized union
7. "Hot cargo" agreements: that is, refusals to handle, use, sell, transport, or otherwise deal in another employer's products

Impasse Panel to take whatever action is necessary to resolve impasses in collective bargaining, and prohibited strikes in the public sector.

COMPANY EXAMPLE

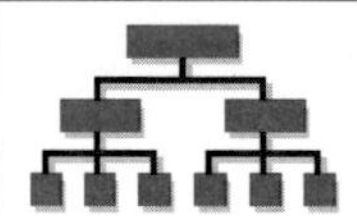

DO LABOR-MANAGEMENT TEAMS VIOLATE FEDERAL LABOR LAW?[26]

After a year of heavy losses, Electromation, Inc., of Elkhart, Indiana, a small electrical-parts maker, skipped wage hikes for its 200 workers. When employees objected, the company set up "action teams"—each with up to six hourly workers and one or two managers—to deal with problems such as absenteeism and pay scales for skilled workers. Soon after, the Teamsters began an organizing drive at the company and filed an objection to the action teams with the NLRB. The Teamsters argued that the teams were simply a company-sponsored union in which management decided who would be on each committee. Such "sham" unions were a common 1930s maneuver by companies to undercut legitimate unions. However, there was no evidence that Electromation knew that the union was organizing its workers when it implemented its action-team plan.

In late 1992, the full NLRB ruled that such teams violated the National Labor Relations Act. In recent years, of course, teams have become quite popular, and they can be found at 80 percent of the 1000 largest U.S. companies. To be legal, such teams must be structured carefully so as not to interfere with

ETHICAL DILEMMA
Are Unfair Practices Unethical?

Are the unfair labor practices shown in Table 12-1 also unethical? Are there circumstances under which activities might be legal (e.g., cutting off health-care benefits for striking workers) but at the same time also be unethical?

collective bargaining issues over wages, hours, or conditions of employment. Here are three safe approaches:

1. Establishment of teams to deal with issues other than working conditions. These issues could include quality, efficiency, productivity, and safety.
2. Establishment of a team or committee specifically for purposes of communicating with employees. For example, the team solicits suggestions from employees but does not negotiate with management about them.
3. Delegation of management authority to a team. For example, a job enrichment team could be established in which the team decides on the job assignments and overtime scheduling for team members. Alternatively, a team consisting of workers and management that has the authority to resolve grievances could be established.

The Organizing Drive

There are three ways to kick off an organizing campaign: (1) employees themselves may begin it, (2) employees may request that a union begin one for them, or (3) in some instances, national and international unions may contact employees in organizations that have been targeted for organizing. In all three cases, employees are asked to sign *authorization cards* that designate the union as the employees' exclusive representative in bargaining with management.

Well-defined rules govern organizing activities:

1. Employee organizers may solicit fellow employees to sign authorization cards on company premises, but not during working time.
2. Outside organizers may not solicit on premises if a company has an existing policy of prohibiting all forms of solicitation, and if that policy has been enforced consistently.[27]
3. Management representatives may express their views about unions through speeches to employees on company premises. However, they are legally prohibited from interfering with an employee's freedom of choice concerning union membership.

The organizing drive usually continues until the union obtains signed authorization cards from 30 percent of the employees. At that point it can petition the National Labor Relations Board (NLRB) for a representation election. If the union secures authorization cards from more than 50 percent of the employees, however, it may ask management directly for the right to exclusive representation. Usually the employer refuses, and then the union petitions the NLRB to conduct an election.

The Bargaining Unit

When the petition for election is received, the NLRB conducts a hearing to determine the appropriate (collective) bargaining unit, that is, *the group of employees eligible to vote in the representation election.* Sometimes labor and management agree jointly on the appropriate bargaining unit. When they do not, the NLRB must determine the unit. The NLRB is guided in its decision, especially if there is no previous history of bargaining between the parties, by a concept called community of interest. That is, the NLRB will define a unit that reflects the shared interests of the employees involved. Such elements include similar wages, hours, and working conditions; the physical proximity of employees to one another; common supervision; the amount of interchange of employees within the proposed unit; and the degree of integration of the employer's production process or operation.[28] Under the Taft-Hartley Act, however, professional employees cannot be forced into a bargaining unit with nonprofessionals without their majority consent.

The *size* of the bargaining unit is critical for both the union and the employer because it is strongly related to the outcome of the representation election. The larger the bargaining unit, the more difficult it is for the union to win. In fact, if a bargaining unit contains several hundred employees, the unit is almost invulnerable.[29]

The Election Campaign

Emotions on both sides run high during a representation-election campaign. However, management typically is unaware that a union campaign is under way until most or all of the cards have been signed. At that point, management has some tactical advantages over the union. It can use company time and premises to stress the positive aspects of the current situation, and it can emphasize the costs of unionization and the loss of individual freedom that may result from collective representation. Supervisors may hold information meetings to emphasize these anti-union themes. However, certain practices by management are prohibited by law, such as:

1. Physical interference, threats, or violent behavior toward union organizers
2. Interference with employees involved with the organizing drive
3. Discipline or discharge of employees for prounion activities
4. Promises to provide or withhold future benefits depending on the outcome of the representation election

These illegal activities are T.I.P.S.—that is, management may not *t*hreaten, *i*nterrogate, *p*romise, or *s*py.

Unions are also prohibited from unfair labor practices (see Table 12-1), such as coercing or threatening employees if they fail to join the union. In addition, the union can picket the employer *only* if (1) the employer is not currently unionized, (2) the petition for election has been filed with the NLRB in the past 30 days, and (3) a representation election has not been held during the previous year. Unions tend to emphasize two themes during organizing campaigns:

- The union's ability to help employees satisfy their economic and personal needs
- The union's ability to improve working conditions

The campaign tactics of management and the union are monitored by the NLRB. If the NLRB finds that either party engaged in unfair labor practices during the campaign, the election results may be invalidated and a new election conducted. However, a federal appeals court has ruled that the NLRB cannot force a company to bargain with a union that is not recognized by a majority of the workers, even if the company has made "outrageous" attempts to thwart unionization.[30] Earlier court rulings did allow the NLRB automatically to certify the union as the sole representative of the bargaining unit if evidence showed that management had interfered directly with the representation-election process.

The Representation Election and Certification

If management and the union jointly agree on the size and composition of the bargaining unit, a representation election occurs shortly thereafter. However, if management does not agree, a long delay may ensue. Since such delays, sometimes over 4 years, often erode rank-and-file union support, they work to management's advantage.[31] Not surprisingly, therefore, few organizations agree with unions on the size and composition of the bargaining unit.

When a date for the representation election is finally established, the NLRB conducts a *secret ballot* election. If the union receives a majority of the ballots *cast* (not a majority of votes from members of the bargaining unit), the union becomes certified as the exclusive bargaining representative of all employees in the unit. Once a representation election is held, regardless of the outcome, no further elections can be held in that bargaining unit for 1 year. The entire process is shown graphically in Figure 12-2.

The records of elections won and lost by unions and management have changed drastically since the 1950s. In the 1950s, unions won over 70 percent of representation elections. By the 1990s, that figure had slipped to less than half.[32] However, unions win 73 percent of elections when they use rank-and-file campaigns, versus just 27 percent when they rely on professional organizers.[33]

The Decertification of a Union

If a representation election results in union certification, the first thing many employers want to know is when and how they can *decertify* the union. Under NLRB rules, an incumbent union can be decertified if a majority of employees within the bargaining unit vote to rescind the union's status as their collective bargaining agent in another representation election conducted by the NLRB.[34]

Since decertification is most likely to occur the first year or so after certification, unions will often insist on multiyear contracts to insulate themselves

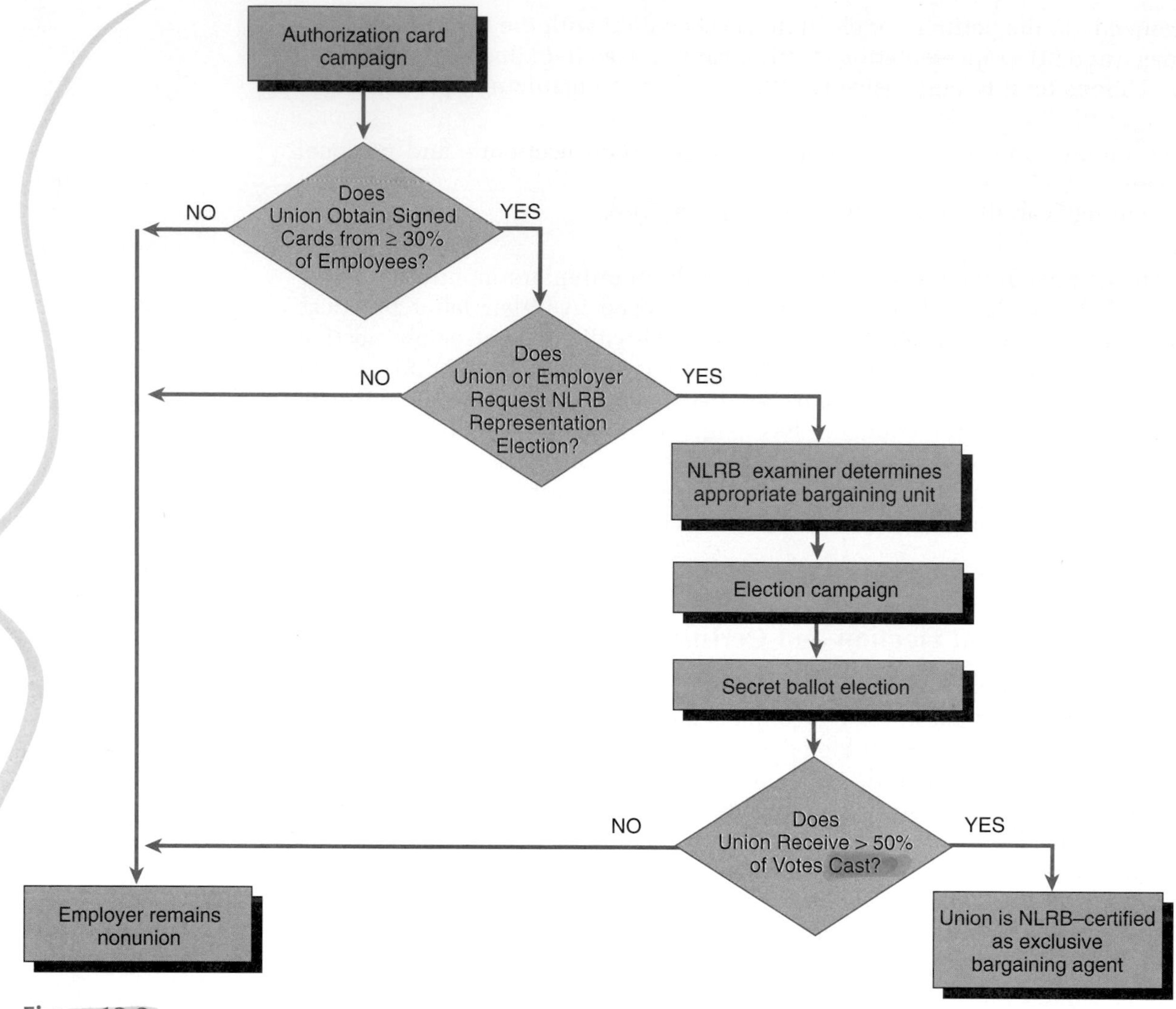

Figure 12-2
Steps involved and decisions to be made in a union organizing campaign.

against it. Once the terms and duration of the labor contract are agreed to by both parties, the employer is obligated to recognize the union and to follow the provisions of the contract for the stipulated contract period. The American Federation of Labor and Congress of Industrial Organizations (AFL-CIO), a 13.1 million–member federation of local, national, and international unions in the United States,[35] estimates that even after winning a certification election, unions are unable to sign contracts a third of the time. For example, after the Service Employees International Union won a representation election at the Hyatt Regency Hotel in New Orleans, it took the union 5 years to negotiate its first contract. By then, most of the original workers had left the hotel, and the union was decertified within 7 months.[36]

A petition for decertification must be supported by evidence that at least 30 percent of employees in the bargaining unit want a decertification election. NLRB cases indicate that two or more of the following types of evidence are necessary:

- Employees have verbally repudiated the union.
- There is a marked decline in the number of employees who subscribe to union dues checkoff, and hence a minority of employees remain on checkoff.
- A majority of employees did not support the union during a strike.
- The union has become less and less active as a representative of employees.
- There was substantial turnover among employees subsequent to certification.
- The union has admitted a lack of majority support.

As with certification elections, once a decertification election is held, a full year must elapse before another representation election can take place.

Once a union is legally certified as the exclusive bargaining agent for workers, the next task is to negotiate a contract that is mutually acceptable to management and labor. The next section examines this process in more detail.

COLLECTIVE BARGAINING: CORNERSTONE OF AMERICAN LABOR RELATIONS

Origins of Negotiation in the United States

The first U.S. strike occurred in the late eighteenth century (the Philadelphia cordwainers), and many other "turnouts" followed during the first half of the nineteenth century. These disputes were neither preceded by nor settled by negotiation. Negotiation is a two-party transaction whereby both parties intend to resolve a conflict.[37] Employers unilaterally established a scale of wages. If the wages were unacceptable, journeymen drew up a higher scale, sometimes inserting it into a Bible on which each worker swore that he or she should not work for less. The scale was presented to the employer, and if he or she did not agree, the workers "turned out" and stayed out until one side or the other caved in. There were no counterproposals, no discussions, no negotiations.

Horace Greeley, who was simultaneously a union sympathizer and an employer, found a better way. In 1850, he told a workers' mass meeting, "I do not agree that the journeymen should dictate a scale, but they should get the employers to agree to some scale." A few years later, Greeley proposed that workers come to negotiations with statistics and arguments supporting the fairness of their cause. He set the United States on the course known to the twentieth century as collective bargaining.[38]

The Art of Negotiation

What constitutes a "good" settlement? To be sure, the best outcome of negotiations occurs when both parties win. Sometimes negotiations fall short of this ideal. A really bad bargain is one in which both parties lose, yet this is a risk that is inherent in the process. Despite its limitations, abuses, and hazards, negotiation has become an indispensable process in free societies in general and in the U.S. labor movement in particular. The fact is that negotiation is the most effective device thus far invented for realizing common interests while compromising on conflicting interests.[39] Any practice that threatens the process of collective bargaining will be resisted vigorously by organized labor.

In general, there are two postures that the parties involved in bargaining might assume: win-lose and win-win. In win-lose, or distributive, bargaining, the goals of the parties initially are irreconcilable—or at least they appear that way. Central to the conflict is the belief that there is a limited, controlled amount of key resources available—a "fixed pie" situation. Both parties may want to be the winner; both may want more than half of what is available.[40]

In contrast, in win-win, or integrative, bargaining, the goals of the parties are not mutually exclusive. If one side pursues its goals, this does not prohibit the other side from achieving its own goals. One party's gain is not necessarily at the other party's expense. The fundamental structure of an integrative bargaining situation is that it is possible for both sides to achieve their objectives.[41] While the conflict initially may appear to be win-lose to the parties, discussion and mutual exploration usually will suggest win-win alternatives.

How do skilled negotiators actually behave? In one study, skilled negotiators were defined in terms of three criteria: (1) they were rated as effective by both sides, (2) they had a "track record" of significant success, and (3) they had a low incidence of "implementation" failures. Of the 48 skilled negotiators studied, 17 were union representatives, 12 were management representatives, 10 were contract negotiators, and 9 were classified as "other." The behavior of this group was then compared with that of an "average" group over 102 negotiating sessions. The following areas were assessed:[42]

- **Planning time.** There were no significant differences between the groups.
- **Exploration of options.** Skilled negotiators considered a wider range of outcomes or options for action (5.1 per issue) than average negotiators (2.6 per issue).
- **Common ground.** Skilled negotiators gave over 3 times as much attention to finding common-ground areas as did average negotiators.
- **Long-term versus short-term orientation.** The skilled group made twice as many comments of a long-term nature as did the average group.
- **Setting limits.** The average negotiators tended to plan their objectives around a fixed point (e.g., "We aim to settle at 81"). Skilled negotiators were much more likely to plan in terms of upper and lower limits—to think in terms of ranges.
- **Sequence and issue planning.** Average negotiators tended to link issues in sequence (A, then B, then C, then D), whereas skilled negotiators tended to view issues as independent and not linked by sequence. The advantage: flexibility.

Face-to-Face Negotiating Behavior

The same study also identified important differences between skilled and average negotiators in terms of their actual behavior toward each other.

- **Irritators.** Certain words and phrases that are commonly used during negotiations have negligible value in persuading the other party but do cause irritation. One of the most prevalent is "generous offer," used by a negotiator to describe his or her own proposal. Average negotiators used irritators more than 4 times more often than did skilled negotiators.

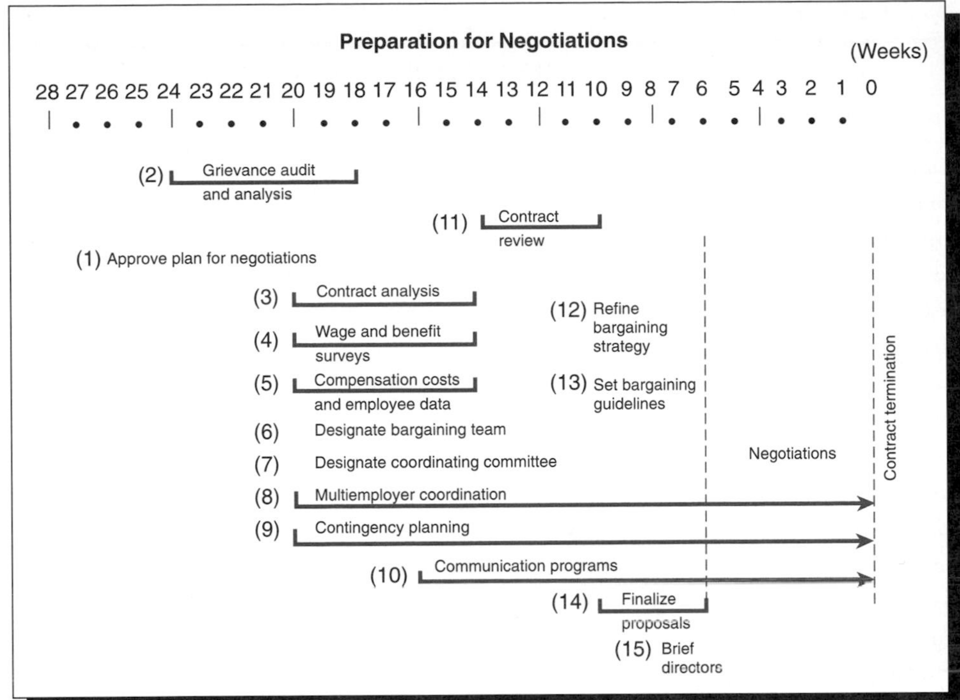

Figure 12-3
Activities and lead times involved in preparation for negotiations.

- **Counterproposals.** Frequently during bargaining, one party puts forward a proposal and the other party immediately counters. Skilled negotiators make immediate counterproposals significantly less frequently than do average negotiators.
- **Argument dilution.** If one party has five reasons for doing something, is this more persuasive than having only one reason? Apparently not. Skilled negotiators used an average of 1.8 reasons; average negotiators used 3.0.
- **Reviewing the negotiation.** Over two-thirds of the skilled negotiators claimed they always set aside some time after a negotiation to review it and to consider what they had learned. In contrast, just under half of average negotiators made the same claim.

What is the bottom line in all this? If you want to become a win-win negotiator, be aware of the behaviors to imitate and those to avoid.

Preparation for Negotiations

Like any other competitive activity, physical or mental, the outcome of collective bargaining is influenced significantly by the preparation that precedes actual negotiations. Mistakes made during union-management negotiations are not easily corrected. Although there is no single "best" set of prebargaining activities or an optimum lead time in which to conduct them, the model shown in Figure 12-3 may provide a useful guide for planning.

In a general sense, planning for subsequent negotiations begins when the previous round of bargaining ends. However, as Figure 12-3 indicates, the formal process begins about 6 months (roughly 24 weeks) prior to the expiration of the current labor agreement. It includes the following 15 activities:[43]

Table 12-2

ANALYSIS OF 2 YEARS OF GRIEVANCES IN ONE COMPANY

Type of grievance	Total
Temporary layoff benefits	98
Transfer clause	64
Supervisor working	60
Noncontractual and local agreement	32
Discharge and discipline	27
Discrimination for union activities	26
Overtime pay	20
Overtime equalization	13
Call-out pay	11
Safety and welfare (safety shoes)	9
Contractor doing bargaining-unit work	9
Pension, supplemental unemployment benefits, and insurance	7
New job rate	6
Daily upgrade	5
Holiday pay	4
Schedule change	3
Report pay	3
Timeliness of grievance	2
Seniority	1
Total grievances during contract	400

1. **Approve the plan for negotiations** with top management, identifying management's objectives, intermediate and long-term plans, significant changes in the production mix, major technological innovations, and so forth.
2. **Conduct an audit and analysis of grievances** under the existing contract to provide such information as the number of grievances by section of the contract, interpretations of contract provisions through grievance settlements and arbitration awards, and weaknesses in contract language or provisions. One such analysis is shown in Table 12-2.
3. **Perform a contract analysis,** including a section-by-section comparison with other benchmark collective bargaining agreements. This is particularly important if the agreements tend to establish patterns in an industry. In addition, a review of demands made by the union during prior negotiations may help identify areas of mounting interest.
4. **Conduct wage and benefit surveys of competitors,** both union and nonunion. These are essential. Include data on changes in inflation, along with an assessment of the structure and operation of employee benefits. Interpret these data with respect to the current and projected composition of the workforce, for example, with regard to age and gender.
5. **Present compensation costs and employee data** in a form that allows management to determine changes in costs. Following are examples of such data:

Average holiday workforce per plant:

8 first shift, 3 second shift, 3 third shift = 14 workers on, 106 off

14 workers × 13 plants × 8 hr × $22.00* = $32,032

106 nonworkers × 13 plants × 8 hr × $11 = $121,264

Total hours worked per year by workforce:

120 workers/plant ×13 plants × 2080 annual hr/worker = 3,244,800 hr/work year

Cost for holiday workers:

$$\frac{\$32{,}032}{3{,}244{,}800} = .010 \text{ cent}$$

Cost for nonworkers who are paid:

$$\frac{\$121{,}264}{3{,}244{,}800} = 0.37 \text{ cent}$$

Total cost of each holiday:

.010 = .037 = .047 cent/hr

*Normal $11/hr × double time.

Figure 12-4
Costing out a holiday.

- Demographic profile of the workforce by sex, age, race, seniority group, shift, and job classification.
- Wage payments and premiums: current rates, overtime premiums, shift-differential payments, report-in and call-in payments. In recent years employers in aerospace, steel, auto, telephone, and other industries have been trying to substitute annual (or lump-sum) bonus checks for raises as a way of controlling labor costs. In companies such as Boeing, workers have been receiving such bonuses since 1983, and they have become a way of life.[44]
- Benefit payments: pay for sickness, vacations, holidays, and civic duties, as well as premiums for pensions, medical, and disability insurance coverage. (An example of one such calculation, costing out a holiday, is shown in Figure 12-4.)
- The costs of benefits that are required by law: unemployment insurance, workers' compensation, Social Security.
- Data on worker performance, including absenteeism, layoffs, promotions, transfers, paid time for union activities, and leaves of absence.[45]

6. **Designate a bargaining team** on the basis of technical knowledge, experience, and personality. Include members from line management (not the CEO), human resources–labor relations staff, and finance-accounting staff (to provide expertise in cost analysis). Unfortunately, evidence indicates that financial officers do not negotiate, evaluate, or even participate in major wage and benefit agreements.[46] This is a costly mistake.

7. **Designate a coordinating committee** to develop bargaining guidelines for approval by top management and to monitor progress during negotiations.

Table 12-3

WORDS TO GRIEVE BY

Ability	Fully	Possible
Absolutely	Habitually	Practical
Adequate	High degree	Properly
Almost	Immediately	Qualification
Capacity	Minimal	Reasonable
Completely	Minimum	Regular
Day	Necessary	Substantially equal
Equal	Normal	Sufficient number
Forthwith	Periodic	With all dispatch
Frequent		

8. **Provide multiemployer coordination** (as appropriate). This may range from a simple information exchange among loosely connected employers to close coordination among organizations (e.g., regional hospitals) that bargain individually with the same union.
9. **Plan for contingencies.** This activity is essential, for there is always the possibility of a bargaining impasse that may lead to a strike. In the event of a strike, here are the items that one company is prepared to deal with:

   Benefits (strikers)
   Notification of company attorneys
   Continuation of operations
   Staffing (continuation of production)
   Notification responsibilities
   General picket report
   Poststrike instructions
   Treatment of nonstrikers
   Strike preparation (sales, production)
   Customer service
   Plant contacts
   Media communication
   Security
   Photographic record
   Strike-incident report
   Reinstatement of strikers
   Vendors

10. **Establish communication programs** designed to facilitate two-way communication between the bargaining team and supervisors. These programs will help bring supervisors' interests into the planning process. During negotiations, informed supervisors can be an effective channel of communication to nonsupervisory employees.
11. **Conduct a contract review.** The coordinating committee should do this, based on all the data assembled thus far. Pay particular attention to:
    - Identification of important differences among contract provisions, workplace practices, and human resource policies.
    - Identification of contract provisions to be reviewed, added, or eliminated (examples of ambiguous contract language that can lead to different interpretations are shown in Table 12-3; we might consider these "words to grieve by").
12. **Refine the bargaining strategy** once the preparatory activities are completed. Modify the strategy established at the beginning of the planning

Table 12-4

MAJOR SECTIONS OF A TYPICAL COLLECTIVE BARGAINING AGREEMENT

Unchallenged representation	Protection of employees
Employee rights	Continuous hours of work
Management rights	Recall pay
No strikes	Distribution of overtime
Compensation	Out-of-title work
Travel	No discrimination
Health insurance	Benefits guaranteed
Attendance and leave	Job classifications
Workers' compensation leave with pay	Promotional examinations
Payroll	Employee assistance program
Employee development and training	Employee orientation
Safety and health maintenance	Performance rating procedures
Layoff procedures	Day-care centers
Joint labor-management committees	Discipline
Seniority	Grievance and arbitration procedures
Posting and bidding for job vacancies	Resignation
Employee benefit fund	Job abandonment
Workweek and workday	Duration of agreement

process to reflect such factors as union demands and strategy, management's objectives, experience with multiemployer coordination, and the likelihood of a work stoppage.

13. **Set bargaining guidelines** for top management's approval. Ensure that the chief negotiator has the authority to reach a settlement within the guidelines. Also establish a procedure to modify the guidelines as needed once negotiations are under way.

14. **Finalize proposals** in writing, along with acceptable variations, to provide flexibility. Recheck the data bank for accuracy, comprehensiveness, and ease of access. Ensure that notices required by contract or by labor law have been issued and acknowledged. Compile bargaining aids (e.g., a bargaining book, data reference sheets, and work sheets), and finalize arrangements for note taking and record keeping.

15. **Brief directors,** as necessary, on the planning process, guidelines, and bargaining strategy. Establish a procedure for additional briefings during negotiations and reinforce the principle that governing-board members should stay out of the bargaining process.

Successful bargaining results in an agreement that is mutually acceptable both to labor and management. Table 12-4 shows some of the major sections of a typical agreement.

Unfortunately, contract negotiations sometimes fail because the parties are not able to reach a timely and mutually acceptable settlement of the

In the U.S., strikers engaged in a lawful protest of unfair labor practices enjoy the highest degree of legal protection.

issues—economic, noneconomic, or a combination of both. When this happens, the union may strike, management may shut down operations (a lockout), or both parties may appeal for third-party involvement. Let's examine these processes in detail.

BARGAINING IMPASSES: STRIKES, LOCKOUTS, OR THIRD-PARTY INVOLVEMENT

Strikes

In every labor negotiation there exists the possibility of a strike. The right of employees to strike in support of their bargainable demands is protected by the Landrum-Griffin Act. However, there is no unqualified right to strike. A work stoppage by employees must be the result of a lawful labor dispute and not in violation of an existing agreement between management and the union. Strikers engaged in activities protected by law may not be discharged, but they may be replaced during the strike. Strikers engaged in activities that are not protected by law need not be rehired after the strike.[47]

Types of Strikes

As you might suspect by now, there are several different types of strikes. Let's consider the major types:

Unfair-Labor-Practice Strikes. These are caused or prolonged by unfair labor practices of the employer. Employees engaged in this type of strike are afforded the highest degree of protection under the act, and under most circumstances they are entitled to reinstatement once the strike ends. Management must exercise great caution in handling unfair-labor-practice strikes because the

Table 12-5

RULES OF CONDUCT DURING A STRIKE

- People working in or having any business with the organization have a right to pass freely in and out.
- Pickets must not block a door, passageway, driveway, crosswalk, or other entrance or exit.
- Profanity on streets and sidewalks may be a violation of state law or local ordinances.
- Company officials, with the assistance of local law enforcement agents, should make every effort to permit individuals and vehicles to move in and out of the facility in a normal manner.
- Union officials or pickets have a right to talk to people going in or out. Intimidation, threats, and coercion are not permitted, either by verbal remarks or by physical action.
- The use of sound trucks may be regulated by state law or local ordinance with respect to noise level, location, and permit requirements.
- If acts of violence or trespassing occur on the premises, officials should file complaints or seek injunctions. If you are the object of violence, sign a warrant for the arrest of the person(s) causing the violence.
- Fighting, assault, battery, violence, threats, or intimidation are not permissible under the law. The carrying of knives, firearms, clubs, or other dangerous weapons may be prohibited by state law or local ordinance.

National Labor Relations Board will become involved and company liability can be substantial.

Economic Strikes. These are actions by the union of withdrawing its labor in support of bargaining demands, including those for recognition or organization. Economic strikers have limited rights to reinstatement.

Unprotected Strikes. These include all remaining types of work stoppages, both lawful and unlawful, such as sit-down strikes, strikes in violation of federal laws (e.g., the prohibition of strikes by employees of the federal government), slowdowns, wildcat strikes, and partial walkouts. Participants in unprotected strikes may be discharged by their employers.

Sympathy Strikes. These are refusals by employees of one bargaining unit to cross a picket line of a different bargaining unit (e.g., when more than one union is functioning at an employer's plant). Although the National Labor Relations Board and the courts have recognized the right of the sympathy striker to stand in the shoes of the primary striker, the facts of any particular situation will ultimately determine the legal status of a sympathy strike.[48]

During a strike, certain rules of conduct apply to both parties; these are summarized in Table 12-5. In addition, certain special rules apply to management. *Management must not:*

- Offer extra rewards to nonstrikers or attempt to withhold the "extras" from strikers once the strike has ended and some or all strikers are reinstated.
- Threaten nonstrikers or strikers.
- Promise benefits to strikers in an attempt to end the strike or to undermine the union.

- Threaten employees with discharge for taking part in a lawful strike.
- Discharge nonstrikers who refuse to take over a striker's job.

COMPANY EXAMPLE

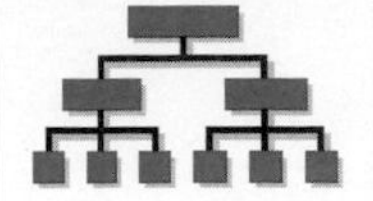

MORE FIRMS KEEP OPERATING IN SPITE OF STRIKES

To an increasing number of companies, "strike" is no longer a frightening word, for they are prepared to continue operating right through a labor walkout. Highly automated firms like American Telephone & Telegraph Company have been operating through strikes for years, but in today's economic climate, where many labor-intensive firms such as Magic Chef, Inc. and Whirlpool Corporation truly believe that their survival depends on not giving in to union demands, such a strategy is revolutionary. Although union officials criticize these management tactics, such actions are producing a flourishing business for security firms. The security firms provide companies with armored cars, vans, and guards to protect nonstriking workers during labor disputes. For example, one security firm helped Dannon Company, the yogurt maker, maintain operations at several New York–area plants during a series of strikes by members of the Teamsters union. The security firm provided about 100 guards to escort company trucks. The guards do not carry weapons, but they are armed with cameras. When strikers know they will be photographed, there tends to be a lot less violence. The cost for the 12-week security service: more than $1 million.[49]

Labor's ultimate weapon, the strike, is mostly failing. The threat of permanent replacement, recent court decisions, growing anti-union sentiment, and a pool of unemployed workers willing to break a strike make it easier for employers to defeat a walkout. As a result, the number of strikes and lockouts has decreased steadily throughout the last two decades to just 37 in 1996.[50] At Caterpillar, Inc., the maker of construction equipment, management forced an abrupt end to a 5-month strike by 12,500 UAW members by advertising for permanent replacements at six plants in Illinois. With an average wage of $17 an hour and an 8.5 percent state unemployment rate, union members knew they would be committing economic suicide if they stayed out. The specter of losing jobs forced the union back to the bargaining table.[51]

Proposed alternatives to strikes, including corporate campaigns and in-plant slowdowns, have had mixed success. During a slowdown, while workers adhere to the minimums of their job requirements, they continue to get paid, thereby frustrating management, but such a work-to-rule strategy could backfire in the long run; if productivity suffers a prolonged decline and a company fails to meet its production schedules, competitors will move in quickly. Then everybody loses. Companies are fighting back by retaliating in kind, firing activist employees and in some cases locking out the entire workforce. A recent NLRB decision that permits companies to replace locked-out workers with temporary employees has strengthened management's hand.[52]

Management's anti-union tactics have been quite successful, but this does not absolve management of the responsibility to treat workers with dignity and respect, to avoid arrogance, and to recognize that it is hard to give up gains that were so difficult to earn in the first place.

The Increasingly Bitter Nature of Strikes

Although the number of strikes has dropped dramatically during the 1990s, their intensity and general nastiness has escalated significantly. Unfair labor practices by both management and labor seem more and more common. For example, when Local 376 of the UAW engaged in a legal strike against Colt Firearms Company, a judge ruled that the company engaged in dozens of unfair labor practices. It changed working conditions, failed to bargain in good faith, offered to settle separately with employees who quit the union, and rejected the union's offer to have strikers return to work under the terms of their old contract. Although the company kept its plants operating by using replacement workers and about 200 union members who crossed the picket lines, a judge ordered that 800 strikers be reinstated in their old jobs.[53]

When the United Mine Workers struck Pittston Company, the company hired replacements and cut off the miners' health-care benefits. Over the course of a bitter 9-month strike, the company was forced to spend about $20 million in security, and the union accumulated $65 million in court fines related to picket-line violence and other violations of court injunctions.[54] By any stretch of the imagination, could this be considered win-win negotiating? A similar pattern of violence ensued in the 1990 strikes at Greyhound, Inc., and the *New York Daily News.* When workers see their jobs being lost to replacement workers, violence—including sniper fire, smashed windshields, and threats against substitute workers—often follows. During the *Daily News* strike, the paper itself became a weapon in the war, as one headline pleaded "Call Off the Thugs."[55]

A 1990 Supreme Court decision in *NLRB v. Curtin Matheson Scientific, Inc.* may undermine a common management strategy. The decision upheld the Board's policy that a company cannot oust a striking union by hiring replacement workers and asserting that the new employees do not support the union. Such a policy had been an effective weapon for management because a company is not required to recognize a union that is not supported by a majority of its employees. In short, employers cannot eliminate unions simply by replacing union workers.[56]

What remains unclear is the extent to which the bitterness of strikes will be reduced. In many ways, broader forces are at work, as both companies and their workers are caught in the maw of an economic vise, the jaws of which represent domestic and international competition.

When the Strike Is Over

The period of time immediately after a strike is critical, since an organization's problems are not over when the strike is settled. There is the problem of conflict between strikers and their replacements (if replacements were hired) and the reaccommodation of strikers to the workplace. After an economic strike is settled, the method of reinstatement is best protected by a written memorandum of agreement with the union that outlines the intended procedure. A key point of consideration in any strike aftermath is misconduct by some strikers. To refuse reinstatement for such strikers following an economic strike, management must be able to present evidence (e.g., photographs) to prove the misconduct.

The most important human aspect at the end of the strike is the restoration of harmonious working relations as soon as possible so that full operations can be resumed. A letter or a speech to employees welcoming them back to work can help this process along, as can meetings with supervisors indicating that no resentment or ill will is to be shown toward returning strikers. In practice, this may be difficult to do. However, keep these points in mind:

- Nothing is gained by allowing vindictiveness of any type in any echelon of management.
- The burden of maintaining healthy industrial relations now lies with the organization.
- There is always another negotiation ahead, and rancor has no place at any bargaining table.[57]

Lockouts

When a collective bargaining agreement has expired and an employer's purpose is to put economic pressure on a union to settle a contract on terms favorable to the employer, it is legal for the employer to lock out its employees.[58] It also is legal for a company to replace the locked-out workers with temporary replacements in order to continue operations during the lockout. However, the use of permanent replacements (without first consulting the union) is not permissible, according to the National Labor Relations Board, because such an action would completely destroy the bargaining unit and represent an unlawful withdrawal of recognition of a duly designated union.[59] Thus, when BASF Corporation ended a 5½-year lockout of the Oil, Chemical, and Atomic Workers union from its sprawling chemical complex in Geismar, Louisiana, the two parties agreed to a 3-year contract. The settlement affected 110 workers, who were reinstated in their old jobs. However, 5½ years earlier, the union had represented 370 workers at the 1200-employee plant.[60]

Third-Party Involvement

A bargaining impasse occurs when the parties are unable to move further toward settlement. However, because there is no clear formula to determine if or when an impasse in negotiations has been reached, litigation often ensues, and a judge must decide the issue.[61] In an effort to resolve the impasse, a neutral third party may become involved. In most private-sector negotiations, the parties have to agree voluntarily before any third-party involvement can be imposed on them. Because employees in the public sector are prohibited by law from striking, the use of third parties is more prevalent there.[62]

Three general types of third-party involvement are common: mediation, fact finding, and interest arbitration. Each becomes progressively more constraining on the freedom of the parties.

Mediation

Mediation is a process by which a neutral third party attempts to help the parties in dispute to reach a settlement of the issues that divide them. The neutral third party does not act as a judge to decide the resolution of the dispute (a process referred to as arbitration).[63] Rather, mediation involves persuading, opening communications, allowing readjustment and reassessment of bargaining stances, and making procedural suggestions (e.g., scheduling, conducting, and controlling meetings; establishing or extending deadlines).

There is no set time when a mediator will go in and attempt to resolve a dispute. By law, the Federal Mediation and Conciliation Service must be notified 30 days prior to the expiration of all labor contracts. However, some unions, such as the United Auto Workers, traditionally refuse mediation, and so many others manage to settle by themselves that the agency estimates that it is involved in only 8000 to 9000 of the country's 100,000 yearly labor negotiations.

Mediators have two restrictions on their power: (1) they are involved by invitation only, and (2) their advice lacks even so much as the umpire's option of throwing someone out of the game. Nevertheless, some mediators will do almost anything to get a settlement.

When 55,000 aerospace workers struck Boeing Corporation, Douglas Hammond, the federal mediator, actually stepped outside his usual role as a neutral middleman and devised the agreement that resolved the strike. There was tremendous pressure to do something: in the Seattle area, personal income had slid $30 million a week during the strike, the White House cited the stoppage as a factor in lower retail sales and industrial production indicators, and calls from the secretary of labor and the Pentagon were becoming routine. Even the U.S. trade deficit was affected because of Boeing's role as a leading exporter.

Had the effort backfired, Mr. Hammond's standing would have been compromised and negotiations thrown back to square one. Why did he succeed? According to the president of Machinists District 751: "In the negotiating room, Doug Hammond didn't duck. He took a bold stand and I admire him." Added Boeing's top negotiator: "He seems to know the timing, when to separate us and when to get us face-to-face. I trust him, and that's the bottom line."[64]

Fact Finding

Fact finding is a dispute resolution mechanism that is commonly used in the public sector at the state- and local-government levels. Disputes over the terms of collective bargaining agreements are more common at these levels since such bargaining ordinarily includes subjects, such as pay and benefits, that are excluded from bargaining with the federal government.

In a fact-finding procedure, each party submits whatever information it believes is relevant to a resolution of the dispute. A neutral fact finder then makes a study of the evidence and prepares a report on the facts. This procedure is often useful where the parties disagree over the truthfulness of the information each is using.[65]

Actually, the term "fact finding" is a misnomer. This is because fact finders often proceed, with statutory authority, to render a public recommendation of a reasonable settlement. In this respect, fact finding is similar to mediation. However, neither fact finding nor mediation necessarily results in a contract between management and labor. Consequently, the parties often resort to arbitration of a dispute, either as a matter of law (compulsory arbitration) or by mutual agreement between union and management (interest arbitration).

Interest Arbitration

Like fact finding, interest arbitration is used primarily in the public sector. However, arbitration differs considerably from mediation and fact finding. As one author noted: "While mediation assists the parties to reach their own settlement, arbitration hears the positions of both and decides on binding settlement terms. While fact finding would recommend a settlement, arbitration dictates it."[66]

Interest arbitration is controversial for at least two reasons: (1) imposition of interest arbitration eliminates the need for the parties to settle on their own because if they reach an impasse, settlement by an outsider is certain, and (2) many municipal employers apparently feel that arbitrators have been too generous in the awards made to public-employee unions. As a result, some states now specify the factors arbitrators must consider in making awards. Some of these, such as comparable wage rates, are items favored by unions; others, such as productivity and the ability of the employer to pay, are items favored by management.[67]

LEGALITIES

DOES THE ADA OVERRIDE SENIORITY RIGHTS?

Does the requirement in the Americans with Disabilities Act for "reasonable accommodation" supersede collectively bargained seniority rights? A federal appeals court ruled on this issue in a recent case that involved an employee of Consolidated Rail Corporation who was diagnosed with epilepsy. Medical restrictions prevented him from returning to his night-time shift. So he sought to invoke a provision in the collective bargaining agreement that permitted an employee with a disability, upon written agreement of the employer and the union, to "bump" a more senior employee or to occupy a more senior position and be immune from bumping by more senior employees. When the union refused to sign the agreement, the employee brought suit under the ADA.

The court rejected the employee's argument, finding that "collective-bargaining seniority rights have a pre-existing special status in the law and that Congress to date has shown no intent to alter this status by the duties created by the ADA."[68]

TRENDS IN COLLECTIVE BARGAINING

Changes in the Economic Environment

While the impact of foreign competition on U.S. firms is well known, two other changes, which are not as well known, have also affected the course of collective bargaining in recent years: nonunion domestic competition and deregulation. New domestic competitors that began and managed to remain unorganized have produced low-cost market competition, which, in turn, has put downward pressure on union wage rates. At nonunion Nucor Corporation, workers are paid a base rate below that of union workers at other steel makers. But they are also paid a production bonus that can exceed 150 percent of base pay. The result: very industrious workers can earn more than $20 an hour—well above union wages. Nucor's total labor costs per hour are about equal to those of other unionized steel makers, but the company gets higher productivity from its workers because it has lower staffing levels and more flexible work rules.[69]

The deregulation of many product markets created two key challenges to existing union relationships: (1) it made the market entry much easier, for example, in over-the-road trucking, airlines, and telecommunications; and (2) under regulation, management had little incentive to cut labor costs, because high labor costs could be passed on to consumers; conversely, labor-cost savings could not be used to gain a competitive advantage in the product market. Under deregulation, however, even major airlines (which are almost entirely organized) found that low costs translated into low fares and a competitive advantage. As a result, all carriers need to match the lowest costs of their competitors by matching their labor contracts.[70] At United Airlines, unions gave $5.5 billion in concessions over 6 years. Why? In return for up to 63 percent of United's stock. This put intense pressure on other airlines to match United's cost structure in order to compete.[71]

High-Priority Issues for Management and Labor

Given the changes noted above, management's top priority is to control the growth of labor costs. To do so, companies are pushing for greater cost sharing of health-care expenses, weakening of cost-of-living clauses, greater links between pay and corporate performance, and more emphasis on lump-sum bonuses that do not step up the wage base. They are also trying to increase flexibility by securing changes in restrictive work rules. Frequently, such changes lead to reductions in the numbers of employees needed to staff ongoing operations.

Unions, on the other hand, are seeking to phase out two-tier wage schemes (which set lower pay for new employees), to resist cuts on health-care benefits, and to gain improved job security (maintenance of employment at the same firm) and "employment security" for their members. In the latter approach, a company that is laying off a worker would train him or her for another job and try to place that worker in another job. As we will see, both management and labor have been willing to compromise on these broad goals in specific instances.

Recent Bargaining Outcomes

In general terms, median first-year wage raises across 693 collectively bargained contracts in 1995 averaged 3.0 percent, up from 2.9 percent in 1994. Lump-sum bonuses appeared in 20 percent of all agreements, up from 16 percent in 1994. However, cost-of-living adjustments appeared in only 6 percent of contracts, down from 7 percent in 1994, and 3-year agreements continue to be the norm.[72]

To be sure, the ever-present threat of foreign competition has put added pressure on firms to reduce their labor costs in order to survive. In many unions, therefore, the focus of bargaining has shifted to emphasize job security to reduce the risk of job loss. For example, in the auto industry, Ford, GM, and Chrysler all agreed to keep their hourly employment levels of United Auto Workers at 95 percent of 1996 levels through 1999 (except for jobs lost to productivity gains, market-share declines, and the sale of uncompetitive plants). In return, the union agreed to $2000 signing bonuses per worker, plus 3 percent wage increases in 1998 and 1999.[73]

For the automakers, the negotiations were not so much about wages and benefits as about international competitiveness—with Toyota, Honda, Mercedes, and BMW all operating nonunion North American assembly operations. The $43 an hour in wages and benefits paid to UAW workers is as much as $15 an hour higher than some Japanese "transplant" operations pay, because of lower benefit levels and younger workforces with almost no retirees at the transplant operations. These factors, combined with greater efficiency in assembly processes, translate to as much as a $1000-per-vehicle advantage over the Big Three. How will the Big Three automakers compete? By making their factories more efficient, designing vehicles that are less labor-intensive, and shedding uncompetitive parts businesses.[74]

As another example, consider the agreement between Rubbermaid, Inc., and the United Rubber Workers Local 302 at the company's 73-year-old plant in Wooster, Ohio. Over a 7-year period the union gave ground on wages and health benefits; it agreed to eliminate automatic cost-of-living increases, reduce overtime pay, and relax rigid work rules. It also agreed to a two-tier wage system that pays new workers substantially less than veteran workers. Why did the union make such concessions? Rubbermaid promised to guarantee the jobs of the workers during the life of the contract.[75] The result: no layoffs in Wooster, despite the fact that the company has 23 other factories that are newer, lower-cost, and nonunion. Both sales and profits have increased substantially at the plant. But instead of granting wage increases, Rubbermaid earmarks about one-third of its profits for dividends to shareholders and nearly two-thirds for investment in new, more efficient machinery that the company considers vital to ensure its survival. These are positive responses to a changing economic environment.

Labor-Management Cooperation

Make no mistake about it: the recent popularity of cooperation stems largely from the sweeping changes in the economic environment that have occurred over the last decade. Another reason is new technology—factory automation, robotics, and more modern production systems. Cooperation offers a pragmatic approach to problems that threaten the survival of companies, the jobs and income security of their employees, and the institutional future of their unions.[76] Progressive unions such as those representing laborers, the machinists, the needle trades, and the steelworkers are at the forefront of a revolutionary change in the way unions view cooperation with management. The unions are asking what kinds of improvements in productivity or quality the employer needs to stay competitive while paying union wages, and then they help the employer achieve its objectives.[77]

For example, the International Association of Machinists (IAM) is now marketing itself as a resource for employers. It runs week-long courses for plant managers and local union leaders on high-performance work systems in its Maryland school. The managers and union officers study side by side, learning everything from the history of high-performance systems to new accounting methods to measure them. The goal: to protect workers' jobs and pay by making their employers more competitive. Unions also want to win for employees more say over their work and how their companies are run.

Following an IAM training module, union leaders and managers from manufacturing to marketing created team systems and joint decision-making councils at a 500-employee unit of Aluminum Company of America—which makes

IMPACT OF UNION REPRESENTATION ON PRODUCTIVITY, QUALITY OF WORK LIFE, AND THE BOTTOM LINE

Is there a link between unionization and organizational performance? Unionization of a workforce often increases control over wage levels by giving monopoly power to the union as the single seller of labor to an enterprise. It also creates a "voice" mechanism for employees by establishing negotiated grievance procedures and the right to bargain collectively.[80]

Economic studies generally show that the existence of a grievance process that acts as a check or balance on management's authority can enhance productivity. One explanation for this is that higher productivity results from lower turnover, which in turn enhances employees' knowledge of the jobs they perform.[81]

If unions actually do raise productivity, why do managements oppose them with such vigor? The answer lies in the impact unions have on corporate profits. A number of studies support the argument that while unions may increase productivity, the wage and benefit increases associated with unionization (20 percent more than those of nonunion workers) often exceed productivity gains.[82]

equipment for the packaging industry. Relations on the shop floor have improved dramatically, and efficiency gains are expected to follow.[78]

Institutionalizing cooperative relationships is no easy task. However, successful efforts have been characterized by features such as the following:[79]

- The reason for the cooperative effort remains strong.
- Benefits derived from the cooperation are distributed equitably.
- The union is perceived as instrumental in attaining program benefits.
- The cooperative effort does not infringe on traditional collective bargaining issues (see the earlier example of Electromation, Inc.).
- The program does not threaten management prerogatives.
- Management has refrained from subcontracting out bargaining-unit work.
- The program does not overlap the grievance procedure.
- Union leaders are not viewed as being co-opted.
- The cooperative effort is protected from the use of bargaining tactics and maneuvers.
- Union leaders continue to pursue member goals on traditional economic issues.

Current Tactics of Management and Labor

Both sides are becoming quite sophisticated in their attempts to win the minds, hearts, and votes of workers during organizing campaigns and also in response to industrial action. For example, when the UAW tried to organize Nissan's car and truck assembly plant in Smyrna, Tennessee, top Nissan officials made no public statements in the contentious organizing campaign. Instead, Nissan made anti-union employees available to journalists to explain their feelings. The company also relied on frequent and forceful anti-union broadcasts on the plant's closed-circuit television network.[83] Workers rejected the union by a 2-to-1 margin.

IMPLICATIONS FOR MANAGEMENT PRACTICE

Given current conditions in the economic environment, a distributive (win-lose) orientation toward labor is simply inefficient. Rather, view your employees as a source of potential competitive advantage. Treat them with dignity and respect, and they will respond in kind. As for the labor movement itself, it too needs to adjust.

Management is adopting aggressive anti-union tactics in response to strikes, by hiring replacement workers and using lockouts. It has also pitted unionized workers against one another. General Motors did this when it said it would close down either a plant in Arlington, Texas, or one in Ypsilanti, Michigan. The 3200 Arlington workers put cooperation with GM ahead of UAW fellowship, voting to allow a three-shift schedule to build cars around the clock without overtime pay and approving other work-rule changes. Workers in Ypsilanti did not offer GM much, and the company closed the plant.[84]

In response to these tactics, unions have taken several specific actions. One is in-plant slowdowns. Rather than strike and risk losing jobs to outsiders hired to replace them, workers stay on the job and carry out their tasks "by the book," showing no initiative and taking no shortcuts. Although the AFL-CIO has endorsed this strategy, results thus far are inconclusive.[85] Another tactic is the "rolling strike," which targets one shop at a time. Moving the action keeps management from easily hiring replacements. Rolling strikes recently were used by state employees in Oregon, clerical workers in Los Angeles, and janitors in Washington, D.C. Such strikes are difficult to combat because they are more like guerrilla warfare than a full-fledged battle. However, in a recent New Jersey supermarket strike, management locked out union members at one unpicketed store for each store picketed.[86]

Nevertheless, one union tactic has worked well. Firms that practice just-in-time inventory management, in which supplies are delivered just when needed, are vulnerable to a strike by workers who make the supplies. This was the case in 1996 at two General Motors brake-parts plants in Dayton, Ohio. The plants supplied 90 percent of GM's brake parts; by striking, the 3000 workers involved effectively shut down the nation's largest carmaker, idling 22 of GM's 29 North American production facilities.[87]

Unions are also trying to broaden their base. Thus only about 11 percent of the 1.3 million members of the Teamsters union actually drive trucks. The remaining membership includes workers as diverse as pilots, zookeepers, and Disney World's Mickey Mouse. The most progressive unions—the Teamsters, the United Brotherhood of Carpenters, UNITE (the needle trades union), the Service Employees International Union—are remaking themselves internally, by changing from servicing current members to recruiting new ones. To free up resources for organizing, many unions are slashing departments and merging locals. Some are laying off and firing staffers who cannot or will not move from servicing to organizing. The carpenters even brought in a management consultant to help restructure the union! Unions that do change get results. For example, since the Teamsters trained 220 local organizers to run rank-and-file campaigns, the union has won 40 percent more elections than in previous years.[88]

Finally, unions are lobbying hard for pro-labor legislation, for example, restrictions on the ability of U.S. firms to shift operations to Mexico or Canada under the North American Free Trade Agreement. By the end of 1996, they claim, NAFTA had cost more than 600,000 American jobs and resulted in large trade deficits with Mexico and Canada.[89] As these few examples demonstrate, it will be a long time before organized labor's obituary is written.

IMPROVING PRODUCTIVITY, QWL, AND PROFITS THROUGH LABOR-MANAGEMENT COOPERATION

Human Resource Management in Action: Conclusion

There are lots of success stories of labor-management cooperation in which established unions have taken leading roles. For example, the Amalgamated Clothing and Textile Workers Union, which represents 6200 workers who assemble copiers at Xerox Corporation, has helped cut costs on the firm's machines by millions of dollars. Three tries at teamwork since 1982 have worked out so well that Xerox is bringing 300 jobs from abroad to a new plant in Utica, New York, where it expects higher quality and savings of $2 million a year. Xerox gives union officials internal financial documents and teaches them statistics in the same classes managers take. Cooperative efforts such as these have produced big gains in efficiency at companies such as National Steel Corporation, Scott Paper Company, and LTV Corporation.

Progressive unions are working with management to raise productivity by jointly sponsoring training programs and agreeing to adopt teams and new work systems.[90] As we have seen, the world has changed dramatically in the last decade. If U.S. labor leaders let today's opportunities for labor-management cooperation slip by, they may not get another chance to be part of the solution to the continuing challenge to improve productivity, quality of work life, and profits.

SUMMARY

At a general level, the goal of unions is to improve economic and other conditions of employment. Although unions have been successful over the years in achieving these goals, more recently they have been confronted with challenges that have led to membership losses. Unions are trying to reverse that decline by organizing more workers.

The National Labor Relations Board, created by the Wagner Act, supervises union organizing campaigns and representation elections. If the union wins, it becomes the sole bargaining agent for employees. Collective bargaining is the cornerstone of the U.S. labor movement, and anything that threatens its continued viability will be resisted vigorously by organized labor. Both sides typically prepare about 6 months in advance for the next round of negotiations. Such preparation involves an analysis of grievances, current wage and benefits costs, and the costs of proposed settlements.

Unfortunately, bargaining sometimes reaches an impasse, at which point the parties may resort to a strike (workers) or a lockout (management). Alternatively, the parties may request third-party intervention in the form of mediation, fact finding, or interest arbitration. In the public sector, such intervention is usually required.

Current trends in industrial relations, such as labor-management cooperation, and new tactics used by management and labor are being fueled by changes in the economic climate. These include foreign competition, domestic nonunion competition, changes in technology, and deregulation. In view of these changes, accommodation of labor and management to each other's needs (win-win bargaining) is more appropriate than the old adversarial win-lose approach.

DISCUSSION QUESTIONS

12-1 Are the roles of labor and management inherently adversarial?
12-2 Discuss the rights and obligations of unions and management during a union organizing drive.
12-3 Discuss key differences in the behavior of successful versus average negotiators.
12-4 Contrast the Japanese system of industrial relations to that of the United States.
12-5 Compare and contrast mediation, fact finding, and interest arbitration.

APPLYING YOUR KNOWLEDGE

Exercise 12-1 *Contract Negotiations at Moulton Machine Shop*

Collective bargaining is the cornerstone of American labor relations. Face-to-face negotiations involving give-and-take on the part of both management and labor representatives are an inherent part of our present system. It is through these negotiations that both sides attempt to understand the positions of the other and attempt to persuade the other side of the fairness of their own demands.

The purpose of this exercise is for you to experience the collective bargaining process and to gain an awareness of the nature and complexity of labor negotiations.

Background Information

Moulton Machine Shop is a 60-year-old shop located near Lake Erie in Pennsylvania. The company manufactures a wide variety of made-to-order products, but its primary business is the repair of mechanical airplane parts and components, a business that it conducts on an international basis. The firm has developed a reputation for quality and timely work on difficult machining projects. The mostly blue-collar workforce at Moulton consists of about 200 workers who were organized 30 years ago by the International Machinists Union (IMU). The labor relations climate at Moulton has been fairly good over the last 20 years (after a rather stormy beginning), with no strikes in the last 9 years. In the past 2 years, however, the number of grievances has increased substantially.

Recent economic conditions have been difficult for Moulton. Over the past 5 years, increased competition from lower-priced foreign-based machine shops has pruned Moulton's profit margins. Overall, sales are down about 10 percent compared with projections made earlier in the year. Moulton's management believes that competition will intensify in the near future, creating even more problems for the firm. The union is aware of the financial situation at Moulton and is sympathetic, but has been very clear in its overtures to management that it intends to fight for an improved contract for its members because they have fallen behind equivalent workers in recent years.

Current Contract Provisions

Clause	Current contract
Wages	Average hourly wage is $11.23.
Benefits	Company-paid medical and life insurance.
Overtime	Time-and-a-half.
Layoffs	A 2-week notice is required to lay off any union member who has been at Moulton more than 2 months.
Vacations	2 weeks for all employees except those with over 20 years' service, who receive 3 weeks.
Holidays	Nine paid per year.
Sick leave	4 paid days per year unless verified by doctor, in which case, can be up to 10 days.
Length of contract	2 years.

Additional Information

1. Hourly wage rates for union members doing similar work elsewhere in the local vicinity average $11.75.
2. A $50 deductible dental insurance plan would cost about $45 per employee.
3. Overtime averaged 185 hours per employee last year.
4. Among competitors, the most frequent vacation, holiday, and sick-leave schedules are as follows: (1) 2 weeks' vacation for starters, 3 weeks after 10 years of service, and 4 weeks after 25 years; (b) 10 paid holidays per year; and (c) 6 paid sick-leave days per year (although there is a wide variation here, with a few firms having no paid sick leave at all).
5. Contract length at similar firms varies from 1 to 3 years.

Procedure

The class should be divided into groups of three. Each group consists of a union negotiator, a management negotiator, and an observer. The instructor will provide a role statement for each negotiator. These role statements should not be shared with the other negotiator or with the observer. Each group's task is to negotiate a contract between Moulton Machine Shop and the IMU. Your instructor will tell you how much time you have available for this task. It is important that you settle this contract in the limited time available so that you can avert a costly strike.

As the negotiations proceed, observers should record significant events. (A sample observation form is depicted below.) When the negotiations end, observers will be asked to report the final agreed-upon contract provisions to the rest of the class and to describe the process by which the negotiations took place in each group.

CONTRACT NEGOTIATIONS OBSERVATION FORM

Clause	**Final settlement**
Wages	______
Benefits	______
Overtime	______
Layoffs	______
Vacations	______
Holidays	______
Sick leave	______
Length of contract	______
Other provisions	______

1. How do the negotiations begin? Which side talks the most in the beginning? Does each side have a clear understanding of the purpose of the negotiations?

2. What behaviors of the negotiators seem to either bring the parties closer together or drive them farther apart?

3. How does the climate of the negotiations change over time? Which side talks the most as the negotiations wear on? Do the parties agree more or less as time passes?

4. How do the negotiations end? Are the parties friendly with each other? Do they both seem committed to the final solution? Are future union-management relations likely to get better or worse as a result of this agreement?

REFERENCES

1. Deshpande, S. P., & Fiorito, J. (1989). Specific and general beliefs in union voting models. *Academy of Management Journal,* **32**, 883–897.
2. Sweeney's blitz (1997, Feb. 17). *Business Week,* pp. 56–62.
3. Greenwald, J. (1993, Dec. 6). A growing itch to fight. *Time,* pp. 34, 35. See also Ayres, B. D., Jr. (1989, Apr. 27). Coal miners' strike hits feelings that go deep. *The New York Times,* p. A16.

4. Kristol, I. (1978, Oct. 23). Understanding trade unionism. *The Wall Street Journal,* p. 28.
5. Serrin, W. (1985, Dec. 5). Union at Stevens, yes; upheaval, no. *The New York Times,* p. A18.
6. Rose, R. L. (1996, Oct. 29). New AFL-CIO president seeks to revitalize old federation. *The Wall Street Journal,* pp. B1, B8. See also Kochan, T. A. (1979). How American workers view labor unions. *Monthly Labor Review,* **103**(4), 23–31.
7. Sweeney's blitz, loc. cit.
8. Doctors' union interests become a spreading syndrome (1997, Feb. 25). *The Wall Street Journal,* p. A1.
9. Bernstein, A. (1996, Nov. 18). Bigger paychecks, yes. Better pay, no. *Business Week,* p. 116. See also Kuttner, R. (1996, Sept. 9). Happy labor day, Joe six-pack. Have some crumbs. *Business Week,* p. 26.
10. Lublin, J. S. (1996, Apr. 11). The great divide. *The Wall Street Journal,* pp. R1, R4.
11. Mellor, S. (1995). Gender composition and gender representation in local unions: Relationships between women's participation in local office and women's participation in local activities. *Journal of Applied Psychology,* **80**, 706–720.
12. Sweeney's blitz, loc. cit.
13. Work week (1997, Feb. 11). *The Wall Street Journal,* p. A1.
14. Greenwald, op. cit., p. 35.
15. Schuster, M. (1990). Union-management cooperation. In J. A. Fossum (ed.), *Employee and labor relations.* Washington, DC: Bureau of National Affairs, pp. 4-44 to 4-81.
16. Fox, J. (1996, Oct. 28). The UAW makes nice. *Fortune,* pp. 28, 29. See also Milbank, D. (1992, May 5). On the ropes: Unions' woes suggest how the labor force in U.S. is shifting. *The Wall Street Journal,* pp. A1, A6.
17. Fox, loc. cit. See also Freedman, A. (1988, May). How the 1980s have changed industrial relations. *Monthly Labor Review,* pp. 35–38.
18. Ibid.
19. Christian, N. M., & Stern, G. (1996, Oct. 30). Workers strike at 2 GM plants, prodding talks. *The Wall Street Journal,* p. A6. See also Local GM labor dispute spins out of control (1996, Mar. 13). *The Wall Street Journal,* pp. B1, B5.
20. Dowling, P. J., & Schuler, R. S. (1996). *International dimensions of human resource management* (3d ed.). Boston: PWS-Kent.
21. Poole, M. (1986). *Industrial relations: Origins and patterns of national diversity.* London: Routledge & Kegan Paul.
22. Japanese union membership (1992, Dec. 30). *The Wall Street Journal,* p. A4. See also Labor letter (1991, Apr. 23). *The Wall Street Journal,* p. A1.
23. Dunlop, J. T. (1988, May). Have the 1980's changed U.S. industrial relations? *Monthly Labor Review,* pp. 29–34.
24. Davis, E. M., & Lansbury, R. D. (in press.). Industrial relations in Australia. In C. J. Bamber & R. D. Lansbury (eds.) *International and comparative industrial relations* (3d ed.). Sydney: Allen & Unwin. See also Fossum, J. A. (1990). Employee and labor relations in an evolving environment. In J. A. Fossum (ed.), *Employee and labor relations.* Washington, DC: Bureau of National Affairs, pp. 4-1 to 4-22.
25. Davis & Lansbury, op. cit. See also Quinlan, M. (1996). The reform of Australian industrial relations: Contemporary trends and issues. *Asia Pacific Journal of Human Resources,* **34**(2), 3–27. See also Sloan, J. (1997, Jan.). What the Workplace Relations Act will mean for business. *Employee Relations Brief, FT Law & Tax, Asia Pacific,* pp. 1–4. Sydney: Pearson Professional Publishing.
26. Chait, H. N. (1993, Winter). Labor law update. *HRM Update,* pp. 1–3. See also Salwen, K. G. (1992, Dec. 18). NLRB says labor-management teams at firm violated company-union rule. *The Wall Street Journal,* p. A12. See also Putting a damper on that old team spirit (1992, May 4). *Business Week,* p. 60.
27. *NLRB v. Babcock & Wilcox* (1956). 105 U.S. 351.
28. Mills, D. Q. (1994). Labor-management relations (5th ed.). New York: McGraw-Hill.

29. NLRB proposal on single units criticized. (1996, Mar.). *HR News,* p. 2. See also Kilgour, J. G. (1983, Mar.–Apr.). Union organizing activity among white-collar employees. *Personnel,* pp. 18–27.
30. Wermiel, S. (1983, Nov. 16). NLRB can't force companies to bargain with minority unions, U.S. court rules. *The Wall Street Journal,* p. 12.
31. Zachary, G. P. (1995, Nov. 17). Long litigation often holds up union victories. *The Wall Street Journal,* pp. B1, B15. See also Prosten, W. (1979). The rise in NLRB election delays: Measuring business's new resistance. *Monthly Labor Review,* **103**(2), 39–41.
32. Unions holding fewer, winning more elections (1992, Dec.). *Mountain States Employers Council Bulletin,* p. 4.
33. Sweeney's blitz, loc. cit.
34. Swann, J. P., Jr. (1983). The decertification of a union. *Personnel Administrator,* **28**(1), 47–51.
35. Rose, loc. cit.
36. Kotlowitz, A. (1987, Apr. 1). Grievous work. *The Wall Street Journal,* pp. 1, 12.
37. Fisher, R., Ury, W., & Patton, B. (1991). *Getting to yes* (2d ed.). New York: Penguin.
38. Ways, M. (1979, Jan. 15). The virtues, limits, and dangers of negotiation. *Fortune,* pp. 86–90.
39. Ibid.
40. Lewicki, R. J. (1997). *Negotiation* (3d ed.). Homewood, IL: Irwin/McGraw-Hill.
41. Ibid. See also Walton, R. E., & McKersie, R. B. (1965). *A behavioral theory of labor negotiations.* New York: McGraw-Hill.
42. Moran, R. T. (1987). *Getting your yen's worth: How to negotiate with Japan, Inc.* Houston: Gulf.
43. Miller, R. L. (1978, Jan.). Preparations for negotiations. *Personnel Journal,* pp. 36–39, 44.
44. Uchitelle, L. (1989, Oct. 12). Boeing's fight over bonuses. *The New York Times,* pp. D1, D6.
45. For more information on labor contract costing, see Cascio, W. F. (1991). *Costing human resources: The financial impact of behavior in organizations* (3d ed.). Boston: PWS-Kent.
46. Fruhan, W. E., Jr. (1985). Management, labor, and the golden goose. *Harvard Business Review,* **63**(5), 131–141.
47. American Society for Personnel Administration (1983). *Strike preparation manual* (rev. ed.). Berea, OH: Author.
48. Ibid.
49. Greenberger, D. (1983, Oct. 11). Striking back. *The Wall Street Journal,* pp. 1, 18.
50. Work week (1997, May 20). *The Wall Street Journal,* p. A1. Rubis, L. (1996, Mar.). Court rejects president's order on strikers. *HR News,* p. 1; Kilborn, P. T. (1992, Apr. 16). Caterpillar's trump card. *The New York Times,* pp. A1, B6. See also Bernstein, A. (1991, Aug. 5). You can't bargain with a striker whose job is no more. *Business Week,* p. 27.
51. Hicks, J. P. (1992, Apr. 21). Still bitter, Caterpillar workers return. *The New York Times,* p. A16.
52. Uchitelle, L. (1993, June 13). Labor draws the line in Decatur. *The New York Times,* pp. F1, F6. See also Kotlowitz, A. (1987, May 22). Labor's shift: Finding strikes harder to win, more unions turn to slowdowns. *The Wall Street Journal,* pp. 1, 7.
53. Colt told to rehire 800 strikers; back pay is to be in millions (1989, Sept. 13). *The New York Times,* p. B3.
54. Swasy, A., & Karr, A. R. (1990, Jan. 2). Pittston, UMW tentatively set labor accord. *The Wall Street Journal,* p. A3.
55. Kifner, J. (1990, Nov. 4). Daily News strike becomes a battle for advertisers. *The New York Times,* pp. 1, 38. See also Kilborn, P. T. (1990, Apr. 9). Money isn't everything in Greyhound strike. *The New York Times,* pp. A1, A12.
56. Wermiel, S. (1990, Apr. 18). Supreme Court upholds policy barring tactic used to oust a striking union. *The Wall Street Journal,* p. A3.
57. American Society for Personnel Administration, op. cit.

58. Mills, op. cit.
59. Ibid.
60. BASF is poised to end 5.5-year U.S. lockout (1989, Dec. 18). *International Herald Tribune,* p. 7.
61. Oviatt, C. R., Jr. (1995, Oct.). Case shows difficulty of declaring negotiating impasse. *HR News,* pp. 13, 16.
62. Fossum, J. A. (1995). *Labor relations: Development, structure, process* (6th ed.). Homewood, IL: Irwin.
63. Mills, op. cit.
64. Wartzman, R. (1989, Nov. 21). Seizing initiative pays off for Boeing strike mediator. *The Wall Street Journal,* pp. B1, B11.
65. Mills, op. cit.
66. Fossum, op. cit.
67. Mills, op. cit.
68. Union contracts and the ADA (1996, Nov./Dec.). *Mountain States Employers Council Bulletin,* p. 2.
69. Milbank, loc. cit.
70. Cappelli, P. (1990). Collective bargaining. In J. A. Fossum (ed.), *Employee and labor relations.* Washington, DC: Bureau of National Affairs, pp. 4-180 to 4-217.
71. United they don't stand. (1997, Mar. 3). *Business Week,* pp. 86, 88. See also This give-and-take may actually fly (1993, Dec. 27). *Business Week,* p. 37.
72. Union increases up (1996, Mar.). *Mountain States Employers Council Bulletin,* p. 5.
73. Auto agendas: Work force guarantee in Ford's UAW accord puts pressure on GM (1996, Sept. 18). *The Wall Street Journal,* pp. A1, A4.
74. Ibid. See also Blumenstein, R. (1996, Nov. 7). UAW delegates endorse pact with GM. *The Wall Street Journal,* pp. A2, A6.
75. Uchitelle, L. (1992, Apr. 19). Blue-collar compromises in pursuit of job security. *The New York Times,* pp. 1L, 18L, 19L.
76. Schuster, loc. cit.
77. Look who's pushing productivity (1997, Apr. 7). *Business Week,* pp. 72, 73, 75.
78. Ibid.
79. Cooke, W. N. (1990). Factors influencing the effect of joint union-management programs on employee-supervisor relations. *Industrial and Labor Relations Review,* **43,** 587–603. See also Schuster, loc. cit.
80. Freeman, R. B., & Medoff, J. (1984). *What do unions do?* New York: Basic Books.
81. Kleiner, M. M. (1990). The role of industrial relations in industrial performance. In J. A. Fossum (ed.), *Employee and labor relations.* Washington, DC: Bureau of National Affairs, pp. 4-23 to 4-43.
82. Labor's surprising reemergence (1997, Feb. 17). *Business Week,* p. 110. See also Linneman, P. D., Wachter, M. L., & Carter, W. H. (1990). Evaluating the evidence on union employment and wages. *Industrial and Labor Relations Review,* **44**(1), 34–53.
83. Levin, D. P. (1989, July 28). Nissan workers in Tennessee spurn union's bid. *The New York Times,* pp. A1, A6.
84. Patterson, G. A. (1992, Mar. 6). New rules: How GM's car plant in Arlington, Texas, hustled to avoid ax. *The Wall Street Journal,* pp. A1, A6.
85. Uchitelle, L. (1993, June 13). Labor draws the line in Decatur. *The New York Times,* pp. 1F, 6F.
86. Labor letter (1993, June 8). *The Wall Street Journal,* p. A1.
87. Burkins, G., & Bleakley, F. R. (1996, Mar. 14). UAW strike hit GM "just in time" to cripple firm. *The Wall Street Journal,* pp. A3, A10. See also GM, UAW dig in as shutdown spreads (1996, Mar. 14). *The Wall Street Journal,* pp. A3, A10.
88. Sweeney's blitz, loc. cit.
89. Crutsinger, M. (1997, Feb. 24). Issue of broader NAFTA to focus on lost U.S. jobs. *The Denver Post,* p. 4A.
90. Labor's surprising reemergence, loc. cit.

13 PROCEDURAL JUSTICE AND ETHICS IN EMPLOYEE RELATIONS

Questions This Chapter Will Help Managers Answer

1 How can I ensure procedural justice in the resolution of conflicts between employees and managers?
2 How can I administer discipline without at the same time engendering resentment toward me or my company?
3 How do I fire people legally and humanely?
4 What should be the components of a fair information practice policy?
5 What is ethical decision making in employee relations? What steps or considerations are involved?

ALTERNATIVE DISPUTE RESOLUTION (ADR): GOOD FOR THE COMPANY, GOOD FOR EMPLOYEES?

Human Resource Management in Action

At the McGraw-Hill Companies, in New York, word came down from chief executive Joseph Dionne: it was time to supplement the open-door policy with a formal, in-house ADR program. He told attorneys in the legal department to develop something that settled disputes quickly, something good for morale.

After 6 months of work with consultants, and meetings with employees and managers, as well as executives from Chemical Bank, Cigna, J. C. Penney, and the Brown & Root construction company—all of whom have ADR programs—McGraw-Hill unveiled its Fast and Impartial Resolution (FAIR) ADR program. The three-step program is voluntary, and starts with bringing in a supervisor or HR representative to resolve a dispute. If that does not work, the next step is mediation with a third party. If mediation is fruitless, the third step is binding arbitration with a written decision. The company pays the costs of mediation and arbitration.

The FAIR program is typical of the programs many organizations are developing, as they move from information fact finding or open-door policies to formal, structured policies. Clearly such programs are beneficial to employers, for they save time and money. According to JAMS/Endispute, based in Irvine, California, it takes up to 6 weeks, from the time that company is contacted, to the time mediation actually begins. The parties spend an average of 12.5 hours in the process, and problems are resolved in up to 90 percent of cases. Says Douglas McDowell, general counsel for the Equal Employment Advisory Council, an employer association based in Washington with about 300 member companies: "We think mediation is a fairly safe way to go. . . . it allows the participants to meet with trained mediators, diffuse the acrimony, and come to a resolution in a voluntary agreement. Once settled, it's binding, which is enforceable."

Houston-based Brown & Root has had about 1100 ADR cases, with 17 going to arbitration. The cost of an arbitration has ranged from about $6000 to $20,000, saving the company 50 percent to 80 percent on the legal costs associated with trials in court. Roughly 75 percent of the cases are resolved within 2 months, as opposed to several years in the courts. In Irvine, California, American Savings Bank's 2-year-old, four-step program is enjoying similar success, reducing legal costs by more than 60 percent.

Challenges

1. What do you see as some key advantages and disadvantages of ADR programs?

Source: Bencivenga, B. (1996, January). Fair play in the ADR arena. *HRMagazine,* pp. 50–56. Guttner, T. (1997, February 10). When it's time to do battle with your company. *Business Week,* pp. 130, 131. Egler, T. D. (1995, July). The benefits and burdens of arbitration. *HRMagazine,* pp. 27–30.

2. Should an employee's agreement to binding arbitration be a condition of employment or a condition of continuing employment?
3. Working in small groups, identify characteristics that would make an ADR program fair for both employees and employers.

The chapter opening vignette illustrates another facet of labor-management accommodation: the use of workplace due process to resolve disputes. It is another attempt to enhance the productivity and QWL of employees. Indeed, the broad theme of this chapter is "justice on the job." The chapter considers alternative methods for resolving disputes, such as grievance (in union and nonunion settings) and arbitration procedures. Also examined are discipline and termination in the employment context. Finally, the chapter examines the growing concern for employee privacy in these four areas: fair information practice in the computer age, the assessment of job applicants and employees, employee searches, and whistle-blowing.

A PERSPECTIVE ON JUSTICE

We begin our treatment by presenting definitions of some important terms that will provide both background and context for our treatment of procedural justice. We then examine the implementation of procedural justice through the development of employee voice systems.

Some Definitions

In this chapter we are concerned with three broad issues in the context of employee relations: (1) procedural justice, (2) due process, and (3) ethical decisions about behavior.

Employee relations includes all the practices that implement the philosophy and policy of an organization with respect to employment.[1]

Justice refers to the maintenance or administration of what is just, especially by the impartial adjustment of conflicting claims or the assignment of merited rewards or punishments.[2]

Procedural justice focuses on the fairness of the procedures used to make decisions. Procedures are fair to the extent that they are consistent across persons and over time, free from bias, based on accurate information, correctable, and based on prevailing moral and ethical standards.[3]

Due process in legal proceedings provides individuals with rights such as the following: prior notice of prohibited conduct; timely procedures adhered to at each step of the procedure; notice of the charges or issues prior to a hearing; impartial judges or hearing officers; representation by counsel; opportunity to confront and to cross-examine adverse witnesses and evidence, as well as to present proof in one's own defense; notice of decision; and protection from retaliation for using a complaint procedure in a legitimate manner. These are constitutional due process rights. They protect individual rights with respect to state, municipal, and federal government processes. However, they normally do not apply to work situations. Hence, employee rights to due process are based on a collective bargaining agreement, on legislative protections, or on procedures provided unilaterally by an employer.[4]

Ethical decisions about behavior concern one's conformity to moral standards or to the standards of conduct of a given profession or group. Ethical decisions about behavior take account not only of one's own interests but also, equally, of the interests of those affected by the decision.[5]

PROCEDURAL JUSTICE IN ACTION: EMPLOYEE VOICE SYSTEMS

For most organizations, the most important thing they can do to ensure procedural justice is to provide individuals and groups the capacity to be heard, a way to communicate their interests upward—a voice system. Voice systems serve four important functions:

1. They assure fair treatment to employees.
2. They provide a context in which unfair treatment can be appealed.
3. They help improve the effectiveness of an organization.
4. They sustain employee loyalty and commitment.[6]

Here are some examples of voice systems that are commonly used:

- Grievance procedures, by which an employee can seek a formal, impartial review of a decision that affects him or her.
- Ombudspersons, who may investigate claims of unfair treatment or act as intermediaries between an employee and senior management and recommend possible courses of action to the parties.
- Open-door policies by which employees can approach senior managers with problems that they may not be willing to take to their immediate supervisor. A related mechanism, particularly appropriate when the immediate supervisor is the problem, is a skip-level policy, whereby an employee may proceed directly to the next higher level of management above his or her supervisor.
- Participative management systems that encourage employee involvement in all aspects of organizational strategy and decision making.
- Committees or meetings that poll employee input on key problems and decisions.
- Senior management visits, where employees can meet with senior company officials and openly ask questions about company strategy, policies, and practices or raise concerns about unfair treatment.
- Question/answer newsletters, in which employee questions and concerns submitted to a newsletter editor and investigated by that office are answered and openly reported to the organizational community.[7]
- Toll-free telephone numbers that employees can use anonymously to report waste, fraud, or abuse.

Table 13-1

CORE CHARACTERISTICS OF EFFECTIVE VOICE SYSTEMS

Elegance—simple procedures, broad application, vested authority, good diagnostic system
Accessibility—easy to use, advertised, comprehensive, open process
Correctness—administered well, includes follow-up, self-redesigning, correctable outcomes
Responsiveness—timely, culturally viable, tangible results, management commitment
Nonpunitiveness—appeal system, anonymity, no retaliation for using the system

Source: B. H. Sheppard, R. J. Lewicki, & J. W. Minton, *Organizational justice: The search for fairness in the workplace.* New York: Lexington Books, 1992, p. 149.

Characteristics of Effective Voice Systems

A thorough review of the literature on voice systems reveals five core characteristics of the most effective ones. These are shown in Table 13-1.

The first criterion is *elegance.* That is, the system should be simple to understand, it should apply to a broad range of issues, it should use an effective diagnostic framework, and finally, those who manage the system should be able to respond definitively to the issues raised.

The second criterion is *accessibility.* Effective voice systems are easy to use, well advertised, comprehensible, open processes. Information is publicized on how to file a complaint. Indeed, research has found that employees view this feature as a key attribute of an effective dispute-handling system.[8]

The third criterion of effective voice systems is *correctness;* that is, the system should provide the "right" answer to problems by being unbiased, thorough, and effective. The more correct a system, the more likely it is that (1) the complainant can provide relevant input about the problem, (2) the organization can investigate and call for more information if it needs it, (3) a system exists for classifying and coding information in order to determine the nature of the problem, (4) employees can appeal lower-level decisions, and (5) both procedures and outcomes make good sense to most employees.[9]

A fourth criterion is *responsiveness.* At the most basic level, responsive systems let individuals know that their input has been received. Thus IBM's "Speak Up" program requires the manager of the function in question to prepare a written response to the employee within 3 days or face severe sanctions. Responsive systems provide timely responses, are backed by management commitment, are designed to fit an organization's culture, provide tangible results, involve participants in the decision-making process, and give those who manage the system sufficient clout to ensure that it works effectively.

Finally, effective voice systems are *nonpunitive.* This is essential if employees are to trust the system. Individuals must be able to present problems, identify concerns, and challenge the organization in such a way that they are not punished for providing this input, even if the issues raised are sensitive and highly politicized. If the input concerns wrongdoing or malfeasance, the individual's identity must be protected so that direct or indirect retribution cannot occur. Employees as well as managers must be protected.[10]

Table 13-2

FORMS OF UNION SECURITY AND THEIR LEGAL STATUS IN RIGHT-TO-WORK STATES

	Legal	Illegal
Closed shop Individual must join the union that represents employees in order to be considered for employment.		X
Union shop As a condition of continued employment, an individual must join the union that represents employees after a probationary period (typically a minimum of 30 days).		X
Preferential shop Union members are given preference in hiring.		X
Agency shop Employees need not join the union that represents them, but, in lieu of dues, they must pay a service charge for representation.		X
Maintenance of membership Employee must remain a member of the union once he or she joins.		X
Checkoff Employee may request that union dues be deducted from his or her pay and be sent directly to the union.	X	

Now let's examine how the theory of procedural justice can be applied in a number of areas of employee relations.

ADMINISTRATION OF THE COLLECTIVE BARGAINING AGREEMENT

To many union and management officials, the real test of effective labor relations comes after the agreement is signed, that is, in its day-to-day administration. At that point, the major concern of the union is to obtain in practice the employee rights that management has granted on paper. The major concern of management is to establish its right to manage the business and to keep operations running.[11] A key consideration for both is the form of union security that governs conditions of employment.

Union Security Clauses

Section 14b of the Taft-Hartley Act enables states to enact right-to-work laws that prohibit compulsory union membership (after a probationary period) as a condition of continued employment. Table 13-2 illustrates the forms that such union security provisions can take and indicates that most of them are illegal in the 21 states that have passed right-to-work laws.

Agency shop agreements appear in about 12 percent of all collective bargaining contracts.[12] May the "service charge" for representation be used to pay for activities such as lobbying for pro-labor legislation, organizing efforts, and political activities *in addition to* collective bargaining? Non-union-member employees of American Telephone & Telegraph Company sued the Communications Workers of American (CWA) over this issue. The Supreme Court ruled that a union may be violating the rights of nonmembers who are required to pay

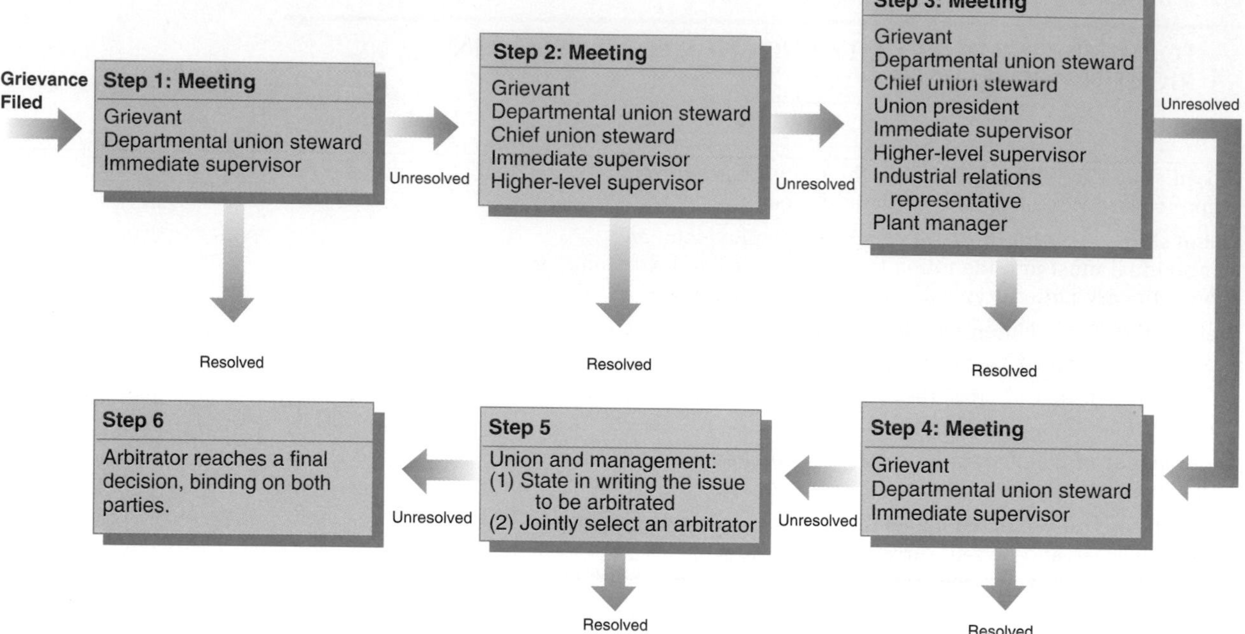

Figure 13-1
Example of a formal grievance procedure in a unionized firm.

agency fees for union representation if it uses those fees for political and other activities not directly related to collective bargaining. How much money goes to activities other than collective bargaining? At the trial-court level, a federal judge ordered the CWA to rebate 79 percent of the agency fees it had collected one year, because the union could only prove that 21 percent of its collections were devoted to collective bargaining.[13]

Grievance Procedures in the Unionized Firm

Occasionally during the life of a contract, disputes arise about the interpretation of the collective bargaining agreement, potential violations of federal or state law, violations of past practices or company rules, or violations of management's responsibility (e.g., to provide safe and healthy working conditions). In each instance, an aggrieved party may file a grievance. A grievance is an alleged violation of the rights of workers on the job.[14] A formal process known as a *grievance procedure* is then invoked to help the parties resolve the dispute. Grievance procedures are the keystone of industrial relations because of their ability to resolve disputed issues while work continues without litigation, strikes, or other radical dispute resolution strategies.[15]

In addition to providing a formal mechanism for resolving disputes, the grievance procedure defines and narrows the nature of the complaint. Thus each grievance must be expressed in writing. The written grievance identifies the grievant, when the incident leading to the grievance occurred (it could, of course, be ongoing), and where the incident happened (or is happening). The written statement also indicates why the complaint is considered a grievance and what the grievant thinks should be done about the matter.[16] A typical grievance procedure in a unionized firm works as shown in Figure 13-1. As the figure indicates, unresolved grievances proceed progressively to higher and higher levels of management and union representation and culminate in voluntary, binding arbitration. Specific time limits for management's decision and the union's approval are normally imposed at each step, for example, 3 days for each party at step 1, 5 days for each party at steps 2 and 3, and 10 days for each party at step 4.

It also is important to note that many unions have a policy that up to step 3 of the procedure, the grievance "belongs" to the employee. That is, the union will process a grievance through step 2 (and is some cases through step 3) at the grievant's request. However, if the grievance is not settled and reaches step 3, it becomes the union's grievance. At that point, the union will decide whether or not the grievance has merit and whether additional time and financial resources of the union should be spent in carrying it forward. Indeed, many local unions let the membership vote formally to decide whether to take a grievance to arbitration.[17] They do this for good reason: the grievance process is expensive.

Costing a Grievance

One study found that to process 500 grievances (the actual number filed in a single West Coast union local over a 1-year period), 4580 labor-hours were required, or an average of 9.1 hours per grievance. Assume that the average total compensation (wages plus benefits) for the grievant, union, and management representatives is $135 per hour (in 1997 dollars), or more than $1200 per grievance. This translates into an annual cost of $600,000 to resolve 500 grievances. However, this figure is conservative, for it reflects only the direct time used for formal meetings on grievances. It does not include such other factors as preparation time, informal meetings, clerical time, and administrative overhead for management and the union.[18] In complex grievance cases that proceed all the way to arbitration (step 6 in Figure 13-1), the cost to the company or union may exceed $6700 per grievance (in 1997 dollars).[19]

Common Grievances and Their Resolution

For the West Coast local just mentioned, the majority of grievances were filed over disciplinary issues: the introductory disciplinary memorandum, suspensions, and termination. Seniority, the basis of many individual work rights for union employees, is often the basis for a grievance. Beyond that, no single category accounts for a large proportion of the grievances filed.

The majority of grievances filed are resolved without resorting to arbitration. Of these, unions and management each win about half the time. However, unions tend to win more grievances related to such issues as the denial of sick benefits, termination, transfer, suspension, and disciplinary memoranda. Ordinarily, the burden of proof in a grievance proceeding is on the union. Since fewer issues of interpretation are involved in the areas that unions usually win, this pattern of grievance resolution is not surprising.[20]

In summary, there are two key advantages to the grievance procedure: (1) it ensures that the complaints and problems of workers can be heard, rather than simply allowed to fester, and (2) grievance procedures provide formal mechanisms to ensure due process and procedural justice for all parties. Research indicates that employees who have access to such a system are more willing to continue working for their organizations after filing a grievance than are employees who do not have access to such a system. On the other hand, the job performance of grievance filers is likely to be lower after they learn the outcome of their grievances.[21]

In addition, the process is not completely objective in that factors other than merit sometimes determine the outcome of a grievance. Some of these factors include the cost of granting a grievance, the perceived need for management to placate disgruntled workers or to settle large numbers of grievances in order to expedite the negotiation process,[22] and the grievant's work history (good performance, long tenure, few disciplinary incidents).[23]

What is the role of the line manager in all this? To know and understand the collective bargaining contract, as well as federal and state labor laws. Above all, whether you agree or disagree with the terms of the contract, it is legally binding on both labor and management. Respect its provisions, and manage according to the spirit as well as the letter of the contract.

Does a High Number of Grievances Indicate Poor Labor Relations?

One study examined the impact of a fact-finding program on the grievance process over a 6-year period. A fact-finding team (made up of an appointed union representative and a supervisor, neither of whom could be a party to the grievance under consideration) was given authority to settle disputes in a public utility in the western United States. The program had three objectives: (1) to encourage a more open system of dispute resolution by requiring the revelation of a series of stipulated facts (neither party could subsequently raise a fact not raised in the fact-finding stage), (2) to encourage resolution of disputes at lower levels in the grievance process, and (3) to resolve disputes in a more timely manner.

Measures were obtained in the utility in question as well as in another western utility in which no such intervention occurred. Monthly data were collected for 36 months prior to the intervention, 24 months during it, and 12 months after its removal. All grievances filed by employees of both utilities over the 6-year period (4130 grievances) were examined. The results showed that the introduction of fact finding led to an increase in the grievance rate and its removal to a decrease back to the baseline level. Fact finding did not lead to a higher winning percentage for either party, but disputes were resolved at lower levels.

The fact-finding system was discontinued after 2 years at the request of both parties. Management felt it was too expensive and that the benefits of the system did not outweigh its costs. However, the key issue for the union was political—the large difference in authority of the union fact finder (appointed) and the union steward (elected).

Was the program effective? Conventional wisdom suggests that large numbers of grievances signal an unhealthy organizational climate, but these results may suggest the opposite—that a large number of grievances signals the presence of a friendly system that is easily accessible and time-efficient. At a minimum, it seems that high grievance rates do not invariably indicate poor labor relations.[24]

Arbitration

Arbitration is used widely by management and labor to settle disputes arising out of and during the term of a labor contract.[25] As the chapter opening vignette illustrated, it is also being used to resolve employment-related cases. In 1994, for example, the American Arbitration Association handled 60,000 cases.[26] Figure 13-1 shows that compulsory, binding arbitration is the final stage of the grievance process. It is also used as an alternative to a work stoppage, and it is used to ensure labor peace for the duration of a labor contract. Arbitrators may be chosen from a list of qualified people supplied by the American Arbitration Association or the Federal Mediation and Conciliation Service.

Arbitration hearings are quasi-judicial proceedings. Prehearing briefs may be filed by both parties, along with lists of witnesses to be called. Witnesses are cross-examined, and documentary evidence may be introduced. However, *arbitrators are not bound by the formal rules of evidence,* as they would be in a court of law.

Following the hearing, the parties may each submit briefs to reiterate their positions, evidence supporting them, and proposed decisions. The arbitrator then considers the evidence, the contract clause in dispute, and the powers granted the arbitrator under the labor agreement, and issues a decision. In the rare instances where a losing party refuses to honor the arbitrator's decision, the decision can be enforced by taking that party to federal court.[27]

Generally an arbitration award cannot be appealed in court simply because one party believes the arbitrator made a mistake in interpreting an agreement.[28] This was recently affirmed by a full federal appeals court in California. A mechanic had been fired for not properly tightening the lug bolts on the wheels of a Mercedes-Benz. An arbitrator ruled that a 120-day suspension, as had been urged by the man's Machinists Union local, was enough discipline. Following extensive precedent, the court ruled that arbitrator awards are extensions of labor contracts, and court deference is the rule.[29]

PRACTICAL EXAMPLE

FINAL-OFFER ARBITRATION IN MAJOR LEAGUE BASEBALL

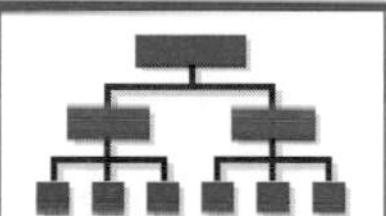

The arbitration process allows players with a minimum level of tenure to submit salary disputes to binding arbitration. The final-offer structure requires both the player and the team to submit a salary figure to the arbitrator, who must then select either the player's or the team's offer. In reaching a decision, the arbitrator must use a set of prescribed criteria, including the player's performance, the player's current salary, the performance of other players in the league, and the amount others are paid.

Several studies have examined the impact of arbitration on perceived equity, motivation, and subsequent performance. Among pitchers, those who lost arbitration allowed more batters to get on base, allowed more earned runs, and struck out fewer batters than did arbitration winners. Further, the size of the difference between salary demands and offers was related to subsequent performance changes (the larger the difference, the worse a player performed), but some of the difference may have been due to player experience (experienced players showed more stable performance from year to year).[30]

Among position players, results indicate that (1) all players perform better prior to arbitration; (2) this increase in performance contributes to the propensity to file for arbitration; (3) players who increase their performance more dramatically than others win arbitration; (4) subsequent performance declines for all players, because exceptionally high performance must eventually regress to the player's average level of ability; and (5) more arbitration losers than winners changed teams and left major league baseball. Even though a greater percentage of losers leave baseball, perceived inequity probably has only a small effect on leaving, because few labor market alternatives exist at these pay levels.[31] These results for pitchers and position players indicate the powerful effects of perceived equity or inequity on subsequent performance.

Grievance Procedures in Nonunion Companies: Workplace Due Process

Grievance arbitration has generally worked well, and this is why many companies have extended it as an option to their nonunion employees. For example, Federal Express Corporation's "guaranteed fair-treatment process" lets employees appeal problems to a peer review board chosen by the worker involved and management. The board rules for employees about half the time. Bosses cannot appeal decisions, but employees can, to a panel of top executives up to and including the chairman of the board.[32] TWA employees take disputes to a panel comprising an arbitrator, a representative from the HR staff, and another employee. One reason for the growing popularity of these programs is that they tend to reduce lawsuits. At Aetna Life & Casualty Company, for example, only 1 of the almost 300 complaints handled by Aetna's program has gone to litigation.[33]

Figure 13-2 illustrates how such a procedure works in one company. This procedure emphasizes the supervisor as a key figure in the resolution of grievances. As a second step, the employee is encouraged to see the department head, an HR representative, or any other member of management. Alternatively, the employee may proceed directly to the roundtable, a body of employee and management representatives who meet biweekly to resolve grievances. Management immediately answers those questions that it can and researches those requiring an in-depth review. The minutes of roundtable meetings, plus the answers to the questions presented, are posted conspicuously on bulletin boards in work areas.[34]

To work effectively, a nonunion grievance procedure should meet three requirements:

1. All employees must know about the procedure and exactly how it operates.
2. Employees must believe that there will be no reprisals taken against them for using it.
3. Management must respond quickly and thoroughly to all grievances.[35]

Workplace due process is one of the fastest-developing trends in industry. In the coming decade, a majority of people-oriented firms are likely to adopt it. But how does a firm begin? Here are four key steps:[36]

1. **Make sure your HR department has lots of expertise in dispute resolution.** It must be able to handle most of the complaints that cannot be resolved by managers and their subordinates; otherwise the "company court" will be inundated with cases. At Bank of America, HR professionals, rather than line managers, investigate cases. They understand the investigation process and

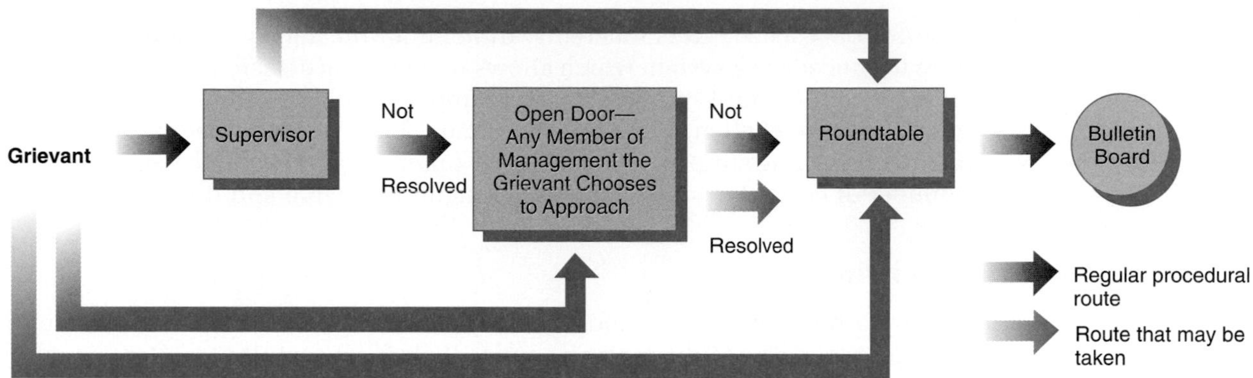

Figure 13-2
Example of a nonunion grievance procedure. This diagram indicates the possible routes a grievant may take to resolve a complaint. The regular procedural route is designed to resolve the grievance at the lowest possible level—the supervisor. However, if the grievant feels uncomfortable approaching the supervisor, the grievance may be presented directly to any level of management via the open-door policy or the roundtable. (*Source:* Reprinted from D. A. Drost & F. P. O'Brien, Are there grievances against your non-union grievance procedure? *Personnel Administrator,* 28(1), 1983, 37. Copyright 1983. Reprinted with permission from *HRMagazine* (formerly *Personnel Administrator*), published by the Society of Human Resource Management, Alexandria, VA.)

the bank's policies better, and they devote the time necessary for a thorough review, which can take as long as a week.[37] At companies such as Polaroid and Citicorp, problem review boards may hear only 12 to 20 cases a year, because of the skill of the HR department in dispute resolution.

2. **Train all managers and supervisors in your company's due process approach.** They simply must know company HR policy because it is the "law" governing company courts and adjudicators. Coach them in how to handle complaints, so that they can resolve problems immediately. And if subordinates take their complaints to the company court, teach your managers to accept reversals as a fact of business life, for in a good due process system, reversals are bound to occur. Three separate studies reported reversal rates that ranged from 20 to 40 percent.[38]

3. **Decide whether you want a panel system or a single adjudicator.** Panel systems enjoy high credibility and, for the panelists, mutual support. About 100 companies, including Bank of America, Control Data, Digital Equipment, and Polaroid, now use peer review panels (the roundtable in Figure 13-2) to resolve disputes over firings, promotions, and disciplinary actions. A panel typically consists of three peers and two management representatives. Most companies do not permit grievants to have outside representation; instead, they provide an HR staff member if help is needed in preparing the case. The panel's decisions are binding on both sides.

   An adjudicator system, in which a single investigator first acts as a fact finder and then changes hats and arbitrates the facts has the advantages of speed, flexibility, and maximum privacy. IBM uses the single adjudicator approach.

4. **Make your due process system visible.** At a minimum, the system should be described in the employee handbook and publicized by HR specialists. SmithKline Beecham goes even further. Periodically, it features its grievance procedure on closed-circuit televisions for all company employees.

The trend toward workplace due process represents an effort by companies to broaden employees' rights in disciplinary matters. A position paper at

Control Data stated: "It is inherently difficult for the management power structure to concede to a system which allows review of its decision making. . . . But any concept of employee justice is incomplete without the presence of some mechanism to challenge the power system."[39] Due process mechanisms build an open, trusting atmosphere; help deter union organizing; and stem the rising number of costly lawsuits claiming wrongful discharge and discrimination.

Discipline

Make no mistake about it: most employees want to conduct themselves in a manner acceptable to the company and to their fellow employees. Occasionally, problems of absenteeism, poor work performance, or rule violations arise. When informal conversations or coaching sessions fail to resolve these problems, formal disciplinary action is called for.

Employee discipline is the final area of contract administration that we will consider. Typically, the "management rights" clause of the collective bargaining agreement retains for management the authority to impose *reasonable* rules for workplace conduct and to discipline employees for *just cause.* As developed in thousands of arbitration cases over the past 60 years, the concept of just cause requires an employer not only to produce persuasive evidence of an employee's liability or negligence, but also to provide the employee a fair hearing and to impose a penalty appropriate to the proven offense.[40] Unions rarely object to employee discipline, provided that (1) it is applied consistently, (2) the rules are publicized clearly, and (3) the rules are considered reasonable.

Discipline is indispensable to management control. Ideally, it should serve as a corrective mechanism to create and maintain a productive, responsive workforce.[41] Unfortunately, some managers go to great lengths to avoid using discipline. To some extent this is understandable, for discipline is one of the hardest HR actions to face. Managers may avoid imposing discipline because of (1) ignorance of organizational rules, (2) fear of formal grievances, or (3) fear of losing the friendship of employees. Yet failure to administer discipline can result in implied acceptance or approval of the offense. Thereafter, problems may become more frequent or severe, and discipline becomes that much more difficult to administer.

As an alternative, some companies are experimenting with a technique called "positive discipline." On its face, it sounds a lot like traditional discipline dressed up in euphemisms. It works as follows: Employees who commit offenses first get an oral "reminder" rather than a "reprimand." Then comes a written reminder, followed by a paid day off—called a "decision-making leave day" (a suspension, in traditional parlance). After a pensive day off, the employee must agree in writing (or orally at some union shops) that he or she will behave responsibly for the next year. The paid day off is a one-shot chance at reform. The process is documented, and if the employee does not change, termination follows.

How has positive discipline worked? At Tampa Electric, which has used it for over 10 years, more employees have improved their job performance than have left the company. Says one power station manager: "Before, we punished employees and treated them worse and worse and expected them to act better. I don't ever recall suspending someone who came back ready to change."[42] These arguments for not imposing punishment are persuasive. But evidence also indicates that discipline (that is, punishment) may be beneficial.[43] Consider the following:

- Discipline may alert the marginal employee to his or her low performance and result in a change in behavior.
- Discipline may send a signal to other employees regarding expected levels of performance and standards of behavior.
- If the discipline is perceived as legitimate by other employees, it may increase motivation, morale, and performance.

In fact, statistical reanalyses of the original Hawthorne experiments suggest that managerial discipline was the major factor in increased rates of output.[44] Department managers in a retail store chain who used informal warnings, formal warnings, and dismissals more frequently than their peers had higher departmental performance ratings (in terms of annual cost and sales data and ratings by higher-level managers). This relationship held even when length of service was taken into account. More frequent use of sanctions was associated with improved performance. Why is this so?

The answer may lie in social learning theory.[45] *Individuals in groups look to others to learn appropriate behaviors and attitudes.* They learn them by modeling the behavior of others, by adopting standard operating procedures, and by following group norms. Individuals whose attitudes or behaviors violate these norms may cause problems. Tolerance of such behavior by the supervisor may threaten the group by causing feelings of uncertainty and unfairness. On the other hand, management actions that are seen as maintaining legitimate group standards may instill feelings of fairness and result in improved performance. Failure to invoke sanctions may lead to a loss of management control and unproductive employee behavior.[46] Finally, do not underestimate the *symbolic* value of disciplinary actions, especially since punitive behavior tends to make a lasting impression on employees.[47]

Progressive Discipline

Many firms, both unionized and nonunionized, follow a procedure of progressive discipline that proceeds from an oral warning to a written warning to a suspension to dismissal. However, to administer discipline without at the same time engendering resentment by the disciplined employee, managers should follow what Douglas McGregor called the "red-hot-stove rule." According to that rule, discipline should be:

Immediate. Just like touching a hot stove, where feedback is immediate, there should be no misunderstanding about why discipline was imposed. People are disciplined not because of who they are (personality) but because of what they did (behavior).

With Warning. Small children know that if they touch a hot stove, they will be burned. Likewise, employees must know very clearly what the consequences of undesirable work behavior will be. They must be given adequate warning.

Consistent. Every time a person touches a red-hot stove, he or she gets burned. Likewise, if discipline is to be perceived as fair, it must be administered consistently, given similar circumstances surrounding the undesirable behavior. Consistency among individual managers across the organization is

DATE: April 14, 1997

TO: J. Hartwig
FROM: D. Curtis
SUBJECT: Written Warning

On this date you were 30 minutes late to work with no justification for your tardiness. A similar offense occurred last Friday. At that time you were told that failure to report for work on schedule will not be condoned. I now find it necessary to tell you in writing that you must report to work on time. Failure to do so will result in your dismissal from employment. Please sign below that you have read and that you understand this warning

[Name] [Date]

Figure 13-3
Sample written warning of disciplinary action.

essential, but evidence indicates that (1) line managers vary considerably in their attitudes about discipline,[48] and (2) they tend to be less concerned with consistency than with satisfying immediate needs within their work units.[49]

Impersonal. A hot stove is blind to who touches it. So also, managers cannot play favorites by disciplining subordinates they do not like while allowing the same behavior to go unpunished for those they do like.

A recent review of arbitration cases and case law suggests two other characteristics of a legally defensible progressive discipline system: (1) *Allow an employee the opportunity to respond,* and (2) *allow employees a reasonable period of time to improve their performance.*[50]

Documenting Performance-Related Incidents

Documentation is a fact of organizational life for most managers. While such paperwork is never pleasant, it is necessary, and in the case of performance-related incidents should conform to the following guidelines:

- Describe what led up to the incident—the problem and the setting. Is this a first offense or part of a pattern?
- Describe what actually happened, and be specific: that is, include names, dates, times, witnesses, and other pertinent facts.
- Describe what must be done to correct the situation.
- State the consequences of further violations.

Conclude the warning by obtaining the employee's signature confirming that he or she has read and understands the warning. A sample written warning is shown in Figure 13-3. Note how it includes each of the ingredients just described.

The Disciplinary Interview

Generally, such interviews are held for one of two reasons: (1) over issues of *workplace conduct,* such as attendance or punctuality; or (2) over issues of *job performance,* such as low productivity. Disciplinary interviews tend to be very legalistic. As an example, consider the following scenario:

You are a first-line supervisor at a unionized facility. You suspect that one of your subordinates, Steve Fox, has been distorting his time reports to misrepresent his daily starting time. While some of the evidence is sketchy, you know that Fox's time reports are false. Accompanied by an industrial relations representative, you decide to confront Fox directly in a disciplinary interview. However, before you can begin the meeting, Fox announces, "I'd appreciate it if a coworker of mine could be present during this meeting. If a coworker cannot be present, I refuse to participate." Your reaction to this startling request is to:

a. Ask Fox which coworker he desires and reconvene the meeting once the employee is present.
b. Deny his request and order him to participate or face immediate discipline for insubordination.
c. Terminate the meeting with no further discussion.
d. Ignore the request and proceed with the meeting, hoping that Fox will participate anyway.
e. Inform Fox that, as his supervisor, you are a coworker and attempt to proceed with the meeting.

Unless your reaction was *a* or *c*, you have probably committed a violation of the National Labor Relations Act.[51]

In *NLRB v. J. Weingarten, Inc.*, the Supreme Court ruled that a *union* employee has the right to demand that a union representative be present at an investigatory interview that the employee reasonably believes may result in disciplinary action.[52] However, in *NLRB v. Sears, Roebuck and Co.* (1985), the Court overturned an earlier decision, ruling that *Weingarten* rights do not extend to nonunion employees.[53] Following is a summary of the Weingarten mandate:

1. The employee must *request* representation; the employer has no obligation to offer it voluntarily. If such a request is made, the union representative may meet with the employee privately before the investigatory interview takes place.[54]
2. The employee must reasonably believe that the investigation may result in disciplinary action taken against him or her.
3. The employer is not obligated to carry on the interview or to justify its refusal to do so. The employer may simply cancel the interview and thus effectively disallow union or coworker representation.
4. The employer has no duty to bargain with any union representative during the interview, and the union representative may not limit the employer's questioning.[55]

If the National Labor Relations Board determines that these rights were violated and that an employee subsequently was disciplined for conduct that was the subject of the unlawful interview, the board will issue a "make-whole" remedy. This may include (1) restitution of back pay, (2) an order expunging from the employee's personnel records any notation of related discipline, or (3) a cease-and-desist order. To avoid these kinds of problems, top management must decide what company policy will be in such cases, communicate that policy to first-line supervisors, and give them clear, concise instructions regarding their responsibilities should an employee request representation at an investigatory interview.[56]

Having satisfied their legal burden, how should supervisors actually conduct the disciplinary interview? They must do *nine* things well:

1. Come to the interview with as many facts as possible. Check the employee's personnel file for previous offenses as well as for evidence of exemplary behavior and performance.
2. Conduct the interview in a quiet, private place. "Praise in public, discipline in private" is a good rule to remember. Whether the employee's attitude is truculent or contrite, recognize that he or she will be apprehensive. In contrast to other interviews, where your first objective is to dispel any fears and help the person relax, a "light touch" is inappropriate here.
3. Avoid aggressive accusations. State the facts in a simple, straightforward way. Be sure that any fact you use is accurate, and never rely on hearsay, rumor, or unconfirmed guesswork.
4. Be sure that the employee understands the rule in question and the reason it exists.
5. Allow the employee to make a full defense, even if you think he or she has none. If any point the employee makes has merit, tell him or her so and take it into consideration in your final decision.
6. Stay cool and calm; treat the subordinate as an adult. Never use foul language or touch the subordinate. Such behaviors may be misinterpreted or grossly distorted at a later date.
7. If you made a mistake, be big enough to admit it.
8. Consider extenuating circumstances, and allow for honest mistakes on the part of the subordinate.
9. Even when corrective discipline is required, try to express confidence in the subordinate's worth as a person and ability to perform acceptably in the future. Rather than dwelling on the past, which you cannot change, focus on the future, which you can.

Employment-at-Will

For the more than 70 percent of U.S. workers who are not covered by a collective bargaining agreement or an individual employment contract, dismissal is an ever-present possibility. *Employment-at-will* is created when an employee agrees to work for an employer but there is no specification of how long the parties expect the agreement to last. Under a century-old common law in the United States, employment relationships of indefinite duration can, in general, be terminated at the whim of either party.[57] Furthermore, under certain situations, successful victims of unjust dismissal can collect sizable punitive and compensatory damages from their former employers. An analysis of 120 wrongful discharge cases that went to trial in California found that the average salary of fired employees was $36,254. Plaintiffs won 67.5 percent of their cases and were awarded an average of $646,855. About 40 percent of the awards were for punitive damages.[58] It is important to note, however, that initial jury awards, while frequently high, are almost always reduced after trial, according to a study by the Rand Institute for Civil Justice. Half of all damage awards in California, for example, are for less than $177,000.[59]

COMPANY EXAMPLE

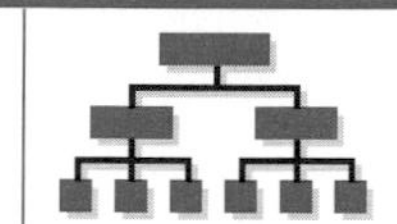

FIRED EMPLOYEE SHOWS CHARACTER DEFAMATION[60]

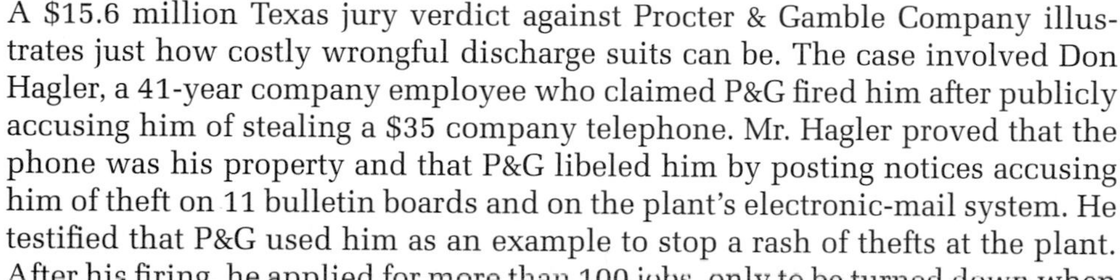

A $15.6 million Texas jury verdict against Procter & Gamble Company illustrates just how costly wrongful discharge suits can be. The case involved Don Hagler, a 41-year company employee who claimed P&G fired him after publicly accusing him of stealing a $35 company telephone. Mr. Hagler proved that the phone was his property and that P&G libeled him by posting notices accusing him of theft on 11 bulletin boards and on the plant's electronic-mail system. He testified that P&G used him as an example to stop a rash of thefts at the plant. After his firing, he applied for more than 100 jobs, only to be turned down when prospective employers learned why he had been fired by P&G. The state court jury agreed with Mr. Hagler and awarded him $1.6 million in actual damages and $14 million in punitive damages.

In recent years, several important exceptions to the "at-will" doctrine have emerged. These exceptions provide important protections for workers. The first—and most important—is legislative. Federal laws limit an employer's right to terminate at-will employees for such reasons as age, race, sex, religion, national origin, union activity, reporting of unsafe working conditions, or disability.[61] However, employment-at-will is primarily a matter of state law.[62]

Such suits are now permitted in 46 states, and in many of them, courts have shown a willingness to apply traditional causes of action—such as defamation, fraud, intentional infliction of emotional distress, and invasion of privacy—to this area of employment law.[63]

State courts have carved out three judicial exceptions. The first is a *public policy exception.* That is, an employee may not be fired because he or she refuses to commit an illegal act, such as perjury or price fixing. Second, when an employer has promised not to terminate an employee except for unsatisfactory job performance or other good cause, the courts will insist that the employer carry out that promise. This include *implied* promises (such as oral promises and implied covenants of good faith and fair dealing) as well as explicit ones.[64] For example, in *Fortune v. National Cash Register Company,* a salesperson (Mr. Fortune) was fired after he sold a large quantity of cash registers. Under the terms of his contract, Mr. Fortune would not receive a portion of his commission until the cash registers were delivered. He claimed he was fired before delivery was made to avoid payment of the full $92,000 commission on the order. The court held that terminating Mr. Fortune solely to deprive him of his commission would breach the covenant of good faith implied in every contract.[65]

The third exception allows employees to seek damages for outrageous acts related to termination, including character defamation. Such acts include so-called retaliatory discharge cases, where a worker is fired for actions ranging from filing a workers' compensation claim to reporting safety violations to government agencies. The Supreme Court has ruled that where state law permits (as it does in 34 states), union as well as nonunion employees have the right to sue over their dismissals, even if they are covered by a collective bargaining contract that provides a grievance procedure and remedies.[66]

For some employers, however, relief is in sight. Since 1988, the California Supreme Court has disallowed thousands of lawsuits by employees seeking punitive damages for wrongful discharge.[67] On the other hand, courts in many states—notably Illinois, Massachusetts, Michigan, and New York—expressly permit punitive damages in certain instances.[68]

To avoid potential charges of unjust dismissal, managers should scrutinize each facet of the HR management system. They should look for example, at the following:

Recruitment. Beware of creating implicit or explicit contracts in recruitment advertisements. Ensure that no job duration is implied and that employment is not guaranteed or "permanent."

Interviewing. Phrases intended to entice a candidate into accepting a position, such as "employment security," "lifelong relationship" with the company, "permanent" hiring, and so forth, can create future problems.

Applications. Include a statement that describes the rights of the at-will employee, as well as those of the employer. However, do not be so strident that you scare off applicants.

Handbooks and manuals. A major source of company policy statements regarding "permanent" employment and discharge for "just cause" is the employee handbook. According to a growing number of state laws, such handbook language constitutes an implied contract for employment. Courts have upheld an employer's prerogative to refrain from making any promises to employees regarding how a termination will be conducted or the conditions under which they may be fired. However, if an employer does make such a promise of job security, whether implied verbally or in writing in an employment document or employee handbook, the employer is bound by that promise.[69]

Performance appraisals. Include training and written instructions for all raters, and use systems that minimize subjectivity to the greatest extent possible. Give employees the right to read and comment on their appraisals, and require them to sign an acknowledgment that they have done so whether or not they agree with the contents of the appraisal.[70] Encourage managers to give "honest" appraisals; if an employee is not meeting minimum standards of performance, "tell it like it is" rather than leading the employee to believe that his or her performance is satisfactory. Document employee misconduct and poor performance, and provide a progressive disciplinary policy, thereby building a record establishing "good cause."[71]

Employment Contracts

As noted earlier, employees with contracts (bargained collectively or individually) are not at-will employees. More and more executives, professionals, and even middle managers are demanding contracts. A survey of 560 of the nation's largest companies revealed that 48 percent of them have written understandings with their high-ranking employees.[72] While getting a contract can be a wise career move, when is the proper time to ask for one—and how?

You should consider asking for a contract in any business where the competition for talent is intense, where ideas are at a premium, or when the conditions of your employment differ in unusual ways from a company's standard practices. A contract assures you of a job and a minimum salary for some period of time, usually 2 to 3 years, during which you agree not to quit. Other typical provisions include your title, compensation (salary, procedures for salary increases, bonuses), benefits, stock options, length of vacation, the circumstances under which you can be fired, and severance pay. However, with all these perks come a handful of restrictive covenants, or clauses, that basically limit your ability to work elsewhere. For example:[73]

- A *no-solicitation* clause prohibits you from recruiting key clients or employees away from your former employer for 1 or 2 years.
- *Payback* clauses require that you not take another job until you have repaid the company any expenses incurred in your relocation and recruitment.
- Less common is a clause that mandates that the company must have an opportunity to *match* any employment offer that you get. If the employer matches a competing offer, you must remain.
- A *no-disclosure* clause prohibits you from divulging trade secrets or other proprietary information to outsiders during your employment at a company or after you leave.
- A *no-compete* clause bars you from working for a competitor for 6 months to 2 years. The clause is valid whether you are fired, your job is eliminated, or you leave voluntarily.

No-compete agreements are most common in such highly competitive industries as computers, pharmaceuticals, toys, biotechnology, and electronics. However, whether or not a contract has been signed, executives are still required to maintain all trade secrets with which their employers have entrusted them. This obligation, often called a "fiduciary duty of loyalty," cannot keep the executive out of the job market, but it does provide the former employer with legal recourse if an executive joins a competitor and tells all. Indeed, that is precisely what McDonald's claimed when it succeeded in muzzling a former market researcher.[74]

COMPANY EXAMPLE

McLITIGATION

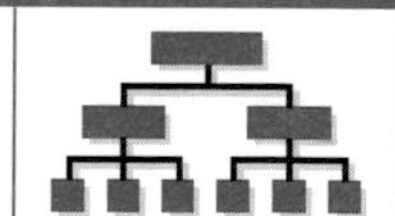

The former employee (we'll call him McEx) was an expert in market research. He quit to join a competitor a few years ago, taking with him a large batch of papers. McDonald's filed suit, alleging that he walked away with company secrets.

Before filing suit and within a few days of his leaving, McDonald's sent a letter to McEx warning him not to divulge any "confidential information" regarding activities such as marketing, advertising, training methods, profit margins, raw materials prices, selling prices, and operating procedures.

The letter further requested a meeting with McEx, during which he would be asked to return any written materials he had taken from McDonald's and also to sign an agreement not to divulge any company trade secrets to his new employer.

When McEx declined to attend the meeting, McDonald's promptly filed suit in McEx's new home state. The company managed to win a temporary restraining order that McEx says effectively meant he could not perform any market research for his new employer. He was thereafter relegated to less important work.

Finally, about 6 months after the suit was filed, the case was settled out of court. McEx agreed not to use information gained on the job with McDonald's in his new job. But the issue had become academic. Disenchanted with his new "nonjob" and aware that his new employer was viewing him more as a problem than as an asset, McEx left his new job. He is now employed by another food chain, not involving fast-food restaurants. In short, companies are now playing hardball when it comes to the disclosure of trade secrets. For both parties, the stakes are high.

Companies say they need no-compete agreements now that growing numbers of acquisitions, bankruptcies, mergers, and layoffs regularly set loose employees with access to trade secrets and other sensitive information. Sometimes, however, judges find that the agreements go too far in restraining employees. In such cases they will modify terms to make them less restrictive (e.g., with respect to geographical boundaries or the length of time an employee is barred from competing).[75]

From the company's perspective, it is important to recognize that employment agreements are governed by state law. Thus a company with facilities in multiple states may have to contend with multiple interpretations of the same agreement. To avoid that, firms generally include a choice-of-law provision, which designates that the laws of a particular state will be used to interpret the contract. Finally, a contract should state that it reflects the entire agreement of the parties, and can be amended only in writing signed by both parties. Doing so prevents employee claims that the employer made oral promises or agreements that expanded his or her rights.[76]

Now let's go back to the negotiation process for employment contracts. In dealing with a prospective employer, do not raise the issue of a contract until you have been offered a job and have thoroughly discussed the terms of your employment. How do you broach the subject? Calmly. Say, for example, "I'd appreciate a letter confirming these arrangements." If the employer asks why, you might point out that both of you are used to putting business agreements on paper and that it is to your mutual benefit to keep all these details straight.[77]

Here are some tips on how to negotiate an employment contract:

1. Keep the tone upbeat. Do not use the words "I" and "you"; talk about "we"—as though you are already aboard.
2. Decide beforehand on three or four "make-or-break" issues (e.g., salary, job assignment, location). These are your "need-to-haves." Also make a list of secondary issues, so-called nice-to-haves (e.g., company car, sign-on bonus).

3. Negotiate the entire package at one time. Do not keep coming back to nit-pick.
4. Be flexible (except on your make-or-break issues); let the company win on some things.

Once you receive the proposed contract, have an attorney review it before you sign. Remember: employment contracts are legally enforceable documents.

Termination

Layoffs were discussed in Chapter 9. The focus here is on how to terminate employees when it becomes necessary to do so. Termination is one of the most difficult tasks a manager has to perform. As noted in the discussion of employment-at-will, disgruntled former employees are winning about two-thirds of court cases contesting their dismissals. Clearly, there is room for improvement on the part of managers. For those fired, the perception of inequity, of procedural injustice, is often what drives them to court.

Sometimes termination is done for disciplinary reasons, sometimes for economic reasons (i.e., downsizing). It is not an infrequent occurrence, since some 2 million workers in the United States are fired every year,[78] and that does not include large-scale layoffs, which claimed 459,000 U.S. jobs in 1996.[79] With respect to layoffs, while the Plant Closing Law of 1988 requires employers of more than 100 workers to grant 60 days' written notice before closing a plant or before laying off more than one-third of a workforce in excess of 150 people, very few firms provide any training to supervisors on how to conduct terminations.

While termination may be traumatic for the employee, it is often no less so for the boss. Faced with saying the words "Your services are no longer required," even the strongest person can experience having the "shakes," sleepless nights, and sweaty palms.[80] So how should termination be handled? Certainly not the way it was at one company that was trying to downsize. At 8:30 A.M. all employees were ordered to their offices. Between then and 10:30 A.M., like angels of death, managers accompanied by security guards knocked on doors, brusquely informed employees that their services were no longer required, gave affected employees a box in which to place their personal articles, and asked the employees to leave the premises within 15 minutes, accompanied by a security guard. Is this procedural justice? Certainly not.

As an alternative, more humane procedure, companies should familiarize all supervisors with company policies and provide a termination checklist to use when conducting dismissals. One such checklist is shown in Figure 13-4.

Before deciding to dismiss an employee, managers should conduct a detailed review of all relevant facts, including the employee's side of the story. To ensure consistent treatment, the supervisor should also examine how similar cases have been handled in the past. Once the decision to terminate has been made, the termination interview should minimize the trauma for the affected employee. Prior to conducting such an interview, the supervisor should be prepared to answer three basic questions: who, when, and where.

Who. The responsibility for terminating rests with the manager of the individual who is to be released. No one else has the credibility to convey this difficult message.

THE TERMINATION CHECKLIST

Documentation

______ If the job is eliminated, gather supporting evidence of a company or department reduction in head-count.

______ If poor performance is the reason, the file should contain copies of several successive poor appraisals that were transmitted to (and usually signed by) the candidate at the time they were prepared.

Clearances

______ Who needs to approve the termination?

Prior Notices

______ Safeguards to prevent leaks to the public
______ Key staff members
______ Board members
______ Key customers
______ Regulatory agency officers

Precautions for New Leaks

______ Ignore the leak
______ Advance the date of termination to immediate
______ Delay the termination with no comment

Terms of Termination

______ Resignation
______ Transfer to special assignment
______ Early retirement
______ Outright termination

Legal Precautions

______ Salary
______ Bonuses
______ Benefits
______ Other obligations
______ Scientists and inventors
______ No-compete agreements

Public Announcements

______ Should it be a standard press release?
______ What should the content of the statement be?

Personal Considerations

______ Medical data
______ Significant dates
______ Family circumstances
______ Personal emotional state

Figure 13-4
The termination checklist. (*Source:* D. H. Sweet, Outplacement. In W. F. Cascio (ed.), *Human resource planning, employment, and placement.* Washington, DC: Bureau of National Affairs, 1989, pp. 246, 247.)

When. This decision may be crucial to the success of the termination process. First of all, consider personal situations—birthdays, anniversaries, family illnesses. Further, most experts agree that Friday is the worst day of the week for terminations. That gives the employee the entire weekend to brood before he or she can take any positive action.[81]

Where. Neutral territory—not the manager's or employee's office. The firing manager should arrange a neutral location so that each party is easily able to leave after the interview.

Following these activities, the firing manager should follow five rules for the termination interview:[82]

1. **Present the situation in a clear, concise, and final manner.** Do not confuse the message to be delivered, and do not drag it out. Say, for example, "Tom,

The Termination Interview

- ______ Think through details.
- ______ When? Not late on Friday.
- ______ Who? It's the line manager's responsibility.
- ______ Where? Best place is in a neutral area or the candidate's office.
- ______ Outplacement consultant on hand?
- ______ Termination letter prepared?

Orderly Transitions of Commitments

- ______ Reassign internal assignments and projects.
- ______ External activities to be reassigned:
  - Customer servicing
  - Convention or professional meetings
  - Speeches and public relations commitments
  - Civic and professional commitments
  - Club memberships
  - Board memberships, e.g., of subsidiaries

Regrouping the Staff

- ______ Announcement to immediate colleagues and support staff
- ______ What they are to be told
- ______ Transfer of assignments
- ______ References
- ______ Reassurances

Termination Letters

- ______ Written evidence to verify the termination
- ______ Summary of important information the candidates may not have listened to, or remembered
- ______ Brief and businesslike confirmation of the facts and the details
- ______ Include:
- ______ • Termination date
  - Severance or bridging pay allowance
  - Vacation pay
- ______ Continuation of benefits:
  - Regular benefits
  - Special benefits, such as pension rights
- ______ Job search support:
  - Logistical
  - Financial
  - Outplacement
  - Transfer of responsibilities
  - Continuation of responsibilities
  - Return of company property
  - Legal documents
  - Conditions of termination?

Source: Reprinted with permission from James J. Gallagher, chairman, J. J. Gallagher Associates, New York, N.Y.

Figure 13-4
(cont.)

no doubt you are aware that the organization has eliminated some jobs, and one of them is yours." Remember: spend only a few minutes, do not make excuses, do not bargain, and do not compromise. Get to the point quickly and succinctly. As one outplacement executive noted: "It's not cruel to cut clean."[83]

2. **Avoid debates or a rehash of the past.** Arguments about past performance may only compound bad feelings that already exist. Do not shift responsibility; the person is your responsibility, and you must accept that as a fact.

3. **Never talk down to the individual.** Your objective should be to remove as much of the emotion and trauma as possible. Emphasize that it is a situation

that is not working and that the decision is made. It is a business decision—do not make excuses or apologies. Be tactful, and by all means, avoid insulting (and unlawful) remarks, such as "At your age I'd be thinking of early retirement."

4. **Be empathetic but not compromising.** "I'm sorry that this has to happen, but the decisions are made. We are going to provide assistance to you [or to each of the people affected]."
5. **What is the next step?** "I'm going to give you this letter outlining the severance arrangements. I suggest you take the rest of the day off and plan on being here tomorrow at 9 A.M. to talk with the benefits people. Also, we have engaged a very successful outplacement firm, and I would like to introduce you to Fred Martin, who, if you wish, will be working with you through your transition."[84]

Be prepared for a variety of reactions from disbelief to silent acceptance to rage. The key is to remain calm and focus on helping the employee confront the reality of the situation. This is best done by maintaining your distance and composure. It does no good to argue or cry along with the employee.

After terminations or layoffs, the work attitudes and behaviors of remaining employees ("survivors") may suffer. If the layoff (or its management, or both) is perceived to be unjust, survivors are likely to feel angry. In addition, they may feel guilty that they, rather than their laid-off coworkers, could have been dismissed just as easily. This layoff-induced stress, with its attendant feelings of anger, guilt, and job insecurity, can be reduced in two ways. One, provide extra social support (e.g., from coworkers and supervisors) to those survivors who are perceived as especially "at risk." Two, provide outplacement support to those who are dismissed; organizations that do so enjoy, as a secondary benefit, reduced postlayoff stress among survivors.[85]

Finally, public disclosure of termination practices (e.g., in the case of layoffs) may actually help displaced employees, since it assures potential employers that economic factors—not individual shortcomings—caused the dismissals.[86] Having examined a very public issue, termination, let us now turn our attention to a related issue, employee privacy.

EMPLOYEE PRIVACY AND ETHICAL ISSUES

Privacy refers to the interest employees have in controlling the use that is made of their personal information and in being able to engage in behavior free from regulation or surveillance.[87] Attention centers on three main issues: the kind of information collected and retained about individuals, how that information is used, and the extent to which it can be disclosed to others. These issues often lead to ethical dilemmas for managers, that is, situations that have the potential to result in a breach of acceptable behavior.

But what is "acceptable" behavior? The difficulty lies in maintaining a proper balance between the common good and personal freedom, between the legitimate business needs of an organization and a worker's feelings of dignity and worth.[88] Although it is not possible to prescribe the *content* of ethical

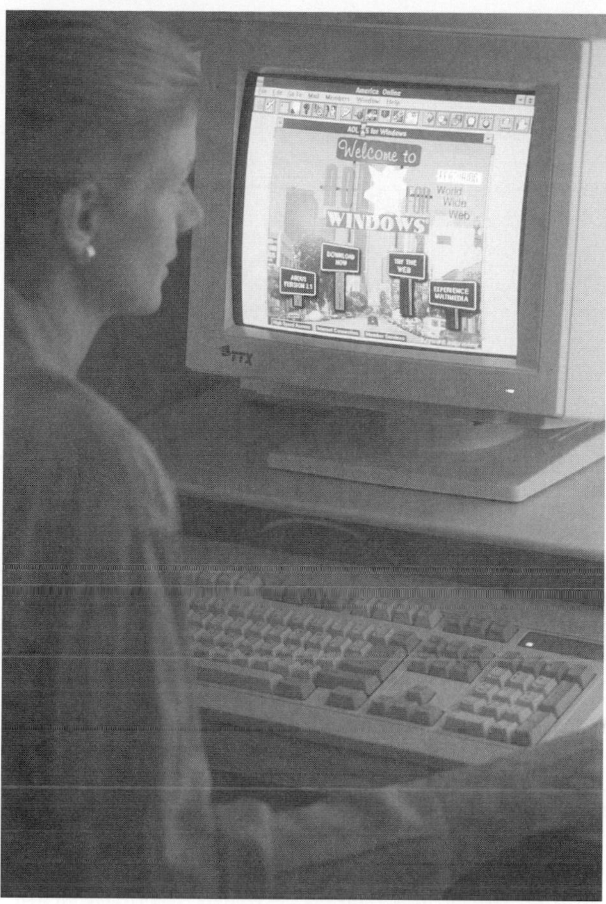

Public computer networks provide access to vast amounts of information, yet personal privacy is a major business and public policy issue.

behavior across all conceivable situations, it is possible to prescribe *processes* that may lead to an acceptable (and temporary) consensus among interested parties regarding an ethical course of action. The remainder of this chapter examines several areas that pose potential ethical dilemmas for employers and privacy concerns for employees or job applicants. Let us begin by considering fair information practice policies.

Fair Information Practices in the Computer Age

The Electronic Communications Privacy Act of 1986 prohibits "outside" interception of electronic mail by a third party—the government, the police, or an individual—without proper authorization (such as a search warrant). Information sent on public networks, such as Compuserve and MCI Mail, to which individuals and companies subscribe, is therefore protected. However, the law does not cover "inside" interception, and, in fact, no absolute privacy exists in a computer system, even for bosses.[89] They may view employees on closed-circuit TV; tap their phones, e-mail, and network communications; and rummage through their computer files with or without employee knowledge or consent 24 hours a day.[90]

ETHICAL DILEMMA
Do Employees Have a Right to Electronic Privacy?[91]

When Alana Shoars arrived for work at Epson America, Inc., one morning, she discovered her supervisor reading and printing out electronic-mail messages between other employees. Ms. Shoars was appalled. When she had trained employees to use the computerized system, she had told them their mail was private. Now a company manager was violating that trust.

When she questioned the practice, Ms. Shoars says she was told to mind her own business. A day later, she was fired for insubordination. Then she filed a $1 million lawsuit for wrongful termination. Although she soon found a job as e-mail administrator at another firm, she still bristles about Epson: "You don't read other people's mail, just as you don't listen to their phone conversations. Right is right, and wrong is wrong."

Michael Simmons, chief information officer at the Bank of Boston, disagrees completely. "If the corporation owns the equipment and pays for the network, that asset belongs to the company, and it has a right to look and see if people are using it for purposes other than running the business." At a previous job, for example, Mr. Simmons discovered that one employee was using the computer system to handicap horse races, and another was running his Amway business on his computer. Both were fired immediately. "The guy handicapping horses was using 600 megabytes of memory," Mr. Simmons said. What do you think? Do employees have a right to electronic privacy?

Safeguards to protect personal privacy are more important than ever. Yet the results of a recent survey of top corporate managers of 301 businesses of all sizes and in a wide range of industries revealed an unsettling fact: fewer than one in five had a written policy regarding electronic privacy—that is, employee computer files, voice mail, electronic mail, or other networking communications. With respect to computer-based employee records, 66 percent of HR managers reported that they have unlimited access to such information, while 52 percent of executives do.[92] What should managers do? Here are some general recommendations for establishing a fair information practice policy:

1. Set up guidelines and policies to protect information in the organization: types of data to be sought, methods of obtaining the data, retention and dissemination of information, employee or third-party access to information, release of information about former employees, and mishandling of information.
2. Inform employees of these information-handling policies.
3. Become thoroughly familiar with state and federal laws regarding privacy.
4. Establish a policy that states specifically that employees and prospective employees cannot waive their rights to privacy.
5. Establish a policy that any manager or nonmanager who violates these privacy principles will be subject to discipline or termination.[93]

Next, managers should articulate, communicate, and implement fair information practice policies by taking the following actions:[94]

1. Avoid fraudulent, secretive, or unfair means of collecting data. When possible, collect data directly from the individual concerned.

2. Do not maintain secret files on individuals. Inform them of what information is stored on them, the purpose for which it was collected, how it will be used, and how long it will be kept.
3. Collect only job-related information that is relevant for specific decisions.
4. Maintain records of individuals or organizations who have regular access to or who request information on a need-to-know basis.
5. Periodically allow employees the right to inspect and update information stored on them.
6. Gain assurance that any information released to outside parties will be used only for the purposes set forth prior to its release.

Companies that have taken such measures, such as IBM, Bank of America, AT&T, Cummins Engine, Avis, and TRW, report that the measures have not been overly costly, produced burdensome traffic in access demands, or reduced the general quality of their HR decisions. Furthermore, they receive strong employee approval for their policies when they ask about them on company attitude surveys. By matching words with deeds, companies such as these are weaving their concerns for employee privacy into the very fabric of their corporate cultures.

Assessment of Job Applicants and Employees

Decisions to hire, promote, train, or transfer are major events in individuals' careers. Frequently, such decisions are made with the aid of tests, interviews, situational exercises, performance appraisals, and other assessment techniques. Developers and users of these instruments must be concerned with questions of fairness, propriety, and individual rights, as well as with other ethical issues.

Developers, if they are members of professional associations such as the American Psychological Association, the Society for Human Resource Management, or the Academy of Management, are bound by the ethical standards put forth by those bodies. Managers who use assessment instruments are subject to other ethical principles, beyond the general concerns for accuracy and equality of opportunity. These include:[95]

- Guarding against invasion of privacy (e.g., with respect to biodata items, four areas seem to generate the greatest concern: self-incriminating items, those that require applicants to recall traumatic events, intimacy, and religion)[96]
- Guaranteeing confidentiality
- Obtaining informed consent from employees and applicants before assessing them
- Respecting employees' rights to know (e.g., regarding test content and the meaning, interpretation, and intended use of scores)
- Imposing time limitations on data (i.e., removing information that has not been used for HR decisions, especially if it has been updated)
- Using the most valid procedures available, thereby minimizing erroneous acceptances and erroneous rejections
- Treating applicants and employees with respect and consideration (i.e., by standardizing procedures for all candidates)

What can applicants do when confronted by a question they believe is irrelevant or is an invasion of privacy? Some may choose not to respond. However,

IMPACT OF PROCEDURAL JUSTICE AND ETHICS ON PRODUCTIVITY, QUALITY OF WORK LIFE, AND THE BOTTOM LINE

As we have seen throughout this chapter, employees and former employees are very sensitive to the general issue of "justice on the job." On a broad range of issues, they expect to be treated justly, fairly, and with due process. Doing so certainly contributes to improved productivity and quality of work life, for grievances are both time-consuming and costly. On the other hand, organizations that disregard employee rights can expect two things: (1) to be hit with lawsuits and (2) to find courts and juries to be sympathetic to tales of employer wrongdoing. Employment-at-will cases illustrate this trend clearly. As for employers contesting such suits, one corporate attorney noted: "Even a victory isn't a victory because the [defendant's] attorneys' fees are at least $50,000 for a typical case."[103] As in so many other areas of employee relations, careful attention to procedural justice and ethical decision making yields direct as well as indirect benefits. The old adage "an ounce of prevention is worth a pound of cure" says it all.

research indicates that employers tend to view such nonresponse as an attempt to conceal facts that would reflect poorly on an applicant. Hence applicants (especially those who have nothing to hide) are ill-advised not to respond.[97] Clearly, it is the employer's responsibility to (1) know the kinds of questions that are being asked of candidates and (2) review the appropriateness and job-relatedness of all such questions.

Whistle-Blowing

Like the blowing of a whistle by a referee to indicate violations of the rules on a playing field, whistle-blowing in a business setting refers to disclosure by former or current organization members of illegal, immoral, or illegitimate practices under the control of their employers. The whistle-blower discloses such practices to people or organizations that may be able to do something about them.[98] Are there contexts or circumstances that actually sanction unethical behavior? Research indicates that individuals can be conditioned to behave unethically (if they are rewarded for it), especially under increased competition,[99] but that the threat of punishment has a counterbalancing influence.[100] More important, when a formal or informal organizational policy is present that favors ethical behavior, ethical behavior tends to increase.[101] Is there a set of characteristics associated with whistle-blowers?

Research with almost 8600 employees of 22 federal agencies and departments revealed that those who had observed alleged wrongdoing were more likely to "blow the whistle" if they:

- Were employed by organizations perceived by others to be responsive to complaints.
- Held professional positions, had long service, and had positive reactions to their work.
- Were recently recognized for good performance.
- Were male (although race was unrelated to whistle-blowing).
- Were members of large work groups.[102]

These findings are consistent with other research that has destroyed the myth that whistle-blowers are social misfits. A study of nearly 100 people who reported wrongdoing in public- and private-sector organizations found that the average whistle-blower was a 47-year-old family man employed for 7 years before exposing his company's misdeeds.[104]

Despite retaliation, financial loss, and high emotional and physical stress,[105] there are at least two reasons why more whistle-blowers are likely to come forward in the future: (1) some 40 states (and the federal government) now protect the jobs of workers who report wrongdoing by their companies,[106] and (2) disclosure of fraud, waste, and abuse by federal contractors can lead to substantial financial gains by whistle-blowers. As a result of recent amendments to the federal False Claims Act of 1863, private citizens may sue a contractor for fraud on the government's behalf and share up to 30 percent of whatever financial recovery the government makes as a result of the charges. Such an incentive helped the government recover more than $1.2 billion from cheaters between 1987 and 1997. On the other hand, only about 11 percent of False Claims Act cases produce a recovery, and defending a claim, even if baseless, can cost $400,000 or more.[107]

Whistle-blowing is likely to be effective to the extent that the whistle-blower is credible and relatively powerful, reports information that is clearly illegal and unambiguous, has evidence that is convincing, and is part of an organization that encourages whistle-blowing and discourages retaliation against whistle-blowers. However, the more an organization depends on the wrongdoing (e.g., by covering up shoddy aircraft maintenance procedures), the less likely that internal whistle-blowing will be effective and the more likely that external whistle-blowing will be effective.[108] If you have a tale to tell, consider these do's and don'ts:[109]

Do make sure your allegation is correct, keep careful records, research whether your state provides protection for whistle-blowers, and be realistic about your future.

Do talk to your family, and be prepared for a worst-case scenario.

Don't assume a federal or state law will protect you as the "good guy." Legal protection for private-sector workers is often inadequate and varies from state to state.

Don't run to the media (check with an attorney first), and **don't** expect a windfall if you're fired. Although some states allow punitive damages, you may be eligible only for back pay and reinstatement—in a place where you probably don't want to work anyway.

Conclusion

Ethical behavior is not governed by hard-and-fast rules. Rather, it adapts and changes in response to social norms. This is nowhere more obvious than in human resource management. What was considered ethical in the 1950s and 1960s (deep-probing selection interviews; management prescription of standards of dress, ideology, and lifestyle; refusal to let employees examine their own employment files) would be considered improper today. Indeed, as we have seen, growing concern for employee rights has placed organizational

IMPLICATIONS FOR MANAGEMENT PRACTICE

Individual managers who disregard employee rights to procedural justice do so at their peril. If you are operating in a unionized setting, know the collective bargaining agreement inside and out. More important, follow both the letter and the spirit of its provisions. In nonunion settings, be sure that decisions about selection, assignment, promotion, discipline, and discharge are based on clear standards and recorded judgments that can be examined when a dispute arises. Study after study confirms the beneficial effects on employee attitudes and performance of procedural justice safeguards.[110] Provide explicit procedures for resolving conflicts and be sure that all employees know how to use them. Finally, treat all people with dignity and respect; think win-win rather than win-lose.

decision-making policies in the public domain. The beneficial effect of this, of course, is that it is sensitizing both employers and employees to new concerns.

To be sure, ethical choices are rarely easy. The challenge in managing human resources lies not in the mechanical application of moral prescriptions but rather in the process of creating and maintaining genuine relationships from which to address ethical dilemmas that cannot be covered by prescription.[111]

Human Resource Management in Action: Conclusion

ALTERNATIVE DISPUTE RESOLUTION (ADR): GOOD FOR THE COMPANY, GOOD FOR EMPLOYEES?

The EEOC, which supports mediation and other forms of ADR, has been outspoken in its long-standing opposition to binding arbitration that is a condition of employment or a condition of continuing employment. In a recent case, for example, a federal judge signed a consent decree that permanently stopped a Houston employer, River Oaks Imaging and Diagnostic, from enforcing its mandatory arbitration agreements. The EEOC charged that River Oaks used arbitration to retaliate against employees who had filed sexual-harassment complaints.

This raises another issue, namely, what does a fair ADR program look like? According to the EEOC, a fair ADR program is voluntary, neutral, confidential, and enforceable. Attorneys and HR professionals add that generally an ADR plan is considered fair if employees are not forced to give up legal rights, such as the right to sue, and if the ADR remedies are the same as those that can be obtained in court, such as obtaining punitive damages. They also support allowing employees to opt into a program after a dispute, rather than requiring arbitration as a condition of employment. In addition to these features, the Society for Human Resource Management suggests the following additional standards of fairness:

- Accessibility
- Opportunity for a hearing before one or more neutral, impartial decision makers
- Opportunity to participate in the selection of decision makers

- Participation by the employee in assuming some portion of the costs of the dispute resolution process

Programs that incorporate features like these are good for employers *and* good for employees. They will encourage both sides to make greater use of ADR in the future.

SUMMARY

The broad theme of this chapter is "justice on the job." This concept includes procedural justice, due process, and ethical decision making. Each of these processes should guide the formulation of policy in matters involving dispute resolution (e.g., through union or nonunion grievance procedures), arbitration, discipline, employment contracts, and termination for disciplinary or economic reasons. Indeed, such concerns for procedural justice and due process form the basis for many challenges to the employment-at-will doctrine.

Two of the most important employment issues of our time are employee privacy and ethical decision making. Three areas that involve employee privacy are receiving considerable emphasis: fair information practices in the computer age, the assessment of job applicants and employees, and whistle-blowing. Although it is not possible to prescribe the content of ethical behavior in each of these areas, processes that incorporate procedural justice can lead to an acceptable (and temporary) consensus among interested parties regarding an ethical course of action.

DISCUSSION QUESTIONS

13-1 Discuss the similarities and differences among these concepts: procedural justice, workplace due process, and ethical decisions about behavior.

13-2 What advice would you give to an executive who is about to negotiate an employment contract?

13-3 Is it ethical to tape-record a conversation with your boss without his or her knowledge?

13-4 How can a firm avoid lawsuits for employment-at-will?

13-5 What are some guidelines to follow in determining a reasonable compromise between a company's need to run its business and employee rights to privacy?

APPLYING YOUR KNOWLEDGE

George Cotter Blows the Whistle — *Case 13-1*

Employees who find themselves in the dicey position of witnessing a breach of ethics, a crime, or a health or safety threat in the workplace need to proceed very cautiously. Protection for federal workers who expose fraud or wrongdoing is fairly broad, but that is not the case for many private-sector workers. A wrong step can leave an employee without a job and without legal recourse. Furthermore, it can ruin his or her reputation and make subsequent employment extremely difficult to obtain.

Take the case of George Cotter, an East Coast regional manager for Selton, a medium-size entertainment company. In 1995, Mr. Cotter noticed that something funny seemed to be going on at his company. Specifically, some higher-level executives were ordering big shipments of free compact discs for recipients who were not, in fact, entitled to them. After doing some legwork to ensure that his suspicions were supported, Mr. Cotter took his findings to higher-level supervisors. In fact, he notified supervisors on three different occasions. His allegation was that the upper-level executives were receiving kickbacks for delivering free compact discs to certain individuals. This was obviously costing Selton Company a large amount of money.

George Cotter expected to be thanked for his discovery. Instead, he got fired, supposedly for not adequately performing his job.

Six months later, Cotter filed a wrongful termination lawsuit with a superior court in his county. The preliminary ruling was in his favor, but Selton Company is presently in the process of appealing the case to the State Supreme Court.

Cotter is not as famous as Ernest Fitzgerald, the Air Force civil servant who identified billions of dollars in cost overruns at Lockheed in 1968, or as the Morton-Thiokol engineers who tried to stop the launch of the space shuttle *Challenger* because weather conditions were too cold. But Cotter is a classic whistle-blower. Unfortunately, Selton's response—firing him—also appears to be classic.

In theory, most managers agree that blowing the whistle is what they want employees to do. But in practice, many "ethical dissenters" can attest to the fact that they are treated like pariahs, if not fired outright, after fingering the wrongdoing in their organizations. The problem seems to be that laws protecting whistle-blowers are extremely spotty. Certain environmental laws and workplace safety regulations have whistle-blower provisions. But most states are loath to interfere with "at-will" employment contracts.

Questions

1. Under what circumstances are employees most likely to blow the whistle?
2. What steps should George Cotter have taken to help ensure that his whistle-blowing was received favorably by the organization and to help protect his job?

REFERENCES

1. Fossum, J. A. (1990). Employee and labor relations in an evolving environment. In J. A. Fossum (ed.), *Employee and labor relations.* Washington, DC: Bureau of National Affairs, pp. 4-1 to 4-22.
2. *Webster's new collegiate dictionary* (1976). Springfield, MA: Merriam-Webster.
3. Greenberg, J. (1987). Reactions to procedural injustice in payment distributions: Do the means justify the ends? *Journal of Applied Psychology,* **72,** 55–61.
4. Wesman, E. C., & Eischen, D. E. (1990). Due process. In J. A. Fossum (ed.), *Employee and labor relations.* Washington, DC: Bureau of National Affairs, pp. 4-82 to 4-133.
5. Cullen, J. B., Victor, B., & Stephens, C. (1989). An ethical weather report: Assessing the organization's ethical climate. *Organizational Dynamics,* **18,** 50–62. See also Nielsen, R. P. (1989). Changing unethical organizational behavior. *Academy of Management Executive,* **3**(2), 123–130.

6. Sheppard, B. H., Lewicki, R. J., & Minton, J. W. (1992). *Organizational justice: The search for fairness in the workplace.* New York: Lexington.
7. Ibid.
8. Ibid.
9. Tyler, T. R., & Bies, R. J. (1990). Beyond formal procedures: The interpersonal context of procedural justice. In J. S. Carroll (ed.), *Applied psychology and organizational settings.* Hillsdale, NJ: Erlbaum, pp. 77–98.
10. Sheppard et al., op. cit.
11. Mills, D. Q. (1994). *Labor-management relations* (5th ed.). New York: McGraw-Hill.
12. Ibid.
13. Noble, K. B. (1988, June 30). Unions limited in use of dues and fees. *The New York Times,* p. 13.
14. Mills, op. cit.
15. Labig, C. E., & Greer, C. R. (1988). Grievance initiation: A literature survey and directions for future research. *Journal of Labor Research,* **9,** 1–27.
16. Ibid.
17. Ibid.
18. Dalton, D. R., & Todor, W. D. (1981). Win, lose, draw: The grievance process in practice. *Personnel Administrator,* **26**(3), 25–29.
19. Kotlowitz, A. (1987, Aug. 28). Labor's turn? *The Wall Street Journal,* pp. 1, 14. See also Kotlowitz, A. (1987, Apr. 1). Grievous work. *The Wall Street Journal,* pp. 1, 12.
20. Mesch, D. J., & Dalton, D. R. (1992). Unexpected consequences of improving workplace justice: A six-year time series assessment. *Academy of Management Journal,* **35,** 1099–1114. See also Dalton & Todor, loc. cit.
21. Olson-Buchanan, J. B. (1996). Voicing discontent: What happens to the grievance filer after the grievance? *Journal of Applied Psychology,* **81,** 52–63.
22. Meyer, D., & Cooke, W. (1988). Economic and political factors in the resolution of formal grievances. *Industrial Relations,* **27,** 318–335.
23. Klaas, B. S. (1989). Managerial decision-making about employee grievances: The impact of the grievant's work history. *Personnel Psychology,* **42,** 53–68. See also Dalton, D. R., Todor, W. D., & Owen, C. L. (1987). Sex effects in workplace justice outcomes: A field assessment. *Journal of Applied Psychology,* **72,** 156–159. See also Dalton, D. R., & Todor, W. D. (1985). Gender and workplace justice: A field assessment. *Personnel Psychology,* **38,** 133–151.
24. Mesch & Dalton, loc. cit.
25. Egler, T. D. (1995, July). The benefits and burdens of arbitration. *HRMagazine,* pp. 27–30.
26. Bencivenga, B. (1996, Jan.). Fair play in the ADR arena. *HRMagazine,* pp. 50–56.
27. Arbitrator overruled (1997, Feb.). *Mountain States Employers Council Bulletin,* p. 4. See also Hill, M., Jr., & Sinicropi, A. V. (1980). *Evidence in arbitration.* Washington, DC: Bureau of National Affairs.
28. Egler, 1995, loc. cit.
29. Labor letter (1989, Nov. 14). *The Wall Street Journal,* p. A1.
30. Hauenstein, M. A., & Lord, R. G. (1989). The effects of final-offer arbitration on major league baseball players: A test of equity theory. *Human Performance,* **2,** 147–165.
31. Bretz, R. D., Jr., & Thomas, S. L. (1992). Perceived equity, motivation, and final-offer arbitration in major league baseball. *Journal of Applied Psychology,* **77,** 280–287.
32. Ewing, J. B. (1989, Oct. 23). Corporate due process lowers legal costs. *The Wall Street Journal,* p. A14.
33. Bencivenga, loc. cit. See also Taking it to arbitration (1985, July 16). *The Wall Street Journal,* p. 1.
34. Drost, D. A., & O'Brien, F. P. (1983). Are there grievances against your non-union grievance procedure? *Personnel Administrator,* **28**(1), 36–42.

35. Ibid.
36. Ewing, loc. cit.
37. Seeley, R. S. (1992, July). Corporate due process. *HRMagazine,* pp. 46–49.
38. Ibid. See also Reibstein, L. (1986, Dec. 3). More firms use peer review panel to resolve employees' grievances. *The Wall Street Journal,* p. 33. See also Olson, F. C. (1984). How peer review works at Control Data. *Harvard Business Review,* **62**(6), 58–61.
39. Seeley, op. cit., p. 49.
40. Wesman & Eischen, loc. cit.
41. Falcone, P. (1997, Feb.). Fundamentals of progressive discipline. *HRMagazine,* pp. 90–94. See also Belohlav, J. (1983). Realities of successful employee discipline. *Personnel Administrator,* **28**(3), 74–77, 92.
42. Baum, L. (1986, June 16). Punishing workers with a day off. *Business Week,* p. 80.
43. O'Reilly, C. A., III, & Weitz, B. A. (1980). Managing marginal employees: The use of warnings and dismissals. *Administrative Science Quarterly,* **25,** 467–484.
44. Franke, R., & Karl, J. (1978). The Hawthorne experiments: First statistical interpretation. *American Sociological Review,* **43,** 623–643. See also O'Reilly & Weitz, loc. cit.
45. Bandura, A. (1986). *Social foundations of thought and action: A social cognitive theory.* Englewood Cliffs, NJ: Prentice-Hall.
46. Trevino, L. K. (1992). The social effects of punishments in organizations: A justice perspective. *Academy of Management Review,* **17,** 647–676.
47. O'Reilly, C. A., III, & Puffer, S. M. (1989). The impact of rewards and punishments in a social context: A laboratory and field experiment. *Journal of Occupational Psychology,* **62,** 41–53.
48. Klaas, B. S., & Feldman, D. C. (1994). The impact of appeal system structure on disciplinary decisions. *Personnel Psychology,* **47,** 91–108. See also Klaas, B. S., & Dell'omo, G. G. (1991). The determinants of disciplinary decisions: The case of employee drug use. *Personnel Psychology,* **44,** 813–835.
49. Klaas, B. S., & Wheeler, H. N. (1990). Managerial decision making about employee discipline: A policy-capturing approach. *Personnel Psychology,* **43,** 117–134.
50. Falcone, loc. cit.
51. Israel, D. (1983). The Weingarten case sets precedent for co-employee representation. *Personnel Administrator,* **28**(2), 23–26.
52. *NLRB v. Weingarten* (1975). 420 U.S. 251, 95 S. Ct. 959.
53. *NLRB v. Sears Roebuck and Co.* (1985, Feb. 27). *Daily Labor Report,* **39,** D1–D5.
54. Weingarten rights include prior consultation (1992, Aug.). *Mountain States Employers Council Bulletin,* p. 4.
55. Employee's "Weingarten" rights limited by NLRB (1993, Jan.). *Mountain States Employers Council Bulletin,* p. 4.
56. Israel, loc. cit.
57. Lorber, L. Z., Kirk, J. R., Kirschner, K. H., & Handorf, C. R. (1984). *Fear of firing: A legal and personnel analysis of employment-at-will.* Alexandria, VA: American Society of Personnel Administration.
58. Geyelin, M. (1989, Sept. 7). Fired managers winning more lawsuits. *The Wall Street Journal,* p. B13.
59. Geyelin, J., & Moses, J. M. (1992, Apr. 7). Rulings on wrongful firing curb hiring. *The Wall Street Journal,* p. B1.
60. Stern, G. (1993, May 5). Companies discover that some firings backfire into costly defamation suits. *The Wall Street Journal,* pp. B1, B7.
61. Spurgeon, Haney, & Howbert, P. A. (1985). *Ready, fire! (aim): A manager's primer in the law of terminations.* Colorado Springs, CO: Author.
62. Koys, D. J., Briggs, S., & Grenig, J. (1987). State court disparity on employment-at-will. *Personnel Psychology,* **40,** 565–577.
63. Stern, loc. cit. See also Geyelin, loc. cit.

64. Hershizer, B. (1984). The implied contract exception to at-will employment. *Labor Law Journal,* **35,** 131–141.
65. Bakaly, C. G., Jr., & Grossman, J. M. (1984, Aug.). How to avoid wrongful discharge suits. *Management Review,* pp. 41–46.
66. Wermiel, S. (1988, June 7). Justices expand union workers' right to sue. *The Wall Street Journal,* p. 4.
67. Yoder, S. K., & Lambert, W. (1990, Dec. 21). California rulings may limit worker suits. *The Wall Street Journal,* p. B6. See also Schlender, B. R. (1988, Dec. 30). California ruling curtails damages in dismissal suits. *The Wall Street Journal,* p. B1.
68. Geyelin, loc. cit.
69. Handbook (1994, Jan.). *Mountain States Employers Council Bulletin,* p. 2. See also Fulmer, W. E., & Casey, A. W. (1990). Employment at will: Options for managers. *Academy of Management Executive,* **4**(2), 102–107.
70. Lorber, L. Z. (1984). Basic advice on avoiding employment-at-will troubles. *Personnel Administrator,* **29**(1), 59–62.
71. Falcone, loc. cit. See also Engel, P. G. (1985, Mar. 18). Preserving the right to fire. *Industry Week,* pp. 39–40.
72. Stickney, J. (1984, Dec.). Settling the terms of employment. *Money,* pp. 127, 128, 132.
73. Baig, E. C. (1997, Mar. 17). Beware the ties that bind. *Fortune,* pp. 120, 121. See also Lublin, J. S. & Scism, L. (1997, May 8). Ex-Aetna executive must restrict duties. *The Wall Street Journal,* p. B7.
74. Personal affairs (1983, June 6). *Forbes,* pp. 174, 178.
75. Baig, loc. cit. See also Wadman, M. K. (1992, June 26). More firms restrict departing workers. *The Wall Street Journal,* pp. B1, B3. See also You'll never eat lunch in this industry again (1991, Nov. 11). *Business Week,* p. 44.
76. Egler, T. D. (1996, May). A manager's guide to employment contracts. *HRMagazine,* pp. 28–33.
77. Stickney, loc. cit.
78. Geyelin, loc. cit.
79. Bernstein, A. (1997, Apr. 7). Who says job anxiety is easing? *Business Week,* p. 38.
80. Bing, S. (1997, Feb. 3). Stepping up to the firing line. *Fortune,* pp. 51, 52. See also Sweet, D. H. (1989a). *A manager's guide to conducting terminations.* Lexington, MA: Lexington Books.
81. Youngblood, D. (1987, June 22). Supervisors offered guidelines to "humane" firing. *Rocky Mountain News,* p. 62.
82. Bing, op. cit. See also Stern, loc. cit. See also Sweet, 1989a, loc. cit.
83. Youngblood, loc. cit.
84. Sweet, 1989a, op. cit., p. 56.
85. Brockner, J., Grover, S., Reed, T. F., & Dewitt, R. L. (1992). Layoffs, job insecurity, and survivors' work effort: Evidence of an inverted-U relationship. *Academy of Management Journal,* **35,** 413–425. See also Brockner, J. (1988). The effect of work layoffs on survivors: Research, theory, and practice. In B. M. Staw & L. L. Cummings (eds.), *Research in organizational behavior.* Greenwich, CT: JAI Press, vol. 10, pp. 213–255.
86. Sweet, D. H. (1989b). Outplacement. In W. F. Cascio (ed.), *Human resource planning, employment, and placement.* Washington, DC: Bureau of National Affairs, pp. 2-236 to 2-261.
87. Piller, C. (1993, July). Privacy in peril. *Macworld,* pp. 124–130.
88. Privacy (1988, Mar. 28). *Business Week,* pp. 61–68.
89. Behar, R. (1997, Feb. 3). Who's reading your e-mail? *Fortune,* pp. 57–70. See also Elmer-Dewitt, P. (1993, Jan. 18). Who's reading your screen? *Time,* p. 46.
90. Brown, E. (1997, Feb. 3). The myth of e-mail privacy. *Fortune,* p. 66. See also Piller, C. (1993, July). Bosses with X-ray eyes. *Macworld,* pp. 118–123.

91. Rifkin, G. (1991, Dec. 8). Do employees have a right to electronic privacy? *The New York Times,* p. 8F.
92. Piller, loc. cit.
93. A model employment-privacy policy (1993, July). *Macworld,* p. 121.
94. Cook, S. H. (1987). Privacy rights: Whose life is it anyway? *Personnel Administrator,* **32**(4), 58–65.
95. London, M., & Bray, D. W. (1980). Ethical issues in testing and evaluation for personnel decisions. *American Psychologist,* **35,** 890–901.
96. Mael, F. A., Connerley, M., & Morath, R. A. (1996). None of your business: Parameters of biodata invasiveness. *Personnel Psychology,* **49,** 613–650.
97. Stone, D. L., & Stone, E. F. (1987). Effects of missing application-blank information on personnel selection decisions: Do privacy protection strategies bias the outcome? *Journal of Applied Psychology,* **72,** 452–456.
98. Miceli, M. P., & Near, J. P. (1992). *Blowing the whistle.* New York: Lexington.
99. Nielsen, loc. cit.
100. Jansen, E., & Von Glinow, M. A. (1985). Ethical ambivalence and organizational reward systems. *Academy of Management Review,* **10,** 815–822.
101. Hegarty, W. H., & Sims, H. P., Jr. (1979). Organizational philosophy, policies, and objectives related to unethical decision behavior: A laboratory experiment. *Journal of Applied Psychology,* **64,** 331–338.
102. Miceli, M. P., & Near, J. P. (1988). Individual and situational correlates of whistle-blowing. *Personnel Psychology,* **41,** 267–281.
103. Barrett, A., cited in Schlender, B. R. (1988, Dec. 30). California ruling curtails damages in dismissal suits. *The Wall Street Journal,* p. B1.
104. Farnsworth, C. H. (1987, Feb. 22). Survey of whistle blowers finds retaliation but few regrets. *The New York Times,* p. 22.
105. Greenwald, J. (1993, June 21). A matter of honor. *Time,* pp. 33, 34. See also Hilts, P. J. (1991, Mar. 22). Hero in exposing science hoax paid dearly. *The New York Times,* pp. A1, B6.
106. Near, J. P., & Miceli, M. P. (1995). Effective whistle-blowing. *Academy of Management Review,* **20,** 679–708.
107. Whistle-blowers on trial (1997, Mar. 24). *Business Week,* pp. 172, 174, 178.
108. Near & Miceli, loc. cit.
109. Dunkin, A. (1991, June 3). Blowing the whistle without paying the piper. *Business Week,* pp. 138, 139.
110. Gilliland, S. W. (1993). The perceived fairness of selection systems: An organizational justice perspective. *Academy of Management Review,* **18,** 694–734. See also Saal, F. E., & Moore, S. C. (1993). Perceptions of promotion fairness and promotion candidates' qualifications. *Journal of Applied Psychology,* **78,** 105–110. See also Schwarzwald, J., Koslowsky, M., & Shalit, B. (1992). A field study of employees' attitudes and behaviors after promotion decisions. *Journal of Applied Psychology,* **77,** 511–514. See also Konovsky, M. A., & Cropanzano, R. (1991). Perceived fairness of employee drug testing as a predictor of employee attitudes and job performance. *Journal of Applied Psychology,* **76,** 698–707.
111. Cascio, W. F. (1998). *Applied psychology in personnel management* (5th ed.). Englewood Cliffs, NJ: Prentice-Hall.

CASE IN THE NEWS

Bargaining in Detroit: One Size No Longer Fits All

By Keith Naughton

Is time running out for the auto industry's long-held tradition of pattern bargaining? Even as United Auto Workers President Stephen P. Yokich celebrated the deal with Ford Motor Co., much of which he expects Chrysler Corp. and General Motors Corp. to meet, that question is increasingly being raised around Detroit.

Trying to squeeze GM, Ford, and Chrysler into a one-size-fits-all contract no longer makes much sense—particularly for the companies. And even the union probably could do better for its members by using a different approach. The system is a vestige of the 1950s, when Detroit ruled the roads. Today, one-third of the market is owned by foreign carmakers not covered by the pattern. The Big Three also face divergent financial and operating problems. Chrysler, for example, spends $600 less to build each vehicle than GM does, and earns 45% more. That productivity gap allows Ford and Chrysler to use the talks as a weapon against GM.

Triennial Contest

In the postwar era, pattern contracts spread across the auto, rubber, steel, and other businesses. The egalitarian ideal made sense in time of U.S. hegemony: By making wages and benefits uniform industrywide, companies competed on product quality, not the backs of their workers. "You took labor costs out of the competitive equation," says ex-UAW President Douglas Fraser.

But foreign competition changed that. Pattern bargaining has been much weakened in every major manufacturing industry except autos. And today, rather that standardizing Detroit's labor costs, pattern talks put them in play more than ever.

Nowhere is that more evident than in the triennial "beauty contest" the Big Three engage in to be named as the UAW's "target." The rush to be first isn't surprising: The winner gets to establish the pattern its rivals must more or less follow. Not only can the lead company craft a deal that best suits its needs but it can stick it to rivals at the same time.

Take the deal Ford struck guaranteeing a minimum employment level only 5% below its current staffing. That's virtually meaningless for Ford, which has hired nearly 10,000 workers since 1992 and plans no big cuts. But Ford knows

Maybe it's time to limit industrywide rules to such issues as wages and standard benefits.

such a pledge hurts GM. Without a 30% cut in its labor force, analysts say GM can't reduce its productivity gap. Says Morgan Stanley & Co. auto analyst Stephen Girsky: "GM is going to have to look to get around the pattern."

Certainly, the UAW knows that, too. And problems at individual companies have led the union to interpret the pattern loosely in past talks. Still, thanks to Ford, GM will have to agree to a restrictive minimum jobs level where none existed before. Analysts say the best GM can hope for is job cuts of 15%—half of what it needs.

When the strongest company sets labor costs for the weakest, it perpetuates and often worsens the laggard's problems. Chrysler and Ford, with the UAW's complicity, drastically slashed their workforces during their brushes with death in the early 1980s. GM never had the management discipline to do so. That left GM's labor costs the highest of the Big Three—one reason why its U.S. auto profits are the lowest.

The irony today: GM seems ready to make some of the tough cuts, but the pattern system intended to protect GM's 220,000 UAW workers may take money out of their pockets. Although the 1982 UAW talks established profit-sharing for workers, GM's weakness means its workers get little compared with those at Chrysler and Ford. "The union has prevented GM from restructuring and cost each of their employees thousands in profit-sharing," says Bear, Stearns & Co. analyst Nicholas Lobaccaro.

"Death Knell"

GM must move fast. Some 2.7 million vehicles sold in the U.S. this year will be made at Japanese transplants. Most of their workers are nonunion—paid an average of $38 an hour in wages and benefits, vs. $43 at GM and $40 at Ford and Chrysler. "The transplant situation is the final death knell for the pattern," says University of Michigan labor economist Sean McAlinden.

Even Yokich has signaled that he is willing to make the pattern more porous to accommodate each auto maker's needs. "What do you call a pattern?" he asked this summer. "Each company is different." But stretching the pattern won't end it. Since the pattern talks increase the union's bargaining clout, the UAW would bitterly fight any attempt to dismantle them. Nor could the companies impose such a change without risking enormous labor strife.

Instead, Fraser says it may be time to construe the industry pattern far more narrowly. Rather than set industrywide rules for a thorny issue such as outsourcing, for example, he says the pattern might be applied only to hourly wages, pensions, health care, and standard benefits. The pattern is likely to survive in some form this year, but with luck, it will be the dying gasp of a 20th century tradition.

Naughton tracks autos from Detroit.

Discussion Questions

1. Pattern bargaining is designed to promote competition based on product quality, and, by making labor costs equal across companies, to take labor costs out of the competitive equation. How does foreign competition affect pattern bargaining?

2. ". . . today, rather than standardizing Detroit's labor costs, pattern talks put them in play more than ever." How? and Why is this so?
3 Resolved: "Pattern bargaining should be preserved in some form." Divide the class into teams that represent affirmative and negative positions on this issue. Allow both sides to make initial statements and then rebuttal statements. Discuss how the points made by both sides have informed students' opinions.

PART 6

SUPPORT, EVALUATION, AND INTERNATIONAL IMPLICATIONS

This capstone section deals with three broad themes: organizational support for employees, evaluation of human resource management activities, and the international implications of human resource management activities. Chapter 14 examines key issues involved in employee safety and health, both mental and physical. Chapter 15 presents the latest methods of assessing the costs and benefits of human resource management activities in a number of areas. Finally, Chapter 16 considers key issues in international human resource management; given the rapid growth of multinational corporations, it is perhaps in this area more than any other that employees and their families need special social and financial support from their firms.

14 SAFETY, HEALTH, AND EMPLOYEE ASSISTANCE PROGRAMS

Questions This Chapter Will Help Managers Answer

1 What is the cost–benefit trade-off of adopting measures to enhance workplace safety and health?
2 Which approaches to job safety and health really work?
3 What should an informed, progressive AIDS policy look like?
4 What are some key issues to consider in establishing and monitoring an employee assistance program?
5 Does it make sound business sense to institute a worksite wellness program? If so, how should it be implemented and what should it include?

*SUBSTANCE ABUSE ON THE JOB PRODUCES TOUGH POLICY CHOICES FOR MANAGERS**

Human Resource Management in Action

Experts estimate that 5 to 10 percent of employees in any company have a substance abuse problem (alcohol or drugs) serious enough to merit treatment. The situation may be even worse. In 1984 and 1985, unbeknown to employees and job applicants, Chevron Corporation carried out anonymous drug testing. About 30 percent of all applicants and 20 percent of all employees tested positive for illegal drug use.

What is an appropriate policy for managers to adopt in these circumstances? Certainly cost pressures are forcing some employers to reexamine their drug and alcohol treatment programs. After noting that the cost of a 21-day detoxification program runs from $4000 to $14,000, one health-care professional commented, "People want to fire other people because they consume a lot of health-care dollars. Those of us in the . . . field are feeling [pressure]. We were feeling it before *Valdez*, and we'll feel it after. In terms of cutting their costs, they go for the most visible, and clearly the most visible are chemically dependent people."

Another professional in the field says that more hard-line companies simply demote people who have been in treatment. "They won't have a written policy, but they'll guide the person into a position of no strategic importance. If asked, the companies won't acknowledge it. They don't want the bad publicity of being a mean guy."

Buoying these hard-liners are some very public drug- and alcohol-related accidents, of which the *Exxon Valdez* oil spill is probably the best known. In the mid-1990s, three Northwest Airlines pilots were convicted of operating a commercial airliner while intoxicated. What should firms do? While dismissal and demotion are two obvious policy choices, rehabilitation is a third.

Among companies that endorse rehabilitation, however, there is considerable debate about whether employees should be returned to their jobs if they are successfully rehabilitated. Standard industry practice is to return people to their jobs after treatment. Exxon, however, bucked the industry trend following the wreck of its oil tanker *Exxon Valdez* (and the environmental disaster that followed). The ship's captain had previously been treated for alcoholism and returned to work. After the accident, a blood test revealed a high level of alcohol in his system. Exxon therefore adopted the policy that, following treatment, known alcohol and drug abusers will not be allowed to return to so-called safety-sensitive jobs, such as piloting a ship, flying a plane, or operating a refinery, although they will be given other jobs. (By late 1996 Exxon was hit with 107 discrimination lawsuits as a result of this policy.[1])

Those who favor returning people to work after rehabilitation argue that it is not only more humane but also more effective. Refusing to return people to work—even in safety-sensitive positions—would be "short-sighted. It will

*Adapted from Firms debate hard lines on alcoholics, *The Wall Street Journal*, Apr. 13, 1989, p. B1. Reprinted by permission of *The Wall Street Journal*,

make sure that no one who's an alcoholic ever gets help," according to the medical director of United Airlines (which regularly returns pilots to their jobs after treatment). "As ubiquitous a disease as alcoholism is, you have two choices: you either have practicing alcoholics in the cockpits, or you have recovering ones." Those who take a more hard-line attitude toward drug and alcohol abuse point out that many companies are thinking through their policies, wondering how much criticism from the community they can tolerate.

Challenges

1. What are some arguments for and against each of these policies on substance abuse on the job: dismissal, demotion, return to the same job following rehabilitation, return to a different job following rehabilitation?
2. Should follow-up be required after rehabilitation? If so, how long should it last and what form should it take?

As the chapter opening vignette shows, managers face tough policy issues in the area of workplace health and safety. As we will see, a combination of external factors (e.g., the spiraling cost of health care) and internal factors (e.g., new technology) are making these issues impossible to ignore. This chapter begins by examining how social and legal policies on the federal and state levels have evolved on the issue of health and safety on the job, beginning with workers' compensation laws and culminating with the passage of the Occupational Safety and Health Act. The chapter then considers enforcement of the act, with special emphasis on the rights and obligations of management. It also examines prevailing approaches to job safety and health in other countries. Finally, it considers the problems of AIDS and business, employee assistance programs, and corporate wellness programs. Underlying all these efforts is a conviction on the part of many firms that it is morally right to improve job safety and health—and that doing so will enhance the productivity and quality of work life of employees at all levels.

THE EXTENT AND COST OF SAFETY AND HEALTH PROBLEMS

Consider these startling facts about U.S. workplaces:[2]

- 17 workers die on the job each day.[3]
- More than 6.5 million workers (roughly 1 of every 12) either get sick or are injured because of their jobs. Of the illnesses that occur, 62 percent are associated with repetitive-stress injuries (RSIs) such as carpal tunnel syndrome. RSIs are classified as illnesses because of their long-term nature.[4] They cost employers $20 billion annually, and have increased 800 percent in the last decade.[5]

- Being hit by an object is the most common workplace injury, followed by sprains, strains, slips, and falls.[6] Falls account for 10 percent of fatal work injuries.
- Low-back injuries account for one-fourth of all workers' compensation claims, and cost an average of $8300, more than twice the average workplace claim.[7]
- 35 million workdays are lost every year.

The number of workdays lost balloons to 75 million when permanently disabling injuries that occurred in prior years are included. The cost? A staggering $40 billion in lost wages, medical costs, insurance administration costs, and indirect costs. At the level of the individual firm, a Du Pont safety engineer determined that a disabling injury costs an average of roughly $25,000 (in 1997 dollars). A company with 1000 employees could expect to have 27 lost-workday injuries per year. With a 4.5 percent profit margin, the company would need almost $15 million of sales to offset that cost.[8] At Southern California Edison, over an 8-year period, the average cost of an injury (disabling or not) was almost $6300 (in 1997 dollars). Of this cost, 41.2 percent represented lost productivity; 30 percent, medical costs; and 28.8 percent, direct, nonmedical costs.[9]

Regardless of one's perspective, social or economic, these are disturbing figures. In response, public policy has focused on two types of actions: *monetary compensation* for job-related injuries and *preventive measures* to enhance job safety and health. State-run workers' compensation programs and the federal Occupational Safety and Health Administration are responsible for implementing public policy in these areas. Let's examine each of them.

WORKERS' COMPENSATION: A HISTORICAL PERSPECTIVE

State governments introduced workers' compensation laws in the early 1900s. Such laws are based on the principle of *liability without fault,* under which employers contribute to a fund providing compensation to employees involved in work-related accidents and injuries. The scale of benefits is related to the nature of the injury. The benefits are not provided because of liability or negligence on the part of the employer; rather, they are provided simply as a matter of social policy. Since the premiums paid reflected the accident rate of the particular employer, states hoped to provide an incentive for firms to lower their premium costs by improving work conditions. The Supreme Court upheld the constitutionality of such laws in 1917, and by 1948, all states had adopted them in one form or another.[10]

For the more than 80 million workers, or 88 percent of the nation's workforce, who are covered, workers' compensation provides three types of benefits: (1) payments to replace lost wages while an employee is unable to work, (2) payments to cover medical bills, and (3) if an individual is unable to return to his or her former occupation, financial support for retraining. For payments to replace lost wages, the legislation typically allows for some percentage of regular wages (60 to 67 percent) up to a maximum amount. However, the benefits actually received are often less than half of regular wages.[11]

By the 1960s, it was becoming apparent that neither the workers' compensation laws nor state safety standards were acting to reduce occupational hazards. Evidence began to accumulate that there were health hazards (so-called silent killers) in the modern work environment that either had not been fully recognized previously or were not fully understood. Research on industrial diseases was beginning to disclose that even brief exposure to certain toxic materials in a work environment could produce disease, sterility, and high mortality rates. This new concern was dramatized by revelations of "black lung" (pneumoconiosis) among coal miners, of "brown lung" (byssinosis) among textile workers, and of the toxic and carcinogenic (cancer-causing) effects of substances such as vinyl chloride and asbestos in other work environments.

In 1990, stress-related awards accounted for nearly 14 percent of occupational disease claims, up from less than 5 percent just 8 years before. Perceptions of exposure to health and safety risks increases worker stress, and such stress is related directly to health-care costs.[12] Workers' compensation has also been awarded for certain adverse physiological reactions to working at computer monitors, such as eyestrain.[13] Thus, in addition to *compensation* for work-related injuries, it became clear that a federally administered program of *prevention* of workplace health and safety hazards was essential. This concern culminated in the passage of the Williams-Steiger Occupational Safety and Health Act of 1970.

THE OCCUPATIONAL SAFETY AND HEALTH ACT

Purpose and Coverage

The purpose of the act is an ambitious one: "To assure so far as possible every working man and woman in the Nation safe and healthful working conditions and to preserve our human resources." Its coverage is equally ambitious, for the law extends to any business (regardless of size) that *affects* interstate commerce. Since almost any business affects interstate commerce, about 6 million U.S. workplaces and 93 million workers are included.[14] However, employers in low-hazard industries with 10 or fewer employees are exempt from regular safety inspections.[15] Federal, state, and local government workers are also excluded since the government cannot easily proceed against itself in the event of violations.

Administration

The 1970 act established three government agencies to administer and enforce the law:

- **The Occupational Safety and Health Administration** (OSHA) to establish and enforce the necessary safety and health standards
- **The Occupational Safety and Health Review Commission** (a three-member board appointed by the President) to rule on the appropriateness of OSHA's enforcement actions when they are contested by employers, employees, or unions

- **The National Institute for Occupational Safety and Health** (NIOSH) to conduct research on the causes and prevention of occupational injury and illness, to recommend new standards (based on this research) to the secretary of labor, and to develop educational programs

Safety and Health Standards

Under the law, each employer has a "general duty" to provide a place of employment "free from recognized hazards." Employers also have the "special duty" to comply with all standards of safety and health established under this act.

OSHA has issued a large number of detailed standards covering numerous environmental hazards. Items covered include power tools, machine guards, compressed gas, materials handling and storage, and toxic substances such as asbestos, cotton dust, silica, lead, and carbon monoxide.

As an example, consider OSHA's bloodborne pathogen standard. Workers exposed to blood and bodily fluids (e.g., health-care providers, first-aid providers) are covered by the rule, but it does not apply to workers who give first aid as "good Samaritans." It requires facilities to develop exposure-control plans, implement engineering controls and worker training, provide personal protective equipment and hepatitis B vaccinations, and communicate hazards to workers.[16]

To date, NIOSH, on the basis of its research, has identified more than 15,000 toxic substances, but the transition from research findings to workplace standards is often a long, contentious process. Currently, it takes 38 to 46 months to set a standard.[17]

Record-Keeping Requirements

A good deal of paperwork is required of employers under the act. Specifically:

- A general log of each injury or illness (OSHA Form 200) (see Figure 14-1)
- Supplementary records of each injury or illness (OSHA Form 101)

Employees are guaranteed access, on request, to Form 200 at their workplaces, and the records must be retained for 5 years following the calendar year they cover. The purpose of these reports is to identify where safety and health problems have been occurring (if at all). Such information helps call management's attention to the problems, as well as that of an OSHA inspector, should one visit the workplace. The annual summary must be sent to OSHA directly, to help the agency determine which workplaces should receive priority for inspection.

OSHA Enforcement

In administering the act, OSHA inspectors have the right to enter a workplace and to conduct a compliance inspection. However, in its *Marshall v. Barlow's, Inc.* decision, the Supreme Court ruled that employers could require a search warrant before allowing the inspector onto company premises.[18] In practice, only about 3 percent of employers go that far, perhaps because the resulting inspection

U.S. Department of Labor

For Calendar Year 19 ______ Page ___ of ___

Company Name	Form Approved O.M.B. No. 1220-0029
Establishment Name	See OMB Disclosure Statement on reverse.
Establishment Address	

Extent of and Outcome of INJURY						Type, Extent of, and Outcome of ILLNESS												
Fatalities	Nonfatal Injuries					Type of Illness							Fatalities	Nonfatal Illnesses				
Injury Related	Injuries With Lost Workdays				Injuries Without Lost Workdays	CHECK Only One Column for Each Illness *(See other side of form for terminations or permanent transfers.)*							Illness Related	Illnesses With Lost Workdays				Illnesses Without Lost Workdays
Enter DATE of death. Mo./day/yr.	Enter a CHECK if injury involves days away from work, or days of restricted work activity, or both.	Enter a CHECK if injury involves days away from work.	Enter number of DAYS *away from work.*	Enter number of DAYS of *restricted work activity.*	Enter a CHECK if no entry was made in columns 1 or 2 but the injury is recordable as defined above.	Occupational skin diseases or disorders	Dust diseases of the lungs	Respiratory conditions due to toxic agents	Poisoning (systemic effects of toxic materials)	Disorders due to physical agents	Disorders associated with repeated trauma	All other occupational illnesses	Enter DATE of death. Mo./day/yr.	Enter a CHECK if illness involves days away from work, or days of restricted work activity, or both.	Enter a CHECK if illness involves days away from work.	Enter number of DAYS *away from work.*	Enter number of DAYS of *restricted work activity.*	Enter a CHECK if no entry was made in columns 8 or 9.
(1)	(2)	(3)	(4)	(5)	(6)	(7)							(8)	(9)	(10)	(11)	(12)	(13)
						(a)	(b)	(c)	(d)	(e)	(f)	(g)						

INJURIES ILLNESSES

Certification of Annual Summary Totals By ______________ Title ______________ Date ______________

OSHA No. 200

POST ONLY THIS PORTION OF THE LAST PAGE NO LATER THAN FEBRUARY 1.

Figure 14-1

OSHA Form 200, log and summary of occupational injuries and illnesses.

is likely to be especially "close."[19] Employers are prohibited from discriminating against employees who file complaints, and an employee representative is entitled to accompany the OSHA representative during the inspection.

Since it is impossible for the roughly 900 agency inspectors (most of whom are either safety engineers or industrial hygienists) to visit the nation's 6 million workplaces, a system of priorities has been established. OSHA assigns top priority to worksites that involve exposure to three risks: confined spaces, lead in construction materials, and tuberculosis. Businesses particularly affected include health-care facilities, nursing homes, construction companies, and manufacturers whose plants contain potentially dangerous chemicals.[20]

At the worksite, inspectors concentrate more on dangerous risk factors than on technical infractions. For example, OSHA fined Samsung Guam, Inc. $8.3 million after a worker fell 50 feet to his death. The construction company had no railings or harness ropes, letting workers walk across steel beams with no protection.[21]

Considerable emphasis has been given to OSHA's role of *enforcement,* but not much to its role of *consultation.* Employers in nearly every state who want help in recognizing and correcting safety and health hazards can get it from a free, on-site consultation service funded by OSHA. The service is delivered by state governments or private-sector contractors using well-trained safety and/or health professionals (e.g., industrial hygienists). Primarily targeted for smaller businesses, this program is penalty-free and completely separate from the OSHA inspection effort. An employer's only obligation is a commitment to correct serious job safety and health hazards.[22]

Penalties

Fines are mandatory where serious violations are found. If a violation is willful (one in which an employer either knew that what was being done constituted a violation of federal regulations or was aware that a hazardous condition existed and made no reasonable effort to eliminate it), an employer can be assessed a civil penalty of up to $70,000 for each violation. An employer who fails to correct a violation (within the allowed time limit) for which a citation has been issued can be fined up to $7000 for each day the violation continues. Finally, a willful first violation involving the death of a worker can carry a criminal penalty as high as $70,000 and 6 months in prison. A second such conviction can mean up to $140,000 and a full year behind bars.[23]

Executives can also receive criminal penalties. Calling their conduct everything from assault and battery to reckless homicide, prosecutors in at least 14 states have sought jail time for employers who ignore warnings to improve safety on the job. States have jailed close to a dozen employers in the 1990s—handing one plant owner a sentence of nearly 20 years after 25 workers died in a fire at his food-processing plant. Investigators found that the high death count had been the result of illegally locked plant doors and the absence of a sprinkler system.[24]

Appeals

Employers can appeal citations, proposed penalties, and corrections they have been ordered to make through multiple levels of the agency, culminating with the Occupational Safety and Health Review Commission. The commission presumes the employer to be free of violations and puts the burden of proof on OSHA.[25] Further appeals can be pursued through the federal court system.

The Role of the States

Although OSHA is a federally run program, the act allows states to develop and administer their own programs if they are approved by the secretary of labor. There are many criteria for approval, but the most important is that the state program must be judged "at least as effective" as the federal program. Currently, 23 states have approved plans in operation.

Workers' Rights to Health and Safety

Both unionized and nonunionized workers have walked off the job when subjected to unsafe working conditions.[26] In unionized firms, walkouts have occurred during the term of valid collective bargaining agreements that contained no-strike and grievance and/or arbitration clauses.[27] Are such walkouts legal? Yes, the Supreme Court has ruled, under certain circumstances:[28]

- Objective evidence must be presented to support the claim that abnormally dangerous working conditions exist.
- If such evidence is presented, a walkout is legal regardless of the existence of a no-strike or arbitration clause.
- It is an unfair labor practice for an employer to interfere with a walkout under such circumstances. This is true whether a firm is unionized or nonunionized.
- Expert testimony (e.g., by an industrial hygienist) is critically important in establishing the presence of abnormally dangerous working conditions.
- If a good-faith belief is not supported by objective evidence, employees who walk off the job are subject to disciplinary action.

OSHA's Impact

From its inception, OSHA has been both cussed and discussed, and its effectiveness in improving workplace safety and health has been questioned by the very firms it regulates. Controversy has ranged from disagreements over the setting of health standards to inspection procedures.[29] Employers complain of excessively detailed and costly regulations that, they believe, ignore workplace realities. Investigations by Congress and by outside researchers have found that OSHA has made no significant, lasting reductions in lost workdays or injury rates.[30] In the opinion of the AFL-CIO, this is due to a lack of enforcement of safety standards and regulations by OSHA. The directors of OSHA argue exactly the opposite: It is precisely because of better record-keeping, brought about in part by stiff fines levied against companies by OSHA, that injury rates have not shown a sustained decline. Another reason is that employers sometimes try to improve their competitiveness at the expense of safety.

COMPANY EXAMPLE

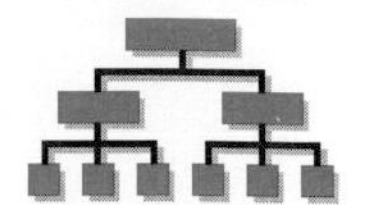

MAINTAINING PRODUCTIVITY AT THE EXPENSE OF SAFETY

Preoccupied with staying in business, many small businesses skimp on safety information and worker training. That can be especially risky because such companies rely more heavily than do big companies on workers who are young or who speak little English. As an example, consider the case of Everardo Rangel-Jasso.

Mr. Rangel-Jasso was crushed to death at Denton Plastics, Inc., in Portland, Oregon. The 17-year-old was backing up a forklift, with a box high on its fork, when he cut the rear wheels sharply and the vehicle tipped over. A posted sign, in English, warned forklift drivers to wear seat belts—but the Mexican youth did not speak English. According to an OSHA investigator, a seat belt might have saved his life.

Employees told OSHA that Hispanic workers learned their jobs through "hand signals and body gestures." Mr. Rangel-Jasso had not received any forklift training and lacked a driver's license and a juvenile's work permit. Federal and state officials levied more than $150,000 in fines against the company, and two senior managers faced criminal indictments. This case is not an isolated incident. A computer analysis of 500,000 federal and state safety inspection records from 1988 to 1992 showed that 4337 workers died at inspected workplaces with fewer than 20 workers, but only 127 died at companies with more than 2500 workers. According to an OSHA administrator: "[At many small businesses] it takes a serious accident or fatality for them to wake up."[31]

Despite these problems, even OSHA's critics have agreed that simply by calling attention to the problems of workplace safety and health, OSHA has caused a lot more awareness of these dangers than would otherwise have been the case. Management's willingness to correct hazards and to improve such vital environmental conditions as ventilation, noise levels, and machine safety is much greater now than it was before OSHA. Critics also agree that, because of OSHA and NIOSH, we now know far more about such dangerous substances as vinyl chloride, PCBs, asbestos, cotton dust, and a host of other carcinogens. As a result, management has taken at least the initial actions needed to protect workers from them.

Finally, any analysis of OSHA's impact must consider the fundamental issue of the *causes* of workplace accidents. OSHA standards govern potentially unsafe *work conditions* that employees may be exposed to. There are no standards that govern potentially unsafe *employee behaviors.* And while employers may be penalized for failure to comply with safety and health standards, employees are subject to no such threat. Research suggests that the enforcement of OSHA standards, directed as it is to environmental accidents and illnesses, can hope *at best* to affect 25 percent of on-the-job accidents.[32] The remaining 75 percent require *behavioral* rather than *technical* modifications.

ASSESSING THE COSTS AND BENEFITS OF OCCUPATIONAL SAFETY AND HEALTH PROGRAMS

Let's face it: accidents are expensive. Aside from workers' compensation costs, consider the "indirect" costs of an accident:

1. Cost of wages paid for time lost
2. Cost of damage to material or equipment
3. Cost of overtime work paid to other workers as a result of the accident
4. Cost of wages paid to supervisors while their time is required for activities resulting from the accident
5. Costs of decreased output of the injured worker after he or she returns to work

6. Costs associated with the time it takes for a new worker to learn the job
7. Uninsured medical costs borne by the company
8. Cost of time spent by higher management and clerical workers to investigate or to process workers' compensation forms

On the other hand, safety pays. For example, the policies and procedures designed to ensure employee safety at Du Pont and ALCOA have produced both safer work environments and cost savings.

COMPANY EXAMPLE

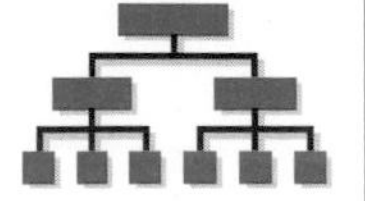

SAFETY PAYS AT DU PONT AND ALCOA

At Du Pont Corporation, safety experts provide feedback while engineers observe workers and then redesign valves and install key locks to deter accident-causing behavior. When injuries do happen, the company reports them quickly to workers to provide a sense of immediacy, trying to show the behavior that caused the accident without naming the offender. It also fosters peer pressure to work safely by giving units common goals—that way, workers are working together instead of independently. Du Pont offers carrots, too. Its directors regularly give safety awards, and workers win $15 to $20 prizes if their divisions are accident-free for 6 to 9 months. The company's incentive for doing this is not altogether altruistic—it estimates its annual cost savings to be $150 million.

At Aluminum Company of America, Inc. (ALCOA), which introduced a "brothers' keeper" slogan in the workplace, all employees must submit safety improvement suggestions, and even the lowest-level workers can stop production lines if they suspect a safety problem. The company's chairman has made safety a top priority as well. Have these efforts paid off? Most assuredly. ALCOA improved its safety record by 25 percent in 3 years and estimates it saves $10,000 to $12,000 in workers' compensation for each accident avoided.[33]

Like many other problems of the marketplace, safety and health programs involve what economists call "externalities"—the fact that not all the social costs of production are necessarily included on a firm's profit and loss statement. The employer does not suffer from the worker's injury or disease and therefore lacks the full incentive to reduce it. As long as the outlays required for preventive measures are less than the social costs of disability among workers, higher fatality rates, and the diversion of medical resources, the enforcement of safety and health standards is well worth it and society will benefit.[34]

ORGANIZATIONAL SAFETY AND HEALTH PROGRAMS

As noted earlier, accidents result from two broad causes: *unsafe work conditions* (physical and environmental) and *unsafe work behaviors.* Unsafe physical conditions include defective equipment, inadequate machine guards, and lack of protective equipment. Examples of unsafe environmental conditions are noise, radiation, dust, fumes, and stress. In one study of work injuries, 50 percent re-

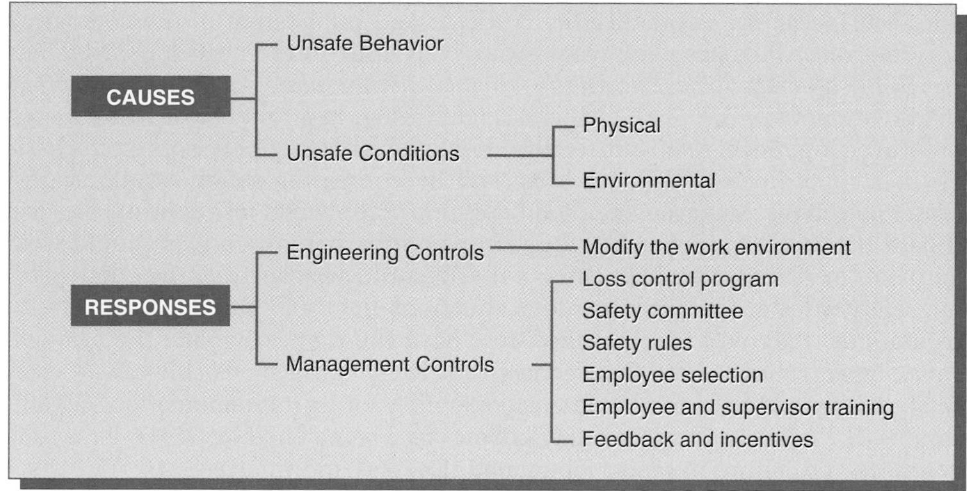

Figure 14-2
Causes of and responses to workplace accidents.

sulted from unsafe work conditions, 45 percent resulted from unsafe work behaviors, and 5 percent were of indeterminate origin.[35] However, accidents often result from an *interaction* of unsafe conditions and unsafe acts. Thus, if a particular operation forces a worker to lift a heavy part and twist around to set it on a bench, the operation itself forces the worker to perform an unsafe act. Telling the worker not to lift and twist at the same time will not solve the problem. The *unsafe condition itself* must be corrected, either by redesigning the flow of material or by providing the worker with a mechanical device for lifting.

To eliminate, or at least reduce, the number and severity of workplace accidents, a combination of management and engineering controls is essential. These are shown in Figure 14-2. *Engineering controls* attempt to eliminate unsafe work conditions and to neutralize unsafe worker behaviors. They involve some modification of the work environment: for example, installing a metal cover over the blades of a lawn mower to make it almost impossible for a member of a grounds crew to catch his or her foot in the blades. *Management controls* attempt to increase safe behaviors. The following sections examine each of the elements shown in Figure 14-2.

Loss Control

Management's first duty is to formulate a safety policy. Its second duty is to implement and sustain this policy through a *loss control program.* Such a program has four components: a safety budget, safety records, management's personal concern, and management's good example.[36]

To reduce the frequency of accidents, management must be willing to spend money and to budget for safety. As we have seen, accidents involve *direct* as well as *indirect* costs. Since the national average for indirect costs is 4 times higher than the average for direct costs, it is clear that money spent to improve safety is returned many times over through the control of accidents. Detailed analysis of accident reports, as well as management's personal concern (e.g., meeting with department heads over safety issues; on-site visits by top executives to discuss the need for safety, as practiced at ALCOA; and publication of the company's accident record), keeps employees aware constantly of the need for safety.

Study after study has shown the crucial role that management plays in effective safety programs.[37] Such concern is manifested in a number of ways: by appointing a high-level safety officer, by offering rewards to supervisors on the basis of their subordinates' safety records, and by comparing safety results against preset objectives. Management's good example completes a loss control program. If hard hats are required at a particular operation, then executives should wear hard hats even if they are in business suits. If employees see executives disregarding safety rules or treating hazardous situations lightly by not conforming with regulations, they will feel that they, too, have the right to violate the rules. In short, organizations show their concern for loss control by establishing a clear safety policy and by assuming the responsibility for its implementation. Organizations that fail to implement safety policies face being fined by OSHA for unsafe practices and failure to report job-related illnesses and injuries.

COMPANY EXAMPLE

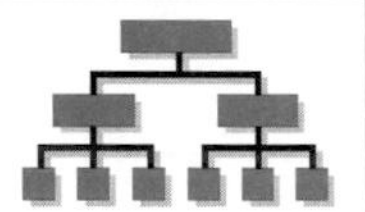

CUTTING CORNERS IN THE MEATPACKING INDUSTRY

IBP, formerly known as Iowa Beef Processors, is the largest meatpacker in the United States. It operates 12 plants that employ 17,000 workers. In 1987, OSHA levied a $25.9 million fine against the company for willfully failing to report more than 1000 job-related injuries and illnesses over a 2-year period. Among the unreported injuries and illnesses cited by the agency were knife cuts and wounds, concussions, burns, hernias, and fractures.

OSHA determined that 1 week before it subpoenaed IBP's records, the company assembled 50 people to "revise" injury and illness logs. According to OSHA, IBP added more than 800 injuries and illnesses that had not been recorded when they occurred. How did OSHA know this to be true? Company workers had previously obtained the unrevised logs and had given them to agency investigators.[38]

In 1988, OSHA tacked on an additional $3.1 million in fines against IBP for requiring employees to perform repetitive motions that can cause nerve damage (carpal tunnel syndrome) that may cripple the hand or wrists so that the victim is unable to grip or pick up objects. The matter was settled in 1989, when IBP agreed to pay a reduced fine ($975,000), while establishing a model job redesign program to combat repetitive-motion injuries.[39]

The Role of the Safety Committee

Representation of employees, managers, and safety specialists on the safety committee can lead to a much higher commitment to safety than might otherwise be the case. Indeed, merely establishing the committee indicates management's concern. Beyond that, however, the committee has important work to do:

- Recommend (or critique) safety policies issued by top management
- Develop in-house safety standards and ensure compliance with OSHA standards
- Provide safety training for employees and supervisors

Use of protective equipment and proper work procedures helps avoid costly, disabling accidents on the job.

- Conduct safety inspections
- Continually promote the theme of job safety through the elimination of unsafe conditions and unsafe behaviors

As an example of recommendations that such a committee might make, consider some possible policies to reduce the incidence of repetitive-motion injuries that have afflicted not only meatpackers and pianists but also telephone and computer operators and supermarket checkout clerks. Aetna Life and Casualty Company installed ergonomically designed chairs with lower-back supports, adjustable seats, and armrests. U.S. West created "Worksmart," a one-on-one telephone operator–training program. Operators' work habits are videotaped and analyzed for work speed and posture. Exercises help stretch hands and wrists, and a metronome helps operators work at a smooth pace.[40] These two approaches, modifying equipment and analyzing the way work is done, are the two most common preventive actions by employers.[41]

Safety Rules

Safety rules are important refinements of the general safety policies issued by top management. To be effective, they should make clear the consequences of not following the rules, for example, by calling for progressive discipline. Evidence indicates, unfortunately, that in many cases the rules are not obeyed. Take protective equipment, for example.

OSHA standards require that employers *furnish* and employees *use* suitable protective equipment (e.g., hard hats, goggles, face shields, earplugs, respirators) where there is a "reasonable probability" that injuries can be prevented by such equipment. Companies often find that it is in their own best interests to do so as well. A 5-year study of 36,000 Home Depot, Inc. employees found that back-support devices reduced low-back injuries by about a third. The study compared the incidence of such injuries before and after the company made corsets mandatory for all store employees.[42] As the following data show, however, "You can lead a horse to water, but you can't make it drink."[43]

- Hard hats were worn by only 16 percent of workers who sustained head injuries, although 40 percent were required to wear them.
- Only 1 percent of workers suffering facial injuries were wearing facial protection.
- Only 23 percent of workers with foot injuries were wearing safety shoes or boots.
- Only 40 percent of workers with eye injuries were wearing protective equipment.

Perhaps the rules are not being obeyed because they are not being enforced. But it is also possible that they are not being obeyed because of flaws in employee selection practices, because of inadequate training, or because there is simply no incentive for doing so.

Employee Selection

To the extent that keen vision, dexterity, hearing, balance, and other physical or psychological characteristics make a critical difference between success and failure on a job, they should be used to screen applicants. However, there are two other factors that also relate strongly to accident rates among workers: *age* and *length of service*.[44] On one hand, regardless of length of service, the younger the employee, the higher the accident rate. On the other hand, accident rates are substantially higher during the first month of employment than in all subsequent time periods, regardless of the age of the worker. And when workers of the same age are studied, accident rates decrease as length of service increases. A recent large-scale study found that workers over age 55 are a third less likely than their younger colleagues to be injured at work seriously enough to lose work time.[45] This is true in industries as diverse as mining, retail trade, transportation, public utilities, and service. The lesson for managers is clear: *new worker equals high risk.*

Training for Employees and Supervisors

Accidents often occur because workers lack one vital tool to protect themselves: information. Consider the following data collected by the Bureau of Labor Statistics:[46]

- Nearly 1 out of every 5 workers injured while operating power saws received no safety training on the equipment.
- Of 724 workers hurt while using scaffolds, 27 percent had received no information on safety requirements for installing the kind of scaffold on which they were injured.

For many office workers, video display terminals are essential tools.

- Of 554 workers hurt while servicing equipment, 61 percent were not told about lockout procedures that prevent the equipment from being turned on inadvertently while it is being serviced.

In nearly every type of injury that researchers have studied, the same story is repeated over and over. Workers often do not receive the kind of safety information they need, *even on jobs that require them to use dangerous equipment.* This situation is unfortunate, but a problem that is just as serious occurs when safety practices that are taught in training are not reinforced on the job. Regular feedback and incentives for compliance are essential.

Feedback and Incentives

Previous chapters have underscored the positive impact on the motivation of employees when they are given feedback and incentives to improve productivity. The same principles can also be used to improve safe behavior. In one study of a wholesale bakery that was experiencing a sharp increase in work accidents, researchers developed a detailed coding sheet for observing safe and unsafe behaviors. Observers then used the sheets to record systematically both safe and unsafe employee behaviors over a 25-week period before, during, and after a safety training program. Slides were used to illustrate both safe and unsafe behaviors. Trainees were also shown data on the percentage of safe behaviors in their departments, and a goal of 90 percent safe behaviors was established. Following all of this, the actual percentage of safe behaviors was posted in each department. Supervisors were trained to use positive reinforcement (praise) when they observed safe behaviors. In comparison with workers in departments that received no training, workers in the departments that received training averaged almost 24 percent more safe behaviors. Not only did employees react favorably to the program, but the company was able to maintain it. One year prior to the program, the number of lost-time injuries per million hours worked was 53.8. Even in highly hazardous industries, this figure rarely exceeds 35. One year after the program, the figure was less than 10.[47]

Newport News Shipbuilding and Dry Dock Company cut its injury rate in half by using a similar behavioral approach to safety management. The company's bottom-up approach empowers employees to correct others' unsafe behavior and take it upon themselves to fix unsafe things they observe.[48] The results of these studies suggest that training, goal setting, and feedback provide useful alternatives to disciplinary sanctions to encourage compliance with the rules. As one safety consultant noted: "It's better to recognize a guy for success than to beat him up for failure."[49]

Job Safety and Health: What Are Companies Doing?

Traditionally, managers tended to think of safety as an important issue primarily in manufacturing. Today, however, 84 percent of U.S. employees work in service-based industries, as well as in high-technology jobs.[50] Many of the new jobs involve video display terminals (VDTs), semiconductor production, or exposure to chemicals. Some companies are proactively dealing with these new challenges.

Between 40 and 50 percent of the U.S. workforce deals with VDTs on a daily basis. Many users complain of a variety of syndromes, including blurred vision, eyestrain, repetitive-motion disorders, and muscular pains in the shoulder, back, or neck.[51] To deal with potential problems associated with VDT viewing, the St. Paul Companies, a large insurance company, recently introduced a program designed to teach VDT users relaxation techniques, workstation organization, and health awareness, including the need for regular eye checkups. The company reported significantly lowered techno-stress levels following the program.[52] Apple Computer, trying to make its computer screens more user-friendly, uses an antiglare treatment that scatters light. Other firms are purchasing antiglare filters for their employees to use.[53]

Another new technology that may produce adverse health consequences is semiconductor production, which involves acids and gases. Such consequences may include a higher rate of miscarriages among women who work in the production process, as well as higher rates of nausea, headaches, and rashes. Digital Equipment, AT&T, Intel, and Texas Instruments all have adopted policies that allow pregnant women to transfer out of production operations without sacrificing pay or seniority.[54]

Companies are also alerting workers exposed to high levels of chemicals or other possible causes of disease. The notification rules come under OSHA's "hazard communication" standard, put into effect in 1988. The rules apply to about 575,000 hazardous chemicals and 320,000 manufacturing businesses, and affect some 32 million workers.[55] They require every workplace in the country to identify and list hazardous chemicals being used ("from bleach to bowl cleaner")[56] and to train employees in their use. Such "right-to-know" requirements have helped avoid situations in which workers are unknowingly being exposed to potentially hazardous materials.

COMPANY EXAMPLE

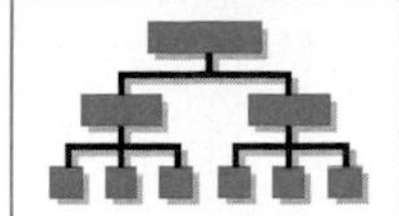

RIGHT-TO-KNOW RULES IN THE CHEMICAL INDUSTRY

Cathy Zimmerman, a 26-year-old lab technician at Hercules, Inc., in Wilmington, Delaware, was pouring chemicals in 1986 when she noticed that the bottles were labeled "mutagen" and "teratogen." She went to her dictionary, which said that a mutagen can alter chromosomes and a teratogen can cause malformations in fetuses. "I said, 'O, my God!'" she recalls. "When I saw that, I talked to my boss and told him I was scared. I didn't want to take a chance."

Mrs. Zimmerman, who was expecting her first child, was transferred to Hercules' flavoring division, where she was able to work with less hazardous materials. But she hopes that a new right-to-know training program required by OSHA will prevent such surprises in the future. "With right-to-know, we'd have gone over it first, before it came into the lab," she says. "We didn't have that before."

Some employees are alarmed to discover that they have been working with certain hazardous chemicals. Others are overwhelmed by the detailed labeling, which they say makes it even harder to distinguish really dangerous materials. Meanwhile some businesses claim that fearful workers are demanding unnecessary and costly changes. At the same time, however, OSHA defends the measure, arguing that heightened awareness, and even anxiety, will help reduce work-related accidents. As one spokesperson for OSHA commented, "I'd rather be anxious and alive than calm and dead."[57]

In the United States there is considerable pressure to improve plant safety. See the International Application on the next page for examples of the situation in other countries.

HEALTH HAZARDS AT WORK

The Need for Safeguards

The National Institute of Occupational Safety and Health has identified more than 15,000 toxic substances, of which some 500 might require regulation as carcinogens (cancer-causing substances). The list of chemical, physical, and biological hazards is a long one. It includes carbon monoxide, vinyl chloride, dusts, particulates, gases and vapors, radiation, excessive noise and vibration, and extreme temperatures. When present in high concentrations, these agents can lead to respiratory, kidney, liver, skin, neurological, and other disorders.

There have been some well-publicized lawsuits against employers for causing occupational illnesses as a result of lack of proper safeguards or technical controls.[64] Thus the U.S. Supreme Court ruled in the case of Karen Silkwood, a former laboratory analyst at a plutonium plant in Oklahoma, that the federal government's interest in nuclear safety did not prevent a jury from awarding damages to Mrs. Silkwood's family for injuries arising from exposure to radiation at her workplace.[65] In another decision, a jury in Cleveland awarded $520,000 to a former government employee who sued the maker of a

INTERNATIONAL APPLICATION
Health and Safety—The Response by Governments and Multinational Firms in Less Developed Countries

In 1984, 45 tons of lethal gas leaked from the Union Carbide (India) Ltd. pesticide plant in the central Indian city of Bhopal, killing more than 3800 people and disabling more than 20,000 in history's worst industrial disaster. Subsequently, the Indian Supreme Court ordered Union Carbide to pay $470 million in damages to victims of the disaster (although dissatisfied survivors could still file claims in the United States as well);[58] and an Indian judge ordered the seizure of all of Carbide's Indian assets as part of continuing criminal proceedings against the company.[59]

These events produced important consequences. U.S. multinational firms found out that liability for any Bhopal-like disaster could be decided in U.S. courts. This, more than pressure from third-world governments, has forced companies to tighten safety procedures, upgrade plants, supervise maintenance more closely, and educate workers and communities in their far-flung empires.[60] In India, despite the outcry against Union Carbide, the country continues to welcome foreign investment and technology.

In Mexico, a gas explosion at Pemex, the state-owned oil monopoly, killed at least 500 people and wounded thousands of others at about the same time as the Bhopal disaster. One year later, little had been done to improve the conditions that caused the explosion. After years of neglect and rampant pollution at Pemex facilities, the government was loath to clamp down because that would focus attention on the main culprit: the Mexican government itself.[61]

Neither the Bhopal nor the Pemex incident had any noticeable effect on multinational investment in Mexico. In fact, all the developing countries in one survey seem to rely on the multinationals, rather than on draconian new regulations, to prevent a repeat of Bhopal. This is true in South Korea, Taiwan, Egypt, and Thailand, for example. In Thailand, a 1993 fire at a toy factory killed more than 240 workers. There were no fire escapes, fire alarms, sprinkler systems, or other safety features. Experts say such negligence is common throughout the region, where labor unions are weak and corruption is often endemic.[62] As these few examples make clear, in many of the less developed countries around the world, foreign investment is a political and economic issue, not a safety issue.

This situation may be changing, for the rapid globalization of business now links manufacturers, investors, and consumers everywhere. Increasingly, consumers can see how their shirts and sneakers actually are made, peering into Indonesian factories and Honduran sweatshops. Under pressure from U.S. consumer and labor groups, firms such as Nike, Kmart, and Wal-Mart announced new codes for overseas contract labor. Thus, after a 1996 audit by Ernst & Young, ordered by Nike, subcontractors now are keener about ensuring that workers wear protective gloves and masks and that fire extinguishers are properly maintained. Yet conditions remain tough. In Indonesia, military police regularly enter factories to keep workers under control. Overtime is mandatory, and workers complain that exhausted colleagues regularly faint from overwork. If consumers refuse to buy goods produced under sweatshop conditions, then economic pressure may force firms to become as much trendsetters in labor as they are in fashion.[63]

fireproofing material that contained asbestos after she was diagnosed as having an asbestos-related disease. The woman had worked in the building for 12 years and sued the original seller of the material 3 years after that.[66]

The U.S. Supreme Court has ruled that the states can prosecute company officials under criminal statutes for endangering the health of employees, even if such hazards are also regulated by OSHA.[67] Nevertheless, some of the criticism against employers is not fair. To prove negligence, it must be shown that management *knew* of the connection between exposure to the hazards and negative health consequences and that management *chose* to do nothing to reduce worker exposure. Yet few such connections were made until recent years. Even now, alternative explanations for the causes of disease or illness cannot be ruled out in many cases. Responsibility for regulation has been left to OSHA.

The primary emphasis to date has been on installing engineering controls that *prevent* exposure to harmful substances. In fact, in a sweeping move in 1989, OSHA established or toughened workplace exposure limits for 376 toxic chemicals. The rules cost employers $788 million a year. While this figure might sound steep, consider that an estimated $30 billion is spent annually just to treat preventable cancer. The benefits? According to OSHA, the new limits should save nearly 700 lives a year and reduce work-related illnesses such as cancer, liver and kidney impairments, and respiratory and cardiovascular illnesses by about 55,000 cases a year.[68] But is cost–benefit analysis appropriate when lives are literally at stake?

The Supreme Court recognized this problem in its 1981 "cotton dust" decision. It held that OSHA need not balance the costs of implementing standards against the benefits expected. OSHA has to show only that it is *economically feasible* to implement the standards. The decision held that Congress had already decided the balance between costs and benefits in favor of the worker when it passed the law.[69] On one issue all parties agree: the nature of cancer itself makes it virtually impossible for workers to protect themselves from exposure to cancer-causing substances. In recent years, another killer has entered the workplace. While its origins lie outside the workplace, businesses cannot ignore either its cost or its consequences. That killer is AIDS.

AIDS and Business

AIDS (acquired immune deficiency syndrome) is a medical time bomb. With 340,000 diagnosed cases in the United States and 1.5 million people with the human immunodeficiency virus (HIV) that causes AIDS, employers are fast having to deal with increasing numbers of AIDS victims in the workplace. Unlike victims of other life-threatening illnesses, such as Alzheimer's or heart disease, the vast majority of those with HIV or AIDS are of working age—between 25 and 44. AIDS is a bottom-line business issue.[70] Consider these facts and prognoses regarding the disease:

- The World Health Organization estimates that by the year 2000, 30 million people will be infected with HIV. Yet AIDS, a killer, can itself be killed through education and the adoption of safe behavior.[71]
- Non-AIDS public-health programs will be curtailed in cities hit hard by the epidemic.
- With no cure in sight for at least 20 years, the Health Insurance Association of America estimates that the AIDS medical bill may be as much as $11 billion a year. The disease has already killed more than 200,000 Americans.[72] In the first half of 1996 alone, 21,700 Americans died from AIDS.[73]
- The cost of treating an AIDS patient from diagnosis to death was $102,000 in 1993. This figure will escalate over time as people with AIDS live longer—largely due to better drugs to fight the disease, and with the growing availability of AIDS-related health care. In 1996, the average time period from infection with HIV to the development of AIDS was 8 to 11 years.[74] The cost of

treating AIDS is higher than the average cost of treating leukemia, cancer of the digestive system, a heart attack, or paraplegia from an auto crash.

- The cumulative costs of long-term disability payments to people with AIDS are expected to exceed $2 billion.
- Direct costs to companies will escalate in three ways: through (1) increased medical premiums to cover their employees with AIDS, (2) increased medical premiums to cover AIDS victims without insurance, and (3) an increased Medicaid burden.
- Indirect costs will also affect the bottom line in at least three ways. One is through lost work time of AIDS patients. Since jobs held by AIDS-affected workers are protected by the Americans with Disabilities Act, others have to do their work while they are out, and the substitute workers may be less productive. Two, productivity may suffer if coworkers refuse to work with an AIDS-infected employee. Three, recruitment costs will increase because AIDS is a lethal disease that is always fatal. Those employees (or coworkers who quit rather than work with an AIDS-infected employee) must be replaced.[75]
- The ADA also prohibits discrimination against job applicants who have the disease.

COMPANY EXAMPLE

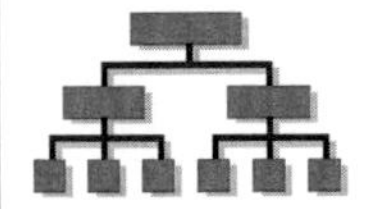

LEVI STRAUSS & COMPANY'S AIDS-RELATED CORPORATE PHILOSOPHIES[76]

1. There is no special AIDS policy. Instead, the company addresses the needs of employees with AIDS and their coworkers within the framework of its general approach to employee relations.
2. There is no preemployment testing of any sort for AIDS, and there are no AIDS screening questions on employment applications.
3. Employees with AIDS are treated with compassion and understanding—as are employees with any other life-threatening disease.
4. Employees with AIDS can continue to work as long as they are medically cleared to do so; they are also eligible for work accommodation.
5. Employees are assured of confidentiality when seeking counseling or medical referral.
6. Company medical coverage, disability leave policy, and life insurance do not distinguish between AIDS and any other life-threatening disease.
7. The company's medical plan supports home health and hospice care for the terminally ill.
8. A case management strategy is implemented whenever an employee becomes critically ill.
9. Managers are held accountable for creating a work environment that is supportive of an employee with AIDS.
10. The company has assumed responsibility for educating employees so that neither unwarranted fear nor prejudice affects the work environment of people with AIDS.
11. Individual, family, or group counseling is available to employees and their families through the company's employee assistance program (EAP) or through outside agencies.

12. The EAP staff conducts department and management counseling sessions on request about issues such as how to handle rumors about AIDS, how to deal directly with people's feelings when a colleague becomes ill with AIDS, what colleagues can do to be helpful to a person with AIDS, and how to deal with grief associated with the death of a colleague.

How do these policies work in practice? According to CEO Robert Haas: "It's a kaleidoscope of combined efforts with literally thousands of people in Levi Strauss & Co. [worldwide] contributing to our broad commitment to employee education, to humane care, to outreach, and to our various publics; and that's a model for how we do business here . . . it creates enormous commitment, better decisions, a lot of energy, and results that speak for themselves."[77]

EMPLOYEE ASSISTANCE PROGRAMS

Another (brighter) side of the employee health issue is reflected in employee assistance programs (EAPs). Such programs represent an expansion of traditional work in occupational alcoholism treatment programs. From a handful of programs begun in the 1940s (led by Du Pont), today more than 80 percent of the largest companies in the United States, and many others in Canada, offer EAPs, as do about a third of all worksites with more than 50 employees.[78] EAPs have been developed and applied in other countries as well, but exact transfer from one culture to another simply will not work. Rather, it is necessary to "fit" the EAP to the social, cultural, economic, and political climates of the countries in question.[79]

By its very title, "employee assistance program" signals a change both in application and in technique from the traditional occupational alcoholism treatment program. Modern EAPs extend professional counseling and medical services to all "troubled" employees. *A troubled employee is an individual who is confronted by unresolved personal or work-related problems.*[80] Such problems run the gamut from alcoholism, drug abuse, and high stress to marital, family, and financial problems. While some of these may originate "outside" the work context, they most certainly will have spillover effects to the work context.

Do Employee Assistance Programs Work?

As a recent large scale review of the cost-effectiveness of EAPs concluded: "There is no published evidence that EAPs are harmful to corporate economies or to individual employees. . . . All of the published studies indicate that EAPs are cost-effective."[81] By offering assistance to troubled employees, the companies promote positive employee relations climates, contribute to their employees' well-being, and enhance their ability to function productively at work, at home, and in the community.[82]

From a business perspective, well-run programs seem to pay off handsomely. In well-run programs, management at various levels expresses support for the program, educates employees about the program and provides necessary training on its use, makes the program accessible to employees, and ensures that it operates in a confidential, credible, and neutral manner.[83] Following are two examples of well-run programs.

General Motors Corporation, whose EAP counsels more than 6500 employees with alcohol problems each year, reports a 65 to 75 percent success rate and estimates that it gains $3 for every $1 spent on care. In addition, blue-collar workers who resolve their alcohol and drug abuse problems through an EAP file only half as many grievances as they did before treatment. McDonnell Douglas's EAP serves about 100,000 employees and 250,000 dependents. It estimates a 4-to-1 return on its investment. Workers treated for alcohol or drug dependency missed 44 percent fewer days of work after the EAP was set up, as compared with pre-EAP years. Turnover among these employees also dropped from 40 percent to 8 percent after the EAP had been in effect for 4 years.[84]

EAPs cost $20 to $30 per employee per year,[85] but, as we have seen, data on their effects are impressive. Nevertheless, it is important to be cautious. Often there is a "rush to evaluate" EAPs and other occupational programs. This can lead to premature claims of success or, equally likely, premature condemnation. *Beware of making strong statements about a program's impact at least until repeated evaluations have demonstrated the same findings for different groups of employees.*[86]

How Employee Assistance Programs Work

There are five steps involved in starting an EAP:[87]

1. **Develop a written statement** of the objectives of the program, consistent with organizational policy. Confirm the company's desire to offer help to employees with behavioral or medical problems, and emphasize that such help will be offered on a personal and confidential basis.
2. **Teach managers, supervisors, and union representatives what to do**—and what not to do—when they confront the troubled employee and when they use the program to resolve job performance problems. Both the supervisor and the steward need to be trained to recognize that they are helping, not hurting, the employee by referring him or her to the EAP.
3. **Establish procedures for referral** of the troubled employee to an in-house or outside professional who can take the time to assess what is wrong and arrange for treatment.
4. **Establish a planned program of communications** to employees to announce (and periodically to remind them) that the service is available, that it is confidential, and that other employees are using it.
5. **Continually evaluate** the program in terms of its stated objectives.

More on the Role of the Supervisor

In the traditional alcoholism treatment program, the supervisor has to look for symptoms of alcoholism and then diagnose the problem. Under an EAP, however, the supervisor is responsible only for identifying declining work performance. If normal corrective measures do not work, the supervisor confronts the employee with evidence of his or her poor performance and offers the EAP. Recognize, however, that classic warning signs, such as chronic tardiness and absenteeism, are not always evident at companies where some employees telecommute, or where workers may be geographically separated from their supervisors. Nevertheless, here are some recommendations on how to proceed:[88]

1. Once you suspect a problem, begin documenting instances in which job performance has fallen short. Absenteeism (leaving early, arriving late for work, taking more days off than allowed by policy), accidents, errors, a slackened commitment to completing tasks, and a rise in conflicts with other employees (due to mood swings) may become evident.
2. Having assembled the facts, set up a meeting. Keep the discussion focused on performance, and do not try to make a diagnosis. Outline the employee's shortcomings, insist on improvement, and then say, "I need to bring you to the medical department, something isn't right here. . . . I'm taking you to the experts."
3. Often managers are scared of potential liability and scared to be wrong. They worry, "Can the person sue me?" As long as the discussion focuses on declining job performance, legal experts say that a defamation claim is highly unlikely. Besides, confrontation without focusing on job performance is usually ineffective anyway.

This approach leaves the diagnosis and treatment recommendations to trained counselors. But you can increase the odds of success, according to the medical director of United Airlines, by "telling them that if performance doesn't improve they'll be disciplined."[89] As difficult as it is, such intervention often works.[90]

Now that we understand what EAPs are, their effects, and how they work, let us examine three of today's most pressing workplace problems. These are alcoholism, drug abuse, and violence.

Alcoholism

Management's concern over the issue is understandable, for alcohol misuse by employees is costly in terms of productivity, time lost from work, and treatment. How prevalent is alcoholism, and how costly is it? At the outset we should note that while many figures are bandied about, a critical review of the development and reporting of knowledge about employee alcoholism treatment programs has shown these estimates to be supported by limited empirical data.[91] Nevertheless, according to the National Council on Alcoholism and Drug Dependence:[92]

- About 18 million Americans have a serious drinking problem.
- Annual deaths due to alcohol number about 105,000.
- Of all hospitalized patients, about 25 percent have alcohol-related problems.
- Alcohol is involved in 47 percent of industrial accidents.
- Fully half of all auto fatalities involve alcohol.

The cost? A staggering $86 billion in costs due to lower productivity and treatment, premature death, and accidents, crime, and law enforcement.

Alcoholism affects employees at every level, but it is costliest at the top. Experts estimate that it afflicts at least 10 percent of senior executives. As an example, consider an executive who makes $100,000 per year, is unproductive, and files large health claims. That cost is certainly far higher than a $10,000 treatment program.[93]

A study done for McDonnell Douglas Corporation shows how expensive it is to ignore substance abuse problems in the workplace. The company found that in the previous 5 years each worker with an alcohol (or drug) problem was absent 113 more days than the average employee and filed $23,000 more in medical claims. Their dependents also filed some $37,000 more in claims than the average family. As we have seen, however, intervention works. Recovered alcoholics frequently credit such programs with literally saving their lives. Companies win, too—by reclaiming employees whose gratitude and restored abilities can result in years of productive service.

Drug Abuse

Drug abuse is no less insidious. It cuts across all job levels and types of organizations and, together with employee alcohol abuse, costs U.S. businesses more than $30 billion in annual productivity losses.[94]

Evidence clearly shows that drug abuse affects on-the-job behaviors.[95] Here is a profile of the "typical" recreational drug user in today's workforce. He or she:

- Is late 3 times as often as fellow employees.
- Requests early dismissal or time off during work 2.2 times as often.
- Has 2.5 times as many absences of 8 days or more.
- Uses 3 times the normal level of sick benefits.
- Is 5 times as likely to file a workers' compensation claim.
- Is involved in accidents 3.6 times as often as other employees.
- Is one-third less productive than fellow workers.

A longitudinal study of 5465 applicants for jobs with the U.S. Postal Service found that after an average of 1.3 years of employment, employees who had tested positive for illicit drugs had an absenteeism rate 59.3 percent higher than employees who had tested negative. Those who had tested positive also had a 47 percent higher rate of involuntary turnover than those who had tested negative. However, there was no relationship between drug test results and measures of injury and accident occurrence.[96] This may not be true in other occupations, however.

Said a construction union leader in California: "Sometimes 90 percent of the crew's been doing uppers. I just leave the jobs when the guys are dopers. Would you want to work on a four-story building knowing the guy with the blowtorch next to you is doing drugs?"[97]

Remember, the Americans with Disabilities Act protects rehabilitated alcohol and drug abusers from discrimination in employment. However, the ADA Technical Assistance Manual specifically states: "Employees who use drugs or alcohol may be required to meet the same standards of performance and conduct that are set for other employees."[98] As we have seen, rehabilitation under an EAP can be effective. From an employment perspective, however, the key issue is documented evidence of decreased job performance.

Violence at Work

What do General Dynamics, Circle K Corporation, and the U.S. Postal Service have in common? They have employees who died violently while at work. Nationally, an average of 20 workers are murdered and 18,000 workers are assaulted each week.[99] Those most at risk are taxi drivers, police officers, retail workers, people who work with money or valuables, and people who work alone or at night. Prehire drug testing, detailed questions about previous employment, and criminal record checks can go a long way toward identifying violence-prone individuals.[100]

Violence disrupts productivity, causes untold damage to those exposed to the trauma, is related to workplace abuse of drugs or alcohol and to absenteeism, and costs employers millions of dollars. In a stressed-out, downsized business environment, people are searching for someone to blame for their problems. With the loss of a job or with some other event the employee perceives as unfair, the employer may become the focus of the disgruntled individual's fear and frustration. Although security measures cannot prevent all harm, there are steps organizations can take to reduce the risk of violence.[101] First, be alert to warning signs. These include:

- **Verbal threats**—take seriously remarks from an employee about what he or she may do. Experts say that individuals who make such statements usually have been mentally committed to the act for a long period of time. It may take very little provocation to trigger the violence.
- **Physical actions**—employees who demonstrate "assaultive" physical actions at work are dangerous. The employer, working with experts trained to assess a possibly violent situation, needs to investigate and intervene. Failure to do so may be interpreted as permission to do further or more serious damage.
- **Behaviors**—watch for changes such as irritability and a short temper. Is the employee showing a low tolerance to work stress or frustrations?[102]

Prevention strategies include the following:[103]

- **Consult specialists**—professionals in the area of facility security, violence assessment, EAP counseling, community support services, and local law enforcement—to formulate a plan for identifying, defusing, and recovering from a violent event.
- **Create and communicate to all employees a written policy** that explains the organization's position on intimidating, threatening, or violent behavior and establishes a procedure for investigating any potentially violent talk or action.
- **Establish a crisis management team** with the authority to make decisions quickly. This group will evaluate problems, select intervention techniques, and coordinate follow-up activities, such as counseling victims and dealing with the media.
- **Offer training and employee orientation**—train supervisors and managers in how to recognize aggressive behavior, identify the warning signs of violence, be effective communicators, and resolve conflict. (Untrained supervisors often escalate violent situations.) Orient all employees on facility security procedures and on how to recognize and report threats of violence in the workplace.

IMPACT OF SAFETY, HEALTH, AND EAPs ON PRODUCTIVITY, QUALITY OF WORK LIFE, AND THE BOTTOM LINE

We know that the technology is available to make workplaces safe and healthy for the nation's men and women. We also know that legislation can never substitute for managerial commitment to safe, healthy workplaces based on demonstrated economic and social benefits. Consider just one example. On the basis of an analysis of 3896 disability cases, Northwestern National Life Insurance Company calculated that the average cost of rehabilitating an employee disabled because of stress was $1925. If he or she is not rehabilitated, companies will need to hold in reserve an average of $73,270 or more to cover disability payments for employees disabled by job-related stress.[104] On balance, commitment to job safety, health, and EAPs is a win-win situation for employees and their companies. Productivity, QWL, and the bottom line all stand to gain.

- **Help employees adjust to change**—for example, in the event of downsizing, a merger, or an acquisition, give employees advance notice. Under the Worker Adjustment and Retraining Act (WARN) of 1988, covered employers are required to give 60 days' notice to employees affected by mass layoffs or plant closings. Keeping employees informed about impending changes and providing additional benefits, such as severance pay or EAP stress-management counseling, can help employees adjust to the change.
- **Be aware of potential risks and respond appropriately.** Remarks such as "I'll kill you" or "I'd like to put out a contract on him" should not be taken lightly. Experts say that in many cases an individual who becomes violent has given multiple clues of potentially violent behavior to a number of people within the organization. However, these warnings were overlooked or dismissed. Be proactive; do not assume the employee does not mean what he or she says, because when employees feel powerless there is a greater likelihood of violence. Report the incident to management for investigation.

CORPORATE HEALTH PROMOTION: THE CONCEPT OF WELLNESS

Consider these sobering facts:

- U.S. companies spend, on average, about 26 percent of their earnings (13.6 percent of their payrolls) on health-care costs.[105]
- Business today pays half the nation's health-care bill. Common backaches alone account for about 25 percent of all workdays lost per year, for a total cost of $15 billion to $20 billion in lost productivity, disability payments, and lawsuits.[106]
- Business spends some $700 million per year to replace the 200,000 employees aged 45 to 65 who are killed or disabled by heart disease.

Keep in mind that health plans do not promise good health. They simply pay for the cost of ill health and the associated rehabilitation. Because 8 of the

10 leading causes of death are largely preventable, however, managers are beginning to look to *disease prevention* as one way to reduce health-care spending. The old saying "an ounce of prevention is worth a pound of cure" is certainly true when one compares the costs of a workshop to help employees stop smoking with the price tag on an average coronary bypass operation.[107]

Is it possible that health-care costs can be tamed through on-the-job exercise programs and health promotion efforts? Convinced that if people were healthier, they would be sick less often, two out of three U.S. businesses with more than 50 employees have some form of health promotion program in place.[108] Do such programs work? In a moment we will consider that question, but first let's define terms and look at the overall concept of wellness.

The process of corporate health promotion begins by promoting health awareness, that is, knowledge of the present and future consequences of behaviors and lifestyles and the risks they may present. The objective of wellness programs is not to eliminate symptoms and disease; it is to help employees build lifestyles that will enable them to achieve their full physical and mental potential. *Wellness programs differ from EAPs in that wellness focuses on prevention, while EAPs focus on rehabilitation.* Health promotion is a four-step process:[109]

1. Educating employees about health-risk factors—life habits or body characteristics that may increase the chances of developing a serious illness. For heart disease (the leading cause of death), some of these risk factors are high blood pressure, cigarette smoking, high cholesterol levels, diabetes, a sedentary lifestyle, and obesity. Some factors, such as smoking, physical inactivity, stress, and poor nutrition, are associated with many diseases.[110]
2. Identifying the health-risk factors that each employee faces.
3. Helping employees eliminate or reduce these risks through healthier lifestyles and habits.
4. Helping employees maintain their new, healthier lifestyles through self-monitoring and evaluation. The central theme of health promotion is "No one takes better care of you than you do."

To date, the most popular programs are smoking cessation, blood pressure control, cholesterol reduction, weight control and fitness, and stress management. In well-designed programs, 40 to 50 percent of employees can be expected to participate.[111] However, it is the 15 percent to 20 percent of high-risk employees who account for up to 80 percent of all claims that are the most difficult to reach.[112] The following section shows why it is important to try to reach high-risk employees.

Linking Unhealthy Lifestyles to Health-Care Costs

A 4-year study of 15,000 Control Data employees showed dramatic relationships between employees' health habits and insurance claim costs. For example, people whose weekly exercise was equivalent to climbing fewer than five flights of stairs or walking less than half a mile spent 114 percent more on health claims than those who climbed at least 15 flights of stairs or walked 1.5 miles weekly. Health-care costs for obese people were 11 percent higher than those for thin ones. And workers who routinely failed to use seat belts spent 54 percent more days in the hospital than those who usually buckled up. Finally, people who smoked an average of one or more packs of cigarettes a day had 118 percent higher medical expenses than nonsmokers.[113] This study was the first to tie health costs to workers' behavior. It was corroborated in another longitudinal study that appeared at about the same time.[114] Together, such results may form the basis for incentive programs to (1) improve workers' health habits and (2) reduce employees' contributions to health-insurance costs or increase their benefits.

COMPANY EXAMPLE

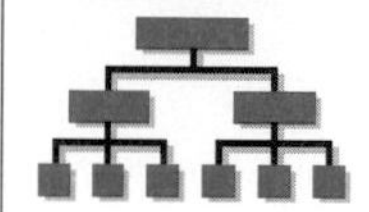

HOW JOHNSON & JOHNSON AND QUAKER OATS REACH HIGH-RISK EMPLOYEES

At J&J, employees get $500 discounts on their insurance premiums if they agree to have their blood pressure, cholesterol, and body fat checked and fill out detailed health-risk questionnaires. Among the more than 150 questions: Do you drive within the speed limit? How often do you eat fried foods? Do you exercise regularly, and if not, why not?

Workers found to be at high risk for health problems receive letters urging them to join a diet and exercise program. Those who refuse lose the $500 discount. Before the discount was offered, only 40 percent of the company's 35,000 U.S. employees completed the health assessments. After the discount was offered, more than 96 percent did.

Quaker Oats Company gives employees up to $140 credit in the company's flexible benefits program if they make a "health lifestyle pledge." The more promises they make, the more benefit credits they earn. Pledging to exercise aerobically three times a week is worth $20 in credit, as is a commitment to wear seat belts. Drinking in moderation and refraining from smoking are worth $50 each. The program runs on the honor system.[115]

Evaluation: Do Wellness Programs Work?

Few controlled studies of wellness programs exist,[116] and the movement's doctrines remind some medical doctors of earlier measures that also seemed as unassailable as apple pie—annual physicals, annual Pap smears, and mass health screening. Unfortunately, none of these provided the huge health benefits that seemed almost guaranteed.

Wellness programs are especially difficult to evaluate, for at least six reasons:[117]

1. Health-related costs that actually decrease are hard to identify.
2. Program sponsors use different methods to measure and report costs and benefits.
3. Program effects may vary depending on when they are measured (immediately versus lagged effects).
4. Program effects may vary depending on how long they are measured.
5. Few studies use control groups.
6. Data on effectiveness are limited in the choice of variables, estimation of the economic value of indirect costs and benefits, estimation of the timing and duration of program effects, and estimation of the present value of future benefits.

ETHICAL DILEMMA
Should Employees Be Punished for Unhealthy Lifestyles?[120]

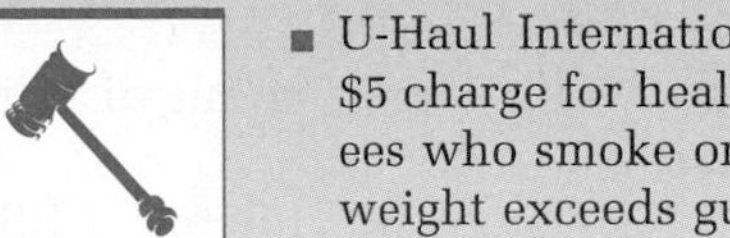

Johnson & Johnson Health Management, Inc., which sells wellness programs to companies, estimates that 15 to 25 percent of corporate health-care costs stem from employees' unhealthy lifestyle conditions. As a result, individuals may not be hired, might even be fired, and could wind up paying a monthly penalty based on their after-hours activities. Here are some examples:

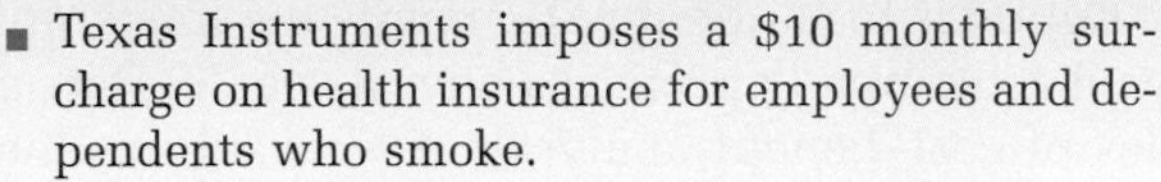

- Texas Instruments imposes a $10 monthly surcharge on health insurance for employees and dependents who smoke.
- Turner Broadcasting will not hire smokers.
- U-Haul International imposes a biweekly $5 charge for health insurance for employees who smoke or chew tobacco or whose weight exceeds guidelines.
- Multi-Developers will not hire anyone who engages in what the company views as high-risk activities: skydiving, piloting a private aircraft, mountain climbing, or motorcycling.

Existing civil rights laws generally do not protect against "lifestyle discrimination" because smokers and skydivers are not named as protected classes. Should employers be able to implement "lifestyle policies"?

At a general level, four key questions need to be answered:

1. Do health promotion programs in fact eliminate or reduce health-risk factors?
2. Are these changes long-lasting?
3. If the changes are long-lasting, will illness and its subsequent costs be reduced?
4. Are the savings great enough to justify the expense?

Based on a number of independent studies, the answers to the first two questions appear to be yes—especially when programs incorporate systematic outreach and follow-up counseling.[118] For example, one longitudinal study measured the following health-risk factors: blood pressure, cholesterol levels, number of pounds over ideal mean weight, seat belt usage, salt intake, dietary fat intake, smoking, alcohol intake, exercise, and stress. Although there was some variation in improvement in various categories, and between age groups, there was nearly a 20 percent improvement in health-risk scores after 18 months, and the gains were sustained at 30 months. While the effect of age on the rate of change diminished over time, the effect of educational level did not. Those with more education had lower health-risk scores at the beginning of the study and also made the most improvement. In general, these results suggest that participation in an organized health promotion program results in improved health.[119]

The answer to the third question also appears to be positive, based on an analysis of 200 corporate wellness programs. The best such programs cut medical claims by up to 20 percent. If such "demand reduction" could be extended to all Americans, according to the researchers, the nation could cut $180 billion from its health-care bill.[121]

With respect to the fourth question, several studies have focused on *costs that would have been incurred if a wellness program had not been available.*

This was the approach taken by the Adolph Coors Company in evaluating its mammography screening program for breast cancer. By calculating exactly how many examinations showed breast cancer in the early stages, Coors was able to calculate the costs avoided, assuming that without mammography the problem would have gone undetected and the cancer would have matured. Coors spent $232,500 to perform 2500 screenings and avoided $828,000 in health-care costs. This yielded a net saving of $595,500, or a return on investment (ROI) of greater than 3.5 to 1.[122]

The medical director at Eli Lilly & Company estimated that an advanced case of breast cancer costs Lilly more than $100,000 a case in lost work time and medical costs. Mammography equipment costs about $80,000. While it might appear that a compelling case can be made for purchasing such equipment, experts estimate that a company needs to employ at least 1000 to 2000 women to justify starting such a program. For smaller companies that cannot afford to buy their own equipment, one option is to contract with mobile mammography screening programs to bring vans to company premises once a year.[123] Here are some other company examples of cost–benefit analyses of worksite wellness programs:

- Travelers Insurance reported saving $7.8 million in benefit costs by using its "Taking Care" program for its 34,700 participating employees. Each dollar spent yielded a return of $3.40.[124]
- Pillsbury claims that every dollar spent on its "Be Your Best" wellness program produced $3.63 in health-related cost savings.[125]
- Adolph Coors company, which has blazed the health promotion trail, claims an average dollar return on investment of more than 6 to 1. Its cardiac rehabilitation program alone saved the company $4.2 million over a 10-year period.[126]
- Small businesses too are saving money by claiming insurance discounts for group-life premiums if they offer some type of wellness program to their employees. Thus Babson Brothers, a dairy-farm equipment maker in Naperville, Illinois, saved $5000, or 5 percent, on its group-life premiums because it has a no-smoking policy and fitness programs.[127]
- A comprehensive review of three large-scale computer simulations of the effects of worksite wellness programs found that such programs may be cost-beneficial, that economic benefits stem primarily from increases in productivity and less so from decreases in health-care costs, and that program effects vary considerably both within organizations (from year to year) and also between organizations.[128]

Wellness Programs and the Americans with Disabilities Act (ADA)

Employers that *require* employees to submit to wellness initiatives, such as health-risk appraisals (questionnaires about one's health history and current lifestyle) and assessments (physical and biomedical tests that screen for specific health conditions), are violating the ADA. This is so because the act forbids employers from conducting mandatory medical exams once an employee is hired, unless the inquiry is "job-related and consistent with business necessity."

IMPLICATIONS FOR MANAGEMENT PRACTICE

In the coming years, we can expect to see three developments in occupational safety and health:

1. More widespread promotion of OSHA's consultative role, particularly as small businesses recognize that this is a no-cost, no-penalty option available to them.
2. Wider use of cost–benefit analysis by regulatory agencies; industry is demanding it, and Executive Order 12292 endorses it.
3. Broadening of the target group for EAPs and wellness programs to include dependents and retirees.

The high costs of disabling injuries and occupational diseases, together with these three trends, suggest that the commitment of resources to enhance job safety and health makes good business sense over and above concerns for corporate social responsibility.

Employers also must be careful when tying financial incentives or disincentives (e.g., cash bonuses, lower health insurance contributions) to test results. The employer can offer an incentive only upon verification that the employee went for the test. The incentive cannot be tied to the test results. Under the ADA, employers cannot discriminate in pay or benefits on the basis of a legally protected disability. In addition, any test results from wellness screening must be kept confidential.

What type of wellness programs do not violate the ADA? Educational wellness programs that encourage people to sign up for tests and instruct them on how to improve their lifestyles.[129] By helping employees to take an interest in their future health, employers should ultimately be able to keep at least a loose lid on claims and major expenses.

SUBSTANCE ABUSE ON THE JOB PRODUCES TOUGH POLICY CHOICES FOR MANAGERS

Human Resource Management in Action: Conclusion

Given the amounts of time and money invested in employees, especially highly skilled knowledge workers, many firms try to rehabilitate those with substance abuse problems. But how do firms get "problem" employees into rehabilitation programs? The most popular approaches are self-referral and referral by family and friends. Among pilots who have gone through the airline industry's alcohol rehabilitation program, in effect since 1973, 85 percent were initially turned in by family, friends, or coworkers.

According to the Air Line Pilots Association, one of the hallmarks of the industry's program is a willingness of people to turn in an alcoholic pilot. That willingness, in turn, depends on knowing that the pilot can return to work. If people know that by turning in a pilot they will also be taking away his or her livelihood, they may not do it.

The key to returning to work, in the opinion of most professionals in the field of substance abuse, is follow-up, because substance abuse is a recurring disease. Prior to the *Exxon Valdez* accident, the company really had no systematic policy on how to handle employees after treatment. The company depended solely on the judgments of local managers.

Under United's program, rehabilitated pilots are monitored for at least 2 years. During this time, the pilot is required to meet monthly with a committee comprising counselors and representatives of both union and management in a kind of group therapy session with other recovering pilots. They may also be required to undergo periodic surprise alcohol or drug tests. United has never had an alcohol-related accident.

Although experts do not always agree on how long follow-up should last, programs most commonly require 6 months of intensive contact, such as weekly meetings, and 1 year after that of monthly contact. Longer-term follow-up may last as long as 4 years.

SUMMARY

Public policy regarding occupational safety and health has focused on state-run workers' compensation programs for job-related injuries and federally mandated preventive measures to enhance job safety and health. OSHA enforces the provisions of the 1970 Occupational Safety and Health Act, under which employers have a "general duty" to provide a place of employment "free from recognized hazards." Employers also have the special duty to comply with all standards of safety and health established under the act. OSHA's effectiveness has been debated for more than a decade, but it is important to note that workplace accidents can result either from *unsafe work conditions* or from *unsafe work behaviors.* OSHA can affect only unsafe work conditions. There are no standards that govern potentially unsafe employee behaviors.

Major concerns of employers today are the possible health hazards associated with high technology, such as video display terminals and semiconductors; diseases related to radiation or carcinogenic substances that may have long latency periods; and AIDS.

In response, OSHA has established or toughened workplace exposure limits for many carcinogenic substances. Management's first duty in this area is to develop a safety and health policy. Management's second duty is to establish controls that include a loss control program, a safety committee, safety rules, careful selection of employees, extensive training, and feedback and incentives for maintaining a safe work environment.

Employee assistance programs represent a brighter side of the health issue. Such programs offer assistance to all "troubled" employees. Under an EAP, supervisors need be concerned only with identifying declining work performance, not with involving themselves in employee problems. Treatment is left to professionals. Finally, health promotion, or wellness, programs differ from EAPs in that their primary focus is on prevention, not rehabilitation. Both EAPs and wellness programs hold considerable promise for improving productivity, quality of work life, and the bottom line.

DISCUSSION QUESTIONS

14-1 Should OSHA's enforcement activities be expanded? Why or why not?
14-2 What advantages and disadvantages do you see with workers' compensation?
14-3 Discuss the relative effectiveness of engineering versus management controls to improve job safety and health.
14-4 If the benefits of EAPs cannot be demonstrated to exceed their costs, should EAPs be discontinued?
14-5 Should organizations be willing to invest more money in employee wellness? Why or why not?

APPLYING YOUR KNOWLEDGE

Skyline Machine Shop — *Case 14-1*

Skyline Machine Shop is a medium-size firm located in San Jose, California. It employs almost 1000 workers when business is good. Skyline specializes in doing precision machining on a subcontract basis for several large aerospace companies. Skilled machinists are always in short supply, and therefore command high salaries and generous benefit packages.

Recently, one of the plant foremen, Len Fulkner, paid a visit to Skyline's personnel manager, Jamie Trenton, to discuss a personnel-related problem.

Fulkner: You know, Jamie, I've been around the barn a time or two. I've seen all kinds of personnel-type problems over the years. But I guess maybe I'm over the hill—53 is no spring chicken you know! The other day I ran into a situation like I've never seen before, and I need your help.

Trenton: What happened Len?

Fulkner: Well, last Thursday one of my best machinists, Harry Boecker, began acting really weird. He seemed in a daze, couldn't seem to concentrate on the part he was milling, and began dropping tools and engineering drawings all over. At first I thought he'd been drinking. But I smelled his breath and couldn't smell anything. When I asked him what was wrong, he mumbled something about "coke."

Trenton: What did you do?

Fulkner: I sent him home for the rest of the day. I didn't know what else to do, but I knew he was a danger to himself and others so I had to get him out of the plant. I hope I did the right thing. I'm really worried about the guy, Jamie. I'd hate to lose a good machinist like that, but I don't know the first thing about drugs or how to handle workers who have been taking them. Can you help me?

The next day, Jamie Trenton had a meeting scheduled with the president of Skyline. Jamie had been thinking for some time about recommending an employee assistance program (EAP) to the president, and her conversation with Len Fulkner convinced her that now was the appropriate time. Quite a few other firms in the San Jose area had instituted EAPs—seemingly with some success. However, Jamie knew that Skyline's president was skeptical of "follow-the-leader" approaches to employee benefit packages.

Questions

1. Did Len Fulkner handle the situation with Harry Boecker correctly? Why or why not?
2. Prepare an outline of a cost–benefit analysis that Jamie Trenton could use in presenting her EAP proposal to Skyline's president. In particular, what categories of benefits might be quantifiable?
3. If Jamie's proposal is accepted, what key steps would you recommend to her in implementing a new EAP at Skyline Machine Shop?

REFERENCES

1. Seligman, D. (1996, Dec. 9). Keeping up. *Fortune,* p. 60.
2. *Accident facts* (1996). Chicago: National Safety Council.
3. Davis, A. (1997, Feb. 26). Treating on-the-job injuries as true crimes. *The Wall Street Journal,* pp. B1, B6.
4. Rubis, L. (1997, Apr.). 1995 drop in workplace injuries includes repetitive motion cases. *HRNews,* p. 9.
5. Thompson, R. W. (1997, Jan.). NY jury breaks RSI ice, holding Digital liable in keyboard case. *HRNews,* pp. 1, 4. See also McLain, J. D. (1996, Apr. 27). Study: Repetitious work's a hazard. *North Coast Times,* pp. D1, D2.
6. Labor letter (1993, Sept. 14). *The Wall Street Journal,* p. A1.
7. Rundle, B. (1996, Oct. 9). Back corsets receive support in UCLA study. *The Wall Street Journal,* pp. B1, B2.
8. Labor letter (1987, Apr. 14). *The Wall Street Journal,* p. 1.
9. Dieterly, D. (1994). *Industrial injury cost analysis by occupation in an electric utility.* Occupational Research Division, Southern California Edison Co.
10. Burtt, E. J. (1979). *Labor in the American economy.* New York: St. Martin's Press.
11. Ledvinka, J., & Scarpello, V. G. (1991). *Federal regulation of personnel and human resource management* (2d ed.). Boston: PWS-Kent.
12. Manning, M. R., Jackson, C. N., & Fusilier, M. R. (1996). Occupational stress, social support, and the costs of health care. *Academy of Management Journal,* **39,** 738–750. See also McLain, D. L. (1995). Responses to health and safety risk in the work environment. *Academy of Management Journal,* **38,** 1726–1743.
13. Olian, J. D. (1990). Workplace safety and employee health. In J. A. Fossum (ed.), *Employee and labor relations.* Washington, DC: Bureau of National Affairs, pp. 4-218 to 4-285.
14. Salwen, K. G. (1993, Nov. 22). White House to proffer ergonomic rule for workplaces, employers' liabilities. *The Wall Street Journal,* p. B6.
15. Marsh, B. (1994, Feb. 3). Workers at risk. *The Wall Street Journal,* pp. A1, A8.
16. New OSHA bloodborne pathogen standards (1992, Sept.). *Mountain States Employers Council Bulletin,* p. 4.
17. Salwen, loc. cit. See also Stepping into the middle of OSHA's muddle (1993, Aug. 2). *Business Week,* p. 53.
18. *Marshall v. Barlow's, Inc.* (1978). 1978 OSHD, Sn. 22,735. Chicago: Commerce Clearing House.
19. Etter, I. B. (1993, Sept.). You can't hide from an OSHA inspector. *Safety & Health,* p. 3; Elliott, S. (1984, June 27). OSHA Region III area director, personal communication.

20. Bowers, B. (1994, Feb. 1). OSHA to mix a little mercy with latest crackdown. *The Wall Street Journal,* p. B2.
21. Work week (1995, Oct. 31). *The Wall Street Journal,* p. A1.
22. U.S. Department of Labor, Occupational Safety and Health Administration (1996). *Consultation services for the employer.* Washington, DC: U.S. Government Printing Office.
23. OSHA penalties increased (1991, Feb.). *Mountain States Employers Council Bulletin,* p. 2.
24. Davis, A., loc. cit. See also The price of neglect (1992, Sept. 28). *Time,* p. 24.
25. U.S. Department of Labor (1983, Mar.). *Program highlights: Job safety and health.* Washington, DC: U.S. Government Printing Office, Fact Sheet No. OSHA-83-01 (rev.).
26. *NLRB v. Jasper Seating Co.* (1988). CA 7, 129 LRRM 2337. See also *Whirlpool Corporation v. Marshall* (1981, Feb. 26). *Daily Labor Report,* Washington, DC: Bureau of National Affairs, pp. D3–D10.
27. *Gateway Coal Co. v. United Mine Workers of America* (1974). 1974 OSHD, Sn. 17,085. Chicago: Commerce Clearing House.
28. Ledvinka & Scarpello, op. cit.
29. Davis, B. (1992, Aug. 6). What price safety? *The Wall Street Journal,* pp. A1, A7.
30. Marsh, loc. cit. See also Trost, C. (1988, Apr. 22). Occupational hazard: A much-maligned OSHA confronts rising demands with a reduced budget. *The Wall Street Journal,* Supplement, p. 25R. See also McCaffrey, D. P. (1983). An assessment of OSHA's recent effects on injury rates. *Journal of Human Resources,* **18**(1), 131–146.
31. Marsh, op. cit., p. A1.
32. Cook, W. N., & Gautschi, F. H. (1981). OSHA plant safety programs and injury reduction. *Industrial Relations,* **20**(3), 245–257.
33. Milbank, D. (1991, Mar. 29). Companies turn to peer pressure to cut injuries as psychologists join the battle. *The Wall Street Journal,* pp. B1, B3.
34. Ashford, N. A. (1976). *Crisis in the workplace: Occupational disease and injury.* Cambridge, MA: MIT Press. See also Burtt, op. cit.
35. Follmann, J. F., Jr. (1978). *The economics of industrial health.* New York: AMACOM.
36. *Inside OSHA: The role of management in safety* (1975, Nov. 1). New York: Man and Manager, Inc.
37. Getting business to think about the unthinkable (1991, June 24). *Business Week,* pp. 104–107; Smith, M. J., Cohen, H. H., Cohen, A., & Cleveland, R. J. (1978). Characteristics of successful safety programs. *Journal of Safety Research,* **10,** 5–15. See also Cohen, A. (1977). Factors in successful occupational safety programs. *Journal of Safety Research,* **9,** 168–178.
38. Shabecoff, P. (1987, Oct. 11). Industry is split over disclosure of job dangers. *The New York Times,* p. 28.
39. Swoboda, F. (1990, Jan. 12). OSHA targets repetitive motion injuries. *Washington Post,* p. A10. See also U.S. fines meatpacker $3.1 million over injuries (1988, May 12). *The New York Times,* p. A20.
40. Repetitive stress: The pain has just begun (1992, July 13). *Business Week,* pp. 142, 143. See also Crippled by computers (1992, Oct. 12). *Time,* pp. 70, 71.
41. Repetitive motion complaints. (1996, Aug. 15). *USA Today,* p. B1.
42. Rundle, loc. cit.
43. U.S. Department of Labor, 1983, op. cit.
44. Older workers in the U.S. less likely to be seriously injured. (1996, Sept.). *Manpower Argus,* p. 8. See also Graham, S. (1996, Jan.). Debunk the myths about older workers. *Safety & Health,* pp. 38–41. See also Siskind, F. (1982). Another look at the link between work injuries and job experience. *Monthly Labor Review,* **105**(2), 38–41. See also Root, N. (1981). Injuries at work are fewer among older employees. *Monthly Labor Review,* **104**(3), 30–34.

45. Leary, W. E. (1982, Aug. 2). Management concern affects mine safety. *Denver Post,* p. 1C.
46. U.S. Department of Labor, 1983, op. cit.
47. Komaki, J., Barwick, K. D., & Scott, L. R. (1978). A behavioral approach to occupational safety: Pinpointing and reinforcing safe performance in a food manufacturing plant. *Journal of Applied Psychology,* **63,** 434–445.
48. Yandrick, R. M. (1996, Feb.). Behavioral safety helps shipbuilder cut accident rates. *HR News,* pp. 3, 11. See also Rever, R. A., & Wallin, J. A. (1984). The effects of training, goal setting, and knowledge of results on safe behavior: A component analysis. *Academy of Management Journal,* **27,** 544–560.
49. Milbank, loc. cit.
50. The perplexing case of the plummeting payrolls (1993, Sept. 20). *Business Week,* p. 27.
51. McLain, D. L., loc. cit. See also Eyestrain tops American office workers' lists of job-related complaints (1991, Nov. 19). *The Wall Street Journal,* p. A1. See also Lorber, L. Z., & Kirk, R. J. (1987). *Fear itself: A legal and personnel analysis of drug testing, AIDS, secondary smoke, and VDTs.* Alexandria, VA: ASPA Foundation.
52. Olian, loc. cit.
53. Eyestrain tops American office workers' lists of job-related complaints, loc. cit.
54. Olian, loc. cit.
55. *Chemical hazard communication* (1988). Washington, DC: U.S. Department of Labor, OSHA #3084 (rev. ed.).
56. Jacobs, S. L. (1988, Nov. 22). Small business slowly wakes to OSHA hazard rule. *The Wall Street Journal,* p. B2.
57. Hays, L. (1986, July 8). New rules on workplace hazards prompt intensified on-the-job training programs. *The Wall Street Journal,* p. 31.
58. McMurray, S. (1991, Oct. 4). India's high court upholds settlement paid by Carbide in Bhopal gas leak. *The Wall Street Journal,* p. B3. See also Damages for a deadly cloud (1989, Feb. 27). *Time,* p. 53.
59. McMurray, S., & Harlan, C. (1992, May 1). Indian judge orders seizure of Carbide assets in country. *The Wall Street Journal,* p. B5.
60. Foreign firms feel the impact of Bhopal most (1985, Nov. 26). *The Wall Street Journal,* p. 24.
61. Ibid.
62. Thailand fire shows region cuts corners on safety to boost profits (1993, May 13). *The Wall Street Journal,* p. A13.
63. Pangs of conscience: Sweatshops haunt U.S. consumers (1996, July 29). *Business Week,* pp. 46–48.
64. *Illinois v. Chicago Magnet Wire Corp.* (1990, Oct. 24). 126 Ill. 2d 356, 534 N.E., 2d 962, 128 Ill.
65. Marcus, A. D., & de Cordoba, J. (1990, Oct. 17). New York court rules employers can face charges in worker safety. *The Wall Street Journal,* p. B9.
66. $520,000 awarded in an asbestos-related illness (1987, Oct. 8). *The New York Times,* p. A21.
67. Wermiel, S. (1989, Oct. 3). Justices let states prosecute executives for job hazards covered by U.S. law. *The Wall Street Journal,* p. A11.
68. Karr, A. R. (1989, Jan. 16). OSHA sets or toughens exposure limits on 376 toxic chemicals in workplace. *The Wall Street Journal,* p. C16.
69. Stead, W. E., & Stead, J. G. (1983, Jan.). OSHA's cancer prevention policy: Where did it come from and where is it going? *Personnel Journal,* pp. 54–60.
70. Hooker, T. (1996, Oct.). *HIV/AIDS facts to consider: 1996.* National Conference of State Legislatures, Denver, CO. See also Alliton, V. (1992, Feb.). Financial realities of AIDS in the workplace. *HRMagazine,* pp. 78–81.

71. Tedlow, R. S. (1993, June 18). *Levi Strauss & Co. and the AIDS crisis.* Harvard Business School, Case #9-391-198.
72. Alliton, loc. cit.
73. Suris, O. (1997, Feb. 28). AIDS deaths drop significantly for first time. *The Wall Street Journal,* p. B1.
74. Hooker, op. cit.
75. Ibid.
76. Tedlow, op. cit.
77. Tedlow, op. cit., p. 17.
78. Seppa, N. (1997, Mar.). EAPs offer quality care and cost-effectiveness. *APA Monitor,* pp. 32, 33. See also Is business bungling its battle with booze? (1991, Mar. 25). *Business Week,* pp. 76–78. See also Sperling, D. (1989, Mar. 9). More employers help foot the detox bill. *USA Today,* p. 5D.
79. Balgopal, P. R., Ramanathan, C. S., & Patchner, M. A. (1987, Dec.). *Employee assistance programs: A cross-cultural perspective.* Paper presented at the Conference on International Personnel and Human Resource Management, Singapore.
80. Berg, N. R., & Moe, J. P. (1979). Assistance for troubled employees. In D. Yoder & H. G. Heneman, Jr. (eds.), *ASPA handbook of personnel and industrial relations.* Washington, DC: BNA, pp. 1.59–1.77.
81. Blum, T. C., & Roman, P. M. (1995). *Cost-effectiveness and preventive implications of employee assistance programs.* Washington, DC: U.S. Department of Health and Human Services.
82. Stone, D. L., & Kotch, D. A. (1989). Individuals' attitudes toward organizational drug testing policies and practices. *Journal of Applied Psychology,* **74,** 518–521.
83. Milne, S. H., Blum, T. C., & Roman, P. M. (1994). Factors influencing employees' propensity to use an employee assistance program. *Personnel Psychology,* **47,** 123–145.
84. Seppa, op. cit. See also Is business bungling its battle with booze? loc. cit.
85. Seppa, loc. cit.
86. Foote, A., & Erfurt, J. (1981, Sept.–Oct.). Evaluating an employee assistance program. *EAP Digest,* pp. 14–25.
87. Ray, J. S. (1982). Having problems with worker performance? Try an EAP. *Administrative Management,* **43**(5), 47–49.
88. How is drinking affecting the workplace? (1993, Aug.). *Mountain States Employers Council Bulletin,* p. 5. See also How to confront—and help—an alcoholic employee (1991, Mar. 25). *Business Week,* p. 78.
89. How to confront—and help—an alcoholic employee, loc. cit.
90. Pollock, E. J. (1996, Sept. 9). In leaner, meaner workplace, bosses get tough on addiction. *The Wall Street Journal,* pp. B1, B2.
91. Weiss, R. M. (1987). Writing under the influence: Science versus fiction in the analysis of corporate alcoholism programs. *Personnel Psychology,* 40, 341–356.
92. Is business bungling its battle with booze? loc. cit.
93. Pollock, loc. cit.
94. Farkas, G. M. (1989). The impact of federal rehabilitation laws on the expanding role of employee assistance programs in business and industry. *American Psychologist,* **44,** 1482–1490.
95. Lehman, W. E. K., & Simpson, D. D. (1992). Employee substance abuse and on-the-job behaviors. *Journal of Applied Psychology,* **77,** 309–321.
96. Normand, J., Salyards, S. D., & Mahoney, J. J. (1990). An evaluation of preemployment drug testing. *Journal of Applied Psychology,* **75,** 629–639.
97. Taking drugs on the job (1983, Aug. 22). *Newsweek,* p. 55.
98. How is drinking affecting the workplace? loc. cit.
99. OSHA issues guidelines on workplace violence (1996, Nov./Dec.). *Mountain States Employers Council Bulletin,* p. 3.

100. Fisher, A. (1997, May 26). Managing. *Fortune,* pp. 165, 166.
101. Mountain States Employers Council and Nicoletti-Flater Associates (1997). *Violence goes to work: An employer's guide* (2d ed.). Denver: Mountain States Employers Council. See also Ferlise, W. G. (1995, Apr.). Violence in the workplace. *Personnel Testing Council of Metropolitan Washington Newsletter,* p. 9.
102. Kilborn, P. T. (1993, May 17). Inside post offices, the mail is only part of the pressure. *The New York Times,* pp. A1, A15.
103. Ferlise, loc. cit. See also Violent employees (1994, Feb.). *Mountain States Employers Council Bulletin,* p. 5.
104. Brody, J. E. (1991, July 10). As benefits and staff shrink, job stress grows. *The New York Times,* p. C11.
105. Lombino, P. (1992, Feb.). An ounce of prevention. *CFO,* pp. 15–22. See also Winslow, R. (1991, Jan. 29). Medical costs soar, defying firms' cures. *The Wall Street Journal,* p. B1.
106. Rundle, loc. cit. See also Hollenbeck, J. R., Ilgen, D. R., & Crampton, S. M. (1992). Lower back disability in occupational settings: A review of the literature from a human resource management view. *Personnel Psychology,* **45,** 247–278.
107. Lombino, loc. cit.
108. Ibid.
109. Epstein, S. S. (1989). *A note on health promotion in the workplace.* Boston: Harvard Business School.
110. Stolberg, S. (1993, Nov. 10). Top underlying cause of death: Tobacco use. *The Denver Post,* p. 2A. See also Kahn, R. L., & Byosiere, P. (1992). Stress in organizations. In M. D. Dunnette & L. M. Hough (eds.), *Handbook of industrial and organizational psychology* (2d ed., vol. 3). Palo Alto, CA: Consulting Psychologists Press, pp. 571–650.
111. Mavis, B. E. (1992). Issues related to participation in worksite health promotion: A preliminary study. *American Journal of Health Promotion,* **7**(1), 53–63. See also Alexy, B. B. (1991). Factors associated with participation or nonparticipation in a workplace wellness center. *Research in Nursing and Health,* **14**(1), 33–39.
112. Lombino, loc. cit.
113. Jose, W. S., Anderson, D. R., & Haight, S. A. (1987). The StayWell strategy for health care cost containment. In J. P. Opatz (ed.), *Health promotion evaluation: Measuring the organizational impact.* Stevens Point, WI: National Wellness Institute, pp. 15–34.
114. Parkes, K. R. (1987). Relative weight, smoking, and mental health as predictors of sickness and absence from work. *Journal of Applied Psychology,* **72,** 275–286.
115. Jeffrey, N. A. (1996, June 21). "Wellness plans" try to target the not-so-well. *The Wall Street Journal,* pp. B1, B6.
116. Terborg, J. R. (1995a, Feb.). *What's working and what's not working in worksite health promotion.* Keynote address presented at the 7th National Health Promotion Conference, Brisbane, Australia. See also Falkenberg, L. E. (1987). Employee fitness programs: Their impact on the employee and the organization. *Academy of Management Review,* **12,** 511–522.
117. Cascio, W. F. (1991). *Costing human resources: The financial impact of behavior in organizations* (3d ed.). Boston: PWS-Kent.
118. Erfurt, J. C., Foote, A., & Heirich, M. A. (1992). The cost-effectiveness of worksite wellness programs for hypertension control, weight loss, smoking cessation, and exercise. *Personnel Psychology,* **45,** 5–27. See also Viswesvaran, C., & Schmidt, F. L. (1992). A meta-analytic comparison of smoking cessation methods. *Journal of Applied Psychology,* **77,** 554–561. See also Gebhardt, D. L., & Crump, C. E. (1990). Employee fitness and wellness programs in the workplace. *American Psychologist,* **45,** 262–272.

119. Fries, J. F. (1992). Health risk changes with a low-cost individualized health promotion program: Effects at up to 30 months. *American Journal of Health Promotion,* **6**(5), 367–380.
120. If you light up on Sunday, don't come in on Monday (1991, Aug. 26). *Business Week,* pp. 68–72.
121. Fries, J. F., Koop, C. E., Beadle, C. E., Cooper, P. P., England, M. J., Greaves, R. F., Sokolov, J. J., & Wright, D. (1993). Reducing health care costs by reducing the need and demand for medical services. *New England Journal of Medicine,* **329**(5), 321–325.
122. Johnson, S. (1988, June). Breast screening's bottom line—lives saved. *Administrative Radiology,* p. 4.
123. Petty, A. (1993, Sept. 17). More women get mammograms at work. *The Wall Street Journal,* pp. B1, B6.
124. Lombino, loc. cit.
125. Rothman, H. (1992). Wellness works for small firms. *Nation's Business,* **77**(12), 42–46.
126. Terborg, J. R. (1995b). Computer simulation: A promising technique for the evaluation of health promotion programs at the worksite. In R. L. Kaman (ed.), *Worksite health promotion economics.* Dallas: Human Kinetics, pp. 193–215. See also Lombino, loc. cit.
127. Wellness can mean a trim bottom line (1993, Aug. 16). *Business Week,* p. 112.
128. Terborg, 1995b, loc. cit.
129. Matthes, K. (1992, Dec.). ADA checkup: Assess your wellness program. *HR Focus,* **69**(12), 15.

15 COMPETITIVE STRATEGIES, HUMAN RESOURCE STRATEGIES, AND THE FINANCIAL IMPACT OF HUMAN RESOURCE MANAGEMENT ACTIVITIES

Questions This Chapter Will Help Managers Answer

1. Does our firm's HR strategy follow from our firm's competitive business strategy?
2. What kinds of employee behaviors and HR activities should we encourage, given our firm's competitive business strategy?
3. How can HR research be useful to a line manager?
4. If I want to know how much turnover is costing us each year, what factors should I consider?
5. Is there evidence that high-performance work policies are associated with improved financial performance?

*ATTITUDE SURVEY RESULTS: CATALYST FOR MANAGEMENT ACTIONS**

Attitude surveys can yield far more than a measure of morale. By relating specific management actions and styles to high employee turnover and lowered profitability, the results of an attitude survey in one company led to concrete directions for change. The changes implied improved productivity, quality of work life, and bottom-line financial gain.

The company is a nationwide retail operation with an exceptional record of growth and profitability. To staff its rapidly expanding management positions, the company hires large numbers of men and women as trainees in store management. However, despite attractive salaries and promotion opportunities, the company was having trouble retaining the new hires. Top management was at a loss to explain why. Turnover among store managers accelerated beyond the most recent hires; managers in whom the company had invested considerable time and money were also quitting. Moreover, there was no apparent pattern to the turnover—some locations were experiencing a great deal, others very little.

Despite continued profitability, there was growing concern among top management that the level of turnover might be detrimental to the company's long-term success. The actual dollar outlay for the cost of turnover was only one aspect of the problem. An additional consideration was the possibility of poor public relations resulting from unhappy former employees. As a consumer-oriented company, the firm was concerned about its public image and the effect that a "bad employer" reputation could have on the patronage of its stores.

The Problem: Turnover versus Profitability

As turnover worsened, the company conducted various statistical analyses and reviewed reports from field managers in an attempt to locate the source of the problem. Several theories were proposed, such as low pay and inconvenient scheduling of work, but none was supported by sufficient evidence to produce change. Indeed, most of the proposed solutions to the turnover problem (e.g., hiring more employees to work fewer hours) were rejected because their anticipated costs would reduce company profitability.

Top management initially felt that high turnover was acceptable because it did not have much of an adverse effect on profits. In fact, many managers believed that turnover actually increased profitability because it kept overall salary costs down. Vacancies caused stores to operate understaffed until replacements were hired, and these new hires were paid lower salaries than their predecessors.

Why an Attitude Survey?

Despite attempts to find it, the root cause of the turnover of store managers remained elusive. The problem could lie anywhere in the management system,

*Adapted from B. Goldberg and G. G. Gordon, Designing attitude surveys for management action, *Personnel Journal,* October 1978, pp. 546–549. Used by permission.

in the types of employees hired, in how they were trained, in how they were managed, or in how their performance was rewarded.

Top management decided to conduct a broad survey among the store managers themselves to determine the cause of the high turnover. The survey's intent was not to determine how to improve morale and thereby to reduce turnover. It was to help management discover the factors contributing to turnover and the concrete and constructive actions that might reduce it. And, because top management believed that high turnover had a positive effect on profitability, another objective of the survey was to determine what could be done to reduce turnover without reducing profitability. This part of the survey yielded some very enlightening results.

Designing the Survey

The company first rank-ordered its profit centers in two ways—(1) according to turnover and (2) according to profitability—on the basis of the results for the most recent 12-month period. A questionnaire was developed through personal interviews with a number of store managers, and hypotheses were advanced concerning the relationship between the attitudes of store managers and turnover. The hypotheses produced further guides for questionnaire design; they also yielded an outline for subsequent data analyses.

The resulting questionnaire covered a broad range of management issues, including:

- Store characteristics (location and volume)
- Biographical characteristics of the store managers
- Recruitment and selection practices
- Training activities
- Working conditions
- Management climate
- Rewards system

The questionnaire was sent to every store manager then working in one of the profit centers identified earlier.

Survey Results

The survey revealed significant differences in the ways store managers were selected, managed, and treated. It also identified a number of fundamental management practices that were counterproductive. For example, some higher-level supervisors never made field visits to work with their store managers.

However, the most revealing part of the survey results had to do with turnover and profitability. Many factors contributing to high turnover were also contributing to lower profitability. The survey revealed six critical areas of human resource management, all interrelated and each related to turnover and profitability.

Challenges

1. What are some of the advantages and disadvantages of a low turnover rate?
2. How can attitude surveys help orient managers toward more effective performance?
3. In the survey-design phase, why do you think the company first ranked each store in terms of its profitability and turnover rate?

In business settings, it is hard to be convincing without data. If the data are developed systematically and comprehensively and are analyzed in terms of their strategic implications for the business or business unit, they are more convincing. The chapter opening vignette demonstrates how a systematic procedure (an attitude survey) designed to collect data on a broad range of management issues could be used to improve management practices. This chapter first presents several alternative competitive strategies and then identifies the kinds of employee behaviors and human resource (HR) activities that are most consistent with each one. The chapter then examines the need for audit and evaluation of HR activities and shows how HR research can help in this effort. Finally, the chapter presents examples of methods used to assess the costs and benefits of HR activities in some key areas.

ORIENTATION

As emphasized earlier, the focus of this book is *not* on training HR specialists. Rather, it is on training line managers who must, by the very nature of their jobs, manage people and work with them to accomplish organizational objectives. Consequently, the purpose of this chapter is not to show how to measure the effectiveness of the HR department; the purpose is to show how to align HR strategies with general business strategies and, having done so, to assess the costs and benefits of relevant HR activities. The methods can and should be used in cooperation with the HR department, but they are not the exclusive domain of that department. They are general enough to be used by any manager in any department to measure the costs and benefits of employee behavior.

This is not to imply that dollars are the only barometer of the effectiveness of HR activities. The payoffs from some activities, such as managing diversity and providing child care, must be viewed in a broader social context. Furthermore, the firm's strategy and goals must guide the work of each business unit and of that unit's HR management activities. For example, to emphasize its outreach efforts to the disadvantaged, a firm might adopt a conscious strategy of *training* workers for entry-level jobs, while *selecting* workers who already have the skills to perform higher-level jobs. To make the most effective use of the information that follows, keep these points in mind.

Chapter 1 identified strategic HR management as a process of getting everybody from the top of the organization to the bottom to do things to implement the strategy of the business effectively—to use people most wisely with respect to the organization's strategic needs. The following sections describe some alternative competitive strategies and then link HR processes to each one.

Alternative Competitive Strategies

The means that firms use to compete for business in the marketplace and to gain competitive advantage are known as *competitive strategies.*[1] Competitive strategies may differ in a number of ways, including the extent to which firms emphasize innovation, quality enhancement, cost reduction, and speed.[2]

While it might appear logical that the different types of strategies require different types of HR practices,[3] the research evidence on this issue is mixed.[4] Lacking clear evidence on this issue, some authors recommend that firms adopt a set of "best practices" regardless of their competitive strategy.[5] Others emphasize the need to focus on activities that are most crucial to the implementation of the competitive strategy chosen.[6] However, these two perspectives are not necessarily mutually exclusive, for a firm's performance may be enhanced even more when best practices are matched to the requirements inherent in a firm's competitive strategy.[7] The important lesson for managers is that *human resources represent a competitive advantage that can increase profits when managed wisely.* Let us now consider alternative competitive strategies in more detail, along with their HR management implications.

Innovation strategy is used to develop products or services that differ from those of competitors. Its primary objective is to offer something new and different. Enhancing product or service quality is the primary objective of the *quality-enhancement strategy,* while the objective of a *cost-reduction strategy* is to gain competitive advantage by being the lowest-cost producer of goods or provider of services. Finally, the objective of a *time-based, or speed, strategy* is to be the fastest innovator, producer, distributor, and responder to customer feedback. Innovation strategy emphasizes managing people so that they work *differently;* quality-enhancement strategy emphasizes managing people so that they work *smarter;* cost-reduction strategy emphasizes managing people so that they work *harder;* and speed strategy emphasizes managing people so that they work *more efficiently* by changing the way work is done.

While it is convenient to think of these four competitive strategies as pure types applied to entire organizations, business units, or even functional specialties, the reality is more complex. As the following example illustrates, various combinations of the four strategies are often observed in practice.

As is well known, Ford Motor Company has emphasized employee involvement since the early 1980s. In October 1978, Philip Caldwell, then president of Ford, made the following statement at a meeting of top executives: "Our strategy for the years ahead will come to nothing unless we ask for greater participation of our work force. Without motivated and concerned workers, we're not going to lower our costs as much as we need to—and we aren't going to get the product quality we need."[8] Elements of both cost-reduction and quality-enhancement strategies are evident in Caldwell's statement.

Employee Behaviors and Human Resource Strategies Appropriate to Each Competitive Business Strategy

Innovation Strategy

Under a competitive strategy of innovation, the implications for managing people may include selecting highly skilled individuals, giving employees more discretion, using minimal controls, making greater investments in human resources, providing more resources for experimentation, allowing and even rewarding occasional failure, and appraising performance for its long-run implications. Innovative firms such as Hewlett-Packard, 3M, Raytheon, and PepsiCo illustrate this strategy.[9]

Because the innovation process depends heavily on individual expertise and creativity, employee turnover can have disastrous consequences.[10] Moreover, firms pursuing this strategy are likely to emphasize long-term needs in their training programs for managers and to offer training to more employees throughout the organization.[11] HR strategy should therefore emphasize the use of highly valid selection and training programs as well as the reduction of controllable turnover, especially among high performers, who are not easy to replace.

The latter approach is being used more and more by firms that are trying to hang on to valued employees as they steer through bankruptcy reorganizations. Such "employee-retention plans" offer incentive bonuses for managers who stay for 1 or 2 years and who meet certain performance criteria. They also offer lucrative severance packages if jobs are cut. Federated Department Stores and Allied Stores, Campeau Corporation's U.S. retailing subsidiaries, used this approach, as did the Braniff, L. J. Hooker, LTV, and Wickes companies. Although the programs are relatively new, early indications are that they work. Why do companies adopt them? Because it does little good for a firm to fight its way out of bankruptcy court if essential employees do not stay around to guide the restructured operations.[12]

Quality-Enhancement Strategy

The profile of behaviors appropriate under this strategy includes relatively repetitive and predictable behaviors; a longer-term focus; a modest amount of cooperative, interdependent behavior; a high concern for quality with a modest concern for quantity of output; a high concern with how goods or services are made or delivered; low risk-taking activity; and commitment to the goals of the organization.[13]

Quality enhancement typically involves greater commitment from employees and fuller use of their abilities. As a result, fewer employees may be needed to accomplish the same amount of work. This phenomenon has been observed at firms such as L.L. Bean, Corning Glass, Honda, and Toyota.[14]

It is well known that the gains in productivity that result from more valid selection or training programs can be expressed in various ways: in dollars, increases in output, decreases in hiring needs, or savings in payroll costs.[15] Since fewer workers may be needed after the implementation of more valid selection or training programs, managers may wish to focus on the change in staffing requirements (as well as the associated cost savings) as one outcome of a quality-enhancement strategy.

Since reliable, predictable behavior is important to the implementation of this strategy, another objective is to minimize absenteeism, tardiness, and turnover. Cost savings associated with any HR programs designed to control these undesirable behaviors should therefore be documented carefully. In a later section of this chapter, we will present methods for doing this.

Commitment to the goals of the organization and flexibility to change can both be increased by constant formal and informal training programs. Changes in commitment and flexibility can then be assessed by measuring employee attitudes over multiple time periods. Finally, other ways to signal concern for the long-term welfare of employees are by actively promoting day-care, employee assistance, wellness, and smoking-cessation programs.

In summary, to be consistent with a quality-enhancement strategy, HR strategy should focus on using highly valid selection and training programs, on promoting positive changes in employees' attitudes and lifestyles, and on decreasing absenteeism and controllable turnover. To assess the effectiveness of strategy implementation, managers must then examine costs and benefits in each of these areas.

Cost-Reduction Strategy

Firms pursuing this strategy are characterized by tight fiscal and management controls, minimization of overhead, and pursuit of economies of scale. The primary objective is to increase productivity by decreasing the unit cost of output per employee. Strategies for reducing costs include reducing the number of employees; reducing wages; using part-time workers, subcontractors, or automation; changing work rules; and permitting flexibility in job assignments.[16]

The profile of employee behaviors under this strategy includes relatively repetitive and predictable behaviors, a comparatively short-term focus, primarily autonomous or individual activity, a modest concern for quality coupled with a high concern for quantity of output (goods or services), emphasis on results, low risk taking, and stability. In addition, there is minimal use of training and development.

Sometimes managers adopt cost-reduction strategies in rather desperate situations, as their firms struggle to survive.[17] More commonly, though, cost reduction is used in combination with other strategies to keep companies prosperous. As an example, consider the response to international competition of Cummins Engine Company, a $2.5 billion manufacturer of diesel engines and related products and services, headquartered in Columbus, Indiana. The company has about 22,000 employees worldwide, and its sales mix is 70 percent U.S. business and 30 percent international. It powers about 60 percent of the trucks on U.S. highways.

Cummins watched with deep concern throughout the 1970s as foreign competition won nearly 100 percent of the U.S. motorcycle market, 30 percent of the U.S. auto market, and a big chunk of the U.S. steel market—all in about 10 years. In the company's view, those gains in market share were mostly won fairly and squarely with better products, quality, prices, and responsiveness to the customer.[18] Those industries are close to Cummins's, and the company vowed to compete aggressively. To do so, it focused on the variables of product, prices, costs, and performance. It spent nearly a billion dollars on product development through the 1980s—triple the company's market value in 1980. To meet world price levels, the company swore off price increases for 5 years. As for performance, managers at every level developed specific goals in the areas of quality, cost, and delivery, and allocated them to work groups throughout the company. Every quarter, the president provided videotaped progress reports to all employees.

What were the results? Financially, the company has lost no domestic business to international competition. Its domestic market share has grown, as has its success in international markets. As one executive noted: "We have experienced, and managed, a full range of human emotions during these years. . . . Our people have been stretched, pulled, and at times really shaken up trying to meet all these challenges; facilities have been closed as operations were consolidated, and many jobs were lost despite our successful efforts to create new ones. . . . This process, of course, continues . . . for it is a game—or war—that can be won but never finished."[19]

Speed Strategy

"The computer, the fax, and the microwave are not going to go away; they are going to get faster or be replaced by new technologies that do even more than they do and are faster yet. Demands by consumers for more choices, and faster,

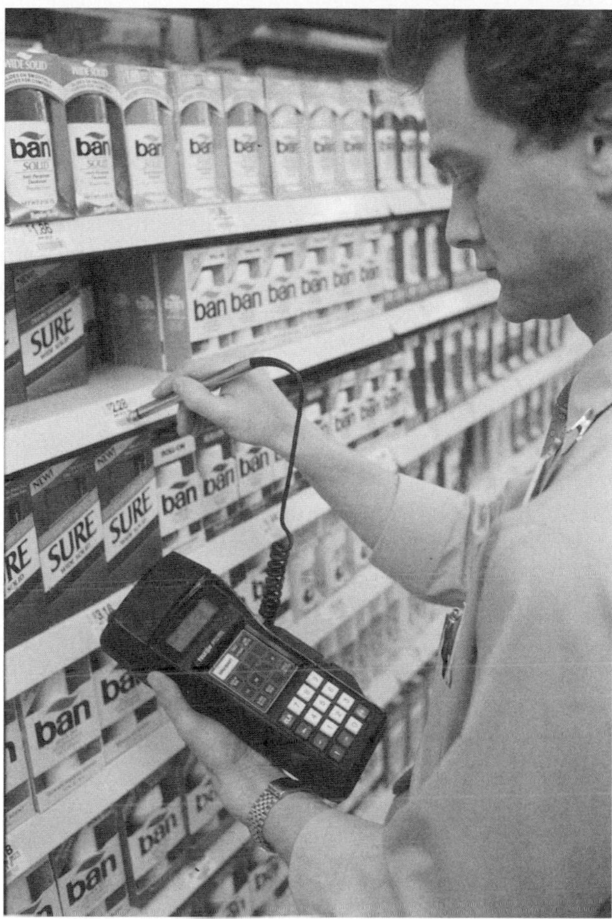

Hand-held computer scanners enhance the speed and accuracy of inventory management. Empowered, well-trained workers manage this process.

more comprehensive services . . . would seem to underline the need for speed in development, production, and delivery of products and services."[20]

The first imperative under such a strategy is to select highly skilled individuals who are committed to speed management and whose beliefs, attitudes, and values related to time are consistent with those the organization is seeking. Both workers and managers must embrace change rather than resist it, company culture must support their efforts, and both work groups and cross-functional teams must share the same norms about time. A fluid, networked organizational structure, rather than the old "command, control, and compartmentalization" system, is most appropriate. Finally, all HR systems, including staffing, training, reward, and performance management, must support the speed-management philosophy.

To appreciate the importance of speed in every function, consider the following changes in development time: new cars—Honda, from 5 years to 3; telephones—AT&T, from 2 years to 1; computer printers—Hewlett-Packard, from 4.5 years to 22 months; and trucks—Navistar, from 5 years to 2.5. When it comes to production, consider these world-class time standards from receipt of the customer's order to finished product: General Electric (circuit-breaker boxes)—from 3 weeks to 3 days; Motorola (pagers)—from 3 weeks to 2 hours; Hewlett-Packard (electronic testing equipment)—from 4 weeks to 5 days; and

Brunswick (fishing reels)—from 3 weeks to 1.[21] In terms of services, consider the bank that decreased the time for loan approval from several days to 30 minutes by creating a team composed of a credit analyst, an experienced collateral appraiser, and a bank procedures expert. The team is empowered to draw on its collective knowledge and experience to respond to the customer almost at once.[22]

General Electric CEO Jack Welch summed up the challenge well: "We have to get faster if we are to win in a world where nothing is predictable except the increasingly rapid pace of change."[23] Managing people effectively in such an environment is a continuing challenge.

HUMAN RESOURCES RESEARCH—THE BASIS FOR AUDIT AND EVALUATION OF HR SYSTEMS

One of the classic functions of management is that of control. In a small business, managers are close to the scene of operations. They can see for themselves exactly what is happening. However, the need for management control becomes greater as managers are farther removed from the scene of operations, as is the case in many firms that do business in multiple locations. To facilitate management control, it is important to conduct HR research to assess the effectiveness of HR systems.

Assessing the Effectiveness of HR Systems

Researchers have attempted to gauge effectiveness in at least six different ways:[24]

- **Judgments about the reputation of HR policies and practices of a given firm** by corporate officers, HR executives, faculty members, placement directors, and leading consultants. Policies and practices examined include open communications, high performance standards, rewards based on performance, use of employee skills and abilities, encouragement of employee participation in work decisions, advancement opportunities, and identification and development of high-potential managers.
- **Human resource accounting**—an approach that considers only the investments made in managers (e.g., recruiting, selecting, and training them) and not the returns on those investments. Valuing managers in this way is what accountants call the "asset model of accounting," for it uses the historical cost of the asset. However, asset models of HR accounting have never caught on widely.[25]
- **Audit of the HR function,** for example, department mission, organization, personnel, labor relations, recruitment and selection, training and development, employee relations, employee benefits, compensation, HR planning, organizational planning and development, equal employment opportunity (EEO), safety, security, facilities, and documentation.
- **HR cost monitoring** in areas such as *employment* (cost per hire, orientation cost), *training and development* (cost per employee, total cost as a percentage of payroll), *compensation* (compensation expense as a percentage of operating expense, total compensation costs), *benefits* (benefits cost as a percentage

of payroll, health-care costs per employee), *EEO* (cost per complaint, cost of litigation), *labor relations* (cost per grievance, cost of work stoppages), *safety and health* (accident costs, costs of citations or fines), *overall HR* (HR costs as a percentage of operating expenses, turnover costs).

- **Competitive benchmarking** using key indicators such as *employment* (average days taken to fill open requisitions, ratio of offers made to number of applicants), *EEO* (ratio of EEO grievances to employee population, minority representation by EEO category), *training* (percentage of employees trained by employment category, training hours per employee), *performance appraisal* (distribution of performance appraisal ratings, reliability of appraisal ratings), *salary administration* (percentage of overtime hours relative to straight time, ratio of average salary to midpoint by grade level), *benefits* (percentage of sick leave to total pay, average length of time taken to process claims), *work environment/safety* (frequency/severity ratio of accidents, ratio of OSHA citations to number of employees), *labor relations* (percentage of grievances settled, average length of time to settle a grievance), and *overall HR effectiveness* (turnover rate, absenteeism rate).
- **Linking the use of high-performance work practices to firm performance.** We will have more to say about this approach in a later section, but in general its objective is to demonstrate that the use of "best practices" in areas such as staffing, training, performance management, incentives, and labor-management relations relates consistently to firm-level measures of financial performance.

Regardless of the approach chosen, it is important to consider two issues: (1) alternative types of outcomes, and (2) level of analysis.

Types of Outcomes

Outcomes may be expressed in quantitative terms (e.g., cost–benefit analysis) or in qualitative terms (e.g., indicators of overall morale, job satisfaction, or reaction to a training program). Alone, each type of outcome is incomplete; both are necessary to describe the rich results of HR programs. Later in this chapter, we will examine how quantitative outcomes can be determined. Now, however, let's consider a qualitative HR research tool that is becoming quite popular—the attitude survey.

To a large extent, the growing popularity of attitude surveys is due to an idea stressed in many popular books on management: it is important to listen to employees. This idea has taken on added significance as more companies endure the organizational trauma of mergers and restructurings or adopt more participative management styles.

As employee surveys become more common, the range of issues on which opinions are solicited is expanding considerably. At Wells Fargo & Company in San Francisco, for instance, employees have been asked about such things as the effectiveness of the bank's advertising, the quality of innovation of its products, and its responsibility to the community.[26]

Surveys are most effective when they are aligned with competitive strategy—that is, when they tap issues that are important to strategy implementation at all levels and when managers commit up front to take action based on survey findings. Doing so helps build bridges between survey feedback and existing change strategies such as total quality management, reengineering, or continuous improvement.[27]

Attitude surveys represent just one type of HR research tool. In addition, the wide availability of computerized employee databases makes it possible to answer a variety of other questions, such as factors that relate consistently to the retention of engineers, the productivity and turnover of salespeople, and the personal characteristics of employees who accept offers of early retirement. Finally, detailed, sophisticated research is being conducted on issues as diverse as the impact of plant shutdowns, worker participation in management decisions, worker ownership, and the impact of quality-improvement efforts. As these few examples show, the range of HR research topics and the methods used to investigate them are limited only by the imagination and ingenuity of the managers and researchers involved.

The Level of Analysis

It is important to distinguish HR activities performed at the corporate level from those performed at the middle-management level or at the operating level.[28] At the corporate level, HR decisions involve the design of policies that meet an organization's strategic challenges, such as business objectives, corporate values or culture, technology, structure, and responses to environmental constraints (e.g., health and safety policies).

At the middle-management level, key HR decisions involve the design of systems or programs that are consistent with policy guidelines and will facilitate the cost-effective achievement of business goals. The primary objective is management control, and it is accomplished by assessing the cost-effectiveness of HR programs.

At the operating level, managers implement HR policies and programs, making decisions that affect the attraction, retention, and motivation of employees. This level includes the hands-on HR practices of line managers (e.g., to reduce absenteeism or controllable turnover) and the day-to-day services provided by the HR function (e.g., recruiting, staffing, training) that directly affect HR outcomes.

Assuming that a manager appreciates the need to align competitive and human resource strategies and desires to assess the costs and benefits of the HR activities that are most relevant to the chosen strategy, how does he or she proceed? Let us begin by examining one approach—behavior costing.

The Behavior Costing Approach

This approach focuses on dollar estimates of the behaviors, such as the absenteeism, turnover, and job performance, of managers. Behavior costing measures not the value of a manager as an asset, but rather the economic consequences of his or her behavior. This is an expense model of HR accounting,[29] and, contrary to popular belief, there are methods for determining the costs of employee behavior in all HR management activities—behaviors associated with the attraction, selection, retention, development, and utilization of people in organizations. It is the approach taken in this chapter to assessing the costs and benefits of the activities of all employees, managerial as well as nonmanagerial. We will apply standard cost-accounting procedures to employee behavior. To

Table 15-1

DIRECT AND INDIRECT COSTS ASSOCIATED WITH MISMANAGED STRESS

Direct costs	Indirect costs
Participation and membership:	Loss of vitality:
Absenteeism	Low motivation
Tardiness	Dissatisfaction
Strikes and work stoppages	
	Communication breakdowns:
Performance on the job:	Decline in frequency of contact
Quality of productivity	Distortions of messages
Quantity of productivity	
Grievances	Faulty decision making
Accidents	
Unscheduled machine downtime and repair	Quality of work relations:
	Distrust
Material and supply overutilization	Disrespect
Inventory shrinkages	Animosity
Compensation awards	Opportunity costs

Source: B. A. Macy & P. H. Mirvis, *Evaluation Review, 6*(3), Figure 4-5. Copyright © 1982 by Sage Publications, Inc. Reprinted by permission.

do this, we must first identify each of the elements of behavior to which we can assign a cost; each behavioral cost element must be separate and mutually exclusive from the others. To begin, let's consider the definitions of some key terms.

Some Definitions

The costing methods described below are based on several definitions and a few necessary assumptions. To begin with, there are, as in any costing situation, both controllable and uncontrollable costs, and there are direct and indirect measures of these costs.

- *Direct measures* refer to actual costs, such as the accumulated, direct cost of recruiting.
- *Indirect measures* do not deal directly with cost; they are usually expressed in terms of time, quantity, or quality.[30] In many cases indirect measures can be converted to direct measures. For example, if we know the length of time per preemployment interview plus the interviewer's hourly pay, it is a simple matter to convert time per interview into cost per interview.

Indirect measures have value in and of themselves, and they also supply part of the data needed to develop a direct measure. As a further example, consider the direct and indirect costs associated with mismanaged organizational stress, as shown in Table 15-1.[31] The direct costs listed in the left-hand column of Table 15-1 can all be expressed in terms of dollars. To understand this concept, consider just two items: the costs associated with work accidents and with grievances. Figure 15-1 presents just some of the direct costs associated with accidents; it is not meant to be exhaustive, and it does not include such

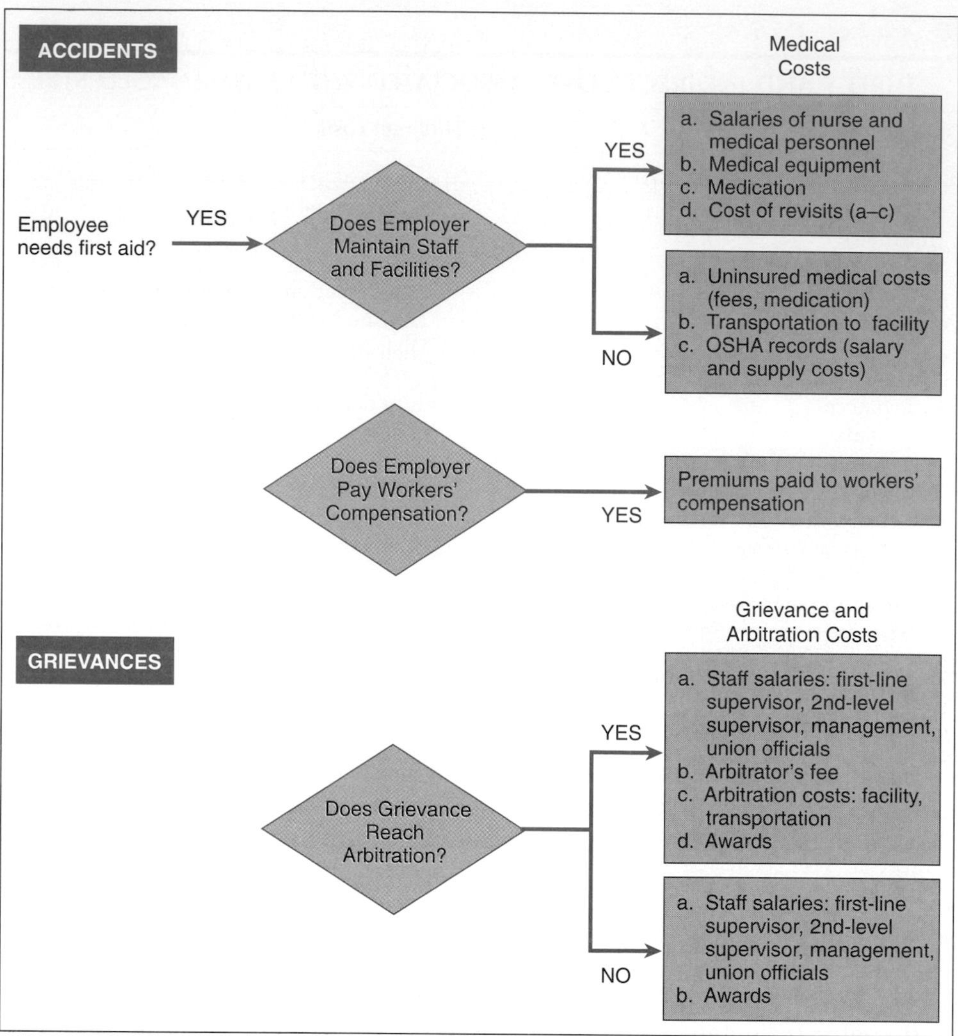

Figure 15-1
The costs of accidents and grievances.

items as lost time, replacement costs, institution of "work to rule" by coworkers if they feel the firm is responsible, the cost of the safety committee's investigation, and the costs associated with changing technology or job design to prevent future accidents. The items shown in the right-hand column of Table 15-1 cannot be expressed as easily in dollar terms, but they are no less important, and the cost of these indirect items may in fact be far larger than the direct costs. Both direct and indirect costs, as well as benefits, must be considered to apply behavior costing methodology properly.

Controllable versus Uncontrollable Costs

In any area of behavior costing, some types of costs are controllable through prudent HR decisions, while other costs are simply beyond the control of the organization. Consider employee turnover as an example. To the extent that people leave for reasons of "better salary," "more opportunity for promotion and career development," or "greater job challenge," the costs associated with turnover are somewhat controllable. That is, the firm can alter its HR management practices to reduce the voluntary turnover. However, if the turnover is due to such factors as death, poor health, or spouse transfer, the costs are uncontrollable.

The point is that in human resource costing, the objective is not simply to *measure* costs but also to *reduce* the costs of human resources by devoting resources to the more "controllable" factors. To do this, we must do two things well:

1. Identify, for each HR decision, which costs are controllable and which are not
2. Measure these costs at Time 1 (prior to some intervention designed to reduce controllable costs) and then again at Time 2 (after the intervention)

Hence the real payoff from determining the cost of employee behaviors lies in being able to demonstrate a financial gain from the wise application of human resource management methods.

The next three sections present both hypothetical and actual company examples of behavior costing in the areas of absenteeism, turnover, and training. Following the examples is a presentation of three macro-level assessments of the financial impact of high-performance work practices. The focus will be on methods and outcomes rather than on alternative HR management approaches that might be used to reduce costs or increase profits in each area. (Such approaches have been discussed elsewhere in the book.)

COSTING EMPLOYEE ABSENTEEISM

In any human resource costing application, it is important first to define exactly what is being measured. From a business standpoint, *absenteeism is any failure of an employee to report for or to remain at work as scheduled, regardless of reason.* The term "as scheduled" is very significant, for it automatically excludes vacations, holidays, jury duty, and the like. It also eliminates the problem of determining whether an absence is "excusable" or not. Medically verified illness is a good example. From a business perspective, the employee is absent and is simply not available to perform his or her job; that absence will cost money. How much money? In 1997 dollars, the cost of unscheduled absences in U.S. workplaces varied from about $290 to $630 *per employee per year.*[32]

A flowchart that shows how to estimate the total cost of employee absenteeism over any period is shown in Figure 15-2.[33] To illustrate the computation of each cost element in Figure 15-2, let us use as an example a hypothetical 1800-employee firm called Mini-Mini-Micro Electronics; hour and dollar amounts for each element are shown in Table 15-2. An item-by-item explanation follows.

Item 1: Total Hours Lost. Assume that employee absenteeism accounts for 1.6 percent of scheduled work hours (the all-company average in the United States in 1996),[34] which will be applied to total scheduled work hours. Also assume an 8-hour day and a 5-day week. Hours of scheduled work time per employee per year may be determined by subtracting 2 weeks' vacation hours and 5 paid holidays from total work hours:

1. Compute total employee-hours lost to absenteeism for the period.

2. Compute weighted-average wage or salary/hr per absent employee.

3. Compute cost of employee benefits/hr per employee.

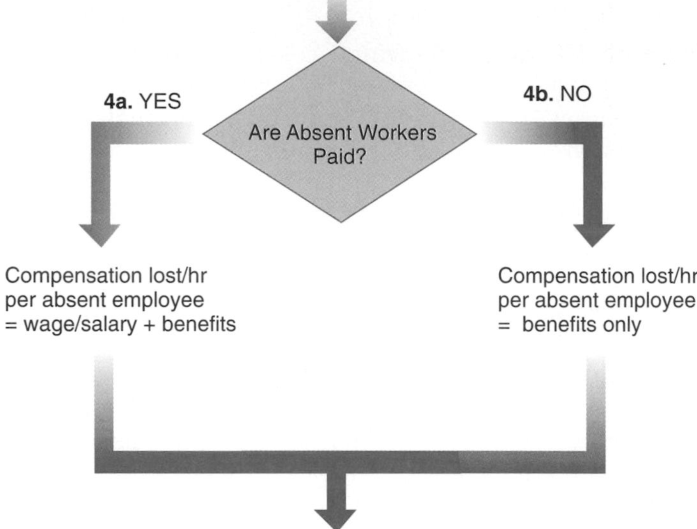

5. Compute total compensation lost to absent employees [(1) x (4a) or (4b) as applicable].

6. Estimate total supervisory hours lost to employee absenteeism.

7. Compute average hourly supervisory salary + benefits.

8. Estimate total supervisory salaries lost to managing absenteeism problems [(6) x (7)].

9. Estimate all other costs incidental to absenteeism.

10. Estimate total cost of absenteeism [(5) + (8) + (9)].

11. Estimate total cost of absenteeism/employee [(10) ÷ total no. of employees].

Figure 15-2
Total estimated cost of employee absenteeism. (*Source:* Wayne F. Cascio, *Costing human resources: The financial impact of behavior in organizations,* 3d ed, 1991. © PWS-Kent Publishing Co., Boston. Reprinted by permission of PWS-Kent Publishing Co., a division of Wadsworth, Inc.).

- Total hours of work per year = 40 hours × 52 weeks = 2080 hours
- 2 weeks of vacation = 40 hours × 2 weeks = 80 hours
- 5 paid holidays = 40 hours × 5 days = 40 hours

$$\text{Scheduled work hours per year per employee} = 2080 \text{ hr} - 80 \text{ hr} - 40 \text{ hr} = 1960 \text{ hr}$$

To calculate total scheduled work hours per year, multiply the hours of scheduled work time per employee by the number of employees:

Table 15-2

COST OF EMPLOYEE ABSENTEEISM AT MINI-MINI-MICRO ELECTRONICS

Item	Mini-Mini-Micro Electronics
1. Total hours lost to employee absenteeism for the period	56,448 hr
2. Weighted-average wage or salary per hour per employee	\$10.159/hr
3. Cost of employee benefits per hour per employee	\$3.556/hr
4. Total compensation lost per hour per absent employee:	
(a) if absent workers are paid (wage or salary plus benefits)	\$13.715/hr
(b) if absent workers are not paid (benefits only)	—
5. Total compensation lost to absent employees [total hours lost × 4(a) or 4(b), whichever applies]	\$774,184.32
6. Total supervisory hours lost on employee absenteeism	8820 hr
7. Average hourly supervisory wage, including benefits	\$18.225/hr
8. Total supervisory salaries lost to managing problems of absenteeism (hours lost × average hourly supervisory wage—item 6 × item 7)	\$160,744.50
9. All other costs incidental to absenteeism not included in the preceding items	\$50,000
10. Total estimated cost of absenteeism—summation of items 5, 8, and 9	\$984,928.82
11. Total estimated cost of absenteeism per employee: Total estimated costs ÷ total number of employees	\$547.18 per employee absence

1960 hr × 1800 employees = 3,528,000 total scheduled work hours per year

To determine total work hours lost to absenteeism, multiply total scheduled hours by 1.6 percent:

3,528,000 hr × 0.016 = 56,448 work hours lost per year

Item 2: Weighted-Average Wage or Salary per Hour per Absent Employee. The two out of every three employers that have a system in place for employees to report their absences can determine the exact wage or salary per hour per absent employee.[35] Others might use the following procedure to estimate a weighted-average wage or salary per hour per absentee:

Occupational group	Approximate percentage of total absenteeism	Average hourly wage	Weighted-average wage
Blue-collar workers	0.55	\$10.45	\$ 5.747
Clerical workers	0.35	8.15	2.852
Management	0.10	15.60	1.560
Total weighted-average pay per employee per hour			\$10.159

Item 3: Cost of Employee Benefits per Hour per Absent Employee. The cost of benefits is included in the calculations because benefits consume, on average, more than a third of total compensation (see Chapter 11). Ultimately, we want to be able to calculate the total compensation lost as a result of absenteeism. Since our primary interest is in the cost of benefits per absentee, we multiply the weighted-average hourly wage by the benefits as a percentage of base pay. (If benefits differ as a function of union-nonunion or exempt-nonexempt status, a weighted-average benefit should be computed in the same manner as was done to compute a weighted-average wage.) For Mini-Mini-Micro, the cost of benefits per hour per absentee is

$$\$10.159 \times 0.35 = \$3.556$$

Item 4: Total Compensation Lost per Hour per Absent Employee. This amount is determined by adding the weighted-average hourly wage and the hourly cost of benefits (assuming that absent workers are paid). Some firms (e.g., Honda USA) do not pay absentees: "No work, no pay." In such instances, only the cost of benefits should be included in the estimate of total compensation lost per hour per absent employee. For Mini-Mini-Micro, where absent workers *are* paid, the compensation lost per hour for each absent employee is

$$\$10.159 + \$3.556 = \$13.715$$

Item 5: Total Compensation Lost to Absent Employees. This amount is simply total hours lost multiplied by total compensation lost per hour:

$$56{,}448 \text{ hr} \times \$13.715/\text{hr} = \$774{,}184.32$$

Note that the first five items shown in Figure 15-2 refer to the costs associated with absentees themselves. The next three items refer to the firm's costs of managing employee absenteeism.

Item 6: Total Supervisory Hours Lost in Dealing with Employee Absenteeism. Three factors determine this category of lost time:

A = Estimated average number of hours lost per supervisor per day managing absenteeism problems
B = Total number of supervisors who deal with absenteeism problems
C = Total number of working days in the period for which absentee costs are being analyzed (including all shifts and weekend work)

The supervisor's time is "lost" because, instead of planning, scheduling, and troubleshooting productivity problems, he or she must devote time to nonproductive activities associated with managing absenteeism problems. The actual amount of time lost can be determined by having supervisors keep diaries indicating how they spend their time or by conducting structured interviews with experienced supervisors.

To calculate supervisory hours lost, multiply $A \times B \times C$. For Mini-Mini-Micro Electronics, the data needed for this calculation are as follows:

Estimate of A = 30 minutes, or 0.50 hour, per day
Estimate of B = 72 supervisors (Of the firm's 1800 employees, 10 percent, or 180, are supervisors, and 40 percent of the 180, or 72, of the supervisors deal regularly with absenteeism problems.)
Estimate of C = 245 days per year

$$\text{Supervisory hours lost in dealing with absenteeism} = 0.50 \text{ hr/day} \times 72 \text{ supervisors} \times 245 \text{ days/year}$$
$$= 8820 \text{ supervisory hours lost per year}$$

Item 7: Average Hourly Supervisory Wage, Including Benefits. For those supervisors who deal regularly with absenteeism problems, assume that their average hourly wage is $13.50 plus 35 percent benefits ($4.725), or $18.225 per hour.

Item 8: Total Cost of Supervisory Salaries Lost to Managing Problems of Absenteeism. To determine this cost, multiply the total supervisory hours lost by the total hourly supervisory wage:

$$8820 \text{ hr} \times \$18.225/\text{hr} = \$160{,}744.50$$

Item 9: All Other Absenteeism-Related Costs Not Included in Items 1 through 8. Assume that Mini-Mini-Micro spends $50,000 per year in absenteeism-related costs that are not associated either with absentees or with supervisors. These costs are associated with elements such as overtime premiums, wages for temporary help, machine downtime, production losses, inefficient materials usage by temporary substitute employees, and, for very large organizations, permanent labor pools to fill in for absent workers.

Item 10: Total Cost of Employee Absenteeism. This cost is the sum of the three costs determined thus far: costs associated with absent employees (item 5) plus costs associated with the management of absenteeism problems (item 8) plus other absenteeism-related costs (item 9). For Mini-Mini-Micro Electronics, the total yearly cost is

$$\$774{,}184.32 + \$160{,}744.50 + \$50{,}000 = \$984{,}928.82$$

Item 11: Per-Employee Cost of Absenteeism. This amount is the total yearly cost divided by the number of employees:

$$\$984{,}928.82 \div 1800 \text{ employees} = \$547.18$$

Interpreting the Costs of Absenteeism

Perhaps the first questions management will ask upon seeing absenteeism cost figures are "What do they mean? Are we average, above average, below average?" Unfortunately, there are no industry-specific figures on the costs of employee absenteeism. Certainly, these costs will vary depending on the type of firm, the industry, and the level of employee that is absent (unskilled versus skilled or professional workers). As a benchmark, however, consider that the average employee in the United States has about seven unscheduled absences per year, while the average British employee has about eight per year.[36]

Remember that the dollar figure just determined (we will call this the "Time 1" figure) becomes meaningful as a baseline from which to measure the financial gains realized as a result of a strategy to reduce absenteeism. At some later time (we will call this "Time 2"), the total cost of absenteeism should be measured again. The difference between the Time 2 figure and the Time 1 figure, minus the cost of implementing the strategy to reduce absenteeism, represents net gain.

Another question that often arises at this point is "Are these dollars real? Since supervisors are drawing their salaries anyway, what difference does it make if they have to manage absenteeism problems?" True, but what is the best possible gain from them for that pay? Let's compare two firms, A and B, identical in regard to all resources and costs—supervisors get paid the same, work the same hours, manage the same size staff, and produce the same kind of product. But absenteeism in A is very low, and in B it is very high. The paymasters' records show the same pay to supervisors, but the accountants show higher profits in A than in B. Why? Because the supervisors in firm A spend less time managing absenteeism problems. They are more productive because they devote their energies to planning, scheduling, and troubleshooting. Instead of putting in a 10- or 12-hour day (which the supervisors in firm B consider "normal"), they wrap things up after only 8 hours. In short, reducing the number of hours that supervisors must spend managing absenteeism problems has two advantages: (1) it allows supervisors to maximize their productivity, and (2) it reduces the stress and the wear and tear associated with repeated 10- to 12-hour days, which, in turn, enhances the quality of work life of supervisors.

COSTING EMPLOYEE TURNOVER

Turnover may be defined as *any permanent departure beyond organizational boundaries*[37]—a broad and ponderous definition. Not included as turnover within this definition, therefore, are transfers within an organization and temporary layoffs. The rate of turnover in percent over any period can be calculated by the following formula:

$$\frac{\text{Number of turnover incidents per period}}{\text{Average workforce size}} \times 100\%$$

Nationwide in 1993, for example, monthly turnover rates averaged about 0.7 percent, or 8.4 percent annually.[38] However, this figure most likely represents both controllable turnover (controllable by the organization) and uncontrollable turnover. Controllable turnover is "voluntary" on the part of the employee, while uncontrollable turnover is "involuntary" (due, e.g., to retirement, death, or spouse transfer). Furthermore, turnover may be *functional,* where the employee's departure produces a benefit for the organization, or *dysfunctional,* where the departing employee is someone the organization would like to retain.

High performers who are difficult to replace represent dysfunctional turnovers; low performers who are easy to replace represent functional turnovers.

The crucial issue in analyzing turnover, therefore, is not how many employees leave but rather the performance and replaceability of those who leave versus those who stay.[39]

In costing employee turnover, first determine the total cost of all turnover and then estimate the percentage of that amount that represents controllable, dysfunctional turnover—resignations that represent a net loss to the firm and that the firm could have prevented. Thus, if total turnover costs $1 million and 50 percent is controllable and dysfunctional, $500,000 is our Time 1 baseline measure. To determine the net financial gain associated with the strategy adopted prior to Time 2, compare the total gain at Time 2, say $700,000, minus the cost of implementing the strategy to reduce turnover, say $50,000, with the cost of turnover at Time 1 ($500,000). In this example, the net gain to the firm is $150,000. Now let's see how the total cost figure is derived.

Components of Turnover Costs

There are three broad categories of costs in the basic turnover costing model: separation costs, replacement costs, and training costs. This section presents only the cost elements that make up each of these three broad categories. Those who wish to investigate the subject more deeply may seek information on the more detailed formulas that are available.[40]

Separation Costs

Following are four cost elements in separation costs:

1. **Exit interview,** including the cost of the interviewer's time and the cost of the terminating employee's time.
2. **Administrative functions related to termination,** for example, removal of the employee from the payroll, termination of benefits, and turn-in of company equipment.
3. **Separation pay,** if applicable.
4. **Increased unemployment tax.** Such an increase may come from either or both of two sources. First, in states that base unemployment tax rates on each company's turnover rate, high turnover will lead to a higher unemployment tax rate. Suppose a company with a 10 percent annual turnover rate was paying unemployment tax at a rate of 5 percent on the first $7000 of each employee's wages in 1996. But in 1997, because its turnover rate jumped to 15 percent, the company's unemployment tax rate may increase to 5.5 percent. Second, replacements for those who leave will result in extra unemployment tax being paid. Thus a 500-employee firm with no turnover during the year will pay the tax on the first $7000 (or whatever the state maximum is) of each employee's wages. The same firm with a 20 percent annual turnover rate will pay the tax on the first $7000 of the wages of 600 employees.

The sum of these four cost elements represents the total separation costs for the firm.

Replacement Costs

The eight cost elements associated with replacing employees who leave are the following:

1. **Communicating job availability**
2. **Preemployment administrative functions,** for example, accepting applications and checking references
3. **Entrance interview,** or perhaps multiple interviews
4. **Testing** and/or other types of assessment procedures
5. **Staff meetings,** if applicable, to determine if replacements are needed, to recheck job analyses and job specifications, to pool information on candidates, and to reach final hiring decisions
6. **Travel and moving expenses,** for example, travel for all applicants and travel plus moving expenses for all new hires
7. **Postemployment acquisition and dissemination of information,** for example, all the activities associated with in-processing new employees
8. **Medical examinations,** if applicable, either performed in-house or contracted out

The sum of these eight cost elements represents the total cost of replacing those who leave.

Training Costs

This third component of turnover costs includes three elements:

1. **Informational literature** (e.g., an employee handbook)
2. **Instruction in a formal training program**
3. **Instruction by employee assignment** (e.g., on-the-job training)

The sum of these three cost elements represents the total cost of training replacements for those who leave.

Two points should be noted: First, if there is a formal orientation program, the per-person costs associated with replacements for those who left should be included in the first cost element, *informational literature.* This cost should reflect the per-person, amortized cost of developing the literature, not just its delivery. Do not include the total cost of the orientation program unless 100 percent of the costs can be attributed to employee turnover.

Second, probably the major cost associated with employee turnover, *reduced productivity during the learning period,* is generally not included along with the cost elements *instruction in a formal training program* and *instruction by employee assignment.* The reason for this is that formal work-measurement programs are not often found in employment situations. Thus it is not possible to calculate accurately the dollar value of the loss in productivity during the learning period. If such a program does exist, then by all means include this cost. For example, a major brokerage firm did a formal work-measurement study of this problem and reported the results shown in Table 15-3. The bottom line is that we want to be conservative in our training cost figures so that we can defend every number we generate.

The Total Cost of Turnover

The sum of the three component costs—separation, replacement, and training—represents the total cost of employee turnover for the period in question. Other factors could also be included in the tally, such as the uncompensated

Table 15-3

PRODUCTIVITY LOSS OVER EACH THIRD OF THE LEARNING PERIOD FOR FOUR JOB CLASSIFICATIONS

Classification	Weeks in learning period	Productivity loss during each third of the learning period 1	2	3
Management and partners	24	75%	40%	15%
Professional and technicians	16	70	40	15
Office and clerical workers	10	60	40	15
Broker trainees	104	85	75	50

Note: The learning period for the average broker trainee is 2 years, although the cost to the firm is generally incurred only in the first year. It is not until the end of the second year that the average broker trainee is fully productive.

performance differential between leavers and their replacements, but that is beyond the scope of this book.[41]

Remember, *the purpose of measuring turnover costs is to improve management decision making.* Once turnover figures are known, managers have a sound basis for choosing between current turnover costs and instituting some type of turnover-reduction program (e.g., job enrichment, realistic job previews).

As examples, consider the results Corning, Inc., found when it tallied only its out-of-pocket expenses for turnover, such as interview costs and hiring bonuses. That number, $16 to $18 million annually, led to an investigation into the causes of turnover and, in turn, to new policies on flexible scheduling and career development.[42]

Merck & Company, the pharmaceutical giant, found that, depending on the job, turnover costs were 1.5 to 2.5 times the annual salary paid.[43] In the retail automobile industry, the cost of turnover (in 1997 dollars) averages more than $24,000 per salesperson.[44] Obviously, there are opportunities in this area for enterprising managers to make significant bottom-line contributions to their organizations. Indeed, one way to reduce turnover, especially among employees who seek opportunities for personal growth and professional development, is to provide training. At firms such as Hewlett-Packard, IBM, and Skyway Express, training is an important component of the competitive strategies of innovation, quality enhancement, and speed.[45] Methods of assessing the costs and benefits of training are described next.

COSTING THE EFFECTS OF TRAINING ACTIVITIES

At the most basic level, the task of evaluation is counting—counting clients, counting errors, counting dollars, counting hours, and so forth. The most difficult tasks of evaluation are deciding which things should be counted and developing routine methods for counting them. Managers should count the things that will provide the most useful feedback. As noted in Chapter 7, managers assess the results of training to determine whether it is worth the cost. Training valuation (in financial terms) is not easy, but the technology to do it is available and well developed.[46] A manager may have to value training in two types of situations: one in which only indirect measures of dollar outcomes are available and one in which direct measures of dollar outcomes are available.

Indirect Measures of Training Outcomes

Indirect measures of training outcomes are more common than direct measures. That is, many studies of training outcomes report improvements in job performance or decreases in errors, scrap, and waste. Relatively few studies report training outcomes directly in terms of dollars gained or saved. Indirect measures can often be converted into estimates of the dollar impact of training, however, by using a method known as utility analysis. Although the technical details of the method are beyond the scope of this chapter,[47] following is a summary of one such study.

In a study of the effects of behavior-modeling skills on the performance of supervisors (see Chapter 7 for a fuller description of behavior modeling), the performance of a trained group of supervisors was compared with that of an untrained group. The two groups were matched as closely as possible on characteristics such as job requirements, geographical location, salary, experience, and age. When posttraining performance appraisal scores for the two groups were compared, the trained group was rated about 12 percent higher than the untrained group.[48]

Using utility analysis to translate the gain in performance into economic terms, the authors found the 1-year net benefit for the 65 supervisors who were trained to be about $35,000. This represents the dollar gain in performance, minus the cost of the training program, adjusted for variable costs (those that rise and fall with changes in productivity, such as sales commissions), taxes, and discounting. These benefits were assumed to accumulate over time, and, assuming that obsolescence did not negate the effect of the training, a net benefit of almost $150,000 was estimated by year 5. Now let's focus on direct measures of training outcomes—by considering a study that examined the impact of training on sales performance.

Direct Measures of Training Outcomes

When direct measures of the dollar outcomes of training are available, standard valuation methods are appropriate. The following study valued the results of a behavior-modeling training program for sales representatives in relation to the program's effects on sales performance.[49]

Study Design

A large retailer conducted a behavior-modeling program in two departments, Large Appliances and Radio/TV, within 14 of its stores in one large metropolitan area. The 14 stores were matched into seven pairs in terms of size, location, and market characteristics. Stores with unusual characteristics that could affect their overall performance, such as declining sales or recent changes in management, were not included in the study.

The training program was then introduced in seven stores, one in each of the matched pairs, and not in the other seven stores. Other kinds of ongoing sales training programs were provided in the control-group stores, but the behavior-modeling approach was used only in the seven experimental-group stores. In the experimental-group stores, 58 sales associates received the training, and their job performance was compared with that of 64 sales associates in the same departments in the control-group stores.

As in most sales organizations, detailed sales records for each individual were kept on a continuous basis. These records included total sales as well as hours worked on the sales floor. Since all individuals received commissions on their sales and since the value of the various products sold varied greatly, it was possible to compute a job performance measure for each individual in terms of average commissions per hour worked.

There was considerable variation in the month-to-month sales performance of each individual, but sales performance over 6-month periods was more stable. In fact, the average correlation between consecutive sales periods of 6 months each was about .80 (where 1.00 equals perfect agreement). Hence the researchers decided to compare the sales records of participants for 6 months before the training program was introduced with the results achieved during the same 6 months the following year, after the training was concluded. All sales promotions and other programs in the stores were identical, since these were administered on an areawide basis.

The Training Program Itself

The program focused on specific aspects of sales situations, such as "approaching the customer," "explaining features, advantages, and benefits," and "closing the sale." The usual behavior-modeling procedure was followed. First the trainers presented guidelines (or "learning points") for handling each aspect of a sales interaction. Then the trainees viewed a videotaped situation in which a "model" sales associate followed the guidelines in carrying out that aspect of the sales interaction with a customer. The trainees then practiced the same situation in role-playing rehearsals. Their performance was reinforced and shaped by their supervisors, who had been trained as their instructors.

Study Results

Of the original 58 trainees in the experimental group, 50 were still working as sales associates 1 year later. Of the remaining 8 associates, 4 had been promoted during the interim, and 4 others had left the company. In the control-group stores, only 49 of the original 64 were still working as sales associates 1 year later. Only 1 had been promoted, and 14 others had left the company. Thus the behavior-modeling program may have had a substantial positive effect on turnover since only about 7 percent of the trained group left during the ensuing year, in comparison with 22 percent of those in the control group. (This result had not been predicted.)

Figure 15-3 presents the changes in average per-hour commissions for participants in both the trained and untrained groups from the 6-month period before the training was conducted to the 6-month period following the training. Note in Figure 15-3 that the trained and untrained groups did not have equal per-hour commissions at the start of the study. While the stores that members of the two groups worked in were matched at the start of the study, sales commissions were not. Sales associates in the trained group started at a lower point than did sales associates in the untrained group. Average per-hour commissions for the trained group increased over the year from $9.27 to $9.95 ($15.74 to $16.90 in 1997 dollars); average per-hour commissions for the untrained group declined over the year from $9.71 to $9.43 ($16.49 to $16.01 in 1997 dollars). In

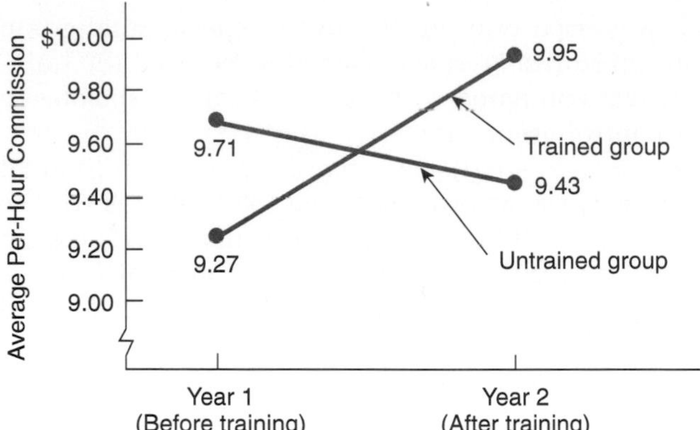

Figure 15-3
Changes in per-hour commissions before and after the behavior-modeling training program.

other words, the trained sales associates increased their average earnings by about 7 percent, whereas those who did not receive the behavior-modeling training experienced a 3 percent decline in average earnings. This difference was statistically significant. Other training outcomes (e.g., trainee attitudes, supervisory behaviors) were also assessed, but, for our purposes, the most important lesson was that the study provided objective evidence to indicate the dollar impact of the training on increased sales.

The program also had an important secondary effect on turnover. Since all sales associates are given considerable training (which represents an extensive investment of time and money), it appears that the behavior modeling contributed to *cost savings* in addition to *increased sales.* As noted in the previous discussion of turnover costs, an accurate estimate of these cost savings requires that the turnovers be separated into controllable and uncontrollable, because training can affect only controllable turnover.

Finally, the use of objective data as criterion measures in a study of this kind does entail some problems. As pointed out earlier, the researchers found that a 6-month period was required to balance out the month-to-month variations in sales performance resulting from changing work schedules, sales promotions, and similar influences that affected individual results. It also took some vigilance to ensure that the records needed for the study were kept in a consistent and conscientious manner in each store. According to the researchers, however, these problems were not great in relation to the usefulness of the study results. "The evidence that the training program had a measurable effect on sales was certainly more convincing in demonstrating the value of the program than would be merely the opinions of participants that the training was worthwhile."[50]

MACROLEVEL ASSESSMENTS OF THE FINANCIAL IMPACT OF HIGH-PERFORMANCE WORK PRACTICES

More and more business leaders seem to recognize that investments in workers are keys to their future competitiveness. Here are some representative comments from two such leaders at a recent conference on the future of the U.S. workplace:[51]

- "For years many of us invested in new machinery to de-skill operations and speed things up. I think the lesson today is we need to start investing in people, for the real technology of the 1990s and the 21st century is our people." (CEO of Levi Strauss & Co.)

- "Technology can be copied and moved readily. If we are going to win, it will be because of the asset of our people, and those people working together are absolutely crucial to our future." (CEO of Boeing, Inc.)

The Growing Use of High-Performance Work Practices

In an effort to enhance their competitiveness, some firms have instituted high-performance work practices. Sometimes this is done in an effort to avoid downsizing, and sometimes it is done in conjunction with downsizing. Such practices provide workers with the information, skills, incentives, and responsibility to make decisions that are essential for innovation, quality improvement, and rapid response to change. They seem particularly appropriate given the attributes that characterize today's economic environment: an unusual reliance on frontline workers; the treatment of workers as assets to be developed, not costs to be cut; new forms of worker-management collaboration that break down adversarial barriers; and the integration of technology and work in ways that will cause machines to serve human beings and not vice versa.[52] In a nationally representative sample of 700 private-sector establishments in the United States, 37 percent had a majority of frontline workers engaged in two or more high-performance work practices.[53] Thus, while the absolute number of firms that have adopted such practices still constitutes a minority, if managers are to be able to argue forcefully for greater investments in people, they must be able to demonstrate that the benefits of implementing such practices outweigh the costs. Do such programs pay off?

High-Performance Work Practices and Organizational Performance

A substantial amount of research has been conducted on the relationship between productivity and high-performance work practices, such as the use of valid staffing procedures, organizational cultures that emphasize team orientation and respect for people, employee involvement in decision making, compensation linked to firm or worker performance, and training. The evidence indicates that such practices are usually associated with increases in productivity (defined as output per worker), as well as with a firm's long-term financial performance.[54] However, these effects are most pronounced when such work practices are implemented together as a system.[55] As an example, let us briefly consider the impact of organizational culture on employee retention and HR costs.

Organizational Culture, Employee Retention, and HR Costs

A recent study investigated the retention rates of 904 college graduates hired by six public accounting firms over a 6-year period.[56] Organizational culture values varied considerably across the six firms, from high task orientation (i.e., high orientation toward detail and stability) to high interpersonal orientation (i.e., high concern for a team orientation and respect for individuals).

New employees stayed an average of 45 months in the cultures emphasizing interpersonal relationships, but only 31 months in the cultures emphasizing work-task values (see Figure 15-4). This is a 14-month difference in median

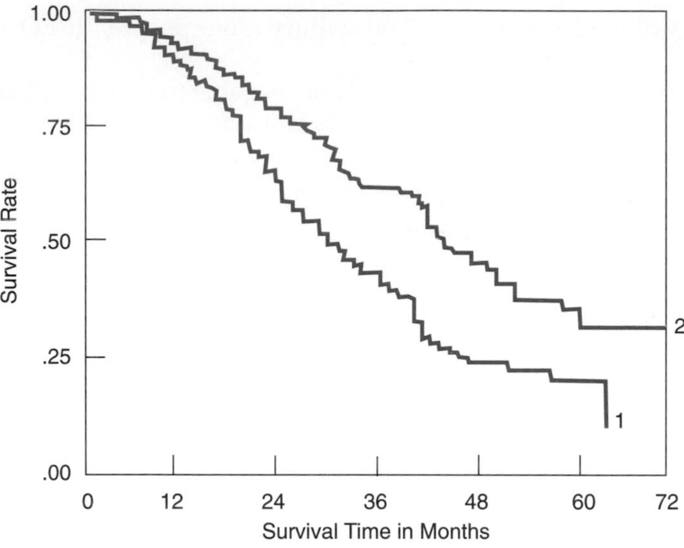

Figure 15-4
Voluntary survival rates in two organizational cultures. (*Source:* J. E. Sheridan, Organizational culture and employee retention. *Academy of Management Journal, 35,* 1992, 1049.)

survival time. The next task was to translate the difference in time into a measure of profits forgone (i.e., opportunity losses).

Using the firms' average billing fees, along with hiring, training, and compensation costs, mean profits per professional employee ranged from $58,000 during the first year of employment to $67,000 during the second year and $105,000 during the third. A firm therefore incurs an opportunity loss of only $9,000 ($67,000 – $58,000) when a new employee replaces a 2-year employee, but a $47,000 loss ($105,000 – $58,000) when a new employee replaces a 3-year employee.

If it is assumed that both strong and weak performers generated the same average level of profits in each year of employment and that annual profits were distributed uniformly between those with 31 and those with 45 months' seniority, it is possible to estimate the opportunity loss associated with the 14-month difference in median survival time. This difference translated into an opportunity loss of approximately $44,000 per new employee [($47,000 – $9,000/12) × 14] between the firms having the two different types of cultural values. Considering the total number of new employees hired by each office over the 6-year period of the study, the study indicates that a firm emphasizing work-task values incurred opportunity losses of approximately $6 to $9 million more than a firm emphasizing interpersonal-relationship values.

High-Performance Work Practices and Financial Performance

A comprehensive study of work practices and financial performance was based on a survey of over 700 publicly held firms in all major industries. The study examined the use of "best practices" in the following areas:

- Personnel selection
- Job design
- Information sharing

IMPACT OF HUMAN RESOURCE MANAGEMENT ACTIVITIES ON PRODUCTIVITY, QUALITY OF WORK LIFE, AND THE BOTTOM LINE

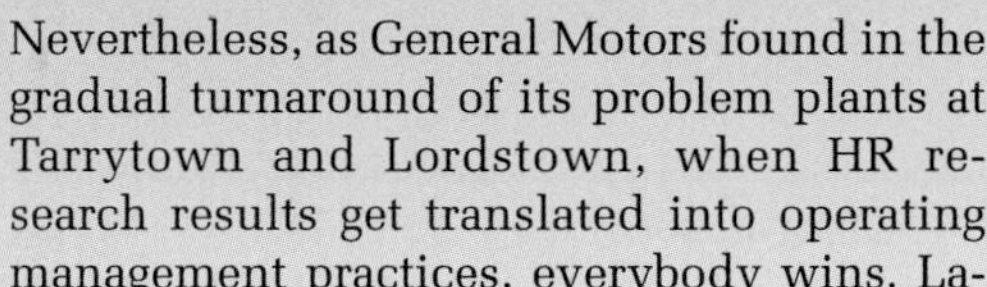

There is a rapidly growing awareness in the business community of the need for HR research. Indeed, there is a growing consensus among managers in many industries that the future success of their firms may depend more on the skill with which human problems are handled than on the degree to which their firms maintain leadership in technical areas. Consider family leave costs as an example. Survey research has shown that the average cost of parental leave is 32 percent of annual salary (39 percent for management employees and 28 percent for nonmanagement employees). The alternative, permanently replacing the employee, costs at least 75 percent of salary.[57]

Awareness alone, however, will not improve productivity, and there are no quick-fix solutions. Nevertheless, as General Motors found in the gradual turnaround of its problem plants at Tarrytown and Lordstown, when HR research results get translated into operating management practices, everybody wins. Labor-management relations improve, productivity goes up, quality goes up, profitability goes up, reworks go down, and the quality of work life becomes more tolerable.

The head of Mazda Motor Corporation captured the essence of HRM when he said: "The most important element in management is the human being, whatever his or her job happens to be." Another executive went a step further, saying: "The corporation that is not in the business of human development may not be in any business. At least not for long."[58]

- Performance appraisal
- Promotion systems
- Attitude assessment
- Incentive systems
- Grievance procedures
- Labor-management participation

On the basis of an index of "best-practice" prevalence, firms using more progressive policies in these areas were generally found to have superior financial performance. The 25 percent of firms scoring highest on the index performed substantially higher on key performance measures, as shown below:

Performance measure	Bottom 25%	2nd 25%	3rd 25%	Top 25%
Annual return to shareholders	6.5%	6.8%	8.2%	9.4%
Gross return on capital	3.7%	1.5%	4.1%	11.3%

The top 25 percent of firms—those using the largest number of "best practices"—had an annual shareholder return of 9.4 percent, versus 6.5 percent for firms in the bottom 25 percent. Firms in the top 25 percent had an 11.3 percent gross rate of return on capital, more than twice as high as that of the remaining firms. After accounting for other factors likely to influence financial performance (such as industry characteristics), the human resource index remained significantly related to both performance measures.[59]

As these examples show, adoption of high-performance work practices can have an economically significant effect on the market value of the firm. How large an effect? Recent work indicates a range of $15,000 to $45,000 per employee,[60] and that such practices can affect the probability of survival of a new firm by as much as 22 percent.[61] The extent to which these practices actually will pay off depends on the skill and care with which the many HR practices available are implemented to solve real business problems and to support a firm's operating and strategic initiatives.

Human Resource Management in Action: Conclusion

ATTITUDE SURVEY RESULTS: CATALYST FOR MANAGEMENT ACTIONS

The survey highlighted six areas of human resource management that were related to effective company performance in terms of turnover and profitability:

1. **Recruitment and selection.** High-profit locations were recruiting many more management trainees from among the nonmanagement employees already working for the company. Hence the high-profit locations were getting store manager trainees who already had experience and an understanding of what the job entailed.
2. **Training.** Classroom instruction was rated favorably by everyone and was not a factor in turnover. The training that did make a difference was on-the-job training. Store managers in high-profit, low-turnover areas reported that they received better in-store training than did their counterparts in lower-profit areas.
3. **Staffing.** Keeping management staff at a minimum was not producing greater profits. It was producing overworked, disenchanted managers who could neither run their stores effectively nor provide the training found to be so important for new store managers. Less effective profit centers had fewer managers, who worked many more hours, had fewer days off, and were bothered more frequently at home about work-related matters when they had a scheduled day off.
4. **Performance management.** Managers in the high-profit, low-turnover areas received performance reviews on a quarterly basis. Store managers throughout the system who received performance reviews less than quarterly wanted to see them conducted more often. In addition, everyone expressed a desire for more informal feedback from superiors about his or her performance. A second aspect of performance management and control was regular store visits by higher-level supervisors. Supervisors in high-profit areas visited their stores more frequently than did their counterparts in low-profit areas.
5. **Climate.** Job security in this company's environment was not associated with compensation or with promotion opportunities. However, it was associated with the needs of the store managers to be treated fairly, to be kept informed, and to have superiors available when needed to help the store managers solve their problems. In less effective profit centers, store managers saw their superiors as less competent at handling problems, they had less confidence that their superiors would back them up in their actions, and they felt that their superiors neglected them in terms of the frequency of store visits and formal performance reviews. They also indicated that they were more apt to hear things first through the grapevine rather than directly from their superiors.

ETHICAL DILEMMA
Survey Feedback: Nice or Necessary?

Is it unethical to ask employees for their opinions, attitudes, values, or beliefs on an attitude survey and then subsequently not to give them any feedback about the results? We know that survey results that are not fed back to employees are unlikely to be translated into action strategies, and that it is poor management practice to fail to provide feedback.[62] Is it unethical as well? (Hint: See the definition of ethical decision making in Chapter 13.)

6. **Management style.** The areas described thus far all point to some basic differences in how the store managers were being managed in different parts of the company. These distinctions became clearer when comparisons were made between high- and low-turnover centers that were highly profitable. In fact, two styles of management seemed to result in high profitability. In high-profit, low-turnover centers, store managers felt that they worked in a delegative and supportive climate, with a strong emphasis on performance and the control of performance; however, these emphases were balanced by a demonstrated concern for the store managers and their needs. In contrast, high-profit, high-turnover areas were characterized as directive and over-controlling in style; considerable emphasis was placed on the achievement of bottom-line results without a strong emphasis on the personal and developmental needs of the store managers.

Top Management's Response to the Survey Findings

On the basis of the survey results, top management established a task force to deal with the problems identified. The task force recommended 28 specific actions with time frames for accomplishment that varied from 1 month to 1 year. These actions ranged from close enforcement of staffing guidelines to development of an improved in-store training package. In time, as expected, turnover began to trend downward.

This study illustrates two important aspects of ensuring the effectiveness of an attitude survey as a management tool. First, the survey dealt with the operational aspects of working life in the company, and it focused on issues over which top management had some control. Hence top management found it an easy task to translate survey findings into direct actions. Second, an attitude survey's credibility with top management rests squarely on its ability to demonstrate that the results are important in some meaningful business sense. In the present study, the message that provoked significant actions was the proof that if certain management practices were adopted, greater profitability and reduced turnover could be expected.

While it is not always possible to relate survey results directly to profits (as it was here), it is possible to approach any survey from the perspective of how the results can contribute to organizational effectiveness. This perspective is a key step in establishing the credibility of the survey.

IMPLICATIONS FOR MANAGEMENT PRACTICE

Many managers do not realize the magnitude of their firm's investment in employees until they adopt a systematic framework for costing human resources. However, to be most useful, such a framework must include three key steps:

1. Understand your organization's, department's, and operating unit's competitive strategies—innovation, quality enhancement, cost reduction, speed, or some combination of these.
2. Make sure that HR activities are consistent with your chosen competitive strategy; for example, if innovation is the objective, do not skimp on training and development activities.
3. Use behavior costing methods to assess the costs and benefits of the HR activities that are most relevant to your chosen competitive strategy.

SUMMARY

In assessing the costs and benefits of HR activities, managers must first understand the competitive strategies of their organizations, departments, and operating units. Some possible strategies are innovation, quality enhancement, cost reduction, and speed. The next task is to align HR strategy with competitive strategy and to emphasize the kinds of employee behaviors that are most appropriate to the chosen strategy. In order to assess the outcomes of HR activities, HR research (which includes both qualitative and quantitative outcomes) may be conducted at corporate, middle-management, or operating levels.

One approach to HR research that is growing in popularity is called behavior costing. Applying behavior costing methodology properly requires that both direct and indirect costs be considered. However, the objective is not simply to measure these costs; it is also to reduce them by devoting resources to show costs that are controllable. The chapter presented behavior costing methods in three key areas of employee behavior—absenteeism, turnover, and employee training—and then examined the financial impact of high-performance work practices on organization-level outcomes. Firms that implement more such practices tend to be more profitable and to provide higher returns to shareholders than those that implement fewer or none of them.

Assessing the costs and benefits of human resource management activities is just one aspect of the broader subject of HR research. The objective of HR research is to contribute to the development and application of improved solutions to employee relations problems and to the more effective use of people in organizations. When HR research results that are targeted on operational problems get translated into practice, everybody wins.

DISCUSSION QUESTIONS

15-1 Discuss three controllable and three uncontrollable costs associated with absenteeism.

15-2 Why should efforts to reduce turnover focus only on controllable costs?

15-3 Discuss the HR activities that are most relevant to the following competitive strategies: innovation, quality enhancement, cost reduction, and speed.

15-4 Given the positive financial returns from high-performance work practices, why don't more firms implement them?

15-5 If attitude surveys are to be taken seriously by management, what key issues should be considered in their design, implementation, and evaluation?

APPLYING YOUR KNOWLEDGE

Absenteeism at ONO, Inc. — *Case 15-1*

ONO, Inc. is an auto supply company with 11 employees. In addition, there are two supervisors and Fred Donofrio, the owner and general manager. Last year, ONO did $2 million in business and earned $100,000 in profits ($150,000 before taxes). The auto supply business is extremely competitive, and owners must constantly be on the lookout for ways to reduce costs in order to remain profitable.

Employee salaries at ONO average $14.00 an hour, and benefits add another 33 percent to these labor costs. The two supervisors earn an average of $20.00 an hour, with a similar level (percentage) of benefits. Employees receive 2 weeks of vacation each year and 12 days of paid sick leave.

Over the last 2 years, Fred Donofrio has noted an increasing rate of absenteeism among his 11 employees (there seems to be no similar problem with the two supervisors). Last week, he asked Cal Jenson, his most senior supervisor, to go through the records from last year and determine how much absenteeism had cost ONO. Further, he asked Cal to make any recommendations to him that seemed appropriate depending on the magnitude of the problem.

Cal determined that ONO lost a total of 539 employee labor-hours (67.375 days) to absenteeism last year (this figure did not, of course, include vacation time). Further, he estimated that he and the other supervisor together averaged 1½ hours in lost time whenever an employee was absent for a day. This time was spent dealing with the extra problems (rescheduling work, filling in for missing workers, etc.) that an absence created. On several occasions last year, ONO was so short of help that temporary workers had to be hired or present employees had to work overtime. Cal determined that the additional costs of overtime and outside help last year totaled $475.

Cal is now in the process of preparing his report to Fred Donofrio.

Questions

1. What figure will Cal Jenson report to Fred Donofrio for the amount that absenteeism cost ONO last year?
2. Is absenteeism a serious problem at ONO? Why or why not?
3. What recommendations for action could Cal Jenson make to Fred Donofrio?

REFERENCES

1. Porter, M. E. (1985). *Competitive advantage.* New York: Free Press.
2. Vinton, D. E. (1992). A new look at time, speed, and the manager. *Academy of Management Executive,* **6**(4), 7–16. See also Schuler, R. S., & Jackson, S. E. (1987). Linking

competitive strategies with human resource management practices. *Academy of Management Executive,* **1**(3), 207–219.

3. Jackson, S. E., & Schuler, R. S. (1990). Human resource planning. *American Psychologist,* **45,** 223–239.
4. Becker, B., & Gerhart, B. (1996). The impact of human resource management on organizational performance: Progress and prospects. *Academy of Management Journal,* **39,** 779–801. See also Gerhart, B., Trevor, C., & Graham, M. (1996). New directions in employee compensation research. In G. R. Ferris (ed.), *Research in personnel and human resources management,* **14,** 143–203. Greenwich, CT: JAI Press.
5. See, for example, Pfeffer, J. (1994). *Competitive advantage through people.* Boston: Harvard Business School Press.
6. Cappelli, P., & Crocker-Hefter, A. (1996). Distinctive human resources are firms' core competencies. *Organizational Dynamics,* **24**(3), 7–22.
7. Youndt, M. A., Snell, S. A., Dean, J. W., Jr., & Lepak, D. P. (1996). Human resource management, manufacturing strategy, and firm performance. *Academy of Management Journal,* **39,** 836–866.
8. Banas, P. A. (1988). Employee involvement: A sustained labor/management initiative at the Ford Motor Company. In J. P. Campbell and R. J. Campbell (eds.), *Productivity in organizations.* San Francisco: Jossey-Bass, pp. 388–416. (Quotation source: p. 391.)
9. Schuler & Jackson, loc. cit.
10. Kanter, R. M. (1985, Winter). Supporting innovation and venture development in established companies. *Journal of Business Venturing,* **1,** 47–60.
11. Jackson, S. E., Schuler, R. S., & Rivero, J. C. (1989). Organizational characteristics as predictors of personnel practices. *Personnel Psychology,* **42,** 727–736.
12. Pollock, E. J. (1990, Mar. 20). Beleaguered firms dangle lures to retain employees. *The Wall Street Journal,* pp. B1, B2.
13. Schuler & Jackson, loc. cit.
14. Taylor, A., III. (1990, Nov. 19). Why Toyota keeps getting better and better and better. *Fortune,* pp. 66–79.
15. Cascio, W. F. (1989). Using utility analysis to assess training outcomes. In I. L. Goldstein (ed.), *Training and development in organizations.* San Francisco: Jossey-Bass, pp. 63–88.
16. Touby, T. (1993, Nov./Dec.). The business of America is jobs. *Journal of Business Strategy,* **14**(6), 20–31.
17. Richman, L. S. (1993, Sept. 20). When will the layoffs end? *Fortune,* pp. 54–56.
18. White, B. J. (1988). The internationalization of business: One company's response. *Academy of Management Executive,* **2**(1), 29–32.
19. Ibid., p. 31.
20. Vinton, op. cit., p. 14.
21. Reitman, V., & Simison, R. L. (1995, Dec. 29). Japanese car makers speed up car making. *The Wall Street Journal,* pp. B1, B5. See also Dumaine, B. (1989, Feb. 13). How managers can succeed through speed. *Fortune,* pp. 54–74.
22. Stalk, G., Jr., & Hout, T. M. (1990). *Competing against time.* New York: Free Press.
23. Dumaine, op. cit., p. 55.
24. Phillips, J. J. (1996). *Accountability in human resource management.* Houston: Gulf Publishing.
25. Turner, G. (1997, Apr.). *Accounting for human resources: A trilogy of excuses.* Paper presented at the 20th annual Congress of the European Accounting Association, Graz, Austria. See also Scarpello, V., & Theeke, H. A. (1989). Human resource accounting: A measured critique. *Journal of Accounting Literature,* **8,** 265–280. See also Baker, G. M. N. (1974). The feasibility and utility of human resource accounting. *California Management Review,* **16**(4), 17–23.

26. Reibstein, L. (1986, Oct. 27). A finger on the pulse. Companies expand use of employee surveys. *The Wall Street Journal,* p. 27.
27. Kraut, A. I. (1996). *Organizational surveys.* San Francisco: Jossey-Bass. See also Does survey feedback make a difference? (1993, Fall). *Decisions . . . Decisions,* pp. 1, 2.
28. Cascio, W. F. (1997, Apr.). HR effectiveness: The structural perspective. In R. Jacobs (Chair), *Measuring HR effectiveness: So how are we doing?* Symposium presented at the 12th annual meeting of the Society of Industrial and Organizational Psychology, St. Louis, MO. See also Tsui, A. S., & Gomez-Mejia, L. R. (1988). Evaluating human resource effectiveness. In L. Dyer (ed.), *Human resource management: Evolving roles and responsibilities.* Washington, DC: Bureau of National Affairs, pp. 1-187 to 1-227.
29. Mirvis, P. H., & Macy, B. A. (1976). Measuring the quality of work and organizational effectiveness in behavioral-economic terms. *Administrative Science Quarterly,* **21,** 212–226.
30. Fitz-enz, J. (1984). *How to measure human resources management.* New York: McGraw-Hill.
31. For a fuller treatment of this issue, see Sauter, S. L., & Murphy, L. R. (eds.). (1995). *Organizational risk factors for job stress.* Washington, DC: American Psychological Association. See also Kahn, R. L., & Byosiere, P. (1992). Stress in organizations. In M. D. Dunnette & L. M. Hough (eds.), *Handbook of industrial and organizational psychology* (2d ed., vol. 3). Palo Alto, CA: Consulting Psychologists Press, pp. 571–650.
32. Unscheduled absence costs up (1993, June). *HRMagazine,* p. 22.
33. Cascio, W. F. (1991). *Costing human resources: The financial impact of behavior in organizations* (3d ed.). Boston: PWS-Kent.
34. Bulletin to management (1996, 4th Quarter). Washington, DC: Bureau of National Affairs.
35. Unscheduled absence costs up, loc. cit.
36. Workplace epidemic: Absenteeism rises for third year in a row (1996, Feb. 27). *The Wall Street Journal,* p. A1. See also Cost of absenteeism for British employers (1995, Dec.). *Manpower Argus,* no. 327, p. 6.
37. Macy, B. A., & Mirvis, P. H. (1983). Assessing rates and costs of individual work behaviors. In S. E. Seashore, E. E. Lawler, P. H. Mirvis, & C. Camann (eds.), *Assessing organizational change.* New York: Wiley, pp. 139–177.
38. Bulletin to management, op. cit.
39. Martin, D. C., & Bartol, K M. (1985). Managing turnover strategically. *Personnel Administrator,* **30**(11), 63–73.
40. Cascio, 1991, op. cit.
41. For more on this subject, see Cascio, 1991, op. cit.
42. Solomon, J. (1988, Dec. 29). Companies try measuring cost savings from new types of corporate benefits. *The Wall Street Journal,* p. B1.
43. Ibid.
44. Ashbach, N. W. (1989, Apr.). *The cost of turnover in the retail automobile industry.* Unpublished manuscript, Executive MBA Program, University of Colorado, Denver.
45. Watson, J. (1993, Feb. 8). CEO of Skyway Express, speech to IBM employees, Denver, CO.
46. Cascio, 1989, op. cit.
47. For more information, see Boudreau, J. W. (1991). Utility analysis for decisions in human resource management. In M. D. Dunnette & L. M. Hough (eds.), *Handbook of industrial and organizational psychology* (vol. 2). San Francisco: Jossey-Bass, pp. 621–745. For a contrarian view, see Skarlicki, D. P., Latham, G. P., & Whyte, G. (1996). Utility analysis: Its evolution and tenuous role in human resource management decision making. *Canadian Journal of Administrative Sciences,* **13**(1), 13–21. See also Latham, G. P., & Whyte, G. (1994). The futility of utility analysis. *Personnel Psychology,* **47,** 31–46.

48. Mathieu, J. E., & Leonard, R. L., Jr. (1987). Applying utility concepts to a training program in supervisory skills: A time-based approach. *Academy of Management Journal,* **30,** 316–335.
49. Meyer, H. H., & Raich, J. S. (1983). An objective evaluation of a behavior modeling training program. *Personnel Psychology,* **36,** 755–761.
50. Ibid., p. 761.
51. Forecasting the future of the American workplace (1993, Sept.). *American Workplace,* **1**(1), 1, 4.
52. Ibid., comments by former U.S. Secretary of Labor Robert Reich, p. 1.
53. Osterman, P. (1994). How common is workplace transformation, and can we explain who adopts it? *Industrial and Labor Relations Review,* **47**(2), 173–188.
54. Terpstra, D. E., & Rozell, E. J. (1993). The relationship of staffing practices to organizational-level measures of performance. *Personnel Psychology,* **46,** 27–48. See also Gerhart, B., & Milkovich, G. T. (1990). Organizational differences in managerial compensation and firm performance. *Academy of Management Journal,* **33,** 663–691.
55. Delery, J. E., & Doty, D. H. (1996). Modes of theorizing in strategic human resource management: Tests of universalistic, contingency, and configurational performance predictions. *Academy of Management Journal,* **39,** 802–835. See also Barney, J. (1995). Looking inside for competitive advantage. *Academy of Management Executive,* **9**(4), 49–61. See also *High performance work practices and firm performance.* (1993, Aug.). Washington, DC: U.S. Department of Labor.
56. Sheridan, J. E. (1992). Organizational culture and employee retention. *Academy of Management Journal,* **35,** 1036–1056.
57. Survey calculates family leave costs (1993, Jan.). *HRMagazine,* p. 40.
58. Gilmour. A. D. (1988). Changing times in the automotive industry. *Academy of Management Executive,* **2**(1), 23–28.
59. Huselid, M. A. (1995). The impact of human resource management practices on turnover, productivity, and corporate financial performance. *Academy of Management Journal,* **38,** 635–672.
60. Davidson, W. N., III, Worrell, D. L., & Fox, J. B. (1996). Early retirement programs and firm performance. *Academy of Management Journal,* **39,** 970–984.
61. Welbourne, T. M., & Andrews, A. O. (1996). Predicting the performance of initial public offerings: Should human resource management be in the equation? *Academy of Management Journal,* **39,** 891–919.
62. Kraut, op. cit.

16 INTERNATIONAL DIMENSIONS OF HUMAN RESOURCE MANAGEMENT

Questions This Chapter Will Help Managers Answer

1 What factors should I consider in sizing up managers, employees, and customers from a different culture?

2 What should be the components of expatriate recruitment, selection, orientation, and training strategies?

3 How should an expatriate compensation package be structured?

4 What kinds of career management issues should a manager consider before deciding to work for a foreign-owned firm in the United States?

5 What special issues deserve attention in the repatriation of overseas employees?

*A DAY IN THE LIFE OF TOMORROW'S MANAGER**

The time is 6:10 A.M., the year is 2010, and another Monday morning has begun for Linda Smith. The marketing VP for a major U.S. appliance manufacturer is awakened by her computer alarm. She saunters to her terminal to check the weather outlook in Madrid, Spain, to which she'll fly late tonight, and to send an electronic voice message to a supplier in Thailand.

Meet the manager of the future, a breed different from her present-day counterparts. She lives in an international business world shaped by competition, collaboration, and corporate diversity. Comfortable with technology, she's been logging on to computers since she was 7 years old. A literature honors student with a joint MBA–advanced communications degree, the 38-year-old joined her current employer 4 years ago after stints at two other corporations—one abroad—and a marketing consulting firm. Now she oversees offices in a score of countries on four continents.

Is this realistic? Absolutely, say chief executives and management consultants. Tomorrow's managers will have to know how to operate in an anytime, anyplace universe. They may land on London time and leave on Tokyo time. While managers who are not cost-conscious and productive will not survive any better in the future than they do now, in the future they will also have to be more flexible, more responsive, and smarter. Managers will have to be nurturers and teachers, instead of police officers and watchdogs.

7:20 A.M.: Ms. Smith and her husband, who heads his own architecture firm, organize the home front before darting to the supertrain. They leave instructions for their computer to call the housecleaning service as well as the gourmet carryout service that will prepare dinner for eight guests Saturday. And they quickly review the schedules for their two small daughters with their nanny.

On the train during the speedy 20-minute commute from suburb to city, Linda Smith checks her electronic mailbox and reads her favorite trade magazine via her laptop computer.

The jury is still out on how dual-career couples will juggle high-pressure work and personal lives. While some experts predict that the frenetic pace will only quicken, others believe that more creative uses of flexible schedules as well as technological advances in communications and travel will allow more balance. Said one expert: "In the past, nobody cared if your staff had heart attacks, but in tomorrow's knowledge-based economy we'll be judged more on how well we take care of people."

Challenges

1. What kinds of employee relations, compensation, and career management issues will Linda Smith encounter at the office?

---

*Adapted from C. Hymowitz, A day in the life of tomorrow's manager, *The Wall Street Journal,* Mar. 20, 1989, p. B1. Reprinted by permission of *The Wall Street Journal,*

2. How might new office technology shape the ways that managers communicate with workers, suppliers, and customers?
3. Given the globalization of companies, will managers intent on rising to the top still be judged largely on how well they articulate ideas and work with others?

Increasingly, the world is becoming a "global village" as multinational investment continues to grow. All the HR management issues that have been discussed to this point are interrelated conceptually and operationally and are particularly relevant in the international context: HR planning, recruitment, selection, orientation, training and development, career management, compensation, and labor relations. In examining all these issues, as well as considering the special problems of repatriation (the process of reentering one's native culture after being absent from it), this chapter thus provides a capstone to the book.

THE GLOBAL CORPORATION: A FACT OF MODERN ORGANIZATIONAL LIFE

The demise of communism, the fall of trade barriers, and the rise of networked information have unleashed a revolution in business. Market capitalism guides every major country on earth. Goods and services flow across borders more freely than ever; vast information networks instantly link nations, companies, and people. The result—twenty-first-century capitalism.[1]

The vehicle for "going global" is often not an acquisition or a financial transaction but, rather, an international alliance, a collaboration between two or more multinational companies that allows them jointly to pursue a common goal. However, alliances cover only some of the activities of the partners. The partners therefore maintain their individual identities and engage in other activities, separate from those of the alliance. As an example, consider the joint venture between Nissan and Ford Motor Company to design and build a minivan. The resulting vehicle is sold as the Mercury Villager by Ford, and as the Nissan Quest by Nissan.

This characteristic distinguishes an international alliance from an international merger or acquisition, in which the identities and activities of the partners are fully merged. Such alliances may take several forms, for example, joint ventures, marketing and distribution agreements, research and development partnerships, or licensing agreements.[2] In the opinion of many, such alliances are an essential component of global business strategy.[3]

One reason that leadership in any one developed market increasingly requires leadership in all is that the developed world has become one in terms of technology. All developed countries are equally capable of doing everything, doing it equally well, and doing it equally fast. All developed countries also share instant information. Companies can therefore compete just about everywhere the moment that economic conditions give them a substantial price advantage. Consider Hong Kong's airline, Cathay Pacific. The airline's computer

Foreign investment by the world's leading companies is a fact of modern life. These billboards in Saigon advertise products from Swiss (Nestlé), Japanese (Hitachi), and American (Xerox) multinationals.

center has moved to Sydney, where the land costs only 1 percent of the price of a comparable site in Hong Kong. Its revenue-accounting back office has been shifted to Guangzhou, China, and even some of its aircraft maintenance is now done in Xiamen on the South China coast, where labor costs only 10 percent to 20 percent of Hong Kong levels. The labor-intensive part of its reservations, such as special meals for passengers, is handled out of Bombay.[4] When customers vote with their pocketbooks, they leave the trappings of nationalism behind.[5]

Signs of Globalization

In this emerging economic order, foreign investment by the world's leading corporations is a fact of modern organizational life. Over 800 multinational companies have regional headquarters in Hong Kong alone![6] Today foreign investment is viewed not just as an opportunity for U.S. companies to invest abroad but also as an opportunity for other countries to develop subsidiaries in the United States and elsewhere. Indeed, a single marketplace has been created by factors such as the following:[7]

- Global telecommunications enhanced by fiber optics, satellites, and computer technology.[8]
- Giant multinational corporations such as Gillette, Unilever, and Nestlé, which have begun to lose their national identities as they integrate and coordinate product design, manufacturing, sales, and services on a worldwide basis
- Growing free trade between nations (exemplified by the 1993 North American Free Trade Agreement between Mexico, the United States, and Canada)
- Financial markets' being open 24 hours a day around the world

- International investment among multinational companies, which totaled $315 billion in 1996 alone, of which $96 billion came from U.S. companies[9]
- Foreign control of more than 12 percent of U.S. manufacturing assets and employment of over 3 million U.S. workers
- The emergence of global standards and regulations for trade, commerce, finance, products, and services

Before proceeding further, let's define some terms that will be used throughout the chapter:

- A **global corporation** is one that has become an "insider" in any market or nation where it operates and is thus competitive with domestic firms operating in local markets.[10] Unlike domestic firms, however, the global corporation has a global strategic perspective and claims its legitimacy from its effective use of assets to serve its far-flung customers.
- An **expatriate** or *foreign-service employee* is anyone working outside her or his home country with a planned return to that or a third country.
- **Home country** is the expatriate's country of residence.
- **Host country** is the country in which the expatriate is working.
- A **third-country national** is an expatriate who has transferred to an additional country while working abroad. A German working for a U.S. firm in Spain is a third-country national.

One of the most important determinants of a company's success in an international venture is *the quality of its executives.* In the words of one international executive: "Virtually any type of international problem, in the final analysis, is either created by people or must be solved by people. Hence, having the right people in the right place at the right time emerges as the key to a company's international growth. If we are successful in solving that problem, I am confident we can cope with all others."[11]

Globalization as a Growth Strategy

Consider these startling facts:

- Over 100,000 U.S. companies are engaged in global ventures, valued at over $1 trillion. U.S. corporations have invested more than $400 billion abroad and employ more than 60 million overseas workers.[12]
- One in five American jobs is tied directly or indirectly to international trade. Merchandise exports are up more than 40 percent since 1986, and every $1 billion in U.S. merchandise exports generates approximately 20,000 new jobs.[13]
- McDonald's operates over 21,000 restaurants in 105 countries, 8928 of which are outside the United States.[14]
- Gillette holds 68 percent of the U.S. market in wet shaving, 73 percent of the European market, and 91 percent of the Latin American market. More than 75 percent of its employees work outside the United States, and more than 70 percent of sales and profits come from overseas operations in 200 countries.[15] It is a partner in joint ventures with razor-blade companies in Russia, Poland,

and China, and it is rolling out its Braun and Oral-B products in eastern Europe and Asia.[16]

- Foreigners hold top management positions in one-third of large U.S. firms and one-fourth of European-based firms. They are even more conspicuous in third-world, developing countries.

It should be clear by now that today's world economy is governed by an entirely new set of rules and that to compete effectively, firms must abandon such outdated assumptions and behaviors as these:

- Believing that there is "one best way" to approach all problems or that for each problem there is only "one best answer"
- Attending only to immediate short-term problems and issues, focusing on details, seeing only the parts and not the whole, ignoring the long term, failing to put problems into a context, and losing sight of the objectives of the overall organization and the economy as a whole
- Failing to be aware of the implicit and unstated assumptions that have guided individual behavior and organizational policies in the past and failing to change them when they are no longer appropriate in the current environment[17]

The following example depicts the global approach: Many U.S. executives were surprised to find out how well Japanese ways worked at Nissan's car and truck plant in Smyrna, Tennessee. The plant features Japanese-style quality controls (small work groups with a big say in problem solving, job rotation every 2 hours, and statistical quality control techniques), just-in-time delivery of parts, and widespread use of industrial robots. Painting is done with West German technology, using robots from Norway. Fiber-optic communications, developed by U.S. aerospace firms, monitor 3000 points in the paint process. The result? After producing 500,000 vehicles, the plant showed two things: (1) U.S. workers are just as productive and skilled as the Japanese, and (2) the plant is one of the most efficient, highest-quality plants in the world.[18]

In the 1980s, as the United States lost market share and jobs in important industries like steel, autos, and electronics, both labor and management in many firms grudgingly acknowledged that they had to change, that they could not continue doing business as usual. They had to reach out to the world at large. Thus, many ideas for managing the General Motors Saturn plant were borrowed from around the world as a result of plant visits by the Group of 99, a team of Saturn workers who traveled 2 million miles to visit some 160 pioneering enterprises, including Hewlett-Packard, McDonald's, Volvo, Kawasaki, and Nissan.[19] As is well known, all these firms have operations in many countries around the globe. Many companies are expanding their operations to serve international markets. At least during the early stages of such expansion they tend to staff their overseas operations with expatriates. One of the first things they learn is that when they do so costs can be astronomical.

The Costs of Overseas Executives

One of the first lessons global corporations learn is that it is far cheaper to hire competent host-country nationals (if they are available) than to send their own executives overseas, for foreign-service employees typically cost 2 to 3

Table 16-1

TYPICAL U.S. EXPATRIATE COMPENSATION PACKAGE (ANNUAL EXPENSE): MARRIED WITH ONE CHILD

Category	U.S. compensation	Overseas compensation
Base salary	$85,000	$85,000
Overseas incentive		15%
Hardship		10%
Housing differential		35%
Furniture		12%
Utilities differential		20%
Car and driver		15%
Cost-of-living adjustment		40%
Club membership		2%
Education		12%
Total	$85,000	$221,850
U.S. tax	24,000	24,000
Net annual compensation	$61,000	$197,850

Note: A complete expatriate package also includes the following: (1) annual transportation to the United States for home leave, (2) storage of U.S. household goods, (3) shipment of some goods to the foreign location, (4) U.S. auto disposal, (5) U.S. house management, (6) interim living expenses, (7) travel to new assignment and return, and (8) annual tax equalization

times the salary of a comparable domestic employee, and often many more times the salary of a local national employee in the assignment country (see Table 16-1).[20]

For example, General Motors typically spends $750,000 to $1 million on an executive and his or her family during a 3-year stint abroad.[21] Consider these 1997 cost-of-living indexes for a two-person U.S. family at the $75,000 income level, where New York equals 100: Mexico City—90, Prague—96, Frankfurt—122, Bombay—141, London—151. Sao Paulo—166, Moscow—192, Beijing—227, Tokyo—258, and Hong Kong—268.[22]

The costs of doing business are often much higher overseas than in the United States. Consider office space as an example. In the United States, rent per square foot ranges from about $21 in Los Angeles to $36 in midtown Manhattan. By contrast, rents expressed in U.S. dollars average about $49 in Paris and Frankfurt and $61 in London. In such Asian cities as Bombay, Beijing, Hong Kong, and Tokyo, dollar rents range from $64 to $101.[23] Of course, these costs fluctuate with international exchange rates relative to the U.S. dollar. On top of the high costs of such items as office space are the costs incurred by a high failure rate among expatriates—between 16 and 40 percent of all Americans sent overseas.[24] For all levels of employees, the costs of mistaken expatriation include the costs of initial recruitment, relocation expenses, premium compensation, repatriation costs (i.e., costs associated with resettling the expatriate), replacement costs, and the tangible costs of poor job performance. When an overseas assignment does not work out, it still costs a company, on average, twice the employee's base salary.

Although the costs of expatriates are considerable, there are compensating benefits to multinational firms. In particular, overseas postings allow managers to develop international experience outside their home countries—the kind of experience needed to compete successfully in the global economy that we now live in.[25]

Nevertheless, it is senseless to send people abroad who do not know what they are doing overseas and cannot be effective in the foreign culture. As the manager of international HR at Hewlett-Packard remarked: "When you are sending someone abroad to work on an important agreement, it is terribly important that they have as much information as possible about how to do business in that country. The cost of training is inconsequential compared to the risk of sending inexperienced or untrained people."[26]

For all these reasons, companies need to consider the impact of culture on international HR management. But what is culture? Culture refers to characteristic ways of doing things and behaving that people in a given country or region have evolved over time. Culture helps people make sense of their part of the world and provides them with an identity.

THE ROLE OF CULTURAL UNDERSTANDING IN INTERNATIONAL MANAGEMENT PRACTICE

Managers who have no appreciation for cultural differences have a *local* perspective. They believe in the inherent superiority of their own group and culture, and they tend to look down on those considered "foreign." Rather than accepting differences as legitimate, they view and measure alien cultures in terms of their own.

By contrast, *cosmopolitan* managers are sensitive to cultural differences, respect the distinctive practices of others, and make allowances for such factors when communicating with representatives of different cultural groups. Recognizing that culture and behavior are relative, they are more tentative and less absolute in their interactions with others.[27]

Such cultural understanding can minimize "culture shock" and allow managers to be more effective with both employees and customers. The first step in this process is increasing one's general awareness of differences across cultures, for such differences deeply affect human resource management practices.

HUMAN RESOURCE MANAGEMENT PRACTICES AS A CULTURAL VARIABLE

Particularly when business does not go well, Americans returning from overseas assignments tend to blame the local people, calling them irresponsible, unmotivated, or downright dishonest. Such judgments are pointless, for many of the problems are a matter of fundamental cultural differences that profoundly affect how different people view the world and operate in business. This section presents a systematic framework, 10 broad classifications, that will help managers assess any culture and examine its people systematically. It does not consider every aspect of culture, and by no means is it the only way to analyze culture. Rather, it is a useful beginning for cultural understanding. The framework comprises the following 10 factors:[28]

- Sense of self and space
- Dress and appearance
- Food and eating habits
- Communication: verbal and nonverbal
- Time and time sense
- Relationships
- Values and norms
- Beliefs and attitudes
- Work motivation and practices
- Mental processes and learning

Sense of Self and Space

Self-identity may be manifested by a humble bearing in some places, by macho behavior in others. Some countries (e.g., the United States) may promote independence and creativity, while others (e.g., Japan) emphasize group cooperation and conformity. Americans have a sense of space that requires more distance between people, while Latins and Vietnamese prefer to get much closer. Members of each culture have their own unique sense of self and space.

Dress and Appearance

This classification includes outward garments as well as body decorations. Many cultures have distinctive clothing—the Japanese kimono, the Indian turban, the Polynesian sarong, the "organization-man-or-woman" look of business, and uniforms that distinguish wearers from everybody else. Cosmetics are more popular and accepted in some cultures than in others, as is cologne or aftershave lotion for men.

Food and Eating Habits

The manner in which food is selected, prepared, presented, and eaten often differs by culture. Most major cities have restaurants that specialize in the distinctive cuisine of various cultures—everything from Afghan to Zambian. Utensils also differ, ranging from bare hands to chopsticks to full sets of cutlery. (Knowledge of food and eating habits often provides insights into customs and culture.) For example, the Chinese emphasize their group orientation by serving food on a single revolving tray from which each individual who is sitting around the dinner table serves himself or herself.

Communication: Verbal and Nonverbal

The axiom "words mean different things to different people" is especially true in cross-cultural communication. When an American says she is "tabling" a proposition, it is generally accepted that it is being put off until a later time. In England, "tabling" means discussing something now. Translations from one language to another can generate even more confusion as a result of differences in style and context. Coca-Cola found this out when it began marketing its soft-drink products in China.

The traditional Coca-Cola trademark took on an unintended translation when shopkeepers added their own calligraphy to the company name. "Coca-Cola," pronounced "ke kou ke la" in one Chinese dialect, translates as "bite the wax tadpole." Reshuffling the pronunciation to "ko kou ko le" roughly translates to "may the mouth rejoice."[29]

In many cultures, directness and openness in communication are not appreciated. An open person may be seen as weak and untrustworthy, and directness can be interpreted as abrupt, hostile behavior. Providing specific details may be seen as insulting to one's intelligence. Insisting on a written contract may suggest that a person's word is not good.

Nonverbal cues can also have different meanings. In the United States, one who does not look someone in the eye arouses suspicion and is called "shifty-eyed." In some other countries, however, looking someone in the eye is perceived as aggression.[30] Just as communication skills are key ingredients for success in U.S. business, such skills are basic to success in international business. There is no compromise on this issue; ignorance of local customs and communications protocol is disrespectful.

Time and Time Sense

To Americans, time is money. We live by schedules, deadlines, and agendas; we hate to be kept waiting, and we like to get down to business quickly. In many other countries, however, people simply will not be rushed. They arrive late for appointments, and business is preceded by hours of social rapport. People in a rush are thought to be arrogant and untrustworthy.

In the United States, the most important issues are generally discussed first when making a business deal. In Ethiopia, however, the most important things are taken up last. While being late for business meetings seems to be the norm in Latin America, the reverse is true in Sweden, where prompt efficiency is the watchword.[31] The lesson for Americans doing business overseas is clear: *be flexible about time and realistic about what can be accomplished.* Adapt to the particular process of doing business that is practiced in the host country.

Relationships

Cultures designate human and organizational relationships by age, gender, status, and family relationships, as well as by wealth, power, and wisdom.[32] Relationships between and among people vary by category—in some cultures the elderly are honored; in others they are ignored. In some cultures women must wear veils and act deferentially; in others the female is considered the equal, if not the superior, of the male.

In some cultures (e.g., Japan, Korea, and to some extent, the United States and Great Britain), *where* one went to school may affect one's status.[33] Often, lifelong relationships are established among individuals who attended the same school. In other cultures (e.g., Switzerland), one's rank in the military may affect one's job level and prospects for promotion. Finally, the issue of nepotism is viewed very differently in different parts of the world. While most U.S. firms frown upon the practice of hiring or contracting work directly with family

INTERNATIONAL APPLICATION
Bargaining with the Japanese[36]

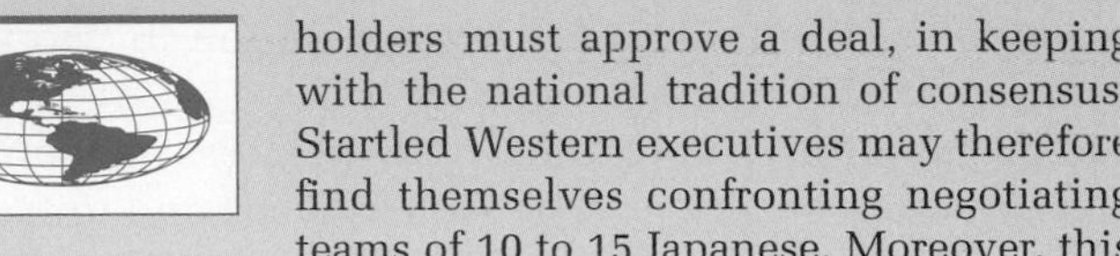

The knot tightens in the Western businessman's stomach as he peers glumly at the Japanese negotiating team across the table. The executive's flight leaves early tomorrow. His home office has been pressing him to complete a deal quickly. But although the talks have dragged on for days, the key issues have barely been discussed. "What is this?" the frustrated businessman wonders. "Don't these people know that time is money?"

Such questions arise frequently when Western executives confront the Japanese. Foreigners eager to do business must often endure endless rounds of what seem to be aimless talks, dinners, and drinks. Still, they have little choice but to put up with the ceremony if they hope to gain access to Japan's vast domestic market.

The exotic set of rituals seen during negotiations is the face Japan presents to the world of business. Japanese negotiators are exquisitely polite and agonizingly vague, yet at the same time they are determined to win the best possible deal. Perhaps the most striking feature of this system of bargaining is the huge amount of time it consumes. One Australian attorney offers the following rule of thumb: allow 5 times as long as usual when doing business in Japan.

Japanese companies negotiate slowly because everyone from junior management to major shareholders must approve a deal, in keeping with the national tradition of consensus. Startled Western executives may therefore find themselves confronting negotiating teams of 10 to 15 Japanese. Moreover, this may be only the beginning. The faces can change from session to session as new experts are added for different topics.

The Japanese are usually minutely well informed about their prospective partners. Said one former official of British Leyland who worked on a joint agreement with Honda, "The Japanese negotiators seemed to know more about our labor and managerial problems than we did."

At first the Japanese seem to have remarkably little interest in the business at hand. Their conversation is likely to dwell at length on social and family concerns rather than on products and prices. They stress personal relations because they are interested in the long-term implications of an agreement. Western executives, on the other hand, may tend to look more a the shorter term. Said one expert, "The American feeling is that it's the horse buyer's fault if he fails to ask whether a horse is blind [i.e., one party's advantage is the other party's disadvantage]; . . . for the Japanese, however, a deal is more of a discussion of where mutual interests lie."[37]

members, in Latin America or Arab countries, it only makes sense to hire someone you can trust.[34]

Values and Norms

From its value system, a culture sets norms of behavior, or what some call "local customs." International managers ignore them at their peril.[35] One example is the impact of values and norms on negotiating styles.

Beliefs and Attitudes

To some degree, religion expresses the philosophy of a people about important facets in life. While Western culture is influenced largely by Judeo-Christian traditions and Middle Eastern culture by Islam, Oriental and Indian cultures are dominated by Buddhism, Confucianism, Taoism, and Hinduism. In cultures where a religious view of work still prevails, work is viewed as an act of service

INTERNATIONAL APPLICATION (cont.) Guidelines for Negotiating with the Japanese

Experts on Japanese business methods offer the following guidelines for foreign negotiators:[38]

1. Before sending a woman to take part in formal talks, be sure she understands that while foreign women will generally be accepted by their male counterparts in Japan, Japanese women are all but barred from the management of big companies, and the important after-hours socializing in Japan is exclusively stag. (This situation is changing slowly,[39] and, understandably, it is difficult for U.S. professional women to accept.)
2. Do not send anyone under age 35 to conduct negotiations. Said a U.S. manager with a high-tech firm, "You are insulting the Japanese by sending a young man to deal with a senior executive, who is likely to be 65."
3. Be wary of mistaking Japanese politeness for agreement. A Japanese negotiator may frequently nod and say "hai" (yes) during talks. But the word also is used to let the listener know that the conversation is being followed, as with the English "uh-huh" or "I see." In short, "yes" does not always mean "yes."
4. Japanese negotiators may confuse outsiders by lapsing into silence to mull a point. Western businesspeople may then jump into that pool of silence, much to their regret. Thus the head of a Japanese firm did nothing when a contract from International Telephone and Telegraph (ITT) was presented for his signature. The ITT manager hastily sweetened the deal by $250,000. If he had waited just a few more minutes, he would have saved the company a quarter of a million dollars.
5. Evasiveness is another characteristic of Japanese negotiators. They hate to be pinned down, and they often suppress their views out of deference to their seniors. Add to this the Japanese tendency to tell listeners what they seem to want to hear, and foreign negotiators can easily go astray.

To be successful, visiting executives never let on what they are really thinking, have unending patience, and are unfailingly polite. In short, they act very Japanese.

to God and people, and is expressed in a moral commitment to the job or quality of effort.[40] In Japan, the cultural belief in loyalty to family is transferred to the work organization. It is expressed in work-group participation, communication, and consensus.[41]

T. Fujisawa, cofounder of Honda Motor Company, once remarked: "Japanese and American management is 95 percent the same, and differs in all important respects." In other words, while organizations are becoming more similar in terms of structure and technology, people's behavior within those organizations continues to reveal culturally based differences.[42]

Work Motivation and Practices

Knowledge of what motivates workers in a given culture, combined with (or based on) a knowledge of what they think matters in life, is critical to the success of the international manager. Europeans pay particular attention to power and status, which results in more formal management and operating styles in comparison with the informality found in the United States. In the United States individual initiative and achievement are rewarded, but in Japan managers are encouraged to seek consensus before acting, and employees work as teams. In one comparison of motivating factors for middle-aged Japanese and U.S. business managers, the Japanese showed more interest in advancement, money, and forward striving. Since these characteristics tend to be closely associated with success, it may be that achievement and advancement motivation are driving forces behind Japanese productivity and "team" action is only their method of disciplining and rewarding it.[43] When a similar survey was conducted among German workers, 48 percent said higher income was the key motivating factor for them, followed by opportunities for promotion (25 percent) and more independence (25 percent).[44]

The determinants of work motivation may not be all that different in developing countries. In Zambia, for example, work motivation seems to be determined by six factors: the nature of the work itself, opportunities for growth and advancement, material and physical provisions (i.e., pay, benefits, job security, favorable physical work conditions), relations with others, fairness and unfairness in organizational practices, and personal problems. The effect of personal problems is totally negative. That is, *the presence of such problems impairs motivation, but their absence does not enhance it.*[45]

Mental Processes and Learning

Linguists, anthropologists, and other experts who have studied the issue of mental processes have found vast differences in the ways people think and learn in different cultures. While some cultures favor abstract thinking and conceptualization, others prefer rote memory and learning. The Chinese, Japanese, and Korean written languages are based on ideograms, or "word pictures." On the other hand, English is based on precise expression using words. Western cultures stress linear thinking and logic, that is, A, then B, then C, then D. Among Arabic and Oriental cultures, however, nonlinear thinking prevails. This has direct implications for negotiation processes. That is, A may be followed by C, then back to B and on to D. Such an approach, in which issues are treated as independent and not linked by sequence, can be confusing and frustrating to Westerners because it does not appear "logical." What can we conclude from this? What seems to be universal is that each culture has a reasoning process, but each manifests the process in its own distinctive way.[46] Managers who do not understand or appreciate such differences may conclude (erroneously and to their detriment) that certain cultures are "inscrutable."

COMPANY EXAMPLE

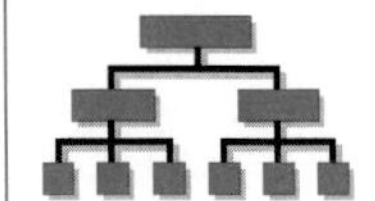

CULTURAL DIFFERENCES AMONG IBMers WORLDWIDE

Geert Hofstede, a Dutch researcher, identified four dimensions of cultural variation in values among IBM employees in 60 countries.[47] He analyzed 116,000 questionnaires completed by respondents matched by occupation, gender, and age at different time periods. The four dimensions were power distance, uncertainty avoidance, individualism, and masculinity.

Power distance refers to the extent that members of a culture accept inequality and whether they perceive much distance between those with power (e.g., top management) and those with little power (e.g., rank-and-file

Effective multinational managers are constantly open to new ideas, trying to learn from cultures other than their own.

workers). Hofstede found the top power distance countries to be the Philippines, Mexico, and Venezuela; the bottom ones were Austria, Israel, and Denmark.

Uncertainty avoidance is reflected in an emphasis on ritual behavior, rules, and stable employment. Countries that score high on this dimension tend to be more ideological and less pragmatic than those that score low. The countries highest in uncertainty avoidance were Greece, Portugal, Belgium, and Japan; the lowest were Singapore, Denmark, Sweden, and Hong Kong. The United States is low on this dimension.

Individualism reflects the extent to which people emphasize either personal or group goals. If they live in nuclear families that allow them to "do their own thing," individualism flourishes. However, if they live with extended families or tribes that control their behavior, collectivism—the essence of which is giving preference to in-group over individual goals—is more likely.[48] The most individualistic countries are the United States and the other English-speaking countries. The most collectivist countries are Venezuela, Columbia, and Pakistan.

Hofstede's fourth dimension, *masculinity,* is found in societies that differentiate very strongly by gender. Femininity is characteristic of cultures where sex-role distinctions are minimal. While the centrality of work in a person's life is greater in masculine cultures, feminine cultures emphasize quality of life. Hofstede found the most masculine cultures to be Japan, Austria, and Venezuela, while the most feminine were Sweden, Norway, and the Netherlands.

This work is valuable because it provides a set of benchmarks against which other studies can be organized conceptually. It also helps us understand and place into perspective current theories of motivation, leadership, and organizational behavior.

SHOULD YOU WORK FOR A FOREIGN-OWNED FIRM IN THE UNITED STATES?[49]

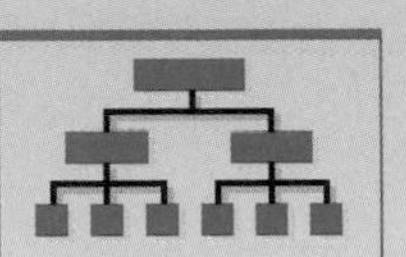

Increasing numbers of American managers are joining foreign-based companies that are doing business in the U.S. market. However, working for such a company can be difficult. Its offices typically are managed by expatriates, who are most comfortable with the culture, language, and customs of their home country and are likely to import international management styles into the U.S. workplace. For their U.S. subordinates, that could mean fewer opportunities for women and a wide range of other cultural differences. Such culturally related problems arise frequently at Japanese companies. Americans emphasize individualism, while for the Japanese, work is a collective effort. Comfortable with silence, the Japanese tend to be reserved in their communication, while Americans put a premium on frankness and the precise use of words. Other difficulties may arise, as they did for a U.S. salesman at Nippon Express U.S.A., when meetings were conducted in Japanese, with no effort made to translate for Americans.

Even if people are linguistically capable, say experts, learning how to praise or criticize someone from a different culture is a difficult skill. Asking a Swiss or German boss for a performance appraisal would probably lead to a very specific answer, while a Japanese, Korean, or Chinese boss would tend to be more vague.

Depending on the corporate culture, the staffing of the U.S. office, and the nationality of the company, it is possible to work for a foreign firm and barely notice cultural differences. Such is the case at Ebel U.S.A. Inc., a U.S. sales agent of a Swiss watch company, or at the Los Angeles office of the National Bank of Canada. Other companies have become so international that they are essentially melting pots. Schlumberger, Ltd., for example, was founded by two French brothers, is incorporated in the Netherlands Antilles, has executive offices in New York and Paris, and does business in more than 100 countries. Says one manager: "When you join Schlumberger, you put your passport away."

Despite the difficulties, there will be healthy payoffs for those who can cross cultural boundaries. Many foreign-owned companies doing business in the United States offer competitive salaries and assignments abroad. In addition, working for a foreign company can promote empathy for other cultures and a skill at working with people from around the world. Those are attractive characteristics in a global job market.

Lessons Regarding Cross-Cultural Differences

There are three important lessons to be learned from this brief overview of cross-cultural differences:

1. **Do not export headquarters-country bias.** As we have seen, the HR management approach that works well in the headquarters country might be totally out of step in another country. Managers who bear responsibility for international operations need to understand the cultural differences inherent in the management systems of the countries in which their firms do business.
2. **Think in global terms.** We live in a world in which a worldwide allocation of physical and human resources is necessary for continued survival.
3. **Recognize that no country has all the answers.** Flexible work hours, quality circles, and various innovative approaches to productivity have arisen outside the United States. Effective multinational managers must not only think in global terms, but also be able to synthesize the best management approaches to deal with complex problems.

HUMAN RESOURCE MANAGEMENT ACTIVITIES OF GLOBAL CORPORATIONS

Before we consider recruitment, selection, training, and other international HR management issues, it is important that we address a fundamental question: is international HR management worthy of study in its own right? The answer is yes, for two reasons—scope and risk exposure.[50] In terms of scope, there are at least five important differences between domestic and international operations. International operations have:

1. More functions, such as taxation and coordination of dependents.
2. More heterogeneous functions, such as coordination of multiple-salary currencies.
3. More involvement in the employee's personal life, such as housing, health, education, and recreation.
4. Different approaches to management, since the population of expatriates and locals varies.
5. More complex external influences, such as societies and government.

Heightened risk exposure is a second distinguishing characteristic of international HR management.[51] Companies are vulnerable to a variety of legal issues in each country, and the human and financial consequences of a mistake in the international arena are much more severe. On top of that, terrorism is now an ever-present risk for executives overseas. The cost of a kidnapping may run $2 to $3 million, and it is estimated that there are 10,000 to 15,000 kidnappings a year worldwide.[52] Not surprisingly, therefore, firms spend 1 to 2 percent of their revenues on protection against terrorism.[53] These risks and costs have had an important effect on how people are prepared for and moved to and from international assignment locations. In light of these considerations, it seems reasonable to ask, "Why do people accept overseas assignments?" Why do they go? As companies' global ambitions grow, fast-track executives at companies such as General Mills, Procter & Gamble, General Electric, and Mobil Oil see foreign tours as necessary for career advancement. As senior executives with years of overseas experience move into top management positions at these companies, they are redefining the image of a successful U.S. executive.[54]

Japanese executives have long accepted the fact that a stint overseas is often necessary for career advancement. After all, their companies depend on exports. Mitsubishi earns more than 50 percent of its revenues abroad, and, at any one time, 1000 of the company's roughly 9800 Japanese employees are posted abroad.[55]

Organizational Structure

Businesses tend to evolve from domestic (exporters) to international (manufacturing and some technology resources allocated outside the home country) to multinational (allocating resources among national or regional areas) to global (treating the entire world as one large company) organizations.[56] As an example of the latter, consider global powerhouse Asea Brown Boveri (ABB). It employs 210,000 people in 25 countries. It combines small-company entrepreneurialism with big-company economies of scale—a global paradox. ABB is at once international and local. It is a global federation of national companies employing and managed by their own nationals—all of whom are plugged into a global network.

Decentralization helps ABB avoid the "big-company syndrome." The company comprises 1000 legal entitles and 5000 distinct profit centers and profit-and-loss balance sheets. With only five managers per profit center and three layers of management, ABB is very flat. The result? A small-company atmosphere in a big company. Within this framework, an elite cadre of 500 global managers assigns contracts, coordinates international purchasing, promotes standardization, and facilitates technology exchange through the corporation.[57]

Organizational structure directly affects all HR management functions from recruitment through retirement. Thus effective HR management does not exist in a vacuum but is integrated into the overall strategy of the organization. Indeed, from the perspective of strategic management, the fundamental problem is to keep the strategy, structure, and HR dimensions of the organization in direct alignment.[58]

Human Resource Planning

This issue is particularly critical for firms doing business overseas, for they need to analyze both the local *and* the international external labor markets as well as their own internal labor markets in order to estimate the supply of people with the skills that will be required at some time in the future. Six other key issues in international HR planning are as follows:[59]

1. Identifying top management potential early[60]
2. Identifying critical success factors for future international managers
3. Providing developmental opportunities
4. Tracking and maintaining commitments to individuals in international career paths
5. Tying strategic business planning to HR planning and vice versa
6. Dealing with multiple business units while attempting to achieve globally and regionally focused (e.g., European, Asian) strategies

In developed countries, national labor markets can usually supply the skilled technical and professional people needed. However, developing countries are characterized by severe shortages of qualified managers and skilled workers and by great surpluses of people with little or no skill, training, or education.[61] The bottom line for companies operating in developing countries is that they must be prepared to develop required skills among their own employees.

Recruitment

Broadly speaking, companies operating outside their home countries follow three basic models in the recruitment of executives: (1) they may select from the national group of the parent company only, (2) they may recruit only from within their own country and the country where the branch is located, or (3) they may adopt an international perspective and emphasize the unrestricted use of all nationalities.[62] Each of these strategies has both advantages and disadvantages.

Ethnocentrism: Home-Country Executives Only

This strategy may be appropriate during the early phases of international expansion, because firms at that stage are concerned with transplanting a part of the business that has worked in their home country. Hence, detailed knowledge of that part is crucial to success. On the other hand, a policy of ethnocentrism, of necessity, implies blocked promotional paths for local executives. And if there are many subsidiaries, home-country nationals must recognize that their foreign service may not lead to faster career progress. Finally, there are cost disadvantages to ethnocentrism as well as increased tendencies to impose the management style of the parent company.[63]

Limiting Recruitment to Home- and Host-Country Nationals

This practice may result from acquisition of local companies. In Japan, for instance, where the labor market is tight, most people are reluctant to switch firms. Thus use of a local partner may be extremely important. Hiring host-country nationals has other advantages as well. It eliminates language barriers, expensive training periods, and cross-cultural adjustment problems of managers and their families. It also allows firms to take advantage of (lower) local salary levels while still paying a premium to attract high-quality employees.

Yet these advantages are not without cost. Local managers may have difficulty bridging the gap between the subsidiary and the parent company, because the business experience to which they have been exposed may not have prepared them to work as part of a global enterprise.[64] Finally, consideration of only home- and host-country nationals may result in the exclusion of some very able executives.

Geocentrism: Seeking the Best Person for the Job Regardless of Nationality

At first glance it may appear that this strategy is optimal and most consistent with the underlying philosophy of a global corporation. Yet there are potential problems. Such a policy can be very expensive, it would take a long time to implement, and it requires a great deal of centralized control over managers and their career patterns. To implement such a policy effectively, companies must make it very clear that cross-national service is important and that it will be rewarded.

Colgate-Palmolive is an example of such a company. It has been operating internationally for more than 50 years, and its products (e.g., Colgate toothpaste, Ajax cleanser) are household names in more than 170 countries. Fully 60 percent of the company's expatriates are from countries other than the United States, and two of its last four CEOs were not U.S. nationals. In addition, all the top executives speak at least two languages, and important meetings routinely take place all over the globe.[65] Regardless of their recruitment strategies, more and more firms are being forced to confront a very serious problem that affects many executives offered overseas assignments: job aid for spouses.

PRACTICAL EXAMPLE

JOB AID FOR SPOUSES OF OVERSEAS EXECUTIVES

In 59 percent of all U.S. families, both the husband and the wife hold jobs. About 41 percent of employees transferred abroad have spouses who worked before relocating. At the same time, global companies are expanding into areas such as central and eastern Europe and the Middle East, where spouses of expatriates face particularly tough obstacles to finding jobs. Here is a scenario likely to become more and more common in the future: A company offers a promotion overseas to a promising executive. But the executive's spouse has a flourishing career in the United States. What should the company—and the couple—do?

Employers and employees are wrestling with this dilemma more often these days. As noted in Chapter 9, job aid for the so-called trailing spouse is already a popular benefit for domestic transfers. Now, 47 percent of employers are also providing information or formal job help to the spouses of international transferees.[66]

HR officers may try to find a job for the spouse within the company, press a spouse's current employer for a foreign post, provide job leads through customers and suppliers, or plow through costly government red tape to get work permits. Particularly when the trailing spouse is female, this kind of aid tends to occur in industries like banking, financial services, pharmaceuticals, and computers, all of which have significant numbers of high-level women executives.

Despite company efforts, it is often very difficult to place spouses abroad. Where there are language barriers or barriers of labor laws, tradition, or underemployment, it can be almost impossible. Certain Middle Eastern nations frown on women working or even driving. In Switzerland and Kenya, expatriate spouses even need permission to work as volunteers.[67] Moreover, an international assignment can slow a spouse's professional progress and sometimes stir resentment. On the other hand, some spouses find their overseas experiences as personally and professionally rewarding as their spouses do. One American tax lawyer received permission to work in Brussels as an independent legal consultant. A German travel executive followed his wife to Britain and, 7 months later, landed a job organizing exhibitions between Britain and Germany. Not surprisingly, however, many experts believe that spousal income loss will be the single most important factor determining an executive's decision to accept or reject an overseas position.[68]

International Staffing

There are two important guidelines in the area of international staffing: (1) do not assume that a job requires the same skills from one location to another, and (2) do not underestimate the effect of the local culture and physical environment on the candidate.[69] In many cultures, tribal and family norms take precedence over technical qualifications in hiring employees. African managers often hire relatives and members of their tribes.[70] Likewise, in India, Korea, and Latin America, family connections are frequently more important than technical expertise. For an expatriate, technical competence along with other factors, such as cross-cultural adaptability and flexibility, increase her or his chances of successful performance abroad.[71]

Selection criteria for international jobs cover five areas: *personality, skills, attitudes, motivation, and behavior.*[72] Personality traits related to success include perseverance and patience (for when everything falls apart); initiative (because no one will be there to indicate what one should try next); and flexibility (to accept and to try new ways).

Highly developed technical skills, of course, are the basic rationale for selecting a person to work overseas. In some cases, unfortunately, technical skills are the *only* criterion for selection. This approach is a mistake, because technical competence per se has nothing to do with one's ability to adapt to a new environment, to deal effectively with foreign coworkers, or to perceive and if necessary, imitate, foreign behavioral norms.[73] In addition to technical skills, candidates should possess skills in communication (both home- and host-country languages, verbal, nonverbal, and written);[74] interpersonal relations (in developing countries, native people will simply walk off the job rather than continue to work with disagreeable outsiders); and stress management (to overcome the inevitable culture shock—frustration, conflict, anxiety, and feelings of alienation—that accompanies overseas assignments).

Tolerant attitudes toward people who may differ significantly in race, creed, color, values, personal habits, and customs are essential for success in overseas work. People who look down smugly on other cultures as inferior to their own simply will not make it overseas.

High motivation has long been acknowledged as a key ingredient for success in missionary work. Who, for example, can forget the zeal of the Protestant missionaries in the book *Hawaii,* by James Michener, as they set out from their native New England? While motivation is often difficult to assess reliably, firms should at the very least try to eliminate from consideration those who are only looking to get out of their own country for a change of scenery.

The last criterion is behavior—especially concern for other members of a group, tolerance for ambiguity, displays of respect, and nonjudgmental behavior. These characteristics may be determined from tests or interviews. For example, the Foreign Assignment Selection Test (FAST) appraises candidates in terms of six critical criteria: cultural flexibility, willingness to communicate, ability to develop social relationships, perceptual abilities, conflict resolution style, and leadership style. Research indicates that most of the FAST criteria are indeed related to expatriate adjustment at work and outside of work in a new cultural environment.[75]

COMPANY EXAMPLE

INTERVIEWING POTENTIAL EXPATRIATES AT AT&T

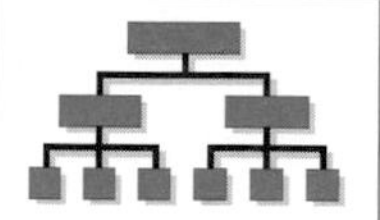

AT&T is a new worldwide player, having experienced exponential growth in overseas markets. At the end of 1986, this U.S. giant had 50 people in 10 countries, and about 1 percent of its revenue came from outside the United States. Eight years later, it had more than 52,000 overseas employees in 105 countries and earned 26 percent of its revenue abroad![76] Here are some typical questions used by AT&T to screen candidates for overseas transfers:[77]

- Would your spouse be interrupting a career to accompany you on an international assignment? If so, how do you think this will affect your spouse and your relationship with each other?
- Do you enjoy the challenge of making your own way in new situations?
- How able are you in initiating new social contacts?
- Can you imagine living without television?
- How important is it for you to spend significant amounts of time with people of your own ethnic, racial, religious, and national background?
- As you look at your personal history, can you isolate any episodes that indicate a real interest in learning about other people and cultures?
- Has it been your habit to vacation in foreign countries?
- Do you enjoy sampling foreign cuisines?
- What is your tolerance for waiting for repairs?

A final issue involves government regulation of staffing activities in foreign countries. In several western European countries, for example, employment offices are operated by the government, and private agencies are not permitted. And in countries such as Holland, Poland, and Sweden, prospective employees have the right to prior knowledge of psychological tests. If they so choose, they can insist that test results not be reported to an employer. In fact, in Sweden, employer, union, peers, and subordinates all participate in the entire selection process for managers—from job analysis to the hiring or promotion decision.[78] These kinds of HR practices and regulations may require global corporations to modify their human resource and industrial relations policies to operate successfully overseas.

Orientation

Orientation is particularly important in overseas assignments, both before departure and after arrival. Formalized orientation efforts—for example, elaborate audiovisual presentations for the entire family, supplemented with presentations by representatives of the country and by former expatriates who have since returned to the United States—are fine, to a point. Instead of trying to convey the "truth about Tokyo," overseas orientation programs should make quite clear that employees and family members will each experience their *own* Tokyos. No matter what they may have heard or read, each person's experiences will be unique.

Some firms go further. Federal Express, for example, actually sends prospective expatriates and their families on familiarization trips to the foreign location in question. While there, they have to "live like the natives do" by taking public transportation, shopping in local stores, and visiting prospective schools and current expatriates. More than 7 out of 10 firms now pay for such trips, up from fewer than 2 out of 10 in 1985.[79]

In fact, there may be three separate phases to orientation.[80] The first is called *initial orientation,* which may last as long as 2 full days. Key components are the following:

- **Cultural briefing.** Traditions, history, government, economy, living conditions, clothing and housing requirements, health requirements, and visa applications. (Drugs get a lot of coverage, for both adults and teenagers—whether they use drugs or not. Special emphasis is given to the different drug laws in foreign countries. Alcohol use also gets special attention when candidates are going to Muslim countries, such as Saudi Arabia.)
- **Assignment briefing.** Length of assignment, vacations, salary and allowances, tax consequences, and repatriation policy.
- **Relocation requirements.** Shipping, packing, or storage; and home sale, rental, or acquisition.

During this time, it is important that employees and their families understand that there is no penalty attached to changing their minds about accepting the proposed assignment. It is better to bail out early than reluctantly to accept an assignment that will be regretted later.

The second phase is *predeparture orientation,* which may last another 2 or 3 days. Its purpose is to make a more lasting impression on employees and their families and to remind them of material that may have been covered months earlier. Topics covered at this stage include:

- Introduction to the language.
- Further reinforcement of important values, especially open-mindedness.
- En route, emergency, and arrival information.

The final aspect of overseas orientation is *postarrival orientation.* Upon arrival, employees and their families should be met by assigned company sponsors. This phase of orientation usually takes place on three levels:

- **Orientation toward the environment.** Language, transportation, shopping, and other subjects that—depending on the country—may become understandable only through actual experience.
- **Orientation toward the work unit and fellow employees.** Often a supervisor or a delegate from the work unit will introduce the new employee to his or her fellow workers, discuss expectations of the job, and share his or her own initial experiences as an expatriate. The ultimate objective, of course, is to relieve the feelings of strangeness or tension that the new expatriate feels.
- **Orientation to the actual job.** This may be an extended process that focuses on cultural differences in the way a job is done. Only when this process is complete can managers begin to assess the accuracy and wisdom of the original selection decision.

Cross-Cultural Training and Development

Prior to 1990, AT&T had no formal process for choosing people for international positions, or for providing training for them. This oversight resulted in a crushing 40 percent of expatriates leaving the company during or after their assignments. Subsequently, the company created an international HR department to handle selection, orientation, training, relocation, legal issues, and labor procedures. It also created an International Career Development Program to maximize the payoffs of overseas assignments.[81]

To survive, cope, and succeed, managers need training in three areas: the culture, the language, and practical, day-to-day matters.[82] Reviews of research on cross-cultural training found that it has a positive impact on an individual's development of skills, on his or her adjustment to the cross-cultural situation, and on his or her performance in such situations.[83] These results suggest that sending a manager overseas without training is like sending David to meet Goliath without even a slingshot.

To a very great extent, expatriate failure rates can be attributed to the culture shock that usually occurs 4 to 6 months after arrival in the foreign country. The symptoms are not pleasant: homesickness, boredom, withdrawal, a need for excessive amounts of sleep, compulsive eating or drinking, irritability, exaggerated cleanliness, marital stress, family tension and conflict (involving children), hostility toward host-country nationals, loss of ability to work effectively, and physical ailments of a psychosomatic nature.[84]

To be sure, many of the common stresses of everyday living become amplified when a couple is living overseas with no support other than from a spouse. To deal with these potential problems, spouses are taught to recognize stress symptoms in each other, and they are counseled to be supportive. One counseling exercise, for example, is for the couples to list periodically what they believe causes stress in their mates, what the other person does to relieve it, and what they themselves do to relieve it. Then they compare lists.[85] Some companies have taken a different tack to grooming global talent. Gillette, Inc., is a good example of a company with a comprehensive training program for international employees.

COMPANY EXAMPLE

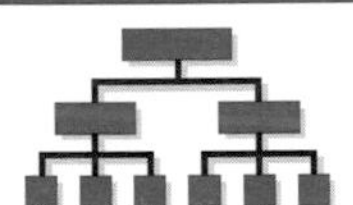

GILLETTE'S INTERNATIONAL TRAINEE PROGRAM[86]

Gillette competes in three major consumer businesses: personal-grooming products for men and women, stationery products, and small electrical appliances. Some of its brand names include Right Guard, Soft & Dri, Braun, Oral-B, Liquid Paper, and Paper Mate. All these consumer product businesses share common traits: they are number one worldwide in their markets, profitable, fast-growing, and anchored by a strong technological base.[87]

Gillette's global deployment of people has created the need for individuals trained specifically to work in operations. The company's International Trainee Program is designed to do just that.

Gillette seeks top business graduates from prestigious universities internationally. In addition, trainees must be:

- Adaptable, having good social skills.
- Younger than 30 years old.
- Mobile and oriented toward an international career.
- Single.
- Fluent in English.
- Enthusiastic and aggressive.

Junior trainees typically work at the Gillette subsidiaries in their home countries for 6 months. After that, Gillette management may choose to transfer

Table 16-2

TRAINING DESIGN RELATED TO STAGE OF GLOBALIZATION

Domestic (export) stage	International stage	Multinational stage	Global stage
Degree of rigor required is low to moderate.	Degree of rigor required is moderate to high.	Degree of rigor required is moderate to high.	Degree of rigor required is moderate to high.
Content emphasis is on interpersonal skills, local culture, consumer values, and behavior.	Content emphasis is on interpersonal skills, local culture, technology transfer, stress management, local business practices, and laws.	Content emphasis is on interpersonal skills, two-way technology transfer, corporate value transfer, international strategy, stress management, local culture, and business practices.	Content emphasis is on global corporate operations/systems, corporate culture transfer, multiple cultural values and business systems, international strategy, and socialization tactics.
Low to moderate training of host nationals to understand home-country products and policies.	Low to moderate training of host nationals; primary focus on production/service procedures.	Moderate to high training of host nationals in technical areas, product/service systems, and corporate culture.	High training of host nationals in global corporate production/efficiency systems, corporate culture, multiple cultural and business systems, and headquarters policy.

Source: J. S. Black, H. B. Gregersen, & M. E. Mendenhall, *Global assignments.* San Francisco: Jossey-Bass, 1992, p. 109.

them to one of the firm's three international headquarters (Boston, London, or Singapore) for 18 months. Assignments usually depend on which world region their subsidiaries are part of. Current trainees come from Argentina, Brazil, China, Colombia, Egypt, Guatemala, India, Indonesia, Malaysia, Morocco, New Zealand, Pakistan, Peru, Poland, Russia, South Africa, Turkey, and Venezuela.

Upon completion of their terms, graduates return to their home countries to assume entry-level managerial positions. If they are successful, they move on to other assignments in other countries. Eventually, they end up back in their home countries as general managers or senior operating managers.

The intent of the program is not to fill short-term vacancies. Rather, the objective is to hire and develop people who want careers with global proportions. As this example shows, the global workforce is a reality now, and it will continue to be so into the twenty-first century.

Integration of Training and Business Strategy

As noted earlier, firms tend to evolve from domestic (exporters) to international (or multidomestic) to multinational to global. Not surprisingly, the stage of globalization of a firm influences both the type of training activities offered and their focus. Table 16-2 summarizes some key design issues that emerge at each stage of globalization.

In general, the more a firm moves away from the export stage of development, the more rigorous the training should be, including its breadth of content. At the multinational and global stages, managers need to be able to socialize host-country managers into the firm's corporate culture and other firm-specific practices. This added managerial responsibility intensifies the need for rigorous training.[88]

International Compensation

Compensation policies can produce intense internal conflicts within a company at any stage of globalization. Indeed, few other areas in international HR management demand as much top-management attention as does compensation.

The principal problem is straightforward: *salary levels for the same job differ among countries in which a global corporation operates.* Compounding this problem is the fact that fluctuating exchange rates require constant attention in order to maintain constant salary rates in U.S. dollars.

Ideally, an effective international compensation policy should meet the following objectives:

- Attract and retain employees who are qualified for overseas service
- Facilitate transfers between foreign affiliates and between home-country and foreign locations
- Establish and maintain a consistent relationship with regard to the compensation of employees of all affiliates, both at home and abroad
- Maintain compensation that is reasonable in relation to the practices of leading competitors[89]

As firms expand into overseas markets, they are likely to create an international division that becomes the home of all employees involved with operations outside the headquarters country. Three types of expatriate compensation plans typically found during this stage of development are:[90]

- Localization
- "Higher-of-home-or-host" compensation
- Balance sheet

Localization refers to the practice of paying expatriates on the same scale as local nationals in the country of assignment. It implies paying a Saudi a British salary and benefits in London, and an American an Argentine package in Buenos Aires. Salary and benefits may be supplemented with one-time or temporary transition payments.

Localization works well under certain conditions, for example, when transferring an employee with very limited home-country experience, such as a recent college graduate, to a developed country. It also works well in the case of permanent, indefinite, or extremely long (e.g., 10-year) transfers to another country.

Higher-of-home-or-host compensation localizes expatriates in the host-country salary program, but establishes a compensation floor based on home-country compensation so that expatriates never receive less than they would be paid at home for a comparable position.

This approach frequently is used for transfers within regions—notably in Latin America and in the European Union—and for assignments of unlimited

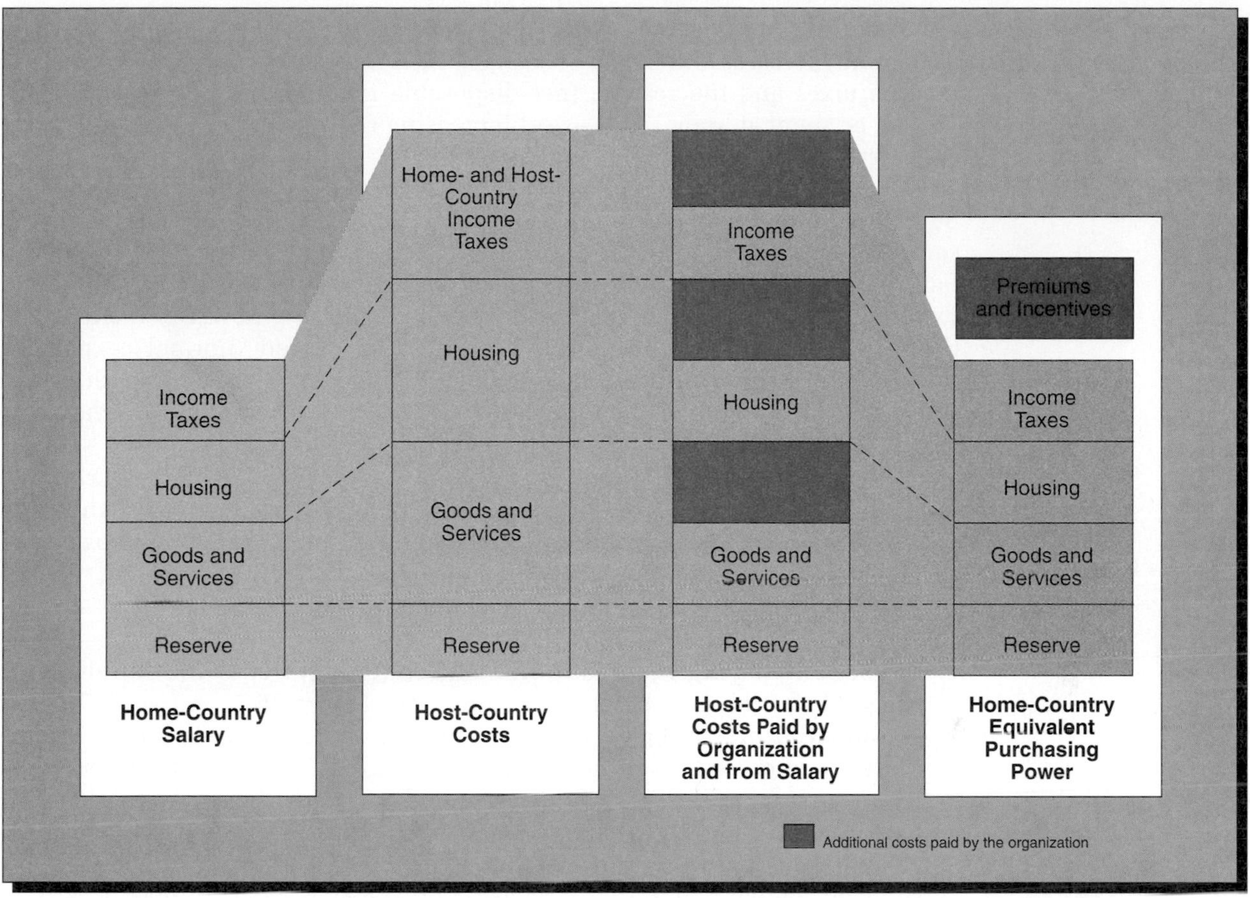

Figure 16-1
The balance sheet approach to international compensation. *Source: Compensation basics for North American expatriates: Developing an effective program for employees working abroad.* Scottsdale, AZ: American Compensation Association, 1995, p. 8. Used with permission.

duration. It is less appropriate for expatriates on a series of assignments of 2 to 3 years each.

The balance sheet approach is by far the most common method used by North American, European, and, increasingly, Japanese global organizations to compensate expatriates. Its primary objective is to ensure that expatriates neither gain nor lose financially compared with their home-country peers. If there is no financial advantage to being in one country instead of another, then this objective will be realized. It also facilitates mobility among the expatriate staff in the most cost-effective way possible.[91]

Nonmonetary differences in the attractiveness of individual assignments (if they are not already reflected in base pay) may be compensated with separate allowances (premiums) and incentives. For example, expatriates often receive "hardship" allowances if they are sent to culturally deprived locations, those with health or safety problems, or other unusual conditions. Figure 16-1 illustrates this approach.

Note the labels at the bottom of each of the four columns of Figure 16-1. The first is "Home-Country Salary." Each of the four categories identified in this column is a "norm" that represents the typical proportion of income that someone at the stated income level and family size spends (e.g., a $75,000-a-year manager with a wife and two small children). Each category behaves differently as income increases and family size changes. In most countries, as income rises, income taxes and the reserve (net disposable income that can be saved, invested, or spent at home) increase at increasing rates, while housing and goods and services increase at decreasing rates.

Host-country costs of income taxes, housing, and goods and services tend to be higher abroad than in most home countries, while the reserve remains the same. The column labeled "Host-Country Costs Paid by Organization and from Salary" demonstrates that if expatriates are responsible for the same level of expenditures abroad as at home and overall purchasing power is maintained, the employer becomes responsible for costs that exceed "normal" expatriate home-country costs. Thus if housing is more expensive abroad than at home, the employer is responsible for the remainder. These differentials are shown as gray blocks within column 3 of Figure 16-1.

The column labeled "Home-Country Equivalent Purchasing Power" illustrates the objective of the balance sheet: to provide the expatriate with the same purchasing power as a peer at home, plus any premiums and incentives necessary to induce an employee to accept a particular foreign assignment.

Two philosophies characterize the balance sheet approach:

1. **Protection**—paying expatriates in home-country currency the supplements suggested by the gray blocks in column 3 of Figure 16-1.
2. **Equalization or "split pay"**—the employer pays the reserve in home-country currency after deducting home-country norms from the expatriate's salary for income taxes, housing, and goods and services. The company pays all income taxes through the expatriate, while making payments to the expatriate in local currency to provide housing and purchasing power for goods and services comparable to the purchasing power of a home-country peer.

The most important advantages of the balance sheet approach are these:

- It preserves the purchasing power of expatriates in a cost-effective manner.
- It facilitates mobility among expatriates.

In an analysis of the international compensation package, two major components are (1) benefits and (2) pay adjustments and incentives. Let's consider each of these.

Benefits

Benefits may vary drastically from one country to another. For example, in Mexico an *acquired rights* law requires that if a benefit, service, or bonus is paid 2 years in a row, it becomes an employee's right. Both India and Mexico mandate profit sharing—10 percent of pretax profits must be distributed to employees.[92] Most developed and emerging economies have some form of national health care supplied by employer- and employee-paid premiums. In Russia, benefits are a major strategic tool for employers, who offer scarce goods and services, medical care, improve housing, and access to quality products.[93] In Europe, employees have various statutory rights that vary from country to country. These include pensions, sick pay, minimum wages, holiday pay, overtime, pay, minimum work time, and dismissal procedures (including legally required severance benefits). In Japan, a supervisor whose weekly salary is modest (by

U.S. standards) may also get benefits that include family income allowances (Toyota provides about $180 per month for the first dependent and about $50 per month for additional dependents), housing or housing loans, subsidized vacations, year-end bonuses that can equal 3 months' pay, and profit sharing.[94]

Global corporations commonly handle benefits coverages in terms of the "best-of-both-worlds" benefits model. Here is how it works: Wherever possible, the expatriate is given home-country benefits coverage. However, in areas such as disability insurance, where there may be no home-country plan, the employee may join the host-country plan.

Most U.S. multinationals also offer various types of premiums and incentives. Their purpose is to provide for the difference in living costs (that is, the costs of goods, services, and currency realignments) between the home country and the host country. Premiums may include any one or more of the following components:

- **Housing allowance.**
- **Education allowance** to pay for schools, uniforms, and other educational expenses that would not have been incurred had the expatriate remained in the United States.
- **Income tax equalization allowance** (as described earlier).
- **Hardship pay,** which is usually a percentage of base pay provided as compensation for living in an area with climactic extremes, political instability, or poor living conditions.
- **Hazardous-duty pay** to compensate for living in an area where physical danger is present, such as a war zone. Such a premium can be as high as 25 percent of base pay in some Middle Eastern and African countries.[95]
- **Home leave**—commonly one trip per year for the entire family to the expatriate's home country. Hardship posts normally include more frequent travel for rest and relaxation.
- **School allowance**—as a rule, companies will pay for private schooling for the children of their expatriates.[96]

Finally, it is common practice for companies to pay for security guards in many overseas locations, such as in Middle Eastern countries, in the Philippines, and in Indonesia.

Pay Adjustments and Incentives

In the United States, adjustments in individual pay levels are based, to a great extent, on how well people do their jobs, as reflected in a performance appraisal. In most areas of the third world, however, objective measures for rating employee or managerial performance are uncommon. Social status is based on characteristics such as age, religion, ethnic origin, and social class. Pay differentials that do not reflect these characteristics will not motivate workers. For example, consider Japan. Although the situation is changing, especially among large companies, rewards are based less on the nature of the work performed or individual competence than on seniority and personal characteristics such as age, education, or family background. A pay system based on individual job performance would not be acceptable since group performance is emphasized and the effect of individual appraisal would be to divide the group.[97] Needless to say, exportation of U.S. performance appraisal practices to these kinds of cultures can have disastrous effects. Despite such differences, research

Table 16-3

SOME CHARACTERISTICS OF PERFORMANCE APPRAISAL SYSTEMS IN THE UNITED STATES, SAUDI ARABIA, AND KOREA

Issue	United States	Saudi Arabia	Korea
Objective	Administrative decisions, employee development	Placement	Develop relationship between supervisor and employee
Done by?	Supervisor	Manager several layers up who knows employee well	Mentor and supervisor
Authority of appraiser	Presumed in supervisor role	Reputation (prestige determined by nationality, age, sex, family, tribe, title, education)	Long tenure of supervisor with organization
Style	Supervisor takes the lead, with employee input	Authority of appraiser is important; never say "I don't know"	Supervisor takes the lead, with informal employee input
Frequency	Usually once/year	Once/year	Developmental appraisal once/month for 1st year; annually thereafter
Assumptions	Objective—appraiser is fair	Subjective appraisal more important than objective; connections are important	Subjective appraisal more important than objective; no formal criteria
Feedback	Criticisms are direct; may be in writing	Criticisms more subtle; not likely to be given in writing	Criticisms subtle and indirect; may be given verbally
Employee acknowledgment and possible rebuttal	Employee acknowledges receipt; may rebut in writing	Employee acknowledges receipt; may rebut verbally	Employee does not see or sign formal appraisal; would rarely rebut
How praised	Individually	Individually	Given to entire group
Motivators	Money, upward mobility, career development	Loyalty to supervisor	Money, promotion, loyalty to supervisor

**Note:* Characteristics of the Saudi Arabian approach to appraisal come from P. R. Harris & R. T. Moran, *Managing cultural differences* (3d ed.). Houston: Gulf Publishing, 1990.
Source: W. F. Cascio & E. Bailey, International HRM: The state of research and practice. In O. Shenkar (ed.), Global perspectives of human resource management. Englewood Cliffs, NJ: Prentice-Hall, 1995, p. 29.

indicates that there are also important similarities in reward-allocation practices across cultures. The most universal of these seems to be the equity norm, according to which rewards are distributed to group members on the basis of their contributions.[98]

When implementing performance appraisal overseas, therefore, first determine the purpose of the appraisal. Second, whenever possible, set standards of performance against quantifiable assignments, tasks, or objectives. Third, allow more time to achieve results abroad than is customary in the domestic market. Fourth, keep the objectives flexible and responsive to potential market and environmental conditions. Table 16-3 illustrates characteristics of performance

ETHICAL DILEMMA
Bribery to Win Business?

In the United States, the Foreign Corrupt Practices Act of 1977 (amended in 1988 to increase criminal fines for organizations and civil sanctions for individuals) prohibits payments by U.S. firms and their managers to win foreign business. The act has cost U.S. companies billions in lost business. In France and Germany, on the other hand, companies may offset payments to foreign officials against tax charges.[102] In Korea, bribes are a way of life. Former president Roh Tae Woo amassed a $650 million slush fund (prior to its exposure and ensuing scandal and reforms in 1995), and even midlevel bureaucrats who wield regulatory powers demand payments. How much? About 1.2 percent of annual sales for big companies, and about 0.8 percent for small- and medium-sized companies.[103] Is this practice ethical?

Korea (and Russia) wish to join the 29 member countries of the Organization for Economic Cooperation and Development (OECD), but they will have to change their ways to do so. In 1997, OECD member countries agreed to negotiate a binding international convention to criminalize the bribery of foreign public officials, "irrespective of the value or the outcome of the bribe, of perceptions of local custom, or of the tolerance of bribery by local authorities."[104]

appraisal in a Western culture (the United States), a Middle Eastern culture (Saudi Arabia), and a Far Eastern culture (Korea). Perhaps the most important lesson of this table is that a foreign manager could be completely misled by assuming that the approach that "works" in his or her own culture will work elsewhere.[99]

More and more U.S. companies that are exploring strategic compensation approaches at home are beginning to adopt similar approaches for their senior executives worldwide. As an example, consider the balance sheet approach to expatriate compensation. It is most appropriate to the business strategies of an organization that is in the export or international stage of globalization. However, as firms evolve from multinational to global, they want their expatriates to understand that the greatest organizational growth—and their fastest career development opportunities—are outside their home or base country. Hence a large part of the compensation of these individuals will be performance-based, not a package of costly allowances and premiums that represent fixed costs.[100]

For these reasons, as the international operations of multinational firms evolve, the firms begin to introduce local and regional performance criteria into their pay plans, and they attempt to qualify the plans under local tax laws. Why do this? In order to create stronger linkages between executives' performance and long-term business goals and strategies, to extend equity ownership to key executives (through stock options), and, in many instances, to provide tax benefits.[101]

Labor Relations in the International Arena

Labor relations structures, laws, and practices vary considerably among countries.[105] Unions may or may not exist. Management or government may dictate terms and conditions of employment. Labor agreements may or may not be contractual obligations. Management may conclude agreements with unions that have little or no membership in a plant or with nonunion groups that wield more bargaining power than the established unions do. And principles and issues that are relevant in one context may not be in others, for example, seniority in layoff decisions or even the concept of a layoff.[106]

In general, unions may constrain the choices of global companies in three ways: (1) by influencing wage levels to the extent that cost structures may become noncompetitive, (2) by limiting the ability of companies to vary employment levels at their own discretion, and (3) by hindering or preventing global integration of such companies (i.e., by forcing them to develop parallel operations in different countries).[107]

One of the most intriguing aspects of international labor relations is multinational collective bargaining. Unions have found global corporations particularly difficult to deal with in terms of union power and difficult to penetrate in terms of union representation.[108] Here are some of the special problems that global corporations present to unions:

1. While national unions tend to follow the development of national companies, union expansion typically cannot follow the expansion of a company across national boundaries, with the exception of Canada. Legal differences, feelings of nationalism, and differences in union structure and industrial relations practices are effective barriers to such expansion.
2. The nature of foreign investment by global corporations has changed. In the past, they tended to invest in foreign sources of raw materials. As a result, the number of processing and manufacturing jobs in the home country may actually have increased. However, in recent years there has been a shift toward the development of parallel, or nearly parallel, operations in other countries.[109] Foreign investment of this type threatens union members in the home country with loss of jobs or with a slower rate of job growth, especially if their wages are higher than those of workers in the host country. This threat is very real in Germany, for example, where labor costs are 25 percent higher than in the United States, and 33 percent higher than in Japan.[110]
3. When a global corporation has parallel operations in other locations, the firms' ability to switch production from one location shut down by a labor dispute to another location is increased. This strategy assumes, of course, that (1) the same union does not represent workers at each plant; (2) if different unions are involved, they do not coordinate their efforts and strike at the same time; and (3) the various plants are sufficiently parallel that their products are interchangeable.

One solution to the problems that global corporations pose for union members is multinational collective bargaining. For this to work, though, coordination of efforts and the cooperation of the unions are required. What is called for is an "international union" with the centralization of authority characteristic of U.S. national unions. Yet two persistent problems stand in the way of such an international union movement:[111]

1. National and local labor leaders would have to be willing to relinquish their autonomy to an international level. This is a major stumbling block because the local union or enterprise union is essentially an autonomous organization.

2. Political and philosophical differences pose a further barrier to any international union movement. For example, a French labor leader committed to a communist form of economic organization is unlikely to yield authority willingly to an international union patterned after the United Auto Workers or any other union committed to the capitalist economic system. Conversely, the leaders of the United Auto Workers are unlikely to relinquish their autonomy to a communist international labor union.

Toward International Labor Standards

In view of the lack of success with multinational collective bargaining, unions have taken a different tack. Labor unions in the United States, for example, are attempting to influence the international labor practices of U.S.-based corporations, arguing that U.S.-based employees are unable to compete with overseas workers who are paid below-market wages and benefits. Toys 'R' Us has been the target of several such campaigns over the past several years, including a "toycott" to force the retailer to stop selling goods allegedly manufactured with prison or child labor in China and a union-led boycott to protest the company's refusal to allow unionization of its workers.[112]

Four forces are driving the trend toward adoption of international labor standards: labor unions, pressure from social advocacy groups, resentment in some developing countries against multinationals, and U.S. and European proposals for linkages between trade policy and human rights. The international labor standards advocated by these groups include:

- Prohibitions in child labor.
- Prohibitions on forced labor.
- Prohibitions on discrimination.
- Protection for workers' health.
- Payment of adequate wages.
- Provision of safe working conditions.
- Freedom of association.

In addition, some developing countries are beginning to hold Western-based multinationals responsible for their foreign labor practices. Vietnam, for example, recently passed a law requiring Vietnamese managers working for a foreign-owned company to be paid at the same rate as any expatriate managers residing in Vietnam.[113] To prepare for the emerging labor standards of twenty-first-century capitalism, managers with international responsibilities should monitor developments closely and begin to consider an appropriate strategic response. Another strategic development is regional trading blocks, of which NAFTA is just one example.

The North American Free Trade Agreement (NAFTA)

Economic competition in the twenty-first century will consist not of scattered countries nibbling at one another, but of major regions operating as economic units on the global playing field.[114] Begun in 1994, NAFTA will eliminate trade barriers on goods and services within the United States, Canada, and Mexico over 15 years. The agreement creates a region of 370 million consumers with $6.5 trillion in output. It is North America's strategic response to the global economy.

How has it worked? The United States has not lost jobs, but neither has NAFTA per se created U.S. jobs. However, employment in the *maquiladora* border factories—which import auto parts and electronics, process them, and send them north again—has boomed. In the first 2 years after NAFTA, maquiladora employment rose 20 percent to 648,000, and it is expected to reach 943,000 by the year 2000. Two-way trade with Mexico—Canada already had its own free-trade pact with the United States—has grown 30 percent.[115] In Mexico, labor, management, and the government are working together toward a common goal: world-class levels of productivity. An illustration of this approach is the case of Volkswagen de México.

COMPANY EXAMPLE

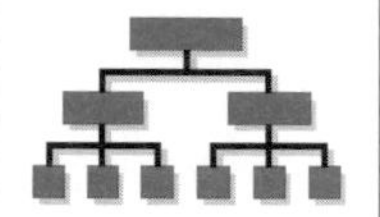

DEALING WITH UNION DISSIDENTS AT VOLKSWAGEN de MÉXICO[116]

Conflict erupted when the government-controlled union at VW, based in Puebla, Mexico, agreed with management on a massive restructuring plan to raise productivity. VW management insisted the new agreement was vital for global competitiveness. This was hardly idle talk, since VW supplies the entire North American market from Puebla. Fearing layoffs, however, a group of dissidents opposed the plan. After weeks of a bitter strike, the government gave VW permission to rip up the union contract. The company promptly fired 14,000 workers and rehired all of them, minus some 300 dissidents, under a new contract. Within days, VW instituted a new HR management system; seniority as a basis for promotion is out, while training, and lots of it, is in. Workers are now promoted according to skills and performance.

Today, the most favored union leaders in Mexico preach the gospel of productivity—and it is paying off. Already Nissan de México is exporting Sentras to Canada and light trucks back to Japan, while Ford's super-efficient Hermosillo plant builds Escorts and Tracers for U.S. consumption.[117]

There were only 51 strikes in Mexico in 1996, but the situation may change as unions become more aggressive in trying to recoup real-wage losses of 40 percent since 1988, largely due to wage-price stabilization agreements that keep wage hikes below the rate of annual inflation. Unions also want to change labor laws that give government boards wide powers to certify elections of union representatives and permit or bar strikes. Said one observer: "We're entering a period in which all the rules of union activity will be rewritten. . . . the unions will be much more militant."[118]

REPATRIATION

The problems of repatriation, for those who succeed abroad as well as for those who do not, have been well documented. All repatriates experience some degree of anxiety in three areas: personal finances, reacclimation to the U.S. lifestyle, and readjustment to the corporate structure.[119] They also worry about the future of their careers and the location of their U.S. assignments. Precisely the same issues have been found in studies of Japanese and Finnish expatriates.[120]

Financially, repatriates face the loss of the foreign-service premium and the effect of inflation on home purchases. Having become accustomed to foreign ways, upon reentry they often find home-country customs strange and, at the extreme, annoying. Such "reverse culture shock" may be more challenging than the culture shock experienced when going overseas.[121] Finally, almost four out of every five returning American expatriates complain that their assignments upon return to the United States are mundane and lack status and authority in comparison with their overseas positions.[122] Possible solutions to these problems fall into three areas: planning, career management, and compensation.

Planning

Both the expatriation assignment and the repatriation move should be examined as parts of an integrated whole—not as unrelated events in an individual's career.[123] To accomplish this objective, firms must define a clear strategic purpose for the move. Prior to the assignment, therefore, the firm should define one or more of the three primary purposes for sending a particular expatriate abroad: executive development, coordination and control between headquarters and foreign operations, and transfer of information and technology.[124] Research shows that unless there is a planned purpose in repatriation, the investment of over $1 million to send an expatriate overseas is likely to be squandered completely.

Increasingly, multinational corporations are seeking to improve their HR planning and also to implement it on a worldwide basis. Careful inclusion of expatriation and repatriation moves in this planning will help reduce uncertainty and the fear that accompanies it.

Career Management

The attrition rate for repatriated workers is among the highest in corporate life, as high as 50 percent.[125] Firms such as 3M, IBM, Ford, and Disney appoint a "career sponsor" (usually a group vice president or higher)[126] to look out for the expatriate's career interests while she or he is abroad and to keep the expatriate abreast of company developments. The development of global electronic-mail networks certainly has made that job faster and easier than it used to be. Sponsors also must be sensitive to the "job shock" the expatriate may suffer when she or he gets back and must be trained to counsel the returning employee (and her or his family as well) until resettlement is deemed complete.[127] To accelerate this process, some firms assemble a group of former expatriates to give advice and offer insights based on their own experiences.[128]

Compensation

The loss of a monthly premium to which the expatriate has been accustomed is a severe shock financially, whatever the rationale. To overcome this problem, some firms have replaced the monthly foreign-service premium with a onetime "mobility premium" (e.g., 3 months' pay) for each move—overseas, back home, or to another overseas assignment. A few firms also provide low-cost loans or other financial assistance so that expatriates can get back into their hometown housing markets at a level at least equivalent to what they left. Finally, there is a strong need for financial counseling for repatriates. Such counseling has the psychological advantage of demonstrating to repatriates that the company is willing to help with the financial problems that they may encounter in uprooting their families once again to bring them home.[129]

Human Resource Management in Action: Conclusion

A DAY IN THE LIFE OF TOMORROW'S MANAGER

8:15 A.M.: In her high-tech office that doubles as a conference room, Ms. Smith reviews the day's schedule with her executive assistant (traditional secretaries vanished a decade ago). Then it's on to her first meeting: a conference via video screen between her division's chief production manager in Cincinnati and a supplier near Munich.

While today's managers spend most of their time conferring with bosses and subordinates in their own companies, tomorrow's managers will be intimately hooked to suppliers and customers and will be well versed in competitors' strategies.

10:30 A.M.: At a staff meeting, Ms. Smith finds herself refereeing between two subordinates who disagree vehemently on how to promote a new appliance. One, an Asian manager, suggests that a fresh campaign begin much sooner than envisioned. The other, a European, wants to hold off until results from a test market are received later that week.

Linda Smith quickly recognizes that this is a cultural, not strategic, clash, pitting a "let's do it now and analyze it later" approach against a more cautious style. She makes them aware that they're not really far apart, and the European manager agrees to move swiftly.

By 2010, managers will have to handle greater cultural diversity with subtle human relations skills. Managers will have to understand that employees do not think alike about such basics as handling confrontation or even what it means to do a good day's work.

12:10 P.M.: Lunch is in Ms. Smith's office today, giving her time to take a video lesson in conversational Japanese. She already speaks Spanish fluently and wants to master at least two more languages. After 20 minutes, she moves to her computer to check her company's latest political-risk assessment on Spain. Although the report indicates that the recent student unrest is not anti-American, she decides to have a bodyguard meet her at the Madrid airport anyway.

Technology will provide managers with easy access to more data than they can possibly use. The challenge will be to synthesize the data to make effective decisions.

2:20 P.M.: Two of Ms. Smith's top lieutenants complain that they and others on her staff feel that a bonus payment for a recent project wasn't divided equitably. Bluntly, they note that while Ms. Smith received a hefty $20,000 bonus, her 15-member staff had to split $5000, and they threaten to defect. Smith quickly calls her boss, who says he'll think about increasing the bonus for staff members.

With skilled technical and professional managers likely to be in short supply, tomorrow' managers will have to share more authority with their subordinates and, in some cases, pay them as much as or more than the managers themselves earn.

IMPACT OF INTERNATIONAL HRM ON PRODUCTIVITY, QUALITY OF WORK LIFE, AND THE BOTTOM LINE

The ways in which a company operates overseas can have fundamental, long-term impacts on all three indicators. Recognize that poor conditions in an organization's international facilities can generate intense negative publicity, if discovered. In a recent poll, 51 percent of consumers surveyed said that a company's record on fairness and quality in hiring influences their buying choices. However, only 16 percent of company executives mentioned this record as a potential factor. Issues such as child and forced labor are particularly inflammatory to Western consumers.

Levi Strauss & Company found a way to minimize the use of child labor in its international facilities without repudiating local custom. It pays would-be child laborers to go to school, and offers them a position in its factories once the children have reached the legal minimum age of 14. Using this strategy, the company is able to maintain commitment to its principles without alienating local families who often depend on their children's wages to survive.[130] The strategy also has the benefits of enhancing productivity, quality of work life, and the bottom line.

While yielding more to their employees, managers in their thirties in 2010 may find their own climb up the corporate ladder stalled by superiors—older baby boomers who do not want to retire. Nevertheless, despite the globalization of companies and the speed of overall change, some things will stay the same. Managers intent on rising to the top will still be judged largely on how well they articulate ideas and work with others. In addition, different corporate cultures will still encourage and reward different qualities—for example, risk taking versus caution and predictability.

6:00 P.M.: Before heading to the airport, Ms. Smith uses her videophone to give her daughters a good-night kiss and to talk about the next day's schedule with her husband. Learning that he must take an unexpected trip himself the next evening, she promises to catch the SuperConcord home in time to put the kids to sleep herself.

SUMMARY

Foreign investment by the world's leading corporations is a fact of modern organizational life. For executives transferred overseas, the opportunities are great, but the risks of failure are considerable. This is because there are fundamental cultural differences that affect how different people view the world and operate in business. The lessons for companies doing business overseas are clear: guard against the exportation of home-country bias, think in global terms, and recognize that no country has all the answers.

Recruitment for overseas assignments is typically based on one of three basic models: (1) ethnocentrism, (2) limiting recruitment to home- and host-country

IMPLICATIONS FOR MANAGEMENT PRACTICE

No one has discovered a single best way to manage. But before a company can build an effective management team, it must understand thoroughly its own culture, the other cultures in which it does business, and the challenges and rewards of blending the best of each.

In the immediate future, there will certainly be international opportunities for managers at all levels, particularly those with the technical skills needed by developing countries. In the longer run, global companies will have their own cadres of "globalites," sophisticated international executives drawn from many countries, as firms like Gillette, Nestlé, and Sumitomo do now. There is a bright future for managers with the cultural flexibility to be sensitive to the values and aspirations of foreign countries.

Finally, there is one thing of which we can be certain. Talent—social, managerial, and technical—is needed to make global business work. Competent human resource management practices can find that talent, recruit it, select it, train and develop it, motivate it, reward it, and profit from it. This will be the greatest challenge of all in the years to come.

nationals, or (3) geocentrism. Selection is based on five criteria: personality, skills, attitudes, motivation, and behavior. Orientation for expatriates and their families often takes place in three stages: initial, predeparture, and postarrival. Cross-cultural training may incorporate a variety of methods and techniques, but to be most effective, it should be integrated with the firm's long-range global strategy and business planning.

International compensation presents special problems since salary levels differ among countries. To be competitive, firms normally follow local salary patterns in each country. Expatriates, however, receive various types of premiums (foreign-service, tax-equalization, cost-of-living) in addition to their base salaries—according to the balance sheet approach. Benefits are handled in terms of the best-of-both-worlds model.

Since global companies operate across national boundaries, while unions typically do not, the balance of power in the multinational arena clearly rests with management. To provide a more level playing field, unions are pushing hard for international labor standards.

An overseas assignment is not complete, however, until repatriation problems have been resolved. These problems fall into three areas: personal finances, reacclimation to the U.S. lifestyle, and readjustment to the corporate structure.

DISCUSSION QUESTIONS

16-1 What advice would you give to a prospective expatriate regarding questions to ask before accepting the assignment?

16-2 Discuss the special problems that women face in overseas assignments.

16-3 How can the balance of power between management and labor be restored in international labor relations?

16-4 Describe the conditions necessary in order for a geocentric recruitment policy to work effectively.

16-5 Should foreign language proficiency be required for executives assigned overseas? Why or why not?

APPLYING YOUR KNOWLEDGE

Expatriate Orientation Role Play — *Exercise 16-1*

American business is increasingly international in scope. Many problems can arise when Americans attempt to conduct business in foreign countries without an awareness of the local culture and customs. The obvious solution to these problems is education and training—in particular, a series of briefings (provided by the HR department) for expatriates before they are sent on overseas assignments.

The purpose of this exercise is to familiarize you with the culture and customs of one foreign country and with the process of developing and implementing a cultural briefing program for expatriates.

Procedure

Select a foreign country in which you have some interest. Then go to your college's library and find several resources that discuss the customs and cultural dimensions of your chosen country that would be important for a businessperson to know.

On the basis of the information you have collected, develop a mock cultural briefing to be given to the rest of the class. Your cultural briefing should cover such topics as traditions, history, living conditions, clothing and housing requirements, health requirements, drug and alcohol laws, and political and economic climate.

Collect visual aids for your briefing. For instance, your library or a campus professor may have slides, videotapes, photos, or visual aids available through on-line services that you can borrow to give students a visual overview of the country you have chosen. A local travel agency may have some brochures that you could pass around as part of your presentation. Another possibility is to develop a brief role play which demonstrates a "rude" American insulting his or her host through ignorance of local customs. Such a demonstration can be built right into your overall cultural briefing.

Be creative! The main idea is to teach the other students in your class about the conduct of business in another country and the importance of a cultural briefing for expatriates before they leave the United States.

REFERENCES

1. 21st century capitalism: New rules for the global economy (1996, Jan. 14). *Business Week,* Special advertising section. See also Thurow, L. (1992). *Head to head.* New York: Warner Books.
2. Cascio, W. F., & Serapio, M. G., Jr. (1991, Winter). Human resources systems in an international alliance: The undoing of a done deal? *Organizational Dynamics,* pp. 63–74.
3. Ohmae, K. (1989, Mar.–Apr.). The global logic of strategic alliances. *Harvard Business Review,* pp. 143–154.
4. Kraar, L. (1997, May 26). The real threat to China's Hong Kong. *Fortune,* pp. 85–94.
5. Ohmae, loc. cit.
6. Kraar, loc. cit.

7. Marquardt, M. J., & Engel, D. W. (1993). *Global human resource development.* Englewood Cliffs, NJ: Prentice-Hall.
8. Revzin, P., Waldman, P., & Gumbel, P. (1990, Feb. 1). World view: Ted Turner's CNN gains global influence and a "diplomatic" role. *The Wall Street Journal,* pp. A1, A10.
9. Solomon, C. M. (1997, Jan.). Global business under siege. *Global Workforce,* pp. 18–23. See also Foreign money keeps flooding into the U.S. (1997, May 19). *The Wall Street Journal,* p. A1.
10. Ohmae, K. (1990). *The borderless world.* New York: Harper Business.
11. Dueer, M., in Greene, W. E., & Walls, G. D. (1984). Human resources: Hiring internationally. *Personnel Administrator,* **29**(7), 61.
12. Marquardt & Engel, op. cit.
13. *Investing in people and prosperity* (1994, May). Washington, DC: U.S. Department of Labor.
14. Gibson, R., & Coleman, C. Y. (1997, Feb. 27). How Burger King finally became a contender. *The Wall Street Journal,* pp. B1, B4.
15. Grant, L. (1996, Oct. 14). Gillette knows shaving—and how to turn out hot new products. *Fortune,* pp. 207–210.
16. Laabs, J. J. (1993, Aug.). How Gillette grooms local talent. *Personnel Journal,* pp. 65–76.
17. Mitroff, I. I., & Mohrman, S. A. (1987). The slack is gone: How the United States lost its competitive edge in the world economy. *Academy of Management Executive,* **1,** 65–70.
18. Golden, S. B., Jr., Manager, training and organization development, Nissan Motor Manufacturing Corp. U.S.A. (1994, Feb. 19). Personal communication. See also Hillkirk, J. (1987, Oct. 28). Nissan gears up in USA. *USA Today,* p. 4B.
19. Gwynne, S. C. (1990, Oct. 29). The right stuff. *Time,* pp. 74–84.
20. Sheridan, W. R., & Hansen, P. T. (1996, Spring). Linking international business and expatriate compensation strategies. *ACA Journal,* pp. 66–79.
21. The fast track leads overseas (1993, Nov. 1). *Business Week,* pp. 64–68. See also The No. 1 reason overseas assignments fail: The spouse hates it. (1997, Jan. 7). *The Wall Street Journal,* p. A1.
22. Where the living is costly (1997, Feb. 3). *Business Week,* p. 30.
23. A global view of office space. (1996, Dec. 16). *Business Week,* p. 26.
24. Black, J. S., Mendenhall, M., & Oddou, G. (1991). Toward a comprehensive model of international adjustment: An integration of multiple theoretical perspectives. *Academy of Management Review,* **16,** 291–317.
25. McClenahen, J. S. (1997, Jan. 20). To go—or not to go? *Industry Week,* pp. 33, 36.
26. Copeland, L. (1984). Making costs count in international travel. *Personnel Administrator,* **29**(7), 47.
27. Hesketh, B., & Bochner, S. (1994). Technological change in a multicultural context: Implications for training and career planning. In H. C. Triandis, M. D. Dunnette, & L. M. Hough (eds.), *Handbook of industrial and organizational psychology,* vol. 4. Palo Alto, CA: Consulting Psychologists Press, pp. 191–240.
28. Harris, P. R., & Moran, R. T. (1990). *Managing cultural differences* (3d ed.). Houston: Gulf Publishing.
29. Ricks, D. A. (1993). *Blunders in international business.* Oxford, England: Blackwell.
30. Copeland, loc. cit.
31. Axtell, R. E. (1996). *Do's and taboos around the world.* New York: John Wiley & Sons.
32. Harris & Moran, op. cit.
33. Dunn, C., Kim, J. H., Kim. Y. N., Koh, S. J., Mann, R., Matthews, W., & Suoo, M. (1997, May). *Human resource management in South Korea.* Working paper, Graduate School of Business, University of Colorado–Denver.

34. Copeland, loc. cit.
35. Ralston, D. A., Gustafson, D. J., Elsass, P. M., Cheung, F., & Terpstra, R. H. (1992). Eastern values: A comparison of managers in the United States, Hong Kong, and the People's Republic of China. *Journal of Applied Psychology,* **77,** 664–671.
36. Negotiation waltz (1983, Aug. 1). *Time,* pp. 41–42.
37. Ibid., p. 42.
38. Ibid. See also Moran, R. T. (1985). *Getting your yen's worth: How to negotiate with Japan, Inc.* Houston: Gulf Publishing.
39. Japan: Women changing at work (1993, Dec. 10). *The Denver Post,* p. 28A.
40. Ibrahim, Y. M. (1994, Feb. 3). Fundamentalists impose culture on Egypt. *The New York Times,* pp. A1, A10.
41. Harris & Moran, op. cit.
42. Adler, N. J., Doktor, R., & Redding, S. G. (1986). From the Atlantic to the Pacific century: Cross-cultural management reviewed. *Journal of Management,* **12,** 295–318.
43. Howard, A., Shudo, K., & Umeshima, M. (1983). Motivation and values among Japanese and American managers. *Personnel Psychology,* **36**(4), 883–898.
44. Employee motivation in Germany (1989, Mar.). *Manpower Argus,* no. 246, p. 6.
45. Machungwa, P. D., & Schmitt, N. (1983). Work motivation in a developing country. *Journal of Applied Psychology,* **68**(1), 31–42.
46. Harris & Moran, op. cit.
47. Hofstede, G. (1991). *Cultures and organizations.* London: McGraw-Hill. See also Hofstede, G. (1980). *Culture's consequences.* Beverly Hills, CA: Sage.
48. Triandis, H. C. (1994). Cross-cultural industrial and organizational psychology. In H. C. Triandis, M. D. Dunnette, & L. M. Hough (eds.), *Handbook of industrial and organizational psychology,* vol. 4. Palo Alto, CA: Consulting Psychologists Press, pp. 103–172.
49. Lancaster, H. (1996, June 4). How you can learn to feel at home in a foreign-based firm. *The Wall Street Journal,* p. B1. See also Odds and ends (1992, Nov. 11). *The Wall Street Journal,* p. B1.
50. Schuler, R. S., Dowling, P. J., & De Cieri, H. (1993). An integrative framework of strategic international human resource management. *Journal of Management,* **19**(2), 419–459. See also Thinking globally: Worldwide marketplace demands farsighted management of human resources. (1997, Feb.). *HR News,* pp. B1–B8.
51. Pasquarelli, T. (1996, Oct.). Dealing with discomfort and danger. *HRMagazine,* pp. 104–110.
52. Solomon, 1997, loc. cit.
53. Dowling, P. J., Schuler, R. S., & Welch, D. E. (1994). *International dimensions of human resource management* (2d ed.). Boston: PWS-Kent.
54. Lublin, J. S. (1996, Jan. 29). An overseas stint can be a ticket to the top. *The Wall Street Journal,* pp. B1, B5.
55. Why Japan's execs travel better (1993, Nov. 1). *Business Week,* p. 68.
56. Sheridan & Hansen, loc. cit. See also Reynolds, C. (1995a). *Compensating globally-mobile employees.* Scottsdale, AZ: American Compensation Association. See also Briscoe, D. (1995). *International human resource management.* Englewood Cliffs, NJ: Prentice-Hall.
57. 21st century capitalism, op. cit.
58. Schuler et al., loc. cit. See also Bartlett, C. A. (1986). Building and managing the transnational: The new organizational challenge. In M. E. Porter (ed.), *Competition in global industries.* Boston: Harvard Business School Press, pp. 367–404.
59. Cascio, W. F. (1993). International human resource management issues for the 1990s. *Asia-Pacific Journal of Human Resource Management,* **30**(4), 1–18. See also Dowling et al., op. cit.

60. Spreitzer, G. M., McCall, M. W., Jr., & Mahoney, J. D. (1997). Early identification of international executive potential. *Journal of Applied Psychology,* **82,** 6–29.
61. Marquardt & Engel, op. cit. See also Safavi, F. (1981). A model of management education in Africa. *Academy of Management Review,* **6**(2), 319–331.
62. Briscoe, op. cit.
63. Reynolds, 1995a, op. cit.
64. Solomon, C. M. (1994, Jan.). Staff selection impacts global success. *Personnel Journal,* pp. 88–101.
65. Ibid.
66. Lublin, J. S. (1992, Aug. 19). Spouses find themselves worlds apart as global commuter marriages increase. *The Wall Street Journal,* pp. B1, B4.
67. Rosen, B. (1995, June 19). Trailing spouses get the chance to re-create their careers abroad. *International Herald Tribune,* p. 9.
68. Ibid. See also Adkins, L. (1990, Oct.–Nov.). Innocents abroad? *World Trade,* pp. 70–76.
69. Black, J. S., Gregersen, H. B., & Mendenhall, M. E. (1992). *Global assignments.* San Francisco: Jossey-Bass.
70. Marquardt & Engel, op. cit. See also Safavi, loc. cit.
71. Jenkins, L. (1995, Summer). Overseas assignments: Sending the right people. *International HR Journal,* pp. 41–43.
72. Cascio, W. F. (1991, Sept.). *International assessment and the globalization of business: Riddle or recipe for success?* Keynote address prepared for the National Assessment Conference, Minneapolis, MN.
73. Mendenhall, M. E., & Oddou, G. (1995). The overseas assignment: A practical look. In Mendenhall & Oddou (eds.), *Readings and cases in international human resource management* (2d ed.). Cincinnati, OH: South-Western, pp. 206–216.
74. Ronen, S. (1989). Training the international assignee. In I. L. Goldstein (ed.), *Training and development in organizations.* San Francisco: Jossey-Bass, pp. 418–453.
75. Black, J. S. (1990). Personal dimensions and work-role transitions: A study of Japanese expatriate managers in America. *Management International Review,* **30**(2), 119–134.
76. Solomon, 1994, loc. cit.
77. Fuchsberg, G. (1992, Jan. 9). As costs of overseas assignments climb, firms select expatriates more carefully. *The Wall Street Journal,* pp. B1, B5.
78. Lévy-Leboyer, C. (1994). Selection and assessment in Europe. In H. C. Triandis, M. D. Dunnette, & L. M. Hough (eds.), *Handbook of industrial and organizational psychology,* vol. 4. Palo Alto, CA: Consulting Psychologists Press, pp. 173–190.
80. Black et al., op. cit. See also Solomon, 1994, loc. cit. See also Conway, M. A. (1984). Reducing expatriate failure rates. *Personnel Administrator,* **29**(7), 31–38.
81. Solomon, 1994, loc. cit.
82. Dowling et al., op. cit.
83. Harrison, J. K. (1992). Individual and combined effects of behavior modeling and the cultural assimilator in cross-cultural management training. *Journal of Applied Psychology,* **77,** 952–962. See also Black, J. S., & Mendenhall, M. (1990). Cross-cultural training effectiveness: A review and a theoretical framework for future research. *Academy of Management Review,* **15,** 113–136.
84. Linowes, R. G. (1993). The Japanese manager's traumatic entry into the United States: Understanding the American-Japanese cultural divide. *Academy of Management Executive,* **7**(4), 21–40. See also Black et. al., op. cit.
85. Chronis, P. G. (1983, Feb. 6). They're learning how to live overseas . . . in Boulder, *Denver Post,* pp. 1C, 8C–9C.
86. Laabs, loc. cit.
87. Grant, loc. cit.
88. Black et al., op. cit.

89. Sheridan & Hansen, loc. cit.
90. Reynolds, 1995a, op. cit.
91. Ibid.
92. Flynn, G. (1994, Aug.). HR in Mexico: What you should know. *Personnel Journal,* pp. 34–44.
93. Milkovich, G. T., & Newman, J. M. (1996). *Compensation* (5th ed.). Chicago: Irwin.
94. Deloitte Touche Tohmatsu International. (1997). *The hidden costs of employment: A comparative study of income tax and additional employment costs across Europe.* St. Albans, UK: Author. See also Milkovich & Newman, op. cit. See also Corporate benefits as a competitive tool in Japan. (1990). *Japan Economic Institute Report.* Washington, DC: Japan Economic Institute.
95. U.S. Department of Labor (1996, July). *U.S. Department of State indexes of living costs abroad, quarters allowances, and hardship differentials.* Washington, DC: U.S. Government Printing Office.
96. Reynolds, C. (1995b). *Compensation basics for North American expatriates.* Scottsdale, AZ: American Compensation Association.
97. Sano, Y. (1993, Feb.). Changes and continued stability in Japanese HRM systems: Choice in the share economy. *International Journal of Human Resource Management,* pp. 11–27.
98. Kim, K. I., Park, H. J., & Suzuki, N. (1990). Reward allocations in the United States, Japan, and Korea: A comparison of individualistic and collectivistic cultures. *Academy of Management Journal,* **33,** 188–198.
99. Cascio, W. F., & Bailey, E. (1995). International HRM: The state of research and practice. In O. Shenkar (ed.), *Global perspectives of human resource management.* Englewood Cliffs, NJ: Prentice-Hall, pp. 15–36.
100. Sheridan & Hansen, loc. cit.
101. Ibid. See also Brooks, B. J. (1988). Long-term incentives: International executives need them too. *Personnel,* **65**(8), 40–42.
102. Bray, N. (1997, May 27). OECD ministers agree to ban bribery as means for companies to win business. *The Wall Street Journal,* p. A2.
103. Glain, S. (1995, Nov. 21). South Koreans say bribes are part of life. *The Wall Street Journal,* p. A11. See also Running scared in Seoul: The scandal may signal the end of the corrupt old ways. (1995, Nov. 27). *Business Week,* pp. 58, 59.
104. Bray, loc. cit.
105. Rothman, M., Briscoe, D., & Nacamulli, R. (eds.). (1993). *Industrial relations around the world.* Berlin: Walter de Gruyter.
106. Gatley, S. (1996). *Comparative management: A transcultural odyssey.* London: McGraw-Hill. See also Gaugler, E. (1988). HR management: An international comparison. *Personnel,* **65**(8), 24–30.
107. Movassaghi, H. (1996). The workers of nations: Industrial relations in a global economy. *Compensation & Benefits Management,* **12**(2), 75–77. See also Dowling et al., op. cit.
108. Mills, D. Q. (1994). *Labor-management relations* (5th ed.). New York: McGraw-Hill. See also Levine, M. J. (1988). Labor movements and the multinational corporation: A future for collective bargaining? *Employee Relations Law Journal,* **13,** 382–403.
109. Sera, K. (1992). Corporate globalization: A new trend. *Academy of Management Executive,* **6**(1), 89–96.
110. Time to leave the cocoon? (1993, Oct. 18). *Business Week,* pp. 46, 47.
111. Levine, loc. cit.
112. International labor standards gain attention. (1997, Mar./Apr.). *Workplace Visions International,* pp. 3–6.
113. Ibid.
114. Gomez, J. A. (1994, Dec. 10). Competition and collaboration in a new marketplace: Implications for U.S. and Canadian managers operating in Mexico. *Proceedings:*

Business Practices under NAFTA: Developing common standards for global business, pp. 12–18. Institute for International Business, University of Colorado–Denver. See also Davis, B. (1995, Oct. 26). Two years later, the promises used to sell NAFTA haven't come true, but its foes were wrong, too. *The Wall Street Journal,* p. A24. See also Bradley, B. (1993, Sept. 16). NAFTA opens more than a trade door. *The Wall Street Journal,* p. A14.

115. Davis, loc. cit.
116. The Mexican worker (1993, Apr. 19). *Business Week,* pp. 84–92.
117. Border crossings (1993, Nov. 22). *Business Week,* pp. 40–42.
118. Templeman, J. (1997, Apr. 28). Mexico's unions are slipping their leash. *Business Week,* p. 57.
119. McClenahen, loc. cit. See also Black, J. S., & Gregersen, H. B. (1991). When Yankee comes home: Factors related to expatriate and spouse repatriation adjustment. *Journal of International Business Studies,* **22**(4), 671–695.
120. Gregersen, H. B., & Black, J. S. (1996). Multiple commitments upon repatriation: The Japanese experience. *Journal of Management,* **22,** 209–229. See also Black et al., op. cit.
121. Gregersen, H B. (1992). Commitments to a parent company and a local work unit during repatriation. *Personnel Psychology,* **45,** 29–54.
122. Dobrzynski, J. H. (1996, Aug. 18). The out-of-sight Americans: Executives pay later for their stints abroad. *International Herald Tribune,* pp. 1, 7.
123. Ibid. See also Before saying yes to going abroad (1995, Dec. 4). *Business Week,* pp. 130, 132.
124. Black et al., op. cit.
125. Work week. (1997, Jan. 7). *The Wall Street Journal,* p. A1. See also Dobrzynski, loc. cit.
126. Taking steps can cut risk of rocky return from overseas stint (1993, Aug. 25). *The Wall Street Journal,* p. B1.
127. Ibid. See also Bennett, R. (1993, Sept./Oct.). Meeting the challenges of repatriation. *Journal of International Compensation & Benefits,* pp. 28–33.
128. Savich, R. S., & Rodgers, W. (1988). Assignment overseas: Easing the transition before and after. *Personnel,* **65**(8), 44–48.
129. Work week, loc. cit. See also Bennett, loc. cit.
130. Strategy suggestions (1997, Mar./Apr.). *Workplace Visions International,* p. 8.

CASE IN THE NEWS

Tearing Up Today's Organization Chart

By Paula Dwyer
Pete Engardio
Zachary Schiller
Stanley Reed

MANAGEMENT

The New Model

It's 7 A.M. Friday in a specially rigged conference room at the head office of GE Appliances in Louisville. CEO J. Richard Stonesifer, a fresh pot of coffee by his side, is ready to roll. The speakerphone hums, and Stonesifer greets his management staff in Asia. Stonesifer and his colleagues chew over sales figures and production glitches and gossip about Whirlpool Corp., their biggest competitor. For the next five hours, Stonesifer follows the sun across the globe, holding phone meetings or videoconferences with aides in Europe and the Americas. These talks "allow us to make immediate adjustments," Stonesifer says. "Customer complaints are never more than seven days from my attention."

Tomorrow's winners will use Western-style accounting, Japanese-style teamwork, advanced communications—and give entrepreneurial local managers a long leash.

Across the ocean, in Richard J. Callahan's London office overlooking fashionable Berkeley Square, a similar scene takes place. The US West International chief picks up his phone and begins a turbocharged conference call with seven division presidents in five countries. They hash over cellular-phone sales in the Czech Republic, forecast long-distance hookups in Russia, and give a thumbs-up to opening an office in Japan.

"Sea Change"

Stonesifer and Callahan have never met and are in very different businesses, but they have a lot in common. Both are trying to manage a revolution. They're racing to stay abreast of markets from Latin America to Russia and China that are accelerating in growth and leaping ahead in sophistication. New markets, rapid advances in communications, and new sources of brainpower and skilled labor are forcing businesses into their most fundamental reorganization since the multidivision corporation became standard in the 1950s. "We're talking about a new order, a sea change, that will go on for the rest of my career," says Callahan. "It's almost like Halley's Comet arriving unannounced."

Senior managers are struggling to adapt themselves and their organizations to the 21st century business world that's rapidly taking shape. Boundaries will be even less important than they are today. The rate of technological progress will accelerate, with breakthroughs in biotechnology or digital electronics coming from such unexpected places as Israel, Malaysia, or China. At the same time, the huge demands of the new middle classes and their governments will revive such supposedly mature businesses as household appliances and power-plant construction.

To tap economies of scale, companies will sell similar products worldwide or offer the same services in dozens of countries, adapted to local needs.

All this means that business opportunities will explode—but so will competition as technology and management know-how spread beyond brand-name companies to new players in Asia and Latin America. With more countries viewing protectionism as economically incorrect, it will be cheaper and easier for expansion-minded CEOs to go on the offense to steal a rival's market. But they'll have to play defense as well—staying alert for upstarts such as Nokia, a Finnish electronics maker that has snatched 20% of the world's mobile-phone market almost overnight.

Thriving in this fast-paced environment requires a new kind of company and a new kind of CEO. Just as much of the world is embracing a liberalized economic model, so businesses of all stripes seem to be converging on a common management model to run their far-flung operations. Although that model is still a work in progress, the outlines of what is likely to be the early 21st century's world standard are beginning to take shape.

This model company will rely on Western-style accounting and financial controls, yet stress Japanese-style teamwork. It will value ethnic diversity, though less from high-mindedness than pragmatism. It will be centrally directed by multicultural, or at least cosmopolitan, executives who will set overall tone and strategy but give entrepreneurial local managers a long leash.

Successful chief executives for the next couple of decades will be those who take advantage of global economies of scale by selling similar products worldwide or offering the same services in dozens of countries. But they must also make sure that their operations blend in locally. That's not only to avoid ruffling feathers but also to find out what their customers want and to gain access to new ideas, tactics, and technologies. They must also encourage information-sharing and innovation throughout their companies and make sure they don't get bypassed—as IBM did by sticking to mainframes.

This model anticipates even more brutal competition than earlier ones. Yet the model values ethical behavior and fair play. It is irreverent about hierarchy, and it even tolerates some organizational unruliness. But its reward structure is crystal clear: Work smartly and produce high-quality goods and services and, in return, the company will give you personal recognition, continuous training, and a good living.

No Clones

Top management at such companies as Ford, IBM, Digital Equipment, and Texas Instruments all have something like this model in mind as they go through costly restructurings. These corporations saw their increasingly important international operations become slow-moving—and at times redundant—clones of corporate headquarters. Little communication or coordination took place among regions. Worse, country organizations sometimes spent more energy competing with each other than they did fighting with rival companies.

In the late 1980s, many multinationals thought the answer to such provincialism was the matrix system. In a typical matrix, a country manager or business-unit boss might report to both a regional boss and a product-group chief rather than straight up the line. The idea is to give the front-line manager a richer flow of information and guidance. By requiring two or more executives to reach a consensus, the matrix also supposedly breaks down geographic barriers and leads to smarter business decisions.

Lately, however, the matrix has taken a lot of heat because it can lead to endless dithering. Digital Equipment Corp. CEO Robert B. Palmer blames the matrix for delaying for years his company's needed shift from minicomputers to PCs. While manufacturing, engineering, marketing, and other groups debated the move, competitors moved way ahead. "The marketplace is too Darwinian to permit that much discussion," says Palmer.

Still, in a world of such complexity, many big companies don't see any alternative to multiple reporting lines. "You can't avoid a matrix, so you'd better learn how to manage in one," says management consultant Gary Hamel.

So companies are trying to fine-tune the matrix to suit their particular goals and corporate cultures. They once-powerful country managers are losing authority at IBM as Chairman Louis V. Gerstner Jr. reorganizes the behemoth's 235,000 employees into 14 customer-focused groups such as oil and gas, entertainment, and financial services. Gerstner wants a big customer to be able to cut one deal with a central sales office to have IBM computers installed worldwide. Under the old system, a corporate customer with operations in 20 countries faced the nightmare of contracting, in effect, with 20 little Big Blues, each with its own pricing structure and service standards.

At Ford Motor Co., CEO Alexander J. Trotman is also waging war on fiefdoms, but the matrix he has designed is more product-driven. In one of the most radical shakeups in corporate history, he's eliminating self-contained country units and the separate vehicles, engines, and components they produce. Now, Ford wants to make cars for the global market, shaving $2 billion in expenses in the process. "There's no point being a multinational unless you leverage economies of scale," says Harvard University professor of marketing John A. Quelch.

World View

Ford isn't alone in pursuing near-global products. Texas Instruments Inc. has worldwide product-development teams that weed out parochial ideas and back ones with global appeal. "We want every product possible to serve the entire world," says Semiconductor Group President Thomas Engibous.

While some companies are centralizing, many others, including AT&T and Owens-Corning Fiberglas Corp., are setting up stand-alone units—or nearly so—to go after business in Asia, especially China. Many companies feel they have to give their people in China a lot of autonomy to let them pursue the opportunities they discern. "Generally, you are dealing with the senior guy locally," says Owens-Cornings' Asia Pacific President Charles R. Bland. "If you have to check back with your boss, it compromises your credibility."

Even if these companies get their architectures right, they will still need to do more. The toughest task is creating the flexible, opportunistic organizations that CEOs say they are after. How a company manages and exploits information is crucial. "The game is shifting from capturing benefits of scale to developing and diffusing the benefits of information," says Christopher A. Bartlett, an international-management specialist at Harvard business school. "It was simple when it was all in the home market, but it is much tougher to use the world as a source of intelligence and expertise." One company trying hard to play the global game is Owens-Corning. It developed a technology for glass-reinforced plastic pipe in a Norwegian joint venture. Now, it is manufacturing the pipes in a global network of plants from Barcelona to Botswana.

But few companies have really mastered the skills of gathering and exploiting information from around the globe. One of the difficulties is getting global teams to talk to each other. US West's Callahan complains that his group running cellular-telephone projects in Eastern Europe doesn't interact enough with a team checking out possible investments in Spain and Latin America. He isn't even satisfied with the level of coordination between his cable-television and telephone staff in Britain, where a US West joint venture offers a combined cable/telephone service over the same lines. He has hired consultants to help break down the cultural barriers. "We've spent years trying to unravel the old way, and we're still not up to snuff," he says.

High-Tech Talk

Having the right sort of E-mail and other information systems is essential if companies are to maximize their talent and intelligence-gathering. GE Medical Systems does 1,000 hours of teleconferencing a year. Frustration with the local phone service has pushed the fast-expanding Mexican cement maker, Cementos Mexicanos, to install an information system that allows it to monitor every component of its multinational empire. "With a keystroke, we can discover how much energy an oven in our Spain operation is consuming," says Informatics Manager Gelacio Iñiguez.

Companies are spending a lot of time and money on these networks. For Unilever PLC, which has 31,000 employees using either E-mail or Lotus Notes, just getting its people trained is a major project. Unilever is experimenting with a program run by Hewlett-Packard Co. that broadcasts a live tutorial session from its studios in the U.S. and Europe to Unilever employees anywhere in the world. A companywide satellite-training network may come next.

Buddy System

Many corporations are finding overseas joint ventures, partnerships, and other alliances to be superb vehicles for gaining market intelligence. For companies with limited capital, such as $700 million Japanese telecommunications-hardware maker Uniden Co., combinations may be the only way to expand overseas. "You can't live in you own world anymore," says Uniden Chairman Yoshio Sakai. "Finding the right partner regardless of nationality is the key to future global success." The company is considering an offer to enter a wireless-communications venture with French conglomerate Matra-Hachette.

Even giants use joint ventures to ease their way into some of the tougher markets. When it wanted to crack China's ice-cream market, Unilever joined forces with Sumstar, a state-owned Chinese investment company. Bob Smith, general manager of the venture, called Wall's (Beijing) Co., says Sumstar's help with the formidable bureaucracy was crucial in getting a high-tech ice-cream plant up and running in the Chinese capital in just 11 months.

SWAT Teams

Along with signing up Chinese heavy hitters, Unilever dispatched a team of Chinese-speaking troubleshooters from the company's 100-country operation. They are helping to build detergent plants, market shampoo and other personal products, and even sell Lipton tea to the world's largest tea-drinking country. Many companies are developing these specialized SWAT units to push into markets rapidly. Texas Instruments has some 200 professionals—dubbed the Nomads—who have set up chip-fabrication plants in Italy, Taiwan, Japan, and Singapore in the past four years. US West's Callahan boasts that he can "put a team into South Africa by Friday" to begin setting up a cellular-phone system. "We're faster than any telephone company in the world."

After the SWAT teams pack up and head home, someone has to run the business. When recruiting executives for overseas assignments, Korn/Ferry International President Richard M. Ferry says companies seek out experienced managers who have lived abroad and enjoyed it, speak several languages, are proficient with technology, and are able to motivate people by other means than issuing orders. "Having a well-stamped passport isn't enough to make an executive a global player," says Ferry.

The best practitioners of the new management model have had the humbling experience of learning that they can't run a China operation from New York. But it's local nationals, not expatriates, whom companies now prefer. Locally hired managers better understand cultural no-no's and can help companies shed their imperialist image. But more important, they often are more in tune with subtle changes in consumer buying habits, customer complaints, and government regulations, all of which can affect operating profits. "I may be head of international," says Levi Strauss International President Peter A. Jacobi, "but to think I can make decisions worth a damn in the Far East is ridiculous."

Many internationally expanding companies are hustling to add foreigners to their payrolls. At McDonald's Corp., often half of the 250 trainees attending a two-week Hamburger University management course in Oak Brook, Ill., are from outside the U.S. Simultaneous translation is provided in 22 languages. This fall, AT&T is launching a program that will bring foreign-based managers to the U.S. for up to two-year stints. Boston-based Gillette Co. scouts out likely talent in 28 countries where it has offices. Candidates are people such as Justyna Pisiewiez, a Polish recruit with a degree from a Beijing university. Along with Polish and Chinese, she also speaks English and Russian. These trainees are first put through a trial run at the local operation that recruited them. Then, they're packed off to Boston, London, or Singapore for an 18-month apprenticeship under an executive mentor before being sent home. They wind up "with a foot in both camps," says Human Resources Director James J. Noone. "We are far more successful when we rely on local people to run the businesses."

After hiring foreign talent, companies must take pains to integrate them. To encourage its Singaporean workers who make paging devices to collaborate with a sister plant in Boynton Beach, Fla., Motorola Inc. flew most of them to a Copper Mountain (Colo.) resort in August for bonding exercises. There, they played Outward Bound-style team-building games, such as helping each other move from one floating platform to another using a single wood plank.

Falling Behind

Unwillingness to give foreigners much clout could put Japanese companies at a disadvantage. Even at Uniden, where only 277 out of 10,000 employees work in Japan, Japanese executives run all foreign subsidiaries, and most key decisions are made at headquarters. Overcentralized management compounds the problem. Taku Ogata, an adviser on China for Nomura Research Institute Ltd. and author of a Japanese bestseller, *The Secret of Success in China,* thinks the unwillingness of Japanese companies to give authority to foreign executives is causing them to fall behind their Western competitors in China. Western companies hire Chinese managers, turn them loose, and reward them lavishly if they do well. By contrast, Japanese companies hesitate to hire Chinese at high levels, and Chinese prefer to work for Western companies, because the pay is much better.

But most Japanese companies are likely to change slowly, if at all. They won't necessarily lose out in the free-wheeling 21st century, but the Japanese may well be at a disadvantage in a hypercompetitive world where rivals borrow the best from their playbook.

The 21st century will be full of uncertainty and risk. As he sits in his London office, U S West's Callahan says he still doesn't know if the organization he's trying to create will perform. "Am I afraid? Yes, I am," he acknowledges. But he also feels privileged, because it's exhilarating to be on the frontier. The next century is going to be a time when the successful manager is a thinker and a risk-taker, not a bureaucrat.

By Paula Dwyer in London, with Pete Engardio in Hong Kong, Zachary Schiller in Cleveland, Stanley Reed in New York, and bureau reports

HOW TO GET YOUR COMPANY READY FOR THE GLOBAL CENTURY

Build for Speed and Flexibility

Flatten Hierarchies

Fewer bureaucrats make for faster reaction times and freer flow of ideas. ABB has only one layer between the top ranks and the business units.

Be on the Lookout for Joint Ventures and Partnerships

They conserve capital, bring you information and technology, and get powerful local players on your side. AT&T is trying to use Unisource, a consortium of European phone companies, to break into the highly protected European telecom market.

Use Teams to Chase New Opportunities and Ensure Cross-Fertilization

Unilever, GE Appliances, and Texas Instruments all use SWAT teams to set up new operations. L. M. Ericsson used teams to beat rivals by developing digital mobile-phone systems for Europe, the U.S., and Japan.

Be Global and Local

Look for Global Products and Economies of Scale

If you are serving global customers, they shouldn't have to cut dozens of separate country deals in separate countries. If you can standardize components, do it. Texas Instruments has a team that combs its operations for ideas with global potential. Ford is centralizing its auto-design process to save money by standardizing parts.

But Don't Overcentralize

No market has a monopoly on the best ideas anymore. ABB designs its tilting trains in Sweden and its locomotives in Switzerland. Intel is doing cutting-edge research in Israel. Motorola designed a new generation of pagers in Singapore.

Open Up the Company

Stay Open-Minded

It's up to the CEO to establish a corporate culture that nurtures innovation. Keep challenging assumptions. Don't get locked into dying businesses. Andy Grove has shifted Intel's focus from memories to microprocessors to systems.

Open Information Channels

Install E-mail and financial-reporting systems that bring everyone into the loop.

Diversify Management

You are unlikely to succeed in places such as India and China without Indian and Chinese executives. But be sure these managers feel that they belong to the company and share its goals. AT&T is launching a program that will bring young managers around the world to the U.S. for three-month to two-year stints.

GETTING "TWO BIG ELEPHANTS TO DANCE"

Alexander J. Trotman / Ford

When he gets a break from a killer travel schedule, Alex Trotman spends his time on the sweeping remake of Ford Motor Co. he launched last April. Looking to the future, the chairman wants to transform Ford from an old-style multinational to a streamlined global company—a task made more difficult by the company's manufacturing complexity. The first step will be merging the once very separate North American and European car operations into one big organization that can capture world economies of scale. The trick, Trotman says, is getting "these two big elephants to dance." Latin America and Asia will be brought in later.

"Ford 2000" is a bold and risky plan. But the British-born Trotman, 61, who ran Ford operations in Europe, Asia and the Pacific, and North America before becoming chairman last fall, says region-bound companies won't be competitive.

The chairman is merging Ford's North American and European operations.

Trotman's most controversial move is integrating Ford's car-development groups across boundaries. Until now, regional fiefdoms designed vehicles for their own markets. That pleased local tastes, but often resulted in costly duplication. Trotman's favorite example: two similar four-cylinder engines, developed for European and North American units, that don't share a single component. Never again, he vows: "We are in an all-out race to make the absolute best use of our worldwide resources."

Ford took a big step in this direction with the Mondeo—its latest try at a "world car." An elaborate system using teleconferencing and shared computer-aided design allowed staffers in Germany, Britain, and the U.S. to work on the project together. The Mondeo is selling briskly in Europe, while the U.S. version, the Ford Contour and Mercury Mystique, are now being launched to critical acclaim. Trotman plans to build on that Mondeo infrastructure to create a whole new global lineup.

By Kathleen Kerwin in Dearborn, Mich.

A FLEET-FOOTED TEAM IN ASIAN FINANCE

Shaukat Aziz / Citicorp

Citicorp has done as much as any major American multinational to diversify its management. Nowhere is this more true than in Asia. Shaukat Aziz, 45, a native of Pakistan, has been in charge of Citicorp's $800 million finance business for all of Asia but Japan since 1992. His colleague Rana G. S. Talwar, an Indian national, heads the consumer business. They are two of the eight non-Americans in the elite group of 15 executive vice-presidents, dubbed the "G-15," who rank directly behind Citicorp Chairman John S. Reed and the bank's five vice-chairmen.

Lately, Aziz' clout has increased. The country managers he supervises have wide latitude to cut financing and investment deals with local corporations and governments. "We can get very quick reactions," he says. Citi must be able to move fast to maintain its solid share of the fast-growing Asian capital markets, where megadeals are clinched in days. These executives have made Citi a major player in virtually every Asian market and often the leader among foreign banks.

Before taking his current job, Aziz held top regional posts in Riyadh, Athens, New York, and London. In Singapore, he sees to it that his country managers—who have worldwide responsibility for all clients based in their territories—work with product managers located around the world to offer currency trading, investment banking, and other services. The goal, Aziz says, is for Citi to be a "customer-driven organization supported by product people."

By Peter Engardio in Hong Kong

AN EVER-QUICKER TRIP FROM R&D TO CUSTOMER

Lars Ramqvist / Ericsson

The key: Design a product and ready it for market—simultaneously.

Lars Ramqvist's first move as CEO of L. M. Ericsson in 1990 was to shut himself in his office for six straight weeks. The new head of Sweden's $10 billion telecommunications equipment maker tried to figure out how to get Ericsson's often fractious business units to work as a team. "We behaved like seven different companies, each calling on the same account," explains the 55-year-old physicist. "Our customers were confused."

Ramqvist decided on a radical overhaul that would centralize sales of all products in each country unit. That way, Ericsson would present a single face to its customers. Ramqvist's restructuring has helped turn Ericsson from a company that was struggling badly a few years ago into one of the world's hottest telecom players. Some analysts see earnings growing at a 25% compound rate over the next five years.

To bind together a sprawling, research-intensive empire, Ramqvist introduced a matrix system with unit managers reporting to both product divisions and corporate headquarters. While executives have to put more time into consensus-building, the matrix has been very effective for sharing information among 40 R&D labs around the globe and getting products to market fast.

For example, when it was moving into digital mobile phones in the early 1990s, Ericsson designed the units and set up the manufacturing and service networks simultaneously. That put it way ahead of competitors. Ericsson is still the only company with digital mobile phones that meet European, American, and Japanese standards.

Ramqvist says such rapid-fire development campaigns will be essential to Ericsson's future success in crucial areas such as asynchronous switching and lighter mobile phones. "Time is important. It's that simple," he says.

By Julia Flynn in London

PUTTING FOREIGNERS IN THE EXECUTIVE SUITE

Tamotsu Iba / Sony

Must a Japanese company cease being Japanese to succeed in the business world of the future? Sony is probably the company that is most closely following such a strategy. With 80% of its sales coming from overseas, Sony has long been Japan's international trailblazer. And although few Japanese companies have admitted foreigners into senior management, an American and a European, Michael P. Schulhof and Jacob K. Schmukli, run Sony's U.S. and European operations and sit on the board of the parent company. "Recruit the best possible local management. From our experience, that's the best direction," says Tamotsu Iba, Sony's executive deputy president and chief planner.

In fact, some observers think Sony could soon become the first Japanese company to be run by a non-Japanese. Iba has his doubts about that, and he stresses that headquarters will still have a big role in decision-making. But he agrees that Sony will continue giving non-Japanese executives more responsibility. "Sony has become a very attractive place for foreigners to work," he says.

One reason that is true is that Sony's Japanese executives tend to speak better English than their counterparts at other Japanese companies. Iba, 58, says this is no accident. "We hire and promote people mainly for their ability to do business," he says. "But if you can't speak English here, you can't fully do your job."

By Robert Neff in Tokyo

Discussion Questions

1. *Business Week* argues that a new, worldwide model of effective management for the twenty-first century is emerging. Describe this model.
2. You are the second in command at a multinational firm. Develop an action plan for the CEO that will encourage continual information sharing and innovation at all levels and locations at which business is done.
3. Develop a blueprint that outlines how multinationals can get the most out of global teams.

Glossary

absenteeism Any failure of an employee to report for or to remain at work as scheduled, regardless of reason.

absolute rating systems Rating formats that evaluate each employee in terms of performance standards, without reference to other employees.

accepting diversity Learning to value and respect styles and ways of behaving that differ from one's own.

acquired rights law A Mexican labor law stipulating that if a benefit, service, or bonus is paid 2 years in a row, it becomes an employee's right.

action programs Programs, including the activities of recruitment, selection, performance appraisal, training, and transfer, that help organizations adapt to changes in their environments.

adjustment The managerial activities intended to maintain compliance with the organization's human resource policies and business strategies.

adverse impact discrimination Unintentional discrimination that occurs when identical standards or procedures unrelated to success on a job are applied to everyone, despite the fact that such standards or procedures lead to a substantial difference in employment outcomes for the members of a particular group.

affirmative action Those actions appropriate to overcome the effects of past or present discriminatory policies or practices or other barriers to equal employment opportunity.

age grading Subconscious expectations about what people can and cannot do at particular times of their lives.

agency shop A union security provision stipulating that although employees need not join the union that represents them, in lieu of dues they must pay a service charge for representation.

alternative dispute resolution (ADR) A formal, structured policy for dispute resolution that may involve third-party mediation and arbitration.

annuity problem The situation that exists when past merit payments, incorporated into an employee's base pay, form an annuity (a sum of money received at regular intervals), allowing formerly productive employees to slack off for several years while still earning high pay.

antidiscrimination rule The principle that holds that employers can obtain tax advantages only for those benefits that do not discriminate in favor of highly compensated employees.

assessment center method A process that evaluates a candidate's potential for management on the basis of multiple assessment techniques, standardized methods of making inferences from such techniques, and pooled judgments from multiple assessors to rate each candidate's behavior.

assessment phase of training The phase whose purpose is to define what the employee should learn in relation to desired job behaviors.

authority For managers at all levels, the organizationally-granted right to influence the actions and behavior of the workers they manage.

baby boomlet Those people born between 1978 and the present—the children of the baby boomers—who have a strong desire for the affluence of their parents' generation, and who will have a major impact on future products and marketing.

baby-boom generation Those people born between 1946 and 1964, currently 55 percent of the workforce, who believe that the business of business includes leadership in redressing social inequities and are currently frustrated by shrinking advancement opportunities.

baby-bust generation Those people born between 1965 and 1977 (which includes the lost generation and the birth dearth generation), who see work primarily as a means to an end, rejecting the notion of loyalty to a corporation, and who value family over work.

balance In a pay system, the relative size of pay differentials among different segments of the workforce.

balance sheet approach A method of compensating expatriates in which the primary objective is to ensure that the expatriates neither gain nor lose financially compared with their home-country peers.

bargaining impasse The situation that occurs when the parties involved in negotiations are unable to move further toward settlement.

behavior costing An approach to assessing human resource systems that focuses on dollar estimates of the behaviors of managers, measuring the economic consequences of managers' behaviors.

behaviorally anchored rating scales (BARSs) Graphic rating scales that define the dimensions to be rated in behavioral terms and use critical incidents to describe various levels of performance.

benchmark jobs Jobs that are characterized by stable tasks and stable job specifications; also known as *key jobs.*

"best-of-both-worlds" benefits In global corporations, an approach to benefits coverage stating that wherever possible, the expatriate is given home-country benefits coverage, but if there is no home-country plan in a certain benefit area, the employee may join the host-country plan.

birth dearth generation Those people born between 1970 and 1977, who, although practical, focused, and future-oriented, are skeptical about solving society's problems.

blended life course A lifestyle with balance in the ongoing mix of work, leisure, and education.

bona fide occupational qualifications (BFOQs) Otherwise prohibited discriminatory factors that are exempted from coverage under Title VII of the Civil Rights Act of 1964 when they are considered reasonably necessary to the operation of a particular business or enterprise.

business game A situational test in which candidates play themselves, not an assigned role, and are evaluated within a group.

career A sequence of positions occupied by a person during the course of a lifetime; also known as one's *objective career.*

career paths Logical and possible sequences of positions that could be held in an organization, based on an analysis of what people actually do in the organization.

career sponsor An individual (usually a group vice president or higher) who is appointed to look out for the expatriate's career interests while she or he is abroad, to keep the expatriate abreast of company developments, and to counsel the expatriate when she or he returns home.

case law The courts' interpretations of laws and determination of how those laws will be enforced, which serve as precedents to guide future legal decisions.

certiorari Discretionary review by the Supreme Court when conflicting conclusions have been reached by lower courts or when a major question of constitutional interpretation is involved.

checkoff A union security provision under which an employee may request that union dues be deducted from her or his pay and be sent directly to the union.

closed shop A union security provision stipulating that an individual must join the union that represents employees in order to be considered for employment.

collective bargaining unit The group of employees eligible to vote in a representation election.

collectivism The extent to which members of a culture give preference to an in-group over individual goals.

compensable factors Common job characteristics that an organization is willing to pay for, such as skill, effort, responsibility, and working conditions.

compensatory damages In civil cases, damages that are awarded to reimburse a plaintiff for injuries or harm.

competency-based pay system A pay system under which workers are paid on the basis of the number of jobs they are capable of doing, that is, on the basis of their skills or their depth of knowledge.

competitive strategies The means that firms use to compete for business in the marketplace and to gain competitive advantage.

conciliation agreement An agreement reached between the Office of Federal Contract Compliance Programs and an employer to provide relief for the victims of unlawful discrimination.

concurrent engineering A design process that relies on teams of experts from design, manufacturing, and marketing working simultaneously on a project.

consideration The aspect of leadership behavior that reflects management actions oriented toward developing mutual trust, respect for subordinates' ideas, and consideration of their feelings.

contract compliance Adherence of contractors and subcontractors to equal employment opportunity, affirmative action, and other requirements of federal contract work.

contrast effects A tendency among interviewers to evaluate a current candidate's interview performance relative to the performances of immediately preceding candidates.

contrast error A rating error occurring when an appraiser compares several employees with one another rather than with an objective standard of performance.

contributory plans Group health-care plans in which employees share in the cost of the premiums.

cosmopolitan managers Managers who are sensitive to cultural differences, respect the distinctive practices of others, and make allowances for such factors when communicating with representatives of different cultural groups.

cost control The practice of keeping business costs at the lowest possible level in order for the business to be competitive.

cost-reduction strategy A competitive strategy with the primary objective of gaining competitive advantage by being the lowest-cost producer of goods or provider of services.

critical incidents In job analysis, vignettes consisting of brief actual reports that illustrate particularly effective or ineffective worker behaviors; a behavior-oriented rating method consisting of such anecdotal reports.

culture The characteristic customs, social patterns, beliefs, and values of people in a particular country or region, or in a particular racial or religious group.

culture shock The frustrations, conflict, anxiety, and feelings of alienation experienced by those who enter an unfamiliar culture.

debarment The act of barring a contractor or subcontractor from any government contract work because of violations of equal employment opportunity and affirmative action requirements.

decertification Revocation of a union's status as the exclusive bargaining agent for the workers.

decision support system (DSS) An interactive computer program designed to provide relevant information and to answer what-if questions; may be used to enhance communication about and understanding of employee benefit programs.

defined benefit plans Pension plans under which an employer promises to pay a retiree a stated pension, often expressed as a percentage of preretirement pay.

defined-contribution plan A type of pension plan that fixes a rate for employer contributions to a pension fund; future benefits depend on how fast the fund grows.

Delphi technique A structured approach for reaching a consensus judgment among experts, consisting of successive rounds in which experts independently generate information that is summarized by an intermediary and fed back to the experts for revision until there is a convergence of expert opinion.

demotions Downward internal moves in an organization that usually involve cuts in pay and reduced status, privileges, and opportunities.

dental HMOs Health maintenance plans for dental care that operate in the same way as medical HMOs.

desirable qualifications In job specifications, those qualities and skills that are advantageous but are not absolutely necessary for the performance of a particular job.

development The managerial function of preserving and enhancing employees' competence in their jobs through improving their knowledge, skills, abilities, and other characteristics.

disability A physical or mental impairment that substantially limits one or more major life activities.

discrimination The giving of an unfair advantage (or disadvantage) to the members of a particular group in comparison with the members of other groups.

distributed practice Practice sessions with rest intervals between the sessions.

distributive bargaining In negotiations, the bargaining posture that assumes that the goals of the parties are irreconcilable; also known as *win-lose bargaining.*

diversity-based recruitment with preferential hiring An organization's recruitment policy that systematically favors women and minorities in hiring and promotion decisions; also known as a *soft-quota system.*

doctrine of constructive receipt The principle that holds that an individual must pay taxes on benefits that have monetary value when the individual receives them.

downsizing The planned elimination of positions or jobs in an organization.

due process In legal proceedings, a judicial requirement that treatment of an individual may not be unfair, arbitrary, or unreasonable.

economic strikes Actions by a union of withdrawing its labor in support of bargaining demands, including those for recognition or organization.

efficiency wage hypothesis The assumption that payment of wage premiums by employers to attract the best talent available will enhance productivity and thus offset any increase in labor costs.

employee assistance programs Programs that offer professional counseling, medical services, and rehabilitation opportunities to all troubled employees.

employee relations All the practices that implement the philosophy and policy of an organization with respect to employment.

employee stock ownership plans (ESOPs) Organizationwide incentive programs in which employees receive shares of company stock, thereby becoming owners or part owners of the company; shares are deposited into employees' accounts and dividends from the stock are added to the accounts.

employment-at-will The employment situation that exists when an employee agrees to work for an employer but there is no specification of how long the parties expect the agreement to last.

engineering controls Modifications of the work environment that attempt to eliminate unsafe work conditions and neutralize unsafe worker behaviors.

enterprise unions Unions in which membership is limited to regular employees of a single company regardless of whether they are blue-collar or white-collar employees.

entrepreneurs Enterprising, decisive managers who can thrive in high-risk environments and can respond rapidly to changing conditions.

equal employment opportunity (EEO) Nondiscriminatory employment practices that ensure evaluation of candidates for jobs in terms of job-related criteria

equal employment opportunity (EEO) (*cont.*) only, and fair and equal treatment of employees on the job.

equity The fairness of a pay system, assessed in terms of the relative worth of jobs to the organization, competitive market rates outside the organization, and the pay received by others doing the same job.

equity norm A reward-allocation practice, common across cultures, in which rewards are distributed to group members on the basis of their contributions.

erroneous acceptance In the selection of personnel, the selection of someone who should have been rejected.

erroneous rejection In the selection of personnel, the rejection of someone who should have been accepted.

essential functions Job functions that require relatively more time and have serious consequences of error or nonperformance associated with them.

ethical decisions about behavior Decisions that concern one's conformity to moral standards or to the standards of conduct of a given profession or group; decisions that take into account not only one's own interests but also, equally, the interests of all others affected by the decisions.

ethical dilemmas Situations that have the potential to result in a breach of acceptable behavior.

ethnic Pertaining to groups of people classified according to common traits and customs.

evaluation phase of training A twofold process that involves establishing indicators of success in training as well as on the job and determining exactly what job-related changes have occurred as a result of the training.

exclusive representation The concept that one and only one union, selected by majority vote, will exist in a given job territory, although multiple unions may represent different groups of employees who work for the same employer.

exempt employees Employees who are exempt from the overtime provisions of the Fair Labor Standards Act.

expatriate Anyone working outside her or his home country with a planned return to that or a third country; also known as a *foreign-service employee.*

experience-based interview An employment interview in which candidates are asked to provide detailed accounts of how they reacted in actual job-related situations.

expert system (ES) An interactive computer program that combines the knowledge of subject-matter experts and uses this information to recommend a solution for the user; may be used to enhance communication about and understanding of employee benefit programs.

external criteria Measures of behavior and results that indicate the impact of training on the job.

fact finding A dispute resolution mechanism in which each party submits whatever information it believes is relevant to a resolution of the dispute, and a neutral fact finder then makes a study of the evidence and prepares a report on the facts.

fairness As it pertains to employee performance rewards, the employees' perceptions that rewards are given honestly and impartially, without favoritism or prejudice; an employee's perception depends on a comparison with the reward received and some comparison standard, such as rewards received by others, rewards received previously, or rewards promised by the organization.

family-friendly firms Organizations with policies, such as on-site child care and flexible work schedules, that take into account the families of employees.

featherbedding Requiring an employer in a labor contract provision to pay for services that are not performed by hiring more employees than are needed or by limiting production.

feedback Evaluative or corrective information transmitted to employees about their attempts to improve their job performance.

femininity The extent to which members of a culture consider sex-role distinctions to be minimal and the dominant cultural values are related to quality of life.

fiduciaries Pension trustees.

financial rewards The component of an organizational reward system that includes direct payments, such as salary, and indirect payments, such as employee benefits.

flexible benefits Benefits provided under a plan that allows employees to choose their benefits from among the alternatives offered by the organization.

flexible-spending accounts Accounts into which employees can deposit pretax dollars (up to a specified amount) to pay for additional benefits.

flextime A strategy that allows any employee the right, within certain limitations, to set his or her own workday hours.

forced distribution A behavior-oriented rating method in which the overall distribution of ratings is forced into a normal, or bell-shaped, curve, under the assumption that a relatively small portion of employees is truly outstanding, a relatively small portion is unsatisfactory, and all other employees fall in between.

foreign-service employee Anyone working outside her or his home country with a planned return to that or a third country; also known as an *expatriate.*

formal recruitment sources External recruitment channels, including university relations, executive search firms, employment agencies, and recruitment advertising.

401(k) plan A defined-contribution pension plan in which an employee can deduct a certain amount of his or her income from taxes and place the money into a personal retirement account; if the employer

401(k) plan (*cont.*) adds matching funds, the combined sums grow tax-free until they are withdrawn, usually at retirement.

gain sharing An organizationwide incentive program in which employee cooperation leads to information sharing and employee involvement, which in turn lead to new behaviors that improve organizational productivity; the increase in productivity results in a financial bonus (based on the amount of increase), which is distributed monthly or quarterly.

generational diversity Important differences in values, aspirations, and beliefs that characterize the swing generation, the silent generation, the baby boomers, the baby-bust generation, and the baby boomlet.

geocentrism In the recruitment of executives for multinational companies, a strategy with an international perspective that emphasizes the unrestricted use of people of all nationalities.

glass ceiling The barrier faced by women in breaking through to senior management positions, so called because although women can see the top jobs, they cannot actually reach them.

global corporation A corporation that has become an "insider" in any market or nation where it operates and is thus competitive with domestic firms operating in local markets.

globalization The interdependence of business operations internationally; commerce without borders.

goals and timetables Flexible objectives and schedules for hiring and promoting underrepresented group members to ensure compliance with equal opportunity employment and affirmative action requirements.

grievance arbitration The final stage of the grievance process, which consists of compulsory, binding arbitration; used as an alternative to a work stoppage and to ensure labor peace for the duration of a labor contract.

grievance procedures Procedures by which an employee can seek a formal, impartial review of a decision that affects him or her; a formal process to help the parties involved resolve a dispute.

group life insurance Life insurance benefits, usually yearly renewable term insurance, provided for all employees as part of a benefits package.

halo error A rating error occurring when an appraiser rates an employee high (or low) on *many aspects* of job performance because the appraiser believes the employee performs well (or poorly) on some *specific aspect.*

hard quotas In an organization's recruitment and selection process, a mandate to hire or promote specific numbers or proportions of women or minority-group members.

headhunter An executive recruiter.

health awareness Knowledge of the present and future consequences of behaviors and lifestyles and the risks they may present.

health maintenance organization (HMO) An organized system of health care, with the emphasis on preventive medicine, that assures the delivery of services to employees who enroll voluntarily under a prepayment plan, thereby committing themselves to using the services of only those doctors and hospitals that are members of the plan.

home country An expatriate's country of residence.

host country The country in which an expatriate is working.

hostile environment harassment Verbal or physical conduct that creates an intimidating, hostile, or offensive work environment or interferes with an employee's job performance.

"hot cargo" agreements Refusals by the management or union members of a company to handle another employer's products because of that employer's relationship with a particular union.

human resource accounting An approach to assessing human resource systems that considers only the investments made in managers and not the returns on those investments.

human resource forecasts The human resource planning activity that predicts future human resource requirements, including the number of workers needed, the number expected to be available, the skills mix required, and the internal versus external labor supply.

human resource planning (HRP) An effort to anticipate future business and environmental demands on an organization, and to provide qualified people to fulfill that business and satisfy those demands; HRP includes talent inventories, human resource forecasts, action plans, and control and evaluation.

in-basket test A situational test in which an individual is presented with items that might appear in the in-basket of an administrative officer, is given appropriate background information, and is directed to deal with the material as though he or she were actually on the job.

in-house temporaries Temporary workers who work directly for the hiring organization, as opposed to those supplied from temporary agencies.

in-plant slowdowns The action of union workers of staying on the job instead of striking, but carrying out their tasks "by the book," showing no initiative and taking no shortcuts.

incentives One-time supplements, tied to levels of job performance, to the base pay of employees, including nonexempt and unionized employees.

income-maintenance laws Laws designed to provide employees and their families with income security in case of death, disability, unemployment, or retirement.

indirect labor Workers who provide essential services to line workers.

individual analysis In the assessment of training needs, the level of analysis that determines how well each employee is performing the tasks that make up his or her job.

individualism The extent to which members of a culture emphasize personal rather than group goals.

informal recruitment sources Recruitment sources such as walk-ins, write-ins, and employee referrals.

initial screening In the employee recruitment and selection process, a cursory selection of possible job candidates from a pool of qualified candidates.

initiating structure The aspect of leadership behavior that reflects the extent to which an individual defines and structures her or his role and those of her or his subordinates toward task accomplishment.

innovation strategy A competitive strategy with the primary objective of developing products or services that differ from those of competitors.

institutional memories Memories (primarily of workers with long service) of corporate traditions and of how and why things are done as they are in an organization.

integrative bargaining In negotiations, the bargaining posture that assumes that the goals of the parties are not mutually exclusive, that it is possible for both sides to achieve their objectives; also known as *win-win bargaining.*

integrity tests Overt (clear-purpose) tests that are designed to assess directly attitudes toward dishonest behaviors and personality-based (disguised-purpose) tests that aim to predict a broad range of counterproductive behaviors at work.

interest arbitration A dispute resolution mechanism in which a neutral third party hears the positions of both parties and decides on binding settlement terms.

internal criteria Measures of reaction and learning that are concerned with outcomes of the training program per se.

international alliance A collaboration between two or more multinational companies that allows them jointly to pursue a common goal.

interrater reliability An estimate of reliability obtained from independent ratings of the same sample of behavior by two different scorers.

inventories Standardized measures of behavior, such as interests, attitudes, and opinions, that do not have right and wrong answers.

job analysis The process of obtaining information about jobs, including the tasks to be done on the jobs as well as the personal characteristics necessary to do the tasks.

job description A written summary of task requirements for a particular job.

job evaluation Assessment of the relative worth of jobs to a firm.

job families Job classification systems that group jobs according to their similarities.

job posting The advertising of available jobs internally through the use of bulletin boards (electronic or hard-copy) or in lists available to all employees.

job sharing An approach that allows two employees to share the job responsibilities normally handled by only one employee, and to receive salary and benefits in proportion to their contribution.

job specification A written summary of worker requirements for a particular job.

just cause As it pertains to arbitration cases, the concept that requires an employer not only to produce persuasive evidence of an employee's liability or negligence, but also to provide the employee a fair hearing and to impose a penalty appropriate to the proven offense.

justice The maintenance or administration of what is just, especially by the impartial adjustment of conflicting claims or the assignment of merited rewards or punishments.

key jobs Jobs that are characterized by stable tasks and stable job specifications; also known as benchmark jobs.

knowledge capital The value of the knowledge possessed by people at all levels of an organization.

labor market A geographical area within which the forces of supply (people looking for work) interact with the forces of demand (employers looking for people) and thereby determine the price of labor.

leaderless group discussion (LGD) A situational test in which a group of participants is given a job-related topic and is asked to carry on a discussion about it for a period of time, after which observers rate the performance of each participant.

liability without fault The principle that forms the foundation for workers' compensation laws, under which benefits are provided not because of any liability or negligence on the part of the employer but as a matter of social policy.

Likert method of summed ratings A type of behavioral checklist with declarative sentences and weighted response categories; the rater checks the response category that he or she thinks best describes the employee and sums the weights of the responses that were checked for each item.

localization The practice of paying expatriates on the same scale as local nationals in the country of assignment.

lockout The shutting down of plant operations by management when contract negotiations fail.

long-term disability (LTD) plans Disability insurance plans that provide benefits when an employee is disabled for 6 months or longer, usually at no more than 60 percent of base pay.

loss control program The program that implements and sustains management's safety policy through provision of a safety budget, maintenance of safety records, management's personal concern, and management's good example.

lost generation Those people born between 1965 and 1969, who feel disenfranchised because they grew up in the shadow of the baby boomers.

maintenance of membership A union security provision stipulating that an employee must remain a member of the union once he or she joins.

managed care A cost-containment strategy for providing health care that relies on a gatekeeper system to gain tighter management control over the cost of health care for employees.

managed health A developing trend toward integrating disability coverage with workers' compensation and, eventually, with group health care; also known as *total health and productivity management.*

managed-disability programs Disability insurance plans that focus on making sure that disabled employees receive the care and rehabilitation they need to help them return to work quickly.

management by objectives (MBO) A philosophy of management with a results-oriented rating method that relies on goal-setting to establish objectives for the organization as a whole, for each department, for each manager, and for each employee, thus providing a measure of each employee's contribution to the success of the organization.

management controls Measures instituted by management in an attempt to increase safe worker behaviors.

managing change The ongoing managerial process of enhancing the ability of an organization to anticipate and respond to developments in its external and internal environments, and to enable employees at all levels to cope with the changes.

managing diversity Establishing a heterogeneous workforce (including white men) to perform to its potential in an equitable work environment where no member or group of members enjoys an advantage or suffers a disadvantage.

market-based pay system A pay system that uses a direct market-pricing approach for all of a firm's jobs.

masculinity The extent to which members of a culture differentiate very strongly by gender and the dominant cultural values are work-related.

massed practice Practice sessions that are crowded together.

meaningfulness In employee training programs, the aspect of factual material that makes it rich in associations for the trainees and therefore easy to understand.

mediation A process by which a neutral third party attempts to help the parties in a dispute reach a settlement of the issues that divide them.

mentor One who acts or is selected to act as teacher, advisor, sponsor, and confidant for a new hire or a small group of new hires in order to share his or her knowledge about the dynamics of power and politics, facilitate socialization, and improve the newcomers' chances for survival and growth in the organization.

merged-gender mortality tables Mortality tables that, rather than treating males and females separately, show the combined number of persons living, the combined number of persons dying, and the merged-gender mortality rate for each age.

merit guide charts Charts that are used to determine the size of an employee's merit increase for a given level of performance; the intersection on the chart of the employee's performance level and his or her location on a pay grade identifies the percentage of pay increase.

merit pay systems Pay systems, most commonly applied to exempt employees, under which employees receive permanent increases, tied to levels of job performance, in their base pay.

meta-analysis A statistical cumulation of research results across studies.

midcareer plateauing Performance by older workers at an acceptable but not outstanding level, coupled with little or no effort to improve performance.

mixed-motive case A discrimination case in which an employment decision was based on a combination of job-related as well as unlawful factors.

mobility premium A one-time payment to an expatriate for each move—overseas, back home, or to another overseas assignment.

modular corporation A new organizational form in which the basic idea is to focus on a few core competencies—those a company does best—and to outsource everything else to a network of suppliers.

mommy wars Personal conflicts experienced by women in the workforce, especially those in demanding executive positions, as they juggle work and family roles.

money-purchase plan A defined-contribution pension plan in which the employer contributes a set percentage of each vested employee's salary to his or her retirement account; annual investment earnings and losses are added to or subtracted from the account balance.

negligent hiring The failure of an employer to check closely enough on a prospective employee who then commits a crime in the course of performing his or her job duties.

no-compete agreements Clauses in a contract that bar an individual from working for a competitor for 6 months to 2 years if he or she is fired, if the job is eliminated, or if the individual leaves voluntarily.

nonfinancial rewards The component of an organizational reward system that includes everything in a work environment that enhances a worker's sense of self-respect and esteem by others, such as training opportunities, involvement in decision making, and recognition.

objective career A sequence of positions occupied by a person during the course of a lifetime; commonly referred to simply as one's *career.*

objective personality and interest inventories Inventories that provide a clear stimulus and a clear set of responses from which to choose.

obsolescence As it pertains to human resource management, the tendency for knowledge or skills to become out of date.

ombudspersons People designated to investigate claims of unfair treatment or to act as intermediaries between an employee and senior management and recommend possible courses of action to the parties.

open-door policies Organizational policies that allow employees to approach senior managers with problems that they may not be willing to take to their immediate supervisors.

operational planning Short-to middle-range business planning that addresses issues associated with the growth of current or new operations, as well as with any specific problems that might disrupt the pace of planned growth; also known as *tactical planning.*

operations analysis In the assessment of training needs, the level of analysis that attempts to identify the content of training—what an employee must do in order to perform competently.

organization In business, a group of people who perform specialized tasks that are coordinated to enhance the value or utility of some good or service that is wanted by and provided to a set of customers or clients.

organization analysis In the assessment of training needs, the level of analysis that focuses on identifying where within the organization training is needed.

organization development Systematic, long-range programs of organizational improvement.

organizational culture The pattern of basic assumptions developed by an organization in learning to adapt to both its external and internal environments.

organizational entry The process of becoming more involved in a particular organization.

organizational reward system A system for providing both financial and nonfinancial rewards; includes anything an employee values and desires that an employer is able and willing to offer in exchange for employee contributions.

orientation Familiarization with and adaptation to a situation or an environment.

outsourcing Shifting work other than the organization's core competencies to a network of outside suppliers and contractors.

overlearning Practicing far beyond the point where a task has been performed correctly only several times to the point that the task becomes "second nature."

paired comparisons A behavior-oriented rating method in which an employee is compared with every other employee; the rater chooses the "better" of each pair and each employee's rank is determined by counting the number of times she or he was rated superior.

paradigm shift In management philosophy, a dramatic change in the way of thinking about business problems and organizations.

parallel forms reliability estimate The coefficient of correlation between two sets of scores obtained from two forms of the same test.

passive nondiscrimination An organization's commitment to treat all races and both sexes equally in all decisions about hiring, promotion, and pay, but with no attempt to recruit actively among prospective minority applicants.

pattern bargaining Negotiating the same contract provisions for several firms in the same industry, with the intent of making wages and benefits uniform industrywide.

Paul Principle The phenomenon that over time, people become uneducated, and therefore incompetent, to perform at a level they once performed at adequately.

pay compression A narrowing of the ratios of pay between jobs or pay grades in a firm's pay structure.

peer nomination A method of peer assessment that requires each group member to designate a certain number of group members as highest or lowest on a performance dimension.

peer ranking A method of peer assessment that requires each group member to rank the performance of all other members from best to worst.

peer rating A method of peer assessment that requires each group member to rate the performance of every other group member.

pension A sum of money paid at regular intervals to an employee who has retired from a company and is eligible to receive such benefits.

performance appraisal A review of the job-relevant strengths and weaknesses of an individual or a team in an organization.

performance management A broad process that requires managers to define, facilitate, and encourage performance by providing timely feedback and constantly focusing everyone's attention on the ultimate objectives.

performance standards Criteria that specify *how well,* not *how,* work is to be done, by defining levels of acceptable or unacceptable employee behavior.

placement In the employee recruitment and selection process, the assignment of individuals to particular jobs.

point-of-service plans Health-care plans that offer the choice of using the plan's network of doctors and hospitals (and paying no deductible and only small copayments for office visits) or seeing a physician outside the network (and paying 30 to 40 percent of the total cost); an in-network gatekeeper must approve all services.

portability Tax-free transfer of vested benefits to another employer or to an individual retirement account if a vested employee changes jobs and if the present employer agrees.

power distance The extent to which members of a culture accept the unequal distribution of power.

preferential shop A union security provision stipulating that union members be given preference in hiring.

preferred-provider organization (PPO) A health-care system, generally with no gatekeeper, in which medical care is provided by a specified group of physicians and hospitals; care from outside the network is available at additional cost to the individual employee.

premium-price options Stock options granted at a price higher than the market price.

prima facie case A case in which a body of facts is presumed to be true until proved otherwise.

privacy The interest employees have in controlling the use that is made of their personal information and in being able to engage in behavior free from regulation or surveillance.

procedural justice Justice that focuses on the fairness of the procedures used to make decisions—the extent that the decisions are consistent across persons and over time, free from bias, based on accurate information, correctable, and based on prevailing moral and ethical standards.

process In a process-based organization of work, a collection of activities cutting across organizational boundaries and traditional business functions that takes one or more kinds of input and creates an output that is of value to a customer.

productivity A measure of the output of goods and services relative to the input of labor, material, and equipment.

profit sharing An organizationwide incentive program in which employees receive a bonus that is normally based on some percentage of the company's profits beyond some minimum level.

progressive discipline A discipline procedure that proceeds from an oral warning to a written warning to a suspension to dismissal.

projective measures Measures that present an individual with ambiguous stimuli (primarily visual) and allow him or her to respond in an open-ended fashion.

promotions Upward internal moves in an organization that usually involve greater responsibility and authority along with increases in pay, benefits, and privileges.

psychological success The feeling of pride and personal accomplishment that comes from achieving one's most important goals in life.

punitive damages In civil cases, damages that are awarded to punish a defendant or to deter a defendant's conduct.

pure diversity-based recruitment An organization's concerted effort to actively expand the pool of applicants so that no one is excluded because of past or present discrimination; the decision to hire or to promote is based on the best-qualified individual regardless of race or sex.

Pygmalion effect The phenomenon of the self-fulfilling prophecy; with regard to training, the fact that the higher the expectations of the trainer, the better the performance of the trainees.

qualified individual with a disability An individual with a disability who is able to perform the essential functions of a job with or without accommodation.

qualified job applicants Applicants with disabilities who can perform the essential functions of a job with or without reasonable accommodation.

quality of work life (QWL) A set of objective organizational conditions and practices designed to foster quality relationships within the organization; employees' perceptions of the degree to which the organizational environment meets the full range of human needs.

quality-enhancement strategy A competitive strategy with the primary objective of enhancing product or service quality.

quid pro quo harassment Sexual harassment that is a condition of employment.

quotas Inflexible numbers or percentages of underrepresented group members that companies must hire or promote to comply with equal employment opportunity and affirmative action requirements.

race norming Within-group percentile scoring of employment-related tests.

realistic job preview (RJP) A recruiter's job overview that includes not only the positive aspects but also the unpleasant aspects of the job.

reasonable accommodations Adjustments in the work environment to allow for the special needs of individuals with disabilities.

recency error A rating error occurring when an appraiser assigns a rating on the basis of the employee's most recent performance rather than on long-term performance.

recruitment A market exchange process in which employers attempt to differentiate their "products" (job opportunities) among "consumers" (job applicants) who vary in their levels of job-relevant knowledge, abilities, and skills.

recruitment pipeline The time frame from the receipt of a résumé to the time a new hire starts work.

redeployment Transfer of an employee from one position or area to another—often resulting from a business slowdown or a reduced need for certain skills and usually coupled with training for the transition to new job skills and responsibilities.

relative rating systems Rating formats that compare the performance of an employee with that of other employees.

reliability The consistency or stability of a measurement procedure.

repatriation The process of reentering one's native culture after being absent from it.

representation election A secret-ballot election to determine whether a particular union will be certified as the exclusive bargaining representative of all the employees in the unit.

required qualifications In job specifications, those qualities and skills that are absolutely necessary for the performance of a particular job.

results-oriented systems Rating formats that place primary emphasis on what an employee produces.

Resumix Human Skills Management System An automated résumé-processing system that uses electronic technology to process résumés, input data into an applicant database, and provide on-line access to résumé and skills information on available job candidates.

retaliatory discharge The situation that exists when an employee is terminated for what she or he considers unreasonable, outrageous reasons; in such cases, the employee may seek damages under an exception to the employment-at-will doctrine.

retention The managerial activities of rewarding employees for performing their jobs effectively; ensuring harmonious working relations between employees and managers; and maintaining a safe, healthy work environment.

reverse discrimination Discrimination against whites (especially white males) and in favor of members of protected groups.

right-to-work laws Laws that prohibit compulsory union membership as a condition of continued employment.

secondary boycott A boycott occurring when a union appeals to firms or other unions to stop doing business with an employer who sells or handles struck products.

selection ratio The percentage of applicants hired, which is used in evaluating the usefulness of any predictor.

seniority Privileged status attained by length of employment.

seniority system An established business practice that allots to employees ever-improving employment rights and benefits as their relative lengths of pertinent employment increase.

sensitivity The capability of a performance appraisal system to distinguish effective from ineffective performers.

"70 percent comfortable" rule Saturn Corporation's guideline for reaching consensus among team members: each team member must feel at least 70 percent comfortable with any decision made by the team.

severance pay Payments, usually based on length of service, organization level, and reason for termination, provided to employees whose employment is terminated.

sexual harassment Unwelcome sexual advances, requests for sexual favors, and other verbal or physical conduct of a sexual nature when submission to or rejection of this conduct explicitly or implicitly affects an individual's employment, unreasonably interferes with an individual's work performance, or creates an intimidating, hostile, or offensive work environment.

silent generation Those people born between 1930 and 1945, who dedicated themselves to their employers, made sacrifices to get ahead, and currently hold most positions of power in the country.

simplified employee pension A defined-contribution pension plan under which a small-business employer can contribute a certain percentage or amount of an employee's salary tax-free to an individual retirement account; the employee is vested immediately for the amount paid into the account but cannot withdraw any funds before age 59½ without penalty.

situational interview An employment interview in which candidates are asked to describe how they think they would respond in certain job-related situations.

situational tests Standardized measures of behavior whose primary objective is to assess the ability to *do* rather than the ability to *know* through miniature replicas of actual job requirements; also known as *work-sample tests.*

skip-level policy An organizational policy that allows an employee with a problem to proceed directly to the next higher level of management above his or her supervisor.

socialization In the employee recruitment and selection process, the introduction of new employees to company policies, practices, and benefits through an orientation program; the mutual adaptation of the new employee and the new employer to one another.

soft-quota system An organization's recruitment policy that systematically favors women and minorities in hiring and promotion decisions; also known as *diversity-based recruitment with preferential hiring.*

spatial relations ability The ability to visualize the effects of manipulating or changing the position of objects.

speed strategy A competitive strategy with the primary goal of being the fastest innovator, producer, distributor, and responder to customer feedback; also known as a *time-based strategy.*

staffing The managerial activities of identifying work requirements within an organization; determining the numbers of people and the skills mix necessary to do the work; and recruiting, selecting, and promoting qualified candidates.

status In an organization, the value ascribed to an individual because of his or her position in the organization's hierarchy.

stock options The right (primarily of executives) to buy a company's stock sometime in the future at a fixed price, usually the price on the day the options are granted.

strategic human resource management (HRM) An approach to human resource management that has the goal of using people most wisely with respect to the strategic needs of the organization, ensuring that people from all levels of the organization are working to implement the strategy of the business effectively.

strategic job analyses Future-oriented analyses that identify skill and ability requirements for jobs that do not yet exist.

strategic planning Long-range business planning that involves fundamental decisions about the very nature of the business, including defining the organization's philosophy; formulating statements of identity, purpose, and objectives; evaluating strengths, weaknesses, and competitive dynamics; determining organizational design; developing strategies; and devising programs.

subjective career A sense of where one is going in one's work life based on one's perceived talents and abilities, basic values, and career motives and needs.

succession plans Internal labor supply forecasts—consisting of setting a planning horizon, identifying replacement candidates for each key position, assessing current performance and readiness for promotion, identifying career development needs, and integrating the career goals of individuals with company goals—that are used to ensure the availability of competent executive talent.

swing generation Those people born between 1910 and 1929, who struggled through the Great Depression, fought in World War II, and rebuilt the American economy after that war.

sympathy strikes Refusals by employees of one bargaining unit to cross a picket line of a different bargaining unit.

system A network of interrelated components.

systemic discrimination Any business practice that results in the denial of equal employment opportunity.

systems approach An approach to managing human resources that provides a conceptual framework for integrating the various components within the system and for linking the human resource management (HRM) system with larger organizational needs.

tactical planning Short- to middle-range business planning that addresses issues associated with the growth of current or new operations, as well as with any specific problems that might disrupt the pace of planned growth; also known as *operational planning.*

talent inventory The human resource planning activity that assesses current human resources skills, abilities, and potential, and analyzes how those resources are currently being used.

team A group of individuals who are working together toward a common goal.

telecommuting An approach, made possible by the use of personal computers, fax machines, and electronic mail, in which an employee works either full-time or part-time from his or her home.

test-retest reliability An estimate of reliability obtained from two administrations of the same test at two different times.

tests Standardized measures of behavior, such as math and vocabulary skills, that have right and wrong answers.

third-country national An expatriate who has transferred to an additional country while working abroad.

"Three-C" logic An approach to organizational design based on the strategies of command, control, and compartmentalization.

time-based strategy A competitive strategy with the primary goal of being the fastest innovator, producer, distributor, and responder to customer feedback; also known as a *speed strategy.*

total health and productivity management A developing trend toward integrating disability coverage with workers' compensation and, eventually, with group health care; also known as *managed health.*

total quality management (TQM) A management approach that emphasizes the continuous improvement of products and processes to ensure long-term customer satisfaction; TQM has a group problem-solving focus that encourages employee empowerment.

tournament model of upward mobility A model of career success based on the assumption that an individual must have a challenging first job and receive quick, early promotions in order to be successful in his or her career; so called because, as in a tournament, everyone has an equal chance in the early contests but the losers are not eligible for the later, major contests.

training Planned programs designed to improve performance at the individual, group, and/or organizational levels.

training and development phase of training The phase whose purpose is to design the environment in which to achieve the objectives defined in the assessment phase by choosing methods and techniques and by delivering them in a supportive environment based on sound principles of learning.

training paradox The seemingly contradictory fact that training employees to develop their skills and improve their performance increases their employability outside the company while simultaneously increasing their job security and desire to stay with their current employer.

transfer The extent to which competencies learned in training can be applied on the job.

troubled employee An individual who is confronted by unresolved personal or work-related problems.

turnover Any permanent departure of employees beyond organizational boundaries.

two-tier wage schemes Wage practices that set lower pay for new employees.

type A behavior patterns Hard-driving, aggressive, competitive, impatient patterns of behavior.

unauthorized aliens Foreign-born U.S. residents not legally authorized to work in the United States.

uncertainty avoidance The extent to which members of a culture feel threatened by ambiguous situations and thus emphasize ritual behavior, rules, and stability.

unequal treatment Disparate treatment of employees based on an intention to discriminate.

unfair-labor-practice strikes Strikes that are caused or prolonged by unfair labor practices of the employer.

union shop A union security provision stipulating that, as a condition of continued employment, an individual must join the union that represents employees after a probationary period.

unprotected strikes Both lawful and unlawful work stoppages, such as sit-down strikes, slowdowns, and wildcat strikes, in which participants' jobs are not protected by law; thus the participants may be discharged by their employer.

utility analysis A method of converting measures of staffing or training outcomes into the metric of dollars.

validity Evidence regarding the appropriateness or meaningfulness of inferences about scores from a measurement procedure.

validity generalization The assumption that the results of a validity study conducted in one situation can be generalized to other similar situations.

variable-pay systems Pay programs that are linked to profit and productivity gains.

vesting Guarantee as a legal right with no contingencies, as of an employee's retirement benefits after a certain length of employment.

virtual corporation A new organizational form in which teams of specialists come together to work on a project and then disband when the project is finished.

virtual workplace A new organizational form based on the idea of working anytime, anywhere—in real space or in cyberspace.

visioning Conceptualizing what should be happening in the future, and having the ability to excite and inspire others in making the vision a reality.

voice systems Organizational systems that provide individuals and groups with the capacity to be heard, with a way to communicate their interests upward.

weighted application blanks (WABs) Statistically significant relationships between responses to questions on application forms and later measures of job performance.

***Weingarten* rights** Rights defined by the Supreme Court in *NLRB v. J. Weingarten, Inc.,* stating that a union employee has the right to demand that a union representative be present at an investigatory interview that the employee reasonably believes may result in disciplinary action; *Weingarten* rights do not extend to nonunion employees.

wellness programs Programs that focus on prevention to help employees build lifestyles that will enable them to achieve their full physical and mental potential.

whistle-blowing Disclosure by former or current organization members of illegal, immoral, or illegitimate practices under the control of their employers.

willful violations Violations of OSHA requirements in which an employer either knew that what was being done constituted a violation of federal regulations or was aware that a hazardous condition existed and made no reasonable effort to eliminate it.

win-lose bargaining In negotiations, the bargaining posture that assumes that the goals of the parties are irreconcilable; also known as *distributive bargaining.*

win-win bargaining In negotiations, the bargaining posture that assumes that the goals of the parties are not mutually exclusive, that it is possible for both sides to achieve their objectives; also known as *integrative bargaining.*

"Work-Out" program General Electric's program to involve every employee in improving efficiency and to foster communication between lower-level employees and bosses.

work-sample tests Standardized measures of behavior whose primary objective is to assess the ability to do rather than the ability to *know* through miniature replicas of actual job requirements; also known as *situational tests.*

workforce utilization A means of identifying whether the composition of the workforce—measured by race and sex—employed in a particular job category in a particular firm is representative of the composition of the entire labor market available to perform that job.

Credits

PHOTO CREDITS

6: Corbis-Bettman; **8:** © Spencer Grant/Stock Boston; **13:** © Ron McMillan/Gamma Liaison; **66:** © Jonathan Lurie/Gamma Liaison; **82:** © PBJ Pictures/Gamma Liaison; **85:** © Nicole Bengiveno/Matrix; **137:** © James Schnepf/Gamma Liaison; **186:** Jerry Marshal; **216:** © Robert Reiehert/Gamma Liaison; **217:** Rueters/Corbis-Bettman; **220:** Randy Matusow; **275:** © John Barr/Gamma Liaison; **317:** Jon Feingersh/The Stock Market; **340:** Richard Wood/The Picture Cube; **354:** © James Schnepf/Gamma Liaison; **384:** AP/Wide World Photos; **441:** © Richard Ilimeisen/Medichrome; **453:** © Grant LeDue/Stock Boston; **504:** © Jim West/Impact Visuals; **547:** © Will & Deni McIntyre/Photo Researchers; **577:** © The Stock Shop; **579:** Gerard Fritz/MONKMEYER; **611:** © Louie Psihyos/Matrix; **643:** © Karen Kasmauski/Matrix; **653:** © Alex Quesada/Matrix

Name Index

Subject Index